shakespearean criticism

"Thou art a Monument without a tomb,
And art alive still while thy Book doth
    live
And we have wits to read and praise to
give."

*Ben Jonson, from the preface
to the First Folio, 1623.*

Mr. WILLIAM
SHAKESPEARES
COMEDIES,
HISTORIES, &
TRAGEDIES.

Published according to the True Originall Copies.

Martin Droeshout sculpsit London.

LONDON
Printed by Isaac Iaggard, and Ed. Blount. 1623.

ISSN 0833-9123

Volume 37

shakespearean criticism

Yearbook 1996

A Selection of the Year's Most Noteworthy Studies
of William Shakespeare's Plays and Poetry

Advisers

Ralph Berry, *University of Ottawa*
William C. Carroll, *Boston University*
S.P. Cerasano, *Colgate University*
Sidney Homan, *University of Florida*
MacDonald P. Jackson, *University of Auckland*
Randall Martin, *University of New Brunswick*
T. McAlindon, *University of Hull*
Yasuhiro Ogawa, *Hokkaido University*

GALE

DETROIT • NEW YORK • TORONTO • LONDON

STAFF

Dana Ramel Barnes, *Editor*

Michelle Lee, *Associate Editor*

Aarti Stephens, *Managing Editor*

Susan M. Trosky, *Permissions Manager*
Kimberly F. Smilay, *Permissions Specialist*
Steve Cusack, Kelly A. Quin, *Permissions Assistants*

Victoria B. Cariappa, *Research Manager*
Julia C. Daniel, Michele P. LaMeau, Tamara C. Nott,
Tracie A. Richardson, Cheryl L. Warnock, *Research Associates*

Mary Beth Trimper, *Production Director*
Deborah Milliken, *Production Assistant*

Gary Leach, *Desktop Publisher*
Randy Bassett, *Image Database Supervisor*
Robert Duncan, Michael Logusz, *Imaging Specialists*
Pamela A. Reed, *Photography Coordinator*

∞™ This book is printed on acid-free paper that meets the minimum requirements of American National Standard for Information Sciences—Permanence Paper for Printed Library Materials, ANSI Z39.48-1984.

Library of Congress Catalog Card Number 86-645085
ISBN 0-7876-1135-2
ISSN 0883-9123

Printed in the United States of America
Published simultaneously in the United Kingdom
by Gale Research International Limited
(An affiliated company of Gale Research)
10 9 8 7 6 5 4 3 2 1

Gale Research

Contents

Preface   vii

Acknowledgments   ix

Comedies

Histories

Tragedies

Romances and Poems

Preface

*S*hakespearean Criticism (SC) provides students, educators, theatergoers, and other interested readers with valuable insight into Shakespeare's drama and poetry. The critical reactions of scholars and commentators from the seventeenth century to the present day are reprinted in the series from hundreds of periodicals and books. Students and teachers at all levels of study will benefit from *SC*, whether they seek information for class discussions and written assignments, new perspectives on traditional issues, or the most noteworthy analyses of Shakespeare's artistry.

Scope of the Series

Volumes 1 through 10 of the series present a unique historical overview of the critical response to each Shakespearean work, representing a broad range of interpretations. Volumes 11 through 26 recount the performance history of Shakespeare's plays on the stage and screen through eyewitness reviews and retrospective evaluations of individual productions, comparisons of major interpretations, and discussions of staging issues. Beginning with Volume 27 in the series, *SC* focuses on criticism published after 1960, with a view to providing the reader with the most significant modern critical approaches. Each of these volumes is organized around a theme that is central to the study of Shakespeare, such as politics, religion, or sexuality.

The *SC* Yearbook

SC compiles an annual Yearbook, collecting the most noteworthy contributions to Shakespearean scholarship published during the previous year. The essays are chosen to address a wide audience, including advanced secondary school students, undergraduate and graduate students, and teachers. Each year an advisory board of distinguished scholars recommends approximately one hundred articles and books from among the hundreds of valuable essays that appeared in the previous year. From these recommendations, Gale editors select examples of innovative criticism that represent current or newly developing trends in scholarship. The 32 essays in the present volume, *SC-37*, the *1996 Yearbook,* provide the latest assessments of the Shakespeare canon.

Organization and Features of the *SC Yearbook*

Essays are grouped on the basis of the genre of the Shakespearean work on which they focus: Comedies, Histories, Tragedies, and Romances and Poems. An article examining the relationship between pastoralism and *The Winter's Tale,* for example, appears in the Romances and Poems section of the yearbook.

- Each piece of criticism is reprinted in its entirety, including the full text of the author's footnotes, and is followed by a complete **Bibliographical Citation.**

- The *SC Yearbook* provides a **Cumulative Index to Topics.** This feature identifies the principal topics in the criticism and stage history of each work. The topics are arranged alphabetically, and the volume and starting page number are indicated for each essay that offers innovative or ample commentary on that topic.

Citing the *SC Yearbook*

Students who quote directly from the *SC Yearbook* in written assignments may use the following general forms to footnote reprinted criticism. The first example pertains to material drawn from periodicals, the second to material reprinted from books.

[1]Michael Neill, "Unproper Beds: Race, Adultery, and the Hideous in *Othello*," *Shakespeare Quarterly*, 40 (Winter 1989), 383-412; reprinted in *Shakespearean Criticism*, Vol. 13, Yearbook 1989, ed. Sandra L. Williamson (Detroit: Gale Research, 1989), pp. 327-42.

[2]Philip Brockbank, "*Julius Caesar* and the Catastrophes of History," in *On Shakespeare: Jesus, Shakespeare and Karl Marx, and Other Essays* (Basil Blackwell, 1989), pp. 122-39; reprinted in *Shakespearean Criticism*, Vol. 13, *Yearbook 1989*, ed. Sandra L. Williamson (Detroit: Gale Research, 1991), pp. 252-59.

Suggestions Are Welcome

The editors encourage comments and suggestions from readers on any aspect of the *SC* series. In response to reader recommendations, several features have been added to *SC* since the series began, including the topic index and the sample bibliographic citations noted above. Readers are cordially invited to write, call, or fax the editors: *Shakespearean Criticism*, Gale Research, 835 Penobscot Bldg., Detroit, MI, 48226-4094. Call toll-free at 1-800-347-GALE or fax to 1-313-961-6599.

Acknowledgments

The editors wish to thank the copyright holders of the excerpted criticism included in this volume and the permissions managers of many book and magazine publishing companies for assisting us in securing reproduction rights. We are also grateful to the staffs of the Detroit Public Library, the Library of Congress, the University of Detroit Mercy Library, Wayne State University Purdy/Kresge Library Complex, and the University of Michigan Libraries for making their resources available to us. Following is a list of the copyright holders who have granted us permission to reproduce material in this volume of *SC*. Every effort has been made to trace copyright, but if omissions have been made, please let us know.

COPYRIGHTED EXCERPTS IN *SC*, VOLUME 37, WERE REPRODUCED FROM THE FOLLOWING PERIODICALS:

Alternative Shakespeares, v. 2, 1996. Copyright © 1996 Terence Hawkes. All rights reserved. Reproduced by permission.—*Cahiers Elisabethains,* v. 49, April, 1996. Copyright © 1996 *Cahiers Elisabethains.* Reproduced by permission.—*College English,* v. 58, February 1996, for "Possible Pasts: Historiography and Legitimation in *Henry VIII*," by Ivo Kamps. Copyright © 1996 by the National Council of Teachers of English. Reproduced by permission of the publisher and the author.—*Comparative Drama,* v. 30, Summer, 1996; v. 30, Fall, 1996. Copyright © 1996, by the Editors of *Comparative Drama.* Both reproduced by permission of the publisher.—*Criticism,* v. 38, Summer, 1996. Copyright © 1996 by Wayne State University Press, Detroit, Michigan 48201-1309. Reproduced by permission.—*ELH,* v. 63, Winter, 1996. Copyright © 1996 The John Hopkins University Press. All rights reserved. Reproduced by permission.—*English Literary Renaissance,* v. 26, Spring, 1996. Copyright © 1996 by *English Literary Renaissance.* Reprinted by permission of the publisher.—*Philological Quarterly,* v. 75, Winter, 1996 for "Shakespeare at Work: The Two Talbots" by E. Pearlman. Copyright © 1996 by The University of Iowa. Reproduced by permission of the author.—*The Review of English Studies,* v. XLVII, August, 1996 for "Apparent Perversities: Text and Subtext in the Construction of the Role of Edgar in Brook's Film of *King Lear*," by J. G. Saunders. Copyright © Oxford University Press, 1996. All rights reserved. Reproduced by permission of the publisher and the author.—*Shakespeare Quarterly,* v. 47, Summer, 1996; v. 47, Fall, 1996; v. 47, Winter, 1996. Copyright © The Folger Shakespeare Library 1996. All reproduced by permission.—*Shakespeare Studies,* v. XXIV, 1996 for "Other Voices: The Sweet, Dangerous Air(s) of Shakespeare's *Tempest*" by Jacquelyn Fox-Good; v. XXIV, 1996 for "Fluellen's Name," by Lisa Hopkins. Copyright © 1996 by Associated University Presses, Inc. All rights reserved. Both reproduced by permission of the respective authors.—*Shakespeare Survey: An Annual Survey of Shakespearian Study and Production,* v. 49, 1996 for "'Have You Not Read of Some Such Thing?' Sex and Sexual Stories in *Othello*" by Edward Pechter. Copyright © Cambridge University Press, 1996. Reproduced by permission of the publisher and the author.—*Studies in English Literature: 1500-1900,* v. 36, Spring, 1996 for "Rethinking Gender and Genre in the History Play" by Martha A. Kurtz; v. 36, Spring, 1996 for "The Political Conscious of Shakespeare's *As You Like It*" by Andrew Barnaby. Copyright © William Marsh Rice University 1996. Both reproduced by permission of the publisher and the respective authors.—*Texas Studies in Literature and Language,* v. 38, Summer, 1996 for "On Not Being Deceived: Rhetoric and the Body in *Twelfth Night*" by Dr. Lorna Hutson. Copyright © 1996 by the University of Texas Press, PO Box 7819, Austin, Texas 78713-7819. Reproduced by permission of the University of Texas Press and the author.

COPYRIGHTED EXCERPTS IN S*C*, VOLUME 37, WERE REPRODUCED FROM THE FOLLOWING BOOKS:

Bishop, T. G. From "Compounding *Errors*" in *Shakespeare and the Theatre of Wonder.* Cambridge University Press, 1996. Copyright © Cambridge University Press 1996. Reprinted with the permission of the publisher and the author.—Cantor, Paul A. From "*King Lear*: The Tragic Disjunction of Wisdom and Power," in *Shakespeare's Political Pageant: Essays in Literature and Politics.* Edited by Joseph Alulis and Vickie Sullivan. Rowman & Littlefield Publishers, Inc., 1996. Copyright © 1996 by Rowman & Littlefield Publishers, Inc. All rights reserved. Reproduced

Comedies

The Political Conscious of Shakespeare's *As You Like It*

Andrew Barnaby, *University of Vermont*

> the purpose of playing . . . [is] to hold as 'twere the mirror up to nature: to show virtue her feature, scorn her own image, and the very age and body of the time his form and pressure.
>
> *Hamlet* (III.ii.20-4)

When in *As You Like It* the courtier-turned-forester Jacques declares his desire to take up the vocation of the licensed fool, he is immediately forced to confront the chief dilemma of the would-be satirist: the possibility that his intentions will be ignored and his words misconstrued as referring not to general moral concerns—the vices of humankind, for example—but rather to specific realities, persons, events (II.vii.12-87).[1] Given that Jacques has just demonstrated a laughable inability to grasp the barbs of a true practitioner of the satiric craft (Touchstone), we must be wary of taking him as a reflexive figure of Shakespeare's own vocation. But the lines undoubtedly show Shakespeare's discomfort with the recent censoring of satiric material (including a well-publicized burning of books in June of 1599),[2] and his own earlier experience with *Richard II,* as well as Ben Jonson's recent jailing for the "seditious and slanderous" content of the *Isle of Dogs,* had certainly made him familiar with the danger posed by those readers who misread the typical as the straight-forwardly topical. Despite his simplemindedness, then, Shakespeare's Jacques does in some way reflect a working playwright's continual anxiety that his works might be misconstrued as deriving meaning not from his intentions but from ideas and events beyond the signifying scope of his labors.

The modern equivalent of this reader-writer conflict resides not in the competing interpretations of author and court censor but in those of author and scholar-critic. But the necessity of facing up to such interpretative discrepancies has for the most part been obscured by the reigning critical methodology in Renaissance studies, New Historicism, and in particular by its inability to formulate a convincing explanatory model for the processes of acquisition by which texts come both to represent and to participate in the larger discursive systems that determine them. Although it would be counterproductive to dismiss the very impressive critical achievements of New Historicism, we might yet need to consider what we are to make of writing itself as a purposeful and perspectively limited activity: what of writers as the agents of meaning within their own textual compositions? what do we do when what we can reconstruct of authorial intention

runs counter to "cultural" evidence? and, more broadly, how precisely can any literary work be understood to signify historical reality?

In taking up these issues, Annabel Patterson has recently argued that it has become necessary to "reinstate certain categories of thought that some have declared obsolete: above all the conception of authorship, which itself depends on our predicating a continuous, if not a consistent self, of self-determination and, in literary terms, of intention." And she adds specifically of poststructuralist criticism of Shakespeare that the "dismissal of Shakespeare as *anybody,* an actual playwright who wrote . . . out of his own experience of social relations" has shown itself to be both incoherent methodologically and reductive at the level of historical understanding.[3] Such out-of-hand dismissal precludes the possibility of understanding how the early modern period actively conceptualized and debated its cultural forms or how an individual writer may have sought to engage in those debates.

The remainder of this essay will focus on how *As You Like It* (and so Shakespeare himself) does consciously engage in debate concerning the crises points of late-Elizabethan culture: the transformation of older patterns of communal organization under the pressures of new forms of social mobility, an emergent market economy, and the paradoxically concomitant stratification of class relations; the more specific problems of conflict over land-use rights, the enclosure of common land and its attendant violence, poverty and vagrancy.[4] In considering how modern historical understanding might itself seek to articulate this engagement, moreover, I shall be arguing that the play's meditation on the unsettled condition of contemporary social relations is precisely, and nothing more than, an interpretative response to the perceived nature of those conditions.

To recognize that what we have in Shakespeare's play can never be anything but a rather one-sided dialogue with social conditions then current is not to deny that the play is, in crucial ways, at once topical and discursively organized. But it is to acknowledge that such topicality and discursivity are necessarily transformed by the historical condition of writing itself. What we are left with, then, is not a symbolic re-encoding of the entire sweep of current circumstances (as if the play could encompass the full historical truth of even one element of Elizabethan culture in its own tremendous complexity). Shakespeare does indeed address the peculiar historical circumstances of late-Elizabethan culture, and that engagement is evidenced in the formal elements of his play (most particularly in its pastoral form, an issue that will be examined in greater detail in subsequent sections). But if *As You Like It* is historically relevant it is so primarily because it can be read as a rhetorical (and so intentional) act in which one writer's sense of things as part of history becomes available to his readers in the purposeful design of the play. It is to an understanding both of that design and of the limitations of current critical practice that the following discussion is directed.

I

The play begins with Orlando's complaining of his mistreatment at the hands of his older brother, Oliver, who has refused to fulfill the charge of their father, Sir Rowland de Boys: it was Sir Rowland's wish that his youngest son receive both a thousand crowns and sufficient breeding to make a gentleman of himself, despite being excluded from the much greater wealth of the estate because of the law of primogeniture. But Oliver has treated Orlando as a servant instead, and, in likening himself to the prodigal son (I.i.37-9), Orlando seeks both to remind Oliver that, unlike his gospel counterpart, *he* has yet to receive his promised inheritance and to register, for the audience as well as for Oliver, the discrepancy between his noble birth and his current circumstances.

In the course of rebuking Oliver for being so remiss in his fraternal duties, Orlando violently, if briefly, seizes his brother. In his finely nuanced reading of the play, Louis Montrose has argued that, in its explosive suddenness and aggressiveness, Orlando's action captures the essential tension caused by the culturally charged nature of the sibling conflict over primogeniture in Renaissance England, where younger sons of the gentry were excluded from the greater wealth of family estates in increasing numbers.[5] Moreover, the symbolic associations of the violence complicate the political inflections of the scene. For, in context, the violence does not just move from younger brother to older brother but also from servant to master and from landless to landowner, and these associations extend the cultural scope of the already politicized conflict. As Montrose suggests, in the broader discursive contextu–alization of the scene, Orlando's alienation from his status as landed gentleman serves "to intensify the differences between the eldest son and his siblings, and to identify the sibling conflict with the major division in the Elizabethan social fabric: that between the landed and the unlanded, the gentle and the base."[6]

Richard Wilson has recently elaborated on this argument by suggesting that the play's central conflicts reenact the particular tensions unleashed in Elizabethan society by the subsistence crisis of the 1590s. According to Wilson, in its "discursive rehearsal" of the social hostilities generated out of the combination of enclosure and famine (especially severe in the years just prior to the play's composition and in Shakespeare's native Midlands), the play becomes complexly enmeshed in the "bitter contradictions of English agricultural revolution," a struggle played out in the various conflicting relations between an enervated aristocracy, a rising gentry, and a newly dispossessed laboring class and effected primarily by the emergence of a new market economy.[7]

As compelling and historically informed as Wilson's reading is, however, it is yet undermined by its vagueness concerning how the play actually represents these issues. That Wilson wants and needs to posit the dialogic encounter of text and context as the site of the play's (and his argument's) meaning is evidenced by his own critical rhetoric. As we have just noted, he refers to the play as a "discursive rehearsal" of a multifaceted sociocultural history; elsewhere he writes that "the play is powerfully *inflected* by narratives of popular resistance"; that "social conflict [over famine and enclosure] *sears* the text"; that Duke Senior's situation in the forest of Arden "*chimes* with actual projects" associated with the capitalist development of the woodlands; that the play "*engages in the discursive revaluation* of woodland" that emerged as part of the rise of a market economy in late-Renaissance England.[8] The problem with this type of phrasing is that it never renders intelligible the processes by which text and context come into contact. We are dealing, in short, with the theoretical problem of how precisely a literary work may be said to allude to, reflect, mediate on, or even produce the historical forces that form its enabling conditions.

To put the issue another way, Wilson's reading is stranded by its inability to assess what we might call the play's signifying capacity. While I am not disputing that the particulars of enclosure and famine (and more generally the social transformation of late-Elizabethan society) constitute the proper historical backdrop of the play, Wilson consistently scants the historical conditions of writing and reception, and he therefore has no means of assessing the work of the text as a site of meaning.[9] Eschewing any reliance on the text's own coherence or Shakespeare's possible intentions as explanatory models, Wilson's argument relies instead on the juxtaposition of select formal elements of the play (plot details, bits of dialogue, character motivation, etc.) with a dense evocation of historical details that appear circumstantially relevant to the play's action. While this mode of argumentation—what Alan Liu has recently termed a kind of critical *bricolage*[10]— yields some perceptive insights into the workings of the play, social reality, and the discursive networks connecting them, what it really produces is a series of strange allegorical encounters in which the play is said to provide shadowy symbolic re-encodings of a broad spectrum of historical realities: legal edicts, demographic statistics, anecdotes from popular culture, institutional practices, persons, events, and even vast structural changes in the organization of English culture.

To get a clearer sense of this method we might consider just a few of his more suspect interpretative findings. For example, according to Wilson, Rosalind's lack of "holiday humor" in I.ii stems not from her father's banishment but from her recognition of a broader crisis of the aristocracy (particularly centered on a new "aristocratic insolvency"), and this even though her own subsequent banishment is read as a symbol of the expulsion of tenant farmers from common lands; and later her cross-dressing becomes an "impudent challenge" both of rural poachers to "the keepers of game" and, more generally, of class and gender trespassers to the patriarchal hierarchy maintained by the Elizabethan upper orders. The "obscure demise" of Orlando's servant, Adam, figures the rising "mortality rate" in rural England due to the late-1590s dearth, even though Adam does not die (he merely disappears as a character—a point to which we shall return). Orlando's carving of his beloved Rosalind's name on the forest trees is said to symbolize a Stuart policy of marking trees as part of the surveying that preceded royal disafforestation; and this is so even though such a policy post-dates the composition of the play and even after Wilson has described Orlando as a gentleman-leader of popular resistance for whom the damaging of trees was a potent sign of protest.[11] In almost all of the examples he gives, the text is so overdetermined by contradictory historical realities that it becomes virtually unreadable; despite his historicizing efforts, Wilson seems to repeat the very argument of those he terms "idealist critics" who see the play as "free of time and place."[12]

The argument's lack of coherence appears to derive primarily from Wilson's attempt to analyze what he calls the play's "material meaning." Although he never says precisely how we are to understand the phrase, his one effort at glossing suggests that it is something known only in the negative, as that which is concealed or evaded by the text's explicit statements.[13] This is an odd notion, given the ease with which Wilson finds the text making explicit statements about the social situation;[14] indeed, given his practice, it makes more sense to take the term "material" in its traditional Marxist sense: the "historical" as located in a culture's dominant mode of production. In the case of *As You Like It* the "material" would then include the cultural struggle over agrarian rights, the conversion of woodland to arable land, and the broader movement of a regulated to a market economy (seen especially in the capitalization of land-use rights), and this "material"

history would provide the base from which the manifestations of superstructure (including the play) would derive meaning.

The problem with this formulation is that it both reduces the play to a straightforward (albeit jumbled) allegory of "history as it really happened" and avoids the theoretical problem of how (or where) the play actually represents this history. Addressing precisely this hermeneutic problem in relation to the Shakespearean text (and so offering a different sense of "material meaning"), Patterson properly asks: "how do words relate to material practice?" And she notes that Shakespeare himself "used both 'abstract' and 'general' as terms to denote his own form of material practice, writing for a popular audience, the 'general,' and abstracting their experience and his own into safely fictional forms."[15] Such a critical stance depends on several related notions: that Renaissance writers were quite capable of comprehending the cultural situation of their own productions; that these productions must be read as forms, that is, as organized, fictionalized, and generically regularized abstractions of perceived realities; that any discussion of form must consider the representational practices by which historical situations are reproduced aesthetically; and that, as abstractions, forms take their meaning from a variety of interpretative exchanges—between author and world as an act of perception, author and reader/audience as a rhetorical act, reader/audience and world as an act of application—and therefore cannot be explained by recourse to the notion of a general, all-encompassing discursive field. To view fictional form as a significant material practice in its own right is to see that it at once signifies historical realities and constitutes its own reality, that it is both constantive and performative; it thus "both invite[s] and resist[s] understanding in terms of other phenomena."[16]

As texts such as Ben Jonson's Preface to *Volpone* suggest, for Renaissance writers this invitation and resistance is played out primarily (though not exclusively) in ethical terms.[17] The citation from *Hamlet* that stands as my epigraph makes a similar point: "to hold . . . the mirror up to nature" is to engage in moral discrimination, distinguishing virtue from vice in acts of praise and blame. Such acts might themselves be understood as historically relevant; indeed, Hamlet's earlier assertion that actors are "the abstract and brief chronicles of the time" (II.ii.524-5) suggests that dramatic representations were expected to speak to contemporary history (albeit in "abstract and brief" form). Leah Marcus takes this point even further in her claims that "local meaning was at the center" of Renaissance literary practices, and that what contemporaries "attended and talked about" concerning a literary work was its "currency . . . , its ability to . . . 'Chronicle' events in the very unfolding." But, as she also points out, Renaissance "poets and dramatists [typically] looked for ways to regularize and elevate topical issues so that they could be linked with more abstract moral concerns."[18] In *As You Like It* that ethical sensibility, "regularizing and elevating" a pressing cultural debate over current social conditions, is marked especially in the play's engagement with the traditions of pastoral, where pastoral must be understood as a form obsessively concerned with the related questions of social standing (the constant re-marking of distinctions between gentle and base) and moral accountability.[19] It is to an attempt to assess the moral and political commitments of the play, as well as the representational strategies it employs to render these commitments intelligible, that we now turn.

II

The three plays that Shakespeare wrote in 1599—*Julius Caesar, Henry V,* and *As You Like It*—are all variously concerned with aristocratic identity, an issue cited, probed, redefined in late-Elizabethan culture in "a vast outpouring of courtesy books, poetry, essays, and even epics," all directed toward "the fashioning . . . of the gentleman or the nobleman."[20] *Julius Caesar* looks at the issue as a crisis of aristocratic self-definition in the face of Tudor efforts at political and cultural centralization; the play examines this crisis and moralizes it in terms of a questioning of the continued possibility of aristocratic excellence (defined primarily in terms of humanist notions of virtuous civic action).[21] *Henry V* explores the relationship between aristocratic conduct and national identity in the context of militarist expansionism, but this focus is extended to an examination of the aristocratic capacity for responsible leadership of commoners and the popular response to that leadership.[22] As critics have recently argued, both plays are concerned with the nature of historical understanding itself, and especially with examining the possibilities and limits of applying knowledge of the past—already an interested rhetorical activity—to present concerns.[23] Like *As You Like It*, then, both plays are interested at once in the vexed relation between aristocratic culture and the broader workings of political society and in the representational and interpretative practices by which fictional accounts serve as mediatory sites of informed public concern over contemporary affairs.

As You Like It returns the meditation on aristocratic conduct to the domestic sphere where, as we have seen suggested, it focuses on the related issues of inheritance practices, agrarian social structure, and the current controversy over land-use rights. Right from its opening scene, in fact, the play introduces us to its particular interest in the problem of aristocratic definition. Indeed, despite Orlando's complaints against the system of primogeniture which denies him his brother's authority, the real source of his frustration is that his "gentlemanlike qualities"—the

very marks of his class, so crucial in a deferential society—have been obscured by his having been "trained . . . like a peasant" (I.i.68-70). Throughout the opening scene, in fact, what Orlando is most concerned with is the possibility that his status might be taken away simply by its not being properly recognized. In its particular locating of Orlando's predicament, then, the play's opening scene initiates a line of inquiry that will both inflect the rest of the play and share in a culturally charged debate: by what markings is it possible to identify the true aristocrat?

But the issues of status and its violation, of place, displacement, and recognition—all so central to the play's comic vision—are not confined to the interactions among the upper orders. For they are raised as part of an exploration of the customary bonds between the upper and lower orders as well. And, as the relationship between landowner and landless servant depicted in the opening suggests, the play also puts in question the nature and meaning of aristocratic conduct toward social inferiors. Shakespeare, we shall see, interlaces the depiction of violated noble status with a depiction of the displacement of laboring classes (represented in the opening scenes by both Orlando and Adam) from their traditional places in the service of the rural nobility.

The play's concern with the related issues of social standing and displacement, aristocratic conduct, and the moral bonds connecting high and low, is further developed in II.iii. Upon returning from Frederick's court, Orlando is secretly met by Adam who warns him of Oliver's villainous plot:

> this night he means
> To burn the lodging where you use to lie,
> And you within it.
>
> (II.iii.22-4)

Amidst the special urgency of the moment, Adam's warning is enveloped in a broader meditation on what has happened in the wake of Sir Rowland's passing. So he addresses Orlando:

> O unhappy youth,
> Come not within these doors! Within this roof
> The enemy of all your graces lives.
> Your brother—no, no brother, yet the son
> (Yet not the son, I will not call him son)
> Of him I was about to call his father—
>
> . . . . .
>
> This is no place, this house is but a butchery;
> Abhor it, fear it, do not enter it.
>
> (II.iii.16-28)

Marking the logical consequence of the sibling conflict set in motion in the opening scene, Oliver's "unbrotherly" act is viewed here as particularly heinous, totally unnatural, a kind of abomination; indeed, as Montrose notes, we hear in this struggle the echoes of the original fratricide, the elder Cain killing his younger brother Abel.[24] But the fratricide is clearly rewritten in the cultural context of Renaissance inheritance practices, for we note that Oliver's "sin" is figured particularly as a repudiation of the familial duties and obligations emanating from a line of inheritance between noble father and noble son. Sir Rowland's heir, in effect, perverts the very link between nature and human social order—the family—and thereby disavows the very foundation of his inheritance. Oliver's unbrotherly dealings mark the violation of more than just the person of his brother; they are symbolically broadened to assimilate the house itself, symbol of both the family and the larger estate as an extension of the family. In dishonoring his place within the family, Oliver threatens the very cultural inheritance that extends a sense of place to those outside the family. Adam thus identifies Oliver's special villainy as a violation of kinship ties that both reenacts human history's primal scene of violence and marks the loss of that "place"—the noble manor—whose very purpose is to locate the various lines of interaction defining the social order.[25]

In II.iii, then, younger brother and elder servant are linked together in their experience of the psychically disorienting effects of displacement, a loss registered particularly in the feelings of estrangement they voice over their impending exile (II.iii.31-5, 71-4). There is something extremely conservative in this nostalgic evocation of tradition, of course, but it is important to insist that the image of "proper" social relations that Shakespeare depicts does not offer merely a moralized restoration of traditional cultural forms but provides rather an extended meditation on the political economy that should at once reveal and sustain the moral economy.

As an example of this concern, Shakespeare's complex adaptation of the gospel parable he so carefully etches into the opening scene deserves greater attention. We noted earlier that at the very outset of the play Orlando's self-figuration as the prodigal son is intended to register the discrepancy between his noble birth and his current circumstances. But the very lack of applicability of the parable to Orlando's case—unlike the prodigal son he has neither squandered his inheritance nor even received it—is even more significant within the play's moral and political vision. This discrepancy is critical primarily because it reconfigures the parable's central focus on the interaction of family members from how each of the two brothers interacts independently with the father to a direct confrontation between them. At the most obvious level, this change has the effect of politicizing the fraternal struggle by making it a conflict over the now-deceased father's patrimony, whereas in the parable the fraternal conflict is less about inheritance per se than with the sibling rivalry over the attentiveness of the still-living father. Shakespeare, that is, transforms a story concerned with the nature of a future "heavenly" kingdom into a decidedly human, indeed, political affair.

More specifically, the retelling provides a completely different context for understanding the roles of the two brothers within the parable. For example, whereas the parable faults (even as it treats sympathetically) the elder brother's uncharitable attitude toward his younger brother, the play, by contrast, renders this animosity, and the behavior that attends it, unsympathetic; indeed, Shakespeare appears to conflate two different parts of the parable by rewriting the elder brother's (now perverse) behavior as the cause of the (now innocent) younger brother's degradation. Living among the hogs and eating husks with them, Orlando appears as the dutiful son, toiling long years without just recompense. Although the play never quotes the parable directly on this point, Shakespeare subtly borrows from the parable the elder brother's complaint to his father—"All these years I have slaved for you and never once disobeyed any orders of yours"—and reassigns the context to Orlando's frustration with Oliver's unfair treatment of him. And as Orlando is no longer responsible for his fallen circumstances, so his situation ceases to represent a moral failing—a lapse in personal ethical responsibility—and comes instead to mark a political and economic awareness of the social mechanisms that lead one into such penury.

Oliver's role is thereby refigured (loosely to be sure) as "prodigal." In the parable, of course, it is the elder brother who laments that while he has never "disobeyed any orders" of the father, his prodigal brother enjoys all the special privileges even after "swallowing up [the father's] property." But Shakespeare makes the true bearer of privilege appear prodigal precisely because, while he has done nothing to earn his portion of the estate (other than being the eldest son), he has enjoyed its benefits without sharing them with his hardworking brother. And even as the play merges the Judeo-Christian primal scene of violence—Cain's killing of his younger brother Abel—with the Christian parable of the difficult demands of brotherly love, it also recontextualizes the elder brother's failure of charity in the political relations not just between elder and younger sons (already politicized in Renaissance culture) but also between masters and servants, landed and landless, gentle and base. Moreover, while the opening scene stages, in the guise of Orlando's violence, a threat to the overturning of traditional authority, the subsequent scenes stage a recognition of what is more precisely in need of transformation: the aristocratic figure who fails to fulfill the obligations of status and custom, and especially to maintain cultural stability by sustaining the moral (and political) value that accrues to social place.

It is within the context of such unbrotherly dealings and their symbolic affiliation with social injustice conceived on a broader scale that Duke Senior's praise of rural life at the opening of act II has its strongest resonance:

> Now, my co-mates and brothers in exile,
> Hath not old custom made this life more sweet
> Than that of painted pomp? Are not these woods
> More free from peril than the envious court?
> Here feel we not the penalty of Adam.
>
> (II.i.1-5)

Exiled to Arden by his usurper-brother, Frederick, Duke Senior moralizes his own violated status as a paradoxically edifying experience, one in which the recovery of a communal (fraternal) ethic, in opposition to a courtly one, marks the return to a prelapsarian condition.

We must pause over such an idealization, of course. For it is possible to read the "pastoral" vision here as merely mystifying the class consciousness it appears to awaken. Montrose asserts, for example, that Renaissance pastoral typically "puts into play a symbolic strategy, which, by reconstituting the leisured gentleman as the gentle shepherd obfuscates a fundamental contradiction in the cultural logic: a contradiction between the secular claims of aristocratic prerogative and the religious claims of common origins, shared fallenness, and spiritual equality among . . . gentle and base alike."[26] For a modern reader especially, the very social structure maintained in Duke Senior's Arden weakens the political force of his claims for ethical restoration. From this limited perspective, that is, Duke Senior bears a remarkable resemblance to the gentleman-shepherd of so many Elizabethan pastorals, who, "in the idyllic countryside" is most determined to "escape temporarily from the troubles of court." As Montrose adds, "in such pastorals, ambitious Elizabethan gentlemen who may be alienated or excluded from the courtly society that nevertheless continues to define their existence can create an imaginative space within which virtue and privilege coincide."[27] The duke's idealization of the leisured life of the country would then, despite its egalitarian appeal, serve to reemphasize the division between baseness and gentility and to celebrate aristocratic values in isolation from a broader vision of how those values serve as the foundation of an entire network of social relations.

We might note further how Duke Senior's aristocratic rhetoric appears to de-radicalize its own most potent political symbol: the image of a prelapsarian fraternal community. As Montrose and others have pointed out, from the Peasants' Revolt of 1381 onward popular social protest in England often challenged class stratification by appealing to a common Edenic inheritance.

Powerfully condensed into the proverb, "When Adam dalf and Eve span, who was then the Gentleman?" such protest offered a radical critique of aristocratic privilege, both interrogating the suspect essentialism inherent in the notion of "degree" and reversing the valuation of labor as a criterion of social status.[28] Duke Senior's speech, however, does neither: it never questions the "naturalness" of his rank within the fraternal community (which never ceases to be hierarchically organized) nor does it champion labor as a morally edifying and communal burden. For Duke Senior, the retreat to a prelapsarian condition becomes rather the site from which to critique court corruption and decadence.

Nevertheless, we should not underestimate the reformist, populist impulse embedded in that critique. For, as act I depicts it, the condition of fallenness that exists in Frederick's court is defined primarily by its persecution of those members of the nobility—Orlando and Rosalind—most popular with the people (I.i.164-71, I.ii.277-83). Moreover, Orlando and Rosalind are conceptually linked to Sir Rowland himself, so universally "esteemed," as Frederick tells us, and so an enemy (I.ii.225-30). Frederick's function as the play's arch-villain is registered therefore, like Oliver's before him, by a lack of respect for the memory of that overdetermined father whose recurrent, if shadowy, presence in the play provides a "local habitation and name" to a broader cultural ideal: the forms of customary obligation that link gentle and base in pastoral fraternity, an evocation of religious communion that emphasizes social dependency and reciprocity even as it does not thereby reject society's hierarchical structure.

Much of the value (both moral and political) associated with that community is symbolized in Duke Senior's phrase "old custom" and its own associations with popular protest. As Patterson remarks, even when such protest did not advocate structural changes in the social order, an appeal to the authority of "origins" (again, often condensed into the recollection of a common Edenic origin) "was integral to the popular conception of *how* to protest, as well as providing theoretical grounds for the 'demands,' for the transformation of local and individual grievances into a political program."[29] *As You Like It* makes it clear that the duke's use of the phrase cannot be seen as privileging the rights of the nobility alone; indeed, Adam's subsequent lament over his exile (II.iii.71-4) is designed to set out the meaning of "old custom" from the perspective of the rural servant. Linking together a sense both of the immemorialness of custom and of its historical embeddedness by reference to his age and associating that further with the original Edenic dispensation through his name, Adam's speech marks how an appeal to customary practices could serve the interests of the lower orders.

In the tradition of popular protest, an idealization of the past could serve as the focal point of protesters' awareness of current social injustice, even as the perception of injustice was rarely separated from an appeal to the moral economy taken to subtend the political one. This ethical evaluation of the mutual interests of the upper and lower orders is powerfully figured in the tableau that closes act II: Duke Senior, Orlando, and Adam gathered together at a life-sustaining meal. Here, the problem of rural poverty (old Adam is starving to death) is answered in the nostalgic evocation of "better days," when paupers were "with holy bell . . . knoll'd to church, / And sat at good men's feasts" (II.vii.113-5). The meal, reimagined as a Sabbath-day feast, symbolizes the restoration of social communion especially as this is founded on those culturally sustaining lines of authority in which servants and masters properly recognize each other with reciprocal "truth and loyalty" (II.iii.70), the very qualities that were the hallmark of the days of Sir Rowland.[30]

In focusing on the paired plights of Orlando and Adam up through the end of act II, the play defines that perception of injustice, and of the moral obligations of the community, from the perspective of the lower orders and their first-hand experience of the effects of enclosure and eviction, dearth and hunger. Moreover, what Wilson misreads as Adam's subsequent "demise" (his disappearance from the play after act II) can be better understood as Shakespeare's attempt to give even more nuanced attention to the plight of the lower orders. In replacing Adam with the shepherd, Corin, as the play's test case, Shakespeare refocuses the issue of the condition of rural laborers in a character whose situation more obviously typifies such conditions in their particular relation to enclosure and eviction, especially in the face of the new commercialization of the land.

Significantly, Shakespeare puts the words describing the bleak prospects for rural living into Corin's own mouth; he thereby suggests a clear-sighted popular consciousness of the current situation. So Corin has earlier described his living in response to Rosalind's request for food and lodging:

> I am shepherd to another man,
> And do not shear the fleeces that I graze.
> My master is of churlish disposition,
> And little reaks to find the way to heaven
> By doing deeds of hospitality.
> Besides, his cote, his flocks, and bounds of
>   feed
> Are now on sale, and at our sheep-cote now
> By reason of his absence there is nothing
> That you will feed on.
>
>   (II.iv.78-86)

Hunger is again the central issue, but the exchange subtly shifts attention away from the almost incidental hunger of disguised aristocrats (who can afford to "buy entertainment" [line 72]) to the plight of the rural laborer whose suffering derives from the very condition of his employment (significantly, in the service of an absentee landlord). As Lawrence Stone summarizes the historical situation described here:

> the aristocracy suffered a severe loss of their landed capital in the late-Elizabethan period, primarily because of improvident sales made in order to keep up the style of life they considered necessary for the maintenance of status. When they abandoned sales of land and took to rigorous economic exploitation of what was left in order to maximize profits, they certainly restored their financial position, but at the expense of much of the loyalty and affection of their tenants. They salvaged their finances at the cost of their influence and prestige.

He adds that as part of a "massive shift away from a feudal and paternalist relationship" on the land, "these economic developments were dissolving old bonds of service and obligation," a process compounded by an "increasing preference [among the nobility] for extravagant living in the city instead of hospitable living in the countryside."[31] A figure for the current destruction of the manorial economy, Corin's master is guilty of all these charges simultaneously: he is absent from the estate; he exploits the (once commonly held) land for profit; he threatens to sell the estate with no concern for his workers' future prospects; he refuses the ethical responsibilities of his class—hospitable living, the sustenance of the customary culture, leadership of the countryside. The scene's concern with the immediate need to allay hunger becomes then a stepping-stone to a broader meditation on hunger's place in the complex socioeconomic transformation of late-Elizabethan culture. From the immediate perspective of the play, moreover, this transformation threatens to become a dangerous social upheaval, the blame for which must be assigned to the moral failure of well-to-do landowners.

As idealistic as it is, then, Celia and Rosalind's offer to purchase the "flock and pasture" and "mend" Corin's wages (II.iv.88, 94) retains an element of popular political consciousness; for it suggests that it is still possible for laborers to reap the rewards of faithful service to masters who know how to nurture traditional lines of authority.[32] Shakespeare's revision of his source text, Thomas Lodge's *Rosalynde,* is particularly relevant on this point, not the least for its demonstration of the deliberateness with which Shakespeare addresses the specific issue of economic hardship among the rural poor. In Lodge's romance, the shepherd (Coridon) offers Aliena and Ganimede the simple comforts of his lowly cottage as part of a traditional extolling of pastoral content:

Marry, if you want lodging, if you vouch to shrowd your selves in a shepheardes cotage, my house . . . shalbe your harbour . . . [A]nd for a shepheards life (oh Mistresse) did you but live a while in their content, you would saye the Court were rather a place of sorrowe, than of solace. Here (Mistresse) shal not Fortune thwart you, but in meane misfortunes, as the losse of a few sheepe, which, as it breeds no beggerie, so it can bee no extreame prejudice: the next yeare may mend al with a fresh increase. Envie stirs not us, wee covet not to climbe, our desires mount not above our degrees, nor our thoughts above our fortunes. Care cannot harbour in our cottages, nor do our homely couches know broken slumbers: as we exceed not in diet, so we have inough to satisfie.[33]

The fact that the sheepcote is for sale (and so, by a stroke of good fortune, available as a home for the wandering noblewomen) is only incidental to Coridon's prospects; the simple pleasures of his life will hardly be affected by a change in masters. Shakespeare, by contrast, revalues Corin's poverty by tying it explicitly to his economic vulnerability in the new commercial market: as one who, as "shepherd to another," does not "shear the fleeces" he grazes. In associating Corin's straitened circumstances—his limited supply of food is not "inough to satisfie"—with his very lack of authority over the estate (and his master's unreliable ownership practices), Shakespeare's revision of the scene emphasizes the real threat of rural dispossession; he thus makes it clear that "pastoral content" can only result from a functional economic relation between servant and landowner: hence, Corin's concern that his new masters actually "like . . . / The soil, the profit, and this kind of life" (II.iv.97-8).

The conflicted relationship between leisured gentleman and base laborer is symbolically played out in the conversation between Corin and Touchstone in III.ii. Although the confrontation is humorous, it also includes a more serious evaluation of the attendant problems of social stratification, marked especially by the lack of respect shown toward common laborers. As Judy Z. Kronenfeld points out, Shakespeare here transforms the typical pastoral encounter in which an "aristocratic shepherd" (a gentleman pretending to be a shepherd) demonstrates courtly superiority by mocking the "clownish countryman" (or what is really a "burlesque version of the countryman").[34] What Shakespeare depicts instead is an encounter between a lowly court servant (now a pretended gentleman) and a sympathetically realistic shepherd. Touchstone's pretense to gentility in the scene hearkens back to his original meeting of Corin in II.iv. There, in the company of Celia and Rosalind, Touchstone responds to Corin's "Who calls" with the demeaning "Your betters, sir" (lines 67-8): the response mockingly raises Corin to the level of the gentlewomen ("sir") only to reassert the difference in social standing ("your betters") and to place Touchstone in that higher circle.

Touchstone maintains the masquerade in III.ii when he attempts to flout Corin's baseness in a condescending display of courtly sophistication (lines 11-85). But, as Kronenfeld notes, the sophistication comes off as mere "court sophistry," and the emptiness of his claims to superiority is thereby exposed as nothing more than a witty social rhetoric covering over an absence of any clearly defined *essential* differences between gentle and base. Shakespeare thus uses the tradition against itself, for the typical encounter of aristocrat (pretending to be a shepherd) and countryman—where the contrast is meant to "reaffirm the social hierarchy"—is rewritten to suggest (albeit humorously) the mere pretense of that contrast.[35] It is possible to read the scene as positing that there are no differences between gentle and base, a position which might include the more radical recognition that class standing itself is merely the result of an ideological manipulation of cultural signs. Within the context of the play as a whole, however, it perhaps makes more sense to read it as a moral commentary on class division and especially on the meaning of aristocratic identity: if gentility is as much a social construct as it is a privileged condition of birth, its maintenance requires that it be continually reconstructed through meritorious signs, and these signs are to be made legible in the virtuous conduct shown toward those whose livelihood depends on how the "gentle" fulfill the obligations of their class.

III

In discussing George Puttenham's *Arte of English Poesie* in the context of Elizabethan pastoral discourse, Montrose cites Puttenham's claim that pastoral was developed among ancient poets "not of purpose to counterfait or represent the rusticall manner of loves and communication: but under the vaile of homely persons, and in rude speeches to insinuate and glaunce at greater matters, and such as perchance had not bene safe to have beene disclosed in any other sort."[36] Puttenham's related concerns with safety and the necessity of dissimulation in a dangerous social environment, the poet's self-awareness as a cultural commentator, and the struggle to make homely fiction serve the higher ends of instruction bring us back to Patterson's contention that Shakespeare's own "material practice" purposely seeks out "safely fictional forms" to achieve its ends. In *As You Like It,* moreover, Shakespeare's practice turns explicitly to pastoral form, which, we might surmise, is deliberately deployed to "glaunce at greater matters" "cleanly cover[ed]" (as Spenser puts it in the *Shepheardes Calender*) by a "feyne[d]" story.[37]

The precise nature of those "matters" and Shakespeare's specific ends may be debated, of course. But it is hard to imagine that they are any less comprehensive than those attributed by Montrose to Puttenham. Puttenham, Montrose writes, conceives "of poetry as a body of changing cultural practices dialectically related to the fundamental processes of social life"; and his "cultural relativism and ethical heterodoxy, his genuinely Machiavellian grasp of policy, are evident . . . in his pervasive concern with the dialectic between poetry and power."[38] It comes as some surprise, therefore, when Montrose later revises this estimation and gives us a Puttenham whose writing only serves the ends of personal aggrandizement within the confined circles of the court, whose sense of his culture's complexity is merely the sophistry of a "cunning princepleaser," and whose grasp of the political purposes of poetry never rises above its merely politic ends. And, as Montrose dismisses the narrowness of Puttenham's courtly orientation, so he dismisses pastoral discourse itself, whose power to "glaunce at greater matters" is suddenly reduced to courtliness in another form: thus, the "dominantly aristocratic" perspective of Elizabethan pastoral becomes but a reinscription of "agrarian social relations . . . within an ideology of the country," which is "itself appropriated, transformed, and reinscribed within an ideology of the court."[39] Pastoral's "greater matters," it seems, are only the matters of the great for whom the masks of rural encomium serve their own (narrowly defined) hegemonic interests. For Montrose, that is, despite pastoral writers' own recognition that their art form is "intrinsically political in purpose," pastoral's central concern with aristocratic identity only serves to mystify the issues of class standing and social relations it appears to raise.[40] As he argues, finally, because Renaissance pastoral "inevitably involve[s] a transposition of social categories into metaphysical ones, a sublimation of politics into aesthetics," it necessarily functions as "a weapon against social inferiors."[41]

Without denying pastoral's aristocratic orientation, we might note that it is only from the reductively binary perspective of the New Historicist that an "elite community" must be opposed to all "egalitarian ideas," or that its members could have "little discernible interest" in the condition of those who serve them.[42] *As You Like It* certainly suggests that such a critical perspective fails to register the possibility of the presence of dissenting voices within the dominant culture. Indeed, if the play is not in full support of the popular voice, it is yet concerned to link an aristocratic crisis of identity to the more vexing problems of the "base." Shakespeare's pastoral world is thus less concerned with celebrating nobles as virtuous than in reexamining the precise nature of aristocratic virtue. And lest we think Shakespeare is the exception that proves the rule, it is instructive to recall the aristocratic Sidney's own brief meditation on pastoral in his *Defence of Poesy*: "Is the poor pipe disdained, which sometimes out of Meliboeus' mouth can show the misery of people under hard lords and ravening soldiers and again, by Tityrus, what blessedness is derived to them that lie lowest from the goodness of them that sit highest?"[43] That "blessedness," moreover, is not presumed to be the reality of his culture but only a symbolic idealization challenging his aristocratic readers to a kind of creative, ethically oriented *imitatio*.

Montrose's Historicism cannot envision this possibility because he denies to Renaissance pastoral writers any critical distance from the courtly aristocracy from which they drew support (including occasional financial support). He goes even further in denying that "the mediation of social boundaries was [even] a *conscious* motive in the writing of Elizabethan pastorals," let alone that a cultural critique might have been leveled "in terms of a *consciously* articulated oppositional culture."[44] Such a dismissal of Renaissance writing as a purposeful, socially engaged activity is typical of New Historicist criticism more generally, which matches a methodological subordination of individual intention to larger "systems" of thought with a tonal condescension toward the capacity of earlier writers to comprehend their own cultural situations. Against this effacement of the subject, I would counter that an interest in the historical conditioning of texts is necessarily concerned with the conditions of their being written and being read, with the social processes by which meaning is formulated and communicated, with acts of knowledge as acts of persuasion, with the "rhetoricity" of texts as the essence of their historicity.[45] The reduction of historical criticism to the impersonal voice—to what Foucault once called the "it-is-said"[46]—precludes the possibility of understanding how the movement of ideas within discursive systems requires real readers and writers whose very activities help reveal to us the contours of historical existence.

Notes

[1] All references to Shakespeare's plays are to *The Riverside Shakespeare,* ed. G. Blakemore Evans (Boston: Houghton Mifflin, 1974).

[2] Celia's earlier remark to Touchstone—"since the little wit that fools have was silenc'd, the little foolery that wise men have makes a great show" (I.ii.88-90)—obliquely refers to this.

[3] Annabel Patterson, *Shakespeare and the Popular Voice* (Oxford: Basil Blackwell, 1989), pp. 4, 24.

[4] For a concise summary of these changing historical circumstances, see Lawrence Stone, *The Causes of the English Revolution, 1529-1642* (New York: Harper and Row, 1972), pp. 58-117.

[5] Louis Montrose, "'The Place of a Brother' in *As You Like It:* Social Process and Comic Form," *SQ* 32, 1 (Spring 1981): 28-54.

[6] Montrose, "'The Place of a Brother,'" pp. 34-5. That the exchange between Orlando and Oliver is more than just the struggle between younger and older brothers is emphasized by Orlando's response to Oliver's insulting question: "Know where you are, sir?" Orlando replies: "O sir, very well; here in your orchard" (I.i.40-1). The condition of "gentility" (marked in the mocking uses of "sir") is clearly tied to the question of who actually owns the property.

[7] Richard Wilson, "'Like the old Robin Hood': *As You Like It* and the Enclosure Riots," *SQ* 43, 1 (Spring 1992): 1-19, 3-5. For a historical overview of the broader cultural, political, and economic issues conditioning this hostility, see Roger B. Manning, *Village Revolts: Social Protest and Popular Disturbances in England, 1509-1640* (Oxford: Clarendon Press, 1988).

[8] Wilson, "'Like the old Robin Hood,'" pp. 4, 5, 9; my emphases.

[9] Wilson's lack of interest in what the text itself does to produce the meanings he finds in it is perhaps not so surprising given his attempt, formulated elsewhere, to theorize the fundamental irrelevance of literature to the forces of history and culture that must always supersede it. See his Introduction to *New Historicism and Renaissance Drama,* ed. Richard Wilson and Richard Dutton (London: Longman, 1992), pp. 1-18. It should be noted that Wilson considers himself a "Cultural Materialist" rather than a "New Historicist," and in that Introduction he seeks to differentiate the critical assumptions governing their respective practices. But the mode of argumentation employed in his essay on *As You Like It* does not bear out the differences he alleges.

[10] Alan Liu, "The Power of Formalism: The New Historicism," *ELH* 56, 4 (Winter 1989): 721-71, 721.

[11] Wilson, "'Like the old Robin Hood,'" pp. 4, 6, 9, 10-11, 13, 18.

[12] Wilson, "'Like the old Robin Hood,'" p. 3 and n. 15. Liu remarks that "the limitation of the New Historicism is that in its failure to carve out its own theory by way of a disciplined, high-level study of the evolution of historically situated language, its discoverable theory has been too assimilable to the deconstructive view of rhetoric as an a-, trans-, or uni-historical figural language" (p. 756). Although his own critical practice employs precisely this kind of formalism, Wilson himself makes much the same complaint about New Historicist critics, whose elision of historical referent in favor of the "textuality of history," he asserts, aligns them with New Critics (*New Historicism and Renaissance Drama,* pp. 9-10).

[13] Wilson first uses the phrase, without defining it, on p. 3 of "'Like the old Robin Hood'"; later he cites

Foucault's observation that "in every society discourse is controlled and redistributed to avert its dangers and *evade its formidable materiality.*" As an instance of this, Wilson notes that "pastoral discourse . . . *will conceal* the real revolution in the forest economy" (p. 17; my emphases). (Inexplicably, although in his Introduction to *New Historicism and Renaissance Drama* Wilson again notes Foucault's claim for the "'formidable materiality' of all discourse" [p. 9], he does so as part of his critique of the overly abstract post-Marxist practice of Foucault and other French intellectuals, especially as this tradition has become the philosophical foundation of American New Historicism.) For discussion of the trope of revelatory "concealment" within post-structuralist criticism, see Richard Levin, "The Poetics and Politics of Bardicide," *PMLA* 105, 3 (May 1990): 491-504, 493-4.

[14] One example: Touchstone's quip to the bumpkin, William, concerning their rival claims on Audrey—"to have, is to have" (V.i.40)—means, we are told, that a new concept of property ownership is now superseding traditional agrarian rights based on the notion of collective possession (Wilson, p. 18).

[15] Patterson, p. 14.

[16] Ibid.

[17] See Preface to *Volpone,* in *Ben Jonson,* ed. C. H. Herford and Percy and Evelyn Simpson, 11 vols. (Oxford: Clarendon Press, 1925-52), 5:18-9. Having been jailed again in 1604, along with Chapman and Marston, for the anti-Scottish sentiments of *Eastward Ho!,* Jonson used the Preface to chastise readers for their propensity for assigning topical meanings to his plays: by substituting local for more general meanings, Jonson thought, his readers would necessarily fail to appreciate the moral lessons of his writing and so not see how his meanings were to be used for their own edification and improvement.

[18] Leah Marcus, *Puzzling Shakespeare: Local Reading and Its Discontents* (Berkeley: Univ. of California Press, 1988), pp. 26, 41.

[19] For discussion, see Louis Montrose, "Of Gentlemen and Shepherds: The Politics of Elizabethan Pastoral Form," *ELH* 50, 3 (Fall 1983): 415-59, esp. 425, 433.

[20] Wayne A. Rebhorn, "The Crisis of the Aristocracy in *Julius Caesar,*" *RenQ* 43, 1 (Spring 1990): 75-111, 81.

[21] For discussion, see Timothy Hampton, *Writing from History: The Rhetoric of Exemplarity in Renaissance Literature* (Ithaca: Cornell Univ. Press, 1990), pp. 198-236.

22 For discussion, see Patterson, pp. 71-92.

23 Hampton, pp. 210-4; Patterson, pp. 83-90.

24 Montrose, "'The Place of a Brother,'" p. 46.

25 On the importance of the noble manor to the aristocratic ethical ideal, see Don E. Wayne, *Penshurst: The Semiotics of Place and the Poetics of History* (Madison: Univ. of Wisconsin Press, 1984).

26 Montrose, "Of Gentlemen and Shepherds," p. 432.

27 Montrose, "Of Gentlemen and Shepherds," p. 427.

28 Montrose, "Of Gentlemen and Shepherds," pp. 428-32; Patterson, pp. 39-46.

29 Patterson, p. 41.

30 For discussion of the cultural importance of the meal as a marker of "serviceable" authority in the Renaissance, see Michael Schoenfeldt, "'The Mysteries of Manners, Armes, and Arts': 'Inviting a Friend to Supper' and 'To Penshurst,'" in *"The Muses CommonWeale": Poetry and Politics in the Seventeenth Century,* ed. Claude J. Summers and Ted-Larry Pebworth (Columbia: Univ. of Missouri Press, 1988), pp. 62-79.

31 Stone, pp. 68, 72, 84.

32 The promise of increased wages for Corin recalls the 500 crowns Adam has saved under Sir Rowland (II.iii.38). Although Orlando goes on to extol Adam's virtue as "the constant service of the antique world, / When service sweat for duty, not for meed!" (lines 57-8), we see that dutiful service rightfully expects proper compensation.

33 Thomas Lodge, *Rosalynde,* in *As You Like It* (A New Variorum Edition), ed. Howard H. Furness (Philadelphia, 1890), p. 338; spelling slightly modernized.

34 Judy Z. Kronenfeld, "Social Rank and the Pastoral Ideals of *As You Like It,*" *SQ* 29, 3 (Summer 1978): 333-48, 344.

35 Kronenfeld, pp. 345, 344.

36 Quoted in Montrose, "Of Gentlemen and Shepherds," p. 435.

37 Edmund Spenser, *The Shepheardes Calender,* "September" (lines 137-9), in *Poetical Works,* ed. J. C. Smith and E. de Selincourt (Oxford: Oxford Univ. Press, 1970), p. 453.

38 Montrose, "Of Gentlemen and Shepherds," pp. 435-6.

39 Montrose, "Of Gentlemen and Shepherds," pp. 438-44, 426, 431.

40 Montrose first makes this point in "'Eliza, Queene of shepheardes,' and the Pastoral of Power," *ELR* 10, 2 (Spring 1980): 153-82, 154.

41 Montrose, "Of Gentlemen and Shepherds," pp. 446-7.

42 Montrose, "Of Gentlemen and Shepherds," p. 427; for broader discussion, see Kevin Sharpe, *Politics and Ideas in Early Stuart England* (London: Pinter, 1989), esp. chaps. 1-2, 6, 10.

43 Quoted in Kronenfeld, p. 334.

44 Montrose, "Of Gentlemen and Shepherds," pp. 427, 432; my emphases.

45 For discussion of the promise of this kind of "rhetorical" criticism, see Liu, p. 756.

46 Michel Foucault, *The Archaeology of Knowledge,* trans. A. M. Sheridan-Smith (New York: Pantheon Books, 1972), p. 122.

Source: "The Political Conscious of Shakespeare's *As You Like It,*" in *Studies in English Literature: 1500-1900,* Vol. 36, No. 2, Spring, 1996, pp. 373-95.

Compounding *"Errors"*

T. G. Bishop, *Case Western Reserve University*

The sea, in fact, is that state of barbaric vagueness
and disorder out of which civilisation has emerged,
and into which, unless saved by the effort of gods
and men, it is always liable to relapse.

W. H. Auden

Let it suffice that we have not arrived at a wall, but
at interminable oceans.

Emerson

The aim of this chapter is to argue that Shakespeare's
Comedy of Errors provides us with an explicitly germi-
nal model of his dramatic practice at once in its narrative, poetic and social dimensions, and that the conclusion of the work turns to the dramatic dynamic of wonder
in order to enact Shakespeare's own recognition of his
practice. In order to approach this intricate nexus, we
must first consider the larger question of the institution
for and out of which Shakespeare wrote, to suggest how
he responded to changes in English society and culture
by reframing the question of the work that narrative
does, in effect retroping old plots in the new context of
the professional theatre. Shakespeare's work is in this
way informed by a revisionary conservatism by which
he self-consciously subjects the stories he inherits to
analysis and critique in order to regenerate them for
present uses. Apparently exiled from the plays, wonder
returns in the end to recoup and transfigure the scattered fragments in a reunion that speaks also to the
function of dramatic narrative in Shakespeare's hands.
The hyperbolic and overdetermined spectacle of wonder thus invoked becomes a site of plenitude informed
in its forcefulness by the resistance of the very skepticism it has had to overcome.

I

Complex factors determine the transition from late
medieval to Elizabethan drama.[1] We need to note first
some significant shifts in the character of performance as a social occasion. The medieval plays . .
. emerge from a community-based, large-scale organization of a recurrent and participatory nature. They
are part of a perennial festival where plans are laid
and expenses defrayed collectively through guilds and
other associations. A substantial part of the purpose
and pleasure of this theatre is likewise communal:
there is a common involvement in a common project
that aims to expound a common knowledge.[2] Though
economic motives could nerve the festivals as potential sources of trade and prestige, they were not
principally commercial ventures. Indeed, the large

cost of mounting them at a time of economic difficulty for many late sixteenth-century towns may have
contributed to their disappearance.[3]

While the influence of the medieval festival plays on
aspects of Elizabethan drama has been disputed, it is
clear that the overall shapes of the two institutions and
of their characteristic products are very different. The
medieval plays are carefully attuned to their particular
institutional context, and hence too specialized to provide a model of dramatic form flexible enough for a
secular, professional theatre. Although Emrys Jones,
for instance, has argued cogently for some similarities
in structure, such as between the Passion of Christ and
the baiting of Gloucester in Shakespeare's *Henry VI
Part Two,* even such striking parallels are largely a
question of local patterns of action rather than of a
general indebtedness in conception.[4]

The institution of the professional acting company,
its attachment to specific patrons, and the eventual
settlement of at least some companies in permanent,
continuously running theatre venues in the later sixteenth century determined a new shape for the social
occasion of performance. At these explicitly commercial concerns, audiences pay the performers not
the project. Performances, even before the monarch,
are in an important way services for customers, and
the nature and quality of the performance impinges
not on the honor of a community, but on the commercial viability of the company and the livelihoods
of its members. The audience need have no quotid-
ian, community-based relation to the actors on which
to draw. Relations "across the footlights" are much
more a nonce affair, to a great extent limited to the
professional occasion itself, and the openness of these
relations to improvisation may well form part of the
matter of the play. "Novelty" of both story and occasion becomes an important element in commercial
success, and accordingly the public theatres of the
late sixteenth century produce and experiment with
new plays at a prodigious rate: as high as twenty new
plays a year in an uninterrupted season, or about one
every two weeks.[5]

The theatre thus occupied a very different place within
the civic life of Elizabethan London from the great
five- and seven-day celebrations recorded intermittently
but consistently there from the late twelfth century.[6]
The Elizabethan public theatre was a focus for *ad hoc*
outings and celebration by individuals or small groups
(apprentices, law students, families) seeking temporary

relief from everyday duties. It could be enjoyed at any time it was open, and was set up to answer, within certain limits, a steady demand. While much of the theatrical calendar was still hitched to traditional time-tables (such as the Lenten inhibitions or the Christmas festivals), there was no longer any discernible shaping connection between the ritual life of the community and its theatrical entertainments.[7] What was offered was a much more local transaction, which might make use of older forms of festivity and communality, but confined their invocation to the space of the "wooden O" and the duration of the performance. Barring disruptions by plague, riot, or political upheaval (though these were common enough), the public theatres could expect to be open for business continuously for long periods, necessitating a constant and renewable appeal to a public who came by choice and on no common timetable. The collective exploration of traditional forms of common life could have only a very limited role in this theatre. *Twelfth Night,* for instance, might be played on its name date or else when you would, since nothing in the play ties it to a particular day. What features survive in it from the calendar association are better understood as tropes for psychological and social processes in general than as specific to a particular ceremonial order. For a certain fee, the ludic privileges of a mobilized Epiphany can be enjoyed at any time of year. This is a key liberation for the full-time professional theatre, but the emancipation also makes the company dependent on securing the audience's assent to the performance and its occasion in ways that become increasingly self-conscious. Medieval plays might roar and browbeat their audiences into silence. The gambits of Elizabethan Prologue and Epilogue, with their often nervous rhetoric of placation and apology and their language of bonds, amends, and amity, suggest a very different relation.

But it is not only the changed lineaments of the social occasion that alter the kinds of plays the Elizabethan theatre nurtures. In the cycle-plays, the performed action and its recognitions are framed by the semiotic complex of the Incarnation and the Eucharist within the institution of the Church. A gesture thither always closes down the potential for either play or skepticism, as none of these authorities can be effectively challenged. Hence in the most experimental or testing plays of this tradition, a gap or rift may open up between the central theological enactment and the elaboration or parody attached to it. In the Wakefield *Secunda Pastorum,* famous for its social protest and gameful pre-plot of the stolen sheep, this disarticulation is particularly plain. As long as the authority of the structuring institutions remains unimpeachable, such rifting cannot itself be addressed in the play. It remains a symptom rather than a topic.

The sixteenth century, however, saw the appearance and development of an increasingly powerful and in-stitutionalized current of what we might now call "cultural criticism." The reformist polemicists against the theatre have often been noted, yet the wider ramifications of the succession of spokesmen, from Gosson and Stubbes to Prynne, have been less considered. Their importance lies as much in how they indicate the progressive factionalizing of English culture at large as in their specific raillery against the playhouses. Such iconoclasm was not confined to anti-theatrical polemic; its wide range suggests the extent to which skepticism was becoming a posture generally available, as much to playwrights as to their opponents, as Christopher Marlowe's turbulent example shows. What we see emerging for the first time is an extensive cultural dialectic of critique and affirmation, much more fraught and much more concerned to entrench itself in particular institutions than heretofore.[8]

This does not mean that older, communal functions entirely disappeared. Though it is obvious that the cycle-plays are not an appropriate formal vehicle for the new theatre, which must find pleasures more "packageable" for an increasingly various economic, social, and intellectual order, it does not follow that their function of exploring the nature and modes of collective self-understanding disappeared. A conservative and tradition-minded society, such as Renaissance England largely was, does not lightly discard social forms and ceremonial structures that have served it well, even in the face of critique. With a playwright of socially conservative preferences, as Shakespeare by and large was, the older uses of performance might re-emerge grafted onto or articulated through another dramatic structure—as happens with holiday customs in *Twelfth Night.* C. L. Barber, for one, argued that the rhythms and forms of traditional popular festivity underlie a great deal of Shakespeare's work in comedy, and that these plays made use of the elements and energies of old holiday, both in the construction of the narrative on stage and in evoking a para-ritual ambience for the contemporary audience. Barber's work showed remarkably clearly the process of co-optation that adapted old communal traditions to new dramatic occasions, and this transition reflects with unusual clarity and detail aspects of the more general movement away from a medieval towards a modern order in sixteenth-century England.[9]

That Barber's central subject was inevitably Shakespeare tells us something in particular about the latter's attitude to older forms of social celebration and regulation. Unlike the more radical voices either of Stephen Gosson or Ben Jonson—both playwrights and later polemicists against the public theatre from political persuasions we might describe as Reformist and Royalist respectively—Shakespeare's brand of conservatism did not seek to root out the cultural forms of the past in order to assert its own claims. It preferred to absorb them, imagining its relation to the past not as polemic opposition but as metaphor and metamorphosis. Such a position is in general nativist rather than international, evolutionary rather than revolutionary. In some ways it is like Sir Edward Coke's insistence that the common law was a peculiar institution and handed down "immemorial customs" *toto divisos orbe Brittannos*. A theatre emerging from such a pragmatically conservative stance does not confront its audience, or even seek to settle with it as an independent contracting party, as Jonson does in inducting *Bartholomew Fair*. Wherever such a theatre goes, like the Chorus in *Henry V*, it wishes to secure the community's collective assent and imaginative implication first. It seeks to make the story and the theatrical occasion theirs for the telling.

We should consider closely what it means to assert that Shakespeare was conservative in this way, and examine the roots and lineaments of this conservatism and its implications for dramatic structures answering his commercial and professional needs. Some possible misunderstandings can be headed off at once by asserting that to be conservative in this sense is to be like neither Spenser nor Jonson. Along with Shakespeare, both of these figures were staunch supporters of the English monarchy, and in that sense "conservative" as we might see the term. But that is hardly an Elizabethan political position: it is more like the point at which Elizabethan (and Jacobean) politics begins. It should be emphasized that there were no significant opponents of monarchy in England in this period, and that such opponents of the current monarch as there were—basically radical Catholics—were staunchly in favor of monarchy as such and themselves divided as to how far they should go in opposing Elizabeth and James. Even the organizers of rebellions and risings were hardly calling for the destruction of monarchy as a basis for civil order: the traditional order was most often what they saw as under threat when they rose. Though what might be called the "preconditions" for the much more radical political ferment of forty years later were perhaps present, it would be mistaken to read those developments back too far as "oppositional" alternatives.

On the other hand, both Spenser and Jonson *were* strongly in favor of various kinds of "reform" in the relations between government and people. Spenser's association with the more ardent Protestant reformers not infrequently brought him into conflict with Elizabethan arrangements, and the kind of apocalypticism displayed in Book One of *The Faerie Queene,* even if oriented towards restoration of the "true Church," required a radical break with much of the recent past which Elizabeth for one was reluctant to make. Jonson, though decidedly of the other religious party and uncomfortable with Spenserian fervencies, also supported a more or less radical revision of the political terms of government towards an imperial profile and away from the more delicate politics of equilibrium and consensus which Elizabeth, along with her ministers, had managed for so long. Though the imperial impulse had been gathering for some time in English politics and law and was by no means a Jacobean invention, it emerged into full articulation with James, and Jonson strongly endorsed it. Recent political criticism of Shakespeare has sometimes overlooked the fact that to be politically "avant-garde" in both Church and State matters in the period meant embracing either Puritanism or Absolutism. The latter stances could also themselves agree in welcoming the image of a strong central figure, as was the case with Prince Henry. At least in the period from 1590 to 1610, "radical" English aesthetics and politics were as often moving towards the imperial monarchy as away from it.

If modern political categories will not help to define Shakespeare as an Elizabethan "conservative," one way of broaching the question is to reflect on the fact—to some extent unusual among his peers—of Shakespeare's lifelong maintenance of relations with the community of his birth. Unsatisfactory though his biographical records are, they are insistently traversed by the thread of Stratford-on-Avon and Shakespeare's concern with the position of his family there. Emphasis on his links with the milieu and politics of the court has tended to obscure this, yet it gives us significant information about Shakespeare's underlying sense of his filiations and community.[10] Also of some significance here may be that Shakespeare was never initiated into the "second home" at the universities, which so often eclipsed the natal community with a prestige language and a sense of the common fellowship of learning. Again, the contrast with Jonson is instructive. There is no sign that Shakespeare, unlike Jonson, sought to overcome his scholarly "deficit" or surmount his humble origins either by prodigious application to learning or by small revisions of name and family history, and this despite the ridicule his lack of "nurture" seems to have cost him at various hands, most notoriously Robert Greene's.[11] But though important aspects of Shakespeare's work remain close to the pattern of rural and small-town life, this does not mean he was not acutely aware of the challenge presented, for instance, by Stubbes's critique of rural summer celebrations. The task was to discern whether and how older functions could be retained, even if performed by new instruments. Coke's attitude is again instructive: he claimed that English judges found within the customary structures of the common law what was necessary to the present case. They did not alter the law in so doing: they revealed more of it, still and always at work.[12]

The idea or pattern of cultural activity embraced by such a view of the world is one that does not insist on radical separation from its community or its own history. Where patterns of communal recognition and reflection such as the cycle-plays disappeared, the emerging professional troupes might be inserted on occasion into their room. A discontinuity of formal and logistic organization need not necessitate one at the level of communal function, and while Chester and York clung stoutly to their traditional plays, and Coventry kept up its cycle into Shakespeare's life-time and subsequently attempted to replace it with a comparable civic drama, other communities might have seen the business more as a matter of "farming out" a community function previously, as it were, performed "in-house."[13] Such a tactic preserves what can be preserved and adapts to a new form or occasion those elements that cannot in a process of impro-visatory adjustment.

There survives one remarkable account tending to confirm that this is more or less what at least some communities did. In 1639 at the age of 75—which makes him Shakespeare's exact contemporary—Ralph Willis included a childhood reminiscence of the stage in his penitential treatise, *Mount Tabor*. Willis's story is well-known but deserves quotation in full:

> In the city of Gloucester the manner is (as I think it is in other like corporations) that when the players of enterludes come to towne, they first attend the Mayor to enforme him what noble-mans servants they are, and so to get a licence for their publike playing; and if the Mayor like the actors, or would shew respect to their lord and master, he appoints them to play their first play before himself and the Aldermen and Common Counsel of the city; and that is called the Mayor's play, where every one that will comes in without money, the Mayor giving the players a reward as he thinks fit to shew respect unto them. At such a play, my father took me with him and made me stand betweene his leggs, as he sate upon one of the benches where wee saw and heard very well. The play was called, *The Cradle of Security*, wherin was personated a king or some great prince with his courtiers of several kinds, amongst which three ladies were in speciall grace with him; and they keeping him in delights and pleasures, drew him from his graver counsellors, hearing of sermons, and listening to good counsell, and admonitions, that in the end they got him to lie down in a cradle upon the stage, where these three ladies joyning in a sweet song rocked him asleep, that he snorted againe, and in the mean time closely conveyed under the cloaths where withall he was covered, a vizard like a swine's snout upon his face, with three wire chains fastened thereunto, the other three end wherof being holden severally by those ladies, who fall to singing againe, and then discovered his face, that the spectators might see how they had transformed him, going on with their singing.

> Whilst all this was acting, there came forth of another doore at the farthest end of the stage two old men, the one in blew with a serjeant-at-armes mace on his shoulder, the other in red with a drawn sword in his hand and leaning with the other hand

upon the others shoulder; and so they two went along in a soft pace round about by the skirt of the stage, till at last they came to the cradle, when all the court was in greatest jollity; and then the foremost old man with his mace stroke a fearful blow upon the cradle, whereat all the courtiers, with the three ladies and the vizard, all vanished; and the desolate prince starting up bare-faced and finding himself thus sent for to judgment, made a lamentable complaint of his miserable case, and so was carried away by wicked spirits. . . .

> This sight tooke such impression in me that, when I came towards mans estate, it was as fresh in my memory as if I had seen it newly acted.[14]

Willis's recollection shows quite clearly the relation between the professional players and the community they play for, aside from its demonstration of the last-ing impact dramatic images could have on the Eliza-bethan spectator, even from what seems to us so bare-bones a piece as *The Cradle of Security*. The perfor-mance is from the first implicated in the hierarchical network of social life, with its mutual privileges and duties. The troupe of actors is both a professional or-ganization and a roving limb of the nobleman who sponsors them: the Mayor has his choice which of these aspects he will regard. For him to sponsor "the Mayor's play" is to assert his pre-eminence, but also to fulfill his duty to promote the honor and well-being of the commonality, presumably at his own expense. To at-tend the play is to acknowledge in return both of these gestures. The play in turn moralizes on the duties and dangers of high place and its failure in vivid, eschatological images, and thus also participates in glossing its occasion. Its appropriateness is complete even down to its suspicious treatment of the female figures elsewhere excluded from Willis's recollection of his civic and personal fathers.

Though Gloucester was larger than Stratford-on-Avon, it seems fair to assume this is the kind of thing which the documented visits to that town of the professional troupes of actors in 1583-4 and 1586-7 involved, and such a context is most likely to have been that in which Shakespeare first encountered the Elizabethan theatre.[15] It is in accord with such a view that he depicts players when he comes to write: his troupes, professional or scratch, are very much aware of the social dimension of their work. Though they tend to be overeager, naive or insufficiently *au fait* with the complexity of their moment (whether the poisoned milieu of *Hamlet* or the aristocratic churlishness of *Love's Labours Lost*), they are always conceived as absorbing into themselves the ambient energies of the occasion they play to. What distinguishes their shortcomings from the work of the Lord Chamberlain's Men is not only a difference in technical skill, but the latter's added resources of de-liberate critique to add to those of fellowship and ser-vice in its repertoire of stances.

II

One recent critic who has sought to address the Elizabethan theatre in this way as an active site of cultural reflection in the moment of performance is Louis A. Montrose. Seeking what he calls "a Shakespearean anthropology," Montrose surveys sixteenth-century English history, emphasizing a galloping disequilibrium and a burgeoning anxiety among a bourgeoisie increasingly unsure of its bearings. From this, Montrose proposes that the Elizabethan theatre became a self-conscious site of surrogate ritual in a world whose reassuring solidity of symbolic practice was being eroded: "I am suggesting . . . that the public theatre absorbs some vital functions of ritual within Shakespeare's society. These functions are not adequately performed by more central and officially sanctioned institutions, and are in some ways inimical to them."[16] This is an exhilarating vista, yet so much remains unspoken as to give one pause. The assertion that Shakespeare's theatre was a species of collective ritual is by no means a new one, going back as it does at least to Francis Fergusson's attempt to assimilate *Hamlet* to a model of Sophoclean drama derived from the Cambridge anthropologists, a claim later refashioned by O. B. Hardison with Christian ritual as the model.[17] The difficulty here is to specify in what the ritual aspect inheres and how it is addressed and understood by the playwright and taken up by the audience. In both Ferguson and Hardison, "ritual" remains in some sense archeological, an inherited rather than a meditated condition. In Montrose's view, its invocation seems a kind of secret or unconscious gesture in response to an equally unformulable discomfort with established religion. At the same time, the underlying assumption about the expressive or cathartic inadequacies of Elizabethan religion is highly speculative: inadequate for whom? one is entitled to ask, and how do we know? Those who objected most vociferously to the established religious order tended to be those who also strongly denounced the theatre. Though it is certainly true that Shakespeare's plays "present exemplary fictions in which human characters are confronted by change within the self, the family, the body politic, the cosmos," it is hard to see this as a historically specific assertion about Elizabethan drama: it does just as well for Euripides, Goethe, Chekhov, or even Brecht.[18]

Montrose's remarks are the more frustrating because he is surely right about Shakespeare's attentiveness to the ritual aspects of the dramatic language and action he inherits, though whether the same description will do for Greene or Jonson (i.e. whether it is really a general condition of Elizabethan drama) is another question. A powerful impulse to draw on the magical and world-shaping energies of ritual does inhabit Shakespeare's plays. But if ritual informs Shakespeare's theatre, it is less because of some non-specific malaise in the churchgoing public that the theatre struggles to identify and physic, and more through a quite specific response to the forms of story and dramatic occasion it inherits. The principal place we should look to establish the historicity of a work such as a play is less to a rather nebulous history of the culture at large, and rather to the textures of the work itself understood as the mediated and meditated product of histories at once formal, institutional, social, and vocational. To reduce any one of these to an epiphenomenon of another is to move away from a full appreciation of the work's history and "historicity" rather than towards it.[19] In the current instance, neither the assertion of O. B. Hardison that "continuity" characterizes the relation between medieval ecclesiastical ritual and Shakespearean drama nor Montrose's stress on "the essential feature of discontinuity" will really do. It is the intertwining of retention and transformation that is the fullest measure of Shakespeare's historical consciousness. Analysis needs to unfold where this process of adaptation is chiefly accomplished: where continuity and discontinuity confront each other in the metamorphic absorption and troping of older modes of dramatic story into newer ones.

The Eucharistic fusion of word and matter that underlies the dramaturgy of the cycles is a crucial instance of how Shakespeare folds received cultural schemas into his theatre's transformed task. There can be no doubt that the power of this ritual event remained active in Elizabethan society. The very persistence of intense controversy around it testifies to that. As they are absorbed into Shakespearean drama, these struggles over the central symbol of the Christian order re-emerge, linked to questions at once of the continuity of English historical experience and of the performance of that experience on stage. This is particularly explicit in *Richard II*, where the central action articulates a struggle between the desire to affirm the miraculous corporeality of sacramental kingship (tied directly to the actor's performance of Richard in and on his body) and a counter-desire to drain the action of that very mystique in favor of a roughcut and contingent pragmatism of office and role. The identification of workable schemas to interpret the body's action becomes a primary goal, but the play entertains the option of a sacramental solution only as a dream whose fullness, like Gaunt's health, is ebbing almost from before the outset. That Gaunt refers to the Incarnation while himself dying, even as the actor playing him is faced with the daunting technical task of performing the famous long aria to "this sceptered isle," indicates the extent to which the political and the dramaturgical are intertwined through the question of "embodiment." Old symbol and new context, nostalgia and critique, icon and actor self-consciously confront one another. All through Shakespeare's career, questions of "embodiment" framed in relation to the sacramental model are central to his thinking-through of the meaning of theatrical performance. But while a deep desire for the tangibility of the body is pervasive, so also is a sense of the difficulty of grasping such a moment. What was merely dichotomy in the *Secunda Pastorum* has become a restive dialectic.[20]

In putting the issue this way, I have in mind a discussion of the self-consciousness of fictive form as representation, in which John Hollander cites the remark of Friedrich Schlegel that "In all its descriptions, this poetry should describe itself, and always be simultaneously poetry and the poetry of poetry." Hollander comments that "a closely guarded poetic secret peers out of the last clause. . . . [which] hides a more powerful assertion—not 'and' but '*because.*'"[21] We could restate and extend this point here by proposing that poetry expresses its historical conditions most fully, since it also there expresses how it does and does not understand them, where it renders those conditions available to itself in deliberate inflection. To read a poem as an act of historical awareness is to attempt to chart its successes and failures in the struggle for consciousness of its own ways of knowing the world in and through itself.[22]

In this dialectic of affirmation and critique in Shakespeare's theatre, the dynamic of wonder becomes crucial. Wonder as a conscious crisis of the integrity of knowledge unfolds at just the point where, according to Schlegel and Hollander, the characteristically poetic is to be sought, so that the self-consciousness characteristic of this emotion generates precisely a double orientation on "poetry and the poetry of poetry." In Shakespeare's work, the outbreak of wonder registers interplay and negotiation between simultaneous desires for continuity and discontinuity, between the impulse to successful solution and the forcefulness of a critique that resists easy satisfaction. In tragedy, wonder's turbulent power stems directly from the force that has destroyed the protagonists and their world, even as it also guarantees the audience's relative protection from that force by the saving grace of figuration. In comedy, even more crucially, wonder absorbs into itself the resistance of skepticism, and its force measures that resistance even as the latter is overcome and sublated. Resistance braces the desire to affirm surviving powers of recognition and articulation, and in particular, the reconstruction and survival of the institutions of continuity, chief among them marriage. A variable tempering of wonder and skepticism against one another across different plays marks out a continuum in Shakespeare's comic practice, along which critical argument has in turn arrayed itself.

The language of doubling and twinning which haunts the instabilities of wonder . . . appears specifically in Shakespeare's plays at the level of plotting in his recurrent preoccupation with stories of twins—including the pretend twins of *Much Ado about Nothing,* the anti-twins Edgar and Edmund, and those twin-like

abstractions Art and Nature in *The Winter's Tale.* What is at stake here is the poetic recognition of the interest the plays and their audiences have in the dialectical mirroring of continuity and discontinuity in one another as motives for theatrical representation. In most cases, the end of the play stages a critical confrontation between these character pairs that is framed by and produces wonder.

In what follows, I will argue that scenes of wondrous speculation, present from the first, articulate in this way much of Shakespeare's concern with the theatre as poetic and social event, and that these scenes focus a particularly Shakespearean self-consciousness in language and action. Careful reading can demonstrate in what way they meditate on continuity as their chief aspiration, one whose difficulty in turn gauges their historical consciousness. In particular these plays use the dynamic of wonder to think through their impulse to absorb and adapt their own cultural history, to be "at once theatre and the theatre of theatre."

III

When Shakespeare chose to frame Plautus' play of the twins of Epidamnum with the venerable romance of the shipwrecked family, he did more than merely complicate the plot: he immeasurably enlarged the scope of the whole dramatic structure. Modern critics have been quick to see the paired stories of the father and his sons as segregated by style or genre or some other consideration, but fixing overrigid boundaries between "frame story" and the central action tends to obscure the links between them in a way the play explicitly refuses.[23] The central action and concern of the opening scene is the power of Egeon's narrative to create a community of mutual interest, even in the face of political and social antagonism. The question of what narrative is *for* is before us from the outset, and the opening tableau sets forth large images of the play's stakes which are then worked out in more elaborate detail through the Plautine material. By fusing Plautus' rambunctious plot with the life-and-death romance of Egeon's quest, and both with allusions to St. Paul (as though Plautus and Paulus were anagrammatic twins), Shakespeare's hybrid tests their respective modes of narration, as though asking "Which kind of story, if any, can help us stave off death?"[24]

This is a weighty question, perhaps too much so for such a slight piece. Yet it is the play's own initial question. Consider the opening tableau. A bound prisoner stands before his judge and asks—for mercy? On the contrary—he asks only for a speedy death:

> Proceed, Solinus, to procure my fall
> And by the doom of death, end woes and all.
>
> (I.i.1-2)

The action, it seems, will be over before it has even begun; the play threatens to contract itself into the few moments needed to utter the sentence and chop off the head. Such an end seems altogether too forbidding and abrupt. Its absoluteness, the anonymity of the speaker, his "fall" with its "doom of death," hint at the image of a more general or final "proceeding" and judgment. His judge continues these intimations in speaking of his Syracusan counterpart whose victims:

> Wanting guilders to redeem their lives
> Have sealed his rigorous statutes with their
> blood. . . .
>
> (I.i.8-9)

These are hints only, but they evoke a complex of images and notions about time, death, and judgment familiar enough to an Elizabethan audience and suggest, without being too explicit about it, that the overall resolution will address some sort of "redemption." We seem to be engaging in a kind of theological oneupmanship on Plautus here. Roman comedy being the work of pagans, it is hardly surprising that such a vocabulary was unavailable to it. But such a play in a Christian society claims it sees further into the life—and death—of things.

These images are unusually stark for opening a comedy, and before their fatality Egeon seems already to have quailed. Duke Solinus for one seems to want the prisoner to begin the play differently. He responds not to Egeon's call for death, but to some imagined plea for mercy: "Merchant of Syracusa, plead no more. / I am not partial to infringe our laws" (I.i.3-4). And though playing stern, he deliberately invites Egeon to re-forge just the ties of sympathy to the community at large that the old man seems most eager to break off. All through the scene, Solinus forces Egeon to return to his story, where Egeon is eager to abridge it, to take it as read. "Gather the sequel by what went before," he insists, as though it were all a self-evident matter of mere logic. Egeon wants to tell us that the world is always fatal, nature and time the twin wheels of a slow, small grinding. There is no point in recounting it all over again: the sentence reaches its period, the great axe falls. That's all there is to it.

Solinus shares this much with Egeon: for him too syntax is an absolute ruler: "passed sentence may not be recalled / But to our honour's great disparagement." Yet Egeon's despair goes deeper and links itself to the general process of time and the bell. Life cures us of itself:

> Yet this my comfort, when your words are
> done,
> My woes end likewise with the evening sun.
>
> (I.i.26-7)

By making him tell the whole tale over, Solinus not only puts off the end Egeon seeks, he works to repair the very social connections Egeon wishes to sunder. Inspired to pity, if not fear, Solinus throws Egeon back on the community for rescue. His task, an almost parabolic one, is to find a redeemer among "all the friends thou hast in Ephesus." This is not to Egeon's liking and he views it as merely one more futile episode in a narrative whose end he has long since longed for: "Hopeless and helpless doth Egeon wend / But to procrastinate his lifeless end." He is a figure of Despair: for him all time is drained of vitality, all story points only deathwards. "Lifeless" is as much an epithet of the speaker as of his expected end.

Does all story, all time uncover only an image of death? Must the rigorous logic of cause and effect lead us to submit to an Iron Law, not "partial to infringement," that stands grimly behind narrative? When is an end not an End? Solinus' "limit" puts these questions before us, so that whenever in the subsequent action we are told what time it is—and we are so insistently—we may recall Egeon's quest. Yet a curious jingle of phonemes all through the course of Egeon's lamentable narrative tells a more lively, lucky "undertale" than their speaker knows. A quartet of terms chimes an arbitrary, serendipitous consonance in the world which brings "hope" and "help" to make "hap" at last "happy."[25] This is not logic. On the contrary, these doublings and echoes are silly happenstance, a gratuitous accident of language. Yet their tale outweighs Egeon's in the end, and from their very plasticity Shakespeare will generate a marvelous world of plenitude, of strange and happy miracle.

Meanwhile, the vision of time as an inhuman controlling law ticking away on its ineluctable path is not confined to the first scene. Such a strict sense of time is taken into the play as an integral part of the basic narrative apparatus of classical comedy. T. W. Baldwin argues that this feature is derived specifically less from *Menaechmi* than from Shakespeare's whole understanding of classical comedy: "Shakespeare already knew these unities; he did not learn them from *Menaechmi;* at least, not at this time."[26] Indeed, the "limit of this day" is so integral to the design of the Antipholus section of the play that its deep connection to the opening scene is often overlooked. Narratively, and to some extent thematically, Egeon's story and that of his sons are segregated, but both put in play a conception of time as one-dimensional, an inflexible linear process in which Death follows Judgment as verb follows subject as two o'clock follows one.

Time as an irreversible sequence of effects organizes both events and conversation for much of the play. As the breakneck, mechanical rhythm of farce comes to orchestrate the action, the intentions of the characters seem more and more to lag behind the onward sweep of the minute hand. From Antipholus of Syracuse's first conversation with a Merchant who rushes off to a business lunch, it is clear that Ephesus keeps as strict a clock as it does a law-court. As with Egeon, though in a less desperate key, time is money, and money is life. The secular, commercial community is bound to time as its vital, regulatory engine. But with Ephesian Dromio's first entrance the mortal clock starts to accelerate and takes on a striking inhumanity:

> Returned so soon! Rather approached too late.
> The capon burns, the pig falls from the spit;
> The clock hath strucken twelve upon the bell;
> My mistress made it one upon my cheek.
> She is so hot because the meat is cold;
> The meat is cold because you come not home;
> You come not home because you have no
>   stomach;
> You have no stomach having broke your fast.
> But we, that know what 'tis to fast and pray,
> Are penitent for your default today.
>   (I.ii.43-52)

Dromio's lines hunt temporal process back along a line of causally related points which has as its latest term the infliction of violence upon him. The traditional vulnerability of the clown's body to attack is here the result of living at the mercy of a rigorous time which servant Dromio's logic maps out rhetorically line by line. Dromio's very name has both the aspect of breakneck speed and linear movement: it means "one who runs," "one who races."[27]

Clowns are always in danger of becoming sorry cogs in a mechanistic universe under whose laws they suffered long before Newton. In *Errors,* the life of the body generally is governed by a remorseless temporal violence. The body, thinks Dromio, itself ties one to time: "Methinks your maw, like mine, should be your clock" (I.ii.66), and later, in a pathetic outburst, this same Dromio sums up his whole life as a series of moments struck into his body one by one:

> I have served him from the hour of my nativity to this instant, and have nothing for my service but blows. When I am cold, he heats me with beating; when I am warm, he cools me with beating. I am waked with it when I sleep, raised with it when I sit, driven out of doors with it when I go from home, welcomed home with it when I return; nay, I bear it on my shoulders, as a beggar wont her brat; and, I think, when he hath lamed me, I shall beg with it from door to door. (IV.iv.29-40)

The body of a Dromio is an object at the mercy of physical laws, like the football one compares himself to (II.i.83). Narration for him is always only one step away from a beating if he is "out of season": "Ay, ay, he told his mind upon mine ear" (II.i.48). In this far-

cical view of things, time, money and violence link up in every "striking" of the bell. Each new event "tells," as a bell, a coin, a blow, consequent on its forebear with clarity and remorseless precision.

Several passages of the play that otherwise seem digressive or excrescent are related to this thematic and metadramatic preoccupation with "telling" time. During one of their periodic interludes, the Syracusan pair conduct a peculiar conversation about the baldness of Father Time. Antipholus observes that "there's a time for all things." Dromio denies this by what might be called his First Law of Time: "There's no time for a man to recover his hair that grows bald by nature" (II.ii.71). The somewhat strained banter that follows includes references to legal remedies for time's trespass and to "the world's end," which Antipholus calls "a bald conclusion." The comic routine, itself only "marking time" in the action, puts before us again a temporal order which goes in one direction only: Egeon's deadly time progressively stripping its hapless, hairless victims.

The play's principal dramatic image for narrative as an expression of the First Law of Time, an image that comes to dominate both action and language, is the line. We could plot the whole play as a set of vectors on a street map of Ephesus, where each intersection would mark a staged incident. This linearity reflects and reflects on the nature of narrative generally. Critical discussions of narrative have always used linear imagery—it seems to be a primary human way of conceiving time—but the real witchcraft of Ephesus seems to lie in the way this narrative design keeps incarnating itself everywhere, coming alive from page to prop-box in the lines, ropes, chains, whips, and snares that gradually entangle and constrict the characters. The opening image of the play is of a man bound for death, and rope-bonds thence proliferate. Dromio's tale of being struck because of a spitted pig is told insistently in serried lines. The verse-writing throughout includes many different kinds of "lines" and line patterns, more than is usual in Shakespeare. Alexandrines, fourteeners, quatrains, couplets, stichomythia ("line-story"), all make their appearance. This may have to do with the "earliness" of the play, but it also fits its preoccupation with its own method of story-telling. "What kind of story gets told in lines?" seems the implied question.

Egeon's opening narrative has begun the process of imagining lines. Maplike, it encourages us to chart the movements of the family across the sea: he ships from Syracuse to Epidamnum, she follows, they return. It is these same lines that he and his son are now attempting to trace or decipher, a linear trajectory forcibly "splitted" when the wooden line to which the family was literally bound—the "small, spare mast"—hit the rock.[28] Shipwrecks are everywhere in romances, but the detail of that splitting mast, original with Shakespeare's version, turns out to be much more than variation on a cliché. It is an image integrally bound up with the poetics of narrative in the play. And it may have an even deeper metadramatic dimension. Lars Engle points out that the mast to which the family are bound is also a secret emblem for the linear design of the action: from end to end the family are strung along their mast in the very order in which they speak: Egeon-Syr. Antipholus-Syr. Dromio-Eph. Dromio-Eph. Antipholus-Emilia.[29]

It is not linear conceptions of time only on which Ephesian social life runs. The whole community is undergirded and held together by a poetics of the line, the bond, the limit, and the boundary. Ephesians are always "drawing the line" at something, as Solinus does when he refuses to "infringe our laws." Each thing, each sign in the city has its appointed place and bonded meaning: the social order, the commercial network, the very town geography are mapped with clarity and semiotic rigor. We dine at the Tiger and host at the Centaur, Adriana stays at the Phoenix, the Courtesan at the Porpentine and so forth. Unfortunately for social and semiotic order alike, walking homophonic puns (or are they metaphors?) are now usurping the names Antipholus and Dromio.

Both the appeal and the danger of a life kept in line are made dramatically concrete in the goldsmith's chain that comes to play such an important part in the action. This prop is first mentioned pat as Adriana is lamenting the fraying of her own bond:

> I know his eye doth homage otherwhere,
> Or else what lets it but it would be here?
> Sister, you know he promised me a chain.
>
> (II.i.104-6)

It is for a moment as though Adriana is speaking of her marriage vow. And when Angelo the goldsmith brings in the prop in question in a later scene, his entrance is likewise carefully timed to crystallize the Syracusan brother's nervous fantasy of a Luciana who,

> Possessed with such a gentle sovereign grace,
> Of such enchanting presence and discourse,
> Hath almost made me traitor to myself.
> But, lest myself be guilty to self-wrong,
> I'll stop mine ears against the mermaid's song.
>   *Enter Angelo with the chain*
>   (III.ii.160-4)[30]

In the succeeding seventeen lines, the word "chain" appears five times, concluding with:

> But this I think, there's no man is so vain
> That would refuse so fair an offered chain.
>
> (III.ii.185-6)

The metaphoric connection between the two offers is sustained by that chain of "chains," just as it comes to represent commercial obligation (and especially the bondage of debt) by a similar verbal obsessiveness in the following scene. There the chain appears no fewer than thirteen times in forty-five lines (IV.i.20-65), interwoven with terms like "bound," "bond," "attach," and with references to the pressing march of time.

The increasing confusion of the plot at this point suggests that the importance of this strand of gold is not only in the various "social bonds" that Adriana, both Antipholuses, and the Goldsmith take it for. The chain also becomes an image of the linkages of assumption and inference which give the play its hilarious, increasingly desperate drive. In short, it is a neatly-imaged "chain of events," comically literal, materializing the audience's own attachment to an increasingly knotty plot. We may even see it as an emblem of metaphor itself, appearing as it does so charged with figurative linkages. As these emblematic and metadramatic functions multiply, this polysemous chain of chains comes to head a class of linear counters in an exploration of acts of linkage for good and ill in the play.

For instance, we might also consider the fortunes of the chain's poor cousin: the "rope's end" for which Ephesian Antipholus sends his Dromio in the middle of the "chain" discussion, and with which he intends to beat his wife. The other Dromio shortly appears sans rope and, when duly berated, offers a bewildered pun on death by the hangman's rope, presumably another "end of the line" joke (IV.i.99). As Antipholus is haled off to prison, this same Dromio is sent to Adriana for bail. When the first Dromio later returns, with his rope, the sequence resumes:

> ANTIPHOLUS To what end did I bid thee hie
>   thee home?
> DROMIO To a rope's end, sir, and to that
>   end am I returned.
> ANTIPHOLUS And to that end, sir, I will
>   welcome you. *Beats Dromio*
>   (IV.iv.15-17)

This rather suggests that Antipholus here whips Dromio with that same rope. But there is yet more. The women appear with the Doctor, and Dromio warns: "Mistress, *respice finem,* respect your end; or rather, the prophecy like the parrot, 'beware the rope's end'" (IV.iv.42-4).[31] The hanging joke is common, but here it seems to have come to life. When he later asserts that "God and the rope-maker bear me witness / That I was sent for nothing but a rope" (IV.iv.91), it looks for a moment as if God has himself turned rope-maker. Pinch decides that "They must be bound, and laid in some dark room" (IV.iv.95).

The notion of "bonds" has thus gradually been extended by the play to cover more and more territory.

Ordinary dead metaphors of being "bound" to do this or go there begin to chafe uncomfortably (e.g. IV.i.3). The play fills with instances of lines, boundaries, and acts of crossing over. The comic scene at the locked gate, for example, turns on a structural boundary that cannot be crossed, across which names themselves start to break their bonds with referents:

> E. DROMIO Maud, Bridget, Marian, Cicely,
> Gillian, Ginn!
>
> S. DROMIO Mome, malt-horse, capon, coxcomb,
> idiot, patch!
>
> (III.i.31-2)

One Dromio here calls names, the other replies in playful parallel with abuse (*abusio*) and name-calling. And what is an insult but a name emphatically *not* ours? Antipholus is dissuaded from breaking down the wall in rage only because it would invite a circulation of bad names for himself and his wife over which he would have no binding or regulatory power:

> If by strong hand you offer to break in,
> Now in the stirring passage of the day,
> A vulgar comment will be made of it;
> And that supposed by the common rout
> Against your yet ungalled estimation,
> That may with foul intrusion enter in,
> And dwell upon your grave when you are
> dead. . . .
>
> (III.i.98-104)

Names are becoming alarmingly deathless succubi that usurp the lives of people. Ephesian "credit" as a whole depends on a one-to-one correspondence between a name and its *nominatum*, but the ever-intersecting paths of the twins function like crossed wires, disrupting the flow of information, mismatching the links that bind all things in their "proper" places. It is here that Antipholus decides to divert the chain from his wife to the Courtesan.

The Plautine poetics of line and limit in Ephesus thus governs at once linguistics, narratology, and anthropology. The alarming implications of this poetics do not go unnoticed or uncriticized by the play. The end-driven regulatory scheme of cause and effect, name and referent, is glossed by a set of references scattered through the play to Biblical, and especially soteriological, history. We have already noted the hints of a "fall and judgment" pattern in the opening scene. These resonances return sharpened when Egeon reappears unsuccessful at the end of his "grace period":

> By this, I think, the dial points at five;
> Anon, I'm sure, the Duke himself in person
> Comes this way to the melancholy vale,
> The place of death and sorry execution,
> Behind the ditches of the abbey here.
>
> (V.i.118-22)

The "melancholy vale" and "place of death" echo the Biblical "valley of the shadow" and "place of the skull" and take their place in a string of allusions through the play to the Fall and consequent sentence of Death. For instance, when Dromio runs to beg Adriana for money to set Antipholus free, he says his master is "in Tartar limbo, worse than hell," the captive of "A devil in an everlasting garment" and "One that, before the judgment, carries poor souls to hell" (IV.ii.32-3, 40). Luciana in her turn has become "Mistress Redemption." When he returns with the bail to find the other Antipholus unarrested, he enquires: "What, have you got the picture of old Adam new-appareled?"

> Not that Adam that kept the Paradise, but that Adam that keeps the prison; he that goes in the calf's skin that was killed for the Prodigal; he that came behind you, sir, like an evil angel, and bid you forsake your liberty. (IV.iii.16-21)

It is St. Paul's "Adam in whom all die" that is in the picture here, the first patriarch in Hell. All the play's talk of fiends and devils in Ephesus suggests a community still under the dominion of "the penalty of Adam," inhabited by fiends of whom "It is written, they appear to men like angels of light" (IV.iii.56).[32] Images of divine judgment haunt the play. Even the glorious figure of Nell (Knell?) the kitchen wench, whose name is not rope enough to measure her body, is an apocalyptic giant: her grime is "in grain. Noah's flood could not do it" and "If she lives til Doomsday, she'll burn a week longer than the whole world" (III.ii.106, 100). The hapless characters enmeshed by the linear poetics of classical comedy are assimilated to St. Paul's Ephesians that were "dead in trespasses and sinnes, Wherein, in time past ye walked, according to the course of this world" (Ephes. 2.1-2).[33] When Dromio fears the devil-Courtesan will "shake her chain, and fright us with it," it is the Devil of Revelation who is behind her, and binding in a pit that is indeed at hand.[34]

That the regulation of the communal order of Plautine Ephesus is in the end a deathward process is made clear by its final champion: the would-be exorcist Dr. Pinch, whose talk is all the fiend and whose very name is constraint. He gets hold of those who have reached the end of their tether, and the "dark and dankish vault" to which he carts them is like enough to hell. But it is his appearance which clinches the matter:

> . . . a hungry lean-faced villain;
> A mere anatomy, a mountebank,
> A threadbare juggler and a fortune teller,
> A needy-hollow-eyed-sharp-looking wretch;
> A living dead man.
>
> (V.i.238-42)

Within necessity's sharp Pinch lurks a figure familiar from countless homilies. St. Paul would have seen through Pinch at once: under his disguise of family therapist, he is Death's point-man in Ephesus.[35]

At the end of the line, the wear and tear of Time on hapless mortality crystallizes in Egeon's final appearance, having failed to secure a community of friends to change his iron bonds for human ones and save his life. In the play's most moving passage, Egeon longs for something more than the body of this death, and the death of this body:

> O time's extremity,
> Hast thou so cracked and splitted my poor tongue
> In seven short years, that here my only son
> Knows not my feeble key of untuned cares?
> Though now this grainèd face of mine be hid
> In sap-consuming winter's drizzled snow,
> And all the conduits of my blood froze up,
> Yet hath my night of life some memory;
> My wasting lamps some fading glimmer left;
> My dull deaf ears a little use to hear.
>
> (V.i.308-17)

This is where the rhetoric of the opening scene pointed, the victimization of "one thing after another" and the partition of community—the tongue like the mast—in cracking and splitting. The play has staged the temporal drive of classical comedy itself as a drive towards death.

Confronting this deadly world of bond and line, its story-books ruled by antique precept, are two alternative sites of imagery: one an equally inhuman contrary, the other a sublation the play hopes will transfigure both contraries alike. The first alternative Egeon's family faced on their "helpful bark" in the dissolute violence of the storm and the all-melting ocean of natural chaos.[36] In this environment we can no more survive than under the iron government of Time's Law. Law in Ephesus opposes and seeks to shape the always incipiently chaotic flux of natural process. To this extent it is presented as fitfully appealing. Errant Antipholus of Syracuse longs for the stable order of bounded social life when he lands on the firm ground of the mart, bringing the very marine dissolution of which Egeon has just spoken with him into Ephesus. A famous speech expresses the pathos of oceanic boundlessness:

> I to the world am like a drop of water
> That in the ocean seeks another drop,
> Who, falling there to find his fellow forth,
> Unseen, inquisitive, confounds himself.
>
> (I.ii.35-8)

Boundary in these lines has become fluid, evanescent, and metamorphic.[37] The pathos of its imminent loss is curiously cosmic, perhaps through the submerged connection between world and drop, as though a person were not less a node than a globe of manifold possibilities, a little Nell made cunningly. Indeed, the threat to Dromio

of Nell's magnitude belongs with this sense of the uncontrollable flux of the world as a potential solvent of personal identity, as too does the element of fear mixed with desire in his master's response to Luciana. For these men, women have too much fluidity about them.

If the contraries of rope and ocean, law and nature, were the only alternatives, it would be a grim lookout. Some mediating term or passage is needed between them. For this transfiguration the play turns to two sources: intellectually to the language of the sacramental, emotionally and dramaturgically to the theatre of wonder with its dialectic of surrender and self-consciousness. Death and earth, the penalty of Adam, is only half the story. Out of Paul's redemptive contrary ("Even so in Christ shall all be made alive") Shakespeare produces a third possibility, a deeper tide towards a breakdown of order not into death but life. Between the two opponents of Time-as-Law there is some commerce: both stress the availability of sudden, improvisatory breakthroughs. Hence the language of wandering and ocean occasionally coalesces with the language of the sacramental under the banner of fluidity. But their two tendencies are fundamentally distinct: one divides and fragments only, where the other does so in order to generate a more vital compounding. Unlike so many of his Protestant contemporaries, but very like those who wrote and performed the medieval cycle-plays, Shakespeare's principal point of connection to theology is not through sin but through the notions of incarnation and the sacramental, where word and matter, spirit and flesh are explicitly confounded in the creation of communal forms of life.

Apart from the hint of "redemption" in the opening scene, various reminiscences of the Incarnation pepper the middle of the play: Dromio refers to his "nativity," there is a character called Balthasar and a merchant who has been waiting since "Pentecost." And when Ephesian Antipholus chooses not to break down the door of his house for fear his credit will suffer, we might see a worldling's distant anti-echo of the liberation and epiphany played out before the infernal gate and its rapscallion Porter.[38] The "undoing" of time's tyranny also appears when Dromio comes to "Mistress Redemption" for bail. First there is a telling reminder of three familiar images for the bondage of time and story:

> ADRIANA Tell me, was he arrested on a band?
> DROMIO Not on a band, but on a stronger thing:
> A chain, a chain! Do you not hear it ring?
> ADRIANA What the chain?
> DROMIO No, no, the bell; 'tis time that I
>   were gone.
>
> (IV.ii.49-53)

Bond, chain, and bell are cardinal images of the world's rigor. But the hint of new, more liberal possibilities follows:

DROMIO It was two ere I left him, and now
the clock strikes one.

ADRIANA The hours come back! That did I
never hear.

DROMIO O yes, if any hour meet a sergeant,
'a turns back for very fear.

ADRIANA As if time were in debt! How
fondly dost thou reason!

DROMIO Time is a very bankrupt, and owes
more than he's worth to season.

Nay he's a thief too: have you not heard
men say,

That time comes stealing on by night and
day?

If 'a be in debt and theft, and a sergeant in
the way,

Hath he not reason to turn back an hour in
a day?

                                    (IV.ii.54-62)

This corresponds to the earlier jokes about Time's
baldness, but now Time is fugitive rather than bailiff.
If Time still steals from us, runs away too fast, he now
begins to show a capacity for the unexpected and transgressive. If Time can run backwards, there is no telling
what may happen. If Time is a thief, we glimpse a
world less dominated by logic, more open to improvisation and even miracle, in which "the day of the Lord
wil come as a thief in the night" (2 Pet. 3.10). This
new vision of time is associated directly with the redemption of Antipholus from his bonds, and when
Dromio hands over the money, he does so with a reference to St. Peter's release from prison, itself instance
and echo of Christ's power to liberate: "Here are the
angels that you sent for to deliver you" (IV.iii.41).[39]

The linear imagery of Ephesus also appears again
strangely shifted and fused with the fluidity of ocean
in Antipholus' evocation of Luciana's hair as a bed
afloat on the surface of the ocean:

Spread o'er the silver waves thy golden hairs,
And as a bed I'll take them, and there lie,
And in that glorious supposition think
He gains by death that hath such means to die:
Let Love, being light, be drowned if she sink.
                                    (III.i.48-52)

The thin meniscus that screens life from death is sustained and made viable by the magically erotic, a power
that will allow Antipholus to float luxuriantly on a raft
of hair, close to but not concerned at the danger of
drowning in nature's deep.[40] Metamorphic Eros occupies the middle ground between rope and water, "error" as fatal mistake and "error" as endless deviation.[41]
This fusion of the erotic with the sacramental is a
combination that comes to be characteristic of
Shakespeare's work. It is by no means always a stable
combination, and can turn bitter in the extreme as it

does for Othello. But in *The Comedy of Errors,* as for
Adriana, the language of ocean is eroticized and attracted towards the sacramental:

For know, my love, as easy mayst thou fall
A drop of water in the breaking gulf,
And take unmingled thence that drop again
Without addition or diminishing
As take from me thyself, and not me too.
                                    (II.ii.126-30)

The breaking gulf as the sacrament of marriage described in Ephesians is Shakespeare's most important
image of lived *contaminatio*.[42] If the gulf breaks, it is
a dynamic and creative fracture, as the bonds of most
Ephesian institutions are not. Its surging energies at
once sustain and mobilize the central social institution.
The crucial importance of Paul's letter to the play thus
comes into clearer focus. Paul's vision of erotic desire
in marriage as a social counterpart to the Word-as-
Flesh undergirds Shakespeare's contamination of
boundary with flux, a move that at once dissolves law
and circumscribes ocean.

The Shakespearean drama of *contaminatio* that unfolds
in *The Comedy of Errors* has, like its classical counterparts in the play, its metanarrative emblems. Consider
again the "chain" as an image of narrative. As a figure
of bondage, it points us to the world of rigor and Old
Law. But as a figure of metaphor, it points on the contrary to a power in language that desires and makes new
pertinencies, new constituencies, new connections with
the world. That the chain's first associations should be
to erotic emotion is therefore deeply appropriate, since
in Shakespeare Love is the sign *par excellence* of the
promise of new community, as well as that under which
all of Paul's unifications occur. The chain thus both
looks to the marriages of the conclusion and recalls the
ropes and mast that bound the shipwrecked family together as the play's first images of bonds that protect
from the blind chaos of mere nature.

The resuscitation of community through clarification
of the vital significance of narrative turns out to be the
play's deepest impulse, and explains the pervasive use
of the Ephesians' epistle. Paul's theology there is oriented especially to the maintenance of community: the
letter is written to bolster and encourage the cohesion
of a Church threatened with fragmentation. Against
Egeon's vision of the tongue "cracked and splitted,"
we can set Paul's image of a body that has overcome
such attrition:

For he is our peace, whiche hath made both one:
and hath broken downe the wal that was a stoppe
betweene us,/ Taking away in his fleshe the hatred,
(even) the law of commaundementes (contayned) in
ordinaunces, for to make of twayne one newe man
in hym selfe, so makyng peace:/ And that he might

reconcile both unto God in one body through (his) crosse, and slue hatred thereby. (Ephes. 2.14-16, Bishops' Bible)

What Shakespeare takes from Paul's writings is less a particular doctrine than a kind of figurative substrate of images and associations in which incarnation is the principal trope for all kinds of unification, including that which creates new community between the play and its audience. This commitment to incarnation as the goal of poetry has a kind of secular "real presence" as its dramatic ideal, and imagines language itself as a ubiquitous informing power. Verbal utterance at this level deeply creates and roots itself in a form of life and experience, where the world fits itself to one's desire and a language can be found that mediates each to the other. Such an ideal language does not constrain, constrict, bully, or scar: language that does that is what Ephesus deals in when it writes its governing signs, as Dromio laments, directly into the flesh in bruising and chaining. The language of Shakespearean incarnation, on the other hand, seeks a sacrament-like function which can express the life of the flesh, and inform that life with its own vitality. Language is in this way itself a creative activity, not a merely secondary one, welling up from some deep source which is also the source of experience. The plasticity of language and the mutability of experience are twin—or one—in their interinanimation. They are a vital unity of a kind usefully imaginable through the older theological conception of the sign that acts.

Shakespeare's poetry does what medieval drama always threatened to do, what Aquinas indicated was always implied by the logic of a sacramental semiosis: it unbinds itself and its shaping power from the Church. At the heart of Shakespeare's drama is a power confident that words can incarnate lives before the eyes of an audience without the institutional apparatus of the Church to guarantee their orthodoxy, and without a structure of dogma external to the dramatic occasion. Though such a stance suggests that the playwright is in direct competition with God, no sense of struggle ever emerges, either in abjection or self-aggrandisement (Marlowe is an instructive comparison here). The universe of verbal creation is capacious enough to allow for both. It follows that one can only with some restriction speak of the Shakespearean project as a "secularization." One could just as easily call it a radical resacralization of the world. For Shakespeare words are all, but a great all inseparable from the continuing life of the world itself, and whose deepest energy springs from the ever-metamorphic reproduction of the world. It is as though Shakespeare read the Bible as an epic poem written by Ovid.

The problem finally to be faced is by what counter-magic the trixiness of metaphor can be reconciled with the hunger for persistence, how the pun can be made flesh. It is here that we encounter the play's own rabbit-out-of-the-hat in the person of Emilia. Nothing in the classical logic of the narrative requires her presence: all that is required is that the two Antipholuses (or even the two Dromios) finally run into one another in the street. In Shakespeare's play, this encounter is shepherded by Emilia, who seems to grasp at once the precise shape of the resolution called for. She becomes its focal point, stands in in her own person for the redemptive figure that the Pauline allusions have led us to expect. Why should the body of the mother, whose labor as mother is explicitly announced as finally accomplished at the point of reunion, replace the body of Christ?[43]

The play is almost explicit about this compounding of Emilia's gestation with the Incarnation. Emilia declares "Thirty-three years have I but gone in travail / Of you, my sons, and till this present hour / My heavy burthen ne'er delivered" (V.i.401-3). That odd time interval corresponds to no chronology mapped out anywhere else in the play, indeed it contradicts Egeon's tale.[44] Shakespeare is notoriously careless about such details, but that will not explain this particular choice of number. The answer is, of course, that thirty-three years was the period of the Incarnation, at the end of which the clock was turned back, the chain broken, and the fatal debt paid.[45] Emilia's "thirty-three years" of "travail" end likewise in liberation from bonds, forgiveness of debt, and redemption of time—all accomplished in the moment of recognition. This image of a labor to deliver the world anew redefines the nature of narrative as a temporal process and supervenes over the old images and mechanisms of plot closure. Its gargantuan—and rather disturbing—pain was after all not towards death, but towards new life, and the Plautine logic which drew us to expect, as early as I.ii, that Antipholus' "thousand marks" would in the end redeem Egeon, is pointedly set aside by Solinus: "it shall not need, thy father hath his life." The late and peculiar completion of the twins' "suspended" nativity translates the characters back in time to a "gossips' feast" to be held in the sacral space of the Abbey, in which all will join to break down "the wal that was a stoppe betweene us." Nativity (rhyming with itself in Emilia's closing speech), incarnation, baptism, marriage: the sacramental counters pile up upon one another, but are also absorbed into the natural image of childbirth, here understood as the redelivery of its own vitality to the community.

The "poetics of incarnation" plays a still deeper role in the scene. It has to do with Shakespeare's feel for our knowledge of the world in our language: how language can deliver the world as a gestated presence to us for naming and recognition. We can glimpse this if we consider again Shakespeare's attraction to fictions of identical twins. Linguistic witchcraft such as metaphor, pun and double reference have materialized throughout the play as twinning. The scene of recognition where the twins finally meet puts flesh on these verbal two-in-one paradoxes, and the dissolution of identity and boundary which Paul's sacramental language imagines is also crystallized for them and us when they stand before one another. Instead of the romance cliché of recognition tokens—what Stephen Gosson sneered at as the "broken ring, . . . handkercher, or piece of a cockle shell"[46]—we have a matching pair of living bodies, a pair that yet comprise or share, so the language seems inclined to claim, one spirit:

> One of these men is genius to the other;
> And so of these, which is the natural man,
> And which the spirit? Who deciphers them?
>
> (V.i.333-5)

Flesh and spirit are each in each here, and cannot be extricated. Romance *anagnorisis* provides the dramatic and emotional occasion to focus a profound feeling both for language as a discoverer of the world and for theatre as a site of knowledge ("theory"). It almost seems that the scene, with its language of mirroring and of confrontation with a miraculous other self, is a response to Paul's famous formulation of how our limited knowledge is to be completed: "for now we see through a glass, darkly, but then face to face." Each twin is both self and other, as the lovers were without knowing it in Plato's *Phaedrus*.

We may seem to have erred far in our turn from the matter of "wonder," but the strange and satisfying paradox of the identical twins who face one another at the play's end returns us to it. It is the first of Shakespeare's many scenes that exploit this feeling of the world made over in wonder, and it shows us just how involved his dramaturgy is with the issues of knowledge and its ground that wonder engenders. In sharing in a mutual wonder "across the footlights," the characters are for the first time equal with the audience, as the secret we have held for so long is now made common knowledge.[47] Each Antipholus (= "reciprocal love") facing himself tastes the audience's delight in the realization of knowledge released, transferred, freely given, incarnate for all to see.[48] The boundaries between stage and audience are deliberately made porous. No one is quite sure of what his or her bearings ought to be: all the characters will assert is that the world has become somehow both theirs to live in and at the same time beyond them, that they can embrace it only between affirmation and denial. Gingerly they explore the world's new shape, linking it together piece by piece, feeling at its edges with the mind's fingertips as skepticism and elation hold one another in tension:

> ANGELO That is the chain, sir, which you
>   had of me.
> ANTIPHOLUS I think it be, sir, I deny it not.
> ANGELO And you, sir, for this chain arrested
>   me.

> ANTIPHOLUS I think I did, sir, I deny it not.
>
> (V.i.378-81)

We can hear language's adequacy to the world being felt out. The double drift of separation and identification that marks theatrical wonder's relation to the world it meets reappears here through the reunited twins. One Dromio at least has a strong sense that he may be seeing himself—one rather gets the impression that it is for the first time: "Methinks you are my glass, and not my brother; / I see by you I am a sweet-faced youth" (V.i.418-19). The discovery of his beauty is a joke, of course, but it also focuses the general sense that the world is a newly beautiful place where the self is potentially at home with itself, where narcissistic delight can be true without being invidious or damaging.

Gestation is the play's final image of itself, replacing the rope of classical poetics and the sea of romance flux with umbilical cords and amniotic fluid. It may also give something of Shakespeare's sense of himself as a nascent playwright. The end of the process that Egeon figured as deathward turns out to be an image of the society and family gradually re-membered into a living body. Re-membering is also the image of the work of the play itself, and of its working *on* itself over the course of the narrative to articulate characteristic procedures and conceptions of Shakespearean drama. If we have always felt that Nell was the play's most striking figure, the end proves this intuition right by revealing her as the play's great comic image of the body that can contain us all, that will by its very material cohesion resist the Flood and postpone death "a week longer than the rest of the world." Nell is the play's early, popular foreshadowing of the figure of the mother produced as the final site of unification. The incarnative imagination casts itself revealingly as a female principle of vivification which stands in for the body of Christ. Feared in Nell as too overwhelmingly material, this principle is embraced in Emilia as the site where the social body can be revealed in its most concrete, but also most wonderful, work of reproduction.[49]

At the end of the play, romance recognition, heterosexual marriage, sacramental semiotics are assimilated to one another as common images of a credible faith in the world.[50] The body of Christ resurrected becomes the body of Emilia delivered. The final attachment of this comic vision to the world rather than to a supernatural aspiration is summed up in the *topos* of reproduction within the verbal order of matrimony. By linking the conservative notion of "legitimacy" with the transformational power of incarnative trope, Shakespeare registers at once inheritance and renewal. The impetus to matrimony that will drive the whole of Shakespeare's writing in comedy is a response therefore not only to social and political conditions, as many have argued, but to questions of cultural and poetic self-consciousness at the widest level.

IV

This sense of comedic resolution as a "fitting together" of contraries—and the discovery of how deeply they may answer each other—can be said to describe not only Shakespeare's attraction to a particular kind of story, but a preoccupation and a sensibility that manifests itself at all levels of his writing. From his consistent attention to erotic experience (both hetero- and homo-), to his predilection for exploiting the unclassical indecorums of the Elizabethan stage, to his notably dense and paradoxical metaphoric language, his impulse is to discover a figurative complement, to push apparent difference towards some deeper reciprocal unity, sometimes imagined beyond language itself, as in "The Phoenix and the Turtle." Consider, for instance, the large number of phrases that condense crucial moments of entire plays in a stark and baffling paradox that demands to be understood, and, even more surprisingly, that we think we can and do understand: "Mine own and not mine own"; "Nothing is but what is not"; "I am not what I am"; "This is, and is not, Cressid"; "A natural perspective that is and is not"; "I confess nothing, nor I deny nothing"; "I did love you once. . . . I loved you not."[51] These are not merely clever paradoxes, inward-looking mirrors, for they are deployed to register their plays' sense of sources of language, feeling or knowledge ever beyond the horizon of the expressible, which only such teasing, even maddening, formulae can index. Rhetorician Puttenham called such figures "The Wondrer" and certainly in their dramatic context they often have the qualities at once of profound representational power and of equally profound self-consciousness that we have associated with the dynamic of that emotion.[52]

To take just one more instance, consider how the paradoxes of doubling and doubt shape this radiant moment of discovery in *A Midsummer Night's Dream:*

DEMETRIUS These things seem small and undistinguishable,
Like far-off mountains turned into clouds.
HERMIA Methinks I see these things with parted eye,
When everything seems double.
HELENA   So methinks;
And I have found Demetrius like a jewel,
Mine own and not mine own.

(IV.i.187-92)

It is not only the heady evaporation of dream mixed with the open-mouthed discovery that "all is true" that makes this so exciting and joyous. It is the gradual discovery, through successive, gingerly approximations, of *just* the language for this very state. Helena's grasp of the right way to word the world in her feeling catches its own quality of stumbling on truth right

there for us: her metaphor crystallizes as the wonderful jewel of itself. We hold it breathless, sparkling in the hand. The possibility of metaphor as the granting of the world we want, our own and not our own, catches up the vibration of erotic desire in its strong toil of grace. In Shakespeare's comedy, language's love for the world can be requited.

Notes

[1] Of general studies dealing with the transition, I have found particularly useful those of David Bevington, *From "Mankind" to Marlowe: Growth of Structure in the Popular Drama of Tudor England* (Cambridge: Harvard University Press, 1962); F. P. Wilson, *English Drama 1485-1585,* ed. G. K. Hunter (Oxford University Press, 1968); Weimann, *Popular Tradition,* and Walter Cohen, *Drama of a Nation* (Ithaca: Cornell University Press, 1985).

[2] This is not to imply that the enterprise was not organized by hierarchies of participation, inclusions, and exclusions—after all, there had to be audiences at least. But the whole process expressed and involved community structures as instruments of logistic management.

[3] For the economic downturn in provincial municipalities at this time, see P. Clark and P. Slack, *English Towns in Transition, 1500-1700* (Oxford University Press, 1976) and Charles Phythian-Adams, "Urban decay in late-medieval England" in Philip Abrams and E. A. Wrigley, eds., *Towns in Societies: Studies in Economic History and Historical Sociology* (Cambridge University Press, 1978), pp. 159-85.

[4] Emrys Jones, *The Origins of Shakespeare* (Oxford University Press, 1977), Ch. 2, pp. 31-84.

[5] Based on figures from Henslowe's diary tabulated in Carol Rutter, ed., *Documents of the Rose Playhouse* (Manchester University Press, 1984). This high rate seems to be more typical of the earlier period, when the theaters were still building up a repertory of reliable hits. See also Andrew Gurr, *The Shakespearean Stage 1574-1642,* 3rd edn. (Cambridge University Press, 1992), pp. 103-4.

[6] See E. K. Chambers, *The Medieval Stage,* 2 vols. (London: Oxford University Press, 1903), vol. 2, pp. 379-83. The longer performances were held at Clerkenwell before huge crowds of nobility and commoners, usually in the middle of the year and especially at the Feast of St. John. Smaller-scale plays and saints' plays were performed by various bodies of clerks and laymen at other sites, especially for saint's-day celebrations. There were also performances for city guild feasts. It is likely that not all of these plays were religious in nature, as C. R. Baskerville has demon-

strated ("Some evidence for early romantic plays in England," *Modern Philology* [*MP*] 14 [1916], 229-51, 467-512). It is worth nothing that "the acting of Christ's Passion" was undertaken as late as the 1610s in Ely House "at which there were thousands present" (Chambers, *Medieval Stage,* p. 382). Stephen Mullaney has lately speculated extensively on "the place of the stage" in London, though to my mind his reading of the theatre as unavoidably "liminal" and therefore transgressive because of its place in "the liberties" over-reads those parts of the City, which also housed both Whitehall and the Law-courts—hardly sites of transgression. See Steven Mullaney, *The Place of the Stage: License, Play and Power in Renaissance England* (Chicago: University of Chicago Press, 1988), esp. Ch. 1.

[7] Some critics have argued the contrary. A recent example is R. Chris Hassell Jr., *Renaissance Drama and the English Church Year* (Lincoln: University of Nebraska Press, 1979).

[8] Besides studies on Marlowe, which have necessarily to grapple with his iconoclasm, several critics have emphasized the theatre's adoption of a posture of "cultural criticism." See e.g. Margot Heinemann, *Puritanism and Theatre* (Cambridge University Press, 1980), Jonathan Dollimore, *Radical Tragedy* (Chicago: University of Chicago Press, 1984), and Graham Bradshaw, *Shakespeare's Scepticism* (Ithaca: Cornell University Press, 1990).

[9] C. L. Barber, *Shakespeare's Festive Comedy* (Princeton University Press, 1959). Barber's work remains important in orienting us on the connections between dramatic form and social custom even if he occasionally cuts the cloth to fit the argument, as with his discussion of the ending of *Twelfth Night*. It is precisely Shakespeare's impulse to revise or criticize the social forms he incorporates into comedy that Barber tends to downplay.

[10] It is worth remembering in this context that the number of people in an average theatre audience was roughly comparable to the number of people in Elizabethan Stratford, so that it was at least a plausible imaginative leap to think of the Globe as a brief, nonce Stratford. See Samuel Schoenbaum, *William Shakespeare: A Compact Documentary Life* (Oxford University Press, 1987), p. 26; A. M. Nagler, *Shakespeare's Stage* (New Haven: Yale University Press, 1958), p. 107.

[11] On Jonson see David Riggs, *Ben Jonson: A Life* (Cambridge: Harvard University Press, 1989). Jonson, of course, made fun of the Shakespeare coat of arms awarded in 1596 and himself claimed descent from Carlisle gentry. That Shakespeare's petition was on behalf of his father is worth thinking about. Even to a cynical eye, it indicates a desire to be seen as a dutiful son (says Lear's Fool: "He's a mad yeoman who sees his son a gentleman before him").

[12] See John Pocock, *The Ancient Constitution and the Feudal Law,* rev. edn. (Cambridge University Press, 1987), pp. 34-8, 274-5, and more recently Richard Helgerson, *Forms of Nationhood* (Chicago: University of Chicago Press, 1992), Ch. 2.

[13] See Gardiner, *Mysteries End;* R. W. Ingram, "1579 and the decline of civic religious drama in Coventry" in *The Elizabethan Theatre VIII,* G. R. Hibbard ed. (Ontario: P. D. Moany, 1980), pp. 114-28. Max W. Thomas discusses Will Kemp's famous dance marathon from London to Norwich in related terms: "*Kemps Nine Daies Wonder:* dancing carnival into market" *PMLA* 107:3 (May, 1992), 511-23.

[14] *Short Title Catalogue of English Books, 1475-1640,* second editiion [*STC*] 25752, sig. F7v-F9r. Quoted in Wilson, *English Drama,* pp. 76-7. Willis later objects by contrast to the corrupting influence of more recent plays.

[15] See Schoenbaum, *Compact Documentary Life,* pp. 115-17.

[16] Louis A. Montrose, "The purpose of playing: reflections on a Shakespearean anthropology," *Helios* 7 (1980), 51-74 at p. 64.

[17] Francis Fergusson, *The Idea of a Theater* (Princeton University Press, 1949), Ch. 4, esp. pp. 114-19; O. B. Hardison, *Christian Rite and Christian Drama* (Baltimore: Johns Hopkins University Press, 1965), pp. 287-92.

[18] Montrose, "Purpose," p. 63.

[19] See the pertinent reflections of Geoffrey Hartman on this question in *Beyond Formalism* (New Haven: Yale University Press, 1970), pp. 42-60 and 356-86.

[20] This connection between religious and theatrical uses of the language of "incarnation" needs more extensive investigatiion. Though critics as diverse as Sigurd Burckhardt, Muriel Bradbrook, Graham Hough, and Murray Krieger, along with Montrose, have all used the term to describe Shakespeare's dramatic language, there has been no sustained attempt to follow its implications. This is the more strange in that the term is clearly one of central historical significance in the period. See Burckhardt, *Shakespearean Meanings* (Princeton University Press, 1968); Bradbrook, *The Rise of the Common Player* (London: Chatto and Windus, 1962); Hough, "The allegorical circle," *Critical Quarterly* 3 (1916), 199-209; Krieger, *A Window to Criticism: Shakespeare's Sonnets and Modern Poetics* (Princeton University Press, 1964).

[21] Hollander, *Melodious Guile,* p. 13.

[22] For ideological criticisms of various stripes, including Marxism and some versions of "New Historicism," this element of self-consciousness has been a stumbling-block, since ideological criticism is heavily invested in the notion that the work has an "unconscious" which the critic uncovers. This difficulty has recurrently given rise to the notion of an "internal distance from ideology" by which poetry enjoys a special status as cultural production. See for instance Pierre Macherey, *A Theory of Literary Production,* trans. Geoffrey Wall (London: Routledge and Kegan Paul, 1978), pp. 90-101; Terry Eagleton, *Criticism and Ideology* (Atlantic Highlands: Humanities Press, 1976), pp. 89-101, and Stephen Greenblatt, *Shakespearean Negotiations* (Oxford: Clarendon Press, 1987), pp. 125-8. Greenblatt in particular puts the matter strongly when he comments (p. 127) that in the "complex, limited institutional independence" of Shakespeare's theatre, "this marginal and impure autonomy, arises not out of an inherent, formal self-reflexiveness but out of an ideological matrix in which Shakespeare's theatre is created and re-created." I am suspicious of that "not/but." Reflexiveness can also operate on the "ideological matrix," including inherited ideologies bound up in the forms of fiction.

[23] Most recently, John D. Cox in *Shakespeare and the Dramaturgy of Power* (Princeton University Press, 1989), p. 64, arranges columns on his page to divide Egeon from his sons once more. But the play is highly suspicious of partitions like this, and always moves to break them down.

[24] See T. W. Baldwin, *On the Compositional Genetics of* The Comedy of Errors (Urbana: University of Illinois Press, 1965). Baldwin demonstrates that Shakespeare used Lambinus' edition of Plautus of 1576 with its commentary, along with T. Cooper's 1565 *Thesaurus* to gloss unfamilar terms in Plautus or Lambinus. It is therefore unlikely that the translation of Plautus' play by "W. W." (1595) was directly related to Shakespeare's composition.

[25] The relevant lines are 37 "happy," 38 "hap," 65 "hope," 103 "helpful," 113 "hap," 120 "mishaps," 135 "hopeless," 138 "happy," 140 "Hapless," 141 "mishap," 151 "help," 157 "Hopeless and helpless." The pattern is striking once remarked. It recurs to some extent at the play's end.

[26] Baldwin, *Genetics,* p. 207.

[27] The name, in the form Dromo, is a common servant name in Terence, but not in Plautus. One of the servants in Lyly's *Mother Bombie* is called Dromio, which is no doubt where Shakespeare gets his name from. Lyly's Dromio does not enact his name, however.

[28] Baldwin (*Genetics,* p. 116) points out that period Bibles contained maps of St. Paul's journeys, so that

a visual element of mapping and lines may well have been part of the imaginative process of composition.

[29] Lars Engle, personal communication. Note that it is not necessary for this to have been noticeable to either audience or readers: it is more like a deep schema confirming the play's concern with linearity as a narrative design. It is even, conceivably, a happy accident. Cf. Patricia Parker, "Elder and younger: the opening scene of *The Comedy of Errors,*" *Shakespeare Quarterly* 34 (1983), 325-7. Parker also notes some of the Biblical references with which I will shortly be concerned, and there are a good many others. In part I hope here to remedy her description of these as "still largely uninterpreted."

[30] The image of Odysseus bound to that other mast to hear the Sirens' singing is relevant here.

[31] The obscure joke about the parrot may go to the breakdown of linguistic mediation here: a parrot repeats its words without intending or knowing their meanings, and therefore can be (in)opportune automatically: it has its jokes thrust upon it, as it were. Here hanging and whipping is all one.

[32] II Cor. 11.14: "And no marvell: for Satan himself is transformed into an Angel of light" (Geneva Bible, 1560; "Angell of light" is the page-heading on Y.Y.ii[r]). Unless otherwise indicated, all Biblical quotations will be from the Geneva Bible.

[33] Echoes of Ephesians turn up in the most unlikely places: as for example when Dromio says of Nell that "If my breast had not been made of faith, and my heart of steel, / She had transformed me to a curtal dog" (III.ii.145-6), echoing Ephes. 6 just after the more often cited passages on marriage. Here an interesting question arises: are Shakespeare's characters to be understood as Christians or pagans? In accordance with a movement towards the sacramental for which I will argue shortly, they seem to move across a border during the play, beginning in the crypto-pagan ambience of romance and thence becoming more and more involved with a Christian vocabulary. "Salvation" in a strict theological sense is not the issue of the play, but the redemption of a viable community is (the impulse the play shares with medieval drama); hence the language of the play draws increasingly on Christian sources.

[34] Rev. 20.1-3: "And I saw an angel come downe from heauen, hauing the kye of the bottomles pit, and a great chaine in his hand./ And he toke the dragon, that olde serpe[n]t, which is the deuil and Satan, and he bounde him a thousand yeres,/ And cast him into the bottomles pit, and he shut him vp, and sealed the dore."

[35] See Baldwin, *Genetics,* pp. 47-56. We should also remember that Paul wrote to Ephesus while in prison

in Rome as the Gospel's "ambassadour in bondage," and his letter uses a language of death and liberation surely not unrelated to the death sentence he always expected. Cf. his speech to the Elders of Ephesus in Acts 20, esp. vv. 22-3.

[36] Cf. Ephesians 14.4: "That we hence forth be no more children, wauering & caryed about with euerie winde of doctrine. . . ."

[37] See Baldwin, *Genetics,* Ch. 12. Also Jonathan Crewe, "God or the good physician: the rational playwright in *The Comedy of Errors,"* Genre 15 (1982), 209-10. Crewe's alternatives, focusing on the "rational" playwright, exclude one who relies on less rational means. A sacramentality that might mediate between the theological and the therapeutic is not discussed as a model for the action.

[38] That Shakespeare was familiar with the scene of the "devil-porter" at the Gate of Hell we know from *Macbeth.* Again, I am not suggesting an allegorical reading here. It is more a question of the trains of thought and association producing the particular texture of the action. The scene is of course more immediately taken from Plautus' *Amphitruo,* but to confound a medieval echo of Hell's gates with the more classical obvious source would be characteristic of the method of this play.

[39] Cf. Acts 12.11.

[40] Though it is impossible that this is a recollection of Longinus' hull that saves the Homeric sailors from drowning, it is remarkable that Antipholus' erotic wonder at Luciana should come up with the same image of imminent yet screened dissolution.

[41] A few lines earlier these same two tangents of "Error" had been brought within sight of one another:

> Lay open to my earthy, gross conceit,
> Smothered in errors, feeble, shallow, weak,
> The folded meaning of your words' deceit.
> Against my soul's pure truth why labor you,
> To make it wander in an unknown field?
>   (III.ii.34-8)

We should recall also the strange epithets used of this Antipholus in the Folio: "Antipholus Erotes" (I.ii.s.d.) and "Antipholis Errotis" (II.ii.s.d.). These may have developed from a suggestive confounding (*contaminatio*) of Plautus' *meretrix* "Erotium" with error and errancy: see Evans's note, *Riverside Shakespeare,* p. 85. The notion of love as a kind of fruitful misprision pervades Shakespeare's work. Are these traces of his "small Latin"?

[42] Ephes. 5.28-31, a passage linking the estate of marriage to the mystical body of the Church, which is

Christ's "owne flesh." Luciana has earlier (II.i) used other sections of this passage to argue for the supremacy of husbands, as has frequently been remarked, but the deeper poetics of the sacramental body in the play's use of the passage have been less noted.

[43] Two relevant connections can only tease us at this point: first that Ephesus was the site of the Great Temple of Diana the Mother in classical times (this was common knowledge, but also particularly available through the tale of Apollonius of Tyre that underlies *Pericles*); second that the Third General Council at Ephesus (A.D. 431) declared as doctrine, contrary to the assertion of Nestorius and his followers, that Christ did develop as a human child in Mary's body, and that she was consequently *theotokos,* the bearer of God. Whether this is design or happy accident on Shakespeare's part we cannot know, but once more we discover the confounding of a classical with a Christian motif in the play. The coincidence of Virgin and Mother in Ephesus is also relevant to *Pericles.*

[44] The opening scene suggests the twins are only 23. See Baldwin, *Genetics,* pp. 107-9.

[45] Lest this seem overly ingenious for such a standard "round figure," there is the page in the Bishops' Bible titled "The order of times," showing the timetable of Paul's evangelical career: its first entry gives the figure "xxxiii" as "The yeres of Christes incarnation." Before this comes a map of "the peregrination or iourney of Saint Paul" (Geneva has one of these also), and after, the opening of Romans. See Bishops' Bible, 1569, sig. K2ᵛ.

[46] Gosson, *Plays Confuted in Five Actions,* quoted in Leo Salingar, *Shakespeare and the Traditions of Comedy* (Cambridge University Press, 1974), p. 73.

[47] Just these connections are revisited in an even more daring fashion in *Twelfth Night,* where the sense of wavering boundary is also present ("Do I stand there?") as though, as in love, the steady "wal" of the self could no longer be policed, and where the reminiscence of a recognition effected by tokens is made marvelously redundant ("My father had a mole upon his brow"), given that the fact of the answering *body* supersedes all symbols: "An apple cleft in twain is not more twin than these two creatures." The daring oscillation of gender identity in that play adds an extra pleat to the dialectic.

[48] Antipholus (usually spelled "Antipholis" in the Folio text until II.ii.110) is probably a metathesis for Antiphilos, a Greek masculine to parallel Latin Antiphila, a name to which Shakespeare had access, and whose gloss as a "significant" name was available, in the learned editions of Terence—e.g. 1552 Paris—perhaps taught to Shakespeare in school. Antipholus thus pre-

sumably implies something like "mutual affection." Baldwin remarks (pp. 100-1) that "Shakespeare evidently expected his Antipholi to signify *amor . . . reciprocus,* 'reciprocal love.'"

[49] That the pair "feared/embraced" should correspond with the class distinction between a kitchen wench and a gentle matron is indicative of how Shakespeare's language remains open to some kinds of transformation but not others. Still, even Nell becomes "a fat friend" at the last.

[50] The feast that failed outside Antipholus' door in III.i opens with a friendly dispute over whether "flesh" or "words" make the successful social occasion (ll. 19-29). Only the play's end brings them together. On the importance of eating in the play, see Joseph Candido, "Dining out in Ephesus: food in *The Comedy of Errors,*" *Studies in English Literature* [SEL] 30 (1990), 217-41.

[51] From respectively: *A Midsummer Night's Dream, Macbeth, Othello, Troilus and Cressida, Twelfth Night, Much Ado about Nothing, Hamlet.* Shakespeare's attraction to paradox, though it is not the first thing that strikes us since his paradoxes are not pointed in an astringently intellectual way, brings him closer to company with Donne and other emergent poets of the 1590s than we might have thought. The difference seems to be in his conception of the ontology of language in general, so that it feels a very different thing in his hands: it is not so much a set of suasive or heuristic tools, still less a suite of ornaments or a pack of social cards (though he can use it in any of these ways), as a capacious surface on which the soul's currents work themselves into expression.

[52] Rosalie Colie's marvelous book on the Renaissance tradition of paradox, *Paradoxia Epidemica* (Princeton University Press, 1966), discusses Shakespeare's use of paradox mostly in the context of "affirming what is 'not'" (Ch. 7) or "reason in madness" (Ch. 15). The sense of affirmation behind apparent contradiction which can often be felt in comedy is less canvassed.

Source: "Compounding '*Errors,*'" in *Shakespeare and the Theatre of Wonder,* Cambridge University Press, 1996, pp. 63-92.

"Would Not the Beggar Then Forget Himself?": Christopher Sly and Autolycus

William C. Carroll, *Boston University*

When Rivers suggests to the future Richard III that he and his followers would follow Richard, "if you should be our king," Shakespeare's Richard recoils in his usual false sincerity, "If I should be? I had rather be a peddler!" (*Richard III* 1.3.148-49). The contemporary depth of disgust in Richard's invocation of his symbolic opposite may also be seen reflected in the Maid's initial encounters with the Peddler in *The Pedler's Prophecy* (1595):

> I never knew honest man of this occupation,
> But either he was a diser, a drunkard, or a
>   maker of shift,
> A picker, a cutpurse, a raiser of simulation,
> Or such a one as runne away with another
>   mans wife.
>
> . . . . .
>
> [A type of men] whose whole trade is idlenesse:
> Dicers, drunkards, makers of strife,
> Very sincks and sentences of all wickednesse.
>
> (A4ᵛ, B)

The low reputation of peddlers in the period derived not only from empirical evidence but from legal theory as well, for the statutes defining vagrants invariably included, like the 1597 law (39 Eliz. I, c.4), "all Juglers Tinkers Peddlers and Petty Chapmen wandring abroad" (*TED*: 2.355).[1] Here we see that though a peddler holds an "occupation," he is *defined* by statute as a vagabond; so too jugglers[2], tinkers, and others. Though they are not on the public dole, do not (usually) beg in the streets, and generally support themselves, such occupations are nevertheless legally and socially condemned. The real objection is that they are "wandring abroad"—literally vagrant (a peddler, one writer said in 1631, is "a wandring starre," *Cater*: 8). They are not bound through guilds to a master-apprentice hierarchical relation, to a fixed place or to a fixed wage.

Such free-lance economic activity was considered harmful in other ways as well. In *Love's Labor's Lost*, for example, Berowne complains of Boyet,

> This fellow pecks up wit as pigeons pease,
> And utters it again when God doth please.
> He is wit's peddler, and retails his wares
> At wakes and wassails, meetings, markets, fairs;
> And we that sell by gross, the Lord doth know,
> Have not the grace to grace it with such show.
>
> (5.2.316-21)

Recasting the dandified Boyet as a peddler is an insult in class terms, but a more concrete objection is that he "utters" or sells whenever the time seems appropriate, earning "retail" at the expense of those who "sell by gross," or wholesale.[3] This violation of economic convention is repeated in the peddler's infiltration of various seasonal festivals and in his seeming ubiquity; as one character in *The Pedler's Prophecy* says, "there be too many such runnagates at these days, / All the whole world with such idle persons doth flow" (C3ʳ⁻ᵛ). The peddler was thus a loose cannon on the economic ship: unregulated, mobile, transgressive. Tinkers were little better. Indeed, "a sort [i.e., gang] of tinkers" (3.2.277) forms part of the mob in *2 Henry VI,* and Robert Greene tells a conny-catching tale of "a tinker, that went about the country" and practiced the "black art" of the picklock (Salgado 1972: 227). "A Tinker," as one writer put it, "is a mooveable: for hee hath no abiding place; by his motion hee gathers heate, thence his cholericke nature" (*Overburian:* 34).[4]

Peddlers and tinkers were simply vagabonds, different from Counterfeit Cranks or Dommerars only in the details of their transgressions. In *The Highway to the Spital-House,* "Copland" and the Porter rank peddlers like any other stereotype of beggar.

> *Copland*
>
> Come none of these pedlars this way also,
> With pack on back, with their bousy speech,
>   Jagged and ragged, with broken hose and
>   breech?
>
> *Porter*
>
> . . . . .
>
> . . . out of the spital they have a party stench.
> And with them comes gatherers of cony-skins,
>   That chop with laces, points, needles and pins.
>
> (Judges: 23-24)

Some master thieves, Gilbert Walker reports in *A Manifest Detection of Dice-Play* (1552), "follow markets and fairs in the country with peddlers' footpacks, and generally to all places of assembly" (Kinney: 83). Awdeley describes both types: "A Swigman goeth with a Pedlers pack" (5), and "a Tinkard leaveth his bag a sweating at the Alehouse, which they terme their Bowsing In[n], and in the meane season goeth abrode a begging" (5). Most tinkers, Dekker says in *The*

Wonderful Year (1603), are "base, rascally . . . with a ban-dog and a drab at their tailes, and a pike-staffe on their necks, [and] will take a purse sooner then stop a kettle," though his story concerns a "devout" one (1963: 1.142). A man disguised as a tinker in Robert Armin's *The History of the two Maids of Moreclacke* (1609) enters *"in a tawny coate like a tinker, and his boy with budget and staffe, Toures tincks upon his pan drinking"* (C3ᵛ). The wandering tinker in Francis Beaumont and John Fletcher's *The Coxcomb* (c. 1609) is more threatening, however, as he enters *"with a Cord"* (2.2.1.s.d.) and his doxy, Dorathy; frustrated by all the locked doors, they circle Viola menacingly, with many sexual comments, and finally bind her, before abandoning her (2.1.28-93).

Harman, as usual, amplifies these two rogue types considerably. If "dronken" tinkers, also called "Prigs," see any old kettles or pewter about, they "quicklye snappeth the same up, and in to the booget [i.e., budget, or pig-skin bag] it goeth round" (59), just as Autolycus, who sings "If tinkers may have leave to live, / And bear the sow-skin budget" (*The Winter's Tale* 4.3.19-20), describes himself as a "snapper-up of unconsidered trifles" (4.3.25-26). Such tinkers, Harman notes, mingle "with a litle worke for a coulour," or pretense, and so "they live with deceite." The "swadder or Pedler," Harman likewise concedes, is "not all evile, but of an indifferent behaviour"; they themselves fear the stronger beggars such as Upright Men because "they have often both wares and money of them" (60). Evidently uneasy with their ambivalent status, Harman nevertheless accepts their mere status as criminal: "But for as much as they seeke gaine unlawfully against the lawes and statutes of this noble realme, they are well worthy to be registred among the number of vacabonds" (60).

With his usual combination of plagiarism and invention, Dekker (in *O per se O*, 1612) describes, in the familiar metaphor, the "swarms of locusts" who flock to the Deerhurst Fair, with a resonant political analogy: "If you look upon them you would think you lived in Henry VI's time, and that Jack Cade and his rebellious ragamuffins were there mustering" (Pendry 1968: 287). Dekker's vision of the fair is like something out of Dante, with more than one echo of *The Winter's Tale* and foreshadowing of Jonson's *Bartholomew Fair*. At Deerhurst, "None here stands crying 'What do you lack?' for you can ask for nothing that is good but here it is lacking. The buyers and sellers are both alike, tawny sunburnt rascals, and they flock in such troops that it shows as if Hell broke loose. The shopkeepers are thieves and the chapmen rogues, beggars and whores" (Pendry 1968: 288). In the usual projection of hierarchy, Dekker also describes how one "is chosen the Lord of the Fair, who is commonly the lustiest rogue in the whole bunch," leading his mob "from alehouse to alehouse" (288) in a drunken inversion of a royal procession. Such fairs always end

in riot and violence, he concludes: "Here lies a rogue bleeding, there is a *mort* cursing, here a *doxy* stabbing with her knife. And thus this fair which begins merrily ends madly, for knaves set it up and queans pull it down" (Pendry 1968: 288). Dekker ironically ends his own book by identifying himself with such vagrants: "Enough of this, and he that desires more pieces of such pedlary ware may out of this little pack fit himself with any colours. *Vale!*" (Pendry 1968: 308).

The peddler and the tinker, then, were as clearly defined vagrant stereotypes as the Counterfeit Crank. In fact, at times, according to one writer, the peddler who fears impressment will resort to all the usual deceits of a Genings: he will "stirre his stumpes: but if that will not serve, he turnes counterfeit cripple, and as one cut off by the stumps, he cants his maimes most methodically: and this practice hee most constantly retaines till the coast be cleare" (*Cater*: 139). Like other vagrants, they blear the honest man's eye: the peddler was a "raiser of simulation," the tinker "live[s] with deceit." These vagabonds employ the standard canting language, "babbling French," as Copland says, but speak as well their own more specialized rhetoric; the Tinker's "tongue is very voluble, which with Canting proves him a *Linguist*" (*Overburian*: 35). They are also associated, like other types of masterless men, with disorderly mobs in country and city, even linked to Jack Cade as potentially rebellious subjects (Cade's wife is also said to be "a peddler's daughter," *2 Henry VI* 4.2.44). Peddlers and tinkers are distinguished from most other vagrants, however, by the fact that they have an "occupation," though "they seek gain unlawfully against the laws and statues of this noble realm," as Harman noted; they are thus marked more by their tendency to rob than to beg. Overbury's Tinker ironically "observes truely the Statutes, and therefore hee had rather steale then begge . . . and [he is] so strong an enemie to idlenesse, that in mending one hole, he had rather make three then want worke" (*Overburian*: 35). In some ways, peddlers and tinkers figure as prototypes of early capitalist entrepreneurs, yet contemporary discourse in general ranks them as petty criminals and inveterate frauds, experienced practitioners of various "black arts," like their cousins the Dommerar and the Abraham Man. Residual feudal values thus criminalize their entrepreneurial economic self-sufficiency, serving as one additional marker of the period's obsession with socioeconomic transgression. Perhaps the most telling description of all is R.M.'s ironic vision of a tinker "in the summer season . . . most frequent to be seene at the Royall Exchange of a Bush or hedge" (C6ᵛ). The central symbol of the emergent new economy, the institution presiding over, but not really controlling, exchange transactions of capital, is thus fused with what is taken to be its economic and philosophic opposite, the tinker, in a metaphor of condescension.[5] Yet the tinker's mobility reflected capital's liquidity—indeed, it proceeded from the same forces—

in ways that were not yet understood. The bourse and the beggar are, once again, two dishes, but to one table.

Given their pedigrees of thievery and deception, then, we might expect that the representations of tinker and peddler in Shakespeare's plays would be as darkly edged as that of Poor Tom, but such is not the case. Instead, Shakespeare seems to move in the opposite direction, offering us the genial warmth of Snout the Tinker in *A Midsummer Night's Dream* rather than, say, a vicious Jonsonian cheat whose trickery mocks the stupidity of his victims. The purpose of this chapter is to consider in some detail the two chief Shakespearean exemplars of this vagrant type, Christopher Sly in *The Taming of the Shrew* and Autolycus in *The Winter's Tale*.

The Taming of a Tinker

Christopher Sly identifies himself to the lord by reciting a comical curriculum vitae that firmly locates him geographically and socially: "Am not I Christopher Sly, old Sly's son of Burton-heath, by birth a peddler, by education a cardmaker, by transmutation a bearherd, and now by present profession a tinker?" (Ind. 2.17-20). And he further cites as a reference "Marian Hacket, the fat alewife of Wincot," to whom he owes the substantial sum of fourteen pence for the ale he has drunk. Stage directions and speech headings of the Folio text of *The Taming of the Shrew,* however, identify him more simply as "Begger" and "drunkard," generic rubrics which include all of Sly's announced "profession[s]." Sly's career path follows a rather low arc, its endpoints of peddler and tinker legally and socially identical. As a "bearherd," however, Sly has begun the first small step toward the world of professional entertainer, a rural version of the quasi-theatrical urban spectacles on display at the Beargarden; perhaps this phase of his career accounts for his garbled allusions to *The Spanish Tragedy* (Ind. 1.9). But Sly's "education" as a "cardmaker"—that is, one who made cards for combing wool—is the most ironic of his occupations, since the enclosure of common lands to pasture sheep, as the More paradigm explained, led to depopulation and an increase in vagrants—hence, to wandering beggars like Sly himself.[6] Sly denies that he is descended from "rogues. Look in the chronicles: we came in with Richard Conqueror" (Ind. 1.3-4), but when the lord tells him he has awakened from a dream, he is happy enough to renounce his "present profession," and in blank verse rather than prose: "Upon my life, I am a lord indeed, / And not a tinker nor Christopher Sly" (Ind. 2.72-73).[7]

I have written elsewhere (1985: 41-50) on the energies of metamorphosis in *The Shrew,* with particular emphasis on the various forms of transformation enacted in the Induction; Sly's attempted metamorphosis into a lord is mirrored in the transformation of the boy page

who dresses like Sly's lady, in the multiple allusions to Ovid's *Metamorphoses* (including the transformations of Cytherea, Io, and Daphne), and in the transforming effects experienced by an audience watching a play (Ind. 1.93-97; 2.127-32). The relation between these modes of transformation in the frame plot and what happens to Kate and Petruchio in the inner plot is a complex issue, the subject of my earlier study and many other critics as well.[8] But here I want to focus more narrowly on Sly's social and economic status and the class issues involved in his metamorphosis into a lord.

The rogue pamphlets of Harman, Dekker, and Robert Greene echo official documents, such as Edward Hext's letter to Burghley in 1596, in describing the histrionic abilities of certain vagabonds, some of whom counterfeit mutilation and degradation, as we have seen, but also others who "play the role" of the proper citizenry, and even infiltrate the legal system. Their role playing is supposedly so perfect that no one can distinguish them by external signs. But Sly is clearly not such a beggar, for he seems to have no histrionic gifts at all, and his lower nature continually reveals itself in his new role. The lord anticipates that Sly,

> . . . if he were conveyed to bed,
> Wrapped in sweet clothes, rings put upon
>   his fingers,
> A most delicious banquet by his bed,
> And brave attendants near him when he wakes,
> Would not the beggar then forget himself?
>   (Ind. 1.36-40)

The expectation is that when Sly awakens, they will "persuade him that he hath been lunatic, / And when he says he is [i.e. now], say that he dreams, / For he is nothing but a mighty lord" (Ind. 1.62-64).

Sly's inability to "forget himself" into a new social role—or at least convince the audience that he can play the part—may remind us of Bottom (another weaver) and his similar incapacity in *A Midsummer Night's Dream,* but it should also be noted that Sly's situation is not exactly identical with those of Dekker's and Fleetwood's rogues, whose counterfeiting reaches only into the ranks of the middling sort. Shakespeare makes Sly attempt something far more difficult, to become "a mighty lord." The social and economic gaps between the tinker and the lord are about as large as could be imagined. Though the tinker is legally condemned for his "profession," the lord has none at all, an "idleness" permissible only in the aristocracy. The lord's avocation is hunting, not for food but for sport. His concern for his overheated dogs, one of whom he would not lose "for twenty pound" (Ind. 1.20), an enormous sum, does not extend to the human being he discovers sleeping: "O monstrous beast, how like a swine he lies! / Grim death, how foul and loathsome is thine image!" (1.33-34). The lord cares for his "dog" but now prepares to trick the "swine" by inverting his social position.

The world of the lord is one of spectacular conspicuous consumption, sensual indulgence, and practiced indolence, as close to the grotesque parody of Sir Epicure Mammon in Jonson's *Alchemist* as it is distant from Sly's "small ale" (Ind. 2.1) here. The lord commands the huntsmen—evidently now not his equals but his social inferiors—to see to the details of the jest:

> Carry him gently to my fairest chamber,
> And hang it round with all my wanton pictures.
> Balm his foul head in warm distilled waters,
> And burn sweet wood to make the lodging sweet.
> Procure me music ready when he wakes,
> To make a dulcet and a heavenly sound.
> And if he chance to speak, be ready straight,
> And with a low submissive reverence
> Say, "What is it your honor will command?"
> Let one attend him with a silver basin
> Full of rosewater and bestrewed with flowers;
> Another bear the ewer, the third a diaper,
> And say, "Will't please your lordship cool
>   your hands?"
> Someone be ready with a costly suit,
> And ask him what apparel he will wear;
> Another tell him of his hounds and horse,
> And that his lady mourns at his disease.
>   (Ind. 1.45-61)

All this because "he is nothing but a mighty lord." Yet it is not Sly's past life that can be thought of as a "dream" here, but rather the one the lord describes, which is a fantasy of hierarchical power and privilege.

The dream of class privilege, soothed by the murmurs of "low submissive reverence," is punctuated by the arrival of the players, who "offer service to your lordship" (Ind. 1.77). They had better receive the lord's patronage, too, otherwise these players will violate the same vagrancy laws—in the same paragraph, in fact—that defined tinkers and peddlers as vagabonds.[9] The lord calls for a play, the players exit to prepare, and the lord instructs that "Barthol'mew my page" be "dressed in all suits like a lady," to pretend to be "Lord" Sly's wife. Again the language emphasizes the comic inversion of the hierarchical, and now specifically marital, power. The page's proper conduct, we are told, should be "such as he hath observed in noble ladies / Unto their lords":

> Such duty to the drunkard let him do
> With soft low tongue and lowly courtesy,
> And say, "What is't your honor will command,
> Wherein your lady and your humble wife
> May show her duty and make known her love?"
> And then with kind embracements,
>   tempting kisses,

> And with declining head into his bosom,
> Bid him shed tears, as being overjoyed
> To see her noble lord restored to health,
> Who for this seven years hath esteemed him
> No better than a poor and loathsome beggar.
>   (Ind. 1.104-22)

Now the "submissive" fantasy of class privilege merges with the patriarchal dream of the "humble wife," easy to "command," dedicated to "duty." These positions are normalized, in the lord's plan, while Sly's ordinary position is no better than, and legally, no different from, that of a "poor and loathsome beggar."

When Sly awakens into his fictive lordship, however, it becomes clear that no matter what "apparel" or "costly suit" he wears, he cannot be mimetically transformed into the elevated social position of the lord. Promises of fantastic sensual indulgences, including erotic Ovidian transformation scenes, are summoned up to encourage the befuddled tinker, but clothes, it is clear, do not make the gentleman, though Sly continues to try. It has often been noted how Sly's attempt to command his "Lady's" obedience anticipates Petruchio's with Kate, but the key passage again brings together both marital and class hierarchies:

> *Sly.* Are you my wife, and will not call
>   me husband?
> My men should call me "lord"; I am
>   your goodman.
> *Page.* My husband and my lord, my lord
>   and husband,
> I am your wife in all obedience.
>   (Ind. 2.102-5)

Sly's wonderfully blunt command—"Servants, leave me and her alone. / Madam, undress you and come now to bed" (Ind. 2.113-14)—is no different from the lord's commands earlier, except that they are not obeyed. Instead, the players are announced, and Sly dispenses mock-aristocratic grace ("Marry, I will let them play it") but also reveals his confusion over the exact nature of this entertainment: "Is not a comonty a Christmas gambold or a tumbling trick? . . . household stuff?" (Ind. 2.133-36). The beggar is thus, as always, a kind of spectacle himself, an object lesson and source of amusement for the lord no less than the official entertainers, the players.

In the anonymous play *The Taming of A Shrew,* as is well known, Sly is seen and heard again at the end of the play, the frame plot closing securely; once more dressed in his "owne apparell," Sly promises to try out the shrew-taming lessons on his own wife. He speaks of his experience as Bottom does in *Midsummer Night's Dream:* "I have had / The bravest dreame to night, that ever thou / H[e]ardest in all thy life" (Bullough: 1.108).

But in *The Shrew,* by contrast, there is no awakening or demystification of Sly, who has vanished textually from the play. In a way, then, Shakespeare at last fulfills the beggar's own fantasy, "I would be loath to fall into my dreams again" (Ind. 2.123), and he remains in the apparel of a gentleman.

Autolycus: A "Gentleman Born"

After Simon Forman saw a performance of *The Winter's Tale* at the Globe on 15 May 1611, he reported the Leontes-Polixenes plot with some care, explicitly noting the abandonment and recovery of Perdita. Yet Forman notoriously did not mention any of the spectacular stage effects from the second half of the play—no Chorus of Time (though he does note that Perdita is sixteen years old), no bear, no eating of Antigonus, no great statue scene; he does not even note Hermione's apparent death, much less her rebirth. But one feature of the second half of the play struck his attention greatly, and he devoted considerable space to it:

> Remember also the Rog that cam in all tottered like coll pixci and howe he feined him sicke & to have bin Robbed of all that he had and howe he cosened the por man of all his money, and after cam to the shep sher with a pedlers packe & ther cosened them Again of all their money And howe he changed apparrell with the kinge of Bomia his sonn, and then howe he turned Courtier &c.

The message of all this was clear to Forman: "Beware of trustinge feined beggars or fawninge fellouss" (Chambers: 2.341). Autolycus is an entirely different kind of "feined beggar" than Poor Tom, of course—not a lunatic but the cheerful peddler, part of the tradition of the merry beggar. He enters singing of the red blood reigning in the winter's pale and the sweet birds, O how they sing.

Although Autolycus's character seems derived primarily from literary sources—something of the picaresque, a little of the Vice (Felperin: 217-18), and a great deal of a tradition that romanticized the freedom and openness of the tramp's life, as we saw in the first chapter—still, the language Shakespeare has created for him receives its life from a number of other wellsprings. The songs link Autolycus with a popular tradition of festive natural celebration; many analogous songs have been reported with the same peddler's cry, "What do you lack?"[10] On the other hand, the language of Autolycus also reveals a strong indebtedness to the conny-catching pamphlets of Robert Greene, not only in the specific trick which Forman recalled (which seems to come from *The Second Part of Conny-catching* [1591]), but in the vocabulary and diction of his language.[11] Autolycus is given many of the specialized terms of the thieves' trade: "doxy," "pugging" (or "prigging"), "die and drab," "prig," "cutpurse," "I

picked and cut most of their festival purses," and so forth. More, his voice is both unique in its colloquial eccentricities and almost Jonsonian in its sharp familiarity with the conventions of thieving: "You might have pinched a placket, it was senseless. 'Twas nothing to geld a codpiece of a purse. I could have filed keys off that hung in chains. No hearing, no feeling, but my sir's song, and admiring the nothing of it . . . had not the old man come in with hubbub against his daughter and the King's son and scared my choughs from the chaff, I had not left a purse alive in the whole army" (*The Winter's Tale* 4.4.612-21).

Autolycus's language is Shakespeare's closest approximation to beggar's cant. He is indeed a merry-hearted, jovial vagabond, but he also knows that "Gallows and knock are too powerful on the highway; beating and hanging are terrors to me" (4.3.28-29). He can flourish now because "I see this is the time that the unjust man doth thrive" (4.4.677-78). In placing his character so precisely in this particular social context, Shakespeare inevitably invokes questions of class privilege and social identity—issues that concern the other characters in Bohemia as much as they do Autolycus.

While much criticism has in the past been concerned with the relative attractiveness of Autolycus as a character,[12] his structural function in the play has also been frequently described in formalist terms.[13] Yet Autolycus appears not in an eternal and unreal springtime but in the particular historical context of Jacobean England. David Kaula has demonstrated how "the terminology Autolycus applies to his wares [e.g., "trumpery," 4.4.600] belongs to the verbal arsenal of anti-Catholic polemical writing in Reformation England" (289), and he argues that as "the cunning merchant of popish wares" (292), Autolycus is intended to be "a counterpart to Perdita" (293), setting up a binary distinction between "the artificial and the natural, the predatory and the charitable, the licentious and the chaste" (294).[14]

One thread of Kaula's argument is directly relevant to my topic here: his observation that "Autolycus' 'popish' associations seem to be limited to his peddler's role" (301). But this association is completely predictable, given the essential transgressiveness of the peddler to begin with. Kaula quotes from several Protestant writers who link Catholic icons with peddlers' wares. One of them is Samuel Harsnet ("the trinkets, toyes, & pedlars ware in the Popes holy budget" [Kaula: 289]), from whose work Shakespeare quotes some years earlier in *King Lear.* Another writer claims, in 1602, that "Romish wares" are

> sent abroad among the common people, both Protestants and Papists in London and in the countrey, & that, by certain women Brokers and Pedlers . . . who with baskets on their armes, shal come and offer you other wares under a colour, and

so sell you these, where they see and know any
likelihood to utter them. . . . under the habit of such,
many young Jesuites, and olde Masse-priests range
abroad, and drawe disciples after them. (Kaula: 291)

Here, there is transgression on many levels: not only
religious and economic, but gender-related as well, for
if anyone should not be errant, it is a woman, even
"certain women." Yet as Alice Clark has noted, "in
some districts the trade [of peddler] was almost [a]
monopoly" of women (206).

In the great fantasy of paranoia, the "people" have
been infiltrated by papists, peddlers, and women, each
of whom works through a disguise, and operates
through deceit, "under a colour." Even when something innocuous is being peddled—ballads, for example,
rather than heresy—the same rhetorical negatives are
invoked, as in one work of 1592, which complains of
the "Ballad-seller, [who] hath a whole Armie of
runnagates at his reversion, that swarme everie where
i n *England,* and with their ribauld songs infect the
Youth of this flourishing Commonweale."[15] Chettle
(also 1592) echoes this vision in Anthonie Nownow's
comment in *Kind-Hartes Dreame.*

> I am given to understand, that there be a company
> of idle youths, loathing honest labour and dispising
> lawfull trades, betake them to a vagrant and vicious
> life, in every corner of Cities & market Townes of
> the Realme singing and selling of ballads and
> pamphletes full of ribaudrie, and all scurrilous
> vanity, to the prophanation of Gods name, and with-
> drawing people from christian exercises, especially
> at faires markets and such publike meetings. (15)

Thus, even these peddlers, often employed by the stationers themselves to distribute their printed commodi-
ties, "swarme," in the usual metaphor, and "infect"
parts of the body politic.

Peddlers were known to frequent "wakes and wassails,
meetings, markets, fairs," as Berowne noted in *Love's
Labor's Lost,* while a "petty Countrey Faire" itself was
said to be little more than "the publication of some few
Pedlers packs distinguisht into Boothes" (Saltonstall: 49);
thus Autolycus's appearance at a sheep-shearing festival is conventional. Wassails, fairs, and sheep-shearing
festivals were public sites outside the normal boundaries of surveillance and control, and thus they were
socially marginal in every sense of the term. Jonson's
Bartholomew Fair (1614) is a catalogue of every
"enormity" imaginable at such a fair.[16] Shakespeare's
Autolycus combines in one character two of Jonson's—
Nightingale the ballad-seller, who works in league with
Edgeworth, the cutpurse. The commercial activity such
peddlers engage in, though statutorily illegal, is considerable and quite welcomed by the customers. Peddlers
such as Autolycus are condemned in part, then, be-

cause they enable a redefinition of the very concept of
the marketplace—no longer closed but open, not static
but fluid, not fixed in its elements but "placeless," in
Michael Bristol's term (1991: 163). They represent, in
short, the transgressive fluidity of capital.

Perhaps the central paradigm of the feudal conception
of work, enshrined (or embalmed) in the London craft-
guilds and in the codifications of the Statute of Arti-
ficers, is the master-apprentice relation. But the peddler, both cause and symptom, heralds a different kind
of economy, in which a different paradigm operates:
"Come to the peddler;/ Money's a meddler, / That doth
utter all men's ware-a" (*The Winter's Tale* 4.4.321-
23). Money talks: money can "utter," both speak and
put on the market, *all* "ware." The peddler is the
embodiment of this medium of exchange, this "meddler." To "meddle" also carries the sense "to mix
(wares) fraudulently" (OED v.1b) and "to have sexual
intercourse (with)" (OED v.5)—perhaps from the standard contemporary pun on "medlar," the pulpy apple
synonymous with the female genitals.[17] Sexual meddling is therefore a refraction of economic meddling.
All these associations may also be seen at play in the
Pedler's speech in John Heywood's *The Foure PP* (c.
1531): "Why, dost thou nat knowe that every pedler /
In every trifull must be a medler?/ Specially in womens
triflinges" (lines 217-19). Money is the "meddler,"
Autolycus says, and the peddler's profession participates in an economy of alleged corruption linked to
several other types of transgression.

Autolycus's personal history, moreover, mimics the
declension from an older to a newer form of service:
"I have served Prince Florizel," he tells the audience,
"and in my time wore three-pile, but now I am out of
service" (4.3.13-14). Now, for Autolycus, "My traffic
is sheets" and "my revenue is the silly cheat" (4.3.23,
27-28). Poor Tom, too, was once "a servingman, proud
in heart and mind" (*King Lear* 3.4.84), but is now
"nothing." Since being "whipped out of the court,"
Autolycus reports (in the third person) of his career
that he has been "an ape bearer, then a process server,
a bailiff. Then he compassed a motion of the Prodigal
Son and married a tinker's wife . . . having flown over
many knavish professions, he settled only in rogue"
(4.3.87-97).

As an accomplished, role-playing rogue, Autolycus has
certainly mastered more than the role of peddler. In his
initial encounter with the Clown, Autolycus does an
excellent version of Nicholas Genings, as he falls to
the ground in apparent agony:

> *Autolycus.* O, that ever I was born! [*He
> grovels on the ground*]
> *Clown.* I' the name of me!
> *Autolycus.* O, help me, help me! Pluck but
>   off these rags, and then death, death!

Clown. Alack, poor soul! Thou hast need of more rags to lay on thee, rather than have these off.

Autolycus. O sir, the loathsomeness of them offends me more than the stripes I have received, which are mighty ones and millions. (4.3.49-57)

Another Shakespearean character also has "the falling-sickness": "He fell down in the marketplace, and foamed at mouth, and was speechless" (*Julius Caesar* 1.2.252-53). But Julius Caesar's infirmity is meant to be real, while Autolycus is anything but speechless. Indeed, he claims that he has been robbed and beaten, "my money and apparel ta'en from me, and these detestable things [his garments] put upon me" (4.3.60-62). Claiming that his "shoulder blade is out," Autolycus picks the Clown's pocket as he is helped to his feet.

This scene's language of "rags," "apparel," "garments," and "horseman's coat" reflects Shakespeare's emphasis on the rogue's shifting, unstable identity and his histrionic gifts.[18] Simon Forman's account of the play, quoted earlier, marked three distinct kinds of "apparel" for Autolycus: first, he "cam in all tottered like coll pixci"[19]; afterwards he came to the sheep-shearing "with a pedlers packe"; and finally, "he changed apparrell with the kinge of Bomia his sonn, and then howe he turned Courtier &c." In this last phase, the beggar and the king(-to-be) once again confront one another, and the mirroring of inversion is played out in an outright exchange of clothing. And like Christopher Sly trying to become a "great lord," Autolycus is to be "turned Courtier." When Camillo and Florizel approach Autolycus to exchange clothing, Camillo remarks that they will exchange only "the outside of thy poverty" (4.4.635). As we have repeatedly seen, though, the outside of poverty is always the least authentic of cultural signs; even the "millions" of "stripes" Autolycus claims to have received were frequently faked, and he never shows them anyhow.

As the gentles speak the language of the theater—"play," "part"—Camillo advises Perdita to "disliken / The truth of your own seeming" (4.4.655-56), a practice she is already unwittingly engaged in, and which is being extravagantly enacted by Autolycus. His self-transformation into a courtier begins when he takes off a false beard ("Let me pocket up my peddler's excrement," 4.4.716-17), and announces himself to the Clown and Shepherd in high astounding terms, almost Falstaffian in their mock-pomposity:

> Whether it like me or no, I am a courtier. Seest thou not the air of the court in these enfoldings? Hath not my gait in it the measure of the court? Receives not thy nose court odor from me? Reflect I not on thy baseness court contempt? Think'st thou,

for that I insinuate to toze from thee thy business, I am therefore no courtier? I am courtier cap-a-pie, and one that will either push on or pluck back thy business there. Whereupon I command thee to open thy affair. (4.4.733-41)

While the Clown thinks "this cannot be but a great courtier," his father the Shepherd reflects more observantly that "his garments are rich, but he wears them not handsomely" (4.4.751-54).

"Garments" and "apparel" continue to be the subject when we next see the rustics at the court of Sicilia. They now wear new clothing and claim the same transformation of social class that Sly and Autolycus did: "See you these clothes? Say you see them not and think me still no gentleman born. You were best say these robes are not gentleman born. Give me the lie, do, and try whether I am not now a gentleman born" (5.2.132-35). These jokes may have been meant to reflect the phenomenon of the great number of newly made "gentlemen" in King James's court, but there is an equally strong connection to Shakespeare's interest throughout the play in whether a "gentleman" is "born" or made, natural or constructed. The Clown reports a comically confusing nexus of kinship relations: "I was a gentleman born before my father; for the King's son took me by the hand and called me brother; and then the two kings called my father brother; and then the Prince my brother and the Princess my sister called my father father" (5.2.140-44). Like the famous debate in 4.4 over the priority and value of art and nature, the Clown's speech further blurs the categories of distinction. Yet clothes, again, do not make the gentleman. In a final irony, Autolycus and the clowns reverse position again, and he enters "courtly" service again to his new "good masters" (5.2.175), the Clown and the Shepherd.

Autolycus is hardly a Grand Rogue or Upright Man in Harman's terms: "On the highway," he admitted, "gallows and knock are too powerful . . . beating and hanging are terrors to me." He projects his memory of such "terrors" onto the rustics in a comic but disturbing set-piece when he threatens them.

> If that shepherd be not in handfast, let him fly. The curses he shall have, the tortures he shall feel, will break the back of man, the heart of monster. . . . Some say he shall be stoned; but that death is too soft for him, say I. . . . He has a son, who shall be flayed alive; then, 'nointed over with honey, set on the head of a wasp's nest; then stand till he be three-quarters and a dram dead; then recovered again with aqua vitae or some other hot infusion; then, raw as he is, and in the hottest day prognostication proclaims, shall be set against a brick wall, the sun looking with a southward eye upon him, where he is to behold him with flies blown to death. (4.4.772-95)

Such tortures far exceed what any beggar might legally receive, though the testimony of some former prisoners in Bridewell, we saw, was chilling enough.[20] The only way to escape such torture, as Autolycus notes, is to approach the prince. Shakespeare's conclusion to this line of action in the play resonates suggestively with the passage in *Lear* that exposes "the great image of authority" (4.6.158ff.). Here, the Clown says of Autolycus, "He seems to be of great authority. Close with him, give him gold; and though authority be a stubborn bear, yet he is oft led by the nose with gold. Show the inside of your purse to the outside of his hand" (4.4.803-7).

The nature and validity of authority, in both legal and social categories, are thus brought into question by the very presence of the beggar: poor implies rich, low implies high, "nothing" implies "all." The lean beggar serves not just as an antithesis to the fat king, but as an opposing principle to all authority that derives from the sociopolitical hierarchy that maintains and justifies the monarchy, the court, and the social gradations ramifying from it. "What authority surfeits on would relieve us," says the First Citizen in the opening scene of *Coriolanus* (1.1.15-16). Here the reality of hunger among the poor is not genially transformed, as it is in the cases of Sly and Autolycus, but fully staged in a Shakespearean version of Bacon's dictum that "the rebellions of the belly are the worst."[21]

> If they would yield us but the superfluity while it were wholesome, we might guess they relieved us humanely. But they think we are too dear. The leanness that afflicts us, the object of our misery, is as an inventory to particularize their abundance. Our sufferance is a gain to them. Let us revenge this with our pikes ere we become rakes; for the gods know I speak this in hunger for bread, not in thirst for revenge. (*Coriolanus* 1.1.16-23)

"The leanness that afflicts" the poor, in the Citizen's dialectic, is at the same time the sign of the patricians' "abundance." The patricians are fat, overflowing, surfeited, indifferent to the poor: they "suffer us to famish, and their storehouses crammed with grain; make edicts for usury to support usurers; repeal daily any wholesome act established against the rich; and provide more piercing statutes daily, to chain up and restrain the poor. If the wars eat us not up, they will" (1.1.78-84). The "statutes" are "piercing," not just in the general sense, but as we have seen, in the literal ways in which beggars' bodies were marked and punished. Yet this rebellion, in Menenius's famous allegory, turns out not to be one of the belly, which is said to signify the beneficent Senators of Rome, but the "great toe," because like it, they are the "lowest, basest, poorest" of the rebellion (1.1.155-56).

Shakespeare's general allusion in this scene to the Midlands Revolt of 1607 has often been noted, per-

haps most brilliantly by Janet Adelman, who illuminates the play's underlying dynamic of rebellion, hunger, and violence.[22] As Manning shows (1988: 229-46), the rising in 1607 began as enclosure riots and soon spread to wider forms of disorder and violence before it was suppressed. Although the contemporaneity of the allusion in *Coriolanus* is clear enough, it is also significant that one of Coriolanus's lines attacking the mob ("You cry against the noble Senate, who, / Under the gods, keep you in awe, which else / Would feed on one another," 1.1.185-87) echoes a line from the similar insurrection scene, probably by Shakespeare, in *The Book of Sir Thomas More*, where "men like ravenous fishes / Would feed on one another" (2.3.92-93). Whether this allusion is understood as a specific one, or as a coincidental reference to the familiar political trope of "big fish eats little fish," it continues the recurring discursive formation of the beggar or masterless man or woman as essentially constituted by his or her body—indeed, as one of the lowest levels on the food chain.

Coriolanus dismisses the hunger of the poor along with their "proverbs": "That hunger broke stone walls, that dogs must eat, / That meat was made for mouths, that the gods sent not / Corn for the rich men only" (1.1.205-8). Hunger and poverty are, if not technically synonymous, nevertheless inevitably linked, and Shakespeare constantly associates the wandering poor with the kind of starvation that leads to political danger. The citizens of Rome in *Coriolanus* "are all resolved rather to die than to famish" (1.1.4-5), and Richard III can think of no greater insult than to call Richmond's troops

> A sort of vagabonds, rascals, and runaways,
> A scum of Bretons and base lackey peasants,
> Whom their o'ercloyed country vomits forth
> To desperate adventures and assured destruction.
>
> . . . . .
>
> These famished beggars, weary of their lives,
> Who, but for dreaming on this fond exploit,
> For want of means, poor rats, had hanged
>   themselves.
>
> (*Richard III* 5.3.316-19, 329-31)

Again, these beggars are in opposition to plenitude, though the "o'er-cloyed country," having much too much its fill of such figures, must vomit them forth; famished themselves, they are paradoxically also a nauseating food to others. And "rebellion . . . hurly-burly innovation . . . [and] insurrection" are fueled, as Henry IV warns, by "moody beggars, starving for a time / Of pell-mell havoc and confusion" (*I Henry IV* 5.1.74-82). Thus the hungry hunger for chaos, which will leave them yet hungrier and more desperate. The same kind of "loud rebellion" threatens in *Henry VIII*, where

The clothiers all, not able to maintain
The many to them 'longing, have put off
The spinsters, carders, fullers, weavers, who,
Unfit for other life, compelled by hunger
And lack of other means, in desperate manner
Daring th'event to th'teeth, are all in uproar,
And danger serves among them.

(1.2.29-37)

This last reference to the social unrest arising from widespread unemployment in the wool industry returns us to Sly and Autolycus, who had adapted to rather than rebelled against their subjection. Sly, we recall, had once worked as a "cardmaker," and Autolycus finds his greatest success as a cutpurse at a sheep-shearing festival—the end product, so to speak, of the socio-agricultural revolution of the enclosure movement which, it was argued, created vast numbers of vagabonds such as Autolycus himself. While Jack Cade was "ready to famish," "so hungry that, if I might have a lease of my life for a thousand years, I could stay no longer," and claims to be "vanquished by famine, not by valor" (*2 Henry VI* 4.10.2, 4-6, 74), Autolycus is a source of plenitude, commercially speaking. "He utters [tunes] as [if] he had eaten ballads" (4.4.184-85), we are told, and his peddler's pack is a "silken treasury" (4.4.350), a cornucopia of consumer products, as eagerly desired "as if my trinkets had been hallowed and brought a benediction to the buyer" (4.4.604-5). Sly, as we saw, was offered a vision of sensual and gustatory plenitude ("A most delicious banquet by his bed," *The Taming of the Shrew* Ind. 1.38) which is inverted in the inner plot in Petruchio's strategy of starving Kate to tame her. The associations she makes by now seem inevitable:

What, did he marry me to famish me?
Beggars that come unto my father's door
Upon entreaty have a present alms;
If not, elsewhere they meet with charity.
But I, who never knew how to entreat,
Nor never needed that I should entreat,
Am starved for meat, giddy for lack of sleep,
With oaths kept waking, and with brawling fed.

(4.3.3-10)

Such deprivation can only be comparable to the life of a beggar, it seems, but Kate's confidence in their receiving "present alms" is not always borne out in Renaissance England: she obviously never met anyone like Timon of Athens, who advises "Hate all, curse all, show charity to none, / But let the famished flesh slide from the bone / Ere thou relieve the beggar. Give to dogs / What thou deniest to men" (*Timon* 4.3.532-35).

Cade's attempted ascent to a kind of peasant kingship and Poor Tom's elevation (as we will see) to the position of "learned justice" are therefore comically mirrored in Sly's and Autolycus's reversals in status from vagabond tinker and peddler to lord and gentleman. These doubled inversions suggest that the beggar's status in these plays is not only to speak the voice of the dispossessed, which they do insistently, and not only to offer a sociopolitical impersonation of the voice and values of those above them, but also to be that force which naturally seeks to *rise,* and so constitutes a deeply politicized energy.[23] The presence of the beggar always engages the question of social class. Even Christopher Sly, the most passive figure in this group, begins to imagine the impossible: "I am a lord indeed, / And not a tinker nor Christopher Sly" (Ind. 2.72-73). But the beggar, in the end, is never permitted fully to "forget himself," and all the mock-elevations are eventually overturned.

Notes

[1] The language of the 1572 statute (14 Eliz. I., c.5) is virtually identical: "all Juglers Pedlars Tinkers and Petye Chapmen" (*TED*: 2.329).

[2] For "juggling," or legerdemain, see Samuel Rid's how-to manual, *The Art of Juggling or Legerdemaine* (1612); Rid plagiarizes freely from Reginald Scot's *The Discovery of Witchcraft* (1584). For a dramatic example of a beggar con-man practicing juggling, see Fletcher and Massinger's *Beggars' Bush* (3.1.62-96), where Prig tricks the "Boores."

[3] The Arden edition of *Love's Labor's Lost* quotes from Gabriel Harvey (1592) and William Covell (1595) in illustrating "by gross" as a term for wholesale, in opposition to "retail" (155). Dekker (1609) has the same conjunction of terms—one sells "by the gross" and another "buys his sport by the penny and like a haggler is glad to utter it again by retailing" (Pendry 1968: 98).

[4] In a more benign characteristic, tinkers were also said to be innately musical, in some accounts even the ur-musicians: "From his Art was Musicke first invented, and therefore is hee alwaies furnisht with a song; to which his hammer keeping tune, proves that he was the first founder of the Kettle-drumme" (*Overburian*: 35); "his Musicke is always a paire of wodden Organs under a Peinthouse, or a Crosse which he loves not to see; beside his daily practice of the voice set and sung to the Tabering on a Kettle" (R.M.: C6ᵛ). Shakespeare makes nothing of this tradition in Sly, and little beyond Autolycus's singing itself.

[5] Dekker says "the theatre is your poets' Royal Exchange," where the Muses are merchants, "players are their factors," and gallants and courtiers are "the soundest paymasters and . . . the surest chapmen" (Pendry 1968: 98). As Knights observes, "It was international finance that first made capital mobile. It was international finance that prepared the way for the doctrine of complete economic freedom. . . . All that Gresham

[who built the Royal Exchange] and the financiers who followed him represented, therefore, would be completely alien to the peasants and small masters who still formed more than three quarters of the population of England. The ideas of the local community were not those of the Royal Exchange, and a clash was inevitable" (44-45).

6 Boose situates the play in the context of "a vast cultural circulation of the anxieties of displacement that arose from the enclosure era" (203), linking the concepts of "husbandry" and the ownership of common lands to the situation of women, particularly Kate. See also Stallybrass on this question. Boose goes on to show how "the disgruntlements of class are being transferred into the space of gender" (213) in *Shrew*. Her reading of Sly overlaps with mine at several points.

7 None of the details of his "profession" is present in *The Taming of A Shrew*.

8 Two recent, and quite different, discussions by Sirluck and Hager (26-33) are useful.

9 Skura offers a fine reading of the Induction, through the trope of the "Player King as Beggar in Great Men's Houses" (99-106). She points out that while the Lord is "necessary to realize Sly's fantasies, . . . Sly is also necessary for the Lord to work out his own" (103).

10 See, for example, *The Pedler's Prophecy:* "What lacke you, what buy you, any good pinnes etc" (D3), as well as the Dekker reference from *O per se O* quoted in the first section of this chapter. Gerrard's song in *Beggars' Bush*—"Bring out your Cony-skins, faire maids to me" (3.1.97-113)—is part of the same tradition. As one writer noted of the peddler, "What doe yee lacke is his ordinary intergatory" (*Cater:* 138).

11 Autolycus's links to the traditions of vagabondage were briefly described in McPeek (237-46). A far more compelling account of Autolycus's historical and social contexts is provided in Mowat's essay, which authoritatively discusses the "texts and infracontexts" of *The Winter's Tale* 4.3 in particular, and of the character in general. Mowat emphasizes the specific use of the term "rogue" to refer to Autolycus (64-66), whereas I believe he is more clearly marked in the tradition of the peddler.

12 Opinion about Autolycus's character has varied considerably. For Knight, Autolycus "is spring incarnate; carefree, unmoral, happy, and sets the note for a springlike turn in our drama" (100). Berlin claims that, as Autolycus is the representative of "the lowest, the underworld . . . the audience feels no sadness about his plight, because he *is* a rogue, because his spirit is essentially merry, and because the audience is not sympathetic toward him at the play's end. Shakespeare

casts no moral opinion against him" (228). Vickers, however, finds that Autolycus's "attitude and especially his images reveal a boasting superiority which is less attractive" (414).

13 Tillyard argues that Autolycus is "organic to the whole country scene, and that it would collapse into an oversweetness of sentiment without him. . . . His delinquencies, like the pastoral realism, keep the earthly paradise sufficiently earthly without disturbing the paradisiac state" (Muir: 86). Frey sees his structural function in similar terms: Autolycus is "a figure who mediates humorously between the claims of Polixenes and those of Perdita and Florizel. He excites a laughter whose result is always to lessen the tension between opposing forces: age and youth, pretension and reality, greed and charity, wrath and forgiveness, lion and lamb" (148). Cox, however, describes in some detail the parallels between Autolycus and Leontes, concluding that "the story of Autolycus, self-robber and self-deceiver, is a springlike variation of the winter story of Leontes" (298).

14 Kaula's argument becomes unconvincing, for me, when it pushes over into explicit allegory: so Perdita's "betrothal to Florizel is meant to represent, on one level of symbolism, the union between Christ and his Bride" (296), and Perdita is equated with "the Virgin Mary" (297). I also see the binary distinctions Kaula lists as deconstructed within the play. Hamilton attempts, with mixed success, to place Autolycus in the historical context of the Union debates of 1604-10: he "is not a Scot exactly, but he is a refiguration and an acknowledgment of a social and political phenomenon in which the Scottish people were implicated and one that was threatening the English system of legitimation" (244).

15 E. de Maisonneuve, *Gerileon of England* (1592), A4; quoted in the Arden edition of *The Winter's Tale* (100).

16 See Stallybrass and White on the cultural significance of Bartholomew Fair.

17 Cf. *Coriolanus* (4.5.49-52): *Third Servingman:* "Do you meddle with my master?" *Coriolanus:* "Ay, 'tis an honester service than to meddle with thy mistress"; and *Romeo* (1.2.39-40): "It is written that the shoemaker should meddle with his yard." For "medlar," see *Romeo* (2.1.35-37), *Measure for Measure* (4.3.172), *As You Like It* (3.2.116-18), and *Timon* (4.3.309-15).

18 See my comments elsewhere on the metamorphoses of Autolycus and those in the play as a whole (1985: 210-25). Mowat points out the inversion of the Good Samaritan story here (61-62).

19 The Arden editor glosses "coll pixci" as "Colle- or Colt-pixie = hobgoblin, particularly in the form of a ragged (tattered) colt which leads horses astray into bogs, etc." (xxii).

[20] The literary source of this torture is probably Boccaccio's *Decameron* 2.9 (Arden *The Winter's Tale*: 132), but oral traditions of contemporary Spanish cruelties might also have been in the background.

[21] Leinwand reminds us that the mob in *Coriolanus* is made up of "citizens" of the "middling sort": "Only their hunger may temporarily align them with either the poor or with those just a step ahead of poverty" (1993: 296).

[22] For an early study, see Pettet; see also Patterson (135-46).

[23] Though they are very different characters, Cade, Poor Tom, Sly, and Autolycus share many common attributes in their language: it is almost exclusively prose, highly colloquial, filled with puns and dramatic irony, semantically and syntactically unstable, invariably refracting the imagery and thematic concerns of the "high" language of the plays. But beyond the obvious political themes *in* their language, the most political aspect of it is that it exists at all. For more on their language, see my essay (1992).

Works Cited

Adelman, Janet. " 'Anger's My Meat': Feeding, Dependency, and Aggression in *Coriolanus*." In *Representing Shakespeare*, ed. Murray M. Schwartz and Coppèlia Kahn. Baltimore: Johns Hopkins University Press, 1980.

Armin, Robert. *Collected Works,* ed. J. P. Feather. London: Johnson Reprints, 1972.

Awdeley, John. *The Fraternity of Vacabondes.* In *The Rogues and Vagabonds of Shakspere's Youth,* ed. Edward Viles and F. J. Furnivall. London, 1880.

Bacon, Francis. *The Works of Francis Bacon,* ed. James Spedding et al. London: Longmans, 1857-74.

Beaumont, Francis, and John Fletcher. *The Dramatic Works in the Beaumont and Fletcher Canon,* ed. Fredson Bowers. New York: Cambridge University Press, 1985.

Berlin, Normand. *The Base String: The Underworld in Elizabethan Drama.* Rutherford, N. J.: Fairleigh Dickinson University Press, 1968.

Book of Sir Thomas More, The. 1911; reprint Oxford: Oxford University Press, 1961.

Boose, Lynda E. "*The Taming of the Shrew,* Good Husbandry, and Enclosure." In *Shakespeare Reread,* ed. Russ McDonald. Ithaca: Cornell University Press, 1994.

Bristol, Michael D. "In Search of the Bear: Spatiotemporal Form and the Heterogeneity of Economies in *The Winter's Tale*." *SQ* 42 (1991): 145-67.

Bullough, Geoffrey, ed. *Narrative and Dramatic Sources of Shakespeare.* New York: Columbia University Press, 1975.

Carroll, William C. "Language, Politics, and Poverty in Shakespearian Drama." *ShS* 44 (1992): 17-24.

———. *The Metamorphoses of Shakespearean Comedy.* Princeton: Princeton University Press, 1985.

Cater-Character, A, Throwne out of a Boxe by an Experienced Gamester (1631), ed. James O. Halliwell. London: Thomas Richards, 1859.

Chambers. E. K. *William Shakespeare: A Study of Facts and Problems.* Oxford: Clarendon, 1930.

Chettle, Henry. *Kind-Hartes Dreame (1592),* ed. G. B. Harrison. London, 1923.

Clark, Alice. *Working Life of Women in the Seventeenth Century.* New York: Harcourt, Brace & Howe, 1920.

Copland, Robert. *The Highway to the Spital-House.* Reprinted in Judges.

Cox, Lee Sheridan. "The Role of Autolycus in *The Winter's Tale*." *SEL* 9 (1969): 283-301.

Dekker, Thomas. *The Dramatic Works of Thomas Dekker,* ed. Fredson Bowers. Cambridge: Cambridge University Press, 1955.

———. *The Non-Dramatic Works of Thomas Dekker,* ed. A. B. Grosart. 1885; reprint New York: Russell & Russell, 1963.

Felperin, Howard. *Shakespearean Romance.* Princeton: Princeton University Press, 1972.

Fletcher, John. *The Dramatic Works in the Beaumont and Fletcher Canaon,* ed. Fredson Bowers. New York: Cambridge University Press, 1985.

Fletcher, John, and Philip Massinger. *Beggars' Bush,* ed. John H. Dorenkamp. The Hague: Mouton, 1967.

Frey, Charles. *Shakespeare's Vast Romance: A Study of "The Winter's Tale."* Columbia: University of Missouri Press, 1980.

Hager, Alan. *Shakespeare's Political Animal: Schema and Schemata in the Canon.* Newark: University of Delaware Press, 1990.

Hamilton, Donna B. "*The Winter's Tale* and the Language of Union, 1604-1610." *ShakS* 21 (1993): 228-50.

Harman, Thomas. *A Caveat or Warening for Commen Cursetors Vulgarely Called Vagabones.* In *The Rogues and Vagabonds of Shakspere's Youth,* ed. Edward Viles and F. J. Furnivall. London, 1880.

Heywood, John. *The Plays of John Heywood,* ed. Richard Axton and Peter Happe. Cambridge: D. S. Brewer, 1991.

Jonson, Ben. *Ben Jonson,* ed. C. H. Herford and Percy and Evelyn Simpson. Oxford University Press, 1925-52.

Judges, A. V. *The Elizabethan Underworld.* 1930; reprint New York: Octagon, 1965.

Kaula, David. "Autolycus' Trumpery." *SEL* 16 (1976): 287-303.

Kinney, Arthur, ed. *Rogues, Vagabonds, & Sturdy Beggars.* Amherst: University of Massachusetts Press, 1990.

Knight, G. Wilson. *The Crown of Life.* 1958; reprint New York: Barnes & Noble, 1966.

Knights, L. C. *Drama and Society in the Age of Jonson.* 1937; reprint New York: Norton, 1968.

Leinwand, Theodore B. "Shakespeare and the Middling Sort." *SQ* 44 (1993): 284-303.

Manning, Roger B. *Village Revolts: Social Protest and Popular Disturbances in England, 1509-1640* Oxford: Oxford University Press, 1988.

McPeek, James A. S. *The Black Book of Knaves and Unthrifts in Shakespeare and Other Renaissance Authors.* Storrs: University of Connecticut, 1969.

Mowat, Barbara. "Rogues, Shepherds, and the Counterfeit Distressed: Texts and Infracontexts of *The Winter's Tale* 4.3." *ShakS* 22 (1994): 58-76.

Muir, Kenneth, ed. *Shakespeare; "The Winter's Tale": A Casebook.* London: Macmillan, 1969.

Overburian Characters, The, ed. W. J. Taylor. Oxford: Blackwell, 1936.

Patterson, Annabel. *Shakespeare and the Popular Voice.* Oxford: Blackwell, 1989.

Pedler's Prophecy, The, ed. John S. Farmer. 1911; reprint New York: AMS Press, 1970.

Pendry, E. D., ed. *Thomas Dekker.* Cambridge: Harvard University Press, 1968.

Pettet, E. C. "*Coriolanus* and the Midlands Insurrection of 1607." *ShS* 3 (1950): 34-42.

Rid, Samuel. *The Art of Juggling or Legerdemaine.* London, 1612.

Salgado, Gamini, ed. *Cony-Catchers and Bawdy Baskets: An Anthology of Elizabethan Low Life.* Harmondsworth: Penguin, 1972.

Saltonstall, Wye. *Picturae Loquentes* (1631). Oxford: Blackwell, 1946.

Shakespeare, William. *Love's Labour's Lost,* ed. Richard David. London: Methuen, 1956 (Arden edition).

——. *The Winter's Tale,* ed. J. H. P. Pafford. London: Methuen, 1966 (Arden edition).

Sirluck, Katherine A. "Patriarchy, Pedagogy, and the Divided Self in *The Taming of the Shrew.*" *UTQ* 60 (1991): 417-34.

Skura, Meredith Anne. *Shakespeare the Actor and the Purposes of Playing.* Chicago: University of Chicago Press, 1993.

Stallybrass, Peter. "Patriarchal Territories: The Body Enclosed." In *Rewriting the Renaissance: The Discourses of Sexual Difference in Early Modern Europe,* ed. Margaret W. Ferguson, Maureen Quilligan, and Nancy J. Vickers. Chicago: University of Chicago Press, 1986.

Stallybrass, Peter, and Allon White. *The Politics and Poetics of Transgression.* Ithaca: Cornell University Press, 1986.

Tudor Economic Documents, ed. R. H. Tawney and Eileen Power. London: Longmans, 1924.

Vickers, Brian. *The Artistry of Shakespeare's Prose.* London: Methuen, 1968.

Source: "'Would Not the Beggar Then Forget Himself?': Christopher Sly and Autolycus," in *Fat King, Lean Beggar: Representations of Poverty in the Age of Shakespeare,* Cornell University Press, 1996, pp. 158-79.

Reification and Utopia in *As You Like It*: Desire and Textuality in the Green World

Hugh Grady, *Beaver College*

Power and the Green World

As You Like It, written and performed sometime between 1598 and 1600, pre-dates the plays discussed hitherto and in some ways seems to come from a different world. And yet this genial comedy can be linked with *King Lear,* and to a lesser extent the other Jacobean tragedies: although this 'most Mozartian' of Shakespeare's plays has long been celebrated for its geniality, a number of critics have also noted—and been puzzled by—the uncannily large number of parallels in structure and themes with what is otherwise its generic opposite, *King Lear.*[1] The resemblance is based on the depiction by both plays of the division of families and the disruption of the polity as a reified power establishes itself at the expense of the customary bonds of traditional culture. Refugees from the disrupted world react through communal solidarity to create a social space as an alternative to that of reified power; in this utopian space eros functions, however, not as a metonymy-metaphor for reification (as in the earlier plays discussed), but as a social force creative of community (albeit one with disruptive tendencies uneasily contained through the problematic solutions of patriarchal marriage). And as the play develops, this space is itself put under interrogation and suspicion, in an open-ended dialogue with the representations of the real which flit in and out of the text of the play in counterpoint to its utopian projections.

In addition, Robert Wilson's cultural materialist reading of the play has recently supplied us with another area of commonality between the two: both plays may be linked to a social subtext constituted by the rioting against enclosure in the Midlands (the area including Shakespeare's Warwickshire) in the 1590s.[2] Wilson has unearthed valuable historical material here, and his argument is illuminating and convincing in its basic outline. In the 1590s the woodlands had become a highly contested political battleground in which squatters were resisting the encroachments of market-driven land enclosures. Armed rebellion erupted in 1596 at Rycote, and the festivals of the following autumn were marked by agitation for 'a rising of the people'.[3] The play *As You Like It,* Wilson argues, with its depiction of social transformation, hunger, and the woodlands as a sanctuary, is the Shakespearean text most marked by consciousness of the famines, riots, and disorders that swept over the English Midlands, with *King Lear* offering more generalized allusions to the same events.

Instead of seeing with Wilson a kind of betrayal in

Shakespeare's comic development of this material, or as part of a larger project of state co-optation of peasant rebellion,[4] however, we can read the play as an enactment of utopian projections based in part on the phenomenon of enclosure, but focusing not on a realistic disclosure of injustice so much as an exploration of utopian alternatives to new reifications of market and state power, one quite material manifestation of which Wilson defines for us. The play's many parallels with *King Lear,* noted briefly by Wilson, can lead us into this topic.

As in the later play, the familial treacheries of brother against brother recapitulate and vary a more socially consequential familial treachery within the state. Power has been reduced to a few brush-strokes here, but we get glimpses of its corrosive effects in ways that anticipate *Lear*'s later tragic developments: families and friendships are split, secret violence is plotted, and power can only maintain itself by violations of the customary boundaries which structure the lifeworld within which it is functioning. And if Wilson is right in constructing for this play a context of peasant rebellion against the capitalization of farming, we have to add to the overt, thematized reification of power a latent, displaced reification of nascent capitalism at work in the disruptions of the customary lifeworld of Midland (and other) peasants as enclosures of formerly common lands cause major social disruption and rebellion.

Of course the play's two-family exposition is also giving us that *sine qua non* of New Comedy, the two lovers whose union so many critics have understood as symbolically unifying and overcoming the tensions investigated in the play—it took Nahum Tate to recognize a similar potential in *Lear* when he had Edgar and Cordelia fall in love and marry at the end of his tragicomic version. Here the spark of love must be struck even as the logic of power unfolds and darkens the proceedings. But, I will argue, the union of erotic polymorphous perversity with the utopian projections of green-world comedy will prove to be the chief contradiction in Arden.

In *King Lear* the temporary triumph of reified power led to the heath-scenes' radical evacuation of traditional values before the play depicted a slow, painful, and equivocal construction of alternative values from the play's lower social strata. In *As You Like It,* in contrast, it is the moment of evacuation that is equivocal and fleeting, the construction of counter-community and alternative values taking centre-stage. If the comedy thus seems less radical than the tragedy, it is certainly in a sense more pragmatic, more interested in exploring alternatives to emerging modernity than in ideology-critique *per se*. What takes the place of Lear's portentous raging and sympathetic identification with poor Tom is a delineation of one possible counter-community—and its problems.

The banished community created by reified power's colonization of the lifeworld if marked early in *As You Like It* with the aura of utopia; the old Duke is already there as the play begins:

> They say he is already in the forest of Arden, and a many merry men with him; and there they live like the old Robin Hood of England. They say many young gentlemen flock to him every day, and fleet the time carelessly, as they did in the golden world. (1. i. 114-19)[5]

In *As You Like It,* as in the late romances, we can find both ideological and utopian holders for that place which the text of *King Lear* signified by the term 'nothing', that place of desacralized, decultured modernity which Shakespeare and many of his contemporaries were investigating imaginatively and which the tragedies I have examined had occupied with worlds in the grip of reification. When we look for how the cultural producers of the Age of Shakespeare, Marlowe, and Jonson imagined alternatives to reification, we could do much worse than to look at the Forest of Arden. There we will find in the first place one of those antinomies of modernized cultures so endemic and basic to our thinking that it has largely been transparent to commentators on this play, or seen in terms of the sentimental 'wisdom' and 'sanity' for which this play has been repetitively celebrated in an older criticism. When we find such evocations, as Gayatri Spivak has said of a different set of texts, we know that ideology is at work—although the play does not stop at this ideological level. But one of the moves of the play's logical unfolding which has endeared it to many in our own times is its generation of those structurally indispensable antinomies of modern systems of meaning and experience, the public and the private.[6] As the young Marx indicated long ago, one of the consequences of the replacement of a feudal by a market society was the separation of the state from civil society proper, and the restructuring of civil society into an atomized realm of competing interests. In this arrangement the state expressed the 'universal' or communitarian aspects of the social order, while civil society tended to fragmentation. Society became bifurcated, into a public state and a private civil society, with only the political classes directly involved in the communitarian project of the state.[7]

When the state becomes desacralized and revealed as a realm of reified power at work instead of a divinely chartered authority for a unified community, and when civil society is revealed as itself informed by the logic and dynamics of the capitalist market-place, with its ruthless class divisions and inequalities, it becomes increasingly difficult for these two realms to function as legitimated arenas for cultural meaning; that is, as Habermas has argued, they are merely 'systems' incapable of functioning as the social structures of traditional pre-capitalist societies had done to re-enforce the cultures of the life-world and provide meaning to life.

The historical response to this situation has been manifold. Habermas famously traced the Enlightenment construction within civil society of a compensatory 'public sphere', which reintroduced an element of the political (this time latently democratic) within the space which had previously been evacuated of the political under the reifications of Absolutism. But Habermas's narrative does not exhaust the social reorganizations which followed from the early modern separation of the public and the private. We should note such disparate social attributes of modernity as the rise of companionate marriage and the transformation of the nuclear family from an economic to a 'meaning-giving' function in modern capitalist society, and the creation or refunctioning of a broad range of institutions—religions, the educational structures, voluntary associations, and the larger, more diffuse institutions of entertainment, art, and culture—in response to a general crisis of meaning observable in Western culture as one of the clearest indications of long-period modernity. In ideological terms, the categories of the various modern humanisms arose to provide normative concepts to substitute for those of evacuated public and religious spheres.

In the early modern period, of course, all those developments were either in birth or still to come. But communal alternatives to reified societies seemed to exist both in the highly hierarchical but mythically re-enforced and legitimated structures of a feudalism whose forms and some of whose realities persisted into the early modern—and, as a new generation of historical critics is teaching us, in the oral cultures and practices of those men and women dislodged by the new agriculture who invoked (often mythical) traditions and customs in support of their own communal response to the disruptions of early reifications. An older criticism focused exclusively on the former as having significance for Shakespearean texts; now, a newer criticism is asserting the relevance for Shakespeare especially of subaltern revolts and their counter-cultures of resistance as a response to the crisis of overall cultural 'meaning' which erupting modernity was precipitating—and which was a central preoccupation of the London theatres.

In *As You Like It,* we watch the construction of such a counter-society—and then an acute analysis of its own problems and contradictions—as Shakespeare keeps true to the interminable textuality of Renaissance sceptical rhetoric even in the gates of utopia.

With all the emphasis in other Shakespearean texts on the cold impersonality of reification as a disruptive reality of early modern culture, it is no surprise to watch privatized, 'human' relations become the centre of alternative values in the counter-society of the Forest of Arden. In this context, the deadly cold of sex-power is replaced by the warmth of libido—aim-inhibited, aim-conscious, and aim-displaced—dispersed throughout the social order—and of hetero- and homoeroticism portrayed as great if dangerous pleasures from which, however, power is not easily or ever completely banished. And to accommodate this thematic sea-change, I will be moving out of the discourses of what Agnes Heller called the 'cold Marxism' of ideology-critique and entering the utopian registers of 'warm Marxism'. This shift in tone and affect, however, does not imply a change in underlying theoretical frame; rather, as Adorno recognized in the moving conclusion of his *Minima Moralia,* the idea of the utopian expresses the dialectical potential for change of a reified social reality; the utopian is the corollary, not the contrary, of the theory of reification.

The genially sentimental relationship of Orlando and Adam can serve to introduce us to the forces behind the building of the utopian community. When Adam resigns his service to Oliver and offers his life savings and service to Orlando, Orlando encodes this act as one from a former time, before the development of a capitalist labour-market:

> O good old man, how well in thee appears
> The constant service of the antique world,
> When service sweat for duty, not for meed!
> Thou art not for the fashion of these times,
> Where none will sweat but for promotion,
> And having that do choke their service up
> Even with the having.
>
> (II. iii. 56-62)

This rhetoric of feudal bonds should not obscure for us, however, that Adam has in fact, by throwing in his lot with Orlando, stepped outside of the customary network of feudal relations; his customary bond, after all, is to the heir Oliver, not to Orlando. Rather than reassert the stability of the regulated feudal labour customs, he has violated them by asserting his own independence and becoming an outlaw with Orlando.

The new bands which tie together this penniless master Orlando and his provider-servant, Adam, are in fact an inversion of the customary feudal relationship, as Orlando recognizes as he explains that he is in no situation to meet his own feudal obligations to Adam:

> But, poor old man, thou prun'st a rotten tree,
> That cannot so much as a blossom yield
> In lieu of all thy pains and husbandry.
>
> (lines 63-5)

When, in Arden, as Orlando sets out to find some nourishment for his weakened companion, he uses terms not of customary obligations, but of personal and familial love, in a metaphor which links their bond with that of both a mother and child and those usurped citizens of the forest lamented by Jaques:

> Then but forbear your food a little while,
> Whiles, like a doe, I go to find my fawn,
> And give it food.
>
> (II. vii. 127-9)

And again his rationale is given in terms other than those of customary obligations:

> There is an old poor man,
> Who after me hath many a weary step
> Limp'd in pure love; till he be first suffic'd,
> Oppress'd with two weak evils, age and
>   hunger,
> I will not touch a bit.
>
> (lines 129-33)

So what do we call this kind of relationship, neither customary nor familial nor natural, but described in terms alternately borrowed first from feudal, then from familial and animalistic lexicons? We lack a precise term for such a relationship because it has become 'natural' in the post-feudal world: we are witnessing the production of what we can best call private relationships, attempted voluntary re-creations of relationships of mutual support which in customary society had had a formal, juridical quality but in the newer conditions of reified societies must be entered into through acts of will and solidarity outside of formal social or political networks. The apparently eternal category of the 'personal' thus emerges as one of three simultaneously created, interrelated components of an emerging and recognizably modern ideology: an evil realm of power, a good realm of the depoliticized 'personal', and a lost realm where they were once unified in an Adamic fullness of meaning. Here Duke Senior clarifies this conceptual production in his conclusion that some category the opposite of the public will be necessary for his utopian experiment:

> And this our life, exempt from public haunt,
> Finds tongues in trees, books in the running
>   brooks,
> Sermons in stones, and good in every thing.
>
> (II. i. 15-17)

But we will need to return to these overdetermined lines in a different context below.

Such small units as that of Adam-Orlando are but the building-blocks of Arden's utopia, however. In a sense, such a fellowship *à deux* remains essentially atomistic and socially isolated, not by itself a real counter-community. But such a counter-community, as Orlando discovers to his great surprise, in fact exists already in Arden.

Orlando had brought with him into the forest something of the same cultural attitude of instrumentalization which his fellow Elizabethans and Jacobeans imported to the New World colonies:

> I thought that all things had been savage here,
> And therefore put I on the countenance
> Of stern commmand'ment.
>
> (II. vii. 107-9)

Nature, as John Locke would define the attitude within a century, is a vast pantry of uses which any man can make his property through his labour—and, as the colonists practised it, through violent appropriations. Instead Orlando finds a community of fellows with whom he forges links of common social situation and common codes of 'civility', 'good manners', 'pity', 'nurturance', and 'gentleness'.

Once more, we find human relations described in the language of class and court ideologies. These are the terms whereby the Elizabethan gentry marked itself out as different, more educated, more human than the common lot of the kingdom. But of course they are also words denoting values of easy social intercourse, of mutual respect, fellow feeling, mutual care, and generosity. In effect the play asks whether these values of a formerly privileged life—alluded to by both the Duke and Orlando—can be refunctioned within the tighter straits of Arden:

> True it is that we have seen better days,
> And have with holy bell been knoll'd to church,
> And sat at good men's feasts, and wip'd our eyes
> Of drops that sacred pity hath engend'red;
> And therefore sit you down in gentleness,
> And take upon command what help we have
> That to your wanting may be minist'red.
>
> (II. vii. 120-6)

Immediately following, we get the Duke's allusions to life as a universal theatre of woeful pageants, and then Jaques begins that most quoted of Shakespearean set-speeches, 'All the world's a stage'. Much attention has been given to the necessity of retheatricalizing this performance and noting the ironizing effect which the entrance of the sainted Adam has on Jaques's reductive descriptions of old men. But we might give some attention as well to the scene's introduction of the theme of theatricality, with its associations, as we saw in the case of *King Lear,* with anti-essentialist Shakespearean scepticism. As a comment on the exiles' project to reproduce the gentry's codes of fellowship and generosity within the 'savage' outlaw world of Arden, the figure of theatricality suggests the possibility and desirability of a cultural rewriting of the 'parts' which 'one man in his time plays';[8] of refunctioning in a new social context of (relative) equality and fellowship something of the ideals which, we soon learn through the song which follows fast upon these lines, were all too often merely that homage which vice pays to virtue in hypocrisy:

> Most friendship is feigning, most loving mere folly.
> Then heigh-ho, the holly!
> This life is most jolly.
>
> (II. vii. 181-3)

Thus, the portrait of Adam, the invocation of ideals of gentility, and the idealization of 'antique days' create within this play that 'golden-age effect' which was in turn re-created in our own century by Modernist notions of the organic society and unified sensibility of the Elizabethan world picture (the Modernist golden age being, in that never-ending escalator trip to the past which Raymond Williams once traced in a justly famous passage,[9] the very age which in Shakespeare is suggested to be a decadent present). In *As You Like It* the idealization of the past carries those values and social practices precisely under frontal attack by the reifications of state and market-place in the Elizabethan epoch. If structures of reification are operating as impersonal, unintentional, yet human and social iron cages around the social being of every social participant, they cause to be idealized all those social communities (imagined or historical) operating in apparently consensual and intentional ways—even, in an insight which Freud would unsentimentally insist upon, those operating through conditions of the domination and subordination of feudalistic social hierarchy.

In short, the creation and celebration of a still-current category of the personal and private is one of the major thematic developments of *As You Like It.* But far from resting at this step, the play moves forward in a fascinating process of cultural house-building in the cleared space of Arden. From the molecular 'private' of Adam and Orlando (and of Rosalind and Celia), we move to a larger, more inclusive community of refugees in the process of founding new social relations out of the material of their older ones—relations radically transformed, however, by the new rough egalitarianism and communal solidarity of the cleared space of Arden.

There is something in this new space of the upside-down world of the festive comedy of C. L. Barber,[10] or, better, because of its greater consciousness and development of the political and social ramifications of its theme, the carnival tradition as described by Bakhtin: Robin Hood, after all, is very much a social

Leveller, and the golden time was the age of Saturn(alia).[11] But as numerous commentators have seen, it is the pastoral much more than the carnivalesque that is evoked as we enter the green world—but a 'pastoral' so critiqued and ironized that the unqualified term becomes misleading. In fact, the pastoral seems one strand of a more unique, *sui generis* complex for which Northrop Frye coined the term 'green-world comedy' forty years ago.[12] Frye's theory of green-world comedy in fact, freed of the infernal machinery and de-historicized timelessness he posited for it in *An Anatomy of Criticism,*[13] is one of the sources towards an adequate understanding of the quite consequential and powerful implications of this wonderful play. But more fully theorized and historicized is the related unique theory of the utopian developed over several decades by the unorthodox (some would say theological) Marxist Ernst Bloch.[14] Bloch's peculiar blend of humanism and futurism can certainly not simply be transported *prêt à porter* to today's post-structuralist theoretical paradigm; but I believe the central idea of the utopian is entirely relevant today. And much of the needed alteration has already been done by Bloch's friend Walter Benjamin, by Horkheimer and Adorno, and in several publications by Fredric Jameson.[15] In addition, I believe, we can see the utopian as implicated in and produced from a Lacanian play of desire within a reified 'real'. Thus, as we will see, the utopian, as a component of a larger post-structuralist sense of textuality and open-endedness, can help rewrite the antinomies of containment and subversion which, as I suggested elsewhere,[16] have outlived their usefulness as illuminating concepts within cultural materialism. Here, then I am less interested in the details of Bloch's immense *œuvre* than in the adaptation of his central concept within a different critical paradigm.

To get at it directly, we can say that the relationship of the reified first world[17] to Arden is one of utopian projection: that is, the play creates an imagined, counterfactual realm of idealizations whose relation to the reified 'real' of the play is that the former imaginatively fills the lack constituted by the play of desire within the real.[18] The utopian is that contradiction in terms, the place for the fulfilment of (finally unfulfillable) desires, an index and reflex of the experienced deprivations of specific social locations and forces. Although Bloch indeed coquetted with a language of 'archetypes' and 'timeless art works' in a dialogue with an older aesthetic paradigm, he consistently grounded specific utopian visions in specific socio-economic situations, insisting on the open-endedness of all utopian constructions, but equally on their determinate relation to the material world of their creations. We might formulate this through a paraphrase of Marx: people create utopias through imagination, but not just as they please; they do not make them under circumstances chosen by themselves, but under circumstances directly encountered, given, and transmitted from the past.

However, Bloch would insist, if Marx was right that 'The tradition of all the dead generations weighs like a nightmare on the brain of the living,'[19] it is equally true that the future creates a space for that other kind of dreaming that is the more direct fulfilment of desires—an idea hardly foreign to a young Marx who could write,

> the world has long dreamed of something of which it only has to become conscious in order to possess it in actuality. It will be evident that there is not a big blank between the past and the future, but rather that it is a matter of *realizing* the thoughts of the past. It will be evident, finally, that mankind does not begin any *new* work but performs its old work consciously.[20]

Although Bloch himself emphasized the idea of a utopian orientation to the future, such an orientation is clearly possible only after Enlightenment creates an idea of progress which only Bacon among the Age of Shakespeare's cultural producers seems fully to embrace. Before the Enlightenment, the utopian resided largely in the past, in the myth of the Garden of Eden or the Golden Age; or if, as in Christianity, it was projected into the future, it was into an unearthly future, by definition outside of modern history.[21]

To anticipate, I want to argue further that Arden's utopian community itself comes under investigation as containing numerous contradictions and problems. Rather than some unmediated access to nature, as Duke Senior imagines at first, utopia turns out to be a refuge from reified power in which what we might call 'linguistic' reifications, inherent in all cultural production, come to the fore. We will need, therefore, unlike earlier Modernist Elizabethan golden age advocates, or even unlike Bloch, to reinsert the utopian or golden age effect back into the textuality from which it was produced—as part of a dizzying array of non-identical conceptualizations and valorizations in play in the interminable, constantly deconstructed dialectics of Arden, to which I now turn.

The Textuality of the Green World

. . . French post-structuralism . . . modelled itself on language as a self-constituting system in-forming human consciousness, but in some sense itself an alien entity at the heart of a (hence paradoxically divided) selfhood. Whereas Lukács had posited a non-reified society as the historical *telos* to which post-capitalist society would give birth, we have seen how Althusser, within a milieu greatly influenced by French structuralism, felt that social structures would always contain an unavoidable residuum of reification—just as human thought will always be limited by the enabling structures of language—or as power is an inescapable enabling condition for all possible societies for Foucault. And Adorno, with his own focus on the 'objectivity' of intersubjective cultural artefacts, similarly resisted what he saw as a Romantic dream of unmediated access to the natural in Lukács's vision of a fully post-reified world.

In *As You Like It,* Shakespeare seems to situate himself among those sceptical of the possibility of a complete overcoming of reification, at least of those linguistic and cultural structures which in-form all possible human creations. Shakespeare's critique of the pastoral[22] seems to be based in his keen sense of the profligacy of signifiers and their uneasy relation to a realm of signifieds. The Romantic-Lukácsian position—here implicitly identified as a logocentrism—seems to be articulated as part of our introduction to Arden by Duke Senior:

> Hath not old custom made this life more sweet
> Than that of painted pomp? Are not these woods
> More free from peril than the envious court?
> Here feel we not the penalty of Adam,
> The seasons' difference, as the icy fang
> And churlish chiding of the winter's wind,
> Which when it bites and blows upon my body
> Even till I shrink with cold, I smile and say,
> 'This is no flattery: these are counsellors
> That feelingly persuade me what I am.'
>
> (II. i. 2-11)

The Duke quite clearly situates utopia in a realm where signification is unproblematic, where the double voice of hypocrisy is impossible because all simply is, without pretence. But the idea seems to self-destruct almost as soon as it is articulated by the Duke,[23] who begins, as numerous commentators have noted, to encounter nature in rhetorical terms, as a persuader and, shortly, the source of a language which must itself be interpreted and 'moralized'. The Duke's apparently simple idea of nature as a realm of unproblematic truth is, of course, full of fruitful problems and has a long provenance and continued ramifications: Walter Benjamin, for example, pointed out that in the cabbala the language of Adam was held to be of just such an essentializing power, all known languages fallen from that happy state and unable fully to represent the world's being, a lack which both philosophy and poetry continually attempt to restore and in fruitful fruitlessness continually fail.[24]

The Duke here loses himself in a similar reverie, his reference to the negation of 'the penalty of Adam' perhaps as much signifying his imagining of a prelapsarian language as in the loss of the eternal spring of Eden named in the following appositive.[25] The claim is paradoxical because the feel of the biting cold which he describes is anything but paradisaical; the sweetness, after all, is one of the

> . . . uses of adversity,
> Which like the toad, ugly and venomous,
> Wears yet a precious jewel in his head.
>
> (II. i. 12-14)

Thus the Duke has not reinvented the lost language of Adam, in which signs fully represent their signifieds, nor has he succeeded in fully separating himself out of the Symbolic order which had named and structured the world for him—a naming which he now sees as the occasion for flattery and falseness, but which he simply negates rather than replaces. In the cleared space of Arden, whose freedom he finds well worth its discomforts, he proves unable, despite his early claim, to re-create the Adamic language; like all of us, he must function within a profligacy of fallen signifieds. If a new world (or counter-society) is to be created, it will have to be formed out of the culture and language imported into the utopian space, and the Duke seems deluded on this point at least at the very beginning. The parallel in this instance is perhaps less with *Lear* than it is with Gonzalo-Montaigne's vision of a golden age in *The Tempest*—a vision put into question as soon as it is articulated; there is even some parallel here with Richard II in his prison cell: the Duke—and all the refugees assembled in the Forest of Arden—immediately structure 'nature' into an idealized realm, not constructed from 'nothing', but built from the shards of an abandoned social realm refunctioned as signifiers of signifiers—as metaphors:

> And this our life, exempt from public haunt,
> Finds tongues in trees, books in the running
>   brooks,
> Sermons in stones, and good in every thing.
>
> (II. i. 15-17)

In metaphor, that tension-filled 'equation' of dissimilars, is recapitulated and heightened the gap between signified and signifier which is characteristic of all languages and which makes this utopian space not Eden but a space for the play of an interminable desire among signifieds now free of their fixed, ideological determinations but still haunted by lack and incompleteness. The green world becomes a space of imagination for utopian construction, but one condemned also to cold, limit, and language itself. Perhaps the Duke, after his initial pure pastoralism, has discovered that melancholy dictum of modernity which Lacan says Freud defined most memorably: that the play of human desire constituting the libido, what he calls 'the whole microcosm' of mental complexity, 'has absolutely nothing to do with the macrocosm; only in fantasy does it engender [the] world'.[26] In any case it is clear that there is ample room and reason for melancholy in Arden, and it is famously supplied, first by the Duke himself, then by the redoubtable Jaques. The gaps among nature, culture, and utopia are represented, perhaps, in the lament on hunting deer introduced by the Duke but amplified and ramified by Jaques. Pregnant as are the Duke's definitions, there is a real sense in which they are, like Richard II's, a denial or displacement, a flight from the social 'real' which the Duke and his men are obsessively projecting on to nature's nameless—and unmoralized—spectacle. Certainly in Shakespeare's *As You Like It,* the Duke's idealism does not fare well as the play's complex dialectics unfold, and for that reason, the return to the world and to political power at the end of the play seems less a betrayal than it does a return to reality. One cannot live in utopia, seems to be one implication of the play, and it is one with which Bloch would have no argument. The usefulness of utopia is rather to serve as a reference point for critical reflection on the non-utopian real to which we are condemned.

The play establishes in the series of packed set speeches during our first trip into the space of Arden that the Forest is a realm of freedom, but one which will be structured by the finite resources and worn, ideological thought-tracks of the cultures which informed the consciousness and behaviour of these exiles. We can read the many references to the march of time in Arden as further indications of the non-Adamic, finite quality of this particular utopia. No wonder so many of the characters are so melancholy. They are trapped in the realm of the (merely) possible, condemned never to experience the Pastoral Absolute. The entire Western tradition of the pastoral, Lacan in effect tells us, is based on the myth of immediate satisfaction of the self in the fullness of nature. And, as Lacan famously argues (and a whole religious discourse ratifies), desire never achieves a terminal point, only the partial satisfactions of an endless series of objects which are essentially substitutes for an unachievable prelinguistic unity. If utopia appears at first as a fulfilment of desire, the very nature of desire guarantees that utopia will never be static, complete, or final. Nor could any play be constructed within a completely static domain of pastoral such as Lacan posits, as Shakespeare, that consummate practical dramatist, well knew. The unique dramatic structure of this play—one where, as a number of critics have observed, plot in the normal sense has given way to a choreography of dialogues on set themes in the forest[27]—amounts to repeated deferments and a chain of desired objects very much in a Lacanian mode. In Arden, in short, you can't always get what you want—but you can get what you need.

Thus the Forest of Arden is no Garden of Eden, and even less a Dantesque Paradiso. Most viewers and readers, for instance, are taken with metasituational Jaques lamenting the re-creation of injustice—and with the Fool's pointed insistence on the continued deprivations of time and the lack of creature-comforts within his utopian space. And, as we will see below, we are given an elaborate demonstration of the problems of eros set loose in a world where gender is an arbitrary, quasi-grammatical, and problematic category. Even with all these limitations, however, we are reminded by the embedded jump-cuts of Elizabethan staging created by the sudden shift of scene from Arden (II. i) back to the court (II. ii), Arden is a far cry from the dreary and dangerous suspicion, envy, and fear of reified court politics, a point reinforced in the congenially sentimental portrait of the aged faithful servant named Adam in silent, indeterminate commentary on his namesake's loss of paradise.

Desire in Utopia

In the plays examined earlier, the dynamics of instrumentalized or reified power worked to deprive experience of the customary social bonds which libido could permeate to create the pleasures of community—or more chillingly, as we saw in the tragedies, desire was refunctioned into structures of acted-out sado-masochism and domination-submission homologous to reified power itself. In Shakespeare, then, the emergence of desire as one of the chief problematics of utopia forms an intertextual dialectic of the utopian with reification. But desire has its own vectors, independent of that dialectic as well: and discourses of love and desire were of course central to court and related upper-class society. What gets explored in Arden, as in so much of the lyric poetry of Elizabethan culture, are love, sex, and desire, mainly as represented by any number of the literary encodings of these dangerous impulses—literary representations which must have been quasi-ideological codes pre-structuring the experience of love for much of the court, the fashionable world, and who knows how deeply into other of the day's complex social strata. Certainly the play links style in love with social station—a good deal of the comedy depends on incongruities of rustic peasants acting out courtly love codes, codes which in turn had been represented as the discourse of idealized shepherds. Here, however, I want to focus on how desire itself emerges as a permeating theme within utopian life, and one which soon brings into bold relief the social constructedness of gender roles within the customary society which has been transported and reproduced within Arden. The character Rosalind, of course, is at the centre of this aspect of the play, the culmination of the Elizabethan romantic heroines and prime exponent of the problematics of gender, sex, and desire within utopian life.[28]

Rosalind's own love relationship with Orlando is, in terms of the codes of courtly love and Protestant marriage which were uneasily but repeatedly united in the literature associated with Elizabeth's court, a relatively ideal and easy one. There is, for example, none of Desdemona's ill-fated violation of paternal approval; Rosalind has fallen in love, fortuitously, with a young man who is the son of her father's close friend (and enemy to the egregious Duke Frederick):

My father lov'd Sir Rowland as his soul,
And all the world was of my father's mind.
Had I before known this young man his son,
I should have given him tears unto entreaties,
Ere he should thus have ventur'd.

(I. ii. 235-9)

An important part of what gets transported from the disrupted customary lifeworld to the utopian space in Arden is this quite conventional, audience-pleasing romance, and this is part of what is responsible for this play's recent reputation among a substantial portion of feminists, cultural materialists, and new historicists for complicity with discourses of patriarchy and power. But within the relaxed space of Arden Rosalind is able to investigate at least some of these discourses, probing and questioning their premises and paradoxes before the 'containing' ending of the play's return to social hierarchy and to Protestant, patriarchal marriage. As we will see, however, this containment is itself unstable; there is an undermining of 'order' throughout the play and in the playfully complex ending which shows the conventions to be socially rather than naturally constructed and calls into question the very institution of patriarchal marriage which had just been apparently endorsed.

Orlando plays his part in this investigation mainly as a comic 'straight man'. The Duke, we have seen, had generated problems of which he seemed unaware in his early speech to his fellow exiles:

And this our life, exempt from public haunt,
Finds tongues in trees, books in the running
    brooks,
Sermons in stones, and good in every thing.

(II. i. 15-17)

Orlando seems to exemplify the gap between signifier and signified which the Duke, in his quest for the Adamic language, ignored, by causing love-poetry to be found in the trees by the device—in one sense literal-minded, in another sense, highly artificial and witty—of hanging his poems amid the leaves of trees;[29] both these senses serve to undermine the 'naturalness' of love-discourse, the first by its naïve logocentrism, the second by its very artificiality.

The disclosed conventionality of heartfelt love-poetry thus exposes one of the chief paradoxes of Elizabethan (and subsequent) discourses of love—and of utopian construction more generally. The 'naturally' heartfelt and uniquely personal turns out, on inspection, to be quite banal and to involve technicalities of metrics and rhyme that would seem the very opposite of the natural flowering of passion which is being celebrated and investigated. Thus the banter and playfulness of this play's disquisition on love actually recapitulates a central

problematic of this era's cultural poetics. The most celebrated and defining qualities of personal experience are at the same time the most conventional, because they are ideologically pre-defined.

This paradox structures the two chief ways to 'read' the 'staged' metaphor of poems as leaves (in turn related to the play's more general exploration of nature and art): in what we take to be the conventional and culturally 'primary' meaning of the comparison, the expression of Orlando's (and Rosalind's) love is the natural consequence of desire in play, the words of love Adamic signifiers of this natural occurrence. But in their mockery of what Orlando presumably intended, Rosalind, Celia, and Touchstone, like good Derrideans, insist on the materiality of the signifier and its slippery relationship to its signified:

CEL. Didst thou hear these verses?
ROS. O yes, I heard them all, and more too, for some of them had in them more feet than the verses would bear.
CEL. That's no matter; the feet might bear the verses.
ROS. Ay, but the feet were lame, and could not bear themselves without the verse, and therefore stood lamely in the verse.

(III. ii. 163-71)

Presumably such artificiality was perceived by the play's most consistent searcher after an (impossible) natural, the melancholy Jaques, in his critical remarks to Orlando:

I pray you mar no more trees with writing love-songs in their barks.

(III. ii. 259-60)

In any case, it is this gap which Rosalind focuses on as, in one of those defining moments of Shakespearean stagecraft, she decides (for no good naturalistic reason, as numerous post-Enlightenment critics have complained) to make the most of her disguise as Ganymede and to 'speak to him like a saucy lackey, and under that habit play the knave with him' (III. ii. 295-7), in the process continually puncturing Orlando's Petrarchan conventionality.

This moment—the metatheatrical exploitation of the boy-actor's portrayal of a female role by in turn having the fictional female feign maleness—has rightly been celebrated in much recent feminist and Postmodernist criticism for its vertiginous theatricality and its pointed alienation-effect regarding gender roles themselves. In *As You Like It,* the playful dialogue of the inverted moment also alienates the love otherwise celebrated in this genial comedy by its further probing into the constructed, 'made', or 'fictional' nature of love-discourse. The result is a complexly layered set of simultaneous affirmations and denials of the genuineness, naturalness, and value of a love-experience whose heady pleasurableness is the largest and most successfully transmitted of several contradictory messages within this magic scene (and its follow-ups) of endlessly deferred desire.

One of Rosalind's chief tactics in her disguised encounters with Orlando is to speak for the interests of the desiring female body against the heroic Petrarchan discourse of Orlando,[30] whether in the unequivocal discourse of one of her riddles—

> Marry, he [Time] trots hard with a young maid between the contract of her marriage and the day it is solemniz'd. If the interim be but a se'nnight, Time's pace is so hard that it seems the length of seven year. (III. ii. 313-17)

—or in the equivocations of her answer, playing with a double meaning of cony (rabbit, cunt) and kindled (born, sexually aroused):[31]

> As the cony that you see dwell where she is kindled. (III. ii. 339-40)

The anti-Petrarchan theme soon gets displaced to the pastoral figures of Silvius and Phebe and then, in a different modality entirely, to Touchstone and Audrey, in a complex play of literary traditions against and within each other.

Desire in Arden may be, as Dusinberre suggested, dangerous, and unruly enough to make the containing round of unlikely marriages at the end plausible to a charmed audience, but patriarchal marriage itself comes in for a great deal of critical scrutiny as well in this play. Rosalind, the main creator of the ring of country copulatives at the end of the play, is also one of its chief critics, not only a debunker of the love of Troilus and Cressida (IV. i. 97-100), but a reciter of numerous commonplaces on the hazards of marriage with women (which lead to protest by Celia), including their likelihood of being found in a neighbour's bed. It is in fact Rosalind who initiates what becomes an elaborate series of jokes and allusions to cuckoldry and the wearing of horns, with her playful warning to Orlando that a snail signifies a husband's inevitable destiny:

> Why horns! which such as you are fain to be beholding to your wives for. But he comes arm'd in his fortune, and prevents the slander of his wife.
>
> (IV. i. 59-62).

This joke is of course heavy in overdeterminations: we have to assume that members of this basically patriarchal society would be full of anxiety on such a subject as cuckoldry, a violation of norms central to the trans-

mission of property between the generations and thus crucial for the system's reproduction; and a number of recent critics have read this motif accordingly. But there is a consistent theme in the cuckoldry motif which this interpretation ignores: all these jokes evoke a communitarian ethos of freer, extra-marital sexual relations. And if such explorations form part of a complex problematic of utopia and the pastoral, and are themselves subject to multiple dialogic interruptions, they also deserve to be unearthed from the protective machinery of joking and the censuring mechanisms of our own and Elizabethan ideology with which they are surrounded, in the Shakespearean text and in subsequent criticism. As we will see, the argument of several of the jokes is that sexual promiscuity is as 'natural' as the horns of the deer, and as with earlier signifyings of the natural in the play, the assertion deconstructs as it is articulated. If the analogy holds true here as well, then, we should classify this strand of the play's textuality as a utopian longing like Duke Senior's nostalgia for a language of transparent meanings. And just as the Duke's evocations, even though they proved questionable, established a critical context by which to judge the flattery and insincerity of the court, we would have to see these as creating a space for rethinking the strictures on human sexuality of English Protestant patriarchy—and its allied ideological cousins, many of them still current.

Touchstone gives one of the central speeches. As he enacts the proverbially corrupt ways of the courtier against the maid-of-the-country Audrey, he links the married state, the horns of the cuckold, and the wealth of a walled town into an enigmatic comparison:

> As horns are odious, they are necessary. It is said, 'Many a man knows no end of his goods.' Right! many a man has good horns, and knows no end of them. Well, that is the dowry of his wife, 'tis none of his own getting. Horns? even so. Poor men alone? No, no, the noblest deer hath them as huge as the rascal. Is the single man therefore bless'd? No, as a wall'd town is more worthier than a village, so is the forehead of a married man more honorable than the bare brow of a bachelor; and by how much defense is better than no skill, by so much is a horn more precious than to want. (III. iii. 51-63).

The main point of the joke would seem to be that cuckoldry is endemic to the married state and nothing to be ashamed of, being the 'dowry' of wives and no fault of their men; and as the fact that only the wealthy need fear theft is no argument for poverty, so the vulnerability of married men to the horns is no argument against marriage.

In his provocative article on the social context for this play supplied by the Midlands enclosure riots of the 1590s, Richard Wilson argued that these lines could be read as Touchstone's advocating an extension of communal charivari tactics (traditionally employed against cuckolded husbands) to those other violators of customary rights the pastoral gentry enclosing the communal lands for sheep-grazing.[32] It seems to me, however, that Touchstone identifies here with the subject-position of the landholder rather than the squatter, and his topsy-turvy-world argument would seem to question the justice of the use of charivari against cuckolded husbands: the sexual profligacy of wives is for him in this playful speech, as it was for Rosalind-Ganymede earlier, a simple given, a property of wives as natural, as Touchstone has it, as the horns of a deer. Both of them would seem to be saying of desire in general what Rosalind later says of a woman's wit:

> Make the doors upon a woman's wit, and it will out at the casement; shut that, and 'twill out at the key-hole; stop that, 'twill fly with the smoke out at the chimney. (IV. i. 161-4)

—until, as she concludes, 'you met your wive's wit going to your neighbor's bed'—where she was going 'to seek you there' (IV. i. 167-71).

To summarize: one textual current of this play—often embedded within the anxiety-based textuality of jokes, but no less significant for that—celebrates a community of sexual freedom, a series of sexual encounters as boundless as the play of desire itself—perhaps something like that with which popular opinion tended to associate the Family of Love, that much attacked and apparently ubiquitous group of Protestant anti-authoritarians with whom Margot Heinemann associated the theme of social egalitarianism in *King Lear* (see above, Chapter 4) and who were popularly associated with libertinage, even though their views on marriage were apparently orthodox.[33] Part of the utopian discourse of the play is an assertion of the naturalness of promiscuous desire: language and desire seem to emerge as the fundamental building-materials of all possible utopias, their paradoxical double inscription in both nature and culture one of the constantly explored subjects of the word-play.

The strange celebration of cuckoldry continues in two songs—the music offering another protective layering, like that of humour, as Touchstone signals when he says of 'It was a lover and his lass' that it has 'no great matter' (V. iii. 35) and is but 'a foolish song' (line 40). And yet this is a play in which the foolish carries a good deal of authority; in Arden of all places we need to pay much more attention than has been traditionally given to the 'conventional' links of country-folks making love in acres of rye and the natural rhythms of the seasons—and the resonances of those simple ideas with the strange assertions of the earlier song:

> What shall he have that kill'd the deer?
> His leather skin and horns to wear.
>   Then sing him home.

> [*The rest shall bear this burthen.*
> Take thou no scorn to wear the horn,
> It was a crest ere thou wast born;
> Thy father's father wore it,
> And thy father bore it.
> The horn, the horn, the lusty horn
> Is not a thing to laugh to scorn.
>
>   (IV. ii. 10-18)

There is clearly a double inscription involved here: the context of the first stanza situates the horns on a deer, taken by a hunter. There probably is, as Richard Wilson argued, allusion to a tradition of plebeian defiance of the attempts of the king, aristocrats, and gentry to reserve certain hunting-grounds and herds for their own use. Several popular uprisings, as Wilson relates, began with wholesale slaughter of protected deer on private parkland. These associations, then, provide part of the context for the 'burthen's' transvaluative argument that the horn is an ancient and honourable crest, not a thing of scorn. But of course in this play the horns must also be the horns of the cuckold, traditionally put on an effigy of a cuckolded husband in the 'rough music' of a 'skimmington' or charivari in which a community of men (and sometimes women and/or men disguised as women) enforced their sense of communal gender relations by punishing a transgressor. Here, however, a community of outlaws instead insist that the horn is an ancient 'crest' of no shame: the 'lusty horn' is to be honoured, not scorned; and in this last turn, the horn seems to metamorphose one more time to become the phallus, that sexual emblem inextricably implicated in a heterosexual profligacy of desire[34] and a prime component in the joyful overdetermination of the play's utopianism. The horn, in short, evokes desire itself.

And additionally, as several recent critics have written, it is not only heterosexuality that is fêted in this strand of the play. The male homoerotics of Rosalind-Ganymede have been described and noted in several places,[35] while an implicitly lesbian sexuality can be discerned in the same material, as Elaine Hobby pointed out;[36] and certainly an eros, whether conscious or not, is at work in the intense relationship of Rosalind and Celia. In fact we can see Rosalind and Celia's friendship not only as potentially lesbian but alternatively as one of a number of the intense and socially crucial human bonds Freud linked to 'aim-inhibited' libido—a force we see at work in the kindness and need of Adam, the fellowship of the Duke and his hospitality to Orlando, and the power of communal ideals and the suppleness of human nature to produce effortless conversions by those subjects of atomistic reification in this play, Oliver and Duke Frederick.

The utopia of *As You Like It* can thus be characterized as a utopia structured by the play of desire as an ameliorative, bonding, and creative force within human life; and while desire is always dangerous, in the sense of unstable and unpredictable, to any real or utopian social construct, including those of this play, we can agree with Valerie Traub that, if the play refuses to enact some 'paradisaical, erotic economy, a utopian return to a polymorphously preverse body unmediated by cultural restraints . . . [and] if *As You Like It* suggests the "folly" of desire, part of that folly is the discipline to which it is subject'.[37]

Of course the play ends[38] with a monumental celebration of marriage as the inevitable and proper vessel for the cultivation of eros (well, not quite, since Rosalind still must speak a deconstructing epilogue, to which I will return below). The unstable chain of mismatched lovers which Rosalind had initiated when Silvius fell in love with her as Ganymede is stabilized when the country copulatives are paired off and wed in proper English Protestant fashion:

> Wedding is great Juno's crown,
>   O blessed bond of board and bed!
> 'Tis Hymen peoples every town,
>   High wedlock then be honored.
> Honor, high honor, and renown
> To Hymen, god of every town!
>
> (V. iv. 141-6)

And yet, the final emphasis on marriage, so overwhelming as a plot-structure device, is destabilized by several different kinds of 'supplements' to marriage's apparent finality in the play. Much has been already written in recent years on the way in which the apparent at-oneness of the marriages is disturbed by the play's epilogue, spoken by 'Rosalind' in a playful coquetting with the gender ambiguity of a boy-actor playing a woman playing a boy, and a playful invocation of promiscuous eros.[39] The result is a reaffirmation of those very qualities (gender-role instability, the promiscuity of desire) which had apparently been 'contained' by the multiple matrimonies. Here, however, let me focus instead on the additional instabilities associated with the unexplained entrance of 'Hymen' into the conclusion.

The brief remarks of several critics linking Hymen to Rosalind's knowledge of magic strike me as unconvincing. Rosalind's claim to magic is made casually, in her role as Ganymede, as a reason for Orlando to believe she might indeed produce the true Rosalind against all appearances (v. ii. 59-68). Consistently, Rosalind has been cast as a figure of deflating common sense whose role has been to assert the realities of the body and the unideal married state against the Petrarchan idealizations of Orlando. Making her somehow 'magic' at the end seems to remystify what this character has so consistently laboured to demystify.

Instead, I think we have to see the entrance of Hymen as a part of the metatheatrical drawing of attention to the illusionism of the comic ending about to unfold. A figure from the masque tradition, Hymen unobtrusively violates the 'realistic' conventions of a play otherwise devoid of fairies or supernatural beings of any sort, as if to signal the distance between the theatrical artifice of the ending and the social 'real' which the play has circulated and investigated.[40] Thus, the message delivered by Hymen—it seems almost a theophany—is enveloped by an aura of a kind of mimetic dissonance, a jarring of two different 'registers' of aesthetic representation that undercuts as soon as it is spoken Hymen's celebration of unity:

> Then is there mirth in heaven,
> When earthly things made even
>   Atone together.
>
> (V. iv. 108-10)

'Atone' was a keyword in High Modernist readings of this play, its etymological components 'at one' suggestive of that Coleridgean mystical unification that played such a central role, as we have seen above, in influential Modernist readings of *Othello* and *King Lear*. In the context of this play, it had seemed the perfect solution to all the textual dissonance provided by the caustic commentaries of the talk of marriage and romance: these could simply be banished to a lower level, the 'final' meaning of the play held to be captured in the mystic unity of Imagination.

In the text, however, the at-one-ment is, specifically, a reference to the series of marriages about to take place in the hasty comic ending directed by Rosalind, an at-one-ment, as we see in the dialogue immediately following, that depends on an artful set of equivocations in which two contradictory things are each (in a specific sense incongruent with the second paired sense) affirmed in turn:

> ROS. [*To Duke Senior.*] To you I give myself,
>   for I am yours.
> [*To Orlando.*] To you I give myself, for I
>   am yours.
>
> (V. iv. 116-18)

In a memorable passage, Malcolm Evans calculated that there must be 172 senses of the words that Hymen then utters to 'bar confusion':

> Here's eight that must take hands
> To join in Hymen's bands,
>   If truth holds true contents.
>
> (lines 128-30)[41]

That is, truth's contents turn out on close examination to be multiple and profligate, in a carnival heteroglossia that again undermines the at-one-ment and the attempt at the tying down of meaning and desire by Hymen. Marriage here becomes linked to that Adamic unity (at-one-ment) whose impossibility and idealization had been announced and abandoned in a few memorable lines by Duke Senior, as we have seen.

By the play's last act we know that communal at-one-ment is an ideal never to be realized even in a utopia free of power politics and the enclosures of a rapidly capitalizing agriculture; in utopia unity inevitably gives way to a carnival of interminable desired signifieds, conflicts between the sexes, and strains among even the (not-so-)natural institutions of marriage and friendship. Patriarchal marriage in particular is seen in this play as taking on the impossible task of 'containing' the uncontainable, the play of desire across an eroticized community of innumerable subject-objects, male and female, homoerotic and heteroerotic. But the badge of the cuckold—within the logic of this most outrageous of the strands of the play's textuality at any rate—is a badge of honour, a carnivalesque emblem of a utopian sexual freedom, and this is not the least of the senses in which the play is as we like it.

Utopian Consequences

The utopian impulses of *As You Like It* are not of course confined to this play alone within Shakespeare's works; they are a component of all the green-world comedies (parallels with *Love's Labour's Lost* and *A Midsummer Night's Dream* come immediately to mind); they often, as we saw with *Othello* and *Lear,* come briefly into view in the tragedies; and they constitute an in-forming dynamic within all the late tragicomedies.

Shakespeare's category of the utopian possesses that rare quality of self-relexivity, of an understanding of some of its own limits and weaknesses, that makes it particularly congenial in our own post-illusion, Postmodernist era. It also represents, as I suggested earlier, a way beyond those outworn antinomies of recent Shakespearean criticism, subversion and containment: the utopian is in effect always already both contained and subversive: relegated to the afterlife, the ideal, to myth, art, folklore, entertainment, and holiday for the most part (it is of course one of the prime contents of the carnivalesque), the utopian seems to coexist with rather than directly challenge the lacks and frustrations the desire for which had helped create it; and yet by giving expression to what has been repressed, the utopian creates a space for, and sometimes gives a name to, the ideologically unthinkable, transmitting it as a counter-memory within the reproductions of the social life of the subaltern classes— and, as in Shakespeare, within what becomes the culture of the ruling classes as well.[42] Utopia influences the social at those Messianic moments, like 1989 in Eastern Europe, when the unthinkable becomes for a time thinkable in one of those revolutionary junctures that permanently change the world (though never quite in the ways its agents imagine).

The capacity of the concept of the utopian to undo the antinomies of containment and subversion depends on the play of desire in the utopian—and it is precisely desire which Marx and the tradition founded by him tended to neglect in its theories of revolution. It is desire, then, in the place of that mysteriously motivated historical demiurge suspected by so many as the ghost lurking within the machinery of Marxism, that we should posit as a needed Postmodernist supplement to the rhetorical chain in a well-known Marxian metaphor which attempts in its own way to understand the coexistence of containment and subversion in the lifeworld: let us then insert desire as an additional term within Marx's Shakespearean encomium to 'our brave friend, Robin Goodfellow, the old mole that can work in the earth so fast, that worthy pioneer—the Revolution'.[43]

Notes

[1] The most developed discussion of the parallels I found—Frank McCombie, 'Medium and Message in *As You Like It* and *King Lear*', *Shakespeare Survey,* 33 (1980), 67-80—argues that the two plays each display the limits of the tragic and comic 'filters' Shakespeare utilized in what McCombie posits as a conscious intertextuality, which extends also to *Cymbeline* and *The Tempest.* See also David Young, *The Heart's Forest: A Study of Shakespeare's Pastoral Plays* (New Haven: Yale University Press, 1972), 81, for a less developed listing of the large number of parallels, constituting what Young calls a 'curious kinship' between the two plays, so different in mood and tone. Both of these works credit earlier studies of *King Lear* as a pastoral or anti-pastoral tragedy for explaining something of the parallel, esp. that of Maynard Mack, *'King Lear' in our Time* (Berkeley: University of California Press, 1965), 65-6.

[2] Richard Wilson, '"Like the Old Robin Hood": *As You Like It* and the Enclosure Riots', *Shakespeare Quarterly,* 43 (Spring 1992), 1-19, notes the parallel between the two plays as a way of getting at the political content of *As You Like It.* The article subsequently appeared as ch. 3 of his *Will Power: Essays on Shakespearean Authority* (New York: Harvester, 1993), 63-82.

[3] Wilson, 'Like the Old Robin Hood', 2.

[4] Ibid. 19.

[5] *As You Like It* in *The Riverside Shakespeare,* ed. G. Blakemore Evans *et al.* (Boston: Houghton Mifflin, 1974). Subsequent citations are from the same edn.

[6] Of innumerable discussions of the centrality of the public-private dichotomy to literary culture, I recom-

mend particularly Susan Wells, *The Dialectics of Representation* (Baltimore: Johns Hopkins University Press, 1985), 165-73.

[7] Karl Marx, *On the Jewish Question,* in *Writings of the Young Marx on Philosophy and Society,* ed. and trans. Loyd D. Easton and Kurt H. Guddat (Garden City, NY: Anchor, 1967), esp. 227.

[8] Steven Mullaney discusses the metaphor of the world as a stage, seeing it as evidence for the era's consciousness of the self as socially constructed, in *The Place of the Stage: License, Play, and Power in Renaissance England* (Chicago: University of Chicago Press, 1988), 71-2 *et passim.*

[9] Raymond Williams, *The Country and the City* (New York: Oxford University Press, 1973), 9-12.

[10] C. L. Barber, *Shakespeare's Festive Comedy: A Study of Dramatic Form and its Relation to Social Custom* (1959; repr. Cleveland, Oh.: Meridian, 1963), 222-39. Characteristically, Barber's emphasis in this Modernist reading is on the 'balance' and 'poise', embodied primarily by Rosalind, between holiday and daily life.

[11] See Peter Stallybrass, '"Drunk with the Cup of Liberty": Robin Hood, the Carnivalesque, and the Rhetoric of Violence in Early Modern England', in Nancy Armstrong and Leonard Tennenhouse (eds.), *The Violence of Representation: Literature and the History of Violence* (London: Routledge, 1989), 45-76, for a fascinating study of the carnivalesque associations of the matter of Robin Hood.

[12] Northrop Frye, *Anatomy of Criticism: Four Essays* (1957; repr. New York: Atheneum, 1968), 182-5.

[13] Fredric Jameson, *The Political Unconscious: Narrative as a Socially Symbolic Act* (Ithaca, NY: Cornell University Press, 1981), 103-50, offers a critique of Frye very much in this mode and one which links him to Bloch's idea of the utopian, to be discussed below.

[14] Perhaps the most apposite of Bloch's major works in this context is the monumental *The Principle of Hope,* first pub. as *Das Prinzie Hoffnung* (1954-9); trans. Neville Plaice, Stephen Plaice, and Paul Knight (Cambridge, Mass.: MIT Press, 1986). See also Ernst Bloch, *The Utopian Function of Art and Literature: Selected Essays* (Cambridge, Mass.: MIT Press, 1988). A very useful introduction with excerpts, to which I am indebted, is Maynard Solomon (ed.), *Marxism and Art: Essays Classic and Contemporary* (New York: Vintage, 1974), 567-87. A more recent treatment, with excellent bibliographical detail of primary and secondary works and an acute analysis of Bloch's strengths and weaknesses, is Ch. 5 of Martin Jay, *Marxism and Totality: The Adventures of a Concept from Lukács to*

Habermas (Berkeley: University of California Press, 1984)—a treatment, however, not much interested in Bloch's relevance to cultural criticism.

[15] The utopian has been a topic in several of Fredric Jameson's works—see his chapter on Bloch in *Marxism and Form: Twentieth-Century Dialectical Theories of Literature* (Princeton: Princeton University Press, 1971), 116-59; 'Introduction/Prospectus: To Reconsider the Relationship of Marxism to Utopian Thought', *Minnesota Review,* 6 (1976), 53-8; 'Reification and Utopia in Mass Culture', *Social Text,* I (Winter 1979), 130-48; and *The Political Unconscious,* 281-99. In addition, the concept of the utopian has been interpreted and further developed in a number of Frankfurt works on the aesthetic; it permeates the work of the like-minded Benjamin, who used his own terminology (like 'Messianic time') to convey concepts closely allied to Bloch's 'utopian'; Horkheimer and Adorno make use of the term and/or concept throughout their work; see particularly the ending of Adorno's *Minima Moralia,* trans. E. F. N. Jephcott (London: New Left Books, 1974), 247, and his posthumous *Aesthetic Theory,* trans. C. Lenhardt (Boston: Routledge, 1984).

[16] Hugh Grady, 'Containment, Subversion—and Postmodernism', *Textual Practice,* 7 (Spring 1993), 31-49.

[17] I make use here of the distinction within Shakespearean comedy between a power-oriented 'first world' and an idealized 'second world' in Elliot Krieger, *A Marxist Study of Shakespeare's Comedies* (New York: Barnes & Noble, 1979), but the theory of comedy put forth there is in many ways the opposite of the Bloch-influenced concepts I work with here. Where Bloch would see a utopian projection with a critical, non-ideological dimension, Krieger sees a specifically aristocratic ideological projection that mystifies the class struggle—although Fredric Jameson would see no inconsistency, arguing that every universalizing ideological viewpoint is necessarily utopian at the same time; *Political Unconscious,* 289-92. For Kreiger, however, Shakespeare is only redeemed because, he argues, the processes of idealization are distantiated and put under scrutiny in the various Shakespearean texts.

[18] I am indebted to Jameson's precedent in dialectically linking reification and the utopian, in 'Reification and Utopia in Mass Culture' and *Political Unconscious,* 288-99. However, the details and theoretical framework of my own linkage of the two differ somewhat from Jameson's: his treatment emphasizes the collectivizing aspects of the utopian, whereas I focus on its relation to the specific lacks and wants of determinate socio-historical situations.

[19] Karl Marx, *The Eighteenth Brumaire of Louis Bonaparte* (New York: International, 1963), 15.

[20] Karl Marx, letter to Arnold Ruge, May 1843; excerpted and repr. in Solomon (ed.), *Marxism and Art,* 58.

[21] Thomas More's *Utopia,* ironically, is not a good example of Bloch's idea of the utopian because of its reproduction of so many of the repressions of its social origins. The Blochian utopian qualities of More's work reside in its cognitive rather than libidinal aspects, and these, in turn, are complex, with anti-utopian dimensions, a quality classically defined in the chapter on More in Stephen Greenblatt's *Renaissance Self-Fashioning* (Chicago: University of Chicago Press, 1980).

[22] Attention to the pastoral element of the play was the dominant approach to *As You Like It* in the High Modernist era, and a range of views on Shakespeare's incorporation and critique of the tradition has been defined; see e.g. Young, *The Heart's Forest.* My own use of the term, as argued below, is influenced by some insightful comments on the pastoral by Lacan.

[23] See Malcolm Evans, *Signifying Nothing: Truth's True Contents in Shakespeare's Text* (Brighton: Harvester, 1986), 155, and Keir Elam, '"As they Did in the Golden World": Romantic Rapture and Semantic Rupture in *As You Like It*', *Canadian Review of Comparative Literature,* 18 (1991), 217-32, for related but somewhat different deconstructive comments on the Duke's speech.

[24] I am giving one of several (not necessarily compatible) ramifications of Benjamin's use of this piece of cabbalistic lore. See, for one instance, Walter Benjamin, 'On Language as such and on the Language of Man', in *Reflections: Essays, Aphorisms, Autobiographical Writings,* trans. Edmund Jephcott (New York: Harcourt, 1978), 314-32, or his *The Origin of German Tragic Drama,* trans. John Osborne (London: New Left Books, 1977), 37-8. This latter work is most relevant in the following passage: 'Adam's action of naming things is so far removed from play or caprice that it actually confirms the state of paradise as a state in which there is as yet no need to struggle with the communicative significance of words. Ideas are displayed, without intention, in the act of naming, and they have to be renewed in philosophical contemplation. In this renewal the primordial mode of apprehending words is restored' (p. 37). The Duke (and Jaques) soon move to a mode of 'philosophical restoration' in the absence of the original Adamic language.

[25] See Robert Schwartz, 'Rosalynde among the Familists: *As You Like It* and an Expanded View of its Sources', *Sixteenth Century Fournal,* 20 (1989), 69-76, for an argument that the Duke Senior is here expressing central tenets of the antinomian 'Family of Love', which taught a doctrine of a possible spiritual regeneration in nature from the effects of original sin. If this is true, I would argue, Shakespeare is putting this doctrine under the same kind of sceptical interro-

gation to which he subjected Montaigne on the Brazilian Indians in *The Tempest.* But fascination with the idea of a freedom of extra-marital sexuality in *As You Like It,* to be discussed below, may also be associated with this group, which, . . . has been linked with the social egalitarianism of *King Lear.*

[26] Jacques Lacan, *The Ethics of Psychoanalysis 1959-1960,* ed. Jacques-Alain Miller, trans. Dennis Porter (London: Routledge, 1992), book VII, p. 92. The whole of ch. 7, with its discussion of the problem of human happiness and desire, is relevant to this play.

[27] Harold Jenkins, '*As You Like It*', *Shakespeare Survey,* 8 (1955), 40-51, and Ann Barton, Introduction to *As You Like It, Riverside Shakespeare,* 365-8.

[28] The cultural significance of Rosalind has been a major topic of feminist and new historicist criticism, engendering numerous disparate interpretations concerning whether she is more proto-feminist or patriarchal. See e.g. Clara Claiborne Park, 'How a Girl can be Smart and still Popular', in Carolyn Lenz, Gayle Greene, and Carol Neely (eds.), *The Woman's Part: Feminist Criticism of Shakespeare* (Urbana: University of Illinois Press, 1980), 100-16; Lisa Jardine, *Still Harping on Daughters: Women and Drama in the Age of Shakespeare* (Totowa, NJ: Barnes & Noble, 1983), 9-33; Linda Woodbridge, *Women and the English Renaissance: Literature and the Nature of Womankind, 1540-1620* (Urbana: University of Illinois Press, 1984), 153-6; Catherine Belsey, 'Disrupting Sexual Difference: Meaning and Gender in the Comedies', in John Drakakis (ed.), *Alternative Shakespeares* (New York: Methuen, 1985), 166-90; Barbara J. Bono, 'Mixed Gender, Mixed Genre in Shakespeare's *As You Like It*', in Barbara Kiefer Lewalski (ed.), *Renaissance Genres: Essays on Theory, History, and Interpretation* (Cambridge, Mass.: Harvard University Press, 1986), 189-212; Phyllis Rackin, 'Androgyny, Mimesis, and the Marriage of the Boy Heroine on the English Renaissance Stage', *PMLA* 102-/1 (Jan. 1987), 29-41; Leah S. Marcus, *Puzzling Shakespeare: Local Reading and its Discontents* (Berkeley: University of California Press, 1988), 98-103; Jan Kott, *The Gender of Rosalind: Interpretations: Shakespeare, Büchner, Gautier,* trans. J. Kosicka and M. Rosenzweig (Evanston: University of Illinois Press, 1992), 11-40; Jean E. Howard, *The Stage and Social Struggle in Early Modern England* (London: Routledge, 1994), 118-21; and Juliet Dusinberre, 'As *Who* Liked It?', *Shakespeare Survey,* 46 (1994), 9-21. For a fuller bibliography on what has become an extensive literature on the multifaceted sexual politics associated with Rosalind and the other cross-dressed Shakespearean heroines, see Ann Thompson, 'Shakespeare and Sexuality', *Shakespeare Survey,* 46 (1994), 1-8. Interestingly, three central cultural materialist-new historicist discussions of Shakespeare's (and other) cross-dressed heroines—Stephen Greenblatt,

Shakespearean Negotiations: The Circulation of Social Energy in Renaissance England (Berkeley: University of California Press, 1988), 66-93; Jonathan Dollimore, *Sexual Dissidence* (Oxford: Clarendon, 1991), 291-306; and Alan Sinfield, *Faultlines: Cultural Materialism and the Politics of Dissident Reading* (Berkeley: University of California Press, 1992), 52-79—all eschew central discussion of Rosalind in favour of Olivia or Portia; and Louis Adrian Montrose, 'The Place of a Brother in *As You Like It:* Social Process and Comic Form', *Shakespeare Quarterly,* 32 (Spring 1981), 28-54, shifts the centre of attention in his reading of the play from Rosalind to Orlando. In contrast, for feminist critics Rosalind tends to be central.

[29] See Dusinberre, 'As *Who* Liked It?', on the connections with Ariosto (and his English translator John Harington) of Orlando, whose hanging of poems from trees mimics a popular poem-hanging episode of *Orlando Furioso* which was also a favourite subject of illustrators.

[30] See e.g. Dusinberre, 'As *Who* Liked It?', who, in a complex argument, finds a body-affirming Rabelaisian discourse in dialogue with a heroic one derived from Ariosto, both strands associated with Ariosto's English translator, and author of a treatise on the water-closet, Sir John Harington. Rosalind is overdetermined, but one of the carriers of the Rabelaisian: 'In *As You Like It,* Shakespeare acknowledges . . . the realities of passion as evasive of self-discipline. Passion is dangerous; it thrives not on liberty but on repression. . . . The energy of the play derives from a constant oscillation, centered mainly in Rosalind herself, between repression and expression, from which powerful fantasies of sexual desire are generated, and circulate through the entire theater, revitalizing both players and audience' (p. 19).

[31] See Elaine Hobby, '"My Affection hath an Unknown Bottom": Homosexuality and the Teaching of *As You Like It*', in Lesley Aers and Nigel Wheale (eds.), *Shakespeare in the Changing Curriculum* (London: Routledge, 1991), 125-42, for a discussion of this and other sexual equivocations, often ignored in traditional annotations of these lines. Similarly, the title comes from another such often ignored *double entendre,* this time one in which 'bottom', according to Hobby, could refer to both penis and posterior.

[32] Wilson, 'Like the Old Robin Hood', 13.

[33] See Schwartz, 'Rosalynde among the Familists'.

[34] Montrose, 'The Place of a Brother in *As You Like It*', 49-50, saw the horn in its phallic mode as involved in constructing male solidarity out of sexual anxiety. Similarly Peter Erickson, *Patriarchal Structures in Shakespeare's Dramas* (Berkeley: University of California Press, 1985), 15-38, sees the phallic horn as primarily affirming male solidarity in the service of patriarchy while Marilyn

Williamson, *The Patriarchy of Shakespeare's Comedies* (Detroit: Wayne State University Press, 1986), 41-53, sees the cuckoldry references of the play as intrinsically misogynist (although she notes that Rosalind gets in some feminist points). None of these critics entertains the possibility of utopian readings of the motifs.

[35] e.g. Valerie Traub, 'Desire and the Differences it Makes', in Valerie Wayne (ed.), *The Matter of Difference: Materialist Feminist Criticism of Shakespeare* (Ithaca, NY: Cornell University Press, 1991), 81-114, and Philip Tracy, '*As You Like It:* Homosexuality in Shakespeare's Play', *College Language Association Journal,* 25 (1981), 91-105.

[36] Hobby writes: 'For a lesbian and feminist reader/ teacher such as me, however, the central focus of the play's concern with order is found in the character of Rosalind. . . . In Rosalind, we are presented with two interwoven challenges to the stability of gender. This is achieved through a juxtaposition of Rosalind's characteristics as young woman with her behaviour when playing the part of a young man; and through a series of jokes about the actual gender identity of the actor playing Rosalind/Ganymede's part'; 'My Affection hath an Unknown Bottom', 134.

[37] Traub, 'Desire and the Differences it Makes', 106.

[38] See Ejner J. Jensen, *Shakespeare and the Ends of Comedy* (Bloomington: Indiana University Press, 1991), for a cogent argument critical of the tendency of 20th-cent. criticism of Shakespearean comedy to privilege the conclusion of plays over the dissonances and contradictions of the works' 'performative comedy'. He particularly faults Barber and Frye for this tendency. I would add that this procedure seems to me a consequence of the Modernist 'spatialization' of the work, which requires an array of its elements frozen in a single instance of time, an instance which has almost always been the work's ending (see Hugh Grady, *The Modernist Shakespeare* (Oxford: Clarendon, 1991), 92-112). Jensen, however, calls for a return to an older paradigm based on immediate theatrical effects—an approach reminiscent in my view of E. E. Stoll's iconoclastic but pre-Modernist criticism—rather than developing what seem to me the Postmodernist implications of his argument: that the ending is always already deconstructed by the textuality of the work.

[39] See particularly Kott, *The Gender of Rosalind,* and Belsey, 'Disrupting Sexual Difference', 180-5.

[40] Jensen, *Shakespeare and the Ends of Comedy,* discusses both Hymen and the epilogue of the play as instances of complex events difficult to 'fix' into a determinate teleological ending, citing the contradictory readings of 20th-cent. critics in support of this view; see pp. 75-8.

[41] Evans, *Signifying Nothing,* 145-90.

[42] Raymond Williams showed many years ago that 'culture' can never be neatly assigned as the exclusive property of a single class; see his *Culture and Society, 1780-1950* (1958; repr. New York: Harper, 1966).

[43] Karl Marx, 'Speech at the Anniversary of the *People's Paper*', in *The Marx-Engels Reader,* ed. Robert Tucker (New York: Norton, 1972), 428.

————————

Source: "Reification and Utopia in *As You Like It*: Desire and Textuality in the Green World," in *Shakespeare's Universal Wolf: Studies in Early Modern Reification,* Clarendon Press, 1996, pp. 181-212.

On Not Being Deceived: Rhetoric and the Body in *Twelfth Night*

Lorna Hutson, *Queen Mary and Westfield College, University of London*

Elder Loveless. Mistres, your wil leads my speeches from the purpose. But as a man—

Lady. A *Simile* servant? This room was built for honest meaners, that deliver themselves hastily and plainely, and are gone. Is this a time or place for *Exordiums,* and *Similes,* and *metaphors?*[1]

"Shakespearean comedy," writes Stephen Greenblatt, "constantly appeals to the body and to sexuality as the heart of its theatrical magic."[2] Without wishing to disparage the enterprise of writing histories of the body, or indeed to underestimate what such histories have accomplished in terms of enhancing our understanding of early modern culture[3], I would like in the following pages to challenge the operation of a certain kind of "body history" within recent Shakespeare criticism. I do not so much want to disagree with Greenblatt's statement as it stands, as to argue that our understanding of how Shakespeare's comedy intervened, both in its own time and subsequently, to modify attitudes to sexuality and to gender has been more obscured than enlightened by the obsession with the "body" as Greenblatt here understands it, and with the kind of body history to which he and others have prompted us to turn.

1. Circulating Arguments: The "Single Sex" Body

I shall focus my argument on Shakespeare's *Twelfth Night,* a play which, for all the curiously metaphoric, even disembodied nature of the language in which it articulates the desires of its protagonists, has nevertheless become the touchstone of this "body" criticism within Shakespeare studies. Yet it is worth remarking that the current critical interest in *Twelfth Night* as a play about the indeterminacy of gender and the arbitrary nature of sexual desire actually began with the contemplation not of the materiality of the body, but with that of the signifier. In much earlier twentieth-century criticism, Shakespeare's comedies have been appreciated as temporary aberrations from an established sexual and social order for the purposes of a thoroughly conservative "self-discovery" and return to the *status quo.*[4] Saussurian linguistics, alerting critics to the way in which meaning in language is always the effect of a play of differences, enabled them to challenge such interpretations on their own terms by arguing that the conservative denouement was inadequate to contain and fix the meanings released by the play of differences. This was especially the case in comedies such as *As You Like It* and *Twelfth Night,* in which the fiction of a woman's successful masquerade of masculinity is complicated by the understanding of its having been originally composed for performance by a boy. Suddenly, instead of being about the discovery of one's "true" identity, or a "natural" social and sexual order, it seemed that what the comedies were about was the ease with which systems of sexual difference could be dismantled, and the notion of gendered identity itself called into question. This was important when it happened—the mid-1980s—because at the same time feminist critics were beginning to draw attention to the misogynistic implications of the transvestite theater, thereby throwing into confusion that venerable tradition of critical delight in the sprightliness of Shakespeare's girls-dressed-as-boys. How could we go on liking Rosalind and Viola in the knowledge that what they really represented was the denial to women of access to the histrionic exchanges in which they excelled and we took pleasure?[5] Just in time poststructuralist criticism saved us from the agony of this dilemma by recuperating the double transvestitism of the comedies as a calling into question of the "fully unified, gendered subject," thereby producing, instead of a patriarchal Shakespeare, a Shakespeare who, in the words of Catherine Belsey, offered "a radical challenge to patriarchal values by disrupting sexual difference itself."[6]

Subsequently, the notion that what the comedies were about was really the indeterminacy of gender was given a new and historically authenticating twist by investigations into the history of biological definitions of gender which seemed to prove that, in the minds of Shakespeare's contemporaries, gender itself was a kind of comic plot, the happy denouement of which could only be masculinity. A special issue of *Representations* on "Sexuality and the social body in the nineteenth century" contained an article by Thomas Laqueur which, though primarily concerned with the politics of nineteenth-century reproductive biology, was nevertheless to have a considerable impact on Renaissance literary studies as a result of what its findings implied about the biological construction of gender in the early modern period. Laqueur drew our attention to a momentous, but overlooked event in the history of sexuality. Sometime in the late eighteenth century, the old belief that women needed to experience orgasm in order to conceive was abandoned. Women were henceforward to be thought of as properly passionless, because passive, participants in the act of sexual reproduction. What this implied was nothing less than a change in the existing physiology of sexual difference: the ancient Galenic model, according to which the hidden reproductive organs of women were merely a colder, imperfectly developed, and introverted type of the penis and testicles, requiring to be chafed into producing their seed, was replaced by the modern notion of the incommensurability of male and female reproductive organs. Laqueur's crucial point, however, was that the need to replace the old Galenic "metaphysics of hierarchy" between the sexes with an "anatomy and physiology of incommensurability" actually anticipated any real scientific understanding of women's reproductive makeup, and must therefore have been motivated not by scientific discovery, but by the need to find a new rationale for the exclusion of women from Enlightenment claims for the equality of men.[7]

I am ignorant of the effect of Laqueur's argument on nineteenth-century criticism, but the impact on Renaissance studies has been considerable. Writing in 1986 Laqueur cites, in a footnote, a paper on Shakespeare's *Twelfth Night* by Stephen Greenblatt, which was first published in 1985 in a collection called *Reconstructing Individualism*[8] and subsequently included in Greenblatt's 1988 *Shakespearean Negotiations* as the essay, "Fiction and Friction." Both authors evince exactly the same ancient and sixteenth- and seventeenth-century medical texts—first and foremost, Galen on the exact parity between male and female reproductive organs ("think of the 'uterus turned outward and projecting': Would not the testes [ovaries] then necessarily be inside it? Would it not contain them like a scrotum? Would not the neck [the cervix], hitherto concealed . . . be made into the male member?"[9]) and then Galen's sixteenth- and seventeenth-century readers, Ambroise Paré, Jacques Duval, Thomas Vicary, Helkiah Croke, and Jane Sharp.[10] They also both cite Montaigne, who twice refers to a story also told by Ambroise Paré about the sex-change of Marie-Germaine, a contemporary inhabitant of Vitry-le-François, who had the misfortune or good fortune to realize her manhood by jumping too energetically over a stream, thus prompting the eruption of the appropriate genitals[11].

Where Laqueur expounded the Galenic model of woman as introverted man in order to expose the politics of nineteenth-century reproductive biology and its denial of female orgasm, Stephen Greenblatt's identical quotations employ the model's stress on the defective "heat" of female reproductive organs, and the "friction" required to activate them, as an allegory for the "theatrical representation of individuality in Shakespeare." "Erotic chafing" writes Greenblatt, "is the central means by which characters in plays like *The Taming of the Shrew, A Midsummer Night's Dream, Much Ado About Nothing, As You Like It,* and *Twelfth Night* realize their identities and form loving unions."[12] One might be forgiven for balking at the definition of *The Taming of the Shrew* as a fiction of "identity," or at the naturalization of its highly pragmatic argument of husbandry as a form of "erotic chafing"; Greenblatt,

however, refrains from pursuing his argument in relation to this or indeed any of Shakespeare's comedies other than *Twelfth Night.* He puts the question of the relation of identity to erotic chafing—of fiction to friction—more persuasively by asking, "how does a play come to possess sexual energy?"[13] The answer is supplied by a reading of *Twelfth Night,* the crux of which is a short speech made by the male twin, Sebastian, after Olivia has realized that his double, with whom she was in love, is a woman and his sister. "So comes it, lady," says Sebastian, "you have been mistook,"

> But nature to her bias drew in that.
> You would have been contracted to a maid;
> Nor are you therein, by my life, deceiv'd:
> You are betroth'd both to a maid and man.[14]

According to Greenblatt, the "nature" to which Sebastian refers is, precisely, the Galenic discourse of the one-gender body. Sebastian's reference to himself as "both a maid and man" consequently invokes the inherent instability of gender as construed by this model, which in turn enables a good, radical-sounding assault on more comfortable readings which essentialize sexual difference. Thus, Greenblatt quotes C. L. Barber's argument that, "the most fundamental distinction that the play brings home to us . . . is the difference between men and women" in order to reinforce, by contrast, the persuasiveness of his view that the fundamental physiological distinction between men and women is precisely what the play can't "bring home," historically speaking. At the end of *Twelfth Night,* as he points out, "Viola is still Cesario—'For so you shall be,' says Orsino, 'while you are a man' (5.1.386)—and Olivia, strong-willed as ever, is betrothed to one who is, by his own account, both 'a maid and a man.'"[15] Notice just how closely this conclusion resembles the poststructuralist reading which found *Twelfth Night* calling into question, "the possibility of a fully unified, gendered subject." And, as with the poststructuralist argument, a crucial legacy of this reading is its obscuring of the need to account, in feminist terms, for the historical fact of the absence of women's bodies from the Renaissance stage. In the light of the Galenic theory of reproduction, concludes Greenblatt, it is easy to see that transvestitism actually "*represents* a structural identity between men and women—an identity revealed in the dramatic disclosure of the penis concealed behind the labia."[16] And the dramatic fiction—an outrage to belief which is nevertheless endowed with generative because persuasive power—becomes analogous to the friction or chafing required, according to this Galenic model, both to warm women into conception, and to stimulate their reticent reproductive organs into realizing their latent virility.

Two years after Greenblatt's "Fiction and Friction" was published, Laqueur's thesis on the political and cultural investments of reproductive biology was published in book form as, *Making Sex: Body and Gender from the Greeks to Freud*. The chapter on the pervasiveness of the Galenic model in Renaissance thought and culture carries an epigraph from *Twelfth Night:*

> Sebastian [To Olivia]
> So comes it, lady, you have been mistook.
> But nature to her bias drew in that.
> You would have been contracted to a maid;
> Nor are you therein, by my life, deceived:
> You are betrothed both to a maid and man.[17]

And he goes on to introduce the substance of his chapter thus:

> Somehow if Olivia—played by a boy, of course—is not to marry the maid with whom she has fallen in love, but the girl's twin brother Sebastian; if Orsino's intimacy with "Cesario" is to go beyond male bonding to marriage with Viola, "masculine usurped attire" must be thrown off and woman linked to man. Nature must "to her bias" be drawn, that is, deflected from the straight path. "Something off center, then, is implanted in nature," as Stephen Greenblatt puts it, which "deflects men and women from their ostensible desires and toward the pairings for which they are destined." But if that "something" is not the opposition of two sexes that naturally attract one another—as it came to be construed in the eighteenth century—then what is it?[18]

The answer, of course, is the one-gender body according to Galen, with all its micro- and macrocosmic correspondences. The reading of a single Shakespeare play—or rather, the reading of *five lines* from a single Shakespeare play—seems to be doing a lot of work in supporting a circular argument about the relevance of body history to the question of how the magic of theater relates to the early modern conception of the body.

In the last five years, Laqueur's and Greenblatt's arguments and examples—Galen, Ambroise Paré, Jacques Duval, Helkiah Crooke, Jane Sharp, and (especially, perhaps) Montaigne—have been repeatedly invoked and quoted to support arguments about the pervasiveness of sixteenth-century fears that women might turn into men and men into women. Stephen Orgel thus accounts for the practice of having boys play women on the English stage by means of a complex argument whereby pathological fears about the chastity of women are weighed against equally pathological "fantas[ies] of a reversal from the natural transition from woman to man," which "are clearly related to anatomical theories of the essential homology of male and female." "Many cases," he writes, "were recorded of women becoming men through the pressure of some great activity."[19] The endnote to this large claim refers not to women, but to alligators, but as the previous note referred the reader to Laqueur's *Representations* article and to Greenblatt's "Fiction and Friction," we can be reason-

ably sure that the "many cases" in question are in fact the single case of Marie-Germaine, cited by both Paré and Montaigne. It is true that both Montaigne and Paré liken the case of Marie-Germaine to other examples; these, however, being drawn from such authors as Pliny and Ovid, scarcely seem to constitute "many cases being recorded" in the times of the authors concerned.[20] Judith Brown's well-researched *Immodest Acts: The Life of a Lesbian Nun in Renaissance Italy* exaggerates less, but still enlarges the evidence: "in a few cases women did not just imitate men, but actually became men," she writes, citing Greenblatt.[21] More recently, Valerie Traub's *Desire and Anxiety: Circulations of Sexuality in Shakespearean Drama*—which contains an interesting and persuasive account of *Twelfth Night*—claims, citing both Greenblatt and Laqueur, that fear of turning into a woman "may have been a common masculine fantasy" in the sixteenth and seventeenth centuries.[22] Traub's critical project involves enlarging Orgel's contention that the homoerotics of the Renaissance stage enabled "fantasies of freedom" for women as well as men[23] by deconstructing the hierarchy of hetero- over homo-erotic readings of the plays, and revealing, as she puts it, "the polymorphous potential of desire itself, which Shakespeare so assiduously evokes and controls." Though such potential might not seem to have much to do with women in an exclusively male theater, Traub argues that boys were available to women as objects of fantasy, and in rejecting what she characterizes as the "feminist" interpretation of the boy player's significance (that is, the boy-player as instrument of the patriarchal control of female chastity) reveals her indebtedness to Greenblatt in preferring to argue that the boy-payer represented, "an embodiment of the metadramatic theme of identity itself: always a charade, a masquerade, other." Laqueur provides further support for Traub's rejection of the idea that an all-male theater in itself argues either indifference to women's intelligent participation, or fear of the effects of such participation upon the reputation of women and their families. On Laqueur's evidence Traub proposes that

> in spite of patriarchal control of female sexuality through the ideology of chastity and the laws regarding marriage, there seems to have been a high cultural investment in female erotic pleasure—not because women's pleasure was intrinsically desirable, but because it was thought necessary for conception to occur.[24]

Once again, as in Greenblatt and in Orgel, the focus on a medical discourse about the body enables a way of speaking of sixteenth- and seventeenth-century dramatic discourse, and of the position that it offered women in the audience, as exhaustively signified by its analogue, erotic arousal.

What bothers me most about these arguments is that while they seem to be historicizing and de-essentializing our ideas about the relationship of gender to sexuality, the "fantasies" and "anxieties" that they identify in early modern dramatic texts take no account at all of the way in which, in sixteenth-century society, a woman's sexual behavior was perceived to affect the honor and therefore the credit and economic power of her kinsmen.[25] Nor do they consider the way in which such traditional conceptions of sexual honor, credit, and wealth were themselves being rapidly transformed by the technology of persuasion—or "credit"—that such dramatic texts as Shakespeare's represented. None of these critics appear to entertain the possibility that the capacity to plot, write, and *be able to make use* of the erudition and wit of a comedy such as *Twelfth Night* might in itself be more central to sixteenth- and seventeenth-century conceptions of what it meant to "be a man" than any theory derived from Galen. Moreover, for all the emphasis on plurality, the "polymorphous potential" and the "unmooring of desire" released by the comedies, there still seems to be a commitment to the twentieth-century "lit-crit" notion that what the comedies are really all about is individual identity. Traub explores how characters negotiate their individual desires in the plays as if they were real people and not even partly figures in a persuasive discourse or agents of a plot, while Greenblatt celebrates "the emergence of identity through the experience of erotic heat" as "this Shakespearean discovery, perfected over a six- or seven- year period from *Taming to Twelfth Night*."[26] It seems that where literary criticism, as it was once conceived, celebrated the saturnalian energies of Shakespeare's comedies for returning us to a "natural" social and sexual order, these theorists of desire want to find a historically specific concept of "nature"—the Galenic one-sex body—that mimics what is actually their essentialized notion of culture as something which is always preoccupied with the theatrical destabilization of "identities"—identity is "always a masquerade, a charade, other." But what if the errors, confusions, and masquerades of comedy were not, in their own time, thought of as dramas of identity? And what if the way in which the plays construct sexual difference in relation to the audience crucially concerned not the sexual object-choice of men or women in the audience[27], but whether or not they were able to make use of the play as a discourse, an argument, to enhance their own agency? When James Shirley wrote the preface to an edition of Beaumont and Fletcher's comedies, published in 1647, he called it the collection of

the Authentick Witt that hath made Blackfriers an Academy, where the three howers spectacle while *Beaumont* and *Fletcher* were presented, were usually of more advantage to the hopefull young Heire, then a costly, dangerous, forraine Travell . . . And it cannot be denied but that the young spirits of the Time, whose Birth and Quality made them impatient of the sowrer ways of education, have from the attentive hearing of these pieces, got ground in point of wit and carriage of the most severely employed

students . . . How many passable discoursing dining witts stand yet in good credit upon the bare stock of two or three of these single scenes![28]

I'd like to suggest that Shirley's final metaphor of young men as prodigals, living on the "credit" of an ability to recommend themselves to strangers, a "stock" of wit which they have learned from plays, might tell us something about the way in which Shakespeare's plays, for all that they invoke the magic of the reproductive body, nevertheless construct sexual difference by appealing to the male (because formally educated) mind.

2. "Nor are you therein, by my life, deceiv'd": Twelfth Night and Gl'Ingannati

My counter-argument depends on the claim that the kind of comic plot from which Shakespeare never wavered—the five-act plot derived from Terence and Plautus—was perceived in his own time to be concerned, not with the emergence of identity, but with men's discursive ability to improvise social credit, or credibility. For all its popular appeal, Shakespeare's drama had a rigorous intellectual basis in the deliberative or hypothetical structure of Terentian comedy as it was rhetorically analyzed in every grammar school.[29] The rhetorical analysis of Terentian comedy, far from being a rigid intellectual straightjacket (as I was implicitly taught at school, where I learned that Shakespeare transcended his contemporaries by ignoring the classical unities) enabled the achievement of a drama that carried emotional conviction as an unfolding narrative of events—"a kind of history," as Shakespeare himself called it—by investing the representation of those events with the impression of an intelligible combination of causality and fortuitousness.[30] Not only were Terentian plots themselves examples of how one might dispose an argument probably; they also offered images of male protagonists who were themselves able, in moments of crisis, to improvise a temporary source of credit (perhaps a disguise, or a fiction of being related to someone rich) that could defer disaster until the terms of the crisis had altered to bring in a fortunate conclusion. The commentaries of the fourth-century grammarian, Donatus, together with those of Melanchthon and other sixteenth-century humanists, were appended to every edition of Terence, with the effect that no schoolboy could escape noticing how the plays demonstrated that uncertain or conjectural arguments were more productive in social exchanges—because more productive of emotional credibility—than the traditional means of assuring of good faith by oaths or other tokens.[31]

The Terentian plot characteristically concerned an illicit sexual union between a well born young man and a prostitute, which in turn betrayed a promise made between his father and neighbor that the son should unite their houses by marrying the neighbor's daughter. Characteristically, too, the plot managed to lend emotional credibility to the highly improbable argument that the prostitute in question was, in fact, the long lost daughter of the neighbor, thereby reconciling in her person the laws of desire and those of social exchange. Donatus's commentary on Terence was discovered in 1433, and its impact on the composition of European drama evident by the early sixteenth century.

Formal effects upon sixteenth-century vernacular drama, however, were complicated by the ideological impacts of the Reformation and Counter-Reformation, both of which revolutionized attitudes to sex, marriage, and the conjugal household in Europe. For example: Terentian comedy articulates a sense in which the space of prostitution is prophylactic; a household of male, citizen relatives is not dishonored by the entry of the heroine whose desirability was initially associated with her marginal status and sexual accessibility to the young hero. The plays therefore represent a society in which official to tolerance of prostitution first sanctions the initial violation of chastity and ensures that, once attached to a citizen household, the woman will be protected by the very institution that once made her vulnerable. The Reformation and the Counter-Reformation, however, brought with them an end to ideologically sanctioned prostitution, so that, as Lyndal Roper writes of Augburg, "any sexual relationship outside marriage, and any occasion on which the sexes mingled . . . might lead to sin."[32] The marginal status once overtly allocated to prostitutes became a covertly allocated category of suspicion embracing all women.

Nevertheless, there were differences in the way in which Catholic and Protestant Europe acknowledged this and reacted to the sexual mores of the Terentian plot. While the writers of Italian *commedia erudita* cynically substituted citizens' wives and daughters for the prostitutes of Roman comedy, northern humanists tempered their enthusiasm for New Comedy as a model of Latinity and eloquence with a distaste for its evident authorization of illicit financial and sexual transactions, that is, clandestine marriages and rhetorical and sartorial impostures of credit. Thus, while Ariosto was claiming to outdo Terence and Plautus with his brilliant *I Suppositi* in which conjectural arguments ("supposes") are manipulated by the dramatist and the heroes to facilitate and subsequently legitimize the defloration of a citizen's daughter, German and Dutch humanists were redeeming the Terentian plot of sexual and financial deception by adapting it to the New Testament parable of the talents and that of the prodigal son.[33] The waste of money and dissipation of male sexual energy, became, in these reforming "Christian Terence" plays, analogous to the danger posed to civil society by the abuse of conjectural argument in what we might call the "technology of credit" represented by the Terentian plot.[34]

I use the word "technology" here to stress the material impact of the pedagogic dissemination of Terentian rhetoric. A pre-capitalist society necessarily guarantees its economic exchanges—exchanges of honor and wealth—by such instruments as oaths, which bind the faith of the contracting parties. The Terentian plot dramatizes a situation in which oaths and gestures of good faith bring about such an impasse as can only be resolved by exploiting the "error" or uncertainty about motive and intention which obtains between the participants in any social transaction. At a formal level, this very exploitation of error or uncertainty was the basis of the Terentian achievement of dramatic verisimilitude. Reformation dramatists were, therefore, concerned to appropriate the power of the Terentian formula to grant verisimilitude to dramatic fantasy, or to bestow credibility upon outrageous hypotheses, without endorsing the suggestion that this rhetorical "technology of credit" be exploited to facilitate deceptive sexual and financial exchanges in real life.

Much has been made, in recent discussions of "desire" on the English Renaissance stage, of the anti-theater writers' objections to the eroticized body of the boy player. These discussions evidently misunderstand the relationship of anti-theater writing to sixteenth-century neo-Terentian drama, with disastrously simplifying effects. Thus, for example, the title of one polemic against the stage, Stephen Gosson's *Playes Confuted in Five Actions* does not go unnoticed, but its relevance is missed; Laura Levine calls Gosson's conception of his attack as a five-act play "confused," while Jean Howard simply notes that Gosson "uses the five-act structure of classical drama to wage war on theatre."[35] The point is that the five act Terentian argument represented, for educated sixteenth-century men, a technology of credit or of probability which, in its dramatic form, was perceived to be implicated in an ethos of betrayal, sexual and otherwise. Gosson's title indicates a need to appropriate dramatic probability for the cause of reform, as it moves from mocking native English drama's ignorance of verisimilitude to condemning the probable arguments of Italian *commedia erudita* for their thematic endorsement of sexual and financial deception:

> When the soule of your playes is . . . Italian baudery, or the wooing of gentlewomen, what are we taught? . . . the discipline we gette by these plays is like to the justice that a certaine Schoolmaster taught in *Persia,* which taught his schollers to lye, and not to lye, to deceive, and not to deceive, with a distinction how they might do it to their friends, & how to their enemies; to their friends, for exercise; to their foes, in earnest. Wherein many of his pupils became so skillful by practise, by custome so bolde, that their dearest friendes payde more for their learning than their enemies. I would wish the Players to beware of this kinde of schooling . . . whilst they

teach youthfull gentlemen how to love, and not to love . . . As the mischiefe that followed that discipline of *Persia* enforced them to make a lawe, that young men should ever after, as householders use to instruct their families: so I trust, that when the Londoners are sufficiently beaten with the hurte of suche lessons that are learned at Plaies, *if not for conscience sake, yet for shunning the mischief that may privately breake into every mans house,* this methode of teaching will become so hateful, that even worldly pollicy . . . shal be driven to banish it.[36] [my italics]

Gosson, of course, had himself been a dramatist; English playwrights were not ideologically immune to the effects of the Reformation, and were themselves torn between admiration for the rhetorical proficiency of Italian *commedia erudita,* and unease at its explicit promotion of an ethos of imposture and deception.

George Gascoigne thus produced an exuberant translation of Ariosto's irrepressible *I Suppositi* but followed it with the composition of an exceptionally harsh prodigal son play in which he argued that he would henceforth be guilty of "no Terence phrase," since "Reformed speech doth now become us best."[37] George Whetstone's two five-act plays concerning the exposition and punishment of illicit sex and the abuse of financial credit in a city like London were prefaced by an acknowledgment of the need for English dramatists to heed the Terentian rhetoric of probability, for the English playwright "grounds his work on impossibilities." The problem, argued Whetstone, was that the available Continental models of a probable drama—*commedia erudita* and "Christian Terence"—were no use to the English dramatist: "at this daye, the *Italian* is so lascivious in his commedies that the worst hearers are greeved at his actions," while "the *German* is too holye: for he presentes on every common Stage, what Preachers should pronounce in Pulpets."[38] As Shakespeare paid both Gascoigne and Whetstone the compliment of rewriting the plays in question, we may reasonably infer that he was aware of the difficulty of dissociating the productivity of the Terentian technology of probability from its implicit endorsement of violations of chastity and betrayals of household honor.[39]

Shakespeare's *Twelfth Night,* for all its currency as a drama of the body and sexual desire, is in fact so remarkably chaste that Elizabeth Barrett Browning's friend, Anna Jameson, writing a political and feminist criticism of Shakespeare in 1832 could exclaim, "how exquisitely is the character of Viola fitted to her part, carrying through her ordeal with all inward grace and modesty!"[40] Jameson was not being naive or repressed about the sexual content of the play: a glance at the Italian or Roman models of any comedy by Shakespeare will reveal how consistently he chastened their arguments, displacing deep into his depiction of female "character" the signs of an inclination towards sexual

betrayal that in his originals were explicit sexual acts. The lawyer John Manningham, seeing a performance of *Twelfth Night* at the Middle Temple in February 1602, noted that it was "much like the commedy of errors or Menachmi in Plautus, but most like and neere to that in Italian called Inganni."[41] Although there is a play called "Inganni," Manningham was almost certainly thinking of *Gl'Ingannati* or "The Deceived," a play by the Accademia degli Intronati di Siena, written as an apology to the ladies for a sketch performed the previous evening, which was Twelfth Night, 1531.[42] *Gl'Ingannati* seems to have enjoyed a reputation for formal excellence only second, or perhaps not even that, to Ariosto. If Machiavelli (who himself translated Terence's *Andria,* the play central to Donatus's analysis) could urge the Tuscans to forget their prejudice against Ferarese Ariosto, for his "gentil composizione," the French Charles Estienne, dedicating his translation of *Gl'Ingannati* to the Dauphin in 1549, argued that this Sienese play surpassed even Ariosto, giving the reader the impression "que si Terence mesmes l'eust composé en Italien, à peine mieux l'eust il sceu difer; inventer ou deduyer."[43] [That if Terence himself had composed it in Italian, he would hardly have known better how to express, invent or handle it.] English readers were probably aware of the play's high literary reputation; the scholarly publisher, Girolamo Ruscelli, included a collection of Italian comedies "buone degne di legersi, & d'imitarsi," [well worthy of being read and imitated] to which he appended a critical apparatus "de' modi osservati in esse da gli antichi, cosi Greci come Latini" [in the manner observed in the case of ancient authors, both Greek and Latin] so as to make them into a book of "eloquentia."[44]

Behind the central plot device of both Ariosto's *I Suppositi* and *Gl'ingannati* (and remotely, therefore, behind Shakespeare's *Taming of the Shrew* and *Twelfth Night*) lay the notorious play by Terence called *Eunuchus,* which concerns a young man's gaining access, on the pretext of being a eunuch, to the house in which a virgin is being kept, whom he proceeds to rape[45]. The subsequent predictable discovery of her citizenship makes her eligible for marriage without making him guilty of the rape of a citizen's daughter, since the house where he performed the rape was a brothel. Renaissance versions of the plot, of course, have to deal with what we might call the "homosocial" aspect of the crime—that is, the outrage to fathers and kinsmen—since the virgin is no longer found in a house of courtesans. Thus, Polinesta's father in *I Suppositi* lifts the genre into pathos with his sorrow at the loss of his daughter's honor in his own house. And in *Gl'Ingannati,* though there is less pathos, the scandal of the daughter's seduction is perhaps even greater, due to the bizarre means by which she is left alone with a man in her bedroom (her father assumed the man was a woman dressed up; maybe it is a reminiscence of this scandalous plot that has Viola asking to be presented "as an eunuch" to Orsino's court at the beginning of *Twelfth Night*[46]).

Gl'Ingannati begins with a contract between two old men, Virginio and Gherardo, whereby Gherardo is to marry Virginio's daughter, Lelia; "Ne pensar ch'io mi sia permutare di quel ch'io t'ho promesso" [Don't think I'll go back on what I've promised] says Virginio; a merchant's credit depends on keeping his word.[47] But his daughter, Lelia—Shakespeare's Viola—has slipped away from her convent and, disguised as a page, has entered the service of Flammineo, with whom she is in love, but who is himself besotted with another, namely Gherardo's daughter, Isabella, the equivalent of Shakespeare's Olivia. Isabella receives letters and "embassies" [imbasciati] from Flammineo by means of his cute page, Fabio (Lelia in disguise) with whom she, of course, falls in love.

It is worth pointing out how much more explicit than *Twelfth Night* this play is about the fact that sexual desire is not gender specific. Indeed, it becomes very clear that what counts, in distinguishing those who may desire and ask, and those who must be passive, is not gender but social status.[48] Thus, when Lelia's nurse, Clemenzia, finds out that, as Flammineo's page, she has been sleeping in the antechamber of his bedroom, she assumes he will ask her to sleep with him.[49] And later, when Isabella's maid, Pasquella, asks Lelia, disguised as Fabio, why on earth "he" doesn't want to sleep with her mistress, Lelia-as-Fabio replies: "a me bisogna servire il padrone, intendi, Pasquella?" [I have to serve the master, you know what I mean, Pasquella?] and Pasquella does understand: "O io so ben che a tu padron non faresti dispiacere a venirci, non dormi forse con lui?" [Oh, I know very well that you don't displease your master by coming here; but you don't, by any chance, sleep with him?]. When Lelia replies, "Dio il volesse ch'io fosse tanto in gratia sua" [I wish I were so much in his favor] Pasquella is puzzled; "Oh non dormiresti piu volentieri con Isabella?" [Wouldn't you rather sleep with Isabella?], she asks. And she makes it clear, in an ensuing speech on the ephemerality of Fabio's good looks, that (as a fellow dependent herself) she regards the arrangement of sleeping with Isabella not so much as more "natural" than simply as more stable, practical, and fortunate in the long term for Fabio.[50]

In good Terentian fashion, the denouement of the play proves that the contract between the old men is not broken, though both are fortunately deceived; their houses are united not by the impotent old Gherardo's marrying Lelia, but by the passionately consummated union of Isabella with Lelia's long-lost twin bother, Fabrizio, who, like Shakespeare's Sebastian, doesn't question his good fortune in happening accidentally upon a rich woman who ardently desires him. But where Shakespeare's Olivia finds out who her lover really is

by means of the words he speaks (which, as we've seen, have been recently been read as proof of the inherent instability of gender in sixteenth-century thinking about the body), Isabella and the audience of *Gl'Ingannati* discover who *her* lover is in a speech which is more explicitly designed to "appeal to the body." Pasquella, Isabella's maid, emerges from the room in which the two old men have locked Isabella and someone who they think is the truant Lelia, in boy's clothes:

PASQUELLA:

Quei due vecchi pecoroni dicevan pur, che quel giovanetto era donna & rinserronelo in camera con Isabella mia padrona, & à me diede la chiave, io volsi entrar dentro, & veder quel facevano, & trovai che s'abbracciavano, & si baciavano insieme, io hebbi voglia di chiarirmi s'era maschio o femina. Havendolo la padrona disteso in sul letto, & chiamandomi ch'io l'aiutassi, mentre ch'ella gli teneva le mani, egli si lasciava vincere, lo sciolsi dinanzi, e a un tratto, mi sentii percuotere non so che cosa in su le mani, nè conobbi se gli era un pestaglioto [pestella], un garotta [carota], o pur quell' altra cosa, ma sia quel che si vuole, e no*n* è cosa che habbia sentita la grandine. Come io la viddi cosi fatta fuggii, sorelle, & serai l'uscio, & sò che per me no*n* vi tornarei sola, & se qualch'una di voi non me'l crede, & voglia chiarirsene, io gli prestarò la chiave.

[PASQUELLA:

those two old sheep insisted that young man was a woman, and shut him in the room with Isabella, my mistress, and gave me the key. I wanted to go in and see what they were doing, and, finding them embracing and kissing together, I had to satisfy myself as to whether the other[51] was male or female. The mistress had him stretched out on her bed, and was asking me to help her, while she held him by the hands. He allowed himself to be overcome, and I undid him in front, and in one pull, I felt something hit my hand; I couldn't tell whether it was a pestle, or a carrot, or indeed something else, but whatever it was, it hadn't suffered from hailstones. When I saw how it was, girls, I fled, and locked the exit! And I know that as far as I'm concerned, I won't go back in alone, and if one of you doesn't believe me, and wants to satisfy herself, I'll lend her the key.][52]

Pasquella then tries to persuade the distraught Gherardo that it isn't true—his daughter isn't really embracing a man: "vedeste voi ogni cosa, e miraste che gli è femina" [Did you see everything? Well, then you can see she's a woman]. But Gherardo is not to be appeased: "svergognato a me," he says, "I am dishonoured."[53] Gherardo has been deceived, despite his own sharp awareness of the nebulous quality of sexual honor and its susceptibility to gossip.

Precisely because they involve citizens' wives and daughters rather than courtesans, Renaissance imitations of Terentian comedy exhibit a strong awareness of the resemblance of the Terentian technology of probability—the uncertain, or conjectural argument—to the everyday gossip that destroys female sexual honor. Ariosto makes this a theme in *I Suppositi,* where the nurse comes out of her house, onto the stage, anxious to avoid the spread of rumor within the walls, and proceeds to announce to the theatre at large that her charge has (probably) been sleeping with a household servant. But here in *Gl'Ingannati* the joke turns on the way that Gherardo's cautious calculations on the risks of mere probability, uncertainty, and conjecture—calculations as to whether an association with the transvestite (and hence probably promiscuous) Lelia would call Isabella's own sexual innocence into question—are overthrown, by the substitution of Fabrizio for Lelia in Isabella's bedroom, which ensures an unequivocally penetrative defloration. "L'ho veduto con questi occhi," says Gherado, "egli s'era spogliato in giubbone, et non hebbe tempo a corprisi . . . Io dico che gli e maschio, e bastarebbe a far due maschi" [I saw it with these eyes . . . he was undressed to his shirt and didn't have time to cover himself . . . I tell you he was a man, and had enough for two men].[54]

The rhetorical deceptions by means of which the play's argument attains its probability—"la façon de disposer & pursuyure leur sens & argumens en icelles, pour donner recreation aux auditeurs" that Charles Estienne so admired[55]—thus come to be associated with this act of penetrative sex. To the ladies in the audience, the prologue comments,

> Questa Comedia per quanto io ne habbia intesto, la chiamano gl'Ingannati, non perche fossero mai ingannati da voi nò, . . . ma la chiamano cosi perche poche persone intervengono nella favola, che nel compimento non si trovino ingannati. Ma e ci son de gli ingannati tra gli altri d'una certa sorte, che volesse Iddio, per il mal ch'io vi voglio, che voi foste ingannate spesso cosi voi, et io fusse l'ingannatore . . . la favola è nuova, . . . ne meno altronde cavata che della loro industriosa zucca, onde si cavorno anco la notte di Beffana le sorti vostre . . .

> [As far I understand it, they've called this comedy "The Deceived" not because they were ever deceived by you, oh no, . . . but they've called it so because there aren't many characters in the plot (favola) who don't, in the end, find themselves deceived. But there is among these deceptions one particular sort which makes me wish (for the malice I bear you) that you might be often deceived, if I were the deceiver . . . the plot is a new one . . . and is extracted from no other source than their busy pumpkin heads, from whence also came the fortunes you were allotted on Twelfth Night.][56]

In this context, it looks as if the most significant single departure from the Italian variants on the plot of *The Eunuch* in *Twelfth Night* is its dissociation of the effectiveness of the original imposture of credit—the original pretense of androgyny or emasculation which effectively gains access to both to the person and to the heart of the wealthy Olivia—from the identification of its triumph as explicitly sexual (Fabrizio proving his virility with Isabella), rather than chastely marital (Sebastian contracted to Olivia). To a chance member of the audience of *Twelfth Night* in the Middle Temple in 1601 who saw the resemblance of Shakespeare's play to *Gl'Inganni* or *Gl'Ingannati,* meaning respectively "the deceits" and "the deceived," Sebastian's speech at the end might well recall these plays' themes and titles:

> So comes it, lady, you have been mistook.
> But nature to her bias drew in that.
> You would have been contracted to a maid;
> *Nor are you therein, by my life, deceiv'd:*
> You are betroth'd both to a maid and man.
>   (V.i.257-61)

"Deceiv'd" surely here recalls its Italian translation, "ingannata," and no less surely, there is an ethical distinction being made here between being "mistook" and being "deceiv'd" that turns on the question of whether or not Sebastian is a "maid." His affirmation before the audience that he is both "a maid and man" is less a signal of his inherent androgyny than an assurance that Olivia, not having experienced the same "inganno" as Isabella, remains chaste, honorable, and a prize worthy his, Sebastian's, having.

To the argument implied here—namely, that the explicit eroticism of *Gl'Ingannati* makes interpretations of *Twelfth Night* that focus exclusively on the body and sexuality look a little contrived—it could be objected that I am being literal-minded about the theatrical representation of desire. It could be argued (and I would agree) that the very reticence and fantasticality of the amorous language of *Twelfth Night* ensures the "circulation" of desire or of sexual energy more effectively than the gleeful voyeurism of *Gl'Ingannati*. If this is so, however, it must also be acknowledged that the same linguistic reticence and latency of meaning which allows us, in the 1990s, to read *Twelfth Night* as a celebration of the polymorphous potential of desire, equally enabled Anna Jameson in 1832 to find in Viola a paradigm of the sexual self-control that qualified women for access to education and political life. For, within Laqueur's argument, Jameson belongs to that category of nineteenth-century women who based their claims for the recognition of women's political capacity on arguments proving their inherent moral strength.[57] If the rest of Laqueur's argument for the importance of the eighteenth-century transition from the endorsement to the denial of female orgasm has substance, then it must follow that Shakespeare's own texts belong among the discourses that have, historically, helped to construct the moral characteristics felt to be appropriate to a biology of *incommensurability*—sexual difference—between the male and female. And this in turn would imply that, in their own time, Shakespeare's comedies were not just—in Stephen Greenblatt's words—fictions which "participated in a larger field of sexual discourses" but were fictions of the Reformation—that is, they were actively transformative of existing sexual discourses, tending to substitute the intimation of female sexual intention for the representation of the act which would implicate both sexes equally.[58]

It is, in fact, possible to trace through Shakespeare's plays a consistency of strategy (though not, of course, of effect) in his chastening of the roles and language of women. Whereas in his Italian and Roman sources, the significance of the "woman's part" to the resolution of the dilemma depends upon her having had sex, in Shakespeare this significance is translated into an implicit, or uncertain argument involving her *disposition* to have sex, or her "sexuality." To modern readers this can give the impression of a more complex "interiority" or "character" because its doubtfulness requires our interpretation. In the fraught context of the emergent commercial theatre of sixteenth-century England, however, Shakespeare's chastening of Italian and Roman dramatic models was motivated by the need to prove that the productively deceptive arguments of a Terentian-style theatre need not, as its enemies suggested, necessarily advocate the breakdown of trust and honor by endorsing every kind of sexual and financial deception in contemporary society.[59]

To attempt a reading of *Twelfth Night* that would seriously try to take account of the play's place in the history of sex and gender would require some elaboration of how, in common with other Shakespeare plays, this comedy makes a theme of being implicated in a humanistic literary culture which, through its privileging of skill in persuasive argument, was in the process of transforming relations of economic and social dependency. Current discussions of the subversive erotics of the Renaissance stage trivialize the economic and social issues at stake in *Twelfth Night* and similar plays by reducing the whole of the humanist literary culture of which the theatre was a product to the most banal version of Greenblatt's "self-fashioning"—a mere "increased self-consciousness about the fashioning of human identity as a manipulable, artful process."[60] "Self-fashioning" thereby becomes synonymous with a quite unspecific notion of "theatricality," which in turn is easily assimilated to the concept of "performativity" articulated by Judith Butler in relation to the category of gender.[61] The sixteenth-century investment in masculine education, which crucially enabled the very instances of "self-fashioning" or of "theatricality" so beloved of current criticism—an education which privi-

leged the dialectical and analysis and imitation of classical texts—is simply left out of the discussion. What we have as a result is a criticism of Shakespeare, Jonson and others that is incapable of accounting for the rhetorical and affective excess distinguishing this drama of the English Renaissance from its Continental antecedents; an excess which, in the case of *Twelfth Night,* permits interpretations as widely divergent as those of Greenblatt, Barber, and Jameson, and which therefore (because of its contribution to the historical "instability" of the play's "identity") surely begs to be interpreted as a thematic aspect of the play's concern with disguise, deception, and "theatricality."

For an example of how even good contemporary criticism effaces the rhetorical content of the play I want to turn to Valerie Traub's argument that the meaning of Viola/Cesario resides principally in the "dual erotic investment" that the play establishes in order to "elicit the similarly polymorphous desires of the audience, whose spectator pleasure would be at least partly derived from a transgressive glimpse of multiple erotic possibilities." In order to "substantiate the play's investment in erotic duality," she continues,

> one can compare the language used in Viola/Cesario's two avowals of love: the first as Orsino's wooer of Olivia, and the second as s/he attempts to communicate love to Orsino. In both avowals, Viola/Cesario *theatricalizes desire,* using a similar language of conditionals toward both erotic objects . . . "If I did love you with my master's flame, / With such a suffr'ing, such a deadly life, / In your denial I would find no sense; / I would not understand it." . . . "My father had a daughter love'd a man, / As it might be, perhaps, were I a woman, I should your lordship." (my italics)[62]

I would not for a moment deny the existence of the "dual erotic investment" which Traub does well to point out. However, another brief glance at *Gl'Ingannati* will show that Shakespeare's text is more remarkable for resisting than exploiting the considerable dramatic potential of any such investment.

Reading *Gl'Ingannati,* Shakespeare would have come across a model for a scene between Olivia and Viola/Cesario. The scene in question requires the audience to share the voyeuristic position of Flammineo's servants who stumble across Isabella and Lelia/Fabio during an intimate exchange of words and caresses. The audience, however, knows that "Fabio" is, for the purposes of the play, a woman (though the part was probably played by a boy).[63] For the servants, then, the scene arouses sexual feeling and a sense of scandal at the betrayal of Flammineo by the "boy" whom he loved and trusted so much; the audience, however, freed from any sense of the latter, is invited to enjoy the transgression of the scene as if it were a kind of affluence; in Traub's words, it becomes "a transgressive glimpse of multiple erotic possibilities."

Isa. Sapete, vorrei. *Lel.* Che vorresti
Isa. Vorrei, accostatevi.
Sca Accostatevi saluticaccio [selvaticaccio] . . .
Isa. Udite, vi volete partire?
Sca. Baciala che ti venga il cancaro.
Cri. L'ha paura di non esser veduta . . .
Isa. Entrate un poco dentro all'uscio.
Sca. La cosa è fatta . . .
Crim. Oime, oime, o seccarecio altretanto a me.
Sca. Non ti diss' io che la bacciarebbe?

[*Isa.* Do you know what I'd like? *Lel.* What
    would you like?
Isa. I'd like you to come closer.
Sca. Get closer, you bumpkin.
Isa. Listen, do you want to go?
Sca. Kiss her, for Christ's sake.
Cri. She's afraid of being seen.
Isa. Come into the doorway a little.
Sca. The thing is done.
Cri. Alas, alas, I'm dry and thirsty—do it to me!
Sca. Didn't I tell you he'd kiss her?][64]

Without denying the possibility of performing the equivalent scene between Olivia and Viola/Cesario in such a way as to maximize its erotic possibilities, I would want to argue that the rhetorical excess which distinguishes Shakespeare's text from the Italian model insists on a far higher level of engagement from the audience *as auditors.* This, in turn, reorients the dramatic meaning of the scene from pleasure in the spectacle of erotic possibility towards complicity in the act of *interpretation* by means of which a reader or auditor lends credibility to the figures, tropes, and fictions in the discourse of another.

Such audience complicity in the bestowal of credibility through interpretation replicates what the scene offers by way of a narrative of "desire." Olivia's desire for Viola/Cesario must become intelligible (unless we ignore the text altogether) through Viola/Cesario's progression away from formal literary models of courtship towards the affective intimacy of a more familiar mode of address, exemplified in the deservedly famous speech which begins, "Make me a willow cabin at your gate" (1.5.273). At this point we have already witnessed Olivia's unenchanted exposure of the economics of the Petrarchan argument, her parody of its facile and opportunistic movement from the praise of natural beauty to the imperatives of husbandry and reproduction: "O sir, I will not be so hard-hearted, I will give out divers schedules of my beauty" (1.5.247-48). Cesario's subsequent readiness to improvise a first-person fiction of abandonment in love represents an ability to extemporize, to seize "the gifts of moment" and so illustrate the crowning glory of classical rhetorical education.[65]

The speech's most obvious analogue in the schoolboy literature which prepared men for such improvisations is that of the impassioned epistolary rhetoric of the women of Ovid's *Heroides,* whose vivid evocations of their writing, and of the cries that echo through the wild and lonely places to which they are abandoned, resemble (in their simultaneous acknowledgment of hopelessness and its contradiction by the emotions aroused in the reader) the curious emotional power tapped by Cesario's entry into a hypothetical desolation of ineffectual texts that nevertheless defy the premise of their ineffectuality. Like Dido writing "without hope to move you," or Oenone, telling Paris how she made Ida resound with howls ("uluati") at his desertion, Viola/Cesario imagines filling the vacant times and spaces of rejection with "cantons of contemned love" and "halloos" of Olivia's name, suddenly evoking a geography of loneliness in a play otherwise suggestive of houses, estates, and urbanity.[66] The implied femininity of Cesario's hypothetically assumed persona here, however, merely complicates the already problematic dramatic hypothesis of a female "Viola" inasmuch as the prominence of Ovid's *Heroides* within the education syllabus for boys implied, as Warren Boutcher has noted,

> a relationship between the path to knowledge and . . . the mastery of the heroical *genus familiare,* with its base in epistolary stories which involve—both in the telling and in the action—intimate access to and power over feminine sensibility.[67]

The "femininity" of the genre, then, is inseparable from its implication in a plot of seduction not unlike that of Petrarchism, except that in this version "femininity" itself—understood as a peculiar susceptibility to artificially induced compassion—is the emotional catalyst of masculine rhetorical success.

Olivia's desire for Viola/Cesario becomes apparent as a response to this speech and is inseparable, in its articulation, from the material expression of belief ("credit") that would exempt the unknown stranger from providing the heraldic display (the "blazon") that would put "his" gentility beyond doubt:

> "What is my parentage?"
> "Above my fortunes, yet my state is well,
> I am a gentleman." I'll be sworn thou art;
> Thy tongue, thy face, thy limbs, actions and spirit
> Do give thee five-fold blazon. Not too fast:
>   soft! soft!
> Unless the master were the man . . .
>
>   (1.5.293-98)

Olivia's desire motivates her affirmation of Cesario's somewhat evasive protestation of gentility on the grounds of "his" exceptional beauty, eloquence, and presence of mind. What this implies, then, is that the capacity to arouse desire resides less in the androgynous beauty of the body, than in the body conceived as the medium of *elocutio* ("tongue . . . face . . . limbs . . . actions . . . spirit"); that is, the apt delivery of the mind's invention. Viola/Cesario *embodies* the capacity of timely and well expressed speech to compel for a mere fiction *credit,* that is the kind of materially consequential belief (in this case, belief in matrimonial eligibility) that is rarely afforded to the "real thing."

The transgressive "glimpse" being offered to a seventeenth-century audience here, I would suggest, is less that of lesbian desire than that of the opportunity for social advancement and erotic gratification afforded by education for any servant of ability entrusted with missions of such intimate familiarity. That the entertainment of such a possibility is necessarily transgressive (though here held at bay from full recognition by the "femininity" of Viola) is evident from the care taken in the Malvolio plot to exploit the audience's revulsion at the very same idea. As a steward, Malvolio shares with Viola/Cesario the distinction of being a household servant whose "civility" of manner is qualification for a position of exceptional trust in the intimate affairs of the household. Olivia's musing, "unless the master were the man," touches the center of the play's concern with the question of social advancement by means of skills and attractions "blazoned" in the execution of service rather than properly inhering in nobility. How can such social advancement be imagined except as an individualistic pursuit of gain, a betrayal of trust, sexual honor, economic dependency, and love?

Leo Salingar and Emrys Jones have shown how comedies of the late 1590s and early 1600s are concerned with establishing the credentials of a notion of "gentility" that operates independently of the feudal structures of lineage and affinity. "The king might create a duke, but not even he could create a gentleman," writes Jones, echoing a sentiment expressed in plays of this period.[68] Gentility thus conceived is less the effect of lineage than of a certain affluence—freedom from manual labor—combined with the type of liberal education that might contribute a civil demeanor in social exchange. The arguments of such comedies therefore require that the discursively and morally cumbersome aspects of the humanist education bequeathed by Erasmus and the grammar schools be adapted to requirements of a style and *habitus* such as Viola/Cesario exhibits: a non-pedantic conversational facility appropriate to the modest enterprises of urban social encounter.

Salingar sees the conflicts played out through this redefinition of humanistic "wit" in terms of an attempt to distinguish between money values and "the values of a leisure class" whose social and financial ambitions are subliminally expressed as the civilized pleasures of courtship. Jones notes in the early 1600s the "crystallisation of a new theatrical formula":

The plays in question are comedies, usually set in some fictitious vaguely foreign court, often with a double-plot of which one part may be romantic and the other more frankly comic. The comic action sometimes takes the form of a persecution, a "baiting" extended through several episodes.[69]

About the same time as the Chamberlain's men performed *Twelfth Night,* the children of the Chapel staged one of the plays to which Jones here refers, *The Gentleman Usher.*[70] In the predicament of its eponymous antihero, Bassiolo, the play comments interestingly on *Twelfth Night,* condensing different aspects of the situations in which Viola/Cesario and Malvolio find themselves. Bassiolo is, like Malvolio, the most trusted servant in the household of Count Lasso, but, like Viola/Cesario, his being familiarly confided in and befriended by a nobleman for whom he undertakes to woo Margaret, Count Lasso's daughter, immediately puts him in a position of both actual and potential betrayal of trust: Vincentio accuses him of behaving, "as if the master were the man" in an erotic sense, but he has already done so in the sense that in his contract of friendship with Vincentio, he is wooing for himself.

Chapman's is, however, a far more conservative play than Shakespeare's. Whereas Viola/Cesario's inspired improvisation on the model of the Ovidian heroic epistle actually gains the sympathetic ear and the heart of Olivia, Bassiolo's verbose and cumbersome attempt at amorous epistles merely earns him the noble lovers' contempt, serving to prove that the adaptation of a liberal education to civilized wooing can only be managed by one whose gentleness of birth is beyond dispute. The play is nevertheless concerned to argue the necessity of complementing the hunting and riding skills traditionally definitive of nobility with "wits and paper learning"[71] of a non-pedantic kind; the Duke's ennobling of his illiterate minion, Medice, proves disastrous, arguing against the social advancement of servants who are unable to acquit themselves plausibly in noble society. At the same time, however, the play finds, in Bassiolo's dilemma between fidelity to his master, and the opportunity offered by Vincentio's pretended confidence in his rhetorical ability, that any servant so accomplished and entrusted is liable to deceive.

The fantastic unlikelihood of the plot of *Twelfth Night* and its apparent preoccupation with issues of gender have distracted critical attention from the play's affinity with such contemporary comedies of civility and social advancement. Yet it might well be argued that the very fantasticality of the fiction of gender in *Twelfth Night* constitutes the play's strategy of engagement with contemporary debates on the legitimacy of the individualistic exploitation of service in order, in Viola's own words, to "make occasion mellow."[72]

Twelfth Night endorses the notion of rhetorical opportunism, or individual enterprise insofar as it expresses the mastery of fortune and of the occasions of civil life as the metaphorical equivalent of heroic enterprise on the high seas. Thus, for example, the rivalry between Viola and Aguecheek for the favor of Olivia is recurrently expressed in a nautical idiom. Viola is spoken of as having "trade" (3.1.76) and "commerce" (3.4.175) with Olivia, "she is the list of my voyage" says Viola (3.1.77). The hapless Aguecheek, for lack of Viola's witty invention and attractive presence, is berated for having "sailed into the north of my lady's opinion, where you will hang, like an icicle on a Dutchman's beard, unless you redeem it by some laudable attempt, either of valor or policy" (3.3.24-28). Fabian's reference here—to a 1598 translation of Gerrit de Veer's report of the ordeal of Dutch explorers trapped for ten months in Nova Zembla, where they "never saw, nor heard of any man"[73]—comically imagines Aguecheek's conversational failure both as a failure to prove his masculinity and as meriting exile altogether from the new medium of masculine self-assertion—the profitable commerce of sociability.

The sociability thus defined as heroically masculine, however, must be purposeful as well as facile; Orsino, as Feste says, is insufficiently discriminating in the object of his discourse: "I would have men of such constancy put to sea that their business might be everywhere and there intent nowhere, for that's it always makes a good voyage of nothing" (2.4.75-78). The pervasiveness of such oceanic metaphors, as well as references to maps and narratives of discovery (Malvolio's smiling face is likened to the 1599 map which displayed the new world "as revealed by actual voyages of discovery"[74]) invests the Renaissance synonymity of "tempest" and "fortune" with specifically economic resonances.[75] From the analogy developed between drinking and the hazards of navigation (Feste tells Olivia that a drunken man is like a drowned man—1.5.132) there emerges a chiastic narrative of rhetorical *oikonomia,* in which the eloquent and beautiful twins exchange near-drowning for domestic security, while the drunken and inept or irresponsible Toby and Aguecheek—initially comfortable with cakes and ale in Olivia's buttery—are finally banished, like the "knaves and fools" they prove to be, to the "wind and the rain" of Feste's song, beyond Olivia's gates.

Oikonomia is rhetorical because linguistic ability is identified with the ability to manage wealth. Maria declares of the wealthy Aguecheek that he is incompetent with his resources, he will "have but a year to all those ducats. He's a very fool, and a prodigal" (1.3.22); this failure in husbandry is then discovered at intervals during the play as Aguecheek's recurrent inability to invent plausible arguments or "reasons" for his words or actions. Aguecheek's companions are always teasing him for the reasons he cannot give; *"Pourquoi?"*

asks Toby when Aguecheek declares his intention to leave at once, but the question bewilders the knight (1.3.89). In a later exchange Fabian joins Toby in demanding evidence of plausibility: "You must needs yield your reason, Sir Andrew" (3.2.2). The letter which Toby urges him to make "eloquent and full of invention" (3.2.41-43) turns out to be as barren as his speech: *"Wonder not . . . why I do call thee [a scurvy fellow] for I will show thee no reason for't"* (3.4.152-53).[76]

When Anna Jameson praised Viola for the moral sensibility she displayed both in the propriety of her fidelity to Orsino, and in "her generous feeling for her rival Olivia," she appropriated for nineteenth-century feminism a seventeenth-century play's concern with calling into question the assumption that eloquent servants, accomplished in the provision of reasons, and entrusted with the intimate affairs of the household, are necessarily opportunists, people who *deceive.*[77] The narrative rationale of the scene I have already remarked upon in *Gl'Ingannati,* in which Flammineo's servants spy upon Isabella and Lelia's kiss, is to enrage Flammineo against the deceitfulness of his favorite, Fabio; a hilarious scene ensures in which the probability of the kiss is itself called into doubt by the incompetence of the servants in relaying to Flammineo their evidence of Fabio's perfidy.[78] The point here, however, is that Lelia/Fabio *has* kissed Isabella; one deceit leads to another, and Lelia finds herself explaining her refusal of further favors to Isabella on the grounds that "too much love" for Isabella has already led her to deceive ("ingannare") her lord.[79] Earlier, however, Lelia/Fabio showed a singular lack of regard for Flammineo's suit, attempting by means of Pasquella to ensure that Isabella would never respond to his affections; Viola, as Jameson notes, is remarkable for resisting the temptation to do this. In Chapman's *Gentleman Usher,* Bassiolo, also in the position of a go-between or an ambassador between lovers, is tempted not only into exploitation of his position of trust, but into presumptions of equality and friendship with the nobleman who employs him, which the play then ridicules with all the fervor of profound social anxiety.

It becomes clear that the twinning of Sebastian and Viola, and the femininity of the latter, occurs in Shakespeare's play not simply (as in other derivatives of Terence's *Eunuch*) for the sake of resolving an erotic impasse by offering a means of gaining access to the cloistered woman, but for the sake of foregrounding an outrageously improbable *hypothesis* about the possibility of combining fidelity in service with rhetorical *oikonomia*—that is, the heroic exploitation of rhetorical opportunity, which typically achieves both economic security and erotic gratification. Terence Cave has noted that the final revelation of "Viola's" identity remains merely hypothetical, contingent on an accumulation of probabilities beyond the scope of the play: "Do not embrace me till each circumstance / Of place, time, fortune do cohere and jump / *That* I am Viola."[80] It could be said that the femininity of Viola is the grounds upon which the fiction of the servant Cesario can prove the success of eloquence in the narrative of social advancement that Sebastian fulfills, while at the same time ensuring this narrative remains quite untainted by what would otherwise be its precondition—the betrayal of the master by his "man." Viola/Cesario, then, represents more than the "dual erotic investment" that exhausts the meaning of Lelia/Fabio, for s/he is the means by which a seventeenth-century audience could be seduced into entertaining unawares the possibility of a positive version of Malvolio, a servant able to exploit the civility that earns the trust and favor of noblewomen to the extent of achieving the "love" that promises contractual equality. When Fabian imagines himself condemning the cross-gartered Malvolio as an "improbable fiction" on the stage, he draws attention to the self-consciousness that marks the play's violation of the Terentian rhetoric of probability, which remains so near the textual surface of *Gl'Ingannati*. Any audience hearing Fabian, however, must feel that the primary violation of probability lies not in the outrageousness of Malvolio's behavior, but in the very existence of the person called Viola, who represents, as Terence Cave has written, "a particularly fruitful violation of the laws of rational discourse no less than sexual decorum," and whose name performs a number of associative tricks, as it "echoes the erotic flowers and music of the opening scene, insidiously rearranges the letters of Olivia's name, and comes close to naming violation itself."[81]

The play's erotic investment in Viola/Cesario is less, I would argue, than its investment in the violation of probability constituted by the twinship of Viola and Sebastian, which first casts the desire and emotion aroused by Cesario into extremity, and then resolves that extremity as a miraculous disproof of the betrayal of trust that would, in the ordinary circumstances of daily life, be its explanation. Thus, for example, where the sodomitic behavior of Fabrizio's traveling companion, the pedant in *Gl'Ingannati*, merely fuels the sexual comedy of that play,[82] the love Antonio feels for Sebastian, while equally open to homoerotic interpretation, is not sidelined by mockery, but rendered able to share on equal terms in a dramatic climax which turns less on the nuptials that unite the two houses than on the proof that not one of the lovers of a beautiful "boy"— neither his wife, nor his master, nor his friend in need— is "therein, by my life, deceiv'd." The "hints of corruption and aggression," which, as Cave notes, recur in the play, accumulate around the common sense perception that the youthful beauty of a stranger is *probably* as deceitful as it is irresistibly attractive.[83]

Certainly Orsino, having charged his lovely ambassador with the ethically problematic obligation to make "discourse" of his "dear faith" and "act" his woes,

reads the apparent consequence—Cesario's contract to Olivia—as presaging the youth's career in similar deceptions: "thou dissembling cub! What wilt thou be / When time hath sown a grizzle on thy case?" (5.1.162-63). The pathos of Olivia's case is more marked, as she interprets Viola/Cesario's love for Orsino as the "fear" rightfully aroused by the consciousness of having betrayed his master. In attempting to prevent Viola/Cesario's protestation of innocence, she exposes the instability of her own grounds for belief in the youth's continued fidelity to her. "Oh, do not swear!" she begs, "Hold little faith, though thou hast too much fear" (5.1.169-170). Most moving of all, however, is Antonio's apology for being obliged by love into an extremity that makes demands of the one he loves. "What will you do, now my necessity / Makes me to ask you for my purse?" he gently enquires (3.4.342-43), only to be moved by Viola/Cesario's nonrecognition, into an outburst against the deceptiveness of the "promise" that was the boy's manner and looks (3.4.369-79).

A contemporary reader, perusing a popular anthology of the period known as *The Paradyse of daynty deuises,* found one poem entitled thus: "Who mindes to bring his ship to happy shore / Must care to know the lawes of wisdomes lore." By this poem he wrote, "rules of wary life," bracketing off for particular annotation a verse referring to trust in friendship. Do not bestow credit on boys, the verse advised, for, "Ful soone the boy thy freendship will despyse / And him for loue thou shalt ungrateful find."[84] As Erica Sheen has pointed out, the protracted denouement of *Cymbeline* features a "boy" called Imogen who refuses to plead for the life of her savior and friend, Lucentio. His moralizing comment, "briefly die their joys / that place them on the truth of girls and boys" does nothing to assuage the audience's impatient desire to resolve his mistake, proving the "truth" that probability and versified common sense would deny.[85] Just so here, in *Twelfth Night,* Antonio's sententious conclusions on beauty and deceit merely fuel the audience's desire to relieve him of the pain of believing he has loved a "most ingrateful boy" (5.1.75). In view of this, Greenblatt's observation that, at the end of the play, "Viola is still Cesario," seems not so much to argue for any specific beliefs about instability of gender, as to be a part of that complex affective structure by means of which a boy proves, most improbably, to be "true" to all the kinds of lovers he might have—right up until the end of the play.

What, then, of the play's place in a history of sex and gender? The least that should be said is that any attempt to de-essentialize and historicize gender by appealing to a Galenic theory of men and women differentiated only by degrees of body heat is of strictly limited value in the analysis of a complicated tradition of comic writing in which what distinguishes men is their privileged access to allusive and intertextual levels of meaning—in other words, their access to active participation in the historical and discursive process of defining the social roles and characteristics of either sex. But something rather more positive may be said about *Twelfth Night* in particular. For here once again Shakespeare has chastened the argument of a neo-Terentian play in such a way as to maximize the interpretative possibilities, and consequently the historical tenacity, of the English dramatic text.

That the meaning of the Viola/Olivia courtship for a seventeenth-century audience resided at least partly in its capacity to seduce them into condoning the social (rather than sexual) transgression elsewhere reviled by the play's mockery of Malvolio is suggested by the history of critical reaction to Shakespeare's conception of Viola. The probability of Lelia's dressing up as Fabio is established in *Gl'Ingannati* in an exchange with her nurse during which she admits that since being kept prisoner by soldiers, she has become sexually suspect irrespective of her conduct: ever since the sack of Rome, she says, "ne credevo poter vivere sì honestamente, che bastasse a far che la gente non havesse che dire" [I didn't see how I could live honestly enough to stop them gossiping].[86] In 1753 Charlotte Lennox, writing a criticism of Shakespeare, objected to the want of any similar argument of probability in relation to Viola's decision to dress as a man:

> A very natural scheme, this for a beautiful and virtuous young Lady, to throw off all the modesty and Reservedness of her Sex, mix among men, herself disguised as one; and prest by no Necessity; influenced by no Passion, expose herself to all the dangerous consequences of so unworthy and shameful a Situation.

The Italian source, she notes, "is much more careful to preserve Probability" than "the Poet Shakespeare."[87]

However, by 1832 the very want of any "probable" argument for Viola's behavior (since any such would reflect upon Viola's modesty) enabled Anna Jameson to celebrate her femininity as the source of the peculiar integrity which characterizes her relations to both master and mistress.[88] The very improbability of Viola, then, serves to break down the identification of rhetorical virtuosity (the capacity to make things probable) *with the sexual conquest of women* that marks the plot of the Italian play. The literal intertwining of the names of Malvolio, Olivia, and Viola has often been pointed out, but it many not be entirely fanciful to recall that the identification of "inganni" (deceptions, probable arguments) with the sexual deception that makes Isabella unchaste is signaled in the prologue of *Gl'Ingannati* with following innuendo:

> Ma e ci son de gli ingannati tra gli altri d'una certa sorte, che volesse Iddio, *per il mal ch'io vi voglio,*

che voi foste ingannate spesso cosi voi, et io fusse l'ingannatore.

> [But there is among these deceptions one particular sort which makes me wish, *for the malice I bear you,* that you might be often deceived, if I were the deceiver.][89]

Here "il mal ch'io vi voglio" is a kind of flirtatious joke on the euphemism for fancying someone, "ti voglio bene." In entertaining ambitious fantasies which suddenly and indecorously make the audience aware that these are also sexual fantasies about Olivia (2.5.47-48), Shakespeare's Malvolio bears the trace of the erotic "mal . . . voglio" by which Fabrizio's economic success is identified as a sexual conquest and extended through innuendo to characterize the terms upon which a female audience may be imagined capable of enjoying the argument of the play.

What was positive for seventeenth-century women about the way in which *Twelfth Night* addressed them, then, was due less to the "high cultural investment in female erotic pleasure . . . because it was thought necessary for conception to occur" than to its opposite:[90] the extent to which, by refusing to subject Olivia to the "mal . . . voglio" of an explicitly sexual encounter with Sebastian on the model of Isabella's with Fabrizio, Shakespeare manages to portray a heroine whose prudence, good judgment, and ability to govern others remain uncompromised even by her contract with the beautiful youth. For in marrying Sebastian, Olivia has arguably yielded to no whim, but carried out the strategic plan first made known to us by Sir Toby Belch: "she'll not match above her degree, neither in estate, years, nor wit" (1.3.106-108). Olivia never wavers from this purpose, and in providing the precedent that it elsewhere pretends to deny—marriage between a noblewoman and one beneath her—the play endorses the real-life example of the highly intelligent Katherine Brandon, Duchess of Suffolk, who, after having been married at fourteen to her forty-nine-year-old noble guardian, later decided to marry none other then her gentleman usher, who was "an accomplished gentleman, well versed in the study of the languages . . . bold in discourse, quick in repartee." There were, as Katherine Brandon's biographer commented, "many reasons why the clever and serviceable gentleman usher who conducted her business . . . should seem to the Duchess a more desirable husband than an ambitious noble."[91] Shakespeare's play, around 1602, contributed to the undoing of the social and sexual stereotyping that would make of that last statement nothing but a dirty joke.

Notes

[1] Francis Beaumont and John Fletcher, *The Scornful Lady, The Dramatic Works in the Beaumont and*

Fletcher Canon, ed. Fredson Bowers (Cambridge: Cambridge UP, 1970), 2:I.i.82-86. This paper was first written for a seminar led by Alison Brown at the Institute of Historical Research; see Alison Brown, "Renaissance Bodies: A New Seminar on the Renaissance," *Bulletin for the Society of Renaissance Studies* 12 (1994): 20-22. I would like to thank Pamela Benson, Alan Bray, Terence Cave, Helen Hackett, David Norbrook, Diane Purkiss, and Erica Sheen for their helpful criticisms and comments.

[2] Stephen Greenblatt, "Fiction and Friction," *Shakespearean Negotiations* (Oxford: Clarendon, 1988), 86, quoted by Valerie Traub, *Desire and Anxiety: Circulations of Sexuality in Shakespearean Drama* (London: Routledge, 1992), 119.

[3] I should acknowledge here my gratitude to Gayle Kern Paster, who, on reading a version of this paper, pointed out that my concern here is more with textual criticism's historicizing of erotic desire rather than with body history *per se.*

[4] For example, see C. L. Barber's still very interesting *Shakespeare's Festive Comedy* (Princeton: Princeton UP, 1959).

[5] See Lisa Jardine, *Still Harping on Daughters* (London: Harvester, 1983), 9-36.

[6] Catherine Belsey, "Disrupting sexual difference: meaning and gender in the comedies," *Alternative Shakespeares,* ed. John Drakkakis (London: Methuen, 1985), 180. For another poststructuralist challenge to traditional readings of the comedies, see Malcolm Evans, "Deconstructing Shakespeare's Comedies" in the same volume.

[7] Thomas Laqueur, "Orgasm, Generation and the Politics of Reproductive Biology," *Representations* 14 (1986), 3.

[8] See Stephen Greenblatt, "Fiction and Friction," *Reconstructing Individualism,* ed. Thomas C. Heller, Morton Sosna, and David E. Wellbery (California: Stanford UP, 1986), 30-52.

[9] Greenblatt 80; Laqueur 4-5.

[10] Greenblatt 74-75, 79, 85, 181; Laqueur 12-16.

[11] Greenblatt 81; Laqueur 13.

[12] Greenblatt, 88.

[13] Greenblatt, 87.

[14] William Shakespeare, *Twelfth Night,* ed. J. M. Lothian and T. W. Craik (London: Methuen, 1975), 5.1.257-61. Further references to this edition will appear in the text.

[15] Greenblatt, 72.

[16] Greenblatt, 82.

[17] Thomas Laqueur, *Making Sex: Body and Gender from the Greeks to Freud* (Cambridge, MA: Harvard UP), 114.

[18] Laqueur, 115.

[19] Stephen Orgel, "Nobody's Perfect: Or Why Did the English Stage Take Boys for Women?" *South Atalantic Quarterly* 88.1 (1989), 13.

[20] The examples Montaigne cites are those of Iphis, from Ovid, *Metamorphoses* IX, 793ff, and of Lucius Constitius, from Pliny, *Naturalis Historia* VII, iv. See Michel de Montaigne, *The Complete Essays,* trans. M. A. Screech (London: Penguin, 1991), 110. In his chapter of "histoires memorables de certains femmes qui sont degenerees en hommes," Ambroise Paré, *Des Monstres et Prodiges,* ed. Jean Céard (Geneva: Libraire Droz, 1971), includes the same example from Pliny, the story of Marie Germaine, and the example of Maria Pateca, told by João Rodrigues in *Amati Lusitani Medici Physici Praestantissimi, Curationum medicinalium centuriae quatuor* (Froben: Basel, 1567), 168. Needless to say, Rodrigues also cites Pliny, confirming a certain sense of circularity and repetition in the gathering of such instances. One might want to argue for a belief in the frequency of the phenomenon from Montaigne's comment, "Ce n'est pas tant de merveille que cette sort d'accident se rencontre fréquent" [It isn't surprising that this sort of accident occurs frequently]. However, as Montaigne attributes the "accident" in question to the power of the imagination, which elsewhere in the same essay becomes responsible for unfounded beliefs in the magic that causes impotence, it is not clear how sceptically he means this. In any case, Montaigne's version of Marie-Germaine's accident does not conform to Paré's analysis, since Montaigne attributes to the power of the imagination the capacity to satisfy itself a sexual longing by producing the desired genitals of the (opposite?) sex—"si l'imagination peut en telles choses, elle est si continuellement et si vigoureusement attaché à ce sujet, que, pour n'avoir si souvent à rechoir en même pensée et âpreté de désir, elle a meilleur compte d'incorporer une fois pour toutes cette virile partie aux filles." This would seem to argue that girls did not already possess "cette virile partie." See Michel Eyquem de Montaigne, *Oeuvres Complètes,* ed. R. Barral (Paris: du Seuil, 1967), 54. An excellent article by Patricia Parker, which came to my notice after I had written this article, criticizes both the functioning of medical discourse and the teleology of masculinity as a "reassuringly stable ground" in the arguments of Laqueur and Greenblatt and points to the

preoccupation of Montaigne's essay with the anxiety that masculinity itself requires supplementation, to repair the "defect in sex" which is impotence. See Patricia Parker, "Gender Ideology, Gender Change: The Case of Marie Germaine," *Critical Inquiry* 19 (Winter, 1993), 335-64.

[21] Judith C. Bown, *Immodest Acts: the Life of a Lesbian Nun in Renaissance Italy* (Oxford: Oxford UP, 1986), 12, 169.

[22] Traub, 51. This seems unlikely, since Paré explicitly says that the mutation can only go one way: "nous ne trouvons jamais en histoire veritable que d'homme aucun soit devenu femme, pour-ce que Nature tend tousjours à ce qui est le plus parfaict, et non au contraire faire ce qui est parfaict devienne imparfaict" [we never find in any true history that any man whatsoever became a woman, because Nature always tends towards that which is the most perfect, and does not on the contrary make what is perfect become imperfect].

[23] Orgel, 10.

[24] Traub, 103, 117, 141.

[25] Thus, Traub, in her concern to refute or modify Orgel's argument that the transvestite theatre was at least in part motivated by a recognition of the value represented by female chastity, misleadingly represents the argument as being about "the fantasized dangers posed by women" (121), which obscures beyond recovery the notion that women's chastity was valuable because it affected *male* honor and, therefore, economic power. The latter argument has been well made in relation to "desire" in the ancient world by John Winkler, *The Constraints of Desire: The Anthropology of Sex and Gender in Ancient Greece* (London: Routledge, 1990), 74-75.

[26] Greenblatt, 88.

[27] The idea that women in the audience fell in love with the players seems to have been common enough; see Beaumont and Fletcher 1.1.46-48, of a waiting maid: "She lov'd all the Players in the last Queenes time once over: she was strook when they acted lovers, and forsook some when they plaid murtherers." Women's susceptibility to the fiction, then, seems to have been laughed at, whereas the ridicule of men turns on the degree of aptitude or otherwise with which they make use of the wit they have heard at plays.

[28] James Shirley, "To the Reader," *Comedies and Tragedies Never Printed before and now published by the Authours Orginall Copies,* Francis Beaumont and John Fletcher (London: Humphrey Moseley, 1647), sig. A3[r].

[29] T. W. Baldwin, *Shakespeare's Five Act Structure* (Urbana: U of Illinois P, 1947); Marvin T. Herrick,

Comic Theory in the Renaissance (Urbana: U of Illinois P, 1950); Georgia S. Nugent, *Ancient Theories of Comedy: The Treatises of Evanthius and Donatus, Shakespearean Comedy,* ed. Maurice Charney (New York: Literary Forum, 1980); Emrys Jones has pointed out how easily Shakespeare's accessibility becomes an argument for his comparative lack of learning, *The Origins of Shakespeare* (Oxford: Clarendon, 1977), 2-4. In this part of my argument, I draw on evidence represented more fully in my book, *The Usurer's Daughter,* (London: Routledge, 1994) chs. 5 and 6.

[30] William Shakespeare, *The Taming of the Shrew,* ed. Brian Morris (London: Methuen, 1981) Induction, line 140.

[31] For Donatus and Melanchthon see note 29, and Joel Altman, *The Tudor Play of Mind* (Berkeley: U of California P, 1978).

[32] Lyndal Roper, *The Holy Household* (Oxford: Oxford UP, 1989), 112.

[33] "E vi confessa in questo l'Autore avere e Plauto e Terenzio seguitato, . . . non solo ne li costumi, ma ne li argumenti ancora de le fabule vuole essere de li antiche . . . imitatore" [And the Author confesses that in this he has followed Plautus and Terence . . . because he wants to be an imitator of the ancients not just in their customs, but in their arguments and plots]: *Tutte le Opere di Ludovico Ariosto,* ed. Cesare Segre (Milan: Mondadori, 1974), 197.

[34] See Marvin T. Herrick, *Tragicomedy, Its Origins and Development in Italy and France* (Urbana: U of Illinois P, 1962), 17-46; John Palsgrave, *The Comedy of Acolastus translated in oure englysshe tongue after such maner as children are taught in grammar schoole,* ed. P. L. Carver (London: EETS, 1937); M. Christopherus Stummelius, *Studentes, comoedia de vita studiosorum* (Frankfurt: 1550).

[35] Laura Levine, *Men in Women's Clothing: Antitheatricality and Effeminization, 1579-1642* (Cambridge UP, 1994), 2; Jean E. Howard, *The Stage and Social Struggle in Early Modern England* (London: Routledge, 1994), 40.

[36] Stephen Gosson, *Playes Confuted in Five Actions* (London: T. Gosson, n.d.) sigs. C6[r]-7[r]. Gosson's example of the schoolmaster is taken from Xenophon, *Cyropaedia* I.6.26-39. The example is used to caution against fraud in civil life but to justify fraud in hunting and war, an argument Machiavelli refers to in *Discorsi sopra la prima deca di Tito Livio, Il Principe e altre opere Politiche,* ed. D. Cantimori (Milan, 1976) III. 39, 455-56.

[37] George Gascoigne, *The Complete Works,* 2 vols., ed. John W. Cunliffe (Cambridge UP, 1910) II. 6.

[38] George Whetstone, *The Right Excellent and Famous History of Promos and Cassandra: Devided into Two Commical Discourses, Shakespeare's Narrative and Dramatic Sources,* ed. Geoffrey Bullough (London: Routledge and Kegan Paul, 1968), 2: 443.

[39] Gascoigne's *Supposes* as *The Taming of the Shrew* and Whetstone's *Promos and Cassandra* as *Measure for Measure.*

[40] Anna Jameson, *Shakespeare's Heroines: Characteristics of Women, Moral, Poetical and Historical* (London: George Newnes Hd., 1897), 130. The first edition was published in 1832; see Clara Thomas, *Love and Work Enough: The Life of Anna Jameson* (London: Macdonald, 1967).

[41] See Shakespeare, *Twelfth Night* xxvi-liii.

[42] See Guido Bonino, "Introduzione: Il teatro a Siena tra Rozzi e Intronati," *Il Teatro Italiano,* 6 vols. (Milan: Einaudi, 1977), II. xxxvi-xliii, 87.

[43] *Les Abusez, comedie faite à la mode des anciens comiques . . . traduit en Françoys par Charles Estienne* (Paris: Estienne Grouleau, 1549), sig. A4ᵛ. On the supremacy of Ariosto, and for Machiavelli's estimation of him, see Aulo Greco, *L'Istituzione del teatro comico al rinascimento* (Naples: Liguri, 1976), 10 and Machiavelli, *Discorso o dialogo intorno alla nostra lingua* in *Tutte le Opere di Machaivelli* a cura di F. Flora e di C. Cordie (Milano, 1950) II. 816.

[44] *Delle Comedie Elette Novamente raccolte insieme, con le correttioni, & annotationi di Girolamo Ruscelli* (Venetia, 1554), 164. Unfortunately, there are few annotations after Bibiena and Machiavelli, and there is nothing interesting on *Gl'Ingannati.*

[45] See Terence, *The Eunuch, Terence,* 2 vols., trans. J. Sergeant (London: Heinemann, 1912). Ariosto explicitly derives his seduction plot from *The Eunuch* (*Opere,* IV.197), but mitigates its scandalous effect by crossing it with Plautus' highminded *Captivi.* Shakespeare in *The Taming of the Shrew* makes several references to *The Eunuch,* which assimilate it to the humanist debate about the ethics of teaching schoolboys the classics, and to the anti-theatre argument that theatre works like pornography, to arouse men to commit sexual crimes. For the centrality of *The Eunuch* to sixteenth-century debates about art and pornography, see Carlo Ginzburg, "Titian, Ovid and Erotic Illustration," *Myths, Emblems, Clues,* trans. John and Anne Tedeschi (London: Hutchinson, 1986), 77-95.

[46] 1.3.56; "Thou shalt present me as an eunuch to him"; compare Terence, "*Chaerea.* o fortunatem istum eunuchum qui quidem inhanc detur domum! . . . *Parmeno.* pro illo te deducam" [*Chaerea.* o what a lucky eunuch to be made a present for that house! . . . *Parmeno.* I could take you instead], *The Eunuch,* in Terence, II. 270-71.

[47] *Il Sacrificio, Gl'ingannati, Comedia degli Intronati celebrato nei Giuochi d'un Carnovale di Siena* (Venetia: Altobello Salicero, 1569) 1.1, fol. 18ᵛ. There is a translation of this play by Geoffrey Bullough in *Narrative and Dramatic Sources of Shakespeare* (London: Routledge, 1958), 2: 286-339, but it omits or censors a fair amount.

[48] On this topic in relation to *Twelfth Night,* see Lisa Jardine, "Twins and Travesties: gender, dependency and sexual availability," *Erotic Politics: Desire on the Renaissance Stage,* ed. Susan Zimmerman (London: Routledge, 1992), 27-38.

[49] "*Clem.* Dimmi un poco, & dove dormi tu? / *Lelia.* In una sua anticamera sola. / *Clem.* Se una notte tentato dalla maladetta tentatione ti chiamasse che tu dormisse con lui, come andrebbe? / *Lelia.* Io non voglio pensare al male prima che venga" 1.3, fol. 26ʳ.

[50] *Gl'Ingannati,* 2.2, fols. 32ᵛ-33ʳ.

[51] This isn't quite accurate as a rendering of "s'era maschio o femina," but any other way would announce the gender of Isabella's partner too soon by assigning a pronoun.

[52] *Gl'Ingannati,* 4.4, fol. 58ᵛ. This is one of the passages that Bullough omits in his translation.

[53] *Gl'Ingannati,* 4.8, fol. 62ᵛ.

[54] *Gl'Ingannati,* 4.8, fol. 62ᵛ.

[55] Estienne, *Les Abusez,* sig. A3ʳ.

[56] *Gl'Ingannati,* "Prologo," fol. 15ʳ.

[57] See Laqueur, *Making Sex,* 194-205 and Barbara Taylor, *Eve and the New Jerusalem* (Virago, 1983), 28. Laqueur and Taylor both refer to the use made by feminists like Jameson of texts such as John Millar's *The Origin of the Distinction of Ranks* (Basel, 1793), which suggested that position of women in any society might be taken as a measurement of its civility and well being. Millar's influence is certainly traceable in Anna Jameson's *Sketches in Canada, or Rambles among the Red Men* (London: Longman, 1852), and is compatible with the project of *The Characteristics of Women* as outlined in the introductory dialogue, 20-31.

[58] Greenblatt, *Fiction and Friction,* 75.

[59] For an account of how this happens in *The Comedy of Errors* and *The Taming of the Shrew,* see "Why do

Shakespeare's women have 'characters'?" *The Usurer's Daughter,* 178-213.

[60] Levine, *Men in Women's Clothing,* 11; see also Howard, *Stage and Social Struggle,* 35. Both Levine and Howard reduce the meaning of "theatricality" to the subversions, sexual and social, effected by the assumption of *disguise,* as if clothes themselves made the theatrical fiction credible and powerful.

[61] Levine, *Men in Women's Clothes,* 8.

[62] Traub, *Desire and Anxiety,* 131.

[63] None of the authorities on sixteenth-century Italian drama that I consulted [Mario Baratto, *La Commedia del Cinquecento* (Venice, 1975); Nino Borsellino, *Rozzi e Intronati* (Rome, 1974); Aulo Greceo, *L'Istituzione del teatro comico nel rinascimento* (Naples, 1976); Marvin Herrick, *Italian Comedy in the Renaissance* (Urbana: U of Illinois P, 1960); Louise Clubb, *Italian Drama in Shakespeare's Time* (New Haven: Yale UP, 1989)] could inform me on this question of staging. However, Pamela Benson very kindly consulted the current expert on Italian theatrical production, Richard Andrews, whose reply suggested that although plays in convents had all female casts, courtesans were famous for improvising scenes in their salons, and there is some evidence that women did play at court and in some touring companies, they were unlikely to have taken parts in a play put on by a learned academy, such as the Intronati di Siena. I would like to thank Pamela Benson and Richrd Andrews for this information.

[64] *Gl'Ingannati,* 2:6, fol. 37ᵛ.

[65] See Terence Cave, *The Cornucopian Text* (Oxford: Clarendon, 1979), 127.

[66] See Ovid, *Heroides and Amores,* trans. Grant Showerman (London: Heineman, 1977), 62-63, 82-83. *Twelfth Night* is implicitly urban, by virtue of the stress placed throughout on "civility"; Olivia, for example, berates Toby as an "ungracious wretch, / Fit for the mountains and barbarous caves, / Where manners were ne'er preach'd" before begging Sebastian to forgive the "uncivil" injury he has sustained at the hands of her kinsman. *Twelfth Night* IV.i.46-52.

[67] Warren Boutcher, "Catching the Court Ear in Sixteenth Century Europe," *The Cambridge Companion to Renaissance Humanism,* ed. Jill Kraye (Cambridge: Cambridge UP, 1995). For the centrality of Ovid's *Heroides* to the sixteenth-century grammar school syllabus, especially as practice in letter writing, see T. W. Baldwin, *William Shakespere's Small Latine and Lesse Greeke,* 2 vols. (Urbana, 1944), 1: 119, 148, 157; 2:239. See also Erasmus, "De Conscribendi Epistolis," *The Collected Works of Erasmus,* ed. J. K. Sowards (Toronto: U of Toronto P, 1985), 25: 22-25.

[68] Emrys Jones, "The First West End Comedy," *Proceedings of the British Academy,* LXVIII (1982), 215-58, 232.

[69] Jones, "The First West End Comedy" 233. See also Leo Salingar, "Wit in Jacobean Comedy," *Dramatic Form in Shakespeare and the Elizabethans* (Cambridge: Cambridge UP, 1986), 150.

[70] The date of *Twelfth Night* is established by Manningham's *Diary* as being before February 1602; see *Twelfth Night* xxvi. Chapman's *The Gentleman Usher* was printed in 1606, and the date of first performance is conjectured to be between 1601 and 1604. See "Textual Introduction," *The Gentleman Usher,* ed. Robert Ornstein, *The Plays of George Chapman: The Comedies,* ed. Allan Holaday (Urbana: U of Illinois P, 1970), 131.

[71] Chapman, *The Gentleman Usher,* 2.1.58.

[72] Charlotte Lennox complains of the improbability of Shakspeare's plots in *Shakespear Illustrated . . . by the author of the Female Quixote* (London: 1753), 244. That Lennox's response was still commonplace in the nineteenth criticism is suggested by Jameson's comment, "The situation and character of Viola have been censured for their want of consistency and probability," *Shakespeare's Heroines* 130.

[73] Gerrit de Veer, *The True and Perfect Description of Three Voyages by the Ships of Holland and Zeland* [1609] (Amsterdam: Theatrum Orbis Terrarum, 1970), sig. A2ʳ. The account was entered on the Stationers' Register in 1598; see *Twelfth Night* xxxii.

[74] Helen Wallis, "Edward Wright and the 1599 world map," *The Hakluyt Handbook,* ed. D. B. Quinn (London: Hakluyt Society, 1974), 73.

[75] See Jones, *The Origins of Shakespeare,* 209-10.

[76] Chapman, in *The Gentleman Usher,* also assumes a relationship between rhetorical skill, household management, and the favour of noblewomen: "You are not knowne to speak well? You haue wonne direction of the Earl and all his house, / The fauour of his daughter, and all Dames / That euer I sawe, come within your sight," Vincentio flatters the steward (3.2.167-70).

[77] Jameson, *Shakespeare's Heroines,* 33.

[78] *Gl'Ingannati,* 2:8, fol. 40ᵛ.

[79] *Gl'Ingannati,* 2:8, fol. 38ʳ.

[80] Terence Cave, *Recognitions: A Study in Poetics* (Oxford: Clarendon, 1988), 279.

[81] Cave, 280.

[82] *Gl'Ingannati,* fol. 53ᵛ, Stragualcia, the pedant's servant, rails, "che voi sete . . . un sodomito, un tristo, posso dire" [I could say you were a sodomite, a miserable specimen].

[83] Cave, *Recognitions,* 280.

[84] Richard Edwardes, *The Paradyse of daynty deuises* (London: Henry Disle, 1578) Bodleian Library Pressmark: Wood 482 (6), fols. 5ʳ-6ᵛ.

[85] *Cymbeline,* ed. J. M. Nosworthy (London: Methuen, 1969) 5.5.106-108. I would like to thank Erica Sheen for pointing out the similarity of this affective moment to that in *Twelfth Night.*

[86] *Gl'Ingannati,* I.ii., fol. 23ᵛ.

[87] Charlotte Lennox, *Shakespear Illustrated . . . by the author of the Female Quixote* (London: 1753), 244.

[88] See above, note 72; Jameson observes that "The situation and character of Viola have been censured for their want . . . of probability," *Shakespeare's Heroines,* 130.

[89] *Gl'Ingannati,* "Prologo," fol. 15ʳ.

[90] Traub, *Desire and Anxiety,* 141.

[91] Lady Cecilie Goff, *A Woman of the Tudor Age* (London: John Murray, 1930), 213.

Source: "On Not Being Deceived: Rhetoric and the Body in *Twelfth Night,*" in *Texas Studies in Literature and Language,* Vol. 38, No. 2, Summer, 1996, pp. 140-74.

Double Dating

Laurie Osborne, *Oakland University/Colby College*

Simultaneity and coincidence are the essential features which connect Viola and Sebastian in *Twelfth Night*. Twins, after all, are born at the same time and coincide in one womb. Indeed, Sebastian identifies himself as Viola's twin, rather than merely her brother: "He [Sebastian of Messaline] left behind him myself and a sister, both born in an hour: if the heavens had been pleased, would we had so ended!"[1] Though Viola never reveals that her brother is her twin until she is mistaken for him, Sebastian begins his existence in the play as a twin and, just as importantly, as a displaced twin. His lament for lost simultaneity is followed in the next scene by Viola's response to her own emotional quandary: "O time, thou must untangle this, not I, / It is too hard a knot for me t'untie" (2.2.39-40). For both twins, time is the deciding factor: Sebastian regrets the failure of simultaneity in his experience while Viola commits herself to time, both when she adopts her male disguise and when she discovers the situation which that disguise has provoked.[2] By rescuing Sebastian, Antonio has, from Sebastian's perspective, disrupted the simultaneity of the twins' experience, which arose from their birth at the same time and was reflected in their crucial similarity of feature. What was once a twinned existence in brother and sister becomes a string of coincidences in Illyria. Whereas before they experienced life at the same time (and would have died at the same time), when the play begins their lives are only coincidentally the same. Both are rescued and befriended by a ship's captain; both set down in Illyria; both decide to serve Duke Orsino; and both are caught in the interplay between Olivia's household and the Duke's. The events which occur to them are similar but no longer identical.

In consequence, a minor but fascinating textual problem develops in *Twelfth Night*. As Dennis Huston succinctly puts it, "Sebastian and Viola collide spatially when they are temporally almost three months apart."[3] The doubled time experienced by the twins arises from two unnecessarily specific temporal references, one which precedes the sequence of scenes which causes the problem and one which follows those scenes. Before Viola leaves the Duke to woo Olivia on his behalf, Valentine, noting how fond the Duke has become of his new page, draws her attention to the fact that "he [the Duke] hath known you but three days" (1.4.2-3). In the middle of the conversation between Viola and Olivia which immediately follows, after she parts company with Olivia in act 1, scene 5 and before she receives from Malvolio the ring Olivia has sent after her in act 2, scene 2, Sebastian lands in

Illyria with Antonio. His first appearance in act 2, scene 1 would cause no controversy except that in act 5 Antonio insists that Sebastian has just arrived that day and has been with Antonio "for three months before" (5.1.92). During the three days in which Orsino has come to trust Cesario, Sebastian has passed three months with Antonio. Sebastian's lament for lost simultaneity is made literal in the context of the major differences between the twins' experiences: Viola becomes enamored of Orsino in three days, and Sebastian becomes the beloved of Antonio in three months.

This temporal disjunction provokes interesting responses from both critics and producers of the play. The standard critical explanation is that the incongruity is not noticeable to a spectator watching the action. As John Dover Wilson puts it, "It is only evident to the careful *reader*; the spectator would notice nothing wrong."[4] When *Twelfth Night* becomes a text to be read rather than a performance which has a promptbook, the discrepancy becomes noticeable; the reader facing the text recognizes the references to time. Perhaps because *Twelfth Night* is so thoroughly a text as well as a play by the early 1700s, a number of productions, as presented in both promptbooks and performance editions, appear to resolve the problem anyway. They either omit all or part of Viola's conversation with Valentine in act 1, scene 4 or, more drastically, move the first scene between Sebastian and Antonio so that it does not intrude between Olivia sending the ring and Viola receiving it. Both resolutions of the double date within *Twelfth Night* are quite revealing, but the ease with which Valentine's reference to three days can be dropped shows how arbitrary the reference is from the start.

Twelfth Night shows an attention to time which rivals that in *As You Like It,* ranging from the sea captain's assertion that he was "bred and born / Not three hours' travel from this very place" (1.2.22-23) to the priest who has married Olivia and Sebastian "since when, my watch hath told me, toward my grave / I have travell'd but two hours" (5.1.160-61). Most often, however, periods of time define the relationships in this play, as if emotional distance or proximity were a temporal consideration. Orsino responds to Olivia's plan to mourn for seven years by imagining how great her love for him will be if she will "pay this debt of love but to a brother" (1.1.34). When Valentine marvels at the three-day bond between Orsino and Cesario, he seems to suggest an instant attraction. Even Malvolio articulates his imagined relationship with Olivia in a specific time frame and plans his life, "Having been three months married to her" (2.5.44). These measures of affection have all the consistency of Cecily and Gwendolen in *The Importance of Being Earnest* when each stakes her claim as Ernest's fiancée by asserting, respectively, the most recent proposal or the first.[5] In the same way, strength of affection in *Twelfth Night* can be measured in one scene by seven year's mourning and in another by three day's acquaintance.

Yet the force of time as a measure of emotional ties most vividly appears in Sebastian's assertions of his feeling for his sister and in Antonio's response to the apparent betrayal of Sebastian. Sebastian's claim of being born within an hour of Viola first introduces simultaneity as a principle of closeness. Their separation in the course of the play, first introduced by Viola and then intensified in Sebastian's claim of twinning, signals a failure of congruent experience. This loss of simultaneity is set against the way relationships in Illyria are figured in terms of varying, and even sometimes contradictory, time frames.

Antonio brings together these two models in response to the twins he perceives as one. He represents "Sebastian's" inexplicable coldness to him by describing how Sebastian "grew a twenty years' removed thing / While one would wink; denied me mine own purse, / Which I had recommended to his use / Not half an hour before" (5.1.87-90). He offers this description in almost the same breath in which he affirms that he and Sebastian have spent the last three months together; the proof of the intensity of their former closeness is that *he* has acted as Sebastian's twin: "No int'rim, not a minute's vacancy, / Both day and night did we keep company" (5.1.93-94). The measure of Sebastian's betrayal is the disjointedness of a half hour transfigured into twenty years' remove. Antonio's claim of his own former simultaneity with Sebastian establishes the twins' newly disparate existences; their relationship and their identities, both temporally defined, have been temporarily suspended. Cesario can only recover her identity as Viola, and Sebastian, first disguised as Roderigo and then taken as Cesario, can only publicly resume his identity as Sebastian when Viola and he once again occupy the same place at the same time.

When Antonio first invokes the model of simultaneity, his claim is dismissed as lunacy. Even so, Orsino's response to him extends the three days of Valentine's remark to three months: "fellow, thy words are madness. / Three months this youth hath tended upon me" (5.1.96-97). Thus begins the process in the final scene whereby the coincidences in *Twelfth Night* begin to produce simultaneity. The odd congruence of Orsino's and Antonio's three-month connection with Cesario, the similar claims on her loyalty from Olivia and Orsino, and the identical grievances of Sir Toby and Sir Andrew are concurrent demands on Viola which build to the ultimate coincidence: "One face, one voice,

one habit, and two persons!" (5.1.214). This final coincidence, which cannot be explained away as Antonio's madness or Viola's duplicity, leads the twins to their dance of mutual recognition. They survey what proofs, what coincidences, link them. Each had a father named Sebastian; the father of each had a mole upon his brow. The final and deciding coincidence is, suitably, temporal—both recall the father who "died that day when Viola from her birth / Had number'd thirteen years" (5.1.242-43).

The most unusual aspect of this proof is frequently overshadowed by Sebastian's inexplicable failure to identify himself as Viola's twin: he does not acknowledge that his father also died on his thirteenth birthday but says, "He finished indeed his mortal act / That day that made my sister thirteen years" (5.1.245-46). His answer apparently violates the parallelism of their mutual catechism ("My father had a mole upon his brow." / "And so had mine" [5.1.240-41]), but actually follows Viola's impulse to identify herself. After all, Sebastian has external verification when he recognizes Antonio and Antonio names him; Viola's identity is the issue, as Sebastian's questions indicate: "what kin are you to me? / What countryman? What name? What parentage?" (5.1.228-29). Her self-identification depends on the internal evidence of memory. The proof she offers is remarkable indeed—the date of her thirteenth birthday is the date of her father's death. Olivia reinforces this return to simultaneity and restored relationships when she offers to be Orsino's sister and asserts that "one day shall crown th'alliance on't" (5.1.317); the twins will marry simultaneously, and Orsino and Olivia will become brother and sister in amity at the same time. The "whirligig of time" (5.1.375) may bring its revenges to Malvolio, but "golden time convents" (5.1.381) to sort out most of the other relationships in Illyria—once the twins are restored to the same time.

Similar concerns for simultaneity and identity, time and connection, are the very principles at work in the determinations of two very different dates for the play in the late eighteenth and early nineteenth centuries. In the late 1700s when Edmond Malone first argued that a chronology of Shakespeare's plays would be useful, texts like *Twelfth Night* which appear only in the Folio posed special problems. In the absence of quartos or other early references, scholars relied on internal evidence to ascertain a play's date. Horace Howard Furness points out in the Variorum edition that a scholar named Thomas Tyrwhitt discovered an apparent topical reference to undertakers; as a result, the play was dated at 1614 when there was considerable parliamentary furor about undertaking, "although this date involved the undesirable conclusion that *Twelfth Night* was the last play that Shakespeare had written."[6] Published references to the 1614 origin of *Twelfth Night* actually begin with Malone's "An Attempt to Ascertain the Order in

Which the Plays Attributed to Shakespeare Were Written," which is included as part of the introductory material in the George Steevens edition of Shakespeare's works in 1778.[7] In discussing the chronology he offers, Malone affirms the 1614 date by challenging readers to discover "among the plays produced before 1600, compositions of equal merit with *Othello, King Lear, Macbeth, The Tempest,* and *Twelfth Night* which we have reason to believe were all written in the latter period" (p. 271). For the next fifty years, most experts considered *Twelfth Night* to be one of the later, if not the last, of Shakespeare's works.

References to the 1614 date of *Twelfth Night*'s composition occur in a variety of places besides Malone's scholarly essay. Perhaps the most pervasive case is *The Life of* WILLIAM SHAKSPEARE: *Collected and Arranged from Numerous Rare and Authentic Documents. Containing* EVERY FACT OF IMPORTANCE *from the Birth of This Eminent Poet to the Close of His Brilliant Career,* written by Joseph Graves in the 1820s. Though Graves acknowledges that all efforts to establish which of Shakespeare's plays was written first have failed, he feels confident enough about some of the sequence to assert that: "we may not hesitate . . . to station 'Pericles, the three parts of Henry VI., Love's Labour lost; The Comedy of Errors; The Taming of the Shrew; King John; and Richard II.;' among his earliest productions, we may with equal confidence, arrange 'Macbeth; Lear; Othello; Twelfth Night; and the Tempest;' with his latest, assigning them to that season of life, when his mind exulted in the conscious plenitude of power."[8] The cover of this *Life of Shakespeare* announces that it is "adapted and printed, for the purpose of binding up with any edition of Shakespeare's Plays." Some editions, particularly *Cumberland's British Theatre* (1830), did indeed bind up Graves's version of Shakespeare's life with the plays. Moreover, others who were producing biographies of Shakespeare echoed Graves, like Charles Symmons, who in 1837 also assumed that Shakespeare wrote *Twelfth Night* "when his mind exulted in the conscious plenitude of power."[9]

Even *The Dramatic Souvenir: Being Literary and Graphical Illustrations of* SHAKESPEARE *and Other Celebrated English Dramatists,* published in 1833, devotes fully half of its "literary illustration" of the play to discussing its composition: "Malone considered *Twelfth-Night* was written at leisure, in 1614, when the author had retired from the Theatre, the very last of his plays, and about three years before his death."[10] These ideas about the date of the play were also accepted by Shakespeare enthusiasts, as John William Cole's intensely annotated edition of Shakespeariana indicates. His copious notes on the available editions and documents associated with Shakespeare testify to his interest in the plays and their author, while he lists in his own hand *Twelfth Night*'s date of composition as 1614.[11]

However, in 1831 John P. Collier completely revised the date of *Twelfth Night*'s composition by publishing his discovery of John Manningham's 1601-2 diary entry, which alludes explicitly to a production of the comedy: "Feb 2, 1601[-2] At our feast we had a play called *Twelve Night or what you will,* much like the comedy of errors, or Menechmi in Plautus, but most like & neere to that in Italian called Inganni. A good practise in it to make the steward believe his lady widdowe was in love with him by counterfayting a letter."[12] This reference seems indeed, as Collier says, "a striking, and at the same time a rarely occurring, and convincing proof" (p. 327). This determination also completely revises the date promoted by Malone and others.

This nominally "absolute" determination of the comedy's date dislocates the text; as a result, later editions had to explain the change. Burton's Theatre Edition, published in 1852, quotes the Oxberry introduction but carefully rectifies the date by offering Collier's discovery, evidently common knowledge by that time (p. V). Other editors, like those of *Chambers's Household Shakespeare* (1840), felt obligated to justify the earlier error: "The dramatic art evinced in *Twelfth Night,* and its general excellence, led to a belief that it was one of the poet's latest productions" (p. I).[13] Far from rendering the comedy more firmly established, the diary entry actually exposes the ways in which even identical texts can vary because of "extratextual" considerations such as their date of composition.

The Tyrwhitt *Twelfth Night* (1614) differs from the post-Manningham *Twelfth Night* (1602) established by Collier because Tyrwhitt depended on the way the playwright's imagination supposedly transformed and reflected the events of his day within the play. Collier, on the other hand, derived his date for the play from the physical evidence of the play's production. Both versions of *Twelfth Night*'s date depend on the crucial mutuality which the play itself considers—coincidence and simultaneity. For Tyrwhitt, and Malone as well, the mention of undertakers in act 3, scene 4 and the furor over "undertaking" in Parliament in 1614 were too great a coincidence for the reference not to be deliberate: "Mr. Tyrwhitt, with great probability, conjectures, that *Twelfth Night* was written in 1614: grounding his opinion on an allusion, which it seems to contain, to those parliamentary *undertakers,* of whom frequent mention is made in the Journals of the House of Commons for that year" (Malone, p. 344). Toby's jesting about undertaking reflected Shakespeare's creative rendering of a topical issue particularly hot in 1614— the two must have occurred simultaneously.

When Collier discovered the Manningham diary, Toby's comment was revealed as an irrelevant coincidence rather than one which denotes simultaneity. The many features which define the comedy Manningham saw— the title *Twelve Night, Or what you will,* the plot's similarity to *The Comedy of Errors,* the trick on a steward involving a letter—coincide in the diary entry dated 1601. Although there is a play by John Marston called *What You Will,* all the circumstances in Manningham's diary combined constitute an even greater coincidence than a single reference to undertakers. Thus the occurrence of Manningham writing in his diary and Shakespeare's company producing *Twelfth Night* must be mutually determinant—the date attached to one can also be attached to the other.

Like the twins, two texts of *Twelfth Night,* one dated 1614 and another dated 1601, look the same but participate in different relationships. These doubled texts enact the situation imagined in Jorge Luis Borges's short story "Pierre Menard, Author of *Don Quixote.*" The narrator claims that Menard's "work, possibly the most significant of our time, consists of the ninth and thirty-eighth chapters of Part One of *Don Quixote* and a fragment of the twenty-second chapter."[14] Menard does not copy the novel; he does not produce a contemporary version or a transcription; he does not write it by reenacting Cervantes's life. He takes up a different challenge—to write *Don Quixote* as Pierre Menard. As a result, the narrator tells us, "The text of Cervantes and that of Menard are verbally identical, but the second is almost infinitely richer" (p. 52). In this story, Borges displays the inherent contradiction between, on the one hand, attempting to anchor the text historically in relation to its author and, on the other hand, claiming that a text transcends its time. By insisting that the second *Don Quixote* is "infinitely richer," Borges imagines that the temporal displacement enriches and changes the text, even though the later version is "verbally identical." The second *Twelfth Night,* dated at 1601, may not necessarily be "infinitely richer" but it has certainly occasioned many more readings of the play, including some analyses explicitly based on the 1601 date, like Leslie Hotson's *The First Night of Twelfth Night.*[15]

For the readers of the early nineteenth century, *Twelfth Night* is a comedy self-evidently from the close of Shakespeare's career. Yet, for the twentieth-century reader, with the benefit of 150 years of scholarship based on the 1601 date, *Twelfth Night* is obviously a middle comedy with connections to *Hamlet* and to the tragedies. Like the two versions of *Don Quixote* in Borges's story—one from the sixteenth century and one from the twentieth—the Folio text of *Twelfth Night* before 1831 and after are typographically identical, but utterly different.

Although *Twelfth Night* seems one of the least problematic works in the Shakespearean canon because we can now establish its date so confidently, the achievement of that fixed date actually reveals the text's multiplicity rather than its singularity. Moreover, the real purpose of dating *Twelfth Night* or any Shake-

spearean play is not so much absolute as relational. The shift of *Twelfth Night*'s date not only exposes the doubled nature of that play, but also calls into question the status of *The Tempest.* The speculation on *The Tempest* as Shakespeare's last play (and final statement) originated at the time when *Twelfth Night*'s date shifted. Malone corrected his own chronology in 1821 to give the date as 1607, and, as Gary Taylor notes, Thomas Campbell at around the same time first put forward the attractive theory about *The Tempest*'s valedictory quality.[16]

When Malone initially published his attempt to discover the order of Shakespeare's plays, he laid out the potential importance of such knowledge: "While it has been the endeavour of all his editors and commentators, to illustrate his obscurities, and to regulate and correct his text, no attempt has been made to trace the progress and order of his plays. Yet surely it is no incurious speculation, to mark the gradations by which he rose from mediocrity to the summit of excellence; from artless and uninteresting dialogues, to those unparalleled compositions, which have rendered him the delight and wonder of successive ages" (pp. 270-71). Malone implied that the idea of giving a chronology to Shakespeare's works had not occurred to anyone before him, even though Nicholas Rowe indicated his own curiosity concerning the dating of the plays as early as 1709 (Taylor, p. 157). Malone also linked chronology to the evolution of Shakespeare's art. Indeed the readers and critics of Malone's day were interested in his chronology and fashioned their own theories of Shakespeare's development. Joseph Graves gave a typical view: "It is probable that such as were founded on the works of preceding authors, were the first essays of his dramatic talent: and such as were more perfectly his own, and are of the first sparkle of excellence, were among his last" (pp. 9-10). Graves, like Malone and others, carried his point by inviting the reader to compare the earlier works with the superior later ones.

The significance of dates, then, is twofold. The comedy's date of composition determines its connections with the other plays, and those connections anchor the text to the author's evolving psyche. As Margreta de Grazia has argued, Malone's purpose in determining the sequence of plays was little more than a small part of his overarching aim to establish Shakespeare as an individual. She further suggests that this treatment of Shakespeare's artistic development becomes a model for the emerging bourgeois subject.[17] That model hinged on the idea that his development registered ever-greater perfection.

Comments on *Twelfth Night* found in performance editions before 1831 underscore this notion. George Daniel's 1830 introduction to the play is particularly fulsome: "It is, therefore, not without emotion that we

approach this last work of Shakspeare's mighty genius. . . . That Shakspeare parted with the world on
terms of friendship, this legacy of his love sufficiently
demonstrates; though, in the Epilogue Song (the last
lines that he ever wrote,) we think we can discover
something that savours of transient bitterness"
(Cumberland, p. 5). Daniel even goes so far as to praise
John Fawcett's acting of Feste by commenting that "he
sang the Epilogue Song with true comic spirit; and
with a harmony and *feeling* as if conscious that the *last
words of Shakspeare* were trembling on his lips"
(Cumberland, p. 7). While asserting *Twelfth Night*'s
privileged position as the last play, these statements
also raise several problems.

Most striking, perhaps, is the reference to the Epilogue
Song, which we are asked to take as Shakespeare's
last words. After all, Malone himself notes that the
song appears "earlier" in Shakespeare's career, in a
slightly different form as one of the Fool's songs in
Lear.[18] If Feste's cryptic song is Shakespeare's final
statement, the various attempts to decipher or dismiss
the song which begin as early as 1774 with Bell's
edition take on new significance: "The epilogue song
gives spirit to the conclusion, tho' there is very little
meaning in it, except a trifling address to the audience
in the last line" (Bell, vol. 5, p. 329).[19] The song
troubled Leigh Hunt as well, who praised Fawcett's
presentation of the Clown's role but disliked the song:
"Yet we do not like to think that this was the last song
which Shakespeare wrote. It has too much of the scorn
of the world and all he has seen in it."[20]

There are also more subtle problems revealed in the
assumptions expressed by Daniel. For example, it is
now common knowledge (with all the uncertainty the
phrase should imply) that Shakespeare left the theatre
well before he left the world. Yet placing the date of
Twelfth Night at 1614 suggests that Shakespeare wrote
the play after retiring from London. *Twelfth Night* is
thus not only the last of his plays but also a work
written after he left the playhouse. Malone goes to
some lengths to explore this most unusual aspect of
Tyrwhitt's date. He develops an elaborate explanation
of why Shakespeare would take up the pen again after
he had abandoned the theatre: "When Shakspeare
quitted London and his profession, for the tranquillity
of a rural retirement, it is improbable that such an
excursive genius should have been immediately reconciled to a state of mental inactivity. . . . To the necessity, therefore, of literary amusement to every culti-
vated mind, or to the dictates of friendship, or to both
these incentives, we are perhaps indebted for the comedy of *Twelfth Night;* which bears evident marks of
having been composed at leisure, as most of the characters that it contains, are finished to a higher degree
of dramatick perfection, than is discoverable in our
author's earlier comick performances" (Malone, p. 344).
Malone perceived a greater perfection in Shakespeare's

characterization in his "last" comedy, underscoring his
notions of Shakespeare's developmental improvement.
Daniel concurred and reinforced this sentiment in the
opening of his introduction: "We have now come to
the last production of the Divine Shakspeare. Having
followed his genius through its bright path of glory,
we arrive at the point where it sets, with a splendour
worthy of its highest meridian" (Cumberland, p. 5).

These comments may seem like little more than amusing, if antiquated, examples of previous misconcep-
tions about Shakespeare, which we can safely ignore.
Nevertheless, the readers of Shakespeare in the late
eighteenth and early nineteenth centuries knew a different *Twelfth Night* from the 1601 text we read now,
whether they subscribed to the bardolatrous view of
the comedy which Daniel offers or thought, as the
Oxberry edition tells us, that "it is not a little singular
that this play should be one of the last of Shakspeare's
productions, a play that has all the joyousness and
revelry of youth about it" (Oxberry, p. ii).

Even though explanations of Shakespeare's developing art have changed considerably, Malone was more
prophetic than he knew. While perhaps no longer a
subject as hotly debated as it was when Malone and
George Chalmers argued about whether Shakespeare
wrote *Twelfth Night* "in 1614 or in 1613" (*Souvenir,* p.
v), the dating of his plays still functions as the unacknowledged foundation for many critical arguments.
Our readings depend upon the coincidences recorded
in Manningham's diary as thoroughly as Malone and
Tyrwhitt relied on a coincidental reference to undertakers. However, as the twins' experiences in the play
and Malone's error point out, coincidences do not
necessarily indicate simultaneity. Current criticism may
take a different model of development, but it derives
comparably from the interconnections between chronologically linked plays and their presumed reflections
of an author's individual evolving psyche.

For example, many psychoanalytic approaches to
Twelfth Night rely on its position in Shakespeare's
development. Leonard Manheim argues that the play is
a wish-fulfillment fantasy restoring the playwright's
son Hamnet, twin to Judith, who died in 1596.[21] In
turn, Thomas MacCary discovers in the plays a model
of male sexual development through homoerotic attraction which he sees most fully expressed in the
mature comedies like *Twelfth Night:* "The late romances
do not share that fervour and obsession so characteristic in the mature comedies like *Twelfth Night*."[22] Joel
Fineman, in his argument about the shifting uses of
doubling at the crucial shift in Shakespeare's career
from comedy to tragedy, implicitly depends on the
contemporaneity of the four plays he considers, *As You
Like It, Hamlet, Troilus and Cressida,* and, of course,
Twelfth Night.[23] Likewise, C. L. Barber and Richard
Wheeler explicitly rely on canon chronology for their

study of Shakespeare's psychology, *The Whole Journey*.[24] For these critics, involved in considering Shakespeare's development, the status of *Twelfth Night* as mature comedy is essential and unquestioned.

Even critics less overtly concerned with Shakespeare's overall psychological development also assume the fixed placement of *Twelfth Night* in the canon. Nowhere in his essay about the problem of identity in the play does Dennis Huston specify the play's date as a concern, yet he opens the essay by explicitly linking the comedy to *Hamlet* and brackets the comedy's treatment of sexuality as "an idea that Shakespeare used twice before as a starting point for comedy—in *Love's Labour's Lost* and *The Taming of the Shrew*—and would use again with more serious overtones in *Measure for Measure*" (p. 283). Matthew Wikander, who juxtaposes psychological and anthropological readings of adolescent experience in *Twelfth Night* with the experiences of the boy-actress in Shakespeare's company, also calls upon *Hamlet* in support of the ambivalence toward the theatre which he reads in the boy-actress facing his uncertain future in the company.[25]

In contrast to the central and sometimes invisible role of the 1601 date in these studies, the 1614 date figures in current criticism only as a curiosity. Both Margreta de Grazia and Gary Taylor mention it in passing, but both are more concerned with the developing uses of Shakespeare as an icon rather than with the development of a particular set of texts. Taylor, for example, dismisses Leigh Hunt's praise of *Twelfth Night* as Shakespeare's last play with the conclusion that, given modern scholarship, Hunt is wrong (p. 157). The 1614 date is simply incorrect and therefore irrelevant. Or is it? After all, Taylor catalogs successive generations of scholars and readers who all discover their own versions of Shakespearean authenticity, and de Grazia explores late-eighteenth- and early-nineteenth-century scholarly recuperations in terms of the emergence of bourgeois subjectivity. Similarly, because revisions of the date relocate and duplicate a text like *Twelfth Night*, the text's relationships to the rest of the canon are more historical constructs than transparent reflections of Shakespeare's development.

The shift in *Twelfth Night*'s date implicitly challenges any absolute assumptions, including our own, about the comedy's position in the Shakespearean canon. The historical contingency of our ideas about Shakespeare's chronology, based on the evidence available now, suggests that the suppositions in our current criticism and the analyses themselves are only provisional. However, the resulting loss of transcendent truth does not negate the value of their readings and assumptions or of ours. Instead the significance of successive understandings of the Shakespearean text derives from their historical specificity, that is, from their placement within

a particular cultural situation and historical moment. Consequently, the 1614 date of *Twelfth Night* is more than a mistake or an oddity; it is one of those historical moments which reveals the multiplicity of Shakespearean plays in general and of *Twelfth Night* in particular. Collier's discovery changed the *Twelfth Night* texts as it changed the comedy's date of composition because the physical texts of the play, which we think of as permanent and limited, always exist only within a multiplicity of contexts, including their several selves.

For some scholars, this multiplicity may seem easily resolved. After all, doesn't the problem disappear if what is "really" changing is the interpretation and not the material text itself? This question raises the implicit issue of the material text and its boundaries. The narrative of *Twelfth Night*'s changing date actually reveals three distinct texts, all of which are (at least potentially) typographically the same. The first is the *Twelfth Night* for which the date of composition is irrelevant and unknowable, mere speculation according to Nicholas Rowe. When Malone introduces the importance of recovering the chronology of Shakespeare's plays, not only does he initiate the creation of the Shakespearean subject, as de Grazia argues, he also creates a second *Twelfth Night*, composed around 1614. With the chronology, what was outside the text and unnoted becomes part of the text and inseparable from its interpretation. As the 1601 date gradually became well known, altering the comedy's position among Shakespeare's plays, the change yielded yet a third *Twelfth Night*. The very typographical sameness of these *Twelfth Night* texts points to the real issue: what is inside and what is outside the text? The uncertainty of the text's limits, which this chapter explores in terms of date, the rest of this book examines in terms of the many physical texts associated with Shakespeare's comedy.

Thus double dating offers my first negotiations between "inside" and "outside" the text. When Jacques Derrida argues that the text is "henceforth no longer a finished corpus of writing, some content enclosed in a book or its margins, but a differential network, a fabric of traces referring endlessly to something other than itself," he suggests that texts endlessly overrun their apparent boundaries.[26] Nonetheless, we assume an inside and an outside to texts like *Twelfth Night*. On the one hand, the shifting grounds of *Twelfth Night*'s date implies that dating is somehow outside the text, changeable, subject to constant revision, victim to chance, coincidence, and time. The double date is an aberration; our current date is correct. On the other hand, the changes that *Twelfth Night* underwent between the early nineteenth century and now, merely because of the dating, suggest that the changeability of *Twelfth Night*'s date is part of the multiple traces which break open the notion of the singular text.

In the shift of dates, the texts of *Twelfth Night* experience a temporal dislocation similar to that the twins experience in Illyria; the 1614 *Twelfth Night* exists in a different time with different connections than the 1601 *Twelfth Night,* even though they both occur in one place—the Folio text. When the coincidences overwhelmingly support the 1602 date, *Twelfth Night* apparently takes on a fixed, determinant date. Comparably, when coincidence supports Sebastian's version of time, identity is restored, as Viola redefines herself in terms of father/author and twin. The mysterious other time which Viola/Cesario occupied during the comedy vanishes, just as the 1614 date of the Tyrwhitt *Twelfth Night* becomes irrelevant and has, in essence, vanished. Perhaps the spectators watching the play, like the critics now discussing the date, would not notice the double time of the twins' experience, yet it is that separation and reunion of the twins in time which underscores the metaphoric force of relative time in many relationships within the play.

As a result, the end of *Twelfth Night* gives a truer picture than the current critical perception of a single *Twelfth Night* fashioned around 1600: Viola and Sebastian are twins, the same in appearance but involved in different relationships. The Tyrwhitt *Twelfth Night,* associated with the late plays and implicated in an early-nineteenth-century theory of Shakespeare's development, and the Manningham *Twelfth Night,* associated with the end of Shakespeare's comic writing and implicated in his psychological development, are the same but different. The existence of the second does not negate or dissolve the experience of the first, any more than the dominance of Sebastian's time and the resulting coincidences negate Viola's earlier experiences in the play. *Twelfth Night* leaves us with both twins, and I argue that this history of double dating leaves us with multiple texts. The odd congruence of the history of *Twelfth Night*'s dating and the stories of the twins within the play is, of course, just coincidence.

For my reading, that coincidence demonstrates that the multiplicity of texts, generated materially through history as Jerome McGann suggests, constantly reworks the boundaries of "the text."[27] The permeable, provisional edges, the Derridean "folds" where suddenly the outside edge touches the inside of the form, open a space which is somehow neither inside nor outside.[28] Reading the "outside" history of Shakespearean texts, as this book does, does not and cannot avoid reading the "inside" of those texts as well. This continuing transgression of the textual edges, which are themselves constantly under construction and erasure, is an essential feature of my critical project. The apparently exterior history of performance editions—considered to be outside proper textual history, irrelevant to reading the play, tangential in critical scholarship—also offers an "interior" history of the comedy: a repetition of loss and return, impossible desire and shifting sexual identity, displacement and continuity, and, inevitably, simultaneity and coincidence.

Notes

[1] William Shakespeare, *Twelfth Night: The Arden Shakespeare,* ed. J. M. Lothian and T. W. Craik (New York: Methuen, 1975), act 2, scene 1, lines 18-20. All further references to the play by act, scene, and line (rather than edition name and date) refer to the Arden edition and appear in the body of the chapter.

[2] Olivia's emotional turmoils are also marked by time as a clock inexplicably strikes in the middle of her confession of love for Cesario and she responds, "The clock upbraids me with the waste of time" (3.1.132).

[3] J. Dennis Huston, "'When I Came to Man's Estate': *Twelfth Night* and Problems of Identity," *Modern Language Quarterly* 33 (1972): 274.

[4] J. Dover Wilson (ed., with Arthur Quiller-Couch), *Twelfth Night, or What You Will* (Cambridge: Cambridge University Press, 1930), p. 163, n. 93.

[5] Oscar Wilde, *The Importance of Being Earnest,* in *Complete Works of Oscar Wilde* (New York: Harper and Row, Publishers, 1989), p. 363.

[6] Horace Howard Furness, Introduction to *The New Variorum Shakespeare: "Twelfth Night"* (New York: American Scholars Publications, 1966), p. viii. Tyrwhitt's contribution to the scholarly production of Shakespeare's works in the eighteenth century has recently received more formal recognition in Arthur Sherbo's *Shakespeare's Midwives: Some Neglected Shakespeareans* (Newark: University of Delaware Press, 1992).

[7] Edmond Malone, "An Attempt to Ascertain the Order in Which the Plays Attributed to Shakespeare Were Written," in *The Works of William Shakespeare,* vol. 1, ed. George Steevens and Samuel Johnson (London: Bathurst, 1778), pp. 269-71. Malone did change his mind and in a later edition gave the date as 1607. I provide the full text of these titles, but regularize the capitalization in both chapters and the bibliography of performance editions.

[8] Joseph Graves, *The Life of William Shakespeare: Collected and Arranged from Numerous Rare and Authentic Documents. Containing Every Fact of Importance from the Birth of This Eminent Poet to the Close of His Brilliant Career. To Which Are Added His Last Will and Testament* (London: Printed and Published by J. Duncombe, n.d.), p. 10.

[9] Charles Symmons, "The Life of Shakespeare," bound up in *The Complete Works of Shakespeare* (Leipzig: Baumgartner, 1837), p. ix.

[10] *The Dramatic Souvenir: Being Literary and Graphical Illustrations of* SHAKESPEARE *and Other Celebrated*

English Dramatists (London: Charles Tilt, Fleet Street, 1833), p. 26.

[11] John William Cole's annotated Shakespeariana is part of the Folger Shakespeare Library's Shakespeare Miscellany (verso to page 68).

[12] J. P. Collier, *The History of English Dramatic Poetry to the Time of Shakspeare,* vol. 1 (London: John Murray, 1831), pp. 327-28.

[13] William Shakespeare, *Twelfth Night: Chambers's Household Shakespeare* (London and Edinburgh: Printed by William and Robert Chambers, n.d. [1840]).

[14] Jorge Luis Borges, "Pierre Menard, Author of *Don Quixote,*" in *Ficciones,* trans. Anthony Bonner, ed. Anthony Kerrigan (New York: Grove Press, 1962), p. 48.

[15] See Leslie Hotson, *The First Night of Twelfth Night* (London: Rupert Hart-Davis, 1954).

[16] Gary Taylor, *Reinventing Shakespeare: A Cultural History from the Restoration to the Present* (Oxford: Oxford University Press, 1989), pp. 171-72.

[17] Margreta de Grazia, *Shakespeare Verbatim: The Reproduction of Authenticity and the 1790 Apparatus* (Oxford: Clarendon Press, 1991).

[18] William Shakespeare, *The Tragedy of King Lear,* in *The Complete Oxford Shakespeare,* vol. 3, ed. Stanley Wells and Gary Taylor (Oxford: Oxford University Press, 1987), act 3, scene 2, lines 74-77.

[19] See Karen Greif, "A Star Is Born: Feste on the Modern Stage," *Shakespeare Quarterly* 39 (1988): 61-78.

[20] *Leigh Hunt's Dramatic Criticism: 1808-1831,* ed. Lawrence Huston Houtchens and Carolyn Washburn Houtchens (New York: Columbia University Press, 1949), p. 231.

[21] Leonard F. Manheim, "The Mythical Joys of Shakespeare: Or, What You *Will,*" in *The Design Within: Psychoanalytic Approaches to Shakespeare,* ed. M. D. Faber (New York: Science House, 1970).

[22] W. Thomas MacCary, *Friends and Lovers: The Phenomenology of Desire in Shakespeare's Comedies* (New York: Columbia University Press, 1985), p. 190.

[23] Joel Fineman, "Fratricide and Cuckoldry: Shakespeare's Doubles," in *Representing Shakespeare: New Psychoanalytic Essays,* ed. Murray Schwartz and Coppélia Kahn (New York: Columbia University Press, 1980), pp. 70-109.

[24] C. L. Barber and Richard Wheeler, *The Whole Journey: Shakespeare's Power of Development* Berkeley: University of California Press, 1986).

[52] Matthew Wikander, "Secret as Maidenhead: The Profession of the Boy-Actress in *Twelfth Night,*" *Comparative Drama* 20 (1986): 349-63.

[26] Jacques Derrida, "Living On," in *Deconstruction and Criticism,* ed. Harold Bloom et al. (New York: Seabury Press, 1979), p. 84.

[27] Jerome McGann, *The Textual Condition* (Princeton: Princeton University Press, 1991), pp. 9-11.

[28] Derrida associates this kind of coincidence with the study of borders in Blanchot's narrative where "the edge of the set [ensemble] is a fold [*pli*] in the set." The fold he discovers, the invaginated structure he describes, where the "inverted reapplication of the outer edge to the inside of a form where the outside then opens a pocket," offers the text as Kleinian bottle, where the outside somehow becomes an inside (Derrida, "Living On," p. 96).

Source: "Double Dating," in *The Trick of Singularity: Twelfth Night and the Performance Editions,* University of Iowa Press, 1996, pp. 1-14.

How to Read *The Merchant of Venice* Without Being Heterosexist

Alan Sinfield, *The University of Sussex*

It has been recognized for a long time that *The Merchant of Venice* is experienced as insulting by Jewish people, who constitute a minority in Western Europe and North America. So powerful, though, is the reputation of Shakespeare's all-embracing 'humanity' that this scandal has often been set aside. Nevertheless, in 1994 a newspaper article entitled 'Shylock, Unacceptable Face of Shakespeare?' described how directors were acknowledging that the text requires radical alterations before it can be produced in good faith.[1] David Thacker at the Royal Shakespeare Company was changing some of Shylock's most famous lines and moving scenes around. And Jude Kelly at the West Yorkshire Playhouse was presenting a Portia ready to embrace racist attitudes in her determination to be worthy of her father and a Jessica weeping inconsolably at the end as she laments her loss of her Jewish heritage.

For some commentators, it is sign of the deterioration of our cultures that minority out-groups should feel entitled to challenge the authority of Shakespeare. Christopher Booker, writing in the *Daily Telegraph* in 1992, complained bitterly about an English Shakespeare Company production of *The Merchant* set in 1930s Italy, with Shylock as a suave, sophisticated modern Jewish businessman confronted by fascists. 'In other words,' Booker writes, 'the producer had given up on any distasteful (but Shakespearean) idea of presenting Shylock as an archetypal cringing old miser. He really had to be more sympathetic than the "Christians".' To Booker this was 'bleatings about racism', whereas 'Shakespeare so wonderfully evokes something infinitely more real and profound . . . a cosmic view of human nature which is just as true now as it was in his own day' (Booker 1992).

The problem is not limited to Jewish people. The Prince of Morocco is made to begin by apologizing for his colour—'Mislike me not for my complexion,' he pleads (II. i. 1), taking it for granted that Portia will be prejudiced. And he is right, for already she has declared her distaste: 'if he have the condition of a saint, and the complexion of a devil, I had rather he should shrive me than wive me' (I. ii. 123-5); and after Morocco has bet on the wrong casket she concludes: 'Let all of his complexion choose me so' (II. vii. 79). And how might gay men regard the handling of Antonio's love for Bassanio, or the traffic in boys that involves Launcelot, the disguised Jessica, the disguised Nerissa and the disguised Portia?

The question of principle is how readers not situated squarely in the mainstream of Western culture today may relate to such a powerful cultural icon as Shakespeare. In a notable formulation, Kathleen McLuskie points out that the pattern of 'good' and 'bad' daughters in *King Lear* offers no point of entry to the ideas about women that a feminist criticism might want to develop; such criticism 'is restricted to exposing its own exclusion from the text' (McLuskie, 1985: 97).[2] This challenge has caused some discomfort: must exclusion from Shakespeare be added to the other disadvantages that women experience in our societies? But it has not, I think, been successfully answered. In this essay I pursue the question as it strikes a gay man.

I Antonio vs. Portia

As W. H. Auden suggested in an essay in *The Dyer's Hand* in 1962, the *The Merchant of Venice* makes best sense if we regard Antonio as in love with Bassanio (Auden 1963; see also Midgley 1960). In the opening scene their friends hint broadly at it. Then, as soon as Bassanio arrives, the others know they should leave the two men together—"We leave you now with better company. . . . My Lord Bassanio, since you have found Antonio / We two will leave you' (I. i. 59, 69-70). Only Gratiano is slow to go, being too foolish to realize that he is intruding (I. i. 73-118). As soon as he departs, the tone and direction of the dialogue switch from formal banter to intimacy, and the cause of Antonio's sadness emerges:

> Well, tell me now what lady is the same
> To whom you swore a secret pilgrimage—
> That you to-day promis'd to tell me of?
>
> (I. i. 119-21)

Bassanio moves quickly to reassure his friend and to ask his help: 'to you Antonio / I owe the most in money and in love' (I. i. 130-1). The mercenary nature of Bassanio's courtship, which troubles mainstream commentators who are looking for a 'good' heterosexual relationship, is Antonio's reassurance. It allows him to believe that Bassanio will continue to value their love, and gives him a crucial role as banker of the enterprise.

Whether Antonio's love is what we call sexual is a question which, this essay will show, is hard to frame, let alone answer. But certainly his feelings are intense. When Bassanio leaves for Belmont, as Salerio describes it, he offers to 'make some speed / Of his return'. 'Do not so,' Antonio replies:

And even there (his eye being big with tears),
Turning his face, he put his hand behind him,
And with affection wondrous sensible
He wrung Bassanio's hand, and so they parted.
(II. viii. 37-8, 46-9)

The intensity, it seems, is not altogether equal. As Auden observes in his poem 'The More Loving One', the language of love celebrates mutuality but it is unusual for two people's loves to match precisely:

If equal affection cannot be,
Let the more loving one be me.
(Auden 1969: 282)

Antonio the merchant, like Antonio in *Twelfth Night* and the Shakespeare of the sonnets, devotes himself to a relatively casual, pampered younger man of a higher social class.

In fact, Antonio in the *Merchant* seems to welcome the chance to sacrifice himself: 'pray God Bassanio come / To see me pay his debt, and then I care not' (III. iii. 35-6). *Then* Bassanio would have to devote himself to Antonio:

You cannot better be employ'd Bassanio,
Than to live still and write mine epitaph.
(IV. i. 117-18)

As Keith Geary observes, Antonio's desperate bond with Shylock is his way of holding on to Bassanio (Geary 1984: 63-4); when Portia saves Antonio's life, Lawrence W. Hyman remarks, she is preventing what would have been a spectacular case of the 'greater love' referred to in the Bible (John 15:13), when a man lays down his life for his friend (Hyman 1970: 112).

That theme of amatory sacrifice contributes to an air of homoerotic excess, especially in the idea of being bound and inviting physical violation. When Bassanio introduces Antonio to Portia as the man 'To whom I am so infinitely bound', she responds:

You should in all sense be much bound to him,
For (as I hear) he was much bound for you.
(V. i. 135-7)

At the start, Antonio lays open his entire self to Bassanio:

be assur'd
My purse, my person, my extremest means
Lie all unlock'd to your occasions.
(I. i. 137-9)

Transferring this credit—'person' included—to Shylock's bond makes it more physical, more dangerous and more erotic:

let the forfeit
Be nominated for an equal pound

Of your fair flesh, to be cut off and taken
In what part of your body pleaseth me.
(I. iii. 144-7)

In the court, eventually, it is his breast that Antonio is required to bear to the knife, but in a context where apparent boys may be disguised girls and Portia's suitors have to renounce marriage altogether if they choose the wrong casket, Shylock's penalty sounds like castration. Indeed, Antonio offers himself to the knife as 'a tainted wether of the flock'; that is, a castrated ram (IV. i. 114).

The seriousness of the love between Antonio and Bassanio is manifest, above all, in Portia's determination to contest it. Simply, she is at a disadvantage because of her father's casket device, and wants to ensure that her husband really is committed to her. The key critical move, which Hyman and Geary make, is to reject the sentimental notion of Portia as an innocent, virtuous, 'Victorian' heroine. Harry Berger regards her 'noble' speeches as manipulations: 'Against Antonio's failure to get himself crucified, we can place Portia's divine power of mercifixion; she never rains but she pours.' Finally, she mercifies Antonio by giving him back his ships (Berger 1981: 161-2; see Hyman 1970; Geary 1984).

Antonio's peril moves Bassanio to declare a preference for him over Portia:

Antonio, I am married to a wife
Which is as dear to me as life itself,
But life itself, my wife, and all the world,
I would lose all, ay sacrifice them all
Here to this devil, to deliver you.

Portia, standing by as a young doctor, is not best pleased:

Your wife would give you little thanks for that
If she were by to hear you make the offer.
(IV. i. 278-85)

It is to contest Antonio's status as lover that Portia, in her role of young doctor, demands of Bassanio the ring which she had given him in her role of wife. Antonio, unaware that he is falling for a device, takes the opportunity to claim a priority in Bassanio's love:

My Lord Bassanio, let him have the ring,
Let his deservings and my love withal
Be valued 'gainst your wife's commandement.
(IV. ii. 445-7)

The last act of the play is Portia's assertion of her right to Bassanio. Her strategy is purposefully heterosexist: in disallowing Antonio's sacrifice as a plausible reason for parting with the ring, she disallows the entire

87

seriousness of male love. She is as offhand with Antonio as she can be with a guest:

> Sir, you are very welcome to our house:
> It must appear in other ways than words,
> Therefore I scant this breathing courtesy.
>
> (V. i. 139-41)

She will not even admit Antonio's relevance: 'I am th'unhappy subject of these quarrels', he observes; 'Sir, grieve not you,—you are welcome not withstanding', she abruptly replies (V. i. 238-9). Once more, self-sacrifice seems to be Antonio's best chance of staying in the game, so he binds himself in a different project: *not* to commit his body again to Bassanio in a way that will claim a status that challenges Portia:

> I once did lend my body for his wealth,
> Which but for him that had your husband's ring
> Had quite miscarried. I dare be bound again,
> My soul upon the forfeit, that your lord
> Will never more break faith advisedly.
>
> (V. i. 249-53)

Portia seizes brutally on the reminiscence of the earlier bond: 'Then you shall be his surety' (V. i. 254). Antonio's submission is what she has been waiting for. Now she restores Bassanio's status as husband by revealing that she has the ring after all, and Antonio's viability as merchant—and his ability to return to his trade in Venice—by giving him letters that she has been withholding.

A gay reader might think: well, never mind; Bassanio wasn't worth it, and with his wealth restored, Antonio will easily find another impecunious upper-class friend to sacrifice himself to. But, for most audiences and readers, the air of 'happy ending' suggests that Bassanio's movement towards heterosexual relations is in the necessary, the right direction (like Shylock's punishment, perhaps). As Coppélia Kahn reads the play, 'In Shakespeare's psychology, men first seek to mirror themselves in a homoerotic attachment . . . then to confirm themselves through difference, in a bond with the opposite sex—the marital bond' (Kahn 1985: 106). And Janet Adelman, in a substantial analysis of male bonding in Shakespeare's comedies, finds that 'We do not move directly from family bonds to marriage without an intervening period in which our friendships with same-sex friends help us to establish our identities' (Adelman 1985: 75). To heterosexually identified readers this might not seem an exceptional thought, but for the gay man it is a slap in the face of very familiar kind. 'You can have these passions,' it says, 'but they are not sufficient, they should be a stage on the way to something else. So don't push it.'

To be sure, Kahn points out that 'it takes a strong, shrewd woman like Portia to combat the continuing appeal of such ties between men' (1985: 107). And Adelman remarks the tendency towards casuistical 'magical restitutions' and the persistence of 'tensions that comedy cannot resolve' (1985: 80). So heteropatriarchy is not secured without difficulty or loss. None the less, when Adelman writes 'We do not move directly . . . to marriage', the gay man may ask, 'Who are "We"?' And when Kahn says 'men first seek to mirror themselves in a homoerotic attachment', the gay man may wonder whether he is being positioned as not-man, or just forgotten altogether. If Antonio is excluded from the good life at the end of the *Merchant,* so the gay man is excluded from the play's address. The fault does not lie with Kahn and Adelman (though in the light of recent work in lesbian and gay studies they might want to formulate their thoughts rather differently). They have picked up well enough the mood and tendency of the play, as most readers and audiences would agree. It is the Shakespearean text that is reconfirming the marginalization of an already marginalized group.

II Property and sodomy

The reader may be forgiven for thinking that, for a commentator who has claimed to be excluded from the *Merchant,* this gay man has already found quite a lot to say. Perhaps the love that dared not speak its name is becoming the love that won't shut up. In practice, there are (at least) two routes through the *Merchant* for out-groups. One involves pointing out the mechanisms of exclusion in our cultures—how the circulation of Shakespearean texts may reinforce the privilege of some groups and the subordination of others. I have just been trying to do this. Another involves exploring the ideological structures in the playtexts—of class, race, ethnicity, gender and sexuality—that facilitate these exclusions. These structures will not be the same as the ones we experience today, but they may throw light upon our circumstances and stimulate critical awareness of how our life-possibilities are constructed.[3]

In *The Merchant,* the emphasis on the idea of being bound displays quite openly the way ideological structures work. Through an intricate network of enticements, obligations and interdictions—in terms of wealth, family, gender, patronage and law—this culture sorts out who is to control property and other human relations. Portia, Jessica and Launcelot are bound as daughters and sons; Morocco and Arragon as suitors; Antonio and Bassanio as friends; Gratiano as friend or dependant, Nerissa as dependant or servant, and Launcelot as servant; Antonio, Shylock and even the Duke are bound by the law; and the Venetians, Shylock rather effectively remarks, have no intention of freeing their slaves (IV. i. 90-8).

Within limits, these bonds may be negotiable: the Duke may commission a doctor to devise a way round the law, friendships may be redefined, servants may get new masters, women and men may contract marriages. Jessica can even get away from her father, though only because he is very unpopular and Lorenzo has very powerful friends; they 'seal love's bonds new-made' (II. vi. 6). Otherwise, trying to move very far out of your place is severely punished, as Shylock finds. It is so obvious that this framework of ideology and coercion is operating to the advantage of the rich over the poor, the established over the impotent, men over women and insiders over outsiders, that directors have been able to slant productions of the *Merchant* against the dominant reading, making Bassanio cynical, Portia manipulative and the Venetians arrogant and racist.

The roles of same-sex passion in this framework should not be taken for granted (I use the terms 'same-sex' and 'cross-sex' to evade anachronistic modern concepts). For us today, Eve Sedgwick shows this in her book *Between Men,* homosexuality polices the entire boundaries of gender and social organization. Above all, it exerts 'leverage over the channels of bonding between all pairs of men'. Male-male relations, and hence male-female relations, are held in place by fear of homosexuality—by fear of crossing that 'invisible, carefully blurred, always-already-crossed line' between being 'a man's man' and being 'interested in men' (Sedgwick 1985: 88-9; see Dollimore 1992: chs 17-18). We do not know what the limits of our sexual potential are, but we do believe that they are likely to be disturbing and disruptive; that is how our cultures position sexuality. Fear even of thinking homosexually serves to hold it all in place. So one thing footballers must *not* be when they embrace is sexually excited; the other thing they mustn't be is in love. But you can never be quite sure; hence the virulence of homophobia.

If this analysis makes sense in Western societies today, and I believe it does, we should not assume it for other times and places. As Sedgwick observes, ancient Greek cultures were different (1985: 4). In our societies whether you are gay or not has become crucial—the more so since lesbians and gay men have been asserting themselves. An intriguing thought, therefore, is that in early modern England same-sex relations *were not terribly important*. In *As You Like It* and *Twelfth Night,* homoeroticism is part of the fun of the wooing ('Ganymede', the name taken by Rosalind, was standard for a male same-sex love-object); but it wouldn't be fun if such scenarios were freighted with the anxieties that people experience today. In Ben Jonson's play *Poetaster,* Ovid Senior expostulates: 'What! Shall I have my son a stager now? An engle for players? A gull, a rook, a shot-clog to make suppers, and be laughed at?' (Jonson 1995: I. ii. 15-17).[4] It is taken for granted that boys are sexual partners (engles) for players; it is only one of the demeaning futures that await young Ovid if he takes to the stage. Moralists who complained about theatre and sexual licence took it for granted that boys are sexually attractive.

'Sodomy' was the term which most nearly approaches what is now in England called 'gross indecency'; it was condemned almost universally in legal and religious discourses, and the penalty upon conviction was death. Perhaps because of this extreme situation, very few cases are recorded. Today, staking out a gay cruising space is a sure-fire way for a police force to improve its rate of convictions. But in the Home Counties through the reigns of Elizabeth I and James I—sixty-eight years—only six men are recorded as having been indicted for sodomy. Only one was convicted, and that was for an offence involving a five-year-old boy.[5]

In his book *Homosexual Desire in Shakespeare's England,* Bruce R. Smith shows that while legal and religious edicts against sodomy were plain, paintings and fictive texts sometimes indicate a more positive attitude. This derived mainly from the huge prestige, in artistic and intellectual discourses, of ancient Greek and Roman culture where same-sex passion is taken for granted (Smith 1991: 13-14, 74-6 *et passim*). Smith locates six 'cultural scenarios': heroic friendship, men and boys (mainly in pastoral and educational contexts), playful androgyny (mainly in romances and festivals), transvestism (mainly in satirical contexts), master-servant relations' and an emergent homosexual subjectivity (in Shakespeare's sonnets). Within those scenarios, it seems, men did not necessarily connect their practices with the monstrous crime of sodomy—partly, perhaps, because that was so unthinkable. As Jonathan Goldberg emphasizes, the goal of analysis is 'to see what the category [sodomy] enabled and disenabled, and to negotiate the complex terrains, the mutual implications of prohibition and production' (1992: 20; see Bray 1982: 79). The point is hardly who did what with whom, but the contexts in which anxieties about sodomy might be activated. So whether the friendships of men such as Antonio and Bassanio should be regarded as involving a homoerotic element is not just a matter of what people did in private hundreds of years ago; it is a matter of definition within a sex-gender system that we only partly comprehend.

Stephen Orgel asks: 'why were women more upsetting than boys to the English?' That is, given the complaints that boy-actors incite lascivious thoughts in men and women spectators, why were not women performers employed—as they were in Spain and Italy? Orgel's answer is that boys were used because they were less dangerous; they were erotic, but that was less threatening than the eroticism of women. So this culture 'did not display a morbid fear of homosexuality. Anxiety about the fidelity of women, on the other hand, does seem to have been strikingly prevalent' (Orgel 1989: 8, 18). Leontes and Polixenes lived guiltlessly together, we are told in *The Winter's Tale,* until they met the women who were to be their wives (I. ii. 69-74). The main faultlines ran through cross-sex relations.

Because women may bear children, relations between women and men affected the regulation of lineage, alliance and property, and hence offered profound potential disruptions to the social order and the male psyche. Same-sex passion was dangerous if, as in the instance of Christopher Marlowe's *Edward II,* it was allowed to interfere with other responsibilities. Otherwise, it was thought compatible with marriage and perhaps preferable to cross-sex infidelity. The preoccupation, in writing of this period, is with women disturbing the system—resisting arranged marriages, running off with the wrong man, not bearing (male) children, committing adultery, producing illegitimate offspring, becoming widows and exercising the power of that position. In comedies things turn out happily, in tragedies sadly. But, one way or the other, Shakespearean plays, as much as the rest of the culture, are obsessively concerned with dangers that derive from women.

'We'll play with them the first boy for a thousand ducats', Gratiano exclaims, betting on whether Nerissa or Portia will bear the first boy-child (III. ii. 213-14). As Orgel remarks, patriarchy does not oppress only women; a patriarch is not just a man, he is the head of a family or tribe who rules by paternal right (1989: 10). To be sure, women are exchanged in the interest of property relations in Shakespearean plays, as in the society that produced them. But the lives of young, lower-class and outsider men are determined as well. In *The Merchant,* as everywhere in the period, we see a traffic in boys who, because they are less significant, are moved around the employment—patronage system more fluently than women. Class exploitation was almost unchallenged; everyone—men as much as women—had someone to defer to, usually in the household where they had to live. The most likely supposition is that, just as cross-sex relations took place all the time—Launcelot is accused, in passing, of getting a woman with child (III. v. 35-6)—same-sex passion also was widely indulged.[6]

Traffic in boys occurs quite casually in *The Merchant.* Launcelot is a likely lad. He manages to square it with his conscience to leave his master, Shylock, but it is unclear where he will go (II. ii. 1-30). He runs into his father, who indentured Launcelot to Shylock and is bringing a present for the master to strengthen the bond. Launcelot persuades him to divert the gift to Bassanio, who is providing 'rare new liveries', for the expedition to Belmont (II. ii. 104-5). The father attempts to interest Bassanio in the boy, but it transpires that Shylock has already traded him: 'Shylock thy master spoke with me this day, / And hath preferr'd thee' (II. ii. 138-9). Nor is Launcelot the only young man Bassanio picks up in this scene: Gratiano presents his own suit and gets a ticket to Belmont conditional upon good behaviour. And when Jessica assumes the guise of a boy, the appearance is of another privileged young man, Lorenzo, taking a boy into his service and giving him

new livery: 'Descend, for you must be my torch-bearer. . . . Even in the lovely garnish of a boy' (II. vi. 40, 45). When the young doctor claims Portia's ring from Bassanio for services rendered, therefore, a pattern is confirmed.

My point is not that the dreadful truth of the *Merchant* is here uncovered: it is really about traffic in boys. Rather, that such traffic is casual, ubiquitous and hardly remarkable. It becomes significant in its resonances for the relationship between Antonio and Bassanio because Portia, subject to her father's will, has reason to feel insecure about the affections of her stranger-husband.

III Friendly relations

Heroic friendship is one of Smith's six 'cultural scenarios' for same-sex relations (1991: 35-41, 67-72, 96-9, 139-43). In Shakespeare, besides the sonnets, it is represented most vividly in the bond between Coriolanus and Aufidius in *Coriolanus:*

> Know thou first,
> I lov'd the maid I married; never man
> Sigh'd truer breath; but that I see thee here,
> Thou noble thing, more dances my rapt heart
> Than when I first my wedded mistress saw
> Bestride my threshold.
>
> (IV. v. 114-19)[7]

Unlike Portia, Aufidius's wife is not there to resent him finding his warrior-comrade more exciting than she.

In his essay 'Homosexuality and the Signs of Male Friendship in Elizabethan England', Alan Bray explores the scope of the 'friend' (Bray 1990). Even as marriage was involved in alliances of property and influence, male friendship informed, through complex obligations, networks of extended family, companions, clients, suitors and those influential in high places. Claudio in *Measure for Measure* explains why he and Juliet have not made public their marriage vows:

> This we came not to
> Only for propagation of a dower
> Remaining in the coffer of her friends,
> From whom we thought it meet to hide our love
> Till time had made them for us.
>
> (I. ii. 138-42)

On the one hand, it is from friends that one anticipates a dowry; on the other hand, they must be handled sensitively. Compare the combination of love and instrumentality in the relationship between Bassanio and Antonio: the early modern sense of 'friend' covered a broad spectrum.

While the entirely respectable concept of the friend was supposed to have nothing to do with the officially abhorred concept of the sodomite, in practice they tended to overlap (see Bray 1990). Friends shared beds, they embraced and kissed; such intimacies reinforced the network of obligations and their public performance would often be part of the effect. So the proper signs of friendship could be the same as those of same-sex passion. In instances where accusations of sodomy were aroused, very likely it was because of some hostility towards one or both parties, rather than because their behaviour was altogether different from that of others who were not so accused.

The fact that the text of the *Merchant* gives no plain indication that the love between Antonio and Bassanio is informed by erotic passion does not mean that such passion was inconceivable, then; it may well mean that it didn't require particular presentation as a significant category. What is notable, though, is that Portia has no hesitation in envisaging a sexual relationship between Bassanio and the young doctor: 'I'll have that doctor for my bedfellow', she declares, recognizing an equivalence (V. i. 33). She develops the idea:

Let not that doctor e'er come near my house—
Since he hath got the jewel that I loved,
And that which you did swear to keep for me.
(V. i. 223-5)

The marriage of Bassanio and Portia is unconsummated and 'jewel' is often genital in Shakespearean writing: the young doctor has had the sexual attentions which were promised to Portia. 'Ring', of course, has a similar range, as when Gratiano says he will 'fear no other thing / So sore, as keeping safe Nerissa's ring' (V. i. 306-7; see Partridge 1955: 135, 179). Portia's response to Bassanio (allegedly) sleeping with the young doctor is that she will do the same:

I will become as liberal as you,
I'll not deny him anything I have,
No, not my body nor my husband's bed.
(V. i. 226-8)

Notice also that Portia does not express disgust, or even surprise, that her husband might have shared his bed with a young doctor. Her point is that Bassanio has given to another something that he had pledged to her. Nor does she disparage Antonio (as she does Morocco). Shylock, for the social cohesion of Venice, has to be killed, beggared, expelled, converted or any combination of those penalties. Same-sex passion doesn't matter nearly so much; Antonio has only to be relegated to a subordinate position.

Bray attributes the instability in friendly relations to a decline in the open-handed 'housekeeping' of the great house. Maintaining retinues such as those Bassanio recruits—young men who look promising and relatives who have a claim—was becoming anachronistic. So the social and economic form of service and friendship decayed, but it remained as a cultural form, as a way of speaking. The consequent unevenness, Bray suggests, allowed the line between the intimacies of friendship and sodomy to become blurred (1990: 12-13). Don Wayne, in his study of Ben Jonson's poem 'To Penshurst' and the country-house genre, relates the decline of the great house to the emergence of a more purposeful aristocracy of 'new men' who 'constituted an agrarian capitalist class with strong links to the trading community'; and to the emergence, also, of 'an ideology in which the nuclear, conjugal family is represented as the institutional foundation of morality and social order'. We associate that development with the later consolidation of 'bourgeois ideology', but 'images and values we tend to identify as middle class had already begun to appear in the transformation of the aristocracy's own self-image' (Wayne 1984: 23-5).

The Merchant of Venice makes excellent sense within such a framework. Portia's lavish estate at Belmont is presented as a fairy-tale place; in Venetian reality Bassanio, an aristocrat who already cultivates friends among the merchant class, has to raise money in the market in order to put up a decent show. At the same time, Portia's centring of the matrimonial couple and concomitant hostility towards male friendship manifests an attitude that was to be located as 'bourgeois'. This faultline was not to be resolved rapidly; Portia is ahead of her time. Through the second half of the seventeenth century, Alan Bray and Randolph Trumbach show, the aggressively manly, aristocratic rake, though reproved by the churches and emergent middle-class morality and in violation of the law, would feel able to indulge himself with a woman, a young man or both.[8]

If I have begun to map the ideological field in which same-sex passion occurred in early modern England and some of its points of intersection in *The Merchant,* I am not trying to 'reduce' Shakespeare to an effect of history and structure. I do not suppose that he thought the same as everyone else—or, indeed, that *anyone* thought the same as everyone else. First, diverse paths may be discerned in the period through the relations between sexual and 'platonic', and same-sex and cross-sex passions. These matters were uncertain, unresolved, contested—that is why they made good topics for plays, satires, sermons and so on. Second, playtexts do not have to be clear-cut. As I have argued elsewhere, we should envisage them as working across an ideological terrain, opening out unresolved faultlines, inviting spectators to explore imaginatively the different possibilities. Anyway, readers and audiences do not have to respect closures; they are at liberty to credit and dwell upon the adventurous middle part of a text, as against a tidy conclusion (Sinfield 1992: 47-51, 99-106). As Valerie Traub remarks, whether these early comedies are found to instantiate dissidence or containment is a matter of 'crediting *either* the expense of dramatic energy *or* comedic closure' (1992b: 120; see Smith 1992).

Generally, though, there is a pattern: the erotic potential of same-sex love is allowed a certain scope, but has to be set aside. The young men in *Love's Labour's Lost* try to maintain a fraternity but the women draw them away. In *Romeo and Juliet* Mercutio has to die to clear the ground for Romeo and Juliet's grand passion. In *Much Ado About Nothing* Benedick has to agree to kill Claudio at his fiancée's demand. *As You Like It* fantasizes a harmonious male community in the forest and intensifies it in the wooing of Orlando and Ganymede, but finally Rosalind takes everyone but Jacques back into the old system. Yet there are ambiguities as well. In the epilogue to *As You Like It* the Rosalind/Ganymede boy-actor reopens the flirting: 'If I were a woman, I would kiss as many of you as had beards that pleased me, complexions that liked me, and breaths that I defied not' (V. iv. 214-17; see Traub 1992b: 128). And Orsino in *Twelfth Night* leaves the stage with Viola still dressed as Cesario because, he says, her female attire has not yet been located. Even Bassanio can fantasize: 'Sweet doctor', he says to Portia when she has revealed all, 'you shall be my bedfellow,—/ When I am absent then lie with my wife' (V.i.284-5).

And why not? Was it necessary to choose? Although the old, open-handed housekeeping was in decline, the upper-class household was not focused on the marital couple in the manner of today. Portia welcomes diverse people to Belmont; Gratiano and Nerissa for instance, whose mimic-marriage reflects the power of the household. *The Two Gentlemen of Verona* starts with the disruption of friendship by love for a woman, but ends with a magical reunion in which they will all live together: 'our day of marriage shall be yours, / One feast, one house, one mutual happiness' (Shakespeare 1969: V. iv. 170-1). In a discussion of *Twelfth Night* elsewhere, I have suggested that Sebastian's marriage to a stranger heiress need not significantly affect Antonio's relationship with him (Sinfield 1992: 73). They might all live together in Olivia's house (as Sir Toby does); she may well prefer to spend her time with Maria and Viola (who will surely tire of Orsino) rather than with the naive, swashbuckling husband whom she has mistakenly married. So Antonio need not appear at the end of *Twelfth Night* as the defeated and melancholy outsider that critics have supposed; a director might show him delighted with his boyfriend's lucky break.

This kind of ending might be made to work in the *Merchant*. R. F. Hill suggests it, and Auden reports a 1905 production which had Antonio and Bassanio enter the house together (Hill 1975: 86; Auden 1963: 233). However, Portia plays a harder game than Rosalind and Viola. She doesn't disguise herself, as they do, to evade hetero-patriarchal pressures, but to test and limit her husband. When disguised as a boy she does not, Geary observes, play androgynous games with other characters or the audience (1984: 58). Antonio is invited into the house only on her terms.

Overall in these plays, Traub concludes, the fear 'is not of homoeroticism *per se;* homoerotic pleasure is explored and sustained *until* it collapses into fear of erotic exclusivity and its corollary: non-reproductive sexuality'—a theme, of course, of the sonnets (Traub 1992b: 123, 138-41). The role of marriage and child-(son-)bearing in the transmission of property and authority is made to take priority. If (like me) you are inclined to regard this as a failure of nerve, it is interesting that the *Merchant,* itself, offers a comment on boldness and timidity. 'Who chooseth me, must give and hazard all he hath'—that is the motto on the lead casket (II. ix. 21). Bassanio picks the right casket and Portia endorses the choice but, as Auden points out, it is Shylock and Antonio who commit themselves entirely and risk everything; and in the world of this play there are penalties for doing that (Auden 1963: 235).

IV Subcultures and Shakespeare

Traub notes a reading of *Twelfth Night* that assumes Olivia to be punished 'comically but unmistakably' for her same-sex passion for Viola. But 'to whom is desire between women funny?' Traub asks (1992b: 93). This was my initial topic: must Shakespeare, for out-groups such as Jews, feminists, lesbians, gays and Blacks, be a way of re-experiencing their marginalization? I have been trying to exemplify elements in a critical practice for dissident readers. Mainstream commentators on the *Merchant* (whether they intend to or not) tend to confirm the marginalization of same-sex passion. Lesbians and gay men may use the play (1) to think about alternative economies of sex-gender; (2) to think about problematic aspects of our own subcultures. But (the question is always put): Is it Shakespeare? Well, he is said to speak to all sorts and conditions, so if gay men say 'OK, this is how he speaks to us'—that, surely, is our business.

With regard to the first of these uses, the *Merchant* allows us to explore a social arrangement in which the place of same-sex passion was different from that we are used to. Despite and because of the formal legal situation, I have shown, it appears not to have attracted very much attention; it was partly compatible with marriage, and was partly supported by legitimate institutions of friendship, patronage and service. It is not that Shakespeare was a sexual radical, therefore. Rather, the early modern organization of sex and gender boundaries was different from ours, and the ordinary currency of that culture is replete with erotic interactions that strike strange chords today. Shakespeare may speak with distinct force to gay men and lesbians, simply because he didn't think he had to sort out sexuality in modern terms. For approximately the same reasons, these plays may stimulate radical ideas about race, nation, gender and class.

As for using *The Merchant* as a way of addressing problems in gay subculture, the bonds of class, age, gender and race exhibited in the play have distinct resonances for us. The traffic in boys may help us to think about power structures in our class and generational interactions. And while an obvious perspective on the play is resentment at Portia's manipulation of Antonio and Bassanio, we may bear in mind that Portia too is oppressed in hetero-patriarchy, and try to work towards a sex-gender regime in which women and men would not be bound to compete.[9] Above all, plainly, Antonio is the character most hostile to Shylock. It is he who has spat on him, spurned him and called him dog, and he means to do it again (I. iii. 121-6). At the trial it is he who imposes the most offensive requirement—that Shylock convert to Christianity (V. i. 382-3). Seymour Kleinberg connects Antonio's racism to his sexuality:

> Antonio hates Shylock not because he is a more fervent Christian than others, but because he recognizes his own alter ego in this despised Jew who, because he is a heretic, can never belong to the state. . . . He hates himself in Shylock: the homosexual self that Antonio has come to identify symbolically as the Jew.

> (Kleinberg 1985: 120)[10]

Gay people today are no more immune to racism than other people, and transferring our stigma onto others is one of the modes of self-oppression that tempts any subordinated group. And what if one were Jewish, and/or Black, as well as gay? One text through which these issues circulate in our culture is *The Merchant of Venice,* and it is one place where we may address them.

Notes

[1] Lister 1994; see Sinfield 1994a: 1-8, 19-20.

[2] For a reply to her critics by McLuskie, see McLuskie 1980: 224-9, and for further comment see Dollimore 1990.

[3] Another way is blatantly reworking the authoritative text so that it is forced to yield, against the grain, explicitly oppositional kinds of understanding; see Sinfield 1992: 16-24, 290-302.

[4] See also Jonson 1995: III. iv. 277-8, V. iii. 580-1. On boys in theatre, see Jardine 1983: ch. 1.

[5] See Bray 1982: 38-42, 70-80; Smith 1991: 47-52.

[6] See Jardine 1992; Zimmerman 1992.

[7] See Sinfield 1994b: 25-37; and Sinfield 1992: 127-42 (this is an extension of the discussion of *Henry V* published first in Drakakis 1985), and 237-8 (on *Tamburlaine*).

[8] Bray 1982; Trumbach 1987, 1989; Sinfield 1994b: 33-42.

[9] See the suggestive remarks in Goldberg 1992: 142, 273-4.

[10] Anti-semitism and homophobia are linked by Fiedler 1974: ch. 2, and by Mayer 1982: 278-85.

Source: "How to Read *The Merchant of Venice* Without Being Heterosexist," in *Alternative Shakespeares,* Vol. 2, edited by Terence Hawkes, Routledge, 1996, pp. 122-39.

Histories

The Peasants' Revolt and the Writing of History in *2 Henry VI*

Geraldo U. de Sousa, *Xavier University*

"Away, burn all the records of the realm: my mouth shall be the parliament of England"
—Jack Cade, *2 Henry VI.*

Jean de Léry, a Frenchman who lived in Brazil for several months starting in 1555, offers an account of the Tupinamba Indians' reaction when they first encountered reading and writing. The Tupinamba, if we are to judge from Léry's narrative, thought the Europeans possessed magical powers:

> They know nothing of writing, either sacred or secular; indeed; they have no kind of characters that signify anything at all. When I was first in their country, in order to learn their language I wrote a number of sentences which I then read aloud to them. Thinking that this was some kind of witchcraft, they said to each other, "Is it not a marvel that this fellow, who yesterday could not have said a single word in our language, can now be understood by us, by virtue of that paper that he is holding and which makes him speak thus?"[1]

Léry's appropriation of Tupinamba language through writing and his performance by putting his culture on display underscore a relationship that denies the Tupinamba the power of representation. As Michel de Certeau argues, the passage presents a difference between the dominant culture and the Other: "between 'them' and 'Us' there exists the difference of possessing 'either sacred or profane' writing, which immediately raises the question of a relation of *power*."[2] The power that Certeau has in mind is that between the ephemeral nature of "voice," which is "limited to the vanishing circle of its auditors," and the permanence of writing. "Writing," he adds, *"produces history,"*[3] hence efforts to control the production, preservation, and dissemination of records. One society has the power to produce history; the other does not. Questions of literacy are thus inextricably bound up with questions of power. Shakespeare, I submit, explores these questions in *2 Henry VI.*

Early modern England, however, unlike the totally oral society of the Tupinamba, was neither an oral nor a fully literate society.[4] Also, earlier assumptions about illiteracy, such as those of Walter Ong, have come under a barrage of challenge. Keith Thomas, for example, disputes Ong's hypothesis that "writing structures thought" and the assumption that "the transition from 'orality' to 'literacy' is represented as a crucial stage in human development, leading to abstract thought, rationality, and 'modernity.'"[5] As Thomas aptly explains, "it would be utterly wrong, therefore, to think that illiterates lived in some sort of mental darkness, debarred from effective participation in the great events of their time."[6]

Literacy, in the late medieval and the renaissance periods, signified different things to various classes and social groups. Many historians define literacy rather narrowly, as Harvey J. Graff indicates, "illiteracy in early modern England, as measured by the individual ability to sign one's name, was widespread but distributed unevenly."[7] In early modern Europe, reading and writing were seen as separate skills: "Some people, we have no way to discover how many, could have been able to read without knowing how to write or even sign their names."[8] "The ability to read," according to Thomas, "was much more widely diffused than the ability to write."[9] Furthermore, those who lacked the skills to read or write "could draw on the services of others for access to the written word."[10] Most important, Thomas observes:

> The spread of literacy in early modern England, therefore, did not noticeably alter the direction in which society was moving anyway. Neither did it have more than a gradual effect upon people's mental habits. What it did do was to consolidate the authority of the educated classes over their inferiors and to impoverish and disparage other forms of expression.[11]

As Thomas concludes, "the uneven social distribution of literacy skills greatly widened the gulf between the classes."[12] Shakespeare addresses this latter point in the Jack Cade episodes in *2 Henry VI.* Ironically, Jack Cade seems aware that the authority of the educated classes rests upon their writing skills.

In that play Shakespeare foregrounds writing as a culturally contested representational code.[13] Unlike Annabel Patterson, I am not concerned with questions of intentionality, in part because of the absence of substantive evidence, although I find her overall conclusion compelling: "Shakespeare's career can, therefore, be seen as a life-long meditation on the structure of English society, during which, not surprisingly, his social attitudes altered."[14] Shakespeare's exploration of literacy in *2 Henry VI,* however, constitutes something deeper than a meditation on English society; he closely studies the connection between writing, history, and power. The play specifically examines such a connection at various moments, but most prominently in Act IV. Jack Cade identifies writing as the power that authorizes and perpetuates social injustices. He sees all writing as oppressive for it confirms traditions and confers privileges from which the illiterate are by definition excluded. He mounts a program to destroy rather than decipher or rewrite the code, thus attempting to restructure English society into a preliterate, ahistorical stage. Literacy, in this context, becomes a metaphor for the power of the dominant culture, the power to make history. Rather astutely, Cade's revolution recognizes the absence of a center in the body politic as warring factions vie for supremacy.

In deciding to foreground literacy, Shakespeare arrived at the inextricable connection between history and writing. The sources that he used offer an important clue to that connection. As Geoffrey Bullough, who has studied Shakespeare's sources in depth, suggests, "2 Henry VI is a well-ordered play which departs from history much less than 1 Henry VI and interweaves the several motifs which it takes over in brilliant fashion." Bullough adds that Shakespeare "is interested both in events and in the people who made history: and he sees the course of the story here as a succession of waves as the tide of evil rises."[15] On the one hand, Shakespeare is trying to follow his sources accurately and thoroughly; on the other, I submit, he departs from those sources in order to explore the questions of literacy. In the process, he seems uncannily aware that writing produces history.

I. Writing as Substitution

In 2 Henry VI, writing retains the power of the dominant culture even when the political structure is on the verge of collapse. Jacques Derrida helps us understand the phenomenon when he writes that in the logocentric structure of representation, the "central presence" cannot be recovered because it "has never been itself, has always already been exiled from itself into its own substitute."[16] He adds, "the substitute does not substitute itself for anything which has existed before it" (p. 280). The implications of such substitutions become apparent when one compares the play to its sources.

Images of writing do not figure prominently in the play's sources. Two examples illustrate how Shakespeare went beyond his sources to underscore the connection between writing and power: the episodes involving Eleanor Cobham, Duchess of Gloucester and those involving Suffolk's handling of Henry VI and Margaret of Anjou's wedding. In The Union of the Two Noble and Illustre Fameiles of Lancastre and Yorke (1548), Edward Hall relates that the Marquess of Suffolk, as King Henry VI's procurator, went to France in March 1444 to arrange Henry's marriage to

Margaret, and he brought her to England in April 1445.[17] This marriage, which to many seemed "unfortunate, and unprofitable to the realme of England," brought about territorial losses for England and also civil strife.[18] England gained no dowry and had to pay a hefty price to Suffolk for fetching Margaret, whom Hall describes as follows: "This woman excelled all other, as well in beautie and favor, as in wit and pollicie, and was of stomack and corage, more like to a man, then a woman."[19] There is no mention of how Suffolk used or misused the proxy that England had entrusted him.

Shakespeare, however, fully explores the image of substitution that the proxy entails, and how writing seems to acquire a power of its own, independent of any referent. In fact, Shakespeare underscores the absence or powerlessness of the referent. Empowered with the King's proxy, Suffolk, the King's procurator, returns from France with Margaret of Anjou, whom he has married as the king's stand-in:

I have performed my task and was
     espoused,
And humbly now upon my bended knee,
In sight of England and her lordly peers,
Deliver up my title in the Queen
To your most gracious hands, that are the
     substance
Of that great shadow I did represent—[20]

But the procurator, usurping in more ways than one the power of the one he represented, generated other writings, the "articles of contracted peace." This agreement, which Gloucester finds highly offensive to national pride, undoes the conquests of Henry V by giving away the duchies of Anjou and Maine and bringing to England an impoverished queen without a dowry. Writing becomes graffiti, which as Gloucester vehemently argues, is scribbled upon the books of memory and the historical monuments:

Fatal this marriage, canceling your fame,
Blotting your names from books of memory,
Razing the characters of your renown,
Defacing monuments of conquered France,
Undoing all, as all had never been.
                                        (I.i.99-103)

The graffiti defaces and mutilates inscriptions and monuments.

The substitute Suffolk effects a complete usurpation, replacing the bridegroom not only as signatory to the marriage contract but also as lover to the bride. This substitution was a calculated move, announced in private before he departed for France at the end of 1 Henry VI: "I will rule both her, the king, and the realm" (V.v.108). Suffolk brings with him not an innocent woman whom he can control, but a passionate lover and a warrior, who becomes the she-wolf of France and a virago. As she replaces one identity with another, Margaret understands the power and permanence of writing. She wants to print her kisses on the body of Suffolk: "O could this kiss be printed in thy hand" (III.ii.109). The actual kiss has less power than its representation. Margaret feels affection not for her husband but for the substitute, who has usurped her heart and whose loss she cannot endure.

Similarly, the power of writing that we see in Suffolk's proxy and the attendant act of substitution becomes apparent in the episodes involving the conspiracy, exposure, and punishment of Eleanor Cobham, Duchess of Gloucester. Once again, the source, when compared to Shakespeare's play, seems conspicuously silent about the connection between writing and power. Edward Hall, in Shakespeare's source, discusses the fall of the Duchess, who "was accused of treason, for that she, by sorcery and enchauntment, entended to destroy the kyng, to thentent to advaunce and to promote her husbande to the croune."[21] She was examined, judged, and convicted, and had to "do open penaunce, in iij. open places, within the citie of London" and later was banished to the Isle of Man (p. 101). Her co-conspirators were two priests, a necromancer, and the witch Margaret Jourdain, "to whose charge it was laied, that thei, at the request of the duchesse, had devised an image of waxe, representyng the kynge, which by sorcery, a little and little consumed entendying therby in conclusion to waist, and destroy the kynges person, and so to bryng hym death" (p. 102).[22] Shakespeare omits any references to the wax effigy; instead he emphasizes how writing exposes and destroys the Duchess and her co-conspirators.

In a world of conflicting points of view, shifting allegiances, and broken traditions, writing represents immense power. The Duke of Gloucester's dream that "this staff, mine office-badge in court, / Was broken in twain" (I.ii.24-25), and his wife's own dream about their coronation in Westminster, though subversive thoughts, remain in the realm of fantasy and wish fulfillment until they are actualized through writing. Working for Suffolk and the Cardinal, the two priests Hum and Southwell arrange a consultation for the Duchess with the conjuror Bolingbroke and the witch Margaret Jourdain. Though an eyewitness to the consultation, Southwell realizes that his verbal account apparently does not suffice and a written report must be produced. With paper and pen in hand, he writes down the Duchess' subversive questions (posed by Bolingbroke) and the spirit's answer. He writes very fast indeed, for when the Duke of York appears shortly after the consultation has ended, the written report is ready for perusal. The Duke of York reads the report aloud: "'The Duke yet lives that Henry shall depose; /

But him outlive, and die a violent death'" (I.iv.60). With this writing in hand, York has Eleanor, Margaret Jourdain, and Bolingbroke tried and sentenced. The illiterate Jourdain and Bolingbroke will be put to death; but the Duchess, after doing her public penance, will be exiled to the Isle of Man.

The stage direction explains the Duchess' punishment: "*Enter Duchess of Gloucester barefoot, and a white sheet about her, with a wax candle in her hand, and verses written on her back and pinned on*" (II.iv.17 ff). The literacy of her enemies is put on display, as she observes:

> Methinks I should not thus be led along,
> Mailed up in shame, with papers on my
>   back,
> And followed with a rabble that rejoice
> To see my tears and hear my deep-fet
>   groans.
>
> (II.iv.30-33)

Even the largely illiterate crowd could hardly miss the meaning of the inscription. The government required that proclamations be read aloud, as an example from the Elizabethan period makes apparent: "considering the multitude of our good people are unlearned, and thereby not able by reading hereof to conceive our mind . . . we will that, beside the ordinary publication hereof . . . all curates in their parish churches shall . . . read this admonition to their parishioners."[23] The impact of the written word would not be lost on the illiterates: "so long as they had access to someone who would read, therefore, there was no reason why others needed to be cut off from the culture of the written word."[24] Even the illiterate "lived in a world which was to a great extent governed by texts."[25]

The Duchess of Gloucester's consultation, a temporal, ephemeral event, generates permanent written records. In this instance and elsewhere, Shakespeare shows that the representation not only replaces but also outlasts the original event behind it. We treasure and safeguard the representation as if it were the original, giving a sense of meaning and permanence to our lives. All literate societies, well aware of this, mount efforts to control the production and preservation of records in archives and other depositories.

II. Records of the Realm

On April 8, 1605, Queen Anne gave birth to a daughter, Mary, who, as David M. Bergeron remarks, "had the distinction of being the first royal child born in England since Jane Seymour gave birth to the child who became Edward VI."[26] The baptism took place on May 5, after "much scurrying about and perusing of historical records in order to recall how a royal child should be baptized."[27] The archival record becomes the authority as to how a custom, long forgotten, should be observed. In *2 Henry VI,* examples abound of attempts to research the archives. Reacting to Margaret of Anjou, the Duke of Gloucester observes: "I never read but England's kings have had / Large sums of gold and dowries with their wives" (I.i.128-29). Salisbury, hearing of the account of the Duke of York's claim to the English throne, recalls what he has read:

> This Edmund [Mortimer], in the reign of Bolingbroke,
> As I have read, laid claim unto the crown;
> And, but for Owen Glendower, had been king,
> Who kept him in captivity till he died.
>
> (II.ii.39-42)

Reading the written record of past events challenges or authorizes present ones. Both of these examples underscore Shakespeare's preoccupation with reading and writing.

Shakespeare conflated Jack Cade's Rebellion of 1450 with the Peasants' Revolt of 1381.[28] He did so, I submit, because he found in the Peasants' Revolt an examination of the power of writing. He read into Cade's rebellion the aspirations of the peasants. Shakespeare's return to the past, in dramatizing the reign of Henry VI, is twofold: events that took place around 1450, and those events that took place in 1381. As Bullough notes, "Perhaps in writing *2 Henry VI* in 1591 Shakespeare wished to suggest a parallel between Henry VI's reign and Richard II's."[29] In the pre-history of *2 Henry VI,* the political and judicial institutions of the state have collapsed, first with the deposition of Richard II and the enthronement of Bolingbroke. The success of Henry V's reign and the accomplishments of his expansionist policy that culminated with the conquest of France have, of course, masked the illegitimacy of his claim to the throne. Both Henry IV and Henry V have generated successful records that have almost erased the initial act of usurpation. By the time we reach *2 Henry VI,* Bolingbroke's usurpation seems like ancient history indeed. Situated somewhere between the old-order monarchy of Richard II and the topsy-turvy criminal world of Richard III, the world of *2 Henry VI* represents a transitional period that struggles to maintain authority and legitimacy. A power vacuum obviously emerges. Shakespeare depicts a society that feels the need to purge the archives of the realm and reexamine the events surrounding both the Revolt of 1381 and the deposition of Richard II in 1399/1400.

Edward Hall portrays a Jack Cade who differs from Shakespeare's in significant ways:

> A certayn yongman of a goodely stature, and pregnaunt wit, was entised to take upon him the name of John Mortymer, all though his name were Jack Cade, and not for a small policie, thinking that by that surname, the lyne and lynage of the assistent house of the erle of Marche, which were no small number, should be to hym both adherent, and favorable. This capitayn not onely suborned by techers, but also enforced by pryvye scholemasters, assembled together a great company of talle personages.[30]

Hall describes Cade as "subtill," "covetous," "sober in communication, wyse in disputyng, arrogant in hart, and styfe in his opinion" (pp.114-15). Although he finds followers in "divers idle and vacabonde persons" and in "a multitude of evil rude and rustical persones" (p. 114), Edward Hall's Jack Cade seems the very antithesis of Shakespeare's. Jack Cade of Hall's Chronicle was suborned by teachers and "enforced by pryvye scholemasters." Shakespeare's Cade, of course, feels nothing but contempt for teachers and schoolmasters.[31] Apparently, Shakespeare did not find Hall's explanation satisfactory, although he accepted his conclusion that Cade was manipulated by the Duke of York (Bullough, p. 113).[32]

The two historic uprisings followed similar courses, although the Peasants' Revolt took an anti-literate stance and Jack Cade's did not.[33] "The Peasants' Revolt was topical in the year 1590/1591 when the Lord Mayor was John Allot, A Fishmonger like the heroic Walworth who slew Wat Tyler."[34] Shakespeare was, however, less interested in historical accuracy than in the question of literacy. The peasants had sought to kill all the lawyers: "This sentiment so excited the rustics that they went to further extremes and declared that all court rolls and old moniments should be burnt so that once the memory of ancient customs had been wiped out their lords would be unable to vindicate their rights over them."[35] At Lambeth Palace, the writer of the *Anonimalle Chronicle* tells us, the rebels "destroyed a great number of the archbishop's goods and burnt all the register books and chancery remembrancers' rolls they found there"; and "set fire to and burnt the fine manor of the Savoy," the palace of John of Gaunt.[36] They also captured the Sheriff of Kent, William Septvans, who "was forced to surrender all his muniments, including judicial records and financial rolls. Wat Tyler burned them publicly."[37] The rebels attempted but failed to enter the king's treasury at Westminster (Fryde, p. 21). When Richard II issued a pardon and commanded someone to read it to the commons, the rebels did not take it seriously; rather, according to the *Anonimalle Chronicle,* they returned to London and "had it cried around the city that all lawyers, all the men of the Chancery and the Exchequer and everyone who could write a writ or a letter should be beheaded, wherever they could be found" (reprinted in Dobson, 160). The rebels of 1381 wanted to destroy all records of the kingdom in attempts to restructure English society. By destroying the records, they hoped also to destroy the collective memory upon which the social, political, and economic structure of the country rested.

Unlike the historical Jack Cade, both the peasants of 1381 and Shakespeare's Jack Cade realize that texts, whose production, dissemination, and preservation they cannot control, govern their lives. These texts, generated by the powerful, constitute the basis for oppression. Shakespeare seems well aware of this. The illiterate must submit written petitions if they want wrongs to be redressed. Ironically, one man, mistaking Suffolk for the duke of Gloucester, submits his petition to the wrong person. Suffolk reads the petition against himself: "Against the Duke of Suffolk, for enclosing the commons of Melford" (I.iii.30-32). Queen Margaret, for example, on hearing the various petitioners, misunderstands what they are saying. Peter Thump complains against his master Thomas Horner "for saying that the Duke of York was rightful heir to the crown" (I.iii.26-27). He also adds that his master called the King "usurer," but Queen Margaret corrects him, "an usurper." In this way, they are all dragged into the question of legitimacy (I.iii.). In a display of power, Margaret *tear[s] the supplication* (stage direction, I.iii.41-42), as she orders the petitioner to "begin your suits anew" (41). With this one gesture, Margaret demonstrates the power to control the production and dissemination of records. Gloucester finally sentences Horner and Thump to settle their dispute in combat. Manipulated by others, Horner gets drunk, and Thump kills him (II.iii.). Similarly, the witch Margaret Jourdain is sentenced to burn at the stake in Smithfield; the Duchess, to exile. In the episode involving Saunder Simpcox and St. Albans' miracle, the authorities again trick the illiterate and expose their ignorance.

In Act IV, Jack Cade leads a revolution to combat *literacy* and the tyranny that it represents. Jack Cade's program does not, in its intent, differ from Margaret's gesture of tearing up a petition and the destruction of records that occurred in 1381.[38] Cade proposes a return to a pre-literate stage:[39]

> Is not this a lamentable thing, that of the skin of an innocent lamb should be made parchment? That parchment, being scribbled o'er, should undo a man? Some say the bee stings; but I say, 'tis the bee's wax: for I did but seal once to a thing, and I was never mine own man.

> (IV.ii.76-81)

Cade condemns the slaughter of innocent lambs to make parchment and the use of bee's wax as a seal. He considers these as abuses of nature. Similarly, as Dick the Butcher points out in an aside, the authorities use even the human skin as a parchment to be written upon, referring to the practice of branding the hands

of thieves with the letter "T": "But methinks he should stand in fear of fire, being burnt i'th' hand for stealing of sheep" (IV.ii.61-62).

Cade presides over two trials, that of the clerk and that of Lord Say, which reveal his ideas about the true source of the problems that England faces. The clerk is accused of being able "to write and read, and cast accompt" (IV.ii.83-84); of "setting boys' copies," i.e., teaching schoolchildren to write; and of carrying "a book in his pocket with red letters in't." When he confesses that he was so "well brought up" that he can write his name, Cade does not hesitate: "Hang him with his pen and ink-horn about his neck" (IV.ii.106-107). Lord Say is similarly accused of "corrupting" the kingdom:

> Thou hast most traitorously corrupted the youth of the realm in erecting a grammar school: and whereas before, our forefathers had no other books but the score and tally, thou hast caused printing to be used, and contrary to the king, his crown and dignity, thou hast built a paper-mill.

> (IV.vii.34-39)

Grammar school, printing, paper-mill—all of these become instruments of tyranny. They also underscore the gulf between the privileged literate and the underprivileged illiterate. Cade does not trust those who talk "of a noun and a verb, and such abhominable words as no Christian ear can endure to hear" (IV.vii.42-43); furthermore, he recognizes that the aristocrats' ability to read and write has caused too much injustice:

> Thou hast appointed justices of peace, to call poor men before them about matters they were not able to answer. Moreover, thou hast put them in prison, and because they could not read thou hast hanged them, when, indeed, only for that cause they have been most worthy to live.

> (IV.vii.43-48)

The illiterate outsiders cannot understand, let alone decipher, the codes of the record keepers. The two-track system of justice discriminates against them: because they cannot read, they cannot claim "benefit of clergy" and escape capital punishment. Literacy represents injustice; illiteracy, righteousness and justice.

Cade envisions a revolutionary state in which food and drink exist for all, where everything becomes communal property (IV.ii.67-68). He will abolish money, and everyone will be apparelled "in one livery" to erase the markers of class and status. But all of this can be accomplished only if he eliminates the common enemy, namely writing: "Away, burn all the records of the realm: my mouth shall be the parliament of England" (IV.vii.14-16). The archives of the state and all writings in the realm constitute a record of customs, traditions, privileges, and titles of property and nobility; hence, they perpetuate injustices.

Cade wants to replace writing with orality, literacy with illiteracy—something that does not depend upon or generate written records. For the fictional genealogy to stick, he must destroy the written records because these lie beyond his control. He claims to be the son of Edmund Mortimer, Earl of March; his mother to be a Plantagenet, the daughter of the Duke of Clarence; and his wife to be descended of the "Lacies." Word of mouth sanctions his newly-invented genealogy, as he fashions an identify for himself. He claims that his mother had twins:

> The elder of them, being put to nurse,
> Was by a beggar-woman stol'n away,
> And, ignorant of his birth and parentage,
> Became a bricklayer when he came of age:
> His son am I; deny it, if you can.
>
> (IV.ii.138-43)

Ironically, he speaks in the blank verse of the oppressors, departing from the prose style characteristic of his class in Shakespeare's plays. He admits in an aside that he has invented this story himself; in a sense, he has invented this identity. After knighting himself Sir John Mortimer, Jack Cade decrees that "henceforward it shall be treason for any that calls me other than Lord Mortimer" (IV.vi.5-6). Immediately, his followers execute a soldier for calling him by his old name.

His self-fashioning depends on orality, a less stable and permanent means than that of his enemies, whose self-fashioned identities depend upon production and control of written records. Though short-lived, Cade's program accomplishes its desired intentions. He verbally authorizes the plundering of the nobility's houses and properties. He provides his followers with what they do not have or can never have: equal rights, food and drink, fancy clothing.

Jack Cade had envisioned a return to a simpler pastoral age replacing the urban landscape with pastures: "in Cheapside shall my palfrey go to grass" (IV.ii.68-69). Instead, abandoned by his followers, he ends up hungry and desperate in Alexander Iden's garden in Kent: "On a brick wall have I climbed into this garden, to see if I can eat grass or pick a sallet [salad] another while" (IV.x.6-7). Here he is killed, and from here he will be taken to the king as a prize. What he does not understand is that those who can read and write, even if temporarily divided by a civil war, also control the means of food production and distribution. His stomach, if not his mind, remains at their mercy.

Cade's social and political consciousness astounds. Annabel Patterson argues that "Cade fails every test for the proper popular spokesman" because the Duke of York manipulates him and because he is "also an impostor aristocrat, a traitor to his class, hawking his false claims to the name of Mortimer by way of romantic fiction, the tale of a noble child stolen from its cradle by a beggarwoman, and now returned to claim its inheritance" (p. 49). Patterson forgets to mention, however, that no one within the play is fooled by Cade's claims; rather, the followers seem very much aware that Cade mocks the very fictions that the aristocracy has perpetuated. What may have started out at the instigation of York gains a life of its own. Cade realizes that while the aristocrats try to destroy one another to reconstitute the center of power, he isolates writing as the number one culprit; for no matter who gains power, they preside over the system contained in the records and all writings of the kingdom. Hence, when the King issues another text—now an amnesty to those who surrender—Cade tells his followers that they are being deceived: "I thought ye would never have given out these arms till you had recovered your ancient freedom: but you are all recreants and dastards, and delight to live in slavery to the nobility" (IV.viii.25-29). In his concerted effort to destroy literacy, this illiterate man presents an astute, though desperate, attempt to affirm his own dignity and to gain rights that the system denies him.

Notes

[1] Jean de Léry, *History of a Voyage to the Land of Brazil, Otherwise Called America,* trans. Janet Whatley (Berkeley: Univ. of California Press, 1990), 134-35. Léry was part of a French expedition in 1555 to colonize the Bay of Guanabara, the site of present-day Rio de Janeiro. For an account of the early French settlements, see Leslie Bethell, ed., *Colonial Brazil* (Cambridge: Cambridge University Press, 1987), 1-39. Léry published his account in 1578. For a fascinating discussion of the passage cited from Léry, see Michel de Certeau, *The Writing of History,* trans. Tom Conley (New York: Columbia University Press, 1988), 209-243. The 1973 Brazilian motion picture, directed by Nelson Pereira dos Santos, entitled *Como Era Gostoso o Meu Francês (How Tasty Was my Frenchman)* dramatizes the experience of the fictional French protagonist Jean, who is not unlike Jean de Léry. For a discussion of this motion picture, see Geraldo U. de Sousa, "Theatrics and Politics of Culture in Sixteenth-Century Brazil," *Journal of Dramatic Theory and Criticism* 8 (1994): 89-102

[2] Michel de Certeau, *The Writing of History,* trans. Tom Conley (New York: Columbia University Press, 1988), 215.

[3] Certeau, p. 215.

[4] Thomas, "Literacy in Early Modern England," in *The Written Word: Literacy in Transition,* ed. Gerd Baumann (Oxford: Clarendon Press, 1986), 98.

[5] Thomas, p. 97. Thomas takes Ong, David Cressy, Jack Goody, and others to task.

[6] Thomas, p. 105.

[7] Harvey J. Graff, *The Legacies of Literacy: Continuities and Contradictions in Western Culture and Society* (Bloomington, Indiana: Indiana University Press, 1991), 153.

[8] Cited in Harvey, p. 153.

[9] Thomas, p. 102.

[10] Thomas, p. 106.

[11] Thomas, p. 121.

[12] Thomas, p. 116.

[13] My thesis echoes James Clifford's statement from another context. Clifford introduces a self-reflective notion of ethnography that sees "culture as composed of seriously contested codes and representations" [Intro. to *Writing Culture: The Poetics and Politics of Ethnography,* ed. James Clifford and George E. Marcus (Berkeley: Univ. of California Press, 1986), 2.

[14] Annabel Paterson, *Shakespeare and the Popular Voice* (Cambridge: Basil Blackwell, 1989), 10.

[15] Geoffrey Bullough, ed., *Narrative and Dramatic Sources of Shakespeare III* (London: Routledge and Kegan Paul; New York: Columbia University Press, 1960), 99.

[16] Jacques Derrida, *Writing and Difference,* trans. Alan Bass (Chicago: Chicago University Press 1978), 280.

[17] See Bullough, III, p. 102.

[18] Bullough, III, p. 103.

[19] Bullough, III, p. 102.

[20] I.i.9-14. All quotations are from the Signet edition of *Henry VI Parts I, II, and III,* gen ed. Sylvan Barnet (New York: Penguin, 1989). *Part II* was edited by Arthur Freeman.

[21] Bullough, III, p. 101.

[22] In *Witchcraft and Religion: The Politics of Popular Belief* (Oxford, U.K.; New York: Basil Blackwell, 1984), Christina Larner points out that a similar attempt was made against King James VI of Scotland. During the trials for treason by sorcery that took place in Scotland from November 1590 to May 1591, "it was alleged that over 300 witches had gathered at various times to perform treason against the king. They were supposed to have raised storms while the King and his bride were at sea, to have attempted to effect his death by melting his effigy in wax, to have indulged in hitherto unheard of obscene rituals in the Kirk of North Berwick in the physical presence of their master, the Devil" (p. 9). We recall that King James went to Denmark to fetch his bride in the fall of 1589 and returned to Scotland in the spring of 1590.

[23] Cited by Thomas, p. 106.

[24] Thomas, p. 107.

[25] Thomas, p. 107.

[26] David M. Bergeron, *Royal Family, Royal Lovers: King James of England and Scotland* (Columbia and London: University of Missouri Press, 1991), 78.

[27] Bergeron, *Royal Family, Royal Lovers,* p. 79. An example from the 19th century illustrates how archives can be searched to resuscitate a tradition or ceremony. After Dom Pedro, Crown Prince of Portugal, proclaimed Brazil's independence in 1822 and was proclaimed Emperor, Brazilians searched the archives to duplicate, in the New World, the coronation ceremonies used by the Portuguese kings. Particularly elaborate was the order of precedence used in the Portuguese court, which was carefully searched and adopted for the coronation of the first Emperor of Brazil. The archives were also searched for the state funeral of President Kennedy, which was carefully modelled on the funeral of President Lincoln.

[28] The most thorough study of Jack Cade's rebellion is I. M. W. Harvey, *Jack Cade's Rebellion of 1450* (Oxford: Clarendon Press, 1991).

[29] Bullough, III, p. 91.

[30] Bullough, III, pp. 113-14.

[31] In *The Ardent Queen: Margaret of Anjou and the Lancastrian Heritage* (London: Peter Davies, 1976), Jock Haswell describes the historic Cade: "He was an Irishman, a one-time soldier in France and, according to some, an outlaw. He called himself John Mortimer, thereby trying to associated [sic] himself with the family of Richard Duke of York, whose mother's name had been Anne Mortimer. He collected a large, well-organized and well-disciplined force of men from the county of Kent, established a military camp on Blackheath and issued a manifesto. He protested against

taxation and corruption and lawlessness in high places" (p. 81). See also "Jack Cade" in Philippe Erlanger, *Margaret of Anjou Queen of England* (London: Elek Books, 1970), 119-25.

[32] Bullough writes: "For the Jack Cade scenes [Shakespeare] seems to have combined elements from Hall's account of this rising with elements from Holinshed's, or Grafton's, description of the Peasants' Revolt of 1381, which Hall did not give" (Vol. III, pp. 90-91).

[33] See Bullough, p. 91. Annabel Patterson argues that "there *was* a cultural tradition of popular protest, a tradition in the sense of something handed down from the past, cultural in the sense that what was transmitted were symbolic forms and signifying practices, a history from below encoded in names and occasions, a memorial vocabulary and even a formal rhetoric" (p. 38).

[34] Bullough, p. 91. A Pageant was staged in honor of John Allot, as David M. Bergeron, *English Civic Pageantry 1558-1641* (London: Edward Arnold Publishers; Columbia, South Carolina: University of South Carolina Press, 1971), explains: "to honour John Allot, Fishmonger, his company selected to devise the entertainment Thomas Nelson, about whom little is known other than that he was a printer and a ballad writer. The show survives in a printed text known simply as *The Device of the Pageant*" (p. 132). He adds, "The pageant-dramatist chooses the Jack Straw-Wat Tyler rebellion, part of the Peasants' Revolt of 1381, a subject treated also in the play *The Life and Death of Jack Straw* (printed in 1593) and later referred to in Munday's 1616 show, *Chrysanaleia*" (pp. 133-34).

[35] R. B. Dobson reprints many of the contemporary documents on the revolt in *The Peasants' Revolt of 1381,* 2nd ed (London: Macmillan Press, 1983), p. 133.

[36] Reprinted in Dobson, pp. 155-56. This is probably the most famous account of the Revolt.

[37] E. B. Fryde, *The Great Revolt of 1381* (London: Historical Association, 1981), 17. Fryde tells us that the destruction of John of Gaunt's papers had a tangible effect: "For years afterwards the administration of John of Gaunt's estates was seriously hampered by the burning of his principal archive at the Savoy" (p. 21).

[38] For a discussion of these and other similar uprisings, see Frederick Engles, *The Peasant War in Germany* (1926; rpt New York: International Publishers, 1976); Peter Blickle, *The Revolution of 1525: The German Peasants' War from a New Perspective,* trans. Thomas A. Brady, Jr. and H. C. Erik Midelford (Baltimore: Johns Hopkins University Press, 1981).

[39] Patterson writes, "a return to origins, then, was integral to the popular conception of how to protest, as well as providing theoretical grounds for the 'demands', for the transformation of local and individual grievances into a political program" (p. 41). She adds that the "peasant ideology" consisted of "its Edenic egalitarianism, its archaism, its claim that the world has grown worse through greed, its psychological awareness of poverty as humiliation, and its declaration that force is justified by 'extremitie'" (p. 46).

Source: "The Peasants' Revolt and the Writing of History in *2 Henry VI*," in *Reading and Writing in Shakespeare,* edited by David M. Bergeron, University of Delaware Press, 1996, pp. 178-93.

Fluellen's Name

Lisa Hopkins, *Sheffield Hallam University*

In Kenneth Branagh's film version of *Henry V,* a special emphasis is placed on Ian Holm's Fluellen. When Branagh's Henry, physically and spiritually exhausted, is struggling to come to terms with the aftermath of the battle of Agincourt, it is only the Welshman's well-meaning but apparently oddly timed eulogy of his country that can penetrate his defences and wrest from him the emotional relief of tears. The ensuing moment of bonding becomes one of the most powerful moments in the film, as Fluellen affords his king a vehicle for the expression of celebration. In making such a cinematographic choice, Branagh has undoubtedly responded to an element already strongly present in the text: unfailingly loyal, unwittingly deputizing for him in the matter of Williams, Fluellen obviously does provide a strong psychological prop for the war-wearied king to lean on. I want to argue, however, that he does so also in ways less obvious than this, which are bound up in the matter of his name.

Fluellen's name is, as everyone knows, a nonsense, a roughly phonetic rendition of the actual Welsh name Llywelyn. The Welsh double ll is notoriously hard for nonnative speakers to pronounce; it was on roughly the same basis as Shakespeare's principles of phoneticization that the Welsh surname Llwyd (meaning grey) became anglicized initially to Floyd, before finally ending up as Lloyd. (Jane Austen's friend Martha, now known universally as Martha Lloyd, is invariably "Floyd" in Austen's letters). Given this, Shakespeare's rendering of Llywelyn as Fluellen is not in itself unreasonable; but the problem could of course have been averted altogether had he adopted the simple expedient of choosing another name, one easier for the English to pronounce (others of his Welshmen include the much more manageable Hugh, Owen, and Davy). That he did choose Llywelyn makes his Welsh captain a highly resonant figure, for Llywelyn was the name of the last Welsh Prince of Wales, Llywelyn yr Olaf (the Last), and also of his grandfather, Llywelyn Fawr (the Great). It may seem strange that a tetralogy which overtly condemns one Welsh rebel against the English crown, in the shape of Glendower, should thus covertly celebrate another; but then the entire teleology of the second tetralogy points it inevitably towards the culmination of the first, and the apotheosis of the Welsh Henry Tudor, whose mythology drew extensively on traditions of Welsh revivalism.[1]

But if Fluellen's name is readily comprehensible as Llywelyn, there is another respect in which it is far more alien to traditions of Welsh nomenclature. No Welshman could have a one-word name; an essential part of his identity would be the patronymic, comprising "ap" (son of) and the name of his father. (For a woman the equivalent would be "ferch," daughter of.) Indeed, few Welshmen of any status would be satisfied with just one indicator of lineage: the majority would append also the name of their paternal grandfather, and quite possible their great-grandfather as well, in ways that utterly frustrated English attempts to make conventional surnames for them—indeed the very name of Tudor was plucked more or less at random from Owen Tudor's full customary style of Owain ap Maredudd ap Tudur.[2] There is ample evidence that Elizabethan dramatists were fully cognizant of this naming system. From Marlowe's Rice ap Howell with his Welsh hooks,[3] to John Ford's Rice ap Thomas in *Perkin Warbeck,* there is consistent practice; there is even an extended joke on the subject, in Ford and Dekker's *The Welsh Embassador,* where an Englishman is impersonating a Welshman, and, when, asked his name, replies, "Tis Reese ap meridith, ap shon, ap lewellin, ap morris, yet noe dancers."[4] Yet Shakespeare, who undoubtedly knew Welshmen personally, chooses to omit the crucial patronymic. Why?

Paternal authority is of course a recurring theme of the second tetralogy. Henry IV, whose father was not king before him, struggles to enforce his control over the kingdom and has a continuously difficult relationship with his own son; at one stage he is driven to wish for that terror of all patrilineal societies, that his heir was a changeling and Hotspur his natural child. The young Hal quests through the first two plays in which he features performing a series of complex psychological substitutions in which the mantle of his 'father' is in a constant process of circulation between Henry IV, Falstaff, Hotspur, Blunt (literally), and the Lord Chief Justice; even the apparently self-sufficient Henry V places heavy reliance on the only visibly surviving member of the older generation, his uncle Exeter (one of the products of John of Gaunt's irregular relationship with Katherine Swynford, from which the Tudors also descended), and he invokes Richard II immediately before the crucial battle. His father's biographer Marie Louise Bruce sees the same kind of dislocation as that represented by the displaced fathers of Shakespeare's play in the relationship of the historical Henry V to Richard II, whom, she says, he "had never ceased to love . . . more than his own father";[5] it is interesting to note that, in a bizarre exchange of women, his eventual marriage with Katherine of Valois made him the posthumous brother-in-law of Richard

II, whose second wife, Isabella of France, had been Katherine's elder sister, and herself originally been intended by the English as subsequently Henry's bride, had she not put up a strenuous resistance.[6] All mention of his mother, Mary Bohun, or his more flamboyant stepmother Joanna of Navarre, accused of witchcraft by his younger brother John of Bedford, is studiously avoided; family psychodramas are played out exclusively amongst men.

Patriarchy, in these plays, both validates and problematizes the society it structures. The name of the father legitimates succession to the throne of England and allows for the successful transformation of Hal at the close of *2 Henry IV;* but his story does not end there, for the opening of *Henry V* itself shows him in a situation precisely inverting that triumphant succession by presenting him as a candidate for the crown of France, England's other, where authority can be claimed only through right of the female. Henry's assertion of his right to France depends on his descent from Isabella, mother of Edward III, who was the daughter of Philip the Fair, and a character with whom Shakespeare and his audience would have been familiar from her appearance in Marlowe's *Edward the Second*. When her three brothers died without male issue, Edward, her son, laid claim to his grandfather's crown, and his son Edward the Black Prince led the English nobility to a series of spectacular victories, such as Crécy and Poitiers, which are referred to with fear by the French nobles of *Henry V*. However, the claim through Isabella opened up several alarming issues. As a wife who murdered her husband, Edward II, she provided all too clear an example of the dangers of women in charge; moreover, her three brothers, although they had no surviving sons, did all have daughters, whose claim was at least as good as hers. Particularly strong, in theory, would have been the position of Jeanne of Navarre, daughter of Isabella's eldest brother Louis X, had not the little girl been widely believed to be a bastard because of the confessed adultery of her mother, Marguerite of Burgundy.

This issue of female fidelity is of course at the heart of French attempts to impose the Salic law:

> . . . the land Salic is in Germany.
> Between the floods of Saale and of Elbe,
> Where, Charles the Great having subdued
>   the Saxons,
> There left behind and settled certain French
> Who, holding in disdain the German women
> For some dishonest manners of their life,
> Established there this law: to wit, no female
> Should be inheritrix in Salic land.[7]

"For some dishonest manners of their life" is surely fairly clear code for unchastity; but of course the remedy will do little to help, for barring women from

the succession cannot secure the legitimacy of their offspring (indeed it is only in a matrilinear society, or through DNA testing, that the transfer of power from ruler to biological heir can ever be assured). The potential slur on Henry V's own claim through the female is apparently nicely distanced by having the opprobrium directed at German women alone, but in reality it is difficult to keep it quite so much at arm's length: Henry's own wicked stepmother, Joanna of Navarre, was the grand-daughter of the very Jeanne of Navarre whose alleged bastardy had precipitated the Hundred Years' War. Indeed, Henry's own wife would contract a liaison of unsubstantiated legitimacy after his death (from which sprang the Tudors) and the first tetralogy is fissured by accusations of adultery ranging from those against Henry VI's wife Margaret to Richard III's indictment of his own mother's honor in a desperate attempt to impugn the legitimacy of his elder brother Edward. In this patrilinear society, every family bears the scars of the actual or possible disruption of the father-son chain.

It is from precisely these uncertainties that Fluellen's name offers a respite. Conspicuously lacking the patronymic, he stands almost alone in the plays in not being identified primarily in terms of his father. Falstaff, whose own name is of course similarly falsified from its original of Oldcastle, can be read as a parallel to him in this instance; but Falstaff, as the possible pun false-staff perhaps implies, is constantly engaged in usurping the role of Hal's father which Fluellen never does (and has, moreover, been read by recent feminist criticism as a representation of the *maternal* rather than of the paternal body).[8] It is perhaps this absence of patrilinear determinants in Fluellen which makes him an enabling mechanism for Henry to claim, however briefly, what is at once the most glorious and the most spurious of his identities, that of the agent of the Welsh revival. Fleetingly gesturing towards Henry VII's position as the son of prophecy, the heir of Arthur, Henry agrees that he wears the leek "for a memorable honour. / For I am Welsh, you know, good countryman" (4.7.99-100), with which Fluellen concurs: "All the water in Wye cannot wash your majesty's Welsh plood out of your pody, I can tell you that" (4.7.101-2). Fluellen's reference to Wye points us squarely in the geographical direction of the origins of Henry's claim to be Welsh: he was born in the gatehouse tower of Monmouth Castle, to that most occluded of figures, Mary Bohun, his mother, whose substantial appanage of Hereford lordships and whose Marcher descent provided him with everything that he is able to claim of this identity, and whose inheritance (together with that of his stepmother, who seems indeed to have been imprisoned expressly to facilitate the release of the money tied up in paying her dower) historically provided the only means by which, in a war-torn country, he could finance taking a wife.[9] The memory of Mary Bohun may be only indirectly invoked at this point, but the reference to Henry's birth means that it is inescapably there; and fittingly enough, it is the fatherless Fluellen who has provided a conduit for this return of the repressed mother.

After this *éclaircissement,* Henry will move on to a remarkable refocusing of his energies and interests to direct his attention fully towards the Princess Katherine. Women will feature in his story in a way they never have before—wenching is notably one of the few pastimes he does not try in Cheapside—and marriage is pulled rather unexpectedly out of the generic hat to make this the only one of the history plays to have a classically comedic teleology. In Branagh's film version, the courtship scene is played for all the numerous laughs it can get, and the last is won when Henry breaks off his ardent wooing with a conscious "Here comes your father" (5.2.270-1). This final appearance of a father in the plays, however, brings with it shades not only of comedy, but of the more repressive and disruptive elements of patriarchy, and also of the threats to it. It is, as the epilogue reminds us, in his role as a father that Henry will register his one significant failure: his weak-minded only son will destabilize England and take it, in circular motion, through all the horrors of the first tetralogy, where French might (mediated, noticeably, primarily through French women) is once again rampant. Moreover, although the entrance into matrimony may look like an achievement of full adulthood which makes redundant the power of the father, it is actually fundamentally conditioned by it. However much his badinage may attempt to disguise it, Henry's interest in Katherine is of course solely dictated by the identity of her father: as daughter of the King of France, she can help to reinforce his own claim to the throne. Her Frenchness here may, in this respect, even paradoxically underline his own Welsh resonances: as a claimant in his own right who nevertheless seeks the additional support of marriage with the daughter of a previous king, he again directly parallels Henry VII in the marriage with Elizabeth of York which provided the conclusion of the first tetralogy as this does of the second.

But the missing element of Fluellen's name may help us to detect an element similarly missing from Katherine's. Her sister, wife of Richard II, had been Isabella of France; she herself is known to history universally as Katherine of Valois, signifying the intervening decline in fortune of her family which causes them to cease to be synonymous with the country they so temporarily rule. As well as strengthening Henry's claim to the throne, therefore, she also, paradoxically, weakens it, firstly through this silent change of title which makes her so much less than her sister had been to Richard II, and secondly by the simple fact that to concede that it needs strengthening is to concede that it is not already sufficient. To complicate the situation still further, there was historically some room for doubt

that the King of France *was* Katherine's father, because of the very strong suspicion that her mother, Isabeau of Bavaria, had committed adultery with her brother-in-law, Louis of Orléans;[10] indeed Queen Isabeau herself gave force to these rumors when she subscribed to the Treaty of Troyes, which disinherited the Dauphin and referred to him as "the so-called Dauphin."[11] Certainly the point may well be hinted at for an audience by the fact that the Dauphin, whose actions initiated events and who has been given such prominence throughout the play, has disappeared so abruptly from the story; and that earlier pointed reference to the "dishonest manners of . . . life" of German women (I.2.49) may also be recalled by anyone who happens to remember "Queen Isabel's" nationality (though Shakespeare could hardly afford to be too pointed here, since Isabeau, through Katherine of Valois's second marriage to Owen Tudor, was an ancestress of Elizabeth I). "Here comes your father" thus implicitly interpellates Charles VI firmly as being in fact Katherine's father, and also carries a hidden agenda of its own, since what Henry wants is actually for Charles VI to function in effect as his *own* father, whose legitimate heir and successor he will be. A record of a life which started with a father wishing for a change of sons thus ends, ironically, with a son wishing for a change of fathers.

The problematics of patriarchy thus played out are negated, exceptionally and briefly, only in Fluellen, the last of Henry's spiritual fathers, who proffers to him a link with the mythical glories of the Welsh past, and, through it, an even more extraordinary connection to that ultimate warrior, Alexander the Great. And yet even in the company of the fatherless Fluellen one can never be totally safe from fathers, since just as memories of the forgotten Mary Bohun struggle to the surface in Fluellen's conversation, so too do those of that discarded father figure, Falstaff:

> As Alexander killed his friend Cleitus, being in his ales and his cups, so also Harry Monmouth, being in his right wits and his good judgements, turned away the fat knight with the great-belly doublet—he was full of jests and gipes and knaveries and mocks—I have forgot his name.
>
> (4.7.40-5)

But though the memory of the father may linger here, the name of the father at least has no power, for Fluellen, though his memory stretches back to tales of Alexander the Great and Cadwaladr, has, fittingly, forgotten it.

Notes

[1] David Rees, *The Son of Prophecy: Henry Tudor's Road to Bosworth* (London: The Black Raven Press, 1985), 98-110.

[2] Ralph A. Griffiths and Roger S. Thomas, *The Making of the Tudor Dynasty* (Gloucester: Alan Sutton, 1987), 31.

[3] Christopher Marlowe, *Edward the Second,* edited by Charles R. Forker (Manchester: Manchester University Press, 1994), II. vii. 45 s.d.

[4] *The Welsh Embassador,* in Fredson Bowers, ed., *The Dramatic Works of Thomas Dekker,* 4 vols (Cambridge: Cambridge University Press, 1961), III. ii. 348.

[5] Marie Louise Bruce, *The Usurper King: Henry of Bolingbroke 1366-1399* (London: The Rubicon Press, n.d.), 248.

[6] Anne Crawford, *Letters of the Queens of England 1100-1547* (Gloucester: Alan Sutton, 1994), 107.

[7] William Shakespeare, *Henry V,* edited by Gary Taylor (Oxford: Oxford University Press, 1982), I. 2. 44-51. All further quotations from the play will be from this edition.

[8] See for instance Valerie Traub, *Desire and Anxiety: Circulations of Sexuality in Shakespearean Drama* (London: Routledge, 1992), 55-56.

[9] Crawford, *Letters,* pp. 112-13.

[10] For an account of how Henry V and his supporters used this rumor, see Marina Warner, *Joan of Arc* (1981) (Harmondsworth: Penguin, 1983), 73; for an extended but coyer discussion of Isabeau's adultery (which credits her with other lovers too) see Peter Earle, *The Life and Times of Henry V* (London: Weidenfeld and Nicolson, 1972), 182-83). Warner also discusses the suggestion that it was Joan's reassurance of Charles VII that he was legitimate which was the ground of the king's faith in her; this idea originates in the sixteenth century and would, if Shakespeare were aware of it, have fed interestingly into the series of echoes of the first tetralogy which disrupt the closure of the second.

[11] Warner, *Joan of Arc, 73.*

_____

Source: "Fluellen's Name," in *Shakespeare Studies,* Vol. XXIV, 1996, pp. 148-55.

Possible Pasts: Historiography and Legitimation in *Henry VIII*

Ivo Kamps, *University of Mississippi*

The methods and politics of history writing intrigued Shakespeare throughout his career as a dramatist. Among his earliest plays, Shakespeare's first tetralogy already offers a full-blown conception of the shape of English history, interlacing Machiavellian ideas, providentialism, and Tudor ideology (see Rackin 27-9). The second tetralogy, culminating in *Henry V*, successfully dramatized a more complex grasp of the past, tarnishing the popular Elizabethan notion of the "great man" who bends history to his will (see Kamps 94-104). Even in a late romance such as *The Tempest* we discover that Shakespeare frames the basic conflict between Prospero and Caliban in terms of Prospero's "history" of his tenure on the island and Caliban's account of the same events (see Barker and Hulme). Other examples of Shakespeare's fascination with things historiographical are plentiful in the Roman plays and throughout his oeuvre, but nowhere is his interst in the nuances of the production of historical accounts more pronounced and more thoughtfully treated than in *Henry VIII* (1613), a dramatic collaboration with John Fletcher. Deeply steeped in the historiographical developments that occurred in sixteenth- and early seventeenth-century England, this play appropriates and dramatizes various contradictory historiographical methods and bespeaks a decisive break with official Tudor ways of thinking about the English past.

I.

In *The Arte of English Poesie* (1589), George Puttenham represents the view of many Elizabethans when he decrees it to be the task of "historical Poesie" to record the "famous acts of Princes and the vertuous and worthy lives of our forefathers" (54). Arthur B. Ferguson, in his influential study, *Clio Unbound,* expands on this notion and suggests that Tudor historians cared little about social customs, institutions, and beliefs, and perhaps even less about secondary and largely informal causes, or anything else that reached "beyond the history of states as told in terms of the acts, the ambitions, and the tragic dilemmas of the actors themselves" (4,5). Alvin Kernan unites these views when he observes that Tudor playwrights appropriate the typical historical pattern for their historical dramas: "a weak or saintly king makes political mistakes and is overthrown by rebellious and arrogant subjects; the kingdom becomes a wasteland and society a chaos in which every man's hand is set against his fellow; after a period of great suffering, reaction against the forces of evil occurs, and a strong and good king restores order" (264). *Henry VIII*, it has been claimed repeatedly, is an aesthetic failure because it lacks a strong king as well as cohesive philosophy of history (Ribner 191).

It must be conceded that Shakespeare and Fletcher's Henry VIII fails to meet expectations raised by both Tudor historiographical practice and historical drama. The king is neither Puttenham's "great man," nor Kernan's "strong and good king [who] restores order." Joseph Candido describes him as a "well-intentioned yet strangely inattentive king" who fails "to address himself to the deep religious and political differences that divide his ministers" (56, 57). He is "blithely superficial" in his approach to the "grave and divisive issues of his reign" and too out of touch "to inspire our confidence in quite the same way that Henry V or even Bolingbroke does" (Candido 57). The central question here is whether Shakespeare and Fletcher are trying to portray the traditional "weak ruler" or aiming at something altogether different.

A second question is whether the play's episodic structure is due to a lack of both a consistent dramatic design and "a coherent and meaningful philosophy of history" (Ribner 291), or is instead a deliberate effort to portray history differently. How we answer these questions hinges on how we view the play's final scene and how we read Archbishop Cranmer's speech at the christening of Princess Elizabeth. Ostensibly at heaven's bidding, the Archbishop of Canterbury foretells the Age of Elizabeth as a golden world. She shall shower on England "a thousand thousand blessings"; "every man shall eat in safety / Under his own vine what he plants, and sing / The merry songs of peace to all his neighbours"; and "God shall be truly known" (*Henry VIII* 5.4.19, 33-35, 35). The nature of this speech is important because after the turmoil portrayed in the play—the opportunistic removal of the loyal Queen Katherine, the equally expedient execution of the Duke of Buckingham, and the timely fall of the powerful and corrupt Cardinal Wolsey—Cranmer tries to restore social order in the Henrician state by proffering a prophetic history of the next seven or eight decades. He links the Elizabethan past (which flows from the Henrician past) to the Jacobean present: "Nor shall this peace sleep with her" because her successor, James I, shall be "as great in admiration as herself," inherit her "blessedness," and "He shall flourish, / And like a mountain cedar, reach his branches / To all the plains about him: our children's children [i.e., James's generation] / Shall see this and bless heaven" (42, 43, 52-

55). In this decidedly teleological oration it is the *promise* of the reigns of Elizabeth I and James I which underwrites the appropriateness of Henry's rule. But what is a promise to Cranmer's audience in 1533 is of course *history* to his audience in 1613. In short, how we respond to the play as a whole depends greatly on how we respond to Cranmer's rendering of Tudor-Stuart history.

Commentators who view the play as an aesthetic success turn to this final scene (and its historiography) to unify its various elements into a meaningful whole. Paul Dean, for instance, contends that while the "falls" of Buckingham, Katherine, and Wolsey and the "rises" of Anne Bullen and Thomas Cranmer are not unrelated, they are best understood "as a translation into dramatic terms of the undulations of the Wheel of Fortune which controls the action" (Dean 177). Dean acknowledges and then unifies the play's episodic structure by invoking the medieval *de casibus* tradition, thus explaining a Jacobean history play in terms of an essentially medieval theory of history. Frank V. Cespedes argues "that the structure of *Henry VIII* is designed to force upon its audience an awareness of two things at once: the fortunate march of English history toward the reign of Elizabeth [and James], and the 'sad,' 'woeful' story . . . of individuals during Henry VIII's reign who unwittingly helped to shape, and perished in the unfolding of, this historical process" (Cespedes 415). Thus the play presents the Jacobean viewer with "a conflict between historical ends and means" (415) of an essentially "'good' historical process" (437). Matthew H. Wikander simply notes that the Buckingham, Katherine, and Wolsey episodes "befog" the "play's historiography," which really "celebrates the stability and continuity of the monarchy in a manner even more providential than that of the Tudor chronicles" (46, 47). If Cranmer constitutes the standard of historical judgment in the play, then Dean's and Cespedes's readings are compelling; but I think we ought to resist granting the Archbishop such special status. Indeed, I want to do what neither the play's detractors nor those who try to save its reputation do, which is consider the possibility that Shakespeare and Fletcher give us not a disunified play about history but a play about disunified history.[1] The latter alternative, rather than harking back to medieval notions of history, looks to the more "modern" world of Jacobean historiography to illuminate the play. Choosing it allows us to see that despite the christening scene's power and pathos, Cranmer's effort to produce dramatic and historical closure is an ideological move that is undercut by other historical "voices" of the play.

Although Frances A. Yates has eloquently argued that the play depicts a return to the John Foxean way of viewing "Tudor reform of the Church as an imperial reform" carried out here by Henry VIII (68, 67-82),

we should not conclude that a nostalgia for things Elizabethan necessarily led a Jacobean audience to embrace uncritically the Archbishop's narrow, medieval, providential conception of history. Since Cranmer is without a doubt the King's mouthpiece (he is instrumental in providing the legal means for the divorce), we do well here to remember Jean Bodin's admonition voiced in the *Method for the Easy Comprehension of History* (translated into English by Thomas Heywood in 1608) against looking for "the truth of history . . . in the Commentaries of Kinges, for they are given to speake largely of their own praises, but to make no use of those Observations which are little or nothing interessed in their praise or disgrace" (12). If this edict applies to Henry, it must also apply to his agent Cranmer. Moreover, I will show there is reason to conclude that Cranmer's unifying historiography sounded archaic and unsophisticated not only to more learned Jacobeans but also to those who were raised on the popular histories of Holinshed, Hall, Grafton, and others. From their own reading of the histories, Shakespeare and Fletcher certainly understood that Cranmer's conception of history was dated, and, to make sure the viewer understood the same, they set Cranmer's ideologically driven "good" historical process in competition with other, more recent methods of historical representation. In the episodes detailing the fortunes of Queen Katherine, the Duke of Buckingham, and Cardinal Wolsey, Shakespeare and Fletcher draw on distinct and at times theoretically incompatible "schools" of Renaissance historical thought. The Buckingham episode confronts questions of eye-witness evidence and hearsay; Katherine's divorce and disgrace foreground questions of historical (and legal) precedent versus innovation; while Wolsey's plunge from power in the play is in part facilitated by an antiquarian appeal to evidence that speaks for itself.

One notable effect of dramatizing these historiographies is a highlighting of their acute differences as knowledge-producing practices—differences that produce not historical clarity or certainty but epistemological ambiguity. Such ambiguity was a relatively new phenomenon in the late sixteenth and early seventeenth centuries. As Phyllis Rackin observes, "Historiographic writing no longer had a direct, unequivocal relation with historical truth. Alternative accounts of historical events and opposed interpretations of their causes and significance now threatened each other's credibility, a process intensified by the development of the printing industry and the spread of literacy" (Rackin 13). What is more, the crown itself began to take an increasingly active role in historiographical argumentation. In the Tudor era, we can trace the alliance between royal legitimation and historiography back to Polydore Vergil's *Anglica Historia* (1534), a work commissioned by Henry VIII's father for the construction not only of a history for England but also of a compelling foundation for the Tudor dynasty. Henry VIII was certainly no less aware than his father of history's political utility. For instance, in his 1533 Act in Restraint of Appeals—a document produced primarily for the specific purpose of establishing England as an autonomous nation independent from Rome—Henry appeals to the authority of "histories and chronicles" to authenticate the position of the monarch. A passage from the 1533 Act reads: "Where, by divers sundry old authentic histories and chronicles, it is manifestly declared and expressed that this realm of England is an empire, and so hath been accepted in the world, governed by one supreme head and king having the dignity and royal estate of the imperial crown of the same, unto whom a body politic . . . be bounden and owe to bear next to God a natural and humble obedience . . . ." (Stephenson and Marcham 304). Richard Halpern observes that James had already argued in *The Trew Law of Free Monarchies* that the kings of Scotland historically (and therefore legally) preceded "any estates or ranks of men . . . any Parliaments . . . or lawes." The kings and no one else, James maintained, erected states, devised and formed governments, and "were authors and makers of the Lawes" (Halpern 223). In the *Trew Law,* James admits "that in the first beginning of Kings rising among the Gentiles . . . men choosed out one among themselves . . . to maintain the weakest in their right," virtually conceding that historically speaking the monarch owes his powers to the people. But he then goes on to explain that this scenario hardly applies to Scotland: "For as our Chronicles beare witnesse, this Ile, and especially our part of it, being scantly inhabited, but by very few, and they as barbarous and scant of ciuility, as number, there comes our first King *Fergus,* with a great number with him, out of *Ireland,* which was long inhabited before us, and making himself master of the countrey, by his owne friendship and force, as well of the *Ireland-men* that came with him, as of the countrey-men that willing fell to him, hee made himself King and Lord. . . . Thereafter he and his successors . . . made and established their lawes. . . . So the trewth is directly contrarie in our state to the false affirmation of such seditious writers, as would perswade vs, that the Lawes and state of our countery were established before admitting of a king . . ." (James I 61-62).

As we witness in *Henry VIII,* such historiographical pluralism is flexible enough to serve the state as it disposes of a Duke with pretensions to the throne, a Queen who is too old to bear a male heir, and an increasingly powerful and autocratic Cardinal. Yet since James I himself increasingly turned to historical argumentation to assert himself unequivocally on such momentous issues as royal prerogative and the crown's relationship to the law of the land, and since, as J. G. A. Pocock observes, "historical criticism became one of the sharpest weapons of monarchy" (17), it is easy to see how any epistemological ambiguity stemming from historiographical eclecticism could also destabi-

lize the monarch's authority on such matters. Hence, in *Henry VIII* the Henrician state first exploits historiographical diversity and then tries to provide historical closure and clarity by attempting to erase or, at the very least, suppress the ambiguities that sprout from that diversity. In the scene depicting Elizabeth's christening, Cranmer's providential account of royal genealogy appropriates and reorders the discontinuous elements of Tudor (and Stuart) royal history under the all-embracing rubric of God's plan for England. The problem of course is that the historiographical eclecticism of the play strongly resists such a totalizing move. Taken as a whole, therefore, the play focuses not on the inevitable outcome of a historical process, as Cranmer submits, but on the various historiographical strategies that can be employed to make the outcome *appear* inevitable. *Henry VIII* draws our attention to the operations by means of which historiography produces a past and the ways in which historiography and historians mystify those operations by sanctifying them.

When *Henry VIII* is viewed in light of its serious interest in the process of historiographical representation, we can begin to extricate the play from the "Elizabethan" context in which so many critics have deemed it aesthetically inferior, and to which others have tried to make it conform. Although, as several critics have observed, Henry VIII does sporadically seem active behind the scenes, he is a far cry from the protagonist of the Elizabethan history play who, in the words of Leonard Tennenhouse, is able to "seize hold of the symbols and signs legitimizing authority and wrest them from his rivals, thus making them serve his own interests" (121). This presentation of the King, however, is quite deliberate. One of the conclusions of this essay is that far from being a successful or failed Elizabethan heroic play (in which a strong protagonist like Henry V or Henry VII triumphs over historical conflict), Shakespeare and Fletcher's account of the reign of Henry VIII precisely emphasizes the impotence of "powerful" individuals in the face of a network of mostly "invisible" and inscrutable historical forces that beset them from all sides.

II. BUCKINGHAM, KATHERINE, AND WOLSEY: "THE CHRONICLES OF THEIR DOINGS"

The judicial proceedings against Buckingham, Katherine, and Wolsey manifest none of the disinterestedness, uniformity, and stability one might hope to expect in a nation of law. Although conducted—at least in name—on behalf of the state, the three trials reveal a variety of motivations and methods of legal protocol, in particular with regard to the composition and treatment of evidence. The purpose of this variety is to show how radically different legal and historiographical discourses are able to exercise power and claim knowledge (or what passes for knowledge) under a single rubric, that of justice or truth or law.

Although many of the events that bear on the fates of these three characters do not lie in the distant past, common historiographical principles apply because, as D. R. Woolf observes, the kind of accounts of "current events, which would now be deemed journalism, were [then] commonly referred to as histories" (16). In understanding the trials of Buckingham, Katherine, and Wolsey it is therefore significant that Renaissance historians were generally dubious about the construction of reliable accounts of current or recent history. Bodin observes: "Sure those that will write of the present, can hardly write truly, but [because] they must touch the credit and reputation of some men" (11). Annabel Patterson, among others, has argued credibly that Bodin's point about the power of men of reputation was not lost on Shakespeare or his contemporaries (Patterson 52-115). And Raphael Holinshed himself, a principal source for *Henry VIII,* openly bemoans the historian's inability to be an witness to all that happens himself and the unfortunate need "to inquire of moderne eie-witnesses for the true setting downe" of what he delivers (Holinshed, Preface).

In *Henry VIII,* the case against the Duke of Buckingham is shaped by the historiographical concerns just described. During a pre-trial hearing held at Cardinal Wolsey's instigation, Henry seals the Duke's fate on the basis of the testimony of a single character, the Duke's former Surveyor. We hear of a formal trial (conducted by the Duke's peers) during which additional witnesses are heard before the Duke is officially sent to the scaffold, but it is the pre-trial hearing before the King that procures the death sentence. The oral testimony of a disgruntled employee is relied on to reconstruct the past speeches and intentions of a character (Holinshed, by contrast, places much greater stress on the "evidence" supplied by other witnesses, and he points out that "inquisitions were taken in diuerse shires of England of him" [Holinshed 658-60]).

Buckingham is arrested on charges of "high treason" against the King's person (1.1.201) only moments after declaring his aim to inform the King of Wolsey's treasonous political strategems. But before turning to the scene in which the Duke's Surveyor brings the "evidence," Shakespeare and Fletcher insert another scene—clearly for the purpose of juxtaposition—in which Wolsey himself stands accused of shadowy dealings. And if we compare the case against Buckingham with the initial assault on Wolsey's reputation, we instantly notice alternative ways of handling historical evidence. Early in act 1, when he is accused of levying unprecedented taxes on the people and thereby causing a popular uprising, the Cardinal bitterly complains that he is "Traduc'd by ignorant tongues, which neither know / My faculties nor person, yet will be / The chronicles of my doing" (1.2.72-74). Wolsey has good reason not to want anyone to narrate the history of his activities, for at the court he has few reliable allies and

many opponents who would not hesitate to bring him down. But with Henry on his side, maybe Wolsey need not worry how his actions are chronicled. Katherine, who appears in the sympathetic role of the people's advocate, and who has little trouble exposing the Cardinal as the driving force behind the exorbitant "commissions, which compels from each / The sixth part of his substance, to be levied / Without delay" (1.2.57-59), is incapable of convincing her husband to acknowledge that Wolsey's unauthorized levy is a sign of his fundamentally corrupt character. The King immediately rescinds the tax measure and in that respect takes the evidence against the Cardinal seriously, but when it comes to the Cardinal himself, the charges against him are, for all practical purposes, treated as if they were, indeed, but slander from the tongues of ignorant accusers. The contradiction is never resolved.

In sharp contrast, Buckingham's pre-trial hearing before the King—the very next event in the same scene—shows us precisely how devastating an effect oral testimony can have on a person's reputation and fate. The Duke stands accused of treason by a single person, his former Surveyor, a man the Duke believes is now on the Cardinal's payroll (1.1.222-23). The Surveyor claims to have heard the Duke "discharge a horrible oath" in which he swore that, "were he evil us'd," he would assassinate the King (1.2.206, 207). The Surveyor, however, offers no material or corroborating evidence. His only attempt to bolster his credibility is to relate how the Duke was incited to these villainous thoughts by a "vain prophecy" (149), which promised that "the duke / Shall govern England" (170-71). Queen Katherine is obviously disturbed by the developments, and she (echoing Bodin) points out that the Surveyor may well be motivated by a desire for revenge against his former master, who dismissed him from "office / On the complaint o' th' tenants" (172-73). The Queen's observation also recalls the earlier complaint against Wolsey, who, like the Surveyor, was charged with wrongdoings by anguished subjects (56-57). The similarity heightens the contrast between the two "trial" scenes, and the difference between the judges. Under roughly similar circumstances, the Duke dismissed his Surveyor, while the King retains his Cardinal. And to top it off, the King pronounces the Duke a "traitor to th' height" (214) solely on the basis of the testimony of a man of dubious motivation and reputation.

Holinshed was clearly not convinced of Henry's justice in this matter (even though he enumerates *more* "evidence" against the Duke). Recalling one of his own guidelines for history-writing, Holinshed concludes his recapitulation of the indictment against Buckingham with the following remarks: "These were the speciall articles & points comprised in the indictment, and laid to his charge: but how trulie, or in what sort prooued, I haue not further to say, either in accusing or excusing him, other than as I find in [Edward] Hall and Polydor[e Vergil], whose words in effect, I haue thought to impart to the reader, and without anie wresting of the same either to or fro" (Holinshed 661). Holinshed does not always show himself such a paragon of historiographical prudence, but here his assessment accords with that of modern historians (see, for instance, Ridley 122-23), and Shakespeare and Fletcher follow the chronicler's lead by inserting a scene in which two gentlemen agree that "By all conjectures" (2.1.41) "the cardinal is the end of this" (40), that is, of the Duke's fall. That the King may be implicated in the biased proceedings against Buckingham is suggested by Henry's words to Cranmer in act 5: "At what ease / Might corrupt minds procure knaves as corrupt / To swear against you? Such things have been done" (5.1.131-33). (The passage is lifted from Foxe's *Acts and Monuments,* but with an interesting addition. The line "Such things have been done" does not appear in Foxe. The addition suggests that Shakespeare and Fletcher want us to recall the Surveyor's testimony against Buckingham. The relevant passage in Foxe reads: "Do you not consider what an easy thing it is to procure three or four false knaves to witness against you? Think you to have better luck that way than your master Christ had?" [896].)

But there is a further consideration to be reckoned with in assessing the "justice" doled out by the King, one that makes it critically perverse to view this episode as merely a clash between "great men." Buckingham himself offers a complex reading of his fate. When first arrested, he stoically professes that

> The net has fallen upon me; I shall
>   perish
> Under device and practice.
>
>   . . . . .
>
> It will help me nothing.
> To plead mine innocence, for that dye is on
>   me
> Which makes my whit'st part black. The will
>   of heav'n
> Be done in all things: I obey.
>   (1.1.203-4, 207-10)

There is an intriguing irony at work here. Buckingham is apparently so convinced of the efficiency of Wolsey's plots ("device and practice") against him that he believes it useless to resist (regardless of his actual guilt or innocence). He also implies, however, that if his impending death is indeed a certainty (and *only* if it is a certainty), then it *must* be God's will that he dies. Consequently, in the Duke's world view, the effectiveness of Wolsey's machination becomes equated directly with providence because *only* providence can be a certainty.

These views do not change as Buckingham's execution draws near. Following the trial he still professes his innocence, but also states that he bears the law (a third facilitator in his downfall) no malice for his death, and that "his vows and prayers / Yet are the King's" (2.1.62, 88-89). The law, he says, "has done upon the premises but justice" (63), and thereby he appears to validate the process which has brought him down, even though he still implicitly challenges the evidence and says he "could wish more Christians" those who have "sought" the judgment against him (64). This dichotomy continues to haunt his final thoughts. "Heaven has a hand in all" (124), he proclaims, but then warns that if you "are liberal of your loves and counsels, / Be sure you be not loose; for those you make friends / And give your hearts to, when they once perceive / The least rub in your fortunes, fall away / Like water from ye" (126-30).

Simultaneously, Buckingham asserts the omnipresence of providence and holds out for the efficacy of an individual's actions. If we posit that the Duke believes his predicament to be shaped by binary powers—divine determinism versus independent human agency—we can only conclude that he has given up on a unified vision of the world in which contradictions are only apparent. This paradoxical view of reality becomes less vexing, however, when we consider Foucault's conception of power as a field of forces without traditional notions of agency, and from which there is no escape: "Where there is power, there is resistance, and yet, or rather consequently, this resistance is never in a position of exteriority to power" (Foucault 95). The apparent paradox is resolved if we do not insist on situating the Duke's views in the context of a binary clash between freedom and determinism. Although Buckingham clings to the prospect that his fate might be an effective example to others—and even implies that if he had known then what he knows now things might be different—this hardly means that if he had not trusted his Surveyor and if he had not been convicted of treason, providence would have been altered in any way. As far as he or any human being can know, *that* would have been providence in all its inscrutable inevitability. The Duke's dilemma rests in his desire to hold out for some form of human agency while he is unwilling to assert his independence of God's ways. Hence, his vision of resistance in the face of Wolsey's plots resides wholly within an always deferred and unknowable providential scheme.

The case against the Duke, then, is conducted according to established legal principles, some of which overlap with those of humanist historians. Henry's divorce proceedings against Queen Katherine—who "like a jewel has hung twenty years / About his neck, yet never lost her lustre" (2.2.31-32)—are of a distinctly different character. In the Duke's trial, we saw the prosecution try hard to follow entrenched principles—although without great rigor vis-à-vis witnesses and evidence—and the Duke saw fit to sanction the trial in the narrow legal context, as well as in terms of providence. In the legal procedures against Katherine, however, law, church, and history all fail the King, leaving him to his own ingenious devices.

Founded generally on the principle of custom and (religious and secular) authority, English society demanded some type of legal precedent in cases of divorce. If the appropriate precedent was not immediately apparent, a historical search for one could follow. Historical inquiry of some sort, therefore, was a routine aspect of most legal cases (many humanist scholars fed right into this ancient practice by arguing that the primary function of history was to guide legal, moral, and political conduct in the present). Shakespeare and Fletcher's Henry explicitly confirms this basic principle in his response to the Wolsey-taxation case. When notified of the Cardinal's scheme, the King instantly revokes his secretary's actions and asserts that

> Things done without example, in their issue
> Are to be fear'd. Have you a *precedent*
> Of this commission? I believe, not any.
> We must not rend our subjects from our
> laws
> And stick them to our will.
>
> (1.2.90-94; emphasis added)

The argument can be expressed simply: nothing can be done without a historical precedent because we, like our subjects, must observe the law. This view, while it gains him admiration from his subjects, does not serve Henry once he has decided to divorce Katherine and marry Anne Bullen. There is no historical precedent upon which the divorce can be granted. Katherine has borne him an heir, and there is no doubt she has been obedient and faithful to him in every conceivable way. Neither Henry's desire for a male heir, nor the burden of a guilty conscience, nor his desire to marry another woman constitute a precedent for divorce in Renaissance England. Therefore, what is required, if the divorce is to take place, is an act of innovation. Traditional legal avenues must be abandoned in favor of unknown territories. But such ventures are not without peril. As J. G. A. Pocock notes apropos of Machiavelli's political historiography, "nothing was more difficult than innovation; if ancient customs existed, they were almost impossible to change; if they did not, they were almost impossible to create" (285). Faced with Rome's refusal to grant special dispensation for the divorce (which was not surprising, since Rome had granted special permission for the marriage between Henry and his late brother's wife), Henry resorts to the creation of "a precedent of wisdom" (2.2.85) by commissioning written opinions on the matter from the theologians of Oxford, Cambridge, and a host of European universities.

The Queen, on the other hand, has the authority of history and custom on her side. Not only does she make a convincing case for having been the perfect Queen and wife (2.4.11-42), she also unwaveringly invokes the historical events and figures that authorized her marriage to Henry.

> The king your father [Henry VII] was reputed
> for
> A prince most prudent, of an excellent
> And unmatch'd wit and judgment: Ferdinand
> My father, King of Spain, was reckon'd one
> The wisest prince that there had reign'd by
> many
> A year before. It is not to be question'd
> That they had gather'd a wise council to
> them
> Of every realm, that did debate this business,
> Who deem'd our marriage lawful . . .
>
> (2.4.43-51)

To Katherine (or to anyone in concord with Tudor law, culture, and decorum), the case against her can only be profoundly baffling. Henry VII—patriarch and founder of the Tudor dynasty—and the King of Spain were the architects of her marriage, Rome gave it its blessing, and an international council imparted its judicial approval. Therefore, with "history" so overwhelmingly on her side, it is not surprising that Katherine rejects what is to her the most unseemly of proceedings and departs from the court prematurely and dramatically (ignoring the King's summons), refusing to submit herself while contending that she has "here / No judge indifferent, nor no more assurance / Of equal friendship and proceeding" (2.4.14-16). Katherine only barely fits the typical Renaissance category of the heroine as patient victim; she endures her fate, but she also boldly defies her King and judge, stretching the definition of the heroine to the breaking point, and remaining noble and sympathetic throughout.

The King's claim consists of a guilty conscience (resulting from a change of heart about the legitimacy of his marriage), the possibility that the absence of "male issue" is evidence of God's censure of the marriage, and the opinions collected by Thomas Cranmer. In other words, in a clear departure from his ruling in the Wolsey-taxation matter, Henry counters Katherine's perfectly solid, legally sound, and traditional defense with an intangible appeal to conscience, providence, and manufactured "evidence." Appropriately, it is precisely at the moment of legal stalemate that we first learn of Henry's desire for the return of "well-beloved Cranmer." "With thy approach, I know / My comfort comes along," he asserts (2.4 236-38). "Approach" here means Cranmer's physical return to the court, but it also denotes his new and alternative "approach" to the divorce, the invention of which is often credited to him.

The innovation lies in the King's method, not in the grounds on which he seeks the divorce. At Blackfriars, he implicitly draws on biblical precedent when he attributes the lack of issue in his marriage to God's disapproval of the union. This type of explanation is a direct allusion to the punitive consequences promised to all who violate Leviticus's prohibition against a union between a man and his deceased brother's wife. However, Henry does not cite his source—which is essential if the argument is to have the force of a precedent—nor is he, sensing "the dilatory sloth and tricks of Rome" (2.4.235), any longer content to have the matter adjudicated by the Pope. Partially, he therefore does seek the divorce on conventional grounds. Yet his actions take the controversy out of the ecclesiastical courts (where it traditionally belongs, thus circumventing the authority of Rome), and transform the King's great matter into a "direct" appeal—legitimized by commissioned opinions—to God's law.

In this way, it is not established authority or church law or custom but individual will and disputation produced by selected university theologians which constitute the legal basis for the King's decision to press ahead with the divorce. The abandonment of both the humanist predilection for precedent and the Catholic deference to authority (as well as Henry's rejection of Katherine's direct appeal to the Pope for judgment [2.2.117]) in favor of theological wranglings here inevitably results in a rewriting of the past: the marriage that was first deemed politically desirable, legal, and holy turns out to be really politically dangerous, illegal, and incestuous.

Buckingham's conviction, then, is based on tainted testimony and the Queen's removal is facilitated by acts of legal and historical innovation. The fall of Thomas Wolsey, however, requires neither the unscrupulous handling of evidence, nor the creation of it. In fact, the removal of Wolsey calls for only the most minimal participation by King or state authority because the Cardinal himself has committed to paper an incriminating chronicle of his doings: an inventory of his inordinate wealth (which extends beyond "possession of a subject"), and a piece of correspondence in his hand "writ to th' Pope against the king" (3.2.124, 287). These documents come into the King's possession and initiate a process of law against the Cardinal that differs greatly from the proceedings conducted against Buckingham and Katherine. The King's use of these written artifacts invokes an antiquarian approach to the past. Antiquarians typically set themselves the task of describing the physical remains (documents, monuments, coins, and other artifacts) of former times. Unlike Renaissance humanist historians, they were unwilling, or at best reluctant, to engage in the writing of narrative history. If it was the humanist's fundamental aim to proclaim history's utility as a pedagogical tool, it was the antiquarian's primary purpose to resuscitate and preserve the past in order to learn about the past itself, not about its relevance to the present. Hence, when an antiquarian like William Camden did try his hand at something that resembles a narrative—"an Historical Account of the first Beginnings of the Reign of Queen Elizabeth" (Camden 3)—he provoked Wallace T. MacCaffrey to charge him with exercising too much interpretive restraint. Camden's

> book is conceived as a monument to the achievement of Queen Elizabeth and her government. This purpose he seeks to accomplish not by praising her merits but, more obliquely, more delicately, by laying out the record of her reign. To him that record is self-evident; its very recital will command the admiration of the world and posterity. What Camden did not quite grasp is that the record by itself, unadorned by interpretation or examination, is intellectually unassimilable by his readers. The relentless flow of historical facts informs their minds without illuminating their understanding.
>
> (MacCaffrey xxxi)

Aside from the value judgment implied in this passage, it is undeniable that Camden's history, and the fruits of antiquarian scholarship in general, were no feast for those nourished themselves on the more user-friendly narratives of Hall, Grafton, Holinshed, and others. What is of concern here, however, is the interpretive temperance attributed to Camden, a temperance which marks the essential character—at least in theory—of the antiquarian enterprise.

Henry's handling of the Wolsey documents emulates, at least in its external manifestations, Camden's interpretive forbearance motivated by the desire to let the artifact *speak for itself*. Henry never directly accuses Wolsey of any misdoings. He interrogates him about his loyalty, duty, and holiness, but never asserts his guilt. Instead, when the Cardinal (who does not know his papers have been intercepted) professes his undying loyalty, the King merely hands him the inculpating documents and leaves. In an emotional soliloquy, it is Wolsey *himself* who reads the papers and declares his own guilt and fall from glory. In the context given, the evidence speaks for itself. However, the playwrights undercut the antiquarian approach at the very same time that they allow Henry to employ it triumphantly. Peter Rudnytsky shrewdly observes that even though the matter of the "crossed letters" derives from Holinshed, it pertains there *not* to Wolsey but to Thomas Ruthall, Henry VII's Bishop of Durham (Rudnytsky 49). Moreover, the case against Wolsey, which, if we limit our consideration to the documents themselves, appears just, is equivocal at its very core. The Cardinal's post-dismissal repentance and regeneration have led many commentators to put a positive spin on his fate by viewing his rise and fall in terms of the *de casibus* genre, but if we consider that Henry may well be turning against Wolsey not because of his indiscretions in general—the King was apparently not all that distressed over the taxation measures—but for a particular indiscretion: opposing the divorce—then we have to abandon a morality-play version of history.

In the proceedings against Wolsey, Katherine, and Buckingham, then, we have three different legal and historiographical approaches to the recovery of past events. And while it may be tempting to compare these approaches qualitatively and rank them according to their capacity to produce truth or justice, it is important to note that they all hold equal purchase in the Henrician state. Shakespeare and Fletcher do not seem interested in valorizing any particular approach. Indeed, Shakespeare and Fletcher arrange their materials so that it is impossible to tell if any of these trials is held to yield truth or justice, or if they merely serve ulterior motives. Yet judgments are doled out, heads roll, and a Queen abdicates.

Despite the antiquarian restraint that marks the Wolsey episode, elusive providence is invoked to explain the inexplicable (as it was in the trials of Buckingham and Katherine). Commenting on the King's discovery of Wolsey's treasonous papers, the Duke of Norfolk asserts that "It's heaven's will; / Some spirit put this paper in the packet / To bless your eye withal" (3.2.128-30). Wolsey first attributes the situation to "negligence," and, subsequently, to a "cross devil" (213-14). The juxtaposition of heavenly "spirit" with "devil" simply demonstrates two ways in which differently motivated characters can construe an act indifferent, an instance of apparent "negligence."

Throughout the play there are speeches suggesting that God withholds from Henry insight into Wolsey's ways, but the Cardinal's stratagems (the arrest of Buckingham just as the Duke is about to apprise the King of Wolsey's intrigues [1.1.190-202] and his ability to control Henry with the "witchcraft" of his tongue [3.2.15-19]) can just as easily and more revealingly be called on to account for Henry's inaction. Moreover, Henry's first detection of Wolsey's "contrary proceedings" is hardly suggestive of a moment in which God lifts a veil from his eyes. Shakespeare and Fletcher do not give the slightest indication that Henry's new awareness is occasioned by a divine stirring. It simply occurs at the close of the trial of the Queen, when Campeius's refusal to pass sentence after the Queen leaves the court leads Henry's political acumen to conclude that "These cardinals trifle with me" (2.4.234).

In all three legal cases, then, providence is invoked, but its invocation inevitably signals a moment of human powerlessness, an instance in which the players lose control over the circumstances of their situation. Buckingham acknowledges providence because he conceives of his fate as imminent and certain. Neither

his innocence (if he is innocent) nor his reason or rhetoric can help him escape Wolsey's net; therefore it *must* be God's will. Likewise the nobles wait patiently for the moment that God lifts the veil from Henry's eyes (2.2.41-43). They see themselves as impotent in the matter. Henry evokes providence to explain why he does not have a male heir, a situation over which he perceives himself as powerless as long as he is married to Katherine. At a loss for a substantial case against his wife, he also appropriates providence as a cause why the divorce must become a reality.

In its exploration of various historiographies active in the legitimation process, *Henry VIII* (in the scenes discussed so far) treats providence either as another tool (in Henry's case) in the political process, or as an ultimate but untraceable metaphysical sign to which characters appeal when they are threatened with marginalization to or elimination from the legitimation process. Buckingham, Katherine, and Wolsey all resist, but their "resistance is never in a position of exteriority in relation to power" (Foucault 95). For them, providence comes to mean something very similar to Foucault's "power." They acquiesce in the realization that the "multiplicity of force relations immanent in the sphere in which they operate" constitutes "their own [inscrutable] organization" (92). They experience these relations as "intentional" but also as "nonsubjective" (94); that is, they do not consider them to be random, but the ultimate inscrutability of God's intention also makes them nonsubjective (in the sense that they do not originate from a knowable subject). Hence, they perceive that "power is [never] exercised without a series of aims and objectives"; yet their surrender to state authority, coupled with a continued dedication to the King, discloses a recognition that the operations of power finally do not result "from the choice or decision of an individual subject" (95), that is, the King's person. Foucault writes that "if it is true that Machiavelli was among the few . . . who conceived the power of the Prince in terms of force relationships, perhaps we need to go one step further, do without the persona of the Prince, and decipher power mechanisms on the basis of a strategy that is immanent in force relationships" (97). Shakespeare and Fletcher, it seems, beat Foucault to it.

III. Historiography and Royal Legitimacy

Judith H. Anderson astutely observes that "looking back from Cranmer's vision to the rest of the play, even in the absence of an intentional signal from the playwright[s], we should have difficulty not wondering whether so nice a vision is not merely rhetorical" (153). At the christening of the infant Elizabeth, Archbishop Cranmer's exalted historical vision of a Golden Age to come is plainly intended to erase the historiographical eclecticism and the inscrutability of history itself that the play has given voice to up until that point. As behooves the king's impromptu historian, the divinely inspired Cranmer presumably affords special insight into the "deep structures" of history by suggesting that while certain historical moments and figures may fade, essential patterns and attitudes remain (see Kastan 137). He craftily links James I to Henry VIII and Elizabeth I through the image of the phoenix, declaring that when "The bird of wonder dies, the maiden phoenix, / Her ashes new create another heir / As great in admiration as herself" (5.4.40-42). The image certainly constitutes a potent compliment to James, not in the least because it designates him the heir not merely of the Queen's crown but also of her "peace, plenty, love, truth, [and] terror" (46). But if we listen closely to the churchman we notice that even in the speech that most eloquently invokes a providential view of Tudor-Stuart legitimacy and continuity (5.4.14-55), the controlling metaphor employed—that of the phoenix—undermines the very genealogy it is meant to reinforce.

The editor of the Arden edition of *Henry VIII* notes that the phoenix is "a common image of the royal succession" (Foakes 175-76n). And so it is, but it is vital to note that the phoenix's power to identify the identity of any particular monarch is wholly retroactive or historical and not predictive or prophetic. The coronation behind, the image of the bird that rises from its own ashes bolsters the authority of the new ruler as the one who replaces the deceased one in the never-dying office of the monarch. But the image of the phoenix can never identify the new ruler *before* he or she has ascended to the throne, not even if the person is designated by law and blood to inherit the crown. The natural body and the corporate body do not merge until *after* the coronation. The phoenix image denotes an abstraction, a quality, "the Dignity" of the monarch as monarch, and "the singularity of the royal office" (Kantorowicz 384); it is simply not designed to select any particular individual to become king or queen. Yet Cranmer's speech, spoken in 1533 (in historical time), is clearly meant to be prophetic. Therefore, insofar as the phoenix refers to "the Dignity," it is incapable of designating a natural body for the office and thus of adding any legitimacy to the individual who will possess the crown in the future to which Cranmer alludes (that is, the Jacobean present).

Such added legitimacy might have been welcome because even James I, at least in his own mind, was not completely secure in his right to the crown of England. His harsh treatment of Arabella Stuart and William Seymour, who married in 1610 without the king's blessing, is a telling instance of James's insecurity. Arabella Stuart, S. R. Gardiner points out, was "also descended from Margaret, the sister of Henry VIII, [and] had a better title, as she had been born in England, whereas James had been born in Scotland. It

was a maxim of the English law . . . that no alien court inherit land in England. If, therefore, James was incapable of inheriting an acre of land south of the Tweed, he was still more incapable of inheriting the whole realm" (Gardiner 79). Seymour was a direct descendant of the Suffolk line to which Henry VIII had bequeathed the crown of England in the event his own offspring—Edward, Mary, and Elizabeth—died without a successor. Since none of Henry's children's children survived after March 24, 1603, the union of Arabella and Seymour consolidated a claim of blood and one of law to the throne of England. James forbade the marriage, and when it came out that the young lovers, though apparently without political ambitions, had married anyway, Arabella was taken into custody and Seymour was sent to the Tower (Gardiner 117).

Therefore, had they wished to do so, Fletcher and Shakespeare could have emphasized James's blood connection to Elizabeth Tudor (Henry VIII's sister Margaret was James's great-grandmother). Even though that blood connection was the very reason that Henry's will (made statute by parliament) barred the Stuart line from the throne of England, mentioning it would have given a sense of the rightness and inevitability of James's reign that the image of the phoenix lacks. Instead, the playwrights have Cranmer make a different, highly controversial genealogical move.

Rather than acknowledging the troublesome blood tie through Margaret Tudor, Cranmer exploits the phoenix as "the image of asexual procreation" (Noling 305) to insinuate a mother-son bond between Elizabeth and James. When the queen dies, the phoenix dies, and from *its* ashes—i.e., not from the queen's—another monarch mysteriously emerges to take her place. In this representational scheme, the reproductive function belongs to the phoenix. Cranmer's deployment of the phoenix image abandons the customary figure of metaphor (which allows for the body politic and body natural to be recognized as distinct even while they are mysteriously one) for the figure of simile. The effect of this rhetorical move is subtle but significant. Cranmer says: "Nor shall this peace sleep with her [Elizabeth]; but, *as* when / The bird of wonder dies, the maiden phoenix, / Her ashes new create another heir / As great in admiration as herself" (5.4.39-42; emphasis added). The choice of simile over metaphor changes the relation between the body natural and the body politic from *identification* to one of *likeness*. In the case of metaphor, two entities temporarily coexist in unity, but in the similetic instance certain traits from one entity (the phoenix) are *transferred* to the other entity (the Queen). In this particular example, then, Cranmer transfers the reproductive function of the phoenix to the body natural of the Queen. It is not the phoenix that creates itself anew, but the Queen who *like* the phoenix from "Her ashes new create another heir." Cranmer's linguistic sleight of hand implies that Elizabeth will give birth to James, which is of course quite ironic, since Elizabeth chose to remain single and childless, but also strangely appropriate because so many of her subjects longed for her to marry and produce an heir and stabilize the succession. Cranmer's provocative move may appeal to an audience's wishful memories and lingering regrets over Elizabeth's denial of their wish.

Perhaps a Jacobean audience may not have grasped the intricacies of Cranmer's maneuver, but its general sense—the intimate association between Elizabeth and James—must have been obvious. Some members of the audience may well have been swayed by the speech, but anyone not caught up in the moment Cranmer is trying to create could instantly recognize how it grossly distorts even the most basic understanding of English royal genealogy.

More blatantly damning to Cranmer's efforts to blend Tudor ideology and providence into a unified and compelling whole may be the *type* or *genre* of his historiographical speech. Given that *Henry VIII* draws heavily on historical sources, sometimes simply versifying Holinshed, it may be somewhat alarming to realize that Cranmer's all-important prophecy does not have a historical source. The speech is entirely made up. There are of course many instances in the play where Shakespeare and Fletcher introduce materials for which we have no source, but Cranmer's speech deserves special attention because, by offering its Jacobean audience a summary representation of the previous eighty years, it draws attention to itself *as a* historiographical representation. To present a fictional speech as history is not necessarily to overstep the legitimate bounds of Renaissance historical representation, but this particular manifestation, we will see, turns out to be suspect.

Driven by a desire to educate their readers, early humanist historiographers studiously imitated the propensity of ancient historians to invent speeches where they felt this was appropriate. Relying on classical precedent, they believed that

> The instructional value of history should be increased not only by the exposition of motives but also by the rhetorical manipulation of material in order to emphasize those elements which have the greatest moral or political significance. The most important rhetorical device is the set speech, which gives intensity to the narrative, and so produces a greater effect upon the reader. Long and important speeches should be constructed according to the rules of ancient oratory. Whenever possible, they should be based on factual evidence, but it is permissible to invent them so long as they are probable, are appropriate to the situation and to the character of the speaker,

or reproduce the supposed essence of actual speeches. They should normally be introduced only into crucial situations and attributed only to eminent personages. They may serve as dramatic vehicles for the historian's exposition of his character's motives, or, indirectly, for his judgment and opinions. (Leonard Dean 4)

Without a doubt, Cranmer's prophecy is such a set speech. In its prophetic mode, his oration hits stock Tudor and Stuart themes—political and religious—and draws freely on both traditional pastoral imagery, biblical allusions, and the religious imagery associated with the Cult of Elizabeth (Roy Strong draws directly on Cranmer's speech in the opening pages of his *The Cult of Elizabeth* [15]). Cranmer's brand of history, therefore, although it strictly speaking belonged to an earlier period, would be recognized *as* historical by a Jacobean audience. And if Shakespeare and Fletcher had opted to shape their play about the reign of Henry VIII wholly in accordance with these early humanist historiographical principles, there would be cause to join with those critics who exalt Cranmer as Shakespeare and Fletcher's official historian.

To embrace any one historiography as true, however, would require us to ignore the competition for privileged historical representation the play dramatizes. Moreover, adopting Cranmer's vision of history means empowering a version of the past that is too simple and omits too much. The Archbishop's Tudor-Stuart genealogy fails to stand up under even the most basic scrutiny. His history pictures an uninterrupted connection between Henry, Elizabeth, and James, tacitly posits Henry's actions leading to the birth of Elizabeth as the original impulse of the Reformation, and links them gracefully to the Jacobean Church of England. His seamless genealogy is silent about the reigns of both Catholic Mary (1553-1558) and Edward VI (1547-1553), nor does it mention that the historical Henry VIII (who declares his daughter's birthday a "Holy-day" [5.4.76]) was to execute her mother and declare Elizabeth a bastard, legally barring her from the succession—all in pursuit of the elusive male heir. The latter events do not take place within the historical parameters of the play, but Shakespeare and Fletcher do allow Katherine a poignant deathbed petition to Henry on behalf of their daughter Mary. She commends, she says, to "his goodness / The model of our chaste loves, his young daughter / (The dews of heaven fall thick in blessings on her)" (4.2.131-33). The mere acknowledgment of Mary's existence challenges the ideological and genealogical continuity of Cranmer's pro-James historiography. But the ultimate irony is of course that Cranmer himself, as everybody knew from Foxe's fantastically popular *Acts and Monuments,* was burned at the stake by Bloody Mary for his heretical Protestant beliefs. The Archbishop's history of England erases his own tragic death.

Another reason not to valorize Cranmer's providential model of history is that, although early humanist historiography still enjoyed some credibility, a number of its essential characteristics had fallen largely in disrepute in the playwrights' day. Despite historiography's erratic development, historians like Francis Bacon, John Selden, William Camden and others became increasingly sophisticated in their methods precisely by bracketing questions of divine truth from historical inquiry, not because they did not value them, but because they considered them neither appropriate nor especially helpful to the fields of human, civil, and political history. The liberal usage of invented speeches had come under constant attack from all but the most old-fashioned historians. In Heywood's translation of the *Method,* Jean Bodin finds fault with "many Historiographers, who in the midst of their discourses, fall off from their entended Narrations, to play Orators or Rhetoritians, so deluding the expectations, and confounding the memories of their readers" (16). Even earlier, in 1574, Thomas Blundeville had published his translation of the Italian treatise on history by Francisco Patrocio and Accontio Tridentio. It is the historiographer's office, Blundeville translates, "to tell things as they were done without either augmenting or diminishing them, or swaruing one iote from the truth. Whereby it appeareth that the hystoriographers ought not to fayne anye Orations nor any other thing, but truely to reporte euery such speach, and deede, euen as it was spoken or done" (Blundeville 164). Similar quotations can be drawn from antiquarians like Camden or even from popular historians like Holinshed and Grafton.

Notwithstanding these various challenges to Cranmer's brand of historiography, *Henry VIII* never rejects the possible existence or power of providence. Nor, however, does it illustrate or exalt that power, or even show a definite instance of its involvement in human history. In a perverse way, providence—the ultimate truth of Christian history—becomes as abstract and remote a concept as Foucault's idea of power, which is so inscrutable that it has to be defined only in terms of its effects or in terms of what it is *not*. Shakespeare and Fletcher are not interested in the origins of power or the meaning of God's providence. Their conception of history is not one that calls for a justification of God's ways to humanity. On the contrary, in *Henry VIII,* when a character turns to providence it is always to escape a particular conception of history that seems suddenly to have been rendered futile and powerless or simply inconvenient. Nonetheless, Shakespeare and Fletcher do not appear to promote a nihilistic view of life; the play never indicates that there is no "actual" history that exists behind or beyond linguistic representation—just that that history is not accessible. In *Henry VIII,* they explore how the *manipulations* of historical discourses, and the nearly inscrutable complex of motives and forces that drives those manipulations, can bring characters to just such

a moment in which they feel only the unknown can account for (though not explain) particular historical circumstances. And since providential history by definition extends to the end of human history, it is significant that it manifests no prophetic power in *Henry VIII.* Cranmer divines the future but, even aside from his historical errors, he is in fact rewriting history for a Jacobean audience. Providence becomes history—ideological history—after the fact, and subsequently takes on a life of its own.

This does not make *Henry VIII* a subversive text in the ordinary sense. The play is not overtly embroiled in specific political controversies of its day (but see Hamilton 163-90), but this hardly makes it an apolitical text. It eschews micropolitics for a more profound and far-reaching consideration of the relationship between political authority and historiography. The theatrical appropriation of historiographical practices and their simulation on stage constituted a potential, if not actual, threat to any party or individual intent on accruing power on the basis of historical argumentation. Shakespeare and Fletcher's drama, for all its complexity, must have had a general demystifying effect. As such, *Henry VIII* must be considered not a flawed imitation of an Elizabethan genre but a uniquely Jacobean response to and enactment of the complex historiographical discourses of its own historical moment.

Note

[1] I follow the Oxford edition in assuming that Shakespeare and Fletcher share the play's authorship (Wells et al.). And I follow Frances Yates in maintaining that Fletcher and Shakespeare would have seen "eye to eye" on "the general approach to historical and contemporary problems in *Henry VIII*" (67). What is more, I share Yates's conviction "that it is not a matter of great importance whether the whole play is actually written by Shakespeare or whether part of it is written by Fletcher." Whether the play—a play about disunified history—is the result of harmonious collaboration or of cross purposes, a Jacobean audience would be presented with the play as it is, not with authorial intention(s).

Works Cited

Anderson, Judith H. *Biographical Truth: The Representation of Historical Persons in Tudor-Stuart Writing.* New Haven: Yale UP, 1984.

Barker, Francis, and Peter Hulme. "'Nymphs and reapers heavily vanish': The Discursive Con-texts of *The Tempest.*" *Alternative Shakespeares.* Ed. John Drakakis. New York: Methuen, 1985. 191-205.

Blundeville, Thomas. *The true order and Methode of wryting and reading Hystories.* Ed. Hugh G. Dick. *Huntington Library Quarterly* 2 (1940): 149-170.

Bodin, Jean. "Of Choice of History, by Way of Preface." Thomas Heywood's translation of Sallust, *The Conspiracy of Cataline* and *The War of Jugurtha* (1608). Trans. Thomas Heywood. New York: Knopf, 1924.

Camden, William. *The History of the Most Renowned and Victorious Princess Elizabeth, Late Queen of England* (1615). Ed. Wallace T. MacCaffrey. Chicago: U of Chicago P, 1970.

Candido, Joseph. "Fashioning Henry VIII: What Shakespeare Saw in *When You See Me, You Know Me.*" *Cahiers Elisabéthains* 23 (1983): 47-59.

Cespedes, Frank. V. "'We are one in fortunes': The Sense of History in *Henry VIII.*" *English Literary Renaissance* 10 (1980): 413-38

Dean, Leonard E *Tudor Theories of History Writing. Contributions in Modern Philology.* No. 1. Ann Arbor: U of Michigan P, 1947.

Dean, Paul. "Dramatic Mode and Historical Vision in *Henry VIII.*" *Shakespeare Quarterly* 37 (1986): 175-89

Ferguson, Arthur B. *Clio Unbound: Perception of the Social and Cultural Past in Renaissance England.* Durham: Duke UP, 1979.

Foucault, Michel. *The History of Sexuality: An Introduction.* Trans. Robert Hurley. New York: Vintage, 1980.

Foxe, John. *The Acts and Monuments.* Ed. M. Hobart Seymour. New York: Robert Carter and Brothers, 1856.

Gardiner, S. R. *History of England from the Accession of James I to the Outbreak of the Civil War 1603-1642.* Vol. I. New York: AMS P, 1965.

Halpern, Richard. *The Poetics of Primitive Accumulation: English Renaissance Culture and the Genealogy of Capital.* Ithaca: Cornell UP, 1991.

Hamilton, Donna B. *Shakespeare and the Politics of Protestant England.* Lexington: U of Kentucky P, 1992.

Holinshed, Raphael. "Preface to the Reader." *Chronicles of England, Scotland and Ireland.* Vol. 2. London, 1808. Unpaginated.

———. *Chronicles of England, Scotland and Ireland.* Vol. 3. London, 1808.

James I. *The Trew Law of Free Monarchies. The Political Works of James I.* Ed. Charles McIlwain. Cambridge: Harvard UP, 1918.

Kamps, Ivo. *Historiography and Ideology in Stuart Drama.* Cambridge: Cambridge UP, 1996.

Kantorowicz, Ernst H. *The King's Two Bodies: A Study in Medieval Political Theology.* Princeton: Princeton UP, 1981.

Kastan, David Scott. *Shakespeare and the Shapes of Time.* Hanover, NH: UP of New England, 1982.

Kernan, Alvin B. "From Ritual to History: the English History Plays." *The Revels History of Drama in English.* Vol. 3. London: Methuen, 1975. 262-99.

MacCaffrey, Wallace T. Introduction. Camden xi-xxxix.

Noling, Kim H. "Grubbing Up the Stock: Dramatizing Queens in *Henry VIII.*" *Shakespeare Quarterly* 39 (1988): 291-306.

Patterson, Annabel. *Censorship and Interpretation: The Conditions of Writing and Reading in Early Modern England.* Madison: U of Wisconsin P, 1984.

Pocock, J. G. A. *The Ancient Constitution and the Feudal Law: A Study of English Historical Thought in the Seventeenth Century.* Cambridge: Cambridge UP, 1987 [reissue].

Puttenham, George. *The Arte of English Poesie.* 1589. Ed. Edward Arber. Kent, OH: Kent State UP, 1970.

Rackin, Phyllis. *Stages of History: Shakespeare's English Chronicles.* Ithaca: Cornell UP, 1990.

Ribner, Irving. *The English History Play in the Age of Shakespeare.* Princeton: Princeton UP, 1957.

Ridley, Jasper. *Henry VIII: The Politics of Tyranny.* New York: Fromm, 1986.

Rudnytsky, Peter L. "*Henry VIII* and the Deconstruction of History." *Shakespeare Survey* 43 (1991): 43-57.

Shakespeare, William, and John Fletcher. *King Henry VIII.* Arden edition. Ed. R. A. Foakes. London: Methuen, 1968.

Stephenson, Carl, and Frederick George Marcham, eds. and trans. *History: A Selection of Documents from A.D. 600 to the Interregnum.* Vol. 1. New York: Harper and Row, 1972.

Strong, Roy. *The Cult of Elizabeth.* Berkeley and Los Angeles: U of California P, 1977.

Tennenhouse, Leonard. "Strategies of State and Political Plays: *A Midsummer Night's Dream, Henry IV, Henry V, Henry VIII.*" *Political Shakespeare: New*

Essays in Cultural Materialism. Ed. Jonathan Dollimore and Alan Sinfield. Ithaca: Cornell UP, 1985. 109-28.

Wells, Stanley, Gary Taylor, John Jowett, and William Montgomery, eds. *William Shakespeare: The Complete Works.* Oxford: Clarendon P, 1986.

Wikander, Matthew H. *The Play of Truth and State: Historical Drama from Shakespeare to Brecht.* Baltimore: Johns Hopkins UP, 1986.

Woolf, D. R. *The Idea of History in Early Stuart England: Erudition, Ideology, and "The Light of Truth" from the Accession of James I to the Civil War.* Toronto: U of Toronto P, 1990.

Yates, Frances. *Shakespeare's Last Plays: A New Approach.* London: Routledge & Kegan Paul, 1975.

Source: "Possible Pasts: Historiography and Legitimation in *Henry VIII*," in *College English,* Vol. 58, No. 2, February, 1996, pp. 192-215.

Rethinking Gender and Genre in the History Play

Martha A. Kurtz, *Southampton College of Long Island University*

Two concepts that have exercised considerable influence over criticism of Elizabethan drama in the past fifteen years are what might be called the hegemony of genre—that is, the idea that the ideological content of a play is predetermined and controlled by the dramatic genre to which the play seems to belong—and the Lacanian dualistic theory of gender in which masculine and feminine are seen as discrete and oppositional identities, the boundaries of which are never blurred and which can never overlap or unite. These two assumptions coalesce in the frequently reiterated premise that the history play as a genre is fundamentally antagonistic to women and the "feminine":

> The myth of the history plays involves fathers and sons. It does not involve mothers, daughters, or wives.

> Antagonists and consorts, queens and queans, witches and saints: women play almost every conceivable role on Shakespeare's historical stage. But there is one role that no woman can play, that of the hero. Aliens in the masculine world of history, women can threaten or validate the men's historical projects, but they can never take the center of history's stage or become the subjects of its stories.

> In the man's world of the history play, the only power the woman can wield is her power to dismay through verbal abuse . . . The curse of the scold is feared almost as much as the drubbing she supposedly administers to her unfortunate man . . . but it achieves nothing.

> Tudor history was not simply written without women; it was also written *against* them. Patriarchal history is designed to construct a verbal substitute for the visible physical connection between a mother and her children, to authenticate the . . . relationships between fathers and sons, and to suppress and supplant the role of the mother.

> The feminine offers too powerful a challenge to the idea of history itself for Shakespeare to deal with it in the history plays. The Otherness of the feminine challenges the ethos of power and conquest through aggression; history as a genre must ultimately base itself on that ethos, no matter how it also criticizes it. If we lose interest in the military-political adventure we have lost interest in history itself as a genre.[1]

An extension of a patriarchal Tudor historiography, the history play is seen by these writers as inherently a "men's world" in which women are the naturally feared and opposing Other whom the genre must minimalize, weaken, and exclude in order to maintain its own generic identity. The domain of the "masculine" is the public life that becomes documented history; its ethos is "power and conquest through aggression." The domain of the "feminine," it is implied, is the opposite of this—the private life that is never documented, the ethos that, whether it renounces aggression or pursues it in distinctively "feminine" ways (deception, manipulation, verbal abuse), is ultimately powerless.

We should be cautious about arguments that make such sweeping claims. "Masculine" and "feminine" are notoriously slippery terms, which are more apt to show the qualities that a particular culture in a particular historical moment assigns to men and women than any unchanging truths about gender, and which reduce the complexities of real men and women to gross oversimplifications. To define the "masculine" as an "ethos of power and . . . aggression" implies that no gentler qualities properly belong to men; if to be "feminine" is to be passive, powerless, and overlooked, then women can never appropriately be powerful or important. Linda Bamber, Phyllis Rackin, and Lisa Jardine are not, of course, speaking about masculinity and femininity in general, but as they are seen in the characters and situations of Elizabethan history plays. We may wonder, however, whether a genre that includes plays as diverse as the *Henry VI* trio and *Sir Thomas More, 1 Henry IV,* and *Woodstock,* is likely to show one point of view about anything, even gender.

There may be some basis for a theory of generic determinism in the case of comedy or tragedy, which by the sixteenth century had a long history of precedents and a few established conventions that undoubtedly did influence the audiences' expectations and the writers' products. The history play, on the other hand, was an invention of the last twenty years of Elizabeth's reign. The playwrights were making it up as they went along; it is difficult to see how they could have been constrained by a genre that they were in the process of creating.[2] Printed histories like Holinshed's chronicle or Foxe's *Acts and Monuments* obviously contributed greatly to the dramatic product, but, in addition to the fact that different chroniclers have demonstrably different biases, we need to remember that many aspects of popular culture also helped to shape most of the so-called "chronicle histories," as undoubtedly did the different personalities, backgrounds, and interests of the individual playwrights. While some history plays may well be based on a patriarchal ethos that marginalizes or demonizes women, it does not follow that such an ethos is the foundation of the genre as a whole.

It is easy, of course, to see where the idea of a generic opposition to women in the history plays has come from. There are few women characters in any of the best-known plays, and even fewer who exercise any kind of political power. Hotspur's Kate seems paradigmatic: her anxious questions left unanswered, her love brushed aside like a child's toy ("Away, you trifler! Love! I love thee not, / I care not for thee, Kate; this is no world / To play with mammets, and to tilt with lips"), she cannot be told where her husband is going or even where he expects her to go, and she is asked to be "content" with a course of events that soon leaves her a grieving widow (1 Henry IV II.iii.91-3, 118).[3] She is not alone. In Richard II, Richard's queen learns of the most important event in her life from a household servant, the gardener—and can only weep and curse helplessly in response, unable to do anything to change the course of events that will lead to her widowhood and exile. She cannot even confront the source of her misery directly, but must take her anger out on the gardener and his plants.[4] Almost equally helpless are the trio of women in Richard III, who lament the husbands and children they have lost to Richard's sinister power, and the French princess Katherine in Henry V, who must marry "as it shall please de roi mon père" and the conquering English king (V.ii.261).[5] There are a few women in Shakespeare's early histories who take action in an attempt to control their own lives, but, as a number of studies have pointed out, they are ultimately defeated and demonized.[6] Joan of Arc and Margaret of Anjou lead men in battle, but Joan is exposed as a whore and burned at the stake, while Margaret becomes first the "tiger's heart wrapp'd in a woman's hide" who commits the most memorable atrocities in a play remembered primarily for its bloodshed and horror, and then the half-mad harridan who haunts the halls of power in Richard III, with no power left of her own except the one she shares with Hotspur's Kate and Richard II's queen—the power to curse (3 Henry VI I.iv.137).[7] However strong such women as Joan or Margaret may be for a time, they are ultimately punished for their audacity in exercising power by being reduced to helpless grotesques who are rejected by the masculine forces of their own dramatic world and by the audience.

Or so the argument goes. Yet, important as it is to recognize the ways in which these women characters are deprived of political power, we should not forget the theatrical effect created by a few women on a stage crowded with men: their gender, highlighted by their costumes, sets them apart and draws a particularly intense attention to everything they say and do, giving them a theatrical power that goes considerably beyond the number of lines they speak or the political power they are able to exercise in their fictional worlds. Kate's role in Henry IV and Isobel's in Richard II are not insignificant simply because the parts are small. Shakespeare seems to go out of his way to emphasize the plight of these helpless women: confined to, but not sheltered by, their domestic existence, they emblematize the suffering that public action often inflicts on private lives. If this is not as gratifying today as portrayals of strong, successful women would be, it nevertheless has the effect of making the women a kind of moral touchstone in the plays. We may be interested in the war and politics that dominate the action, but we cannot fully approve of them when Kate and Isobel are standing by to remind us of the senseless suffering these masculine activities create.[8] In productions of Richard III the women—particularly Margaret—are riveting. Their language is almost hypnotic in its intensity and, with the possible exception of the weak-willed Anne, they clearly have the moral high ground. They are the only ones who see Richard as we see him and say what we want to hear said about him, and they, not Richmond, provide a focal point for the audience's sympathies throughout the play. In the end, of course, they are justified and Richard is defeated.[9] In the Henry VI plays Margaret can be seen as a different kind of critique of the values of the masculine world of war: what is horrifying in men is more vividly horrifying in her because it is unexpected. We can see the nightmare violence for what it is more clearly in a woman than in a man because we are less accustomed to it there, the way a cigarette looks more shocking in a child's mouth than an adult's.[10] Joan's leveling cynicism about the heroics of war has much the same popular appeal as Falstaff's, and if she is satirized and demonized in the last act, the audience will not necessarily forget all that has gone before.[11] Each of these women is different in character and social position from the others, but each exercises considerable theatrical power on the audience, and each implies a criticism of the masculine characters and their struggles for political power and conquest.

These are the women in the best-known histories.[12] If, as I am arguing, we need to approach the history plays with fewer preformed notions about patriarchal history and the unbending determinism of genre and gender, and more openness to the plays' theatricality and the power that the women in them may exercise on the plays' audiences, we also need to expand our definition of the genre to include plays other than those by Shakespeare. There are many to choose from; in the space that remains I will look at two, Woodstock and Sir Thomas More, each of which complicates in different ways the simple ideas about gender so often attributed to the history plays.

It would be hard to find a more conventionally "feminine" woman than *Woodstock's* Queen Anne. She is beautiful, tactful, kind, and good. When Richard marries her in the first act, she pleases everyone by her delight in England and her desire to become English ("[L]et me be englishèd: / They best shall please me shall me English call" [I.iii.48-9]).[13] She spends her time sewing garments to give to the poor (II.iii). She not only rides sidesaddle herself, she is responsible for introducing that "feminine" approach to exercise to other English ladies, thus—the play's hero declares—teaching them "womanhood" (I.iii.53-61). She is called "virtuous" so often that it begins to sound like another name.

Like Shakespeare's Kate or Isobel she has relatively little to say—about eighty lines—and she spends much of her time in distress: over her husband's bad relationship with his uncles, his extravagance, the condition of the kingdom's poor, and so on. Midway through the play she dies. Yet she is an important character. Her femininity, far from being marginalized or discredited, is treated by the play's central character, Woodstock, as a potentially powerful force for good. He is delighted that she has taught ladies to be more feminine by riding sidesaddle, but it is not only women whom he hopes she will influence. "Afore my God," he declares to his brothers on the king's wedding day,

> I have good hope this happy marriage,
>   brothers,
> Of this so noble and religious princess
> Will mildly calm his headstrong youth, to
>   see
> And shun those stains that blur his majesty.
>
> (I.i.183-7)

Richard's "headstrong" ways include extortion, reckless expenditure, and, ultimately, kidnapping and murder. In a world in which the character of one man could mean the difference between life and death for his subjects, a woman's ability to influence her husband takes on political as well as private significance.

Richard, unfortunately, proves to be hard to "calm." Although he is always affectionate to his wife, he continues to raise taxes to feed his extravagant personal tastes, which include huge feasts and expensive new clothes. Anne, meanwhile, is shown with the ladies of her court packing up "shirts and bands and other linen"—some of it sewn by the queen herself—to send to the poor, and we learn that she has sold her jewels and plate to help relieve the suffering caused by her husband's taxation (II.iii.1.s.d.; 21-3). Her "housewifery" and charity are highly praised by everyone who hears of them, and pose an obviously desirable alter-

native to the insensitivity and selfishness of the king (II.iii.63). They are also politically powerful. When she is dying, later in the play, Woodstock laments the probable results:

> Her charity hath stayed the Commons' rage
> That would ere this have shaken Richard's
>   chair
> Or set all England on a burning fire.
> And—'fore my God—I fear, when she is
>   gone
> This woeful land will all to ruin run.
>
> (IV.ii.58-62)

While this popular uprising never occurs, Woodstock's fear of it is a measure of the importance he attaches to Anne's popularity. In the end we find that her influence extends even to the king. Despite his selfishness and cruelty he is so devastated by his wife's death that he suddenly repents of having ordered Woodstock's murder and tries, though unsuccessfully, to have it stopped. With typical extravagance, he orders the house where Anne died to be pulled down:

> Down with this house of Sheen, go ruin all!
> Pull down her buildings, let her turrets
>   fall:
> For ever lay it waste and desolate
> That English king may never here keep
>   court,
> But to all ages leave a sad report,
> When men shall see these ruined walls of
>   Sheen
> And sighing say, Here died King Richard's
>   queen.
>
> (IV.iii.157-63)

Like the rebellion Woodstock fears, the ruined palace suggests the importance of Anne to the survival of the kingdom.

Anne's goodness, particularly in the emblematic scene with the shirts and linen, clearly establishes the positive values of the play as something we might call "feminine." They are not associated exclusively with women, however. Anne's concern for the poor and her willingness to sacrifice her jewels to help them is matched by her great ally throughout the play, Woodstock, who is called "Plain Thomas" in acknowledgment not only of his blunt speech, but also of his preference for frieze coats and plain hose. When pressed by his brothers, he agrees to put on richer clothes for Richard's wedding day and astonishes his nephew by his "golden metamorphosis / From homespun housewifry"; the last word links Woodstock with women in general and the queen in particular (I.iii.75-6). "Plain Thomas" remains uncomfortable in his best clothes, however, and when twitted by Richard about his usual dress, he defends it vehemently:

Ay, ay, mock on. My tother hose, say
  ye?
There's honest plain dealing in my tother
  hose.
Should this fashion last I must raise new
  rents,
Undo my poor tenants, turn away my
  servants,
And guard myself with lace; nay, sell more
  land
And lordships too, by th'rood. Hear me,
  King Richard:
If thus I jet in pride, I still shall lose;
But I'll build castles in my tother hose

. . . . .

Tother hose! did some here wear that
  fashion
They would not tax and pill the Commons
  so!

(I.iii.102-12)

The last lines are a direct dig at Richard and his favorites, whose exotic and expensive costumes are a highly visible sign of their selfishness throughout the play. Vanity and extravagance, so often considered feminine sins, are in this play assigned exclusively to men, while simplicity and unselfishness, feminized by the term "housewifry," are associated with both the women of the play and its male hero.

"Housewifry" is, in an important sense, what this play is about. Its concern is not so much with public action—with what Linda Bamber calls the "military and political adventures" that she believes are the ethos of the history play as a genre—but with the private lives of public people and their use (and abuse) of domestic economy. Unlike his counterpart in Shakespeare's *Richard II,* this Richard is not interested in pursuing wars abroad or political maneuverings at home; he only wants to build new buildings and tear down old ones, to try on new clothes and give parties for his friends. His sins are largely a result of his poor housekeeping, the selfish extravagance which forgets that a king's or a lord's private indulgences affect the lives of others. The queen, on the other hand, is a good housekeeper, while Woodstock remembers that a lord's rich clothing spells financial ruin for his dependents and that castle building is best done in plain hose.

If the king prefers parties to politics and war, Woodstock and his brothers also prefer private life—though theirs is a simpler and more wholesome one than the king's. In act III, they retire to Woodstock's country house at Plashey after being dismissed from the court. "I lived with care at court, and now am free," Lancashire declares, and York agrees:

Come, come, let's find some other talk, I
  think not on it:
I ne'er slept soundly when I was amongst
  them,
So let them go.

(III.ii.6-9)

The description of Plashey is irresistible:

This house of Plashey, brother
Stands in a sweet and pleasant air, ifaith:
Tis near the Thames, and circled round with
  trees
That in the summer serve for pleasant fans
To cool ye; and in winter strongly break
The stormy winds that else would nip ye
  too.

(III.ii.9-14)

If there is an emotional heart of the play, this is it. Domesticity, associated with both women and men, is the ethos of this play, not the public world of action and corruption.

As in other histories, however, the private world is not invulnerable. In *Richard II* it is the weeping queen who reminds us of its dangers; in the *Henry IV* plays, it is Hotspur's Kate. In *Woodstock,* it is a man—Woodstock himself, who is seized from his domestic retreat and carried to his death by a party of masked men that includes the king. The kindly duke's fate seems oddly connected to the absence of his lady. Just before the maskers arrive the duchess is called away to attend to the queen, who has been taken sick. Woodstock urges his wife to hurry, yet she resists; like so many women in the history plays, she has had foreboding dreams of her husband's death and does not want to leave him. Woodstock dismisses her fears and hurries her out of the house, but when he is left alone he is obviously unsettled:

And, but th'important business craves such
  haste,
She had not gone from Plashey House
  tonight.

(IV.ii.52-3)

While there is little she could have done to prevent the kidnapping, the scene leaves one with the impression that Woodstock has lost some kind of defense—an impression doubled when we learn that there are few servants left at Plashey, as "most of my attendants [are] waiting on her [the duchess]" (IV.ii.130). Left without his wife and most of his household, Woodstock is peculiarly vulnerable, and no one should be surprised when the king strikes. Although her spoken part is tiny the duchess, like Queen Anne, seems to carry a symbolic importance far greater than the number of her lines. *Woodstock* is a play more concerned with the need for kindness and domestic economy than with war games and masculine heroics; when the women are gone, "this woeful land will all to ruin run."

The women of *Woodstock* are feminine in conventional ways, but other characters respect them and their values are reflected in the play's central male figure; they are neither demonized nor marginalized, despite the smallness of their parts. In the opening scenes of *Sir Thomas More,* on the other hand, we meet a woman who is in many ways their opposite. Outspoken, brash, violent, and vulgar, Doll Williamson—like Joan of Arc or Margaret of Anjou—has been described as a shrewish transvestite whose violation of all the constraints conventionally placed on feminine behavior mark her as "comic" and "monstrous," while her close brush with death on the gallows is said to teach the usual lessons about the evils of rebellion and the value of submission to (masculine) authority.[14] Yet such a reading ignores the context in which Doll appears—a scene in which authority behaves so outrageously that Doll's outrageous behavior seems the only reasonable response.

When the play opens, two foreigners are wreaking havoc on London's citizens by stealing the food from their mouths and the wives from their beds, all the while sanctioned by an arrangement between their ambassador and the Privy Council that grants them immunity. While one man takes a pair of doves from a carpenter who has just bought them, another tries to drag away the carpenter's wife—Doll Williamson. Confronted by several citizens, the foreigners refuse to pay for the birds and continue to try to take Doll Williamson with them, boasting that they will have any woman they want, "and she were the mayor of London's wife" (I.i.47).[15] We learn that one of these men has seduced "the goldsmith's wife . . . whom thou enticedst from her husband with all his plate," and then took the goldsmith to court and "mads't him, like an ass, pay for his wife's board" (I.i.10-3). The Londoners are naturally infuriated, and respond with rough poetic justice by burning the houses of the men who have attacked their own home lives.

The most impressive figure in the scenes, however, is Doll. While her husband and his friends are at first "curbed by duty and obedience," and believe "[y]ou may do anything, the goldsmith's wife, and mine now, must be at your commandment," she does not submit passively to attack (I.i.51, 42-4). "Purchase of me? Away ye rascal! I am an honest plain carpenter's wife and though I have no beauty to like a husband, yet whatsoever is mine scorns to stoop to a stranger. Hands off then when I bid thee," she orders de Bard when he first tries to drag her off (I.i.4-7). When he threatens her, she calls him "dog's face" and, a little later, tells him to "[t]ouch not Doll Williamson, lest

she lay thee along on God's dear earth," and orders him to give the doves back to her husband (I.i.9, 60-5). Her threats are effective: de Bard drops her arm abruptly and leaves, to "complain to my lord ambassador" (I.i.69-70). As the Londoners' resentment rises, she continues to urge the men to take action, and puts on armor herself to "make a captain among ye, and do somewhat to be talk of for ever after" (I.i.134-5).

Doll is not alone. Although she is the only female character to appear on stage in this part of the play, the audience is always conscious of her as part of a whole community of women, all of them willing to speak out and fight back against the foreigners' abuse. She speaks, not simply about herself, but about all women: "Hands off proud stranger, or [by] Him that bought me, if men's milky hearts dare not strike a stranger, yet women will beat them down, ere they bear these abuses"; "Ay, and if you men durst not undertake it, before God we women [will]"; "I'll call so many women to mine assistance, as we'll not leave one inch untorn of thee. If our husbands must be bridled by law, and forced to bear your wrongs, their wives will be a little lawless, and soundly beat ye" (I.i.55-58, 95-6, 64-8). Far from being marginalized, women are the dominant power in this part of the play.

These opening scenes give voice to popular grievances, not conservative disapproval of anarchy. Hatred of foreigners, so often seen as a link between these scenes and London's anti-stranger riots of 1593, is coupled with an explosive resentment against class privileges and the arrogance of caste: the foreigner who steals Williamson's doves adds insult to injury when he tells the workingmen that "Beef and brewis may serve such hinds," and asks, "[A]re pigeons meat for a coarse carpenter?" (I.i.23-4).[16] Doll responds to his tone as much as to his actions when she tells him, "And you sir, that allow such coarse cates to carpenters, whilst pigeons which they pay for must serve your dainty appetite: deliver them back to my husband again" (I.i.61-4). Throughout the scene she voices the self-respect and self-assertion we badly want to see in these English citizens who are so outrageously abused. If we laugh, it is not at her but at the ineffective men in the scene—both the law-abiding Englishmen "brideled by law," whose "milky hearts dare not strike a stranger," and the Lombards who are so easily defeated by a little resistance, and who run off like whining children to complain to their ambassador about it.[17] If she transgresses the boundaries of conventional feminine behavior by being neither silent nor submissive, most of the audience will surely be behind her all the way.

Our allegiance becomes more dangerous, of course, as Doll moves from defending her chastity—a motive that even the most orthodox men might find hard to blame—to burning houses. It has been argued that she and the other rioters are deliberately and systematically undermined in the scenes that follow, until they are no longer sympathetic and we side easily with the authorities.[18] Yet while Doll is certainly a diminished figure in the famous scene by Hand D—her two lines suggest that she is now capable of thinking of nothing except "Shrieve More" 's kindness to her brother, "Arthur Watchins"—when Hand S resumes his part she is once again at center stage, as attractive as before. It is remarkable how often her importance in the gallows scene has been overlooked or minimized by modern critics, who focus on Lincoln as "the prime instigator" and main interest of the riot and its aftermath.[19] Yet, except for the interposed scenes written by Hands C and D, Doll dominates the riot from beginning to end. Lincoln is allowed four lines before his death; his speech is a model of orthodoxy, instructing the onlookers to learn from him the value of obedience, meekness, and submission. Doll has five or six times as many lines, all of them noticeably lacking in either meekness or submission. She urges Lincoln to die like a man—"Bravely, John Lincoln, let thy death express / That as thou livedst a man, thou diest no less" (II.iv.50-1)—and she speaks his epitaph, undoing the effect of his speech by inviting us to admire, not condemn, what the rioter has earlier said and done:

> Farewell John Lincoln; say all what they can:
> Thou livedst a good fellow, and diedst an honest man.
>
> (II.iv.71-2)

Doll continues to hold our attention as she asks, and is granted, the favor of dying before her husband, and then addresses him and her friends at length. "Here I begin this cup of death to thee," she tells her husband,

> Because thou shalt be sure to taste no worse
> Than I have taken, that must go before thee.
> What though I be a woman, that's no matter,
> I do owe God a death, and I must pay him.
> Husband, give me thy hand, be not dismayed
>
> . . . . .
>
> Only two little babes we leave behind us,
> And all I can bequeath them at this time
> Is but the love of some good honest friend
>
> . . . . .
>
> *Will.* Why, well said, wife, i'faith thou cheerst my heart,
> Give me thy hand, let's kiss, and so let's part.

> *Doll.* The next kiss, Williamson, shall be in heaven.
> Now cheerly lads, George Betts, a hand with thee,
> And thine too, Ralph, and thine, good honest Sherwin.
> Now let me tell the women of this town
> No stranger yet brought Doll to lying down.
> So long as I an Englishman can see,
> Nor French nor Dutch shall get a kiss of me.
> And when that I am dead, for me yet say
> I died in scorn to be a stranger's prey.
>
> (II.iv.109-32)

Dramatic, pathetic, heroic, and defiant to the last, this speech—longer and more colorful than Lincoln's—is the climax of the Ill May Day scenes. The playwright pulls out all the emotional stops, making Doll the focus of our sympathetic attention and anxiety right up to the moment before she is to step off the platform, when a messenger arrives with the king's pardon, obtained by More's intervention at the last moment. The crowd all throw up their hats with relief, and Doll, typically, gets the last word:

> And Doll desires it from her very heart,
> More's name shall live for this right noble part.
>
> (II.iv.155-6)

The men in this scene are little more than extras. Doll emerges as the hero of the whole affair—a hero who is at once masculine and feminine. "Lusty," defiant, physically tough, she could as easily have been played by a man as a boy, yet even when she is in men's clothing we are never allowed to forget that she is a woman; her concern for her husband and her children in her speech before the gallows surely feminizes her as much as her costume and her actions masculinize her. Truly androgynous, she is one of the attractive Amazons who drew so much popular attention during the 1590s and early 1600s, yet unlike the majority of such figures, she is never "reintegrated into conservative ideology" by being demonized or returned to helpless femininity,[20] and she exercises real power. As we have seen, Lisa Jardine has argued that the history play is a "men's world" in which "the only power the woman can wield is her power to dismay through verbal abuse . . . but it achieves nothing." Doll, however, is clearly effective in winning her freedom and gaining her revenge; although she is arrested with the other rioters and almost hanged, in the end she is released scot-free.

Doll is not the play's only star, of course. She dominates the stage during the first two acts, but the riot introduces the play's title figure, Thomas More, and shows the path by which he moves from relative obscurity to the highest office in the land, the king's reward for his service in calming the rebellion. His entrance moves the play onto a new emotional plane. If Doll is a woman who sets aside traditionally "feminine" behavior to take a violent part in public affairs, More proves to be a man of public affairs with a gentle and decidedly domestic cast of mind. As in *Woodstock,* these "feminine" qualities are celebrated throughout the play as the hero's greatest strengths.

When the Privy Council receives news that the citizens of London are rioting, Surrey remembers "Master More, / One of the sheriffs, a wise and learned gentleman" (I.iii.85-6) and hopes that

> He . . .
> May by his gentle and persuasive speech
> Perhaps prevail more than we can with
>   power.
>
> (I.iii.88-90)

Surrey's hope proves well founded; More does indeed subdue the rioters without show of force. "Gentleness" is his winning suit. His oration is best known for its praise of order and obedience, based on the premise that the king is God's representative on earth, a rebellion against the king a rebellion against God:

> For to the king God hath his office lent
> Of dread, of justice, power and command,
> Hath bid him rule, and willed you to obey.
>
> (II.iii.106-8)

But although these abstract arguments, with their emphasis on male authority and public order, impress the crowd, they do not bring the riot to an end. A different note, more intimate and personal, is struck at the beginning and end of the speech, in which More imagines

>   the wretched strangers,
> Their babies at their backs, with their poor
>   luggage
> Plodding to th'ports and coasts for
>   transportation,

and asks the Londoners what treatment they would want to receive if they were to become such homeless exiles (II.ii.80-2, 133-51). This wins the day: "Faith, 'a says true; let's do as we may be done by," all the citizens exclaim after he reminds them that they too could become homeless, and so they agree to lay down their weapons and go to prison to await the king's mercy (II.iii.152). The appeal to compassion and domestic experience—supposedly "feminine" qualities— proves to have more power than either physical force or what today would be called the "masculine" appeal to abstract reasoning and authority.

Such domestic thinking characterizes More, like Woodstock, throughout the play. His "housekeeping" is praised from beginning to end, first by Doll ("A keeps a plentiful shrievalty," "Th'art a good housekeeper") and then by his own servants; it is one of the reasons that the rioters are willing to listen to him at all (II.iii.47, 63; V.ii.15-7).[21] Scott McMillin has pointed out that the middle part of the play is a series of interior scenes, demarcated on the stage by the curtained space called for in the stage direction before I.ii and contrasted with the public spaces called for at the beginning and end of the play.[22] Within these interior spaces, More is shown "at home"—greeting his friend Erasmus with a practical joke, fussing over the preparations of a banquet for the Lord and Lady Mayor of London (he arranges the chairs himself, and worries about being away from the guests at the same time as his wife), and bringing his wife the news that, as a result of his refusal to sign the king's "articles," he has resigned his office of chancellor and his public life. More's response to his "fall" from public to private life is, typically, cheerful:

> No wife, be merry, and be merry all,
>
>   . . . . .
>
> Let's in, and here joy like to private friends;
>
> (IV.ii.84-6)
>
> [H]e that ne'er knew court courts sweet
>   content;
>
> (IV.iv.29)
>
> Here let me live estranged from great men's
>   looks:
> They are like golden flies on leaden hooks.
>
> (IV.iv.107-8)

(His preference for a private, domestic life over a corrupt public one, so familiar from Jonson and other classically trained poets, recalls as well *Woodstock* and the uncles' satisfaction in their banishment from their nephew's court.) Later More will think of the Tower as "my strong house," rather than "my prison" (V.i.32), and will ask his family,

> Why do you weep? Because I live at ease?
> Did you not see, when I was chancellor,
> I was so cloyed with suitors every hour
> I could not sleep, nor dine, nor sup in
>   quiet?
> Here's none of this, here I can sit and talk
> With my honest keeper half a day together,
> Laugh and be merry. Why then should you
>   weep?
>
> (V.iii.68-74)

He thinks of himself as a "guest" of the Lieutenant of the Tower, sending thanks to "your good lady" for her entertainment of him there (V.iv.18-9). Even the scaffold is conceived of as a comfortable home: "Here's a most sweet gallery, I like the air of it better than my garden at Chelsea" (V.iv.63-4). This is not just escapism: the domestic cast of mind that calms a public rebellion is powerful enough to bring peace to More himself, even in the face of death.

Like Woodstock, the hero of this play is both a public and a private man. He is frequently shown with his private family—his wife, daughters, son-in-law, and servants—but he enjoys equally warm relations with a kind of extended, public family that includes Doll's brother, a group of actors, a poor old woman, and even a pickpocket ("[Y]ou know that you are known to me / And I have often saved ye from this place," he tells Lifter in court, before finding a way to save the condemned thief's life [I.ii.52-3]), as well as mayors and sheriffs. His most private moments tend to be interrupted by calls to public business, as his banquet is interrupted by a call to the court, or his conference with his family by the arrival of the Council to demand that he sign the "articles" or go to prison; while his ability to personalize public life, establishing intimate relations with people like Doll through his kindness to her brother, is shown to be the real source of his political strength.

If there is no firm boundary between public and private life in this play, the distinction between "feminine" and "masculine" is equally ambiguous. More is certainly the head of his household, and at the banquet he tells his wife firmly:

> [G]ive you direction
> How women should be placed, you know it
>   best.
> For my lord mayor, his brethren, and the rest,
> Let me alone, men best can order men.
>   (III.ii.29-32)

At other times he separates himself from a femininity which he defines as weakness, as when he urges his son-in-law not to mourn:

> If you will share my fortunes, comfort then:
> An hundred smiles for one sigh; what, we
>   are men.
> Resign wet passion to these weaker eyes,
> Which proves their sex, but grants [them]
>   ne'er more wise.
>   (IV.iv.55-8)

Yet Doll has shown that women need not be weak, and More does not always dissociate himself from the feminine. In his retirement, he calls his daughters "you that like to branches spread / And give best shadow to a private house" (IV.iv.6-7), and in his last meeting with his family he urges them:

> Ever retain thy virtuous modesty.
>
> . . . . .
>
> Live all, and love together, and thereby
> You give your father a rich obsequy.
>   (V.iii.115-22)

Privacy and modesty have been two of More's most obvious characteristics throughout the play; these lines suggest that his daughters are his spiritual as well as his material heirs. Known for his "gentle and persuasive speech" rather than force and aggression (I.iii.89), rooted in domestic life and surrounded by women in scene after scene, the hero of this history play is as "feminine" as he is "masculine," and is celebrated as both.

Yet if More is meek and gentle as he goes to his death, he is also defiant. He refuses to the end to bend his conscience and sign the king's "articles," preferring death to submission, although he continues to declare that "his majesty hath been ever good to me" (V.iv.71-2). The final scene on the scaffold inevitably recalls the scaffold scene at the end of act II and sets up a series of unsettling parallels. The one most frequently noted is that between More and Lincoln, the rebel who actually died reiterating what More had preached to the crowd of rioters—"Obedience is the best in each degree" (II.iv.59).[23] Yet More does not finally take his own advice. The more striking similarity in many ways is to Doll, the real focus of attention on the earlier scaffold, as More is on the final one. The stoicism and humor that she showed then are repeated in More at the play's end, when he jokes about what the king will do with his head and how his headache will be cured (V.iv.75-9, 83-4). His defiance echoes hers as well, although it is more quietly expressed.

The parallel between More and Doll suggests a more disturbing similarity in this play: between the foreigners whom Doll resists so vigorously, and the king whom More less obviously, but with no less courage, defies. Both attack private life, the foreigners by seizing men's food and men's wives, the king by choosing to assert his will over a man's private conscience and so destroying the happy family circle with which More is so much identified. When the king is merciful, pardoning the attractive rebels of the opening scenes, he is imaged as a mother, who

> in the arms of mild and meek compassion
> Would rather clip you, as the loving nurse
> Oft doth the wayward infant, than to leave
>   you.
>   (II.iv.160-2)

When he chooses to execute More, however, he joins *Woodstock's* King Richard as the enemy of the family, of women (all the women in the play are aligned with

More), and of conscientious men. At the core of these histories is an ethos, not of masculine "military adventure" or "aggression" and "conquest," but of a private and domestic life which belongs to both sexes and which is seen as opposed to, and threatened by, the hostile and destructive power of the crown.[24]

I am not arguing that all Elizabethan histories have such a domestic center, that women in Elizabethan society enjoyed equality with men, or that there was a politics or a drama that could, by today's standards, reasonably be called feminist. I am suggesting that the obvious disenfranchisement of most Elizabethan women from political power and the brief roles allotted to them in the historical and political drama did not mean that they were necessarily insignificant in such drama. In some plays, at least, the "feminine" is as powerful a force as the "masculine," both in the audience's sympathies and, at times, in the fictional world of the play itself: the women in Shakespeare's histories are used to critique the excesses of the men who rule their lives, while women in other histories exercise forms of power that are validated, not demonized, by the playwrights who created them. Nor are the masculine characters portrayed exclusively in terms of aggression and lust for power: Woodstock and More are celebrated for their gentleness, their compassion, and their "house-wifery," not their military prowess. Neither gender nor genre limits the ability of the audiences of these plays to identify with and support masculine and feminine heroes alike. The history play of the 1590s was not a totalitarian, hegemonic genre that enforced the code of a patriarchal society, but a new and experimental form within which individual playwrights might articulate a range of ideas, radical as well as conservative, about men and women and their place in public life.

Notes

[1] Linda Bamber, *Comic Women, Tragic Men: A Study of Gender and Genre in Shakespeare* (Stanford: Stanford Univ. Press, 1982), p. 163; Phyllis Rackin, *Stages of History: Shakespeare's English Chronicles* (Ithaca: Cornell Univ. Press, 1990), p. 147; Lisa Jardine, *Still Harping on Daughters: Women and Drama in the Age of Shakespeare* (Brighton: Harvester; Totowa NJ: Barnes and Noble, 1983), p. 118; Rackin, p. 161; Bamber, p. 142.

[2] Indeed, one may question whether the "history" ever really became a clearly defined dramatic genre, and if it did, what conventions and boundaries governed it. It is, however, a convenient term for plays based on what was known as English history, and I use it in that sense.

[3] William Shakespeare, *The First Part of King Henry IV,* ed. A. R. Humphreys, Arden Shakespeare (London: Methuen, 1960). Bamber sees Kate here as "merely

. . . a kind of contrast or background from which the hero rides off to his adventure," a "supernumerar[y] in a world of men" (p. 142).

[4] "Isolated from the arena of power, she can foresee the outcome of the historical action before it occurs, and she can report it after it is complete, but she can do nothing at all to affect its course" (Rackin, p. 163).

[5] William Shakespeare, *King Henry V,* ed. J. H. Walter, Arden Shakespeare (London: Methuen, 1954). See Bamber, p. 138, and Marilyn L. Williamson, "'When Men are Rul'd by Women': Shakespeare's First Tetralogy," *ShakS* 19 (1987): 41-60, 56, on the helplessness of the women in *Richard III,* and Bamber, p. 143; Leah S. Marcus, *Puzzling Shakespeare: Local Reading and Its Discontents* (Berkeley: Univ. of California Press, 1988), p. 94; and Lance Wilcox, "Katherine of France as Victim and Bride," *ShakS* 17 (1985): 61-76, on Katherine.

[6] See, among others, Theodora A. Jankowski, *Women in Power in the Early Modern Drama* (Urbana: Univ. of Illinois Press, 1992), pp. 77-102; Bamber, pp. 135-8, 140; Marcus, pp. 80-3, 94; Rackin, pp. 153-8, 197-8; and Williamson, pp. 41-2.

[7] William Shakespeare, *The Third Part of King Henry VI,* ed. Andrew S. Cairncross, Arden Shakespeare (London: Methuen, 1964).

[8] Kate and Isobel are joined by Mortimer's Welsh wife, with her evocative tears; the anxious (if comic) duchess of York; and Doll Tearsheet and Mistress Quickly—all victims in one way or another of the values of the masculine world. One can, of course, argue that sympathy with these characters is a result of a modern, politicized feminist consciousness, but the similarity between Kate and Brutus's wife Portia—and the difference in the ways they are treated by their husbands—suggests that Shakespeare did not necessarily share Hotspur's view of women as unworthy of men's confidence, while the war Hotspur raises against King Henry is certainly not endorsed by the play.

[9] Rackin acknowledges that the women in *Richard III* are "all gifted with the power to prophesy and curse and articulate the will or providence," but seems to feel that this power is negligible (p. 177). For a point of view similar in some ways to mine, see Madonne M. Miner, "'Neither mother, wife, nor England's queen': The Roles of Women in *Richard III,*" in *The Woman's Part: Feminist Criticism of Shakespeare,* ed. Carolyn Lenz et al. (Urbana: Univ. of Illinois Press, 1980), pp. 48, 52. It is not always noticed that Elizabeth beats Richard at his own game at the end of the play, seeming to give in to his request for her daughter's hand ("Relenting fool, and shallow, changing woman!") but actually betrothing her to Richmond. William Shakespeare,

King Richard III, ed. Antony Hammond, Arden Shakespeare (London: Methuen, 1981), IV.iv.431, IV.v.6-8.

[10] Bamber, on the other hand, argues that "Margaret's actions are unnatural because unwomanly"—in other words, that they would be natural in a man—and Angela Pitt says that she is "totally evil and unnatural because she lacks womanly qualities. In their place she has those that are the glory of a man but grotesque in a woman" (Bamber, p. 137; Pitt, *Shakespeare's Women* [Newton Abbott: David and Charles; Totowa NJ: Barnes and Noble, 1981], p. 153; cf. Jankowski, p. 102). Monstrosity is not confined to women, however: Margaret is more than matched by Richard III, while Clifford, York, and Cade are far from humane.

[11] Joan's earthy appeal has often been acknowledged. See Gabriele Bernhard Jackson, "Topical Ideology: Witches, Amazons, and Shakespeare's Joan of Arc," *ELR* 18, 1 (1988): 40-65, for a particularly fine discussion of the ways in which Joan's portrait is complicated by attractive ambiguities.

[12] Eleanor and Constance in *King John* are also strong characters who operate in the public arena. Rackin acknowledges this, but agrees with Virginia Mason Vaughan that their disappearance midway through the play is "a necessary condition for the restoration of patriarchal historical discourse" (pp. 177, 184 n. 45). One could, however, argue that the loss of the women is one of the causes of the darkness that most audiences agree falls over the play in its last acts.

[13] *Woodstock: A Moral History,* ed. A. P. Rossiter (London: Chatto and Windus, 1946). References will be to this edition and will appear parenthetically in the text. I have silently emended Rossiter's sometimes confusing punctuation.

[14] Charles R. Forker and Joseph Candido, "Wit, Wisdom, and Theatricality in *The Book of Sir Thomas More,*" *ShakS* 13 (1980): 85-104, 100.

[15] *Sir Thomas More: A Play by Anthony Munday and Others,* ed. Vittorio Gabrieli and Giorgio Melchiori (Manchester: Manchester Univ. Press, 1990). References will be to this edition and will appear parenthetically in the text.

[16] Gabrieli and Melchiori believe that the name of one of the foreigners—Caveler—was "suggested by the pun on 'caviller,' a quibbling disputant," but it may be meant to be pronounced "cavalier," with aristocratic implications (p. 60, note 14.1).

[17] If we had been meant to laugh at Doll, the playwrights could easily have called for her to dress in bits and bobs of old kitchen gear like Ambidexter in *Cambyses:* "Enter the VICE, with an old capcase on his head, an old pail about his hips for harness, a scummer and a potlid by his side, and a rake on his shoulder" (Thomas Preston, *Cambyses, King of Persia,* in *Drama of the English Renaissance,* vol. 1: *The Tudor Period,* ed. Russell A. Fraser and Norman Rabkin [New York: Macmillan, 1976], ii.1.s.d.). Doll's arrival in II.i dressed for battle "in a shirt of mail, a headpiece, sword, and buckler" suggests that she is to be taken seriously (*More* II.i.1.s.d.). She and her community of women participate in the longstanding folk tradition that actually tolerated "unruly women" as critics of authority. See Natalie Z. Davis, "Women on Top," *Society and Culture in Early Modern France* (Stanford: Stanford Univ. Press, 1975), pp. 124-51.

[18] Scott McMillin, *The Elizabethan Theatre and "The Book of Sir Thomas More"* (Ithaca: Cornell Univ. Press, 1987), p. 141. Richard Helgerson agrees: while he finds it significant that the rebels are initially presented seriously, "no less significant is the fact that the resistance crumbles," and "[i]n revisions of the original text, the rebellion is systematically carnivalized" (*Forms of Nationhood: The Elizabethan Writing of England* [Chicago: Univ. of Chicago Press, 1992], p. 221).

[19] Gabrieli describes her as "heroic," but most writers echo Judith Doolan Spikes in focusing on Lincoln (Vittorio Gabrieli, *"Sir Thomas More:* Sources, Characters, Ideas," *Moreana* 23 [1986]: 17-43, 39; Spikes, "*The Book of Sir Thomas More:* Structure and Meaning," *Moreana* 11 [1974]: 25-39, 28).

[20] Jackson argues that such treatment was conventional even in admiring treatments of the "woman warrior" (pp. 59-60).

[21] "Housekeeping" refers to his hospitality, of course, not to domestic chores, but it conveys the importance of the home to More.

[22] McMillin, pp. 96-112.

[23] See, for instance, Gabrieli and Melchiori, pp. 6, 31.

[24] There are other similarities between the two plays: both exist only in manuscript and both bear signs of censorship. Richard Helgerson assumes that both were Philip Henslowe plays, which, he argues, tended to be concerned more with "the innocent suffering of common people and their defenders," and less with "civil war or foreign conquest" than Shakespeare's histories (pp. 234-5).

Source: "Rethinking Gender and Genre in the History Play," in *Studies in English Literature: 1500-1900,* Vol. 36, No. 2, Spring, 1996, pp. 267-87.

The Limits of Modernity in Shakespeare's *King John*

Steve Longstaffe, *S. Martin's College Lancaster*

Deborah Curren-Aquino, summing up fifty years of critical engagement with Shakespeare's *King John,* identifies a radical break with earlier views of the play in "the tendency in post 1940 scholarship to describe *John* as ambivalent, ambiguous, suspicious, sceptical, questioning and ideologically subversive".[1] The form and tone of *John,* in other words, are recognisably modern. Few critics have gone as far as Sigurd Burckhardt, who in the 1960s asserted that the play documented Shakespeare's *own* modernity, defined as the recognition that order, or "justice and truth at the heart of things", was of human, rather than divine, origin.[2] Burckhardt's position, though not his confidence that he could show that "when he wrote *King John,* or quite possibly in writing it, Shakespeare became a 'modern'", is echoed in Virginia Vaughan's claim of 1989 that the play "like Shakespeare's other history plays" depicts a crucial point in the inauguration of "the relativism of the modern age".[3] But for the most part, writers on *John* have avoided such grand narratives of epistemological shifts, and found the play's modernity to be historically produced in a much more local way: as part of a Shakespearian negotiation with chronicle, source play, or the history play genre. What *John* is sceptical about, in other words, is other historical accounts of John's reign, especially regarding their relationship to what might still be termed Tudor ideology. For many critics, Shakespeare's *John* is in antagonistic relation to such "sources" as the anonymous Queen's Men's play *The Troublesome Reign of King John* and the 1587 *Holinshed,* interrogating the writing of history of which these two texts, and the history play as a genre, were part.

Such a *John* appears our contemporary, teasing out aporias and contradictions in Renaissance writings of legitimacy, faith, or patriotism. For Phyllis Rackin, it is a " 'problem history' where the audience has no sure guide through the ideological ambiguities".[4] Larry Champion identifies it as "an open-ended chronicle play with historical process transformed into human process, stripped bare of Tudor providentialism and reduced to an individual self-interest that only in its best moments might be communally enlightened".[5] Guy Hamel argues that Shakespeare's "assault on formulas [. . .] reveals itself in almost every departure from *The Troublesome Reign*".[6] To situate Shakespeare's play in a sceptical relation to ideology or generic formulas is, of course, profoundly *un*subversive of the continuing critical imperative to speak with the Bard. The modern Shakespeare, as Stephen Greenblatt has

pointed out, must subvert only that which is no longer subversive. The *John* worthy of modern critics' engagement is produced by a common critical strategy, which is most clearly visible in the conclusion of one of the play's editors that "it would be a crippling limitation of the power of *King John* to tie it too closely to the situation of the 1590s".[7] It is in its implication in the religious politics of the period of the Spanish war that *John* is most clearly un-modern; it is part of the wartime anti-Catholic polemic, something which has been played down in order to produce a modernity which legitimates a continual critical return to the play, and to a lesser extent, to Shakespeare.

It is not surprising that there has been relatively little interest in *John*'s brand of Protestant nationalism of late, for, as David Aers has pointed out, many influential contemporary critics of early modern writing "display a marked lack of interest in Christian traditions, Christian practices and Christian institutions".[8] Mid-century critics, following E. M. W. Tillyard's characterisation of the play as "but Mildly Protestant in tone", stressed the "moderation" of the play's anti-Catholic sentiments, whilst identifying an assertion of Protestant nationalism.[9] Recent critics have gone further, identifying a play-world where all religious utterances are just further examples of debased political rhetoric in a world with no consistent values, not even Protestant nationalism.[10]

But how debased is this rhetoric? Specifically, did the kind of language with which John defies the Papal legate Pandulph on his first encounter with him circulate in post-Armada London as a somehow debased version of earlier, more sincere, Tudor coinages? To stretch the 1980s monetary rhetoric further, I suggest that, on the contrary, play rhetoric directed against foreign Catholics wishing to overthrow an English monarch was on the gold standard during this period of war with Spain. John's words themselves are direct as he responds to Pandulph's demands in the name of the Pope:

> Thou canst not, cardinal, devise a name
> So slight, unworthy and ridiculous,
> To charge me to an answer, as the pope.
> Tell him this tale; and from the mouth of
>   England
> Add thus more, that no Italian priest
> Shall tithe or toll in our dominions;
> But as we, under God, are supreme head,
> So under Him that great supremacy,

Where we do reign, we will alone uphold
Without th' assistance of a mortal hand:
So tell the pope, all reverence set apart
To him and his usurp'd authority.[11]

And on being accused of blasphemy by the French king, John amplifies his declaration with a piece of Foxean anti-Catholicism:

Though you and all the kings of
   Christendom
Are led so grossly by this meddling priest,
Dreading the curse that money may buy
   out;
And by the merit of vild gold, dross, dust,
Purchase corrupted pardon of a man,
Who in that sale sells pardon from himself,
Though you and all the rest so grossly led
This juggling witchcraft with revenue
   cherish,
Yet I alone, alone do me oppose
Against the pope, and count his friends my
   foes.

                                        (3.1 88-97)

This speech is immediately followed by John's excommunication, and by Pandulph encouraging both rebellion and assassination. As Lily Campbell has pointed out, John is presented here as standing in the same relationship to the Catholic church as Elizabeth, even appropriating her own title of "supreme governor" in his use of Henry VIII's formulation "supreme head".[12] The clarity of John's position here is momentary, however; he does not reach these vituperative heights again. Indeed, he resigns his crown to Pandulph later on. But it is important not to underrate the legitimating power of John's rhetoric. Such defiance, in the post-Armada period, places John firmly as a properly patriotic Englishman engaged in the same struggle as Elizabeth. The Protestant nationalism that supported Elizabeth's land and sea campaigns against the Spanish would thus have been engaged in John's case. Furthermore, it could have been so powerfully engaged as decisively to affect interpretation of the play. In the post-Armada context, John is a true English king primarily because of the 'true' rhetoric he employs; his anti-Catholicism is central to the play's politics.

King John is consensually dated to the period between 1587, when the second edition of Holinshed appeared, and 1598, when Francis Meres mentioned in print a Shakespearian *King John,* though it is impossible to know whether that play was the one first printed in 1623.[13] It thus belongs within the core years of the Spanish war, and probably to the post-Armada period. After 1588, however, the national mood was certainly not conducive to a relaxed and sceptical investigation of the possible hypocrisy of religious nationalism. The defeat of the Armada, far from engendering a lasting

sense of invulnerability to foreign Catholic invasion, fed a sometimes apocalyptic wartime paranoia.[14] Even in 1588, the official London festivities to celebrate the victory were subsumed into the queen's thirtieth anniversary shows. Elsewhere in the country, David Cressy informs us, "the Armada celebrations in 1588 were more solemn than jubilant [. . .] the festivities were conducted in a minor key".[15] London, though its strategic importance meant that it was carefully governed, had its share of hardship, and had to cope with returning soldiers threatening to loot Bartholomew Fair in 1589, and with royal demands for men, ships, and money at a time when the capital was also struggling with plague and dearth.[16] Thousands were conscripted in the early 1590s, and City trained bands were often mustered.[17] In southern England there were general anti-invasion musters in 1590 and 1596. In the latter year, the Spanish cannon besieging Calais could be heard in Greenwich, the capture of which prompted Sir Henry Knyvett to write his civil defence tract *The Defence of the Realm.* The Spanish raided Cornwall in 1595, and sent another Armada in 1597.[18]

Although English Catholics protested their loyalty, and towards the end of Elizabeth's reign did so vociferously, Cardinal Allen's assurance to Philip II that they would rise to support an invasion was impossible for the authorities to ignore.[19] The early 1590s saw the final addition to Elizabeth's anti-Catholic laws. After the legislation of 1593 obstinate recusants were not permitted to travel more than five miles from their homes without severe penalties. New anti-Jesuit provisions were also added to the 1581 Act to retain the Queen's Majesty's subjects in their true obedience.[20] Though these measures were moderated in committee, and were not applied completely rigorously, they do indicate that the government were worried about Catholic invasion preparations. The church, naturally, was hardly irenic at this time. Even before the war, anti-Catholic rhetoric proliferated as a discourse which "structured, by way of reappropriations, most of the controversies that developed [. . .] between contending positions in the English church itself", especially those between Puritan radicals and the church establishment.[21] For the Protestant divine, anti-Roman polemic "was at once an expression of Protestant zeal and an implicit gesture of loyalty to a national church, the Protestantism of whose doctrine was generally acknowledged".[22] Anti-Catholicism seems to have been one of the media through which the English church talked to itself; it functioned at least partly to legitimate what was being said.

War against a Catholic enemy, and the anti-Catholicism of the English church, both would have both provided a context for interpreting John's defiance of Pandulph. In addition, anyone familiar with recent historical accounts of John's reign would have expected to see him presented as a legitimate king undermined by circumstances and Catholic conspiracy. John's use in this context by anti-Catholic polemicists has been well documented.[23] Foxe's account in the *Acts and Monuments* limits itself to religious matters, and places John within the perspective of the struggle between the true church and antichrist. Holinshed's account emphasises that the contemporary sources are Catholic and therefore biased, "scarselie can they afoord him a good word [. . .] the occasion whereof [. . .] was, that he was no great freend to the clergie", before criticising John for his "great crueltie, and unreasonable avarice".[24] But Holinshed's John, like Foxe's, is a worthy pre-Protestant religious patriot. Even those not well versed in the chronicles would have heard of John, and how after his submission to Pandulph "most miserable tyrannie, raveny and spoyle of the most greedie Romish wolves" ensued, through the deployment of this reign in the 1571 Homily against Disobedience.[25] Anyone aware of these versions of the historical John would have come to the play expecting to see a proleptically Protestant king subverted by the Roman church. Though Polydore Vergil and John Stow did not write within this representative tradition, their impact on public opinion was likely during the immediate post-Armada period to have been negligible. John does appear in the *Huntington* plays of the later 1590s as a wicked tyrant, but in these plays there is no attempt to address the political agenda of *King John*. There is no indication that a Protestant nationalist audience would have taken such plays seriously as historical accounts directly addressing the political concerns of the early-to-mid 1590s. Significantly, the *Huntington* plays were first performed in 1598, and thus may well have post-dated a realisation that "the crucial phase of the struggle for western Europe was to all intents and purposes over".[26]

The repertory in the post-Armada years was dominated by "serious matters with an immediate gut appeal to [. . .] militarism", in the words of Andrew Gurr.[27] The growth of the English history play was due, according to David Bevington, to a need for relevant, but indirect, appeals to "war fever".[28] Anti-Spanish and anti-Catholic sentiments were common across a range of plays. John's resistance to Pandulph in Shakespeare's drama would have functioned metonymically to link him to contemporary anti-Spanish and anti-Catholic sentiment, and to the Protestant histories and other polemical deployments of the historical John's reign. The ubiquity and strength of anti-Spanish and anti-Catholic sentiment, furthermore, could well have operated so as to produce a strong cathexis for these sentiments and their utterer in the play, conditioning responses to, and interpretations of, it. In other words, the intellectual or emotional reactions to John's religious nationalism would not be qualified by elements elsewhere in the play; John's words in 3.1 would themselves qualify the responses to the rest of the play, including some of its ambiguities, suspicions, scepticisms and questions.

Recent critics read John's rhetoric very differently. For many, the religious nationalism of his speeches function not to mobilise anti-Catholic and anti-Spanish sentiment, but to indicate that such a rhetoric, and such a mobilisation, is more fully present elsewhere, in the *The Troublesome Reign*. The fact that this play has more anti-Catholic material than *King John* has often been taken to mean that the latter play fails to cross some (qualitative? quantitative?) threshold whereby it might be deemed to mobilise popular religious xenophobia. Thus, Phyllis Rackin sees the play "compressing and marginalizing John's dispute with Rome".[29] For M. M. Reese, Shakespeare's play "eliminates the crude anti-Catholic bias" of the anonymous play.[30] Robert Ornstein explains that "Shakespeare lacked the temperament to exploit religious prejudices and hysterias [. . .] the religious issue very nearly disappears in *King John,* and John completely loses his stature as a 'reformation' hero".[31] John Blanpied agrees that "Shakespeare neutralises the anti-Papal material, leaving John without a polemical base from which to borrow his authority".[32]

For many, the result of this compression, and consequent neutralisation and marginalization, is a play which, in the words of Virginia Vaughan, presents "politics, not polemics".[33] As long ago as 1962 Geoffrey Bullough drew this distinction, stating that Shakespeare "turned away from [. . .] sectarian propaganda to emphasise more purely political motives".[34] Such a construction of Shakespeare's *John* (and, of course, *John's* Shakespeare) as drawing a distinction between real politics and un-sophisticated (and explicitly anti-Catholic) rabble-rousing has received much critical support, though earlier writers attribute it to a Shakespearian distaste for "bias" or "rant", or a preference for complexity over simplicity, and later ones more to a textual refusal of the easy closure which a more foregrounded religious element would have allowed or perhaps necessitated.[35] The dominance of Christianity in Renaissance England is perhaps the most effective reminder of Renaissance difference; conveniently, Shakespeare manages to play down that difference and provide a transcendent scepticism for our age of suspicious reading.

As can be seen from Blanpied and Ornstein, the playing down of the religious element also means a John robbed of the legitimating power of religious nationalism. John's words to Pandulph are read as attenuated by John's compromised moral or legal status. Deborah Kehler states that "in the light of his false claim, John's use of divinity to serve his own ends is transparent", while for Philip Edwards "what seems an admirable quality of sturdy national courage is questioned by the moral quality of the speaker, and by his eventual fate in the play".[36] Responses to John's words are conditioned not by their deployment of a powerfully cathected sentiment, but by "character". Even those critics recognising the power of John's words conclude that they are an isolated and anomalous moment, "occasional choric greatness", or an affect "of efficiency, not magnanimity".[37] At best, for Larry Champion, the anti-Catholic John is just one of the "equally persuasive views of the usurper, the would-be murderer, the terror-stricken capitulator, the sufferer, the patriot, and the kingly defender of his nation".[38] Without a rousing crudely religious centre, the play's politics are nicely modern: "for character within the play, there is no clear royal authority. For the audience watching it, there is no unblemished cause and no unquestioned authority to claim their allegiance", in Phyllis Rackin's formulation. David Womersley, though he sees the play as clearly conservative in its conclusions, agrees that it "confronts the question of how one lives in a world without value".[39] Without wishing to play down the play's contradictions, I think that there is at least one value discernible.

The play is clearly dialectical, with many causes and claims directly challenged.[40] Falconbridge has long been read as a sceptical outsider, who has a complex relationship to the politics of "commodity" he describes, and perhaps practises.[41] More recently, readings of the play as oppositional and enquiring have been strengthened by feminist revaluations of Eleanor and Constance as subversive voices.[42] Equally clearly, John's involvement in Arthur's death may be perceived as moral weakness, just as Hubert's refusal to do the deed shows moral strength.[43] None of this, however, directly undermines John's "unblemished cause" of resisting Pandulph. Although he is criticised for much else within the play, the only voices raised against John's defiance are Pandulph's and those foreign kings' loyal to him, which is only to be expected, as they are the targets of John's ire.

The main reasons for the widespread critical perception of the play as modern in its politics are mentioned by Kehler and Edwards above: that John is illegitimate, that he is lacking in "moral quality", and that he later gives his crown, effectively, to the Pope. Of these, the "moral" argument is least persuasive. Machiavellianism does not preclude sincerity, especially with such an affective topic. Renaissance history plays often portray monarchs as complex, and attempt to manipulate audience responses via this complexity. Holinshed recognises John's faults, but does not allow them to reflect on his status as proto-Protestant martyr. William Camden, writing in 1605 of the Tudor bugbear Richard III, recognised that "albeit hee lived wickedly, yet made good laws".[44] The other two points require more detailed engagement. John's submission to the Pa-

pacy at the end of the play could well have "cancelled" his earlier robust anti-Papalism. Through an analysis of the representative strategies used for John's cession I will argue that it may not have done so. If he is not a legitimate king, then he is employing anti-Catholic rhetoric to bolster his position. He need not be shown to believe his own words. If this were so, John's use of religious rhetoric is on a par as a cynical manipulation of language with Richard III's political use of witchcraft accusations in Shakespeare's play and the anonymous *True Tragedy of Richard III*.

John is not illegitimate just because his opponents say he is. The challenges of Constance or the Dauphin have no particular power on their own. Yet for many critics, whether or not they engage with *John's* "modernity", it is axiomatic that John is an illegitimate king, that he is a usurper in possession of the crown when the right lies with Arthur (and, some have added, the true kingliness with Falconbridge).[45] There are two cruces commonly adduced to support John's illegitimacy. Both can be read differently.

The first is a critical exchange in the play's first scene, where John and Eleanor discuss the implications of the French challenge just made on Arthur's behalf. Eleanor reproaches John for not dealing with the question sooner, as "This might have been prevented and made whole/With very easy arguments of love,/Which now the manage of two kingdoms must/With fearful-bloody issue arbitrate" (1.1.35-8). John replies "Our strong possession and our right for us", to which Eleanor retorts, "Your strong possession much more than your right,/Or else it must go wrong with you and me./So much my conscience whispers in your ear,/Which none but heaven, and you and I, shall hear" (1.1.39-43). Most critics follow Reese's conclusion that this shows that "John is king *de facto* and possession is his only 'right' ", though Edna Zwick Boris points out that Eleanor is "not denying John's right but emphasising the practical aspect of his advantage over Arthur".[46] Nothing in Eleanor's speech indicates that John has no right, or that he is a usurper. Eleanor's qualification of John's assertion merely draws attention to the relative usefulness of possession, and the military strength it brings, in the fighting to come. Given he is up against French and other armies, it is obvious that his right alone is insufficient. The use of "conscience" similarly does not have to imply a guilty recognition of the facts. Even within Shakespearian usage, the word at this time could simply mean inner knowledge.[47] Eleanor does not wish others to hear because a public acknowledgement of the relative uselessness of John's right is inappropriate to the dignity of his court, especially just after he has been challenged by Chatillon.

Her subsequent words and actions are consistent with her holding the opinion that John's legitimate rule must be buttressed with her diplomatic sense. She refers to the will of Richard I, which in Holinshed plainly entitles John to the throne, in her confrontation with Arthur's mother: "I can produce/A will that bars the title of thy son" (2.1.470-1). Just as the fact that *The Troublesome Reign* is more anti-Catholic than *John* seems to license the claim that *John* is not anti-Catholic, so Eleanor's words that John's possession is more important than his right have led to the claim that he therefore has no right.

The other key moment for John's illegitimacy, and for the play's exploration of the consequent instability of political legitimacy, is Falconbridge's reaction to Arthur's corpse at the end of the fourth act. Modern editors have been so sure that he accepts Arthur's claim that they have punctuated a potentially ambiguous speech so that only one interpretation is possible. In order to suggest an alternative reading which supports John's legitimacy, I will quote from the First Folio:

> Bast. Go, beare him in thine armes:
> I am amaz'd me thinkes, and loose my
>   way
> Among the thornes, and dangers of this
>   world.
> How easie dost thou take all *England*
>   vp,
> From forth this morcell of dead Royaltie?
> The life, the right, and truth of all this
>   Realme
> Is fled to heauen: and *England* now is
>   left
> To tug and scamble, and to part by th
>   teeth
> The vn-owed interest of proud swelling
>   State:
> Now for the bare-pickt bone of Maiesty
> Doth dogged warre bristle his angry crest,
> And snarleth in the gentle eyes of peace:
> Now Powers from home, and discontents
>   at home
> Meet in one line: and vast confusion
>   waites
> As doth a Rauen on a sicke-falne beast,
> The iminent decay of wrested pompe.
> Now happy he, whose cloake and center
>   can
> Hold out this tempest. Beare away that
>   childe,
> And follow me with speed: Ile to the King:
> A thousand businesses are briefe in hand,
> And heaven it selfe doth frowne vpon the
>   Land[48].

                                              (4.3.139-55)

Editors of the recent Penguin, Oxford and Cambridge editions concur in seeing the fourth line as addressed to Hubert, who has now picked up Arthur as Falconbridge commanded, and in punctuating the passage so that "From forth . . ." begins a new sentence.[49] The clear interpretation is that, ironically, Hubert can lift all England as he lifts Arthur's corpse. Arthur is referred to as "England" at 2.1.91 and 202 by Philip of France. All the life, truth and right of England, which resided in Arthur, has fled (like Astraea) to heaven, and all that remains for the country left behind is a dogfight over the remaining in bones of power. Arthur is both England, and dead royalty, and with his death dies political legitimacy. "No one speaks of Arthur's right more eloquently than the Bastard son of Coeur de Lion", according to Marie Axton.[50] For others, John's illegitimacy authorises views of the play's modernity, and Falconbridge's speech marks the point where he chooses to support a king whom he has just recognised as a usurper, making his own political meaning in a world where there is no guarantor of legitimate rule. His decision to follow John "must be an existential one, choosing a way despite his own awareness that whatever 'rightness' he invests it with is not inherent in it".[51]

It is possible, however, to read the speech differently. If the "thou" of the fourth line is not Hubert, but the heaven to which Arthur's soul has presumably fled, Arthur need not be acknowledged as rightful monarch at all. Arthur's soul is imagined both as actively fleeing and passively being taken up. Arthur's body, in a familiar metaphor, is a "realme" from which the ruler ("England", as Arthur is English) has gone. Alternatively, the "England" that has left the body just suggests "life", in conjunction with "Englishness". Either way, Arthur's right is to the realm of his own body. Falconbridge then shifts to the larger realm, also lacking a ruler, but for the different reason that "powers from home, and discontents at home" are in conflict. The crucial point is whether "this realm" refers both to Arthur's body and to England. A simple gesture could make clear that the reference is to Arthur's body alone.

Falconbridge is critical of John, but this need not impugn his legitimacy, as the terms he uses recall those used by the nobles disapproving of John's recrowning in 4.2. Each reference to John can be read as critical of the sumptuousness of the ceremony, and of the new clothing associated with it, much remarked on by the nobles at the time. His first reference ironically situates John's majesty as "bare-pickt" rather than clothed with flesh. "Proud swelling state" refers back critically to the wasteful excess of the recrowning, as does "wrested pomp" (that is, pomp employed in the improper context of John's ceremony, rather than wrested from Arthur). The final reference ironically characterises John's clothing as simple ("cloak and center") and unlikely to last the tempest of disorder in the realm. Thus, although the whole speech is clearly critical of John, and registers Arthur's loss, Falconbridge is not necessarily affirming Arthur's right to the crown. Falconbridge's words are difficult to understand, but an audience accepting John's legitimacy need not have understood him to challenge this right, and it is possible to imagine a performance which makes clear that John is legitimate King. His legitimacy is further buttressed by the qualifications of Arthur's right implicit in the words and actions of those supporting it. A claim supported by a man who carries on his back the spoils of a dead Richard I is not likely to have impressed an Elizabethan audience, even if they responded positively to the bemused and passive "boy" who at one point states "I would that I were laid low in my grave./I am not worth this coil that's made for me" (2.1.164-5).

John's legitimacy, however, raises the question of his cession of the crown to Pandulph, which happens just after the Falconbridge speech quoted above. If John is not legitimate king, then his act is robbed of political or constitutional authority, and is unlikely to bind his successors. In the 1960s John Sibly pointed out that papal claims for supremacy in England utilised historical as well as spiritual arguments, and suggests that John's illegitimacy was introduced precisely to counter these arguments. He begins from the premise that technically, John was not a usurper until Arthur's death, as he could still have resigned the crown when Arthur reached his majority, and sees Falconbridge's words before the recrowning as recognising that John is now a usurper:

> it is *immediately* after the 'flight to heaven' of any 'right' John may have had in the realm, that he 'surrenders' his crown. To an Elizabethan audience, this must very forcibly have demonstrated that John had just given up what he had no right to give at all; and Pandulph had 'restored' what he had no right to receive in the first place.[52]

The cession of the crown is merely an index of the current balance of power, and for a Protestant audience devalues a morally bankrupt and/or illegitimate John still further.[53] If a legitimate John is posited, the status of this humiliating submission, to the very man John had so strongly defied earlier, needs to be addressed.

The mere representation of John's submission need not have functioned simply to condemn him, despite the commonsense appeal of this position. The *Homily Against Rebellion* draws different conclusions. Here John's submission to Pandulph is the clearest example, in its awfulness, of the chaos into which rebellion throws the country. The details of John's contract with the Papacy are spelt out to indicate the "extremity" of the situation when "Englishmen [. . .] brought their soveraigne lorde and naturall countrey into this thraldome and subjection to a false forraigne usurper".[54] John's legitimacy emphasises the indignity of his submission. Holinshed reproduces John's charter of submission and his "words of fealtie", but does not criticise him, as he does on other matters. Foxe is slightly more difficult to interpret. A paragraph of the 1563 edition, omitted from the 1583 second edition, explains John's reasons for submitting as fear of the French king, and the perception that nothing else "could be found to avoid the present destruction both of his person and the realm also". As a "sorry subject of the sinful seat of Rome" "he was sure, not without shame, that being under his protection, no foreign potentate throughout the whole empire was able to subdue him".[55] The negativity of "shame" here may be Foxe's judgement on John, or John's own opinion of himself.

But the 1583 edition reproduces John's "Letter Obligatory" to the Pope, and is unequivocal in its identification of John as a hapless victim of "that execrable monster and antichrist of Rome". Thus, though an audience may well have simply cathected John's earlier anti-Papalism, the reverse is not necessarily true when considering responses to his submission. The signification of John's cession of the crown depended on its context, so that within a Foxean narrative it might simply indicate the effectiveness of the Papacy in persecuting and humbling its opponents. It is also important to recognise that John's cession of the crown in Shakespeare's play employs different dramatic strategies to his earlier confrontation, and that these strategies may well have directed an audience towards a response the final result of which would be to confirm John as legitimate.

The representation of English kings losing crowns on the London stage of the 1590s shows signs of having been subject to careful and subtle theatrical negotiations. Though recent critics have retreated from the once-commonplace conclusion that because the 1608 quarto of Shakespeare's *Richard II* was the first to feature his deposition it must have been censored, there is still the possibility that the first quarto of 1597, or the play as performed, was cut, or that Richard's abdication/deposition was somehow 'unwritable' at this period.[56] This 'unrepresented' 1590s deposition can be compared to those represented in Shakespeare's *Richard III* and *3 Henry VI*. The 1595 quarto of the latter presents Henry's resignation of his throne to the joint protectors Warwick and Clarence in a scene half the length of its 1623 First Folio equivalent, in which Henry accepts the arrangement so that "the people of this blessed land/May not be punished with my thwarting stars" (4.6.21-2). The 1590s quarto "underrepresents", rather than omits, Henry's deposition. In *Richard III* deposition is directly represented only in a stage direction in which Richard fights Richmond and is slain. Although the visitations Richard receives in his sleep before the battle can be argued to be a displaced representation of a deposing tribunal, to whose conclusions Richard involuntarily assents, the death of the king in this instance is underrepresented in that it is a *fait accompli*.

'Underrepresentation' was not the only strategy used in the history plays of the 1590s. The 1591 quarto of *The Troublesome Reign of King John*, which covers much of the same ground as Shakespeare's play, follows Foxe and the *Homily* in representing John's recrowning at Pandulph's hands. As with the two earlier texts, its principal strategy is to attempt to limit interpretation by presenting the deposition/abdication as primarily signifying John's helplessness in the face of Popish prelates' persecutions, the final wrong turning in a Troublesome Reign. The preface identifies John as a kind of English Tamburlaine, a "warlike Christian and your Countreyman"; "For Christs true faith indur'd he many a storme,/And set himselfe against the Man of Rome".[57] This John, as in Shakespeare's play, defies Pandulph on their first meeting, and orders Falconbridge to ransack the abbeys, though *The Troublesome Reign* shows the action where Shakespeare only alludes to it. John recrowns himself in front of his nobles, explaining that he does this not because he has been deposed, but because he is checking the "assured witnes of your loves" in a ceremony to bind the nobles to him, (*Troublesome Reign*, 1555).

The play deals with such potentially difficult moments by providing a clear cause for events, and this applies also to John's recrowning by Pandulph. He prepares to meet the legate by assessing his situation under the Papal interdict, recognising that his sins are too great for him successfully to banish Popery (though he looks forward to it happening), and resolving to "finely dissemble with the Pope" (*2 Troublesome Reign*, 275) as the realm's chaos is caused by Papal interference. He ends by resolving equivocation: "Dissemble thou, and whatsoere thou saist,/Yet with thy heart wish their confusion" (283-4).

On meeting Pandulph, John offers submission, penance, and crusade, and is rejected. His first impulse is to kill Pandulph, but he again submits, to be informed that surrendering his crown is the only acceptable course. John resolves to fight rather than do so. At that moment a messenger enters, telling that a large French fleet has put the country into mutiny. On hearing this, John's resistance collapses. He later receives his crown back "as tenaunt to the Pope" (637), berates himself ("Shame be my share for yeelding to the Priest"), and in his last speech traces this act as increasing his troubles: "Since John did yeeld unto the

Priest of Rome/Nor he nor his have prospred on the earth" (707, 1075-6).

The dramatic strategy of *The Troublesome Reign* is to try to contain the implications of John's submission to the Pope by inserting it into a master narrative, the course of the ancient struggle between Roman and native Christianity (Protestantism). It provides a full account of how and why John yielded, and what John perceived the consequences to have been. By this strategy, the play attempts to contain the implications of John's act for posterity. Because the causes of the deposition easily fit into the Foxean picture of the embattled proto-Protestant subverted by Papal wiles, to represent the deposition itself is not necessarily to provide a subversive undoing of John's status as proto-Protestant hero. This strategy might be called "directive representation": the deposition is shown, but attempts are made to limit an audience's perception of its meaning.

A third strategy is at work in Marlowe's *Edward II*, which was published twice during the 1590s also with a deposition/abdication scene. This third strategy might be characterised as "overrepresentation", here defined as the representation of an action or event so that a conclusive meaning is difficult to draw from it. It is not clear, for example, from Edward's abdication/deposition scene why he has given up the crown, whether he has a choice, or whether he is in a fit state to understand what he is doing. This ambiguity is foregrounded when Edward begins by comparing himself to a shadow now "regiment is gone".[58] He then asks if he must resign his crown as Mortimer will take it, is told that it will rather pass to his son, denies this, is asked again whether he will resign, gives his crown to Leicester, takes it back just until night, is asked again for it, refuses, gives it back to protect his son's right on a reminder from Leicester, calls upon another to take it from him, hands it over, and sends a handkerchief wet with his tears to queen Isabel. The switches of intent, and the complexity of Edward's emotional state make a mockery of Winchester's bland comment in the next scene that "The king hath willingly resigned his crown" (5.2.28). Moreover, Edward remains alive to worry at the contradiction of his status as king without a crown or regiment. Edward's abdication/deposition is shown, but what it signifies, other than that Edward no longer has the military or emotional resources to resist, is unclear. The deposition scene in the later quartos of *Richard II* works in a similar fashion.

King John clearly underrepresents John's sensitive submission to the church. Where *The Troublesome Reign* attempts to direct attention from the constitutional consequences by focusing on John's reasons for, and reactions to, his swearing fealty, *King John* takes only 65 lines (during which John also hears of the effects of Arthur's death upon the rebels) to cover the period between the first mention of the idea and Falconbridge's rejection of it as an "inglorious league". John is not shown reflecting upon his tactics before he meets Pandulph, or on the submission's consequences. Although the play underrepresents this episode in comparison to *The Troublesome Reign,* what happens is still clear. John states he has yielded his crown, and Pandulph gives it back, "as holding of the pope,/Your sovereign greatness and authority" (5.1.3-4). Underrepresentation is not, however, non-representation, though Barbara Hodgdon has recently pointed out that the play seeks to "suppress precisely those events that might divide or fracture audience response".[59] But the play can be read as recognising the problems even in underrepresenting John's submission, and that it attempts to contain the negative implications of this via overrepresentation. It does not follow the Foxean strategy of presenting the recrowning with minimal comment and leaving the reader to point the moral; rather, it makes it difficult to understand, and thus subject to recuperative qualification by John's easily intelligible speeches in 3.1.

Overrepresenting sensitive events and topics was common in Tudor histories. A. R. Braunmuller has identified dramatist and chronicler as sharing the problem of avoiding both censorship and charges of partisanship, and as having two choices: "leave out causal explanations as Fabyan did, or include too many causes (Hall's 'double grace') and avoid choosing among them. Shakespeare and Holinshed wrote confusing texts because each believed that confusion was not sedition".[60] Braunmuller's useful formulation of the available strategies is confirmed in Holinshed's preface to the reader: "I have in things doubtfull rather chosen to shew the diversitie of their writings, than by over-ruling them, and using a peremptory censure, to frame them to agree to my liking: leaving it nevertheless to each mans judgement, to controll them as he seeth cause".[61]

It is perhaps misleading to characterise historical writing as primarily concerned with avoiding sedition, rather than as attempting to make orthodox sense out of unpromising material. Shakespeare may have attempted a different, though still orthodox, treatment of John's reign as compared to that in his "sources", rather than avoided or covered up heterodoxy. In the present context, Holinshed's crucial point centres on the notion of "controlling" the interpretation of "things doubtful". Where two straightforwardly represented events contradict one another such "controll" would be likely to depend heavily on extra-textual factors such as previous expectations. Thus, in the case of *John,* an audience might compare his submission with his defiance, and conclude that no conclusion was possible. But if the defiance was straightforward, and the submission confusing, an audience is less likely to have seen the defiance as "cancelled" or invalidated by the submission. The defiance would be central to a re-

sponse to the play, and the submission marginal. Though *John* underrepresents John's submission in comparison with other texts, the issues upon which an interpretation depend are overrepresented: the validity of a recrowning, whether John can give away his crown, and what significance such an action has.

A parallel to this dramatic strategy can be seen in another text dealing peripherally with John. Thomas Wilson, writing in 1600 of the state of England, states that it is "an absolute Imperiall Monarchy held neither of Pope, Emperor, nor any but of God alone, and so hath bene ever since the year of the World 2855, which was 1108 years before Christ".[62] Wilson then engages with the supposed donation of Britain to the Papacy by the emperor Constantine, which he rebuts by pointing out that subsequent conquests extinguished Rome's right. The only other threat to this independent England is John's submission: "after this, K John did resign the Crowne to Pandolphus, the Pope's legate, and did receive it againe from him, to hold it of the Pope, paying yearly a certain Tribute; but then is easily answered (though it be the Pops strongest clayme) that King John was but an usurper, and being distressed besides with the Barons' Warres, he was forced to do yt to have the Pope's help, but his act was never confirmed by the States of the Country and therefore frivolous".[63]

This passage, written for private circulation and not printed until 1936, stresses the constitutional importance of an engagement with John's submission, though this is not a question Holinshed, Foxe or the *Homily* addressed. Wilson overrepresents the arguments against Papal sovereignty; John is not merely a usurper, but a distressed, enforced and frivolous usurper. The tactic here is not to provide one conclusive refutation, but to produce the impression that the cumulative force of all explanations is strong enough to show John's submission as irrelevant to the current situation. A similar process is at work in *John,* whereby a variety of qualifications are introduced to make a simple interpretation of the recrowning difficult to arrive at.

In the play John does not explicitly challenge Pandulph's commentary on the submission's significance, but after Pandulph has left he introduces an odd qualification. Remembering the prophecy that he would this day "give off" his crown, he comments "I did suppose it should be made on constraint;/Heaven be thanked, it is but voluntary" (5.1.28-9). Given that one of the foci of *The Homily's* treatment of John's recrowning is on the indignity of the English king being forced to submit, this statement can be seen as an attempt by John to reiterate his independence of Pandulph, so that the recrowning is a tactic, a piece of equivocation meaning nothing to John. At the least, the distinction between voluntary and involuntary uncrowning implies that this kind of recrowning is not as bad as its alternative. This muddle can be read as either denoting John's personal muddle (he has lost the crown but tries to persuade himself he hasn't) or as a piece of obliquity for which there is no clear interpretation (though the implication is that the recrowning is not what Pandulph thinks it is). Falconbridge's prompt criticism of John's "inglorious league" (5.1.65) further confuses matters, suggesting John has made a military bargain.

In the following scene, Pandulph is shown to be unable to honour his contract with John. Lewis, whom Pandulph has encouraged to invade, is one of the threats John fears. His first words after the truncated recrowning ceremony are to enjoin Pandulph to go "to meet the French,/And from his holiness use all your power/To stop their marches 'fore we are inflamed" (5.1.5-7). Not only is Pandulph unable to provide what John needs; he is also met with a forceful declaration of royal independence of the Papacy: "I am too high-born to be propertied,/To be a secondary at control,/Or useful serving-man and instrument/To any sovereign state throughout the world/[. . .] must I back/Because that John hath made his peace with Rome?/Am I Rome's slave?" (5.2.79-82, 95-7). Thus, although Pandulph clearly presents the recrowning as signifying John's subservience to the Pope, it is followed by an obscure distinction drawn by John, Falconbridge's perception that a purely political league has been made, and Lewis' declaration that he (and by implication, John) is royal and thus nobody's "slave". Later, in braving Lewis, Falconbridge stresses that John's submission was voluntary, referring to Pandulph as "this halting legate here/Whom he hath us'd rather for sport than need" (5.2.174-5).

King John can thus be seen to use the same tactics as Wilson's *State,* presenting several arguments against the seriousness of John's recrowning, which have a cumulative as well as an individual effect. It might even be said that much of the last third of the play is constructed to contradict Pandulph's claims of the significance of the recrowning, for only two scenes before John receives the crown back from Pandulph, he recrowns himself, and is criticised for so doing. In Act 4 John enters "once again crowned" (4.2.1). Though his nobles defer to John's right to do as he likes, the ceremony is presented, in the words of Pembroke as "superfluous: you were crowned before/And that high royalty was ne'er plucked off,/The faiths of men ne'er stained with revolt/Fresh expectation troubled not the land/With any longed-for change or better state" (4.2.4-8). Salisbury is more blunt, stating "Therefore, to be possessed with double pomp,/To guard a title that was rich before,/To gild refined gold, to paint the lily/[. . .] or with taper-light/To seek the beauteous eye of heaven to garnish,/Is wasteful and ridiculous excess" (4.2.9-11, 14-16). The nobles' criticisms emphasise John's sumptuous excess, as well as

his political overcompensating: "In this the antique and well-noted face/Of plain old form is disfigured", "so new a fashion'd robe" "startles and frights consideration" (4.2.21-22, 27, 25). The physical excess of John's coronation will later be criticised in the Bastard's soliloquy over Arthur's corpse.

But just as prominent are the political arguments. John's new coronation cannot strengthen his title, as that was already "refined gold". He is trying to increase the light of the sun (himself) with a candle. Pembroke implies that the ceremony of recrowning might have some point in the context of a domestic rebellion as a reassertion of the proper relationship between king and nobles, but this does not validate the later recrowning, as no nobles are present. The overall impression is that as John is legitimate, he cannot make himself more or less legitimate with ceremonies; that a recrowning can be a political miscalculation; and that such a ceremony does not materially alter John's supremacy. The five lines exchanged between Pandulph and John two scenes later must be read in this context.

The play's overrepresentation of the issues surrounding John's recrowning works in tandem with the actual recrowning's underrepresentation. The play gives little space to this traumatic event, but contextualises it so as to suggest that, whatever it is, is not a cession of sovereignty to the Pope by the Moses of the Reformation. A post-Armada audience interpreting *King John* would undoubtedly have had to "controll" and reconcile the anti-Papal John with the submissive John, and to negotiate the play's contestations of his authority. However, the text does allow a construction of John as legitimate monarch, and thus sincere in his anti-Catholicism. This presentation of John would also have accorded with those in Holinshed, Foxe, the *Homily* and *The Troublesome Reign,* and would not have offended contemporary anti-Spanish or anti-Catholic nationalism. The model offered by critics identifying the play as "modern", in contrast, situates the play as against the grain of most influential historical accounts, the predominant "war fever" of the theatrical repertory, and the likely mood of wartime London. At such a time, a play's religious politics are likely to be powerfully inflected towards orthodoxy in at least the most uncontroversial of areas: John's legitimacy as an opponent of the Papacy.

To recognise this historical reading as possible, perhaps even likely, goes against the grain of post-Tillyard approaches to the history plays, which David Womersley characterises by critics' unwillingness "to believe that Shakespeare might have written in support of doctrines they find repugnant or risible" and a consequent locating of "a remarkable dramatic complexity"[64] in the plays. The reinvention of the history plays described from a different perspective by

Womersley and Curren-Aquino has helped to continue Shakespeare's dominance of the Renaissance canon as continually relevant politically, something which happens surprisingly frequently by the traditional critical/polemical tactic of presenting Shakespeare, or his texts, as rising above the simplicity and polemic of contemporary "sources". I have attempted to show how it is possible to read *King John* as irrelevant to modern political concerns, and that in at least one important respect Shakespeare is not our "ambivalent, ambiguous, sceptical, questioning and ideologically subversive" contemporary.

Notes

[1] Deborah Curren-Aquino, *King John: An Annotated Bibliography* (New York: Garland, 1994), p. xxvi.

[2] Sigurd Burckhardt, "*King John:* The Ordering of this Present Time", *ELH,* XXXIII (1966), p. 133.

[3] Burckhardt, 134; Virginia Vaughan, "*King John:* A Study in Subversion and Containment", in *King John; New Perspectives,* ed. Deborah Curren-Aquino (London and Toronto: Associated UP, 1989), p. 62.

[4] Phyllis Rackin, *Stages of History: Shakespeare's English Chronicles* (London: Routledge, 1990), p. 66.

[5] Larry Champion, *"The Noise of Threatening Drum": Dramatic Strategy and Political Ideology in Shakespeare and the English Chronicle Plays* (London and Toronto: Associated UP, 1990), p. 98.

[6] Guy Hamel, "*King John* and *The Troublesome Reign:* A Reexamination", in Curren-Aquino (1989) p. 54.

[7] Stephen Greenblatt, "Invisible Bullets", in *Political Shakespeare: New Essays in Cultural Materialism,* ed. Jonathan Dollimore and Alan Sinfield (Manchester: Manchester UP, 1985), p. 29; *King John,* ed. Robert Smallwood (Harmondsworth: Penguin, 1974), p. 12.

[8] David Aers, "A Whisper in the Ear of Early Modernists", *Culture and History 1350-1600: Essays on English Communities, Identities and Writing,* ed. David Aers (Hemel Hempstead: Harvester Wheatsheaf, 1992), pp. 195-6.

[9] E.M.W. Tillyard, *Shakespeare's History Plays* (London, 1944; repr. Harmondsworth: Penguin, 1986), p. 220; see also M.M. Reese, *The Cease of Majesty* (London: Arnold, 1961), p. 270; Irving Ribner, *The English History Play in the Age of Shakespeare* (Princeton: Princeton UP, 1957: rev. edn, London: Methuen, 1965), pp. 121-2; David Bevington, *Tudor Drama and Politics* (Cambridge, MA: Harvard UP, 1968), p. 200.

[10] This argument is developed thoroughly in Deborah

[10] (cont.) Kehler, "'So Jest With Heaven': Deity in *King John*", in Curren-Aquino (1989) p. 101.

[11] *King John* ed E.A.J. Honigmann (London: Methuen, 1954), 3.1.75-86. Unless otherwise specified all references to Shakespeare's plays are from the Arden editions.

[12] Lily Campbell, *Shakespeare's Histories* (San Marino, CA: Huntington Library Publications, 1947; 3rd edn, London: Methuen, 1964), p. 154.

[13] C.W. Heiatt, "Dating *King John*", *N&Q,* xxxv (1988), p. 463 dates the play to 1593/4; Roslyn Knutson, *The Repertory of Shakespeare's Company 1594-1613* (Fayetteville: Arkansas UP, 1991), p. 75 suggests 1596-97; L.A. Beaurline's edition of *King John* (Cambridge UP, 1990), p. 210 plumps for 1590; A.R. Braunmuller's edition (Oxford UP, 1989), p. 15 chooses 1595-96; Smallwood, p. 10 also supports 1593/4, and Honigmann, p. lviii 1590/1.

[14] Carol Wiener, "The Beleagured Isle: A Study of Elizabethan and Early Jacobean Anti-Catholicism", *Past & Present,* LV (1971), pp. 52-3; R.B. Wernham, *After the Armada* (Oxford: OUP, 1984), pp. 453-60.

[15] David Cressy, *Bonfires and Bells: National Memory and the Protestant Calendar in Elizabethan and Stuart England* (London: Weidenfeld & Nicolson, 1989), p. 119.

[16] Peter Clark, "A Crisis Contained? The Condition of English Towns in the 1590s", in *The European Crisis of the 1590s* ed. Peter Clark (London: Allen & Unwin, 1985), p. 55.

[17] Clark, p. 46.

[18] R.B. Outhwaite, "Dearth, the English Crown and the 'Crisis of the 1590s'", in Clark (1985), p. 25; Henry Knyvett, *The Defence of the Realm* (Oxford: Clarendon Press, 1906).

[19] A. Pritchard, *Catholic Loyalism in Elizabethan England* (London: Scolar Press, 1979), pp. 6-8, 12.

[20] T.E. Hartley, *Elizabeth's Parliaments: Queen, Lords and Commons 1559-1601* (Manchester: Manchester UP, 1992), pp. 98-101.

[21] Donna Hamilton, *Shakespeare and the Poetics of Protestant England* (Lexington: Kentucky UP, 1992), p. 4.

[22] Peter Lake, *Moderate Puritans and the Elizabethan Church* (Cambridge: Cambridge UP, 1982), p. 6.

[23] See Carole Levin, *Propaganda in the English Ref-*

ormation: Heroic and Villainous Images of King John (Lewiston/Queenston, NY: Edwin Mellen Press, 1988).

24 Raphael Holinshed, *Chronicles of England, Scotland and Ireland,* Vol. II (London, 1807; repr. New York: AMS Press, 1965), pp. 339, 319.

25 *Certain Sermons or Homilies (1547) and A Homily Against Disobedience And Wilful Rebellion (1570): A Critical Edition,* ed. Ronald Bond (Toronto and London: Toronto UP, 1987), p. 243.

26 Wernham, p. 555.

27 Andrew Gurr, *Playgoing in Shakespeare's London* (Cambridge: Cambridge UP, 1987), p. 135.

28 Bevington, p. 195.

29 Rackin, p. 187.

30 Reese, p. 270.

31 Robert Ornstein, *A Kingdom for a Stage* (Cambridge, MA: Harvard UP, 1972), p. 88.

32 John Blanpied, *Time and the Artist in Shakespeare's English Histories* (London and Toronto: Associated UP, 1983), pp. 100-101. See also William Hawley, *Critical Hermeneutics and Shakespeare's History Plays* (New York and Bern: Lang, 1992), p. 70.

33 Vaughan, 1989, p. 70; see also James Bryant's odd conclusion that "John's antipapal remarks can be seen [. . .] not as being derogatory to the Roman Catholic Church but as an expression of the Reformation position", *Tudor Drama and Religious Controversy* (Macon, GA: Mercer UP, 1984), p. 133.

34 *Narrative and Dramatic Sources of Shakespeare,* ed. Geoffrey Bullough (London: Routledge & Kegan Paul, 1962), Vol. IV, p. 22.

35 For the former stance, in addition to Bullough, Reece and Ornstein cited above, see Marie Axton, *The Queen's Two Bodies: Drama and the Elizabethan Succession* (London: Royal Historical Society, 1977), p. 108; Philip Edwards, *Threshold of a Nation* (Cambridge: Cambridge UP, 1979), p. 115, and Bevington, p. 198. For the latter position, see Hawley, p. 70; Champion, p. 96; Hamel, p. 55.

36 Kehler, p. 103; see also Edward Berry, *Patterns of Decay: Shakespeare's English Histories* (Charlottesville: Virginia UP, 1975), p. 115.

37 Reese, p. 275; Emrys Jones, *The Origins of Shakespeare* (Oxford: Clarendon Press, 1977), p. 239.

38 Champion, p. 96.

39 Rackin, p. 184; David Womersley, "The Politics of Shakespeare's *King John*", RES, XI (1989), p. 502. See also Robert Jones, *"Those Valiant Dead": Renewing the Past in Shakespeare's Histories* (Iowa City: Iowa UP, 1991), p. 60 and Beaurline, p. 51.

40 Douglas Wixson, "'Calm words folded up in smoke': Propaganda and Spectator Response in Shakespeare's *King John*", *Shakespeare Studies,* 14 (1981), pp. 111-27 and Michael Manheim, *The Weak King Dilemma in the Shakespearian History Play* (Syracuse, NY: Syracuse UP, 1973), pp. 116-60.

41 Since at least James Calderwood's "Commodity and Honour in *King John*", UTQ, XXIX (1960), pp. 341-56.

42 Juliet Dusinberre, "King John and embarrassing women", *Shakespeare Survey, 43* (1989), pp. 37-52; Carole Levin, "'I trust I may not trust thee': Women's Visions of theWorld in Shakespeare's *King John*", in *Ambiguous Realities: Women in the Middle Ages and the Renaissance,* ed. Carole Levin and J. Watson (Detroit: Wayne State UP, 1987), pp. 219-34; Rackin, pp. 146-200.

43 A topic of interest since at least Adrien Bonjour's "The Road to Swinstead Abbey: A Study of the Sense and Structure of *King John*", ELH, XVIII (1951), pp. 253-74.

44 William Camden, *Remains Concerning Britain,* ed. R. Dunn (Toronto and London: Toronto UP, 1984), p. 246.

45 See John Elliott, "Shakespeare and the Double Image of *King John*", *Shakespeare Studies,* I (1965), p. 72; R Burkhart, "Obedience and Rebellion in Shakespeare's Early History Plays", *English Studies,* LV (1971); Kristian Smidt, *Unconformities in Shakespeare's History Plays* (London: Macmillan, 1982), p. 73; John Loftis, *Renaissance Drama in England and Spain* (Princeton: Princeton UP, 1987), p. 74; Bonjour, p. 257; Reese, p. 263; Manheim, p. 131; Edwards, p. 115, Levin, 1987, p. 221; Hamilton, p. 43; Berry, p. 115; Bevington, p. 243; Honigmann, p. xxvii; Beaurline, p. 47; Hawley, p. 64; Hodgdon, p. 27; Robert Jones, p. 48; Rackin, p. 162; Kehler, p. 103; Dusinberre, p. 44.

46 Reese, p. 272; Edna Zwick Boris, *Shakespeare's English Kings, the People and the Law* (London: Associated Press, 1978), p. 133.

47 *Cymbeline,* 1.6.114-6.

48 *Mr William Shakespeare's Comedies, Histories and*

Tragedies, facsimile prepared by H. Kökeritz (New Haven and London: Yale UP, 1954), pp. 17-18.

[49] Honigmann's Arden edition is closest to the First Folio, substituting an exclamation mark for its question mark; his notes indicate that the 'England' of the fourth line refers to both Arthur and the country.

[50] Axton, p. 109.

[51] Robert Jones, p. 60; see also Womersley, p. 502 and Smallwood, p. 38.

[52] John Sibly, "The Anomalous case of King John", *ELH,* XXXIII (1966), p. 421.

[53] Emrys Jones, p. 256; Robert Jones, p. 57; Calderwood, p. 97; Bonjour, p. 264; Champion, p. 92.

[54] Bond, p. 243.

[55] *Acts and Monuments,* Vol. II (London: Seeley Burnside & Seeley, 1843), p. 332. I have checked that this passage is not present in the 1583 edition.

[56] J. Leeds Barroll, "A New History for Shakespeare and His Time", *SQ,* XXIX (1988), pp. 441-64.

[57] *The Troublesome Reign of King John,* ed. Bullough, "To the Gentlemen Readers", p. 72. All quotations from *The Troublesome Reign* are from this edition.

[58] *Edward the Second,* ed. W Moelwyn Merchant (London: Benn, 1967), 5.1.26.

[59] Hodgdon, p. 30.

[60] A.R. Braunmuller, *"King John* and Historiography", *ELH,* LV (1988), p. 318.

[61] Holinshed, "Preface to the Reader". [*Chronicles,* Vol. II].

[62] Thomas Wilson, *The State of England Anno Dom 1600,* ed. F. Fisher, *Camden Miscellany, XVI* (London, 1936), p. 1.

[63] Wilson, p. 2.

[64] Womersley, p. 499.

Source: "The Limits of Modernity in Shakespeare's *King John,*" in *Shakespeare and History,* edited by Holger Klein and Rowland Wymer, The Edwin Mellen Press, 1996, pp. 91-118.

"A Monster Great Deformed": The Unruly Masculinity of Richard III

Ian Frederick Moulton, *Arizona State University West*

In recent years, largely due to the work of feminist critics and queer theorists, the dynamics of gender in the early modern period have been subjected to a thorough re-evaluation. In general this body of work stands as a successful and convincing attempt to shift attention from the center to the margins and to validate the experiences, lives, and struggles of those who did not belong to the male elites that were theoretically and materially at the apex of early modern society. In this paper, rather than exploring possibilities at the margins, I wish to concentrate on incoherence at the center by examining some of the fault lines that existed in the practice and gender ideology of masculinity in early modern patriarchy. Sodomy may have been (and may still be) an "utterly confused category,"[1] but to a lesser degree all ideologies of gender are confused, in that they represent contingent responses to a host of social and cultural imperatives, many of which are conflicting or are themselves confused.

One of the greatest structural problems facing any patriarchal society is the control of the masculine aggressivity, violence, and self-assertion that constitute patriarchy's base. Although patriarchy depends on male homosocial ties and masculine aggressivity for its organization and enforcement, the masculine values inculcated by patriarchal societies can themselves pose a threat to patriarchal order.[2] In early modern London a considerable amount of official energy was devoted, with uneven results, to curbing unruly masculine aggression. Tensions raised by the war with Spain and by rapid population growth led to thirty-five outbreaks of disorder in the capital between 1581 and 1602. While most of these disturbances were described by contemporaries as riots of "apprentices," the disorderly crowds also included servants, masterless men, and discharged soldiers and sailors.[3] Although public order in London was generally under the jurisdiction of the City government, the crown was sufficiently fearful of civil unrest in the capital to interfere on many occasions in order to preserve the peace. After a particularly notorious assault by apprentices on Lincoln's Inn in 1590, Elizabeth issued a proclamation that enjoined all masters to keep their apprentices within their houses and imposed a nine o'clock curfew on all apprentices in the surrounding parishes.[4] Concerned about the frequency with which common people were carrying arms, especially pistols or "dagges," Elizabeth issued proclamations throughout her reign in an attempt to curb the practice.[5] The unauthorized carrying of pistols was said to lead to "disorders, insolencies, robberies, and murders," both in London and in the countryside. Also forbidden in these proclamations were the wearing of concealed firearms and "Shooting in any such small Pieces, within two myles of any house where her Maiestie shall reside."[6] While such ordinances, like those issued against vagrant soldiers,[7] were aimed primarily at curbing the violence of lower-class men, in 1613 James issued ordinances against duelling in an effort to end the "odious" practice of private quarrels to the death among young men of "worthie Families."[8]

To focus on patriarchy's inability to control the masculine aggressivity it fosters is not to claim that unruly men are the primary victims of patriarchy but rather to point out an important structural incoherence in any society organized around the supremacy of aggressive masculinity. As Norbert Elias and others have argued, the transition of the male elite from a warrior to a court culture in the sixteenth and seventeenth centuries was marked by an increasing sublimation of affect and the gradual appearance of "pacified social spaces . . . normally free from acts of violence."[9] Manuals of aristocratic conduct such as Castiglione's enormously popular *Book of the Courtier* are largely devoted to negotiating the gap between ideologies of masculinity based on physical force and the novel social situation of the Renaissance court, in which graceful dancing and measured speech were as crucial to a successful courtier as fencing and riding.[10]

While the evolution in manners which Elias describes is an enormously complex process whose implementation is always contested and never completed, in late sixteenth-century England anxieties about unruly masculine aggression were exacerbated by the contemporary political situation. The monarch, who ought to incarnate patriarchy symbolically in the body politic of the kingship, was not a man but a woman, Elizabeth I, whose body natural was feminine and who was incapable of producing a male heir because of her advanced age. Worse, from 1588 to Elizabeth's death in 1603, England was at war with Spain, and thus for fifteen years the national conduct of the most masculine of pursuits, warfare, was in the hands of an elderly woman. That Elizabeth proved herself an able if reluctant leader of a nation at war did not diminish anxieties about her gender or about the uncertain succession. And while in retrospect the 1588 defeat of the Spanish Armada marked the high point of the conflict, this was certainly not apparent at the time: 1589 saw the launching of an English fleet against Spain, and in both 1596 and 1597 Spain launched against England armadas as large as the one of 1588. On land the war was fought by English troops in France, the Low Countries, and Ireland.[11]

While the queen and her more seasoned councillors prudently saw the war with Spain as a calamity to be borne as well as could be, many of her male courtiers—the earl of Essex chief among them—were eager to prove themselves warriors and saw the conflict not as a potential national disaster but as an unprecedented opportunity for individual initiative and personal glory.[12] Lacking the resources to prosecute the war with a national army and navy, Elizabeth was forced to rely on private initiatives, led by courtiers and financed by joint-stock companies, to launch attacks on Spanish interests.[13] The English response to the Spanish threat was thus characterized by tensions between the female monarch and powerful, ambitious, and semi-independent male subjects.

The Elizabethan public stage reacted quickly to the war with Spain and the various enthusiasms and anxieties it provoked. The vogue for English history plays is almost exactly contemporaneous with the war. There were history plays in England both before 1588 (such as Bale's *Kynge Johan,* Norton and Sackville's *Gorboduc,* and Thomas Preston's *Cambises*) and after 1603 (Ford's *Perkin Warbeck,* among others); but as a genre on the popular stage, the English history play flourished after the success of Marlowe's *Tamburlaine* (1587-88). Following Elizabeth's death and the end of the war in 1603, there was a "rapid decline" in both the quality and quantity of history plays.[14] In the early 1590s, arguably the most influential writer of history plays was the young William Shakespeare, whose first four histories—the three parts of *Henry VI* and *Richard III*—had proved enormously popular.[15] While these plays dealt with English wars of the fifteenth century, they also addressed concerns and anxieties provoked by the contemporary war with Spain: they focus on the dangers of feminine rule, the problem of an uncertain succession to the crown, the threat of foreign invaders, and the excesses of unruly or self-serving captains.

During the war itself—and in historical studies long afterwards—the tensions within the English ruling class between a queen "parsimoniously" waging a defensive war and dashing young captains advocating an invasion of Spain were often read in terms of conventional gender ideology—an indecisive, cautious, weak (and old) woman is set against active, bold, strong (and young) men.[16] It is not surprising, therefore, that Shakespeare's first tetralogy consistently reads the political struggles for the English crown in terms of gender. As studies of the first tetralogy by Leah S. Marcus and Phyllis Rackin make clear, political disorder in the *Henry VI* plays stems largely from feminine misrule.[17] Over the course of the three *Henry VI* plays,

effeminate rulers and mannish women destabilize the traditional patriarchal power structure and gender hierarchy of England, leaving the realm in chaos. Marcus, for example, gives an extended reading of the relation in *1 Henry VI* between Joan La Pucelle and Elizabeth, arguing that Shakespeare's staging of Joan addresses various anxieties about Elizabeth's role as a military leader in the war with Spain.[18]

Far less attention, however, has been paid to the workings of gender in *Richard III,* the concluding play of the tetralogy. Here masculine aggression runs rampant in the figure of Richard, who refuses to subordinate himself to traditional patriarchal power structures and lines of succession. In contrast to the feminine and effeminized disorder staged in the *Henry VI* plays, a specifically masculine disorder plagues the kingdom in *Richard III* until proper patriarchal proportion is reintroduced with the accession of the earl of Richmond as Henry VII. In what follows I will argue that Shakespeare's characterization of Richard III functions as both a critique and an ambivalent celebration of excessive and unruly masculinity and, in so doing, highlights the incoherence of masculinity as a concept in early modern English culture.

As the conflict between York and Lancaster progresses in the *Henry VI* plays, the patriarchal system itself seems to be in a state of collapse. Traditional gender values are inverted: it is a time of "perpetual shame," in which one finds "Women and children of so high a courage / And warriors faint!" (*3HVI,* 5.4.50-51).[19] The usurping power of strong, "mannish" women, such as Queen Margaret and Joan La Pucelle, has its corollary in the effeminate weakness of the English male elite, a weakness especially evident in the two rival monarchs, Henry VI and Edward IV. In the gender economy of early modern England, there is room for only one master: if women are mannish, men will necessarily become effeminate, and vice versa.

The reciprocal relationship between mannish women and effeminate men in the gender economy of early modern England is perhaps most clearly set forth in the pamphlet controversy over gender slippage which flared in the early 1620s. The *Haec-Vir* tract of 1620 concludes by blaming the mannishness of women on male effeminacy:

> Now since[,] . . . by the Lawes of Nature, by the rules of Religion, and the Customes of all ciuill Nations, it is necessary there be a distinct and speciall difference betweene Man and Woman, both in their habit and behauiours: what could we poore weake women doe lesse (being farre too weake by force to fetch backe those spoiles you haue vniustly taken from vs) then to gather vp those garments you haue proudly cast away, and therewith to cloath both our bodies and our mindes . . . ?[20]

The rhetoric of this passage is designed to downplay women's power by claiming that women assume authority only when men relinquish it, but in Shakespeare's first tetralogy mannish women are presented as active. Joan and Margaret are not "poore weake women." If effeminate men can produce mannish women, mannish women can produce effeminate men. Though the Yorkists attempt to blame the collapse of traditional gender order on Margaret, the plays make it clear that both of the male rulers themselves bear a burden of responsibility for the gender confusion and social disorder that plague the realm. For in quite different ways, but to much the same effect, both Henry VI and Edward IV are intolerably effeminate.

Henry VI's coming to the throne as an infant is a cause for great concern among his councillors (*1HVI*, 1.1.35-43; 4.1.192). Beyond the practical dangers of having a child monarch—conflict among the regents, uncertainty concerning the succession, and a general division of authority—a boy-king is also dangerously gendered. In early modern England aristocratic boys were not separated from their sisters and given distinctively masculine attire until the "breeching age" of six or seven years. Before that age upper-class male children were attended almost exclusively by women and were not differentiated by dress from girls. They participated in "the common gender of childhood," a gender marked as universally female and subordinate.[21] Coming to the throne when he is "but nine months old" (*3HVI*, 1.1.112), Henry VI becomes king before becoming masculine. Given a hierarchy of gender which sees ability to rule as a fundamentally masculine attribute, this situation is dangerously unstable.

In crucial ways Henry VI's developmental transformation from effeminate boy to masculine adult is never made, and this masculine weakness provides a domestic corollary to the external feminine threat posed to English patriarchy by the Amazonian foreigners Joan and Margaret.[22] The king's lack of manly resolve as a betrayal of patriarchal order is most clearly revealed when he gives away his heirs' rights to the crown, disinheriting his own son in order to placate the duke of York (*3HVI*, 1.1.170-80). Henry's failure to assert not only his own prerogative but also the rights of his male children leads one of his most ardent supporters, the hypermasculine Lord Clifford, to argue at length that the king is unnatural (*3HVI*, 2.2.9-42).

If Henry is utterly ineffective in asserting his rights through diplomacy, he is even less potent in war. King Henry is the very embodiment of "effeminate peace" (*1HVI*, 5.4.107), and Margaret and Clifford refuse even to let him on the battlefield with his own troops. "The Queen hath best success when you are absent," Clifford tells the king (*3HVI*, 2.2.74). Worse, Henry's effeminacy is potentially infectious. Margaret warns him that his "soft courage makes [his] followers faint" (*3HVI*,

2.2.57); and when captured by Warwick, his very presence as a captive is a liability: Warwick laments that "the coldness of the King" has "robbed my soldiers of their heated spleen" (*3HVI*, 2.1.122, 124). Since heat was characteristic of masculinity, cold of femininity, Henry's effeminate coldness chills the entire army.[23]

While Edward IV, who seizes the throne from Henry, seems the antithesis of his predecessor, he proves an equally effeminate ruler. In early modern England a man could show himself effeminate by being too devoted to women as well as by acting like a woman.[24] While Henry remains a perpetual child, tenderhearted, weak, asexual, and innocent,[25] Edward's effeminacy is manifested in his excessive sexual attraction to women. As his brother Richard pointedly reminds him, "You love the breeder better than the male" (*3HVI*, 2.1.42). The final cycle of disorder in the *Henry VI* plays is set in motion by Edward's impetuous marriage to Elizabeth Grey (*3HVI*, 3.2), which humiliates the powerful earl of Warwick (sent to the French court to negotiate a more prudent marriage) and alienates Edward's brother Clarence (who had hoped to marry Lady Grey himself). "In your bride," Richard warns Edward, "you bury brotherhood" (*3HVI*, 4.1.55). Although Edward eventually manages to regain Clarence's allegiance, defeat Warwick, and secure his hold on the crown, there are strong suggestions that he is finally undone by effeminate weakness. In *Richard III* Lord Hastings reports that Edward's doctors fear for his life because he is "sickly, weak, and melancholy" (all signs of effeminate weakness of spirit). Richard, always critical of his brother's inordinate affections, replies that the king has "overmuch consumed his royal person" and coyly asks whether Edward is still in bed (*RIII*, 1.1.135-42). Thus, although their weakness is figured in vastly different ways, both Edward and Henry blast their reigns with effeminate marriages. And destabilizing effeminacy afflicts not only Henry VI and Edward IV but many in the male ruling class, from Henry's regent, Gloucester, who has a proud wife (*1HVI*, 1.1.39), to the unfortunate Lord Hastings, whose corruption is publicly blamed on his affections for Mistress Shore (*RIII*, 3.5.31, 48-51).

Two parallel scenes in the *Henry VI* plays provide an index to the progressive decay of patriarchal order in the course of the tetralogy. In *1 Henry VI*, as Rackin suggests, the crisis of the patriarchy is clearly evident in the heroic deaths of Talbot and his only son, each of whom refuses to leave the line of battle while the other remains in danger (*1HVI*, 4.5-4.7). By making the slain young Talbot his father's only son (even though the historical Talbot had several children), Shakespeare rewrites history so that Talbot's line dies out, thus stressing the self-destructive tendencies within a patriarchal ethic that prizes the preservation of family honor above the lives of individual family members.[26]

As exemplary subjects of the patriarchy, Talbot and his son embody an idealized system of orderly masculine bonds—not only within generations of their own family but also in their comradeship with members of other great families such as Salisbury and Bedford. The strength of this masculine warrior society comes precisely from its cohesion as a community. Deprived of his companions and troops in his confrontation with the French countess of Auvergne, Talbot appears puny, misshapen, and insignificant: "a child, a silly dwarf! . . . [a] weak and writhled shrimp" (*1HVI,* 2.3.22-23). It is Talbot's comrades who make him a great and mighty man: "These are his substance, sinews, arms, and strength" (*1HVI,* 2.3.64). The death of Talbot and the extinction of his line come to represent the decline of the male bonds, both lateral and hierarchical, that constitute English strength. Even the most renowned English warrior clan is powerless to stem the tide of chaos overwhelming England's ruling classes. And, as David Riggs observes, no other characters in the first tetralogy emulate Talbot's example.[27]

If, at the beginning of the tetralogy, patriarchy is revealed as dysfunctional and incapable of passing its values to future generations, by 2.5 of *3 Henry VI* the basic structures of patriarchy are shattered: no longer do fathers and sons share the same ideals and fight side by side; instead the hapless king witnesses the horrible spectacle of fathers killing sons and sons killing fathers. Aristocratic masculine aggressivity—which is presented as doomed, if admirably heroic, in the case of Talbot and his son—has degenerated utterly. In the absence of strong masculine royal authority, English manhood, unruled and untamed, turns to devour itself. It is this unregulated, destructive masculine force that is personified in the twisted and deformed body of Richard III.

Though it is clearly a continuation of the historical narrative of the *Henry VI* plays and was included among the histories in the First Folio, on all its quarto and Folio title pages *Richard III* is, like Marlowe's *Tamburlaine,* identified as a tragedy.[28] The play's generic classification is not without significance for its treatment of gender. As Catherine Belsey, Bruce R. Smith, and others have argued, tragedy is a genre that, perhaps more than any other in early modern England, is gendered male.[29] Thus it is significant that the shift from history to tragedy in the first tetralogy comes at the point where masculine aggression, not feminine assertiveness, becomes the focus of the drama. Like Tamburlaine, Richard is consistently characterized in strongly masculine terms, and his hypermasculinity is closely tied to his aggressive pursuit of power over effeminate pleasure. In the great soliloquy in *3 Henry VI* in which he first articulates his "soul's desire" for the crown, Richard firmly rejects the possibility of finding "heaven in a lady's lap" and decides instead that for him "this earth affords no joy . . . / But to

command, to check, to o'erbear" (*3HVI,* 3.2.128, 148, 165-66). In the famous opening of *Richard III,* Richard forcefully expresses his disgust with "idle pleasures" in a speech that, in its reiterated movement from "stern alarums" to "merry meetings," from "dreadful marches" to "delightful measures," from violence to pleasure, and from rage to joy, provides an anatomy of effeminization (*RIII,* 1.1.131, 7-8).[30]

Though Richard and Tamburlaine's love of war might seem to us monstrous in itself, their sentiments were shared by many Englishmen at the time the plays were first performed. In his famous antitheatrical tract *The Schoole of Abuse* Stephen Gosson attacks the effeminate corruption of English manhood in terms much the same as those Richard uses: he laments the decline of the "olde discipline of Englande" and complains that "our wreastling at armes, is turned to wallowyng in Ladies laps."[31] Similar opinions are voiced in Phillip Stubbes's *Anatomie of Abuses* as well as in Sir Thomas Hoby's popular translation of Castiglione's *Book of the Courtier.*[32]

Just as the dissolution of patriarchal order grows progressively worse in the course of the tetralogy, so Richard grows progressively more monstrous. Though he is born deformed and much is made of his unnatural birth, Richard is not, when he first appears, as monstrous as he will later become. In *2 Henry VI* Richard is a minor character; and while he baits Clifford and slays Somerset in battle (*2HVI,* 5.1.151-56; 5.2.66-71), he shows none of his later cunning or ruthless lust for mastery. In the tragedy that bears his name, Richard is eager only to increase and consolidate his personal power at any cost; but in the early scenes of *3 Henry VI,* Richard is clearly shown to be capable of affection and deeply devoted to his father. Rhapsodizing on his father's bravery in battle, he exclaims, "Methinks 'tis prize enough to be his son" (*3HVI,* 2.1.20), and although this outburst could not provide a greater contrast to the Richard who later claims his only "heaven [is] to dream upon the crown" (*3HVI,* 3.2.168), there is no reason to doubt the sincerity of his remark. Richard's devotion to his father marks him as an orderly subject of the patriarchy and as a member of a masculine community, linked by bonds of loyalty to both his father and his brothers.

The death of Richard's father at the hands of Margaret and Clifford is the occasion for a complete transformation in Shakespeare's representation of Richard. York's death comes to serve as an emblem for his son Richard's alienation from the patriarchal masculine community, and the change in Richard's social position is manifested by a precise physical change. If Warwick's army is chilled by Henry's effeminate coldness, here Richard is overcome with surfeit of masculine heat which makes it physically impossible for him to weep. This shift in Richard's humoral makeup is described in remarkable detail:

I cannot weep, for all my body's moisture
Scarce serves to quench my furnace-burning
   heart;
Nor can my tongue unload my heart's great
   burden,
For selfsame wind that I should speak
   withal
Is kindling coals that fires all my breast,
And burns me up with flames that tears
   would quench.
To weep is to make less the depth of
   grief.
Tears, then, for babes; blows and revenge
   for me!

                     (*3HVI*, 2.1.79-86)

This moment is crucial enough in Richard's development as a character for Shakespeare to recall it in detail in *Richard III*: Richard tells Anne that when his father died, though "all the standers-by had wet their cheeks / Like trees bedashed with rain—in that sad time / My manly eyes did scorn an humble tear" (*RIII*, 1.2.165-67).[33]

In the humoral physiology of the early modern period, the human body was conceived as a "semipermeable, irrigated container" of fungible liquids—blood, sperm, bile, phlegm, tears, sweat.[34] As John Donne asserted in a Lenten sermon of 1623, "every man is but a spunge, and but a spunge filled with teares."[35] To be healthy, the fragile balance of liquid humors in the body had to be carefully maintained according to an economy of heat and cold which differed for men and women: men ought ideally to be relatively hot and dry, women to be moist and cold. In figuring his heart as a fiery furnace, Richard clearly describes the processes by which his metabolic equilibrium is being thrown out of balance. An excess of masculine heat is parching his body: he is drying up. His inability to cry prevents his body from maintaining a healthy humoral balance.

Although throughout *Richard III* weeping is seen as characteristic of women, children, and effeminate lovers (e.g., 1.2.157-58; 2.2; 4.4.201-2), it is important to realize that weeping as such was not uniformly conceived of as unmanly in early modern culture. Just as in the patriarchal cultures of antiquity, men were traditionally permitted, even expected, to weep on just the occasion when Richard proves unable to—the death of a comrade in battle.[36] Thus Richard's own father weeps for the death of his youngest son, crying, "These tears are my sweet Rutland's obsequies, / And every drop cries vengeance for his death" (*3HVI*, 1.4.147-48). York's reading of his own tears as a sign of vengeance demonstrates that the dichotomy between weeping and manliness, between mourning and vengeance, is not a cultural imperative but rather a paradigm that Richard chooses to adopt.[37]

After his father's death Richard's physical abnormality—his monstrosity—obtains inwardly as well as outwardly: his humoral imbalance, his excessive heat, is just as monstrous as his crooked back and withered arm. His physical monstrosity manifests itself as social monstrosity. While York lives, Richard's devotion to his father marks him as an orderly subject of the patriarchy; though he (and his family) are in rebellion against the monarch, Richard accepts patriarchy as such. His loyalty is to the father of his family rather than to King Henry, who has failed so singularly as father of the country. But Richard's inability to mourn York's death marks a perverse turning away from patriarchal principles.[38] Left without a father to subordinate himself to, Richard fights for himself alone. As he proudly declares after killing Henry VI,

I have no brother, I am like no brother;
And this word "love," which graybeards call
   divine,
Be resident in men like one another
And not in me. I am myself alone.

                     (*3HVI*, 5.6.80-83)

Richard believes his deformity sets him apart from others, but instead it is his aggressively masculine singularity that constitutes his monstrosity. His ambition, his prowess as a warrior, his viciousness, his cruel intelligence—the same masculine qualities that made him an asset to the Yorkists as a group—become monstrous when cut loose from the structure of bonds between male warriors which constitutes English ruling-class society. The alienation of Richard's masculinity from the patriarchal order that ought to channel its energies gives his physical deformity significance; indeed it is only after his father's death that he begins to lament his condition and to devise various explanations and genealogies for it (*3HVI*, 3.2.146-95; 5.6.68-83).

From the death of York onward, much is made in the tetralogy of Richard's deformity and his monstrous birth: he was a premature child, "an indigested and deformèd lump," born with teeth "to signify [he came] . . . to bite the world." His birth was heralded by horrid omens, and his "mother felt more than a mother's pain" (*3HVI*, 5.6.51, 54, 49). In early modern England the birth of a deformed child was inevitably seen as portentous,[39] and in Richard's case his deformed body figures his masculinity as both perverse and dangerous for the nation. Some indication of the degree of cultural fascination with monstrous births in the late sixteenth century can be seen in such texts as Stephen Batman's lengthy tract titled *The Doome warning all men to the Iudgemente,* a compendium of "all the straunge Prodigies" and "secrete figures of Reuelations" from the time of Adam and Eve to the day the book was published.[40] Batman casts all human history as a chronicle of reiterated warning, in which every so-called aberration of nature—from rhinoceroses to still-births, from floods to dreams (including Richard's dream of "deformed Images" on the evening of the battle at Bosworth[41])—is a divine portent filled with inescapable and terrifying significance.

As contemporary broadside ballads about deformed infants and animals can attest, deformity is invariably read as a warning against sin—sins often understood as erotic in origin and national in scope. For example, a 1568 broadside setting forth "The forme and shape of a monstrous Child, / born at Maydstone in Kent" is subtitled "A warnyng to England." The broadside reads each deformity of a male infant's body as representing a specific corruption of the English nation: a disfigured mouth indicates filthy speech; a hand with no fingers indicates idleness; and so on. The last part of the malformed body to be thus anatomized is "the hinder part," which "shew vs playne, / Our close and hidden vice."[42] While the erotic overtones of this secret vice are clear enough, neither the prose description of the baby nor the accompanying woodcut mention or show any deformity of the boy's "hinder part." It is as if even "normal" genitals constituted a deformity, a sign of sinfulness and the Fall.

Often a deformed or "monstrous" child was read as a sign that its parents' sexual union had been sinful.[43] As another broadside announcing a monstrous male child conceived out of wedlock puts it, "nature iust enuyed / Her gyft to hym, and cropd wyth mayming knyfe / His limmes, to wreake her spyte on parentes sinne."[44] In the French surgeon Ambroise Paré's 1573 treatise *On Monsters and Marvels*, monstrous births are frequently attributed to aberrant or unnatural erotic practices, such as having intercourse during menstruation. The imagination of women during sex could result in monstrosity: a white woman thinking of a "Moor" could give birth to a dark-skinned child. And if a pregnant woman sat in an "indecent posture," she could deform the fetus she carried.[45]

In broadside ballads the specific nature of a child's deformities is often read as a sign of England's sexual sins. A 1566 broadside that describes "two monsterous children," a boy and a girl, "having both their belies fast ioyned together, and imbracyng one an other with their armes," interprets their "imbracyng" as a warning against the nation's "secret sinnes." The sheet goes on to compare the twins to the "monstrous" races rumored to inhabit "Affrique land" and argues that because England has embraced the "mischeefs great" of foreign and savage lands, the deformities common to such regions are now found in England itself.[46] Another sheet from the same year describes a girl born with rufflike folds of skin on her neck, a deformity that is—predictably—construed as a warning against women's rich and erotically enticing apparel:

Deformed are the things we were,
 Deformed is our hart;
The Lord is wroth with all this geere,—
 Repent for fere of smarte! . . .
And thou, O England, whose womankinde
 In ruffes doo walke to oft,
Parswade them stil to bere in minde
 This Childe with ruffes so soft.[47]

The tendency to conflate eroticism and deformity is conveyed especially graphically in an anonymous erotic poem circulated in manuscript in England in the early seventeenth century, in which the male lover's penis is described as

A monster great deformed, that had on[e] eye
Was full of hayre and had a naked head
most strongly vayn'd, and the top, being
 redd
hee draweth forth, and In on[e of]'s handes
(Apt for the sport) hee shaking of it
 stande[s].[48]

Here the indisputable sign of masculine gender, the organ whose possession grants authority to rule, is seen as a deformed monster that can be mastered only with great effort.

In their writings on deformity, both Michel de Montaigne and Francis Bacon relate physical malformation to excesses and deficiencies in erotic ability. Montaigne speculates that

'He knowes not the perfect pleasure of Venus, *that hath not laine with a limping Woman.'* . . . and it is as well spoken of men as of women: For the Queene of the Amazons answered the Scithian, that wooed her to loves-embracements. . . . *The crooked man doth it best.*

Physical deformity was also thought to cause a shift in the erotic economy of the body. Montaigne asserts that the disabled of both sexes have superior sexual abilities and enlarged genitals:

ancient Philosophy . . . saith, that the legs and thighs of the crooked-backt or halting-lame, by reason of their imperfection, not receiving the nourishment, due unto them, it followeth that the Genitall parts, that are above them, are more full, better nourished and more vigorous. Or else, that such a defect hindring other exercise, such as are therewith possessed, do lesse waste their strength and consume their vertue, and so much the stronger and fuller, they come to *Venus* sports.

For those skeptical of such theoretical speculations, Montaigne offers a more practical explanation of the phenomenon:

I would have saide, that the loose or disjoynted motion of a limping or crooke-backt Woman, might adde some new kinde of pleasure unto that businesse or sweet sinne.[49]

Where Montaigne sees "crooked men" as sexual athletes, for Bacon physical deformity is a sign of perverse desire. In his essay "Of Deformity," Bacon claims scriptural authority for the notion that deformed persons are *void of natural affection,*[50] a phrase that appears twice in the Pauline epistles in the King James Bible, though in neither case does it refer to the physically deformed. In 2 Timothy, those "without natural affection" are characterized as "lovers of pleasures more than lovers of God." In Romans, Paul is more specific: the phrase refers to those "men [who], leaving the natural use of the woman, burned in their lust one toward another; men with men working that which is unseemly"[51]—or, in the parlance of the early modern period, sodomites. Through these explicit Pauline references, Bacon draws attention to the sexualized nature of deformity—a person who is physically deformed may also be erotically perverse.

Bacon also contends that, if the genitals do not function properly, erotic energy will circulate in other channels, and he cites eunuchs as an example of how "deformity is an advantage to rising [in social standing]."[52] That which is unable to raise itself physically may rise socially instead. Clearly this is the social dynamic of Richard's deformity. Given the fungibility of all body fluids in humoral physiology, perhaps Richard's semen has dried up along with his tears. Certainly, despite his concern to buttress his rule with dynastic marriages, he gives no thought to progeny. A phallic "monster great deformed," perpetually engaged in erecting himself, he is, as many commentators have noted, utterly barren, able to destroy and corrupt but not to create. Thus, detached from patriarchal economies of reproduction, the very phallic power on which patriarchal order depends becomes monstrously destructive.

It is in this context that one must read the frequently reiterated trope of Richard as a wild boar (*RIII,* 3.2.11, 28-33, 72-73; 4.5.1-3; 5.3.156). While a white boar was historically Richard III's heraldic emblem, the image of a "bloody, and usurping boar," who rampages through "summer fields and fruitful vines" and "makes his trough" in the "emboweled bosoms" of his innocent foes (*RIII,* 5.2.7-10) cannot but recall Shakespeare's *Venus and Adonis,* in which a youthful and effeminate Adonis flees an aggressive Venus only to be gored to death by a monstrous boar who is the very embodiment of bestial masculinity. As Peter Stallybrass and Allon White suggest, the boar, and indeed the pig in general, is a creature who occupies a special place in the symbolic topography of early modern European culture. Kept in the home and fed

on scraps, an animal whose pink skin "disturbingly resemble[s] the flesh of European babies," the pig was a "creature of the threshold" which "overlapped with, and confusingly debased, human habitat and diet alike. Its mode of life was not different from, but alarmingly imbricated with, the forms of life which betokened civility."[53]

Curiously, those ballads on prodigious births which do not describe human babies tend to describe pigs. A broadside of 1570, for example, entitled "A meruaylous straunge deformed Swyne," makes an explicit link between deformity, swinishness, and treason:

> Judge ye againe that hate your prince,
>   And seeke the realme to spoyle,
> What monstrous Swine you proue at length,
>   For all your couert coyle.[54]

In a similar register Margaret calls Shakespeare's Richard an "abortive, rooting hog" (*RIII,* 1.3.228), and Batman describes Richard's corpse after Bosworth as "caried to *Leicester* like a hogge." What more appropriate emblem for crooked Richard, the "indigested and deforméd lump," alienated from civilized society?

The social disruptiveness of Richard's aggressive masculinity is reflected in his utter contempt for women. Hatred, scorn, and fear of the feminine are fundamental to his character and go far beyond the violent hatred of the maternal which Janet Adelman has rightly seen as crucial to his self-fashioning.[55] Elizabeth of York is a "relenting fool, and shallow, changing woman" (*RIII,* 4.4.431); Margaret, a "withered hag" (*RIII,* 1.3.215). Clarence's imprisonment is blamed on the "mighty gossips in our monarchy" (*RIII,* 1.1.83), and Richard, when not blaming his mother for it, attributes his own deformity to female witches (*RIII,* 3.4.68-72). Feeling himself incapable of loving women, Richard endorses a (demonstrably false) opposition between effeminate love and masculine conquest and makes his "heaven to dream upon the crown."

In his relentless pursuit of power, however, not even so great a misogynist as Richard can afford to ignore women. For in a patriarchal society in which property and social status are passed from father to son, women are crucial to male power.[56] The importance of women's reproductive labor in the perpetuation of the patriarchal order is reflected in the fact that for many of Shakespeare's kings, courtship is a crucial act, which, as much as any other, defines the nature and legitimacy of their rule. As Jean Howard notes, in the second tetralogy the performative nature of courtship is stressed to an extent not evident in the earlier sequence of plays. Howard contrasts Hal's wooing of Katherine with the marriage of Richmond and Elizabeth which concludes the first tetralogy and argues that, because theirs is a strictly dynastic marriage and not an affective one, no wooing scene need be staged.[57] But while both Richmond and Elizabeth are securely positioned in the patriarchal order, Richard is alienated from it; so for him performative courtship is crucial.[58] As he himself puts it when planning his second marriage, "I must be married to my brother's daughter, / Or else my kingdom stands on brittle glass" (*RIII,* 4.2.60-61). Whereas his effeminate brother Edward put lust before policy in his ill-considered marriage to Elizabeth, Richard's wooing, both of Anne (*RIII,* 1.2) and of Elizabeth's daughter (*RIII,* 4.4), is an act of pure *Realpolitik,* in which he is motivated neither by lust nor affection: he will wed Anne, he says, "not all so much for love / As for another secret close intent / By marrying her which I must reach unto" (*RIII,* 1.1.157-59).

Richard endeavors to triumph over the discourses of erotic pleasure by subordinating them entirely to his desire for power. In his incredible seduction of Lady Anne, he skillfully employs the language of affection, sexual desire, and physical obsession (a language he despises as an indication of effeminate weakness) to achieve specific political ends.[59] By offering Anne his sword, he stages a calculated (and illusory) gender reversal, offering her an opportunity to exercise phallic power which he assumes in advance she will be incapable of accepting. Anne succumbs because she allows her political quarrel with Richard to be expressed in a discourse of erotic seduction which, while it gives her the illusion of power over her helpless "effeminate" suitor, actually constructs her as feminine and passive, Richard as masculine and active. As Linda Charnes suggests, once Anne has accepted the gender binaries inherent in Richard's conventional discourse of seduction, her failure to accept the role of masculine avenger which Richard mockingly offers her leaves her with no recourse but submission.[60] Faced with an opponent less willing to reconfigure the political as the erotic, Richard's gambit would have a vastly different outcome: a woman less willing to submit to conventional gender hierarchies (Margaret, say) would certainly plunge the sword through Richard's heart. Indeed, one of Richard's greatest errors is to assume that all women conform to gender stereotypes to the same extent as Anne. Richard always reads gender in essentialist terms, and thus, although his seduction of Lady Anne is successful, he elsewhere underestimates his female opponents.[61]

Richard III, of course, ends with the re-establishment of balanced patriarchal order in the figure of Richmond. It is made clear at every point that Richmond— unlike Richard—sees society in terms of broad kinship networks. He calls his captains "fellows in arms, and my most loving friends" (*RIII,* 5.2.1) and pointedly refers to his stepfather and ally in Richard's camp as "our father Stanley" (*RIII,* 5.2.5). His social vision includes the feminine in subordinate roles; he rules

women but does not reject or despise them. He respects his mother as well as his father (*RIII,* 5.3.80-82). Where Richard in his final address to his troops sees women as valuable property to be kept out of the enemy's hands ("Shall these enjoy our lands? Lie with our wives? / Ravish our daughters?" [*RIII,* 5.3.336-37]), Richmond offers a vision of a stable world held together in the present and the future by familial bonds of masculine duty and feminine and filial loyalty:

> If you do fight in safeguard of your wives,
> Your wives shall welcome home the
>   conquerors;
> If you do free your children from the sword,
> Your children's children quits it in your age.
>   (*RIII,* 5.3.259-62)

Richmond's moderate views may reinscribe comforting traditional hierarchies, but as every reader or viewer of the play knows, he is a flat, unmemorable character, far less vivid and compelling than the unruly monster killed on Bosworth Field. If early modern English drama from *Tamburlaine* to *Hamlet* and *Coriolanus* constructs the narrative of independent masculine aggression as a tragedy, in which an unruly, singular, yet compelling protagonist is inevitably destroyed by larger social forces, the flatness and unbelievability of Richmond suggest that on a larger cultural level the problems of unruly masculinity did not admit of easy resolution. The gap between courtly and warrior ideals resisted any simple gesture toward closure. Monstrous Richard can—indeed must—be killed, but his death is figured as a tragic loss, and no convincing successor can be imagined.

Notes

[1] This description of sodomy appears in Michel Foucault, *The History of Sexuality. Volume I: An Introduction,* trans. Robert Hurley (New York: Vintage, 1980), 101.

[2] See Lyndal Roper, *Oedipus and the Devil: Witchcraft, sexuality and religion in early modern Europe* (London and New York: Routledge, 1994), esp. chaps. 5 ("Blood and codpieces: masculinity in the early modern German town" [107-24]) and 7 ("Drinking, whoring and gorging: brutish indiscipline and the formation of Protestant identity" [145-67]). In particular Roper addresses the custom of *Zutrinken,* or competitive drinking, a "cornerstone of artisan brotherhood" (152) which led inevitably to drunken disputes. She also explores the general disjunction between the cultural ideal of the *Hausvater* and the actuality (revealed in ordinances of discipline and court records) of "drunken, brutish, debauched masters" (154). She discusses the efforts to abolish the wearing of elaborate codpieces and generally stresses the need for patriarchal social structures to control not only the potentially unchaste

bodies of women but also the "anarchic and undisciplined" bodies of men (117-20 and 153). On the opposition in early modern Italy between licit culture "focusing on marriage, family, and a morally ordered society" and the various illicit cultures (organized around such activities as adultery, whoring, and sodomy) associated with adolescent males, see Guido Ruggiero, "Marriage, love, sex, and Renaissance civic morality" in *Sexuality and Gender in Early Modern Europe: Institutions, texts, images,* James Grantham Turner, ed. (Cambridge: Cambridge UP, 1993), 10-30, esp. 16.

3 On riots and disorder in London and the social composition of the London "crowd," see Roger B. Manning, *Village Revolts: Social Protest and Popular Disturbances in England, 1509-1640* (Oxford: Clarendon Press, 1988), 187-219, esp. 191-93. Manning claims that in the late sixteenth century London suffered an "epidemic of disorder" and calls the Apprentices' Insurrection of 29 June 1595 "perhaps the most dangerous urban uprising of the century" (200-201). Manning differentiates the riots in Elizabeth's reign from the later Shrove Tuesday riots (c. 1606-41) in which theaters and brothels were sacked by apprentices in a ritual of festive misrule (192). The earlier disturbances were aimed not at relatively marginal figures such as prostitutes and actors but at local officials, such upper-class institutions as the Inns of Court, and aliens, including foreign ambassadors. See also Ian W. Archer, *The Pursuit of Stability: Social Relations in Elizabethan London* (Cambridge: Cambridge UP, 1991), 1-9 and 216; and Andrew Gurr, *The Shakespearean Stage 1574-1642,* 3d ed. (Cambridge: Cambridge UP, 1992), 14-15. On the representation of unruly apprentices in contemporary literature, see Mark Thornton Burnett, "Apprentice Literature and the 'Crisis' of the 1590s," *The Yearbook of English Studies* 21 (1991): 27-38.

4 See "By the Queene. Where the Queenes most Excellent Maiestie, being given to vnderstand of a very great outrage lately committed by some Apprentices . . . ," 24 September 1590 (STC 8196).

5 See "By the Quene. Forasmvch as contrary to good order . . . ," 17 May 1559 (STC 7898); "By the Queene. A Proclamation prohibiting the vse and cariage of Dagges, Birding pieces, and other Gunnes, contrary to the Law," 21 December 1600 (STC 8276); "By the Queene. A Proclamation against the common vse of Dagges, Handgunnes, Harqvebuzes, Calliuers, and Cotes of Defence," 26 July 1579 (STC 8113); and "By the Queene. A Proclamation against the carriage of Dags . . . ," 2 December 1594 (STC 8240). Similar proclamations had been made in the reigns of Henry VIII, Edward VI, and Mary.

6 See the proclamations published on 21 December 1600 (STC 8276) and 26 July 1579 (STC 8113).

7 See the proclamations of 13 November 1589 ("By the Queene. A Proclamation against vagarant Souldiers and others" [STC 8188]), 5 November 1591 ("By the Queene. The Queenes Maiesty vnderstanding of the common wandering abroad of a great multitude of her people . . ." [STC 8210]), and 28 February 1591 ("Whereas the Queenes Maiestie doth vnderstand, notwithstanding her late Proclamation concerning such persons as wander abroad . . ." [STC 8218]). On masterless men, see Manning, 157-86.

8 "A Pvblication of his Maties Edict, and severe Censvre against Priuate Combats and Combatants," 1613 (STC 8498); "By the King. A Proclamation against priuate Challenges and Combats: With Articles annexed . . . ," 18 November 1613 (may not have been promulgated until 4 February 1614 [STC 8497]).

9 Norbert Elias, *State Formation and Civilization,* Vol. 2 of *The Civilizing Process,* trans. Edmund Jephcott, 2 vols. (Oxford: Basil Blackwell, 1982), 235.

10 See Baldesar Castiglione, *The Book of the Courtier,* trans. Sir Thomas Hoby (London, 1561).

11 The most recent study of the war between England and Spain is Wallace T. MacCaffrey, *Elizabeth I: War and Politics 1588-1603* (Princeton, NJ: Princeton UP, 1992). See also G. R. Elton, *England under the Tudors* (London: Methuen, 1974), 376-84; and John Guy, *Tudor England* (Oxford and New York: Oxford UP, 1988), 331-51.

12 On Essex's early career, see MacCaffrey, 453-94; on Essex's ambitions for personal glory and their exacerbation of his conflict with the Cecil faction in the Privy Council, see esp. 476-78. On Essex's participation in the Portuguese expedition of 1589, against the will of the queen, see MacCaffrey, 462-64; and Elton, 378.

13 On the financial limitations of the English war effort, see MacCaffrey, 59-69.

14 Irving Ribner, *The English History Play in the age of Shakespeare* (New York: Barnes and Noble, 1957), 266. Ribner provides an extensive survey of the genre, though he does not relate the popularity of the history play to the war with Spain.

15 The popularity of the *Henry VI* plays can be judged in part by the contemporary allusions made to them. In *Piers Pennilesse* (1592), Thomas Nashe defends the English theater by using the example of Talbot—in all probability a reference to *1 Henry VI (The Works of Thomas Nashe,* ed. Ronald B. McKerrow, 5 vols. [London: Sidgwick and Jackson, 1904-10], 1:212). Robert Greene paraphrases *3 Henry VI,* 1.4.137, in his

famous attack on Shakespeare as having a "Tygers hart wrapt in a Players hyde" (*Greenes Groats-Worth of witte . . .* [London, 1592], F1ᵛ). The popularity of *Richard III* is demonstrated by the six quarto editions published between 1597 and 1622. Even after publication of the 1623 Folio, two more quartos of *Richard III* were published (1629, 1634). On the publication history of *Richard III,* see Antony Hammond, ed., *King Richard III,* Arden edition (London and New York: Methuen, 1981), 1.

[16] On the view held by historians such as E. P. Cheyney and J. Corbett that Elizabeth was "constitutionally incapable of conducting a war" and which accuses her of "indecision, procrastination, variability of mind, and cheeseparing parsimony," see Elton, 358-59, esp. 358. Though Elton defends Elizabeth's conduct of the war, he does not address the way in which all the faults of which she is accused fit neatly into conventional notions about the failings of women in positions of leadership.

[17] See Leah S. Marcus, *Puzzling Shakespeare: Local Reading and Its Discontents* (Berkeley: U of California P, 1988), 67-96; Phyllis Rackin, *Stages of History: Shakespeare's English Chronicles* (Ithaca, NY: Cornell UP, 1990), 148-58.

[18] See Marcus, 51-105.

[19] Quotations of Shakespeare's plays in this essay follow *The Complete Works of Shakespeare,* ed. David Bevington, 4th ed. (New York: Harper-Collins, 1992).

[20] *Haec-Vir: Or The Womanish-Man* (London, 1620), C2ᵛ.

[21] See Stephen Orgel, "Nobody's Perfect: Or, Why Did the English Stage Take Boys for Women?" *South Atlantic Quarterly* 88 (1989): 7-29, esp. 10-11; and Lawrence Stone, *The Family, Sex and Marriage in England 1500-1800* (New York: Harper and Row, 1977), 409-10.

[22] In Margaret and Joan femininity is allied with foreignness, but native Englishwomen, too, are seen in these plays as unruly and disorderly. Duchess Eleanor, wife of Humphrey of Gloucester, employs the witch Margery Jourdan in an attempt to further her plots against Margaret (*2HVI,* 1.4). On the links between foreignness and effeminacy in the first tetralogy, see Marcus, 76-78.

[23] On the notion that women were colder than men in humoral theory, see Ian Maclean, *The Renaissance Notion of Woman: A Study in the Fortunes of Scholasticism and Medical Science in European Intellectual Life* (Cambridge: Cambridge UP, 1980), 30 and 33-35.

[24] On the dynamics of effeminacy in early modern England, and its associations with both boyishness and uxoriousness, see Valerie Traub, *Desire and Anxiety: Circulations of sexuality in Shakespearean drama* (London and New York: Routledge, 1992), 134-36.

[25] I do not mean by this description to conflate early modern representations of childhood with later notions that children are essentially "innocent" and asexual. My point is that young children, while they might enjoy sexual stimulation and be aware of adult sexual practices, were not as strongly differentiated by gender as were adolescents and adults; nor were prepubescent children directly involved in the economy of reproduction which was so crucial to discourses of both gender and sexuality in early modern Europe.

[26] See Rackin, 155.

[27] See David Riggs, *Shakespeare's Heroical Histories: Henry VI and Its Literary Tradition* (Cambridge, MA: Harvard UP, 1971), 149.

[28] For the quarto and Folio title pages, see Kristian Smidt's parallel edition of the texts, *The Tragedy of King Richard the Third: Parallel Texts of the First Quarto and the First Folio with Variants of the Early Quartos* (New York: Humanities Press, 1969), 28-29. In *Palladis Tamia* (London, 1598) Francis Meres lists *Richard III* (as well as three other history plays: *Richard II, King John,* and *Henry IV*) among Shakespeare's tragedies (Oo2ʳ). On the relations between Shakespeare's Richard, Marlowe's Tamburlaine, and other similar figures in contemporary English drama, see Riggs, 62-92. On the conventional view of Richard and Tamburlaine as scourges, see Hammond, ed., 103.

[29] Catherine Belsey, *The Subject of Tragedy: Identity and difference in Renaissance drama* (London and New York: Methuen, 1985); and Bruce R. Smith, "Making a difference: Male/male 'desire' in tragedy, comedy, and tragi-comedy" in *Erotic Politics: Desire on the Renaissance Stage,* Susan Zimmerman, ed. (New York and London: Routledge, 1992), 127-49. Smith examines the opposition in early modern English culture between English/masculine tragedy and Italian/feminine comedy and explores the effect of this opposition on the representation of homoerotic desire. He argues that "the homoerotic difference in comedy is gender; in tragedy it is power status. . . . romantic comedy turns on gender difference that ends in likeness; tragedy, on gender likeness that ends in difference" (141). See also Linda Bamber, *Comic Women, Tragic Men: A Study of Gender and Genre in Shakespeare* (Stanford, CA: Stanford UP, 1982), who argues that tragedy is a masculine genre, comedy a feminine one. Bamber is critiqued by Jonathan Goldberg, "Shakespearean inscriptions: The voicing of power" in *Shakespeare and*

the Question of Theory, Patricia Parker and Geoffrey Hartman, eds. (New York and London: Methuen, 1985), 116-37; and also by Dympna Callaghan, *Woman and Gender in Renaissance Tragedy: A Study of* King Lear, Othello, The Duchess of Malfi *and* The White Devil (Atlantic Highlands, NJ: Humanities Press International, 1989), 37-41.

Phyllis Rackin has argued that tragedies, unlike histories, were perceived as effeminating because they caused men to weep ("Engendering the Tragic Audience: The Case of *Richard III,*" *Studies in the Literary Imagination* 26 [Spring 1993]: 47-65, esp. 47-50). As I argue below, weeping was not always considered unmanly in early modern culture; it was often seen as an appropriate response to a great man's fall. Rackin's own reading of *Richard III* stresses Richard's "solitary [masculine] individualism" as a tragic hero (62).

[30] This speech echoes Tamburlaine's disgust at his sons' amorous weakness; see Christopher Marlowe, *Tamburlaine the Great,* Part II, ed. J. S. Cunningham (Manchester: Manchester UP, 1981), 1.3.21-32.

[31] Stephen Gosson, *The Schoole of Abuse* (London, 1579), B8[r-v].

[32] See Phillip Stubbes, *The Anatomie of Abuses* (London, 1583); Stubbes contends that effeminacy can be caused by soft and luxurious clothing and argues that music will transnature a young man "into a womã, or worse" (C[1][v]-C2[r], O5). On Castiglione and fears of effeminacy in early modern Europe, see Thomas Laqueur, *Making Sex: Body and Gender from the Greeks to Freud* (Cambridge, MA: Harvard UP, 1990), 125-26. See also Patricia Parker, "Gender Ideology, Gender Change: The Case of Marie Germain," *Critical Inquiry* 19 (1993): 337-64.

[33] This passage occurs only in the Folio text of the play; see Hammond, ed., 333.

[34] Gail Kern Paster, *The Body Embarrassed: Drama and the Disciplines of Shame in Early Modern England* (Ithaca, NY: Cornell UP, 1993), 8.

[35] John Donne, *The Sermons of John Donne,* ed. George R. Potter and Evelyn M. Simpson, 10 vols. (Berkeley and Los Angeles: U of California P, 1959), 4:337. See also Paster, 8-9.

[36] In the *Iliad* weeping at such moments is common: Patroclus weeps at the misfortune of the Achaians at the very moment he makes the heroic plea to be allowed to fight in Achilles's armor (Homer, *The Iliad,* trans. A. T. Murray, Loeb Classical Library, 2 vols. [London: William Heinemann; Cambridge, MA: Harvard UP, 1934], Bk. 16, ll. 1-45). Achilles mocks his friend's tears at first, but he later weeps bitterly at Patroclus's

death (Bk. 18, ll. 1-75). And when old Priam weeps for Hector, Achilles joins him in tears, thinking of the death of his own father (Bk. 24, ll. 507-12). Aeneas, in Book 2 of the *Aeneid,* is also reduced to tears. While the occasions on which men might honorably cry have always been relatively limited in Western cultures, Anne Vincent-Buffault argues in her study of weeping in eighteenth-century France that it was not until the later nineteenth century that European men were expected never to cry for any reason (*The History of Tears: Sensibility and Sentimentality in France* [London: Macmillan, 1991], 241-47).

[37] York is not the only warrior who weeps openly and unashamedly in the tetralogy: "rough Northumberland" weeps at the sight of York's torments (*3HVI,* 1.4.27, 150-51, 169-71); and Warwick admits that when he heard of York's death, he "drowned these news in tears" (*3HVI,* 2.1.104).

[38] Janet Adelman also sees the death of Richard's father as crucial to his later development, though she reads his reaction in a different register than I do. Adelman argues that York's death "deprive[s] Richard of his father's protection and thrust[s] him back toward his mother"; his hatred of the maternal body leads in this reading to his isolation from his brothers (*Suffocating Mothers: Fantasies of Maternal Origin in Shakespeare's Plays,* Hamlet *to* The Tempest [New York and London: Routledge, 1992], 3-4, esp. 3).

[39] On birth defects as a sign of divine judgment, see Keith Thomas, *Religion and the Decline of Magic* (New York: Scribners, 1971), 89-96; and Linda Charnes, *Notorious Identity: Materializing the Subject in Shakespeare* (Cambridge, MA: Harvard UP, 1993), 22-24. In addition to those cited in subsequent notes, broadside ballads announcing and interpreting the birth of deformed children or animals in the late sixteenth century include "The true description of a monsterous Chylde, borne in the Ile of Wight . . ." (London, 1564 [STC 1422]) and "The shape of ii. mōsters, MDlxii" (London, 1562 [STC 11485]), reprinted in *Black-Letter Ballads and Broadsides* (London: Joseph Lilly, 1870), 63-66 and 45-48.

[40] Stephen Batman, *The Doome warning all men to the Iudgemente* (London, 1581).

[41] Of Richard's dream, Batman writes: " . . . the night before the Battayle that was fought at *Bosworth* in *Leicestershire* the 22. of August, in his sleepe he had a fearefull dreame, wherein to him it seemed that he saw deformed Images like terrible Devils, which pulled and haled him, not suffering him to take any rest, which strange vision greatly apalled his former courage: notwithstanding his hope of victorie, he was slaine as a rebell and caried to *Leicester* like a hogge" (281).

[42] "The forme and shape of a monstrous Child, borne at Maydstone . . ." (London, 1568 [STC 17194]), reprinted in *Black-Letter Ballads and Broadsides,* 194-97.

[43] On the relation of the circumstances of conception to birth defects in early modern thought, see Paster, 168-72.

[44] "The true report of the forme and shape of a monstrous Childe borne at Muche Horkesleye . . ." (London, 1562 [STC 12207]), reprinted in *Black-Letter Ballads and Broadsides,* 27-30. In this case the fact that the parents married before the child came to term has no mitigating quality on their implied guilt. That both parents are alleged to have had healthy children through previous marriages suggests that it was their union, not either person taken individually, that was wicked. See also "The true fourme and shape of a monsterous chyld, whiche was borne in Stony Stratforde" (London, 1565 [STC 7565]).

[45] See Ambroise Paré, *On Monsters and Marvels,* trans. Janis L. Pallister (Chicago and London: U of Chicago P, 1982), 3-5 and 38-42, esp. 4.

[46] "The true description of two monsterous children, laufully begotten betwene George Steuens and Margerie his wyfe . . ." (London, 1566 [STC 17803]), reprinted in *Black-Letter Ballads and Broadsides,* 217-20.

[47] "The true Discripcion of a Childe with Ruffes, borne in the parish of Micheham in the countie of Surrey" (London, 1566 [STC 1033]), reprinted in *Black-Letter Ballads and Broadsides,* 243-46.

[48] Ashmole MS 38 is a large collection of miscellaneous English poetry, compiled in the early years of the seventeenth century by one Nicholas Burge, who in 1661 (according to two letters to Ashmole [Ashmole MS 1131]) was one of the Poor Knights of Windsor. The poem, entitled "Ex Ausanio Gallo Cento," is dated 5 February 1627 and appears on page 149.

[49] Michel de Montaigne, "Of the Lame or Crippel" in *The Essayes of Michael Lord of Montaigne. Translated by John Florio* (1603), ed. Israel Gollancz, 6 vols. (London: J. M. Dent, 1897), 6:147-65, esp. 161-62.

[50] Francis Bacon, "Of Deformity" (1625) in *The Essays or Counsels, Civil and Moral of Francis Bacon,* ed. Samuel Harvey Reynolds (Oxford: Clarendon Press, 1890), 308-13, esp. 308.

[51] *The Holy Bible,* Authorized King James Version (Oxford: Oxford UP, 1970), 2 Timothy 3:3-4 and Romans 1:27.

[52] Bacon, 309.

[53] Peter Stallybrass and Allon White, *The Politics and Poetics of Transgression* (Ithaca, NY: Cornell UP, 1986), 47.

[54] "A meruaylous straunge deformed Swyne" (London, 1570 [STC 19071]), reprinted in *Black-Letter Ballads and Broadsides,* 186-90.

[55] See Adelman, 2-4.

[56] See Lisa Jardine, *Still Harping on Daughters: Women and Drama in the Age of Shakespeare* (Sussex: Harvester Press; Totowa, NJ: Barnes and Noble, 1983), 68-102; and Rackin, *Stages,* 158-64.

[57] See Jean E. Howard, *The Stage and Social Struggle in Early Modern England* (London and New York: Routledge, 1994), 149.

[58] Performance in *Richard III* is demonized in a way that it is not in the second tetralogy. Whereas in the figure of Richard performance is *merely* deceit, much of the second tetralogy can be read as an attempt to recuperate performativity in the person of Hal; see Howard, 151-52.

[59] Rebecca W. Bushnell reads Richard's self-representation as an object of desire as effeminizing, but in doing so, she confuses a false image of passivity (which Richard cynically manipulates in the pursuit of power, not erotic pleasure) for Richard's own gender position; see *Tragedies of Tyrants: Political Thought and Theater in the English Renaissance* (Ithaca, NY: Cornell UP, 1990), 123. Richard may present himself as Anne's victim, but he never really places himself in her power. It is his Machiavellian manipulation of erotic discourse, rather than his putative position in it, which constitutes the source of his power in the scene.

[60] In the most compelling reading of Anne's seduction in recent years, Charnes contends that Richard woos Anne through the dead and effeminized body of Henry VI, whose wounds, bleeding afresh at Richard's presence, are linked metaphorically to Anne's own open, desiring female body; Anne's very disgust for Richard is so powerful as to constitute a perverse attraction (see 33-51). In the course of the confrontation between Richard and Anne, Henry's penetrated body (which Charnes convincingly links to the wounded body of Christ in late-medieval Corpus Christi traditions) "is translated from a political-theological sacrifice into a sexual one" (45). Charnes argues that by engaging in erotic discourse with Anne, Richard reintegrates himself in the social world from which he has hitherto been alienated by his physical deformity, and she compares Richard's feigned renunciation of the masculine role in his courtship to the "suspension of

sheer phallic prerogative" which characterizes the space of the erotic in Shakespeare's comedies (40 and 46).

While I am not always convinced by Charnes's larger argument that Richard as a character is in a constant dialogue with his "notorious identity" as one of the most famous villains of Tudor historiography, I find her reading of Anne's seduction compelling, and it has greatly influenced my own thinking about the scene.

[61] For example, before his first confrontation with Margaret's forces in *3 Henry VI,* Richard sneers, "A woman's general. What should we fear" (*3HVI,* 1.2.68).

That Margaret trounces Richard's troops in the following battle teaches him nothing. His certainty that Elizabeth of York is a "relenting fool, and shallow, changing woman" is similarly overconfident, in that it is far from clear she is sincere in her coerced agreement to let Richard marry her daughter.

Source: "'A Monster Great Deformed': The Unruly Masculinity of Richard III," in *Shakespeare Quarterly,* Vol. 47, No. 3, Fall, 1996, pp. 251-68.

The Many-Headed Monster in *Henry VI, Part 2*

Margaret E. Owens, *University of Toronto*

The spectacle of the severed head is so common a feature of Elizabethan and Jacobean history plays that it invites identification as the emblem (or perhaps fetish) that most prominently characterizes the genre. Visual representations of severed heads occur in a broad range of history plays, including Thomas Lodge's *The Wounds of Civil War,* George Peele's *Edward I,* William Shakespeare's *Henry VI, Parts 2 and 3, Richard III,* and *Macbeth,* George Chapman's *Caesar and Pompey,* Thomas Dekker's *Sir Thomas Wyatt,* and John Fletcher and Philip Massinger's *Sir John van Olden Barnavelt.*[1] The reasons for the prevalence of the severed head in the history play are not difficult to determine. The display of the head serves as a striking, unmistakable image signifying not only the defeat and demise of the victim, but, more crucially, the loss or transfer of political power which is consolidated through this act of violence.[2] The political symbolism of the image is clearly evident in the closing scene of Marlowe's *Edward II* in which the newly crowned Edward III orders that Mortimer's head be placed on top of the murdered king's hearse. The resulting ceremonial tableau not only symbolizes the avengement of murder but also encapsulates the transit of power through the course of the play, from Edward II to Mortimer and finally back to Edward's dynastic line.

In its use of the severed head as an icon for political power, the Renaissance theatre was undoubtedly mirroring or reproducing the visual rhetoric of contemporary state punishment. To some extent, dramatists of the period seem to have shared the state's assurance that the spectacle of the traitor's severed head figured as a sign of closure and containment. For instance, in Peele's *Edward I* the king's officers parade *"Lluellens head on a speare"* as a vivid emblem of the English defeat of the Welsh rebels.[3] *2 Henry VI,* however, appears to question the closure and monologism of the stage image which Peele and other dramatists deployed with such apparent ease. With its conspicuous fixation on the severed head, *2 Henry VI* stands out among the Elizabethan history plays. In this play, the horrific yet familiar image is endowed with extraordinary prominence, a pressure so intense as to draw attention not only to its impact as a theatrical spectacle but also its implications as a cultural sign.

Taken beyond its usual status as a fleeting, almost incidental, stage emblem, the severed head emerges as a multiaccentual ideological sign (to adopt the termi-nology of V. N. Voloshinov), that is, a sign whose meanings are contested "by differently oriented social interests."[4] The ideological sign, according to Voloshinov, is characterized by its semiotic instability or polyvalence, which is manifest in a socio-political struggle over the sign's meaning: "The ruling class strives to impart a supraclass, eternal character to the ideological sign, to extinguish or drive inward the struggle between social value judgments which occurs in it, to make the sign uniaccentual."[5] Nowhere is the effort of hegemonic authorities to contain polyvalence more evident than in the case of the severed head, an icon which early modern European states sought to limit to a uniaccentual and ostensibly uncontestable signification. The treatment of this spectacle in *2 Henry VI,* however, tends to expose the inevitable failure of this effort to contain the semiosis of the fragmented body. In this paper, I will chart the battle over the signification of the severed head which is so visibly played out in *2 Henry VI,* a semiotic contest in which the sheer numerical proliferation of the head may be read as an index of its proliferating meaning.

In the course of *2 Henry VI,* the severed heads of four different characters are represented onstage. While the image of the severed head is evoked verbally (1.2.29)[6] long before it is given a visible presence (4.1.141sd), the context of its introduction, in Gloucester's account of his dream, tends to frame the image as a prophetic verbal emblem:

> Methought this staff, mine office-badge in court,
> Was broke in twain; by whom I have forgot,
> But, as I think, it was by th' cardinal;
> And on the pieces of the broken wand
> Were placed the heads of Edmund, Duke of Somerset,
> And William de la Pole, first Duke of Suffolk.
> This was my dream; what it doth bode, God knows.
>
> (1.2.25-31)

Though Gloucester may be loath or unable to interpret the dream, the Elizabethan audience, familiar with proleptic dramatic devices, would likely have recognized the duke's report as supplying a vivid icon of the political chaos to ensue during "The Contention of the two famous Houses of Yorke & Lancaster." Granted, the picture conveyed by the dream is never precisely realized on the stage; it is Lord Say and his son-in-law, not Suffolk and Somerset, who end up mounted on pikes.[7] But it is the nature of the prophetic vision to be somewhat skewed or oblique. In any case, the dream is deadly accurate in identifying Gloucester's downfall as the key event that unleashes the violence of civil war.

As Gloucester's dream indicates, the severed head in this play is not simply an element in the verbal and visual rhetoric of Senecan horror; rather this icon is encoded with specifically political meanings, readily identifiable to the Elizabethan audience. From the perspective of the state, the foremost significance is the destruction of the traitor, hence the importance of displaying the severed heads of executed traitors on the gates of London. Such grim displays served as triumphal spectacles celebrating the state's success in defeating a potential threat. This ritual display was as much militaristic as penal, resembling the collection of heads by warring factions on the battlefield, a practice that Elizabethan England typically disavowed and projected onto a host of cultural Others, including Celts, New World Indians, and Turks.[8]

Although at first glance, and certainly from the vantage point of state authority, the severed head might appear to be the most terminal or fixed of signifiers, decapitation was a malleable and definitely overcoded sign, which operated in a variety of registers or discursive contexts. For instance, within the discursive tradition of the Body Politic topos, decapitation was often refigured as a somewhat different form of dismemberment, a surgical amputation carried out on the diseased body of the commonwealth. In "The Trew Law of Free Monarchies" James I admits that "it may very well fall out that the head will be forced to garre cut off some rotten members . . . to keep the rest of the body in integritie: but what state the body can be in, if the head, for any infirmitie that can fall to it, be cut off, I leaue it to the readers judgement."[9] In this tradition, the removal of the traitor's head is metaphorically displaced, refigured as the amputation of an expendable "member" of the Body Politic. The execution of the traitor is thus imagined as a surgical procedure which ultimately benefits, rather than endangers, the health of the nation.

Those who invoke the Body Politic topos often place limits on its interpretation and application, just as James I stipulates that the monarch, as head of state and hence as the most vital of the Body's members, cannot be "cut off" without dire consequences ensuing. The insistence with which such limits are asserted bespeaks an anxiety which the vocabulary of medical intervention could not dispel. Such efforts to replace the threat of political crisis with a sense of order and control seem only to invoke the spectre of monstrosity which always lurks within the contours of the Body Politic. The writers of treatises on the Body Politic seem morbidly fascinated with disease and deformity so avidly do they detail the potential for the body to slip from soundness to monstrosity. For instance, Edward Forset, in *A Comparative Discourse of the Bodies Natural and Politique* (1606), warns that "the parts" of the Body Politic may "be prodigiously dislocated or transferred from their proper to other vnfitting places, whereof oftentimes the whole bodie getteth the name of a monster mishapen and distorted."[10]

The spectre of monstrosity that is always already inscribed in the Body Politic topos is graphically conjured up on the stage in *2 Henry VI*.[11] However, the amputations normally advocated as a means of suppressing or pruning monstrous growths prove in this play to be implicated in the very production of monstrosity. Through its iteration of verbal and visual images of decapitation, the play implicitly exposes the tropic equation of beheading and surgical excision as a mask for the dangerous consequences that may ensue from strategic acts of violence. Beheading in this play is a sign not of the orderly extirpation of civil dissension but of its uncontrollable proliferation.

In Gloucester's account of his dream, with its doubled image of beheading, the severed head has already begun to multiply. The intimation that the image will continue to proliferate is affirmed in the Duchess of Gloucester's remark on the extent of her own ambition, less than 40 lines after her husband's revelation of his dream:

> Were I a man, a duke, and next of blood,
> I would remove these tedious stumbling-
>   blocks
> And smooth my way upon their headless
>   necks.
>
>   (1.2.63-65)

Also underlined in this remark is the implication that decapitation in this play will signify something other than the state's vigilance in upholding civil order. Indeed Gloucester's vision eventually acquires a visible reality in a succession of beheadings inflicted on members of the ruling elite, as well as on a pretender who claims noble descent. The cumulative effect is to summon up a picture of disembodied heads jostling for power, a situation ultimately arising from the failure of the king to establish with any conviction his authority as the legitimate head of state.

In the proliferation of severed heads on the stage, we witness a version of that much feared Elizabethan bogeyman, the "many-headed monster," an image depicting the violent deformation of hierarchical order. As Christopher Hill observes in "The Many-Headed Monster in Late Tudor and Early Stuart Political Thinking": "The idea that to be many-headed is the same as to be headless is easier to conceive metaphorically than literally."[12] In *2 Henry IV*, this equation is expressed in a pattern of visual effects. Typically, the topos of the many-headed monster (variants include "beast" and "multitude") was applied to popular uprisings. As Hill emphasizes, the formula almost invariably reflects "Dread and hatred of the masses."[13] Yet in *2 Henry VI*, the topos carries a significantly different import to the extent that the nobility, more so than the masses, are presented as the creators, as well as the victims, of the many-headed monster. As Michael Hattaway emphasizes in his analysis of the Jack Cade uprising: "This is no mere riot, but an occasion when aristocratic rebellion is the catalyst for popular revolt."[14]

The visual images of decapitation, which are confined to the second half of the play, implicitly *realize* a discourse that prevails in the first half. By the time we begin to witness bodies being mutilated before our eyes, we have already become accustomed to the rhetoric of dismemberment. One of the most egregious elements in this rhetoric is anatomization, which turns up repeatedly in this play as a type of set speech. For instance, Gloucester shrewdly anatomizes the conspirators ranged against him, as if they comprised a single diseased body:

> Beaufort's red sparkling eyes blab his
>   heart's malice,
> And Suffolk's cloudy brow his stormy hate;
> Sharp Buckingham unburdens with his
>   tongue
> The envious load that lies upon his heart.
>   (3.1.154-57)

In the following scene, Gloucester is himself anatomized when Warwick examines the duke's lifeless body for evidence of homicide:

> But see, his face is black and full of blood,
> His eye-balls further out than when he
>   lived,
> Staring full ghastly like a strangled man.
>   (3.2.168-70)

The murder of Gloucester is the turning-point in the pattern of verbal and visual imagery; from this point on, the gap between rhetoric and (corpo)reality narrows. Characters are no longer simply threatened with violence, as when Margaret warms to the prospect of seeing Gloucester "quickly hop without thy head" (1.3.132); bodies are now literally chopped and lopped, and heads are handled, mishandled, and exchanged for monetary reward. With Gloucester's downfall, language undergoes a metamorphosis, acquiring a nightmarish literality.

The first character to lose his head following Gloucester's murder is Suffolk. Captured by some mariners after a fight at sea and subjected to a summary trial for a long list of crimes against the state, Suffolk is led offstage to execution. In the Folio, one of the killers reenters *"with the body."*[15] A gentleman who has been treated more mercifully by the mariners is onstage at this point to register shock at the "barbarous and bloody spectacle" (4.1.144) and to voice his determination to bring the body to the king.

While the display of the mutilated corpse is relatively brief at the site of execution, a more sustained and extraordinary exhibition of Suffolk's remains occurs several scenes later, when Margaret is shown cradling the head through an entire scene.[16] Implicit in this spectacle is a bizarre analogy that equates the severed head with a suckling infant, a parallel underlined by Margaret's remark, "Here may his head lie on my throbbing breast" (4.4.5).[17] This stage picture ironically fulfils the death fantasy that Suffolk had evoked at his parting from the queen:

> If I depart from thee I cannot live;
> And in thy sight to die, what were it else
> But like a pleasant slumber in thy lap?
> Here could I breathe my soul into the air,
> As mild and gentle as the cradle-babe
> Dying with mother's dug between its lips.
>   (3.2.388-93)

Presumably, the horrific realization of Suffolk's fantasy is intended to underline the perverse nature of his liaison with the queen, a relationship so unhealthy (to the extent that it threatens the unity and stability of the nation) as to engender a death's head instead of a child. An ironic backdrop to Henry's attempts in this scene to deal with the Cade rebellion, the presence of the severed head proves particularly portentous when Henry warns Lord Say, "Jack Cade hath sworn to have thy head" (4.4.19).

Symptomatic of Henry's ineffectuality is the speedy fulfilment of Cade's threat against the head of Lord Say. As with Suffolk, the decapitation follows an *ad hoc* trial, in which Say attempts to defend himself against the rebels' charges that he "sold the towns in France" (4.7.17) and "most traitorously corrupted the youth of the realm in erecting a grammar school" (4.7.26-27). According to the topsy-turvy logic of this popular uprising, Say's "pleading so well for his life" (4.7.91) strengthens Cade's resolve to kill him. And, with an almost Tamburlainean flourish, Cade extends the punishment to Say's son-in-law, commanding his followers to "break into his son-in-law's house, Sir James Cromer, and strike off his head, and bring them both upon two poles hither" (4.7.94-96).

The brief interval during which the beheadings are assumed to be taking place is filled by Cade's punning reflections on the subject of heads, in which a plan to impose a head tax on peers transmutes into a claim on the maidenheads of brides: "The proudest peer in the realm shall not wear a head on his shoulders, unless he pay me tribute; there shall not a maid be married, but she shall pay to me her maiden-head ere they have it" (4.7.103-6). Cade's musings are broken off by the entrance of an unspecified character *"with the heads"* (111sd),[18] and Cade proceeds to direct the deployment of these gruesome properties as if they were puppets or effigies being displayed in a street pageant: "Let them kiss one another, for they loved well when they were alive. Now part them again, lest they consult about the giving up of some more towns in France. Soldiers, defer the spoil of the city until night; for with these borne before us, instead of maces, will we ride through the streets, and at every corner have them kiss. Away!" (112-17). Cade's treatment of the heads bears a striking resemblance to carnivalesque rituals of humiliation, such as the skimmington riding or charivari, which, in the most typical scenario, involved the parading of a cuckolded or browbeaten husband (either in person or in effigy) by a crowd of neighbours making rough music. In his study of "ridings," Martin Ingram points out that "the practice of charivaris seems to have rested on a folkloric tradition that the populace had the right to supplement the legal system."[19] To the extent that the parade of severed heads draws on festive traditions, it is symptomatic of Cade's association with, if not his deliberate manipulation of, carnivalesque rhetoric and practices.[20] However, in this instance, as Alexander Leggatt puts it, "what we see is mostly the anarchy that is the dark side of carnival."[21] According to François Laroque, this is the risk accompanying "the liberating dynamic of festivity";[22] under certain conditions, "festivity . . . become[s] an instrument of torment, an occasion of sacrifice, even an abettor of the forces of evil. In these circumstances, the delirium of festivity goes beyond the mere destruction of objects, in the form of property and wealth, and the frenzied consumption of food, and leads on to the unleashing of violence and massacre."[23] The parading of the heads, including the mimed kissing, is no invention on the playwright's part but a faithful dramatization of Hall's account: "with these two heddes, this blody butcher entered into the citie agayn, and in despyte caused them in euery strete, kysse together, to the great detestacion of all the beholders."[24]

Implicit in the play's reenactment of Cade's triumphal pageant seems to be a shrewd understanding of the political/sexual semiotics of this type of violent street-theatre.[25] Cade's reference to "maces" (4.7.116), specifically identifying the heads on poles as symbols of the rebels' claim to authority, is crucial, as it draws a direct connection between this spectacle of mutilation and Gloucester's dream of the severed heads mounted on the broken ends of his staff of office. Linking these two moments is the symbolic mutilation, or

castration, of Gloucester, when Margaret forces him to give up his staff of office, and gloats at seeing "a limb lopped off" (2.3.42) the Lord Protector. An equation is thus implicitly drawn between losing the staff of office and suffering dismemberment. The decapitations inflicted on Say and Cromer serve as a visible sign of their loss of status, and concomitantly of the rebels' claim to power. In other words, the mutilated and humiliated bodies of aristocrats are flaunted by Cade's crew as the very sign of their own newly won power. Using a central carnivalesque strategy of reducing abstraction to corporeality,[26] of uncovering the dirty secrets hidden by the mask of euphemism and idealism, the rebels demystify the ceremonial mace, exposing its true nature as nothing more than a sign whereby the ruling elite asserts its power over the bodies of the lower orders. In early modern England, to hold office was essentially to hold the right to decapitate and to castrate, in both the figurative and literal senses. The phallic mace is thus raised as a sign not only of the holder's power but also of his ability to disempower.

The pattern of imagery linking the staff of office with decapitation and dismemberment appears to be consistent with the equation advanced by Freud in his essay "Medusa's Head": "To decapitate = to castrate."[27] Cade's punning on heads/maidenheads while the beheadings are taking place demonstrates the tendency for a discourse of sexual competition to refigure political struggle within the context of popular rebellion.[28] The intersection of sexual competition and violence provides a highly charged semiotic code through which political issues are embodied and contested. Supporting the notion that the decapitation of Say is a displaced, or transcoded, form of castration is Cade's allegation against the Lord Treasurer, voiced several scenes earlier: "I tell you that that Lord Say hath gelded the commonwealth and made it an eunuch" (4.2.140-42). Say's punishment, then, mirrors (at one remove) his crime against the commonwealth. The motif of sexual competition is reinforced in the quarto version, where Cade's speech about heads and maidenheads is immediately followed by the entrance of a sergeant, who accuses one of the rebels of having ravished his wife. Cade responds to the complaint by ordering the accused, Dick the Butcher, to punish the plaintiff:

> Go Dicke take him hence, cut out his toong
>   for cogging,
> Hough him for running, and to conclude,
> Braue him with his owne mace.
>
> (1850-52)

Yet another reference to the capture of a mace, combined with a threat to excise a tongue (an homology for the phallus), underlines the castrative nature of punishment in this play.

The seizure by the lower orders of the apparatus of punishment typically plays a central role in popular risings. (Perhaps the mock punishments that figure so prominently in festive traditions can be seen as contained, non-threatening rehearsals of the more serious attempts to appropriate judicial authority.) As Regina Janes emphasizes in her article on the semiotics of beheading in Revolutionary Paris, an atmosphere of exuberance accompanied the violent punishments inflicted by the masses against the *ancien régime*:

> When the rabble cut off the heads of the king's officers, they have redefined themselves as the sovereign people. Literally and physically, they have seized the ultimate power of the sovereign. Instead of learning, they teach. It is a disturbing lesson to those identified with the old order; it is an invigorating lesson to those who identify with the new. . . . The lesson of the heads is that there has been a fundamental change in social hierarchies and the distribution of power. . . . Taking a head transforms the *menu peuple* from the passive "source of sovereignty" to the active executor of sovereign power.[29]

Cade and his crew imitate but also alter, and hence travesty, the modes of punishment inflicted by the crown. Instead of mounting the heads on poles at the Tower or on London Bridge, as static symbols signalling the stability and permanence of the monarchy, the rebels animate the heads, treating them as dynamic symbols of a nascent regime engaged in the process of creating and establishing itself.

Cade's triumphal pageant, however, rapidly disintegrates, along with his leadership. The illegitimate beheader is himself beheaded in a peculiarly private act of punishment inflicted by a loyal citizen, Alexander Iden. Again we witness an *ad hoc* trial in which a self-appointed judge sentences a traitor to decapitation. When Alexander Iden learns that the intruder he has mortally wounded is "that monstrous traitor" Cade (4.10.59), he resolves to dispose of the corpse in an appropriately degrading fashion:

> Hence will I drag thee headlong by the
>   heels
> Unto a dunghill, which shall be thy grave,
> And there cut off thy most ungracious head
> Which I will bear in triumph to the king,
> Leaving thy trunk for crows to feed upon
>   (4.10.73-77)

The meeting of Iden and Henry is largely an elaboration on the chronicle sources. Hall records that Iden "brought his [Cade's] ded body to London, whose hed was set on Londo[n] bridge."[30] According to Holinshed, Cade's body was "brought to London in a cart, where he was quartered; his head set on London bridge, and his quarters sent to diuerse places to be set vp in the

shire of Kent."[31] Whereas in the sources the disposal of the traitor's body follows conventional judicial practice, the dramatization offers a military ritual in which Cade's severed head figures as a spoil of war. The difference in emphasis is in keeping with the focus of the play in the closing scenes as the escalating factionalism breaks out into civil war.

To Henry, the severed head of the traitor testifies to the intervention of divine justice:

> The head of Cade! Great God, how just art
>   Thou!
> O let me view his visage, being dead,
> That living wrought me such exceeding
>   trouble.
>   (5.1.68-70)

But at another level, Henry is shockingly blind to the symbolism of the spectacle that he is participating in, even creating, as he requests a closer look at Cade's visage, perhaps even reaching out to hold the head. Henry seems oblivious to a policy practised by more canny monarchs, that of maintaining a rigid segregation between the sacred body of the sovereign and the polluted body of the traitor. Though mangled and lifeless, the corpse of the traitor remains a source of magical contagion, a ritual object too abominable to be brought into close proximity to the monarch. Presumably, this is the reason English monarchs did not attend state executions (other than their own, of course). Henry, however, stares into the lifeless face of the would-be usurper, creating a scandalous tableau which evokes a sense not so much of balance restored as of the precariousness of his own power. In showing this interest in the rebel's head, Henry inadvertently bestows on Cade an unwarranted honour. And what does he hope to learn by gazing into the face of his enemy? In the Quarto, Henry goes so far as to conduct a physiognomic analysis of the head, in which he details the features that betray Cade's combative nature:

> A visage sterne, cole blacke his curled
>   locks,
> Deepe trenched furrowes in his frowning
>   brow,
> Presageth warlike humors in his life.
>   (2022-24)

While this post mortem does not clear up any mysteries, it does reinforce Henry's confidence that the world follows predictable patterns. But he would be better off applying his analytical skills to the physiognomy of the living, namely York.

Admittedly, Henry's encounter with the head of the traitor, especially in the shorter, Folio version, may be relatively brief. After all, the king also shows some interest in the bearer of the trophy, though it takes a bit of prompting on Buckingham's part before Henry gets around to bestowing the rewards of a knighthood and a thousand marks. In the Quarto, Henry follows his analysis of Cade's visage with an order for the removal of the head, "Here take it hence" (2025), which suggests that the king has been holding the head himself, and now hands it over to an attendant or back to Iden. The Quarto also includes an exit for Iden immediately following his expression of gratitude to the king for the rewards bestowed (2037). In the Folio, the order for the removal of the head and the exit for Iden are both absent. If Iden does not leave the stage with Cade's head, that gruesome property may remain visible—possibly mounted on a pike behind the king—through the remainder of the scene, thereby serving as an ironic backdrop during the ensuing challenges to Henry's authority.

If the head of Cade is visible in the background, the recurrent references to heads in this scene (5.1) acquire a bizarre resonance. One such reference occurs immediately following the knighting of Iden, when Henry attempts to prevent Somerset, accompanied by Margaret, from entering York's field of vision. (York has agreed to dismiss his troops on the condition that the king imprison Somerset in the Tower.) Margaret scoffs at her husband's efforts to conceal Somerset: "For thousand Yorks he shall not hide his head, / But boldly stand and front him to his face" (5.1.85-86). If we recall that Somerset, according to Gloucester's dream, is destined to lose his head, the queen's choice of synecdoche seems unfortunately apt.

An even more scandalous appeal to this type of synecdoche occurs in York's outburst over Henry's breach of faith:

> King did I call thee? No, thou art not king,
> Not fit to govern and rule multitudes,
> Which dar'st not, no, canst not rule a traitor.
> That head of thine doth not become a
>   crown;
> Thy hand is made to grasp a palmer's staff
> And not to grace an awful princely sceptre.
> That gold must round engirt these brows of
>   mine,
> Whose smile and frown, like to Achilles'
>   spear,
> Is able with the change to kill and cure.
> Here is a hand to hold a sceptre up
> And with the same to act controlling laws.
>
>   (5.1.93-103)

York deploys the rhetorical strategy so characteristic of this play, the anatomy, to pose Henry's deficiencies against his own fitness for rule. According to this rhetorical scheme, the man best equipped to rule is the one who possesses a head and hand capable of wielding the symbols of sovereignty. At a figurative level, York's speech decapitates Henry as a usurper; the king's head implicitly joins Cade's. What emerges, especially as a consequence of the sight of Cade's head onstage, is a vision of jostling heads, all competing to wear the crown. How quickly Henry's spectacle of triumph, signalled by the display of the traitor's head, has been eclipsed by York. Clifford insists that York himself should lose his head for openly challenging Henry's rule: "He is a traitor: let him to the Tower / And chop away that factious pate of his" (5.1.134-5). Although York is invulnerable at this point, in the sequel his head will suffer the same fate as Cade's. In a sense, York has unwittingly anticipated that outcome by figuratively anatomizing himself, along with Henry.

So insistent is the verbal and visual imagery of decapitation in 2 *Henry VI* that one might be tempted to speculate that the dramatist(s) took a deliberate risk, indulging in an exercise in theatrical audacity of a kind we more typically associate with Marlowe. Only one of the three displays of severed heads in 2 *Henry VI* is based directly on chronicle material; the other instances, involving the heads of Suffolk and Cade, are pure inventions. Perhaps the incident from the chronicle involving Say and Cromer suggested the notion of using the severed head, especially in its monstrous proliferation, as a powerful icon for the "disintegrative energies"[32] afflicting the world of the play.

If we were to invoke an interpretive grid along the lines of Stephen Greenblatt's subversion-containment model,[33] we might conclude that in 2 *Henry VI*, as in the contemporary treatises on the Body Politic, monstrosity is conjured up chiefly in order to legitimate the hierarchical organization of the state. I do not wish, in the confines of this paper at least, to ruminate on whether any subversive agenda lies behind the 2 *Henry VI*, and, if so, whether it is ultimately contained or neutralized.[34] What is clear is that the play, especially in its dramatization of the Cade episode, reveals that the state has no monopoly on the semiosis of violent spectacle. The representation of monstrosity in this play carries a potentially radical edge in so far as it dramatizes a struggle for ownership of the symbolic apparatus of the state, most conspicuously, the mace and the severed head. The treatment of the symbolism of beheading in 2 *Henry VI* participates in a pervasive effect of this tetralogy, a tendency which Donald G. Watson identifies as "the exposure of [the] iconicity of kingship."[35] More so than in any other history play of the period, the severed head in 2 *Henry VI* functions as a site of contestation rather than as a sign of order restored. As this play seems to insist, the removal of heads does less to contain disruptive energies than it does to unleash them. And what does this imply about the surgical procedures advocated in political treatises: the lopping of infected limbs, the pruning of monstrous growths? Given the grotesque fecundity of the severed head in this play, we might conclude that the efforts of would-be surgeons of the Body Politic are liable to promote rather than to prevent the body's relentless slide into monstrosity.

Notes

[1] This list is by no means exhaustive. I am using a broad definition of the history play, encompassing not only chronicle history but also classical history, foreign history, and topical plays.

[2] For discussions of the semiotics of decapitation in the Renaissance history play, see Martha Hester Fleischer, *The Iconography of the English History Play* (Salzburg: University of Salzburg, 1974), Frank Ardolino, "Severed Heads and Brazen Heads: Headhunting in Elizabethan Drama," *Journal of Evolutionary Psychology* 4 (1983): 169-81, David H. Thurn, "Sovereignty, Disorder, and Fetishism in Marlowe's *Edward II*," *Renaissance Drama* 21 (1990): 115-41, and Karin S. Coddon, "'Unreal Mockery': Unreason and the Problem of Spectacle in *Macbeth*," *English Literary History* 56 (1989): 485-501.

[3] George Peele, *Edward I*, ed. W. W. Greg (Oxford: Malone Society Reprints, 1911), 2632.

[4] V. N. Voloshinov, *Marxism and the Philosophy of Language*, trans. Ladislav Matejka and I. R. Titunik (Cambridge, Mass.: Harvard University Press, 1986), 23.

[5] Voloshinov, 23.

[6] William Shakespeare, *The Second Part of King Henry VI*, ed. Michael Hattaway (Cambridge: Cambridge University Press, 1991). Subsequent references are to this edition, unless otherwise stated.

[7] The Quarto of 1594 has "The heads of the Cardinall of *Winchester*, / And *William de la Poule* first Duke of Suffolke" (223-4) mounted on the ends of the staff. All quotations from the first Quarto are taken from *The First Part of the Contention Betwixt the Two Famous Houses of York and Lancaster* (1594), ed. William Montgomery (Oxford: Malone Society Reprints, 1985). In "The Original Staging of *The First Part of the Contention* (1594)," *Shakespeare Survey* 41 (1989): 13-22, William Montgomery argues that text of *The Contention* likely derives from a London production.

[8] On the tendency for Elizabethans to demonize these groups as mutilators, headhunters, and cannibals, see Christopher Highley, "Wales, Ireland and *1 Henry IV*, *Renaissance Drama* 21 (1990): 91-114, and Stephen Orgel, "Shakespeare and the Cannibals," *Cannibals, Witches, and Divorce*, ed. Marjorie Garber (Baltimore: Johns Hopkins University Press, 1987), 40-66.

[9] James I, *The Political Works of James I*, ed. Charles Howard McIlwain (New York: Russell and Russell, 1965), 65.

[10] Edward Forset, *A Comparative Discourse of the Bodies Natural and Politique* (Farnborough, UK: Gregg, 1969), 50.

[11] A number of recent studies have examined the Body Politic trope in Shakespearean drama; see, especially, Zvi Jagendorf, "*Coriolanus*: Body Politic and Private Parts," *Shakespeare Quarterly* 41 (1990): 455-69; Gillian Murray Kendall, "Overkill in Shakespeare," *Shakespeare Quarterly* 43 (1992): 33-50, and Claire McEachern, "*Henry V* and the Paradox of the Body Politic," *Shakespeare Quarterly* 45 (1994): 33-56. For the history of the Body Politic topos, see David George Hale, *The Body Politic: A Political Metaphor in Renaissance English Literature* (The Hague: Mouton, 1971).

[12] Christopher Hill, "The Many-Headed Monster in Late Tudor and Early Stuart Political Thinking," *From the Renaissance to the Counter-Reformation*, ed. Charles H. Carter (New York, Random House, 1965), 298. Freud, in his essay "Medusa's Head," in volume 18 of *The Standard Edition of the Complete Psychological Works of Sigmund Freud*, ed. James Strachey et al. (London: Hogarth Press, 1955), 273, makes a similar claim from a psychoanalytic perspective: "a multiplication of penis symbols signifies castration."

[13] Hill, 298.

[14] Michael Hattaway, "Rebellion, Class Consciousness, and Shakespeare's *2 Henry VI*," *Cahiers Elisabéthains* 83 (1988): 17.

[15] *The Norton Facsimile: The First Folio of Shakespeare*, ed. Charlton Hinman (New York: W. W. Norton, 1968), 2312. All quotations from the Folio are taken from this edition. In the Quarto, there is no direction calling for the display of Suffolk's body.

[16] This scene represents a departure from the chronicle sources. According to Edward Hall, *The Union of the . . . Families of Lancastre and Yorke* (1548), Suffolk's captors "left his body with the head vpon the sandes of Douer, which corse was there founde by a chapelayne of his, and conueyed to Wyngfelde college in Suffolke, and there buried"; quoted from *Hall's Chronicle* (London: J. Johnson, 1809), 219. All subsequent references to Hall are to this reprint.

[17] For some intriguing commentary on this speech, including its peculiar anticipation of Cleopatra's death scene, see Ann Pasternak Slater, *Shakespeare the Director* (Brighton: Harvester, 1982), 92-93.

[18] The Quarto has "Enter two with the Lord Sayes head, and sir Iames Cromers, vpon two poles" (1854-55).

[19] Martin Ingram, "Ridings, Rough Music and the 'Reform of Popular Culture' in Early Modern England," *Past and Present* 105 (1984): 93.

[20] C. L. Barber, in his seminal study, *Shakespeare's Festive Comedy: A Study of Dramatic Form and its Relation to Social Custom* (Princeton: Princeton University Press, 1959), laid the groundwork for viewing Cade as a Lord of Misrule. The connection between seasonal festivity and political uprisings has been the subject of a number of recent studies. For a brief survey of "English materials" relating to this issue, see Thomas Pettitt, "Here Comes I, Jack Straw:' English Folk Drama and Social Revolt," *Folklore* 95 (1984): 3-20.

[21] Alexander Leggatt, *Shakespeare's Political Drama* (London: Routledge, 1988), 17.

[22] François Laroque, *Shakespeare's Festive World: Elizabethan Seasonal Entertainment and the Professional Stage,* trans. Janet Lloyd (Cambridge: Cambridge University Press, 1991), 303.

[23] Ibid., 270.

[24] Hall, 221. In a recent article, "Jack Cade and Shakespeare's *Henry VI, Part 2,*" *Studies in Philology* 92 (1995): 18-79, Ellen C. Caldwell provides a detailed account of the documentary record concerning Cade's uprising and offers an assessment of the relevance of this material to the social conditions of the 1590s.

[25] Regina Janes, in her article "Beheadings," *Representations* 35 (1991): 25, recounts an almost identical incident which occurred during the French Revolution: "Among the more popular subjects of revolutionary prints was the double decapitation of Bertier de Sauvigny and his father-in-law Foulon. Thrusting the head of Foulon on its pike into Bertier's face, the crowd had chanted, "Baise papa, baise papa" (Kiss papa, kiss papa). . . . " Janes labels the incident an "oddly oedipal drama"; undoubtedly the spectacle was aimed at mocking the basic principles of the aristocratic, patriarchal order, specifically the succession of wealth, power, and status along familial lines.

[26] For the seminal account of this carnivalesque dynamic, see Mikhail Bakhtin, *Rabelais and His World,* trans. Hélène Iswolsky (Bloomington: Indiana University Press, 1984).

[27] Freud, 273.

[28] For an important study of the symbolism of castration and decapitation in Revolutionary France, see Neil Hertz, *The End of the Line: Essays on Psychoanalysis and the Sublime* (New York: Columbia University Press, 1985), 161-93.

[29] Janes, 24.

[30] Hall, 222.

[31] Raphael Holinshed, *Chronicles of England, Scotland, and Ireland* (1587); quoted from volume 3 of *Holinshed's Chronicles of England, Scotland, and Ireland* (London: J. Johnson, 1807-8), 227.

[32] John W. Blanpied, *Time and the Artist in Shakespeare's English Histories* (Newark: University of Delaware Press, 1983), 55.

[33] Stephen Greenblatt, "Invisible Bullets," in *Shakespearean Negotiations: The Circulation of Social Energy in Renaissance England* (Berkeley and Los Angeles: University of California Press, 1988), 21-65.

[34] In "The Powerless Theater," *English Literary Renaissance* 21 (1991): 49-74, Paul Yachnin argues that this type of critical debate is misconceived given that "the production of generalized and two-faced political meaning" was "a central feature of Elizabethan and Jacobean drama." For a summary of recent contributions to the debate concerning the handling of the Cade material in 2 *Henry, VI,* see Caldwell, 67-70.

[35] Donald G. Watson, *Shakespeare's Early History Plays: Politics at Play on the Elizabethan Stage* (London: Macmillan, 1990), 99.

Source: "The Many-Headed Monster in *Henry VI, Part 2,*" in *Criticism,* Vol. XXXVIII, No. 3, Summer, 1996, pp. 367-82.

Shakespeare at Work: The Two Talbots

E. Pearlman, *University of Colorado, Denver*

The enactment of the deaths of Talbot and his young son John in *The First Part of Henry the Sixth* is by all odds Shakespeare's first great theatrical success and therefore an event of great importance in the dramatist's progress. The evidence for this proposition is to be found in *Pierce Penilesse His Supplication to the Divell,* written in late 1592, where Thomas Nashe allows himself this expressive fancy:

> How would it have ioyed brave *Talbot* (the terror of the French) to think that after he had lyne two hundred yeares in his Tombe, hee should triumphe againe on the Stage, and haue his bones newe embalmed with the teares of ten thousand spectators at least (at several times), who, in the Tragedian that represents his person, imagine they behold him fresh bleeding.[1]

The words "fresh bleeding" specify that audiences shed their copious tears at the very moment that Talbot, the almost mythically heroic Earl of Shrewsbury, had retired, wounded, from the siege of Bordeaux and was about to breathe his last. It was a moment of high drama, says Nashe (perhaps hyperbolically), so true and at the same time so affecting that it drew tears from the eyes of ten thousand Londoners. How did Shakespeare achieve so powerful an effect, and why is it that the impact of this once famous scene is largely invisible to moderns, for even the play's admirers—and *1 Henry VI* does not enjoy as celebratory a criticism as some—do not attribute to Talbot's ruin the extraordinary emotive power that Nashe describes? Indeed, why does the modern version of Shakespeare's text seem both pallid and confused when compared to Nashe's great encomium?

In our texts, the "Bordeaux sequence" in which Talbot meets his death is comprised of six consecutive scenes. In the first (4.2), Talbot attempts to relieve a French siege and finds himself hemmed in by enemy troops. In the next (4.3), York, leader of the faction that bears his name, denies responsibility for the danger into which Talbot has been led; this is followed by a mirror scene (4.4) in which Somerset, chief of the Lancastrians, puts the blame for the impending disaster on the Yorkists. In the first battle scene (4.5), Talbot urges his son to fly the field, and in the second (4.6), Talbot rescues his son from danger and, puzzlingly, yet again urges him to fly. Finally, old Talbot dies embracing his dead son (4.7).

In the course of the sequence that so affected Elizabethan audiences, a single event is dramatized two consecutive times—the repetitions a curious departure from Shakespeare's usual economy. In both act 4, scene 5 and scene 6, Talbot the father and John Talbot the son choose loyalty to each other—even at the cost of certain death in combat—to the safety of flight. The apparent blemish usually passes without comment, perhaps because editors and critics tacitly dismiss it as a mark of what they seem to regard as Shakespeare's still immature craftsmanship. But it is worth considering that the obvious redundancy may not be an error of artistry but a flaw of transmission. There are a number of well-known cases in Shakespeare's works in which scholars assert that both a preliminary and a later form of an action have been accidentally preserved—such as the successive reports of Portia's death in *Julius Caesar* and the erroneous printing of two versions of Berowne's great manifesto, "O, we have made a vow to study, lords" [4.3.313ff][2] in *Love's Labour's Lost*—and the duplicated scene of battle may very well be another such instance. The Folio text may in fact proffer both an initial draft (4.6) and a much improved revision (4.5) of the scene of the Talbots' deaths.[3]

So, at least, it has been proposed. In his 1952 Cambridge edition of *1 Henry VI,* John Dover Wilson reacted very strongly to what he surmised to be an imperfection in the text: "these two scenes pursue the same course; 4.6 being virtually a repetition of 4.5. Not only is the action almost identical (the father urging the son to save himself by flight; the son refusing to desert his father: both going forward into battle resolved to die together), but the two speakers repeat the same arguments, even at times in nearly the same words."[4] Yet this response has not been credited by scholarship, perhaps because it had the misfortune to be embedded in an extravagantly disintegrationist context in which Dover Wilson also hazarded that the less highly developed of these two scenes (4.6) was written "by Greene, though possibly by Peele or Nashe" (xlvi-xlvii). At almost the same time that Dover Wilson offered his theory, the very level-headed J. P. Brockbank proposed a similar but more elaborate interpretation of the textual anomaly: "Shakespeare seems to have read Hall's more dramatic account of the death of Talbot and his son (Holinshed omits Talbot's speech). In consequence, perhaps, he was dissatisfied with his own [first] version and rewrote it. Both scenes may have been accidentally left in the manuscript . . . and so printed in the folio, standing in modern texts as 4.6

(the old) and 4.5 (the new)."[5] Whether or not Brockbank divined the actual order of events may be ultimately unknowable, but his proposition—that two successive versions of one scene are preserved in the Folio—makes perfect sense of an otherwise mysterious superfluity. Nevertheless, Brockbank's now forty-year-old intuition has been left unexamined.

Is there evidence in the Folio, not yet brought to light, to support the hypothesis that the one version of the scene revises and therefore supersedes the other? And if the Wilson-Brockbank thesis is tenable, does it then become possible to track the playwright as he made his progress from source through draft to revision?

Shakespeare seems to have designed the climactic moments of *1 Henry VI* in order to make a moralistic point of Talbot's death. The scenes that preface Talbot's end are thick with ideological analysis; the insistent—perhaps even too insistent—moral is that the life of the heroic Talbot has been sacrificed to petty and shameful internecine squabble. Speaking for the party of the white rose, York indicts "that Villaine Somerset" for delaying the "supply / Of horsemen, that were leuied for this siege" (4.3.9-11; TLN 2118-20). On the Lancastrian side, Somerset complains that "This expedition was by *Yorke* and *Talbot* / Too rashly plotted" (4.4.2-3; TLN 2067-680); meanwhile, a choral voice (2 Mes.) adds that "while the Vulture of sedition, / Feedes in the bosome of such great Commanders, / Sleeping neglection doth betray to losse" (4.3.47-49; TLN 2057-59) the memorable conquests of the heroic King Harry. Sir William Lucy makes the point plainer still when he denounces both houses: "The fraud of England, not the force of France, / Hath now intrapt the Noble-minded *Talbot*" (4.4.36-37; TLN 2101-2). It would seem that Shakespeare planned to lay on the moral with a trowel: the noble Talbot falls prey to a "yelping kennell of French Curres" (4.2.47; TLN 1998) because he has been betrayed by English factionalism. Shakespeare seems to have embarked on a reasonable although perhaps excessively didactic course.

Certainly the glorious Talbot could sustain such a moral, for he had come to embody the idealized heart of English chivalry. Defending the "Sacred name of Knight" (4.1.40; TLN 1786), Talbot had stripped the garter from Falstaff's craven knee. When the Countess of Auvergne attempted to play Delilah to his Samson (or, in her formulation, Tomyris to his Cyrus), Talbot had revealed himself to be not only a soldier wedded to his trade and impervious to female assault, but in his own patriotic view the agent, or shadow, of the "substance, sinewes, armes and strength" (2.3.62; TLN 906) of his fellow soldiers. He had been a superb and fearless but one-dimensional warrior, the scourge and terror of the French, a "walking legend,"[6] "an ideal of aristocratic conduct"[7] whose very name struck fear in enemy hearts. With the death of Talbot, the play appears to proclaim, the quintessence of idealized English chivalry became a forfeit to English discord.

Nevertheless, Shakespeare turned away from the obvious and predictable and instead set out on a course that was both more adventurous and more challenging, and ultimately, as both Nashe and history affirm, more memorable. Rather than reinforce the public themes of misgovernment and sedition and patriotism, Shakespeare seized upon a brief anecdote that opened the possibility of exploring the hitherto unsearched private side of his exemplary knight. Holinshed had not only reported how Talbot had been shot, but also that he spoke with his son, Lord Lisle, shortly before the battle:

> . . . after [Talbot] perceiued there was no remedie, but present losse of the battell, he counselled his sonne the Lord Lisle, to saue himselfe by flight, sith the same could not redound to anie great reproch in him, this being the first iournie in which he had beene present. Manie words he vsed to persuade him to have saued his life: but nature so wrought in the son, that neither desire of life, nor feare of death could either cause him to shrinke, or conueie himselfe out of the danger, and so there manfullie ended his life with his said father. (Holinshed 640b)

In these sentences Shakespeare found the kernel of the dialogues between the veteran soldier and his neophyte son to which Nashe would draw attention. Of course there was the difficulty that up until this moment in the play, Talbot had not been portrayed as a father nor had there been the even the slightest hint of a wife or family—let alone a beloved son. But Shakespeare was not to be deterred by the hobgoblin of consistency. If Talbot must acquire paternity in his last moments on earth, why then, so be it. Nor was Shakespeare reluctant to invent and then almost immediately discard an entirely new character—young John Talbot (Holinshed's Lord Lisle)—whose modest lustre was to glow for only the briefest moment.

Shakespeare also read the more circumstantial account of the siege of Castillon in his ancillary source, Edward Hall's *Union of the Two Noble and Illustrate Famelies* (1548). There he discovered that the industrious Hall had blazed a trail that already included a long and emotional oration in which Talbot urged his son to fly the field.

> Oh sonne sonne [says Talbot in Hall's *Union*], I thy father, which onely hath bene the terror and scourge of the French people so many yeres, which hath subuerted so many townes, and profligate and discomfited so many of them in open battayle, and marcial conflict, neither can here dye, for the honor of my countrey, without great laude and perpetuall fame, nor flye or departe

without perpetuall shame and continualle infamy. But because this is thy first iourney and enterprise, neither thi flyeng shall redounde to thy shame, nor thy death to thy glory: for as hardy a [sic] man wisely flieth, as a temerarious person folishely abidethe, therefore the fleying of me shalbe the dishonor, not only of me and my progenie, but also a discomfiture of all my company: thy departure shal saue thy lyfe, and make the[e] able another tyme, if I be slayn to reuenge my death and to do honor to thy Prince, and profyt to his Realme. (Hall *fol.* clxv verso-clxvi)

And Hall then concluded, in words that Holinshed would copy almost exactly, that young Talbot was too noble to heed his father's petition—for "nature so wrought in the sonne, that neither desire of lyfe, nor thought of securitie, could withdraw or pluck him from his natural father" (Hall *fol.* clxvi).

Taking advantage of the opportunity that the chroniclers had dropped in his lap, Shakespeare supplemented the play's public and didactic themes with private anecdote and emotion. From Hall's telling of the story, Shakespeare borrowed not only a number of useful ideas but also the specific design of the first version (4.6) of the encounter between Talbot and his son. The shape of the draft replicates Holinshed's template: the father entreats (of the fifty-seven lines in the draft, Talbot speaks forty-two lines—thirty-two in a single elongated oration); the son, shadowy and evanescent in his first incarnation, denies, and then the two soldiers exit to die nobly together. In both versions, the scene stresses family loyalty and emotion rather than the more abstract themes of feudalism and patriotism. It appears that at just the moment that Shakespeare came to the crucial scenes of the play, he was prompted by Hall's imaginative lecture to reassess the emphatic moralizing that prefaces Talbot's death.

If Shakespeare's first step was to complement public with private, his next—if in fact 4.5 revises 4.6—was to re-think the characters. For while the draft leans heavily on Hall and is consequently very much dominated by Talbot's rhetorical and physical authority, the revision,—a step removed from its chronicle source— presents a father who has aged and has resigned himself to his fate and a son who has now become proportionately more vigorous. If it may be posited that the revision (4.5) was a later insertion, then in the original design, Talbot would have appeared in the first scene (4.2) of the Bordeaux sequence leading his overmatched and doomed troops into combat and would not have returned to the stage until the beginning of 4.6 when the battle was in full force. In the first of these scenes (4.2), Talbot had been portrayed, as he had been throughout the play, as the inspirational soldier. In that initial appearance, he had climaxed his speech with an invocation: "God, and S. *George, Talbot* and Englands right, / Prosper our Colours in this dan-

gerous fight" (4.2.55-56; TLN 2006-7). As if to affirm the continuity of character and action, the draft begins exactly where act 4, scene 2 had concluded: "Saint *George,* and Victory; fight Souldiers, fight" (4.6.1; TLN 2173). Similarly, Talbot had left the stage as a superhero still performing prodigious feats of derring-do; he continues his success with sword and lance in the draft—as the "authorial" stage directions that preface the scene make clear: *Alarum: Excursions, wherein Talbots Sonne is hemm'd about, and Talbot rescues him* (4.6 d; TLN 2169-71).

But the intervening scene, the revision, is of an entirely different character. It takes its cue not from the invocation to God and St. George with which act 4, scene 2 ends, but from the more elegiac note struck in act 4, scene 3. There York had mourned the inevitable disaster awaiting not only Talbot but also the son who has come so inopportunely to Gascony: "Alas," moans York, "what ioy shall noble *Talbot* haue, / To bid his yong sonne welcome to his Graue" (4.3.39-40; TLN 2049-50). While the draft was hyperbolic, the revision has become distinctly valedictory. Talbot is now portrayed as older and wearier, inclined rather to lay down the sword than to deliver his son from French treachery. "O yong *John Talbot,*" he begins,

> I did send for thee
> To tutor thee in stratagems of Warre
> That *Talbots* name might be in thee reuiu'd,
> When saplesse Age, and weake vnable limbes
> Should bring thy Father to his drooping Chaire.
>
> (4.5.1-5; TLN 2114-18)

For the first time in the play, the Earl of Shrewsbury becomes reflective: "But O malignant and ill-boading Starres, / Now thou art come vnto a Feast of death, / A terrible and vnauoyded danger" (4.5.6-8; TLN 2119-21). Even more surprisingly, the soldier whom the playwright has kept singularly shielded from the softer emotions now reveals himself to be a loving father: "Therefore deere Boy," he says to his son, "mount on my swiftest horse, / And Ile direct thee how thou shalt escape / By sodaine flight. Come, dally not, be gone" (4.5.9-11; TLN 2122-24). Shakespeare has clearly made an effort to re-invent Talbot and to establish in the revision a more serene mood than either his preceding (4.2) or succeeding (4.6) scenes offer. The result is a striking discontinuity in tone; at the end of act 4, scene 2 and at the beginning of act 4, scene 6, Talbot is all strut and bellow and warmongering, but in the interpolated act 4, scene 5 he is much altered; there, weary age, beset by "malignant stars," embraces his "dear boy" while falling backward onto a "drooping chair." The scourge and terror of the French has become weak, affectionate, even stoical—and yet these same traits, acquired in the one scene—the revision—mysteriously evaporate in the next—the draft. Unless, of course, act 4, scene 6 was intended for the wastebasket and only accidentally preserved.

To return to the draft: the long speech (4.6.10-41; TLN 2181-2212) on which Talbot now embarks constitutes the heart of the scene as originally composed. It divides into three distinct sections: a discussion of soldiership, a discussion of virginity and bastardy, and finally, a passage of sententious couplets. Each of these sections is reprised in the revision, although the first of them offered very little worthy of preservation. In these initial lines, when Talbot expresses emotion for his son, he does not profess a father's love to a long-lost child but rather the loyalty of one soldier to another: Talbot rescues young John; John admires his father's "Warlike Sword"; Talbot explains that his veteran soldiership has been reinvigorated and that "Leaden Age, / Quicken'd with Youthfull Spleene, and Warlike Rage, / Beat down *Alanson, Orleance, Burgundie*" (12-14; TLN 2183-85). In the more highly developed revision, the Talbots are no longer soldered by soldiership but are linked by more private and personal affections. Only a single phrase from the draft survives in the 'revision': "Leaden Age" has been transmuted into "sapless Age."

In the second part of this long speech, Shakespeare grapples unsuccessfully with a metaphor that equates military and sexual initiation. Talbot reports that he condemned the "irefull Bastard *Orleance*" because he "drew blood" and therefore "had the Maidenhood" (15-16; TLN 2186-87) of his son. But answering innuendo with innuendo, Talbot asserts that he "encountred" Orleans with "blowes" and "quickly shed / Some of his Bastard blood" (16-18; TLN 2189-91). Shakespeare then shifts the argument to the closely related subject of legitimacy. To the Bastard of Orleans, Talbot had said

> Contaminated, base,
> And mis-begotten blood, I spill of thine,
> Meane and right poore, for that pure blood
>   of mine
> Which thou didst force from *Talbot,* my
>   braue Boy.
>
> (21-24; TLN 2192-95)

Talbot asserts that the legitimate blood of his son is superior to the contaminated blood of the Bastard. The metaphor clearly signifies that the chivalry of the English is purer than that of the French; it also hints obliquely that the Bastard can symbolically or metaphysically both violate and infect young Talbot with his "sword" (although vague syntax makes it difficult to construe the lines with confidence).[8] But then Shakespeare seems to lose interest in the signification of blood and abruptly breaks off the discussion: "Here

purposing the Bastard to destroy, / Came in strong rescue" (25-26; TLN 2196-97). Maidenhead, wounds, blood, and bastardy are all brought to the fore in the draft (4.6) but the metaphor never quite bears fruit. In the comparable section of act 4, scene 5, Shakespeare severely prunes these excesses. The Bastard himself has disappeared, but bastardy remains the issue; now the threat to John Talbot's life is not the Bastard's sword but illegitimacy itself. Bastardy, the revision announces, is so fearful a bogey that young John Talbot must sacrifice his life to free himself from its taint. It is a cruel paradox:

> O, if you loue my Mother,
> Dishonor not her Honorable Name,
> To make a Bastard, and a Slaue of me:
> The World will say, he is not *Talbots*
>   blood,
> That basely fled, when Noble *Talbot* stood.
>
> (4.5.12-15; TLN 2126-30)

Bastardy and legitimacy, inchoate in the draft, crystallize in the revision. Because John Talbot is unspotted, he can be subsumed in his father; consequently, it would appear, it is now no more possible that John Talbot can be "seuered" from Talbot than that Talbot can "[him] selfe in twaine diuide" (49; TLN 2162). Young Talbot's immaculate legitimacy, demonstrated by his eagerness to die in its defense, allows him in some mysterious way to assimilate his father's virtues. It is not a particularly difficult idea, but it is curious that Shakespeare came to it by such a long and winding road.

The third section of Talbot's long speech in the draft contains a miscellany of ideas that Shakespeare quarried for the revision. An instance: in the draft, Shakespeare plays with the notion that it is superfluous for both father and son to die. In the original, Talbot phrases it thus: "Oh, too much folly is it, well I wot, / To hazard all our liues in one small Boat" (4.6.33-34; TLN 2204-5). It is a particularly flabby couplet: "well I wot" is empty syllables, and the rewriting of the proverb about venturing all one's goods in a single bottom introduces a bit of naval imagery but is hardly worth the detour. In the revision, the critique of supererogatory death is more economically rendered:

> *Talb.* If we both stay, we both are sure to
>   dye.
> *Iohn.* Then let me stay, and Father doe you
>   flye.
>
> (4.5.20-21; TLN 2133-34)

And again, in the draft, Talbot delivers himself of a crowded piece of zeugma in which one preceding and four succeeding nominatives compete to govern a single intransitive verb:

In thee thy Mother dyes, our Households
  Name,
My Deaths Reuenge, thy Youth, and
  Englands Fame.

                              (4.6.37-38; TLN 2209-10)

In the comparable section of the revision, the identical
idea has been much simplified and refocussed:

Talb. Shall all thy Mothers hopes lye in one
  Tombe?
Iohn. I rather then Ile shame my Mothers
  Wombe.

                              (4.5. 35-36; TLN 2147-48)

In yet another case, Talbot says "Flye, to reuenge my
death when I am dead, / The helpe of one stands me
in little stead" (4.6.30-31; TLN 2201-2). Once again,
this distich could hardly have satisfied the young poet.
In the first line, the phrase "Reuenge my death when
I am dead" is flabby and redundant; in the second, the
grammatical subject "Helpe of one" is only obscurely
linked to its verb "stand," while the phrase "in little
stead" is woefully bland. The 'revision' is far more
vivid and animated:

Talb. Flye, to reuenge my death, if I be
  slaine.
Iohn. He that flyes so, will ne're returne
  againe.

                              (4.5.18-19; TLN 2131-32)

In his particular instance, the draft and revised versions are strikingly close. Having decided to rewrite
Talbot's speech, it would seem, Shakespeare inspected
it to determine if there were lines worth preserving.
He extracted "Flye, to reuenge my death when I am
dead," discarded the limp subordination and supplied
the more concrete "if I be slaine." He went on to
delete the weak rhyming line and substitute the vigorous rejoinder that he put in the mouth of young John
Talbot. The only alternative is that Shakespeare either
forgot or was indifferent to the fact that he had already written the couplet shared by father and son and
not only reproduced it in part but also allowed it to
decline into the bloodless version found in the draft.
This does not seem to be credible; such sloppiness is
not generally Shakespeare's way.

In addition to plundering Talbot's long speech, Shakespeare also adapted at least one phrase from young
Talbot's comparatively brief response. In the draft,
young Talbot says "And if I flye, I am not *Talbots*
Sonne" (4.6.51; TLN 2222). This line reappears in the
revision as a series of staccato questions: "Is my name
Talbot? and am I your Sonne? / And shall I flye?"
(4.5.12-13; TLN 2125-26). Unless the one scene replaces the other, Shakespeare must have been extraor-
dinarily lax to allow so near a repetition to stand.

There may also be a second echo of Talbot's reply in
the revision. In the draft, John Talbot concludes, "Then
talke no more of flight, it is no boot, / If Sonne to
Talbot, dye at *Talbots* foot" (4.6.52-53; TLN 2223-
24). In the comparable lines of his revised speech, the
son does not threaten to die at Talbot's foot but instead kneels to him and solicits death: "Here on my
knee I begge Mortalitie, / Rather then Life, preseru'd
with Infamie" (4.5.32-33; TLN 2146-47). In both
cases, the root idea is better dead than fled; bended
knee now replaces boot and foot. But other pieces of
John Talbot's speech were unsalvageable; what could
possibly be done with the anticlimactic "Before young
Talbot from old *Talbot* flye / The Coward Horse that
beares me, fall and dye" (4.6.45-46; TLN 2217-18)?
Better to let coward horses lie. To review; once Shakespeare decided to do away with 4.6, he looted whatever was useful—ideas, words, phrases, gestures,
metaphors—and rewrote them in the newer version.
In instance after instance, he replaced a confused or
slack expression with one that was sharper and more
certain.

Even so, in terms of the overall redesign of the scene,
Shakespeare's salvaging of remnants is far less important than his embrace of an entirely new rhetorical
strategy. In the draft he had been content with a speech
of advocacy by the father and a shorter speech of
denial by the son. In the more dynamic revision, Shakespeare raised the rhetorical level by distilling arguments for and against flight into a dazzling set of
rhymed distichs in which old Talbot proposes and
young Talbot disposes.

Talb. Shall all thy Mothers hopes lye in one
  Tombe?
Iohn. I, rather then Ile shame my Mothers
  Wombe.
Talb. Vpon my Blessing I command thee
  goe.
Iohn. To fight I will, but not to flye the
  Foe.
Talb. Part of thy Father may be sau'd in
  thee.
Iohn. No part of him, but will be shame in
  mee.
Talb. Thou neuer hadst Renowne, nor canst
  not lose it.
Iohn. Yes, your renowned Name: shall flight
  abuse it?
Talb. Thy Fathers charge shal cleare thee
  from yt staine.
Iohn. You cannot witnesse for me, being
  slaine.
  If Death be so apparant, then both flye.
Talb. And leaue my followers here to fight
  and dye?
  My Age was neuer tainted with such
  shame.

> *Iohn.* And shall my Youth be guiltie of such
> blame?
>
> (4.5.34-47; TLN 2147-60)

It is true that stichomythia is a stylized and non-mimetic form of conversation, and it is something of a paradox that Shakespeare employed an artificial and exaggerated rhetoric to breathe life into the play's most intimate concerns. Although Shakespeare lost interest in stichomythia as he developed as an artist, in the early part of his career he did not hesitate to employ it in such crucial and emotional moments as the wooing of Lady Elizabeth Grey by Edward IV in *3 Henry VI* and of Anne by Richard of Gloucester. There is a later but still elaborate passage in *Romeo and Juliet* when Paris and Juliet meet outside Friar Lawrence's cell. But stichomythia is more than mere rhetorical exuberance: in its very essence it proclaims an equivalence between speakers. As they appear in the revision, father and son are equally intelligent, equally witty, equally succinct, equally moral. Inasmuch as young John Talbot is barely realized in the draft, his death could not deeply engage the passions of the audience. But in the revision, Shakespeare passed the rhetorical initiative to the young Talbot who now not only answers his father stroke for stichomythic stroke but ultimately overwhelms him with a flurry of sentences and sayings. Time after time, young Talbot asserts that his sacrifice is entirely voluntary. When Shakespeare recast the scene, he not only gave room for young Talbot to prosper as a maker of tropes, but at the same time demilitarized and humanized old Talbot himself. As young Talbot grew as a character, so Talbot's love for him became more credible to the audience, and as love became more believable, so too does the impact of his grief. By the end of the sequence, when, at last, Talbot's "old armes" become "yong *Iohn Talbots* graue" (4.7.32; TLN 2263)—as Lear's will be Cordelia's—Shakespeare had shouldered the guns and drums and flourishes of Bordeaux into the arena of tragedy.

One last example of Shakespeare refining the raw material of the draft: after young John offers to die at his father's foot, Talbot brings the scene to a close with a pair of allusive couplets:

> Then follow thou, thy desp'rate Syre of
> Creet,
> Thou *Icarus,* thy life to me is sweet:
> If thou wilt fight, fight by thy Fathers side,
> And commendable prou'd, let's dye in pride.
>
> (4.6.54-57; TLN 2225-28)

Ovid's inexpressibly lovely tale of Daedalus and Icarus is pertinent for a number of reasons. In the *Metamorphosis,* father and son fly from Crete; in *1 Henry VI,* the Talbots think to fly the field of battle. Daedalus teaches the "hurtfull art"[9] of flying; Talbot teaches the art of war. Icarus is a type of the overreacher; instead of keeping to his pre-arranged flight plan, he conceives in mid-voyage a "fond desire to flie to heauen" (8.301), but "the neerenesse of the sunne" (302) causes his waxen wings to melt and, falling, "he drowned in the waue" (306). The "ouer-daring *Talbot*" (4.4.5; TLN 2069) is also, intermittently, an overreacher. And so for four lines in the draft, Talbot appears as Daedalus—the Cretan sire—and young John Talbot becomes Icarus. But in this first pass, Shakespeare reaped only a portion of what Ovid's tale could ultimately be made to yield.

In the very next scene of the Bordeaux sequence (4.7)—or the part that would follow directly after the revision if the draft had been properly discarded—Shakespeare introduced a far fuller allusion to Daedalus and Icarus. As it appears on the Folio page, it is separated from the analogous passage in act 4, scene 6 by just a dozen lines—an inconceivably maladroit repetition. It is not impossible that after writing his unsatisfactory first version, Shakespeare realized that Ovid's story of Daedalus and Icarus demonstrated strengths that his allusion to it did not capture. In the *Metamorphosis,* emotions are portrayed with little disguise or dissimulation. Old Daedalus feelingly expresses his love when he fixes the feathers on his son's back: "His aged cheekes were wet, his hands did quake, in fine he gaue / His sonne a kisse, the last that euer he aliue should haue" (284-85). Perhaps Shakespeare heard with new ears the sorrow in Daedalus' voice as Icarus plunged into the sea, when the "wretched father (but as then no father) cride in feare: / O *Icarus, O Icarus,* where art thou: tell me where, / That I may finde thee, *Icarus*" (308-10). Perhaps he did hear something wonderful—because both the emotion and the vocabulary of the ancient narrative are rejuvenated in the newly re-imagined Talbot, who, searching for his son, fearfully cries (at the beginning of 4.7), "Where is my other Life? mine owne is gone. / O, where's young *Talbot?* where is valiant *Iohn?*" And when Shakespeare relates at last the circumstances of John's death—and this is surely the particular speech that moistened the eyes of ten thousand spectators—he once again made use of Ovid's example to conduct his audience as far down the trail of tears as his early competence was so far capable. When, Talbot says, he had been rescued by his son (in the draft, with its alternate emphasis, it was the father who saved the son), young John could not rest content. Instead,

> great rage of Heart,
> Suddenly made him from my side to start
> Into the clustring Battaile of the French:
> And in that Sea of Blood, my Boy did
> drench
> His ouer-mounting Spirit; and there di'de
> My *Icarus,* my Blossome, in his pride.
>
> (4.7.11-16; TLN 2241-46)

The last prepositional phrase—"in his pride"—supplants the very similar conclusion of the original—"let's dye in pride" (4.6.57; TLN 2228). One more time, the father steps aside to let the son take center stage. The compound adjective "ouer-mounting" ties young Talbot to young Icarus; "Sea of Blood"—a prosy anticipation of the incarnadine seas fifteen years into the future—binds the field of battle to Ovid's Mediterranean. Allusions that merely ornament the draft inhabit the revision. "My Boy . . . My *Icarus,* my Blossome" marks out territory that will some day be Shakespeare's alone. The word "Blossome" cajoles a last reluctant sob from the audience. Acting to expand the emotional range of his play, Shakespeare courageously places near-sentimentality in the mouth of the character who just seconds ago had threatened the French with "Leane Famine, quartering Steele, and climbing Fire" (4.2.11; TLN 1961). Blossom, we may say, speed thee well!

Nor was Shakespeare quite finished with Daedalus and Icarus:

> *Enter with Iohn Talbot, borne.*
> *Seru.* O my deare Lord, loe where your
>   Sonne is borne.
> *Tal.* Thou antique Death, which laugh'st vs
>   here to scorn,
> Anon from thy insulting Tyrannie,
> Coupled in bonds of perpetuitie,
> Two *Talbots* winged through the lither Skie,
> In thy despight shall scape Mortalitie.
>   (4.7.17-22; TLN 2247-53)

"Lither Skie"? In Golding's Ovid, the wax that glued the feathers to Icarus's body was "lyth" (303); appropriating a device of Latin poetry, Shakespeare transfers the epithet from wings to sky.[10] Two *Talbots* "winged"? The participle functions as an adjective to fuse the English soldiers to their ancient precedents. In these very promising lines, classical and Christian images have been wondrously syncretized to permit the Talbot souls to soar heavenward on pagan wings. Just as Shakespeare had earlier made use of Hall's long invented speech to free himself from excessive didacticism, so now he employed Ovid's more passionate art to loosen the grip of chronicle history itself.

To sum up: there are a number of reasons to believe that act 4, scene 6 is a first, less mature version of act 4, scene 5. One: prima facie; as Dover Wilson and Brockbank noticed, the repetition of scenes is an uneconomical and absurd reduplication. Two scenes where one might suffice is a careless and inexplicable lapse. Two: act 4, scene 6 is close to Hall in format (a long speech followed by a brief reply), while act 4, scene 5 invents a new and more complex design; that the first scene would depart from a source to which the second adheres is inherently improbable. Three: in

act 4, scene 5, Talbot is weary and thoughtful and emotional; in act 4, scene 6 he reverts to the warrior mode of act 4, scene 2 and is unaffected by intervening changes in character and tone. Four: act 4, scene 5 continually ransacks the draft for ideas and phrases, a procedure that makes sense only if Shakespeare had already given up on his first version. Five: in case after case, expressions in the revision are more succinct and pertinent than the corresponding expression in the draft. Six: the character of young Talbot is far more fully realized in the revision than in the draft—the alternative is that Shakespeare enhanced the character in one scene and diminished it in the next. Seven: the emotional appeal of a highly figured rhetoric, so prominent in act 4, scene 5, inexplicably disappears in act 4, scene 6. Eight: Shakespeare pushes his chronicle play toward tragedy in the revision; there is no such impulse in the draft. Nine: having decided to abandon act 4, scene 6, Shakespeare gleaned its Ovidian material and re-used it in act 4, scene 7 with a verve and intensity undetectable in the "draft."

It is now possible to recover a possible chronology of the composition of the Bordeaux sequence. Shakespeare first set out in a didactic spirit but his imagination was fired by Holinshed's and more particularly by Hall's attention to young Lord Lisle, Talbot's son. He drafted a first unsatisfactory version of the scene in imitation of the chronicles. Then he rewrote the scene using the first version as a source for a greatly improved performance that adds dimension to the characters and flamboyance to the language. Still not satisfied, Shakespeare turned to Ovid and under his influence composed the ambitious introduction to act 4, scene 7. It is impossible to say exactly when all this was done, but a good guess is that it took place before the early performances to which Nashe refers and that it was certainly completed by the middle 1590s when Shakespeare lost interest in stichomythia.

What can be learned from this exercise? At this late date, it is superfluous to kick the corpse of "warbling his native woodnotes wild." It has long been clear that Shakespeare was not only analytical and persevering, but was also an opportunistic craftsman ready to leap in a new direction when an occasion presented itself. Considering the dramatic traditions from which he emerged, Shakespeare needed to be constantly vigilant in order to prevent his play from lapsing into allegory. At some point in the making of *1 Henry VI,* it is possible to surmise, he may have become aware that the Bordeaux sequence contained far too much heavy-handed ideological machinery. Hall's anecdote presented a wonderful opportunity to correct his course and steer the play from abstractions to emotions.

In comparison to Shakespeare's later efforts, the death of the Talbots is hardly a distinguished piece of writing. The characters impress rather than deceive, and although the language is energetic and rapidly paced, the paradoxes and figures in which the Talbots speak are nevertheless stiff and archaic. Yet Nashe testifies that Londoners found these scenes both moving *and* realistic: audiences were so dazzled by the play that "in the Tragedian that represents his person, [they] imagine they behold [Talbot] fresh bleeding." It is paradoxical that although Shakespeare abandoned his source to invent the witty stichomythic exchanges, and then departed once again to incorporate Ovidian emotion, it was when he was most free and most adventuresome that he won praise for his accurate representation of the past. The play's first audiences seem to have construed stylized artificiality as augmented realism. Such a lesson would not have been lost on the playwright.

When Shakespeare gave exemplary and superhuman Talbot ordinary and familiar human feelings, he not only pleased his audience but also began to redraw the boundaries of the history play. By the end of the century, Shakespeare had mastered the technique toward which this play struggles—the interpenetration of public and private themes—and had discovered that there was far more to historical drama than the vauntings and flytings, the sennets and excursions, and the beard-to-beard challenges that fill so much of the first Henriad. To see where his path would lead, it is only necessary to recall the first scene of *1 Henry IV* when Shakespeare, having revealed in the king's opening address that England was threatened within and without, toggles economically from state to family with the single line, "It is a conquest for a prince to boast of" (1.1.77). Shakespeare's struggle with the writing and rewriting of the Talbot scenes taught him how to collapse the genres, how to slip the noose of the chronicles, and how to subordinate the facts of history to the idea of history.

One final thought: the Talbot deaths introduce a theme that would reverberate throughout Shakespeare's plays. Father and son join in battle not only here but in a number of places along the route. At Crecy (in *Edward III*—for those who believe the play to be Shakespeare's), the king rather cold-heartedly refuses to aid his son, the beleaguered Black Prince, and insists that youth prove its worth in the field. Shakespeare inverts the anti-Oedipal Talbot formula in *3 Henry VI* in the scene of the Son who has killed his Father and the Father who has killed his Son. There is an interesting variant at Shrewsbury where Hal rescues his downed father from the Douglas. The event in all of Shakespeare's plays that is most similar to the Talbot deaths occurs in *Henry V* when Exeter narrates the affecting story of the cousins Suffolk and York who died in each other's arms at Agincourt. York (as reported by Exeter) distinctly echoes Talbot:

> 'Tarry, my cousin Suffolk,
> My soul shall thine keep company in heaven.
> Tarry, sweet soul, for mine, then fly abreast,
> As in his glorious and well-foughten field
> We kept together in our chivalry.'
>
> (4.6.15.19)

Once again Shakespeare integrates sacrifice, family, chivalry, and heavenly flight in order to solicit shamelessly the tears of the spectators:

> The pretty and sweet manner of it forced
> Those waters from me which I would have stopped,
> But I had not so much of man in me,
> And all my mother came into mine eyes,
> And gave me up to tears.
>
> (4.6.28-32)

Talbot is also echoed in *King Lear* when Gloucester and Edgar and a bastard son are all present at Dover. And finally, a most intriguing reprise of the pattern appears in *Macbeth*. At Dunsinane, Macduff is a father who has lost his son and "the boy Malcolm" (5.3.3) a son who has lost a father. As surrogate father and surrogate son, they join to overthrow the tyrant. In the same play there is still another pair of father-son soldiers—the Seywards. Old Seyward, "[A]n older and a better soldier none / That Christendom gives out" (4.3.191-2) and young Seyward, one of "many unrough youths that even now / Protest their first of manhood" (5.2.10-11), fight England's battle in a foreign land. Once again, youth dies without protest and age embraces the sacrifice. These many iterations leave open the possibility that when Shakespeare dramatized the Talbot deaths, both his choice to do so as well as the great leap forward in the intensity of his presentation may have been governed not only by a daring and discriminating analysis of character, rhetoric, and audience, but also by social forces and subterranean motives of which even the playwright himself was unaware.[11]

Notes

[1] *The Works of Thomas Nashe,* ed. R. B. McKerrow. 4 vols. (London: Sidgwick & Jackson, 1910), 1:212.

[2] Quotations to plays other than *1 Henry VI* are drawn from *William Shakespeare: The Complete Works,* ed. Alfred Harbage (Baltimore: Penguin, 1969).

[3] The play's most recent investigator concludes that "the text was set up from holographic fair copy" (*The First Part of King Henry VI,* ed. Michael Hattaway (Cambridge U. Press, 1990), 195. I have accepted his analysis. I have also made the following assumptions (not all of which are essential to my argument): a) that

Shakespeare wrote *1 Henry VI* in its entirety; b) that *1 Henry VI* precedes *2* and *3 Henry;* c) that *1 Henry VI* is either the first or among the very earliest of Shakespeare's surviving writings; d) that Nashe's description of Talbot refers to Shakespeare's *1 Henry VI* and not to any other Henry play; e) that *1 Henry VI* is recorded in Henslowe's *Diary* under the name *harey the vi.*

[4] *The First Part of King Henry VI,* ed. John Dover Wilson (Cambridge U. Press, 1952), xlvii.

[5] Cited from Brockbank's unpublished 1953 Cambridge dissertation in *The First Part of King Henry VI,* ed. Hattaway, headnote to 4.6.

[6] So wittily denominated by Emrys Jones in *The Origins of Shakespeare* (Oxford: Clarendon Press, 1977), 155.

[7] David Riggs, *Shakespeare's Heroical Histories* (Harvard U. Press, 1971), 25.

[8] The adjectives "mean" and "poore" follow and have been divorced from the noun they modify; in the intervening phrase—"I spill of thine"—a genitive floats unmoored to a substantive. Syntactic clarity has been sacrificed to the "thine / mine" chime.

[9] See *The XV Bookes of P. Ouidius Naso Entituled Metamorphosis* (trans. Arthur Golding), London: Robert Waldegrave, 1587 (STC 18959), where the story appears on pages 105-6. Line numbers are drawn from *Shakespeare's Ovid: Being Arthur Golding's Translation of the Metamorphosis.* ed. W. H. D. Rouse (London: Centaur Press, 1961). The phrase "hurtfull art" appears on line 291.

[10] Unless, as Hattaway (4.7.21n) hints, Shakespeare recalled the insatiable Erisicthon, who "instead of food devours the lither ayre" (*Metamorphosis* 8.1027).

[11] Bibliographical tangles in the lines surrounding these scenes have aroused the suspicions of textual editors right from the start; these tangles may be explained by the notion that 4.5 revises 4.6. The scene (4.3) that precedes the battle begins with the stage direction, *Enter a Messenger that meets Yorke.* York and this first messenger converse; then, *Enter another Messenger* (4.3.16 sd; TLN 2026). It is the second messenger who provokes editorial anxiety. The first time he speaks, he is called *2 Mes,* and the second, third and fourth times, he is merely *Mes.* But to this same messenger, York, as he leaves the stage, unaccountably says "*Lucie* farewell" (43; TLN 2053). And why "Lucie"? Until York uttered his farewell, there had been no Lucy; in fact, according to the sources, there was no one of that name in the English expeditionary force in France. How does it happen that York sud-

denly decided to call the Second Messenger "Lucie." Moreover, what explanation can be offered for the fact that, having brought the character onto the stage, the Folio then brings the scene to a close without a providing Mes./2 Mes./Lucie with an Exit (the required stage direction was correctly added in F2)?

The provocative "Lucie" then becomes even more mysterious. Just ten lines into the scene that follows (4.4), an unnamed Captain who has accompanied Somerset and his armies onto the stage makes the announcement that "Heere is Sir *William Lucie,* who with me / Set from our orematched forces forth for ayde" (4.4.10-11; TLN 2075-76). The Captain's lines make it absolutely clear that both he and the character named Sir William Lucy whom he introduces have just come from the camp of Talbot. Sir William Lucy explains that "L. *Talbot,* / . . . ring'd about with bold aduersitie, / Cries out for noble Yorke and Somerset" (13-15; TLN 2277-79). But once again there is illogicality: how can Sir William Lucy possibly be imagined to have come from Talbot in 4.4 when the "Lucie" of 4.3 has just seconds ago been seen in the company of York? Clearly, there is a dropped stitch, for no audience can be expected to believe that the same character has been present in two very different places in two consecutive moments. (The matter becomes not only puzzling but absurd if the F1 stage directions are taken seriously, for, inasmuch as there is no Exit for Mes/ 2 Mes./ Lucie at the end of 4.3 and no Entrance for Sir William Lucy at 4.4, the character could not have gone anywhere or come from anywhere, but must have remained on stage for the duration.) It is quite a labyrinth. It seems as though there should be two separate characters, Mes./ 2 Mes. in 4.3. and Sir William Lucy in 4.4, and that the first of these was latterly labelled "Lucie" in error.

In addition to the confusion just before the two father-son (4.5 and 4.6) scenes, there is a second and related textual anomaly in 4.7 that also involves the same enigmatic messenger. While this time Sir William Lucy is accorded the decency of a proper entrance (*Enter Lucie* [4.7.50sd; TLN 2284]), his first words have arrested the attention of editors since Pope. The Folio reads:

> *Lu.* Herald, conduct me to the Dolphins
> Tent,
> To know who hath obtain'd the glory of the
> day.
>
>   (51-52; TLN 2285-86)

The disturbing hexameter suggests that *Lu.* was designed to amend an original speech heading *Herald* and that the manuscript must once have read:

> *Herald.* Conduct me to the Dolphins Tent to
> know
> Who hath obtain'd the glory of the day.

Shakespeare, it is presumed, meant to change the speaker's name from a generic herald to specific Lucy but somehow the extra syllables survived to spoil the Folio pentameter. Once again "Lucie" appears to be a troublesome afterthought. A reasonable inference from these snags in the text is that there were originally two very minor unnamed characters—a messenger and a herald—whose lines were at some point grafted onto the character named Sir William Lucy who first came into being in 4.4. Shakespeare therefore allowed York to call the character "Lucie" in 4.3 and he substituted *Lu.* for Herald in 4.7. It would seem then, that Shakespeare's concentration of attention on the father-son scenes represents a departure from his original plan. How belated a departure? After, it would seem, an early version of the conversation between York and the messenger in 4.3 was first drafted. By the time Shakespeare had worked and re-worked the scenes of the Talbots' battlefield encounter, young Talbot had materialized and then developed into a significant character; he could not simply appear on stage until the audience had been prepared for his arrival. Shakespeare was therefore compelled to return to 4.3 and to add the foreboding exchange (2044-57) between York and Messenger. So 2 Mes./Mes./Lucie says: "This seuen yeeres did not *Talbot* see his sonne, / And now they meete where both their liues are done" (4.3.37-38; TLN 2047-48). And then York responds, in the sad and subdued mood of the 'revision,'

> Alas, what ioy shall noble *Talbot* haue,
> To bid his yong sonne welcome to his
>   Graue:
> Away, vexation almost stoppes my breath,
> That sundred friends greete in the houre of
>   death.
>   *Lucie* farewell. . . .
>
>   (39-43; TLN 2049-53)

Surely it can be no coincidence that the lines that introduce the audience to John Talbot are the exact same lines that transform Second Messenger into "Lucie." Having invented Sir William Lucy in 4.4, Shakespeare may have forgotten, when he came to insert the lines that prepare for young Talbot's appearance, that the character in 4.3 was merely an unspecified Mes. (or 2 Mes.) and he inadvertently allowed York to call Mes./2 Mes by a name to which he was not entitled. Moreover, to pile speculation upon speculation, it would appear that Shakespeare intended to excise a short section of the scene when he made the addition. It is not unlikely that the lines that introduce young Talbot and "Lucie" replace TLN 2040-43, so that York's concluding phrase—"Long all of Somerset, and his delay" (4.3.46; TLN 2057) would supersede rather than awkwardly replicate its too approximate anticipation—"All long of this vile Traitor Somerset" (33; TLN 2043).

Since this essay was completed, Gary Taylor's "Shakespeare and Others: The Authorship of *Henry the Sixth, Part One*," described as "forthcoming" in Wells and Taylor's *William Shakespeare: A Textual Companion* (Oxford: Clarendon, 1987) has at long last seen the light of day (in *Medieval and Renaissance Drama in England* 7 [1995], 145-205). Taylor attributes portions of *1 Henry 6* to Nashe and to two other unidentified authors; he does not question Shakespeare's authorship of the Bordeaux sequence.

Source: "Shakespeare at Work: The Two Talbots," in *Philological Quarterly,* Vol. 75, No. 1, Winter, 1996, pp. 1-22.

Princes, Pirates, and Pigs: Criminalizing Wars of Conquest in *Henry V*

Janet M. Spencer, *Wingate University*

"The figure who exceeds the law as its master and the one who exceeds it as transgressor," Christopher Pye explains of Henry V and the traitors Cambridge, Grey, and Scroop, "are indeed bound by an unspoken—perhaps unspeakable—knowledge about the origins of power."[1] In Shakespeare's *Henry V,* Henry takes great pains to conceal his capacity to exceed the law by seeking religious legitimation of, or by displacing moral responsibility for, decisions based ultimately on royal prerogative. And for a great number of producers, theatergoers, and literary critics he succeeds admirably.[2] Nevertheless, his decisions to exercise royal power mark him as a figure of legal excess, an identity given specific significance by the "figures and comparisons" drawn between England's warrior-king and the celebrated conqueror whom Fluellen calls "Alexander the Pig."[3] The play provides numerous explicit allusions to Alexander the Great, supporting Fluellen's assertion that "there is figures in all things" (4.7.33). But the episode from Alexander's life that best voices the intuitive, unspoken knowledge about the origins of power, Alexander's encounter with the pirate Dionides, is partially suppressed by an ambiguous series of variations capable of unspeaking the dangerous knowledge it confesses. Even so, the anecdote hovers over the central acts of the play, trailing its associations with debates concerning the morality of wars of conquest and, more important, with what conquest's defiance of law reveals about the origins of power. The pirate anecdote was a commonplace used by Augustine, John of Salisbury, Chaucer, Gower, Lydgate, Boccaccio, Erasmus, and other Continental authors; Shakespeare's familiarity with it shapes the exchange between Enobarbas and Menas in *Antony and Cleopatra.*[4] In the story Alexander's men seize a pirate who, when brought to Alexander for judgment, defends himself by equating the thefts of pirates with those of conquerors, "barring the fact," as Erasmus tells the tale, "that [conquerors] have greater forces and a bigger fleet to harass a larger part of the world with their plunderings."[5] Though the story's moral varies from one version to another, all contain its two key elements: Dionides's comparison of conquerors to pirates and Alexander's pardon of that indictment. These elements encode the polar limits at which a sovereign could exercise the royal prerogative to transcend the law: war's deployment of force to exceed the law of nations and the pardon's restraint of force to override civil law's right to execute convicted felons. Although Shakespeare avoids replicating the pirate anecdote too closely, he frames the conquest of France with Henry's pardons of free speech—that of

the unnamed soldier in Act 2 and that of Michael Williams in Act 4. And despite Falstaff's absence from the play, he maintains the presence of Henry's former compatriots in crime. In an important sense the structure of the anecdote clarifies the structure of the play and, more interestingly, allows the play to voice otherwise unspeakable knowledge about the origins of power.

Despite the European pursuit of territory throughout the sixteenth and seventeenth centuries, the morality of conquest could not simply be assumed; the primary justification for war was, in fact, recovery of territory lost through conquest. Theodor Meron explains that most of the rules of *jus gentium* concerned warfare. These laws supplemented the laws of chivalry which regulated the individual conduct of Christian knights—not Christian nations—at war. Although, as Meron observes, both the Hundred Years' War and Shakespeare's theatrical accounts of it precede the emergence of modern international law, the requirements of a just war were carefully articulated in multiple sources and formed important criteria for determining cases involving ransom and booty in European courts of chivalry. "A just war," Meron explains, "could legitimize criminal acts and create a legal title to goods whose taking in other circumstances would be considered robbery."[6] Although in courts of chivalry the claim to a just cause might legitimize criminal acts, in humanist discussions of war the association between criminal acts and war criminalizes the latter as often as it exonerates the former. Erasmus asks, "What is war, indeed, but murder shared by many, and brigandage, all the more immoral from being wider spread?"[7]

Oddly enough, however, the immorality of wars of conquest could, in fact, be asserted either to defend or to critique the status quo of monarchical power. Whether a conflict was ultimately designated a just war of recovery or an unjust act of expansionism boiled down to the issue of legitimate title to the territory in question, an issue decided in practice more often by the outcome of the conflict than by any other criteria. Of basing just cause on just claim, Erasmus reasons:

> Someone may say, 'Do you want princes not to assert their rights?' I know it is not for such as myself to argue boldly about the affairs of princes, and even if it were safe to do so, it would take longer than we have time for here. I will only say this: if a claim to possession is to be reckoned sufficient reason for going to war, then in such a

disturbed state of human affairs, so full of change, there is no one who does not possess such a claim. What people has not, at one time or another, been driven out of its lands or driven others out? . . . How often has there been a transfer of sovereignty, either by chance or by treaty?[8]

Applications of Dionides's bold comparison probed beyond the problem of king as conqueror to touch the idea of kingship itself. This related issue of just title—not to a particular territory but to the idea of monarchical rule itself—simmered beneath discussions of forms of government.[9] Although the pirate anecdote usually supported egalitarian arguments, it appears as a defense of monarchy in Charles I's scaffold accusation that parliament was guilty of "a great robbery" in waging an unjust war of conquest against him:

> Now, sirs, I must show you both how you are out of the way and [I] will put you in the way. First you are out of the way, for certainly all the way you ever have had yet—as I could find by anything—is in the way of conquest. Certainly this is an ill way. For conquest, sirs, in my opinion is never just, except there be good just cause, either for matter of wrong or just title. And then if you go beyond it, the first quarrel that you have to it, that makes it unjust at the end that was just at first. But if it be only matter of conquest, then it is a great robbery; as a pirate said to Alexander the Great that he was the great robber, he [the pirate] was but a petty robber. And so, sirs, I do think the way that you are in is much out of the way.[10]

In contrast, the anecdote's most influential use to critique monarchy occurs in Augustine's *De Civitate Dei*. Augustine positions the anecdote in a context that exposes the dangerous knowledge of the roots of power which Dionides and Alexander share. An English translation printed in 1610 reads:

> Set iustice aside then, and what are kingdomes but faire theeuish purchases? because what (*a*) are theeues purchases but little kingdomes? for in thefts, the hands of the vnderlings are directed by the commander, the confederacie of them is sworne together, and the pillage is shared by the law amongst them. And if those ragga-muffins grow but vp to be able enough to keepe forts, build habitations, possesse cities, and conquer adioyning nations, then their gouernment is no more called theeuish, but graced with the eminent name of a kingdome, giuen and gotten, not because they haue left their practises, but because that now they may vse them with-out danger of lawe: for elegant and excellent was (*b*) that Pirates answer to the *Great Macedonian Alexander,* who had taken him: the king asking him how he durst molest the seas so, hee replyed with a free spirit,

> *How darest thou molest the whole world? But because I doe it with a little ship onely, I am called a theefe: thou doing it with a great Nauie, art called an Emperour.*[11]

Instead of having the pirate executed for his crimes and his effrontery, Alexander pardons him, offering him a command in his own navy—a move that rewards or, perhaps, appropriates the pirate's dangerous knowledge that his own daring use of force has much in common with power "graced" or legitimized by "the eminent name of a kingdome." The crucial difference between the two is, as Augustine explains, that a sovereign may exercise his power "with-out danger of lawe."

By Christopher Pye's—and Augustine's—logic, excesses of law, whether by prince or pirate, become explorations of the relationship between justice and power. The prince's two chief means of setting the law aside lie paradoxically in these polar opposites: the ability to unleash violence in the prosecution of war or to tame it by pardoning the justly condemned felon. Even these poles of royal prerogative should perhaps be perceived more as important symbols of royal ability to exceed the law than as real measures of absolutist power; the prerogatives to war or to pardon were rarely exercised by sovereign will in isolation from aristocratic consent. Pardons typically followed aristocratic suits for clemency, and, without a standing army, early modern monarchs intent on war were still dependent upon late medieval means of raising, equipping, and fielding their armies.

Moreover, between these acknowledged poles of excess lay a range of prerogatives that existed in uneasy tension with legal restraints on the crown. Early modern England was a constitutional monarchy, but the relationships between sovereign and subject, crown and law were defined by a sense of subjects' traditional rights and an accumulation of common-law precedents, not a written constitution. As such, the "constitutional" prerogatives and limitations on the sovereign were open to negotiation, coercion, and even litigation—contests that the crown could, in fact, lose. In short, monarchs' ability to exceed the law was circumscribed first by what they dared, second by what their eminence allowed them. The difference between piracy and monarchy, Dionides suggests, rests more with the latter than the former. Any single royal offense might have to be tolerated by subjects; a pattern of abuses would upset the delicate balance between crown and parliament. And dependence on parliament for funds—an appropriation legitimized by the process of consent, however much it sometimes resembled piracy—curbed a monarch's tendency to flout the law too blatantly or too often. Nevertheless, carefully displayed excess of law performed a crucial role in maintaining the fiction of a socially useful and politically necessary distinction between sovereign and subject which legitimized the very existence of monarchy itself.

The anecdote about Alexander and Dionides offers dangerous, unspeakable knowledge because it threatens to collapse the apparent opposition between force and mercy; it reveals power's capacity to exceed law and to arrogate a fictional difference between subject and sovereign in order to legitimate that excess. Of Henry V's determination to follow his father's advice "to busy giddy minds / With foreign quarrels" (*2 Henry IV*, 4.5.213-14), Erasmus might well observe:

> There are those who go to war for no other reason than because it is a way of confirming their tyranny over their own subjects. For in times of peace the authority of the council, the dignity of the magistrates, and the force of the laws stand in the way, to a certain extent, of the prince's doing just what he likes. But once war has been declared, then all the affairs of the State are at the mercy of the appetites of a few. Up go the ones who are in the prince's favour, down go the ones with whom he is angry. Any amount of money is exacted. Why say more? It is only then that they feel they are really kings.[12]

This account of a prince's willfulness realized in war may accord most with Richard II's expropriation of Gaunt's revenues, use of blank charters, and devotion to the "caterpillars" of the commonwealth; yet Henry's French campaign serves much the same function of affirming his power: "No king of England, if not king of France" (2.2.193).

By 1500 only wars levied by a prince, not by a feudal overlord, could be deemed legally just in suits argued before courts of chivalry, and English monarchs, like their French cousins, had acquired a monopoly to set the law aside by issuing a public pardon. Such displays of mercy, frequently contrasted with the use of force, were proclaimed as evidence of the prince's likeness to God. According to Portia, mercy

>   becomes
> The throned monarch better than his
>   crown.
> His sceptre shows the force of temporal
>   power,
> The attribute to awe and majesty,
> Wherein doth sit the dread and fear of
>   kings;
> But mercy is above this sceptred sway,
> It is enthroned in the hearts of kings,
> It is an attribute to God himself;
> And earthly power doth then show likest
>   God's
> When mercy seasons justice. . . .
>   (*Merchant of Venice*, 4.1.188-97)

As a display of the Christian virtue of mercy, the royal pardon was one of the prince's safest means of exercising—and hence reasserting—the prerogative to exceed the strict bounds of law; pardons asserted the power to abrogate the sentence of justice without the risk of registering a judgment on the justice of the sentence itself.[13] Pardons simply "set iustice aside."

Portia's speech contrasts the externalization of force with the hidden nature of mercy. Force is revealed in the external trappings of majesty, in the scepter and crown as "attribute[s] to awe and majesty"; mercy is driven "above this sceptred sway" and inward, "enthroned in the hearts of kings," where it becomes an invisible, inscrutable "attribute to God himself." From the secret recesses of the royal heart, mercy can be made manifest at will, allowing "earthly power" to "show likest God's." But, like the attributes of sorrow in *Hamlet* ("actions that a man might play" [1.2.84]), the display of mercy bears no necessary correlation to "that within which passes show" (l. 85).[14] The externalization of internal states must always be distrusted. Mercy may be the act that shows most like God, but its underlying motivation and the use to which it is put may be an exercise in pure *Realpolitik*. The two interpretations of the Dionides anecdote which developed during the Middle Ages base conflicting representations of Alexander's internal state on the same incident. The secular moral, seeking to maintain Alexander's status as a positive exemplum of the successful ruler who first rules himself, praises his clemency and self-control as demonstrated in his pardoning of slander. Augustine's interpretation, however, emphasizes the similarities the pirate perceives between himself and the great conqueror: both seize what they want, disregarding established codes of justice or ethical concern for others; only the grander scale of the conqueror's theft effaces and reinscribes the legal code. From Augustine's perspective, Alexander's pardon seems a triumphant reveling in the power of conquest; his Alexander gloats over the comparison between himself and the pirate, countenancing the critique of conquest's justness in order to exult in the impunity that the power of his army grants him. The secular moral extols Alexander's restraint of power—an internal self-control that legitimates his authority—while the Augustinian interpretation condemns his exultation in his power by equating it with theft.

Augustine's association of robber-kingdoms and "the authority of a prince" resists the legitimation of royal power associated with the secular interpretation and instead criminalizes kingdoms based on conquest. But is the Augustinian tradition at work in *Henry V?* If so, how does it operate and to what effect? The familiarity of Dionides's analogy between pirates and emperors may help to explain the play's repeated emphasis on the comic crew's thievery and prior association with the king; for those who recognize in Hal's repeated willingness to pardon slanderers a covert refer- ence to the Alexander materials—a recognition autho- rized by Fluellen's assertion that "there's figures in all things"—the presence of Pistol, Nym, and Bardolph in France raises questions about the legitimacy of Henry's campaign and perhaps his reign: they conjure up ear- lier visions of Hal when he was but a madcap "petty thief." But how extensive is the play's critique?

We may begin to answer this question by recalling that metaphor and simile often derive as much power from the differences they yoke as from the likenesses they assert; Shakespeare's text generates significant differences between Henry and Alexander. Judicious attention to this balance of likeness and difference seems to be the chief burden of Judith Mossman's recent article exploring the connection between Henry V and Plutarch's Alexander.[15] Her argument cites par- allels between the lives of these two figures and also between the purposes and methods of their chroni- clers. Her theoretical observations, however, seem to allow for greater complexity of artistic treatment than her interpretation of *Henry V* ultimately demonstrates or even allows. Acknowledging that "Plutarch's char- acter of Alexander . . . has been considered one of the biographer's most straightforwardly heroic portraits," Mossman argues that "this, in fact, is an oversimpli- fication. Plutarch certainly hymns Alexander's heroical, epical qualities, but he also takes the opportunity to portray the king's darker side."[16] Mossman notes that

> Plutarch himself encourages us to compare his subjects with a wide variety of historical and mythological models, thereby giving himself scope to develop different aspects of the subject's character. The great advantage of such compar- isons is their potential complexity. A comparison with Achilles, for example, can suggest heroic bravery, stubborn intransigence, tragic self- determination, even homoerotic attraction. A series of comparisons with Alexander has the potential for equal polyvalency.[17]

Though Mossman emphasizes a theoretical complex- ity, in practice she nevertheless finds it "hard to imag- ine an ironic reading of the play that would satisfac- torily explain why Shakespeare would have wanted to subvert Henry" and wonders "what sort of play one is left with if one assumes that *Henry V* sets out to denigrate its central character."[18] Mossman's reading of the relationship between Shakespeare's play and Alexander's career cites many parallels that I acknowl- edge; however, her conclusion that these parallels in- evitably work to demonstrate Henry's superiority to Alexander seems too willing an acceptance of the assessments of the Chorus, Fluellen, and Henry him- self to the exclusion of other voices, disallowing Shake- speare the complexity she finds attractive in Plutarch. She accepts Henry's pronouncement at face value: "'We are no tyrant, but a Christian king,' Henry says

(1.2.241), echoing the opinion of Erasmus and other writers that the Christian is almost inevitably superior even to the excellent and virtuous pagan."[19] Yet in *Dulce bellum inexpertis* Erasmus offers a scathing critique of war which actually inverts the expected relationship between Christian and pagan, exclaiming "All go to war, the decrepit, the priest, the monk, and we mix up Christ with a thing so diabolical! . . . For where is the kingdom of the devil if not in war? Why do we drag Christ into it, when he would be less out of place in a house of ill fame than in a war?"[20] Of the comparison between Christian and pagan, Erasmus explicitly states:

> If you compare Christian monarchs with pagan ones, how weak our cause seems to be! They had no ambition but glory. They took pleasure in increasing the prosperity of the provinces they had subdued in war; where people were barbarous, without letters or laws, living like wild animals, they taught them the arts of civilisation; they populated the uncultivated regions by building towns; they improved unsafe places by construc- ting bridges, quays, embankments, and by a thousand other amenities they made man's life easier, so that it became a fortunate thing to be conquered. . . . The things which are done in wars between Christians are too obscene and appalling to be mentioned here. The fact is that we only copy the worst of the ancient world—or rather we outdo it.[21]

Near the conclusion of his essay, Erasmus adds, "a Christian, if he were truly Christian, would take every means to avoid, avert and stave off a thing so hellish, so foreign to the life and teaching of Christ."[22] Anyone familiar with Erasmus's view of war must necessarily find Henry's claim to be "no tyrant, but a Christian king" ironic, or at least deeply and purposefully am- bivalent. Given this alternative sixteenth-century view of war, that it "is sweet to those who have not tried it,"[23] the audience may be invited to compare the Chorus's claim that Henry is the "mirror of all Chris- tian kings" (2.Cho.6) against its subsequent command for attentive viewing: "Yet sit and see,/ Minding true things by what their mock'ries be" (4.Cho.52-53).

The interpretive complexity and potential ambivalence the Chorus invokes is fully present in Fluellen's analo- gies. The Welshman did, after all, assert the ubiquity of "figures" immediately before alluding to Alexander's drunken murder of his friend Cleitus—only to have his turn to emphasize difference preempted by Gower's counterassertion that "Our King is not like him in that" (4.7.42). Like Alexander, displaying both control of the law and of the injured self, Henry is merciful to underlings who question his use of power, both the unnamed slanderer in Act 2 and Michael Williams in Act 4. And, as in the Dionides anecdote, the context of Henry's pardons underlines the more explicitly forceful dimension of mastery of the law—the successful conquest of foreign territory. Unlike Alexander, however, Henry repeatedly denies association with thieves and thievery. In doing so, Henry denies his dependence upon the raw power in which Alexander gloated, although he, too, derived his title from it. The differences become clear once the analogy touches Henry closely. When Fluellen informs the king about Bardolph, Henry denies any relationship, coldly condemning his former companion in crime to execution, confirming the sentence of law which only he has power to overturn: "We would have all such offenders so cut off" (3.6.107-8).[24]

Traditional readings interpret Henry's action as further evidence of his reformation. In Augustinian reading, however, Henry would not dare pardon Bardolph lest he risk acknowledging that the root of his own royal power is identical to the pirate's, that his French war is itself an affair of questionable legitimacy, designed to distract "giddy minds" from his own questionable legitimacy as king. After he has been confronted by the misgivings of Bates, Court, and Williams before the battle of Agincourt, Henry confesses his dangerous knowledge of his true source of power:

> Not to-day, O Lord,
> O, not to-day, think not upon the fault
> My father made in compassing the crown!
> I Richard's body have interred new,
> And on it have bestowed more contrite
>   tears,
> Than from it issued forced drops of blood. . . .
>   More will I do;
> Though all that I can do is nothing worth,
> Since that my penitence comes after all,
> Imploring pardon. . . .
>
>   (4.1.292-97, 302-5)

Just cause is predicated upon just title. Knowledge that his own source of power was derived from his father's willingness and ability to exceed the law haunts Henry throughout his career on stage. While Alexander fully embraces what he knows of the origins of power, the Lancastrian monarchs must pretend they do not know what they so clearly practice. To borrow Richard's wry concession to his cousin Bolingbroke, "they well deserve to have / That know the strong'st and surest way to get" (Richard II, 3.3.199-200).

Henry knows that the disrupted succession undermines theories of divine legitimation associated with the legal fiction of the king's two bodies, yet he cannot free himself from the need for such theological legitimation because it distinguishes between his own mode of exceeding the law and that of pirates, thieves, and usurpers.[25] His first soliloquy in 1 Henry IV (1.2.195-217) reveals his strategy to restore legitimacy to the crown his father has usurped by staging his own trans-

figuration. Subsequently, this apparent reformation is recounted by Canterbury in language that initially implies belief in the medieval concept of the king's two bodies but then concedes the Reformation view that such "miracles are ceas'd; / And therefore we must needs admit the means / How things are perfected" (Henry V, 1.1.67-69). It is in this context of Canterbury's praise for Henry's reformed character that the play's earliest allusion to Alexander occurs. Shakespeare's development of the allusion sets a precedent for deliberately ambiguous uses of other Alexandrian anecdotes and allusions. As with Fluellen's comparison later in the play, the archbishop's intention is one of praise; but the existence of an alternative version of the anecdote creates a space for a less flattering interpretation. Canterbury, enumerating Henry's unanticipated range of accomplishments, says, "Turn him to any cause of policy, / The Gordian knot of it he will unloose, / Familiar as his garter" (1.1.45-47).

Plutarch records two versions of Alexander's encounter with the Gordian knot.[26] In one, Alexander rises above the challenge through cunning by removing the shaft around which the knot is tied before tackling it; in the other, Alexander resorts to force, slicing through the intricacies of the knot with his sword. In Canterbury's handling of the legend, Alexander's violence is effaced. According to Plutarch, the Phrygians had elected the peasant Gordius as their king in response to an oracle that the first man to approach Jupiter's temple in a wagon could heal their misfortunes. The Gordian knot, which fastened the yoke to the shaft of the wagon, became the focal point of a new oracle which prophesied that whoever untied it would rule over all of Asia. After Alexander either removed the shaft or cut through the knot, he then declared himself the fulfillment of the oracle. But in so doing, Alexander appropriated a popular local legend to legitimate the violence of conquest. Canterbury, preferring the innocent, domestic image of unloosening a garter, suppresses the guile of the one version and the violence of the other.[27] While it is clear from the context that Canterbury privileges the version in which Alexander's superior intelligence enables him to overcome the knot's challenge, the policy associated with the king he praises is a form of violence, specifically that urged by his father: "Be it thy course to busy giddy minds / With foreign quarrels." Furthermore, Canterbury's praise of Henry is as tainted by self-interest in protecting Church revenue as Alexander's appropriation of the oracle, and both participate in attempts to lend religious legitimation to wars of conquest.

To display his royal clemency, the attribute whereby an "earthly power doth then shew likest God's," Henry uses pardons along with other appeals to religious sentiments to legitimate both his execution of justice against his English subjects and his prosecution of war against the French. However, parallels between the structure of Shakespeare's play and the bifold nature of Alexander's encounter with Dionides undermine this project of religious legitimation. The anecdote yields options of viewing Alexander as either the gracious dispenser of mercy or the sinner chiefly in need of it. Previous uses of the anecdote enable Shakespeare to encode limits on Henry's ability to identify with one half of the power structure to the exclusion of the other. The anecdote appears in sources such as Tertullian's *Apology,* Augustine's *De Civitate Dei,* and John of Salisbury's *Policraticus;* Cicero, Tertullian, Augustine, and Erasmus use it to examine the justice of warfare and kingship. All these sources are relevant to the structure of *Henry V.* Cicero's editors place the anecdote in the context of the orator's discussion of justice, reconstructing the passage from Tertullian's citation of it:

> For unless I am mistaken, every kingdom or empire is acquired by war and extended by victory, and furthermore, the chief element in war and victory is the capture and overthrow of cities. Such acts are impossible without doing injury to the gods, for the destruction of the city's walls is likewise the destruction of its temples; the murder of its citizens involves likewise the murder of its priests; and the plundering of secular wealth includes also the plunder of sacred treasures. Hence, the irreligious acts of the Roman people equal the number of its trophies; every triumph over a people is a triumph over its gods; the collections of booty equal in number the surviving images of captive gods.[28]

Tertullian's purpose here is to disprove "the claim of the Romans to signal piety, and the contention that their empire was extended through the favor of the gods."[29] Those sharing Shakespeare's "smalle latine" would likely have been familiar with Augustine and Erasmus, if not Cicero or Tertullian. Thus these comments on the essential impiety of conquest recast in heavy irony Henry's order to execute anyone guilty of plunder (3.6.107-13) and his command "be it death proclaimed through our host / To boast of this, or take that praise from God / Which is his only" (4.8.114-16).[30] For Tertullian, Bardolph's theft, like the pirate's, would be a petty instance of impiety compared to Henry's conquest of France. The haunting applicability of Tertullian's critique of conquest increases the epic tone of the Chorus's presentation of Henry's humility and piety in refusing the outward trappings of a triumphal entry into London:

> . . . So let him land,
> And solemnly see him set on to London.
> So swift a pace hath thought that even now
> You may imagine him upon Blackheath;
> Where that his lords desire him to have
>   borne
> His bruised helmet and his bended sword

> Before him through the city. He forbids it,
> Being free from vainness and self-glorious
>   pride;
> Giving full trophy, signal, and ostent
> Quite from himself to God.
>   (5.Cho.13-22)

The transfer of glory—and therefore responsibility—from the king to God is a legitimating sleight-of-hand that Cicero, Tertullian, Augustine, and Erasmus will not allow. The play's alternating scenes balance aristocracy and underworld, merciful pardon and violent greed, coveting honor and ascribing it to God. This structure reproduces the dialogical strategy of a philosophical tradition that questions imperialistic claims to piety by equating conquest with piracy.

Henry's attempts to use religion or to displace responsibility to justify his French campaign strain against scenes that, especially when set against the background of Alexander and the pirate, work to criminalize it. In his first appearance, the council scene in Act 1, Henry practices both strategies. He displaces authority for his decision to invade France onto the archbishop, whose self-interest in the affair has already been dramatized in the prior scene, charging him to "take heed how you impawn our person, . . . For we will hear, note, and believe in heart, / That what you speak is in your conscience wash'd / As pure as sin with baptism" (1.2.21, 30-32). The Salic law barring claims through the female line—the Gordian knot of Canterbury's speech—is both unraveled and violently bisected by the archbishop's exposition. In this monologue Canterbury initially disclaims the law's relevance to the French throne, but then he cites three French monarchs who supported their claims despite it—each a usurper grasping for any source of legitimacy (ll. 50-55, 64-65, 69, 77-78). Henry, perhaps discomfited by these precedents, repeats his charge, "May I with right and conscience make this claim?" and receives the blame-shifting clarity of response he requires, "The sin upon my head, dread sovereign!" (ll. 96-97). The interchange does not deny the association between conquest and sin; it merely asserts that it is pardonable and displaceable, enabling the archbishop to endorse the campaign, which both legitimates it and exonerates Henry from responsibility for the deaths it will cause.

The scene culminates with a second episode that couples the two strategies as Henry receives the French ambassador, who asks "leave / Freely to render" the Dauphin's message (ll. 237-38). Henry's response couples an assertion of his religious devotion with a veiled threat reminding the ambassador of his power: "We are no tyrant, but a Christian king, / Unto whose grace our passion is as subject / As is our wretches fett'red in our prisons" (ll. 241-43). This assertion of grace and self-control conflates the troublesome poles of power and mercy—the key attributes of legal excess (in the Dionides anecdote) and of divinity (in Portia's appeal). Henry uses the Dauphin's taunt as another opportunity to shift the burden of moral responsibility for this war away from himself, instructing the ambassador to "tell the pleasant prince this mock of his / Hath turn'd his balls to gunstones, and his soul / Shall stand sore charged for the wasteful vengeance / That shall fly with them" (ll. 281-84). Despite Henry's attempts to displace responsibility for the French campaign, his taste for conquest rings throughout his final two speeches in this scene, rendering such conviction to his statement "we have now no thought in us but France" that his subsequent qualification, "Save those to God, that run before our business" (l. 303), seems something of an afterthought, if a strategic one.

The structure of the pirate anecdote underlies this scene, with its balanced attention to Henry's willingness to countenance the Dauphin's scornful message and his ultimate goal of attaining French territory; but the pirate anecdote becomes even more explicit in the pardon scenes of the play's middle acts. Henry's pardon of the unnamed soldier "That rail'd against our person" serves multiple functions in this scene. Shakespeare has transformed the structure of the Dionides anecdote by dividing the recreant into two characters, one to be pardoned and the other to be executed. In doing so, he moves the scene Henry has scripted much closer to the biblical parable of the unmerciful servant (Matthew 18:23-35). By maneuvering the traitors Cambridge, Grey, and Scroop into speaking against the mercy offered to a common "railer," Henry entraps them into taking responsibility for their own executions: "The mercy that was quick in us but late, / By your own counsel is suppress'd and kill'd" (2.2.79-80). By distinguishing between treasonous speech and treasonous actions, he displays himself as merciful and magnanimous, not fearful but bold and trusting. By making the traitors responsible for their own condemnation, however, Henry manages to preempt the attention their betrayal could have drawn to his own questionable claim to France—and, for that matter, to England. He concludes the scene by turning the entire affair into another opportunity to proclaim religious legitimacy for his project of conquest: "We doubt not of a fair and lucky war, / Since God so graciously hath brought to light / This dangerous treason lurking in our way / To hinder our beginnings" (ll. 184-87). Like John of Salisbury, who attached a positive moral to the incident between Alexander and the pirate, Henry has structured this encounter with the traitors to privilege his mercy; Augustine's disparaging moral, adopted by Chaucer and Gower in the alternative tradition of interpretation, seems repressed along with the other "dangerous treason lurking" in Henry's "beginnings."[31] Henry would subsume such concerns under his providentialist rhetoric; the viewer familiar with his previous stage history or with the dual interpretations

of Alexander's encounter with Dionides (especially in the context of Augustine's and Erasmus's views of wars of conquest) might draw other conclusions.

In Act 3 Henry has another opportunity to pardon. This time, however, the offense is not slanderous speech but theft. Shakespeare has again deftly separated the offenses conjoined in Alexander's pirate; he allots the intemperate speech to Williams in Act 4, thus enabling Henry to appear magnanimous in pardoning the one and justly rigorous—or hypocritical—in condemning the other. The only actual robbery reported and punished in *Henry V* is committed by one of the king's former companions; Pistol reports that Bardolph "hath stol'n a pax, and hanged must 'a be" (3.6.40). Pistol asks Fluellen to intercede for Bardolph's life, but Fluellen responds by saying "for if, look you, he were my brother, I would desire the Duke to use his good pleasure, and put him to execution; for discipline ought to be used" (ll. 54-56). Fluellen nonetheless reports Bardolph's danger to the king, who responds:

> We would have all such offenders so cut off: and we give express charge that in our marches through the country there be nothing compell'd from the villages; nothing taken but paid for; none of the French upbraided or abus'd in disdainful language; for where [lenity] and cruelty play for a kingdom, the gentler gamester is the soonest winner.
>
> (ll. 107-13)

Henry, the "mirror of all Christian kings," may conquer an entire kingdom, but he will tolerate no petty piracies.[32]

Historically, the object taken from the church was not a pax but a pyx; J. H. Walter explains the difference:

> The pyx is the box in which the consecrated wafers are kept; the pax is a small metal plate with a crucifix impressed on it. In the celebration of mass in the early Christian Church a kiss of peace was given to the communicants by the priest. In the thirteenth century a metal plate or tablet was kissed by the priest instead and then passed to the congregation to kiss in turn. Shakespeare, who surely must have known the difference, may have substituted "pax" for some reason not now clear.[33]

Of course, a compositor setting the type may have made the substitution, not appreciating the difference. However, a soldier facing a battle against desperate numerical odds might be motivated to steal a pyx—especially one of "little price"—not by greed but by desire to prepare for the possibility of death in battle. Desecration of the sacrament or theft of the pyx was explicitly forbidden in Henry V's Ordinances of War (1419), a prohibition repeated in Henry VIII's Statutes and Ordinances for the Warre (1544).[34] Viewing the play, members of the audience might well hear *pyx,* the item most associated with church pillage in wartime, regardless of what the actor said. Nevertheless, if only as a matter of personal artistic satisfaction, the alteration reflects the slippery view of kingship recorded in the plays of the second tetralogy. The pyx, designed to contain the Reserved Host, invokes the incarnational theology of transubstantiation; the substitution of the pax, an object designed to represent the historical event of the crucifixion of Christ rather than to contain his body, may register a demystification not only of the sacrament but also of the theological underpinnings of the doctrine of the king's two bodies. The pyx contained the mystery, the body of Christ; the pax merely represented it.

In the opening scene of *Henry V,* Canterbury tries to account for Henry's sudden transformation in terms associated with the mystery of the king's two bodies:

> The breath no sooner left his father's body,
> But that his wildness, mortified in him,
> Seem'd to die too; yea, at that very moment,
> Consideration like an angel came
> And whipt th' offending Adam out of him.
>
> (1.1.25-29)

By the scene's end, however, Canterbury finally accedes to Ely's more pragmatic explanation of Henry's transformation, an explanation attributing the change instead to Henry's ability to "obscure" his "contemplation / Under the veil of wildness" (ll. 63-64); Canterbury agrees, "It must be so; for miracles are ceas'd" (l. 67). Henry is indeed the mirror of all Christian kings: pure reflection, royal representation. The stolen pax, like the pirate's identification with Alexander the Great, reveals dangerous knowledge of the source of power.

The issues involved in the more complex encounter between Henry and Williams in Act 4 should also be framed by this debate concerning the nature of the prince, a debate that might itself be elucidated by reference to an episode in the Alexander materials. For the theologians and moralists, the most controversial aspect of Alexander's career related to his claims to divinity, but the Alexander materials also contain a significant number of disclaimers.[35] According to some reports, Alexander (or, in others, his mother) claimed that he was descended from Jupiter; Plutarch deals lightly with the problem by quoting Alexander's mother, Olympias, as saying "will *Alexander* neuer leaue to make me suspected of *Iuno*?" Plutarch's explanation for the contradictions presents a picture of Alexander not as a megalomaniac but as a consummate politician:

> To conclude, he shewed him selfe more arrogant
> vnto the barbarous people, and made as though
> he certainly beleued that he had bene begotten of

some god: but vnto the Grecians he spake more modestly of diuine generation. . . . we maie thinke that *Alexander* had no vaine nor presumptuous opinion of him selfe, to thinke that he was otherwise begotten of a god, but that he did it in policie to kepe other men vnder obedience, by the opinion conceiued of his godhead.[36]

Only in his account of the events following Alexander's murder of Cleitus does Plutarch become genuinely censorious of his subject's claims to divine origin. Even here, however, Plutarch partially displaces blame on an advisor's attempt to goad Alexander to overcome his guilt and grief over Cleitus's death. Plutarch reports that Anaxarchus, entering the room, cried out:

> See, yonder is *Alexander* the great whom all the world lookes apon, and is affraid of. See where he lies, weeping like a slaue on the ground, that is affraid of the law, and of the reproche of men: as if he him selfe should not geue them law, and stablish the boundes of iustice or iniustice, sithence he hath ouercome to be Lord and master, and not to be subiect and slaue to a vaine opinion. Knowest thou not that the poets saie, that *Iupiter* hath Themis, to wit, right and iustice placed of either hand on him? what signifieth that, but all that the prince doth, is wholy right, and iust?[37]

Anaxarchus appeals to Alexander's identification with Jupiter in order to persuade him that the rights of conquest have placed him above censure, above law and justice.[38] A conqueror, he exists to exceed the law.

The tension that develops from these diverse accounts of Alexander's claims to divinity is recapitulated in Tudor and Stuart discourses concerning the nature of the relationship between subjects and their sovereign and between the sovereign and the nation's laws. Are all the actions of the prince "lawful and just" by virtue of divine right, or is the prince's superiority primarily a ruse, a representation, designed "in policie to kepe other men vnder obedience, by the opinion conceiued of his godhead"? Using the doctrine of the king's two bodies was a means of subsuming the all-too-apparent reality of mere human mortality under the rhetoric of divine right. As the Reformation in England opted for the representational view of the sacraments, however, the mythic, incarnational features of the doctrine of the king's two bodies began losing much of their legitimating power before the divine-right-minded Stuarts came to power. Within the common-law tradition, divine legitimation was based on lineal descent and applied to issues of inheritance and succession; it did not license rule without law.

The legitimation of monarchy, especially once natural succession has been interrupted, requires a means of differentiating between subject and sovereign—and between pirates and princes. In *Henry V* the king conceals his sovereign identity under a subject's cloak, passing among his men unrecognized in order to justify the cause for which they are prepared to fight.[39] Ironically, it is the king who, in this scene, is guilty of royal Arianism and would deny the difference between himself and his subjects, claiming, "though I speak it to you, I think the King is but a man, as I am. . . . all his senses have but human conditions. His ceremonies laid by, in his nakedness he appears but a man" (4.1.101-5).[40] This representational view of kingship is not accepted by Williams, who argues that the king's reckoning will be heavy if his cause is unjust and later provokes Henry again by insisting upon the difference between common foot soldiers and the king:

KING HENRY   I myself heard the King say he would not be ransom'd.

WILLIAMS   Ay, he said so, to make us fight cheerfully; but when our throats are cut, he may be ransom'd, and we ne'er the wiser.

KING HENRY   If I live to see it, I will never trust his word after.

WILLIAMS   You pay him then. That's a perilous shot out of an elder-gun, that a poor and a private displeasure can do against a monarch! You may as well go about to turn the sun to ice with fanning in his face with a peacock's feather. You'll never trust his word after! come, 'tis a foolish saying.

KING HENRY   Your reproof is something too round, I should be angry with you, if the time were convenient.

(ll. 190-204)

William's image for the monarch recalls the image Henry himself used in warning to the French ambassador, saying "I will rise there with so full a glory / That I will dazzle all the eyes of France, / Yea, strike the Dolphin blind to look on us" (1.2.278-80). And yet Williams's insistence on the absolute gulf that exists between the "poor and private displeasure" of a subject and a monarch angers Henry, who makes it a quarrel of honor between them.

Having set Fluellen up to take his place in the promised fight with Williams, Henry forces Williams to mouth his own representational view of majesty in order to escape martial law for offering violence to the king:

KING HENRY   How canst thou make me satisfaction?

WILLIAMS   All offenses, my lord, come from the heart. Never came any from mine that might offend your Majesty.

KING HENRY   It was ourself thou didst abuse.

WILLIAMS   Your Majesty came not like yourself. . . . witness the night, your garments, your lowliness; and what your Highness suffer'd under that shape, I beseech you take it for your own fault and not mine; for had you been as I took you for, I made no offense; therefore I beseech your Highness pardon me.

(4.8.45-56)

Williams ignores the facts that he has, at the least, offended the king's majesty verbally by doubting the justness of his cause and trustworthiness of his word (4.1.134, 199-201); Henry also ignores these facts, in keeping with his tolerance of slander. The wording of Williams's excuse allows Henry to save his majesty and merely wear it, too—the very thing (as Plutarch noted approvingly of Alexander) Henry is inclined to do in making much of his majesty before the class-obsessed French but pretending to belong to the "happy few, we band of brothers," among his own men. But this anamorphic portrait of majesty privileges one of its versions; in order for Henry to affirm Williams's submission to his sovereignty, he must also accept the blame for Williams's offense: "what your Highness suffered under that shape, I beseech you take it for your own fault and not mine." Henry may appear the victor, but the debate has returned to the issue of a prince's responsibility for his men's actions and, by extension, for his own.

The most important action Henry undertakes in this play is to wage a war of conquest against the French. He may seek religious legitimation for his actions, and he may seek to displace responsibility for them onto others; in the final analysis, however, "if the cause be not good, the King himself hath a heavy reckoning to make" (ll. 134-35). In pursuing a foreign war, Henry exceeds the law by pressing his prerogative into issues of debatable moral legitimacy, issues that threaten to expose the origins of power. Knowledge of those origins can be dangerous for both pirates like Bardolph and playwrights like his creator; such danger necessitates artistic strategies of suppression, revision, division, but not wholesale evasion. The anticlimactic final act juxtaposes scenes featuring Pistol being beaten by Fluellen for having flouted Welsh customs and Henry flouting French customs while bartering his martial advantage for a marital one that will seal his claim to the French throne—under the very terms denied by Act 1's exposition of the Salic law. Henry's ceremonial entrance immediately follows the exit of Pistol, confessing this intention: "To England will I steal, and there I'll steal" (5.1.87)—a sequence that underscores the king's associations with thieves and cutpurses, the underworld that lives in excess of the law. Henry himself endorses this mode of being when he claims a kiss, contrary to custom, from Katherine: "Dear Kate, you and I cannot be confin'd within the weak list of a country's fashion. We are the makers of manners, Kate" (5.2.269-71). Both Henry and Pistol, like Alexander and Dionides, live in excess of the law; Henry, unlike Alexander, conceals that common bond, claiming to be the "maker," not the breaker, of manners.

In the event, Henry's stolen kiss proves prophetic of another foreign king who would trace a title through a great-grandmother, another king whose son would lose what the father had won. Like Henry, James VI of Scotland did not believe a king could "be confin'd within the weak list of a country's fashion." In his treatise *The Trew Law of Free Monarchies,* James traced civilization in Scotland to the arrival of King Fergus, who, "comming in among barbares, first established the estate and forme of gouernement, and thereafter made lawes by himselfe," claiming, therefore, that in Scotland "kings were the authors and makers of the Lawes, and not the Lawes of the kings." With an eye turned southward, he extends his claim that kings precede (and therefore exceed) law by telling a tale of conquest:

> For when the Bastard of *Normandie* came into *England,* and made himselfe king, was it not by force, and with a mighty army? Where he gaue the Law, and tooke none, changed the Lawes, inuerted the order of gouernement, set downe the strangers his followers in many of the old possessours roomes, as at this day well appeareth a great part of the Gentlemen of *England,* beeing come of the *Norman* blood, and their old Lawes, which to this day they are ruled by, are written in his language, and not in theirs: And yet his successours haue with great happinesse enioyed the Crowne to this day; Where of the like was also done by all them that conquested them before.[41]

James concludes that the king is the "ouer-Lord of the whole land: so is he Master ouer euery person that inhabiteth the same, hauing power ouer the life and death of euery one of them." To James the origin of royal authority lies in force, be it the conqueror's mighty army or the king's "power ouer the life and death" of his subjects. In brief, James concludes that "the King is aboue the law."[42]

Shortly before Elizabeth's death, Sir John Harington, the ailing queen's favored godson, sent a lantern to the Scottish king, cryptically inscribed "Remember me, lord, when thou comest into thy kingdom." The crucifixion allusion legitimates the king's yet unacknowledged authority by identifying him with Christ but, simultaneously, reinscribes the association between the king and thieves. Years later on the scaffold, in attempting to turn the pirate anecdote against a conquering parliament, the best Charles I could manage was a construction that diminished his own role to that of the lesser thief. The association of pirates and conquerors, thieves and kings, served this age sometimes as a means of questioning the morality of warfare, sometimes as a way of considering the legitimacy of royal titles. At rare moments it served to speak a dangerous knowledge about the origins of power.

Notes

[1] Christopher Pye, *The Regal Phantasm: Shakespeare and the Politics of Spectacle* (London and New York: Routledge, 1990), 133.

[2] It seems especially difficult to stage a production critical of Henry, but see Chris Fitter, "A Tale of Two Branaghs: *Henry V,* Ideology, and the Mekong Agincourt" in *Shakespeare Left and Right* (Ivo Kamps, ed. [New York: Routledge, 1991], 259-76), for an assessment of Kenneth Branagh's two interpretations of Henry, first in Adrian Noble's sober examination of war in his 1984 RSC production and later in Branagh's 1989 film. Fitter likens Branagh the director to a "literary Oliver North," who "has deliberately shredded vital documentation, provided by the text and the RSC production, and his Henry therefore emerges as a familiar figure: the handsome military hero and godly patriot at the heart of an establishment coverup" (260).

Richard Dutton surveys critical responses to *Henry V,* most of which manage to redeem Hal on some level even if they acknowledge his flaws or soften harsher judgments by positing an inherent ambivalence in the play's structure; see "The Second Tetralogy" in *Shakespeare: A Bibliographical Guide,* Stanley Wells, ed. (Oxford: Clarendon Press, 1990), 337-80.

[3] Quotations in this essay of *Henry V* and all other Shakespeare plays follow *The Riverside Shakespeare,* ed. G. Blakemore Evans (Boston: Houghton Mifflin, 1974).

Philip Edwards's *Threshold of a Nation: A study in English and Irish drama* (Cambridge: Cambridge UP, 1979) also deals with the play's relation to contemporary issues of conquest and imperialism.

[4] *Antony and Cleopatra,* 2.6.86-96. I am indebted to an anonymous referee for both the reminder of the relevance of this passage to my argument and for subsequent references to the adages of Erasmus. I am also heavily indebted to George Cary's discussion of medieval interpretations of Alexander the Great in *The Medieval Alexander* (Cambridge: University Press, 1956). Cary details a series of contradictory morals drawn during the medieval period from the life of Alexander the Great, noting in general a trend toward positive interpretations (except in Germany) as secular moralists established independence from theologians.

[5] Erasmus, *The 'Adages' of Erasmus: A Study with Translations,* trans. Margaret Mann Phillips (Cambridge: University Press, 1964), 240.

The anecdote has been traced back to Cicero's *De republica;* it appears in a unique but severely damaged manuscript copy of that work held by the Vatican Library. Editors have partially reconstructed the passage through analyses of citations to it in the work of later authors.

[6] Theodor Meron, *Henry's Wars and Shakespeare's Laws: Perspectives on the Law of War in the Later Middle Ages* (Oxford: Clarendon Press, 1993), 41. For a balance of pacifist and realist arguments about the ethics of war, see J. R. Hale, *Renaissance War Studies* (London: Hambledon Press, 1983); Hale, *War and Society in Renaissance Europe, 1450-1620* (New York: St. Martin's Press, 1985); and Philip C. Dust, *Three Renaissance Pacifists: Essays in the Theories of Erasmus, More, and Vives* (New York: Peter Lang, 1987). Consult Meron for a more precise treatment of the relationships between *Henry V*, the historical events, and contemporary legal interpretations of war ethics. Meron concludes that "Shakespeare's attention to historical detail and rules of law in international relations and diplomacy is truly impressive" (214).

[7] Erasmus, 320. According to R. J. Schoeck, this adage first appeared in the 1515 edition of the *Adagiorum Chiliades,* was printed separately over a dozen times during the sixteenth century, and was translated into English in 1533; see *Erasmus of Europe: The Making of a Humanist 1467-1500* (Edinburgh: Edinburgh UP, 1990), 238.

[8] Erasmus, 340-41.

[9] Shortly following the passage quoted above, Erasmus, despite his disclaimer that "it is not for such as myself to argue boldly about the affairs of princes," qualifies the notion of sovereignty by insisting that "we call rule what is really administration. No one can have the same rights over men, free by nature, as over herds of cattle. This very right which you hold, was given you by popular consent. Unless I am mistaken, the hand which gave can take it away" (341). The view of sovereignty here is clearly a contractual/consensual one, not one based on divine or natural right.

[10] *King Charls his Tryal at the High Court of Justice,* 2d ed. (London, 1650), quoted here from *The Trial of Charles I: A Documentary History,* David Lagomarsino and Charles T. Wood, eds. (Hanover, NH, and London: UP of New England, 1989), 141-42. How much the anticonquest sentiments in Charles I's speech and in the 1610 reprinting of Augustine (cited below) may owe to the pacifist nature of Stuart rule is at present a matter of conjecture.

[11] *St. Avgvstine, of the Citie of God* (London, 1610), 159. At least fifteen Latin editions of *De Civitate Dei* were published between 1468 and 1580, some including commentary. This number does not include translations or collections in which *De Civitate* does not appear in the title.

[12] Erasmus, 349.

[13] For historical background on the use of pardon to assert prerogative power, see Natalie Zemon Davis, *Fiction in the Archives: Pardon Tales and Their Tellers in Sixteenth-Century France* (Stanford, CA: Stanford UP, 1987). I have explored her argument in relation to the comic framing of royal pardons in *Richard II* and *Measure for Measure* in "Staging Pardon Scenes: Variations of Tragicomedy," *Renaissance Drama* n.s. 21 (1990): 55-89.

[14] Jonathan Goldberg's study of the strategies of discourse shared by monarchs and authors repeatedly makes the point that such representations always lie at one remove, are always coincidences that do not quite coincide yet occupy "the heart of the relationship of literature to royal power" (*James I and the Politics of Literature: Jonson, Shakespeare, Donne, and Their Contemporaries* [Baltimore and London: Johns Hopkins UP, 1983], 39).

[15] Judith Mossman, "*Henry V* and Plutarch's *Alexander,*" *Shakespeare Quarterly* 45 (1994): 57-73.

[16] Mossman, 58.

[17] Mossman, 63.

[18] Mossman, 58.

[19] Mossman, 61.

[20] Erasmus, 321-22.

[21] Erasmus, 335.

[22] Erasmus, 351.

[23] Erasmus, 308.

[24] Hal's betrayal of Bardolph may seem callous, but it also holds implications for a prince's responsibilities for the actions of his subjects, and so should be examined in conjunction with Hal's later scenes with Williams. See Meron's chapter "Responsibility of Princes" (64-74) and his assessment of Bardolph's sentence (114-15 and 122).

[25] On the king's two bodies, see Marie Axton, *The Queen's Two Bodies: Drama and the Elizabethan Succession* (London: Royal Historical Society, 1977);

and Ernst H. Kantorowicz, *The King's Two Bodies: A Study in Mediaeval Political Theology* (Princeton, NJ: Princeton UP, 1957).

[26] Ambivalent cultural materials such as this, readily available to audiences, were subject to conflicting interpretations regardless of an author's intention. While David Quint argues that Curtius was the more popular source for Alexander's life during the Renaissance, Curtius records only the use of the sword, not the alternative version the archbishop refers to in this scene ("'Alexander the Pig': Shakespeare on History and Poetry," *Boundary 2* 10 [1982]: 49-68).

[27] Canterbury does not specify the garter to be the ceremonial symbol of the Order of the Garter, worn below the left knee; however, given that the Order's founder, Edward III, is both Henry's great-grandfather and the source, through both conquest and maternal descent, of his claim to France, Canterbury may be attempting to associate policy and honor. Rather than resolving the ambiguity of the allusion to Alexander's career, the recognition of this possible association may heighten it by raising questions central both to this particular play and to the tetralogy, questions involving the legitimacy of the Salic law, on the one hand, and, on the other, the nature of honor and the legitimacy of Lancastrian claims to Edward III's throne.

[28] Marcus Tullius Cicero, *On the Commonwealth,* ed. George Holland Sabine and Stanley Barney Smith (Columbus: Ohio State UP, 1929), 207-8.

[29] Quoted in Cicero, 208, n. 47.

[30] Of this command, Phyllis Rackin comments that "the stridency of the threat exposes the anxiety that produced it, the keen sense of the absence of divine right that Henry attempts to fill by the exercise and mystification of earthly power" (*Stages of History: Shakespeare's English Chronicles* [Ithaca, NY: Cornell UP, 1990], 79-80).

[31] On Chaucer's and Gower's interpretations of the Dionides encounter, see Cary, 95-98.

[32] Meron assigns the severity of the thief's punishment to "the specially sacrilegious nature of the offence— laying hands on the box where the Holy Sacrament was kept," noting that it was "no less holy by one whit if it [were] consecrated by a French priest" (122).

[33] *Henry V,* ed. J. H. Walter (London: Methuen, 1954), 3.6.41n.

[34] See Meron, 144 and 150.

[35] In general the theologians emphasized Alexander's blasphemous pride in assuming titles suggesting divinity, but the moralists discredited or de-emphasized the accounts; see Cary, 110-16, 125-35, 152-54, and 181-89.

[36] Plutarch, *The Lives of the Noble Grecians and Romanes,* trans. Thomas North (London, 1579), 723 and 737-38.

[37] Plutarch, 751.

[38] Anaxarchus's evil advice to Alexander forms a sober reprise of the Dionides moral concerning the criminal's and the monarch's ability to exceed the law.

[39] On the disguised-king motif, see Anne Barton, "The King Disguised: Shakespeare's *Henry V* and the Comical History" in *The Triple Bond: Plays, Mainly Shakespearean, in Performance,* Joseph G. Price, ed. (University Park: Pennsylvania State UP, 1975), 92-117; and Annabel Patterson, *Shakespeare and the Popular Voice* (Cambridge, MA: Basil Blackwell, 1989), 89-92.

[40] Henry's royal sleight-of-hand is apparent in stage productions. The cloak conceals his true identity only from the soldiers onstage; the audience is free to note the difference between a disguised king claiming "the King is but a man, as I am" and a disclosed prince confessing "I am but a man, as you are."

[41] James I, *The Political Works of James I,* ed. Charles H. McIlwain (Cambridge, MA: Harvard UP, 1918), 62-63.

[42] James I, 63.

Source: "Princes, Pirates, and Pigs: Criminalizing Wars of Conquest in *Henry V*," in *Shakespeare Quarterly*, Vol. 47, No. 2, Summer, 1996, pp. 160-77.

Henry V and the Chivalric Revival

Robin Headlam Wells, *University of Hull*

"O for a Muse of fire!" What more appropriate way to begin an epic celebration of England's greatest warrior-king than an invocation to Mars, the baleful god of war with 'famine, sword and fire' straining like leashed greyhounds at his heels (Prol. 1-8)?[1] Praised by his contemporaries as the flower of knighthood,[2] the historical Henry V was the epitome of English chivalry; and chivalry is essentially a martial ideal, a code of values that glorified military prowess as the supreme achievement of the virtuous knight.[3] For the medieval chevalier like Shakespeare's Duke of Exeter (4.6.7-32) death on the battlefield in the arms of a brother soldier while in the service of his liege is a consummation devoutly to be wished.

It is this chivalric ideal that the "warlike Harry" epitomizes. Shakespeare's holy warrior has "an aspect of iron" (5.2.239); his god is a 'God of battles' (4.1.285); and when he invades France he comes "In thunder and in earthquake, like a Jove" (2.4.100). Even as a wooer, he loves "cruelly" (5.2.211). But despite the celebratory tone of the Prologue, *Henry V* is no simple endorsement of chivalric ideals. The history of chivalry in late medieval and early modern England is a complex one, and Shakespeare's play embodies the ambivalent attitudes towards war and military heroism which that history inevitably reflects.

Flower of chivalry

Henry V is chiefly remembered for his extraordinary victory at Agincourt. But hardened at an early age to the rigours of border conflict, he showed a passion for war and a contempt for "the cursyd vice of slouthe and ydlenesse"[4] even before he became king. Shortly before his accession he commissioned a translation of the greatest war story of the ancient world. The result was John Lydgate's *Troy Book,* a translation of Guido delle Colonne's *Historia Destructionis Troiae.* Like Shakespeare, Lydgate begins his story with an invocation to Mars, patron of chivalry and the "causer [. . .] Of werre and stryf":

> O myghty Mars, that wyth thy sterne lyght
> In armys hast the power & þe my3t,
> And named art from est til occident
> The myghty lorde, the god armypotent,
> That, wyth schynyng of the stremes rede,
> By influence dost the brydel led
> Of cheualry, as souereyn and patrown . . .

> Now help, o Mars, þat art of kny3thod lord,
> And hast of manhod the magnificence![5]

In his prologue to the *Troy Book* Lydgate explains that it was Henry's own enthusiasm for "verray kny3thod", "the prowesse of olde chiualrie" and "al that longeth to manhood" that was responsible for the prince's interest in the Troy story (I. 69ff.).

Though Henry's early death meant that his political vision, enshrined in the Treaty of Troyes (1420), of a joint kingdom united under English rule would never be realized, it did wonders for his heroic reputation. As Edward Hall writes in his *Chronicle,* Henry's "fame by his death as liuely florisheth as his actes in his life wer sene and remembred".[6] Already by the middle of the fifteenth century he had become part of English national mythology. When William Worcester wrote a book supporting Edward IV's renewal of the war with France he recalled Henry's "gret manhode" and exhorted Edward to remember the "victorious conquestis of youre noble predecessour".[7] And as Henry himself had hoped to inspire patriotic sentiments by making the Troy story available to English readers, so Worcester, in urging his countrymen to take up arms, adjures them to recall the siege of Troy as an example of true chivalry:

> let be brought to mynde to folow the steppis in conceitis of noble courage of the mighty dedis in armes of the vaillaunt knight Hector of Troy, whiche bene enacted in the seige of Troy for a perpetuelle remembraunce of chevalrie.[8]

Contemporary opinion about Henry and his policies was divided.[9] Thomas Hoccleve, while praising Henry as the "floure of Chivalrie",[10] concludes his epideictic *Regement of Princes* with a philippic on the evils of war between Christian states.[11] Even Lydgate, despite the militaristic tone of his invocation to the *Troy Book,* seems to have had reservations about his patron's military ideals. At the end of Book IV he interpolates a long complaint addressed to Mars, the "first meuer of anger and of hate", deploring the ruinous consequences of war (IV. 4440ff.), a theme that he repeats in the concluding lines of the *Siege of Thebes,*[12] written, significantly, after the Treaty of Troyes when contemporaries had good reason for thinking that Henry's policies had been completely vindicated. Modern historians continue to disagree about Henry's character and achievements. M.H. Keen sees Henry's reign as a "record of tremendous English achievement."[13]

But G.L. Harriss argues that his "messianic streak" led to "unjustifiable aggrandizement which was beyond English resources to sustain and which would ultimately face England with the crisis of its failure".[14] Desmond Seward, Henry's harshest modern critic, claims that "for all his brilliance, Henry V's ambition ended by bankrupting and discrediting his son, and by ruining his dynasty".[15]

Henry's reputation as the mirror of Christian chivalry owes much to his brother Humphrey, Duke of Gloucester, who commissioned the Italian historian Tito Livio to write his life (*Vita Henrici Quinti*), to the anonymous *Gesta Henrici Quinti* and to William Worcester, author of the chauvinistic *Boke of Noblesse*. In the sixteenth century the myth of Henry as the "floure of kynges passed"[16] was kept alive by the chroniclers Fabyan, Grafton, Hall and Holinshed. Their patriotic view of Henry found ready acceptance in militant Protestant circles, and is reflected in the crudely jingoistic *Famous Victories of Henry V*. When a new play about Henry appeared shortly after the *Famous Victories* was first printed, describing how the country's youth, gripped by war fever, abandons the "silken dalliance" of peace to follow the "mirror of all Christian kings" into battle (*H5*, 32.chorus.1ff.), it was clear that the Henry myth was in no danger of being allowed to die. At least that is what many twentieth-century critics of Shakespeare's play have assumed. For J.H. Walter Shakespeare's Henry combines the character and action of the epic hero with the moral qualities of Erasmus' Christian prince;[17] for Norman Rabkin he is "the kind of exemplary monarch that neither Richard II nor Henry IV could be, combining the inwardness and the sense of occasion of the one and the strength of the other with a generous humanity available to neither";[18] for Gary Taylor he is "a study of human greatness."[19]

It is true that Shakespeare's portrait of Henry is in many ways a notably sympathetic one. Henry's rhetoric is exhilarating; his courage in battle is exemplary; his piety seems indisputable and his honour bright. By the final scene of the play any lingering doubts about the legitimacy of his claims to France are easily forgotten in the superficially playful charm of the wooing of Katharine. When even the French king and queen seem delighted with "brother England" and the terms of his proposed alliance, what reason is there to doubt the integrity of this now plain-speaking soldier with a heart that "never changes, but keeps his course truly" (5.2.161-2)? But, as many critics have pointed out, this concluding scene of international and domestic harmony, almost like a comedy in its stylized conviviality,[20] is profoundly ironic. Unlike the typical romantic comedy, which ends with an unfulfilled promise of future happiness, the final chorus of *Henry V* takes us back to a future that is already past. We know all too well that not one of Henry's hopes will be realized:

Katharine will never be a "soldier-breeder"; the king himself will not live to see old age; the peace between England and France will hold only a few years. As the chorus reminds us of the English blood that will soon be shed, it is difficult to suppress memory of all the other disquieting events we have witnessed in the play: the scheming clergy so eager to support a war that is conveniently in their own interests; Henry's brutal threats to the citizens of Harfleur; the patently unsatisfactory argument with Williams; the cold-blooded killing of the prisoners. Was Shakespeare, as one modern historian has suggested, the "prisoner of his time",[21] endorsing the militaristic views of the war party in Elizabethan politics? If so, then why did he apparently go out of his way to sow doubts in our minds concerning the integrity of his hero and the wisdom of Henry's policies?

The chivalric revival

To suggest that Shakespeare was the intellectual prisoner of his time is to imply that Elizabethans were united in their endorsement of the militaristic values that Henry V stood for in the popular imagination. This is not true. A brief review of changing attitudes towards the chivalric ideal in fifteenth- and sixteenth-century England may go at least some way towards explaining the anomalies in Shakespeare's play.

Henry V was written at a time when chivalric values, after a period of self-conscious anti-militarism, were once more in fashion.[22] Originating in the Middle Ages as the code of values of a military aristocracy, chivalry placed paramount emphasis on physical courage and military prowess as the guarantors of justice and honour. Where this involved dynastic rights of the kind that were at issue in the Hundred Years War, chivalry provided justification for aggressive international action. In exhorting Edward to defend his territorial rights, William Worcester appeals to "ye noble Englisshe cheualrie [. . .] to take armes and enterprinses, seeing so many good examples before yow of so many victorius dedis in armes done by youre noble progenitoures".[23] One of chivalry's most enduring legacies to the future was the honour code, a system of values characterized above all by a stress on competitive assertiveness. As Mervyn James explains, the honour code both legitimized and provided moral reinforcement for "a politics of violence".[24] It was this medieval code of values that the Essex circle hoped to revive. To his admirers the Earl of Essex was a symbol of national pride, the "Faire branch of Honor" and "flower of Cheualrie".[25] The earl was the centre of a dissident aristocratic movement that wanted to reform the commonwealth and restore military values to a society grown generally "unwarlicke, in love with the name, and bewitched with the delight of peace".[26] Drawing on the aristocratic charisma of its leader, it called for a return to the heroic values of the past. In doing so it was self-consciously rejecting a generation of anti-chivalric thinking.

With changing methods of warfare and the gradual disintegration of the feudal system of land tenure in which chivalry was rooted, the old martial values were in decline at end of the fifteenth century. "O ye knyghtes of Englond", complains Caxton in his *Book of the Order of Chyvalry* (an expanded translation of Ramón Lulls' *Libre del Orde del Cauayleria*) "where is the custome and usage of noble chyvalry that was used in those days".[27] What Arthur B. Ferguson calls "The Indian Summer of English Chivalry" is the literary rearguard action of men like Malory and Hawes, who wanted to revive an antiquated system of values that bore increasingly little relationship to contemporary social and military reality. By the second decade of the sixteenth century, that system was effectively dead. What had killed it was humanism.[28]

Fundamental to Renaissance humanism is a new sense of historical change. For the generation of More and Erasmus, a medieval culture of violence had no place in the new world of enlightened civic humanism. The sword and shield of Erasmus' Christian knight are those, not of the medieval warrior, but of St Paul's metaphoric "armour of God" (Eph. 6:13).[29] Erasmus is the most uncompromising of the sixteenth-century pacifists.[30] He concedes that war may be justified under exceptional circumstances; for example a Turkish attack against a Christian state. But wars between Christian states are inexcusable. In a barely concealed attack on the expansionist policies of the young Henry VIII, Erasmus denounces such wars as unmitigated folly:

> Almost all wars between Christians have arisen from either stupidity or wickedness. Some young men, with no experience of life, inflamed by the bad examples of our forbears told in the histories that fools have compiled from foolish documents, and then encouraged by flatterers and stimulated by lawyers and theologians, with the consent and connivance of bishops, and even at their desire—these young men, I say, go into war out of rashness rather than badness; and then they learn, to the suffering of the whole world, that war is a thing to be avoided by every possible means.[31]

Erasmus' friend More, though equivocal as always, was clearly satirizing chivalric attitudes when he described how the Utopians despise the notion of honour in battle, counting "nothynge so much against glorie, as glory gotten in war".[32] As C. S. Lewis disapprovingly puts it, "the military methods of More's Utopians are mischievously devised to flout the chivalric code at every turn".[33] The powerful influence of Erasmus' thinking can also be seen in Sir Thomas Elyot's *The Governour*. Though not a pacificist, Elyot upholds the humanist emphasis on the primacy of learning. Comparing social values in the modern world with the

"doctryne of auncient noble men", he claims that the reason for the decay of learning in the modern world is contempt for education among the aristocracy. Elyot's model of princely virtue is Henry I, known as Henry Beau Clerke for his learning. Contrasting him with his brother Robert, "a man of moche prowesse, and right expert in martial affayres", Elyot praises Henry as the superior leader because his wisdom and learning enabled him to add "polycie to vertue and courage".[34] In drawing up a scheme of education for a newly emerging governing class Elyot omitted from his list of physical exercises suitable for noblemen any discussion of the tournaments that for Castiglione's courtier are a way of acquiring martial prowess.[35] For Elyot honour is to be won, not through battle, but through public service. The purpose of studying "morall philosophie" is to create a just society based on "vertues, maners, and ciuile policie".[36] Later in the century Elizabeth's tutor Ascham showed a similar scorn for the militaristic element in medieval chivalry when he complained that Malory's *Morte D'Arthur* was nothing but "open mans slaughter and bold bawdrye".[37]

It was the pacifist element in English civic humanism with its contempt for chivalric values that Sidney, and later Essex, wanted to reform. Though it cannot be said that the sixteenth century saw very significant advances in the social position of women, humanist education did at least provide the foundation for sexual equality: as Elizabeth's own example showed, women could also be scholars. By contrast, the honour code is unequivocally masculine; its appeal is, as William Worcester puts it, to "corage, feersnes, manlinesse and strength",[38] sentiments that are echoed by the Elizabethan armorist Gerard Legh when he defines honour as "glory gotten by courage of manhood".[39] In his *Apologie* of 1598 Essex compares the unheroic present with the "those former gallant ages" when England did not hesitate "to atchieve great conquests in France".[40] When Essex wrote his *Apologie* the simmering rivalry between the two main factions in the Privy Council was rapidly approaching crisis point.[41] On one side were the Cecils, astute and scheming politicians, but concerned above all to preserve peace, both at home and abroad. On the other was Essex, arrogant, mercurial, paranoid and desperate for military glory. Where the Cecils instinctively favoured civilian rule, Essex would have liked to have done away with civil magistracy altogether and to have replaced it with martial law. His dream was a military society ruled by an aristocratic élite. Matters came to a head with the Treaty of Vervins (May 1598): the Cecils urged acceptance of Spain's proposals; Essex, hoping no doubt that history would repeat itself and that a war faction would once again triumph as it had done in 1513, insisted on an all-out offensive against the dominant power on the continent: "now, now is the fittest time to make warre upon the Spaniard," he wrote in the *Apologie*.[42]

If the glamorous and bellicose young Henry VIII was a source of practical inspiration for the Elizabethan war faction, the great Lancastrian ancestor on whom he conspicuously modelled himself[43] enjoyed an almost mythical reputation in the popular mind. For the Essex faction Henry V was the perfect symbol of national pride. Here was not only an an inspirational type of what Lydgate calls "the prowesse of olde chiualrie", but also an embodiment of just the kind of aggressive military action that Essex himself so passionately advocated. Samuel Daniel, who praises Essex in the *Civil Wars* as a rare example "Of ancient honor neere worne out of date",[44] imagines the ghost of Henry V returning (like Hamlet's father) to reprove the present age for its neglect of the "wondrous Actions" of the heroic past. In defending Henry's campaigns, he puts the emphasis, not on the reassertion of hereditary rights, but on "ioyes of gotten spoyles", "thoughts of glorie" and "conquests, riches, Land, and Kingdome gain'd" (V, stanzas 1, 3, 40). For Essex's admirers the "dreadful and yet lovely" Henry was the supreme example of chivalric heroism, inspiring both "terror and delight" (V, stanza 2).

Such blatantly militarist sentiments inevitably attracted criticism. There is, of course, always a danger of reading modern assumptions into the debates of the past. But if our own century has particular reason to be wary of charismatic military leaders, the sixteenth century was both fascinated and repelled by the cult of the megalopsyche. As Paul Siegel argues, humanists were fully aware of the opposition between their own ideal of honour through public service and commitment to civic ideals, and what they regarded as a false cult of neo-chivalric honour.[45] Sidney's friend Hubert Languet is typical of those humanists who had profound reservations about the culture of violence fostered by militant Protestantism. Warning him of the temptations of seeking honour through military achievement, Languet wrote to Sidney: "It is the misfortune, or rather the folly of our age that most men of high rank think it more honorable to do the work of a soldier than of a leader, and would rather earn a name for boldness than for judgment".[46] Essex received similar, though less friendly, advice from the Privy Council when it debated the Spanish peace proposals in 1598. Warning the Earl of the dangers of his obsession with war, the treasurer reminded him of the psalmist's prophecy: "Men of blood shall not live out half their days".[47]

When Shakespeare wrote *Henry V* the revival of chivalric military values had not yet reached its farcical anticlimax in the Essex rebellion. But as the final chorus allusions to the Earl's anticipated return from Ireland indicate, Essex and the values for which he stood were the subject of angry political argument.[48] By beginning the play with an invocation, not to one of the nine liberal arts, but instead to the patron god of chivalry, attended by "famine, sword and fire", Shakespeare was giving a sure signal that he meant to engage with the topical matter of martial versus eirenic values. Cultural Materialism suggests that the question that criticism should ask about Shakespeare's plays is whether they are for or against authority; as Jonathan Dollimore puts it, do they "reinforce the dominant order, or do they interrogate it to the point of subversion?"[49] But topical though it was in the late 1590s, neo-chivalric militarism is not an issue that will divide along simple authoritarian versus populist lines. Essex was certainly the centre of a dissident party that threatened Elizabeth's authority. But the rebellion of 1601 was an aristocratic, not a populist movement. As in 1513, the main beneficiaries of a land war in Europe would have been a nobility eager for offices and appointments as well as the usual financial spoils; for the common soldier the reward of victory would no doubt have been much like that of Pistol: no honours and titles, but a life of begging and stealing (5.1.74-83). In his recent Arden edition of *Henry V* T.W. Craik refers to Essex as a popular hero.[50] Though it is true that the earl was lionized by his followers, it is clear from the self-defensive tone of his *Apologie* that his love of war aroused deep suspicion among his opponents; indeed his sanity was seriously doubted.[51] When he made his ill-fated march on the City in February 1601 the people of London, instead of rallying to his cause, stood by in silent amazement as he led his little cavalcade up Fenchurch street crying "for the Queen, for the Queen".[52] Rather than asking whether Shakespeare is "for" or "against" Henry as a representative figure of authority, it would probably make more sense to consider what this exceptionally ambivalent play has to say about the factional issue so clearly announced in its opening lines.[53]

War and chivalry

Modern criticism is divided on the question of whether the play wants us to see Henry V as Christian hero or deceitful Machiavel. Because Henry is a natural autocrat, post-structuralist historicism sees him, perhaps predictably, as the latter. In one of his most influential essays[54] Stephen Greenblatt argues that throughout the three plays in which he appears Henry is a Machiavellian "juggler" and "conniving hypocrite". The final play of the series, says Greenblatt, "deftly registers every nuance of royal hypocrisy, ruthlessness, and bad faith".[55] Ruthless Henry undoubtedly is, but to accuse him of bad faith is to deny him his most outstanding and most dangerous characteristic, namely his frank and single-minded fidelity to his cause.

For Greenblatt *Henry V* is a classic instance of the way authority produces and contains subversion. Insofar as it is concerned to illustrate a transhistorical paradigm of power politics, Greenblatt's essay is, strictly speaking, a-historicist. For all its rhetorical persuasiveness, it suffers from the inevitable limitations of its analogical methodology. When flexible use is made of the text,[56] and when external appeal is made, not to proven source material or contemporaneous political debate, but to unconnected "reiterations" of an *a priori* principle, it becomes difficult either to prove or disprove his thesis. A more truly historicist case for seeing Henry as a dissimulating Machiavel has recently been made by Steven Marx.[57] The idea of the benign Machiavel using deception for the good of the state is not a new one in Shakespeare criticism.[58] But Marx goes, not just to Machiavelli, but to one of Machiavelli's own sources for his political analogues. Noting the presumably intentional parallel between the miracle of Agincourt and God's deliverance of Israel (the "Non nobis" that Henry orders to be sung after the battle is the Latin title of Psalm 115 celebrating the defeat of the Egyptian armies at the Red Sea), he argues that the Old Testament provided Renaissance humanists with a political history as rich and revealing as those of the classical world. Citing a number of biblical figures who use trickery to defeat their enemies, Marx suggests that Shakespeare shows Henry deliberately and cynically using holy war as a political device to inspire faith in his followers and credulity in his enemies.

Based as it is on proven sources rather than on tendentious readings of entirely unconnected texts, Marx's argument is a much more powerful one than Greenblatt's. But again the play itself does not provide convincing support for the claim that Henry is unscrupulously manipulating religion for political ends. Modern historians speak of the historical Henry's "messianic streak"[59] and his religious bigotry.[60] Even Allmand, his most admiring biographer, describes him as "a man with an obsession".[61] Shakespeare's Henry also has that obsessive, single-minded zeal that is characteristic of many religious converts.

It is true that in *Henry IV* the prince uses deception to enhance his reputation, announcing at the beginning of Part 1 that he will "falsify men's hopes" by "redeeming time" when people least expect it (*1H4*, 1.2.204-10). Whether or not his reformation at the end of Part 2 is authentic, he appears, when we see him at the beginning of *Henry V*, to have all the characteristics of the reborn Christian. From the conversation between Canterbury and Ely in the first scene we learn that Henry does indeed seem to be the "new man" described by the sixteenth-century chroniclers:[62]

> Never was such a sudden scholar made;
> Never came reformation in a flood,
> With such a heady currance, scouring
>   faults;
> Nor never Hydra-headed wilfulness
> So soon did lose his seat, and all at once,
> As in this king
>
> (1.1.32-7).

As well as showing an impressive grasp of theological and political matters, the reborn king is a compelling orator, especially on the subject of war. "List his discourse of war," says Canterbury, "and you shall hear / A fearful battle rend'red you in music" (1.1.43-4). It is Henry's passion for war that particularly interests the bishops. Seeing in this a way out of the church's own problems, Canterbury makes the king an offer: if he will guarantee the security of church lands, the clergy will support a re-opening of the war against France. But before Henry will agree to this proposal he insists on satisfying himself that he does have a legitimate claim to the French crown. The ground is thus prepared for the notorious debate on Salic Law.

If it was Shakespeare's intention to portray Henry as the mirror of Christian kings and to justify his aggressive military policies, Canterbury's exposition of Salic Law seems an odd way of going about it. To establish the legality of Henry's claim to France Shakespeare could easily have had a group of courtiers discussing the Plantagenet dynasty. One of them might begin by reminding the court that English kings had ruled the Angevin empire since time immemorial (that is to say, since the 11th century); another might say that Edward III had a better claim to the French throne than anyone else, better certainly than Philip VI; a third might rejoin that Philip's confiscation of the Duchy of Aquitaine in 1337 was quite illegal; a fourth might point out that when Henry's father met the Dukes of Berry, Bourbon and Orléans in Bourges in 1412 all had agreed that Aquitaine was rightfully English. All this could have been done quickly and emphatically. Alternatively, Shakespeare could have followed the example of the *Famous Victories of Henry V* where the question of Henry's legal claims to France is dealt with in two sentences. In response to the king's request for advice Canterbury simply says "Your right to the French crown of France came by your great-grandmother, Isabel, wife to King Edward the third, and sister to Charles, the French King. Now, if the French King deny it, as likely enough he will, then must you take your sword in hand and conquer the right".[63] What could be simpler? The king has a clear legal right and he must defend it.

By contrast, Shakespeare reproduces more or less word for word from Holinshed a forensic argument of such tortuous casuistry that no theatre audience could possibly follow it. Holinshed's own view of Canterbury's tactics comes across fairly clearly. Winding up what Holinshed calls "his prepared tale", the Archbishop shifts to a different register as he exhorts Henry to "advance forth his banner to fight for his right" and "spare neither bloud, sword, nor fire" in defence of his inheritance. Parliament responds to this emotive rhetoric with cries of "Warre, warre; France, France". Carried away by its own jingoism, the House forgets the more mundane question of church lands and votes enthusiastically for war. Holinshed comments dryly: "Hereby the bill for dissoluing of religious houses was cleerelie set aside, and nothing thought on but onelie the recovering of France, according as the archbishop had mooved".[64]

With his keen interest in the unscrupulous use of political oratory—*Julius Caesar* was probably written in the same year as *Henry V*—Shakespeare clearly saw the dramatic potential of such material. But if Canterbury's motives are dishonourable, this does not mean that Henry is necessarily a conniver. Indeed he is insistent that the archbishop explain the crown's legal position "justly and religiously" (1.2.10). Warning him not to "fashion, wrest, or bow" the facts to suit convenience (14), Henry soberly reminds the court of the consequences of going to war. In contrast to Canterbury's casuistical exposition of Salic law, the king's response is a simple question: "May I with right and conscience make this claim?" (96). As in Holinshed, Canterbury's reply is an emotive appeal to national pride:

> Gracious lord,
> Stand for your own; unwind your bloody
>   flag,
> Look back into your mighty ancestors.
> Go, my dread lord, to your great-grandsire's
>   tomb,
> From whom you claim; invoke his war-like
>   spirit . . .
>
>   (100-4).

Taking up the archbishop's theme, Ely urges Henry to think of "exploits and mighty enterprises" (121). Unlike Hamlet, whose reaction to an appeal to dynastic honour is an impassioned declaration of vengeance, Henry remains cool, quietly reminding the court of the need to prepare, not only for a foreign campaign, but also for the possibility of an attack from Scotland. The debate concludes with the Archbishop's emollient parable of the bee hive. Obedience to the rule of nature, says Canterbury, is the key to social harmony: just as members of a bee hive work together under the direction of a king, so national success depends on each member of society working for the common good.

Canterbury's parable is meant as an illustration of the general principle that Exeter has just stated in the preceding speech. "Government," says Exeter,

> though high, and low, and lower,
> Put into parts, doth keep in one consent,
> Congreeing in a full and natural close,
> Like music
>
>   (180-3).

Musical harmony is a key metaphor in political debate in this period.[65] In formulating their constitutional ar-

guments both apologists for and critics of the crown appeal to the laws of a nature whose characteristic feature is "harmonicall agreement" and "due proportion". As the encyclopaedist Pierre de La Primaudaye explains,

> A citie or ciuill company is nothing else but a multitude of men vnlike in estates or conditions, which communicate togither in one place their artes, occupations, workes, and exercises, that they may live the better, & are obedient to the same lawes and magistrates . . . Of such a dissimilitude an harmonicall agreement ariseth by due proportion of one towards another in their diverse orders & estates, even as the harmonie in musicke consisteth of unequal voyces or sounds agreeing equally togither.[66]

That Exeter's appeal to these familiar Pythagorean principles should make Canterbury think of bees is not in itself surprising. The association is conventional. The *inscriptio* of an early 17th-century emblem illustrating the principles of social harmony explains that

> As busie Bees unto their Hive doe swarme,
> So do's th' attractive power of *Musicke*
>   charme [. . .]
> This *Harmony* in t'humane *Fabricke* steales
> And is the sinewes of all Common-weales.[67]

The significant thing about the archbishop's little clerical homily is not its content—which is conventional enough—but the context in which it is made and the lesson that Canterbury draws from it. The mythological figure who embodies Exeter's harmonist principle is Orpheus. As Puttenham explains, Orpheus' legendary ability to tame wild beasts with his music is a figure for the civilizing influence of the arts and their ability to restrain the brutal passions of our fallen nature.[68] His antithesis in Renaissance mythography is Hercules. Orpheus is a symbolic representative of the arts of peace, Hercules those of war.[69] Both figures are claimed by mythographers as founders of civilization and represent opposing ideals of community.[70] The irony of Canterbury's speech is that he should appeal to harmonist principles, not in order to defend the Orphic arts of peace, but to argue for war. In what seems no less of a *non sequitur* than Hector's abrupt *volte face* at the end of his eloquent exposition of natural law in *Troilus and Cressida* (2.2.163-93), the archbishop concludes his parable of social harmony with a call to arms: "Therefore to France, my liege" (1.2.213).

Behind Canterbury's speech lies a long debate on the arts of war and peace.[71] At the end of the play there is another reminder of that debate. In an extended natural image, ironically of great beauty, the Duke of Burgundy reflects sadly on the way peace, the "nurse of arts", has been "mangled" by war. As nature reverts to wildness, so humanity seems to return to its primal savagery:

> as our vineyards, fallows, meads, and
> hedges,
> Defective in their natures, grow to wildness;
> Even so our houses and ourselves and
> children
> Have lost, or do not learn for want of time,
> The sciences that should become our
> country;
> But grow, like savages—as soldiers will,
> That nothing do but meditate on blood . . .
> (5.2.54-60).

But Henry, unlike the effeminate Richard II, is no "nurse of arts". Above all he is a holy warrior. Having satisfied himself that he has good legal and religious grounds for going to war, he announces his decision. With calm deliberation he declares that once France is his he will either bend it to his will or "break it all to pieces" (224-5). When the French ambassadors arrive he informs them that he is "no tyrant, but a Christian king". J.H. Walter has shown that Shakespeare knew Erasmus' *Education of a Christian Prince* well and was probably working closely with it when he wrote *Henry V*.[72] But Henry's notion of what it means to be a Christian king could not be more different from Erasmus'. For Erasmus clemency is one of the prince's cardinal virtues.[73] So too is it for Shakespeare's Portia. If mercy "becomes / The throned monarch better than his crown" it is because "It is an attribute of God himself" (*The Merchant of Venice,* 4.1.184-90). By contrast, Henry sees himself as the scourge of a vindictive God. In retaliation for the Dauphin's insult, Henry tells the ambassadors to warn their prince that

>   his soul
> Shall stand sore charged for the wasteful
> vengeance
> That shall fly at them; for many a thousand
> widows
> Shall this his mock mock out of their dear
> husbands;
> Mock mothers from their sons, mock castles
> down;
> And some are yet ungotten and unborn
> That shall have cause to curse the
> Dauphin's scorn.
> But this lies all within the will of God,
> To whom I do appeal; and in whose name,
> Tell you the Dauphin, I am coming on,
> To venge me as I may and to put forth
> My rightful hand in a well-hallow'd cause
> (282-93).

It would be difficult to think of a more aptly ironic comment on such cold savagery than Exeter's "This was a merry message" (298).

Dramatically the whole scene is of crucial importance in establishing one of the play's central thematic concerns, that is, the dangers of single-minded idealism. Many critics and historians—including, I suspect, Holinshed—are suspicious of Canterbury's motives. Legally his arguments may be sound,[74] but the effect of his speech is not to clarify matters but to confuse them. That Henry himself seems to be satisfied with the archbishop's exposition of Salic Law does not mean that he is a "conniving hypocrite." What we see in this scene is a king first confirming that he has a "well-hallow'd cause", and then coolly and openly informing his enemies what they can expect if they dare to oppose his will. The truly frightening thing about him is the sense he has of the absolute rightness of his cause. Having "whipp'd th' offending Adam out of him" (1.1.29), he is now a man driven by a powerful sense of missionary zeal. Though he claims to be a Christian king, it is really Mars who is his true god, and Henry is his scourge.

By contrast, the clergy with whom he deals are not idealists inspired by a divine mission, but cynical politicians who are prepared to see England go to war rather than lose their lands. Defending Canterbury's speech against the usual charges of tedium and incomprehensibility, Gary Taylor argues that the archbishop's performance is "both comprehensible and dramatically necessary": comprehensible because Elizabethans were apparently interested in Salic Law and were used to listening to long speeches, and dramatically necessary because if you want to build up to a thrilling climax (Henry's riposte to the Dauphin) you have to begin at a low pitch.[75] Taylor needs to defend the archbishop's speech because he believes that Shakespeare approved of Henry's policies and wanted to justify them. Dramatically, however, what comes over most strongly in these crucial opening scenes is not the transparent justice of Henry's cause, but the inherent danger of unholy alliances between unscrupulous cynicism and single-minded idealism, a motif that Shakespeare was later to develop to devastating effect in another tale about an idealistic soldier and a Machiavellian cynic.

But Henry is no Othello; a steely self-control is one of his most impressive characteristics. It is not just that he is good at mastering his feelings; as he admits when he learns of the killing of the luggage boys, normally he is simply not prone to strong emotions. But in this case anger is an entirely appropriate response. The other occasion when he allows his anger to show is in the argument with Williams.

The disguised king who shows his true humanity by mingling with his people in a brief interlude of benevolent deception is a common motif in Elizabethan fiction.[76] It is just such a stereotype that the chorus evokes as he asks us to imagine Henry passing among his "ruin'd band" of soldiers and raising their spirits with his "cheerful semblance and sweet majesty" (4. Chorus, 40). But the reality is rather different. Instead of cheering his men, Henry quarrels with them, provoking Bates to call him and Williams a pair of "English fools" (4.1.220). It is Bates who triggers the argument by innocently suggesting that at a moment like the present the king is probably wishing he were anywhere but at Agincourt. Henry tells him that, "his cause being just and his quarrel honourable" (127), it is unlikely that the king would want to be anywhere else. Bates is not interested in challenging the point, but Williams immediately picks it up: "But if the cause be not good, the king himself hath a heavy reckoning to make" (133-4).

We thus return to the play's central politico-religious problem. In an apocalyptic image of dismembered bodies joining together at the day of judgment, Williams speculates on the horror of dying unattended on the battlefield in the knowledge that wives and children are left unprotected and debts unpaid. If the cause for which these men are about to die is not a good one, he says, "it will be a black matter for the king that led them to it" (133-45). Unknowingly Williams has touched on something that is dear to Henry's heart. Little wonder that he becomes angry, for who is Williams, a common soldier, to question the scourge of God? Henry's response is a long speech absolving the king of any responsibility for the souls of men who die with "irreconciled iniquities" (156); such men, he tells Williams, cannot expect to escape the wrath of God, for "war is his beadle, war is his vengeance" (174-5). Williams and the king are clearly talking at cross purposes: one is thinking about soldiers dying with unprotected dependents; the other is concerned to obey the will of a vindictive "God of battles". Henry's theology is harsh and, so far as Williams is concerned, irrelevant. But it is not pronounced in bad faith. If Henry fails to answer Williams' worries it is because he is apparently incapable of understanding the concerns of a common soldier. As he admitted when he threatened the citizens of Harfleur with "heady murder, spoil, and villainy" (3.3.32), "What is it then to me" if the innocent suffer? "What is't to me?" (15; 19). Henry's mind is on loftier things than the sufferings of common people. As we hear him pray to his God of battles at the end of the scene there is no question of his sincerity. Henry's fault is not "juggling" hypocrisy, but a missionary idealism that is incapable of doubting its own validity. If there is a moral in this play it must be "beware of men with visions".

The debate with Williams does not show Henry to good advantage. But the following morning he is in his true element. His rallying cry to his troops in the Crispin's day speech is not a piece of cynical bravado, but an expression of unaffected joy in doing the one thing that, for the chevalier, gives meaning and purpose to life:

> We few, we happy few, we band of
>   brothers;
> For he to-day that sheds his blood with me
> Shall be my brother
>
>   (4.3.60-2).

For the medieval knight war provides the ultimate test of his virtue; it is something for which his whole training in the chivalric arts has been a preparation. This is why Henry tells Westmoreland that he would not wish for any additional men, since that would diminish the glory of the hour:

> I would not lose so great an honour
> As one man more, methinks. would share
>   from me
> For the best hope I have. O do not wish
>   one more!
>
>   (31-3).

War does not just provide a test of a knight's prowess; to die well is his supreme reward. Johan Huizinga quotes a passage from Jean de Bueil's *Le Jouvencel* (c. 1466) that captures wonderfully the idealized sentiments that war is capable of inspiring:

> It is a joyous thing, is war [. . .] You love your comrade so in war. When you see that your quarrel is just and your blood is fighting well, tears rise to your eye. A great sweet feeling of loyalty and of pity fills your heart on seeing your friend so valiantly exposing his body to execute and accomplish the command of our Creator. And then you prepare to go and die or live with him, and for love not to abandon him. And out of that there arises such a delectation, that he who has not tasted it is not fit to say what a delight it is. Do you think that a man who does that fears death? Not at all; for he feels so strengthened, he is so elated, that he does not know where he is. Truly he is afraid of nothing.[77]

Idealization of battle is the very core of medieval chivalry. It is the knight's moment of true glory. Exactly the same sentiments as those described by Jean de Bueil are expressed in Exeter's account of the deaths of Suffolk and York in Act 4, Scene 6. This speech is a moving piece of theatre. In dramatic contrast to the disorder and confusion among the demoralized French (scene 5), we are now given a picture of heroic self-sacrifice and sublime emotion as two noble warriors, brothers in chivalry, are united in death. Exeter reports how, tenderly kissing the torn and bleeding face of his companion in arms, York cries

> 'Tarry my cousin Suffolk.
> My soul shall thine keep company to
>   heaven;
> Tarry, sweet soul, for mine, then fly a-
>   breast;

As in this glorious and well-foughten field
We kept together in our chivalry'
                                        (4.6. 15-19).

Holding Exeter's hand, the dying York asks him to
commend him to the king. Then he kisses the lips of
his dead companion once more;

And so espous'd to death, with blood he
    seal'd
A testament of noble-ending love
                                        (26-7).

No conventional love scene in Shakespeare is so affecting. Indeed so powerful is Exeter's story that even
Henry is almost moved to tears—almost, but not quite
(4.6.33-4). If this battle scene had been written in the
fifteenth century it might just have been possible to
take it seriously. A century later it is the purest kitsch.

As if to signal the fact that Exeter's romantic chivalry
is no more than theatrical sentimentality, this mood of
maudlin heroism is abruptly broken by an alarum signalling that the French have regrouped. With brutal
efficiency Henry immediately orders the prisoners to
be killed. Since the prisoners are actually on stage at
the time the order is given, Gary Taylor is probably
right in suggesting that the killing would have taken
place in front of the audience.[78] Whether or not circumstances on the battlefield at Agincourt meant that
it was tactically necessary to kill the prisoners is something that no theatre audience would have time to
consider. Dramatically, though, its impact is stark.
This time it is Gower who provides the commentary.
Supposing, wrongly, that Henry had ordered the killing
of the prisoners in retaliation for the slaughter of the
luggage boys, he says, "O, 'tis a gallant King!" (4.7.10).

The dangers of idealism

One effect of the meeting between Henry and his bishops at the beginning of the play is to make us warm
to Henry's integrity. Confronted with such blatant
cynicism, it is not difficult to admire the man of honour.
As Robert Ashley writes in a treatise entitled *Of Honour*
(c. 1600):

By honour are vertues kindled and incouraged, by
honour are vices eschewed, by honour ignoraunce,
error and folly, sloth and sluggishness, hatred and
fear, shame and ignoraunce, and all evill affeccions
are alayed.[79]

Henry is a man inspired by a heroic ideal. At Agincourt
his integrity and his valour are set off to even greater
advantage by the foolish boasting of the Dauphin (3.7).
When the man of honour is as gifted an orator as
Henry, the combination of missionary zeal and impassioned eloquence is almost irresistible. Against our better

judgment we respond to his inspiring words, forgetting for the moment the cruel reality behind the noble
rhetoric. Yet repeatedly the play brings us back to that
reality. Even as the Act 2 Chorus describes how
England's youth are fired with thoughts of war, and
"honour's thought/Reigns solely in the breast of every
man", he tells us that they follow Henry to battle like
"English Mercuries" (2, chorus 3-4; 7).

Mercury is, of course, the messenger of the gods,
noted both for his celerity and for his eloquence (not
a quality normally associated with soldiers). But like
so many of his Olympian clients he has a double nature. He is both peacemaker—the caduceus is a symbol of peace, order and government—and thief.[80] Is
Henry a peacemaker or a thief? It depends on one's
point of view. Lydgate described the historical Henry
as a "prince of pes" resolving an ancient dynastic
dispute (*Troy Book,* V. 3416); Shakespeare's Henry
also sees himself as a peacemaker. Ironically it is on
the eve of a battle in which some ten thousand men
are about to lose their lives that Henry reflects on his
peacemaking role. As he ponders the cares of office
he thinks ruefully how the peasant little knows "what
watch the king keeps to maintain the peace" (4.1.279).
But Erasmus saw Henry's campaigns as a classic
example of the folly of attempting to extend territory.
To him the chivalric ideals that endorsed them were
simply a means of promoting war under a veneer of
glory.

What Shakespeare thought about Henry we can only
guess. However, it is interesting that, having given us
a heroic image of chivalrous English warriors setting
off to do battle for their country's honour, he immediately produces some English Mercuries of a rather
different kind. The subplot of *Henry V* looks very
much like a parody of the play's heroic main plot.[81] Its
characters are pilferers, fools and braggarts motivated
by self-interest and an absurd sense of 'manly' pride.
The ironic parallel between Henry's exploits and those
of his soldiers is underlined by Fluellen's comparison
of him to Alexander the Great: "If you mark Alexander's
life well, Harry of Monmouth's life is come after it
indifferent well" (4.7.33-4). There are several allusions
to Alexander in the play (1.1.46; 3.1.19; 4.7.13ff.). But
the anecdote from Alexander's life that is most damaging to Henry is the general's meeting with a pirate
he has taken prisoner. In St Augustine's version of the
story Alexander asks Dionides how he dare "molest
the seas". Dionides replies: "How darest thou molest
the whole world? But because I doe it with a little ship
onely, I am called a theefe: thou doing it with a great
Nauie, art called an Emperour".[82] In the light of Erasmus'
deprecation of war between neighbouring rulers when
disagreements could easily be settled by arbitration,[83]
Bardolph's complaint at the pointless brawling of his
companions sounds very much like an oblique comment on his betters. As Nym and Pistol quarrel over

a meaningless point of honour, he asks: "why the devil should we keep knives to cut one another's throats?" (2.1.88-9).

If, as Fluellen says, "there is figures in all things" (4.7.35), we have to ask what the function of these sub-plot scenes is with their foolish squabbling, petty thieving and preposterous heroics. Is it to show Henry's "gret manhode"[84] to advantage, revealing "true things by what their mock'ries be" (4, Chorus, 53)? or is it to suggest that for all Henry's noble rhetoric his foreign policy is merely thievery on an international scale? Paradoxically it is both. In his study of medieval chivalry Huizinga suggests that "the quest for glory and honour goes hand in hand with [. . .] hero worship".[85] Only by evoking a sense of the extraordinary glamour of the chivalric ideal in such a way as to make us experience for ourselves the irresistible appeal of its rhetoric is it possible to show the true danger of charismatic heroism.[86] Gary Taylor is right to describe *Henry V* as a study of human greatness. His contemporary biographers were unanimous in seeing him as the flower of English chivalry. But the question that the play forces audiences—both sixteenth-century and modern—to ask is whether the world can afford heroes of this mould.

Compared with Richard II, Henry is a model of kingly authority. But though his own sense of the indisputable rightness of his cause is beyond question, historians have not been unanimous in endorsing that view. One scholar describes his legacy as "a false ideal of foreign conquest and aggression, a reckless contempt for the rights and feelings of other nations, and a restless incapacity for peace".[87] Whatever we may think of the ethics of Henry's policies, their practical result was national impoverishment, both economic and artistic. (In contrast to the literary glories of Richard's reign Henry's is an artistic waste land.) In a study of military leadership John Keegan writes of the sterility of the heroic society. A society that is preoccupied with "the repetitive and ultimately narcissistic activity of combat" is incapable of developing to the full its creative and artistic potential. Keegan's conclusion is that humankind "needs an end to the ethic of [military] heroism in its leadership for good and all".[88]

There are, of course, other kinds of heroism. Having anatomized the warlike Herculean hero in a series of tragedies,[89] Shakespeare turns, at the end of his career, to an entirely different kind of leader. Like the idealized James, for whom he is an epideictic model of both praise and warning, Prospero is a reluctant pacifist who learns that "the rarer action is / Is in virtue than in vengeance" (5.1.27-8). Above all Prospero is a type of the creative artist. By contrast, the heroes of the martial and political tragedies are destructive figures. They are charismatic leaders who are either responsible for the collapse of the state whose safety

they are supposed to be guarding, or else place it in extreme jeopardy. Like them, Henry V is a profoundly paradoxical figure, a national hero who is indirectly responsible for a national disaster.

Notes

[1] Quotations from Shakespeare are from *The Complete Works,* ed. Peter Alexander, London: Collins, 1951.

[2] In the Envoy to his *Troy Book* John Lydgate praises Henry as the "sours & welle" of knighthood, see *Lydgate's Troy Book,* edited by Henry Bergen, 4 vols (London: Early English Text Society, 1906-35), V.1. Thomas Hoccleve describes him as the 'welle of honur' and 'flour of Chivalrie', *Hoccleve's Works,* 3 vols, edited by Frederick J. Furnival, (London: Early English Text Society, 1892-7), 1.41.

[3] See Maurice Keen, *Chivalry,* New Haven and London: Yale UP, 1984; J. Huizinga, *The Waning of the Middle Ages,* (1924; repr. Harmondsworth: Penguin, 1982), chapter 4; Malcolm Vale, *War and Chivalry: Warfare and Aristocratic Culture in England, France and Burgundy at the End of the Middle Ages,* London: Duckworth, 1981.

[4] *Lydgate's Troy Book,* Prol. 83.

[5] Ibid., 1.11.1-7; 36-7.

[6] *Hall's Chronicle,* (1548; repr. London, 1809), p. 113.

[7] William Worcester, *The Boke of Noblesse,* with an introduction by John Gough Nichols, (London: J.B. Nichols, 1860), p. 20.

[8] Ibid. p.20.

[9] J.R. Lander, *Conflict and Stability in Fifteenth-Century England,* (London: Hutchinson, 1969), p.61.

[10] See above, note 2.

[11] *Hoccleve's Works,* 3.192-3.

[12] *Lydgate's Siege of Thebes* III.4645ff., 2 vols, ed. by Axel Erdmann and Eilert Ekwall (London: Early English Text Society, 1911-1930) II, 191.

[13] M.H. Keen, *England in the Later Middle Ages: a Political History* (London: Methuen, 1973), p. 377.

[14] G.L. Harriss, ed., *Henry V: the Practice of Kingship* (Oxford: Oxford UP, 1985), pp. 24; 209. See also Harold F. Hutchison, *Henry V: a Biography* (London: Eyre & Spottiswoode, 1967), pp. 222-4.

[15] Desmond Seward, *Henry V as Warlord* (London: Sidgwick & Jackson, 1987), p. 218.

[16] *Hall's Chronicle,* p. 113.

[17] J.H. Walter, ed., Introduction to Arden edition of *Henry V* (London: Methuen; Cambridge, MA.: Harvard UP, 1954), p. xvi.

[18] Norman Rabkin, *Shakespeare and the Common Understanding,* (1967; repr. Chicago and London: Chicago UP, 1984), p. 98. However, Rabkin later revised this view: see *Shakespeare and the Problem of Meaning* (Chicago and London: Chicago UP, 1981), pp. 33-62.

[19] Gary Taylor, ed., Introduction to *Henry V,* (Oxford and New York: Oxford UP, 1982), p. 72.

[20] In *Shakespeare and the Common Understanding,* pp. 99-100, Rabkin compares the play to a comedy.

[21] Christopher Allmand, *Henry V* (London: Methuen, 1992), p. 434.

[22] See Arthur B. Ferguson, *The Chivalric Tradition in Renaissance England,* Washington, London and Toronto: Folger Shakespeare Library, 1986. See also Sydney Anglo, ed., introduction to *Chivalry in the Renaissance* (Woodbridge: Boydell Press, 1990), pp. xi-xvi; Ferguson, *The Indian Summer of English Chivalry: Studies in the Decline and Transformation of Chivalric Idealism,* Durham, NC: Duke UP, 1960; Richard C. McCoy, *The Rites of Knighthood: The Literature and Politics of Elizabethan Chivalry* (Berkeley, Los Angeles and London: California UP, 1989); Roy Strong, *The Cult of Elizabeth,* London: Thames & Hudson, 1977; Frances Yates, *Astraea: The Imperial Theme in the Sixteenth Century* (London and Boston: Routledge & Kegan Paul, 1975), pp. 88-111.

[23] Worcester, *The Boke of Noblesse,* p. 29.

[24] Mervyn James, *Society, Politics and Culture: Studies in Early Modern England,* (1978; repr. Cambridge: Cambridge UP, 1986), p. 309.

[25] Edmund Spenser, *Prothalamion,* 146, *The Poetical Works,* edited by J.C. Smith and E. de Selincourt (London, New York and Toronto: Oxford UP, 1912), p. 602.

[26] Robert Devereux, Earl of Essex, *An Apologie of the Earl of Essex* (London, 1598), Sig.D2ᵛ.

[27] Ramón Lull, *The Book of the Ordre of Chyvalry,* transl. William Caxton (c. 1483-5), (London: Early English Text Society, 1926), p. 122.

[28] The following paragraph is largely based on Ferguson, *The Chivalric Tradition in Renaissance England* (see above, note 22).

[29] Desiderius Erasmus, *Enchiridion Militis Christiani: An English Version,* ed. Anne M. O'Donnell, SND (Oxford: Early English Text Society, 1981), ch. 2, "The wepons of a chrysten man", pp. 41-55.

[30] See Philip C. Dust, *Three Renaissance Pacifists: Essays on the Theories of Erasmus, More, and Vives* (New York: Peter Lang, 1987), pp. 13-61.

[31] *The 'Adages' of Erasmus,* edited with a translation by Margaret Mann Phillips, (Cambridge: Cambridge UP, 1964), p. 348.

[32] Thomas More, *Utopia,* with an introduction by John O'Hagan (London and Toronto: Dent, 1910), p. 91.

[33] C.S. Lewis, *English Literature in the Sixteenth Century Excluding Drama* (London, Oxford and New York: Oxford UP, 1954), p. 29.

[34] Sir Thomas Elyot, *The Boke Named the Governour,* ed. Foster Watson, (London: Dent, 1907), p. 49.

[35] Baldassare Castiglione, *The Book of the Courtier,* transl. Sir Thomas Hoby, ed. W.H.D. Rouse (London: Dent, 1928), p. 41.

[36] *The Governour,* p. 69.

[37] Roger Ascham, *The Scholemaster* in *English Works,* ed. W.A. Wright (Cambridge: Cambridge UP, 1904), p. 231.

[38] Worcester, *The Boke of Noblesse,* p. 9.

[39] Gerard Legh, *The Accedens of Armory* (1562; repr. London, 1597), fol. 13.

[40] *An Apologie,* Sig. D3ᵛ.

[41] See Wallace T. MacCaffrey, *Elizabeth I: War and Politics 1588-1603* (Princeton: Princeton UP, 1992), pp. 453ff.; see also R.B. Wernham, *The Making of Elizabethan Foreign Policy, 1558-1603* (Berkeley, Los Angeles and London: California UP, 1980), passim.; John Guy, *Tudor England* (Oxford and New York: Oxford UP, 1988), pp. 439ff.

[42] *An Apologie,* Sig. D4.

[43] See Dominic Baker-Smith, 'Inglorious glory': 1513 and the Humanist Attack on Chivalry" in *Chivalry in the Renaissance,* ed. Anglo (see above, note 22), p. 135.

[44] Samuel Daniel, *The Civil Wars,* II. stanza 130, ed. Lawrence Michel (New Haven: Yale UP, 1958), p. 312.

[45] Paul N. Siegel, "Shakespeare and the Neo-Chivalric Cult of Honor", *The Centennial Review,* 8 (1964), p. 43.

[46] Hubert Languet, *The Correspondence of Sir Philip Sidney and Hubert Languet,* edited by S.A. Pears (London, 1845), p. 138.

[47] Quoted by MacCaffrey, *Elizabeth I: War and Politics,* p. 516.

[48] What Shakespeare intended by the allusion to Essex is an unresolved puzzle. Was it a provocative reminder of Essex's popularity? or a warning of his ambitions? or was it, as Annabel Patterson suggests (*Shakespeare and the Popular Voice* [Cambridge, MA and Oxford: Blackwell, 1989], p. 87) a 'well meant' attempt at mediation between the queen and her general? Since the play was presumably written before Essex had disgraced himself in Ireland, the latter suggestion does not seem plausible. Given the unreliability of the Chorus as a commentator (see Andrew Gurr, ed., Introduction to *King Henry V* [Cambridge: Cambridge UP, 1992], pp. 6-16) it would seem more likely that Shakespeare was making a discreetly ironic comment on militaristic values by comparing one well known model of chivalric honour with another.

[49] Jonathan Dollimore, "Critical Development: Cultural Materialism, Feminism and Gender Critique, and New Historicism", in *Shakespeare: a Bibliographical Guide,* ed. Stanley Wells (Oxford: Clarendon Press, 1990), p. 414.

[50] T.W. Craik, ed., Introduction to *King Henry V* (London and New York: Routledge, 1995), p. 3.

[51] P.M. Handover, *The Second Cecil: The Rise to Power 1563-1604 of Sir Robert Cecil, later first Earl of Salisbury,* (London: Eyre & Spottiswoode, 1959), p. 187.

[52] Handover, p. 222; Robert Lacey, Robert, *Earl of Essex: An Elizabethan Icarus,* (London: Weidenfeld & Nicholson, 1971), p. 290.

[53] The standard work on Shakespeare and war is Paul Jorgensen, *Shakespeare's Military World,* (Berkeley and Los Angeles: California UP, 1956). For an important recent discussion of Shakespeare's treatment of militarism see Steven Marx, "Shakespeare's Pacifism", *Renaissance Quarterly,* 45 (1992), pp. 49-95.

[54] Arthur F. Kinney describes "Invisible Bullets" as "perhaps the most important and surely the most influential essay of the past decade in English Renaissance cultural history" (*Rogues, Vagabonds and Sturdy Beggars: A New Gallery of Tudor and Stuart Rogue Literature,* ed. Kinney (Amherst, MA: Massachesetts UP, 1990), p. 1.

[55] Stephen Greenblatt, *Shakespearean Negotiations: The Circulation of Social Energy in Renaissance England* (Oxford: Clarendon Press, 1988), pp. 41; 56.

[56] On Greenblatt's rhetorical strategies, analogical method and flexible treatment of texts see Tom McAlindon, "Testing the New Historicism", *Studies in Philology,* 92 (1995), Fall issue.

[57] Steven Marx, "Holy War in *Henry V*", unpublished paper read at the annual conference of the Shakespeare Association of America, Albuquerque, 1994.

[58] John F. Danby, *Shakespeare's Doctrine of Nature: A Study of 'King Lear'* (London: Faber & Faber, 1961), pp. 81-101.

[59] Harriss, *Henry V,* (note 14 above), p. 24.

[60] Lander, *Conflict and Stability in Fifteenth-Century England.* Lander describes Henry as "a bigot of near-heroic mould whose intense religiosity equalled only his intense legalism over feudal property rights" (p. 58).

[61] C.T. Allmand, "Henry V the Soldier, and the War in France" in *Henry V,* ed. Harriss, p. 129. Cf. Lander, who writes of 'the obsessive character of his kingship' (*Conflict and Stability,* p. 208).

[62] For discussion of Pauline allusions in Henry IV see J.A. Bryant, "Prince Hal and the Ephesians", *Sewanee Review,* 67 (1959), pp. 204-19; D.J. Palmer, "Casting off the Old Man: History and St Paul in Henry IV", *Critical Quarterly,* 12 (1970), pp. 267-83. See also Robin Headlam Wells, *Elizabethan Mythologies: Studies in Poetry, Drama and Music* (Cambridge: Cambridge UP, 1994), pp. 44-62.

[63] *The Oldcastle Controversy: Sir John Oldcastle, Part I and the Famous Victories of Henry V,* Revels Plays edn., ed. Peter Corbin and Douglas Sedge (Manchester and New York: Manchester UP, 1991), p. 175.

[64] *Holinshed's Chronicles,* 3.66.

[65] See Headlam Wells, *Elizabethan Mythologies,* pp. 6-7 and passim.

[66] Pierre de La Primaudaye, *The French Academie* (London: 1586), p. 743.

[67] *The Mirrour of Maiestie: or, The Badges of Honovr* (1618), facsimile copy ed. Henry Green and James

Croston (London:, 1870), Sig. F2. The beehive analogy is a commonplace in classical, medieval and Renaissance political writing (see J.H. Walter's notes on 1.2. in his Arden edition of *Henry V*, p. 22). As Andrew Gurr has shown in the *Education of a Christian Prince*, which Shakespeare is known to have used when he was writing *Henry V*, Erasmus uses the beehive analogy to caution the prince against the temptation to enlarge his territories—see "*Henry V* and the Bees' Commonwealth", *Shakespeare Survey*, 30 (1977), pp. 61-72.

[68] George Puttenham, *The Arte of English Poesie*, ed. by Gladys Dodge Willcock and Alice Walker, (Cambridge: Cambridge UP, 1936), p. 6.

[69] In the *Boke of Noblesse* William Worcester says that the labours of Hercules "were written in a figure of a poesy for to courage and comfort alle noble men of birthe to be victorious in entreprinses of armes" (p. 21).

[70] Puttenham follows Horace (*Ars poetica*, 391-401) in representing Orpheus, together with Amphion, as the founder of civilisation, see *The Arte of English Poesie*, p. 6). But in *The Arte of Rhetorique* (ed. G.H. Mair (Oxford: Clarendon Press, 1909) Thomas Wilson ascribes this role to Hercules (Sig. Avii). In the famous pacifist essay "Dulce bellum inexpertis" Erasmus refers to Hercules as the founder of war. See *The 'Adages' of Erasmus*, (see above, note 31),. p. 317.

[71] See Dust, *Three Renaissance Pacifists*.

[72] Introduction to *Henry V*, (note 17 above), pp. xvii-xviii.

[73] *The Education of a Christian Prince*, (note 67 above), p. 209.

[74] See Theodor Meron, *Henry's Wars and Shakespeare's Laws: Perspectives on the Law of War in the Later Middle Ages* (Oxford: Clarendon Press, 1993), p. 27ff.

[75] Introduction to *Henry V*, (note 19 above), pp. 34-8.

[76] Anne Barton, 'The King Disguised: Shakespeare's *Henry V* and the Comical History' in *The Triple Bond: Plays, Mainly Shakespearean, in Performance*, ed. Joseph G. Price (University Park and London: Pennsylvania State UP, 1975), pp. 92-117.

[77] *The Waning of the Middle Ages*, p. 73.

[78] Introduction to *Henry V*, (note 19 above), p. 32.

[79] Robert Ashley, *Of Honour*, ed. Virgil B. Heltzel (San Marino, Ca.: The Huntington Library, 1947), p. 30.
[80] On Mercury as a symbolic representative of peace, government and control see Douglas Brooks-Davies, *The Mercurian Monarch: Magical Politics from Spenser to Pope* (Manchester: Manchester UP, 1983), p. 2; see also Edgar Wind *Pagan Mysteries in the Renaissance* (London: Faber, 1958), p. 91n2. On his thieving habits see the Homeric *Hymn to Hermes;* see also Ovid, *Metamorphoses*, II.685ff.; II.815ff.

[81] Graham Bradshaw writes brilliantly on what he calls 'dramatic rhyming' in *Henry V* in *Misrepresentations: Shakespeare and the Materialists* (Ithaca and London: Cornell UP, 1993), pp. 63-80.

[82] St Augustine of Hippo, *Of the Citie of God*, trans. J. Healey (London, 1610). For this point I am indebted to Janet M. Spencer, 'The Execution of Justice and the Justice of Execution: Criminalizing Wars of Conquest in *Henry V*', unpublished paper read at the annual conference of the Shakespeare Association of America, Albuquerque, 1994.

[83] *The Education of a Christian Prince* (above, note 67),. pp. 252-3.

[84] See above note 7.

[85] *The Waning of the Middle Ages*, p. 68.

[86] One of the most persuasive analyses of charismatic heroism and its dangerous power is Joseph Conrad's: see Robin Headlam Wells, '"The question of these wars': *Hamlet* in the New Europe" in *Shakespeare in the New Europe*, ed. Michael Hattaway, Derek Roper and Boika Sokolova (Sheffield: Sheffield Academic Press, 1994), p. 105. Emrys Jones discusses charismatic heroism in *Scenic Form in Shakespeare*, Oxford: Clarendon Press, 1971. A theatre audience, says Jones, is a "charmed crowd": just as a crowd can turn law-abiding citizens into credulous barbarians, so intelligent, civilized people become susceptible in the theatre to feelings which in other circumstances they would probably disown (pp. 6; 132).

[87] Charles Plummer, ed., Introduction to Sir John Fortescue, *The Governance of England* (London: Oxford UP, 1885), p. 8.

[88] John Keegan, *The Mask of Command* (London: Jonathan Cape, 1987), pp. 312-3; 350.

[89] See Eugene M. Waith, *The Herculean Hero in Marlowe, Chapman, Shakespeare and Dryden*, London: Chatto & Windus, 1962.

Source: "*Henry V* and the Chivalric Revival," in *Shakespeare and History*, edited by Holger Klein and Rowland Wymer, The Edwin Mellen Press, 1996, pp. 119-49.

Tragedies

No Spectre, No Sceptre: The Agon of Materialist Thought in Shakespeare's *Julius Caesar*

Stephen M. Buhler, *University of Nebraska-Lincoln*

Postremo cur sancta deum delubra suasque
discutit infesto praeclaras fulmine sedes,
et bene facta deum frangit simulacra suisque
demit imaginibus violento volnere honorem?

(Lucretius, *De rerum natura* 6.417-20: Lastly, why
does he shatter holy shrines of the gods, and
even his own illustrious habitations, with the fatal
thunderbolt, why smash finely-wrought images
of the gods and rob his own statues of their
grandeur with a violent wound?)[1]

In *Julius Caesar,* Shakespeare depicts a cosmological
as well as a political struggle. The correspondential
order of things is manipulated on all sides of an increasingly bloody conflict, and the downfall of one
faction occurs when its members stop manipulating
that order and begin, partly and then thoroughly, to
credit it. For that reason alone the play lends itself
well to criticism of what might be called "naive Till-
yardism."[2] A workable argument along such lines
would be similar to the one offered in the above passage. Lucretius asks why, if Jove desires to command
reverence and to reinforce pious practices, he would
so often destroy the sites associated with that piety
with his own thunderbolts; a cultural materialist might
ask why, if Shakespeare indeed wanted to affirm the
validity of the cultural edifices reinforcing the dominant ideology, he would so often leave major components of these constructs in ruins.[3]

Without becoming the dominant discourse of our time,
critical approaches such as those advanced by Jonathan
Dollimore in *Radical Tragedy* have themselves now
come under nearly as strong an attack as Tillyard's
once had. In a recent study of the skeptical in Shakespeare, Graham Bradshaw distinguishes between "dogmatic" and—in something of a pre-emptive strike aimed
at Dollimore's work—"radical" modes of skepticism.
He equates the former with "the terminal, materialistic
nihilism of a Thersites, Iago, or Edmund"; this list
could also include Cassius, whose skepticism is
grounded in Epicurean philosophy. "Radical" skepticism is described as self-reflexive: it "turns on itself—
weighing the human need to affirm values against the
inherently problematic nature of all acts of valuing."[4]
The radical nature of this skepticism further problematizes belief as well, for in the examples of Edmund and
of Cassius we see skeptics repenting. Bradshaw,
though, does not account for the disturbing hollowness that marks these returns to more conventional
values and beliefs. The unsettling effect does not stem

from any lack of sincerity or even dramatic credibility,
but rather from the impotence and ineffectuality that
accompany the characters' penitence. Edmund's remorse comes too late to save Cordelia or ultimately
Lear himself. In his return to what Lucretius terms the
antiquae religiones (5.86), the old superstitions, Cassius
has emulated his Stoic friend too well. He has not
"tried to be better" than his professed philosophy would
permit, as some critics have alleged, but has rather
abandoned its principles, acting upon erroneous judgments of events as a result. In his own suicide Brutus
repays Cassius' tribute in kind.

The correspondential order receives less than simple
affirmation in *Julius Caesar* and the play consequently
participates in what has been described as anti-essentialist strains at work in Renaissance culture. I cannot
agree with the accusation that critics such as Dollimore
are guilty of anachronism when they attach the term
materialism to such strains of thought. John D. Cox
has suggested that in the intervening centuries "philosophical materialism" has been identified with critiques
of political culture: to apply the term with all its modern associations to the Renaissance is anachronistic
and misleading.[5] But while the term itself may not have
had wide currency in the period, the ideas the term
represents and their "modern" associations are not as
inappropriate as Cox contends. Materialist philosophies
were openly considered in the Renaissance and were
judged both upon their supposed and actual political
ramifications and upon the kind of challenges they
presented to established social orders.[6]

Julius Caesar engages fully with the classical and
Renaissance debates over philosophical materialism and
its political import. It does so not only through its
depiction of Cassius, the play's professed materialist,
but also through its portrayal of Brutus, his political
ally and philosophical adversary whose idealism contributes to the failure of the tyrannicides' cause. The
classical heritage of political philosophy is a powerful
presence in *Julius Caesar,* and the tension and friendship which exist between the Stoic Brutus and the
Epicurean Cassius provide both sources of that power
and bases for the play's analysis of power. Two important studies of the play, by David C. Green and
Robert S. Miola, neglect to point out fully the political
importance of these philosophical allegiances. What
results in Green's case is a Tillyardian assurance that
"Shakespeare respects the monarchical authority which
Caesar for him represents." Miola provides the more
sophisticated view that "no trustworthy source of

sovereignty arises" in the play, but he still hears the political debate as only "a confusing cacophony of claims and counterclaims."[7] The choice, however, is not merely one between naive order and problematic chaos, or between dominant ideology and polyvocal, heteroglossic subversion: there are strictly discernible voices in the political culture of Shakespeare's age and the historical period depicted in the play. *Julius Caesar* permits us to hear their counsel and to see the possible results of following or rejecting those policies.

James R. Siemon has noted that the play "fosters analysis and interpretation," most notably of the macrocosmic portents, "to a degree far beyond that encouraged in any other of the early plays,"[8] and he points to Cassius' shifting reinterpretations of the storm in 1.3 as a crucial if "disconcerting" instance of the play's intellectual provocation. Siemon, though, sees Cassius as wavering between different readings which nevertheless are similarly grounded in a faith that these prodigies can "clearly reveal their 'true cause'" and show themselves to be "not arbitrary events but iconic signs" (p. 127). In this reading the play focuses upon an inconstancy and arbitrariness in such icons of which Cassius himself is unaware. But as an Epicurean, Cassius would be very mindful of precisely this question of the arbitrary nature of cosmological correspondences, and Shakespeare— following his Plutarchan sources—highlights Cassius' philosophical affiliations. Much of the play's success in placing correspondential schemes under scrutiny is due both to this character's initial insistence on such questioning and to his ultimate abandonment of the interrogative project.

II

Shakespeare and his contemporaries learned about the Epicurean analysis and rejection of the *polis* and its claims to validation through both natural and supernatural arguments from a variety of sources, both sympathetic and critical. In the former camp one finds Lucretius' *De rerum natura,* which explores not only Epicurus' scientific theories but their foundation in the sage's efforts to keep aloof from the state and from state religion, and the *Lives of the Eminent Philosophers* compiled by Diogenes Laertius, who concludes his survey with a dogged defense of the much-maligned philosopher. Critics who nonetheless provide a wealth of often-accurate detail about Epicureanism include Cicero, himself a player in the events depicted by Shakespeare, and Plutarch, who constantly reminds his readers of the philosophical affiliations of the principal conspirators, Cassius and Brutus. Along with these widely available—and widely read—classical sources, Shakespeare had more contemporary reasons to be interested in the skeptical analysis of religion and its relation to political power. The playwright alludes to these reasons at the end of

Act 2, scene I of *Julius Caesar,* after Brutus has agreed to join and to lead the conspiracy.

All the other self-declared tyrannicides have left, when the aged and ailing Caius Ligarius visits the resolved Marcus Brutus. In playing tribute to his newly-acknowledged leader, Ligarius directs the following simile at Brutus: "Thou, like an exorcist, hast conjured up / My mortified spirit" (2.1.323-24).[9] The precise terms of the compliment here are Shakespeare's alone, and do not appear in the Plutarchan original, *Brutus* II. In the witty praise of Ligarius there is more than a hint of problematization and outright criticism of Brutus' character and of the political scene in Rome. As Stephen Greenblatt has reminded us in connection with *King Lear,* exorcism was not only a highly suspect practice to a great many of Shakespeare's contemporaries, but a profoundly unsettling one as well. Commentators such as Samuel Harsnett, in his *Declaration of Egregious Popish Impostures,* as he justified Protestant suspicion and skepticism, may have been operating on the tactical assumption that "[t]o glimpse the designing clerical playwright behind the performance [that is exorcism] is to transform terrifying supernatural events into a human strategy."[10] Greenblatt further argues that "acknowledging theatricality kills the credibility of the supernatural" in ways beyond the polemicist's control, in ways that often "unsettle all official lines" of denominational and factional authority (pp. 109, 128). A crucial point of contention in *Julius Caesar* is control over the systems of interpretation which recognize what is and is not supernatural validation. While the polemicist might paradoxically lose control in trying to insist on making such distinctions, the dramatist gains power by examining the struggle over interpretive control. Central to this struggle is the intellectual rivalry between friends and allies: Cassius, the Epicurean scoffer at portents, and Brutus, the Stoic believer in the organic integrity of the cosmos, and therefore in divination.[11]

Mark Rose has discussed the epithet *exorcist* in the context of the play, and deftly traces its impact on the rest of the passage with Ligarius: all the imagery involving decrepitude and disease follows as a consequence of the term. Can Brutus, as exorcist, heal the body politic by casting out the spirit of Caesar or will he invoke—indeed reinscribe—that spirit? With his now impolitic sympathies for the last strong man, Ligarius seems to be thinking as much of the spirit of Pompey as his own spirit being revived, and might therefore intend fully his use of the term *conjured.* As Rose succinctly states this aspect of the problem: "'exorcise' can mean to raise a spirit as well as to expel one. . . . Is Brutus an exorcist or a conjurer?"[12] In many ways, however, the distinction is an artificial one in Shakespeare's time as well as in the play: all exorcisms and conjurations were subject to empirical and moral skepticism. One consequence of the epithet "exorcist" is to call into question Brutus' desirability and suitability as a leader. Throughout Shakespeare's plays as well as in the "official" Protestant religio-political view, the term suggests self-deception at best and charlatanism at the worst.[13] One may wonder, then, what kind of legitimacy could possibly accrue to a regime taking its direction from Brutus. Yet another consequence is more expansive: the term contributes to the play's questioning of all authoritative structures and personalities in the late Republic.

This is, after all, a play in which Cassius very deliberately endeavors to show how both the powerful and those who challenge that power can "transform terrifying supernatural events" into political strategies. It is also a play in which the title character himself comments on the frailty of human bodies and minds, "Men are flesh and blood, and apprehensive" (3.1.67), using the later term much as Theseus does in *A Midsummer Night's Dream* when he distinguishes between what Imagination may "apprehend" and what Reason "comprehends" (5.1.6-7).[14] Caesar's words glance here at the very foundations of the Epicurean critique of political culture: the *polis* is supported by the cult of the gods, which is in turn sustained by humankind's apprehensive dread of its own mortality. The Epicurean solution recommends cultivating a detached and skeptical stance toward the *polis*. The Shakespearean program enables us to investigate the interrelations between philosophical allegiances, political *praxis,* and the skeptical detachment which, paradoxically, can link the first two most effectively.

The *De rerum natura* is a prime source here, and Shakespeare's use of Lucretius in Cassius' disquisition on thunder should come as no surprise. In borrowing from this work the playwright strengthens his character's involvement with Epicurean thought by incorporating elements from the classical world's most famous surviving work on Epicureanism, a work which is itself a product of the time that *Julius Caesar* depicts. Lucretius' skepticism toward the supernatural origin of thunder is connected with his sense that from the outset the cult of the gods was a justification for political society. The gods not only help to explain mysterious natural events, but also extend the long arm of punitive law into the next world, into the supernatural realm: this is, Lucretius suggests, the reason why religion has spread over great nations—"*causa deum per magnas numina gentis / pervulgarit*" (5.1161-62).[15] So Lucretius does more than urge his readers to distinguish between the true attributes of divinity and those attributes which are the products of what in another context Epicurus calls "vain imaginings."[16] He also cautions his readers against believing in the civic ramifications of the cult of the gods. By their very nature ataraxic and impassive, the gods cannot possibly be angry at supposed violations of the natural and civic order; one may reject, then, any claim (or curse) that such anger will follow such a disturbance.

Cassius acts out Epicurus' defiance of the cult of the gods, as described by Lucretius. The *De rerum natura* proclaims that nothing could keep Epicurus from opposing Superstition: "*quem neque fama deum nec fulmina nec minitanti / murmure compressit caelum*" (1.68-69: neither fables of the gods could quell him, nor thunderbolts, nor heaven with menacing roar). Cassius continues in this vein, as he informs Casca:

> For my part, I have walk'd about the
>   streets,
> Submitting me unto the perilous night;
> And thus unbraced, Casca, as you see,
> Have bar'd my bosom to the thunder-stone;
> And when the cross blue lightning seem'd
>   to open
> The breast of heaven, I did present myself
> Even in the aim and very flash of it.
>
>   (1.3.46-52)

Casca is understandably shocked, having earlier confessed to Cicero his fear that the thunder indicates that humankind—including his own droll self—has been "too saucy with the gods" (1.3.11). He believes it to be the role and even the duty of humankind "to fear and tremble/When the most mighty gods by tokens send/Such dreadful heralds to astonish us." In response to Casca's pious dismay at his behavior, Cassius announces that such heralds need not be interpreted along the lines of Caesarian *pietas.* He demonstrates this by reading these signs as "instruments of fear and warning/ Unto some *monstrous state*" (70-71). I emphasize the last two words to call attention to Cassius' insistence on linking politics with ways of viewing and reading the spectacular. *Monstrous* here retains its full Latinate associations with "showing" and with the wondrous and portentous, along with its obvious utility for expressing Cassius' moral indignation; *state* in this context refers to Rome as a political entity.

After revising the customary and corresponding reading of celestial events, Cassius can then attribute all interpretations of the night's prodigies to the exigencies of human polity. Caesar himself is, in Cassius' estimation,

>   a man
> Most like this dreadful night
> That thunders, lightens, opens graves, and
>   roars
> As doth the lion in the Capitol—
> A man no mightier than thyself, or me,
> In personal action, yet prodigious grown,
> And fearful, as these strange eruptions are.
>
>   (1.3.72-77)

There is, Cassius implies, nothing inherently meaningful or ominous in these events, nothing which should inspire divine awe; no supernatural agency is needed to explain them. Similarly, Caesar's remarkable successes do not betoken divine favor since all-too-human factors suffice as explanation. Cassius suggests that an understanding of how nature truly operates, and of how human nature is prevailed upon, can keep one from being mystified by even the most dramatic of celestial or political phenomena. He thus provides a clearer philosophical rationale for his earlier sneer at *"immortal* Caesar" and his dismay that "this man/Is now become a *God*" (1.2.60 and 115-16).[17] Already seeing the cult of the gods and absolute forms of authority as sharing a common origin, Cassius readily perceives Caesar engaged in a latter-day application of the same principles. While this might strike us as unlikely, since Caesar's credulity rivals that of Gloucester in *Lear,* one should note that Caesar (like Gloucester) is very selective in his superstitions: those that are most aggrandizing are the ones he comes to hold most tenaciously.

III

At this point Cassius functions not only as an Epicurean scoffer, but also as a kind of proto-Harsnett, debunking Roman superstition and pointing out the political consequences of credulous belief.[18] Another conspirator, Decius Brutus, uses his own insight into the interworkings of religious and political authority in persuading Caesar to come to the Capitol. In an argument remarkable for its mediation between ancient beliefs and contemporary controversies, he interprets Calphurnia's dream in terms strongly reminiscent of the "old religion" in England before promising an imminent offer of royal power. Toward the blood issuing from Caesar's statue in the dream, Decius advises, "great men shall press/For tinctures, stains, relics, and cognizance" (2.2.88-89). Caesar responds favorably to this ceremonial language and transfers credence from Calphurnia's alarmist response to the complaisance Decius Brutus advises. Cassius, though, loses the interpretive control that his co-conspirator practices upon Caesar and that he himself displays with Casca: he eventually comes to believe in the involvement of the supernatural in both physical and human events. This is suggested even by the context in which Cassius' rejection of the supernatural appears: before Cassius arrives on the scene, Cicero laconically observes that "men may construe things after their fashion,/Clean from the purpose of the things themselves" (1.3.34-35). Cicero's words imply that there is a determined and determinable purpose at work in these prodigies, although his composure in the face of these wonders can suggest as much the wryly skeptical observer as the man of firm faith.

Later on, as Cassius looks ahead to the battle at Philippi, he tells Messala of his newfound respect for divina-

tion: "You know that I held Epicurus strong,/ And his opinion; now I change my mind,/ And partly credit things that do presage" (5.1.76-78). After describing the departure of the auspicious eagles and the arrival of dire birds of ill omen at his camp, Cassius concludes that his army is "ready to give up the ghost" (88). Even his repeated insistence that he believes in all this but *partly* is undercut by the dramatic irony of his haunted language, which increasingly hints at the supernatural as well as the natural. He describes himself as "fresh of *spirit,* and resolv'd/To meet all perils very constantly" (90-91). In his address to Brutus before battle, he goes so far as to assert that "The gods to-day stand friendly" (93) to their cause. In short, Cassius is undergoing a reversion to the *antiquae religiones*. He is haunted not only by the oracular birds and the shifting language of transcendence, but also by his sense that he has come full circle upon the date of his birth, that his "life is run his compass" (5.2.25).

IV

In the dramatic logic of *Julius Caesar,* Cassius' newly superstitious turn of mind leads him directly to credit Pindarus' misinterpretation of the evidence, to believe that Titinius has been captured. One of the most important ways in which Shakespeare departs from Plutarch is in suggesting that Cassius' apostasy from Epicureanism leads to his fall into error and subsequent destruction. Cassius forgoes the philosophy's emphases on natural explanations and on direct observation. Plutarch, less attuned to the philosophy, enjoys something of a grim joke at Cassius' and Epicureanism's expense when Cassius, the persistent believer in empirical knowledge, suffers from weak vision and misinterprets what occurs.[19] But Shakespeare ascribes the misinterpretation directly to Pindarus, thereby showing Cassius' mistake to be *not* relying on his own perceptions, *not* observing the tenets of his erstwhile philosophy. Despite his grief-stricken cry, Cassius has not lived to see his best friend taken before his face (5.2.35); deviating from his initial principles, he acts in accordance with what he has been told, rather than what he himself has observed. As Messala subsequently puts it in the same scene, such an error "show[s] to the apt thoughts of men/The things that are not" (68-69). Cassius' acceptance of the supernatural order initiates the credulity that culminates in his suicide. That death turns the tide of battle against the originally anti-superstitious defenders of the Republic.

Nearly two decades ago Jean Auffret noted some of the discrepancies between Plutarch's presentation of Cassius and his philosophy and Shakespeare's own portrayals.[20] Commenting on the character's defiance of the thunderous omens, Auffret saw the connection between this scene and Lucretius' discussion of thunder and its psychological effects. While Auffret takes the philosophic background seriously, he does not consider fully the politics of that background. He takes the Lucretian passage out of its strongly political context and allows the old tradition that Lucretius fought and finally succumbed to melancholic madness to color his reading both of the passage and of Cassius' character. In Auffret's reading of the scene, "Cassius gets infected with the terror he describes—and so does Lucretius—, but his hysteria prepares us for his breakdown at 4.3.92-106 [where Cassius admits to Brutus how deeply pained he is that they are at odds] and his suicide" (p. 71). The "breakdown" Auffret detects in Act 4 is, rather, a demonstration of the strong friendship Cassius feels toward Brutus, and of the strong devotion with which Cassius accepts the Epicurean privileging of friendship. As we have seen, Cassius is far from "hysterical" in the scene with Casca; he effectively uses Epicurean skepticism to undermine political orders that claim legitimacy on supernatural grounds. Shakespeare's attribution of this rhetorical strategy to an Epicurean character has more contemporary precedents as well, and these precedents often take advantage of the parallels between the Renaissance conception of the Epicure and of the Machiavel.

At first this seems a patently risible connection when one considers both Epicurus' and Lucretius' resolve to avoid the corridors of power, termed the *angustum iter ambitionis* (the narrow—petty and constricting—road of ambition) in the *De rerum natura* (5.1132). But the association between Epicure and Machiavel can be justified partly by the historical phenomenon of Epicureanism's popularity among the well-to-do and the powerful during the era which spanned the passing of the Republic and the foundation of the Empire.[21] Men of letters seemed particularly vulnerable. In addition to Lucretius' proselytizing, the Epicurean leanings (or at least training of Vergil and Horace) announce the philosophy's appeal. We can also see, in reaction, Cicero's tireless campaign against Epicureanism in works such as *De finibus* and *De natura deorum*. J. D. Minyard's comments in connection with Caesar and Epicureanism may also indicate Renaissance suspicions toward the philosophy: "Acceptance of Epicurean mechanical materialism and disregard of Epicurean moral conclusions would give someone a great field for action in the world, freeing him from fear and laying on him no obligations except to his own rationalizing sophistication" (p. 18). Such a suspicious attitude provides the rationale for Cicero's references to Epicureanism throughout the oration *In Pisonem*.[22]

V

It was often thought in the Renaissance that those who embraced Epicurean skepticism toward divine and political orders did so for their own selfish ends. Such characters were regularly depicted on the English stage: the name of the Machiavel, at this time, was Legion.

So Cassius might be dismissed as philosophically and dramatically suspect, as he draws upon a marginalized body of thought to further his own ends. He freely translates the signs which seem to warn against Caesar's death as calling for Caesar's murder, and in a move which presages Iago's confidences to the audience in *Othello,* he freely admits that he is "inventing" the public call for Brutus to take action against Caesar. In Plutarch the letters which appeal to Brutus are authentic (*Brutus* 9.3-4); in the play Cassius not only pens the appeals himself but has one planted upon the iconic statue of "old Brutus," the founder of the Republic. Shakespeare's Cassius comes close to Iago in his stage-management of perception and most closely reminds us of the ensign in the lines, "If I were Brutus now and he were Cassius, / He should not humor me" (1.2.314-15). But we also find in the Renaissance—such as with the exposure of fraudulent exorcisms—a sense that anyone who believes in supernatural explanations for purely natural events joins the lunatic, the lover, and the poet in being of imagination all compact. So Cassius' rigorous debunking of the burgeoning Caesarian cult and his turning its tactics upon itself need not have been viewed with horror. The rich ambivalence of the character and his philosophy can be found in these famous lines: "The fault, dear Brutus, is not in our stars, / But in ourselves, that we are underlings" (1.2.140-41). While the final clause suggests personal ambition and a personal *animus* against Caesar, the rest of the sentence not only conforms to Epicurean resistance toward astral determinism but also accords nicely with Christian—especially Reformed Christian—dismissals of astrology. At least where political and religious values other than one's own are concerned, philosophical skepticism is acceptable, and its historical bases can often be explored with impunity.[23]

In addition, Cassius' suicide in response to the supposed capture of his friend is philosophically as well as psychologically consistent. After his heartfelt expressions (in 4.3) of pain at Brutus' criticisms of him, and of joyful relief when he and Brutus are reconciled, it comes as no surprise that Cassius considers friendship such a life-and-death issue. In fact the importance of Brutus' friendship to Cassius personally as well as politically leads Cassius to defer to Brutus' oft-mistaken judgments and misperceptions. But the bond between friends is also of prime value in Epicurus' ethics: what replaces the political relationship that exists between and among human beings in the wake of the Epicurean renunciation of the *polis* is exactly friendship. Admirers of Epicurus point to this as evidence that the philosophy is not solipsistic or hedonistic; critics make similar concessions or point out the apparent inconsistency between a commitment to one's own personal pleasure and a concern for that of others.[24] Failure to recognize the centrality of friendship in the Epicurean scheme of things has not only led

Auffret to judge Cassius as psychologically unstable in his devotion to Brutus, but has also led Allan Bloom to see Cassius in these scenes as being in open conflict with Epicureanism:

> The man whose doctrine insisted that all action is selfish turns out to be the truest and most sentimental of friends. He even dies for friendship. . . . This is no true Epicurean; it is rather a man who has schooled himself in a teaching which ran counter to a fund of common goodness and ordinary political weakness within him. In Cassius, we see the case of a man who thinks worse of himself than he ought to and does so because he has accepted a philosophy which depreciates, discourages, and explains away what is good in him. In the final crisis, this arbitrary shell breaks, and the true man emerges. But it is too late. [25]

Such pronouncements reflect both an unshakable prejudice toward Epicurean philosophy and a determined unwillingness to consider it either on its own terms or in the terms set out in Shakespeare and his sources. Despite Bloom's own training in philosophy, there is little sense here of the complexity at work in the classical philosophical traditions. Instead we have a reductive, even monolithic model of that tradition in which the moral and political significance of a philosophy is determined and held in stasis by its adversaries. Certainly a glance at Diogenes Laertius' definition of the Epicurean sage—"And he will on occasion die for a friend"[26]—should restrain any surprise at Cassius' responses and any conclusion that the philosophy suppresses human good. Cassius is, after all, confronted by the impending loss of men for whom he cares deeply; he faces emotional estrangement from Brutus and responsibility for Titinius' capture. What has been described in these scenes as "Cassius' generosity of spirit"[27] is not only a matter of personality but also of philosophical principle. Shakespeare shows that what is most admirable in Cassius is sustained by his philosophy; what results in his and his compatriots' destruction is precipitated by a fall from the Epicurean "faith."

VI

Brutus attributes Cassius' death to Caesar's spirit, which "walks abroad, and turns our swords/In our own proper entrails" (5.3.95-96). It is not only Ligarius' "mortified spirit" which Brutus conjures up. While "Caesar's spirit, ranging for revenge" is first invoked by Antony (3.1.270), Brutus himself invokes the preconditions for the eventual triumph of both "Caesar" and the entire correspondential construct:

> Between the acting of a dreadful thing
> And the first motion, all the interim is
> Like a phantasma, or a hideous dream.

> The genius and the mortal instruments
> Are then in council, and the state of man,
> Like to a little kingdom, suffers then
> The nature of an insurrection
>
> (2.1.63-69)

And Brutus is the one who eventually calls the apparition he had seen before at the battle at Philippi by Caesar's name. Despite the stage direction of the First Folio—"*Enter the Ghost of Caesar*"—the play leaves open to question the identity and ontology of the apparition which Brutus sees. While Plutarch judges both that the apparition was the responsibility of Caesar's "great guardian-spirit [daimon]" and that "the phantom that appeared to Brutus showed that the murder of Caesar was not pleasing to the gods," he also has the image describe itself as Brutus' own "evil genius."[28] Shakespeare follows this account ("Thy evil spirit") and suggests something of a physiological explanation by having Brutus share in the bad eyesight Plutarch assigns to Cassius. Brutus, the only one to see the spectre, identifies the apparition only in the final scene, after blaming Cassius' suicide on that mighty spirit and before ordering Strato to help him in taking his own life. Despite Cassius' skeptical opinion expressed earlier, that in conjuration the name of "Brutus will start a spirit as soon as Caesar" (1.2.147)—that is, never—Brutus carries out his early wish to "come by Caesar's spirit" (2.1.169) even though he must "dismember Caesar" and dismember his own faction and cause in the process. We should qualify David Bevington's understanding that Brutus is here "victimized by the unshakable flaw of rebellion [which] must force aside the very institutions of legitimate power that it had hoped to preserve" [29] with a realization that in Shakespeare's play neither Brutus nor Cassius can shake off their rivals' claims to supernatural bases for power. They fall victim to the politically-grounded cult of the gods Lucretius militates against in the passages Cassius echoes and enacts.

Perhaps the most crucial deviation from Plutarch's account is the deletion of any hint of Cassius' skeptical reading of Brutus' apparition. In the *Brutus,* just before he comments upon "the superstitious fears which were gradually carrying even Cassius himself away from his Epicurean doctrines," Plutarch describes how Cassius tries to assuage his friend's fears that they have transgressed the limits of the political, natural, and supernatural orders:

> "In our sect, Brutus, we have an opinion that we do not always feel or see that which we suppose we do both see and feel. . . . For the mind of man is ever occupied; and that continual moving is nothing but an imagination."[30]

This attitude, too, has an analogue in the *De rerum natura.* Working from the super-subtle images it received from the distant, detached, ataraxic gods, the human mind was able to embellish and intensify the impressions, through the power of the imagination:

Quippe etenim iam tum divom mortalia saecla egregias animo facies vigilante videbant, et magis in somnis mirando corporis auctu. his igitur sensum tribuebant propterea quod membra movere videbantur vocesque superbas mittere pro facie praeclara et viribus amplis.

(5.1169-74: The truth is that even in those days the generations of men used to see with waking mind, and still more in sleep, gods conspicuous in beauty and of marvellous bodily stature. To these therefore they attributed sensation, because they appeared to move their limbs and to utter proud speech in keeping with their splendid beauty and vast strength.)[31]

Lucretius suggests, moreover, that anxiety over a shakily established order gave strong impetus for these attributions, since this explanation is prefaced by his account of the earliest foundations of political society.

While Plutarch permits Cassius to retain no small measure of Epicurean skepticism toward transcendent orders even at this juncture, Shakespeare's compression of events allows for little in the way of recusancy. The only signs of resistance are his claims to place only partial credence in the omens and his sharing with Brutus a farewell "for ever, and for ever" (5.1.116, 119), still confident, perhaps, in his philosophy's belief that death is the cessation of consciousness and existence. While Brutus here may be flirting with his friend's philosophy, his earlier encounters with Epicurean materials show his distance from its principles. Brutus' insistence that by making Caesar the conspirators' sole target they will "carve him as a dish fit for the gods" (2.1.179) hints at the crimes of Tantalus. Epicurean philosophy interprets both the crime and punishment of Tantalus in ways which make him the type of the superstitious individual. In one version of the myth he serves his son Pelops as a meal to the gods out of desperation at not having enough (or anything special enough) to entertain them properly.[32] In another version, much noted by Epicureans, Tantalus is eternally threatened by a rock hanging over him—that is what prevents him from satisfying either hunger or thirst.[33] Brutus argues that the manner and singularity of Caesar's death must be pleasing to the gods, and he is more than ready to perceive supernatural expressions of their apparent disfavor. He and Cassius slip into superstitious belief, dragging their friends and allies down with them. Skepticism seems to have passed out of Cassius altogether and to have possessed—at least in part—the playwright and the audience. In this "spirit" we may even read Brutus' Stoicism as the source for his Senecan taste in bloody-minded, vengeful, and psychologically-driven ghosts;[34] in the same spirit we may raise serious questions about the philosophical orientations of other characters as well.

It is Antony, we recall, who first invokes Caesar's spirit directly in his soliloquy after the death of Caesar. We can relate this invocation to similar ones in Shakespeare's Henriad: Richard's and Carlisle's incantatory "hauntings" of Bollingbroke and his descendents with the spectre of the deposed rightful king.[35] Antony is able to recall Caesar's ceremonial rejection of the crown—with advantages—and use it against Caesar's supplanters. This tactical skill parallels Richard's ability to use the relinquishing of the crown against his enemies and Cassius' previous ability to manipulate appearances to politic ends. Interestingly, Caesar opines early on that "Cassius has a lean and hungry look," and suggests that we associate Antony with the "fat/Sleek-headed" men who sleep (well into the morning) the sleep of the sensually indulgent. Cassius is here identified with the asceticism of authentic Epicurean teaching and Antony with the Epicure of popular imagination.

While adapting his Plutarchan source, Shakespeare may well be echoing Horace's assessment of himself as a fat, sleek pig of Epicurus' herd.[36] Antony, we soon learn, is no mere sensualist. It is Antony who, with Octavius, shows chillingly ataraxic detachment in negotiating which rivals and allies are to be executed and which spared; the two strongest pillars of the triumvirate partake aggressively in the role of Machiavel. We might also note the "friendship" Antony invokes in this scene is far removed from the depth of personal feeling for which Cassius ultimately dies. Yet Cassius does recognize Antony as a kindred spirit, if an enemy: he judges Antony to be a "shrewd contriver" (2.1.158), an estimation grandly fulfilled in Antony's manipulation of the crowd—using relics, significantly, to maximum effect. "Let it work" is Antony's own laconic, Iago-like comment on the mob violence he has unleashed (3.2.260) while triumphantly overshadowing Cassius' own machinations. This aspect of Antony's Epicureanism should be added to our understanding of the Epicurean elements at work in *Antony and Cleopatra* that have been observed by both Barbara Bono and Hilary Gatti.[37]

VII

Shakespeare shares in his age's widespread mistrust of what motivates those who reject a correspondential relation between the cosmic and political orders. Through the drama of both personality and philosophy, however, he repeatedly ponders the validity of that relation: *Julius Caesar* does not echo Plutarch's belief that in these events we can clearly see that "Heaven wish[ed] to remove from the scene the only man who stood in the way"[38] of change from republican to imperial governance. A similar complexity informs *King Lear*. Edmund may pay the price for sneering at all bonds of sympathy and then repent, albeit ineffectually. But Edgar, like the exorcists Harsnett wishes to expose, still has to invent proofs of such bonds for the benefit of his disillusioned father. Through its encounters with Plutarch and Lucretius, *Julius Caesar* shows "Caesar's spirit" extending the religious *realpolitik* reportedly expressed by James I as "no bishop, no king" to the genuinely radical skepticism of "no spectre, no sceptre." Decius Brutus' ability to link in Caesar's mind the "tinctures, stains, relics, and cognizance" of Calphurnia's dream with the promise of a kingly crown—and all as a ploy to lure Caesar to his death—is but one instance of Shakespeare pondering these political and metaphysical equations.

We can detect Renaissance versions and analogues of what our age calls cultural materialism not only in fissures in the correspondential facade. They can be found clearly in the ideas considered, debated, and dramatized in texts written and read during the period. The history of ideas, then, can lead us to a better grasp of historicized ideas, of the shifting social and political significances invested in intellectual and philosophical systems. The political materialist strain of Epicurean thought, which held a sometimes horrified fascination for readers and writers in the Renaissance, demands that some discrimination be made between Bradshaw's "materialistic nihilism" and skeptical inquiries into the grand scheme of correspondences that Tillyard thought was the age's World Picture. That same philosophical strain also indicates that *materialism,* with much of the term's more recent meaning, was part of the age's political consciousness as well as its unconscious.

Notes

[1] All quotations from Lucretius are taken from the Loeb Classical Library edition, translated by W. H. D. Rouse and revised by Martin Ferguson Smith (Cambridge, Mass., 1982).

[2] E. M. W. Tillyard, *The Elizabethan World Picture* (London, 1943), has been a prime *locus* of debate as well as a target. Even student guides written by traditional scholars have questioned Tillyard's contentions, as in Isabel Rivers, *Classical and Christian Ideas in English Renaissance Poetry* (London, 1979), p. 2: "the blending of these elements did not create one uniform world picture."

[3] See, for example, Jonathan Dollimore, *Radical Tragedy: Religion, Ideology, and Power in the Drama of Shakespeare and his Contemporaries* (Chicago, 1984), esp. pp. 189-217. Alan Sinfield addresses the political significances at work in stagings as well as interpretations of *Julius Caesar* in *Faultlines: Cultural Materialism and the Politics of Dissident Reading* (Oxford, 1992), pp. 10-21.

[4] Graham Bradshaw, *Shakespeare's Scepticism* (Brighton, 1987), p. 39. Similar—but far less nuanced—criticisms of cultural materialist readings have been offered by Robin Headlam Wells, *Elizabethan Mythologies: Studies in Poetry, Drama, Music* (Cambridge, 1994), pp. 12-15.

[5] John D. Cox, *Shakespeare and the Dramaturgy of Power* (Princeton, 1989), pp. x-xi. David Cressy has detected other kinds of "anachronism and dislocation" in *Radical Tragedy* stemming from its theoretical foundations in Foucault's often ahistorical work; see "Foucault, Stone, and Social History," *English Literary Renaissance* 21 (1991), 125.

[6] Cox observes that Augustinian Christianity often resisted claims of transcendentally-sanctioned political authority. Yet he is not always attuned to the problematics of Augustine's views on political authority, since what Cox calls "Christian political realism" often translates into quietism. Epicureanism's original strictures against involvement with political culture are themselves profoundly quietist.

[7] David C. Green, *"Julius Caesar" and Its Source,* Salzburg Studies in English Literature 86 (Salzburg, 1979), p. 20. Robert S. Miola, "*Julius Caesar* and the Tyrannicide Debate," *Renaissance Quarterly* 39 (1985), 288.

[8] James R. Siemon, *Shakespearean Iconoclasm* (Berkeley, 1985), p. 125.

[9] All references to Shakespeare's plays are taken from *The Riverside Shakespeare,* ed. G. Blakemore Evants *et al.* (Boston, 1974).

[10] Stephen Greenblatt, *Shakespearean Negotiations* (Berkeley, 1988), p. 107. John L. Murphy considers some of the more pragmatic political ramifications of the events Harsnett chronicles in *Darkness and Devils: Exorcism and "King Lear"* (Athens, Ohio, 1984), pp. 153-70.

[11] For classical applications of the principle, see Thomas G. Rosenmeyer, *Senecan Drama and Stoic Cosmology* (Berkeley, 1989), p. 79: Seneca's interest in divination is related to Stoicism's conservative view that "the world is full of signs guaranteed by the benevolence of the gods."

[12] Mark Rose, "Conjuring Caesar: Ceremony, History, and Authority in 1599," *English Literary Renaissance* 19 (1989), 297.

[13] Greenblatt, pp. 114-16, briefly discusses exorcism in *The Comedy of Errors, Twelfth Night,* and *All's Well That Ends Well.* While Harsnett's *Declaration* was not published until 1603, the cases which he describes date from 1585-1586.

[14] The connection between Caesar's and Theseus' language has been drawn by Bradshaw, p. 41. Since his study avoids considerations of philosophical backgrounds, it touches on skepticism or materialism in *Julius Caesar* only briefly.

[15] This assertion that punishment can only curb and channel violent ambition—not extirpate it—provides another possible link between Epicurean and Augustinian political theories.

[16] From Epicurus' Principal Doctrine 30; see Diogenes Laertius, *Lives of the Eminent Philosophers,* 10:149. In the translation by R. D. Hicks for the Loeb Classical Library edition (Cambridge, Mass., 1925), the phrase is rendered as "illusory opinion."

[17] Miola, p. 275, argues that "Shakespeare takes pains to corroborate Cassius' opinion of Caesar's unnatural usurpation." I would suggest, though, that Cassius reacts not so much to Caesar's "unnaturalness," but rather to Caesar's claims to supernatural power and significance.

[18] Rose, pp. 292 and 295, suggests striking analogies between the militant republicans in Shakespeare's Rome and the militant reformers in Shakespeare's London: virtually all of Caesar's political opponents, most notably Cassius and Casca, express themselves in antiritualistic terms. Siemon, p. 143, also sees the Reformist "desire to reveal certain cultural and social patterns as both historically real and yet ultimately arbitrary in nature" reflected in *Julius Caesar.* He does not, however, observe similar desires motivating characters *within* the play or appearing as part of the philosophic temper of the age the play represents.

[19] See the excerpts from Sir Thomas North in *Shakespeare's Plutarch,* ed. T. J. B. Spencer (Baltimore, 1964), p. 159; in the Loeb edition of Plutarch's *Parallel Lives,* vol. 6, trans. Bernadotte Perrin (Cambridge, Mass., 1918) the passage is found in *Brutus* 43.3. Green, p. 106, also notes this difference between Shakespeare and Plutarch.

[20] Jean Auffret, "The Philosophical Background of *Julius Caesar,*" *Cahiers Élisabéthains* 5 (1974), 69-71.

[21] This popularity has been examined by J. D. Minyard in his monograph, *Lucretius and the Late Republic* (Leiden, 1985), esp. pp. 18-20 and 33-70.

[22] Cicero, *In Pisonem* 28: "Audistis profecto dici philosophos Epicureos omnis res, quae sint homini expetendae, voluptate metiri; rectene an secus, nihil ad nos aut, si ad nos, nihil ad hoc tempus; sed tamen lubricum genus orationis adulescenti non acriter intellegenti et saepe praeceps." (You surely have heard it said that the Epicurean philosophers evaluate by pleasure all the things for which men strive. Whether that is truly said is nothing to us, or if it be anything to us, it is nothing to the present matter. But for all that it is a slippery kind of message for a youth of no sharp wit and always a dangerous one.) I have used the C. F. W. Mueller edition of Cicero's *Scripta,* (Leipzig, 1893-1908), vol. 3, part 2, 189. For the polemical function of "Epicureanism" in this oration, see Phillip DeLacy, "Cicero's Invective against Piso," *Transactions and Proceedings of the American Philological Association* 72 (1941), 49-58.

[23] I am reminded of how Greenblatt, p. 65, formulates both Elizabethan and twentieth-century attitudes: "There is subversion, no end of subversion, only not for us." But I am more skeptical than he is of both the will-to-containment (in Shakespeare, his contemporaries, and ourselves) and its supposed effectiveness in squelching analyses of one's own culture and political structure.

[24] Phillip Mitsis, *Epicurus' Ethical Theory: The Pleasures of Invulnerability* (Ithaca, 1988), pp. 98-101; source texts include Diogenes Laertius 10.118 and 120, and Cicero, *De finibus* 1.20.65-69. Charles Wells has connected Cassius' fierce devotion to friendship with Epicurean precepts; see *The Wide Arch: Roman Values in Shakespeare* (New York, 1992), p. 81.

[25] Allan Bloom, with Harry V. Jaffa, *Shakespeare's Politics* (New York, 1964), pp. 103-04. As Darryl J. Gless sharply challenges Bloom's reading of the play, he also notes that, in spite of "relentless invocations of the classics, Bloom's convictions receive neither documentation nor specific argument"; see "*Julius Caesar,* Allan Bloom, and the Value of Pedagogical Pluralism," in *Shakespeare Left and Right,* ed. Ivo Kamps (New York, 1991), p. 187.

[26] Diogenes Laertius, 10.120; translation by Hicks.

[27] Vivian Thomas, *Shakespeare's Roman Worlds* (London, 1989), p. 57.

[28] These passages appear in Plutarch, *Caesar* 69.2 and 69.5 in vol. 7 of the Loeb *Parallel Lives* (London, 1919). North, generally following Amyot, describes *genius* as "great prosperity and good fortune" in Caesar's case, and as "ghost" and "ill angel" in the case of Brutus' apparition. See *Shakespeare's Plutarch,* pp. 99-100; and Plutarch, *Les vies des hommes illustres,* trans. Jacques Amyot, ed. Gérard Walter 2 vols. (Paris, 1951), 2:485-86.

[29] David Bevington, *Tudor Drama and Politics* (Cambridge, Mass., 1968), p. 249.

[30] In this case, I have quoted the clearer rendering in Perrin's translation of *Brutus* 39.3; but see also *Shakespeare's Plutarch,* p. 152.

[31] *Shakespeare's Plutarch,* pp. 149-50; *Brutus* 37.1-3.

[32] Servius Grammaticus, *Commentarius in Aeneidos* 6.603. Miola, p. 285, argues that the "dish fit for the gods" passage in *Julius Caesar* is an expression not only of piety but ultimately of fear, since it continues the play's descent "into a strange, unfathomable universe, wherein characters continually misconstrue and misunderstand [the gods'] wishes."

[33] Lucretius, *De rerum natura* 3.978-83:

> Atque ea nimirum quaecumque Acherunte profundo prodita sunt esse, in vita sunt omnia nobis. nec miser inpendens magnum timet aere saxum Tantalus, ut famast, cassa formidine torpens; sed magis in vita divom metus urget inanis mortalis

> (And assuredly whatsoever things are fabled to exist in deep Acheron, these all exist for us in this life. There is no wretched Tantalus, as the story goes, fearing the great rock that hangs over him in the air and frozen in vain terror; rather it is in this life that the fear of gods oppresses mortals without cause).

See also Cicero, *De finibus* 1.18.62, where Cicero's Epicurean interloculor, Torquatus, alludes to Tantalus and his fearful stone.

[34] Marjorie Garber has suggested that the "Ghost of Caesar" has both a generic source in Senecan tragedy and an intradramatic basis in Brutus' psychological

state; see *Dream in Shakespeare: From Metaphor to Metamorphosis* (New Haven, 1974), p. 50. A further connection might be made with the Ghost of Tantalus in *Thyestes* 107-21: his very presence, prompted by a Fury, "infects" his descendents' house; that infection is signalled by omens. Thyestes recalls these signs, especially the late, hesitant dawn, when he discovers how Atreus has taken vengeance upon him (1035-36). See Rosenmeyer, pp. 136-59, on "Sickness, Portents, and Catastrophe" in Senecan drama, especially pp. 140-42.

[35] As in the persuasive reading by Harry Berger, Jr., in *Imaginary Audition* (Berkeley, 1989), pp. 66-73.

[36] Horace, *Epistolae* 1.4.16.

[37] Barbara Bono, *Literary Transvaluation: From Vergilian Epic to Shakespearean Tragicomedy* (Berkeley, 1984), esp. pp. 173-83. Hilary Gatti, "Epicurean Elements in Elizabethan Drama," a paper given at the Sixteenth Century Studies Conference in Tempe, Arizona, October 1987.

[38] *Brutus* 47.4. North, convinced that Rome "could no more abide to be governed by many lords" (that is, could no longer stand republicanism), declares that divine intervention was meant to keep Brutus from becoming the "only absolute governor" in the wake of the Republic's fall; see *Shakespeare's Plutarch,* p. 165.

————————————

Source: "No Spectre, No Sceptre: The Agon of Materialist Thought in Shakespeare's *Julius Caesar*," in *English Literary Renaissance,* Vol. 26, No. 2, Spring, 1996, pp. 313-32.

King Lear: The Tragic Disjunction of Wisdom and Power

Paul A. Cantor, *University of Virginia*

What is the price of Experience do men buy
  it for a song
Or wisdom for a dance in the street? No it
  is bought with the price
Of all that a man hath his house his wife
  his children.

        —William Blake, *The Four Zoas*

I

Many critics regard *King Lear* as the greatest of Shakespeare's plays and also as his most tragic. Indeed, many would claim that it is the most tragic play ever written. And yet, curiously, in most critical accounts of the play it is difficult to see why we should even regard it as tragic at all, whether we are using an Aristotelian or a Hegelian definition of tragedy. In the view of most critics, Lear is basically a pathetic old man, vain and foolish, rash in his judgment and incapable of controlling his emotions—and he is all these things from the very beginning of the play.[1] This characterization seems to preclude viewing Lear on the Aristotelian model of a tragic hero, as someone raised above the ordinary level of humanity, except in the most conventional sense of his social status. Moreover, in the view of the majority of critics, the play charts the growth of Lear's wisdom, as he learns the emptiness of worldly glory and comes to embrace the love of his daughter Cordelia as the one true value in his life.[2] As consoling as this vision of Lear's education through suffering may be, it leaves us with a sense that the dramatic issues of the play can in the end be fully resolved. But if that is the case, then Lear cannot be in a tragic situation as Hegel defines it, that is, he is not caught in the clash of two legitimate principles, a situation from which there is no simple escape, no matter how much he learns. In concrete terms, critics generally do not view Lear as caught between genuinely conflicting loyalties, his political and his personal obligations; on the contrary, in their reading of the play, Lear would simply be right to abdicate the throne and retire into private life.

In short, in the view of most critics, at the beginning of the play Lear is simply mistaken in both his attitudes and his actions, and the course of the drama should in effect teach him the error of his ways.[3] This reading of *King Lear* makes it an edifying play, but it drains it of its tragic power by oversimplifying Shakespeare's understanding of the complexities of political life. Ultimately, this kind of reading threatens to reduce *King Lear* to a form of melodrama, a story of the straightforward conflict of clearly identifiable and separable forces of good and evil, in which the outcome is tragic only in the sense of being disastrous for the main characters. Above all, many critics end up undermining the stature of King Lear as a tragic figure by suggesting that with a little more wisdom he could have avoided the catastrophes in his life. Critics may go on speaking of the grandeur of Shakespeare's achievement and of Lear as a character, but if the standard readings of the play were correct, a more honest reaction would resemble that of Groucho Marx, when, in a meeting almost as improbable as Lear's encounter with Tom o' Bedlam, he was attempting to explain the play to T. S. Eliot:

> I said the king was an incredibly foolish old man, which God knows he *was;* and that if he'd been *my* father I would have run away from home at the age of eight—instead of waiting until I was ten. . . . I pointed out that King Lear's opening speech was the height of idiocy. Imagine (I said) a father asking his three children: Which of you kids loves me the most?[4]

I am sure that most critics would, as Eliot evidently did, reject this characterization of *King Lear,* but the question remains: is there anything in their readings of the play that would allow them to counter this view of its hero? As convinced as critics are of the greatness of *King Lear* as a work of art, they evidently have a hard time giving an account of the play that explains that greatness. In the delightfully insouciant way in which Groucho projects himself into the world of *King Lear,* he unwittingly reveals the problem with many interpretations of the play. In our eagerness to identify with Shakespeare's characters, we run the risk of bringing them down to our own level. The Lear described in many critical essays sounds less like Shakespeare's monarch than the middle-class recreations of Lear in the nineteenth-century fiction of writers like Balzac and Turgenev.[5]

From this perspective, the turning point in the criticism of *King Lear* was Harry Jaffa's brilliant analysis of the opening scene of the play, in which he shows that Lear has a sophisticated scheme in mind for dividing up his kingdom, one in which he hopes to secure the bulk of his land for Cordelia, together with an alliance with the House of Burgundy.[6] As Jaffa shows, Lear's plan, far from being the product of senility, is, if anything, too clever for his own good. I will not go over the details of Jaffa's subtle analysis; suffice it to say here that he points the way to understanding Lear as a tragic figure. The king is not behaving like a doddering old fool in the opening scene, but attempting a remarkable political feat: to pass on his royal inheritance in a way that will avoid the defects of following the conventional rules of primogeniture. Lear fails in his plan, but in Jaffa's view, he fails nobly and hence tragically. Jaffa's reading is true to the text of the play and also to the impression Lear in fact makes on stage in the opening scene. Far from coming across as a pathetic old man, Lear projects a commanding presence in his first appearance, dominating the action and, for all his errors, towering over the other figures on the stage.

In another essay on *King Lear,* I have tried to extend Jaffa's analysis, analyzing the process of education the king undergoes when he loses power.[7] Like Jaffa, I try to show that Lear's errors are not, so to speak, *vulgar* errors; they do not simply proceed from stupidity or lack of thought. I argue that, in tragic fashion, Lear's failings are bound up inextricably with his greatness. Precisely what makes him powerful as a king incapacitates him for seeing the truth about himself and his kingdom. In part this outcome results from his being surrounded by hypocrites and flatterers, who reinforce his self-image and his confidence in the justice of his rule. But as Shakespeare presents it, the problem runs deeper. Lear's errors are a kind of occupational hazard of his kingship. In order to exercise command, he must project an aura of authority, and this need in turn dictates that he have a high opinion of himself, thus fatally tempting him to overestimate his capabilities in such tasks as disposing of his kingdom.

The powerfully tragic vision of *King Lear* is rooted in Shakespeare's understanding of political life, its limitations and its demands. The play turns on what I will call the disjunction of wisdom and power. When Lear is in command as king, he is tragically cut off from the wisdom he needs to rule justly. He gains access to this wisdom only when he loses power, but that process in turn incapacitates him for further rule. In this essay, I will examine largely the second half of *King Lear,* and trace what happens to Lear when he learns the truths to which his position as king initially blinded him. Acts 4 and 5 are crucial to a full understanding of Lear as a tragic figure, but most critics fail to follow the subtle turns Shakespeare portrays in the king's attitudes, because they do not think through the implications of Lear's radically changed view of the world. In many accounts of the play, Lear's education is presented as an unequivocal good, as if there were nothing problematic about his experience. These accounts in effect present private life as simply superior to public life, suggesting that Lear has everything to gain and nothing to lose when he is thrust out of power. Without questioning Lear's legitimate gains in wisdom in the course of the play—indeed I have dis-

cussed them at length elsewhere—I want to explore here the possibility that *King Lear* is tragic precisely because of the complexity of the process Shakespeare is portraying in the king's development. Lear's gains in wisdom come at the expense of his initial grandeur and hence his ability to rule. In the unsettling logic of the world of *Lear,* the characters pay a terrible price for the wisdom they gain, and none more so than Lear himself.

II

Lear's process of education reaches its crisis in act 3, especially with his encounter with Edgar disguised as Tom o' Bedlam, and the insights he gains and even articulates as a result are indeed remarkable. It is tempting but far too simplistic to treat Lear's shattering experience in act 3 as a kind of civics lesson or a seminar at a school of public administration. However much Lear grows in wisdom in act 3, he could not simply translate that wisdom back into a form of rule. For one thing, the wisdom Lear gains in act 3 has a questionable character. In trying to articulate what Lear learns, it is easy to distort the nature of his experience, presenting in an organized and coherent form insights that in fact come to Lear in fits and starts. Lear gains many insights in act 3, but we cannot grasp what he is going through if we do not see how deeply unsettling and disorienting these truths are for him, shattering his self-image and his whole view of humanity. However disturbing it may be to admit, the Lear of act 3 is in no condition to walk back into the court and resume command of his kingdom. What is precisely characteristic of Lear in act 3 is that he cannot hold together the two images of human nature he observes in Edgar as first Tom o' Bedlam and then as the "noble philosopher" (3.4.172), and that is the deepest reason why his experience on the heath at least momentarily unfits him for rule. Lear is agonizingly wrenched back and forth between images of the lowest degradation of the human body and images of the highest development of the human soul. Obsessed with his insights into the extremes of humanity, Lear understandably loses sight of the middle range, but that is precisely the realm where politics ordinarily takes place.[8]

Shakespeare repeats this pattern in Lear's appearances in act 4. The juxtaposition of scenes 6 and 7 shows Lear recapitulating his encounter with the lower and higher sides of human nature, and once again he is unable to integrate his widely diverging images of humanity. Encountering the blind Gloucester in act 4, scene 6, Lear dwells obsessively on the animal side of man and above all woman:

> Behold yond simp'ring dame,
> Whose face between her forks presages
>   snow;

That minces virtue, and does shake the
 head
To hear of pleasure's name—
The fitchew nor the soiled horse goes to't
With a more riotous appetite.
Down from the waist they are Centaurs,
Though women all above;
But to the girdle do the gods inherit,
Beneath is all the fiends'.

                    (4.6.118-27)[9]

This vision is the equivalent of Lear's earlier view of the "bare, fork'd animal" in Tom o' Bedlam (3.4.107-8), as he effaces the distinction between human being and beast. Because Lear is convinced that all human beings are consumed by sexual appetites, he refuses to see anyone punished anymore for violating the conventional rules of sexual conduct:

I pardon that man's life. What was thy
 cause?
Adultery?
Thou shalt not die. Die for adultery? No,
The wren goes to't, and the small gilded fly
Does lecher in my sight.

                    (4.6.109-13)

In Lear's refusal to support conventional marriage contracts, we see what the political consequences would be of the new doctrine of natural justice he learns during the storm on the heath. As ruler he would no longer have any legitimate basis for punishing any of his subjects or enforcing any law. Once Lear views all human beings as alike in their animal urges, for him the difference between legally constituted authorities and criminals dissolves: "see how yond justice rails upon yond simple thief. Hark in thine ear: change places, and handy-dandy, which is the justice, which is the thief?" (4.6.151-54). Though Lear once embodied the majesty of the law in his own person, he loses faith in all authority once he concludes that conventional appearances hide an inner corruption:

Thorough tatter'd clothes small vices do
 appear;
Robes and furr'd gowns hide all. Plate sin
 with gold,
And the strong lance of justice hurtless
 breaks;
Arm it in rags, a pigmy's straw does pierce
 it.
None does offend, none, I say none.

                    (4.6.164-68)

Speeches such as this continue Lear's impulse in act 3 to reject a conventional view of political reality in the name of what is natural to human beings. In particular he displays the same hostility to clothing because it hides the truth about humanity.[10]

Lear's speeches in act 4, scene 6 are very powerful and express some fundamental truths about politics; Edgar is moved to comment on the king's words: "O, matter and impertinency mix'd, / Reason in madness" (4.6.174-75).[11] But before we are tempted simply to equate Lear's viewpoint here with Shakespeare's, we need to look more critically at what the king says. Shakespeare deliberately builds an error into Lear's reflections in this scene: "Let copulation thrive; for Gloucester's bastard son / Was kinder to his father than my daughters / Got 'tween the lawful sheets" (4.6.114-16). These lines should give us pause; Lear's preference for the natural over the conventional child is clearly as mistaken as his earlier tendency to accept conventional professions of love over his true daughter's natural feelings. Like Lear's two auditors at this moment, Edgar and Gloucester, we know how misguided the king's praise of Edmund is. Modern interpreters seem disposed to follow Lear in his thoroughgoing disillusionment with politics and human nature in this scene,[12] but Shakespeare took pains to prevent us from wholly identifying with Lear's one-sided view of man as beast. Even Lear momentarily recognizes the diseased character of his imagination in this scene (4.6.130-31).

Indeed, Lear's jaundiced view of women as all "centaurs" is immediately contradicted by Cordelia's appearance in the next scene. Lear's reunion and reconciliation with his true daughter is one of the most beautiful and moving scenes Shakespeare ever wrote. Act 4, scene 7 provides the dreamlike answer to Lear's nightmare vision of humanity in act 4, scene 6. From his obsession with human carnality in act 4, scene 6, Lear moves to a vision of human spirituality. He is barely aware of his own body in this scene ("I will not swear these are my hands," [4.7.54]) and in his eyes Cordelia has transcended the physical level: "You are a spirit, I know" (4.7.48). By trying to kneel to Cordelia, Lear is finally willing to reverse their relative positions of power. In act 1, scene 1, Cordelia could not express her true love for her father because his power over her stood in the way, threatening to obliterate the distinction between a sincere profession of devotion and the hypocritical and self-serving flattery of her two sisters. Now that Lear has lost his power and admits to being nothing but "a very foolish fond old man" (4.7.59), Cordelia can no longer be accused of any base motives in her love for her father. In rallying to his cause, she, like Kent and the Fool, has nothing to gain and everything to lose. Free of the conventional political roles that complicated and distorted their relationship earlier, Lear and Cordelia are finally able to be simply father and daughter.

Indeed in view of the reversal of their customary positions in this scene—the fact that Lear is willing to kneel to Cordelia—it is arguable that they are liberated even from the conventional roles of parent and child, and face each other as human being to human being in a condition of equality.[13] Lear and Cordelia move beyond any kind of conventional moral accounting, as she rejects his seemingly justified assumption of guilt for their breach:

> *Lear:* I know you do not love me, for your
>   sisters
> Have (as I do remember) done me wrong:
> You have some cause, they have not.
> *Cordelia:*   No cause, no cause.
>
> (4.7.72-74)

In act 4, scene 6, Lear rejected conventional morality out of contempt for human nature and on the basis of the lowest possible view of human beings as indistinguishable from beasts. In act 4, scene 7, Lear and Cordelia rise above conventional moral considerations just as they appear to rise above the level of their bodies.

Shakespeare's juxtaposition of act 4, scene 6 and act 4, scene 7 conveys a deeper wisdom than Lear is able to encompass in either scene alone: the two scenes embody alternative and complementary visions of what is natural to humanity. It is a sad commentary on our times that we are all too eager to acknowledge that Lear is talking about what is natural to the human condition in act 4, scene 6. But on reflection, we can appreciate that in some sense of the term the behavior of Lear and Cordelia in act 4, scene 7 is also a paradigm of nature, now thought of in terms of human perfection, rather than some kind of lowest common denominator of humanity. The simplicity of their dialogue in this scene, the fact that they speak in brief, declarative sentences, above all, the fact that they are finally speaking *to* each other, no longer *at* each other, lends what can be called a natural quality to their interaction here. Neither act 4, scene 6 nor act 4, scene 7 tells the whole truth about the human condition, and to accept one at the expense of the other is to risk falling prey to an overly cynical or an overly idealistic understanding of human nature. Shakespeare was guilty of neither.

However contradictory the images of humanity presented in act 4, scene 6 and act 4, scene 7 may be, the two scenes have one thing in common: in both Lear effectively rejects political life. In act 4, scene 6 his cynical view of humanity undermines all claims to legitimate authority by political figures. In act 4, scene 7 his idealistic view of the human condition leaves all ordinary political considerations far below. The juxtaposition of these two scenes thus points to an important truth about politics. In act 4, scene 6 Lear talks about human beings as if they were all body and no spirit; the result of this view of human nature as purely animal is to eliminate every possible justification for political action. In act 4, scene 7 Lear talks about

himself and Cordelia as if they were all spirit and no body; the result of this contrary view of human nature as purely spiritual is to eliminate every need for political action; Lear and Cordelia pass beyond the world of good and evil. The conjunction of these two scenes suggests that either of these views is one-sided and hence incomplete. As the bifurcation of vision throughout acts 3 and 4 of *King Lear* suggests, man is a composite being, a perplexing mixture of body and spirit. It is precisely for this reason that human beings require political life: to deal with the problems created by the tension between body and spirit. Neither animals nor angels require politics.

We can now see more fully why Lear's gains in wisdom in acts 4 and 5 come at the expense of his ability to rule. At the beginning of the play Lear is the captive of many illusions about himself and his world, but his very overestimation of his own powers is what gives him the aura of authority he needs to command his subjects. The Lear of act 4, scene 6 has learned a great deal about his own limitations, but the result is that he has developed a universal contempt for political authority. He has lost all faith in the ability of political action to improve the human condition, or even to control its worst excesses of passion. The Lear of act 4, scene 7 is simply indifferent to politics; having achieved a spiritual communion with Cordelia in an intensely private moment, he no longer has any interest in public life. Failing to integrate his antithetical visions of humanity in act 4, scene 6 and act 4, scene 7, Lear is unable to grasp the fundamental truth that the political authority he despises and rejects in act 4, scene 6 would be necessary to protect the fragile spirituality he comes to cherish in act 4, scene 7.

III

Lear's loss of his ability to rule is not simply to be traced to the change in his opinions about politics in acts 3 and 4. Shakespeare also focuses on the matter of Lear's temperament. The Lear of act 1, scene 1 is headstrong and rash; those are not the virtues of a philosopher, but they are the qualities of the kind of man who often succeeds in getting other men to obey his will. When we say that Lear has a kingly temperament, we mean in part that he is a spirited man, capable of what he himself calls "noble anger" (2.4.276). His capacity for indignation is one of the forces that attaches him to political life and fuels his ability to get things done. Lear's tendency to identify his personal cause with justice pure and simple is unphilosophic and leads to many of his errors in judgment. Nevertheless, his pride and titanic overestimation of himself are also what makes an admirable man like Kent say that he can see authority written on Lear's face (1.4.26-30).

Thus the more Lear comes to think of himself as an ordinary man, sharing the weaknesses of his fellows, the less capable he becomes of inspiring their awe and hence their obedience. To be sure, Kent, the Fool, and Cordelia come to love Lear more in his defeat and humiliation, but that is precisely a private reaction on their parts and not the same as political loyalty. The Lear we see in the second half of the play has become temperamentally unfit to rule England. We must realize that Lear's learning in the play is not a purely intellectual process; it is not a matter of Lear picking up a textbook in political science and calmly reading about what went wrong with his administration. Lear's education in self-knowledge is a soul-wrenching experience. It rips asunder the deepest fibers of his being. For Lear's titanic ego to be shaken, he must be painfully humiliated, and that is the terrifying process we witness in acts 1 and 2, as his wolfish daughters strip away every shred of dignity he has left. With all his pride, Lear resists this process:

> You see me here, you gods, a poor old
> man,
> As full of grief as age, wretched in both.
> If it be you that stirs these daughters'
> hearts
> Against their father, fool me not so much
> To bear it tamely; touch me with noble
> anger,
> And let not women's weapons, water-drops,
> Stain my man's cheeks!
>
> (2.4.272-78)

Lear realizes that nothing less than his manhood is at stake in this scene, and he futilely wishes that he had the power to act like a manly king and take vengeance on all those who have slighted his dignity. When Lear is confronted by the cruelty of his daughters, he is torn between the contradictory emotions of anger and grief. His anger is rooted in his pride as a king, and makes him ashamed of the grief he feels as an ordinary human being. As Lear himself recognizes, the tension he experiences between wanting to express his grief as a wronged father and the need he feels as a king to suppress any such public display of weakness eventually causes his mind to snap: "O Fool, I shall go mad" (2.4.286).

As much as we are moved by seeing what Lear gains in the process of his education, we should not blind ourselves to what he loses. The Lear of act 4, scene 7 is a broken man, his pride in himself and in his regime shattered. He is a wiser man in this scene, more capable of love, and in many important respects this Lear is preferable to the one we saw in the opening scene of the play. But not in all respects. Unlike the Lear we saw in act 1, scene 1, the Lear of act 4, scene 7 could not walk into any room and just by his regal bearing command the instant respect of any human being in range of his voice. A king who expects to be obeyed cannot go around proclaiming: "I am old and

foolish" (4.7.84). We may admire Lear for this frank admission of his weakness, but we must also recognize its consequences for his ability to rule in the future as anything other than a figurehead. The Lear of act 4, scene 7 is completely without anger; as the Doctor says: "the great rage, / You see, is kill'd in him" (4.7.77-78). It may be a relief for us as audience to see this calm descend upon Lear, but we must recognize that with his rage, something else is for the moment killed in Lear: his pride. And, bound up as it is with his spiritedness, Lear's pride was the source of his greatness as well as of his failures as a king. Up to this point in the play, even in his madness, Lear has displayed an acute awareness of everything going on around him. If anything, he has been too ready to see affronts to his dignity in his subjects' actions, but that hypersensitivity has been profoundly linked to Lear's concern for justice. In act 4, scene 7, he ceases to be aware of his surroundings; he even has to be reminded that he is in Britain (4.7.75). With Lear's "great rage" goes his "noble anger," and with that, his ability and even his desire to govern his kingdom.

In short, we must realize that Lear cannot absorb the kind of unnerving truths he learns about himself and remain the same man. The Lear we see in act 4, scene 7 is profoundly changed from what he was in act 1, scene 1. His newfound wisdom and self-awareness are purchased at the price of his original grandeur.[14] We may ultimately judge the result worth the exchange, but we should not deny that Shakespeare is confronting us with a kind of choice. Shakespeare's tragic world is profoundly disturbing to us. We do not like to think about the tragic disjunctions he presents. We would like to think that it is possible to be a powerful ruler and a wise man at the same time. Perhaps it is possible, and in the case of Henry V Shakespeare offers an example of a man who seems to unite wisdom and power (Prospero is another such case).[15] But even if it is possible, the conjunction of wisdom and power is surely not easy to achieve, and in *King Lear* Shakespeare most fully explores the problems of bringing the two together. When Lear is in power, he is blind to his own limitations, not just out of stupidity, senility, or simple error, but because, as Shakespeare shows, there is something in the very nature of kingship that blinds even and perhaps especially a successful ruler to fundamental truths about his situation. When Lear finally gains access to those truths, it is only through a process that disillusions him about politics in general and shatters the very spirit that made him a commanding figure. That is why *King Lear* is such a tragic play, perhaps the most profound of all tragedies. It offers no easy way out of Lear's dilemma. Shakespeare uncovers a deep and abiding tension between the preconditions of power and the preconditions of wisdom.

IV

The Lear we see in act 5 has recovered his sanity, but he is still a far cry from the regal figure we first saw in act 1. He has become totally absorbed in his private bond with Cordelia:

> Come, let's away to prison:
> We two alone will sing like birds i' th'
>   cage;
> When thou dost ask me blessing, I'll kneel
>   down
> And ask of thee forgiveness. So we'll live,
> And pray, and sing, and tell old tales, and
>   laugh
> At gilded butterflies, and hear poor rogues
> Talk of court news; and we'll talk with them
>   too—
> Who loses and who wins; who's in, who's
>   out—
> And take upon's the mystery of things
> As if we were God's spies; and we'll wear
>   out
> In a wall'd prison, packs and sects of great
>   ones,
> That ebb and flow by th' moon.
>
>   (5.3.8-19)

This is a beautiful speech, and we want to rejoice in Lear's newfound happiness with his daughter. But Lear here betrays his complete indifference to conventional politics; what once was his greatest concern has been reduced to the level of gossip, a mere matter of "who loses and who wins; who's in, who's out." Lear now looks down upon politics as a realm of merely transitory triumphs. He seems to have achieved a kind of philosophic detachment from life, which allows him to see human affairs as if from a contemplative height. But Lear's indifference to politics extends even to an indifference to his own freedom, and hence he seems happy to endure what formerly would have struck him as the ultimate humiliation: to be imprisoned by his enemies. Lear is now content to live like a bird in a cage; as attractive as this image may seem, there is something demeaning about it as well: the majestic lion of a king has been reduced to a tame house pet.[16] As if to remind us that Lear may be indifferent to politics but cannot escape its power, Shakespeare punctuates the king's lyrical fantasy with Edmund's curt and peremptory order: "Take them away" (5.3.19). We may applaud Lear's rising above his earlier conventional devotion to political life, but the fact is that his indifference to power in this scene is about to lead directly to the death of Cordelia. If basically decent men like Lear renounce political life, however justified they may be in their contempt for corruption in high places, no one will be left to defend the Cordelias of this world. Thus if Lear comes to understand the supreme worth of Cordelia, he cannot simply abandon

political life to men like Edmund, who will ruthlessly stamp out all that Lear legitimately has come to value in the realms that transcend politics.

It is thus characteristic of the complexity of the movement of *King Lear* that Shakespeare has Lear at least partially rediscover the value of political life just before his death. Lear does not go to the grave still believing that there is no difference between a human being and an animal; on the contrary, he powerfully asserts the superiority of Cordelia to other forms of life: "Why should a dog, a horse, a rat, have life, / And thou no breath at all?" (5.3.307-8).[17] Recapturing his sense of human excellence, the man who in act 4 could see no reason to punish any malefactor, returns in act 5 to his role as judge and executes the subordinate sent by Edmund to eliminate Cordelia: "I kill'd the slave that was a-hanging thee" (5.3.275). With his unique grasp of psychology, Shakespeare chooses just this moment for Lear to recapture a bit of his old pride and anger, and at the same time to recall his youth, as he responds to the confirmation of his surprisingly valiant deed: "I have seen the day, with my good biting falchion / I would have made them skip" (5.3.277-78).

This is a fascinating moment, as we finally get the briefest glimpse of the young King Lear. Nearing the end of his life, Lear thinks back presumably to the earliest days of his political career, remembering what he forgot in his plan for dividing the kingdom, that the ability to do justice must ultimately be backed up by the sword. Lear's execution of the man who killed Cordelia tells us as much about the nature of justice as his speeches about the hollowness of authority back in act 4, scene 6. It is not that his final act cancels out the truths he articulated earlier; it is only that his deeds bring out the partiality of his speeches. To get at Shakespeare's understanding of justice, we cannot identify it with any single statement by his characters, but must take into account the pattern of the whole play, both deeds and speeches.

The fact that Lear thinks back to his youth at the conclusion of the play provides a clue to its structure; as Edmund's line "The wheel is come full circle" (5.3.175) suggests, the end of *King Lear* harks back to the beginning. At the start of the play the British regime, like Lear himself, has grown old. At the end of the play, the regime renews itself. Like Lear recalling the powerful sword strokes of his youthful arm, the regime must get back in touch with its foundation in the ultimate guarantor of political right: military force. At the beginning of the play, as a result of Lear's peaceful reign and his unquestioned authority, his regime has lost touch with political reality and he himself thinks that he can maintain control even while turning military power over to his children. Act 5 takes us back to the brute facts of political life and reminds us that in the end the deepest political divisions can be settled if not healed only by war.

This consideration explains why the trial by combat of Edmund and Edgar figures so prominently in act 5. Edgar has an airtight legal case against Edmund and one might imagine that their conflict would be settled in a court of law, where a juridical process could establish Edmund's guilt unequivocally. But Shakespeare shows a more primitive form of justice, trial by combat, because the thrust of act 5 is to keep reminding us that angels may dispense with violence in settling their disputes, but human beings cannot. The point is not that might makes right; we have seen the limitations of that savage principle in the destruction of Cornwall, Regan, Goneril, and now finally Edmund, whose careers in evil all go to prove the self-defeating and self-destroying character of a purely low-minded conception of justice.[18] But what Edgar's resort to the sword shows is that right cannot be entirely divorced from might. It is not that the good cause always triumphs in battle, only that if the good cause is to triumph, it ultimately must be in battle (recall that Lear must resort to force in this scene as well).

Edgar has had to learn how to turn some of the weapons of evil men and women against them in order to protect what he values in life.[19] Starting the play as a naive young man, untutored in the deceptive ways of the world, Edgar has had to don one disguise after another in the course of the play to come to terms with the evil in the world. Though he remains almost comically scrupulous in dealing with his enemies,[20] the Edgar at the end of the play can at least no longer be called naive. When Edgar kills Edmund in combat he establishes his right to rule in the realm, and seems to have absorbed whatever was best in his enemy, much as Prince Hal does when he defeats Hotspur.

The fact that Edgar can stake out a claim to rule only with a sword reminds us of the violence at the basis of politics, and we have more confidence in the capacity of this temperamentally mild man to maintain political order once we have seen that he can answer the savagery of evil antagonists with some brute force of his own. But it would be a mistake to fall into a totally cynical reading of the end of *King Lear,* arguing that the good party has had to become as savage as the evil in order to overcome it. The Edgar at the end of the play is not the same Edgar we saw at the beginning, but he has not become an Edmund. In general, in the end the good characters maintain their distinction from the evil, in part because they have been spared the necessity of descending to the barbaric level of their antagonists by the fact that the evil characters have largely destroyed each other. Edgar and Albany never display the lust for power that is the hallmark of their counterparts Edmund and Cornwall.

At most they have learned the need for political action to counter the machinations of their enemies, but that means that they resort to morally dubious actions with a marked reluctance. Unlike Edmund, Edgar never takes pleasure in deceiving others, and he never glories in evil deeds. Hence the end of the play forms a sharp contrast to the beginning:

> *Albany:*   Friends of my soul, you twain
> Rule in this realm, and the gor'd state
>   sustain.
> *Kent:*   I have a journey, sir, shortly to go:
> My master calls me, I must not say no.
> *Edgar:*   The weight of this sad time we
>   must obey,
> Speak what we feel, not what we ought to
>   say:
> The oldest hath bourne most; we that are
>   young
> Shall never see so much, nor live so long.
>   (5.3.320-27)

At the beginning of *King Lear* we are in a world where many of the characters, though not all, are hungry for power; at the end we see characters who apparently cannot wait to hand over power to others. The course of the action has evidently been a sobering experience for decent men like Albany, Kent, and Edgar. No one of them is Plato's philosopher-king—Edgar perhaps comes closest—but they have developed some of his reluctance to rule. As Edgar acknowledges in the final lines, even his experience cannot match the journey Lear went through in the course of the play,[21] but the way in which he accepts rule as a duty imposed on him and not something he eagerly sought shows that he has come to share some of Lear's doubts about political life. Because of his consciousness of the limits of power, Edgar will presumably rule more moderately.

After a period of political chaos, we see a regime refounded at the end of *King Lear*. Like all regimes, its foundation may ultimately be traced back to an act of violence, but given the character of its founders, we may reasonably expect that it will not be a violent regime. All signs in fact point to the inevitability of entering a diminished and tamer world. The precondition for refounding the regime has been the elimination of the evil extremes of humanity who threatened all conventional order. But the extremes of good in Britain have been destroyed as well; Lear, Cordelia, and the Fool are dead, and Kent apparently does not have long to live. A political regime tends to compress the range of humanity, trying to force people into conventional molds, to moderate their passions, to move them toward a comfortable center. The world Edgar will rule will be a safer world, but it will be a world without Lear's grandeur or Cordelia's beauty. That is another way of saying that it will no longer be a heroic or a tragic world. The moderation—one might even say the mediocrity—of the characters left standing at the end of the play is the truest measure of the greatness of King Lear and the tragic nature of his story. No ending of a Shakespeare play captures more perfectly the fundamental contrast at work in tragedy between the ordinary human beings who are content to stay within the limits of the conventional world and the heroic souls who try to go beyond them.

Notes

[1] In his *Shakespeare Our Contemporary,* trans. Boleslaw Taborski (Garden City, N.Y.: Anchor Books, 1966), 130, Jan Kott makes explicit what many critics assume about Lear: "He does not see or understand anything. . . . Lear is ridiculous, naive and stupid."

[2] The classic statement of this view is to be found in A. C. Bradley, *Shakespearean Tragedy* (1904; rept. New York: Meridian Books, 1955), 258-60. See especially Bradley's attempt to state the moral of the play on p. 260: "The good are seen growing better through suffering. . . . The judgment of this world is a lie; its goods, which we covet, corrupt us. . . . Let us renounce the world, hate it, and lose it gladly. The only real thing in it is the soul, with its courage, patience, devotion. And nothing outward can touch that." For a similar view of *King Lear,* see G. Wilson Knight, *The Wheel of Fire* (1930; rept. New York: Meridian Books, 1957), 195-201, and Reuben A. Brower, *Hero and Saint: Shakespeare and the Graeco-Roman Heroic Tradition* (New York: Oxford University Press, 1971), 415. For a more recent statement of this position, see Barbara Everett's essay, "*King Lear*: Loving," in her *Young Hamlet: Essays on Shakespeare's Tragedies* (Oxford: Clarendon Press, 1989), 59-82.

[3] See, for example, Knight, who speaks of "the absurdity of the old King's anger" in the first scene, describes him as "cutting a cruelly ridiculous figure" and as "selfish, self-centered," and characterizes him as "a tremendous soul . . . incongruously geared to a puerile intellect" (*Wheel of Fire,* 161-62).

[4] Letter to Gummo Marx, June 1964, in Groucho Marx, *The Groucho Letters* (New York: Simon & Schuster, 1967).

[5] Knight says that *King Lear* "resembles a Hardy novel" (*Wheel of Fire,* 202). Shades of Groucho, Knight remarks: "It is, indeed, curious that so storm-furious a play as *King Lear* should have so trivial a domestic basis" (161). So curious that one might question whether the basis is really trivial or domestic.

[6] Harry V. Jaffa, "The Limits of Politics: *King Lear,* Act 1, Scene 1," in Allan Bloom, *Shakespeare's Poli-tics* (New York: Basic Books, 1964), 113-45. This essay was originally published in *The American Political Science Review* 51 (1957): 405-27. Briefly stated, Jaffa's thesis is that the intent of Lear's original plan was to give Cordelia the bulk of his kingdom (the middle portion), while giving Goneril the extreme northern and Regan the extreme southern portion, regions their husbands already controlled as feudal lords. Lear intends to marry Cordelia to the Duke of Burgundy, a foreign power strong enough to give her support but not strong enough to conquer and absorb Britain (as the King of France might). Jaffa is the only critic of the play to have articulated the strategy of Lear's original plan, but he was not the first to note that Lear enters act 1, scene 1 with a division of the kingdom already worked out (after all, maps have been drawn up and Lear's counselors Gloucester and Kent are evidently already aware of the details when the play opens). See Samuel Taylor Coleridge, *Shakespearean Criticism,* ed. Thomas Middleton Raysor (London: J. M. Dent, 1960), 49-50, Bradley, *Shakespearean Tragedy,* 202-3, and Kenneth Muir, *Shakespeare: King Lear* (Harmondsworth: Penguin, 1986), 32, 55. For a further elaboration of Jaffa's analysis of Lear's plan, see David Lowenthal, "*King Lear,*" *Interpretation* 21 (1994): 393-96.

[7] "Nature and Convention in *King Lear,*" to be published in Joseph Knippenberg and Peter Lawler, eds., *Poets, Princes, and Private Citizens: Literary Alternatives to Postmodern Politics* (Lanham, Md.: Rowman & Littlefield, 1996).

[8] Compare Apemantus's criticism of Timon of Athens: "The middle of humanity thou never knewest, but the extremity of both ends" (4.3.300-1).

[9] All quotations from Shakespeare are taken from G. Blakemore Evans, ed., *The Riverside Shakespeare* (Boston: Houghton Mifflin, 1974).

[10] On the significance of clothing in act 3, see Lowenthal, "*King Lear,*" 403.

[11] For a similar analysis of Lear's speeches in act 4, scene 6, see Lowenthal, "*King Lear,*" 407-9.

[12] See, for example, Knight, who speaks of Lear "penetrating below the surface shows to the heart of human reality" here (*Wheel of Fire,* 192), or Derek Traversi, *An Approach to Shakespeare* (Garden City, N.Y.: Anchor Books, 1969), vol. 2, 164, who sees Lear revealing "the true state of man" in this scene.

[13] The idea of breaking with the conventional parent-child relationship and replacing it with something more "natural" is presented earlier in the play in demonic form when Cornwall tells Edmund after he betrays Gloucester: "thou shalt find a dearer father in my love"

(3.5.24-25). Here the conventional bond between father and son is replaced by a bond of pure self-interest between villains; in the case of Lear and Cordelia, the conventional bond is replaced by a higher bond of spiritual love.

[14] One must be very careful in formulating one's estimation of King Lear. Even as perceptive a critic as Bradley, who has a better feel for what is tragic in *King Lear* than almost anyone else who has written on the play, gets carried away with his own rhetoric: "there is no figure, surely, in the world of poetry at once so grand, so pathetic, and so beautiful as [King Lear]" (*Shakespearean Tragedy,* 228). It is very difficult to be grand and pathetic *at once*. What is precisely characteristic of Shakespeare's portrayal of King Lear is that he shows a grand political man at the beginning of the play, who becomes a figure of great pathos in his reunion with Cordelia. The dramatic movement of *King Lear* is so extraordinary, the contrast between Lear at the beginning and at the end of the play is so great, that we must be wary of making statements that conflate what I might refer to as the public and the private Lears.

[15] See my essays "Shakespeare's *The Tempest:* The Wise Man As Hero," *Shakespeare Quarterly* 31 (1980): 64-75 and "Prospero's Republic: The Politics of Shakespeare's *The Tempest,*" in John Alvis and Thomas West, eds., *Shakespeare as Political Thinker* (Durham, N.C.: Carolina Academic Press, 1981), 239-55. For a brief but insightful comparison of *King Lear* and *The Tempest,* see Lowenthal, *"King Lear,"* 416.

[16] Bradley is aware that a change has occurred in the Lear of act 5; of his utterances toward the end of the play, Bradley writes: "We feel in them the loss of power to sustain his royal dignity" (*Shakespearean Tragedy,* 234). But Bradley blurs the issue by trying to redefine magnanimity in Christian terms: "what remains is 'the thing itself,' the soul in its bare greatness" (234).

[17] On this point, see Lowenthal, *"King Lear,"* 413.

[18] This outcome fulfills Albany's ominous prediction at 4.2.49-50. For the self-destructive character of evil, see Lowenthal, *"King Lear,"* 409.

[19] For a different view of what Edgar learns in the course of the play, see Joseph Alulis, "The Education of the Prince in Shakespeare's *King Lear," Interpretation* 21 (1994): 373-90.

[20] Consider, for example, Edgar's hesitation in opening the letter from Goneril to Edmund when it falls into his hands (4.6.259-61).

[21] I take "the oldest" in Edgar's speech to refer to Lear; some critics feel the words refer to Kent. This suggestion seems unlikely; usually at the end of a Shakespearean tragedy, the highest-ranking character surviving speaks of the tragic hero of the play. In any event, the closing lines round out the play effectively. The play opens with a discussion of how the difference between two men has been obscured in a political settlement. It closes with lines stressing the way in which one man is distinguished from his fellows; moreover the criterion by which he is distinguished is the depth of his experience, more specifically how much he has been able to "see." Edgar's respect for wisdom is reflected in the fact that he values age (with its greater experience) over youth; at the beginning of the play, Edmund spoke out for youth over age. (On the issue of youth vs. age in the play, see Lowenthal, *"King Lear,"* 399.) Finally, in the first scene of *King Lear* hypocrisy governed the court; at the end Edgar is calling for a new honesty when he enjoins: "Speak what we feel, not what we ought to say." In sum, Edgar's final words manifest a new regard for truth.

Source: *"King Lear*: The Tragic Disjunction of Wisdom and Power," in *Shakespeare's Political Pageant: Essays in Literature and Politics,* edited by Joseph Alulis and Vickie Sullivan, Rowman & Littlefield Publishers, Inc., 1996, pp. 189-207.

Timon of Athens (1606-08)

Victor Kiernan, *University of Edinburgh*

If the unrestricted competition, the struggle of each against all, that was taking hold of Shakespeare's England may be seen through a glass darkly in earlier plays of his, in *Timon of Athens* it comes openly, raucously, into the foreground. Here the new social system is firmly established: it is in control of the State, able to dictate its own laws and mould social conduct. A story to crystallize this new mode of life could not be easy to find, and the one Shakespeare hit on gave him a poor drama, though a good enough platform for social criticism. Not all the text we have can be from his pen, though agreement is hard to reach about what is authentic and what is not. If critical opinion of late has favoured a view of the Folio text as derived from 'a not-quite-finished manuscript of Shakespeare' probably dating from 1607 (Soellner 186, 201), it has surely been too easy-going. Many have thought it, with its frequent unmetrical lines and crudities, and its prose in particular, a rough draft only (e.g. Muir, *Sequence* 187-8). If so, it tells us something of Shakespeare's working methods, and indicates that composition did not always come easily to him. One suggestion has been that a good deal had to be cut out because the Essex rising of 1601 made the staging of any kind of revolt indiscreet (Jorgesen 279-80). But Alcibiades' *coup d'état* is shown in full and given the author's blessing. Essex has probably been blamed for too many things.

A different guess might be a wholesale shift of time and place, for political reasons, such as Massinger made when he transferred his *Believe As You List* from modern Portugal to ancient Rome. Another conceivable interpretation would be that Shakespeare was seized by an impulse to return to narrative poetry, this time in the lately fashionable vein of satire, as a means of working off his feelings about contemporary abuses. Oscar J. Campbell finds in *Timon* some of the same 'satirical devices' made use of in several plays by Jonson (183). But if this was the case Shakespeare found his material swelling too much, and could not help drifting back to drama, with a poet's sketch in the opening scene of an intended work on the fall of someone resembling Timon—perhaps Shakespeare's own plan, turned into a kind of dumb-show introduction.

Soellner finds the play 'deliberately anchored in a pessimistic intellectual tradition' (12); Hazlitt, who may be said to belong to this tradition himself, and had a good share of Timon's misanthropy, declared the play to be 'written with as intense a feeling' as any work of Shakespeare (47). In this light it is tempting to see Timon as the successor of Lear, as Bradley did (*Tragedy,* 246-7; cf. Farnham 7). Both men have succumbed to the sweet poison of flattery; both come to grief through too liberal giving, one bestowing his kingdom, the other his fortune, on undeservers. Timon may have been given some furious tirades for which there was no room in *King Lear,* but with none of the wild grandeur of the Lear story to justify them. Lear is driven out into the wilderness; Timon turns his back on the city and walks out into a desert conveniently close by, to discharge his storms of invective. Shakespeare's disgust with mankind, which strains *King Lear* to the limits of dramatic form, here overflows them altogether; it is a play virtually without a plot. Timon has far too little warrant for his indiscriminate excommunication of mankind, and—lacking inspired madness—even less opportunity than Lear to have acquired the detailed familiarity with human depravity which he suddenly displays. It is clearly the author himself who is finding vent for feelings of his own, inflamed by awareness of similar indignation among many others. There is no lack of evidence elsewhere that Shakespeare sometimes suffered from such inflamed moods, at the opposite pole from his keen relish at other times of life among his fellow-men. It was a fundamental of his nature to be compounded from opposites and contraries.

Lear's ordeals finally emancipate him from self-absorption; Timon's do not. His only way out will be the escape from life that Gloucester learned to renounce. He undergoes no 'genuinely tragic remoulding' (Maxwell, cited by Lerner, 271; cf. Hunter, *Studies* 254). Probably Timon was too well known a character for even Shakespeare to be able to alter much. Dekker was writing in 1609 of 'Timonists' who 'truly loath this polluted and mangy-fisted world' (*Hornbook* 18; cf. 75). Timon was seen, that is, as typifying the alienation of man from man that people were growing uneasily conscious of, not as a bringer of new ideas for curing the malady. In the play he may condemn men's heartlessness towards one another, but it is always their treatment of *him* that infuriates him. *King Lear* is concentrated on the miseries of the poor, *Timon of Athens* on the callousness of the rich; not much, however, or not manifestly, towards the poor. Here the levelling tendency apparent in the two previous plays becomes a morbid one, downward instead of upward. Men are equal in being equally worthless; when Timon wants all 'degrees, observances', ranks, swept away (IV.i. 18-20) it is not for the sake of enfranchisement, but to set mankind free to destroy itself. Lear's frantic denunciations of the human race are palliated by his age, whereas Timon seems to be in the prime of life.

We can suppose Shakespeare to have abandoned work on the play, leaving it perhaps to be cobbled up by a 'prentice hand, when he realized that it was not flowering into a true drama. A hero without distinct personality, raging at a set of ingrates who are only names to us, could not be lifted from the ground by even a whirlwind of poetry. There is something in Timon of Hamlet, unpacking his heart with words, but unlike Hamlet he has no specific mission to urge him on, and no impulse to do anything more than talk. His world is too degenerate to be worth saving; his jeremiads are on a par with those of the pulpit against a human nature incurably defective. They miss the crucial fact that what is wrong is not, at bottom, human nature, but the institutions it has locked itself into. Shakespeare does end by pointing this out, in however rough and ready a manner, not through Timon, but through Alcibiades.

Tragedy cannot for Shakespeare be confined within any circle of personal life, eventful though this may be: it must cast huge shadows of collective concern. A hero's fate and that of his fellow-men must in some fashion be bound up together. In *Timon* this vital factor is for a long time missing. True, the protagonist has been at some time in the past a true hero, a pillar and protector of the city, both with his purse and with his sword, against foreign attack. But we learn this belatedly; through the first two Acts he shows merely as a rich man indulging his foolish whims. It would almost seem as if Shakespeare suddenly perceived this, and brought in Timon's services of bygone years as an afterthought. They are what entitles him, he believes, to call on the Senate for an immense subsidy when he goes bankrupt (II.ii.193 ff.), and to charge the government as well as his friends with ingratitude.

Romantic love had become for Shakespeare a very questionable ideal; he turns now to another fashionable Elizabethan cult, romantic friendship, and finds it even more fallacious. It meant much to him, but only, in his maturity, when cemented by shared principles and sense of duty. In *Julius Caesar* it is the threatened breakdown of a noble friendship that affects us most painfully of all. In Athens things are too one-sided. Appealed to by an associate, in jail for debt, Timon declares that he is not one to desert 'My friend when he most needs me', but little guesses how his friends will behave when he needs *them*. In Shakespeare's calendar ingratitude was always a sin, 'more strong than traitors' arms' against Caesar (*JC* III.ii.186). Timon's misfortune is foretold in *Hamlet*—'who not needs, shall never lack a friend' (III.ii.188); he is as deeply

outraged by his abandonment as Coriolanus, deserted on political grounds.

Timon is alone in the world, without kith or kin, so that his friends mean everything to him. He is a nobleman, often addressed as 'Lord Timon'; a great landowner, living in a pipe-dream nourished by his riches and his ardently generous nature. 'We are born to do benefits', he proclaims, finding a 'precious comfort' in the thought of friends, 'like brothers, commanding one another's fortunes!' (I.ii.94 ff.). His healthy social instinct, formerly dedicated to the commonweal, is now frittered away in useless waste. His philosophy of mutual aid is a kind of collectivism, but of an élitist kind, limited to a clique of men rich enough to exchange valuable gifts. It is, though Timon does not rationalize it so, a method of mutual insurance, such as the poor have always been compelled to practise among themselves. There is no thought of aid to those really in want. It is with savage irony that the disillusioned Timon, in his grace before meat, begs the gods to 'Lend to each man enough, that one need not lend to another': lending and borrowing must always breed rancour. He includes 'the common tag of the people' among those 'suitable for destruction' (III.vi.72 ff.). It was an obtuse critic, of a century ago, who hailed the play as a demonstration that socialism, community of goods, cannot work (Smeaton 434).

There is something in Timon's self-deception, all the same, of Shakespeare's haunting nostalgia for a lost Golden Age, free of private property with its dividing and corroding taint—that property which on a modest scale he himself felt obliged to devote so much of his life to putting together. In this play he is setting against the acrid self-interest of the new age an opposite conception (however much it leaves out) of how life ought to be lived. Timon has never expected to be reduced to poverty: he thinks his wealth inexhaustible, and in any case counts on always having faithful friends to buoy him up. Still, he has a laudable indifference to possessions, except as a means of making others happy; and he accepts voluntary penury rather than return to riches bereft of the sanction of any ties of brotherhood.

Yet the ideal glow he basks in at first is no more than a feeble glow-worm light. As Soellner notices (54), he is an isolated figure even in his palmy days. He has no genuine friend, no confidant to turn to; a strong contrast with Brutus's many loyal friends, and one that reveals Timon's lack of judgment. Costly gifts are no substitute for a communion of beliefs, political allegiances, high purposes. Rome too was an oligarchy, but its best minds dwelt on a vastly higher level than is to be found in Athens. Hugging the dear friends whom he has never tested, Timon is one of Shakespeare's Don Quixotes, a fantasist of the past. There survives in his daydreams at least a negative truth, that 'civilized' life, perennially athirst for gain, corrupts human beings and makes any advance to truly civilized life impossible. Constructive social thinking would for long be out of sight; Shakespeare can only dodge insoluble riddles by going out into the wilderness with Timon in an unavailing protest against the reign of Mammon.

Timon has been called a memorial to the old spirit of open-handed feudal bounty (Siegel 17); but Machiavelli had long since warned readers of *The Prince* against throwing away their money and taking the highroad to despised poverty. Spendthrift habits, of the Rake's Progress sort, were beggaring a wide swathe of the English landed classes. Another factor here must have been simple inability to count. Numeracy was spreading much more slowly than literacy, and ignorance of the use of Arabic numerals and decimals, of even the most straightforward arithmetic, was still common in England (Thomas, 'Numeracy'). Doubtless the Merchant of Venice could count well enough, but he had been wont to lend money without interest; Timon outdoes him by refusing to accept money lent to Ventidius when the latter's son, now well off, wants to return it (I.ii.1 ff.). There is an ostentation verging on vulgar display in his lavish gifts. He can only keep it up now with borrowed money; all his vast estate is gone, as he is at last forced to learn from his steward. Antonio found no one to lend him money when *he* was in dire straits; and Timon's creditors and critics think of his extravagance as Shylock did of Antonio's. It cannot be supposed that Shakespeare, himself a hardworking man careful of his funds, admired Timon's folly. Some lines in *Troilus and Cressida* show what kind of giving he approved: Troilus is generous, 'Yet gives he not till judgment guide his bounty' (IV.v. 102).

Timon's denunciations of mankind are still more excessive than Lear's, yet no one is to blame for leading him astray but himself. He has been flattered, or buttered up, no doubt, but so are all rich men; and he is one of the plutocrats who have been enjoying life in the Athens whose wickedness he now excoriates. No sooner is he angry with his false friends than he is ready to curse everyone wholesale, including women, who have done him no injury that we know of, and commoners. 'Timon will to the woods' (IV.ii.35 ff.), but not in the resigned spirit of *As You Like It,* or the hopeful spirit of the Romances. His maledictions may be magnificent, but there is something in them of the Byronic, or the spoiled child. He does not call on his fellow-men to improve, but to vanish from the earth. He runs some risk at times of sounding like a thunderous echo of the crusty cynic Apemantus. He cannot speak for mankind against its oppressors; all its better qualities he is blind to. He urges Alcibiades to massacre every soul in the city. There is nothing of Lear's devouring remorse, first for his foolishness and then for his wrong-doing or neglect. We can only feel good-

will for Timon by reflecting that he is really condemning not the individuals he thinks have wronged him, but the accumulated cankers and corruptions of society. It is Shakespeare, in however unbalanced a mood of *saeva indignatio,* who is speaking to us.

He can indeed find fault, through Apemantus, with his hero's 'unmanly melancholy' (IV.iii.203-4), a phrase recalling the prominence of 'manly' and 'manliness' in *Macbeth*. Yet Timon can in his way impress us as a tragical figure, because an embodiment of the better, if wasted, qualities of a passing age, horrified by the new age into which he is shaken from his dream; and those qualities have earned him the staunch fidelity of a humble few. It is not merely personal mortification, but the shattering of a faith, that transforms him overnight into a half-crazed misanthropist. Some such loss of cherished illusions is part of the experience of every tragic hero, and therefore also of ours as spectators. Timon could be rich again if he chose, but there can be no way back to Athens for him, any more than for Lear to a throne he has learned to despise. For him only death remains, and he looks forward to it in splendid poetry (IV.iii.372-3; V.ii.213 ff.). He will have a grave washed daily by the tide: he must leave behind not only earth's vile inhabitants, but the infected soil that breeds them.

Shakespeare might be in principle an admirer of republicanism, but his Athens is a very unattractive republic. He must have had in mind his own London, very much a little republic as far as its domestic affairs went, and governed by an oligarchy of the rich. In this play alone Shakespeare shows us a bourgeoisie in power, and his senators have an evident resemblance to the aldermen familiar to us from the works of other playwrights. These London dignitaries were never on cordial terms with the theatres, and Shakespeare's choice of plot allowed him to retaliate against them by proxy.

Timon and his milieu epitomize a time when propertied classes are in a shifting condition, individuals rising or falling, novel sources of wealth being found; when opportunity and insecurity reign jointly, and profit or bare survival can both depend on credit. Little distinction is made between friends whom Timon has enriched and businessmen he has borrowed from to keep up his wasteful style of living. He has inhaled enough of the commercial air of the times to feel that his 'honour' is injured by his failure to pay his debts (II.ii.41)—a notion that Falstaff would have laughed heartily at. It is a sign of how much his outlook has altered that when he discovers gold it does not occur to him to use it for clearing off his debts.

The senators who refused to rescue him from bankruptcy are 'old fellows', he complains, their blood cold and 'caked' (II.ii.211 ff.). Athens is a home of the new or nascent capitalism, but the only mode of enrichment singled out is the most opprobrious, one that any writer could attack and be sure of having the public on his side,—usury. But money-lending in the modern sense of credit, or provision of capital for useful enterprise, was becoming an indispensable part of the economy, which the playwrights were apt to overlook. A senator who has lent money to Timon, and wants it back, may not be a monster, but a rational man of affairs, who sees that Timon's 'raging waste' must soon ruin him. 'My reliances on his fracted dates', he tells his assistant, 'have smit my credit', and though he holds Timon in esteem he has no wish to follow him downhill (II.i.4, 20 ff.). Timon is soon beset by duns, employees of other 'usurers'. There can be no lending of money nowadays 'upon bare friendship, without security' (III.i.39-40); even the gods would find it hard to borrow from men (III.vi.73-4). There is no room for pity in business affairs, 'For policy sits above conscience' (III.ii.87-8). A banker today would say, or think, just the same.

Hitherto Timon has found nothing objectionable in the ways by which money circulates among the prosperous; and of course as a landlord he has found it quite natural that others should dig the soil while he collects rents from them to be spent on feasting and junketing. This is something he never feels any need to think about. Still, Shakespeare can invite us to sympathize with him in spite of his egregious folly. He brings in a group of 'strangers' to express this feeling and protest against all cut-throat money-making (III.ii.64 ff.). 'Religion groans at it.' At bottom the issue presented is between two classes, two eras, and their philosophies.

Timon had many forerunners in inveighing against the encroaching power of money. Erasmus, who spent a good deal of time in England, had elevated Plutus, god of wealth, to primacy on Olympus, as the deity at whose nod 'All public and private affairs are decided' (103). In earlier plays of Shakespeare pecuniary values creep in through many channels, among them the Bastard's tirade on 'Commodity', or profit, in *King John*. Now their blight is intensified into Timon's ferocious denunciation of Gold, the real villain of the play. Kenneth Muir counts two hundred allusions to it, and points out that Shakespeare's play followed close on Jonson's plays about avarice, as the motive force of an acquisitive society (*Singularity* 66, 68). Its contagion can no longer be closed up, shut off, in any single personality like Shylock; it is an impersonal, omnipresent social force. Timon's worthy servant longs for his master's false friends to be compelled to swallow molten gold, a penalty traditionally inflicted on the greedy in hell (III.i.49).

All time-honoured social principles are being subverted by the unfettered pursuit of riches; this play is a manifesto against what is happening. Timon himself has been a casualty, long before his fall; it is his exorbitant fortune that has turned his wits. He has been trying to bribe people, with lavish gifts, into being his bosom friends, and been rewarded with nothing better than flattery—always, like ingratitude, one of Shakespeare's targets. It seems from what his honest steward says that his house has often been the scene of noisy, 'riotous' revelry (II.ii.154 ff.), which must have detracted from the respect earned by his public services. Such feudal profligacy recalls the revelry of Lear's knights, which so disgusted Goneril. 'O, the fierce wretchedness that glory brings us!' the steward is left to lament: this is where 'pomp' and 'state' lead to (IV.ii.31 ff.). Great wealth, like overmuch power, is dangerous both to the possessor and to those whom it enables him to enslave. Timon comes to see this very clearly, of everyone except himself. More than once he thinks of gold, like Erasmus, as the 'god' of this new age (IV.iii.380; V.i.48-9). Even when he is about to make ready his grave and epitaph, he turns back to apostrophize gold—that 'ever young, fresh, loved, and delicate wooer', and destroyer—the 'sweet king-killer', the 'divorce' between father and son, that magnet that can join together things impossibly incongruous (IV.iii.375 ff.).

Timon may seem emotionally involved, to an unnatural degree, with his male friends, though not with any one of them in particular, and to be indifferent to women until, as soon as he is soured, he feels a maniacal loathing for them. There are no reputable women in the play; it might have seemed indecent to bring any onto the stage that is to be drenched by Timon's torrents of abuse. There could be no partner for such a man; he must be alone, like Lear, to pour out his vituperations. These are not so much of government or institutions, as of individual vice, especially sexual. But public and private depravity go together, whether we are to conclude that government corrupts or is corrupted by those it rules.

In the passages from *Timon* quoted with most relish by Marx, the black magic of gold, and the sexual debasement it can cause, stand out together. In a society ruled by gold there can be little room for love. At best it can be looked back on by a mercenary old father as no worse than a fit of youthful silliness: the man for his daughter must have money (I.i.112 ff.). Gold can join couples, and it can drive them apart: it is the 'bright defiler of Hymen's purest bed' (IV.iii.376-7). For the first and only time in Shakespeare we see and hear of women only at their tawdry worst. The only speaking parts, both small, are those of a pair of trollops kept and openly paraded by Alcibiades. 'We'll do anything for gold', one of them assures Timon (IV.iii.150), speaking, we must suppose, for her sisters in general. They provoke another outburst from Timon, and bode ill for their protector's future as reformer of Athens; but by the time he appears under the walls they have disappeared.

In Timon's fevered imagination, at least, sexual vice overflows all bounds of class, age, rank; lust is the great leveller. In a not very Shakespearian colloquy, but with some resemblance to the brothel-scenes in *Measure for Measure* and *Pericles,* a 'Fool' apparently attached to some such establishment is asked the meaning of 'whoremaster': he replies that the term may denote any male from thirteen to eighty, lords, lawyers, philosophers, and, most of all, knights (II.ii.104 ff.). Disgust with everything sexual is carried to an extreme. Intercourse is seldom alluded to without mention of disease as well. Timon can welcome immorality as helping to hasten the extinction of the human race. He bestows gold on Alcibiades' women, adjuring them to further this good work (IV.iii.134 ff.).

Of any interest in social reform he shows only an occasional flicker. There are touches of the puritanical, as when he censures wine and gluttony as likely to cloud or 'grease' men's minds; he goes on to talk disparagingly of 'the subtle blood o' the grape' (IV.iii.193-4, 422 ff.). We have heard things like this in *Hamlet* and *Othello.* In one long speech he sounds as if suddenly transformed into a revolutionary agitator, calling on debtors to cut their creditors' throats, servants to steal, all law and order to be thrown to the winds (IV.i.1 ff.)—as they were by Laertes' anarchical mob. Lear wanted authority dissolved, Timon wants class war to take its place, but, apparently, without any plan or leadership.

Timon winds up by extending his curse to 'the whole race of mankind', of most of which he can scarcely know much. Earth, the all-mother, 'sick of man's unkindness', should no longer breed 'ingrateful man', but only venomous creatures like adders, or savage beasts (IV.iii.176, ff.). Human beings will outdo the devil himself, Timon's man Servilius remarks. Apemantus seems to hint at recent English history as confirming his belief that a great man's neighbour at table is 'the readiest to kill him; 't has been proved' (I. ii.42 ff.). No remedy is to be looked for from the educated, who have a full share in the iniquities of the mass. Timon sees 'boundless theft' practised by the liberal professions. Lawyers in particular indulge in 'uncheck'd theft' (IV.iii.420 ff.). They are also oppressive. 'Religious canons, civil laws, are cruel': what can we expect war to be? (IV.iii.60-61). Many in Shakespeare's audience would have said Amen to this; lawyers were second only to usurers in the Englishman's list of social plagues. Alcibiades the soldier speaks apprehensively of 'the law, which is past depth' to those who rashly plunge into it (III.v.12-13). As for the medical faculty, its 'antidotes are poison' (III.iv.424-6). In all this, as in Lear's curses on mankind, the fundamental Christian doctrine of total de-

pravity, rendered still more strident by Puritanism, must be borne in mind. Without it such maledictions would have sounded hysterical, as they do to us today. All men and women were corrupted, according to the Churches, by the sin of Adam; *society* is corrupt, Shakespeare is saying, because of the unbridled greed and egotism which have come to be the breath of its life.

The play opens with a poet and painter waiting, along with skilled craftsmen, for a chance to sell Timon their wares. Shakespeare must have recalled his early days of dancing attendance on a rich patron and offering homage; a memory that, as Armstrong said, must have disgusted him (155). Since then he had shaken off this degradation by taking the public, with all its shortcomings, for his chief patron. Both poet and painter deplore Timon's reckless spending. But artists must live, and these two are as acquisitive as any other toadies when, getting word of his discovery of gold, they hurry out from Athens hoping to lay their hands on some of it. He overhears them talking, and quickly sends them packing; though it is to his credit that he recognizes in poetry a species of 'alchemy', able to turn base materials into gold (V.i.1 ff., 111). And whatever shifts artists may be reduced to in a soulless society, the poet's intended composition, approved by the painter, amounted to a warning against Timon's blindness, unlikely to have wrung many thanks from him. Artists are finding the new climate unpropitious, we may conclude.

Apemantus is a dull creature on most days of the week, with nothing to do in Athens except snarl at the gay world he sees in Timon's mansion, where his admission speaks well for its owner's tolerance. He has somehow got himself an education, which has left him an intellectual without occupation. Embitterment like his was no small ingredient in the cauldron of English social feeling. He has turned satirist, and occasionally shows wit. He has good warrant, after watching Timon's banquet, to ask 'what need these feasts, pomps, and vain-glories?'—and to sneer at elaborate upper-class etiquette as turning men into creatures more like 'baboon and monkey' (I.i.239 ff.). After Timon's fall Apemantus is seen in a better light, and is capable of some true eloquence. He claims a contentedness with poverty superior to never-satisfied grandeur; Timon retorts that he was born poor, and would have been a debauchee if he could (IV.iii.239 ff.). In their altercation in the wilderness Apemantus sensibly points out that Timon knows no mean, no moderation, but has always been at one of two opposite extremes. (IV.iii.300 ff.). But their talk falls off into an undignified exchange of abuse, sinking from poetry into prose.

Timon illuminates class-society in a few words when he says that life is brief, but sweet

to such as may the passive drudges of it
Freely command.

                                        (IV.iii.253-5)

His catalogue of human ills includes, like Hamlet's, the 'pangs of love', but not poverty (V.i.195 ff.). The lives he adds joy to are those of his fellow-aristocrats; we hear of no donations to the poor, no benefactions such as both lords and opulent merchants often preened themselves on. If he had sought companions among humbler folk, as Hamlet did, his disillusionment would have been less crushing. Here as in ancient Britain, simple virtue has taken refuge among the poor. Every-one makes promises nowadays, says the painter, but fulfilment lags very far behind, except among 'the plainer and simpler kind of people' (V.i.22-5). Timon has no ear for such talk. In one of Shakespeare's most terrible utterances he recommends his steward to give no charity to beggars,

> But let the famish'd flesh slide from the
> bone.

                                        (IV.iii.521)

There were famines in Shakespeare's Europe, one of the worst in Ireland, as there are today in our world. Through Timon's ravings Shakespeare is telling us that this is how the rich do, too often, treat the poor. Through Lear he has told us something of how they *ought* to treat the poor. Misfortune has turned the two men's minds in contrary directions.

In *King Lear* we meet good men of both high rank and low. Timon has faithful adherents only among the lower ranks, as if Shakespeare had lost hope of all grandees. To his servants Timon has doubtless been an indulgent master, in the old style of the great house-hold, and their devotion to him is unbroken. Cast adrift, their 'hearts wear Timon's livery' still (IV.ii.18). Even the servants of the ruined man's creditors, sent to dun him, feel how basely his old associates are behaving (III.iv.22 ff.). Having vainly done his best to dissuade Timon from his fatal liberality, the steward gives his humbler fellows a share of his savings, and goes out to Timon's cave to offer the rest to him, together with his free service. For once Timon feels his now 'dangerous nature' almost subdued, and admits to the 'perpetual-sober gods' that there is one good man left alive. His steward, he knows, could have done better for himself by deserting and betraying him: many get employment with new masters 'Upon their first lord's neck' (IV.iii.485 ff.)—another piece of social realism.

By way of parody (and a reminiscence perhaps of his burlesque brigands in *Two Gentlemen of Verona*), Shakespeare brings into his procession of visitors to Timon's new abode a group of 'banditti' (IV.iii.392 ff.). They try to pass themselves off as soldiers, in distress as many always were, but Timon sees what they are, or it may be is implying that there is not much difference between the two occupations. They call their trade a 'mystery'—mastery, craft; a joke, like Falstaff's 'vocation' of highway robbery, that Shakespeare never tired of. When Timon assures them that all men are thieves, he comes close to saying 'Property is theft'. He urges them to go to Athens and break into shops: they take this as differently meant, and are moved to thoughts of giving up their anti-social life. Here, still more evidently, Shakespeare is teaching back-handedly.

Religion, like all else, is in a bad way. Gold can 'knit and break religions' (IV.iii.34); priests are among those who ignore 'the general weal' in their chase after private gain. A servant speaks of 'those that, under hot ardent zeal, would set whole realms on fire' (III.iii.31), fanatics bent on stirring up broils. Amid this hubbub morality is abandoned to the lowly and unassuming. 'Man was wished to love his enemies', the good steward reminds us (IV.iii.459). There is frequent invoking of 'the gods'. Timon calls on them to confound mankind. They are 'righteous', the steward believes (IV.ii.4); he does not ask why they have made so unrighteous a world. As in *King Lear,* such epithets tell us what virtues human beings feel their rulers most lack.

Nature partakes far more now of human malignity than of heavenly innocence. Apemantus's warning to Timon of how little 'these moss'd trees/That have outlived the eagle' will care about his wishes contains some of the play's superbest poetry (IV.iii.221 ff.). Timon himself makes no attempt to idealize Nature. All living things prey on one another; here again allusions to the political jungle are thinly disguised. For good measure Timon goes on to accuse even sun and moon, earth and sea, of thievery (IV.iii.326 ff., 429 ff.).

We expect a Shakespearian tragedy to work towards events crucial to the public weal or woe. It is never the hero who is commissioned in the end to launch a reconstruction, as new kings could be in the Histories with their simpler requirements. Hamlet and Lear can catch sight of the needs of a new age, but they must leave it to others to provide for them. Timon is so hopelessly overwhelmed by the evils surrounding him that he cannot even dream of reformation; the only cure for mankind is to be wiped out. Change cannot be inaugurated by any legitimate means, or by insur-rection, but only by a *coup d'état*. Its leader Alcibiades is an admirer of Timon, which supplies a degree of continuity. With his army on the march, the Senate begs Timon to come back to Athens, assume full power, and save the city, as he saved it once before from foreign attack. He repels its deputies harshly, but twice in the colloquy rises into a mood of tragic serenity. His thoughts are on his coming death, his sea-washed tomb. 'Lips, let sour words go by, and language end' (V.i.183 ff.): we can fancy we are hearing Shakespeare, in his mood of this play, bidding farewell to poetry, like Prospero, reconciled to life, later on.

Unlike all the other heroes, Timon disappears unseen, careless of how he will be remembered, and leaving no more of a message than the necessity of root and branch change. Salvation from a mutinous army chief is a very new departure in Shakespeare's political thinking, though Fortinbras and Albany are in their own ways forerunners, and Antony and, more distinctly, Octavius successors. Shakespeare is far from wishing to romanticize war, as he had sometimes done before. Timon talks with aversion of 'contumelious, beastly, mad-brain'd war' (V.i.171); a far cry from Othello's glorification of it. There is in Alcibiades' closing speech a return to something like the notion, so frequently met with in Shakespeare, that peace breeds maladies which only war can cure (V.iv.80-82); but the gist is now rather that each must be kept in its proper place. As to army service, Shakespeare is making explicit what he must always have been conscious of more or less: the sacrifices of war fall on the soldier, the benefits go to his sleek employers (III.v.108 ff.), a ruling class as Timon has called them of 'large-handed robbers', who 'pill [pillage] by law' (IV.i.11-12).

Plutarch's portrait of Alcibiades was a mixture of praise and blame; he was not much admired in England (Soellner 51-2). Like his disgruntled men he deems himself ill-rewarded, but the issue over which he takes up the cudgels is a comrade's condemnation by the Senate for killing a man in a fight. It is the only occasion when Shakespeare debates the ethics of duelling seriously; his old problem of Honour comes up afresh. In Alcibiades' view the culprit showed a noble disposition by fighting, because his 'reputation' (so much heard of in that military play *Othello*) had been 'touch'd to death', or traduced. A senator states judiciously the case against duelling: it is 'valour misbegot', or mere revengefulness, and for a man to risk his life without need is folly. It emerges, moreover, that though a bold soldier this man was often drunken and riotous. How many good soldiers are not, Shakespeare—always severe on drunkenness—may be asking? What will an army be, Alcibiades asks, if courage is to be stifled, or why keep an army at all if it is right to swallow injuries (III.v.18 ff.)?

Once again we are witnessing a clash between the outlooks of two eras, two dominant classes. Alcibiades wants law to be its old feudal self, flexible and pliable, taking account of individual claims to favour; the Senate answers him, as it answered Timon's appeal for financial aid, in a spirit of cold, formal legalism. Justice has no room for pity; mercy only encourages law-breaking (as it did in *Romeo and Juliet*): 'We are for the law; he dies.' No person is entitled by his services to ask for law to be set aside. 'My wounds ache at you', the general protests. He is banished for his persistence, and breaks out in fury, telling his masters to banish their own 'dotage',

and the practice of usury 'That makes the Senate ugly'. He is left resolving to stir up the soldiers against their employers, who have been enriching themselves by money-lending while he has been out fighting, like his men, for miserly pay (III.v.95 ff.).

Alcibiades marching on Athens has a resemblance to Coriolanus marching on Rome; but his intention as it takes shape is a far better one. It is truly revolutionary, the overturning of a selfish government of the rich. The trumpets sounding his 'terrible approach' (V.iv.1-2) reverberate like Bolingbroke's 'brazen trumpet' outside Richard II's crumbling castle. England, like Athens, must have harboured some hankerings for an armed saviour; if Essex had come back from Ireland a triumphant conqueror, as Shakespeare had predicted in *Henry V*, he might have had better fortune. Alcibiades' philippic against the senators and their abuse of power, now grown intolerable, is a powerful expression of patience worn out (V.iv.3 ff.). New spokesmen of the Senate assure him that his enemies have died of 'shame'. It is not very clear what is the dividing line between sheep and goats; but those now in the lead offer dignified submission, and appeal to Alcibiades' feeling for his 'Athenian cradle'. He responds in statesmanlike tones: only a few of the most guilty will be punished, the army will be kept in order, Athens can make a new beginning. Forgiveness, so often spoken of in the tragedies, has a place here too; he proclaims a 'more noble meaning' than revenge (V.iv.40 ff.), very much as Prospero, with his enemies in his grasp, chooses to be guided by his 'nobler reason'. Alcibiades is thus faithful to the maxim he had urged in his dispute with the Senate, that justice should be tempered with equity and mercy.

England's evolution had gone far enough, this play shows, for political judgments of considerable maturity to be made. More clearly than ever Shakespeare is recognizing the decay of an old social order, without welcoming the new one taking its place. Each has its better attributes, which he would like to see combined in one whole. His Alcibiades is among the earliest sketches of a populist dictator, with army backing, coming to purge society and promote justice and progress, as in Cromwellian England only forty years later, and as in so many outdated fantasies of our modern world. The senators offering surrender address Alcibiades as 'Noble and young' (V.iv.13); it is fitting that those in Shakespeare who undertake this vanguard role should be young men like him—Fortinbras, Edgar, Malcolm, Octavius. Their youth augurs a new springtime of rejuvenation for their people. Athens is opening its gates to the future.

Source: *"Timon of Athens* (1606-08)," in *Eight Tragedies of Shakespeare: A Marxist Study,* Verso, 1996, pp. 140-53.

"Untired Spirits and Formal Constancy": *Julius Caesar*

Geoffrey Miles, *Victoria University of Wellington*

Returning to Shakespeare, the end (in both senses) of this study, it may be appropriate to return to the lines which I quoted at the beginning of the first chapter:

> Let not our looks put on our purposes;
> But bear it as our Roman actors do,
> With untired spirits and formal constancy.
>
> (2. 1. 224-6)

On the surface Brutus is simply urging his fellow conspirators to conceal their true intentions; but the words he uses are heavily loaded. 'Formal constancy' means (as John Dover Wilson noted) 'consistent decorum': playing one's part without slipping out of character.[1] 'Untired spirits' suggests a more Stoic kind of constancy: souls which do not tire but steadfastly withstand adversity. The Ciceronian and Senecan forms of constancy are thus linked. At the same time, both are enclosed within a theatrical metaphor: they are the qualities of 'our Roman actors'. The specifying of *Roman* actors, which may allude to the passage on actors in *De officiis* (1. 114), also seems to imply a logical connection between being Roman and constant and being an actor. At the same time, the perverse attribution of 'constancy' to actors, whose job is to play a number of roles, suggests a potential incongruity between the two halves of the line—between the inner spiritual strength of an 'untired spirit', and the public hypocrisy of assuming a merely 'formal' constancy. This incongruity is underlined by a submerged pun: 'untried'—in the context of 'put on', 'actors', and 'formal'—suggests the wearing of theatrical 'tires' or costumes.[2] Untired spirits, then, are souls which appear naked and undisguised, not assuming a 'formal' appearance. The tensions between the two halves of the line mirror the central tension of the play, not simply between Ciceronian and Senecan constancy, but between the elements in both of inner truth and of external role-playing.[3]

These tensions are central to Shakespeare's first exploration of Roman constancy. Stoic constancy of the Senecan brand has long been recognized as important in *Julius Caesar*.[4] The relevance of Ciceronian decorum has not been noted, in spite of extensive discussion of the play's images of acting and the theatre.[5] Nor—though *Julius Caesar* has long been seen as a 'problem play', deeply concerned with issues of knowledge, judgement and error, rhetoric and persuasion—has the ironic relevance of the Stoic and Neostoic concept of 'opinion' been perceived.[6] I hope in this chapter to show how Shakespeare constructs Roman constancy as a blend of Senecan *constantia sapientis* and Ciceronian decorum, and how both rest upon and are vitiated by the domination of Rome by opinion. The public temper of Rome is hostile to self-knowledge, in both the individual and the universal sense; in this society decorum becomes a determined playing of inauthentic roles, while aspirations to the heroic stature of the Senecan *sapiens* founder in the gap between claim and reality.

Before I develop this reading, however, a fundamental objection must be faced. Some recent critics have denied the relevance of Stoicism of *Julius Caesar,* on the grounds that, as Plutarch makes clear on the first page of his Life, the historical Brutus was not a Stoic:

> Now touching the GRAECIAN Philosophers, there was no sect nor Philosopher of them, but he heard and liked it: but above all the rest, he loved *Platoes* sect best, and did not much geve him selfe to the new or meane Academie as they call it, but altogether to the old Academie (p. 1054, 2. 1-2)

—that is, the school of Antiochus of Ascalon, which eclectically fused Platonic, Stoic, and sceptical ideas. The debate about Brutus' philosophical position has focused in particular on his reference, in his confused explanation of his attitude to suicide, to 'that philosophy / by which I did blame cato for the death / Which he did give himself' (5. 1. 100-2). J. C. Maxwell pointed out in 1970 that, though commentators generally explained the 'philosophy' as Stoicism, the Stoics (Cato's school) in fact notoriously approved of suicide, whereas Plato condemned it.[7] Subsequent critics have argued inconclusively over the passage and its implications.[8] The most forceful challenge to Stoic readings of the play is that of Gilles Monsarrat, who argues that 'it is unreasonable to father on Shakespeare a philosophic misconception from which his main sources must have preserved him': Shakespeare's Brutus 'is never a Stoic and not always stoical'. More broadly, complaining that ' "Stoicism" is almost like a disease in many critical discussions of *Julius Caesar*', Monsarrat suggests that critics like Anson and Brower 'mistake "Romanity" for "Stoicism" '.[9]

For my purposes—concerned as I am with 'constancy' rather than with Stoic philosophy in general—this controversy seems something of a blind alley. I am not concerned (as for instance Vawter is) to argue that Shakespeare had a scholarly knowledge of Hellenistic philosophy, or a precise understanding of the subtle distinctions between the thought of the Stoics and of the Old Academy—which was, in fact, primarily Stoic in its ethical doctrines.[10] In 5.1 he may indeed have himself been confused about the nature of Brutus' 'philosophy' (the source passage in North is, as already noted, deeply ambiguous)—though if so he turns the confusion to dramatic account. But in any case, I do not think Shakespeare's primary concern in this passage is to distinguish between Cato's Stoicism and Brutus' Platonism; he is much more concerned with the problematic relationship between constancy and suicide. Being 'constant'—a Platonic as well as a Stoic virtue—can be held to require either a Senecan suicide, or (in Plato's famous image) a steadfast sticking to one's post.[11] Either a Stoic or a Platonist could reasonably take up either position, and Brutus' wavering between the two serves not so much to pin a philosophical label on him as to illuminate the ambiguity of constancy as a principle.

More generally, however, it seems undeniable that to represent the 'Romanity' of Brutus, and to a lesser extent of other characters, Shakespeare draws upon the Stoic traditions descending from Seneca and Cicero, and attributes to them attitudes and actions which his audience would clearly have identified as 'stoical'. The objections of Maxwell and Monsarrat to loose assertions about 'Stoicism' are valid; but to deny, on that ground, the illumination which Stoic traditions can throw on the play seems excessively purist.

'A thing unfirm': the world of Julius Caesar

Shakespeare is of course not in any sense original in associating Rome with constancy. The equation of Roman and Stoic virtue had been a commonplace ever since Cicero. Many of the traditional Roman virtues, as defined by the Romans and by later tradition, can be seen as radiating from the central virtue of constancy: fortitude, justice, temperance, *fides, gravitas,* all involve steadiness and steadfastness, a refusal to be shifted from one's duty. Rome itself, the Eternal City, is an archetype of stability and permanence, with its straight roads and marble columns and arches, enduring even in ruins—though those ruins also imply the limits of worldly constancy. Rome's solidity, rationality and order are embodied in the 'Roman' simplicity and clarity of *Julius Caesar*'s structure and language.

These Roman qualities are set, however, against a background of mutability, uncertainty, and mystery. It is most potently embodied in the storm, in which Rome is invaded by supernatural disorder: wild beasts roam the streets, the dead walk, and normality is transformed to 'monstrous quality' (1. 3. 68). 'Are you not moved,' Casca demands of Cicero, 'when all the sway of earth / Shakes like a thing unfirm?' (3-4). The subliminal pun suggests that Rome's 'sway', its civilized political order, rests on shaky foundations.[12]

The storm is all the more terrifying because, though it seems meaningful, its meaning is obscure. Characters suggest incompatible explanations: it is a sign of civil war in heaven or divine anger with mankind (Casca, 1. 3. 11-13), of the unnaturalness of Caesar's tyranny (Cassius, 1. 3. 68-77), of Caesar's impending death (Calphurnia, 2. 2. 30-1) or some other catastrophe (Caesar, 2. 2. 28-9), or simply a natural phenomenon. Cicero, who takes the last view (1. 3. 30), sums up:

> Indeed it is a strange-disposèd time;
> But men may construe things after their
>   fashion,
> Clean from the purpose of the things
>   themselves.
>
>   (1. 3. 33-5)

In a play centrally concerned with the problems of knowledge, judgement, and factual and moral error, Cicero's may be taken a choric comment applicable to much more than the storm.[13]

The disorder and uncertainty of the storm scenes colour the imaginative world of *Julius Caesar* to a surprising degree. All the major characters are complex and changeable, moved by feelings they do not fully understand; the play has a strong undercurrent of powerful, repressed emotions, reflected in imagery of fire, blood, and violence.[14] Similarly, the macrocosm of Rome rests on the dangerously volatile and emotional plebeians. Rome itself is in a process of change from an old to a new order. The characters attempt to control this process, but we know in hindsight that their predictions are wrong and their actions tragically misguided; they move and act in darkness, unsure of anything. Looking into the future near the end of the play, Brutus and Cassius see only that 'the affairs of men rest still incertain' (5. 1. 95), and Brutus utters a heartfelt prayer:

>   O that a man might know
> The end of this day's business ere it
>   come!
> But it sufficeth that the day will end,
> And then the end is known.
>
>   (5. 1. 123-6)

His response to the uncertainty of life is a Stoic fatalism: since it is impossible to predict or control the future, one must be prepared to accept with courage and calmness 'the worst that may befall' (96).

The world of *Julius Caesar* is indeed one which naturally leads to Stoicism. Though in theory Stoic ethics rests on a dogmatic theory of knowledge, in practice the close association between Stoicism and scepticism suggests that it can equally be a response to ignorance. The most dramatic example of this is Montaigne's Pyrrho, the sceptic who resorted to an arbitrary and inflexible consistency in a world where no rational certainty was possible. Shakespeare's Romans, in rather the same way, try to create their own constancy within a mutable world. They do this partly through the permanence and stability of Roman institutions, and partly through aspiring as individuals to the virtue of constancy: to be unmoved, unchanged, always the same, rationally consistent and predictable, in a changing world. The ideal of Shakespeare's Romans is to be, in Casca's words, 'not moved, when all the sway of earth shakes like a thing unfirm'.[15]

'True fixed and resting quality': Senecan constancy

To be unmoved is the virtue of the Stoic *sapiens,* and this Senecan ideal is most splendidly evoked by Caesar just before his murder:

> I could be well moved if I were as you.
> If I could pray to move, prayers would
>   move me.
> But I am constant as the northern star,
> of whose true fixed and resting quality
> there is no fellow in the firmament.
>
>   (3. 1. 58-62)[16]

In declaring that he will not be 'moved', Caesar is making at least three claims: that he will not change his mind, is unmoved by emotion, and cannot be shaken by external pressures. The most obvious sense is the assertion of immovable will. Caesar refuses to change his decision about Cimber's banishment, and so 'turn preordinance and first decree' into childish capriciousness (38-9). Brutus later takes a very similar stand in refusing (with *wonderfull constancy',* as North commented) to pardon Lucius Pella (4. 2. 55 ff.). In either case, since the play withholds the facts about Cimber and Pella, we may commend their firmness of principle or condemn their obstinacy. It is clear that both Brutus and Caesar find a positive virtue in not changing their minds, refusing to be 'moved' in the sense (often used in the play) of 'urged' or 'persuaded'. Brutus is typical in expressing to Cassius his reluctance to '[b]e any further moved' (1. 2. 167-8). The plebs, by contrast, are 'moved' (3. 2. 264) only too easily, and literally, by Antony's rhetoric.[17]

'Move' also, in these instances, implies the arousal of emotion. Caesar is denying that he 'bears such rebel blood' (40) as to be moved by emotive appeals. Brutus acknowledges that Caesar shares his own Stoic ideal of rationality: 'I have not known when his affections swayed / More than his reason' (2. 1. 20-1). It does not occur to him that to deny all 'affections' (emotions or friendships) may be as tyrannical as to be governed by them.[18] Having himself acted on these principles in sacrificing his personal affection for Caesar to the public good, he is contemptuous of Cassius' appeals to love or anger:

> Go show your slaves how choleric you are,
> And make your bondmen tremble. Must I
>   budge? . . .
>   By the gods,
> You shall digest the venom of your spleen,
> Though it do split you.
>
>   (4. 2. 99-100, 102-4)

The man who refuses to be moved by his own passions will not 'budge' in the face of Cassius'.[19] He insists that emotions must be suppressed, even if the effect of that suppression is as painful and self-destructive as Portia's burning coals.

Brutus' Stoic view of emotion is most clearly seen in his advice to the conspirators on the frame of mind in which they must kill Caesar:

>   And, gentle friends,
> Let's kill him boldly, but not wrathfully . . .
> And let our hearts, as subtle masters do,
> Stir up their servants to an act of rage,
> And after seem to chide 'em.
>
>   (2. 1. 171-2, 175-7)

Brutus sums up the Senecan view that the wise man will do what is right 'boldly' but dispassionately. But the simplicity of this doctrine runs into confusion as Brutus, uneasily aware that you cannot kill a man in a spirit of calm reasonableness, ascribes the necessary emotion to the body rather than the heart or soul. The disjunction seems not only implausible but repellently hypocritical: Brutus' simile puts him in the position of one who orders a crime and then disclaims responsibility for it.[20]

The play thus, in a very traditional way, calls into question Stoic *apatheia.* As Antony tells the plebeians, 'You are not wood, you are not stones, but men' (3. 2. 143); Stoic-stockish impassivity is neither humanly attainable nor desirable. In fact, as I have suggested, Shakespeare's Romans are not passionless. The plebs are governed by emotion; so is Antony, though he is also capable of manipulating both his own feelings and theirs to political ends; and the mob violence which results powerfully demonstrates the dangers of unrestrained passions. Restrained passions, however, can be equally dangerous. Those patricians who, unlike Antony, hold to the Roman code of rationality are in fact more strongly influenced by feelings than they are prepared to acknowledge. Immovable Caesar vacillates between the demands of fear, ambition, and dread of ridicule; shrewd Cassius sacrifices his tactical judgement to his reluctance to oppose the grieving Brutus; Brutus himself seems unaware how far his decision to kill Caesar is motivated by personal and family pride. The play has an almost Freudian sense of how emotion can work all the more powerfully because it is repressed.

The effect of Stoic constancy, then, is not to eradicate emotion but to repress it. When the word 'constancy' is explicitly used, it is most often in the context of concealment. Brutus' exhortation to 'formal constancy' comes as he advises the conspirators to conceal their true thoughts and feelings; when he urges Cassius to 'be constant' (3. 1. 22) it is because Cassius' panic threatens to reveal the plot. Portia makes 'strong proof of [her] constancy' by giving herself 'a voluntary wound' and concealing her pain (2. 1. 298-9)—proving herself more constant than Brutus, who has been unable to hide his perturbation from her. Later, fearful of letting slip a betraying word under the strain of waiting for news, she prays,

> O constancy, be strong upon my side;
> Set a huge mountain 'tween my heart and
>   tongue.
>
> (2. 4. 6-7)

Constancy is here conceived not as freedom from suffering but as repression of it; its function is to stop up the passage between feeling and expression. The power of the image is increased by the ambiguity of 'upon my side', which suggests an oppressive weight pressing upon the chest and heart.[21] Constancy in *Julius Caesar* is not so much a superhuman imperviousness to pain as an ability to pretend to be impervious—like Seneca's gladiator who, though wounded, 'maketh shew that it is nothing' (*Const.* 16. 2).

The third sense of being 'unmoved' is the Stoic claim of indifference to external evils. Cassius sums up this doctrine when he tells Brutus, rather glibly, 'Of your philosophy you make no use, / if you give place to accidental evils' (4. 2. 199-200). The essence of stoic philosophy is to enable us to endure 'accidental evils' steadfastly, without 'giving place' to them, in the knowledge that such things are indifferent. Brutus uses the Stoic term when he claims to look on honour and death 'indifferently' (1. 2. 89),[22] and Cassius picks it up when he tells Casca, 'I am armed, / And dangers are to me indifferent' (1. 3. 114).

The most obvious 'accidental evil', as in these passages, is death. Both Caesar and Brutus declare it indifferent. Caesar insists that it is not death ('a necessary end') but the fear of death that is an evil: 'Cowards die many times before their deaths' (2. 2. 32, 36). Brutus explains the Senecan technique of meditation on its inevitability: 'With meditating that she must die once, / I have the patience to endure it now' (4. 2. 244-6).[23] We are made aware, however, that Brutus' Stoic indifference to Portia's death is assumed, and a note of strained overstatement in Caesar's lines makes us suspect that he, too, does not find the fear of death as incomprehensible as he claims (2. 2. 34-7). Brutus' true feelings about death are perhaps revealed in the dialogue over Caesar's body:

> BRUTUS. Fates, we will know your pleasures.
> That we shall die, we know; 'tis but the
>   time
> and drawing days out that men stand upon.
> CASCA. Why, he that cuts off twenty years
>   of life
> cuts off so many years of fearing death.
> BRUTUS. Grant that, and then is death a
>   benefit.
> So are we Caesar's friends, that have
>   abridged
> His time of fearing death.
>
> (3. 1. 99-106)

Caught in Casca's 'sophistical trap', Brutus skids from the claim that death is indifferent to the claim that it is positively desirable.[24] Senecan Stoicism, as we have seen, is always tempted towards a death-wish; Shakespeare's Romans too are tempted to see death as a positive relief from the strain of 'so many years of fearing death' and denying their fear.

Immovable will, passionlessness, indifference to pain and death: all of these aspects of Stoic constancy add up to a claim to rise above humanity, to 'escape man', in Montaigne's phrase. This aspiration is reflected especially in an exaltation of mind and spirit over body, seen in Brutus' reluctance to sleep (4. 2. 281-2) and Portia's voluntary wound; its ultimate act is suicide, the destruction of the body to preserve the mind. Set against it is the physical weakness of the characters: epilepsy, fever, deafness, short-sightedness, ague, insomnia, fainting, illnesses real and pretended. Episodes such as Caesar's epileptic fit at the moment of being offered the crown, and the fatal myopia of the 'great observer' Cassius (1. 2. 203), suggest nature reminding the Romans (again in Montaigne's words) of the 'mortalitie . . . and insipiditie' of the human condition, by forcing them to acknowledge flaws 'inexpugnable unto our reason, and to the Stoicke virtue' (2. 2).[25]

The most extreme statement of this aspiration to divinity is, again, Caesar's Northern Star speech. As John Anson first pointed out, Caesar here echoes Lipsius' claim to 'that great title, the neerest that man can have to God, *To be immooveable*'.[26] He represents himself as the pole star (3. 1. 60), the one unmoving point in a mutable world, and as Mount Olympus (74), an image of immovable bulk but also one which combines the connotations of Seneca's two images of constancy: the rock and the god. Caesar is thus more than human, while the rest of mankind, who are 'flesh and blood, and apprehensive' (67), possess only the lower attributes of humanity, in Lipsius' words 'the filth of the bodie and contagion of the senses'.[27] Indeed, as Anson noted, he betrays that he does not see himself as 'flesh and blood' when he declares that his blood cannot be 'thawed' or 'melt[ed]' (41-2); like the icy Angelo (another character who, as his name suggests, aspires to rise above humanity), Caesar 'scarce confesses / That his blood flows' (*MfM* 1. 3. 51-2). Ice-cold and stone-hard, Caesar represents himself as the monstrous Stoic-stock of the anti-Stoic tradition. The hollowness of the claim, already implied by his vacillations in the previous scene, is made brutally clear when 'Olympus' and 'the Northern Star' are reduced to a 'bleeding piece of earth' (257) on the Senate floor.

The constancy of Brutus, Caesar's mirror-image,[28] is subjected to a less brutal critique. Though less prone than Caesar to claim godlike status, Brutus too seeks to rise above humanity by achieving an impossible degree of consistency, rationality, and imperturbability, 'armed so strong in honesty' that external threats pass by him 'as the idle wind' (4. 2. 124-5). It is an admirable ideal, yet its effect in practice is often to make him rigid, cruel, and (most of all) dishonest—since, although he cannot in fact be absolutely constant, he must pretend to himself and others that he is so.

Brutus (despite the claims of some anti-Stoic critics) is clearly neither evil nor mad; for that matter, even Caesar's invocation of the Northern Star is splendid as well as bombastic. The play's treatment of Senecan constancy is not unsympathetic; but it is shown to be a flawed ideal, not humanly attainable, and therefore liable to involve its adherents in continual pretence and self-deception. In Montaigne's formula, it is 'a profitable desire; but likewise absurd'.

Roman opinion

Shakespeare's treatment of Stoic constancy is essentially traditional. What is more original in the play is his sense of the relationship between constancy and Rome: the paradox that such a heroically individualistic, heaven-aspiring ideal should arise out of a society whose values are public-spirited and earthbound, and the deeper irony that, in fact, an ideal which rests on pretence is thoroughly appropriate to a society governed by appearances and 'opinion'.

In *Julius Caesar* virtue is defined as Romanness. The characters are obsessively conscious of their national identity: the words 'Rome' and 'Roman' occur seventy-three times, not merely as labels but often with a moral significance.[29] Cassius tells the conspirators to 'show yourselves true Romans' (2. 1. 222)—that is, courageous and loyal. Brutus urges Messala, 'as you are a Roman [i.e. honest], tell me true,' and Messala replies, 'Then like a Roman [i.e. bravely] bear the truth I tell' (4. 2. 241-2). To 'be a Roman' in this sense, to live up to the virtues the word implies, is the highest possible praise: Brutus' epitaph for Cassius is 'last of all the Romans' (5. 3. 98). To fail to live up

to them, for instance by breaking a promise, is to be no true Roman but guilty of 'bastardy' (2. 1. 135-9). Genuine as the Roman virtues are, there is something faintly absurd in this elevation of a place-name into a moral norm. Its self-referentiality also raises moral problems: if virtue is identified as Roman, and Romanness as virtue, by what standards can Rome itself be judged?

Similar problems are raised by another of the play's keywords, 'honour'. What is 'Roman' and hence praiseworthy is defined by the opinions of other Romans, by honour and reputation. But what is honour? Brutus identifies it with 'the general good':

> If it be aught toward the general good,
> Set honour in one eye and death i'th' other,
> And I will look on both indifferently;
> For let the gods so speed me as I love
> The name of honour more than I fear death.
> CASSIUS. I know that virtue to be in you,
>   Brutus,
> As well as I do know your outward favour.
> Well, honour is the subject of my story.
>   (1. 2. 87-94)

But the honour that is the subject of Cassius' story is (as his image betrays) an 'outward' matter of public recognition; he harps on the contrast between the 'honours that are heaped on Caesar' (135) and the 'dishonourable graves' (139) to which others like himself are relegated. By his deliberate confusion of personal honourableness with public honours, he shows how Brutus' 'honourable metal may be wrought / From that it is disposed' (309-10).[30] Later, in the Forum, Antony hammers the word 'honourable' itself into another shape, so that the crowd revile Brutus' honour as villainy. Brutus, who begged them to 'Believe me for mine honour' (3. 2. 14), can have no easy answer, for how can 'honour' be defined except as that which others regard as honourable?[31]

Such questions, as we have seen, were being urgently debated in the late sixteenth century by Neostoics and sceptics like Montaigne. In their terms, the Rome of *Julius Caesar* may be defined as a society governed by 'opinion'. It erects its own standards into moral absolutes, and is dominated by the fallible and fickle judgements of public opinion. The problematic quality of *Julius Caesar,* and its preoccupation with questions of truth and judgement, are thus thematically related to its Roman setting. Not that such problems are exclusively Roman; but the Romans are peculiarly prone to them because their pagan and secular world lacks absolute values. Relying purely on human reason, they fail to recognize how far they are in fact guided by opinion; as Montaigne remarked in the 'Apologie', the two can be hard to distinguish in their 'inconstant vanitie and vaine inconstancy'.

The 'public temper of Rome' (in Eliot's phrase) means that truth is constituted by judgements arrived at through a process of public observation, discussion, and persuasion. Characters continually observe and attempt to 'construe' one another's behaviour and character, as Cassius observes and construes Brutus (1. 2. 34, 47), Caesar and Antony observe Cassius, and everyone observes Caesar.[32] They also continually attempt to persuade one another. The Rome of *Julius Caesar* echoes with rhetoric; not only in the great public scenes but in private encounters and even in soliloquy, characters use language to persuade others (or themselves) to a desired opinion.[33]

In such a society there is a constant temptation to confuse what seems true (or can be made to seem true) with what is true. 'Fashion it thus' (2. 1. 30), Brutus tells himself, construing Caesar's actions after his own fashion. The conspirators want Brutus in their plot because, as Casca puts it,

> he sits high in all the people's hearts,
> And that which would appear offence in us
> His countenance, like richest alchemy,
> Will change to virtue and to worthiness.
>   (1. 3. 157-60)

Metellus similarly argues that Cicero's 'silver hairs will purchase us a good opinion' (2. 1. 143-4). Their assumption that what matters is how the conspiracy is seen by others is unconsciously echoed by Brutus a little later, when he urges the conspirators to kill Caesar without anger:

>   This shall make
> Our purpose necessary, and not envious;
> Which so appearing to the common eyes,
> We shall be called purgers, not murderers.
>   (177-80)

Of course, the fact that the murder *appears* necessary does not *make* it so—any more than the fact that the murderers 'seem to chide' their rage means that they are in fact passionless.[34] Brutus has temporarily lost sight of the distinction he later passionately regrets: 'That every like is not the same, O Caesar, / The heart of Brutus ernes to think upon' (2. 2. 128-9). The Romans of *Julius Caesar* are fatally prone to overlook the difference between 'like' and 'the same'.

The most critical way in which opinion displaces knowledge in the play is the failure of self-knowledge. Shakespeare's Romans are more concerned with the way in which others perceive them than with their own self-awareness—a flaw which, I have suggested,

is inherent in both Senecan and Ciceronian Stoicism. The issue is most clearly defined in a passage of Socratic dialogue between Brutus and Cassius:

> CASSIUS. . . . Tell me, good Brutus, can you
>   see your face?
> BRUTUS. No, Cassius, for the eye sees not
>   itself
> But by reflection, by some other things.
> CASSIUS. 'Tis just;
> And it is very much lamented, Brutus,
> That you have no such mirrors as will turn
> Your hidden worthiness into your eye,
> That you might see your shadow. I have
>   heard
> Where many of the best respect in Rome—
> Except immortal Caesar—speaking of Brutus,
> And groaning underneath this age's yoke,
> Have wished that noble Brutus had his
>   eyes.
>
>   (1. 2. 53-64)

Cassius proposes, and Brutus accepts, that it is impossible to see yourself except as reflected in the eyes of others. Self-knowledge can be gained only through the opinions held of you by others, whose opinions in turn are validated by the 'respect' in which *they* are held . . . The sense of endless regression is underlined by Cassius' imagery, which echoes the discussions of honour by Cicero (in *Tusculans* 3) and later writers such as Du Vair. For Cicero, true honour is the accurate reflection of virtue, but false honour, popular reputation, is a mere shadow. Cassius' word 'shadow', which hovers between the two meanings, suggests that the distinction is itself a somewhat shadowy one.[35]

Brutus, in a flash of insight, objects

> Into what dangers would you lead me,
>   Cassius,
> That you would have me seek into myself
> For that which is not in me?
>
>   (65-7)

Cassius brushes aside the question; his task is to induce Brutus to abandon his own sense of his 'self', and accept instead the image of Brutus the tyrannicide reflected in Cassius' glass. In the orchard scene we see this process completed, as Brutus is drawn to accept 'the great opinion / That Rome holds of his name' (1. 2. 318-19), as embodied in the cryptic and forged letter which he has to 'piece . . . out' by the light of 'exhalations whizzing in the air' (2. 1. 51, 44). It is a wonderfully suggestive image of the corruption of self-knowledge by 'opinion'. From now on Brutus will, as Cassius wishes, have and be governed by 'that opinion of [him]self / Which every noble Roman bears of [him]' (92-3).

This failure in self-knowledge of the play's most introspective character is symptomatic of a world in which people see their actions most clearly as reflected in the eyes of others. It is not surprising that one of the recurring images is that of the theatre, where characters' performances are judged by an audience: Casca sees Caesar's refusal of the crown as a performance clapped and hissed by the people (1. 2. 258-61), and Cassius and Brutus, standing over Caesar's body, speculate how future audiences will respond when the 'lofty scene' is 'acted over' (3. 1. 112-19). The most striking of these images, Brutus' charge to the conspirators to emulate the 'formal constancy' of 'Roman actors', suggests how constancy in this world becomes defined as a form of performance. But the link between constancy and Roman acting, of course, had already been made by Cicero.

'A Roman's part': Ciceronian decorum

The peculiar quality of Roman constancy in *Julius Caesar,* I have suggested, derives from the mingling of its Senecan and Ciceronian definitions. While Senecan Stoic constancy involves an element of pretence, it is Cicero who explicitly recommended his readers to model their behaviour on 'Roman actors'. Shakespeare's Romans, however, take from Cicero's image not its ostensible point—the need to choose appropriate roles—but rather its implications of externality and performance.

For Cicero, every human being has three *personae* or roles which must be played consistently—the role of a human being, the role of oneself as an individual, and the social role—but the first two must take precedence over the last. In *Julius Caesar*—from the opening lines in which Flavius and Murellus berate the plebeians for violating decorum by appearing on the street 'without the sign of [their] profession' (1. 1. 4-5)—the social role is primary.[36] Shakespeare's Romans are less concerned with *play[ing] the man well and duely* (in Montaigne's phrase), or with knowing themselves, than with being consistently Roman, playing 'a Roman's part' (5. 3. 88).

Even individual identity becomes a social role. Names such as 'Brutus' and 'Caesar' become the labels of a *persona,* a publicly defined role which the bearer of the name must play.[37] We see this most clearly in the device which John W. Velz has usefully labelled 'illeism', by which characters refer to themselves (or their listeners) in the third person.[38] Illeism is used most often by Caesar—'Caesar is turned to hear' (1. 2. 19), 'Caesar shall forth' (2. 2. 10), 'Shall Caesar send a lie?' (2. 2. 65)—but also by Brutus, Cassius, Antony, Casca, Portia, and others. Its effect is to suggest the speaker looking at himself or herself from the outside. When Caesar says, 'Caesar should be a beast without a heart / If he should stay at home today for fear' (2. 2. 42-3), he means that this is what others would say of him. When Brutus says that 'poor Brutus, with himself at war, / forgets the shows of love to other men' (1. 2. 48-9), he is concerned with how his friends will 'construe' his neglect of them.

In such cases the name stands for an ideal self which the speaker must consistently live up to. Caesar must be valiant, Brutus wise, Portia constant, in order to be themselves. 'Shall Caesar send a lie?' implies that Caesar, being Caesar, cannot stoop to such an act. Portia tells Brutus that he is acting out of character ('I should not know you Brutus'), and, when he tries to use illness as an excuse, responds unanswerably, 'Brutus is wise, and were he not in health / He would embrace the means to come by it' (2. 1. 254, 257-8). Brutus, being Brutus, cannot act as unwisely as he claims to be doing.

The relationship between person and name is defined most sharply by Caesar. Advised by Antony not to fear Cassius, he retorts,

> I fear him not.
> Yet if my name were liable to fear,
> I do not know the man I should avoid
> So soon as that spare Cassius.
>   (1. 2. 199-202)

He goes on to analyse shrewdly why Cassius is dangerous, yet ends by insisting, 'I rather tell thee what is to be feared / Than what I fear, for always I am Caesar' (212-13). 'Caesar' by definition cannot fear. In asserting 'always I am Caesar', Caesar is making the Stoic claim to be *unus idemque inter diversa,* always the same. This is not exactly a claim to be 'true to himself' (in a sense he is being false to himself, since his earnest denials betray that he does indeed fear Cassius), but rather to be true to his role. 'Caesar' is a publicly assumed role, which Caesar the man must play with decorum and 'formal constancy'. The range of actions possible to him is circumscribed by his role; to allow others to say 'Lo, Caesar is afraid' (2. 2. 101) would be a violation of decorum.

To see one's actions in this way from the outside can be a means of avoiding personal responsibility. When Caesar announces what 'Caesar' thinks, he is not expressing his personal feelings but issuing a press statement about a public figure. His shifts in 2. 2 between third person ('Caesar shall forth') and first person ('I will stay at home') suggest his wavering between the vulnerable human being and the immutable public Caesar. Similarly Brutus, while debating with himself over the murder, speaks of himself as 'I'; having made the decision, he slips self-protectively into the third person:

O Rome, I make thee promise,
If the redress will follow, thou receivest
Thy full petition at the hand of Brutus.
                                                    (2. 1. 56-8)

Representing himself as Rome sees him, as a public figure, he avoids the personal implications of the direct statement 'I shall kill Caesar.'

In some ways the Romans of *Julius Caesar* are acting out Cicero's concept of decorum. They see themselves as actors, conceive of virtue as the consistent playing of a part, and are intensely concerned with *aequabilitas,* believing that 'ther is nothing more seemely than an evennesse in all mans lyfe, and everye of his doinges'. They neglect, however, the rest of Cicero's sentence: ' . . . which you can not keepe, if you counterfette an others nature, and lette passe your owne' (1. 111). Lacking self-knowledge, they try instead to act artificial parts imposed on them by their society, the expectations of others, and their own moral aspirations. Casca, an extreme and semi-comic example, seems a man without a self, who changes his *personae* (obsequious courtier, laid-back cynic, superstitious omen-monger, Stoic patriot) as rapidly as he changes his opinions.[39] Others show a clearer tension between natural self and role: Caesar shows fitful glimpses of human warmth and weakness behind the mask of being 'always . . . Caesar'; 'gentle Portia' (2. 1. 277) is crushed by her attempts to live up to the role of Brutus' wife and Cato's daughter.

The tension is clearest in Brutus, the gentle philosopher who turns himself into a political assassin, despite his sense that he is being made to 'seek within [him]self for that which is not in [him]'. He is drawn away from his true self by temptations which Cicero warns against: family tradition, the influence of others, the pressure of public opinion, and, most of all, what Cicero singles out as the greatest enemy of true decorum: the desire to take up a noble role without considering whether one is fitted for it—'for neither is it to anye purpose to fight againste nature nor to ensue any thynge that ye can not atteine' (1. 110). The strain of Brutus' fight against his own nature finally leads him to embrace death with relief.

The most successful characters in *Julius Caesar* are those who eschew consistency and treat their roles as masks to be manipulated and discarded. Both Cassius (in the earlier scenes) and the theatre-loving Antony play with the possibility of alternative roles: 'If I were Brutus now, and he were Cassius . . . ' (1. 2. 314); 'But were I Brutus, / And Brutus Antony . . . ' (3. 2. 221-2). Refusing (in Montaigne's words) to treat a 'vizard or apparance' (3. 10) as a 'real essence', they avoid the rigidity of a Brutus or a Caesar. Of course, the flexibility of an Antony has its own dangers. *Antony and Cleopatra* will suggest that the future belongs to Octavius, who maintains his role perfectly because, as far as we can see, he has no identity outside it.

'Like Brutus, like himself'

The Roman idea of constancy in *Julius Caesar,* with its blend of Senecan steadfastness, Ciceronian consistency, role-playing, and concern for public opinion, is perhaps most sharply summed up in the traditional phrase: to be 'like oneself'. The phrase is only used in the last act, and it is in these final scenes that the meaning of constancy is most clearly defined, as Brutus faces its final test, death.

The problems involved in being constant are sharply highlighted in Brutus' double response to the death of Portia. At the end of the quarrel in 4. 2, Brutus, who has been rigidly self-contained in the face of Cassius' passion, bursts into surprising rage at the poet's interruption. Cassius teases him with the lapse from his customary 'philosophy', and Brutus responds (with an odd blend of stark grief and Stoic pride), 'No man bears sorrow better. Portia is dead' (4. 2. 201). The revelation, which forces us to re-evaluate what had up to this moment seemed Brutus' inhuman coldness, is the play's most dramatic demonstration of constancy as the repression of pain. It is illuminated, too, when we learn that Portia, who was so proud of her ability to 'bear . . . with patience' (2. 1. 300), died of '[i]mpatience' of Brutus' absence (4. 2. 204), and by a method horribly appropriate to the Stoic suppression of emotion: swallowing fire (206-10).

A little later, the question of Portia's death is raised again. This time Brutus claims ignorance:

> BRUTUS. Now as you are a Roman, tell me true.
> MESSALA. Then like a Roman bear the truth I tell;
> For certain she is dead, and by strange manner.
> BRUTUS. Why, farewell, Portia. We must die, Messala.
> With meditating that she must die once,
> I have the patience to endure it now.
> MESSALA. Even so great men great losses should endure.
> CASSIUS. I have as much of this in art as you,
> But yet my nature could not bear it so.
>   (241-9)

In this public response Brutus is at once maintaining decorum, the behaviour appropriate to 'a Roman' and to Brutus, and staging a Senecan 'example of constancy' for the benefit of others like Messala. But in the process of maintaining formal constancy he is forced to dissemble his true feelings and tell a flat lie.

The ambiguity of Cassius' half-admiring, half-appalled comment hinges on the meaning of 'art'. Its primary, ostensible meaning is 'The learning of the schools' (*OED* 3)—that is, 'I am as well trained as you in Stoic ethical theory, but I couldn't bear to put it into practice like this.'[40] There is, however, a secondary meaning shared only between Cassius and Brutus: 'Studied conduct or action . . . artfulness' (*OED* 13)— 'I thought *I* was a good hypocrite, but how can you bear to act at a moment like this?' Many critics, equally appalled, have explained away the duplicate revelation as a confusion produced by rewriting.[41] I see it rather as central to Shakespeare's portrayal of constancy: as a genuinely noble ideal which nevertheless rests on unnatural suppression of feeling and on 'artful' pretence, both directed toward satisfying the opinions of others.

The possibility of suicide for Brutus himself is first raised in his conversation with Cassius in 5. 1. I have already looked at this problematic passage in relation to the ambiguity of North and the question of 'that philosophy'; here I would note how Shakespeare links these ambiguities to questions about decorum. Brutus shifts from a fumbling first-person attempt to explain his position ('I know not how, / But . . . ') to a firm third-person declaration that 'Brutus . . . bears too great a mind' to be led in triumph. The illeism suggests that he has slipped from Stoic philosophy to Roman decorum. Philosophy may claim that it is more constant to endure defeat, but as 'Brutus' and a 'noble Roman' he cannot endure such humiliation; to live on in defeat would be for him, as for Cato in Cicero's discussion (1. 112), a violation of decorum. To preserve the integrity of his *persona,* he must die.

The link between death and decorum is heavily stressed in the scenes which lead up to Brutus' death. Titinius dies with the words: 'this is a Roman's part' (5. 3. 88). In 5. 4 this idea of playing a part to the end, and dying in character, is linked with an echoing insistence on names. Young Cato 'proclaim[s his] name about the field' (3) until he is cut down and Lucillius declares that he will 'be honoured, being Cato's son' (11). Lucillius himself meanwhile is more literally playing a part: 'And I am Brutus, Marcus Brutus, I' (7).[42] When his pretence is discovered, he tells Antony,

> I dare assure thee that no enemy
> Shall ever take alive the noble Brutus.
> The gods defend him from so great a
>   shame.
> When you do find him, or alive or dead,
> He will be found like Brutus, like himself.
>   (5. 4. 21-5)

The context, with its motifs of names, honour, and acting, throws a light on the implications of the traditional Stoic formula. Acting 'like himself', Brutus, as much as Lucillius, can be seen as a man playing the role of Brutus.[43]

Senecan constancy and decorum finally mingle in Brutus' death scene. His justification for death is Stoic: it is 'more worthy' to choose death, actively asserting one's freedom, than to wait to be killed (5. 5. 24).[44] Under the Stoicism, though, there is a sense that death is positively welcome. When Brutus declares, 'my bones would rest, / That have but laboured to attain this hour' (41-2), he implies the 'teleological fallacy' (life is merely a preparation for death); but we also hear a note of sad futility (has my labour come only to this?) and of relief that the labour is over. The same note of relief is heard in his last words: 'Caesar, now be still. / I killed not thee with half so good a will' (50-1). At the same time he reveals his continued concern with honour and reputation, assuring his followers that he will 'have glory by this losing day' (36), and reassuring himself that Strato, the instrument of his death, is 'a fellow of a good respect' whose life has 'some smatch of honour in it' (45-6). After his death, Strato and Lucillius sum up:

> MESSALA. . . .   Strato, where is thy master?
> STRATO. Free from the bondage you are in,
>   Messala.
> The conquerors can but make a fire of him,
> For Brutus only overcame himself,
> And no man else hath honour by his death.
> LUCILLIUS. So Brutus should be found. I
>   thank thee, Brutus,
> That thou hast proved Lucillius' saying true.
>   (53-9)

This coda brings together the themes of constancy, decorum, honour, and death. Brutus' suicide has proved his Stoic constancy: asserting his freedom and his invulnerability to external evils, he has set his spirit free and left only his despised body to the conquerors. He has died, in Seneca's term, for the sake of *dignitas:* by dying well he escapes the peril of an evil life, ensures he cannot be forced to change or compromise, and remains himself to the end. Thus he preserves not only Senecan constancy but also decorum. Lucillius recalls for us his earlier prediction; Brutus has been 'found . . . like himself', consistent in character to the end.

Nevertheless, the hints of relief and regret in Brutus' dying words remind us that the role he has been playing, with increasing strain, was not necessarily his true self. He has maintained his role to the end and died in the way Lucillius and others expected. Roman opinion will honour him for dying 'like himself'—but, as he himself said, every like is not the same.[45]

The death of Brutus embodies the complexity of 'constancy' in *Julius Caesar.* He simultaneously fulfils the demands of Stoic ethics, remaining 'constant as the Northern Star' in the face of defeat and death, and of Roman decorum, maintaining 'formal constancy' and playing his part consistently to the end; in both ways he has been 'always the same' in life, and will remain so in fame after his death. Both ideals, however, involve the strain of pretending to be what he is not, and concealing and suppressing his human weakness. It is not surprising that Brutus welcomes death. Only in death can he end the strain of pretence, and achieve in fact the condition he aspires to: absolute changelessness and immovability, a complete freedom of the mind from the body's weakness, and a complete identification between himself and his public role. Ultimately, to play 'a Roman's part' *is* to die.

Notes

[1] *Julius Caesar,* New [Cambridge] Shakespeare (Cambridge, 1949), note ad loc.; he does not explicitly make the connection with Cicero. 'Formal' means 'in outward form or appearance' (*OED* 1c), but with overtones of more pejorative senses: merely in outward appearance (2c), preoccupied with forms (8). Compare the use of 'form' with implications of pretence and deceit in 1. 2. 299 ('*puts on* this tardy form') and 4. 2. 40 ('this sober form . . . hides wrongs').

[2] *OED* 'Tire' v³ 2b ('To attire, clothe duly'); cf. 'tiring-house', the theatrical term for the backstage area. I have not seen this pun previously noted.

[3] Few critics have looked in detail at these lines. One exception is Jonathan Goldberg, *James I and the Politics of Literature* (Baltimore, 1983), 164, who notes the contradiction between 'resplendent transcendence' and 'the duplicitous form of the actor', but distracts from the central problem by creating unnecessary difficulties over the contrast between genuine and assumed looks.

[4] . . . Robert Ornstein, 'Seneca and the Political Drama of *Julius Caesar*', *Journal of English and Germanic Philology [JEGP]* 57 (1958), 51-6, is not on constancy, but relates to a comment in Seneca's *De beneficiis* (2. 20) on Brutus' political naïvety.

[5] Earlier critics regretted the stiffness of the characters ('more orators than men': Mark Van Doren, *Shakespeare* (London, 1939; New York, 1955), 153). But MacCallum's perception in 1910 (*Shakespeare's Roman Plays*) of a distinction between character and role in Caesar ('he must affect to be what he is not', 231) and Brutus ('a kind of pose', 241) has been taken up by most later critics, many of whom see role-playing as related to the political and ethical nature of Rome. Some of the more important discussions are L. C. Knights, 'Personality and Politics in *Julius Caesar*'

(1965; repr. in his *'Hamlet' and Other Shakespearean Essays* (Cambridge, 1979), 82-101); Peter Ure, 'Character and Role from *Richard III* to *Julius Caesar*', in his *Elizabethan and Jacobean Drama,* 22-43; Matthew Proser, *The Heroic Image in Five Shakespearean Tragedies* (Princeton, 1965), 10-50; Stampfer, *Tragic Engagement,* 77-99; John W. Velz, ' "If I Were Brutus Now": Role-playing in *Julius Caesar*', *Shakespeare Studies* 4 (1969), 149-59; Kaufmann and Ronan, *'Julius Caesar',* esp. 20 ('Stoicism is a form of acting'), 37-43; Simmons, *Pagan World,* ch. 3 ('*Julius Caesar*: Our Roman Actors', 65-108); Thomas F. Van Laan, *Role-playing in Shakespeare* (Toronto, 1978), 152-61; Goldberg, *Politics of Literature,* ch. 4 ('The Roman Actor', 164-76); Ralph Berry, 'Communal Identity and the Rituals of *Julius Caesar*', in his *Shakespeare and the Awareness of the Audience* (London, 1985), 75-87; Edward Pechter, '*Julius Caesar* and *Sejanus*: Roman Politics, Inner Selves and the Power of the Theatre', in E. A. J. Honigmann (ed.), *Shakespeare and His Contemporaries* (Manchester, 1986), 60-78.

[6] R. A. Foakes, 'An Approach to *Julius Caesar*', *Shakespeare Quarterly [SQ]* 5 (1954), 259-70, was perhaps the first to note the thematic importance of knowledge and error: 'All is the result of a self-deception, an obsession with names and an ignorance of reality' (270). The epistemological theme has been developed by Ernest Schanzer, *The Problem Plays of Shakespeare* (London, 1963); Mildred E. Hartsock, 'The Complexity of *Julius Caesar*', *PMLA* 81 (1966), 56-62; René E. Fortin, '*Julius Caesar*: An Experiment in Point of View', *SQ* 19 (1968), 341-7; D. J. Palmer, 'Tragic Error in *Julius Caesar*', *SQ* 21 (1970), 399-409 (which Stoically derives error from passion); Wilders, *Lost Garden,* ch. 5 ('Knowledge and Judgement', 79-101). Chang ('Renaissance Historiography') and Rice ('Judgment') relate the theme to Renaissance scepticism, and Vawter, 'After Their Fashion', to Stoic views on fate and divination (an emphasis rather different from mine).

[7] 'Brutus's Philosophy', *Notes and Queries* 215 (1970), 128.

[8] Mark Sacharoff, 'Suicide and Brutus' Philosophy in *Julius Caesar*', *Journal of the History of Ideas* 33 (1972), 115-22, lays out the problems but comes to no convincing conclusion; R. F. Fleissner, 'That Philosophy in *Julius Caesar* Again', *Archiv* 222 (1985), 344-5, unconvincingly suggests that 'that philosophy' is Cato's not Brutus'; Wymer, *Suicide and Despair,* 152, argues that, in the light of Neostoic disapproval of suicide, Shakespeare could still have considered Brutus a Stoic; Martindale and Martindale argue that 'Shakespeare deliberately blurs the issue' (*Shakespeare and the Uses of Antiquity,* 168), though they see this as a weakness in the play.

[9] Monsarrat, *Light from the Porch,* 139-44 (141, 143, 144). In a long footnote (141-2 n.) Monsarrat effectively dismantles Vawter's claim that the historical Brutus was a Stoic.

[10] Long, *Hellenistic Philosophy,* 224.

[11] *Phaedo* 61c; see also Wymer, *Suicide and Despair,* 10-11.

[12] The pun is noted by Dover Wilson and Arthur Humphreys (Oxford Shakespeare edn., Oxford, 1984).

[13] See Jane Bligh, 'Cicero's Choric Comment in *Julius Caesar', English Studies in Canada,* 8 (1982), 391-408, who surveys earlier comments to the same effect.

[14] On imagery, see G. Wilson Knight, *The Imperial Theme* (London, 1931; 3rd edn., 1951), 32-62 ('The Torch of Life') and Charney, *Shakespeare's Roman Plays,* ch. 3. Knight's 'The Eroticism of *Julius Caesar*' (63-95), though eccentric, brings out the elements of irrationality and disorder which conflict with Roman order in the play, and recent criticism has increasingly focused on these: e.g. Spevack's introduction ('What truth . . . exists in the play is connected with the "irrational" ', 26); Mark Rose, 'Conjuring Caesar: Ceremony, History, and Authority in 1599', *English Literary Renaissance* 19 (1989), 291-304 ('The world of this play is fundamentally mysterious', 298).

[15] This causal relationship is not always recognized: e.g. Vawter cites Casca's words as showing that constancy is impossible, but does not add that they also show why it is so desirable ('Division', 184).

[16] There is no hint for this speech in Plutarch. The possible influence of earlier theatrical versions of Caesar as a bombastic Senecan tyrant-figure was explored by Harry Morgan Ayres, 'Shakespeare's *Julius Caesar* in the Light of Some Other Versions', *PMLA* 25 (1910), 183-227, and Joan Rees, '*Julius Caesar*: An Earlier Play and an Interpretation', *SQ* 4 (1955), 135-41.

[17] 'Move[d]' is also used in this sense at 1. 1. 61; 1. 3. 120; 3. 1. 236; 3. 2. 224. The sense of 'persuaded' is clearest in 1. 3; elsewhere it has clear emotional overtones. Kaufmann and Ronan, *'Julius Caesar',* 24, note the centrality of the word 'move', without distinguishing its senses; Michael E. Mooney, ' "Passion, I See, Is Catching": The Rhetoric of *Julius Caesar', JEGP* 90 (1991), 31-50, comments on its use in contexts of persuasion.

[18] Levitsky, 'Elements', 242, is clearly wrong to assume that Brutus is criticizing rather than praising Caesar, but the misreading does suggest the potential moral ambiguity of his praise. On Brutus and reason, see Vawter, 'Division', 182, though his comments are extreme.

[19] *OED* and editors define 'budge' as 'flinch', but the idea of movement is clearly implied.

[20] See Kaufmann and Ronan, *'Julius Caesar',* 40.

[21] Shakespeare elsewhere uses 'sides' (of the body) in the context of repressing powerful emotions: e.g. *TN* 2. 4. 92; *Lear* (F text) 2. 2. 370.

[22] Brutus' phrasing is suggestively ambiguous. The following lines make it clear that he means 'I am indifferent to death if it comes accompanied by honour'; but the more literal reading, that honour (fame, popular approval) is as 'indifferent' as death, is clearly also a plausible Stoic position.

[23] Benjamin Boyce, 'The Stoic *Consolatio* and Shakespeare', *PMLA* 64 (1949), 771-80, deals with Shakespeare's often ironic use of such Stoic responses to death.

[24] The phrase is Harley Granville-Barker's, *Prefaces to Shakespeare* (London, 1963; first pub. 1930), ii. 227.

[25] On the motif of sickness see Knight, *Imperial Theme,* 40-2 ('Nearly everyone in the play is ill'); Foakes, 'Approach', 198-9.

[26] Anson, 'Politics of the Hardened Heart', 14-18. This paragraph is strongly indebted to Anson, though I diverge from his subsequent argument.

[27] Vawter ('Division', 177) and most editors, like the *OED,* take 'apprehensive' to mean 'intelligent' (*OED*'s sense 4); I prefer, with Humphreys, to take it as meaning primarily 'capable of perception' (*OED* 2). It seems incongruous in this context for Caesar to praise human beings in general for being intelligent.

[28] Critics who have noted the parallelism of Caesar and Brutus include Norman Rabkin, 'Structure, Convention and Meaning in *Julius Caesar', JEGP* 63 (1964), 240-54, and Simmons, *Pagan World,* 87.

[29] Foakes, 'Approach', 267-9; Berry, 'Communal Identity', in *Awareness.* Word counts here and elsewhere are taken from Marvin Spevack (ed.), *A Complete and Systematic Concordance to the Works of Shakespeare,* 6 vols. (Hildesheim, 1968-70).

[30] This passage is well discussed by Simmons, *Pagan World,* 95-8.

[31] On 'honour' I am indebted to Norman Council, *When Honour's at the Stake: Ideas of Honour in*

Shakespeare's Plays (London, 1973), ch. 3 (60-74). Gary Miles illuminatingly discusses the actual importance of honour in Roman culture, though he oddly concludes that Shakespeare failed to understand, or at least to communicate, 'why his Roman subjects identified public performance and personal worth as completely as they did' ('How Roman', 282).

[32] Leggatt has some shrewd comments on the ways in which 'appearances matter' in the play (*Shakespeare's Political Drama,* 141-3).

[33] On rhetoric, see Gayle Greene, ' "The Power of Speech To Stir Men's Blood": The Language of Tragedy in Shakespeare's *Julius Caesar'*, *Renaissance Drama* 11 (1980), 67-93; John W. Velz, *'Orator* and *Imperator* in *Julius Caesar:* Style and the Process of Roman History', *Shakespeare Studies* 15 (1982), 55-75; Anne Barton, *'Julius Caesar* and *Coriolanus:* Shakespeare's Roman World of Words', in Philip H. Highfield Jr. (ed.), *Shakespeare's Craft* (Carbondale, Ill., 1982), 24-47 (who argues that rhetoric in this play is 'unequivocally poisonous', 40); and Mooney, 'Rhetoric'.

[34] See Kaufmann and Ronan, *'Julius Caesar',* 40.

[35] William O. Scott, 'The Speculative Eye: Problematic Self-Knowledge in *Julius Caesar',* *Shakespeare Survey* 40 (1988), 77-89, discusses this passage, though with the effect of darkening rather than illuminating it. Like other commentators Scott compares *Tro.* 3. 3. 90-118, where the same idea is treated with more overt irony.

[36] Barbara L. Parker, ' "A Thing Unfirm": Plato's *Republic* and Shakespeare's *Julius Caesar',* *SQ* 44 (1993), 30-43 (36), links this episode with a passage in Plato's *Republic* (4. 434) where carpenter and cobbler typify the masses who must not be allowed to meddle in government. If she is right, the play opens with an allusion to Plato's view that a just community depends on each citizen consistently playing a single role, and hence a gesture towards the Platonic assumptions at the root of the whole constancy tradition. (This is not to accept Parker's wider interpretation of Shakespeare's politics as Platonic.)

[37] Foakes, 'Approach', 264-7; Madeleine Doran, 'What Should Be in that "Caesar"?: Proper Names in *Julius Caesar'*, in *Shakespeare's Dramatic Language* (Madison, 1976), 120-53; Berry, *Awareness, 79* (the name as 'a kind of externalized self').

[38] Velz, 'Ancient World', 10. Velz also discusses the device in 'If I Were Brutus Now', but his political

interpretation (someone must 'be Caesar') is different from mine.

[39] The inconsistencies of Casca's characterization have often been criticized (e.g. by Granville-Barker, *Prefaces,* ii. 212), but in a play so concerned with constancy they are surely as deliberate as those of Cleopatra. For his changes of opinion, note e.g. 2. 1. 142, 152.

[40] For the use of 'art' to mean (Stoic) philosophy, compare Thomas Lodge's *The Wounds of Civil War* (ed. J. W. Houppert, Regents edn., London, 1969), where Marius' question, 'What mean have they left me to cure my smart?' is answered by the echo 'Art' (3. 4. 46).

[41] Most earlier 20th-cent. editors saw this passage as an earlier version of the scene intended to have been replaced by 4. 2. 195-210, and often bracketed it (e.g. Dover Wilson, T. S. Dorsch (Arden, London, 1955)). More recent editors tend to accept that both versions were intended to stand (e.g. the complete Oxford; Humphreys, 79-81), though Spevack, in a confusingly inconclusive discussion, seems to incline towards the duplication theory (149-50). Thomas Clayton, ' "Should Brutus Never Taste of Portia's Death but Once?": Text and Performance in *Julius Caesar',* *Studies in English Literature, 1500-1900* 23 (1983), 237-58, surveys the debate and convincingly defends the existing text.

[42] Other editors give the line (unassigned in F) to Brutus himself; the difference does not seriously affect my argument.

[43] Foakes ('Approach', 267) notes the importance of the episode but not the significance of 'like himself'; Brower (*Hero and Saint,* 233) connects the phrase in passing with Brutus' 'noble role' but does not develop the insight.

[44] This Stoic idea is not explicit in Plutarch's account.

[45] Wymer, *Suicide and Despair,* ch. 7, esp. 150-4, discusses Brutus' suicide in terms very close to my own, noting the sense of 'tragic . . . self-defeat' (135), the tension between inwardness and public persona, and the un-Roman sense of 'dejection [and] weariness' (154).

Source: "'Untired Spirits and Formal Constancy': *Julius Caesar,*" in *Shakespeare and the Constant Romans,* Clarendon Press, 1996, pp. 123-48.

Hamlet

Peter B. Murray, *Macalester College*

In some influential post-structuralist commentary on Shakespeare's representation of character, Hamlet is regarded as psychologically incoherent, and humanist critics are said to project onto the inscription of this character the notions of inwardness and an essential self which were fully developed only in the century following the composition of the play.[1] Francis Barker argues that Hamlet is unable to define the truth of his subjectivity directly and fully because his interiority is merely "gestural," so that at his center there is "nothing" (36-7; cf. Belsey, *Subject* 41). Contrary both to the views of the post-structuralists and to the view attributed to humanist critics, I will argue that Hamlet is not psychologically incoherent but has the divided and only partially self-aware and self-controlling subjectivity that in Shakespeare's time was said to characterize human beings. Hamlet is unable to define the truth of his subjectivity directly and fully because he has a complex interiority that makes self-knowledge difficult. Thus this character is himself able to think about how his thinking may be in error. After all, his own statements that his inaction is caused by cowardly thinking are the main source of the theory that he rationalizes to delay revenge (esp. 4.4.32-46; cf. Belsey's opposed view of how to interpret Hamlet's soliloquies, *Subject* 50, 52).

Regarding the general question of how to think of the text of a play in responding to a character, there is certainly a sense in which a character exists only in the performance of an actor; but on the other hand insofar as we are aware of the actor performing, we are aware, too, that he or she is performing a text. The text is the starting point for both actor and reader. As Harry Berger argues, we infer a character from the text of a play, and this has an important corollary: "a character or dramatic person is the effect rather than the cause of his or her speech and of our interpretation" (147). Whether we are actors, audience, or readers, however, according to the Elizabethan ideas developed in Chapter 1, our imaginations will mostly assimilate scripted speeches and actions to imagined persons who, like real persons, are the cause of their speech and action. And because we respond to imagined persons *as if* they were real, we infer "inner" thoughts and feelings from scripted words and deeds in the process of interpreting the characters as the effect of these phenomena in the way Berger says.[2]

As explained in Chapters 1 and 3, the text is—and was for the Elizabethans—a score for a performance, and a critic who has seen many performances may be able to perform the analysis of the psychology of a character by responding to the text and to memories of performance as evoked by reading the text. My readings have been arrived at in this way, but what I write is based on the potentialities and the constraints for any kind of interpretation that I find inscribed—or implied by what is inscribed—in the text. When I say a character thinks or may think this or that, I mean that the text implies such thoughts, and I do not assume that the character is a real person. The "I find" and "may" here indicate my recognition that any interpretation is inevitably subjective and uncertain, however much one tries to achieve objectivity by taking into account the interpretations of many others and all of the relevant contexts.

In sum, when I infer what Hamlet thinks and feels, I regard him as an imagined person created by Shakespeare to be entered into imaginatively by an actor and imagined or construed by an audience. The audience needs to be able to respond to Hamlet as an imagined person in order to respond appropriately to the play *Hamlet*.[3] For the tragic effect, we must remain sympathetic even when Hamlet does dreadful deeds, and this requires an understanding of his character and situation so that we can see both the qualities that move him and how these lead to tragic error. Hamlet intends to act for the sake of dignity and integrity and the obligations of love, duty, and justice. If he acts wrongly, it is because, as he responds to his very complex and painful situation, his sensitivity and intensity distort his concern for these values, resulting in an error he is unable to see. He has keen awareness, but paradoxically this awareness, joined with his sensitivity and intensity, results in a self-absorbed blindness in crucial situations.

Of course this is only one possible interpretation of Hamlet's character, even using a behaviorist analysis. One strength of a behaviorist analysis is that it suggests that motivation is multiple as well as complex—that thought and action have as many motives as they have reinforcing consequences—so that a single reading can include a number of interpretations usually found only in competing readings (or such motivation is sometimes referred to without much analysis as "overdetermined"). Because a behaviorist analysis focusses on what a character specifically experiences from moment to moment, it is an analysis that could be especially helpful to an actor seeking a psychological understanding to use as a basis for performance.

The explication of text in a behaviorist interpretation occupies so much more space than does the accompanying technical psychological analysis that at times the interpretation may appear not to be specifically behaviorist. I have tried to strike a balance between showing that a behaviorist analysis can be written without excessive use of technical terminology, and explaining phenomena in technical terms sufficiently to show how a behaviorist analysis works. I will count on a reader's recognizing that certain terms having a common-sense meaning have a similar but more specific meaning in behaviorist psychology. In Chapter 2 I have explained Skinner's powerful analysis of the relations between emotions, thoughts, and actions. That chapter explains the technical use of terms such as "avoidance," "escape," "aversive," "reinforced" or "reinforcing," and "evoke": an event or thought evokes a "response" a person is "disposed" to because it has been made probable by conditioning. "Disposed" is used similarly in the proto-behaviorist tradition—we are disposed to act a certain way because of our habituation. Readers will also be able to tell that my analysis is behaviorist in its ways of discussing what a character sees and does not see, how certain thoughts are displaced by others, how absorption in a point of view affects thinking, how intentions arise and change, how intentions and emotions affect and are affected by actions, and so forth. Thus it should be clear that a distinctive psychology is being used even when technical terms are not employed, as is also the case in some psychoanalytic essays on literature.

I analyze Hamlet in detail in order to demonstrate how his character is psychologically coherent throughout the play. I discuss the play *Hamlet* first because none of Shakespeare's works has more to do with ideas about intention, motivation, and action, with the psychology of role-playing and the link between the psychology of acting and of personal life,[4] and with the proto-behaviorist ideas about habit and character. The play contains statements that refer to all the most important ideas in the proto-behaviorist tradition. Early in the play Hamlet draws on the traditional idea that we are creatures of nature but also of habituation. He explains that as a custom which is a vice causes a whole people to lose the respect of others, individuals lose respect "for some vicious mole of nature in them," or "By their o'ergrowth of some complexion," or "by some habit, that too much o'erleavens / The form of plausive manners . . ." (1.4.24-30). When Hamlet arraigns his mother in the closet scene, he suggests that her habitual vice may have "braz'd" her heart so she cannot feel the evil of her life with Claudius (3.4.34-8). In the graveyard scene, Horatio refers to the related principle that habituation makes unpleasant activities become easy in explaining that the Gravedigger sings because he has become accustomed to his work (5.1.65-9). The closet scene, again, has the most complete statement of the psychology of habits in

Shakespeare. When Hamlet urges his mother not to go to bed with Claudius, he explains that although custom or habit is a monster in making us unaware of the evil in our vices, by the same token if she acts virtuously she will come to think virtuously, too (3.4.162-72). Attitudes follow behavior.

Each of these passages poses a question about Hamlet. Is he one in whom a "complexion" such as the humor of melancholy "o'ergrows" to break down "the pales and forts of reason" or in whom "some habit . . . too much o'erleavens the form of plausive manners"? In the closet scene, is Hamlet becoming "braz'd" so that he is callous to the death of Polonius as he turns from stabbing him to speak daggers to his mother about *her* sins? Does such conduct as the role-playing of the antic disposition change him? In the graveyard and at the end of the play have gravemaking and thoughts of death come to have "a property of easiness for him"?

Now, I am certainly not the first to suggest that the psychology of habits may be important in *Hamlet*.[5] A. C. Bradley repeatedly uses the word "habit" in discussing Schlegel's and Coleridge's ideas about Hamlet. He says that in their view Hamlet's excessive thinking "proceeds from an original one-sidedness of nature, strengthened by habit, and perhaps, by years of speculative inaction" (85). Bradley's thesis is that Hamlet's "imaginative and generalising habit of mind" causes his melancholy over his mother's conduct to affect "his whole being and mental world." Hamlet's "speculative habit" helps cause him endlessly to dissect the proposed deed, and the frustration and shame of his delay make him even more melancholy (93). Bradley sees Hamlet becoming caught up in a vicious circle of thought, feeling, and inaction that deepens his melancholy and renders him less and less able to act. Bradley tends to attribute most of Hamlet's feelings, attitudes, and behavior to his melancholy (99), regarding the antic disposition mostly as an effect, as a form of inaction, not also as an important cause, an "act" having an important effect on Hamlet.

Some nineteenth-century interpreters of *Hamlet* did think of the psychology of habits in connection with the antic disposition as an "act," however. C. A. H. Clodius wrote in 1820 that Hamlet's pretended madness "eventually becomes a habit" so that he is "really melancholy and insane" (2:280), and this view was echoed by Hartley Coleridge in 1828 (2:198). Clodius's reading is an interesting effort to synthesize the poles of the nineteenth-century debate on the question of whether Hamlet's madness is real or feigned. This question could then—before Freud's thinking displaced the older psychology—still evoke the answer that what is feigned may become real through habituation. Although I do not think Hamlet becomes mad by pretending to be mad, I will argue that his "habit" of mourning and his antic disposition do affect him, directly in a way related to the psychology of habits and indirectly through his interpretation of others' responses to his behavior.

It is a convention of dramatic literature that the audience should make inferences about characters' dispositions and motives and even about some influences in their earlier lives based on what they do and say and what others say about them: consider what is conveyed by Hamlet's anguished "Must I remember?" (1.2.143) Hamlet's first soliloquy expresses dispositions that we see repeatedly in the play and that we can only imagine have been shaped by his upbringing and education (1.2.129-59). His life at Wittenberg may have heightened a disposition to reflect on experience. He has also developed a concern for Christian values and for the values of noblemen, and it is important that in his situation these two sets of values oppose each other. Hamlet's earlier life has also of course shaped his attitudes toward his father and mother. Hamlet regards his father as noble, and he remembers his mother to have seemed so until she wed Claudius (139-45). In its context, Hamlet's exaggerated idealization of his father as a "Hyperion" is especially reinforced because it emphasizes the baseness of Claudius as a "satyr" (139-40).

Hamlet's ways of thinking and acting have depended on his being reinforced for regarding his father and mother as ideal models whose position held great promise for their son, "Th'expectancy and rose of the fair state" (3.1.154). Because his father is dead and the monarchy is now corrupted by his mother and uncle, the activities of a prince are no longer reinforced for Hamlet. This, along with his grief and outrage, has caused him to fall into a lethargic depression in which "all the uses of this world" seem "weary, stale, flat, and unprofitable" (1.2.133-4). Further, his mother's conduct, especially, has made noble thoughts aversive as they remind him of what she has done (143, 146). In proto-behaviorist terms, we see that it is his character—his disposition ingrained in habits—to think idealistically, valuing honesty, loyalty, love, and noble action. Because he is strongly disposed to think in this way—reinforced by self-esteem—he continues to do so, which means that now his own thoughts add to his torment.

The offensive behavior of Claudius and Gertrude moves him to such great shame, scorn, despair, and rage that in the soliloquy he does not directly express grief for his father. However, real grief must accompany what he says to let him be reinforced by a sense of justification in his outrage over his mother's having mourned so briefly. And Hamlet's grief itself is indirectly expressed in his sense of loss and his idealization of his father.

Hamlet's expression of a wish to die is evidence less of self-rejection than of concern for self-respect—the wish is reinforced as a thought of escape from life's anguish and indignity. The Prince's outraged sense of honor clashes with his Christian values as he finds it reinforcing to think he does not kill himself only because God forbids it. The thought of suicide seems mostly a gesture of protest: he articulates it only in explaining why he cannot do it. Hamlet does not blame himself for any of the wrongs that have occurred. On the contrary, there are hints of self-righteousness in his attitudes. His princely concern for self-respect and noble ideals makes it especially reinforcing for him to think that all the shame comes from his mother and her world.

Yet Hamlet does feel his life has been stripped of value, does feel some contempt for himself because he feels helpless, unable even to speak to remedy what his mother has done. Hence this soliloquy expresses a peculiar mingling of contempt for self with self-respect and self-righteousness. Hamlet's thoughts of how he is sullied primarily evoke a heightened bitterness and vehemence of response from his disposition to affirm his ideals and to scorn those who are truly base. The scorn he expresses is strongly reinforced when it generalizes to all the world and all women because then it all the more expresses the superiority of his father and his ideals and justifies his thinking that he cannot prevail against his foes. This kind of thinking creates the danger that Hamlet will find it reinforcing to think everyone associated with his mother's world is corrupt, or to exaggerate their actual corruption. Also, insofar as he may respond to attacks on his self-respect by seeking grounds to affirm it, he will be strongly reinforced for selectively seeing what he himself does and thinks in an approving and even self-righteous way.

There is no clear evidence that anything Hamlet says here is specifically shaped by Oedipal or pre-Oedipal motives; that is, there is no evidence that his strong idealization of his father is a reaction formation or that his emotional agitation over his mother's conduct is a result of repressed sexual wishes or anxieties. It is impossible, however, to rule out such interpretations, since his feelings about himself and his mother and father and about what his mother and uncle have done may support them. Perhaps we should conclude that here the pre-Oedipal and Oedipal background from Hamlet's early life does not contribute much to the specific shape of what he expresses beyond the conscious manifestations of idealizing his father and being emotionally involved with his mother's nature and behavior.

There are indications that Hamlet avoids reaching the most aversive conclusions about his mother. He may say all women are frail because it is less painful to think this than to think his own mother is an exceptionally frail woman. Also, he could have interpreted

Gertrude's brief effusion of tears before her speedy marriage to Claudius as less frail than hypocritical. Such an interpretation could then have led Hamlet to suspect adultery and, given his hatred of his uncle, murder. Hamlet's strong emotional absorption in his response to the open wrong he sees—his mother's hasty remarriage to a base man—may also contribute to blocking any suspicious thoughts that might occur if he were more detached. He wants to believe the worst of his mother because she has hurt him so terribly, but because she is his mother and can hurt him so much, he does not want to believe the very worst of her.

Hamlet's not dwelling on his grief when alone prompts us to compare his emotions in the soliloquy with his earlier protestations to his mother that he feels grief to the depths of his being (1.2.76-86). Hamlet's continued mourning is customary, for Claudius concedes as much in his first speech (1-4). But is it only his father's death that motivates Hamlet's mourning in defiance of his mother and uncle? This question goes to the heart of the play's exploration of the causes of human behavior and the connection between an intention and an act. In traditional terms, we want to know whether Hamlet intends or has an "unconscious wish" to punish Gertrude and the King by constantly reminding them that they are wrong to have mourned so briefly and married so hastily. If we infer an intention to punish, we may see hypocrisy in Hamlet's claim that he knows not seems and is grieving to the very core of his being. That is, he does not explicitly say he feels only grief but implies this while merely saying he has inside him more than can be shown. If we see what "passes show" as including an intention to punish Gertrude and Claudius, we may think Hamlet is a sly role-player in his speech claiming he knows not seems.

A behaviorist reading can provide a different kind of answer. Hamlet's mourning is reinforced by several consequences, among them punishment of his mother and Claudius, though he may only think of his feelings for his father. Thus mourning is reinforced because Hamlet does indeed feel grief, and mourning for his father is the only expression of his ideals and character that he feels he can enact. However, the mourning does vex the King and Queen, and Hamlet is aware of this. Hence, since his anger at them causes punishing them to be reinforced, their vexation inevitably reinforces Hamlet's mourning. If it would be aversive for Hamlet to think he mourns in order to punish them, then it is not likely that this thought will occur to him or, if it does, that he would believe it. His protestations that he knows not "seems" indicate that it would be aversive for him to think his mourning is not wholly for the sake of his father.

Here I think the play strongly evokes empathy with Hamlet, and a behaviorist analysis validates this re-

sponse by saying that while his mourning is motivated partly because it punishes the King and Queen, Hamlet is not necessarily conscious of this at all, that his scorn of seeming, along with everything else he says here, indicates he is not a conscious seemer himself. But Hamlet's character may change as a result of the combination of his painful circumstances and his own disposition and behavior. His mourning may become obsessive through a process that proto-behaviorism related to becoming habituated to the behavior, as is perhaps implied in the reference to Hamlet's "customary suits of solemn black" (1.2.78).[6] Hamlet may be caught up in a vicious circle, something like the one Bradley proposes, in which (1) his father's death motivates sincere grieving, (2) this behavior becomes strong because it is reinforced by several results, as explained above, (3) these strong expressions of grief induce more grief (as a conditioned response) and an increased tendency to be unsocial and solitary, and (4) solitariness in turn increases melancholy. And so on and on until Hamlet is completely obsessed with his grief and anger, at which point, in Elizabethan terms, the habit or "adustion" of melancholy and choler would make him not only sad and angry but long in deliberation, full of doubts but obstinate once he has made up his mind, deceitful, and suspicious or fearful of others without factual basis, and so forth—all the symptoms of melancholy that scholars have made familiar to us because they seem to fit Hamlet at times (e.g. see excerpt from Bright in Hoy 100-11).

When Horatio and the soldiers enter at the conclusion of Hamlet's soliloquy in 1.2, it takes a moment for Hamlet to recognize his friend (160-1). Then as he greets Horatio we see that Hamlet's disposition as a noble prince and a friend is still strong. He is gracious to Horatio, interpreting generously his embarrassed answers about why he has come to Elsinore, inviting him to criticize Gertrude's behavior and then quickly confirming his friend's reply (163-83). Hamlet's response to the news that his father's spirit has appeared shows that in these circumstances he can make a quick resolution to act in a risky way. He immediately decides to join the watch that night, saying "If it assume my noble father's person, / I'll speak to it though hell itself should gape / And bid me hold my peace" (244-6). There is a note of bluster in this, as though Hamlet is rising to meet a challenge rather than expressing a resolution habitual to his character, but meeting a ghost is not the sort of challenge one accustoms oneself to meet. Hamlet is eager especially because in his frustration he finds it very reinforcing to take action that links him with his father and confirms his feeling that the world is corrupt (255-8).

As they wait that night for the ghost to appear, Horatio's question about the King's drinking is answered by Hamlet in terms that, as I suggested earlier, may apply to himself (1.4.12-38). Many critics have suggested this, of course, and sometimes the speech is interpreted as an explicit statement of something like a theory of the "tragic flaw." Interestingly, it becomes such a statement through the way it is only indirectly such a statement. That is, Hamlet is not explaining how "one defect" in a trait or habit causes the doom of men who are otherwise noble. Rather, his point is that such a flaw causes such men to suffer dishonor. Hamlet's disposition to be a noble prince causes such loss of nobility to be the kind of doom that moves him to feel the tragic qualm.

The Ghost appears, and Hamlet responds in fear, love, and awe, as we would expect on the basis of what we have seen of his characteristic dispositions. Hamlet rejects his companions' warnings of danger and follows the Ghost because he is strongly disposed both to be with his father and to think he has nothing to lose in dying (64-5). Hamlet may also be brave in his habitual character, but it takes more than habitual courage to follow a ghost into the midnight darkness.

In the next scene, once he understands that Claudius has murdered his father, Hamlet is eager to obey the call to revenge. His cry of "O my prophetic soul! My uncle!" (41), does not necessarily indicate that he has earlier suspected his uncle of murder, however. Each of Hamlet's responses to the Ghost before this line indicates more a questioning attitude than an eager suggestion that the Ghost should quickly confirm what he already thinks (7-8, 25-6, 29). Hamlet may speak of his prophetic soul thinking or wishing he had suspected his uncle of murder, or perhaps he means that his hatred of his uncle was an intuitive response to the man's villainous nature. "O my prophetic soul!" may refer specifically to his suspicion at the end of 1.2 that there has been "some foul play" (256). Foul play may be what was prophesied, and "My uncle!" may express a mixture of surprise and confirmation of an intuition that is reinforced because of his hatred.

Hatred of his uncle makes it very reinforcing for Hamlet to believe the Ghost and to accept the command to revenge (1.5.92-112). Hamlet's passionate tone here can be explained by his fierce hatred of Claudius, by the overwhelming nature of what he has just experienced, by his gladness to be released from frustration in having a noble deed to perform, and by his being able to act for his father. As a result of all these reinforcing consequences, Hamlet represses whatever doubts he might otherwise feel. Thus he is not consciously whipping himself into a vengeful rage. There is a highly theatrical quality to his reaching for hyperbole, his rhetorical questions and assertions, and in general the near-fustian quality of the entire speech. But I think this character, who is now so strongly disposed to nobility and honesty, will speak in such a hyperbolic way only if he is entirely absorbed in the feeling and its rhetoric. The speech is an immediate response to an overwhelming experience and he is in a state of vengeful rage from the start.

What Hamlet swears in this speech is to obey the Ghost's final injunction, "Remember me" (91). Both he and the Ghost mean that he should remember his father partly in order to remember to take revenge. Ironically, Hamlet keeps this vow and yet delays revenge: cognitive acts do not in themselves produce physical action. That Hamlet assumes a person simply does what he thinks to do is also suggested in his earlier asking the Ghost to tell him about his murder quickly so he can "sweep" to revenge "with wings as swift / As meditation or the thoughts of love" (29-31). The irony here is very clear—Hamlet does sweep to his revenge on wings as swift as meditation; he does not yet realize that meditation and the thoughts of love can move slowly. The obviousness of this irony is a sign we should take the error into account as implying a question about the relation between thoughts and deeds.

In Hamlet's vow to think of nothing but the Ghost's command and to wipe out of his mind all he has ever learned, there is a danger he will become obsessed. In his excited state, Hamlet is strongly reinforced for thinking that absolute single-mindedness regarding his purpose is fitting. Such single-mindedness would not only be dangerous psychologically but also morally and practically in making him unable to gain perspective on what he is to do. However, Hamlet's vowing to think only of revenge is part of his excited hyperbole, and once his excitement passes, he can be expected to recover the disposition to reflect on his situation.

Until nearly the end of this scene Hamlet remains in an excited, almost hysterical state. The forceful assurance he gives Horatio and Marcellus that the Ghost is honest shows he continues to be powerfully reinforced for believing the Ghost's story. Hamlet's belief is actually strengthened by his past thinking, which he has *not* wiped away, including his own earlier hatred of his uncle. Indeed, Hamlet's phrasing suggests that he affirms the Ghost's honesty so forcefully in part because the Ghost has validated this hatred, though Hamlet does not indicate awareness of such a motive:

> HOR.   There's no offence, my lord.
> HAM. Yes by Saint Patrick but there is, Horatio,
> And much offence too. Touching this vision here,
> It is an honest ghost, that let me tell you.
>   (141-4)

When Hamlet finally comes down from his state of excitement, his words suggest that his speech to the

Ghost also helps to calm himself: "Rest, rest, per- turbed spirit" (190). Following this he is more gra- cious to Horatio and Marcellus, more the friend he was in 1.2. As he begins to think less excitedly of what he has vowed to do, Hamlet's feeling about his mission changes: "The time is out of joint. O cursed spite, / That ever I was born to set it right" (1.5.196- 7). He accepts the necessity of taking revenge but sees what he is to do as a vast and burdensome un- dertaking. This is a realistic perception, and so we can easily sympathize with him. These words may go far toward explaining the difficulty he experiences in bring- ing himself to kill Claudius.

It is just before Hamlet becomes calm that he tells Horatio and Marcellus that he may "put an antic dis- position on" (1.5.180). As many critics have suggested, Hamlet may say this first of all because in the continu- ing excitement of his "wild and whirling words" he is already in an antic disposition (139). Whether he also has a purpose related to his revenge in saying this is uncertain, since he never explains why he puts on the antic disposition. To explain the behavior, then, we can look for the consequences that reinforce it, with the understanding that Hamlet may not be aware of all these. This understanding can help explain how Ham- let can say in his soliloquy at the end of Act 2 that he does not know why he has not yet killed Claudius. If he could see how the antic disposition interferes with turning himself toward revenge, he might be able to understand his delay.

Let us review the possible reinforcing consequences of the antic behavior, any of which Hamlet may think of as a purpose for it at some time. First, Hamlet may hope that the antic role will protect him, though its actual effect is to draw the King's questioning atten- tion. Second, it may be Hamlet's intention to move the King in this way so that his reactions will reveal his guilt. Third, the King's indulgence of the antic humor may help to catch his conscience by disarming what- ever suspicions he might otherwise have regarding Hamlet's staging a play about a royal murder. Fourth, the antic disposition enables Hamlet to feel detached from the Court and to evoke or expose folly, base- ness, and treachery in Polonius, Rosencrantz, and Guildenstern. Thus the antic behavior enables Hamlet to manipulate and dominate his foes. It also enables him to speak freely though in a somewhat disguised manner what he really feels, perhaps functioning in this way as a safety-valve allowing him to express his deep bitterness in a form that is less aversive for him than the deep bitterness itself. In addition, the antic role gives Hamlet time to consider what to do, and hence also allows delay of a deed he may find aversive even if he feels strongly committed to doing it.

The antic role may be a way to avoid acting, but of course the antic role itself is an "act," and Hamlet's

expressions of scorn in this role could cause him to become absorbed in this activity, tending to displace action as a revenger, a role that calls for using daggers rather than merely speaking them. In behaviorist terms, since the antic role does enable him to speak daggers, it would certainly be reinforced as a form of revenge, and absorption in it might be reinforced very strongly because it also enables him to avoid the aversive as- pects of thinking about blood revenge.

Although the antic role is marked by an alienated de- tachment, this could be more a detachment from oth- ers than from self. It has often been suggested that Hamlet is an eiron who has a self-detachment enabling him to see himself well. If instead he becomes ab- sorbed in the righteously alienated viewpoint of the antic role, he might see only those of his own faults that allow him to retain a fundamentally self-protective view of himself. The antic role gives Hamlet the im- pression that he has a detached, objective perspective on others, but this impression could be reinforced because it masks from himself a use of the role to confirm his worst suspicions of everyone. As men- tioned earlier, since his feelings about Claudius and Gertrude strongly dispose him to see evil in anyone he links with them, Hamlet would find it reinforcing to interpret any strange responses of characters such as Polonius as evidence they are false to him. Revealing or finding evil in others could further arouse hatred in Hamlet, and his preoccupation with their evil could heighten any tendency in him toward self-righteous- ness, a tendency reinforced by self-esteem. The more detached and isolated from others he becomes, the less he would be able to engage in role-taking (taking others' points of view) or in fellow-feeling of the sort depending on the acknowledgement of faults or frail- ties similar to theirs in himself. Thus through playing this role, he might become increasingly suspicious and crafty, hostile and self-righteous, his penetrating intel- ligence narrowed so that although he expresses pro- found insights, he fails to consider matters of great importance adequately.

On the other hand, insofar as Hamlet is not absorbed in the antic role's viewpoint, the process of "acting" feelings that are partly sincere and partly "put on" could tend to blur his emotional reality for himself and turn him into one who self-consciously performs his emotions. In this sense Hamlet may become an actor: through putting on an antic disposition he may become less an antic than one who puts on. This would inter- fere with his ability to identify with any role, and hence help to explain his difficulty in becoming a revenger. But although a number of critics write that Hamlet needs to be able to fuse himself fully with the role of revenger, it is not clear that the play suggests this would be a desirable result either morally or psy- chologically or even practically. It seems more impor- tant for us to see whether Hamlet remains true to his noble character and whether he taints his mind in revenge (1.3.78, 1.5.85).

Turning from hypotheses about the antic disposition to the text, we should consider more specifically the shape of the antic behavior. Although the court thinks Hamlet is mad, we can take it for granted from his behavior when he is alone or with Horatio or the players that he is not simply insane in the sense of being out of touch with reality. Thus Hamlet is pretending to be mad when he seems to be unable to recognize Polonius or remember whether he has a daughter (2.2.174, 182). This episode also suggests an alternative interpretation which has frequently been offered, that Hamlet is not so much pretending to be insane as he is playing the Fool, using his reputation of madness as the Fool uses his reputation of natural "idiocy" as a mask preventing the others from fully understanding and taking offense at his pointed witticisms. I do not mean to suggest that Hamlet has a *playful* involvement with the antic disposition. Even when he may act as if he thinks he does, I think the text shows he is confined by his antic role in a bitterly narrow perspective.[7]

Statements of other characters describing the antic disposition give the impression that at least some of Hamlet's behavior is more mad than Foolish; in the behavior we actually see, on the other hand, Hamlet is more Fool than madman. The most bizarre conduct the audience sees is in 4.2 and 4.3. Then it is not entirely certain that Hamlet controls his behavior fully as he does such things as play hide-and-seek with Rosencrantz and Guildenstern and the others who are trying to make him tell where Polonius's body is. Hamlet's behavior in these scenes, however, comes too late to influence greatly our impression of the antic disposition.

In Act 2 Ophelia's description of his conduct in her chamber especially gives us an idea of the behavior which convinces other characters that he is mad (2.1.75-100). We cannot tell whether Hamlet controls this behavior as part of what he deliberately "puts on" in his antic role. His pallor suggests genuine feeling, but his disordered attire and knocking knees are more "playable." There is a strong expression of what troubles him in his "look so piteous in purport / As if he had been loosed out of hell / To speak of horrors" (82-4). These lines imply virtual identification with the Ghost and its mission, an obsession with "horrors" that is sickening Hamlet's thoughts and emotions. He expresses the depth of his anguish in a "sigh so piteous and profound / As it did seem to shatter all his bulk / And end his being" (94-6). Hamlet thus reveals to Ophelia something of what he cannot put into words for her, his preoccupation with horrors loosed from hell that he feels are ending his being. He is evidently reinforced for sharing his suffering with Ophelia as

someone who will pity him. He would also be reinforced for inflicting pain upon her, since she has refused to see him and since his bitterness may now extend to her as a woman and hence frail.

It is clear, then, that Hamlet's conduct is not always and only foolery. During the period of the antic disposition, Hamlet's behavior from the outset has elements of both Fool and madman, as in the near hysteria from which it arose at the end of Act 1. In either of these modes the antic disposition would enable Hamlet to express his emotions in a way that is not well controlled while being reinforced by the thought that this behavior *is* under his control. The behavior is so strongly reinforced by its effect on the court that any thought which justifies it to himself and explains it as sane will also be strongly reinforced: I must be in control of this behavior because I know I am putting it on: "I essentially am not in madness, / But mad in craft" (3.4.189-90). Hamlet means he only pretends to be mad, but he lacks control of this claim itself, since he does not intend the ironic meaning that he may indeed become mad in craftiness, enjoying the "sport" he finds in plot and counter-plot.

We first see Hamlet put on the antic manner in his dialogue with Polonius in 2.2. Hamlet plays the Fool as he says that Polonius is a fishmonger: the joke is that Polonius thinks Hamlet is too mad to recognize him and does not see he is being called a whoremaster (174). But in the light of Hamlet's recent behavior, even a lesser fool than Polonius might think that Hamlet is mad. Indeed, most of Polonius's responses here simply reflect his presumption of Hamlet's madness: if Hamlet says something sane, Polonius can only respond that "Though this be madness, yet there is method in't" (205-6). Polonius has learned to think a certain way and is therefore reinforced for interpreting whatever happens as confirming what he thinks.

But is not something like this occurring in Hamlet's thinking, too? He presumes that Polonius is a fool, and he is strongly reinforced for thinking that the old man's responses merely confirm this conviction (219). For another example, when Hamlet later induces him to say that a cloud is shaped like a camel and a weasel and a whale, Polonius must think he is humoring a madman. Yet Hamlet manipulates Polonius's responses to confirm that he is a fool (3.2.367-75). Each man finds it reinforcing to think himself intelligent and the other mad or foolish, and each is partly right, partly wrong. Hamlet's tone with Polonius in 2.2 suggests that he finds it very reinforcing to give full credit to his wit as the cause of his triumph. Since it would be aversive for Hamlet to see how truly mad he has seemed or to acknowledge any validity in Polonius's point of view, he does not do the role-taking that could enable him to see how his earlier mad conduct affects Polonius's responses.

At the end of this dialogue, Hamlet expresses a death-wish when he says he would not part with anything more willingly than Polonius, "except my life, except my life, except my life" (215-17). Hamlet's feeling about Polonius may partly prompt him to say at this moment that he wishes to die. "These tedious old fools" (219) inhabit the unweeded garden of Hamlet's world and add to his weary despair of life (1.2.133-5). Ironically, insofar as Hamlet is responsible for the mode of his dialogue with Polonius, he is himself the creator of the tediousness. Hamlet's antic behavior contributes to the folly and falseness he rails against in the antic role, so that a vicious circle is created in which he is increasingly alienated and less able to see how he partly causes what he sees as contemptible in others. The more he scorns them, the more he will find it reinforcing to see that he is right to scorn them. This in turn will make it progressively less likely that he will be disposed to see that their behavior with him is in part shaped by his own behavior.

We see this pattern develop further in Hamlet's following dialogue with Rosencrantz and Guildenstern. These friends of his (and Hamlet himself insists that they have been good friends: 2.2.224, 284-6) have been told that Hamlet is mad, and so far as they know, the only purpose of the King and Queen in sending them to Hamlet is to help him recover by finding out what is troubling him (2.2.1-39). There is no hint here that they think of themselves as the King's spies: this is Hamlet's inference and it is important to see how he arrives at it. In the first part of their dialogue he expresses a gladness to see them and a willingness to engage in witty repartee, yet they are aware he receives them "with much forcing of his disposition" and with what appears to them a "crafty madness" through which he evades their inquiries (3.1.12, 8). Hamlet's first greeting seems to express surprise as well as friendliness, and when they respond with witty remarks on their relation to Fortune, he continues the dialogue at the level of banter about the parts of Fortune instead of bringing them closer as friends by asking more personal questions (2.2.224-36). Soon we hear the main tone of the antic voice in the bitterly wise wit of his melancholy assertions that Fortune is a strumpet, that if the world is becoming honest doomsday must be near, that the world and especially Denmark are prisons, and that the seeming great of the world are but the outstretched shadows of beggars (235-65).

In the midst of this, Hamlet explains that the reason he sees Denmark as a prison is that his thinking has made it so (249-51). In saying this, Hamlet implies that the cause of his suffering is more in his mind than in the facts of his situation, distorting if not falsifying what he believes. He again implies that his problem is only in his melancholy state when he says he suffers from "bad dreams" and not from thwarted ambition (254-6).

Clearly Hamlet holds his friends at arm's length, concealing the true causes of his griefs. Yet he suddenly demands that they "deal justly" with him and "be even and direct" in answer to his question about whether they were sent for by the King and Queen (276, 287). Because they hesitate so long in answering this question, he begins to think of them as being on the King's side and against him (290-1, 294-5). There is no sign he takes into account that his supposed madness, his forcing his disposition, and his failure to be even and direct have made it difficult for them to be even and direct.

Hamlet sees himself from his own point of view, as a sane person justified in self-concealment and suspicions of others, and his righteous tone suggests that he does not take their role in order to observe himself from their point of view. Hamlet himself needs what he expects the players to provide for the King and Queen, a mirror to be held up so he can see all the features of his antic behavior that so strongly influence others' responses to him. He creates the impression that he is mad, but evidently expects his friends to respond to him as a normal person. Rosencrantz and Guildenstern do not know what to expect or how to deal with a friend who is mad, and it is reasonable to infer that they should be played as anxious in their repartee from the start.

If Hamlet errs here, the error is a main cause of the deaths of Rosencrantz and Guildenstern, so let us look more closely at the evidence that Hamlet judges them unfairly. When he asks if they were sent for, his choice of words in asking them to "deal justly" implies that he will regard an acknowledgement that they were sent for as a confession (2.2.274-6). This makes it difficult for them to answer honestly, and as they hesitate to speak, he says their looks confess that they were sent for, implying that this fact taints their friendship (278-9). In addition, Hamlet apologizes so strenuously for the poverty of his thanks for their visit that they may find what he says unconvincing (272-4). If the Prince were to take the role of these two "indifferent children of the earth" (227), he might not speak of himself as a beggar. Moreover, there is a sarcastic thrust at them in his remark that "sure, dear friends, my thanks are too dear a halfpenny" (273-4). Although this may mean his thanks are of little worth, the words imply that even such thanks are too good for them if they were sent for. Addressing them as "dear friends" in the midst of all this can make Hamlet seem an insincere friend himself, and he is surely dishonest if he exaggerates the closeness of their friendship to coerce them to be honest: "by the rights of our fellowship, by the consonancy of our youth, by the obligation of our ever-preserved love . . ." (284-7).

Rosencrantz and Guildenstern's responses to Hamlet's questions show they have been put on the defensive and are uncertain how to answer. They do not lie: "To visit you, my lord, no other occasion" is not a lying answer to his question "what make you at Elsinore?" (270-1). The answer equivocates about whether they were sent for, but they do finally acknowledge that they were (269-92). They are only as false to Hamlet as he is to them in not being "even and direct." Their reluctance to be more direct can perhaps be largely explained by the nature of the truth: they believe he is mad and they want to help his family cure him. Alas, Rosencrantz and Guildenstern "have not craft enough to colour" their discomfort (280), nor Hamlet, absorbed in his craft, enough perspective to interpret their discomfort justly: "there is nothing either good or bad but thinking makes it so" (249-50). The result is truly tragic, for Hamlet's disposition to be concerned for honesty and loyalty is what heightens the crafty wariness of his antic attitude so that his perception is severely narrowed.

As the scene continues, Hamlet behaves in a friendly manner with Rosencrantz and Guildenstern, but this manner appears to mask a preoccupation with his private concerns. In the dialogue about the players, Hamlet immediately hints at the reason why he warms to this topic: "He that plays the king shall be welcome" (318). A little later he commiserates with the boy actors because they are required to "exclaim against their own succession" (349). Also, he compares the triumph of the boys over the adult actors to Claudius's succeeding his father in the affections of the people (357-64). When he then formally welcomes Rosencrantz and Guildenstern to Elsinore, the terms he uses suggest more concern for social propriety than a wish to be truly a friend (366-71). Next he hints that his madness is not real, but his words about hawks and handsaws are mystifyingly antic enough to confuse his friends and perhaps even to make them think he is mad (372-5). The hint that he merely feigns madness is probably lost completely when he then plays the antic strongly for Polonius.

Hamlet again lays aside his antic manner when he welcomes the players and asks for a recital of Aeneas's narrative of the revenge slaying of Priam. As the First Player performs, the text does not indicate whether Hamlet's conscience as a revenger is caught, or whether he sees how Gertrude's conscience might be caught by the grief of Hecuba for her slain husband. However, when he stops the Player, he comments on how the theater reflects the realities of the time, and he sets in motion the use of a play to catch the conscience of the King (519-36). This suggests that in his request for a recital about Priam's slaying, Hamlet continues to be preoccupied with his own situation.

When Hamlet is alone a few lines later, he does not respond directly to the grief of Hecuba or to the ruth-less action of the revenger, but to the passion of the actor. Hamlet may seem to say it is "monstrous" that the Player has been moved so greatly by the "force" of a mere "conceit" in a fiction (545-54), but I think the context of these words suggests that this is not his real point. In saying that the actor forces his soul to his conceit and thereby produces emotion, Hamlet says no more than writers on rhetoric and poetry said about the power of vivid language to move a speaker, as explained in Chapter 1. What Hamlet finds monstrous is that he himself has not been moved even though he has great personal cause, and the monstrosity of this is especially revealed through comparison with the actor, who is moved by a mere fiction. This comparison, and the self-judgment it prompts Hamlet to make, is indicated at the start of this speech, as he begins to speak of the actor: "O what a rogue and peasant slave am I! / Is it not monstrous that this player here . . ." (544-5). Hamlet uses the comparison to lash himself with thoughts of how the actor would be moved to an amazing height of passion if he had cause for revenge, while he, Hamlet, has been dull and muddy-mettled, peaking like John-a-Dreams (561-4). Hamlet attacks himself vehemently because doing so is less aversive than failing to oppose his shameful state. That is, because he is strongly disposed to be noble, he feels guilty, which makes it negatively reinforcing for him to punish himself.

When Hamlet asks himself what has caused him to delay his revenge, all he thinks of is cowardice, but he *asks* if he is a coward: he speaks of cowardice as what "must" be holding him back, since he has failed to act, not as what he knows he has felt (566-76). This invites us to try to see for ourselves why he has delayed, and, needless to say, critics have offered many possible explanations, usually explanations suggested by the whole pattern of his action in the play. In my reading, the speech suggests that the psychology of acting helps to account for Hamlet's delay and his inability to explain it to himself.

The key to this idea is to see how Hamlet has not so completely differed from the actor as he thinks he has. I have argued that Hamlet is absorbed in his antic role and that this absorption could tend to displace the thoughts that might lead to his taking revenge.[8] In effect, there has been a reshaping of vengeful behavior into the expression of hostile suspicions and witty verbal attacks that are reinforced strongly because they punish his foes and avoid more aversively bitter thoughts about his dreadful situation. Since he is making his foes suffer, an act of blood revenge can seem less urgent except when he stops to reflect. He can think and speak hatefully, but the role in which he does this is not one that leads to plotting and acting revenge. While Hamlet is absorbed in the antic role, he cannot see the full effect of the role on himself: "Am I a coward?" (566).

It is not true, then, that Hamlet has failed to act; he has acted, but more as an actor than in acts leading to violent revenge. What an actor actually does and does not do points to another aspect of Hamlet's relation to the actor that he does not seem to see. When he speaks of what the actor would "do" if he had a revenge motive, he seems to mean that the actor would do terrifying deeds, but all he literally says is that the actor would display great emotion. Actors emote and they speak daggers, but the theatrical mode of action does not include actual stabbing. This may imply that any role undertaken in an actorly way will not lead to "real" action even if strong emotion is felt. Condemning himself for not being like the actor, Hamlet suggests the way he is like the actor in asserting that he "can say nothing" (564), as if speaking is what is demanded of him. Of course he means that he cannot even say anything against the evils he sees, let alone do anything. If he saw the opposite irony, that he has said a great deal, he would attack himself for it at this point, rather than later in the speech when he does see it. In this again he shows how absorbed he is in his own conceit as he does not see how he is like the actor in the way his conceit moves his soul to "say" much in a great outpouring of passion.

It is sometimes suggested that in this soliloquy Hamlet attempts to whip himself into a passion so he can "put on" the revenger role. But in concentrating on how he is unlike the actor, Hamlet does not suggest that he thinks he is imitating the actor in his passion. Indeed, nothing Hamlet says suggests he has the deliberate intention of working himself into a vengeful passion, and in such a passionate tirade, what is said expresses what is felt and thought unless there are indications to the contrary. It is true that his expression of rage is reinforced because it works up his hatred of Claudius, but if Hamlet were *thinking* of working himself into a vengeful passion, he would likely emphasize his reasons to hate his foe more than he does. He does mention early in his self-condemnation that a "damn'd defeat was made" upon his father, but the passive construction implies that his anger even in saying this is not immediately directed against the agent of this damnable act (566), and following this for several lines his anger is entirely directed against himself. At this moment Hamlet's thought and feeling are turned away from pursuing revenge because, ironically, thoughts about his failure to take revenge absorb him in an expression of shame that threatens to perpetuate the failure it reacts against.

Hamlet expresses his shame by imagining someone insulting him as a nobleman might mock a coward. If this shows that Hamlet is especially concerned about how others judge him, it may suggest that his self-condemnation is not fully internalized. It seems clear, however, that the person who insults Hamlet is Prince Hamlet himself. Up to this point, the text gives no hint

that anyone else alive knows he has any reason for such shame. Thus he evidently attributes his view of himself and his ideals of noble action to an imaginary interlocutor (his father?) in order to punish himself severely for his shameful inaction. In the process of condemning himself, Hamlet finally states what he has failed to do, and so his anger is more or less automatically directed against Claudius, too (574-7). But immediately he rejects such passionately vengeful verbal assaults as inappropriate (578-83)—another likely indication that he has not been intentionally whipping himself up into such a passion thinking that it would move him toward revenge.

Hamlet's reason for rejecting his passionate speech is not that he thinks his emotion is like an actor's and hence invalid and unlikely to lead to action. Instead, he continues to focus on how his behavior is shameful, saying he has been "like a whore" in unpacking his heart with words (581-3). Hamlet's repetition of base terms for prostitutes implies that he means they are base, weak people who curse their lot but do not change what they do, and he thinks that his cursing shows him to be like them, that his cursing will not lead to action. Thus Hamlet does not consciously relate his rejection of unpacking his heart with words to his ideas about the actor, does not think he has behaved like an actor. He has not been markedly histrionic here in an unconscious sense, either. He has the motive and the cue for the passion he expresses in the soliloquy and is not responding with emotions in excess of what his whole situation provokes. All the world's a stage at this moment especially in the sense that Hamlet as the tragic character he is—and is becoming—feels and thinks in a way that absorbs him in a perspective preventing him from seeing fully how this very absorption affects him.

Hamlet rejects his passion when his guilt and shame, which first turned him toward passion, turn him away from passion as itself shameful. There is psychological complexity here, as Hamlet first responds to the actor and then to his own response to the actor. A secondary cause of Hamlet's rejection of passion may be that the strong expression of a behavior causes it to weaken so that another becomes prepotent and replaces it. Or in Elizabethan terms, perhaps Hamlet has expended his passion so that he only has the energy needed to *think* of what he should do (cf. 3.2.191-2, 4.7.113-17).

As Hamlet withdraws from absorption in passion into cool thinking, he examines his idea of using "The Murder of Gonzago" to catch the conscience of the King. As many critics have suggested, it may be that Hamlet no sooner finishes condemning himself for having delayed revenge than he finds a rationalization for further delay. This view does not depend on his rationale for the delay being a poor one; rather, even if a rationale is sound, it is a rationalization if it is in part reinforced as an avoidance of behavior that would be aversive. Yet our suspicion that Hamlet rationalizes should be tempered by relief that he has thought to raise the question whether he can trust the Ghost's word, and hence for the first time moves toward a resolution of the moral issues concerning the revenge (2.2.594-600).

Interpreters often assume that delay is bad, if not because it prevents revenge, then because for Elizabethans it was a sign that Hamlet has a weak character. However, most writers in the tradition I have reviewed say furious anger, not delay, is a weakness and they recommend delay in order to gain time to cool off and think better about what to do—even if revenge is still to be pursued as a result of careful thinking. Some writers recommend almost any rationale or rationalization to prevent angry, unthinking revenge.[9] Thus although in the *Nicomachean Ethics* Aristotle recommends a moderate anger that can be controlled by reason to carry out forceful actions such as revenge (1125b-6b, 1149a-b), most writers thought anger is difficult to restrain, that it tends to become immoderate and take control from reason.

Seneca writes on the danger of injustice to others in anger because in that emotional state we defend harsh judgments and resist any evidence or thought opposed to our hostility ("On Anger" bk 1, ch. 18, sec. 1-2; ch. 19, sec. 1). In anger a person acts rashly, meaning in haste and without due consideration. In his essay on "How One Ought to Governe His Will," Montaigne especially condemns angry, rash action as lacking discretion and therefore being ineffective, but he too couples angry indiscretion with injustice, and this second fault of rashness is important in the long tradition of writings on this subject (3:259, cf. Plutarch "On the Control" 458c-60c). Hamlet makes an issue of rashness by going against the traditional view and praising it as having assisted him in sending Rosencrantz and Guildenstern to death (5.2.6-11). The issue is whether rash "indiscretion" does serve him well when he judges others, or whether his anger makes it reinforcing for him to condemn those he thinks are evil on the basis of inadequate evidence.

In his exposition of the Sermon on the Mount, Augustine writes of rashness as the sin of condemning others for the mote in their eye while ignoring the beam in one's own eye. He says that "those parties especially judge rashly respecting things that are uncertain, and readily find fault, who love rather to censure and to condemn than to amend and to improve, which is a fault arising either from pride or from envy . . ." (bk 2, ch. 19, sec. 63). If anger is of long duration, it hardens into hatred, and then a person "cannot wish to convert" his foe (sec. 63). When men who hate reprove evil in others, "they are acting a part which

does not belong to them; just like hypocrites, who conceal under a mask what they are, and show themselves off in a mask what they are not" (sec. 64). Especially troublesome are those "who, while they take up complaints against all kinds of faults from hatred and spite, also wish to appear counsellors." And then follows a passage which scholars think Shakespeare might well have drawn on for important statements on this theme in *Measure for Measure:*

> And therefore we must piously and cautiously watch, so that when necessity shall compel us to find fault with or rebuke any one, we may reflect first whether the fault is such as we have never had, or one from which we have now become free; and if we have never had it, let us reflect that we are men, and might have had it; but if we have had it, and are now free from it, let the common infirmity touch the memory, that not hatred but pity may go before that fault-finding or administering of rebuke. . . . (Sec. 64)

Jesus's statement that how we judge others determines how God will judge us means that the "very same rashness wherewith you punish another must necessarily punish yourself" (ch. 18, sec. 62).

Hamlet's behavior repeatedly invites comparison with Augustine's hate-filled reprover who does not see how his hatred compromises the integrity of his view of others and who is finally punished through his own rashness. In Act 3 his preaching as "Virtue" to his mother's "Vice" while he stands unrepentant over the body of a man he has rashly killed may be an instance of reproving another for evil while disregarding a greater evil of one's own. I will especially argue that Augustine's ideas about rashness help to explain the psychology of Hamlet's dooming Rosencrantz and Guildenstern and how he is then killed when he judges Laertes to be like himself and a noble youth.

In considering Hamlet's soliloquy at the end of Act 2, however, my main point about rashness is that the dangers of indiscretion probably justify Hamlet's delay. But the dangers of indiscretion are also manifest in the thinking Hamlet does when he cools off in this soliloquy and speaks of his scheme for using "The Murder of Gonzago." He speaks more coolly, but his hatred for Claudius is still at a peak. In wanting to test the conscience of the King, Hamlet thinks well insofar as it is true that the Ghost might be a devil lying to him in order to tempt him to murder. But Hamlet does not think of the corollary to this that Elizabethans would easily have thought of, that the devil can tell truths to tempt us to evil—as Macbeth learns, for example. Even if his uncle is guilty, it may be damnable for Hamlet to kill him, especially if this is done as a hate-filled act of private revenge and not as a political act to displace a regicide from the throne.

Hamlet's failure to think this through can be explained as avoidance. In the first part of the soliloquy he reaches a passionate conviction that he must take revenge, and he has a scheme to allay his anxiety that he might damn himself. But his hatred of Claudius makes it reinforcing to think in a biased way: he says not that he will test the conscience of the King, but that he will "catch" it—he speaks as if he has already found the King guilty (2.2.601). Claudius needs only to flinch at the sight of a staged murder to doom himself (593). When Hamlet is thus disposed it would be aversive for him to consider further whether his scheme will really resolve the moral question about revenge. Now, especially, when he has felt great shame for taking no action, and when his hatred of Claudius has been roused to a peak of intensity, it will be reinforcing to think only of actions which clearly lead to revenge or clearly end the need for revenge. He feels good about this resolution of his dilemma, and it would arouse great anxiety to think that his scheme may fail in some way.

This reading does not preclude the possibility that while Hamlet is strongly disposed to *think* here that he wants to take revenge, the plan he has hit upon is reinforced also because it rationalizes avoiding revenge. The strong conscious desire to kill Claudius may thus co-exist with factors tending to cause Hamlet not to kill him. Hamlet may have a revulsion against killing, he may hate the thought of the whole sordid business, he may fear failure and death, or death as a result of killing, as he evidently fears damnation. And he may delay because he unconsciously identifies Oedipally with his uncle.

In the "To be or not to be" soliloquy, Hamlet is still in the relatively calm if intensely absorbed state that marked the end of the 2.2 soliloquy. Just before Hamlet begins to speak in 3.1, we learn that Claudius, the villain, has a conscience which functions in a straightforward way, causing him pain when he is reminded of his guilt (49-54). Hamlet, however, questions the value of conscience by arguing that it prevents the enactment of important undertakings (56-88). This contrast of course does not show that the villain has a better conscience than the protagonist, but it raises an interesting question about how to compare them. The King's speech may mostly serve to show that a suffering conscience is no guarantee of moral behavior and so prepare us to accept Hamlet's probing toward a more sophisticated view of conscience in the soliloquy.

Because this soliloquy has been interpreted in many ways, it will help to provide a summary of what I think is the most obvious way to read the surface meaning of the speech, as a basis for further discussion.[10] Ostensibly, the question is whether to live or die, and the criterion for the answer is which is nobler if to live is to suffer life's torments passively and to die is to fight against myriad evils and be killed in the unequal contest against the King (56-60). Hamlet finds death desirable so long as he can think of it as a peaceful state of dreamless sleep (60-4). He is perhaps too absorbed in his reverie to think of the Ghost (78-80), but perhaps Hamlet's experience with that spirit evokes the thought that death can be a state of nightmare torment (65-8). The fear of this torment is all that keeps us from committing suicide to escape life's pains (66-83). Thus conscience makes cowards of us all by making us fear punishment for suicide or for carrying out "enterprises of great pitch and moment" such as "taking arms" against a foe. The resolution to act is sickened into pallid thinking about the possible consequences of our actions (83-8).

Although Hamlet's judgment of conscience is negative, it may arise from a more honest conscience than most. Hamlet acknowledges that he longs to escape the evils of the world and that he refrains from suicide or revenge not because he feels they are morally wrong, but because such acts may be punished after death. In this Hamlet is honest about his conscience, saying he does not deeply accept its moral judgments, yet is afraid to disobey it. Hamlet errs, however, in saying that fear makes "us all" obey conscience. Since Claudius has just mentioned his conscience, we note that it has not kept him from doing evil, and various enterprises proceed apace in Hamlet's world undaunted by conscience.

Indeed, Hamlet reveals here a more potent conscience than most. Although his frustration may make it reinforcing to condemn his conscience as mere cowardice, he says he has felt compelled to obey it. His concern not to cause his own damnation is serious, for he has referred to it in each of his major soliloquies, in 1.2, at the end of 2.2, and again here. Originally this concern may have been an opportune rationalization to justify the avoidance of deeds—suicide or revenge—he could not bring himself to perform for other reasons. But in order to work as a rationalization, this concern had to be believable to Hamlet as an intention. Therefore as an intention it can act as a rule guiding his behavior as long as it and the behavior it guides continue to be reinforced. There may be another rationalization here, too. Torn between his nobility and his morality, Hamlet's saying all humans suffer his malaise lets him see his problem as a general one he should not blame himself for too much.

Perhaps Hamlet is both drawn to and diverted from taking revenge because it will lead to his death: drawn to revenge because it will lead to death as escape (60), diverted from it if this makes him see revenge as a form of suicide and hence a cause of damnation. Also, he may think of a mode of revenge that will result in his death (taking arms against a sea of troubles), because suicidal behavior—not including consciously suicidal thoughts—is strongly reinforced even when he intends to think of a revenge action. In this sense suicide may be a theme from the very beginning of the speech, and it can be linked with Hamlet's desire for nobility, which is also expressed in the heroic imagery of taking arms against a sea of troubles.

The strength of noble thoughts for Hamlet can perhaps especially be seen in his discounting conscience as mere cowardice. His disposition to be concerned about integrity and virtue suggests that he would usually value conscience, but when behavior that violates his conscience is strongly reinforced as noble, his thinking alters. Hamlet illustrates very richly the way thought and action can change with changing circumstances and with changes in the behavior that is prepotent.

A psychological analysis should also take into account Hamlet's agony of soul in this soliloquy. Conscience in the sense of "consciousness" achieves a victory here as Hamlet is able to open his eyes wide to the painful conditions of human life as he sees them. Even if he has unknowingly made his world seem worse to him than it is, he shows the tragic figure's capacity to question deeply and to suffer heroically. Hamlet exemplifies Marsilio Ficino's tragic conception of Promethean man, great in his intellectual capacity, but in his use of intellect "uncertain, vacillating, and distressed," "made wretched by the . . . most ravenous of vultures, that is, by the torment of inquiry" (208).

This is the first of two scenes in which Hamlet speaks a monologue while another character seems to be praying (cf. 3.3). Comparison of the two speeches leads to the question of why Hamlet no longer thinks of fears of damnation in the prayer scene. The scene with Ophelia that follows the "To be or not to be" soliloquy is also paralleled in the scene with his mother that follows the prayer scene. Comparison of Hamlet's bitter attacks on Ophelia and Gertrude strengthens the impression that his disposition toward his mother at least partly shapes his response to Ophelia: "Frailty, thy name is woman" (1.2.146). Hamlet does not attack Ophelia only because he is bitter at his mother, however. Ophelia returns his love-tokens, and he shows that this hurts him when he replies by denying he has ever given her anything (3.1.93-6). This reply hurts Ophelia, and her response appears to be an effort to retaliate, since she says he has proved "unkind" (97-102). Then this speech of Ophelia's, in turn, may well evoke Hamlet's attack, which begins immediately in his line "Ha, ha! Are you honest?" (103). He may think she is dishonest because she accuses him of being unkind when she is the one who ended their courtship, or because he senses the falseness of her pose of religious devotion when she has brought all the tokens he has given her and has a self-righteous

couplet ready that rhymes her "noble mind" with his having proved "unkind" (100-1).

Hamlet's feelings toward his mother and Ophelia heighten each other here. His mother's behavior has disposed him to be angry at all women as frail, and hence to be reinforced for attacking them. Then he is hurt by Ophelia's rejection and angered by her dishonesty, which in turn may make him think more specifically of his mother. Thinking of his mother presumably increases his anger, and it evidently contributes greatly to the specific things he says—many of his particular accusations seem to be much more strongly evoked by his mother's conduct than Ophelia's (esp. 111-15, 136-51). Thus Hamlet and Ophelia at first attack each other in a vicious circle of hurt provoking greater hurt, and Hamlet's bitterness toward his mother feeds his responses to Ophelia and is fed by Ophelia's responses to him, so that his attack is savagely in excess of anything Ophelia has done to provoke him.

Insofar as Ophelia's rejection hurts Hamlet, it appears not only that he loved her once, as he says at one point (115), but also that he still feels love for her. In telling her to go to a nunnery, he intends to help her escape from corruption and from the evil he feels welling up in himself (121-31). Although "nunnery" could mean "brothel" here as part of his attack on Ophelia, the context each time he uses this word suggests that she should go to the nunnery to *escape* from evil. Hamlet is profoundly ambivalent toward Ophelia here: he knows their love cannot survive what is to happen, and he is bitter at his mother, Ophelia, and himself for complicity in creating their hopeless situation. Indeed, his attack on Ophelia may be an expression of ambivalence, since it may partly be reinforced as behavior that will end her love for him and so lessen her suffering as well as his for the loss of their love. Hamlet's behavior can be reinforced both by this consequence and by the hurt inflicted on Ophelia.

This analysis of why Hamlet unleashes his tirade against Ophelia obviates the need to assume that at some point he realizes they are being spied upon: if Ophelia's behavior seems dishonest to him, he may infer on this basis that they are being watched. But does Hamlet behave as though he thinks they are being watched? Does he shape his attack to create a certain impression on an audience, perhaps the usual impression that he is mad? The evidence that he tries to affect a hidden audience more directly, such as his reference to his vengefulness and the statement that one who is married will not live, can instead be used to argue that he is *not* aware of having a hidden audience, since these lines betray his secret purpose (125, 150). But the crucial point is that if Hamlet pretends at all, this does not prevent his becoming caught up in an emotional tirade. In this scene he is first so absorbed in his meditation that he does not notice Ophelia; then when he does notice her, he is drawn from his meditative mood into a nearly hysterical state, and he remains at this pitch of intensity until just before his exit.

Hamlet's instructions to the actors and his dialogue with Horatio in 3.2 show that when he is not with those who provoke his passion or evoke his antic role he is capable of normal behavior. He may especially urge the players to hold the mirror up to nature in their acting (1-35) because their performance must be natural enough to catch the conscience of the King by mirroring his guilty image. Although Hamlet is moved in expressing his admiration and affection to Horatio, his emotion is not unbalanced and it subsides immediately when he begins to explain his purpose for staging "The Murder of Gonzago" (54-87). Hamlet is presumably moved to praise Horatio as a man who is not passion's slave partly in response to the pain of his own passionate behavior. Yet, whatever regret he feels for his passion does not seem to include regret that it has most recently hurt Ophelia. He plays cruelly with her feelings as part of his antic performance for the court following this dialogue with Horatio (108-49). Telling Horatio that "I must be idle" as the others enter (90), Hamlet indicates that he quite deliberately puts on the antic disposition, yet his wit has a hectic quality suggesting he is caught up in the excitement of his expectation of triumph over Claudius. In this excitement he finds it especially reinforcing to gloat in the power of his wit to make everyone squirm, and Ophelia is easy for him to victimize.

Hamlet identifies the murderer in the play-within-the-play as the "nephew to the King" (3.2.239). In some interpretations this reveals that Hamlet unconsciously identifies with Claudius as the murderer who killed his father. This is possible, but there are also more immediate causes to consider. Hamlet now thinks that he wants to kill the King and so may speak in a way that identifies himself with the murderer of the King because it would be reinforcing for him to kill King Claudius, and he may not notice the import of his words if it would be aversive for him to see that he reveals his purpose. He can be unaware that he identifies himself as the murderer, for his statement about the murderer's identity is evidently a fact in "The Murder of Gonzago," and he need only see this to explain his behavior to himself. Further, his excitement and his hatred could make frightening the King so reinforcing that Hamlet blurts out these words without noticing how they undermine his avowed purpose in staging the play by making it uncertain whether the King's emotional response to the play is guilt or fear.

Once again it is also possible that Hamlet, without being aware of it, recoils from killing the King, so that the statement that the murderer is the nephew of the King is reinforced because it warns Claudius of the threat Hamlet poses. Since Hamlet thinks he wants to kill the King, however, he would find it aversive to think he recoils from the deed, so awareness of this will likely be repressed. Saying the murderer is the nephew of the King may then be reinforced because frightening the King is one kind of revenge still possible for Hamlet. According to this view Hamlet is ambivalent: two opposed behaviors are strong in him, to revenge and not to revenge, and each controls what he says and does in some degree.

Others in the court think the play threatens or falsely accuses Claudius, and the only reason Hamlet can be so sure of his interpretation of Claudius's reaction is that he knows what others do not, that the play mirrors the Ghost's story. But this suggests that Hamlet's interpretation is at least partly based on a prejudgment and on his hatred of the King which makes it reinforcing for him to find confirmation of the King's guilt. Horatio's agreement with Hamlet's view might show that the King's reaction is unambiguously a guilty one except that Hamlet has shared his knowledge and his prejudgment with his friend. Horatio is not embroiled in Hamlet's personal passions, but he has the same "reasons" to see the King as guilty. To Horatio, as to Hamlet, the King's reaction to the play itself is the thing to watch and there is no reason to relate Hamlet's remark about the nephew of the King to the moment of testing the King's conscience. When the King reacts strongly to the murder, Hamlet and Horatio therefore see no reason to doubt that his reaction is guilt and not fear, or horror that Hamlet should falsely accuse him of so awful a crime. Yet the courtiers who are ignorant of the Ghost's "facts" and Hamlet's reason to focus on the play by itself will interpret the episode as a whole, so that Hamlet's remarks about the play appear to convey his purpose for staging it. The play scene shows how much our responses to events depend on complex contingencies of character, situation, and point of view.

Although Hamlet's situation may lead him to err about the King's reaction to the play, the King is nevertheless guilty and presumably should be punished. But Hamlet's thinking about Claudius also affects his thinking about others, and his actions against them are not so justified. His treatment of Rosencrantz and Guildenstern here seems especially erring. Between 2.2 and late in the play scene, they have reported their observations of Hamlet to the King and Queen (3.1.1-28), but in that episode there is no sign they are evil spies or that their report is not intended to help the King and Queen cure their friend. Rosencrantz and Guildenstern think Hamlet is suffering from melancholy and hence needs to be helped by friends in a manipulative way,[11] and nothing the King and Queen say to them suggests any motive other than to restore Hamlet to health.

The dialogue of Rosencrantz and Guildenstern with Hamlet following the play-within-the-play shows how tragedy arises from mutual misunderstanding. Hamlet thinks he has proven the King's guilt, and in his excitement he does not seem to understand that his friends think he has threatened to kill the King instead (as they say in 3.3.8-23). Their speeches to Hamlet have a tone of impatience and rebuke. In the first part of the dialogue, Guildenstern's impatience gradually increases as Hamlet interrupts with what his friend can only perceive as irresponsible wit (3.2.289-310). Guildenstern feels that Hamlet has behaved outrageously and he dares to be openly critical of these interruptions (300-1, 306-10). On his side, Hamlet is offended by his friends' manner and by their taking what appears to be the King's point of view. Unable to see the possible alternative causes of his friends' conduct, Hamlet evidently infers betrayal. This inference would be reinforced because it fits his earlier suspicions of them and his general view that all at court are corrupt.

The episode reaches its crisis when Rosencrantz half-exasperatedly and half-imploringly says "My lord, you once did love me" (326). But it is too late—Hamlet now interprets everything by his inference that his old friends have betrayed him (327-63). What seems a sincere if desperate and pathetically ill-timed plea for Hamlet to let his friends help him evokes a response that they are only trying to trap him and to play upon him. Guildenstern's last effort to reach Hamlet is "O my lord, if my duty be too bold, my love is too unmannerly" (339-40). This statement expresses the traditional idea that an honest friend or courtier who loves his prince should tell him boldly but courteously when he does wrong and should seek to help him improve his conduct (Castiglione 297; bk 4). The statement is certainly not too hard to explicate for a person of Hamlet's wit—Guildenstern claims that he has been doing his duty and that if he has been too bold in doing it, he is motivated by his love of Hamlet, which transcends mere courtesy and custom. Hamlet's response epitomizes the tragic theme of the scene: "I do not well understand that" (341). When Polonius enters, once again there is mutual misunderstanding caused partly by Hamlet's absorption in his own point of view. As explained earlier, Hamlet thinks he shows Polonius to be a fool by playing the Fool while Polonius evidently thinks of himself as humoring a madman (367-76). Hamlet remarks that these men are pushing him to the extremity of the role of Fool (375), but once again his absorption in the narrow viewpoint of his antic disposition, coupled with his excited and threatening behavior, contributes to the folly of what happens.

Thus Hamlet is tightly enclosed in his alienated vision by the end of the scene, when he asks to be left alone. The first lines of his soliloquy echo the imagery of hellish midnight in the speech of Lucianus, suggesting that Hamlet has now come to think as the murderer does, that the nephew of the King has become Lucianus (249-54, 379-83). This parallel prompts comparison of the revenger's psychology with the murderer's, and we may wish we could find that Hamlet is exaggerating his murderousness as a way to work himself up to kill Claudius. But Hamlet is already worked up to a demonic pitch at the start of the soliloquy, and in his second sentence he begins to cool as drinking hot blood is something he merely says he "could" do (381). Following this he thinks only of how he should behave when he goes to his mother.

But why does Hamlet go to Gertrude instead of killing the King now that he is convinced his revenge is just and he feels ready to do bitter business? The first lines of the soliloquy imply that he takes for granted that in his present mood he is already prepared to act vengefully, and it seems this is why his attention so quickly focusses on the need to separate his violent intentions regarding the King from his purposes regarding his mother. Hamlet sees the danger of killing her, too, in his rage, but not the reverse of this, that thoughts about not using daggers on his mother, but speaking them, may divert him from stabbing the King.

The vehemence of Hamlet's attack on Gertrude in the closet scene suggests that the main cause of his deciding, in this soliloquy, to go to her and not to the King is that speaking daggers to her is powerfully reinforced. Then, too, his mother has asked to see him now. Her request could function as a conscious pretext for delaying his revenge if going to her is partly reinforced because it enables him to escape from anxiety associated with killing his uncle. Nothing Hamlet says in this soliloquy suggests, however, that he perceives himself to be delaying revenge in a sense that casts doubt on his strength of purpose.

Hamlet's monologue in the prayer scene is an extreme example of absorbed thinking that narrowly focuses only on one way of analyzing a situation (3.3.73-96). He analyzes what revenge demands if he is to seek full retribution for what his father has suffered, but the analysis becomes more and more passionate as it proceeds, and he does not consider what he will do to himself by deliberately seeking to damn Claudius. Since Hamlet is familiar with ideas about self-damning acts, we may infer that he has heard (or could figure out for himself) that to seek someone's damnation is such an act. Earlier he has repeatedly expressed a concern that he should not damn himself. Now, however, his newly confirmed hatred of Claudius makes it so reinforcing to think of damning his foe that such thoughts are entirely absorbing, entirely prepotent over thoughts which would lead away from such a goal, so that any concern about damning himself is repressed.

Nonetheless, killing Claudius could still be aversive to Hamlet for any or all of the reasons reviewed earlier and also, at this moment, because it would be horrible to kill a person in the attitude of prayer. Hamlet's passionate determination to damn his uncle may then be regarded as a rationalization, enabling him to delay revenge and also to avoid thinking he does so for any purpose except to punish Claudius more severely. If, however, Hamlet's idea that he wants to damn his uncle is at all a rationalization, it is a passionate one and may become his purpose. Indeed, even if this rationale were a totally false explanation of Hamlet's behavior, once it occurs to him and is strongly reinforced as his purpose because of his anger and because it justifies his delay, it can guide future behavior as an intention—a discriminative stimulus. The reinforcement of this way of thinking could cause it to become strong behavior for Hamlet to seek the damnation of his foes.

The view that Hamlet spares the King at prayer partly because he so urgently wants to confront his mother appears to be confirmed in the closet scene. Hamlet's purpose and his anger so totally absorb him that he is nearly oblivious of all else. He brushes aside his mother's efforts to lecture him (3.4.8-19); her wrongdoing, not his, is the issue. He says he will set up a mirror to show her the innermost parts of herself, but he has no mirror to show him how his rage might evoke her cry for help (3.4.17-21). In some performances, Hamlet draws his sword to keep his mother from leaving, or still has it in his hand from the preceding scene, and he unthinkingly holds it up so its blade can be like a mirror turned toward her. Somehow it seems to Gertrude, as she cries out, that Hamlet's speaking daggers is about to become physical action. Then Polonius, too, cries out, startling Hamlet in his rage so that he reacts "rashly" and stabs through the arras. The act of stabbing is powerfully reinforced because Hamlet is in such a rage, and the person stabbed might be almost any of the several people he now hates. This stabbing could also be reinforced because it strikes at a foe while avoiding the aversive process of preparing a purposeful revenge. Indeed, this stabbing could conceivably be reinforced as well because it might allow Hamlet to avoid a purposeful revenge altogether by resulting in his being restrained from future action. In any case, Hamlet's words suggest that he does not consciously think it is the King behind the arras as he stabs. His mother asks him what he has done and he says he does not know; then he asks whether it was the King (25-6). At most he hoped it was the King as he stabbed.

When his mother reproaches him for his "rash and bloody deed" (27), Hamlet minimizes what he has done, not only to avoid guilt but also because he is now so strongly reinforced for speaking daggers to her that he will not let anything divert him. His deed is, he allows, "Almost as bad" as hers of killing a king and marrying his brother (28-9). His absorption in her evil will not

let Hamlet see how his killing Polonius undercuts his righteous indignation, showing him to be rash in the sense of attacking others' vices while overlooking his own. Gertrude's surprise at the accusation of murder (30) appears to convince Hamlet that she did not know of that crime, since after this he reproaches her only for her marriage to Claudius. If Hamlet no longer thinks she is guilty of murder, then evidently his thoughts about her relationship with Claudius are enough to absorb him intensely. On the other hand, if he continues to think she is guilty of murder, his preoccupation with this relationship is so strong that thoughts of the murder are crowded out.

Hamlet also judges rashly in putting all the blame on Polonius for his own death. Hamlet says Polonius was a "wretched, rash, intruding fool" (31), but if he saw how these words could apply to himself he would not use them so scornfully of Polonius. Hamlet's statement that Polonius has been too "busy" may also apply to himself (33). In the Elizabethan translation of Plutarch's moral essays by Philemon Holland, a person who looks for evil in others while not seeing his own faults is called a busybody ("Of Curiosity").

"I took thee for thy better" again reveals more about Hamlet than about his victim (32). Hamlet now finds it reinforcing to believe that when he stabbed he thought it was the King behind the arras. Moreover, these words say the King is Polonius's "better," suggesting that Hamlet vaguely rationalizes Polonius's death as not very significant because he is a social inferior. Hamlet's thinking here is at least as strongly rooted in princely ideology as in morality, since he does not believe Claudius is morally better than Polonius. Later the same kind of judgment is part of Hamlet's attitude toward Rosencrantz and Guildenstern, when he speaks of their "baser nature" as contrasted with Claudius as well as himself (5.2.60-2).

Hamlet brushes aside his mother's anguish over what he has done and insists that she should let him wring her heart (3.4.34-5). Hard as his own heart has been toward Polonius, he now suggests that "damned custom" has "braz'd" her heart so it is "proof and bulwark against sense" (36-8). Especially in the context of the other ironies here, these lines suggest that as "custom" or habit is hardening Hamlet to hate and scorn most of the people in his world, he is losing his sensitivity to others' suffering and his ability to see from any point of view but his own.

Gertrude's responses show that he "roars" and "thunders" in his tirade against her (52; cf. 39-40). Later in the scene Hamlet claims that he is "cruel only to be kind" (180), that he speaks daggers only to bring Gertrude to repentance. But he does not assert this intention until the Ghost makes him look to his own behavior as well as hers. Before going to her chamber he has said he would be cruel to her, would speak daggers to her so she would be "shent" (3.2.387-90). Editors have usually been kind to Hamlet by glossing "shent" as "rebuked," "reproved," or "censured." The *Oxford English Dictionary* tells us, however, that to shend is to disgrace, to put to shame or confusion; to blame, revile, or scold; to destroy, ruin or injure, including to disfigure, corrupt, infect, soil, and defile. That Hamlet intends something like this in saying he will shend her is clear when he says the shending must be only in words and not also in murderous deeds that would confirm the thrust of his words (389-90).

Before the Ghost comes, there is no indication Hamlet intends to do anything except force his mother to see her inmost evils in order to hurt her. He may also have a dim intention to bring her to repentance, but if he does have such an intention, it is in some degree a rationalization, since in his extreme anger his behavior is of a sort that seems more calculated to "Make mad the guilty" than to enlighten her (2.2.558). Hamlet gives no hint of any compassionate understanding; indeed, he takes the view that Gertrude's behavior has been well-nigh incomprehensible in human terms (3.4.63-81). When she says Hamlet has succeeded in making her see her corrupt nature, he continues to stab with his imaginings of her vile sexual encounters with Claudius (88-94). She replies that his "words like daggers enter in my ears," confirming that he has sufficiently spoken daggers to her if he is attacking her only so she will repent (94-96). Yet when she says this, Hamlet intensifies his attack (96-103).

If Hamlet's purpose were to bring her to repentance, he would by now begin to preach as he does later in the scene when this becomes his stated purpose. As it is, his attack is ended only by the Ghost, who expresses fear for what the "conceit" Hamlet has forced on his mother's soul may do to her, and urges him to help her (112-15). To argue thus that Hamlet's attacking Gertrude is reinforced because it punishes her is not to say this is the only cause of his behavior. The Oedipal attachment makes speaking daggers to her be reinforced as a way to create emotional intimacy between them as they break down together. In addition, hurting his mother, especially speaking daggers to her, could be reinforced as a form of sexual sadism.

The re-appearance of the Ghost causes thoughts of using daggers to become prepotent over speaking them for Hamlet. Even before the Ghost speaks, its presence reminds Hamlet of its command and he thinks of how he has been "tardy" in his revenge (107-9). Hamlet's saying he is "laps'd in . . . passion" is interestingly ambiguous: he probably means he has let the passion for revenge lapse in himself, but part of the cause for this is that he has lapsed into passion, has failed to act as much because of the passions he *has* experienced as because he has lacked passion.

The Queen sees no Ghost and so her thoughts are turned from her own sins to Hamlet's madness. The situation is similar to the start of the scene, as Gertrude and Hamlet see each other to be erring, but they are now more compassionate toward each other and more aware of a need to respond to the other's point of view. Gertrude pities her son for his madness, and because she does not see the Ghost, Hamlet thinks he must explain his behavior to show that he is sane and therefore to be listened to when he tells her about herself (142-51). It would be very reinforcing for Hamlet to believe his explanation that his purpose has only been to move her to repentance (151-7)—especially after the Ghost has urged him to help her—and not that he spoke earlier in vengeful rage.

Thus Hamlet may sincerely think he was cruel "only" to be kind (180), yet his thinking this is also a defensive rationalization. His rationalization becomes extreme when he asks Gertrude to forgive his "virtue" and personifies himself as Virtue in deploring how Virtue must beg pardon and bow and "woo" to be allowed to help Vice reform (154-7). He did not speak in a submissively courteous tone earlier, and the body of Polonius lying on the stage shows that Hamlet is wildly mistaken to regard himself as so near to Virtue.

Hamlet urges Gertrude to reform by habituating herself to sexual abstinence (159-72). He knows that being moved to repentance is not enough, that if she is really to change, her sexual behavior must be habituated so she will no longer desire Claudius. Ironically, Hamlet's statement also applies to the way he himself is changing through his own actions and thoughts, becoming brazed to killing and perhaps "mad in craft" (190). At the moment, however, his intention to reform Gertrude and his thinking of himself as virtuous make it reinforcing for him to repent the killing of Polonius (174-9). Hamlet accepts responsibility for his deed (178-9), and he also speaks of his revenge as a punishment of himself. In this he shows how aversive he finds the Ghost's command: "heaven hath pleas'd it so, / To punish me with this and this with me, / That I must be their scourge and minister" (175-7).

This part of what he says also weakens his repentance insofar as he claims that he did Heaven's will in slaying Polonius. For the first time Hamlet hints that revenge requires the death of more than Claudius, and it seems he thinks this way chiefly because such thoughts allow him to feel justified for killing Polonius. It would be much less aversive to think Heaven has used him to punish Polonius, and through him the King, than to think he has killed a foolish old man in a wild rage. It may even be less aversive to think of himself as a damned agent of God—one meaning of "scourge"—than to think he is a damned agent of his own murderous rage in an act that foolishly dooms himself and has no moral or political value at all. If this reading is correct, Hamlet's concern with his mother's repentance and his turning to repentance himself have deeply ironic consequences insofar as his repentance leads him to see the death of Polonius as providential.

The plurality of evil ones who are to die is next expanded to include Rosencrantz and Guildenstern. Hamlet thinks they know he is to be killed when they reach England, for he speaks of destroying them with the weapon they mean to use against him (206-11). Their dialogue with Claudius in 3.3 shows, however, that they believe Hamlet is to be sent to England because he has threatened the King: there is no evidence anywhere that they think the King's sealed commission orders Hamlet's death.

The nature of Hamlet's error in wanting to kill Rosencrantz and Guildenstern is revealed when he takes pleasure in anticipating their destruction, speaking of the "sport" of hoisting the engineer with his own petard, and saying "'tis most sweet / When in one line two crafts directly meet" (208, 211-12). To find it "most sweet" to pit deadly craft against deadly craft is to be essentially "mad in craft" in proto-behaviorist terms, for the pleasure shows that such craftiness is becoming a habit and therefore a characteristic of Hamlet. By the end of the scene, these thoughts have led Hamlet away from repentance for slaying Polonius: as he removes the body he expresses a sportful, mocking contempt that minimizes the importance of the slaying (213-18). In addition, once Hamlet's preoccupation with his mother is out of the way here, his intensely pleasurable anticipation of destroying Rosencrantz and Guildenstern is prepotent over any movement toward killing the King. Hamlet accepts his being sent to England, and here he seems almost to welcome it as an occasion to kill his former friends. Thinking of this kind may well be reinforced partly because it allows him to avoid killing Claudius.

This analysis of the closet scene illustrates how a behaviorist interpretation can unfold the moment-to-moment dynamics of a drama. Particularly valuable is what such an analysis suggests about the importance of thoughts and intentions and how they change. At one moment Hamlet may not have a very clear intention in mind, as perhaps in his rage at the beginning of the scene. Then when the Ghost has prompted him to cease this rage and his mother's doubts of his sanity make it highly reinforcing for him to explain himself, he thinks of an acceptable rationale for his behavior. He is reinforced in believing this rationale by the assurance it gives him that he has behaved sanely and even virtuously. Hence it becomes his sincere intention to reform his mother, and this intention guides his behavior as he tells her how to reform. This brings him to thoughts of his own need to repent, but then he finds it reinforcing to think his actions are fulfilling the intentions of Heaven and he widens his revenge to include Polonius. Once Polonius is seen as having fallen under Heaven's doom, the revenge can widen further, to include Rosencrantz and Guildenstern. Thus intentions can control behavior, but the intentions are part of the behavior and are subject to the same contingencies of reinforcement as other activities.

This view of Hamlet does not mean he is insincere in his concern for virtue or his mother. He intensely feels what he says at each moment; indeed, it is the intensity of his sincere thinking which so absorbs him. And it is not that Hamlet behaves in merely contradictory ways. The changes in his behavior reflect a coherent character, a character having the complexity to be moved in complex ways as the action unfolds.

In my initial discussion of the antic disposition I said that some of Hamlet's behavior in Act 4, scenes 2 and 3 may be out of control. Thus his saying that he has "Safely stowed" Polonius's body seems out of touch with reality if he thinks he has adequately disposed of the body by putting it in the lobby upstairs. Hamlet has evidently been absorbed in hiding the body and thinking about its being safely stowed, for when he is called he expresses surprise, as if he has been wakened from preoccupation: "Safely stowed. [*Calling within.*] But soft, what noise? Who calls on Hamlet? O, here they come" (4.2.1-3). Most of what Hamlet says in these scenes, however, has the tone of the antic wit at its highest pitch of controlled intensity, and any element of apparent madness may reflect hectic excitement. Certainly Hamlet now has cause to play the antic disposition as madly as possible to give the impression that he has not "murdered" Polonius but killed him in a mad fit. Hamlet's concern with seeking cover by hiding the body of Polonius and then hiding himself in his antic disposition blocks any action against the King. Hamlet's anxiety about confronting his foes after he has killed Polonius evidently makes self-concealment prepotent over other behavior.

Hamlet's soliloquy in response to the sight of Fortinbras's army invites comparison with the soliloquy at the end of Act 2. Again Hamlet's disposition to act nobly makes it reinforcing to punish himself when he sees someone who acts vigorously with less cause than he himself has to act (4.4.32-66). As before, he suspects himself of cowardice, but now he denies that he lacks will and strength and more explicitly blames his disposition, as an intellectual and a Christian moralist, to think about outcomes. As a subject in the psychological sense, he is divided between the disposition to nobility and honor and the disposition to think morally. He defends reason as given by God, but disparages careful foresight as more cowardly than wise. Hamlet does not question the validity of the reasoning he did earlier so much as he suggests that his thinking was to justify a delay caused mostly by fear: "some craven scruple / Of thinking too precisely on th'event—

/ A thought which, quarter'd, hath but one part wisdom / And ever three parts coward—" (40-3). Hamlet here accuses himself of what we call rationalization. There are references to rationalization in other works of Shakespeare,[12] but Hamlet is one of the few characters to ever see it in himself.

Yet Hamlet has little insight here. When he thinks of cowardice as an explanation of his delay, he examines himself no further. The accusation of cowardice is especially painful to a prince, and hence is especially reinforced as punishment. Hamlet wants to discredit himself, but his conclusion that he has been a coward, though it may have some truth, allows him to avoid probing for other causes of delay, some of which might discredit him more. Thus he uses Fortinbras as a model to torment himself with the thought that he has failed to act greatly when his honor is at stake: "a father kill'd, a mother stain'd, / Excitements of my reason and my blood" (57-8). His emotion makes it reinforcing for him to think that henceforth his thoughts must "be bloody or be nothing worth" (66)—he does not want any "thinking too precisely on th'event" to block the bloody deed of revenge. Evidently he intends no longer to think of how he may damn himself or others in what he does, since such thoughts about consequences have especially delayed his revenge. But Hamlet's passionate concern for honor in thinking about "th'event" makes it reinforcing for him to renounce the kind of thinking necessary for truly honorable action. Ironically, to avoid the dishonor of thinking himself a coward, he may think in a way that leads him to act dishonorably in the treacherous means he uses to destroy Rosencrantz and Guildenstern.

Hamlet does not appear again until he returns from the voyage to England, but in 4.6 his letter to Horatio shows he is not a coward in the ordinary sense, for he was the first to board a pirate ship when it attacked. We cannot say, however, that he did this in order to return to Denmark for revenge. Hamlet's apparent purpose was to help repel the pirates, and he became a prisoner when the pirates then broke off the fight (4.6.15-18).

Hamlet and Horatio enter in the graveyard scene as the First Gravedigger sings of his youth and love while digging Ophelia's grave:

HAM. Has this fellow no feeling of his
        business a sings in grave-making?
HOR. Custom hath made it in him a property
        of easiness.
HAM. 'Tis e'en so, the hand of little
        employment hath the daintier sense.
                                              (5.1.65-9)

These lines refer to the proto-behaviorist idea that the most unpleasant activities become easy and even pleasant through habituation. The passage recalls Hamlet's suggestion that his mother has been so "braz'd" or hardened to sin by habit that she may be incapable of sensing the evil of what she has done (3.4.35-8). In 5.1 perhaps more than in the closet scene the statement about habituation raises a question about Hamlet, inasmuch as the Gravedigger is less a character than a figure whose primary function is to be a mirror held up to Hamlet's antic disposition as this disposition fades.

Thus the statement about the Gravedigger's habituation leads to the question whether Hamlet now finds it easy to jest about death, too. If Hamlet comes to terms with death here, he does so on the basis of a hardening of his sensitivities in which he excludes awareness of matters that might cause him pain. By now Hamlet has killed Polonius with his own hand, has used his hand to write Rosencrantz and Guildenstern's death warrant, and has fought the pirates in hand-to-hand combat, so perhaps his hand is no longer the "hand of little employment" that has "the daintier sense" of death. Hamlet may be insensitive in part because he avoids thinking of the deaths of Polonius and his father: the graveyard evokes no remark at all about either of them.[13]

Hamlet's response to death here shows no grief or compassion until his personal relationship with Yorick begins to bring death closer to him. Until then, the single exception tends to confirm this generalization, for it comes at the start in what Hamlet says about the Gravedigger's insensitivity that lets him treat a skull as though he did not know it "had a tongue in it, and could sing once" (74). After this through line 115 there is no sign that Hamlet responds to death as destroying a creature capable of song. Hamlet's comments on death in these lines take a sardonic view of life as a base pursuit of worldly goods that death shows to be futile. Although a similar view is found in Christian thinking, there the idea is to renounce worldly values for the sake of the soul. Nowhere in this scene does Hamlet express any hope, or any concern for the human soul. In this part of the graveyard scene, Hamlet's only regret seems to be that death ends all distinctions of social class. He comments that the Sexton's spade striking Lady Worm's skull is "fine revolution," and he continues, "Did these bones cost no more the breeding but to play at loggets with 'em? Mine ache to think on't" (87-91). We hear this complaint again when the Gravedigger insolently equivocates in answering his question of who the grave is for, and Hamlet says that "the age is grown so picked that the toe of the peasant comes so near the heel of the courtier he galls his kibe" (135-8). Yet even in these complaints Hamlet gives the impression that he feels detached from individual human lives and deaths.

Hamlet shows he is detached, too, in the way his concern about the Gravedigger's insolence diverts him from the question about whose grave is being dug, immediately after he has been told it is for a woman, to the question of how long the fellow has been digging graves (130-8). We know that this is Ophelia's grave, and as we respond to the structure of this scene we are waiting for Hamlet to be jolted out of his impersonal attitude by the news of her death. Hence the statement that a woman had died prompts us to think Hamlet should ask who it is—not be so easily diverted—if he is really concerned and not merely curious in his questioning.

Even when the Gravedigger unearths the skull of Yorick, Hamlet responds with personal feeling only briefly. Soon Yorick's skull becomes an impersonal symbol to use in expressing the traditional warning that the life of the flesh is transitory, that we should remember death (178-89). Again, Hamlet says nothing of the soul; instead he follows the skull into the earth and comments on the "base uses" to which "we may return" (196-209). Hamlet's thinking continues to be narrowly focussed even in the words that express the part of the traditional *memento mori* idea he does utter: "Now get you to my lady's chamber and tell her, let her paint an inch thick, to this favour she must come. Make her laugh at that" (186-9). Hamlet has no intuition that *his* lady is already dead. Only his ignorance lets him speak this way: he has not fully hardened into a person who can laugh at death, for when Ophelia's body is brought in he is overcome with emotion.

Hamlet's use of Yorick's skull as a symbol and his speaking of his lady as a social type lead him back to his concern about how death makes noble bones ache: "Dost thou think Alexander looked o' this fashion i'th' earth?" (191-2). Hamlet's perception that death brings human greatness to "base uses" moves him to a deep sense of loss that he counters with irony: "O that that earth which kept the world in awe / Should patch a wall t'expel the winter's flaw" (208-9). These lines do not express an acceptance of death that frees Hamlet to act but a tragic prince's concern with death as the destroyer of human greatness. Paradoxically, Hamlet's disposition as tragic prince has displaced concern for the soul, choked off compassion for the loss of song, and provoked scorn of petty worldlings.

When Hamlet asks "Why, may not imagination trace the noble dust of Alexander till a find it stopping a bung-hole?" (196-8), Horatio's reply, "Twere to consider too curiously to consider so" aptly indicates how Hamlet's thinking has led him away from what he most needs to think about if he is to act effectively or greatly (199). In ancient, medieval, and Renaissance writers "curiosity" is often used to mean a vice of inquiring about things in a way that leads to the wrong kind of knowledge. Even so free a thinker as Montaigne sometimes uses "curiosity" in this sense (esp. "Apologie" 2.199, "Upon Some Verses" 3:95, 97). Hamlet's think-

ing that minimizes character and spirit as essential greatness does not lead him to think about the fundamental moral and human qualities which his particular greatness depends on. The narrowness of Hamlet's thinking is emphasized by the juxtaposition of his concern for greatness with the entrance of Ophelia's funeral procession. She is a pathetic, not a tragic figure, a victim of the struggle between "mighty opposites." As her body is carried on stage, Hamlet's sensibility could not be further from an intuition of her death.

When he sees that Ophelia is dead, Hamlet becomes so emotionally distracted that for a time he loses his ability to recognize how his killing Polonius has affected Laertes and Ophelia (5.1.239-42, 247-56, 283-5). That Hamlet actually cannot think how he may have offended Laertes—"Hear you, sir, / What is the reason that you use me thus? / I lov'd you ever" (283-5)—may also show how strongly he represses awareness that he has killed Polonius. Laertes has forcefully reminded Hamlet that he killed Polonius (239-42), and it may be part of the point that Laertes's description of Hamlet as a "cursed" one who has committed a "wicked deed" presents the Prince with an image of himself which he cannot recognize. When he later says that the image of his own cause shows him the portraiture of Laertes's (5.2.77-8), Hamlet sees the parallel between himself and Laertes as revengers, but evidently does not see how from Laertes's point of view he appears only as Claudius does to himself, as the murderer of his father—Laertes knows nothing of Hamlet's revenge cause. Again Hamlet interprets a mirror held up to him in a way that reflects his absorption in his own point of view.

Insofar as Hamlet's failures in 5.1 are caused by the overwhelming shock and anguish he feels upon learning of Ophelia's death, sympathy for him is evoked throughout this episode, even in response to his seemingly empty protestations of what he would do to show his love for her. Hamlet is reinforced for thinking and speaking in a way that powerfully expresses his love for Ophelia and thereby not incidentally denies any guilt for her death. This is not to say, however, that he deliberately puts on emotional shows, since Hamlet most needs to convince himself, and he will not be convinced by emotional protestations he sees he is putting on. At the end of his tirade he realizes that he has spoken rant—it has become characteristic of Hamlet to recoil from his own emotionality—but it is in his next speech that he is least in touch with reality, asking Laertes how he has offended him (283-5).

The crucial evidence that Hamlet feels what his words claim he feels about Ophelia is the way he speaks with righteous indignation as though he were simply a faithful lover who has a right to object when his lady's grieving brother expresses great love for her (261-6). In this Hamlet is so preposterously oblivious to the realities that he is probably sincere. In saying he will match Laertes's expressions of grief, Hamlet does not see that Laertes's grief is heightened to a furious passion by vengeful anger. Hamlet says "I will fight with him upon this theme / Until my eyelids will no longer wag" (261-2), meaning the theme of who loved Ophelia more, but this is not the theme upon which Laertes wishes to fight.

Hamlet is calm at the beginning of 5.2, perhaps partly because of the influence of Horatio and partly because passion spends itself (see esp. 5.1.279-83; cf. 3.2.189-92, 4.7.109-14). Here a crucial question is what to make of Hamlet's belief that he has been guided by providence in having Rosencrantz and Guildenstern killed in England. I have explained that according to the traditional meaning of rashness, it is doubtful that Hamlet should praise rashness as a mode of providential action. Hamlet's belief that Rosencrantz and Guildenstern have betrayed his friendship is what makes him so bitter toward them. The evidence, however, does not so clearly support Hamlet's suspicions as to justify sending them to death with no chance of defending themselves. And if they did not know the content of the King's sealed orders, once he destroyed those orders Hamlet had no need to have them killed for fear they would have sought to contrive his death in England.

The text of 5.2.6-48 and the relation of this to what Hamlet says at the end of the closet scene indicate that Hamlet was guided by habit, not providence, when he stole the King's commission and forged a replacement. In part Hamlet believes he was guided by providence because before he could address his "brains" regarding what they should do, they began to write a new scenario (30-1) in the forged commission: that is, he wrote intuitively, without thinking first. But his action here carries out his earlier intention to use craft to destroy Rosencrantz and Guildenstern through the means that were to be used for his own destruction (3.4.206-11). The thought of forging a commission for their deaths is precisely what could be expected to occur intuitively to Hamlet when he finds a commission for his death and is disposed to hoist the engineer with his own petard. There is also evidence that Hamlet acted intuitively on the basis of habit in the suggestion that he took pleasure in forging a new commission—he certainly is excited and pleased as he tells Horatio about it (5.2.38-55). Hamlet's pleasure suggests that he was "mad in craft," habituated to its "most sweet" "sport," so that he is insensitive to the reality of what he has done.

Hamlet's thinking seems paranoid when he says he was "benetted round with villainies" (29). Although the sealed commission has proven only the King's

villainy, Hamlet forged orders that would harm only Rosencrantz and Guildenstern. This was an opportunity for Hamlet to act as the rightful King of Denmark, but what he says does not indicate he thought of this, and what he wrote was a parody of the voice of Claudius in the original commission, using fair words to cover a treacherous deed (32-47). Hamlet indicates no awareness that he has come to be at all like Claudius in craftiness or that his actions have been base. He especially shows insensitivity to the substance of his act when he emphasizes the style of handwriting he employed. His perception of what is base here is that he once thought it "baseness" to write clearly, so he labored to un-learn his ability to write in a clear hand (32-6). Yet his earlier learning—the habit of being able to write clearly—still survives, and this habit enabled him to write "fair" or clear copy. That he applies his concern for what is "fair" only to clarity of handwriting parallels the insensitivity of his reference to "baseness." And perhaps it is significant that even fairness in handwriting was an earlier habit Hamlet has practiced to overcome.

When Hamlet turns to "Th'effect" of what he wrote (37), his concern is more with the statesman's rhetorical style than with the substance of his command (38-47). Hamlet is gleeful as he tells of piling up clauses to parody this style, and as he puns on "as" and "ass" (43). This speech contains eight lines of mock-rhetoric and one-and-one-half lines telling what he commanded, that Rosencrantz and Guildenstern should be "put to sudden death / Not shriving-time allow'd" (46-7). Horatio's question about how he sealed the forged commission evokes the response that "even in that was heaven ordinant" (47-8). The "even" here suggests Hamlet finds it reinforcing to think Heaven was ordinant in the action he has just been narrating. He feels that Heaven has approved of what he has done when he says his indiscretion has served him "well" and this shows there's a Divinity that shapes our ends (8-10). Moreover, his entire narrative has a self-satisfied tone, and he goes on to say that the fate of Rosencrantz and Guildenstern does not "come near" his conscience (58).

But if Heaven was ordinant in Hamlet's sending Rosencrantz and Guildenstern to death without shriving time—an evil if not Satanic act—this could only mean that Heaven used Hamlet as an evil instrument of its vengeance. Since Rosencrantz and Guildenstern may have been guilty of betraying Hamlet, he may have been justified in having them executed and also in having this done "Without debatement further more or less" so they could not argue that he was the one to be killed (45). But Hamlet could have stopped here or he could have used other words to emphasize and enforce his point than "not shriving time allow'd." In their context these words go beyond callousness to suggest that Hamlet feels some gratification at having found justification for letting Rosencrantz and Guildenstern be damned. He draws attention to the nature of his act by his following claim that Heaven has guided him. However guilty Rosencrantz and Guildenstern may be, in a Christian context they should not be deprived of a rite that *they,* at least, might think could save their souls. Hamlet's judgment is deeply tragic as his sense of destiny and right lead him into this dreadful error.

Hamlet does not claim that when he acted on board the ship he thought Heaven was guiding him. He says he did not think about what he was doing, but simply did it intuitively. This may suggest that his idea about providence is a rationalization after the fact to explain and justify his intuitive behavior. Once he has sent Rosencrantz and Guildenstern to death, Hamlet would find it very reinforcing to believe that Heaven directed his actions, but he indicates that he was conscious of his crafty wit at the time he forged the lethal commission, and this challenges his claim that he was not guiding his own conduct. Yet his self-satisfied tone indicates Hamlet is sincere now in thinking providence guided him, and because he believes this, faith in providence can guide his future action.

Ironically, Hamlet's reliance on rashness as providential contributes to his doom. As we saw in the earlier discussion of rashness, Augustine wrote that the rash judge is doomed through his rashness: he judges unjustly, not seeing the "beam" in his own eye while condemning others for "motes," and he is punished through his rash misjudgment of others. Hamlet is killed through his blind trust of Laertes, which is partly caused by his adoption of rashness as providence. Convinced that there is "special providence in the fall of a sparrow," Hamlet now refuses to avoid the potential danger of the fencing match with Laertes (208-20). Hamlet trusts Laertes in a way that expresses the most erring aspect of his rashness. In the graveyard scene he spoke of Laertes as "a very noble youth" (5.1.217), and now he confirms that opinion in saying to Horatio he is sorry he "forgot" himself to Laertes in the graveyard and will "court his favours" (5.2.75-8). This shows that Hamlet still forgets himself to Laertes: Hamlet's reason for being sorry about his earlier behavior is that he sees himself and Laertes to have causes which are the image or portrait of each other, suggesting that Hamlet is inclined to identify with Laertes and to judge him accordingly. But if Hamlet saw his own actions in a clearer light, he would know that he has destroyed Rosencrantz and Guildenstern not nobly but treacherously, so if Laertes is the image of Hamlet, he may be expected to be treacherously vengeful. Thus Hamlet does not expect Laertes's treachery partly because he does not see his own.

To recapitulate the entire ironic pattern of Hamlet's rashness: he judged Rosencrantz and Guildenstern rashly, interpreting their conduct without enough attention to the effect of his behavior on them, assuming they knew they were taking him to his death in England and presuming the nobility and hence justice of his own view. Then this rash judgment led him to doom them rashly, and to avoid guilty thoughts of this he finds it reinforcing, according to the psychology of cognitive dissonance reduction, to think even more strongly than before that his judgment of them was right. This intensifies his sense of himself as noble and hence helps to induce a rash misjudgment of Laertes when he identifies with him. In this sense, the too-harsh judgment of Rosencrantz and Guildenstern is part of what leads to the too-uncritical view of himself and Laertes. To look at it another way, Hamlet's rash judgment of himself helps to induce his opposite misjudgments of Rosencrantz and Guildenstern as base and of Laertes as noble.

In the dialogue with Osric, the subject is for a time Laertes and his fine qualities, but Hamlet mostly attends to Osric's affectedly elaborate style of speech. In a peculiar way, Osric is another mirror in which Hamlet does not see himself. It is partly because they are both admirers of Laertes that, instead of questioning the substance of what Osric says, Hamlet imitates and parodies his speech (106-23). This echoes Hamlet's account of how he parodied the rhetoric of royal commissions, in which he did not consider the deeper implications of imitating the King. Hamlet says that Osric has collected many things to say by rote or habit, but has no character that can be the source of things to say when he is tested beyond what he has collected (184-91). This, like the play's other statements about habit, invites us to consider whether it applies to Hamlet. Whatever habits Hamlet may have, as his trial reaches its climax in the duel scene what do we see has become of his character? Habits of virtue and vice become characteristics, but has Hamlet become a person whose words and thoughts, however sincere, are habitually rationalizations and other forms of self-justification? Has he become evil or false through the ways he has treated others?

Let us take a wider look at Hamlet's thinking in the last scene. He now insists he should kill the King; indeed, he says he would be damned if he did not end the King's evil deeds (63-70). Here Hamlet comes close to claiming a right in law to execute justice on Claudius. But in giving Claudius's original commission to Horatio to read "at more leisure" (26), Hamlet apparently does not think of using this proof of the King's treachery and criminal injustice to further his cause. Evidently Hamlet's new belief that "divinity" "shapes" his course lets him think he does not need to plan any action of his own (10-11, 73-4, 215-20). His thinking that providence will guide his revenge would be strongly reinforced not only because he has been unable to plan revenge but also because thinking that providence is guiding him enables him to avoid anxiety about what he has done to Rosencrantz and Guildenstern.

Yet even if it is in a sense "self-deceiving" for Hamlet to believe he has acted nobly and that providence guides him here, the most important question is whether these beliefs help him to confront his final trial with integrity and courage. Hamlet is aware of peril and he shows courage in his statement that "The readiness is all" (208-20). On the other hand, because Hamlet's disposition to regard death as a state of "felicity" (352) may be one cause of his readiness, his trust of the King and Laertes in the fencing match might be more suicidal than courageous. Now, it appears to me—as to most interpreters—that following the dialogue with Osric the play primarily emphasizes Hamlet's nobility. His rash judgment of Laertes as noble may be predicated on a faulty self-perception, but—again—even an erring notion sincerely believed in can become an intention guiding future action, and so his perception of Laertes and himself as noble guides him back toward nobility. The one constant in all this, and it is a crucial one, is that Hamlet is always disposed to do what he *thinks* is noble.

In his speech asking Laertes's forgiveness for slaying his father, Hamlet is noble to Laertes in acknowledging he has done him wrong and in appealing to Laertes's own gentlemanly honor and "most generous thoughts" for pardon (222-3, 227, 238). Still, this could be rhetoric calculated to manipulate Laertes by appealing to his vanity. Also, there seems to be more self-exculpation than honesty in Hamlet's saying his madness and not he killed Polonius (226-35), even though Hamlet could have come to believe he was mad when he killed Polonius because this enables him to avoid more aversive explanations of the act. The most important basis for believing that Hamlet intends to make a true peace with Laertes is that he has stated this intention to Horatio in a context suggesting sincerity (75-80). In sum, although Hamlet's apology to Laertes is surely in part reinforced because it placates a man who might kill him, Hamlet's intention is almost as surely to give an accounting that will be acceptable to a noble person and will preserve his own image of himself as noble. Thus Hamlet may use manipulative rhetoric but avoid the aversive awareness that he is being manipulative.

Of course in this speech Hamlet conceals crucial facts because he thinks he cannot publicly explain that his cause is the image of Laertes's and that he killed Polonius in a moment of vengeful rage at the King and his mother. Even if Hamlet thinks he deliberately lies in saying his madness and not he killed Polonius, he could be reinforced as a person disposed to be noble if he thinks this is a guiltless lie because the real truth, if he could tell it, would put him in an even better light. Perhaps because Hamlet cannot demonstrate his nobility by explaining to Laertes the facts of his past

action, he speaks in a way that expresses his noble character in tone and manner.

Hamlet also acts nobly in fencing with Laertes, showing courage and bending his best efforts to win the match. His not examining the foils despite his suspicion that he is in peril (208-20) may indicate that his conduct is reinforced partly because he is disposed to die. However, not examining the foils also shows he trusts Laertes and so is further evidence he is the noble man the King counted on him to be (4.7.133-5). Hamlet's surprisingly aggressive fencing suggests that despite his brotherly intentions he is strongly reinforced for attacking Laertes. The possible sources of reinforcement here are many: Hamlet intuits his danger and the King's purpose; also, the fencing is an opportunity to take violent action showing the King what he can do and indirectly attacking the King. Hamlet could even attack Laertes as an image or portrait of himself, if this would be reinforcing, without conscious awareness of this as a supplemental source of strength for his action.

Hamlet acts aggressively, too, in things he says. It is disingenuous for him to say that Laertes's skill will contrast brilliantly with his own ignorance (5.2.252-4), for he has told Horatio he expects to "win at the odds" (206-7). More significant, when he has scored two hits to none for Laertes, Hamlet tauntingly suggests that Laertes wants to shame him by not fighting his hardest (301-3). This remark comes at a crucial moment, for Laertes has just indicated in an aside that his conscience makes him reluctant to stab Hamlet (300). In taunting Laertes, Hamlet intends to provoke him to his best effort, but he does not know of this conflict of conscience. Laertes is evidently angered by the taunt (304), tries again to score a hit on Hamlet, fails, and then immediately stabs him when they are not fencing (3056). If Laertes's determination to stab Hamlet has been strengthened by Hamlet's taunt, there is tragic irony in Hamlet's success as a fencer moving him to a moment of hubristic insolence that seals his fate. The tragic irony is intensified in the way the blindness of Hamlet's hubris is caused by his inability to take the role of the other, to put himself in the place of the very man he thinks is an image of himself.

Until Laertes treacherously stabs him, Hamlet has been trusting, and the violation of that trust moves him to a controlled anger and a disposition to take revenge that governs his behavior through the killing of Claudius. Obviously when Hamlet kills Claudius his revenge is for himself and his mother as well as for his father, which allows us to speculate that Hamlet might not have taken revenge even now for his father's death alone or if he himself were able to continue living. But such speculations should not be allowed to obscure the main impression created in Hamlet's slaying of the King, that he acts in a purposeful and composed manner with a sense of full justification. He is noble in his exchange of forgiveness with Laertes, in his concern that Horatio should report his cause "aright," and in turning his dying thoughts to the future of Denmark (337, 344-5, 360-3).

Whatever changes Hamlet undergoes in the course of the play, it is most important that it is always his characteristic disposition to act nobly: he never becomes unjust in Aristotle's sense of *being* such a person. There is something to the Gravedigger's assertion that an act has three branches, "to act, to do, to perform" (5.1.11-12). In the *Nicomachean Ethics* Aristotle writes that it is "possible for a deed to be unjust without yet being an 'unjust act' if the element of voluntariness is absent" (1135a). Hamlet would act unjustly only if he performed an unjust deed in the way an unjust person does—for the sake of what he knows is an unjust end because he thinks he should act unjustly for the sake of a wrongful motive. In this sense Hamlet never acts unjustly and therefore never becomes an unjust person. Although his deeds and thoughts may become unjust, he never intends to act or think unjustly as an unjust person would. He may acquire the habits and therefore the characteristics of judging rashly and acting craftily, but he does not acquire the habit of thinking he is right to act unjustly—indeed, he does not ever think that what he does is unjust.

These ideas are important, I think, for understanding the complexity of Hamlet's divided subjectivity—the way his intentions and his thinking, his underlying character and his habits, relate to each other in complex and dynamically variable ways as he responds to his changing circumstances. Moreover, if the analysis here has been persuasive, it will be clear that to respond to Hamlet with tragic compassion we must understand him as an imagined person whose behavior can be studied for what it reveals about how and why he thinks, feels, and acts as he does. Only with such an understanding, whether arrived at intuitively or through a psychological analysis, can we see how profoundly erring deeds and perceptions can arise from an intense, sensitive, and anguished concern for love, duty, nobility, and justice.

Notes

[1] For the view that Hamlet is psychologically incoherent, see Barker 39-40, Belsey, *Subject* 41-2, and Weimann, "Mimesis," and for an important earlier essay that has contributed to this view, cf. Booth. Ferry sees Hamlet as having an inwardness we can recognize as like our own (2-3), but she is not specifically concerned with the cultural materialist concepts of the subject: see my discussion of these concepts in Chapter 1, 5-22 and my notes there. Ferry argues that the tradition before Shakespeare provides very little sense

of the sort of inward life we find in Hamlet. For powerful defenses of the view that Hamlet's character has a certain identity within its great variability, see Frye; Marvin Rosenberg, *The Masks of Hamlet,* esp. ix-xv. Cf. Friedman; Morin; see Cruttwell for an earlier essay with this view, esp. 121-8.

On Hamlet as a subject, cf. also Edward Burns 139-58; Eagleton, *William Shakespeare* 70-3; William O. Scott; States, *Hamlet;* Wilks 100-24; Luke Wilson. Wilks's use of Renaissance ideas of conscience, reason, and passion to analyze Hamlet's moral struggle converges with my analysis on a number of points.

I am not persuaded that the variability of Hamlet can in part be attributed to revisions in the second quarto edition making him a *different character* from the Hamlet of the first folio edition (see David Ward and also Werstine on this possibility). Thus I use the conflated text of *Hamlet* ed. by Jenkins, not least because I want to discuss the Hamlet of our cultural and critical tradition.

In his book on much the same topic as mine, *Character: Acting and Being on the Pre-Modern Stage,* Edward Burns defends the (near) "absence of psychology" from his "discourse of character" by analyzing Hamlet's response to Horatio's questions about the Danish custom of drinking (155-8). In Burns's reading, Hamlet locates all the "forces and effects" of the subject "outside it," and thus "The subject position, the 'I' from which a Shakespeare 'character' speaks is . . . separate from, anterior to his or her 'character' (in the sense of the word known to Shakespeare) . . ." (157-8). This may justify, as Burns says, not analyzing Shakespeare's characters in terms of a post-romantic notion of the subject which "would locate the reality of" psychological forces such as humoral temperament, reason, and habit "within the individual subjectivity" (158). His logic, however, leads not to a dismissal of *psychology* but to an analysis based on *pre-modern* psychology and its formulations of the sort of divided subjectivity Hamlet describes. In premodern discourse we typically find humoral temperament and reason within individual subjectivity, and we certainly find habit within both individual subjectivity and character, with character as habit a crucial source of subjectivity *and* its expression.

Thus Burns employs an inadequate analysis of premodern psychology, and he also errs in treating Hamlet's speech as a representative explanation of that psychology. Perhaps most importantly, Burns tends to take Hamlet's discourse as Shakespeare's. This is a general tendency in his analyses, deriving from his tight focus on character construction as a rhetorical practice. Rather than tracing the psychological tradition in relation to character, acting, and being, Burns comes to Shakespeare by way of Theophrastian character description, ancient biographical writing, the *Psychomachia* of Prudentius, and the Tudor allegorical drama. Thus Burns tends to write of Hamlet as *constructing* a subject position or an interiority in his metaphors and his grammar (147, 153; cf. 154, 157-8). Burns argues that Hamlet's use of the infinitive in "To be or not to be," and also his of "we" in this soliloquy, show that the speech is an "almost subjectless utterance." Only the "we" suggests "a subject position," and it "evades any sense of a *particular* subject, any urgent individualism, or special subjectivity" (154). But Hamlet's grammar is not used by him or Shakespeare to construct a subject position in Burns's sense; Hamlet's grammar is an *expression of* his subjectivity as constructed by Shakespeare in the rhetorical mode of mimesis. Thus Hamlet as speaker expresses his thoughts and feelings about his dilemma, so that the use of the infinitive and "we" conveys Hamlet's *characteristic* tendency as a subject to think and hence express himself in a generalizing and philosophical manner. The speech also conveys Hamlet's characteristic concern for nobility, and much more—see my analysis in this chapter.

² For the defense of reading as a mode of character construction and the relation of reading to acting, also see Buzacott 1-13, 88-91, 137; Cole, *Acting as Reading;* Desmet; Goldman, *"Hamlet";* Marvin Rosenberg, *Masks of Hamlet* ix-xv.

³ A. C. Bradley held that "the psychological point of view is not equivalent to the tragic . . . ," but that to comprehend Hamlet's tragedy it is necessary to understand how and why he thinks and feels as he does (101-2). See again note 2 in Chapter 1.

⁴ It is impossible to cite all those who have discussed Hamlet's character, but for discussions that at least implicitly consider the psychology of role playing in relation to Hamlet which have not been cited earlier in this chapter regarding this psychology, see esp. Abel 41-58; Allman 211-54; Battenhouse 252-62; Calderwood, *To Be,* esp. 18-50, and "Hamlet's Readiness"; Calhoun; Cartwright 89-137; Charney, *Hamlet's* 15-34, *Style* 267-95; Danson 22-49; Draper 95, 103-5; Eagleton, *Shakespeare* 39-65; Ellrodt 41-8; Garber, *Coming of Age* 198-205; Goldman, *Shakespeare and the Energies* 79-93, *Actor's Freedom* 146-57 and *Acting and Action* 17-45; Gorfain, "Toward"; Gottschalk; Granville-Barker 1: 245-50; Greene, "Postures"; Joan Lord Hall 34-48; Hedrick; Peter Holland; Lanham 129-43; Harry Levin, esp. 111-26; Mack, "Engagement" 286-87 and "World"; Mann, esp. 44-53; Nardo 15-34; Paris, "Hamlet"; Rabey; Righter 142-7; Harold Rosenberg 68-102; Marvin Rosenberg, *Masks of Hamlet,* esp. 167-85; Siemon 108, 116; Soellner 135-8, 172-94; Ure, "Character" 21-8; Van Laan 171-80; Walcutt, esp. 20-32; Weimann, "Mimesis"; David Young 9-44.

⁵ A number of critics since Bradley have made more than passing mention of the psychology of habits in their interpretations of *Hamlet* and Hamlet: see Battenhouse 255-9; Calderwood, "Hamlet's Readiness"; Hankins 210-13; McDonald 342-8; Shenk 189-64, Siemon 108, 116; Skulsky 25-6, 44-5; Stirling 72; Walcutt 23-32; Whitaker 271-3. Cf. Parker, who alludes indirectly to the psychology of habits, 108-9.

For Coleridge's thesis on Hamlet and habit, see 158; cf. 175. That habit could have its full traditional meaning for Coleridge is seen in a comment that Claudius does not have the "guilt of habit" because his conscience still speaks (170). Cf. Hazlitt's statement that Shakespeare "has kept up the distinction . . . between the understandings and the moral habits of men" (237).

⁶ John Keble quotes the Puritan Thomas Cartwright as opposed to wearing mourning clothes because he believed that all outward expressions of mourning provoke a deepening of grief (1:491n). And this was not only the Puritans' idea, for we saw in Chapter 1 that Montaigne believed outward expressions of grief, even insincere ones, induce the feeling. Montaigne's favorite, Plutarch, says in his "Consolation to His Wife" that mourning clothes and other outward displays of sorrow, such as shearing one's hair, make the mind "dispirited, cramped, shut in, deaf to all soothing influences, and a prey to vain terrors' (609F-10A).

⁷ Here I agree with Nardo's view that to be in "deadly earnest" is opposed to being playful, but I disagree with her view that Hamlet is playful: see Nardo 10-11, 15-34.

As the reader will see, my analysis also finds no basis in the text for the actor to make us aware that he is "playing" Hamlet in any way that would detach him from the character. Hamlet's self-absorption is unusually intense and should be strongly communicated by the actor to the audience. Hamlet comments on the drama and himself in theatrical terms, but the nature of his comments can always be plausibly construed as expressing his own perspective. This is not to say that we should not infer further metatheatrical commentaries from the text, but these are authorial irony.

⁸ Now of course if Hamlet were an actual person, it might not be realistic to think of him as so absorbed in his antic disposition when he thinks of his foes that he tends not to think of what to do for revenge. However, we are analyzing the text of *Hamlet,* in which nearly all that exists of this character after he says he will put on an antic disposition until the news of the actors is his playing that role.

⁹ For these writers it does not matter that a reason to delay may be self-deceiving or even evil so long as it

diverts one until more thought is possible. Thus Montaigne writes of how he diverted a young man from revenge by spurring his ambition to seek honor in rising above revenge in a noble forgiveness, and he says he once diverted himself from revenge with a love affair ("Of Diverting" 3:56-7). Bacon says that in anger the best way to make oneself delay is to think that the time for revenge has not yet come ("Of Anger" 511). Seneca writes that one may tell a person to delay revenge in order to take a heavier revenge later, apparently with the understanding that when the anger has passed, the heavier revenge will not be sought ("On Anger" bk 3, ch. 39, sec. 3). There is a variation on the theme of this kind of thinking in Sidney's *Arcadia* when Pyrocles is about to commit suicide and a voice, possibly that of "his good angel," urges him first to seek *revenge,* in order to divert him from his suicidal purpose (483; bk 3, ch. 22, sec. 7).

[10] On most important questions, my reading agrees with that of Jenkins in the Arden ed, 484-93.

[11] Robert Burton writes of how a friend should keep a melancholy person busy, and, if all else fails, resort to threats and even whipping: 331-3; pt. 2, sec. 2, mem. 6, subs. 2.

[12] See Walley on *Lucrece,* esp. 483-4, and in the plays see passages such as *Tro.* 2.2.164-74.

[13] Hamlet speaks here to other characters, so we cannot assume he says what he feels. However, he generally speaks what he feels to Horatio. Further, the text does not suggest he has any other thoughts, but it does indicate considerable absorption in the narrow line of thought his speech conveys.

Works Cited

Abel, Lionel, *Metatheatre: A New View of Dramatic Form* (New York: Hill, 1963).

Allman, Eileen Jorge, *Player-King and Adversary: Two Faces of Play in Shakespeare* (Baton Rouge: Louisiana State University Press, 1980).

Bacon, Francis, "Of Anger," *The Essays or Counsels, Civil and Moral. The Works of Francis Bacon,* ed. James Spedding, Robert Leslie Ellis, and Douglas Denon Heath, 1857-74, vol. 6 (New York: Garrett, 1968) pp. 510-12, 14 vols.

Barker, Francis, *The Tremulous Private Body: Essays on Subjection* (London: Methuen, 1984).

Battenhouse, Roy [W.], *Shakespearean Tragedy: Its Art and Its Christian Premises* (Bloomington: Indiana University Press, 1969).

Belsey, Catherine, *The Subject of Tragedy: Identity and Difference in Renaissance Drama* (London: Methuen, 1985).

Booth, Stephen, "On the Value of *Hamlet,*" *Reinterpretations of Elizabethan Drama,* ed. Norman Rabkin (Selected Papers from the English Institute, New York: Columbia University Press, 1969) pp. 137-76.

Bradley, A. C., *Shakespearean Tragedy: Lectures on Hamlet, Othello, King Lear, Macbeth,* 2nd ed. (1905; New York: St Martin's; London: Macmillan, 1966).

Burns, Edward, *Character: Acting and Being on the Pre-Modern Stage* (New York: St Martin's, 1990).

Burton, Robert, *The Anatomy of Melancholy* (New York, 1847).

Buzacott, Martin, *The Death of the Actor: Shakespeare on Page and Stage* (London: Routledge, 1991).

Calderwood, James L., "Hamlet's Readiness," *Shakespeare Quarterly,* 35 (1984): 267-73.

Calderwood, James L., *To Be and Not to Be: Negation and Metadrama in Hamlet* (New York: Columbia University Press, 1983).

Calhoun, Jean S., "*Hamlet* and the Circumference of Action," *Renaissance News,* 15 (1962): 281-98.

Cartwright, Kent, *Shakespearean Tragedy and Its Double: The Rhythms of Audience Response* (University Park: Pennsylvania State University Press, 1991).

Charney, Maurice, *Hamlet's Fictions* (New York: Routledge, 1988).

Charney, Maurice, *Style in Hamlet* (Princeton: Princeton University Press, 1969).

Cole, David, *Acting as Reading: The Place of the Reading Process in the Actor's Work* (Ann Arbor: University of Michigan Press, 1992).

Coleridge, Samuel Taylor, *Coleridge on Shakespeare,* ed. Terence Hawkes (1959) (Harmondsworth: Penguin, 1969).

Cruttwell, Patrick, "The Morality of Hamlet—'Sweet Prince' or 'Arrant Knave'?," *Hamlet,* ed. John Russell Brown and Bernard Harris (Stratford-upon-Avon Studies 5, London: Arnold, 1963), pp. 110-28.

Danson, Lawrence, *Tragic Alphabet: Shakespeare's Drama of Language* (New Haven: Yale University Press, 1974).

Desmet, Christy, *Reading Shakespeare's Characters: Rhetoric, Ethics, and Identity,* ed. Arthur F. Kinney (Massachusetts Studies in Early Modern Culture, Amherst: University of Massachusetts Press, 1992).

Draper, John W., *The Humors and Shakespeare's Characters* (Durham: Duke University Press, 1945).

Eagleton, Terence, *Shakespeare and Society: Critical Studies in Shakespearean Drama* (New York: Schocken, 1967).

Eagleton, Terry, *William Shakespeare* (Oxford: Blackwell, 1986).

Ellrodt, Robert, "Self-Consciousness in Montaigne and Shakespeare," *Shakespeare Survey,* 28 (1975): 37-50.

Ferry, Anne, *The "Inward" Language: Sonnets of Wyatt, Sidney, Shakespeare, Donne* (Chicago: University of Chicago Press, 1983).

Friedman, Donald, "Bottom, Burbage, and the Birth of Tragedy," *Reconsidering the Renaissance: Papers from the Twenty-First Annual Conference,* ed. Mario A. Di Cesare (Medieval and Renaissance Texts and Studies 93, Binghamton: Medieval and Renaissance Texts and Studies, 1992) pp. 315-26.

Frye, Northrop, "The Stage is All the World," *Northrop Frye: Myth and Metaphor. Selected Essays, 1974-1988,* ed. Robert D. Denham (Charlottesville: University Press of Virginia, 1990) pp. 196-211.

Garber, Marjorie, *Coming of Age in Shakespeare* (London: Methuen, 1981).

Goldman, Michael, *Acting and Action in Shakespearean Tragedy* (Princeton: Princeton University Press, 1985).

Goldman, Michael, *The Actor's Freedom: Toward A Theory of Drama* (New York: Viking; Toronto: Macmillan, 1975).

Goldman, Michael, "*Hamlet*: Entering the Text," *Theatre Journal,* 44 (1992): 449-60.

Goldman, Michael, *Shakespeare and the Energies of Drama* (Princeton: Princeton University Press, 1972).

Gorfain, Phyllis, "Toward a Theory of Play and the Carnivalesque in *Hamlet,*" *Hamlet Studies,* 13 (1991): 25-49.

Gottschalk, Paul A., "Hamlet and the Scanning of Revenge," *Shakespeare Quarterly,* 24 (1973): 155-69.

Granville-Barker, Harley, *Prefaces to Shakespeare,* vol. 1 (Princeton: Princeton University Press, 1947) 2 vols.

Greene, Thomas, "The Postures of Hamlet," *Shakespeare Quarterly,* 11 (1960): 357-66.

Hall, Joan Lord, *The Dynamics of Role-Playing in Jacobean Tragedy* (New York: St Martins, 1991).

Hankins, John Erskine, *The Character of Hamlet* (1941) (Library of Shakespearean Biography and Criticism. Freeport, NY: Books for Libraries, 1971).

Hazlitt, William, *Characters of Shakespeare's Plays. The Round Table* [and] *Characters of Shakespear's Plays* (London: Dent; New York: Dutton, 1936) pp. 171-361.

Hedrick, Donald K., " 'It is No Novelty for a Prince to be a Prince': An Enantiomorphous Hamlet," *Shakespeare Quarterly,* 35 (1984): 62-76.

Holland, Peter, "*Hamlet* and the Art of Acting," *Drama and the Actor,* ed. James Redmond (Themes in Drama 6. Cambridge: Cambridge University Press, 1984) pp. 39-61.

Jenkins, Harold, "Longer Notes," *Hamlet,* by William Shakespeare (London: Methuen, 1982) pp. 421-571.

Keble, John, ed., *The Works of Richard Hooker,* 2 vols (New York, 1849).

Lanham, Richard, *The Motives of Eloquence: Literary Rhetoric in the Renaissance* (New Haven: Yale University Press, 1976).

Levin, Harry, *The Question of Hamlet* (New York: Oxford University Press, 1959).

Mack, Maynard, "Engagement and Detachment in Shakespeare's Plays," *Essays on Shakespeare and Elizabethan Drama in Honor of Hardin Craig,* ed. Richard Hosley. (Columbia: University of Missouri Press, 1962) pp. 275-96.

Mack, Maynard, "The World of *Hamlet,*" *Yale Review,* 41 (1952): 502-23.

Mann, David, *The Elizabethan Player: Contemporary Stage Representation* (London: Routledge, 1991).

McDonald, Charles O., "*Decorum, Ethos,* and *Pathos* in the Heroes of Elizabethan Tragedy, with Particular Reference to *Hamlet,*" *Journal of English and Germanic Philology,* 61 (1962): 330-48.

Montaigne, [Michel de], "Of Diverting and Diversion," *The Essayes of Michael Lord of Montaigne,* trans. John Florio, 3 vols (London: Dent; New York: Dutton, n.d) 3:51-62.

Morin, Gertrude, "Depression and Negative Thinking: A Cognitive Approach to *Hamlet,*" *Mosaic,* 25 (1992): 1-12.

Nardo, Anna K., *The Ludic Self in Seventeenth Century English Literature* (Albany: State University of New York Press, 1991).

Paris, Bernard J., "Hamlet and His Problems: A Horneyan Analysis," *Centennial Review,* 21 (1977): 36-66.

Parker, M. D. H., *The Slave of Life: A Study of Shakespeare and the Idea of Justice* (London: Chatto, 1955).

Rabey, David Ian, "Play, Satire, Self-Definition, and Individuation in *Hamlet,*" *Hamlet Studies,* 5 (1983): 6-26.

Righter, Anne, *Shakespeare and the Idea of the Play* (1962) (Harmondsworth: Penguin, 1967).

Rosenberg, Harold, *Act and the Actor: Making the Self* (New York: NAL and World, 1970).

Rosenberg, Marvin, *The Masks of Hamlet* (Newark: University of Delaware Press; London: Associated University Presses, 1992).

Scott, William O., "The Liar Paradox as Self-Mockery: Hamlet's Postmodern Cogito," *Mosaic,* 24 (1991): 13-30.

Seneca, [Lucius Annaeus], "On Anger," *Moral Essays,* trans. Richard M. Gummere, 3 vols (The Loeb Classical Library, Cambridge: Harvard University Press; London: Heinemann, 1917-25); 1: 107-355.

Shenk, Robert, *The Sinner's Progress: A Study of Madness in English Renaissance Drama* (Salzburg Studies in English Literature. Elizabethan and Renaissance Studies 74, Salzburg: Institut fur Englische Sprache und Literatur, Universitat Salzburg, 1978).

Sidney, Sir Philip, *The Countesse of Pembrokes Arcadia* (Cambridge: Cambridge University Press, 1912); vol. 1 of *The Complete Works of Sir Philip Sidney,* ed. Albert Feuillerat, 4 vols, 1912-26.

Siemon, James Edward, "Disguise in Marston and Shakespeare," *Huntington Library Quarterly,* 38 (1975): 105-23.

Skulsky, Harold, *Spirits Finely Touched: The Testing of Value and Integrity in Four Shakespearean Plays* (Athens: University of Georgia Press, 1976).

Soellner, Rolf, *Shakespeare's Patterns of Self-Knowledge* (Columbus: Ohio State University Press, 1972). States, Bert O., *Hamlet and the Concept of Character* (Baltimore: Johns Hopkins University Press, 1992).

Stirling, Brents, *Unity in Shakespearean Tragedy: The Interplay of Theme and Character* (1956) (New York: Gordian, 1966).

Ure, Peter, "Character and Role from Richard III to Hamlet," *Hamlet,* ed. John Russell Brown and Bernard Harris (Stratford-upon-Avon Studies 5, London: Arnold, 1963) pp. 9-28.

Van Laan, Thomas F., *Role-playing in Shakespeare* (Toronto: University of Toronto Press, 1978).

Walcutt, Charles C., "*Hamlet*—The Plot's the Thing," *Michigan Quarterly Review,* 5 (1966): 15-32.

Walley, Harold R., "*The Rape of Lucrece* and Shakespearean Tragedy," *PMLA,* 76 (1961): 480-7.

Ward, David, "The King and *Hamlet,*" *Shakespeare Quarterly,* 43 (1992): 280-302.

Weimann, Robert, "Mimesis in *Hamlet,*" *Shakespeare and the Question of Theory,* ed. Patricia Parker and Geoffrey Hartman (London: Methuen, 1985) pp. 275-91.

Werstine, Paul, "The Textual Mystery of *Hamlet,*" *Shakespeare Quarterly,* 39 (1988): 1-26.

Whitaker, Virgil K., *Shakespeare's Use of Learning: An Inquiry into the Growth of His Mind and Art* (San Marino, CA: Huntington, 1953).

Wilks, John S., *The Idea of Conscience in Renaissance Tragedy* (London: Routledge, 1990).

Wilson, Luke, "*Hamlet,* Hales v. Petit, and the Hysteresis of Action," *ELH,* 60 (1993): 17-55.

Young, David, *The Action to the Word: Structure and Style in Shakespearean Tragedy* (New Haven: Yale University Press, 1990).

Source: "*Hamlet,*" in *Shakespeare's Imagined Persons: The Psychology of Role-Playing and Acting,* Barnes & Noble Books, 1996, pp. 57-102.

"Have You Not Read of Some Such Thing?"
Sex and Sexual Stories in *Othello*

Edward Pechter, *Concordia University*

Why does Othello suddenly abandon his affectionate trust in Desdemona for a conviction of betrayal? This question, by placing the protagonist's understanding at the play's centre, takes us back to Bradley's first words about the play in *Shakespearean Tragedy:* 'the character of Othello is comparatively simple, but . . . essentially the success of Iago's plot is connected with this character. Othello's description of himself as "one not easily jealous" . . . is perfectly just. His tragedy lies in this—that his whole nature was indisposed to jealousy, and yet . . . unusually open to deception'.[1] Bradley has long been discredited—a story with which we are all familiar. In 1993 L. C. Knights's 'How Many Children Had Lady Macbeth?' repudiated the notion of treating dramatic characters as the authors and origins of their own histories, autonomous agents with lives outside the dramatic action.[2] Knights's essay coincided with a redirection of Shakespeare studies from character to language, from the 'whole nature' of the protagonist to the coherent artifice of the play itself. Wilson Knight's 'spatial hermeneutics' figures notably in this move away from Bradley, as part of a 'modernist paradigm';[3] psychological integrity is fragmented into linguistic patterns that re-achieve wholeness in a self-reflexive rather than representational text. If a play begins to resemble *Les Demoiselles d'Avignon,* it makes more sense to speak of the structural relation of geometric forms—image patterns contributing to symbolic coherence in a dramatic poem—than about which if any of the characters has a noble nature.

We no longer indulge in the Bradley-bashing that was routine during this period; we ignore him now, the consequence of yet another shift that has rendered his kind of commentary apparently irrelevant. In Richard Rorty's view, there is no such 'thing as "human nature" or the "deepest level of the self" . . . socialization, and thus historical circumstance, goes all the way down'.[4] Rorty wants to collapse the distinctions between depth and surface, inner and outer.[5] If modernists reconceived representation, renouncing the mirror of nature for an abstract and self-referring aesthetic text, a view like Rorty's seems to abandon the concept of representation altogether, denying that there is any stable substance out there (or in here) to be imitated, and that the aesthetic text itself exists with any authority beyond that given by a contingent historical process. From another angle, however, current critics have not abandoned representation but universalized it. If everything is a text, then nature (including the 'whole nature' of Othello's 'character')

and art (including *Othello*) are just different cultural constructs or discursive practices—of many, two. As a consequence, we cash in the question of Othello's jealousy for an enquiry into the sex-gender system; and *Othello* as an object of interest leads us not to Shakespeare or heroic tragedy, authors or theatrical genres, but to the literary system and its contribution to the production and reproduction of cultural value. Hence Valerie Traub, in her state-of-the-art book about *Circulations of Sexuality in Shakespearean Drama:* 'I am less interested in the ways works of art are empowered than in the ways characters are represented as negotiating and struggling *for* power, the extent to which they are granted or denied agency—in short, the ways their subjectivity is constructed through representational means [and] the "processes whereby sexual desires are constructed, mass-produced, and distributed" '.[6]

In conducting this breathless Cook's Tour, I have bypassed some picturesque complications. As W. B. Worthen points out, the typical 'actorly reading' of Shakespeare remains, in contrast to academic criticism, 'notably trained on questions of "character" [as] integrated, self-present, internalized, psychologically motivated'.[7] As with acting, so with teaching Shakespeare: drop into most Shakespeare classes and you will hear Bradley-speak. Since academic criticism is a different mode of understanding from teaching or acting, we should not expect an identity of interests and assumptions. At the same time, the remoteness of academic discourse from two such influential ways of representing Shakespeare as pedagogy and theatre is remarkable. Even more remarkable are the residues of Bradley surviving in academic criticism itself. As Margaret Mikesell points out, the 'renewed criticism of Bradleyan traditions in the early 1950s' often rested in the very methods that were being repudiated, treating 'Othello and Iago as characters [with] the personalities of real people'.[8] This is still the case. 'It is important, of course', Ania Loomba declares, 'to guard against reading dramatic characters as real, three dimensional people'; but these words follow a description of Othello as shedding his alienated 'insecurity' for a 'conception of his own worth' that 'slowly comes to centre in' and then depart from Desdemona's choice—a description that would sit comfortably in the pages of *Shakespearean Tragedy*.[9]

Why does Bradley haunt us, like a half-remembered, maybe even unread text? In one of the first attempts to recuperate Bradley for critical practice, A. D. Nuttall, pointing to an odd discrepancy between the frequently nonsensical claims of Knights's attack and the general acceptance of his claims as self-evidently true, remarked that 'the whole debate may be complicated by the presence of unacknowledged historical factors', a 'pre-rational historical reaction' against 'the over-heated Victorian age'.[10] This shrewd suggestion allows us to understand Bradley-bashing as an overdetermined gesture by which Shakespearians could assert their authentic modernity, liberated from the naiveties of eminent Victorianism. But the 'unacknowledged historical factors' may extend deeper than Victorian sentiment. Consider Michael Bristol who, after proposing recently that audiences should 'efface their response to . . . Othello, Desdmona, and Iago as individual subjects endowed with personalities and with some mode of autonomous interiorized life', has to admit the difficulty of such an effacement, 'not least because the experience of individual subjectivity as we have come to know it *is* objectively operative in the text'.[11] From this perspective, an interest in Othello's character is not merely a hangover from Bradley or nineteenth-century novels, some recently acquired detritus to be jettisoned, but part of a continuing engagement going back to the origins, as best we can determine them, of our interest in the Shakespearian text.

The explanatory narrative I synopsized earlier has a lot going for it: by accounting for Bradley's irrelevance in terms of a naive representability underwritten by an old-fashioned assumption of personal integrity, it makes use of powerfully central concepts in the development of modern thought—'master-problems', in Perry Anderson's phrase.[12] At the same time, these concepts may be serving as screens in the composition of a story generated out of wish-fulfilment as well as disinterested analysis, motivated by a desire to bring about the disappearance we claim to be describing as an accomplished fact. Bristol's 'efface', in concert with 'unacknowledged' and 'pre-rational' in Nuttall, suggest that the uncanny residual presence of Bradley in current criticism is the consequence of denial. We need to reconsider our relation to Bradley, and to the long tradition of commentary which lies behind *Shakespearean Tragedy,* not in order to restore his eminence but to understand our own situation.[13] And *Othello* seems like a particularly appropriate play on which to base this reconsideration, for as Edward Snow has argued, from its irascible inauguration ('Tush, never tell me! . . . 'Sblood, but you'll not hear me!') to its agonized terminal gesture ('The object poisons sight; / Let it be hid'), 'repression pervades the entire world' of the play.[14]

Once more, then: how to explain Othello's reversal of feelings about Desdemona, from 'Perdition catch my soul / But I do love thee' to 'O curse of marriage' within only a few minutes time (3.3.91-2, 272)? I am quoting from the Temptation Scene which, parading before us familiar ideas and feelings from the play's opening, suggests that Othello's alteration should be understood as part of a lucid sequence. At the beginning of the play, Othello speaks self-confidently of his marriage: 'my demerits / May speak unbonneted to as proud a fortune / As this that I have reached' (1.2.22-4); now he begins to doubt 'mine own weak merits' (3.3.191). This acknowledgement, trivial in itself, precipitates a rush of startling reversals. Brabantio's warning, 'Look to her, Moor, if thou hast eyes to see. / She has deceived her father, and may thee', had prompted a secure dismissal early on: 'My life upon her faith' (1.3.292-4). Now in the face of Iago's reiteration, 'She did deceive her father, marrying you', Othello becomes worried: 'And so she did' (210, 212). In the scene's turning point a moment later, Othello suddenly takes the initiative, 'And yet how nature, erring from itself—' and Iago, himself cautious so far, spots an opportunity so desirable that he interrupts Othello to seize it:

> Ay, there's the point; as, to be bold with you,
> Not to affect many proposèd matches
> Of her own clime, complexion, and degree,
> Whereto we see in all things nature tends.
> Foh, one may smell in such a will most rank,
> Foul disproportions, thoughts unnatural!
>
> (232-8)

At the end of this speech, a shaken Othello dismisses Iago, but too late to reverse the process that will lead to catastrophe.

Nature is the crucial idea here, and again we hear echoes of the beginning: 'and she in spite of nature, / Of years, of country, credit, everything, / To fall in love with what she feared to look on!' (1.3.96-8). For Brabantio, nature should have drawn Desdemona to young Venetians of her own rank, 'the wealthy curlèd darlings of our nation' (1.22.69), and her attraction to Othello, 'against all rules of nature' (1.3.101), must be the perverse consequence of witchcraft. The perplexing questions and ambivalent feelings raised by this claim,[15] unresolved in themselves, migrate into a narrative conclusion: Othello denies witchcraft, Desdemona acknowledges she was half the wooer, Brabantio drops the case. But the question returns here in its own conceptual terms, moving Othello to adopt the same cultural stereotypes articulated earlier by Brabantio and now reiterated by Iago as defining his own nature.

> Haply for I am black,
> And have not those soft parts of
> conversation
> That chamberers have; or for I am declined
> Into the vale of years—yet that's not
> much—
> She's gone. I am abused, and my relief
> Must be to loathe her.
>
> (3.3.267-72)

As Arthur Kirsch says, 'Othello eventually internalizes Iago's maleficent sexual vision and sees himself with Iago's eyes', repellent in 'his age and color', thus 'becom[ing] convinced that Desdemona's manifest attraction to him is itself perverse'.[16] Kirsch's story represents something like a current consensus,[17] but if the meaning of Othello's transformation is thus clear, the motive remains mysterious. Why should Othello, against all evidence and self-interest, buy into the view Iago offers of himself and Desdemona? Othello himself sees the foolishness—'Exchange me for a goat / When I shall turn the business of my soul / To such exsufflicate and blowed surmises' (3.3.184-6)—but proceeds to make the investment nonetheless.

All this, however, assumes what is at issue—namely, that Othello is free to make up his mind, not just about Desdemona but about himself, as though he has secure possession of a stable core of autonomous being. The play seems to encourage our current scepticism about such an assumption, drawing attention to the way belief rests on and is shaped by cultural clutter—stories, superstitions, social stereotypes, clichéd aphorisms, vague memories, dreams, the immediate influence of overheard aimless chatter and snatches of old songs.[18] Such influences are particularly potent in times of stress. Brabantio's jump to the witchcraft conclusion is a good example: 'Have you not read, Roderigo, / Of some such thing?' (1.1.175-6). Iago is the source of this clutter, Burke's voice whispering at the ear,[19] burrowing under the threshold of conscious reflection and lodging the vinous poison of mistrust, disgust, abhorrence. He represents what we now call ideological interpellation, or what Renaissance commentators, describing the world from inside a theological rather than a sociological lexicon, understood as diabolical possession. As such, Iago is the origin and the content of Brabantio's dream ('This accident is not unlike my dream'), which Brabantio has no choice but to believe ('Belief of it oppresses me already' [1.1.144-5]), because Iago's white (or is it black?) noise subtends and determines belief. He has already turned Cassio inside out by the time of the Temptation Scene; Othello is a more ambitious project, but Iago's success should seem predictable as well as amazing.

Othello's alien status gives us a familiar current context to understand his story: the immigrant novel. Othello's metaphorical transformation happens literally to Saladin Chamcha in *The Satanic Verses*: he turns into a goat.

> His thighs had grown uncommonly wide and powerful, as well as hairy. Below the knee the hairiness came to a halt, and his legs narrowed into tough, bony, almost fleshless calves, terminating in a pair of shiny, cloven hoofs, such as one might find on any billy-goat. Saladin was also taken aback by the sight of his phallus, greatly enlarged and embarrassingly erect, an organ that he had the greatest difficulty in acknowledging his own.[20]

Finding himself in a kind of asylum along with other embodied clichés of an exotic colonial domain—a manticore, some water-buffalo, slippery snakes, 'a very lecherous-looking wolf'—Chamcha asks, ' "But how do they do it?" ' ' "They describe us" ', the manticore tells him. ' "That's all. They have the power of description, and we succumb to the pictures they construct." '[21] Rushdie's description of *The Satanic Verses*—'the move from one part of the world to another and what that does to the various aspects of one's being-in-the-world'[22]—can make Othello's transformation the centrepiece of an altogether plausible narrative. First he has the power to describe himself, inhabits his own narrative, but moving to Christian Europe he becomes displaced from his 'perfect soul' (1.2.31) and begins to occupy a different story, until finally his blackness serves to figure not a royal-heroic self but bestial sexuality.

But should we be reading Othello as the abject victim at the centre of an immigrant novel? The play was produced in an early colonialist culture, substantially ignorant of much that we have come to know of colonial and postcolonial experience. More to my formalist purposes here, *Othello* lacks the accumulation of finely attenuated nuance required to work in the manner of an immigrant novel, the sense of 'dilatory time' (2.3.363) that Iago, a master narratologist, understands as necessary for such a mode. This problem is insoluble (plays are not novels), but *Othello* goes out of its way to exacerbate it, compressing Cinthio's expansive narrative into an action that seems to occupy a mere two days, beginning at night with the elopement, arriving the next day at Cyprus, proceeding to the Temptation Scene on the day after, and concluding with the murder that night. We have bumped into the famous 'double-time' problem—'the gap', as John Bayley puts it, 'between the swift dramatic time of the plot and the lingering fictional time of the domestic psychology . . . between the impact of the *coup de théâtre* on our emotions, and the effect of the analysis of love and jealousy upon our minds'.[23] It is easy to demonstrate that the impact of swift time is misleading, but the impression remains, and in Morgann's famous adage, 'In Dramatic composition, the *Impression* is the *Fact*.'[24] We must understand Othello's transformation not as the '*eventual* internalizing' of Kirsch's narrative, nor as something that '*slowly*' or '*finally*' comes about, as in Loomba's or my own rewriting of the play, but as issuing from his experience in the very brief interval that seems to elapse since the beginning of the action.

According to Stanley Cavell, *Othello* makes us think 'not merely generally of marriage but specifically of the wedding night. It is with this that the play opens.'[25] 'Even now, now, very now, an old black ram / Is tupping your white ewe' (1.1.88-9). This coupling, the first concrete image we are offered upon which to load (or lodge) the play's matter, may not describe what really happened, or even what happened at all. As many critics have argued, the uncertainty when or even whether Othello and Desdemona consummate their marriage serves to generate anxious speculation on our part, sustained by the pressure of a highly eroticized language which enacts to the mind's eye various images of the deed about whose actual performance we remain unresolved.[26] This irresolution lasts until Othello's invitation on the first Cyprus night: 'Come, my dear love, / The purchase made, the fruits are to ensue. / The profit's yet to come 'tween me and you' (2.3.8-10); but even as Othello's disarmingly ingenuous couplet gives rest to one kind of anxious uncertainty, *have they or haven't they?*, its alarming specificity creates another: *what now will it be like?* This interest is displaced by the flurry of business with Iago, Cassio, Roderigo, and Montano; but Cassio's violent story sustains as well as displaces our interest in Othello and Desdemona's lovemaking, occurring (presumably) 'even now, now, very now'; especially when Iago's astounding simile to describe the disturbance re-evokes that opening image:

> Friends all but now, even now,
> In quarter and in terms like bride and groom
> Devesting them for bed; and then but now—
> As if some planet had unwitted men—
> Swords out, and tilting one at others' breasts
> In opposition bloody.
>
> (2.3.172-7)

The Temptation Scene follows and the play gives us the dramatic impression—the fact—of its occurring the next morning. By means of *post hoc ergo propter hoc,* a mode of narrative understanding implicit in Morgann's Law of Dramatic Composition, we are encouraged to locate the origins of Othello's transformation in his sexual consummation: it is the cause, it is the cause.

The impression is powerfully confirmed at just this pivotal point of the Temptation Scene when Othello's sudden loathing situates itself with specific reference to Desdemona's body:

> O curse of marriage,
> That we can call these delicate creatures ours
> And not their appetites! I had rather be a toad
> And live upon the vapour of a dungeon
> Than keep a corner in the thing I love
> For others' uses. Yet 'tis the plague of great ones;
> Prerogatived are they less than the base.

> 'Tis destiny unshunnable, like death.
> Even then this forkèd plague is fated to us
> When we do quicken.
>
> (3.3.272-81).

The 'corner in the thing I love' directs us to Desdemona's genitals. The forkèd plague alludes to the cuckold's horns, but its demonstrative specificity, '*this* forkèd plague', so soon after 'keep a corner', summons the groin to the mind's eye, like the 'bare, forked animal' in *Lear* (3.4.101). And like the 'simp'ring dame, / Whose face between her forks presages snow' later in the same play (4.5.116-17), Desdemona's whole being seems for a bizarre moment drawn down and compressed into her private part: she is both the thing and the thing in the thing.[27] Similarly graphic details inform Othello's speech to and about Desdemona later on:

> OTHELLO But there where I have garnered up my heart,
> Where either I must live or bear no life,
> The fountain from the which my current runs
> Or else dries up—to be discarded thence,
> Or keep it as a cistern for foul toads
> To knot and gender in! Turn thy complexion there,
> Patience, thou young and rose-lipped cherubin,
> Ay, here look grim as hell.
> DESDEMONA I hope my noble lord esteems me honest.
> OTHELLO O, ay—as summer flies are in the shambles,
> That quicken even with blowing. O thou weed,
> Who are so lovely fair, and smell'st so sweet,
> That the sense aches at thee—would thou hadst ne'er been born!
>
> (4.2.59-71)

As Kittredge points out,[28] *thence,* the repeated *theres* and finally *here* emphatically situate our attention; the sequence reduces Desdemona to an 'it' at once vague and grotesquely specific, especially when the rose-lipped cherubin now looks out, his face between the forks, from the place he was looking *at* a moment earlier. The proliferating evocative power of these passages performs a similar compression upon Othello's life story. 'When we do quicken' in the first passage conflates birth and desire (quickening as tumescence) and locates both in the place of betrayal—the place in the second passage where life is both given and denied ('discarded'), and where desire is at the same time awakened and repelled (the summer flies that quicken with blowing); as though birth, desire, and betrayal—the entire trajectory of any male's affective career in the tragic (or satiric) mode—are simultaneously present in this same loved and loathed thing.

Writing about 'the thing *denied our sight* throughout the opening scene',[29] Cavell described an image of sexual coupling; but as Patricia Parker notes, the focus in these passages is much more concentrated upon 'the "privities" of woman opened simultaneously to scientific "discovery" and the pornographic gaze'.[30] Like many recent critics for whom *Othello* enacts a primal scene (see note 26), Parker suggests that the play entices its spectator into the quasi-erotic pleasures of a dominant position from which to determine meaning; but we can be sceptical about 'the gaze', both generally and as an approach to this play.[31] Rich as they are in vivid detail, these passages multiply and condense incompatible images and contradictory significances to produce an effect not of mastery—a privileged vantage from which to fix meanings, as in a stable visual field—but of giddiness verging on nausea. The 'mind now floods', as Graham Bradshaw says of the rapid sequence of images in the second passage—'fountain', 'cistern', 'it'—unarrestably until we are allowed (or required) to pause at the climactic image of the copulating toads.[32] They are the most memorably vivid presence here, as was the solitary toad in the earlier passage, but in neither do the toads function primarily in terms of visual representation. In the dungeon of the Temptation Scene, 'that dank corner of the emotional prison',[33] you are less likely to see anything than to feel what Othello later describes as 'the slime / That sticks on filthy deeds'[34]; or to smell the damp and stagnant air, 'the vapour', as he says here, we must breathe in to sustain life. With the cesspool and the slaughterhouse, the cistern and shambles, this evocation of malodorous fumes intensifies into the overwhelming specificity of excrement and rotting flesh—the aroma that seems to generate Flaubert's curious question about one of his whores: 'Have you . . . sniffed at the fog of her clitoris?'[35]; what Eliot, in the pre-Pound version of *The Waste Land,* called 'the good old hearty female stench'.[36]

Following a long line back to Plato, Renaissance commentators on the senses designated sight and hearing as the higher faculties, consigning smell, along with taste and touch, to the carnal modes of knowledge.[37] In *Civilization and Its Discontents,* Freud imagines a primal scene in which primitive humanity stands upright, discovers its nakedness, and transfers its sensory allegiance from smell to sight.[38] Such stories underwrite Hans J. Rindisbacher's claims about smell as 'strongly connected with sexuality', the 'very animal function', the 'oldest unsublimated medium', within which we experience the 'force of individual attraction between the sexes'.[39] The play's evocation of smell may be understood as a way around the problem Iago describes:

> But how, how satisfied, my lord?
> Would you, the supervisor, grossly gape on,
> Behold her topped? . . .
> It were a tedious difficulty, I think,
> To bring them to that prospect.
>
>   (3.3.399-403)

Ocular proof may be impossible, but it is olfactory proof, anyway, that provides the most powerfully convincing testimony about what really happened on the wedding night. This evidence finally allows us to answer my original question why Othello reverses his feelings about Desdemona: it is *because of her nasty smell.*

This conclusion is even sillier than Rymer's: if not 'the *Tragedy of the Handkerchief*',[40] then of the vaginal douche—the 'clyster-pipes', as Iago says, blowing reechy kisses from his fingers into the air (2.1.179). Like Rymer—unresponsive to the handkerchief's symbolic resonances: the wedding sheets, stained with blood and sexual fluids[41]—we are being too literal. The smells do not tell us what really happened in Othello and Desdemona's consummation, but what Othello thinks happened. Smells are notoriously transient—as here: the stench of the shambles does not prevent Othello's registering her 'smell . . . so sweet', nor the sweetness the stench of her deed ('Heaven stops the nose at it' [4.2.79]) a moment later.[42] And smells are notoriously subjective. As Marston's Cockledemoy says, 'Every man's turd smells well in his own nose.'[43] But this is not to say that the meanings of smell are determined uniquely by an autonomous individual sensorium. Any somatic base for smell is located beneath the semantic threshold of meaning or consequence. Since all sensory experience belongs to the moment, we need, as Rindisbacher says, 'acculturation and particularly language' in order to 'give it a temporal dimension, add past and future, loss and longing, hope and despair'.[44] This dependence is particularly strong in the case of smells, whose very evanescence seems capturable only through the memories and historical associations which language can evoke.[45] The transience and subjectivity of smell thus bring us back to the verbal or cultural constructedness of the subject itself. The 'foul and the fragrant' qualities detected by an individual's nose are the product, as Alain Corbin says, of the 'social imagination'.[46]

From this perspective, the meaning of Cockledemoy's words matters less than their aphoristic tone. He sounds as though he is quoting, and so he is—Montaigne, Erasmus, perhaps on back to Aristotle.[47] Eliot implies a similarly general familiarity as with 'the good old hearty female stench'; *oh, that stench,* we are asked to respond; *of course.* Cassio's description of Bianca, 'Tis such another fitchew! Marry, a perfumed one!' (4.1.143) works the same way. The polecat is 'noted for its rank odour and lechery', Sanders tells us, and the phrase *such another* is 'a common idiom meaning "one just like all the others" '.[48] Eliot may have had a private waste land and individual talent, Shakespeare his secret sorrows and period of sex nausea, but language like this derives its authority elsewhere. 'Love has pitched his mansion in / The place of excrement.'[49] Crazy Jane's words to the bishop may recall her particular sexual experience, but like the 'saws of books' Hamlet tries to wipe from the tables of his memory after meeting the ghost (1.5.100), they resonate a sententious generality. *Has she not read of some such thing?* Perhaps the good old hearty male tag, *inter urinas et faeces nascimur,* we are born between piss and shit. The aphorism is sometimes attributed to St Augustine—wrongly, it seems, and unlike Cockledemoy's, its origins cannot be determined; but the very anonymity helps to produce the sense of an impersonal authority, independent of any particular author or individual source: 'True he it said, what ever man it sayd'.[50]

Othello's disgust in the Temptation Scene is embedded deeply in the same aphoristic generality. ''Tis the plague of great ones', he says and, describing the curse of marriage, affirms the collective wisdom of the plural pronoun, speaking for all married men ('that we can call these delicate creatures ours') and for all heroes ('even then this forkèd plague is fated to us / When we do quicken'). This is the tone of the canny insider, and though new to Othello's speech, it is not new to us. This is Iago's tone. His speech has been from the beginning a tissue of sententious topoi—as here: 'I know our country disposition well' (3.3.205). This is Hamlet's pun on 'country matters', 'a fair thought to lie between maids' legs' (3.2.111, 113), and it may be said to originate the explicit focus upon female sexual parts. The double meaning—I know how our Venetian women dispose of their cunts; I know how our Venetian cunts dispose of themselves—substantiates the gross synecdoche realized a moment later in Othello's speech: transforming women into the things that make them women. But if Othello assimilates Iago's innuendoes, it is through the suave confidence with which they are communicated: 'This fellow . . . knows all qualities with a learned spirit / Of human dealings' (3.3.262-4). Iago speaks from the cultural centre. The manticore was right. Iago has 'the power of description', and Othello 'succumbs to the pictures' Iago constructs. As Kirsch said, Othello comes 'eventually' to 'see . . . with Iago's eyes'—or smell with his nose, or (as in Rushdie's Heideggerian phrase) to reconstitute his 'being-in-the-world' to accord with Iago's.

Whatever the play's impressions upon us, it seems we cannot escape from an understanding in which Othello's sexual knowledge of Desdemona is not the origin but the consequence of his transformation, not the cause but the effect—specifically, an effect of discourse. 'It is not words that shakes me thus', Othello says later

in a spastic trance that seems to re-enact his lovemaking with Desdemona (4.1.40). But it is words, the story woven of social, racial, and sexual stereotypes in which his knowledge—of himself, Desdemona, everything—is embedded. How it came to be embedded thus we are not told; the play does not record the process of this transformation. It provides a beginning, up to and including 'Perdition catch my soul / But I do love thee', and an ending, starting with 'O curse of marriage', separated by only a few minutes playing time. In lieu of an extended narrative middle, the play gives us intensely charged erotic images, requiring us to imagine Othello's lovemaking with Desdemona; but whatever (and however) we can register disperses itself into stories about sexual feelings and actions, and still other stories (about military promotions, for instance) to which sexual feelings and actions do not seem immediately relevant. The cause for Othello's transformation must be there, in these hints of an immigrant novel the play requires us to invent.

Like Bradley's kind of criticism, the problem I have been struggling with has been relegated to the status of error, and then to oblivion. This story begins with Eliot's charge of *'bovarisme'* in Othello's final speeches.[51] Leavis projected this view backward to reveal an Othello who 'has from the beginning responded' with a self-dramatizing egotism: 'the essential traitor is within the gates'. As a consequence, Bradley's view of a not-easily-jealous Othello becomes 'sentimental perversity'.[52] For current critics too, Othello is vulnerable from the beginning—not, though, because of some peculiar (and presumably corrigible) failure on his part but as the necessary consequence of a general condition. The essential traitor is now 'always already' within the gates. In one version of the current story, we focus on the inherent vulnerability of Othello's alien status, Loomba's 'insecurity', or the 'self-doubt of this displaced stranger' which, according to Neill, 'opens him so fatally to Iago's attack'.[53] From another angle, Othello suffers not from his cultural background but his gender. According to Janet Adelman, male desire 'inevitably soils that object' in which it invests itself and therefore 'threatens to "corrupt and taint" [Othello's] business from the start'.[54] In the Lacanian description, Othello's fate is determined by desire itself, irrespective of gender. 'If language is born of absence', Catherine Belsey tells us, 'so is desire, and at the same moment. This must be so . . . Desire, which invests the self in another, necessarily precipitates a division in the subject.'[55] In Stephen Greenblatt's strong and influential version, Othello's transformation is simply the 'clearest and most important' example of social construction as a general condition: 'In *Othello* the characters have always already experienced submission to narrativity.'[56]

Greenblatt builds from a perception of Othello's Senate speech as 'a narrative in which the storyteller is constantly swallowed up by the story'. This anxiety is then displaced onto Desdemona, as in the lovers' ec-static Cypriot reunion:

OTHELLO O my fair warrior!
DESDEMONA   My dear Othello.
OTHELLO It gives me wonder great as my content
To see you here before me. O my soul's joy,
If after every tempest come such calms,
May the winds bellow till they have wakened death,
And let the labouring barque climb hills of seas
Olympus-high, and duck again as low
As hell's from heaven. If it were now to die,
'Twere now to be most happy, for I fear
My soul hath her content so absolute
That not another comfort like to this
Succeeds in unknown fate.
DESDEMONA   The heavens forbid
But that our loves and comforts should increase
Even as our days do grow.

(2.1.183-96)

Like many others, Greenblatt recognizes in this passage two distinct registers for experiencing pleasure.[57] Othello's speech describes violent movement building to a climax so intense, 'content so absolute', that an intuition of disappointment follows: maybe never again, a sort of *post coitum tristis*. By contrast Desdemona registers pleasure not as the short sharp shock of termination, but as a slow and gradual increase, unfolding without any evident anxiety or much differentiation into an indefinite future. But does it follow from this, as Greenblatt claims, that Desdemona's promise of a daily increase is actually a threat because it 'denies the possibility of [Othello's] narrative control' and 'devour[s] up his discourse' in a way that eventually drives him to murder?[58] Whatever ominous premonitions we may sense, the lovers' greeting in Cyprus ends in blissful fulfilment. 'Amen to that, sweet powers!' he says in response to her prayer for an endless daily increase of love and comfort, thereby accepting her version; but with 'I cannot speak enough of this content. / It stops me here, it is too much of joy', he immediately reaffirms his own. Then finally—'And this (*they kiss*) and this, the greatest discords be / That e'er our hearts shall make' (196-20)—he transforms their 'discords' into kisses, as though unresolved differences, far from disrupting the pleasure of their union, become the source of its security.

So too with the Senate speech. Like all life stories, Othello's describes displacement: growing up, leaving home, enslavement, religious conversion; but these

potential traumas are represented (if at all) not as rupture but as continuity, the accumulation of undifferentiated experience. That his journey goes from 'boyish days / To th' very moment' of the telling (1.3.131-2) suggests not the risk of engulfment but the confident assumption of a capacious future, an unperturbed sense that he will continue to assimilate and structure the material of his life into the daily increase Desdemona later describes. (Indeed, one reason why Desdemona's later words fail to threaten Othello is that he can already experience his life in this female-gendered register.) On the first page of the 'personal history' that bears his name, David Copperfield acknowledges uncertainty whether he will 'turn out to be the hero of my own life', deferring to a text behind his own control: 'these pages must show'.[59] But Othello seems somehow to have eluded this problematic split between narrator and narrative subject. 'Such was my process', he says (141), referring at once to his experience and his relation of that experience, his life and his life story. He cannot be swallowed up by his narrative, because he and his narrative are perfectly identical. How can we know the storyteller from the story?

A protagonist of 'perfect soul' such as this or one anxiously vulnerable and radically flawed from the beginning, as in Greenblatt and other recent accounts of the play: what is at stake in this disagreement? Consider Hazlitt, who opens his commentary on *Othello* by declaring that 'tragedy purifies the affections by terror and pity. That is, it substitutes imaginary sympathy for mere selfishness. It gives us a high and permanent interest, beyond ourselves, in humanity as such. . . . It makes man a partaker with his kind.'[60] Hazlitt, writing in a book called *The Characters of Shakespeare's Plays,* helped develop the tradition that culminated in Bradley.[61] By treating Othello's character as the play's motivational centre, and by emphasizing Othello's 'perfect soul' at the beginning, I have been trying to reconnect with this tradition; but I have no wish to reaffirm Bradley's apparent faith as such in the transcendent humanity of heroic individuals, or to imitate the methods apparently generated out of that faith. By abstracting dramatic characters from their relationship in the dramatic action to produce individualized portraits, Bradley sought to guarantee that our fascination with Iago never interferes with our admiration for Othello.[62] This strategy, however, systematically sanitizes and diminishes the play's power, for while it assures a full measure of pity for Othello's collapse, it avoids terror and any intuition of our own complicity in the events leading to the catastrophe—a guilty complicity that must underlie all the testimony from critical and theatrical traditions of this play's intolerable experience.

On the other hand, consider the tone of normative certainty in the current view: 'always already', 'inevitably', 'necessarily', 'this must be so'. *Cosí fan tutti*. These critics are worldly and insouciant; they know their culture disposition well. As I am by no means the first to remark, the anti-heroic reading of the play winds up sounding like Iago.[63] This is not a bad thing. The play writes us into Iago's perspective at the beginning and in one way or another succeeds in sustaining this alliance, no matter how unholy we understand it to be, up to the end. Current versions should help to account for precisely that sense of guilty complicity Bradley refused; but by moulding the protagonist to conform to a normative shape, they manage to make an equal (though opposite) refusal. For by treating Othello as an exemplary subject, trapped in the prisonhouse of language or the impossible condition of male desire, current versions leave only his alien status as extraordinary; and once this status is defined as the immigrant protagonist's inherent and necessary vulnerability, we are left with nothing more than abjection: *l'homme moyen sensuel*—not a transcendent 'humanity as such' but a derisory 'human, all too human'.

A fall from this height, like Gloucester's from what he supposes to be Dover Cliff, evokes some pity, perhaps, but no fear, and (since we see it coming) not even much surprise. That Bradleyan and anti-Bradleyan assumptions arrive at similar conclusions might suggest that differing beliefs about character are less than fully determining. It matters, of course, whether we come to the play as humanists or constructionists, but watching *Othello* does not require us to solve conceptual problems, like the relative weight of nature and culture, from a position of absolute ontological conviction.[64] To the extent that such conviction commits us to stability and consistency of understanding, it may be the last thing we need. Consistency led Bradley into a maundering pathos, but at least he knew where to start. For unless we are prepared to respond to Othello's existence at the beginning with 'imaginary sympathy', responding with affection and wonder to a marvelous strangeness emanating from a different bodily place, black or tawny, and a world elsewhere—unless, that is, we can see Othello's visage in his mind, we will never be able to acknowledge the play's tragic power.

Theatrical impressions, heroic tragedy, pity and terror: all these acknowledge a major investment on my part in mode, genre, and above all artistic effect. Unlike Valerie Traub, who in the passage I quoted early on declares a relative lack of interest 'in the ways works of art are empowered', I have been writing from inside the traditional vocabulary of literary aesthetics. Traub's diminished interest represents a strong claim often made in current criticism that the sceptical scrutiny of this vocabulary—seeing through aesthetics to the literary system of which it is part, and finally to the cultural system that is said to generate and contain

it (as well as everything else)—produces powerful results. According to Traub, since sexual taboos, 'prohibitions on incest or homosexuality, for instance', are 'arbitrary political constructs and thus open to transformation', then 'by deconstructing and refiguring the anxieties that regulate and discipline erotic life', we can 'contribute modestly to the project of carving out space within the social structure for greater erotic variety'.[65]

This is not a very plausible story; it is hard to believe that a politically inflected deconstruction, or any other way of studying Shakespeare, can contribute, even modestly, to a greater erotic variety. How, then, can we account for the proliferation of such claims on the current critical scene? Here, by way of an answer, is one story: in these austere times, we inhabit an increasingly production-driven research culture, characterized by the felt need to pursue socially useful projects. The functional value of these projects is defined by the functionaries who hold us accountable to themselves in the name of their own accountability to a construct called 'the public' or 'the taxpayer'. In this environment of 'targeted research', we are all cultural workers—willy nilly, though some of us do make love to our employment. As such, we experience submission to the relentlessly instrumental narrativity of the regulators and so find ourselves pointing to imaginary profits on the bottom line. It would be quixotic to inveigh against such strategic claims; after all, the regulators control the purse strings, and they have the power of description. Now, however, it seems we have succumbed to their pictures, promising such payoffs not just strategically to our administrators, but with genuine conviction to each other and even to ourselves.

Hazlitt too was doing targeted research, aiming at 'a high and permanent interest, beyond ourselves, in humanity as such'. In returning to Hazlitt and to Bradley, I am not suggesting that Hazlitt's target is inherently superior, or any more accessible to literary study. Responding with 'imaginary sympathy' to *Othello*'s power will not lead us necessarily to realize humanity as such, erotic variety, or any of the other goals in our various agendas (at least not without the anguished self-disgust Burke described as 'our filthy purgation'[66]). The relation between literary study and ethics, Richard Lanham's ' "Q" question', has gone without satisfactory answer since Plato, because there is no single answer.[67] Stanley Fish is right: like virtue, literary study is its own reward.[68] With a masterpiece like *Othello*, this is more than enough.

Notes

[1] A. C. Bradley, *Shakespearean Tragedy: Lectures on 'Hamlet', 'Othello', 'King Lear', 'Macbeth'* (1904; rpt. London, 1964), p. 151.

[2] This essay is available with some minor revisions in Knights's *Explorations: Essays in Criticism Mainly on the Literature of the Seventeenth Century* (1947; rpt. New York, 1964), pp. 15-54.

[3] The phrases are taken from Hugh Grady, *The Modernist Shakespeare: Critical Texts in a Material World* (Oxford, 1991), esp. chapter 2.

[4] *Contingency, Irony, and Solidarity* (Cambridge, 1989), p. xiii.

[5] More precisely, Rorty wishes to displace these distinctions from the status of ontological categories, where they inscribe a foundational difference between Reality and Appearance, and put them into service for a rough-and-ready pragmatist use, specific to a particular context.

[6] *Desire and Anxiety: Circulations of Sexuality in Shakespearean Drama* (New York and London, 1992), p. 4.

[7] 'Invisible Bullets, Violet Bears: Reading Actors Reading', in Edward Pechter, ed., *Textual and Theatrical Shakespeare: Questions of Evidence* (Iowa City, 1996), pp. 210-29, p. 212.

[8] Margaret Lael Mikesell, Introduction, Part I, in Mikesell and Virginia Vaughan, eds., *'Othello': An Annotated Bibliography* (New York, 1990), pp. xi-xxiv, p. xvii.

[9] *Gender, Race, Renaissance Drama* (Manchester, 1989), pp. 54-8.

[10] 'The Argument about Shakespeare's Characters', *Critical Quarterly,* 7 (1965), 107-20, p. 109.

[11] 'Charivari and the Comedy of Abjection in *Othello*', in Linda Woodbridge and Edward Berry, eds., *True Rites and Maimed Rites: Ritual and Anti-Ritual in Shakespeare and His Age* (Urbana and Chicago, 1992), pp. 75-97, p. 85 (Bristol's emphasis). For a powerful argument that Shakespeare not only sustains but originates modern notions of subjectivity, see Joel Fineman, *Shakespeare's Perjured Eye: The Invention of Poetic Subjectivity in the Sonnets* (Berkeley and Los Angeles, 1986).

[12] 'It is clear', Anderson tells us, writing about theory since World War Two, 'that there has been one master-problem around which *all* contenders have revolved[:] the nature of the relationships between structure and subject in human history and society'. See *In the Tracks of Historical Materialism* (Chicago, 1984), p. 33 (Anderson's emphasis).

[13] I am hardly the first to try to bring either Bradley or the concept of character back into consideration.

In addition to Nuttall, see the discussions in John Bayley, *The Characters of Love: A Study in the Literature of Personality* (London, 1960), chapter 1, esp. pp. 33-47; and the chapters in S. L. Goldberg, *An Essay on 'King Lear'* (Cambridge, 1975), pp. 34-67; and E. A. J. Honigmann, *Shakespeare: Seven Tragedies: The Dramatist's Manipulation of Audience Response* (London, 1976), pp. 4-15. For more recent discussion, coming at the question from widely divergent positions, see Christy Desmet, *Reading Shakespeare's Characters: Rhetoric, Ethics, and Identity* (Amherst, 1992); Alan Sinfield, 'When Is a Character Not a Character? Desdemona, Olivia, Lady Macbeth, and Subjectivity', in *Faultlines: Cultural Materialism and the Politics of Dissident Reading* (Berkeley and Los Angeles, 1992), pp. 52-79, esp. p. 62; and Bert O. States, *Hamlet and the Concept of Character* (Baltimore and London), 1992.

[14] 1.1.1 and 4; 5.2.374-5. See Edward A. Snow, 'Sexual Anxiety and the Male Order of Things in *Othello*', *English Literary Renaissance,* 10 (1980), 384-412, p. 384.

[15] The perplexing questions centre on the competing claims of nature and culture. The ambivalent feelings can be located in terms of the contradictory generic signals many commentators have associated with this play (Susan Snyder, for instance, in *The Comic Matrix of Shakespeare's Tragedies: 'Romeo and Juliet', 'Hamlet', 'Othello', and 'King Lear'* (Princeton, 1979)): if we are watching a comedy, then we are on the side of young love in general and female desire in particular; if tragedy, then the claims of established patriarchal authority demand our primary allegiance. In '*Othello* and Colour Prejudice', G. K. Hunter suggests that the play provokes racist feelings only to require their repudiation (*Dramatic Identities and Cultural Tradition: Studies in Shakespeare and His Contemporaries: Critical Essays* (Liverpool, 1978), pp. 31-59). A. J. Cook describes a similar change in our feelings about Desdemona in 'The Design of Desdemona: Doubt Raised and Resolved', *Shakespeare Studies,* 13 (1980), 187-96.

[16] *Shakespeare and the Experience of Love* (Cambridge, 1981), p. 32.

[17] See Edward Berry, 'Othello's Alienation', *Studies in English Literature,* 30 (1990), 315-34; and David Bevington, 'Introduction' to his edition of *Othello* (1980; rpt. Toronto and New York, 1988), p. xxviii. For a version of this argument written before materialism and constructionism became generally current and including some astute commentary on the question of character, see G. M. Matthews, '*Othello* and the Dignity of Man', in Arnold Kettle, ed., *Shakespeare in a Changing World: Essays* (New York, 1964), pp. 123-45.

[18] In this regard, Lisa Jardine comments brilliantly on Iago's misogynist clichés at the beginning of Act 2. See 'Cultural Confusion and Shakespeare's Learned Heroines: "These are old paradoxes" ', *Shakespeare Quarterly,* 38 (1987), 1-18.

[19] See Kenneth Burke, '*Othello*: An Essay to Illustrate a Method', *Hudson Review,* 4 (1951), 165-203. I am profoundly indebted to Burke both for local detail and the general argument I am making here. See also Joel Altman, ' "Preposterous Conclusions": Eros, *Enargeia,* and the Composition of *Othello*', *Representations,* 18 (1987), 129-57; and Patricia Parker, 'Preposterous Events', *Shakespeare Quarterly,* 43 (1992), 186-213.

[20] Salman Rushdie, *The Satanic Verses* (New York, 1988), p. 157.

[21] Ibid., p. 168. The *Othello* subtext in Rushdie is clearly intentional. See Paul A. Cantor, '*Othello*: The Erring Barbarian among the Supersubtle Venetians', *Southwest Review,* 75 (1990), 296-319.

[22] John Banville, 'An Interview with Salman Rushdie', *New York Review of Books* (4 March 1993), 34-6, p. 34.

[23] Bayler, *The Characters of Love,* p. 134.

[24] *Morgann's Essay on the Dramatic Character of Sir John Falstaff,* ed. William Arthur Gill (1912; rpt. Freeport, 1970), p. 4. Harley Granville-Barker tries to demonstrate that double time solves a problem of audience belief, but since it is Shakespeare who creates the problem, Granville-Barker's argument winds up going round in circles. See *Prefaces to Shakespeare* (1946; rpt. Princeton, 1963), vol. 4, pp. 141-7. Graham Bradshaw has tried to explain away the problem, but his claims, which depend upon a hefty investment in Bianca's pre-dramatic career in Venice, are implausible. See *Misrepresentations: Shakespeare and the Materialists* (Ithaca and London, 1993), pp. 147-68.

For versions of the distinctions at work in the double time of *Othello,* consider Paul Valéry's discussion of the way 'our poetic pendulum travels from our sensation toward some idea or some sentiment, and returns toward some memory of the sensation and toward the potential act which could reproduce the sensation'. See *The Art of Poetry,* trans. Denise Folliot in Jackson Mathews, ed., *The Collected Works of Paul Valéry* (London, 1958), vol. 7, p. 72. See also Kenneth Burke's distinction between plots driven by lyrical associationism and by rational extension in *The Philosophy of Literary Form* (1941; rpt. Berkeley and Los Angeles, 1973), pp. 30-2.

[25] *Disowning Knowledge in Six Plays of Shakespeare* (Cambridge, 1987), p. 132.

[26] For critics (many of them following in Cavell's wake, as I am) who claim that *Othello* 'refers us to a hidden scene of desire that . . . is a focus of compulsive fascination for audience and characters alike', see (in alphabetical order): Janet Adelman, *Suffocating Mothers: Fantasies of Maternal Origin in Shakespeare's Plays, 'Hamlet' to 'The Tempest'* (New York and London, 1992); Lynda E. Boose, ' "Let it be hid": Renaissance Pornography, Iago, and Audience Response', in Richard Marienstras and Dominique Guy-Blanquet, eds., *Autour d' 'Othello'* (Paris, 1987), pp. 135-43; and 'Othello's Handkerchief, "The Recognizance and Pledge of Love" ', *English Literary Renaissance,* 5 (1975), 360-74; Arthur Little, Jr, ' "An essence that's not seen": The Primal Scene of Racism in *Othello*', *Shakespeare Quarterly,* 44 (1993), 304-24; Katharine Eisaman Maus, 'Horns of Dilemma: Jealousy, Gender and Spectatorship in English Renaissance Drama', *ELH,* 54 (1987), 561-83; and 'Proof and Consequences: Inwardness and Its Exposure in the English Renaissance', *Representations,* 34 (1991), 229-52; Michael Neill, 'Changing Places in *Othello*', *Shakespeare Survey 37* (1984), pp. 115-31; ' "Hidden Malady": Death, Discovery, and Indistinction in *The Changeling*', *Renaissance Drama,* 22 (1991), 95-121 (from which the quotation about the 'hidden scene of desire' at the beginning of this note is taken (p. 98); and 'Unproper Beds: Race, Adultery, and the Hideous in *Othello*', *Shakespeare Quarterly,* 40 (1989), 383-412; Patricia Parker, 'Dilation, Spying and the "Secret Place" of Woman', *Representations,* 44 (1993), 60-95; 'Fantasies of "Race" and "Gender": Africa, *Othello,* and Bringing to Light', in Margo Hendricks and Parker, eds., *Women, 'Race', and Writing in the Early Modern Period* (New York and London, 1994), pp. 84-100; and 'Shakespeare and Rhetoric: "Dilation" and "Delation" ', in Parker and Geoffrey Hartman, eds., *Shakespeare and the Question of Theory* (London, 1985), pp. 57-74; and Peter L. Rudnytsky, 'The Purloined Handkerchief in *Othello*', in Joseph Reppen and Maurice Charney, eds., *The Psychoanalytic Study of Literature* (Hillsdale, N.J., 1985), pp. 169-90.

[27] Cf. Neill: Desdemona is 'not merely the precious "thing", the stolen treasure of love's corrupted commerce, but herself the lost place of love' ('Changing Places', p. 128).

[28] George Lyman Kittredge, ed., *Othello* (Boston, 1941), p. 211.

[29] *Disowning Knowledge,* p. 132.

[30] 'Fantasies of "Race" ', p. 87.

[31] Laura Mulvey, who established the idea of 'the gaze' ('Visual Pleasure and Narrative Cinema', *Screen,* 16 (1975), 6-18), twice subsequently cautioned against applying it to all movies ('Afterthoughts on "Visual

Pleasure and Narrative Cinema" Inspired by *Duel in the Sun', Framework,* 15-17 (1981), 12-15; and 'Changes', *Discourse,* 7 (1985), 11-30. All this material is now conveniently available in *Visual and Other Pleasures* (Bloomington and Indianapolis, 1989).) We should be even more sceptical about transferring 'the gaze' to theatre, and even more sceptical yet again when the theatre was produced in such a remote period. Notions of ocular proof associated with experimental science were developing in the Renaissance, as were notions of true perspective in painting and a single privileged vantage point in the masque. These ideas, however, had not achieved anything like their subsequent authority. They competed with other ideas about perception and different epistemological theories. Renaissance ideas about poetry and theatre, moreover, often repudiated the primacy of the visual, an integrated objective stage *gestalt,* and a single controlling point of view. In support of these claims, see Desmet, *Reading Shakespeare's Characters,* pp. 112-13; Barbara Freedman, *Staging the Gaze: Postmodernism, Psychoanalysis, and Shakespearean Comedy* (Ithaca, 1991); Terence Hawkes, *Shakespeare's Talking Animals: Language and Drama in Society* (London, 1970), p. 43 and p. 130; James R. Siemon, *Shakespearean Iconoclasm* (Berkeley and Los Angeles, 1985); Wylie Sypher, *The Ethic of Time: Structures of Experience in Shakespeare* (New York, 1976), pp. 116-20; Rosemond Tuve, *Elizabethan and Metaphysical Imagery: Renaissance Poetic and Twentieth-Century Critics* (Chicago, 1947); and Robert Weimann, *Shakespeare and the Popular Tradition in the Theater: Studies in the Social Dimension of Dramatic Form* (Baltimore and London, 1978). There have been others, apart from Mulvey herself, who have warned against overinvesting in the idea of the gaze (see Edward Snow, 'Theorizing the Male Gaze: Some Problems', *Representations,* 25 (1989), 330-41; and Stephen J. Greenblatt, *Learning to Curse: Essays in Early Modern Culture* (New York and London, 1990), pp. 175-81); nonetheless, critics carry on with the gaze sometimes in full knowledge of Mulvey's disclaimers. Its power seems to be irresistible.

[32] Bradshaw adds that *'flooded* seems the right word [until] the images smash against *dries up,* and reform into the wrenchingly gross, unhinging image of "it"— "it!"—as a foul *cistern' (Misrepresentations,* p. 179). Lawrence Danson talks about the 'fluid metaphors . . . suggested by Othello's figuring Desdemona as either "fountain from which [his] current runs" or "cistern for foul toads to knot and gender in". In *Cymbeline* the idea of the wife as a watery site is complexly joined with the idea of the wife as property—the one idea, as we would expect, confounding the other, since you can't *keep* things that flow like a fountain or breed like a cistern' (' "The Catastrophe is a Nuptial": The Space of Masculine Desire in *Othello, Cymbeline,* and *The Winter's Tale', Shakespeare Survey 46* (1994), pp. 69-79, p. 75).

[33] Neill, 'Changing Places', p. 130.

[34] 5.2.155-6. For remarks on the powerful sense of sexual disgust in 'this appalling line', see William Empson, *The Structure of Complex Words* (London, 1964), pp. 226-7; and Snow, 'Sexual Anxiety', p. 388.

[35] Quoted by Francine du Plessix Gray in 'Splendor and Miseries', *New York Review of Books* (16 July 1992), 331-5, p. 334.

[36] Valerie Eliot, ed., *The Waste Land: A Facsimile and Transcript of the Original Drafts Including the Annotations of Ezra Pound* (London, 1971), p. 23.

[37] 'Love regards as its end the enjoyment of beauty; beauty pertains only to the mind, sight, and hearing. Love, therefore, is limited to these three, but desire which rises from the other senses is called, not love, but lust or madness.' Sears R. Jayne, ed. and trans., *Marsilio Ficino's Commentary on Plato's Symposium* (Columbia, Missouri; 1944), p. 130.

[38] According to Freud, the civilizing of human sexuality since prehistory, said to reside in the stability of family arrangements, involved 'the diminution of the olfactory stimuli by means of which the menstrual process produced an effect on the male psyche. Their role was taken over by visual excitations, which, in contrast to the intermittent olfactory stimuli, were able to maintain a permanent effect . . . The diminution of the olfactory stimuli seems itself to be a consequence of man's raising himself from the ground, of his assumption of an upright gait; this made his genitals, which were previously concealed, visible and in need of protection, and so provoked feelings of shame in him.' *Civilization and its Discontents,* trans. James Strachey (New York, 1962), p. 46. For a suggestive discussion of Freud and of various associations, especially in the nineteenth century, between smell and the primitive, see Hal Foster, ' "Primitive" Scenes', *Critical Inquiry,* 20 (1993), 69-102.

[39] *The Smell of Books: A Cultural-Historical Study of Olfactory Perception in Literature* (Ann Arbor, 1992), p. 13, p. 160 and p. 231.

[40] *A Short View of Tragedy,* in Curt A. Zimanky, ed., *The Critical Works of Thomas Rymer* (New Haven, 1956), p. 160.

[41] Cf. Boose, 'Desdemona's Handkerchief'. Rymer, though, seems to have taken the point almost despite himself; consider the following remarks, intended to make fun of the play's concentration on such a trivial thing as the handkerchief: *'Desdemona* dropt the Handkerchief, and missed it that very day after her Marriage; it might have been rumpl'd up with her Wedding sheets: And this Night that she lay in her wedding

sheets, the *Fairey* Napkin (whilst *Othello* was stifling her) might have started up to disarm his fury, and stop his ungracious mouth' (p. 162). Or, just earlier: 'Had it been *Desdemona*'s Garter, the Sagacious Moor might have smelt a Rat; but the Handkerchief is so remote a trifle, no Booby, on this side *Mauritania,* cou'd make any consequence from it' (p. 160). One might say that, though blind, Rymer could register the meaning well enough as taste and smell. Rudnytsky argues that 'Rymer's comparison of the handkerchief to a "Garter" comes to seem particularly inspired' as suggesting its fetish-like quality ('The Purloined Hand-kerchief', p. 185). Peter Davison is picking up similar olfactory resonances in his remark that Rymer's point about the garter and smelling a rat is very *'pungently put'* (*Othello*. The Critics Debate Series (Basingstoke, 1988), p. 83 [my emphasis]). Davison, who remarks on the 'surprising . . . *personal* acrimony' in *Othello* criticism (p. 10), suggests that 'the peculiar vicious-ness that animates some critics . . . may stem from what in *Othello* subconsciously disturbs them' (p. 53). This suggestion seems plausible, especially in con-junction with all the anecdotes from the play's theat-rical history of audiences so upset that they felt moved in some way to intervene in the action. In this context, Rymer's tone of furious resistance is interesting and revealing. He may not be a good critic, but he is not the perverse anomaly he is sometimes taken to be.

⁴² By contrast, the primary visible qualities can be fixed in a quantitatively determinate space (this tall, that shape, even such-and-such a colour). As a con-sequence of its greater stability, ocular proof may seem like a more realistic and even worthwhile project than olfactory proof. It was, arguably, beginning to acquire such authority in the Renaissance—but only beginning to, and not for everybody (my point in note 31).

⁴³ John Marston, *The Dutch Courtesan*, ed. M. L. Wine. Regents Renaissance Drama Series (Lincoln, Nebraska; 1965), 3.3.45.

⁴⁴ *The Smell of Books*, p. 4.

⁴⁵The 'auratic phenomenon' of smell 'is almost purely linguistic, despite its evident lack of terminological grounding, in fact precisely because of it. The con-nectors in the "smell *like* . . ." or the "smell *of* . . ." are the true linguistic places of the olfactory, empty of sensual quality themselves, functional particles, pro-viders of linkage, connections, bonds. [The] short-coming of language for the olfactory thus turns out to be the true reflection of the liminal and transgressive qualities of that sensory mode' (Rindisbacher, *The Smell of Books,* pp. 330-1).

⁴⁶ *The Foul and the Fragrant: Odor and the French Social Imagination* (Cambridge, Mass.; 1986). The book was originally called *Le Miasme et la Jonquille,*

so the phrase is actually the translator's, perhaps think-ing of 'l'imaginaire'.

⁴⁷ In an unpublished essay, 'The Adverse Body: John Marston', Ronald Huebert points out that Marston found the adage in Florio's Montaigne, 'where it appears as a bathetically unheroic couplet: "Ev'ry mans ordure well, To his own sense doth smell." ' According to Huebert, Florio would have found it 'not in Montaigne's racy French', but in a Latin epigram, 'Stercus cuiusque suum bene olet', itself a mistranslation of Erasmus's Adage 2302, 'suus cuique crepitus bene olet'. For the presumed origins in Aristotle, see John Weightman, 'How Wise Was Montaigne?' *New York Review of Books* (5 November 1992), 32-5, p. 33.

The idea still commands belief. Freud claimed that the social factor in the repression of anal erotism is 'at-tested by the circumstance that, in spite of all man's developmental advances, he scarcely finds the smell of *his own* excreta repulsive, but only that of other people's' (*Civilization and its Discontents,* p. 47, Freud's emphasis). And Weightman reports that 'When, quite recently, I heard it said of a world-famous but rather self-righteous musician, "He thinks his own shit doesn't smell", I took the expression to be a typically rude Australianism' ('How Wise?' p. 33). Its current authority has a different rhetorical register—or two different registers—from the aphoristic mode. For Freud, inhabiting a culture more respectful of scien-tific empiricism than of familiar topoi, the authority is represented not as a maxim but as data—some-thing 'attested by circumstance'. Weightman seems to imply that a bumptious colonial's language may be more authoritative, closer to the true core of tradi-tion, than the polite diction of the metropolitan cen-tre.

⁴⁸ Norman Sanders, ed., *Othello*. New Cambridge Shake-speare (Cambridge, 1984), p. 147.

⁴⁹ 'Crazy Jane Talks with the Bishop'. *The Collected Poems of W. B. Yeats* (New York, 1959), pp. 254-5.

⁵⁰ *Spenser's 'Faerie Queene',* ed. J. C. Smith (Oxford, 1909), vol. 2, p. 121 (Book 4, Canto 10, 1). The misattribution may originate with Freud, to infer from Traub, who passes it along in *Desire and Anxiety* (p. 58 and p. 156). St Augustine is a likely candidate, considering how frequently he participated in this tra-ditional repugnance for the female body. The aphorism can serve also to celebrate the carnivalesque body ('Fair and foul are near of kin'—the main tone in Yeats's poem). For recent commentators who have appropriated the maxim without any attribution, see Greenblatt, *Learning to Curse,* p. 60; Norman Mailer, *Tough Guys Don't Dance* (New York, 1984), p. 116; and Gail Kern Paster, *The Body Embarrassed: Drama and the Disciplines of Shame in Early Modern En-*

gland (Ithaca, 1993), p. 210. Mailer is a particularly interesting writer in this context. He writes obsessively about different excremental-sexual smells and has developed a whole metaphysics about the proximity of female orifices (Mailer's Manichaenism is a subject about which doctoral dissertations are presumably being written even now, now, very now). He even invented a witty neologism for the perineum (employing the plural pronoun whose rhetorical power I shall be describing in a moment): 'we boys out on Long Island used to call [it] the Taint'—presumably for its suggestions of rotten meat, like Othello's 'shambles', but explicitly because ''taint vagina, 'taint anus, ho, ho' (*Tough Guys,* p. 93).

51 'Shakespeare and the Stoicism of Seneca', 1927; rpt. in *Selected Essays*. New Edition (New York, 1950), pp. 107-20, p. 111.

52 'Diabolic Intellect and the Noble Hero', 1937; rpt. in *The Common Pursuit* (Harmondsworth, 1969), pp. 136-59, p. 139, p. 141.

53 'Changing Places', p. 127.

54 *Suffocating Mothers,* p. 63 and p. 65. Adelman's generously detailed notes indicate the depth and range of this object-relations approach among current critics.

55 'Desire's Excess and the English Renaissance Theatre: *Edward II, Troilus and Cressida,* and *Othello*', in Susan Zimmerman, ed., *Erotic Politics: Desire on the Renaissance Stage* (London and New York, 1992), pp. 84-102, p. 86 and p. 95.

56 *Renaissance Self-Fashioning: From More to Shakespeare* (Chicago, 1980), p. 237. Adelman uses the same phrase about 'the impossible condition of male desire, the condition always already lost' (*Suffocating Mothers,* p. 69).

57 Adelman makes the point and provides references to five others who interpret the passage in similar ways, ibid., pp. 72-3 and p. 278.

58 *Renaissance Self-Fashioning,* p. 238 and p. 243.

59 For an interesting discussion of Dickens's opening, see A. D. Nuttall, *Openings: Narrative Beginnings from the Epic to the Novel* (Oxford, 1992), pp. 172ff.

60 In P. P. Howe, ed., *The Complete Works* (London, 1930), vol. 4, p. 200.

61 Of course this tradition does not vanish abruptly with Bradley. Helen Gardner's 1955 British Academy lecture gave it perhaps its purest expression (the clarity of afterlife—Minerva's owl flies at twilight): *The*

Noble Moor (rpt. Folcroft, Pa., 1969). And there continue to be generously responsive acknowledgements of Othello's romantic-heroic stature in Jane Adamson, *'Othello' as Tragedy: Some Problems of Judgment and Feeling* (Cambridge, 1980); Bayley, Cavell, Kirsch, and Mark Rose ('Othello's Occupation: Shakespeare and the Romance of Chivalry', *English Literary Renaissance,* 15 (1985), 293-311). In one recent commentary in this mode, Thomas Clayton's tone of bemused disaffection from current critical norms fairly reflects the view that such celebratory criticism has become, like Bradley himself, self-evidently obsolete. See ' "That's she that was myself": Not-so-famous Last Words and Some Ends of *Othello'*, *Shakespeare Survey 46* (1994), pp. 61-8.

62 Bradley clearly knows what he is doing and why. About Iago he asks, 'How is it then that we can bear to contemplate him; nay, that, if we really imagine him, we feel admiration and some kind of sympathy? . . . Why is the representation tolerable, and why do we not accuse its author either of untruth or of a desperate pessimism? To these questions it might at once be replied: Iago does not stand alone; he is a factor in a whole; and we perceive him there and not in isolation, acted upon as well as acting, destroyed as well as destroying. But, although this is true and important, I pass it by and . . . regard him by himself' (pp. 190-1).

63 For others who make this point, see Bayley (pp. 129-30) and Kirsch (p. 31). Calderwood is particularly given to the canny insider's tone, as witness the words I emphasize in the following passages from *The Properties of 'Othello'* (keyed to the order of the four versions of contemporary criticism as I described them above): (1) The alien's abject dependency and Iago's inevitable triumph: 'But *after all what should we have expected?* The Moor is a stranger' (p. 68). (2) The impossible condition of male desire: 'This masculine appropriation of women in Venice helps explain why Othello's faith in Desdemona succumbs with such surprising ease to Iago's beguilements. He loses faith in part because he never really had any. Though he endows his wife with heavenly qualities, deep down he suspects, *like any other husband,* the sorry truth' (p. 31). (3) Lacan: 'To see yourself in another, as he does—*as we all do* in our psychological extensions of Lacan's mirror stage—is to divide as well as unify the here/thereness of the body/self' (p. 105). (4) The submission to narrativity: '*Normally* the speaking subject is enormously in excess of the grammatical subject; we *are* [Calderwood's emphasis] far more than we can say' (p. 58).

64 The play leaves the question open. Though asking us to credit Othello's nobility, it does not insist that we understand this nobility as necessarily self-generated. Maybe he is formed by his birth, social position,

family and early environment. 'I fetch my life and being / From men of royal siege', he tells us early on (1.2.21-2). Maybe he is climatologically constructed (not a ridiculous notion in the Renaissance), as Desdemona suggests explaining his temperamental indisposition to jealousy: 'the sun where he was born / Drew all such humours from him' (3.4.30-1).

[65] *Desire and Anxiety,* p. 8.

[66] '*Othello',* p. 200.

[67] See 'The "Q" Question', *South Atlantic Quarterly,* 87 (1988), 653-700, modified and incorporated in *The*

Electronic Word: Democracy, Technology, and the Arts (Chicago, 1993).

[68] 'Why Literary Criticism is Like Virtue', *London Review of Books* (10 June 1993), 11-16.

Source: "'Have You Not Read of Some Such Thing?' Sex and Sexual Stories in *Othello,*" in *Shakespeare Survey: An Annual Survey of Shakespeare Studies and Production,* Vol. 49, 1996, pp. 201-16.

Coriolanus and the Failure of Performatives

John Plotz, *Harvard University*

> Young people today can be said to be in a situation where ordinary common sense no longer suffices to meet the strange demands life makes. Everything has become so intricate that mastering it would require an exceptional intellect. Because skill at playing the game is no longer enough; the question that keeps coming up is: can the game be played at all now and what would be the right game to play? (*welches ist das rechte Spiel?*)
>
> —Wittgenstein[1]

I. INTRODUCTION: WHOSE TRAGEDY?

Neither the tragedy "of a people that has lost its hero" as Brecht argues, nor simply that of the lone figure of Coriolanus himself, *Coriolanus* is the tragedy of the gap that looms between the private "true" Self and a public realm of tacitly accepted opportunistic mendacity.[2] The public world in *Coriolanus* is—very like that of *Richard III*—characterized by language deployed solely for *future effect*. When Coriolanus proposes that words and deeds ought to flow directly from the soul of the speaker, and be weighed by how well they correspond with that speaker's (true) inner being, his challenge only uncovers an unease already inherent in this linguistic model. The idea that truth can derive only from inwardness—that *authentic* interiority is a viable alternative to shallow public life—must already be present in a world view that imagines the public sphere to be inherently deceitful. The play's truth-free political realm contains the seeds of tragedy before Coriolanus has even earned his name.

Franco Moretti has pointed out that Shakespearean tragedy ultimately "disentitles the absolute monarch to all ethical and rational legislation," but *Coriolanus* suggests that the impetus to "absolute" monarchy is the need to counteract an equally abhorrent condition, the state of "absolute freedom" of language.[3] The two states—"free politics" and "absolute monarchy"—are seen as mirrors to each other. And, as Moretti's observations on the banality of the endings of Shakespeare's tragedies suggest, no "third way" of finding authoritative, satisfying meaning in the world is capable of replacing this mutually abhorring, yet complementary dyad. Coriolanus's criticism uncovers a *hamartia* that society would just as soon ignore—but his criticism cannot work as a cure.

Yet the very fact of his rebellion launches a corrosive assault on a world that is not entirely alien to our own. All the characters in *Coriolanus* are aware, underneath, that the linguistic games they are playing are fraudulent, that their talk is half to deceive others and half to keep themselves comfortably numb to their own motives: only Coriolanus says out loud what others keep under their hats. Admittedly, this turns out to be an irrational course of action in a world in which the dominant view of language is that it ought to be used to achieve one's interests, and that the nagging sense of an "integral" man beneath the words ought to be suppressed. But, as Adorno said, in an irrational world the irrational response may be the only rational one.[4]

It may seem absurd to argue that Coriolanus is no worse than the world around him, because he is certainly no saint. A prickly monster (that is, a marvel, as well as a horror) who won't hear himself flattered, who loathes the plebeians (as well as the patricians) of his own city, Coriolanus sees no need to concede, explain, or negotiate in any of his dealings. He famously cannot even hear himself banished, but must—taking the "true" Rome into himself—respond "I banish you" to the "real" Rome outside and around him.[5] What could it mean to recuperate this man, to turn the blame for the tragedy back onto Coriolanus's *polis,* his family, finally onto the whole structure of the play? Coriolanus's fault is the most glaring in the play; surely that means the fault is all his?

So two important recent critics of the play argue, influentially and extremely revealingly.[6] But I want to ask what happens if we take seriously the critique of Coriolanus's universe implied in his words, evaluate his response to what he perceives as a flawed world around him, and ask whether any part of his criticism rings true. Whether his actions are rational and ethical or not, Coriolanus acts out a caustic and at times compelling diagnosis of what is wrong with a society where people consciously say things they do not "mean" for the purpose of persuading others of things it is to the speaker's advantage they believe. To the extent that Coriolanus succeeds not in simply rejecting but in scathingly rebuking the Rome that cannot tolerate him, this play manages to make visible a gaping wound in the Roman *polis,* and thus implicitly a wound in Shakespeare's own world. This tragedy might be read as Shakespeare's expression of a dictum of Adorno's: "The wrong life can't be lived rightly."[7]

Coriolanus lives too deeply embedded in the life of a lie to be able to dig himself out with the half-truth he comes up with. But even if his excavation fails (and it does fail him), the critique he offers is something that has been naggingly present in this world of public deceit all along. The *internal* truth he offers simply inverts, like a camera obscura, the acceptable public lies all around him. Understanding the play requires, then, not an evaluation of the success and failure of Coriolanus himself, but rather an exploration of the play's criticism of the political and linguistic norms of its own universe. A play may succeed even where its hero failed. And may even succeed in doing exactly what its hero has failed to do.

II. SIDING WITH THE PUBLIC: THE PROBLEM WITH RECENT CRITICISM

Coriolanus tells the story of a world that, absent some sort of resistance, is filled with characters who deploy language for *future gain*. For these characters, all language is designed to persuade rather than to represent, so there is no notion of the truth-value of speech. All that is measured is its success. This theme emerges elsewhere in Shakespeare: the all-pervading verbal deceit of Richard III in *Richard III* would suit him to inhabit Coriolanus's universe. When he responds to Anne's "I fear me (thy tongue and heart) are false" with "then never man was true" he touches on what irks Coriolanus. Since everyone around him, including his mother, preaches and practices fraudulence, there may be no way to live truthfully.[8] A more precise comparison might be to the complete fraudulence of Richard and his lackeys in More's *History of Richard III,* against which, as Greenblatt convincingly demonstrates, silence or sanctuary are the only viable responses, both of limited efficacy.[9] The genius of *Coriolanus* is that it surpasses both More's and Shakespeare's *Richard III*s in its attempt to map the dual pathology of a world split between "spectacular" public deceit and alienated, (though not silent) private selfhood.

Just because the play reveals a different way to imagine these problems, however, does not mean it reveals that different way *to us*. Recent criticism of the play has overlooked so important a strand of *Coriolanus*'s meaning so persistently that it almost seems worth invoking the time-honored Party line, "It's no accident . . . ." The most influential critics who address the antagonism between its two rival theories of meaning-making get *Coriolanus* seriously wrong; in part because they haven't made an effort to understand Shakespeare in his time; in part because they're too eager to press their own agendas onto him.[10] Both Stanley Cavell's "*Coriolanus* and Interpretations of Politics (Who does the Wolf Love?)," and Stanley Fish's "How to Do Things with Austin and Searle,"—although their axiomatic assumptions and intents differ radically— offer readings of *Coriolanus* that hinge on Coriolanus's unwillingness or inability to follow the rules his society has enacted. To Cavell this seems yet another instance of a Shakespearean tragic hero's refusal to "acknowledge" what the intuitive realist must grasp: that he must find a way to embrace without question the love offered him by some key human being (or beings) in order to affirm his place in the realm of the human. Coriolanus must learn to accept the love of his mother and wife: his inability to do so unsuits him for participation in the *polis* of Rome.

To Fish, similarly, the fault lies entirely within Coriolanus, but the deviation from rule-following marks not so much a psychological *aporia* as a spanner in the societal works: Coriolanus cannot grasp the nature of a proper performative and hence he is outcast from a society baffled by the "excessive" demands he puts on language. To both Cavell and Fish, this is a play about a serious failure on Coriolanus's part, and more generally about the obligations of an individual to shape him or herself to the meanings society has instituted. To Fish, this play speaks to the power of "interpretive communities," and addresses an illegitimate threat to the sort of meaning such a community attempts to instantiate.

This paper sets out to show, firstly, that the stable community Coriolanus is supposed to accept is a morass of deception that could not possibly offer the sort of readily workable reality that both Cavell and Fish posit. Secondly, it will attempt to explain how Fish's theory of the power and legitimacy of "interpretive communities," and Cavell's intuitive realism should have led them to misread this play. In doing so, I hope to shed light on the structural weaknesses of the model of interpretive communities, and to reveal more clearly some of its political implications and applications.

III. ROOTED AND ROTED SPEECH

It is customary to start a discussion of *Coriolanus* with a list of his personal flaws. Let us instead map the world that Coriolanus feels betrayed by, its practices and its personae. Stephen Greenblatt's remarkable discussion of the universe of spectacle and dissimulation described in More's writing provides a helpful paradigm. More describes a universe in which, as Greenblatt writes, "everyone is profoundly committed to upholding conventions in which no one believes."[11] Greenblatt expands that conception in his discussion of the way collaborative fictions such as coronation, public approbation, and bishopric inauguration are criticized in More's writing, even as More himself willingly participated in the fraudulent ceremonies his public persona demanded.[12] More's writing thus applies a corrective to Machiavelli. The speech of public deceit preached, practiced, and derided in More is not entirely meant to deceive; rather, it is a sort of social glue that allows the transactions of (unequal) power to be transacted with a minimum of outright fuss and contradiction and the maximum of pleasant, mendacious, but common amelioration.

That seems to me a fair account of the lurid deceits preached and accepted in *Coriolanus,* deceits that may be *de jure* forbidden, but are the *de facto* norm: the promises of friendship broken, the pious justifications for lying to the plebeians or to the patricians, and Aufidius's banal final speech in which he really expects the Volscians to believe his humble contrition for a murder he has spent weeks planning and has just finished committing!

Whether or not one sees these as true parallels to More's universe, it is immediately apparent that the Rome in which Coriolanus finds himself is political in the worst sense of that word. Shakespeare envisions a continual war of each against each. There is in *Coriolanus* no shared public space to which Coriolanus can return, because all space is occupied by words used to spur others to actions, words to quiet others from dissent, words to perform public ceremonies in which no one really believes. It is for this reason that Cavell is wrong to say that "a political reading is apt to become fairly predictable once you know whose side the reader is taking, that of the patricians or that of the plebeians."[13] An astute political reading (and this includes Brecht's) recognizes at once that there are at least seven sides at various points in the play, in battles that include: Aufidius vs. Coriolanus; Patricians vs. Plebeians; Tribunes vs. Patricians; Plebeians vs. Plebeians; Rome vs. Coriolanus; Coriolanus vs. himself; Volumnia vs. Coriolanus; and so on. All are battles over interest, and over what words mean—all are political confrontations. No one knows who is in charge, and hence words are artfully and *disingenuously* deployed to gain power.

That this world is "political" does *not* mean, as Cavell, Fish, and the more optimistic practitioners of discourse theory may be tempted to assume, that all conversation tends to create and then sustain a public sphere from which *interests* are removed.[14] That sort of political world is imagined in *Coriolanus* in an aesthetic (theatrical) register, but only at one very strange and striking moment discussed below. In general, the play is filled with an exceptionally unscrupulous sort of politics-as-usual, where interest rules and deceit has the drop on sincerity any day.

In order to demonstrate the ordinary forms of deceit practiced in this public realm I will skip the obvious scoundrels: the tribunes (whose elaborate stage-directions for moving the plebs through Rome and cuing their shouts tribe-by-tribe ranks as one of Shakespeare's rawest parodies of the theatrical gone astray), Aufidius, and the ineffectual senators. Instead, I will focus on two sites of political confrontation. The first of these is the staging of a linguistic spectacle where both

sides know perfectly well what is going on, and share in the illusion; the second is one of the great moments of the play, in which one character attempts to inculcate in another the principles of political deceit necessary to get ahead.

Meninius, self-styled dearest friend to Coriolanus, is one prime proponent of manipulative mendacity, as the parable of the belly ought to demonstrate (he is the only Shakespearean character to have either a fart or a belch as a line [1.1.109-10]).[15] But his mendacity in delivering that parable, like the implicit deception More discerns and participates in, is somewhat more complicated than first appears. Meninius's fable of the belly might well be read as exemplary, not of mere hoodwinking (Machiavellian manipulation of the credulous masses), but of elegant language providing convenient cover for baser political motivations. Meninius tells the belly parable just when the crowd is mustering the courage to join a rebellion already in progress, possibly with loss of life. The elaborate parable's purpose is to slow the rush of the mob (that is conceded on both sides), but whether it succeeded quieting the crowd remains in doubt until Coriolanus (*né* Marcius) brings the news that the other plebs have won their battle already. Thus the story turns out to have been entirely academic, and no one has to lose face. On the one side, the crowd has professed interest in the admonitory anecdote, but can still celebrate their victory—won by proxy by the other citizens. On the other side, Menenius congratulates himself for having had a frank and cordial exchange of views with the enemy, and—pointlessly—held them back. This may seem a cynical reading of that episode, but it is true to the spirit of the play as a whole: the actions of one's enemies—and one has no friends, only allies— are judged only by what they accomplish.

The second example of the deceit inherent in the structure of this world is Volumnia's speech to her son Coriolanus, pleading with him to lie in order to get what he (and she) wants. Before discussing this in detail, I should note that Cavell is only the latest critic to see Coriolanus's relationship with Volumnia as key to his psychological problems and his inability to cope with the world. Cavell's position is worth bearing in mind when we see what Volumnia expects of her son.

When Coriolanus has to bargain for his consulship in the market-place, having been challenged by the tribunes, Volumnia assures him that "I would dissemble with my nature, where my fortunes and my friends at stake required I should do so in honor" (3.2.62-64). And she goes farther than that, spelling out the formula I take as the form and archetype for all speech in this politicized world, this world where the absolute freedom of speech is linked to the absolute impossibility of verifying, justifying, or remaining true to one's words:

Now it lies you on to speak
To th' people: not by your own instruction,
Nor by th' matter which your heart prompts
   you,
But with such words that are but roted in
Your tongue, though but bastards and
   syllables
Of no allowance to your bosom's truth.
Now this no more dishonors you at all
Than to take in a town with gentle words,
Which else would put you to your fortune
   and
The hazard of much blood.

                (3.2.54-63)

This speech, simultaneously one of the most moving and shocking moments in the play, is pitched to appeal particularly to Coriolanus. Volumnia's edge (and in this world all advancement hinges on having such an edge) is that, being his mother, she has got a slightly better idea of how to pull his strings than others do. This skill works to her advantage at the end of the play (though certainly not to his). Here it is not sufficient because she, like all his "friends," fails to recognize how far Coriolanus has deviated from their universe, and how ridiculous his unwillingness to compromise makes her look.

Unlike most of Rome, Volumnia dimly understands that Coriolanus, trained to be a martial hope for this city, will have a different conception of what words can do: that they are to him "the matter which your heart prompts you" (3.2.56).[16] However, she tries to rid him of that idea by preaching what the whole city already knows: words are not used to *express* but to *get* things. It is a bit alarming that, in the face of such sly "policy" by Volumnia, Cavell still wants to claim Coriolanus's problem is his psychological inability to reconcile himself to her love and her laws. Still more alarming is to imagine that Shakespeare here idealizes the sort of opportunistic deceit Coriolanus's mother proposes, or that the play "thinks of this creation of the political, call it the public, as the overcoming of narcissism, incestuousness and cannibalism."[17] If Coriolanus spurns his mother (and motherland) after this scene, the decision cannot be called inexplicable. If Coriolanus's narcissism consists of a rejection of the love of a mother who tells him that even she speaks out of policy (that even her love to him is calculated, and her words designed to elicit useful responses), then it is hard to see how this "creation of the political" could be the invigorating revelation Cavell thinks it is.

IV. DESERT AND NOT DESIRE: CORIOLANUS'S RESPONSE

Indeed, Coriolanus's reaction to his mother's speech can only strengthen the case for our seeing his self-consuming tragedy as a reaction to a world full of "roted" and manipulative speech. Coriolanus cries out against the "harlotry" of unrooted language in some of the most moving passages in the play. Three times his mother tries to shame him into lying to the plebs so he can hold on to power. Two times he refuses, and finally, near heartbreak—those who have just discovered that they are bastards in the truth are always heartbroken—he replies:

Pray be content.
Mother, I am going to the market-place.
Chide me no more. I'll mountebank their
   loves,
Cog their hearts from them and come home
   beloved
Of all the trades in Rome.

                (3.2.132-36)

What a thing to tell your mother. Coriolanus does not even assume he will come home beloved of her (he has no reason to trust her anymore) but of those he despises.

Coriolanus's actions, misinterpreted throughout as *self-interested* (even though it is clear he stands to gain from conforming, not from fulminating: the pun in "I'd rather serve in my way than sway with them in theirs" [2.1.198-99] captures this point marvelously), are indeed a sort of hideous, misdirected response to the deceit he sees practiced. But it is my contention they are understandable, or at least explicable. Operating on the assumption that, as Meninius says, "What his breast forges, that his mouth must vent" (3.1.156) Coriolanus goes through the world believing his thoughts and deeds (as *he* recollects them—this is "mine own desert") are linked unproblematically to the words that *should* and do come out of his mouth. So at the confrontation in the marketplace—in which he says he is there not to beg for the consulship, but because his actions by rights should lead inevitably to his becoming consul—he is not behaving as unreasonably as it may seem. He is merely *inverting* a model that says language is all based on expectations of future reward, and replacing it with the idea language represents past mental states or accomplishments. "Mine own desert" brought me, he says, "not mine own desire" since "'twas never my desire yet to trouble the poor with begging" (2.3.66-67). Of course this is a deliberate insult to the poor citizens (he means that they usually do the begging and not he) but one can see his point. All marketplace negotiations envision language as begging, cajoling, or enticement. They look to future gain rather than revealing what happened in the past, and in the speaker's soul.

Coriolanus's ideas about language, I am arguing, constitute a cogent objection to Fish's claim that "reality is a matter of public specification." In fact, when Coriolanus pokes and pries in his awkward way at the social world surrounding him, the ongoing deceptive revision of public specification turns out to be fantastically *unreal*. "Part of Coriolanus's tragedy is that he is forever seeking a level of intuition deeper—more essential or more real—than that stipulated by the public conventions of language," writes Fish.[18] However, faced by the sort of all-encompassing deliberate deception we have seen everywhere but in Coriolanus himself, is he really to blame for that assumption? The language others use is *self*-evidently false. The correct response, in Fish's book and I fear Cavell's, would be that there is no level deeper than *public* speech. But how do we know until we try?[19] In this case, it is immediately obvious that Coriolanus can go deeper in at least one respect: every person in this world is aware of being (in Greenblatt's words) "profoundly committed to upholding conventions in which no one believes," but only Coriolanus is willing to say as much.[20]

Yet the act of saying it, or acting out the cognitive dissonance already embedded within that universe, will do something. To act out the antithesis of a profoundly and systematically distorted theory of language is to nudge that theory, to make somewhat more visible the very fissure that is already present—that between private belief and public performance. That is what Coriolanus does, and only those who assume that the system of meaning as-is must be right (present might makes right) are incapable of perceiving that a pathological deviance may also, in the right frame, function as a corrective.

Any theory holding that meaning can only be created and validated by interpretive communities has this fatal flaw: it leaves no space for the possibility of small changes, or of any immanent critique to a society, or of absurd parody that undermines everything without substituting anything. Indeed, it has no space for anything but a crash that topples the semantic order. Thus every change of "communal interpretation" seems to come like an inexplicable revelation.

Because Fish is so concerned to certify the courtesies and ceremonies whereby a community validates any act and gives meaning to it—because Fish is unwilling to admit that Shakespeare may be depicting a world where some things in the public realm are *wrong*—he is quick to excoriate Coriolanus in all his clashes with those who are (or are supposed to be) his friends. This is an understandable attitude, for it is a sort of empirical given in our, or we might suppose any, world that most people will treat us right most of the time. Understandable or not, however, it is an attitude that simply does not apply to *Coriolanus*. In *Coriolanus* even one's allies may be applying to one's actions a set of criteria that it would destroy one's self-respect (which is to say, one's sense of one's own identity as separate from the community around one) to accept.

For instance, Fish argues it is unproblematic that Cominius should rebuke Coriolanus for not allowing him openly to reward Coriolanus (and lay bare Coriolanus's wounds to the troops) so that "Rome can know the value of her own" (1.10.20-21). Fish reads Cominius's rebuke as follows: "In your concern to protect your modesty, to hold yourself aloof from 'good report' you neglect the reciprocal courtesies that make a society civil."[21] But what is Coriolanus's rationale for that apparent discourtesy, that unwillingness to hear himself praised and rewarded? It is not all that irrational: Coriolanus wants it known that he, like all good men (no matter what side they fight for, interestingly enough) has performed a task to the utmost of his ability, *for the sake of the task,* and not for any *subsequent reward*. The reward should be in the action itself.

> I have done as you have done, that's what
> I can; induced as
> you have been, that's for my country.
> He that has but effected his good will
> Hath overta'en mine act.
>
>   (1.10.16-19)[22]

This passage, usually dismissed as part of Coriolanus's hubristic unwillingness to hear himself praised (so as to avoid the imputation that he fought for the sake of praise), in fact further evidences Coriolanus's belief that the most important duty in a world of deception and lack is to enact to the fullest the deed that is contained within one—to give utterance to all of which one is capable. His theory of action, in other words, is like his theory of speech: it emanates from a dialectical interaction between the contents of one's soul and the precise situation at hand, and it must speak to one's prior sense of what one has been and is, not to what one hopes to gain or to become.[23]

Thus Coriolanus's protests that he has been bettered by any soldier who's *wholly* done his duty—that is, performed all the deeds he is capable of, be he kern or king—strike me as true. Anyone wedded to this denominative theory of deeds and language would feel that he or she—superior though he or she might be to the general mass of untrue rabble—was still not doing *all* that was within himself or herself. When he says that "Rome must know the value of her own" (1.10.20-21), Cominius in fact gets the point exactly wrong. Reckoning up Coriolanus's value to Rome again suggests what may benefit the "interest" of the state, but Coriolanus could care less about that: caring to do one's best (to behave with *virtus*) is not the same as caring to get the best out of a situation.

V. WHO'S BANISHED?

One of the great problems created by Coriolanus's resistance to the standard forms of meaning in his universe is that every speech-act becomes fraught with misunderstanding. Ultimately this is one of the greatest accomplishments of the play: the glowing impossibilities opened up by a line like "I banish you" (3.3.124), or "pray be content, Mother . . . I'll mountebank their loves" (3.2.132-3) are, to borrow Walter Benjamin's phrase, like the strait gate of redemption through which at any moment the messiah might enter.[24] However, just because these woundings of language are so strange, so jarring, we need to be extremely careful about declaring them, as Fish does, either "valid" or "invalid." The accomplishment of *Coriolanus* is precisely to shed a devastating light on the Roman banishment of Coriolanus *without* implying that Coriolanus himself is capable of fully reciprocating the act of banishment. The play depicts the banishment of Coriolanus by Rome as an ineffective attempt to get rid of a nagging anxiety about the nature of the public space, an anxiety that will linger in the "private selves" of the citizens of Rome even after the loud naysayer Coriolanus is gone. But the second banishment—Coriolanus banishing Rome—shows the "truly private" man's inability to comprehend the full meaning of social life. That social life creates—out of people, history, books, weapons, and whatever else it takes—a shared public space in which performatives *work,* whether they are justified or not. So in the end neither of these banishments makes much "sense," though the staging of the dual banishment does *create* sense within the frame of the play.

That is, once we have understood Coriolanus's belief that all of Rome has "mountebanked" its love, and "cogged" itself, it is entirely understandable that he will lash back at his expulsion with: "I banish you. And here remain with your uncertainty" (3.3.124-25). The latter sentence especially is vintage Coriolanus. He is trapped in a world where every speech is by his lights "uncertainty": since things are said *prospectively,* by considerating others' actions in the public world, rather than *retrospectively,* by consulting with one's own soul. Nothing could make more sense than for him to believe he retains all that is good and true about Rome in his breast.

But nothing could be more wrong for a future critic than to assume Coriolanus really *does,* in any meaningful way, turn the paradigmatic tide at this point, and establish a new realm of meaning. Cavell astutely senses this: he recognizes that Coriolanus has given up the world by giving up his Rome, site of all his disagreements and confrontations—though Cavell believes that Rome could have saved Coriolanus had he conformed to its rules.

Stanley Fish, however, who throughout his article downplays and disparages the validity of any individual's protest against the legitimacy of the interpretive community, does a sudden and inexplicable backflip when

it comes to discussing "I banish you." Fish claims that Coriolanus's declaration, though misguided, has the effect of introducing a new authority claim into the world. "One can constitute a state simply by declaring it to exist. . . . A single man plants a flag on a barren shore and claims everything his eye can see in the name of a distant monarch or for himself . . . In the case of Coriolanus, the declaration of independence is more public, but has the same content."[25] But if Fish was wrong to call Coriolanus's original criticisms of the state invalid because they emanate from a bitter and maladjusted outcast, he's still wrong (or still wronger) to assert that Coriolanus's new unauthorized performative can craft a new world simply by rhetorical efficacy. "Life is lived over the head of the individual" writes Adorno: in *Coriolanus* the city is made up not just of enacted consent, but houses, weapons, the senate, wealth, and genealogical stability.[26] Against all that Coriolanus has only a theory about language which is exactly as wrong about the world as the model it bids to replace—*exactly as wrong* since it is nothing but the flip side of a delusionary split between an inherently false public sphere and a true inner self. Fish believes that, in order to work, a challenge to the status quo power must be constitutive of some new world order. But Coriolanus's challenge, which plays out the underside of the prevailing assumptions about language and power, is not newly constitutive, merely *critical.* To conflate the critical and the authoritative speech-act is both dangerously to underestimate the efficacy of a socioeconomic regime and dangerously to exaggerate, as well as misunderstand, what a critical voice can hope to say and do.

Even after one has realized that Coriolanus is justified in having some problems with how the world is ordered, one must also see that the too-close resemblance of his critique to the world it assaults is its fatal weakness. To hold, as it were, a mirror up to nature is a useful corrective to the life wrongly lived. If you get back a true mirror-image, however, you still have not found a solution. Coriolanus's response to the web of words aimed at futurity—to propose that words be grounded in one's past or one's body—is not itself a satisfactory substitute for the world he is surrounded by. *Coriolanus* does not suggest that we ought to abandon the fallacy of manipulative language only to adopt its complementary Coriolanian fallacy: that words and deeds can be judged solely by their truth to the motives of he who performed them. If we believe—and clearly this position is cribbed somewhat from Stoicism—that any deed bravely done is its own reward and its own proof of rightness, we posit a solipsistic universe in which other human beings are mere accidents of cognizance, useful only as motives to our actions.

Fish's asseverations to the contrary, no new world is called into being by Coriolanus's hubristic dissent from the old: indeed this play is striking for its ability to reveal problems with one system of belief without gerrymandering into place a fully formed alternative. Coriolanus's self-consumption (as Cavell demonstrates) and his failed tyranny of one are vigorous enough evidence that the play recoils as much from Coriolanus's solution as it does from the unreliable, "interest"-obsessed mendacity of the other characters, against which Coriolanus imagines himself to be fighting.[27]

VI. A THIRD WAY? NOT UTOPIA, NOT SILENCE

But what then are we to posit *between* the two ways of meaning? It is all very well to follow Adorno in denouncing the wrong life, but it does seem hard to make ethics, or indeed even aesthetics, out of a damaged world. This is a problem that Shakespeare had earlier, in writing *Richard III*. Still earlier Thomas More reckoned with a similar set of concerns in his *History of Richard III*. All the solutions posited in those two works, however, are carefully foreclosed in *Coriolanus*.

As Stephen Greenblatt's *Renaissance Self-Fashioning* shows, one of More's central concerns was with the modicum of necessary deceit built into a courtly system based on elaborate rituals and performatives in which no one truly believed. Greenblatt brings up a vital fact about that sort of world of fatuous mutual flattery: no one is taken in, and as a result it's possible, even probable, to feel that one has a *real life elsewhere:* for More it was in his solitary study, or his dreams of a "strait cell." For Coriolanus that possibility of retreat is clearly exemplified in the world he strives to invent—where we are all true to that *real self inside.*

Greenblatt realizes, however, that More was profoundly troubled by that notion of a real self below the performance, because he knew that a world riven by that contradiction (a public spectacle no one believed in and private selves no one expressed) could never successfully turn itself inside out. The inner man was symbiotically linked to a deceitful outer life, and to make that inner man into the public persona (which Coriolanus has in mind) would be an impossibility, since that private "authentic" self was actually *an artifact of a world constituted by fraudulence in public interchange.*

Coriolanus is oblivious to this fact. He assumes that he can sweep the current state of public interchange away and replace it with a skinless society: we would all wear our hearts on the outside. However this is nothing but a mirror of the prevailing model of *necessary* public fraudulence. Coriolanus too assumes the public space is necessarily deceitful, and that's why he proposes that truth be linked to the "inner man" alone, and all faith in the public sphere—which has shown itself too dependent on sleazy power relations—be

jettisoned. This does work wonderfully to lay bare the assumptions of the public sphere as it is lived in his play—and may even be read farther as a challenge to all attempts (such as John Rawls's in *A Theory of Justice*) to postulate a public space in which interest politics would not necessarily condition public conversation.[28] But the critique contained in Coriolanus's ideas is no more a "real" alternative than is More's solution—a utopia in which the private would be reduced to a mere "cipher" in the face of a benevolent universal and truthful public administrative apparatus.[29]

More had one additional weapon against the mendacious public realm, a weapon that one might expect would also have appealed to a character like Coriolanus. That weapon was silence, or its theological cousin, sanctuary. Throughout his work—and in his life as well—More struggled to envision ways in which silence could *mean* something as a protest against authority. For example, in *The History of Richard III* it seems that the belief in sanctuary may provide a form of silent salvation for one persecuted by that tyrant of perpetual duplicity, Richard III. At one crucial point in the narrative the former Queen, Elizabeth, has sought sanctuary in Westminster, not to denounce the King or organize rebellion, but to live out of his and the world's way. Finally, however, she is forced to relinquish her children to Richard III's men. She gives them up because she recognizes the futility of silence and sanctuary as a defense: it has enabled her to learn so little about the world that she doesn't even know whether or not to believe those (liars) who come to break sanctuary. All she can do is to cede her children: "so well she waste it (Sanctuary) was either nedeles or boteles."[30] That is, sanctuary is either pointless (the children won't be harmed) or ineffective (if the king wants to, he will move even against sanctuary). As it turns out, sanctuary was "boteles": the children are to be killed. The salient point in More's account is that, *from within sanctuary,* Elizabeth had no way of knowing this was to be their fate. One might want to argue that the mere fact of More setting down this description of her "boteles" quest for sanctuary serves as a sort of signpost towards a better world to come. But More's own life is an object lesson in all that silence or sanctuary cannot fend off. Years later, More's own silence (about Henry's new religious notions) did not save him from the scaffold.

Coriolanus too contemplates the possibility that silence might pose some sort of counter to a world where all speech is already duplicity. That he calls his wife "my gracious silence" acknowledges that she does not bear the guilt of duplicity that all other Romans do. But if to do nothing and to be nothing remains a possibility for a woman, it is impossible for Coriolanus. We should not need More to remind us that silence or sanctuary may halt or retreat from, but never "sway" the world. *Coriolanus* reminds us that we ought not mistake a silent protest for a reconfiguration of the world—silence may be made to speak, but it won't say much.

VII. A THIRD WAY? LICKING LANGUAGE

There is in *Coriolanus,* however, at least one palpable site of alternative resistance to both the Coriolanian and the opportunistic theories of language. Interestingly enough, it is contained in the first passage in *Coriolanus* that Fish chooses to discuss, though Fish misses the core of its meaning. It comes when the citizens (that is, the plebs) are debating whether or not they *will,* and whether or not they *may,* reject Coriolanus if he stands for consul:

> First Citizen: Once, if he do require our voices, we ought not to deny him.
>
> Second Citizen: We may, sir, if we will.
>
> Third Citizen: We have power in ourselves to do it, but it is a power that we have no power to do. For if he show us his wounds and tell us his deeds, we are to put our tongues into those wounds and speak for them; so if he tell us his noble deeds, we must also tell him our noble acceptance of them. Ingratitude is monstrous.

> (2.3.1-9)

What the third citizen says is remarkable. He corrects the previous two speakers: we are not beholden to Coriolanus on command, as the first has slavishly suggested, but neither are we free, as the second (a follower of the casuistical tribunes) suggests, to deny him out of hand. Fish misses that correction completely: he says of the second speaker's remark: "it indicates how fragile are the bonds that hold a civil society together: in fact men break the bonds whenever they like."[31] Well, in fact they don't, as any inhabitant of a modern capitalist democracy well knows: those bonds are too far over our heads for any "whenever we like" feeling of rebellion to translate into effective resistance to the system. We are too tied to our duties and places for grumblings to translate themselves in that way.[32]

Fish is right to say that the third citizen goes on "to explain what restrains them from exercising this freedom," but again he goes astray, and fatally, in explaining the nature of the third citizen's speech: "Were it not for the dialogue and dramatic situation, this might well be a textbook discussion of the force and necessity of collective rules."[33] But the third citizen's speech is precisely a *demand* for a "dramatic situation" in which Coriolanus and the citizens will both "play their parts" in the governance of the state. Remove the "dramatic situation" from "we are to put our tongues into these wounds and speak for them" and you've missed a posited Third Way.

It may be that this *radical theatricality* is a sort of linguistic interaction that evades both Coriolanus's stoicism and Volumnia's "roted syllables." The third citizen puts his duty to Coriolanus (and the state) this way: it is our duty to evaluate Coriolanus's claim, and yet to do so feelingly, really putting our thoughts into his deeds. For if the claim tests out as true, by evidence of words and wounds, then indeed the "many-headed multitude" will in this case unite: "we are to put our tongues into his wounds and speak them." That is, true service to the city will *compel* the *polis* to make a true response, but only when all citizens are made into (aesthetic) participants in Coriolanus's action. Asking tongues to speak wounds is asking the *polis* to enter, but enter fully, unabashedly, into the theater of Coriolanus's spectacular body. If Coriolanus's actions are correctly *represented* (by his words and wounds) in the right public space, those actions do not merely provide gist for interpretation by the watching citizens, they actually *force* a reciprocal action of validation on the citizen's parts. The citizen imagines becoming part of Coriolanus's wounded body, and so coming to speak, not against him, but both for him and from him. The citizens are in thrall to the city, in other words, but only if that city performs rightly towards them—and only if by city is meant a vast public arena in which "political" performance may take place. Hence when Sicinius says "what is the city but the people?", the people actually correct him by inverting the terms: "True, the people are the city," reminding him that their power as "people" comes only by accepting their place within the city (3.1.200-1).

Here, then, could be an answer, a way that the civil society Cavell and Fish both assume already exists could in fact be *made-up.* However, this possibility of a theatrical, yet genuine, form of linguistic interaction does not stand a chance in the realpolitik of the play. The possibility of consent implied by this scene and the later scene in which the citizens tell Coriolanus that "the price (of the consulship) is to ask it kindly" (2.3.71) is simply too weak. Too weak to stand up to the combined manipulations of the tribunes—who talk the people into demanding a replay—and the smoldering wrath of Coriolanus, who is so gung-ho on flaunting his inner essence he can't bring himself to brook a repetition of this almost tender moment. The moment in which he was *truly* on display as no one else ever is throughout the play passes—compared to this scene, Volumnia's begging at the end is more manipulation than revelation. No, this is all there is: one moment in which Coriolanus seems to have spoken honestly and won honest approval. Then without even much of a struggle the one possibility for civility is easily erased, and the conflict between Rome and the skinless Coriolanus picks up where it left off, with only one winner possible.

Still, that one moment of possibility, fragile and insubstantial, does exist. In it, Shakespeare is suggesting that language can be made to be *present,* in the present tense, in human interaction—neither a tool for extracting gain from the future, as Volumnia explains it, nor a slave of past actions and mental states, as Coriolanus sees it. It's reasonable at this point, I think, to invoke Stephen Greenblatt's important notion of "salutary anxiety."[34] Shakespeare's decision to raise and then to foreclose on this one possibility of an acceptable compromise between Rome and Coriolanus may be designed both to tap into and to engender a profound uncertainty about how one fits into the world, and how difficult it is both to do one's duty and to know oneself. Doubtless Greenblatt is right to see this engendering of anxiety as a useful form of social conditioning (one that made people want to go back to the theater, among other things), but I'd like to assert as well that the anxiety created by this play reveals a remarkably deft sense of the dangers inherent in two quite different forms of political legitimation: spectacular assent and absolute rule. The dual failure of Coriolanus and his political adversaries must certainly have served the purpose of making theatergoers more obedient (because more anxious) citizens of a realm in which political meaning was in flux despite the best efforts of a powerful monarch. It also signals, however, a willingness to look at a problematic form of life and to confront the necessity, as well as the difficulty, of finding a new way to navigate between two impossibilities. The failure of the proposed theatrical middle, then, can be viewed partly as a reflection on how "better" models for human interaction will not work in certain historical circumstances (how the socioeconomic environment controls us as much as the intellectual one does). It can also be viewed partly as an attempt to shift the burden of meaning-making onto the audience.

The third way we are offered, which we might have dreamed up on our own (as we would have dreamed of Coriolanus . . .) fails, and fails rapidly, in a world where the grasp of authority on power is as strong as its grasp on meaning-making is weak. That a more sensible use of language will fail to rebel successfully against a less sensible one is a great insight of this play: an insight that Fish, with his model of rhetorical might-makes-right, misses. In fact, the failure of a new language is one of the things that makes *Coriolanus* a deeper play than *Richard III.* In *Richard III,* the wily Richard, a propagator of just the sort of mendacity we see in *Coriolanus,* is decisively defeated by blunt and boring Richmond, whom we know to be virtuous and trustworthy *because* he can't talk well. The immanent logic seems to be: if you get power without showing off, or performing verbal flummery, obviously you are a good guy. *Coriolanus,* in which the middle ground of plausible meaning is effortlessly defeated, presents a far more comprehensive puzzle to

the determined reader: where is or was the good in the play? Or does any good it might contain arise interstitially, in the reading or seeing of it, in the tragedy of a society gone so amuck that even to rebel against it is to reinforce its evils?

VIII. CONCLUSION: WELCHES IST DAS RECHTE SPIEL?

Coriolanus shifts the burden of redescribing the world onto the audience, since any meaningful escape from the world Shakespeare has created can arise only intellectually not theatrically: it can be inferred but it is not mimetically presented. But the interpretations of Cavell and Fish suggest that any such attempt at inducing salutary anxiety, if it is indeed contained within the play, has failed in our day. Far from using the play to see the world in some new light, Stanley Fish doesn't even seem particularly concerned with the play's salutary anxiety: if you believe his account, *Coriolanus* goes to show all's right with the world as long as lone cranks don't look too closely at its seams.

Stanley Cavell as well, though he shows tremendous psychological insight in explicating Coriolanus's nature, fails to understand that anxiety about the trustworthiness of language is being passed on to the audience. Cavell is right to see Coriolanus as wasting away under some sort of self-consumption, right to see that his unwillingness to accept the truth and the love his society offers dooms him to something that looks very much like narcissism, solipsism, or skepticism—possibly even cannibalism. But what Cavell cannot do is entertain the possibility that this "traumatic reaction" may be justified. That Coriolanus may have found something radically wrong with his world seems unimaginable in Cavell's philosophy. Cavell's brand of "realism" seems unwilling to imagine—as Wittgenstein *is* willing—that it is the times that are out of joint. Cavell finally wants Coriolanus's criticism of the world to stem from his failure to make accommodations with (or in) the world. I suggest rather that this is a situation like the one Wittgenstein had in mind when he said: "Don't we have the feeling that someone who sees no problem in life is blind to something important, even to the most important thing of all?"[35]

Cavell rightly sees in certain circumstances a single individual may not be able to sway the world around him, but his response is to aver that the individual must mold himself to the world's conditions, no matter how unjust or inhuman those conditions may be, simply because we must face a made world. Shakespeare raises a different possibility: accept that you cannot remake the world, but speak of where it goes wrong in any case. If such speech could *only* succeed, as Fish imagines, by causing a communally sanctioned move from one coherent belief system to another (a "paradigm shift" in collective "interpretation"), then the plaintive snarl that seeks to destroy without rebuilding would be nothing more than a glorious paradox. However, the desire to lay one's grievances before the bar of the world may take on a variety of forms, some of which are better described as *critical* than as constitutive. They range in More and Shakespeare from silence, to seeking sanctuary, to insisting words pour from your mouth like coins, to staging a tonguing of the hero's wounds. None of these actions, and none of the plays about these actions, are either aiming at, nor do they succeed in, revolutionizing thought. They only make uncomfortable the thought that prevails.

Shakespeare stages the results of a bankrupt economy of meaning facing its own nemesis. That the nemesis Coriolanus—who was never intended to succeed—does not succeed should not be taken as proof that the fault lay in Coriolanus's soul. The fault lay in all of us and all around us, the telling it fell to Coriolanus.[36]

Notes

[1] Ludwig Wittgenstein, *Culture and Value,* trans. Peter Winch (Chicago: Univ. Chicago Press, 1980), 27e.

[2] Bertolt Brecht, "Study of the First Scene of Shakespeare's 'Coriolanus,'" *Brecht on Theatre,* ed. and trans. John Willett (New York: Hill and Wang, 1964): 252-65, 258.

[3] Franco Moretti, "A Huge Eclipse," in *Forms of Power and the Power of Forms,* ed. Stephen Greenblatt (Norman: Univ. of Oklahoma Press, 1982): 7-40, 7-8. Stephen Greenblatt hints interestingly that this complementary juxtaposition of "absolute freedom" and "absolute rule" may have been more generally at work in the culture in his discussion of William Strachey's account of the 1609 shipwreck of a fleet bound for Jamestown. Faced with the distressing liberty of Bermuda, plentiful food and waning discipline, the captain had to resort to the "manipulation of anxiety" in order to negotiate the difficult transition "from dreams of absolute freedom to the imposition of absolute control." My contention is that *Coriolanus* goes this one better, by passing from freedom (the licentious use of language without regard to truth) to attempted absolutism (Coriolanus's imperial arrogation of meaning-making to himself) back into a state of persistent anxiety about negotiating a world in which neither of these alternatives quite works. A world, that is, filled with the "salutary anxiety" of which Greenblatt writes (*Shakespearean Negotiations,* [Berkeley: Univ. of California Press, 1988], 154).

[4] Theodor Adorno, "The Stars down to Earth," *The Stars down to Earth and Other Essays in the Irrational in Culture,* ed. Stephen Crook (London: Routledge, 1994), 114.

[5] William Shakespeare, *Coriolanus,* ed. R. B. Parker (Oxford: Clarendon Press, 1994), 3.3.124. Henceforth cited parenthetically in the text by act, scene, and line.

[6] Stanley Fish, "How to do Things with Austin and Searle," *Is There a Text in the Class?* (Cambridge: Harvard Univ. Press, 1980), 197-245; and Stanley Cavell, "Coriolanus and Interpretations of Politics (Who does the Wolf Love?)," *Disowning Knowledge* (Cambridge: Cambridge Univ. Press, 1987), 143-78.

[7] Theodor Adorno, *Minima Moralia: Reflections from Damaged Life,* trans. E. F. N. Jephcott (London: Verso, 1974).

[8] William Shakespeare, *Richard III,* ed. D. J. Wilson (Cambridge: Cambridge Univ. Press, 1954), 1.2.194-95.

[9] Thomas More, *History of King Richard III,* ed. Richard Sylvester (New Haven: Yale Univ. Press, 1963); Stephen Greenblatt, *Renaissance Self-Fashioning* (Chicago: Univ. of Chicago Press, 1980), 13.

[10] This essay engages with the critical approach employed by Cavell and Fish, to the neglect of other criticism. That criticism includes articles such as: Kenneth Burke, "*Coriolanus*—and the Delights of Faction," *Arts in Society* 2 (1963); D. J. Gordon, "Name and Fame: Shakespeare's Coriolanus," *Papers Mainly Shakespearean,* ed. G. I. Duthie (Edinburgh: Oliver and Boyd, 1964): 40-57; Norman Rabkin, *Shakespeare and the Common Understanding* (New York: Free Press, 1967), 120-49; Carol Sicherman, "Coriolanus: The Failure of Words" *ELH* 39 (1972); and Janet Adelman, "'Anger is my Meat': Feeding and Dependency in *Coriolanus*," (1978), rept. Adelman, *Suffocating Mothers: Fantasies of Maternal Origins in Shakespeare's Plays, Hamlet to the Tempest* (New York: Routledge, 1992), 130-64. More recent articles include: T. McAlindon, "*Coriolanus*: An Essentialist Tragedy," *Review of English Studies* 44 (1993); Shannon Miller, "Topicality and Subversion in William Shakespeare's *Coriolanus*," *Studies in English Literature* 32 (1992); Arthur Riss, "The Belly Politic: Coriolanus and the Revolt of Language," *ELH* 59 (1992); Albert Cook, "Some Observations on Shakespeare and the Incommensurability of Interpretive Strategies," *New Literary History* 22 (1991); and Coppelia Kahn, "Mother of Battles: Volumnia and Her Son in Shakespeare's *Coriolanus*," *differences* 4 (1992).

[11] Greenblatt, *Renaissance,* 13.

[12] It may of course be argued that no ceremony can properly be labelled "fraudulent," since ceremony gestures only at itself. But in a society where ceremonies are meant to correspond to higher truths (religious ones, in More's case), they are deceitful if used only

as a form of validation for temporal authorities. More's writing seems to suggest that knowing acquiescence in ceremonies whose real purpose is at odds with their purported purpose is a necessary ingredient in any public life.

[13] Cavell, 145.

[14] In *The Human Condition* (Chicago: Univ. of Chicago, 1958), Hannah Arendt argues that the political sphere can function as a space evacuated of personal ambition and the selfish desires of separate subjective selves. Her model, like Plutarch's in his account of Coriolanus's life, is that of the ancient Greek city-state, and her leading "virtue" (again, like Plutarch's) is the desire and ability to engage in a rational conversation (what Jürgen Habermas will call "communicative rationality" [*The Theory of Communicative Rationality: Volume One, Reason and the Rationalization of Society,* trans. Thomas McCarthy (Boston: Beacon Press, 1984), esp. 397-99]). *Coriolanus* by contrast assumes the worst about such discursive sites. Coriolanus himself postulates truth only interior to the self, while the practitioners of political life no longer have truth as a desideratum: power or influence is all.

In his account of Coriolanus, Plutarch's solution to the clash between Coriolanus and the Roman people (over the people's right to try a senator) might have come straight from Arendt. If the plebeians were only granted the power of trial, they "would not use this power harshly or severely, but would show their moderation and humanity. . . . They would feel themselves so much honored and compensated by the privilege of being able to try a senator, that they would lay aside their resentment as soon as this prerogative came into their hands." (Plutarch, *Makers of Rome,* trans. Ian Scott-Kilvert [London: Penguin, 1965], 33). That is, if one opens a conversation, those who converse will do so rationally, according to the rules implicit in the conversational process itself. *Coriolanus* offers no such compromise.

[15] In his notes to the Oxford Shakespeare, Parker says it is either a ludicrous contortion or (as played nowadays) a belch, but a fart is not ruled out by any modern commentary.

[16] As Plutarch remarks, the fact that the Romans combined all "virtue" under the rubric of *virtus,* which means first and foremost military valor, suggests that Rome was unsuited to the kind of political interaction that characterized the Greek citystate (19). Jonathan Dollimore has written interestingly on this question in "Virtus Under Erasure," *William Shakespeare's Antony and Cleopatra,* ed. Harold Bloom (New York: Chelsea House, 1988): 137-48. Also see Phyliss Rackin, "*Coriolanus:* Shakespeare's anatomy of *Virtus,*" *Modern Language Studies* 13 (1983): 68-79.

[17] Cavell, 167.

[18] Fish, 206.

[19] I am not proposing some sort of "private language." However, in any linguistic community there may be several levels of meaning. In this community, for example, there is a distinction between "wartime" words and words used "truly." Coriolanus's complaint is that the society's language is on a permanent wartime footing, and he proposes to break through to the oft-invoked but never utilized alternative vocabulary of truth.

[20] Greenblatt, *Renaissance,* 13.

[21] Fish, 210.

[22] This might usefully be compared to Joseph Conrad's "Introduction" to *The Secret Agent* (1907; London: Penguin, 1971): "The world generally is not interested in the motives of any overt act but in its consequences. Man may smile and smile but he is not an investigating animal" (7). This criticism of the world's shallow interest in results rather than motives could only have come from a person who, like Coriolanus, measures all his words and his deeds on a scale of *prior* intent. However, the end of that same preface describes the *act of writing* as free of all sense of past motivation and future gain. "There have been moments during the writing of the book when I was an extreme revolutionist, I won't say more convinced than they, but certainly cherishing a more concentrated purpose than any of them had ever done in the whole course of his life. I don't say this to boast. I was simply attending to my business. In the matter of all my book I have simply attended to my business. I have attended to it with complete self-surrender. . . . It would have bored me too much to make-believe" (11). This alternative is also imagined in *Coriolanus*—the *present* of language or of action becomes its own reward and redemption.

[23] While readying this paper for publication, I discovered Leonard Tennenhouse's lucid survey of the struggle in *Coriolanus* between "the new order" of linguistic authority and the former primacy of "physical action" ("*Coriolanus*: History and Crisis of the Semantic Order," in *Drama in the Renaissance,* ed. Clifford Davidson [New York: AMS, 1985]: 217-31, 223). Tennenhouse reads Coriolanus as a "source of disorder in the new state precisely because he is the impractical and impolitic ideal of the old state" (227). In my reading, Coriolanus represents something *immanent* within what Tennenhouse calls a new order, rather than residual from some older theory of meaning. But Tennenhouse's analysis of Coriolanus's distrust of speech—on the grounds that "action is the only public expression that has significance"—seems to me exactly right. Tennen-

house interestingly turns, as Cavell does, to psychology in order to explain the failure of Coriolanus to topple the reign of the linguistic: "his universe of discourse is so fully grounded in a primary narcissism that he can say 'I banish you' when he is banished because he has become in his perversely moral world an autonomous body politic" (227).

[24] Walter Benjamin, "Theses on the Philosophy of History," *Illuminations,* ed. Hannah Arendt (New York: Schocken, 1969), 264.

[25] Fish, 207.

[26] Theodor Adorno, *In Search of Wagner,* trans. Rodney Livingston (London: New Left Books, 1981), 87.

[27] Fish himself belongs to the party of interest that Shakespeare so successfully satirizes in this play. Fish argues, in *Is There a Text in the Class?* (especially 197-245), that successful persuasion in the classroom (and thus, successful construction of meaning) involves showing students that it is in their interest to believe what the teacher has propounded. Reality follows interest when it does not follow persuasion.

[28] Seyla Benhabib's compelling *Situating the Self: Gender, Community, and Postmodernism in Contemporary Ethics* (New York: Routledge, 1992), works towards salvaging the possibility of communicative action as a product of rational intercourse between explicitly *embodied* and situated selves, a development in political philosophy that casts a fresh light on the various *non*aesthetic middle ways between authoritarian and permanently fluid conceptions of political speech.

[29] For "cipher" see Greenblatt, *Renaissance,* 42.

[30] More, 41.

[31] Fish, 203.

[32] Though I find it an illuminating passage in many ways, I read Cavell's discussion of withheld and implied consent in *The Claim of Reason* (New York: Oxford Univ. Press, 1979) as making a similar mistake about the *magnitude* of the political realm, and the possibility of *commensurability* between critique and revolution (22-29). We in this country now, like Shakespeare in his time and nation, do not live in a *polis.* Even in Shakespeare's day the state was big enough that a single cavil did not tip seats of power. To assume that withheld consent in an ideal state equals an annulment of power is to allow ideal states to mislead you about actual ones. At its worst, this sort of idealized Thoreauvian resistance tends toward political apathy and discourages real resistance, intellectual and otherwise.

[33] Fish, 203.

[34] Greenblatt, *Shakespearean,* 147-60.

[35] Wittgenstein, 27e.

[36] This article has benefitted immeasurably from conversations with Judith and Paul Plotz, Lisa Hamilton, Liberty Aldrich, Alex Star, and the members of Marc Shell's course on kinship in Shakespeare, among them Neel Choudhury, Sophia Padnos, and Lianne Farber. I am also grateful to Helen Vendler, Elaine Scarry, and Philip Fisher for their comments, and to the Harvard drama colloquium, where this paper was first presented—especially to Scott Gordon and Amy King.

Source: "*Coriolanus* and the Failure of Performatives," in *ELH,* Vol. 63, No. 4, Winter, 1996, pp. 809-32.

"Apparent Perversities": Text and Subtext in the Construction of the Role of Edgar in Brook's Film of *King Lear*[1]

J. G. Saunders, *Chichester University College*

In an otherwise eulogistic review of Peter Brook's film of *King Lear* ('the best of all Shakespeare movies'), a review which affirmed the need for *imaginative* interpretation of Shakespeare's texts ('The point is simple: these texts, if we are to hold on to their greatness . . . have to be reborn in the imagination of another'), Frank Kermode listed Edgar's speaking of some of Edmund's libels against him, and the transposition of Edgar's terrible words over the dying Edmund ('The gods are just . . . ') to the dying Cornwall, as two of the film's 'apparent perversities'—wondering whether Brook himself could explain 'what he was up to'.[2] I intend to show that the role of Edgar was central to Brook's reading of *King Lear* and that the textual liberties which he took in constructing Edgar's character and role were integral to the subtextual, *imaginative* processes leading to the film's composition. In so doing, I hope to demonstrate that Brook's treatment of Shakespeare's text was in some respects much more audacious and less reverential than Kermode and other commentators seem to have realized.

Text

Brook's attempt to break from the tyranny of the *King Lear* text is well documented in a statement which the film's producer, Lord Birkett, made for Roger Manvell.[3] First, they (Birkett and Brook) cut from the text certain passages which they regarded as 'completely unnecessary'. Then, after making further cuts, they presented their script to Ted Hughes, asking him to treat it as though it were a 'foreign classic' and to translate it into his own idiom—'into a language which seemed to him to be expressive of the story as he saw it, in his own right as a poet'. They hoped that by working on a modern script they would be able to achieve the kind of freedom available to foreign directors such as Kozintsev and Kurosawa, for whom Shakespeare's text did not have the inhibiting 'quality of Holy Writ'. From this experiment they discovered 'that there are passages, obviously the greatest passages in the play, which have a force and emotional power that no translation, no paraphrase, can possibly match'. Kermode congratulated Brook on having discovered for himself the power of the text—'the whole play, and its verse'—though he continued to lament the loss of several cherished moments. However, he is one of a number of commentators whose familiarity with the sound of the *King Lear* text may have prevented them from noticing the textual manipulations which occur when the verbal text in the film serves a predominantly narrative function.

Brook's most striking textual liberties occur in the sequence where Edmund dupes his brother Edgar, in the film a single episode, introduced by a Brechtian title:

> GLOUCESTER'S CASTLE
> Edmond, bastard son of the Duke of Gloucester, plots against his brother Edgar.

The concentrated 'plot' which follows is constructed out of short passages of text taken from two quite separate scenes in the play—Act I, scene ii, and Act II, scene i. In order to appreciate Brook's audacity in cutting and adapting Shakespeare's text to suit his own narrative purpose, it is necessary to consider the structure of these two scenes in some detail. Act I, scene ii would, in the conventions governing French scenic structure, be divided into four short scenes. It begins with Edmund's soliloquy in which he asks WHY BASTARD (1) and descants on his illegitimacy. Gloucester then enters and Edmund traps him into reading THE LETTER (2), purported to be written by Edgar. Gloucester reflects on the breakdown of order and then leaves. Edmund again soliloquizes, this time on the EXCELLENT FOPPERY (3) of those who link behaviour with planetary influence. Edgar enters and discovers that SOME VILLAIN (4) has done him wrong. Act II, scene i, is made up of four more sub-scenes. First Curran tells Edmund of Cornwall's imminent arrival and hints at LIKELY WARS (5) between Cornwall and Albany. Then when Edgar enters, Edmund tells him he must FLY THIS PLACE (6). After Edgar has flown, Edmund tells his father how he saw his brother CONJURING THE MOON (7) and how he tried to persuade him to join in Gloucester's murder. Finally Cornwall arrives and commends Edmund for having a nature of SUCH DEEP TRUST (8).

In the reconstruction of Brook's film narrative which follows, I have used the capitalized short phrases and numbers given above as an easy means of identifying the source of each textual fragment. The bold-type descriptions of setting and action are cut to a minimum. Line numbering of Shakespeare's text is from the Riverside Shakespeare.

> *Edgar and Edmund talk as they ride.*
> Edg.
> How now, brother Edmund, what serious contemplation are you in?
> Edm.
> I was thinking, brother, of a prediction Iread this other day, what should follow these eclipses.

Edg.

And do you busy yourself with that?

Edm.

I promise you, the effects he writes of
succeed unhappily, as of unnaturalness
between the child and the parent,
death, dearth, dissolution, divisions,
menaces.

(I. ii. 138-46) (SOME VILLAIN, 4)

Edg.

When we are sick in fortune—we make
guilty of our disasters, the sun the moon
and stars as if we were drunkards, liars
and adulterers by planetary influence.

(I. ii. 116-22) (EXCELLENT FOPPERY, 3)

Edm.

Why brand they me with baseness.
Bastardy? Base?

(I. ii. 9-10) (WHY BASTARD, 1)

My father coupled with my mother under
the Dragon's tail and I was born under
Ursa Major, so that it follows that I am
rough and lecherous. I should have been
that I am, had the maidenliest star in the
firmament twinkled on my bastardizing.

(I. ii. 128-33) (EXCELLENT FOPPERY, 3)

*The brothers are looking at their sleeping
father.*

Edg.

When sons are at perfect age and fathers in
decline the father should be put in care of
the son.

Edm.

And the son manage the revenue.

(I. ii. 72-4) (THE LETTER, 2)

Edgar leaves.

It's the policy of reverence for age that
makes the world bitter.

(I. ii. 46-7) (THE LETTER, 2)

A messenger comes to Edmund's room.

Mess.

The Duke of Cornwall and Regan, his
Duchess will be here this night.

Edm.

How comes that?

Mess.

I know not. *The messenger leaves.*

(II. i. 3-6) (LIKELY WARS, 5)

Edm.

The better best.

This weaves itself perforce into my
business.

Briefness and fortune work.

(II. i. 14-15) (LIKELY WARS, 5)

Edmund hides a letter.

If this letter thrive, Edmund the bastard
shall top the legitimate.

(I. ii. 19-20) (WHY BASTARD, 1)

Edmund is looking at Edgar sleeping.

Edm.

Legitimate Edgar, I must have your land.

(I. ii. 16) (WHY BASTARD, 1)

Edmund pauses outside his father's room.

Edm.

Now Gods stand up for bastards.

(I. ii. 21) (WHY BASTARD, 1)

Edmund wakes his father.

Edm.

(Father.)

Edmund is talking to Gloucester.

Edm.

I swore he could by no means.

Glou.

By no means what?

Edm.

Persuade me to the murder of your
lordship.

I told him the revenging gods
'Gainst parricides did all the thunder bend,
Spoke with how strong a bond
The child was bound to the father.

(II. i. 43-8) (CONJURING THE MOON, 7)

Glou.

My son Edgar.

(I. ii. 56) (THE LETTER, 2)

Edm.

I threatened to discover him; he replied,
'Who would put any trust or faith in thee
Thou unpossessing bastard?'

(II. i. 66-7) (CONJURING THE MOON, 7)

Glou.

He cannot be such a monster to his father
who so tenderly and entirely loves him.

(I. ii. 94-7) (THE LETTER, 2)

Edm.

I dare pawn down my life for him.

He's done this to feel my affection to
your honour and no other pretence of
danger.

Glou.

Think you so?

(I. ii. 85-9) (THE LETTER, 2)

Has he never before sounded you in this matter?

Edm.

I have heard him maintain it to be fit that sons of perfect age and fathers in decline, the father should be put in care of the son and the son manage the revenue.

Glou.

Villain, villain, unnatural brutish villain.

(I. ii. 75-7) (THE LETTER, 2)

Edm.

If your honour judge it meet.
I'll place you where you shall hear us confer of this.

(I. ii. 90-1) (THE LETTER, 2)

Edmund hides Gloucester and wakes Edgar.
Edm.

(Edgar!) When saw you my father last? Parted you on good terms? Saw you no displeasure in him? Bethink yourself wherein you may have offended him.

(I. ii. 152-60) (SOME VILLAIN, 4)

Edmund leads Edgar into Gloucester's hearing and shows him the letter.
Edm.

(What does it say?)
Edg. (reads)

If our father would sleep till I waked him you should enjoy half his revenue for ever and live the beloved of your brother. Edgar.

(I. ii. 52-5) (THE LETTER, 2)

Edmund hurries Edgar away.
Glou.

(Help! Murder! Help! Murder!)
Edgar and Edmund talk in Edmund's room.
Edg.

When came you to this?
Edm.

I found it thrown in at the casement of my closet.

(I. ii. 58-61) (THE LETTER, 2)

Edg.

Some villain hath done me wrong.
Edm.

That's my fear.

(I. ii. 165-6) (THE LETTER, 2)

Have you not spoken against the Duke of Cornwall
And of his coming hither now in the night in haste,
And Regan with him? Have you nothing said

Against the Duke of Albany?
Edg.

Not a word.

(I. ii. 23-7) (FLY THIS PLACE, 6)

Edm.

I've told you what I've seen and heard but faintly. Nothing like the image and horror of it.

(I. ii. 174-6) (SOME VILLAIN, 4)

Edmund helps Edgar escape and cuts his arm.
Edm.

Light, ho! here! stop! stop! torches! torches!

(II. i. 31, 36, 32) (FLY THIS PLACE, 6)

Glou.

Where is the villain?
Edm.

There stood he in the dark sir, his sharp sword out.

(II. i. 37-9) (CONJURING THE MOON, 7)

Glou.

Pursue him. Go after, ho.

(II. i. 43) (CONJURING THE MOON, 7)

Edm.

(There!)
Gloucester bandages Edmund's arm.
Glou.

Loyal and natural boy. Of all my lands I'll work the means to make thee heritor.

(II. i. 84-5) (CONJURING THE MOON, 7)

A number of features of the above text warrant discussion. Most obviously, as the derivations show, it is a collage of some thirty fragments taken from seven separate textual units. Though most of the text derives indirectly from an edition of *King Lear,* a few words and phrases which are printed in brackets (such as 'What does it say', 1.57 and 'Help! Murder! Help! Murder!', 1.60) are interpolations. Less obvious, perhaps, are a number of changes which render Shakespeare's language somewhat more accessible to a modern audience. These include 'planetary influence' (ll. 10-11) for 'spherical predominance', 'coupled' (1.12) for 'compounded', 'I was born' (ll. 12-13) for 'my nativity was', 'put in care of the son' (l. 17) for 'as a ward to the son' and 'make thee heritor' (ll. 77-8) for 'To make thee capable'. Much more complex are a number of changes in speech allocation which are linked to a major plot difference between play and film.

When, at line 8, Edgar makes his comment on Edmund's professed view of the significance of eclipses, his words in the film text are taken from Edmund's second short soliloquy (EXCELLENT FOPPERY, 3) in which he comments cynically on his father's superstition. More complicated is the textual derivation of Edgar's claim at line 16 that fathers in decline should be wards to their sons. In the play texts these words are spoken by Edmund to Gloucester, prefixed by the claim that he has often heard the idea expressed by Edgar. In Brook's text, at line 48, Edmund does speak the lines as in the play: 'I have heard him maintain it to be fit that sons of perfect age and fathers in decline, the father should be put in care of the son, and the son manage the revenue.' In the film Edmund is speaking some truth—but possibly not the whole truth, for the words 'And the son manage the revenue' (l. 18) had previously been spoken by Edmund, not Edgar, the two brothers sharing the sentiment in a duet. After Edmund has said 'and the son manage the revenue' the first time, Edgar leaves and Edmund's next line, 'It's the policy of reverence for age that makes the world bitter' (l. 19) has an even more complicated derivation. In the play the words belong to the part of Gloucester. However, they are from the letter that he reads—a letter ostensibly written by Edgar but, as a part of Edmund's stratagem, actually written by Edmund. In the film, the letter, itself, is not read by Gloucester. It is read by Edgar, on Edmund's instruction, and overheard by Gloucester. This leads to one further change in allocation. At line 61 the bemused Edgar asks 'When came you to this?' and Edmund tells him 'I found it thrown in at the casement'. In the play texts this small exchange takes place between Gloucester and Edmund. In the film Gloucester is unaware of the existence of the letter. However, the idea of placing Gloucester in a position where he can overhear Edgar does come from Shakespeare ('If your honour judge it meet, I will place you where you shall hear us confer of this, and by an auricular assurance have your satisfaction, and that without any further delay than this very evening' (I. ii. 90-3)). In the play, these words are, in terms of plot, quite redundant. They seem like an echo from *Othello* where Iago does provide his victim with 'an auricular assurance' of a kind the unseeing Gloucester doesn't need. What in the play turns out to be a false trail becomes the basis of the narrative in the film.

In the section on Subtext which follows, I attempt to provide an explanation for Brook's treatment of the text in this episode, but first I want briefly to consider the second of Kermode's 'apparent perversities'—the transference of Edgar's uncompromising judgement on his father to the dying Cornwall. In Shakespeare's *King Lear* text(s) a tendency to stand back and moralize is a feature of the roles of both Edgar and Cordelia. These moments have a medieval theatricality, the character concerned highlighting the moral significance of a tableau or a moment of action which has just passed. Omissions in Edgar's role include his two philosophi-

cal soliloquies, 'When we our betters see bearing our woes' (III. vi. 102-15) and 'Yet better thus, and known to be contemn'd' (IV. i. 1-9), and a number of shorter passages where he reveals his moral concern. These include the following:

> Why I do trifle thus with his despair
> Is done to cure it.
>
> (IV. vi. 33-4)

> O, matter and impertinency mix'd,
> Reason in madness!
>
> (IV. vi. 174-5)

and, most notoriously:

> The gods are just, and of our pleasant vices
> Make instruments to plague us:
> The dark and vicious place where thee he
>   got
> Cost him his eyes.
>
> (V. iii. 171-4)

In giving these lines to Cornwall, Brook may have been highlighting the idea that they have a choric significance transcending the character of the actual speaker. Whatever Brook's motive, an insight such as this would have been completely inappropriate as the culmination of the relationship between Edgar and Edmund which Brook had invented as an integral part of his film and it is the nature of this relationship which forms the basis of the section which follows.

Subtext

The importance of subtextual imagining in establishing Edgar's role and relationships had emerged as a feature of the rehearsal process which helped shape the stage version of *King Lear* which preceded Brook's work on his film. Charles Marowitz, his assistant director, described how he and Brook had identified the relationship between Edgar and Poor Tom as one of the play's major problems.[4] The problem became more complicated when they found that Brian Murray, the actor who then played Edgar, suffered from an 'inner stiffness', which accentuated his difficulty in changing from courtier to Bedlam beggar and which resulted in a clash in acting styles between Edgar and Edmund (then played by James Booth). To assist the two actors in finding their own solutions, Marowitz had devised a series of subtextual improvisations to develop the relationship between the brothers. In one, Edmund as a Franciscan friar had to give Edgar confession and in so doing provide theological arguments for his forfeiting his lands for the good of his soul. In another, Edgar recounted a series of horrible nightmares to Edmund who (still a clergyman) had to explain that the dreams were a divine instruction for him to murder his father. These Stanislavskian role-plays were supplemented by some Brechtian exercises devised to enable Edgar to create a distance between himself and Poor Tom. These involved speaking Poor Tom's part in the third person (prefaced by 'he said') and using a mask to distinguish the moments when the persona of Poor Tom was to be dominant. In the processes which led to the making of the *King Lear* film, these 'problems' were to be explored in rather different ways.

In his interview with Roger Manvell, Lord Birkett described the process which led to the construction of 'the final film script' as follows. First, Peter Brook wrote a narrative version of the story with no dialogue. Then from this narrative they (producer and director) worked out 'a very precise storyline' for the film with 'a very careful estimate of the weight' they 'wanted to put on each episode, each character, and each theme of the piece'. Then, with this more detailed subtextual narrative as a basis, they cut and adapted the text to produce 'the final script'. In the Folger Shakespeare library there are two draft shooting-scripts which correspond to the last two stages of this process. Draft 1 is dated 9 September 1968 and has a brief note explaining that '[a]s the dialogue exists already in the original play, but will need eventually to be cut and adapted, here it is merely indicated'. It divides the film's action into 152 sequences, each new sequence marking a change of time and/or location. Draft 2 is dated 5 December 1968. It incorporates text into the narrative, omitting some of Draft 1's sequences, altering others, and adding several new sequences.

Both drafts provide a rich source of information on Brook's attitude to both major and minor characters. In some ways the commentary is similar to a lengthy set of stage directions written by a dramatist like Shaw who knows all and tells all. It is particularly revealing in its revelations concerning Edgar's relationship with Edmund and (more surprisingly) a network of subtextual linkings between Edmund and Poor Tom.

In both screenplays Edgar's relationship with Edmund is foregrounded in a number of sequences which have been almost entirely erased from the final film. Sequence 3 reads as follows:

3. EXT. LANDSCAPE. DAY

Last, we see the face of a young man, EDGAR. We hear the wind. He is scanning the horizon. In the distance a wide plain. In his eyes, a searching look. A speck becomes a galloping horseman. EDGAR's face lights up with pleasure and excitement.

On the galloping horse, another young man, EDMUND. Same age, almost a twin. A face also full of life. He is surveying the land as he rides. As he sees his brother, his expression is at first one

of dislike, which he rapidly converts into one of seemingly candid joy.

He leaps off his horse and throws himself into his brother's welcoming arms. They embrace.

FINAL TITLES

So, even before the final titles, in the screenplays the story of Edgar and Edmund was given prominence. The narrative and commentary which follow develop the relationship between the brothers in ways scarcely hinted at in the text. Sequence 13 provides a second subtextual encounter between the two. In Draft 1 the sequence reads as follows:

13. EXT. GLOUCESTER'S CASTLE. DAY.

EDGAR and EDMUND both on horseback are playing a dangerous game, each trying to snatch up and carry away a dead fox. It leads them into wild horsemanship: EDGAR scoops up the dead animal and EDMUND pursues him. Drawing level with his brother, he struggles with him, until by superior strength and skill, he topples EDGAR out of the saddle. EDGAR, laughing, yields the carcass: EDMUND looks down triumphantly. In the distance, he sees GLOUCESTER's coach approaching the castle and gallops towards it.

In order to emphasize Edmund's dominant malevolence, the last lines are altered in Draft 2 as follows:

In the distance, he sees GLOUCESTER's coach approaching the castle. He charges at EDGAR's riderless horse, frightening it away, then turns and gallops towards the castle, leaving his brother chasing his horse across the heath.

In sequence 15, where Edmund serves Gloucester, Kent, and the assembly with wine, we learn that he is 'one of the family, yet half a servant'. In sequence 17, in Gloucester's study, his claim to be 'rough and lecherous' is made before Edgar, who 'laughs in admiration, envious of his half-brother's worldliness'. A new sequence (19) is added to Draft 2 where the two brothers look at their drunken father and, with dialogue based on Edmund's later claim that he has often heard Edgar speak subversively of sons and fathers, the two (as in the final verbal text of the film) mockingly suggest that 'the father should be put in care of the son' (Edgar) and that 'the son manage the revenue' (Edmund). In the draft shooting-scripts a textual and subtextual portrait of Edgar emerges as a young man eager to impress his more worldly brother and the sharing of 'libels' forms a part of the relationship. They show Edgar (the great role-player) playing at being a sophisticated young cynic. Given that the Stanislavskian 'If' governing Brook's production included this interpretation of Edgar among its 'given circumstances', it is a short step to imagining that Edmund had, indeed, 'heard him *oft* [the authentic Quarto and Folio reading] maintain it to be fit that, sons at perfect age and fathers declin'd . . . ' etc. So Edmund's completing of Edgar's lines might be seen more as a sign of tired familiarity than as a shared speech. The text, here, may have led to a subtext which recreated the text.

In the draft shooting-scripts Edmund's servantdom is an important dimension of his role (a dimension which has left a faintly discernible trace on the final film). The servants' quarters feature importantly in Edmund's stratagem, since it is here that he hides Edgar before arranging his escape. By imagining Edmund as a servant, Brook was building a web of subtextual relationships from Edgar's lines as Poor Tom ('A servingman! proud in heart and mind', III. iv. 85) and Edmund's claim to be 'rough and lecherous' (I. ii. 131), a claim echoed in Poor Tom's 'serv'd the lust of my mistress' heart, and did the act of darkness with her' (III. iv. 87-8). This web of textual and subtextual associations takes on its full significance in the draft shooting-scripts when Edgar as Poor Tom finds himself face to face with Lear. Sequence 93 in Draft 1 reads as follows:

> To give body to his madness, EDGAR plays a role, a role that has surged out of his imagination that is strangely like his brother, a role in which he claims to be a dangerous, proud, seductive servant, a role in which he gives free reign to everything that is normally opposed to his nature.

The sequence continues to make clear the links between such imaginings and Stanislavskian acting theory—the need to create a subtext in order to give role-play its authenticity: 'Like an actor, he is totally identified with his role, yet still free to observe what goes on around him.' The arrival of Gloucester forces Edgar to the edge of his sanity and more fully into the role of Poor Tom: 'he continues his improvisations and now he is inspired, speaking strange words whose meaning he cannot even guess.'

In the shooting-scripts the roles of both brothers are developed and commented on. While Edgar begins to explore 'his own obscure erotic imagery' (sequence 95), Edmund is enjoying his new status and power. In sequence 104, in the 'curtainless interior' of Goneril's coach, he makes love to her while she murmurs 'The difference of man and man'. He is pictured in sequence 107 'riding into his courtyard as Duke of Gloucester' where some servants 'are immediately obsequious, some resentful'. In sequence 129c, he is 'making love to REGAN'. Goneril delivers to him her love-letter which in 129e he reads aloud to Regan, 'while stroking and humping her'. In the drafts Edgar's killing of Oswald is marked as a decisive stage in his

development. 'This is perhaps the most intense moment of all for him—this is the point in his own journey that he never expected to reach—he has killed a man' (sequence 123). He is about to kill his brother. When he does so, the subtextual commentary makes it quite clear that this was to be a very different ending from that of the earlier Stratford production, where Edmund's lines of repentance were cut. The drafts describe Edmund's last moments as follows:

> Now the two brothers look into one another's face, a long, long, look, while EDMUND's life drains away.

> It is as though some strange understanding passes between them. The contorted look on EDMUND's face—the contorted look we have seen in death locked on CORNWALL, GONERIL and REGAN—slowly softens. He whispers something. EDGAR bends closer. He whispers again. It is almost inaudible, 'Some good I mean to do . . . '. EDGAR puts his ear very close to his brother's mouth. 'The captain . . . has commission . . . to hang . . . Cordelia . . . quickly . . . send in time'.

There is no trace of this moment of repentance in the film. Edmund's last words are 'The wheel has come full circle, I am here'. However, the expressions on the two brothers' faces do hint at 'some strange understanding' and this leads me on to a brief consideration of the relationships between what Birkett called 'the final script' and the film which eventually emerged, a relationship a good deal more complex than that between the *King Lear* Quarto and Folio texts.

Birkett himself goes some way towards accounting for differences. He told Manvell that 'certain events took on an extra importance as we came to shoot them, and certain events seemed less impressive by comparison, so that a certain amount of adaptation went on throughout'.[5] Brook himself has spoken scathingly about the very concept of 'a final script', contrasting the freedom of rehearsals in the theatre with the tyranny of the script in most film production, where 'it's terrifying to find that all manner of things one has scribbled into the script as local colour, notes one has made as a reader for oneself, possibilities to try out, have been taken deadly seriously and that months later someone will hold you to them'.[6] He went on to distinguish between a director's 'surface whims' and 'deeper intentions', suggesting that fidelity to the film script was likely to honour the former while ignoring the latter. Many of the details suggested in the two film scripts are not even hinted at in the final film. There are no subtextual encounters between Edgar and Edmund. The relationship between the two brothers leading to Edgar's flight is treated in the single sequence discussed above. Whether or not the missing moments were no more than 'surface whims' is a matter for speculation, since during the process of editing much material was cut. Brook described this last stage in a letter to the Russian director Kozintsev,[7] who was in the process of completing his own film of *King Lear:*

> Now in the editing, we are searching to interrupt the consistency of style, so that many-levelled contradictions of the play can appear. As a result, we are cutting more and more ruthlessly, eliminating more and more text, so that the film which was 3 hours long, then 21/2 hours a few weeks ago, is now shrinking to about 2 hours and a quarter!

When the film finally emerged it had shrunk to 2 hours and 12 minutes. Though, according to Birkett, he and Brook had initially 'wanted in Lear to achieve the same sort of effortless effect as a modern thriller', after the first screening of the edited film Brook realized that in his attempt to 'interrupt the consistency of style' he had produced a film whose ellipses provided major difficulties of comprehension for 'an average audience'. (It was only at this stage that he decided to introduce the narrative explanatory titles which have subsequently been admired for their Brechtian audacity.)

While working on the relationships between the two film scripts and the finished film, I wrote to Peter Brook to ask him if he would comment on a number of changes in the film which are not hinted at in the drafts. One of these centres on the character of Edgar. It is the moment in the film where Lear first encounters Edgar as Poor Tom. Lear and the viewer see Edgar in a series of shots which rapidly alternate between his face, speaking in close-up, and full shots of his near-naked body. It is a violent sequence where lighting and sound-track assist in producing a series of burning epiphanies, the images of Edgar being disconcertingly unrelated to his words ('A servingman proud in heart and mind', etc.). Most viewers see the Edgar of this sequence as a kind of Christ figure (an association triggered by his bearded face, his posture, and his wearing of an unambiguous crown of thorns). When asked to comment on the 'Christ-like parallels' in this sequence, Brook replied as follows:

> 'Christ-like parallels . . . ' this is post facto interpretation that of course everyone is free to make. But one doesn't direct a play or a film as a commentary, one tries to make the essential spirituality of Edgar emerge through his state and his actions: at that point he joins all naked hermits of history—the Middle and Far East as well as the Middle Ages are full of them—Christianity hasn't the monopoly.

The references to Edgar's 'essential spirituality' and the concern with the religious traditions and practices of 'the Middle and Far East' suggest that Brook's sense of *King Lear*'s mystical significance might have been developing even while he was working on the film. Several features[8] of the film's subtext do not square with the many readings which find the film unyielding in its nihilism.[9] Both film scripts end, as they began, with the focus on Edgar. The second draft has a hint of humanism in its final image. 'The future is his. He cannot avoid it. He has a crown on his head.' The last moments of the film itself are, however, closer in form and in feeling to the very different words which conclude the first draft: 'He is alone in the desert. Then this picture also vanishes, until nothing has left a trace.' I asked Brook if he would be prepared to comment on the differences between the film's ending, with its muted hints of transcendence, and the ending of his Stratford production. His answer was, perhaps appropriately, enigmatic: 'Nothing! This is not a refusal to comment, but an explanation: nothing, nothingness is one of the great zeros out of which the play rises and to which it returns.'

Notes

[1] Brook's *King Lear* was first shown in 1971. It was distributed in video format in 1986 by RCA/Columbia.

[2] F. Kermode, 'Shakespeare and the Movies', in G. Mast and M. Cohen (edd.), *Film Theory and Criticism: Introductory Readings* (Oxford, 1974), 322-32.

[3] R. Manvell, *Shakespeare and the Film* (New York, 1971), 136-43.

[4] C. Marowitz, '*Lear* Log', *Encore*, 41 (1963), 21-33.

[5] Manvell, *Shakespeare and the Film*, 138.

[6] 'Interview with Peter Brook: Penelope Houston and Tom Milne', *Sight and Sound* (Summer 1963), 109-10.

[7] G. Kozintsev, *'King Lear' The Space of Tragedy* (London, 1976), 240.

[8] Most noticeably, in the closing moments of the film there are two tantalizing glimpses of Cordelia. In the first, on the line 'Cordelia, Cordelia! stay a little', Lear sees an image of her which lasts only for a moment. The second glimpse provides a more complex perceptual problem. On the line 'And my poor fool is hanged' the audience sees both Lear and Cordelia in medium shot facing the camera. This time the shot is unambiguously from the audience's viewpoint, since Lear is looking at the camera and not at Cordelia. 'Does Lear' as he dies 'see Cordelia's spirit or is this a final madness?' The question comes from Brook's own shooting-scripts, as does the answer, 'We can never know'.

[9] The judgements and the rhetoric of most commentators highlight the film's cruel nihilism: A. Jorgens, *Shakespeare on Film* (Bloomington and London, 1977), sees the film as 'a bleak existential tale of meaningless violence in a cold, empty universe' (pp. 236-7); M. Mullin, 'Peter Brook's *King Lear:* Stage and Screen', *Literature and Film Quarterly,* 11 (1983), argues that the film shares the same vision as the earlier stage production: 'Nihilistic, bleak, hopeless, ugly, full of horror and lacking pity' (p. 195); P. Kael, in her *New Yorker* review of 12 Dec. 1971, finds 'no apparent light sources', just 'blind, godless desolation' shown in 'nightmare images of blindness and nothingness'. Of the earlier commentators, only W. Chaplin, 'Our Darker Purpose: Peter Brook's *King Lear*', *Arion* (Spring 1973), seems to have seen the images of Cordelia in the closing moments of the film: 'Lear stalks the presence of the living Cordelia on a white beach' (p. 174). Very much against the trend in interpretation, Chaplin sees the film's ending as essentially holy: 'With his daughter he has passed, now, like Oedipus, into a hallowed mystery . . . he has turned in Brook's iconology into the pure sanctity of the light' (p. 175).

Source: "'Apparent Perversities': Text and Subtext in the Construction of the Role of Edgar in Brook's Film of *King Lear*," in *The Review of English Studies,* n. s., Vol. XLVII, No. 187, August, 1996, pp. 317-30.

Romances and Poems

"What means Sicilia? He something seems unsettled": Sicily, Russia, and Bohemia in *The Winter's Tale*

R. W. Desai, *University of Delhi*

The opening scenes of *The Winter's Tale* bring together royalty from three different regions in Europe: Leontes, king of Sicily, which is in the extreme south, in the Mediterranean region; his wife, Hermione, daughter of the Emperor of Russia in the northeast; and Polixenes, king of Bohemia, now the Czech Republic, also in the northeast. This joining of geographical regions has its counterpoint in the contemporary joining of the regions of literary and other forms of cultural discourse. New Historicism has challenged the long established assumption, theorized by New Criticism, that "Art" is an autonomous aesthetic region which transcends the society, ideology, and culture that forms its matrix. Denying this, New Historicism insists upon a different methodology, a cultural criticism that refuses to see literature and history as two distinct entities since such differentiation is a product of our own phenomenological cultural conditioning which can be altered if our perspective is shifted. My purpose here is to attempt to shift our perspective on *The Winter's Tale* to show how Renaissance notions of ethnicity play a crucial part in the play's aesthetic.

I

In this article I shall survey rapidly various Eurocentrist views on race and ethnic differentiation present during Shakespeare's lifetime, and trace their presence in *The Winter's Tale*. These views seem in general to be in consonance with one another, and if they demonstrate how easily stereotypes came to be perpetuated from one period to the next during the sixteenth and seventeenth centuries, this need not surprise us, since in our own experience today such cultural stereotyping continues unabated. In Norway as recently as 1972 when the last referendum on joining the European Union was held, the opposition's catchy slogan was: "Would you want your daughter to marry a Sicilian?"

Hitherto *The Winter's Tale* has been viewed exclusively for its thematic concerns, no attention being paid to the racial and anthropological features that the play implicitly addresses. For example, though it has of course been remarked that Shakespeare interchanges the countries of origin of Leontes, the jealous husband, and Polixenes, the putative rival—Sicily and Bohemia, respectively, thus radically altering these details as given in Greene's *Pandosto*—the possible reasons for this intriguing transposition have not been investigated, as far as I am aware. Such an investigation, taking into account the ideological connotations involved, will, I think, bring to light the underlying assumptions of the Elizabethans on matters of race and ethnicity. (In any attempt to reconstruct attitudes to cultural issues, whether in the past or the present, some over-simplification and generalization are unavoidable. Having said this, it should not be necessary to punctuate every assumption here made with the warning that it is speculative.)

I shall argue that the superiority claimed by the northern Europeans over their southern counterparts is a significant element in the multiculturalism that *The Winter's Tale* embodies. Yet, at the same time, I shall try to show that though initially seemingly subscribing to this popular belief, the play's final message is not its confirmation but rather its questioning and its rejection—up to a point at least. Viewed in this multicultural context, the play seems to embody a discourse in which populist notions are challenged, disjunction is harmonized, and irreconcilable contradictions are transcended. Still, at the play's end, total harmony has not been achieved, and traces of certain elements which the narrative seemed to efface are still disturbingly present.

In making the jealous husband, Leontes, a Sicilian belonging to the Mediterranean type of culture, Shakespeare may have been exercising discretion. His acting company having become the King's Men after the accession of James I to England's throne, Shakespeare may have been reluctant to offend the new monarch by showing a northern European consumed by an irrational sexual jealousy. As is well known, *The Winter's Tale* was one of the plays presented as part of the festivities devised to celebrate the marriage of the king's daughter, Princess Elizabeth, to Frederick, elector palatine of the Rhine, which took place in 1613. In 1619 Frederick was crowned king of Bohemia, the country ruled by Polixenes in *The Winter's Tale*.

Before examining the multiculturalism that the triad of countries—Sicily, Bohemia, and Russia—releases into the play, it seems desirable to resolve the puzzle of the time period in which the play is located. The Oracle at Delphos would define the period as pre-Christian and classical, while the explicit reference to Julio Romano (V.ii.97)[1] would of course advance the period to the mid-sixteenth century. I shall argue that the latter is the intended time-slot, the former classical time-slot being assimilated into the Renaissance time-frame quite effortlessly. As Sukanta Chaudhuri has recently shown, it was in the Renaissance that, uniquely, an earlier age of Greek and Roman classicism was seen as unfolding and, as it were, realizing itself again in course of the Renaissance. . . . Hence Renaissance man can live simultaneously in two worlds—widely separated in date. . . . He is shaped by two parallel operations of process, two developing contexts of thought and writing widely separated in the calendar, while the intervening "Middle" ages recede into the background. The three-part chronology of classical, medieval and Renaissance was devised in the Renaissance itself: a rare instance of an age happily defining its own time-referents and having them accepted by posterity. This permitted a very real though profoundly unchronological linkage of the first and third elements, mental proximities that have nothing to do with distance in space or time.[2]

Hamlet too, we recall, is set in a post-Martin Luther period, as the reference to Wittenberg indicates, yet the play has a Roman dimension as well, as is suggested by names such as Claudius, Horatio, Marcellus, Francisco, and Barnardo. Accordingly, I shall explore in this paper prevailing views in England on race and ethnicity during the sixteenth century, particularly as they were directed toward Sicily, Bohemia, and Russia.

II

Julio Romano died in 1546. Assuming that Paulina intended her audience to believe that the "statue" was created during the last years of his life, then Hermione, now in her mid-forties, would have been in her late twenties at the time of her banishment, and this would place her date of birth at around the early 1500's so that her father, the Emperor of Russia, a detail she specifically mentions (III.ii.119), would have been Ivan III, known as Ivan the Great (1462-1505). But even more immediate for, and better known to, Shakespeare and his audience would have been the exploits of Ivan IV, also known as Ivan the Terrible (1533-84). An English contemporary, Sir Jerome Horsey, related the sack of Novgorod in vivid terms:

> he chargeth it with 30 thowsand Tartors and tenn thowsand gonnors of his guard, withowt any respect ravished all the weomen and maieds, ranzacked, robbed, and spoilled all that wear within it of their jewells, plate, and treasur, murthered the people yonge and olde, burnt all their howshold stuff, merchandices, and warehowses of wax, flæx, tallow, hieds, salt, wynes, cloth, and silks, sett all one fier, with wax and tallow melted down the kennells in the streats, together with the bloud of 700 thowsande men, weomen and children, slaine and murthered; so that with the bloud that rann into the river, and of all other livinge creaturs and cattell, their dead carcacess did stoppe as it wear the stream of the river Volca, beinge cast therin. Noe historie maketh mencion of so horrable a massacre.[3]

For Shakespeare's audience watching the play, Hermione's father, "the Emperor of Russia," could quite easily have meant a telescoped image of the two Ivans. Queen Elizabeth had in fact established such close trade and cultural links with Ivan the Terrible that the king of Poland had written cautioning her against such a friendship:

> We seemed hitherto to vanquish him onely in this, that he was rude of arts, and ignorant of policies. . . . [W]e that know best, and border vpon him, do admonish other Christian princes in time, that they do not betray their dignity, liberty and life of them and their subiects to a most barbarous and cruel enemy. . . .[4]

Accordingly, when Hermione wishes that her emperor father "were alive, and here beholding/ His daughter's trial," but "with eyes/ Of pity, not revenge" (III.ii.120-23), her lament is more than pathos: her reference to "revenge" implies the military power that the country to which she belonged possesses and could exercise to defend her against the false charge leveled against her by her husband. In Shakespeare's source, Greene's *Pandosto,* the Emperor of Russia is not the father of Bellaria (Hermione) but of the wife of Egistus (the wife of Polixenes, who, in Shakespeare's play, does not enter the action at all). Evidently the changes made by Shakespeare would have had immediate political meaning for his viewers.

Ivan the Great was the first Muscovite ruler to designate himself "Grand Prince of all Russia." His first wife died in 1472, and he then married Zoe Palaeologa, the niece of the last Byzantine emperor. But though of Byzantine descent, Zoe Palaeologa had been raised in Italy, a circumstance that helps to explain why Hermione (Zoe's daughter in Shakespeare's play) is the wife of Leontes, king of Sicily. Through the marriage of Zoe to Ivan, Italian influences made themselves felt in Russia. An Italian architect designed the Upenski Cathedral in the Kremlin, and a new Italianate palace was also built there. Russia, in fact, had entered the English consciousness a decade before the birth of Shakespeare when Sebastian Cabot's expedition sailed into the White Sea by the northeast route. The explorers were well received by Ivan IV and were entertained with great hospitality. In 1555 Ivan granted a monopoly of trade in the White Sea to an English company called the Muscovy Company, and in 1566 Queen Elizabeth's emissary Anthony Jenkinson wrote: "I came before the Emperours Majestie, sitting in his seate of honour, and having kissed his hand and done the Queenes Majesties commendations, and delivered her Graces letters and present, he bad me to dinner, which I accepted, and had much honour done unto me both then and all the time of my abode in Russia."[5] In England there was great interest in Russia during this period. A Russian deputation was at the English

Court in 1582-83, and this, as is well known, is reflected in the last act of *Love's Labor's Lost.*

III

The Elizabethan interest in Russia extended to Russians' physical characteristics, which would likely have figured in stage representations of Muscovites. Anthropologically the Russians, like the Czechs and Slovaks, belong to the Slavic peoples. "The Great Russians are mostly of the characteristic Moujik type with a squarish face and heavy features, reddish-blond hair and orange-brown . . . eyes. These in the main are the Muscovites of history."[6]

Turning to Leontes, king of Sicilia and the husband of Hermione, we note that he would have belonged to the Mediterranean type, the physical characteristics of which are "wavy or curly black hair, an average stature of about 5 feet 3 inches, slender build, long head and narrow oval face, straight nose rather inclining to be broad; the eyes are very dark."[7] Thus Leontes would be a distinct contrast to Hermione in appearance, and this distinction should be made by directors of stage and film productions of *The Winter's Tale.* What exacerbates Leontes' insecurity and sexual jealousy could well be the physical and cultural affinity that Polixenes has with Hermione. Polixenes, king of Bohemia, is, like Hermione, of Slavic descent. The Czechs and the Slovaks both belong to the western branch of the Slavic peoples. Around the fifth century A.D. both tribes migrated south and settled in what became Czechoslovakia, with the Czechs in Bohemia in the west and the Slovaks in Slovakia in the east.

But the affinity between Polixenes and Hermione is more than merely anthropological; it is cultural as well. Hermione's easy familiarity with Polixenes, so galling to Leontes and so grievously misunderstood by him, springs not from a perversity of nature but from his misinterpretation of the social mores and customs of northern Europe to which they belong. That in the company of Polixenes Hermione is revealing a facet of her personality totally unknown to Leontes is implied in his aggrieved recollection of her restraint when she was wooed by him:

> Why, that was when
> Three crabbed months had sour'd
>   themselves to death,
> Ere I could make thee open thy white hand,
> And clap thyself my love; then didst thou
>   utter
> "I am yours for ever."
>
>   (I.ii.101-05)

And it may not be too far-fetched to suggest that Leontes' "thy white hand" is ironic, the adjective having resonances suggestive of racial difference. Shakespeare had already explored this subject in *Othello,* a play whose striking correspondences with *The Winter's Tale* have been noted in Shakespearean criticism. A dark complexion, often associated with the south, carried connotations of cultural and social inferiority, as may be seen, we recall, in Beatrice of *Much Ado about Nothing,* a play also often regarded as a precursor of *Othello* and *The Winter's Tale,* and whose setting is Messina, one of the chief cities of Sicily. Beatrice wryly attributes her failure to find a husband to her complexion: "Thus goes every one to the world but I, and I am sun-burnt. I may sit in a corner and cry 'Heigh-ho for a husband!'" (II.i.318-20).

The sexual freedom enjoyed by women of the north was something totally denied to the women of the south. The striking opening sentence of Maria Pia di Bella's essay "Name, Blood and Miracles: The Claims to Renown in Traditional Sicily" states this well: "As is well known, honor looms large in the daily life of Mediterranean peoples. . . . The elements that constitute the honor of the group and the criteria by which it is granted seem to be . . . the chastity of its women; . . . the courage of its men on the battlefield and, whenever their point of honor is at stake, in the home community; their ability to defend their women from blemish."[8]

In contrast to the restrained behavior of the women of the south, the freedom exercised by northern women was easily misconstrued as licentiousness by the southerners. The following passage from Robert Burton is only one of many drawing a distinction between the two cultural practices: concerning "those northern inhabitants," Burton writes:

> Altomarus, Poggius, and Munster in his description of Baden, reports that men and women of all sorts go commonly into the baths together, without all suspicion; "the name of jealousy" (saith Munster) "is not so much as once heard of among them." In Friesland the women kiss him they drink to, and are kissed again of those they pledge. The virgins in Holland go hand-in-hand with young men from home, glide on the ice, such is their harmless liberty, and lodge together abroad without suspicion, which rash Sansovinus, an Italian, makes a great sign of unchastity.[9]

Burton's book was not published until 1621, but as Anthony Gerard Barthelemy points out, it "codifies opinions that were in currency long before its publication."[10]

Act I, scene ii of *The Winter's Tale,* when enacted on Shakespeare's stage so as authentically to represent physically visible differences between the national origins of Leontes, Hermione, and Polixenes, would have encoded a semiotics that the audience would have intuitively grasped and understood, as easily as we today, for example, understand what long and un-kempt hair, a frayed shirt, tattered jeans, and open sandals denote. As Allesandro Serpieri points out, drama has a semiotics of its own, quite distinct from a literary text:

> A semiotic reading of the dramatic text must be aware not only of the cultural pragmatics of its historical context, but also of the potential pragmatics of the *stage* relationships that are inscribed in the strictly verbal make-up of the text itself in accordance with the codes and conventions (both general and historical) of the genre. In a word, critical enquiry into the contextual values of the drama should be carried out with a view to its specific semiotic complexity, a complexity quite distinct from that of literary genres, which are not conditioned by directions for a more-than-verbal use.[11]

In addition, I would like to argue for a further differential between Sicily and Bohemia that aggravates Leontes' aggression, is partly responsible for Polixenes' long nine-month visit to Sicily, and is the reason for his hasty and terrified flight from the country without the observance of the customary protocol. During the sixteenth century, Sicily was prosperous economically and enjoyed political stability, while Bohemia was in both these respects in a state of decline. True, much earlier, in the fourteenth century, Bohemia had emerged as a powerful nation under Charles I, whose reign was considered a golden age. Charles University in Prague, named after him, was the first university to be founded in eastern Europe. But by the sixteenth century Bohemia had all but lost her intellectual supremacy in Europe. Internecine conflict on religious and political issues had divided the country, and the tyranny of the Bohemian nobles had pressed the masses of the population into virtual serfdom. In 1618 occurred the famous Defenestration of Prague, and, as already noted above, the Hapsburgs, beginning with Frederick, son-in-law of James I of England, took control of the country by invitation and ruled it for three centuries thereafter.

In contrast to Bohemia's economic and political distress, Sicily during this period was flourishing. The granary of Europe, she exported vast quantities of grain to the north. "[T]he ever-growing demand for grain in the cities of northern Italy, Provence, Catalonia, helped transform extensive areas of Sicily and Apulia into large farms concentrating on the cultivation of wheat for export."[12] In fact, by the beginning of the seventeenth century the whole of Italy was one of the most highly developed regions of western Europe, with an exceptionally high standard of living for that time. It hardly needs to be pointed out that during this period the Renaissance in Europe had reached its peak in Italy, and the cultural gap between Italy and Russia was at its widest. Foreign travelers were amused at

the barbarous and revolting behavior of the Muscovites, as the following account shows: "Filthily dirty, clad in long, cumbersome garments which prevented all free movements, unkempt hair down to their shoulders, and matted beards, they behaved hoggishly at table dipping their black and greasy fingers indiscriminately into plates and dishes, always eating too much and drinking noisily and greedily out of unwashed vessels."[13] The economic power and cultural prestige of Italy in comparison to the rest of Europe—and to Bohemia in particular—is reflected in the play's opening scene in which Archidamus, a Bohemian courtier, confesses with obvious embarrassment that Bohemia cannot possibly match Sicilia's lavish style of hospitality:

> Verily I speak in the freedom of my knowledge: we cannot with such magnificence—in so rare— I know not what to say—We will give you sleepy drinks, that your senses (unintelligent of our insufficience) may, though they cannot praise us, as little accuse us. (I.i.11-16)

The assertion of superiority on the part of the court of Leontes over Polixenes and his entourage that gives rise to the "insufficience" of Bohemia is seen in the bullying infliction of the forms of hospitality by Leontes upon his reluctant guest, who has long outstayed his welcome and is now on sufferance. Literature does not merely reflect reality; it encapsulates and assimilates it, often so thoroughly that text and context are indistinguishable. To capture this "political unconscious" (Frederick Jameson's coinage and the title of his best known book) we must look not so much at political history as seen in the letters, diaries, and sermons of the period but rather at what was happening on the Elizabethan and Jacobean stage.

IV

Traditional approaches to *The Winter's Tale* have regarded Greene's *Pandosto* as its main source, and no doubt this is true in terms of plot and narrative. But, as I have tried to show, the changes Shakespeare makes are related to culture and politics. That the plays of Shakespeare use their main sources as mere frames within which to incorporate contemporary discourses is now generally accepted. This development in critical practice indicates a welcome and long overdue departure from the too simplistic notion held by many that Ben Jonson was the more widely read and intellectually superior author, while Shakespeare, lacking a university education, used his dramatic instinct to produce plays that were theatrically successful. Fortunately, this kind of patronizing concession to Shakespeare is no longer fashionable. That he must have known the works of Montaigne, Machiavelli, and other well-known Renaissance philosophers is of course well established, but it is equally likely that he knew the work of the French writer Jean Bodin (1530-96), one of the most influential geographers of the time.

Since in this century England entered the nautical age on a wide scale, geography was the science of the future, the equivalent of computer science today. In the preface to his *History of Travel* Richard Willes commented:

> There was a time whan the arte of grammar was so muche esteemed. . . . Than was it honourable to be a Poet . . . that tyme is paste. There was a tyme whan Logike and Astrology weeried the heades of young schollers . . . that tyme is past. Not long since happy was he that had any skil in the Greke language. [However, now] all Christians, Iewes, Turkes, Moores, Infidels and Barbares be this day in loue with Geographie.[14]

Bodin's immensely popular *Methodus* aimed at establishing a correlation of culture with climate and topography, these studies including politics and ethnography as well.

> Between 1566 and 1650 the *Methodus* was issued in thirteen Latin editions, the *République* translated into four languages and published frequently in abridged form. That the proud position of history was to be short-lived and that the Cartesians were to denounce it as unreliable—a collection of myths, and a conglomeration of errors—is relevant only on the Continent, where historical pyrrhonism rose to its highest level and where Bodin's name was seldom mentioned. In England the reception of his work was different. There, from 1580 to the end of the first quarter of the seventeenth century, the French scholar enjoyed a reputation for brilliance and high originality. He not only was known to all serious English students of history and geography but was admired, quoted, and imitated. William Harrison, the author of the *Description of England* in 1577, mentioned him, as did Holinshed, Sidney, Nash, Spenser, Bolton, Hobbes, Wheare, Heylyn, Burton, Carpenter, and Hakewill. "You cannot stepp into a schollar's studye," said Gabriel Harvey, "but (ten to one) you shall litely [sic] finde open either Bodin *de Republica* or Le Royes *Exposition*. . . . " Robert Burton, at one time a teacher of geography, referred to him many times in the *Anatomy of Melancholy* (1621).[15]

Here is one such reference by Burton, in which, quoting Bodin, he contrasts the freedom between the sexes practiced by the northern Europeans with the restraints imposed on them by Italian culture, this difference having a geographical cause: "Bodine . . . ascribes a great cause to the country or clime, and discourseth largely there of this subject, saying, that southern men are more hot, lascivious, and jealous than such as live in the north; they can hardly contain themselves in those hotter climes, but are most subject to prodigious

lust. . . . Germany hath not so many drunkards, England tobacconists, France dancers, Holland mariners, as Italy alone hath jealous husbands."[16] Today the "correct" response is to dismiss such generalizations as conventional stereotypes, but perhaps all that has happened is that we push our feelings underground. Earlier centuries were more outspoken, as can be seen in Shakespeare's creation of characters like Shylock and Don Armado, the "fantastical Spaniard" of *Love's Labor's Lost.*

One of Bodin's intents was to explain the cultural diversity which, he believed, was originally non-existent, for mankind began as a homogeneous unit. Basing his conclusions on observation and on a vast assemblage of documentation, Bodin points out that the people of the south are "of a contrarie humour and disposition to them of the North: these are great and strong, they are little and weake; they of the north, hot and moyst, the others cold and dry; the one hath a big voyce and greene eyes, the other hath a weake voyce and black eyes; the one hath a flaxen haire and a faire skin, the other hath both haire and skin black; the one feareth cold, the other heate."[17] As Terence Hawkes has drily remarked, "All nations execrate their enemies, and the discourse of denigration has a long and monotonous history in Europe, on all sides, and towards all cultural groups."[18]

But Bodin does not quite conform to this kind of a predictable pattern: he is original and interesting because he often refuses to adopt the expected stance. Thus he speaks frequently and approvingly of the good effects of the mingling of races and cultures—"The fusion of peoples changes the customs and nature of men not a little"[19]—and this, he says, gives rise to new states and new cities.

Like Bodin, *The Winter's Tale* is much occupied with genetic fusion. Perdita, herself a product of the union of Sicily and Russia—though she is unaware of this—is critical of cross-breeding and has to listen to Polixenes' celebrated speech in which he extols the ingenuity of genetic engineering in improving the breed:

> You see, sweet maid, we marry
> A gentler scion to the wildest stock,
> And make conceive a bark of baser kind
> By bud of nobler race. This is an art
> Which does mend Nature—change it rather—but
> The art itself is Nature.
>
> (IV.iv.92-97)

Polixenes' later repudiation of his own philosophy, as seen in his vicious denunciation of Perdita, prompted by the fear of plebeian blood contaminating that of his royal family, would seem to suggest that the play satirizes the belief in the purity of blood. But it must

also be noted that the play is not a complete overturning of conventional beliefs, for Perdita, we know, is
actually not a plebeian at all, and her union with Florizel
is not the same as King Cophetua's choice of a beg-
gar-maid, a story that Shakespeare knew very well
(see *Love's Labor's Lost* IV.i.65-66, *2 Henry IV*
V.iii.102, and *Romeo and Juliet* II.i.14). Thus, though
it challenges notions of class and blood superiority,
The Winter's Tale does not totally repudiate them, and
even the challenge is couched in terms that are muted,
not strident. After all, Shakespeare by this time was
writing for a chiefly aristocratic audience.

V

What light, if any, does this dimension of multiculturalism shed on Perdita in terms of her development towards womanhood? Physically, she is the image
of her mother, as is remarked by the Third Gentleman
(V.ii.36-37) as well as by Leontes, who almost falls in
love with her (V.i.226-27). Thus we are in a sense
seeing Hermione all over again, except that Perdita's
behavior is just the opposite of her mother's. Whereas
Hermione, a Russian princess, was free and familiar
with her guest Polixenes, Perdita, half-Russian and
half-Sicilian, is "retired" when her guests, including
Polixenes, arrive and is reprimanded for this by her
putative father, the Old Shepherd (IV.iv.62). "Sir,
welcome./ It is my father's will I should take on me/
The hostess-ship o' th' day. You're welcome, sir"
(IV.iv.70-72). In the restrained conduct of Perdita,
"now grown in grace" (IV.i.24), we witness a reenactment of the Polixenes-Hermione relationship, but
this time with a new and transformed Hermione as
hostess. It is a flashback, so to speak, but with a
difference, a marvelous piece of dramatic legerdemain.

One final observation: it must have been evident to
Shakespeare's audience that, following the death of
Mamillius, the prophecy of the Oracle—"the king shall
live without an heir, if that which is lost be not found"
(III.ii.134-36)—had been fulfilled with the discovery
of Perdita, whose marriage to Florizel would result in
heirs both for Sicilia and Bohemia, thus reconciling the
two countries that had been estranged. With Mamillius'
death, the crown would ultimately pass on to his
nephew, or niece, Perdita's offspring; similarly, with
Queen Elizabeth's death, the English crown had passed
on to her nephew, James VI, son of her cousin, Mary
Queen of Scots.

In *The Winter's Tale* the prospect of heirs being born
is projected in the image of the "branch" and in the
possibility of the King having "no son" (I.i.24, 45), a
curious innuendo made in the play's opening scene in
the face of the fact that the King *does* have a son. But
looked at in the light of the contemporary political
scene, this and the play's ending would, of course,
have reminded the members of Shakespeare's audi-

ence of what they had themselves not long before
experienced: the anxiety of seeing their recent monarch Queen Elizabeth dying without an heir and also
the relief they felt at the throne being then painlessly
filled by James VI of Scotland, coming to England as
James I, thus effecting reconciliation between two
long-standing antagonists, England and Scotland, and
uniting them under a single crown. For that audience,
politics and history had become drama.[20]

Notes

[1] References to *The Winter's Tale* are to *The Riverside
Shakespeare,* ed. G. Blakemore Evans *et al.* (Boston:
Houghton Mifflin, 1974).

[2] Sukanta Chaudhuri, ed., *Renaissance Essays for Kitty
Datta* (Calcutta: Oxford Univ. Press, 1995), pp. 26-
27.

[3] *Russia at the Close of the Sixteenth Century,* ed.
Edward A. Bond (London: Hakluyt Society, 1856), p.
162.

[4] *The First Forty Years of Intercourse Between En-
gland and Russia, 1553-1593,* ed. George Tolstoy (St.
Petersburg, 1875), p. 30, as quoted in Jesse D.
Clarkson, *A History of Russia* (New York: Random
House, 1961), pp. 113-14.

[5] Richard Hakluyt, *The Principal Navigations, Voyages, Traffiques, and Discoveries of the English Nation* (London: J. M. Dent, 1907), II, 73. For a fascinating account of the company's financial success in
England during the reign of Ivan the Terrible, see
Richard Wilson, "Visible Bullets: Tamburlaine the Great
and Ivan the Terrible," *English Literary History,* 62
(1995), 47-49, 60-62.

[6] Julian S. Huxley and A. C. Haddon, *We Europeans:
A Survey of 'Racial' Problems* (New York: Harper,
1936), p. 179.

[7] Ibid., p. 140.

[8] Mario Pia di Bella, "Name, Blood and Miracles: The
Claim to Renown in Traditional Sicily," in *Honor and
Grace in Anthropology,* ed. J. G. Peristiany and Julian
Pitt-Rivers (Cambridge: Cambridge Univ. Press, 1992),
p. 151.

[9] Robert Burton, *The Anatomy of Melancholy,* introd.
Holbrook Jackson (London: Dent, 1932), III, 265 (Pt.
3, Sec. 4, Mem. 1, Subs. 3).

[10] Anthony Gerard Barthelemy, *Black Face, Maligned
Race: The Representation of Blacks in English Drama
from Shakespeare to Southerne* (Baton Rouge and
London: Louisiana State Univ. Press, 1987), p. 155n.

[11] Allesandro Serpieri, "Reading the Signs: Towards a Semiotics of Shakespearean Drama," in *Alternative Shakespeares,* ed. John Drakakis (London: Methuen, 1985), p. 122.

[12] David Abulafia, *Commerce and Conquest in the Mediterranean, 1100-1500* (Aldershot: Ashgate, 1993), p. 21.

[13] C. Marsden, *Palmyra of the North: The First Days of St. Petersburg* (London: Faber and Faber, 1942), p. 27.

[14] Richard Willes, *History of Travel;* as quoted by C. S. Lewis, *English Literature in the Sixteenth Century* (Oxford: Clarendon Press, 1954), p. 308.

[15] Margaret T. Hodgen, *Early Anthropology in the Sixteenth and Seventeenth Centuries* (Philadelphia: Univ. of Pennsylvania Press, 1964), pp. 282-83.

[16] Burton, *Antatomy of Melancholy,* III, 264 (Pt. 3, Sec. 3, Mem. 1, Subs. 2).

[17] Jean Bodin, *The Six Bookes of a Commonweale,* trans. R. Knolles (London, 1606), as quoted by Hodgen, *Early Anthropology,* p. 279.

[18] Terence Hawkes, "Swisser-Swatter: Making a Man of English Letters," in *Alternative Shakespeares,* ed. Drakakis, p. 36.

[19] Bodin, *The Six Books of a Commonweale,* as quoted by Hodgen, *Early Anthropology,* p. 282.

[20] I am grateful to André Beteille of the Delhi School of Economics for several valuable suggestions in the preparation of this article.

Source: "'What means Sicilia? He something seems unsettled': Sicily, Russia, and Bohemia in *The Winter's Tale*," in *Comparative Drama,* Vol. 30, No. 3, Fall, 1996, pp. 311-24.

Two Distincts, Division None: Shakespeare and Fletcher's *The Two Noble Kinsmen* of 1613

Philip J. Finkelpearl, *Wellesley College*

The Two Noble Kinsmen, Shakespeare and Fletcher's adaptation of Chaucer's "The Knight's Tale," can be dated in 1613 with some precision.[1] The date is of some importance because several distinguished scholars have recently linked the play to the marriage of Princess Elizabeth and to other events of the same year.[2] Here, in an essay honoring the most rigorous biographer Shakespeare has ever had, I want to consider the precise sense in which *The Two Noble Kinsmen* can be related to topical matters.

This marriage of Elizabeth to Frederick V, Elector Palatine of the Rhine, was central to the plans of the recently deceased Henry, Prince of Wales, for creating a Protestant alliance to curb the Catholic Habsburgs' power. For the marriage the prince had devised, according to Roy Strong, "a splendid series of spectacles, expressly designed to establish the Stuart court in the eyes of Europe as the fount of revived Protestant chivalry."[3] Although the project never fully materialized because of the prince's death, Strong shows that the prince's aims can be detected in various surviving works. One of these was a wedding masque about Virginia by George Chapman for the Middle Temple and Lincoln's Inn that endorsed the anti-Spanish, anti-Catholic, and Protestant aspects of British imperialistic expansion. Another masque, commissioned for the same occasion by the Inner Temple and Gray's Inn and performed a few days after the wedding, was by Francis Beaumont. The preface Beaumont wrote for the published text of his masque indicates that his aims were similar to Chapman's. He designed the dance of mythological figures representing the Rhine and the Thames in the first antimasque and of "Common People" in the second antimasque (later adapted for *The Two Noble Kinsmen*) to register approval of the match. In the main masque Beaumont presented the political message of the prince through an elaborate fiction about the revival of the Olympic games since "The *Olympian* games portend to the Match, Celebritie, Victorie, and Felicitie."[4] "Victorie," it seems fair to say, is not a term normally associated with marriage. From the viewpoint of would-be heroes—young students at the Inns of Court were particularly critical of King James's pacific foreign policy—"Olympian games" on foreign fields, preferably battlefields, were in desperate need of revival and would be a highly desirable by-product of this match.[5]

Since *The Two Noble Kinsmen,* written after the princess's marriage, included a passage from Beaumont's marriage masque and opens with a masque celebrating the marriage of a prince and princess, it has spawned conjecture—there is no document specifically making the connection—that the play was one of the many dramatic celebrations of the courtly occasion. However, Beaumont, who would have been the natural continuator of the impulses behind the masque, had nothing to do with the play. Indeed, the astonishingly prolific, very young playwright—in 1613, twenty-eight years old but responsible for part or all of at least twelve plays over the past six years—produced no more work for the theater. It had been generally assumed that his marriage to an heiress in 1613 had obviated the need to write for a living, but recently I discovered that soon after the masque Beaumont suffered an incapacitating "apoplexe," or a stroke. He lingered until 1616, dying about a month before Shakespeare.[6]

This unexpected turn of events must have created a problem for the King's Men. That they were experiencing some kind of serious trouble seems to be confirmed by the last line of the prologue of *The Two Noble Kinsmen,* which speaks apprehensively about the possibility that if this play does not succeed, "Our losses fall so thick we must needs leave" (32).[7] After *The Tempest* in 1611 all evidence points to Shakespeare's spending most of his time in Stratford and curtailing, if not altogether stopping, his writing. His retirement would hardly have seemed financially disastrous to the company at a time when Beaumont and Fletcher were at the height of their popularity and capable of producing work at the same prodigious rate as Shakespeare. Now, suddenly, with Beaumont's stroke the production line was in danger of slowing down. This development may, perhaps, account for the reappearance in 1613 of shareholder Shakespeare as a writer, albeit in the new, reduced role of collaborator. Within the year his name is linked (with varying degrees of certainty) with Fletcher's in as many as three collaborative plays: the lost *Cardenio, Henry VIII,* and *The Two Noble Kinsmen.*

It is instructive to observe the nature of the product that emerges from the union of the greatest of all solo writers with the most successful of all dramatic collaborators. The seamless texture of a "Beaumont & Fletcher" production is a commonplace, occasioning Coleridge's confession, "I have never been able to distinguish the presence of Fletcher during the life of Beaumont, nor the absence of Beaumont during the survival of Fletcher."[8] This could never be said about *The Two Noble Kinsmen.* Whether it is the difference in spelling by Shakespeare and Fletcher of a character's name ("Pirithous" vs. "Perithous") or the repetition in a Shakespeare episode of what had already happened in one by Fletcher (cf. 4.1.23 and 5.6.36) or the rather arbitrary insertion of Beaumont's masque dance, there is evidence—and much more could be cited—of a product hastily cobbled together by partners as distant as Stratford and London.

Nonetheless, the final effect is of a hard-won unity. Initially *The Two Noble Kinsmen* seems as though it might become another vehicle for the propagation of Prince Henry's neochivalric activism. In the first act, allotted to Shakespeare, the legendary warrior Theseus, unlike the indecisive, humiliatingly pacific reigning King of England, demonstrates the validity of the constant praise he receives for his unrivaled military prowess. Like "a deity equal with Mars" (1.1.227) he decides to forsake his bride on their wedding day to perform a chivalric act. As in Chaucer, at the entreaty of some queens widowed by the cruel ruler Creon he wages a swift, successful war on Thebes. Unlike the amiable Theseus of *A Midsummer Night's Dream,* although sprung from the same source in Chaucer, here he is revered as a kind of Coriolanus: "O Jove, your actions, / Soon as they move, as aspreys do the fish, / Subdue before they touch" (1.1.137-39). Valor in the form of a remorseless brutality is for him the chiefest virtue, as we hear in his praise of the two noble kinsmen, Palamon and Arcite, whom he captured in the recent war:

By th' helm of Mars, I saw them in the
 war,
Like to a pair of lions smear'd with prey,
Make lanes in troops aghast. . . .

  . . . . .

The very lees of such millions of rates
Exceed the wine of others. . . .

  . . . . .

    their lives concern us,
Much more than Thebes is worth.
     (1.4.17-19, 29-30, 32-33)

As I have been describing this introductory section by Shakespeare, it sounds like an echo of Jonson's *Prince Henry's Barriers* (1610), an event designed by the prince to announce to the world what he hoped to stand for. There, England's greatest warrior kings are extolled in terms like those lauding Theseus: Richard Coeur de Lion "armed with wroth and fire / Ploughing whole armies up with zealous ire," Edward the First, who "lets no less rivers of blood," the Black Prince, "Mars indeed."[9] But despite the glorification of a mortal Mars, Theseus the Slaughterer, in *The Two Noble*

Kinsmen certain passages make us wary about Shakespeare's tone. When a weeping queen urges Hippolyta to kneel for "no longer time / Than a dove's motion when the head's pluck'd off" (1.1.97-98), we are uncertain whether this new unit of time is meant as an admirably cold-blooded expression by a precursor of the Marquis de Sade or as the language of a desperate widow whose sensibility has been corrupted by the atrocities she has experienced. And how are we to feel about the total immersion in barbaric military values of Theseus' recently conquered Amazonian queen, Hippolyta?

Hippolyta. . . . We have been soldiers, and
 we cannot weep
When our friends don their helms, or put to
 sea,
Or tell of babes broach'd on the lance, or
 women
That have sod their infants in (and after eat
 them)
The brine they wept at killing 'em.
     (1.3.18-22)

In that same passage in which Theseus rates Palamon and Arcite's worth as exceeding that of millions of normal men, he directs his surgeons to heal these paragons so that he can imprison them for life! By the fifth act we are so impressed by the purity of Theseus' chivalric nature that Shakespeare can risk a laugh at the expense of this tunnel-visioned warrior's terms of commendation for a potential husband: "he is a good one / As ever strook at head" (5.3.108-9). One passage encapsulates the glorious defect in Theseus' values. When praised for having gone to war in an honorable cause rather than spending his marriage night with his wife, he responds, "As we are men / thus should we do, being sensually subdu'd / We lose our human title" (1.1.230-32). To be godlike, Martian, requires repression of natural instincts. Theseus is at once ponderous, holier than thou, and a paragon.[10]

Through such shadings we realize that Shakespeare is constructing his usual complex dialectic. From the first Theseus' sister-in-law Emilia tries to act as "a counter-reflect 'gainst / My brother's heart, and warm it to some pity" (1.1.127-28). But her function expands in 1.3, one of the most remarkable passages in Shakespeare's late work. She hears of the great friendship between Theseus and Perithous and without warning breaks into an emotional, "high-speeded" (1.3.83) contrast between the mature love of two lifelong male friends and the love she experienced at eleven with another girl of the same age. The male relationship has been grounded in "judgment" and responds to the friends' immediate personal needs. The two girls, "things innocent"—they have scarcely acquired enough identity to be called humans, as Emilia explains—

Lov'd for we did, and like the elements
That know no what nor why, yet do effect
Rare issues by their operance, our souls
Did so to one another.

(1.3.61-64)

Emilia then describes the identity, the fused oneness, of the two lovers. Whether a flower, a hat, or a tune, if one of them owns it, the other assimilates, imitates, or appropriates it:

Had mine ear

Stol'n some new air, or at adventure
  humm'd one
From musical coinage, why, it was a note
Whereon her spirits would sojourn (rather
  dwell on)
And sing it in her slumbers.

(1.3.74-78)

We are in the area of mystical love explored in the sonnets and particularly in *The Phoenix and the Turtle,* where the lovers are "two distincts, division none":

The flow'r that I would pluck

And put between my breasts (O then but
  beginning
To swell about the blossom), she would
  long
Till she had such another, and commit it
To the like innocent cradle, where phoenix-
  like
They died in perfume.

(1.3.66-71)

Emilia's friend Flavina died young, and the lovely equation of the deaths of the girl and the roses, two "phoenixes," validates by its eloquence Emilia's belief "That the true love 'tween maid and maid may be / More than in sex dividual" (1.3.81-82); and the seeming formlessness of Emilia's innocent outburst highlights the stiff artificiality of the world that surrounds her.

Emilia's passage sounds the keynote for a play that is structured around differences of age, gender, values, social class, and ways of loving. This theme is explicitly stated in the bridge that Shakespeare constructs in 2.1 to the contributions of Fletcher that begin with 2.2 and continue through most of the play until the fifth act. As we have seen, Theseus had been goaded into fighting and defeating Creon's Thebes, in the process capturing and imprisoning Palamon and Arcite. In 2.1 at Palamon and Arcite's jail we hear praise of the two "noble sufferers" from the daughter of their jailer. She exclaims—doubtless casting a glance at her pedestrian if not ignoble wooer, who is also present—"It is a holiday to look on them. Lord, the diff'rence of men!" (2.1.55-56). Shakespeare's Palamon and Arcite are

angry, idealistic moralists, proud of their purity yet wary of the inevitable corruption. In the prologue (generally ascribed to Fletcher) the worry is expressed that Chaucer might find the play "witless chaff" and resent the treatment "lighter / Than Robin Hood" that has been accorded to his "fam'd works" (19-21). There is some justification for the prologue's concern because Fletcher's portrayal of the kinsmen, in particular, shows a comic dimension to their chivalrous confrontations. Fletcher's Palamon and Arcite are self-consciously noble rhetoricians, sentimentally lamenting their exile from a Thebes that Shakespeare's pure knights had detested. When we view them alone together for the first time, the cousins' despair gradually modulates to rapture at the prospect of a life in prison, away from the corruption of this world and the possible disruption of their great friendship:

Palamon. Is there record of any two that
  lov'd
Better than we do, Arcite?
Arcite.   Sure there cannot.
Palamon. I do not think it possible our
  friendship
Should ever leave us.
Arcite.   Till our deaths it cannot.

(2.2.112-15)

At this moment the lovely Emilia appears in the courtyard below their cell. Palamon catches sight of her, as does Arcite a moment later, they are both completely smitten by her image, and their friendship immediately comes apart:

Palamon. I saw her first.
Arcite.   That's nothing.
Palamon.   But it shall be.
Arcite. I saw her too.
Palamon.   Yes, but you must not
  love her.

(2.2.158-62)

Here, without doubt is a broadly comic (*and* Fletcherian) moment that cuts through all the high-sounding talk, and it is not an isolated one. In the ensuing exchange Arcite defends his right to love Emilia, despite Palamon's microsecond priority in viewing her:

Arcite.   Because another
First sees the enemy, shall I stand still,
And let mine honor down, and never
  charge?
Palamon.   Yes, if he be but one.
Arcite.   But say that one
Had rather combat me?
Palamon.   Let that one say so,
And use thy freedom; else, if thou pursuest
  her,

Be as that cursed man that hates his
   country,
A branded villain.
Arcite.   You are mad.
                                   (2.2.193-200)

Emilia as an enemy soldier, Arcite as a traitor to his
country! In the same scene Palamon has two other
extravagant fantasies. In the first he wishes he were
an apricot tree that could supply Emilia with fruit "Fit
for the gods to feed on" (2.2.239). He would "make
her / So near the gods in nature, they should fear her"
(241-42). Then, Palamon concludes, "I am sure she
would love me" (243). When a few lines later he
learns that Arcite has been freed, he has another mad
fantasy:

Were I at liberty, I would do things
Of such a virtuous greatness that this lady,
This blushing virgin, should take manhood
   to her
And seek to ravish me.
                                   (2.2.56-59)

A virgin lady ravishing a man because she is so struck
by his virtue! The inseparable partner of the author of
The Knight of the Burning Pestle is beginning his
portion of the play by shamelessly "camping up" the
old, revered "Knight's Tale," in the process adding
some surprising and amusing shadings to Shakespeare's
"pair of lions."

Fletcher's treatment of Palamon and Arcite in the rest
of the play continues to be two-edged but his tone is
generally graver. As strict adherents of the chivalric
code, their conduct is completely regulated for them.
They *must* act as nobly and honorably as possible
while pursuing Emilia to the exclusion of all else. Not
surprisingly considering the emphasis of the play,
"must" appears more frequently in *The Two Noble
Kinsmen* than in any other play in Shakespeare's canon,
almost twice his average.[11] Critics have attacked Fletcher
for failing to differentiate the protagonists, but that is
the point. Adherence to the code makes the two cousins nearly interchangeable automatons, and one may
discern a deeper implication in their actions. Although
the knightly code may originally have been designed to
curb uncivilized instincts, here it sanctions and digni-
fies the urge for revenge, murder, and suicide. In 3.6
the cousins arm each other for single combat with
extravagant, "noble" courtesy, and each tries to cede
advantages in the combat to the other. Then they fight
with a "mad" (122) impulse to annihilate each other—
all this, we must recall, for a girl whom Palamon, at
least, has never met. When separated by Theseus,
who happens upon them in combat, they now try to
outdo each other in a show of indifference for their
lives, each pleading to be punished if the other is, each
refusing freedom if it means abandoning the quest for

Emilia, each eager to be killed if Emilia prefers the
other. To Theseus and his court with their identical
values this fanatical commitment to love or death appears magnificent. "These are men!" (3.6.265) exclaims Pirithous, and we must agree with all this implies, with the full spectrum from admiration of their
purity of commitment to revulsion at their exhibition-
istic machismo.

It is left to Theseus, the legendary embodiment of the
heroic life, to sanction the kinsmen's noble values by
the solution he ordains for their dilemma. Of course,
they must engage in a chivalric encounter, but they
must find "three fair knights" to fight along with them.
The winner "shall enjoy her; the other lose his head,
/ And all his friends" will also be executed (3.6.296-
97). The Spartan harshness of the *four* executions
does not, significantly, derive from Chaucer: its invention is one of the clearest signs that the play is viewing
the honor code skeptically and, perhaps, is supporting
King James's recent decree (1613) against dueling.
When Emilia hears the admiring descriptions of the
cavaliers, whose extravagant sense of noblesse oblige
has made them partners in her lovers' fight, she underlines the outlandish stringency of the conditions:
"Must these men die too?" (4.2.112). Fletcher's Emilia
is consistent with Shakespeare's portrayal—soft-hearted,
gently questioning the harsh tenets of her civilization—
but even her sister, the Amazonian warrior Hippolyta,
notes the disproportion between the stakes and the
penalty. Such a group of men as those pledged to
fight, she says, "would show / Bravely about the titles
of two kingdoms. / 'Tis pity love should be so tyrannous" (4.2.144-46). Both love and her husband are
pitiless and tyrannous, and thus in their world of
"must's," she acknowledges, "It must be" (148). A
comment in the subplot wryly makes the same point
about courtly values. Asked whether Theseus' conditions for settling Palamon and Arcite's differences are
"good," someone comments, "They are honorable, /
How good they'll prove, I know not" (4.1.29-31).
Honorable behavior is not automatically "good."

This is not the only connection between the subplot
and the main plot. Comprising about 20 percent of the
play, with no basis in "The Knight's Tale" and attributed almost completely to Fletcher, this nearly independent story of the pathetic fortunes of the Jailer's
Daughter makes a powerful judgment about heroes
who live their lives on the high wire. Like her father's
captives, she, too, has contracted a passion—a hopeless one in her case because of her social position—
for Palamon. In a succession of soliloquies alternating
with the main plot, we hear that her love is an un-
quenchable sexual hunger: "O for a prick now, like a
nightingale, / To put my breast against" (3.4.25-26).
Eventually she goes mad out of sexual frustration.
After much Victorian prudery about the sort of "trash"
we would expect of the lubricious Fletcher, this sub-

plot and particularly the character of the Daughter have come to be appreciated in recent years as stage-worthy and moving: "Infinitely more interesting than Ophelia. A terribly credible character for us, now," according to the distinguished British actress Imogen Stubbs who played the Daughter in the 1986 Royal Shakespeare Company production at the Swan Theatre.[12]

The Daughter's scenes are counterpointed to ones showing Palamon and Arcite's rivalry, the mad helplessness of animalistic love being set against the mad automatism of courtly love. It is unclear which is worse for humans: to be subdued by one's senses or by one's "godlike" aspirations. But Fletcher exploits the contrast in another way by showing the world of difference between the treatment of love madness in the cousins' heroic, and the Daughter's pastoral, worlds. In 3.5, just before Theseus' harsh but equable solution to the noble kinsmen's problem, we are shown the Daughter's humane return to society and her family. She has been aimlessly wandering around the countryside in search of Palamon and is suddenly spotted by a troop of country folk—they call themselves "mad boys" (3.5.24)—who in the manner of *A Midsummer Night's Dream* are preparing a morris dance to entertain Theseus and his court. They are in desperate need of another woman because "Cicely the sempster's daughter" has not appeared. Suddenly they see the Daughter, obviously mad:

> *First Countryman.* A mad woman? We are made, boys!
> *Schoolmaster.* And are you mad, good woman?
> *Jailer's Daughter.* I would be sorry else.
>
> (3.5.76-78)

In her sorry state, madness has been her only protection, but now in an open, unquestioning manner, the Countrymen, mad boys that they are, incorporate her madness into theirs. The morris dance in *The Inner Temple Masque* was so admired by the king that he "called for it againe at the end"; Beaumont intended it to create "a spirit of Countrey jollitie."[13] Perhaps the motive in inserting the dance into the play may have been merely commercial, a much-needed added attraction for the King's Men, reeling from their recent "losses." However, the effect is similar to that of the "bergomask" in *A Midsummer Night's Dream,* its "Countrey jollitie" a healthy madness that momentarily clears the air.

The Jailer's Daughter had seemed destined to play the mad Ophelia, but while we hear of her further sufferings, we never see her alone again and can no longer imagine her destined for a tragic fate. In her next appearance (4.1), just after Theseus has established the bloody conditions that will cure the cousins' mad-

ness and after we hear her "Wooer" describe how he saved the Daughter from drowning, she enters, as obsessed by Palamon as ever. Now, however, she is back in a warm family circle that literally "humors" her by pretending to be on a ship taking her to Palamon:

> *All.* Owgh, owgh, owgh! 'Tis up! The wind's fair.
> Top the bowling! Out with the mainsail!
> Where's your whistle, master?
> *Brother.*   Let's get her in.
> *Jailer.* Up to the top, boy!
> *Brother.*   Where's the pilot?
> *First Friend.*   Here.
> *Jailer's Daughter.* What ken'st thou?
> *Second Friend.*   A fair wood.
> *Jailer's Daughter.*   Bear for it, master.
> Tack about!   *Sings.*
> "When Cynthia with her borrowed light," etc.
>
> (4.1.147-53)

The family's frantic, desperate "play therapy" offers a uniquely moving moment in Jacobean drama.

But it is the manner in which Fletcher has the Daughter's madness cured that best distinguishes two rhythms of life, two kinds of civilization. The family's doctor sees that the Daughter's trouble is "not an engraff'd madness, but a most thick and profound melancholy" (4.3.48-50). The symptom being a kind of schizophrenia, he prescribes a form of therapy that has adherents today. The family must enter her fantasy world and act the parts she assigns them: "It is a falsehood she is in, which is with falsehoods to be combated" (4.3.93-4). This may involve actions that under ordinary circumstances would be considered immoral. Her old "wooer" must *play* the part of Palamon:

> *Doctor.* . . . do any thing,
> Lie with her, if she ask you.
> *Jailer.*   Ho there, doctor!
> *Doctor.* Yes, in the way of cure.
> *Jailer.*   But first, by your leave,
> I'th' way of honesty.
> *Doctor.*   That's but a niceness.
> Nev'r cast your child away for honesty.
> Cure her first this way, then if she will be honest,
> She has the path before her.
>
> (5.2.17-23)

After the father leaves, this amoral medical empiricist repeats his contempt for the Jailer's unscientific, moralistic qualms: "You fathers are fine fools. Her honesty! / And we should give her physic till we find that—" (5.4.28-29). At the very moment when the climactic battle between the forces of Palamon and Arcite is in preparation—"the noblest sight / That ev'r was seen" (5.2.99-100)—the Wooer, pretending to be Palamon, is preparing to take the Daughter to bed. The "therapy" works, and we hear that the cured Daughter is planning to marry her faithful lover. "Honesty," meaning (as often for Beaumont and Fletcher) unthinking adherence to unnatural precepts, is a "niceness" like love unto death; it is a concern of the heroic world.[14] For the rest, those who do not aspire to "nobility" or godhead, it is enough to satisfy natural appetites and keep the noiseless tenor of their way.

The structure of *The Two Noble Kinsmen* is unusual in that a double plot, largely Fletcher's, is enfolded by Shakespeare's contribution. Only rarely is he concerned with plot or character development. While Fletcher dramatized a contrast between "kinds" of humans, Shakespeare wrapped the human predicaments in broader, cosmological implications. At the opening of the play he establishes the martial, chivalric atmosphere of Athens, but he also keeps reminding us of the higher forces that master our destinies, such as, "Th' impartial gods, who from the mounted heavens / View us their mortal herd, behold who err / And in their time chastise" (1.4.4-6), "This world's a city full of straying streets, / And death's the market-place, where each one meets" (1.5.15-16). When Shakespeare resumes control of the action in the fifth act, he once again raises matters to a higher power, particularly in the magniloquent prayers by the combatants to their tutelary deities before the battle. Arcite's to Mars is as spine-tingling as it is bone-chilling. One thrills to the evocation of a power "whose breath blows down / The teeming Ceres' foison; who dost pluck / With hand armipotent from forth blue clouds / The mason'd turrets" (5.1.52-55). Yet intermixed with the rousing tribute to militarism are passages that may seem less attractive to us than they do to Arcite. The god he unreservedly admires "makes the camp a cestron / Brimm'd with the blood of men" (46-47); he "heal'st with blood / The earth when it is sick, and cur'st the world / O' th' plurisy of people" (64-66). Palamon's great prayer to Venus describes her as even more powerful: "What godlike power / Hast thou not power upon?" (5.1.89-90), but (again in seemingly unconscious derogation) what this love goddess inspires in men is behavior that is humiliating, horrid, or disgusting: "sovereign queen of secrets, who has power / To call the fiercest tyrant from his rage / And weep unto a girl" (5.1.77-79); "thy yoke / [is] . . . heavier / Than lead itself, stings more than nettles" (95-97). Finally, Emilia's exquisite prayer is to a Diana whose purity makes her utterly ineffectual amid such brutal powers: "O sacred, shadowy, cold, and constant queen, / Abandoner of revels, mute, contemplative" (5.1.137-38). Emilia desires to remain outside the sexual world (with much good reason, we are made to feel), but against the two supreme powers, she hopelessly realizes, Diana is impotent: "I shall be gather'd" (170).

The bleak conclusion to the play is thus a natural development from the stress Shakespeare has been placing in act 5 on the role of the gods:

> *Theseus.* . . . O you heavenly charmers,
> What things you make of us! For what we
>   lack
> We laugh, for what we have are sorry, still
> Are children in some kind.
>
> (5.4.131-34)

However different the members of the "mortal herd" (1.4.4-6) may appear from ground level, we are all alike, ludicrous, helpless "things." The somber conclusion by Theseus is apparently Shakespeare's last written utterance. Of course, we have no more right to identify Shakespeare with Theseus than we do with Prospero or Leontes, but at this concluding moment the sentiment sounds ominously closer to Gloucester's view of us as "flies to wanton boys" than to that of the Victorian Bard on the heights bidding a serene farewell to us as "precious winners all."

In any case, *The Two Noble Kinsmen* was a collaboration based upon complementarity. Throughout his career Fletcher laughed at mad lovers and overly rhetorical poseurs; questioned the implications of some of the most prominent cant terms of the time, especially "noble"; and viewed critically the inflexibility of the honor code and hence of the duel. Shakespeare, too, had treated such matters, particularly in *Coriolanus,* where his fifty-eight uses of "noble" remorselessly anatomize the entire spectrum of its meanings from "large-spirited" to "fascistic." Here, however, Shakespeare primarily viewed this play about mad lovers from perspectives we expect in his late plays: on earth that of the idealized love of the Emilia-Flavina relationship and above, virtually from their eighth sphere, that of the marble-hearted "heavenly charmers."

Thus we are left with my initial problem, how this play fits into the theatrical offerings of 1613. It was a play produced at the Blackfriars with an "upscale" audience ready to leap upon any possible contemporary allusion and written by the two most prominent playwrights of the time. It was also a play that began with a masque celebrating a royal marriage, that included a much-admired dance from an actual marriage masque for the princess, and that stressed Prince Henry's favorite topics—honor and chivalric values—written amid other theatrical works that directly celebrated the marriage. Such a play obviously has connections to its time and place, to the topics of the day. But what does it say about them? Certainly it is not a clear endorsement nor is it a criticism of Prince Henry, the king, the princess, or the Protestant political agenda. On the other hand, subtly, tangentially, complexly, it does deal with such topics.[15] We are made to thrill at the magnificence and purity of purpose of the worshipers of Venus and Mars in their various manifestations both high and low while laughing at their confusions, their superficiality, and their ultimate impotency. In part, the richness of the play is made possible by the generous inclusiveness of the Elizabethan dramatic form that can contain divergent but overlapping artistic impulses from dissimilar artists. With a clear opportunity to write something that could cater to power, that could flatter and support official doctrine, Shakespeare and Fletcher demonstrated (as was frequently the case in Jacobean drama, *pace* some New Historicists!) the essential independence of the greatest dramatists.[16] With utter indifference to external pressures they sniffed their way all around the issues with no "irritable reaching after fact and reason." Even at the end of his career Shakespeare with much support from his new partner made his old players, as always, "tell all."

Notes

[1] It adapts a dance from a masque of 20 February 1613 by Beaumont, and Jonson alludes to it in 1614. Despite Paul Bertram's powerfully argued claims for Shakespeare's unassisted authorship in *Shakespeare and The Two Noble Kinsmen* (New Brunswick: Rutgers University Press, 1965), I accept the traditional ascription of joint authorship (for which there is much corroboration) first registered in the Stationers' Register in 1634 and on the title page of the quarto of the same year. There is remarkable unanimity of agreement about the authorship of individual scenes: here I follow the Riverside Shakespeare.

[2] See Eugene Waith, ed., *The Two Noble Kinsmen* (Oxford: Clarendon Press, 1989); Glynn Wickham, "The Two Noble Kinsmen, or A Midsummer Night's Dream, Part II?," in *The Elizabethan Theatre VII*, ed. G. R. Hibbard (Papers given at the Seventh International Conference on Elizabethan Theatre, Waterloo, 1977) (Hamden, Conn.: Archon Books, 1980), 167-96; M. C. Bradbrook, "Shakespeare as Collaborator," *The Living Monument* (Cambridge: Cambridge University Press, 1976), 227-41.

[3] *Henry, Prince Of Wales* (London: Thames and Hudson, 1986), 175. Further page references to this book are in the text.

[4] *The Maske of the Inner Temple and Grayes Inne,* ed. Fredson Bowers in Bowers, gen. ed., *The Dramatic Works in the Beaumont and Fletcher Canon* (Cambridge: Cambridge University Press, 1966), 1:128, lines 36-38.

[5] See my *Court and Country Politics in the Plays of Beaumont and Fletcher* (Princeton: Princeton University Press, 1990), 206-11, for a more detailed discussion of the masque and Beaumont's politics.

[6] Ibid., 41-42, 255-58.

[7] All quotations are from Stanley Wells and Gary Taylor, eds., *William Shakespeare: The Complete Works* (Oxford: Oxford University Press, 1986). I insert without notice some readings from the Quarto (notably 4.1.145) where the Oxford edition's emendation is unnecessary. Some have guessed that "losses" refers to the fire of 1613 that leveled the Globe during a production of *Henry VIII.* Some have suggested that the plural "losses" makes possible a reference to Prince Henry's death; or, I would add, to Beaumont's stroke or to the 1613 death of Shakespeare's last surviving brother Richard.

[8] *Coleridge on the Seventeenth Century,* ed. Roberta F. Brinkley (Durham, N.C.: Duke University Press, 1955), 650.

[9] I have been quoting and paraphrasing from Strong, *Henry, Prince of Wales,* 141, 143-44.

[10] See Talbot Donaldson, *The Swan at the Well: Shakespeare Reading Chaucer* (New Haven: Yale University Press, 1985), 67, for a view of Theseus as "untouchable by human feelings." For a radically different view see Waith, *Two Noble Kinsmen,* "the emphasis on pity in the play supports the idealism of the principal characters."

[11] My figures derive from Marvin Spevack, *A Complete and Systematic Concordance to the Works of Shakespeare* (Hildesheim: Georg Olms, 1968-80). The nearest rival, *The Winter's Tale,* has 16 percent fewer "must's." In the 2,350 lines of "The Knight's Tale" "must" occurs only five times.

[12] Ronnie Mulryne, *This Golden Round: The Royal Shakespeare Company at the Swan* (Stratford-upon-Avon: Mulryne and Shewring Ltd., 1989), 110.

[13] "The Maske of the Inner Temple," ed. Bowers, 134.

[14] For an extended justification of this generalization about Beaumont and Fletcher, see my *Court and Country Politics,* esp. chap. 10 on *The Maid's Tragedy.*

[15] The same may be said of the other Shakespeare-Fletcher collaboration sometimes linked, such as in the Arden edition, to the princess's marriage, *Henry VIII.* Balanced against the rehabilitation of Henry VIII at the end and the nostalgic tribute to Queen Elizabeth is pervasive criticism of the governance of a despotic king, an evil counselor, and a corrupt clergy.

[16] I am asserting a position that I argue at length in "The 'Comedians' Liberty': Censorship of the Jacobean Stage Reconsidered," *English Literary Renaissance* 16 (1986): 123-38.

Source: "Two Distincts, Division None: Shakespeare and Fletcher's *The Two Noble Kinsmen* of 1613," in *Elizabethan Theater: Essays in Honor of S. Schoenbaum,* edited by R. B. Parker and S. P. Zitner, University of Delaware Press, 1996, pp. 184-99.

Other Voices: The Sweet, Dangerous Air(s) of Shakespeare's *Tempest*

Jacquelyn Fox-Good, *Illinois Institute of Technology*

Most recent criticism of *The Tempest* has insisted upon the play's "worldliness," its status as a production of an imperial culture that was—at just the time (1611) the play was written and first performed—colonizing islands like the one Prospero inhabits and subjecting natives like Caliban. As is now quite familiar, these readings foreground the play's ideological and historical contexts, which have both "written" the play and "been written" by it. This emphasis is a crucial value of this approach, which must be seen, at least, as an interrogation of the long-dominant "idealist readings" of the play and of Prospero "as an exemplar of timeless human values," of the "profit" of language, "civilization," forgiveness, all of which finally achieve (in this humanist vision) "a *harmoniously* reconciled new world" (italics mine).[1]

"Harmony" (and related musical metaphors like "concord" and "resolution") occur frequently in such humanist readings, and may even epitomize—by virtue of their "idealism" and apparent "aestheticism"—the kinds of assumptions most subject to ideological critique. According to a colonialist reading, interpreting the play with such metaphors amounts to complicity in the play's strategic "effacement" and "euphemisation" of Prospero's power. Paul Brown, whom we might take as representative of the colonialist position, argues that *The Tempest's* music mystifies and thus tacitly justifies Prospero's power over his subjects, drawing an aesthetic veil over his colonial "project." According to Brown, the play's use of "harmonious music to enchant, relax, and restore," along with its "observation of the classical unities" and its "constant reference to pastoral," underline the play's "aesthetic and disinterested, harmonious and nonexploitative representation of power."[2]

It is *The Tempest's* music that I wish to foreground and investigate in this essay, and it seems useful to begin by noting that music has been rendered subordinate by the two most prominent threads of critical treatment of the play. Humanism conflates "harmony" and music with social "concord" and reconciliation; new historicist/materialist readings make the same conflation but are critical of it, regarding music in its presumed "aestheticism" as a colonialist tool for masking and reproducing the dominant discourse.

At the heart of both arguments lies a naive claim about music, one that has only recently come under scrutiny, even within the academic study of music, where one might expect to find such scrutiny under-

taken. Susan McClary, a musicologist who has been at work to develop a feminist criticism of music, would say that it is *especially* within the academic disciplines of music scholarship (history, theory, ethnomusicology) that such scrutiny has failed to develop, the result of tight "disciplinary" and ideological "control" over the study of music.[3] Until very recently, none of these disciplines within music scholarship had seriously raised any questions about musical signification.[4] Music has been analyzed structurally, its "history" told chronologically and positivistically, but it has generally been assumed to float free of its historical contexts, to be transhistorical, transcendent (a "universal language"), so meaningful as to be inscrutable, meaningless.

These assumptions about Western music in general have of course been manifest in criticism of music in Shakespeare. The "reading" (hearing) of Shakespeare's music that I shall argue for in this essay developed initially as a response to the inadequacy of the critical response to Shakespeare's music that has prevailed—in literary criticism and music scholarship—for most of this century. A brief outline of these responses will suggest not only the critical context for my own argument but will reveal some of the assumptions (or failure to recognize assumptions) that this essay will critique. Music—and particularly music in drama—has been insufficiently theorized; I will offer some theoretical observations here, using them as the basis for some new ways of hearing Shakespeare's music, particularly in *The Tempest*.[5]

Shakespeare's music has by no means been ignored; it has, rather, long been the topic of much literary and music scholarship. In addressing music in Shakespeare, however, *literary* critics have made two basic errors. First, they have regarded Shakespeare's songs not as music but chiefly as poems, more noticeable, perhaps, but as mainly continuous with Shakespeare's *written* texts. Shakespeare's songs are routinely anthologized as poems; if the *music* of the songs appears at all in printed editions of the plays it generally does so only in appendices. Critics who avoid this first difficulty usually fall into the second: they consider the songs as music, but music not enacted but abstracted, as an *idea,* and one that always connotes or symbolizes essentially the same things or performs the same function. The materiality of music dissolves, is made to point to a transcendent signified. Thus W. H. Auden, in an influential interpretation, says Shakespeare uses instrumental music "as an auditory image of a supernatural or magical world."[6] Similarly, music is often said to denote a feeling like joy or peace or, most commonly, a concept metaphorically associated with music. This concept is summarized in the word "harmony" (variously articulated, as in musical/spiritual/political/social/cosmological harmony) and sometimes appears in other terms that employ musical metaphors, such as personal "resolution" and social "concord." Thus in a 1965 book, Clifford Leech concludes that the music of Feste's final songs in *Twelfth Night* counteracts its "negative" images ("tosspots and their drunken heads"). Although the song offers, he says, a "painful narration," "we leave the theatre with a tune in our ears, and the harmony of *Twelfth Night* is after a fashion maintained."[7]

It is this simplistic equation of music with "harmony" that enables different critics to offer virtually identical comments about different songs in different plays. A song's words may be about happiness, sadness, love or pain or loss, but such states are invariably either undercut or reinforced by the song's always "harmonious" music. Thus, Charles Frey, writing nearly twenty years after Leech, can say that all the songs in *As You Like It*

> are dialectical in that, on the one hand, against leisure and love, they admit rough weather and faithlessness but, on the other, they are all occasions for merriment. . . . Despite winter, feigning friendships, foolish loves, the songs insist [partly through their "lyric art"] that "This life is most jolly. . . . "

Frey sees the centrality of song in the play as one aspect of its larger movement toward reconciliation, the "possibility of *harmonizing* a shifting of likings" (italics mine).[8]

Interpreting Shakespeare's music as a univocal symbol, frequent in response to the comedies, has been even more insistent in response to the last plays, where the significance of "harmony" appears to expand from the social into the supernatural realm, and where music on stage is heard as "music of the spheres," the earthly register of divinity. As Shakespeare's "most musical" play, *The Tempest* is clearly the best case in point. G. Wilson Knight found in the play the key polarities around which he organized his long-influential book, *The Shakespearean Tempest* (1932). In all of Shakespeare's plays, he argues, the tempest (symbolizing disorder) opposes music (symbolizing order), which is invariably "harmonious" and "positive."[9] In a 1958 essay, John P. Cutts, a major contributor to the scholarship on music in Shakespeare, particularizes this view: *The Tempest's* music is "equivalent to music of the spheres" heard on a "golden-age island. . . . , where strife and friction are allayed and everything is wrapped in a serene air of celestial harmony."[10] As David Lindley has pointed out more recently, despite

the general revaluation of *The Tempest* which has seen the older view of it as a celebration of reconciliation replaced by a critical consensus stressing its inconclusiveness, ambiguity and doubt, the music has consistently been accepted as imaging and enacting ideals of harmony and concord, whether or not those ideals are finally attained.[11]

As I have already suggested, little has changed in what there is of *music* scholarship on Shakespeare, either. The major contributors mainly emphasize bibliography and history, about which they have provided much crucial information (about sources, manuscripts, instrumentation, use in the theater), but they offer limited and relatively unsophisticated commentary on music's dramatic function within the plays.[12] Critics who strive for a more interdisciplinary approach, a more markedly "literary" criticism of the play's music, take so broad a view that they are unable to say much in detail about particular songs or plays.[13]

Against the view of Shakespeare's music as transhistorical, transcendent, univocal, more signified than signifying, more soul than body, I take a different theoretical approach. This approach is informed by a body of related theoretical work: by Roland Barthes's theories of signification in music and, more fundamentally, by the response of French feminism and post-colonialism to music as (an)other discourse, a language constituted in the "wild zone" occupied by a "muted" group (that of the female or racial other).[14] The view I develop here has partly derived from but also suggests a reading of *The Tempest*. It presents a new way of understanding the effects of its music and also of assessing several of the play's most problematic aspects, including the extent of Prospero's power and his relation to Ariel and Caliban.

In basic outline, my premises are these. Music is, in general, a construction of (and itself participates in constructing) the sociocultural order of which it is a part. It is, in complex ways, representational, and by means (style, texture, harmony, rhythm) that can be described, although such description should not be *reductive,* should not give the impression that music is transparent or can be "fixed" by the word. Thus I presuppose not that music *expresses* feeling but that it is "expressive of it."[15] Such feeling as music is expressive of is affiliated, especially in the Renaissance, with specifically *sexual* feeling, desire, eroticism, the body. Music, particularly vocal music, gathers this expressiveness in part from its mode of production, which may be writing but is mainly performance, *embodiment.* Music's expressive capacity is inflected, moreover, by a range of contexts, a range that must obviously be extended when music is heard within a nonmusical ("literary") text.

These premises can be distilled to two essential emphases: first, music's materiality, its sounds, and second, music's expressive capacities. These suggest to me that music is a "signifying process," in Julia Kristeva's complex sense, a sense useful in this context because Kristeva invokes music in order to articulate it. That is to say: Music must itself be regarded as a kind of "language"—subject to the Law of the Father, to what Kristeva calls (following Lacan) the Symbolic Order. Yet music, nevertheless, more nearly approximates (and is more porous, more open to) the instinctual drives organized in/by the semiotic order, or the *chora,* which is nonverbal, prelinguistic, *non-expressive,* "full of movement," yet articulated, "regulated" by the body of the mother.[16] Kristeva borrows *"chora"* (Gk. for "enclosed space" or "womb") from Plato (*Timaeus*), but the word of course also bears musical associations ("chorus"; "chord") with it; Kristeva defines the *chora* partly by analogy *with* music: "the *chora* is analogous only to vocal or kinetic rhythm."[17] Music, then, does not "float" in an endless play of signifiers, nor does it simply point to a transcendent signified. Rather, it (especially vocal music) *passes through* a voice, a body, one shaped and constructed—like music itself—by dramatic, political and cultural contexts.

The music that "passes through" the "air" of *The Tempest* helps explain why anyone who has seen even a mediocre performance of the play has felt what can be loosely described as its "atmosphere." Indeed, reference to this atmosphere, and attempts to characterize it, amount to something like a standard feature of *Tempest* criticism, especially in its precolonialist phase. Hazlitt wrote that the play "had the wildness of a dream";[18] Coleridge called it "this almost miraculous drama"[19]—a mood captured more recently by Michael Goldman in the play's own language, as the "strange and wonderful *Tempest.*"[20] Colonialist readings of the play also acknowledge these qualities, although of course not to valorize but to expose them, as part of a "strategy by which sovereign power might at once be praised and effaced as *power* in a colonialist discourse."[21]

"Atmosphere"—dreamlike, magical, and thereby either wonderful or tyrannical or the latter by means of the former—is central to the experience of this play, and music is, and was for Shakespeare, too, one of the essential means of *producing* that atmosphere. As is well known, Shakespeare's stage, although it relied on various means of visual representation (costume, properties) employed little or no scenery, so that what one "saw" depended a great deal on what one heard in the "infinite variety" of Shakespeare's language. Music must have been for Shakespeare a highly effective means of dramatizing the atmosphere *The Tempest* requires. At court, where the play was first performed in 1611, he certainly possessed the means of producing the music

he wished to use.[22] More importantly, he could use music to give to his play's atmosphere a more material presence than his flexible stage or his language alone could provide, yet not so much materiality as to limit or falsify what the language did want audiences to imagine.

In any case, considering music in its theatrical context requires an emphasis on its materiality. As I have already made clear, however, what has been advanced, instead, has been its supposed transcendence and immateriality. To some extent, this view has followed from the fact that for the Elizabethans, music *was,* at least in part, "transcendent." It functioned as a potent symbol, a component of the complex ancient traditions of Plato and Pythagoras and later of Boethius. These traditions do read music as harmony, within and between the heavens ("music of the spheres"), the elements (*musica mundana*), and the body and soul (*musica humana*) and as possessing—by means of its connection to the divine—emotional effects and curative powers.[23]

But *The Tempest* radically deconstructs this kind of musical symbolism by several means, which I shall explore in the middle sections of this essay. It does so, first, through the particular ways in which characters and stage directions refer to and describe music in the play; secondly, through the play's actual songs (words and music);[24] third, by means of the space music occupies in the text; and finally, through the broad, often contradictory range not just of philosophical meanings but also of sociocultural constructions and practices of music. These meanings still resonate for twentieth-century listeners and have been articulated and deepened by post-structuralist theory, particularly by the responses of French feminism (especially those of Kristeva and Hélène Cixous) to music and song.

There is indeed much music in *The Tempest,* including Stephano's "scurvy tunes" (2.2.45-52) and Caliban's freedom song (2.2.175-182),[25] Ariel's "songs" (2.1.375-87; 397-406), his "solemn music" (2.1.183) and "music and song" (2.1.298), and his tune played on tabor and pipe (3.3.123); the singing of goddesses (4.1.106-17); various instances of "solemn" and "strange music" (2.1.183; 3.3.22) or "soft music" (3.3.83 and 4.1.58) or "heavenly music" (5.1.52). Much of the music comes to the human characters mysteriously; they hear it distinctly but often cannot say where it originates. The characters do, however, suggest how the music *sounds:* it seems frequently, as in Ariel's first song ("Come Unto These Yellow Sands") to come "dispersedly," from all over the stage/island (1.2.382, 384), eliciting Ferdinand's questions: "Where should this music be? I'th'air, or i'th'earth?" (1.2.388-89). The characters frequently describe the island's music simply as "sound" (1.2.406) or "noise" (2.1.324) or "humming" (2.1.315). Caliban's description is the most memorable and expressive: "Be not afeard," he tells Stephano and Trinculo,

> the isle is full of noises,
> Sounds, and sweet airs, that give delight
>   and hurt not.
> Sometimes a thousand twangling instruments
> Will hum about mine ear; and sometime
>   voices,
> That if I then had waked after long sleep,
> Will make me sleep again, and then in
>   dreaming
> The clouds methought would open and
>   show riches
> Ready to drop upon me, that when I waked
> I cried to dream again.
>
>   (3.2.140-48)

Caliban's description is elusively suggestive, but at least one thing it should make clear is that *The Tempest*'s music is not simply, as so many have said, harmonious, the "very symbol of order."[26] For one thing, this conclusion would seem to require that the play end with a consort (or some similar enactment of "harmony"). It does not; indeed, for so musical a play, music is apparently absent at its close. But even if these distinctions between "harmony" or "concord" and "discord" are not pressed into claims about the play's harmonious ending, they remain too simple to account for the felt experience of music in the play. The island's music is pleasing, "marvelous sweet," (3.3.19) and often "harmonious" (4.1.119); it frequently crystallizes into recognizable forms—"ditties," tunes," and "solemn airs." The pun spoken by Ferdinand and by Caliban—"sweet airs"—connects music in the form of "airs" with the air itself. Thus, the island's music is in part what makes Adrian feel that "the air breathes upon us here most sweetly" (2.1.49), and this sweet "air" can also assume the shape of "airs," the songs Ariel sings and the "solemn music" Prospero sometimes commands. Yet the play's music is chiefly characterized not by order but by *dispersion*. Most often, it is not orchestrated or given form; rather, it is everywhere, seeming to constitute the very air of the island.

What makes music, especially song, a medium particularly suited for these effects of dispersion, shiftiness, explosiveness is suggested in Roland Barthes' discussion of singing (music and language) in his "The Grain of the Voice" (1972) and *The Pleasure of the Text* (1973). In trying to conceive an "aesthetic of textual pleasure," Barthes invents a category he calls "writing aloud," which is "not expressive" (not, that is, in the "service of communication, representation") but is carried by the "*grain* of the voice," an "erotic mixture of timbre and language." What Barthes hears in the grain is "the articulation of the body, of the

tongue, not that of meaning, of language," but of materiality and sensuality. In such "writing"/hearing, the signified is "shifted" a great distance, and the "anonymous body of the actor is thrown into [Barthes's] ear."[27] The grain is, for Barthes, a "dual production" of language and music, and it is just this duality, or rather the *space,* the site where its parts encounter or rub against each other, that produces *significance, jouissance.*[28]

Barthes helps shift attention to the *"playing"* of music, to how it sounds (not to what it "means" or "says") and to how it makes the hearer feel. And as we shall see, this emphasis on the body, on the voluptuousness of the signifiers and the erotic relation between singer and hearer does a great deal to account for our response to the material "sounds and sweet airs" of *The Tempest,* to the music that composes and decomposes itself in the island's "sweet air."

Our response derives not only from the way music is described in the play but from the songs themselves. An excellent example is Ariel's "Full Fathom Five," the play's most famous song and one of only two in the play for which original music survives and which thus allows us to consider its musical effects.

> Full fathom five thy father lies,
> Of his bones are coral made;
> Those are pearls that were his eyes;
> Nothing of him that doth fade,
> But doth suffer a sea-change
> Into something rich and strange.
> Sea-nymphs hourly ring his knell.
>   (Burden) Ding dong.
> Hark, now I hear them, ding dong bell.[29]

The song has been read as a virtual epigraph for the play, a summary of Shakespeare's chief thematic preoccupations, with suffering, change, rebirth.[30] Heard not just as words but as words and music and voice, however, the song has more complex effects. In what follows here, I hope to suggest how the song exemplifies the "dispersed" or multivalent quality that characterizes so much of the play's music, in a way that begins to suggest what the effects of this dispersion might be.

David Lindley has argued that "Full Fathom Five" catches us in a "double response" between our awareness of music's "emblematic significance" in Renaissance drama—its potential for pointing to a Platonic "truth"—and our awareness that the words of the song are *untrue* (Alonso is not really dead). Music symbolizes truth; the song's words are untrue. Thus the song makes us conscious (in Lindley's words) "of the compromise with truth that Prospero's designs necessitate."[31] There is more than doubleness here, however, and it arises not from a contradiction between verbal untruth and musical truth but from the complex interplay of feelings created by the song's words and *actual music*.

Johnson's song begins decisively in G major (with five iterations of the tonic note in the first two measures), lending it a full, open quality not suggestive of trouble or death. Its rhythms move smoothly, not heavily; as its words speak of death, it remains steady and soothing. The song begins also to speak not just of death but of change, and although the effects of this change are to depersonalize and dehumanize Alonso ("father" becomes "bones" become "coral"), they are also to render him beautiful, like pearls, "rich and strange." It is the song's music that *enacts* and seems to provide a medium for this transformation, pulling against the verbal statements of death and stasis (however lovely its forms). It does this by moving within and against its own formal harmonic constraints. In the fourth measure, ("of his bones") the melody seems to be shifting its ground to D, moving from the tonic to a secondary dominant to the dominant ("made" in m. 5), thereby suggesting a brief tonicization of the dominant key (D Major) before the next two measures continue in G. The allusion to D (m. 4) would amount to little, but it recurs; measure 5's "nothing of him," which begins in G, then again suggests D major, this time more strikingly (by means of the sharp-# in the melody). The more substantial shift here creates the expectation that the song has modulated to the dominant key, a modulation that coincides with the apotheosis of Alonso into coral and pearls. The song's next section (m. 10-18) begins again in G, but then introduces chords that sound, especially to modern ears, first like part of G but then like C Major.[32] What results, however it is described, is a striking harmonic change, even more so because it sounds at precisely the moment that Ariel sings of suffering a "sea change."

The music of "Full Fathom Five" partly enacts, and so elaborates, interprets, and extends the song's words; but it also pulls against them—that is, it differentiates the experience of the song from its words alone. Although both words and music make "assertions" about death and transformation, the words seem to define transformation primarily as what moves us from bones to coral, eyes to pearls, what precedes or leads us from death to another kind of finality. But the music seems rather to catch us up in the process of transformation, as something opposed to finality, as an "end" (without end) in itself, and not merely as a means to an end. The song's music does not refer to or summarize "sea change" but rather enacts it (melodically/harmonically) involving the hearer in that process with more immediacy.[33]

The song's words and music can be said to create a multivalence of feeling that is not resolved (something Coleridge called a "hovering between images"), sus-

pending us in a gap, of the kind Barthes seems to have in mind when he writes of "displacing the fringe of contact between music and language."[34] The song's words emphasize death, intensify and beautify its finality; its music enacts transformation, change, possibility. "Full Fathom Five" sings about "sea change"; it is itself, by means of its music, a kind of sea change, inhabiting a middle realm, in neither air nor earth, but in the sea Ariel is singing about—a liminal, fluid, shifting medium with continuous potential for change and rebirth.

This hearing of music as "dispersed," even fragmented, as a locus of instability, complicates significantly the account of music's function in *The Tempest*. First, it particularizes the point I have already made about music's offering Shakespeare a means to constitute his play's "atmosphere." The play's particular *kind* of music, which is "dispersed" and "humming" and then takes formal shape as an "air" or "ditty," is one powerful reification of a world in which all manner of things—spirits, banquets, goddesses—take shape and then disperse, seem present then absent, appear and disappear at will.

The will in question, of course, is presumably that of Prospero, for whom music also serves a complex function. The play's "humming" sometimes seems an externalization of the "beating" (4.1.164) of Prospero's mind. Beyond this, many have regarded the play's music chiefly as the expression and the instrument of Prospero's power. This seems a curious statement, however, for although he sometimes "commands" or "requires" music, Prospero never performs or sings it himself. And although this might be taken as more evidence of his mastery (his power to enslave others to perform his "work(s)"), it nevertheless means that music is not wholly identified with him, but inhabits a separate space, possesses, perhaps, a separate "identity."

It does so by two means. First, the songs, as music, possess a substantive difference from the verbal text that surrounds them. This difference frequently generates the impression that songs and music exist in the margins (or between the lines) of this and others of Shakespeare's plays. (Music did often serve in medieval and early modern drama as or as part of an "interlude.") This effect is powerfully reinforced by the marginal status of those who usually sing: in his earliest plays, Shakespeare usually brings on stage singers who serve only that role, who are not characters more fully implicated in his plots. Even later, as this practice begins to shift, songs are still more frequently sung by "others"—by women (Desdemona, Ophelia), fools (Lear's, Touchstone, Feste), spirits (Puck, Ariel), servants/slaves (Caliban). It is in part this marginality that enables these voices to exert the pressure of critique, even subversion, against the dominant even oppressive "central" figures in these plays (Othello/Lear/Prospero, for example). What results is a "marginal discourse"; *The Tempest*'s music, dispersed, fluid, marginal, approximates Kristeva's conception of the semiotic *chora,* a conception that can further clarify its function, especially in relation to Prospero. Music is "a *jouissance* which breaks the symbolic chain, the taboo, the mastery," which resists, finally defies, Prospero's attempts (in the drama that often seems his monologue) to appropriate, control, or repress it.

Yet Shakespeare's music gathers subversive energy not only from its marginal position in the text but also from the fact that it *is* music, given the way in which music's substance and meaning have been so consistently constructed in the Western tradition. In this construction we can glimpse one reason that Shakespeare's singers are female or feminized—for song and music are themselves thought to be of a "feminine nature." As Susan McClary and others have observed, Western music shares with women a social construction of "irrationality" and the either divine (ineffable) and/or bestial (mad, unreasonable, or unreasoning) status which that irrationality confers. Such irrationality, of course, is irrevocably bound to the body, making music, like women, dangerously erotic and seductive.

This bond between music, women, and the body was especially strong and explicit in the English Renaissance. Recent Renaissance scholarship has become increasingly interested in sixteenth-and seventeenth-century Puritan anti-theatrical tracts, full of warnings about the dangerous seductiveness of the theatres, which were rife with eroticism and seductive temptations to sin—off stage, in an audience that included women, and on stage, in boy actors whose female disguises violated biblical injunctions against cross-dressing and titillated male viewers with a disturbing homoerotic appeal.[35]

But additionally, these writers regarded the theaters as the sites of *numerous* moral dangers—"dicing, dancing, plays, and interludes"[36]—and of those who performed them—"poets, pipers, players and jesters."[37] Among these dangers, music may have posed the most insidious threat, because it possessed, in Stephen Gosson's characterization, for example, the most "goodly outside." For Gosson, music's beauty and its "right use" reside in a Platonic idea[l] which has become disfigured in the process of "descending," both epistemologically (from essence to existence) and historically (from ancient purity to modern "abuses"). Regarding epistemology: they who wish to profit well in the "arte of musicke" will not debase it (or themselves) by wrenching it from the metaphysical into the physical realm, but "shut [their] fidels in their cases and looke up to Heaven":

the order of the spheres, the infallible motion of the planets, the juste course of the yeere, the varietie of the seasons, the concorde of the elements and their qualities . . . concurring together to the constitution of earthly bodies, and sustenaunce of every creature.[38]

And regarding history: the ancients (Chiron, Homer, Apollo) practice "right musicke," "perfect harmony";[39] the moderns have broken the ancient rules, exceeded all bounds, "coin[ed] strange precepts."[40]

To represent the fall of music Gosson introduces the example of "Phaerecrates, a comicall poet," who personifies (modern) Musicke as a woman "with her clothes tattered, her fleshe torne, her face deformed, her whole bodie dismembered." When Justice asks her "howe she came in that plight," she replies that

Melanippides, Phrynis, Timotheus and such fantastical heads had so disfigured her lookes, defaced her beautie, so hacked her and hewed her, and with many stringes given her so many woundes, that she is stricken to death, in daunger to peryshe.[41]

The figure itself (of music as woman), along with the rape implied by its use in this passage, suggests the dense matrix within which music and woman are bound, including of course the "woman's part[s]," both her sexuality and her emotion. First, music is itself a temptation, especially to women, for whom Gosson expresses particular concern, not only because "[they] are citizens," but also "because [they] are weake."[42] In one part of the book, Gosson directly addresses the "gentlewomen" in his audience, for fear that in going to the theater, they will be corrupted, seduced, lose "credit."[43] Yet "woman" is simultaneously endangered, ("weake") and the danger itself. She is the hearer whom music can tempt, and she is Music "herself," a repository of ideal virtue and beauty that has been "defaced," ravished *because* it/she is beautiful. That which chiefly defines, gives value to woman—her sexuality—makes her, at once, powerless (able to be seduced) and dangerously powerful (able to seduce and destroy virtue, including her own). Women and "female nature" or qualities, then, are not just likened to but located within the deadly, seductive center of music, which thereby becomes as well, both effeminate and feminizing. "Plutarch complayneth," reports Gosson,

that ignorant men, not knowing the majestie of auncient musicke, abuse both the eares of the people, and the arte it selfe, with bringing sweet comfortes into the Theaters, which rather *effeminate the mind* as prickes unto vice, then procure amendement of maners as spurres to vertue (italics mine).[44]

Thus in what Barthes calls the "grain"—"the body in the voice as it sings, the hand as it writes, the limb as it performs"[45]—and in which he takes his (erotic) pleasure, these Renaissance moralists also feel this physical, sexual power. But they account it, like "Woman," dangerous.

In *The Tempest* this context lends additional significance to Ferdinand's response to Ariel's first songs. As so often in Shakespeare, the death (symbolic or real) of a parent permits the transfer and transformation of a character's affection to a lover, involving, not least of course, the awakening of sexual desire. Ariel's songs, especially "Full Fathom Five," are both the occasion and the impetus for this awakening in Ferdinand, an awakening that is polarized, like music, between the divine and the sensual. The song seems at first to "allay" his "passion," leading him to think it is "no mortal business" (1.2.406) and that Miranda is "the goddess / On whom these airs attend": but it also incites (or least coincides with) his sexual desire for Miranda, his "wondering" about her status not only as a goddess but also as a mortal, sexual being, a "maid" and a "virgin" (1.2.448).

More significantly, despite the impression the *text* may give that the play's songs are sung by a disembodied voice (an "invisible" Ariel), they are, rather—in performance—nearly always sung by the "airy spirit" that the audience *can* see. (M. C. Bradbrook notes the use on the Elizabethan stage of special costumes to signify a character's invisibility[46]; in my own experience of seeing performances of this play, attempts to make Ariel more "spiritlike" or "airy"—by costuming him in dance leotards or see-throughy gauze—usually produce the contrary effect, of making him seem all the more *physical* and *bodily*.) In any case, the overall result is that nearly all of *The Tempest*'s songs are sung not by a disembodied but by an *embodied* voice; and the body is that of an "asexual boy,"[47] or, rather, of a body whose indeterminate gender feminizes "him,"[48] affiliates him more nearly with the female body.[49] What strengthens this affiliation, as Orgel observes, is that all the roles played by Ariel (for Prospero) are feminine ones: sea nymph, harpy, Ceres.[50]

This means that the songs and music in this play occupy not just a textual but also a physical, even sexual space, one that is separate and also different from the space occupied and controlled by Prospero. Although music may appear to be an expression and instrument of Prospero's power and is one of the many things he attempts to "require" (5.1.51) control, and command,[51] music and sound exceed his grasp, constitute a significant constraint upon, even a subversion of his considerable power. We may further understand the workings of this process by two means, which are linked in the way that both have been used, especially by recent readers and rewriters of *The Tem-*

pest, to speculate about what is missing from, suppressed or subjected in the play: the absent mother of Miranda (Prospero's absent wife), and the colonized other (Caliban). For both, music becomes a means of figuring, if in a ghostly, decomposed, "humming" way, what is dead, absent, suppressed, and of giving voice to it, to what remains (like "woman" in Western culture) *outside* representation.[52]

A suggestive way to theorize this connection in *The Tempest* (between music and an apparently absent female or maternal body) is suggested by French Feminism, specifically in Hélène Cixous's account of *l'écriture feminine*. She defines this, in one instance, as writing that privileges the *voice,* whose source is the mother, the maternal body, a *nameless* voice which Cixous nevertheless names as "a song before the Law, before the breath [*le souffle*] was split by the symbolic, reappropriated into language under the [phallogocentric] authority that separates."[53] For Cixous, the song both flows from and *is* the mother's body; this Voice is the fluid(s) that flow from that body: "Voice: inexhaustible milk."[54] This description conjoins the feminized singer of *The Tempest*'s songs with the dispersed, fluid quality of those songs, by which means they become strongly suggestive of what Coppélia Kahn has termed "the maternal subtext" located beneath (or alongside) the "patriarchal structures" on the "surface" of the text. What Kahn locates as the "psychological presence of the mother [in the text] whether or not mothers are literally represented as characters"[55] becomes manifest in *The Tempest* and in Prospero in a number of ways. To be clear, I should emphasize that I speak here not specifically of *Prospero*'s mother (or even only of his wife, whose absence from the play is conspicuous) but in Kahn's more general sense of the Mother, whose psychological, social and biological functions constitute her power, a power patriarchal Renaissance culture sought to control and to bring into the service of lineage and primogeniture.

In this play, Prospero works, in effect, to "reconceive"[56] both his child and himself, by means of appropriating the female (pro)creative act of childbearing, labor, delivery. He praises Miranda for helping him to endure his suffering at sea. "Thou didst smile," he tells her,

> Infused with a fortitude from heaven,
> When I have decked the sea with drops full salt,
> Under *my burden groaned,* which *raised* in me
> An undergoing *stomach,* to *bear up*
> Against what should ensue. (italics mine)
> (1.2.155-58)

Stephen Orgel and Janet Adelman have similarly interpreted Prospero's appropriation, one driven in part by the common suspicion about women's infidelity, which Prospero invokes obliquely in this same scene to assure Miranda that he is her father: "Thy mother," he says, "was a piece of virtue" (1.2.56) It would have been more likely, this implies, that she was not. This anxiety about women's virtue receives its fullest expression in the representation of Sycorax, the play's evil mother, now dead, yet alive in Prospero's memory, an embodiment of "all the negative assumptions about women that he and Miranda have exchanged."[57] Prospero's attempt to become and (as Adelman reads the play) to *control* the Mother,[58] then, depends upon his demonizing and banishing her (as Sycorax) from the island. Kahn, Orgel, and Adelman all address the inevitable failure of such control, but they find this failure at the play's end, when Lear (like Prospero) must weep "women's weapons—water drops" (*King Lear,* 2.4.279) and when Prospero (like Lear) must yield to the "women's emotions"—forgiveness, kindness, "virtue"—that those tears signify. Yet the failure to suppress or control the female, or, rather, her irrepressible power, manifests itself throughout *The Tempest.* Miranda's mother is powerfully absent partly because the Mother is struggling to be present, her presence displaced onto Prospero's childbirth metaphor; fragmented into the "four or five women" that Miranda remembers once "tended [her]" (1.2.47); dissolved into the fluids—tears, tempest, sea—so central to the experience of this play, into the medium of music and song, the maternal voice, that beats and hums in the island's air.

Given this emphasis on the maternal, the most significant song Ariel sings (the original music for which does not survive) and the most significant role he plays may be that of *Ceres* in the masque. Ceres is of course the primal mother, goddess of nature and fertility, who here sings of

Earth's increase, foison plenty,
Barns and garners never empty,
Vines with clust'ring bunches growing,
Plants with goodly burden bowing;
Spring come to you at the farthest,
In the very end of harvest!
Scarcity and want shall shun you;
Ceres' blessing so is on you.

(4.1.110-117)

Ceres is, as Prospero tells Ferdinand, one of the "spirits, which by mine art / I have from their confines called to enact / My present fancies" (4.1.119-20). The interruption of the masque by Prospero's sudden memory of the "beast Caliban"'s "conspiracy" has usually been understood to suggest the failure of Prospero's art to construct a barrier against "reality" or his own failure as he again (as in Milan) becomes too "rapt in secret studies" (1.2.77) to attend to "government" in the political realm.

But Prospero's masque—as it in effect reconstitutes the Mother in the figure of Ceres and in the medium of song—is not dissolved by "outside realities" but from internal pressures: although he "calls" upon Ceres, her power exceeds his rational, artistic control, both the "confines" in which he has held her and the art by means of which he now tries to represent her. She has come to bestow a marriage blessing, yet she also speaks of having undergone precisely the experience that Prospero is here attempting to prevent, partly by means of the masque itself: the seduction and abduction of a daughter, the result in Ceres's case of a "plot" by Venus and Cupid. The word "plot" (4.1.88) uttered by Ceres during the masque is reiterated by Prospero when he refers (as the masque dissolves fifty lines later) to the "plot" of Caliban. The two plots are *linked* by the "beastliness" of appetite, desire and lust. The masque, then, cannot enable Prospero to overcome his anxiety about Miranda's sexuality or to forget Caliban and his conspiracy; rather, it ensures that he remembers them. And what presses in upon Prospero here is less the "plot" itself and more what drives it: the body, which here most obviously assumes the "deformed shape" of the "beast Caliban." The body of the "beast" is linked with that of the female, by this scene, and more fundamentally by *sound.*

The character in the play who most loudly sings against Prospero and his power to suppress or subjugate is the slave Caliban. Rereadings of the play, and various *rewritings* from the point of view of Caliban, have within the last couple of decades made Prospero and Caliban an almost standard trope[59] of colonization, "figures portrayed as self-and-other, the West and the Rest of Us, the rationalist and the debunker, the colonizer and the indigenous."[60] What in the text has given these writers a position from which to respeak or rewrite Caliban's story is in part *his* position in relation to Prospero, who subjects him by means of paternalism, assumptions of racial superiority, linguistic conversion, "art," and violence. Yet although Caliban has learned Prospero's language (his "profit on't is [he] know[s] how to curse"), it is not only within the discourse of colonialism that Caliban can speak. He possesses an(other) language of his own, as well: music. It is Caliban's distinctive sound, the grain of his voice, that empowers him in ways even Prospero cannot subjugate.

Caliban's experience and knowledge of music include not only the "sweet airs" that Ariel sings but also the island's more unmediated pre- and extra-linguistic "sounds" and "noise," the humming of its "twangling instruments," its "voices." It is partly this knowledge of his native place that enables Caliban to exceed the limits or constraints of his subjected status. For Caliban's world thereby possesses what Stephen Greenblatt has called "opacity," Shakespeare's acknowledgement of "independence and integrity" in "Caliban's construction of reality."[61] Greenblatt finds this quality in the words Caliban uses;[62] I locate it, rather, in the *sounds* (among them musical ones) that he makes and that he understands or is "in tune" with.

Caliban's distinctive *sound* is one he possessed when he was "his own king" and that he does not relinquish even when he *knows* Prospero's language, which he then uses in order to curse his master. This sound, then, is clearly separate from Prospero, as seems demonstrated partly by the way in which Caliban plans to overthrow Prospero, not just politically but linguistically—telling Stephano first to "possess his books," the play's metonym not only for Prospero's art and cunning but for language, the word itself. Without Prospero's language, Prospero will be "but a sot as [Caliban is]," but Caliban's sound will persist: after Caliban soothes Stephano's fear of the island's sound, Stephano is pleased to discover that he shall "have [his] music for nothing." "When Prospero is destroyed" (3.3.150-51), replies Caliban. When Prospero is destroyed, music shall remain.

Caliban's sound is thus not merely "opaque" and self-preservative in Greenblatt's sense but is also a sound of protest and resistance, asserting "a potent force . . . that can not be comprehended or controlled by Western philosophy."[63] This last statement is that of Houston Baker, who relies on "the *sound* of Caliban"[64]— for Baker, the first representation of a "vernacular" voice in Western literature—in order to characterize two strategies of expression by African-Americans: "mastery of form" and "deformation of mastery." The first of these depends on the *mask* (a "cryptic" one), a disguise worn to conceal, inside the master's forms, one's political task. Deformation wears a different mask ("phaneric"), "meant to advertise, to *display* in the manner of a go(ue)rilla," whose "deformation is made possible by his superior knowledge of the landscape and the loud assertion of possession he makes."[65] Caliban deforms. He knows, has always known the "form" of his "indigenous vale/veil"[66]: as he reminds Prospero, "I did show thee all the qualities o'th'isle, / The fresh springs, brine pits, barren place and fertile" (1.2.339-41). Caliban's "loud assertions" *sound* alien, but only to intruders, who regard as "crude hooting" what is, in Baker's view, really "racial poetry."[67]

Baker's praise of Caliban's vernacular sound is part of a theoretical polemic that urges the use of African-American vernacular as a means of "deforming," of speaking *outside* and beyond the traditional Western dualism still inscribed in critical discourse. The explicitly political aim of Baker's reading, like that of other postcolonial readings, suggests the *cultural* basis of his theory; in this it differs from the biological or psychoanalytic bases within which French feminists have theorized what is distinctive about the sound of the other. Yet Baker, too, shifts his position toward a

kind of essentialism by asserting the *primacy* of Caliban's sound: Caliban is thus an "instructor in a first voice," in "tune" with "*first* meanings" and "'natural' forms," with sounds that are "truly *foundational*" (italics mine).[68] This formulation recalls Cixous's virtually mythic "song before the law." Both Baker and Cixous over-simplify song and music, which are not merely primal sound, but the oversimplification reveals a more crucial point of connection: both Baker and Cixous wish to identify, or invent, a language of/for the colonized; both discover this (*l'écriture féminine;* "racial poetry") in sound or music. Yet this conception risks confining music's signification to the "natural" in much the way it has long been confined to the "divine." What is needed, again, is to regard music as a signifying process and to listen to the grain of its voice.

By Caliban's "sound," for example, Baker seems chiefly to mean his "hooting" tone and the native knowledge that gives him the confidence for that tone, but there are more precise ways to characterize Caliban's sounds. The one song Caliban sings himself is sung "drunkenly," evoking from Trinculo just the response—"A howling monster! A drunken monster!" (2.2.187)—that Baker argues the "intruders" will have. The original music for this song does not survive, but the song's words and their sounds are both deformational and transformational, creating a song of protest and of freedom.

> *No* more dams I'll make for fish,
> *Nor* fetch in firing
>   At requiring
> *Nor* scrape trenchering, *nor* wash dish
> Ban Ban Ca-Caliban
> Has a new master. Get a new man!

The first four lines assert "no" or "nor" four times; Caliban is refusing to serve and, in the fifth line, to be *named*. He deconstructs his name, fracturing it into its hardest (labial and glottal) sounds and emphasizing the negation and the curse contained in the meaning of "ban." (Caliban's name literally *contains* a curse— "ban," which was used in the Renaissance to mean "to curse" or "to anathematize"[69]—and might therefore be said to *be* a curse—one he here lets loose and so partly frees himself from). In the sixth line, "no/r" becomes, by way of alliteration and near rhyme, "new"; refusal to serve, to be named, to speak the (old) master's language thus begets a "*new* man." For the other, negation of the master and his signs is a form of affirmation. "Freedom, high day!" The song's message of "freedom" becomes comic, of course, given Caliban's expressed intent to "get a new master" (the drunken Stephano). Still, the song's effect, on the events of the play and on Prospero, nevertheless remains disruptive and transformational.

Such disruption is one particular realization of what I have been arguing is music's more general function as a signifying process in *The Tempest:* as, itself, a language that is nevertheless differentiated from the word and thus seems pre- or extra-linguistic and therefore separate from language and, more specifically, from Prospero's rational control. As Caliban most strikingly shows, music exerts pressure on such control, on resolution, especially through its dispersed grain and through its evocation of the body in its most threatening forms, as sexual, as female, as beastly, or deformed.

Because these assertions about the function of music, particularly in *The Tempest,* significantly revise the conventional thinking about Shakespeare's music, it might be sufficient to conclude with them. But the more particular argument here, concerning the "pressure" that music exerts on Prospero, raises questions about consequences: does Prospero respond to or even feel this pressure? Does music's subversive energy participate in any way in the apparent "change" in Prospero at the play's end?

There is no question that Prospero speaks of yielding, in many ways, by the play's end: he chooses "virtue" rather than vengeance (5.1.28); abjures his art and his "book," (5.1.33-57) and is thus left with his "own" "strength" (5.1.320); passes his dukedom to his daughter and Ferdinand even as he repossesses it; contemplates his own death (5.1.311). The first of these shifts, the decision to forgive his enemies, is precipitated by Ariel:

> *Ariel.*   Your charm so strongly works 'em
> That if you now beheld them, your
>   affections
> Would become tender.
> *Prospero.*   Dost thou think so, spirit?
> *Ariel.*   Mine would, sir, were I human.
> *Prospero.*   And mine shall.

This is significant, for it is Ariel that most nearly embodies music as I have been describing it here. The voice of the other makes itself heard, and it seems, finally, to be registered within Prospero in some way. There are other indications of this: in the "female voice" that emerges when Prospero abjures his art, using the words of Medea from Ovid's *Metamorphoses.* And finally, in Prospero's epilogue, spoken in a meter used elsewhere in the play only by Ariel, in his short speech before the masque (4.1.44-45) and in his songs. The meter is catalectic trochaic tetrameter, conveyed in the songs' rhythms by the relatively longer note values accorded to accented beats (as in "Those are pearls that were his eyes.") There is no "heavenly music" or conclusive "harmony" at the play's end; there is only, in the rhythms of the epilogue, vestigial music, suggesting that music's rhythms have in some way left their traces in Prospero's words.

Music compels Prospero to hear it, but it retains, finally, an "other" location in the play. This separation is felt rather keenly in the play's concluding moments, especially in Ariel's last song and in Prospero's final meeting with Caliban. As Prospero "discases" himself, exchanges his magic robe for that of his dukedom, Ariel is once again singing, but not—this time—at Prospero's command:

> Where the bee sucks, there suck I,
> In a cowslip's bell I lie;
> There I couch while owls do cry;
> On the bat's back I do fly
> After summer merrily.
> Merrily, merrily shall I live now
> Under the blossom that hangs on the
>   bough.

(5.1.88-94)

The simultaneity of Prospero's change of "identity" with Ariel's song suggests, on the one hand, that Prospero participates in the music's shifting, transformational energies (its fluidity, his "changing"); on the other hand, it reasserts separation (Ariel sings of nature in which he will soon be free; Prospero re"encases" himself). Ariel's freedom song recalls Caliban's but has moved beyond protest for freedom to what such protest has led to: an unsubjugated *living within* one's native place (with bees, cowslips, an owl's cry, bat's back, blossoms, boughs) and native sounds. "When Prospero is destroyed" (3.3.151) (or removed), music remains, and it remains, like Ariel, in *motion.* The song's words help evoke this sense of movement, by reference to Ariel's flight and to his constantly changing position (from "cowslip" to "bat's back" to "under the blossom"). The song's music—its "lively" tempo, rhythms, harmonies—materializes this movement.

The song's first section moves rapidly between tonic and dominant both within and between phrases, a vacillation that opens up to one of the possibilities within it. (This occurs, for example, in measure 4, in a modulation to the dominant, which has already been used so prominently in relation to the tonic.) The song generates a sense of movement between possibilities that are essentially constituted of the same materials, such that transformation is always immanent (and imminent). In measures 8-10, for example, the chord set to "af" (in "after") can function in either D or G major; we hear a kind of magical transformation take place within it, as one thing becomes another (we hear it first in D, the key in place during the second phrase, and almost at once in G, to which we are returned by the C natural in the chord set to the word's second syllable ["ter"]).

Movement is heightened in the song's second section, partly with a quickened tempo and a shift into a more rapid-seeming triple meter. Moreover, Johnson now takes the harmony more swiftly from one key to the next, beginning again in G, modulating to D, briefly suggesting D minor, then returning to G. These successive and now more rapid movements between tonic and dominant intensify the feeling that the song/singer is opening up, pressing against and breaking out of the established key. This sensation—of energies breaking out—helps realize Ariel's longing for release. And it is this sense of release, a movement *outward,* that resists the play's (and Prospero's) final attempts to maintain control. For although Prospero has relinquished his power in some ways, he seems in others to be reasserting it, shifting to another kind of rational, logocentric control. He predicates his forgiveness, for example, on a decision to "take part with my nobler *reason* 'gainst my fury" (5.1.27-28). He stages the end of his "project," drawing everyone into a circle, an emblem of his wish to make all *one* at the play's end, to incorporate them, to achieve resolution. The wish for such incorporation (related to the urge of the text and perhaps of Shakespeare for comic closure) is manifested in Prospero's taking Ferdinand into the family (thereby also marrying two dukedoms), in the physical "embrace" of Alonso (5.1.109), in the forgiveness (and acceptance, albeit somewhat forced) of Antonio and, most significantly for my purposes, in the "acknowledgment" of Caliban: "This thing of darkness I / Acknowledge mine" (5.1.275-76).

The most benign reading of this line is that Prospero "owns" or owns up to Caliban, in the sense of *admitting* Caliban is part of Prospero's party on the island (not of the ship's, in distinction from Stephano and Trinculo, whom Alonso "must know and own"). He may also of course be testifying that he "owns" Caliban in the economic sense, as his slave, property. The line is frequently read psychologically, as Prospero's acceptance of that within himself (his own "darkness," his destructive, vengeful appetites, especially sexual ones) which Caliban ("misshapen," "demi-devil," "bastard," unregenerate, inhuman "thing") is seen to externalize and embody. (Shakespeare's line break is suggestive here: "This thing of darkness *I/*"). Now, when Caliban speaks, he does not curse, but says he will be "wise hereafter, / And seek for grace" (5.1.294-95). Yet the deformational power of Caliban, the grain of his voice—as this has resonated with the play's dispersed and humming music—continues to resist, to pose its opacity against Prospero's wish to appropriate it.

Shakespeare was never, of course, the only author of his plays: some were clearly written in collaboration; all become collaborative work in the course of theatrical production. In *The Tempest,* "Shakespeare's music" was mainly Robert Johnson's—not wholly outside Shakespeare's artistic control, but nevertheless the work of another. It is tempting to speculate that Shakespeare came increasingly to regard music, which ap-

pears most prominently in the last plays, as a means of figuring that which could not be "figured," that which seemed to him beyond his power to represent: the force of the body, the experience of women, of the alien or the other, the imponderable depths of his "own" physical, sexual, and mortal being, this thing of darkness which he could acknowledge but never really know.

Notes

[1] Meredith Anne Skura, "The Case of Colonialism in *The Tempest," Shakespeare Quarterly,* 40, no. 1 (Fall 1989): 42-69; rpt. in *Caliban,* ed. Harold Bloom (New York and Philadelphia: Chelsea House, 1992), 221-48. Skura's essay contains a useful summary of historical and new historicist approaches to the play, and a well-selected bibliography.

[2] Paul Brown, "'This Thing of Darkness I Acknowledge Mine': *The Tempest* and the Discourse of Colonialism," in *Political Shakespeare: New Essays in Cultural Materialism,* ed. Jonathan Dollimore and Alan Sinfield (Manchester: Manchester University Press, 1985), 64.

[3] Susan McClary, *Feminine Endings: Music, Gender and Sexuality* (Minnesota: University of Minnesota Press, 1991), especially 3-7, and "Reshaping a Discipline: Musicology and Feminism in the 1990s," *Feminist Studies* 19, no. 2 (Summer, 1993): 399-423; see also McClary's earlier essay, her "Foreword: The Undoing of Opera: Toward a Feminist Criticism of Music," introd. to Catherine Clément, *Opera, or the Undoing of Women,* trans. Betsy Wing (Minneapolis: University of Minnesota Press, 1988), ix-xviii.

[4] McClary is not the first from within academic music to make this complaint. Joseph Kerman makes a plea for a real music *criticism,* complaining that musicologists are respected "for the facts they know about music. . . . , not for their insight into music as aesthetic experience" (*Contemplating Music: Challenges to Musicology* [Cambridge: Harvard University Press, 1985], 12-14). For another suggestion about what an "interpretive criticism" of music might be (and a bibliography of works by some who attempted it), see Anthony Newcomb, "Sound and Feeling," *Critical Inquiry* 10 (June, 1984): 614-43. McClary also wants interpretation of music, but of a particular kind, emphasizing ideological and cultural critique. A few recent examples of such work include McClary's *Feminine Endings,* Richard Leppert's *Music and Image: Domesticity, Ideology and Socio-cultural Formation in Eighteenth-Century Music* (Cambridge: Cambridge University Press, 1989), and Rose Subotnik's *Developing Variations: Style and Ideology in Western Music* (Minneapolis: University of Minnesota Press, 1991).

5 The theoretical discussion I present here extends arguments I have made elsewhere, in "Ophelia's Mad Songs: Music, Gender, Power," in *Subjects on the World's Stage: Essays on British Literature of the Middle Ages and Renaissance* (University of Delaware Press, 1995), 332-66, and also in "'Ringtime': Sexual and Musical Play in Shakespeare's *As You Like It*," forthcoming in *Ars Lyrica* (Journal of the Lyrica Society for Word-Music Relations).

6 W. H. Auden, "Music in Shakespeare," in *The Dyer's Hand and Other Essays* (New York: Vintage, 1968), 507.

7 Clifford Leech, *"Twelfth Night" and Shakespearian Comedy* (Toronto: University of Toronto Press, 1965), 55.

8 Charles Frey, "The Sweetest Rose: *As You Like It* as Comedy of Reconciliation," in *Experiencing Shakespeare: Essays on Text, Classroom and Performance* (Columbia: University of Missouri Press, 1988), 20.

9 G. Wilson Knight, *The Shakespearean Tempest* (London: Oxford University Press, 1932). Knight's comments on *Love's Labor's Lost* and *Twelfth Night* typify his overall approach. In the former, the song "When Daisies Pied" moves significantly, he thinks, from spring to winter, "yet song is, nevertheless, music. The pain is dissolved in music" (83). Similarly, in *Twelfth Night,* "all tragic and tempestuous things are finally blended in the music of Feste's final song, with its refrain. . . . Which song presents a microcosm of the play: tempests dissolved in music" (127).

10 John P. Cutts, "Music and the Supernatural in *The Tempest*" (1958); rpt. in *Shakespeare: The Tempest: A Casebook,* ed. D. J. Palmer (London: Macmillan, 1968), 196.

11 David Lindley, "Music, Masque, and Meaning in *The Tempest,*" in *The Court Masque,* ed. David Lindley (Manchester: Manchester University Press, 1984), 47.

12 For history and sources, the two most useful books in this category are Peter J. Seng's standard work, *The Vocal Songs in the Plays of Shakespeare: A Critical History* (Cambridge: Cambridge University Press, 1967) and F. W. Sternfeld's *Music in Shakespearean Tragedy* (London: Routledge and Kegan Paul; New York: Dover, 1963). See also Edward Naylor, *Shakespeare and Music,* rev. ed. (London: Dent; New York: Dutton, 1931) and other work by John P. Cutts, "Jacobean Masque and Stage Music," *Music and Letters* 35 (1954): 185-200; "Robert Johnson: King's Musician in His Majesty's Public Entertainment," *Music and Letters* 36 (1955): 110-25; "An Unpublished Contemporary Setting of a Shakespeare Song," *Shakespeare Survey* 9 (1956): 86-89; "The Original Music of a Song in *2 Henry IV, Shakespeare Quarterly* 7 (1956): 385-92; "A Reconsideration of the 'Willow Song,'" *Journal of the American Musicological Society* 10 (1957): 14-24; ed., *La musique de scène de la troupe de Shakespeare* (Paris: Centre National de la Recherche Scientifique, 1959; rev. 1971). (Cutts has also written on the masque more generally and on Ben Jonson.) John Stevens's book, *Music and Poetry in the Early Tudor Court* (London and New York: Methuen, 1961, 1978) is generally regarded as the standard work on the topic for this period; his "Shakespeare and the Music of the Elizabethan Stage" (in *Shakespeare in Music,* ed. Phyllis Hartnoll [London: Macmillan; New York: St. Martin's, 1964], 3-48) provides a useful summary, particularly of stage practice. Stevens's work falls into the broader category of "studies in poetry and music," of which Louise Schleiner has more recently provided a bibliography in "Recent Studies in Poetry and Music of the English Renaissance," *English Literary Renaissance* 16, no. 1 (Winter, 1986): 253-68.

13 In this category see especially the multi-volume work by John H. Long, *Shakespeare's Use of Music,* 3 vols. (Gainesville: University of Florida Press, 1955-1971), Winifred Maynard's *Elizabethan Lyric Poetry and Its Music* (Oxford: Clarendon Press, 1986), especially chapter five, "Ballads, Songs and Masques in the Plays of Shakespeare" (151-223), and Mary Chan's *Music in the Theatre of Ben Jonson,* with some consideration of Shakespeare (Oxford: Clarendon Press, 1980). The most comprehensive attempt to organize what's known about music and Shakespeare (a connection broadly defined) is the recent *Shakespeare Music Catalogue,* ed. Bryan S. Gooch and David Thatcher (Oxford: Oxford University Press, 1990).

14 This terminology is Edward Ardener's, from "Belief and the Problem of Women," in *Perceiving Women,* ed. Shirley Ardener (New York: Halsted Press, 1978); qtd. in Elaine Showalter, "Feminist Criticism in the Wilderness," in *The New Feminist Criticism: Essays on Women, Literature, and Theory,* ed. Elaine Showalter (New York: Pantheon, 1985), 262-63.

15 This distinction comes from Alan Tormey's *Concept of Expression: A Study in Philosophical Psychology and Aesthetics* (Princeton: Princeton University Press, 1971), 39-40 and 106-110). I owe its application to music to Peter Kivy's important work on musical aesthetics. See especially *The Corded Shell: Reflections on Musical Expression* (Princeton; Princeton University Press, 1980).

16 Julia Kristeva, "The Semiotic *Chora* Ordering the Drives," in *Revolution in Poetic Language,* trans. Margaret Waller, 1974; rpt. in *The Kristeva Reader,* ed. Toril Moi (New York: Columbia University Press, 1986), 93-98.

[17] Kristeva, "The Semiotic Chora," 94.

[18] William Hazlitt, *Characters of Shakespear's Plays,* ed. Ernest Rhys. (London: Dent; New York: Dutton, 1906), 89.

[19] Samuel Taylor Coleridge, "The Ninth Lecture," *Shakespearean Criticism,* vol. 2, ed. Thomas Raysor (London: Dent; New York: Dutton, 1961), 138.

[20] Michael Goldman, *Shakespeare and the Energies of Drama* (Princeton: Princeton University Press, 1972), 137-39.

[21] Brown, 63.

[22] One of Shakespeare's chief resources there would certainly have been the composer of *The Tempest*'s songs, Robert Johnson. There is ample evidence of his connection with the court of James I and the masques and plays that were an integral part of it. The son of John Johnson (a lutanist in Elizabeth's court), Robert Johnson (c. 1582-1633) became a lutanist in James's court in 1604. As John Cutts has detailed, extant settings from 1607-1617 show that during this period, Johnson was writing music continuously for Black-friars' productions of the King's Men ("Robert Johnson: King's Musician," 110). He composed music not only for Shakespeare's plays (Cutts discusses songs from *The Tempest* as well as from other late plays), but also for plays and masques by Jonson, Chapman, Beaumont, Fletcher and Middleton.

[23] For a summary of these ideas about music, see Catherine M. Dunn, "The Function of Music in Shakespeare's Romances," *Shakespeare Quarterly* 20 (1969): 390-405. Mary Chan provides a more thorough account of these ideas in her *Music in the Theatre of Ben Jonson.*

[24] I restrict my discussion of actual music to that which is original—that is, to Robert Johnson's settings of two of Ariel's songs, "Full fathom five" and "Where the bee sucks." (More information on the sources of these songs follows in later notes.) I exclude from discussion a piece that some regard as original to the play: a dance entitled "The Tempest" in a collection of masque music (British Library Add. MS 10444). I side with those who disagree with W. J. Lawrence's assertion (*Music and Letters* 3 [1922]: 49-58) that this music belongs to Shakespeare's play. For a summary of information about this controversy, see Orgel, 221.

[25] All references are to *The Tempest* of the Oxford Shakespeare, ed. Stephen Orgel (Oxford: Oxford University Press, 1987).

[26] Rose Abdelnour Zimbardo, "Form and Disorder in *The Tempest*," *Shakespeare Quarterly* 14 (1963), 50.

[27] Roland Barthes, *The Pleasure of the Text* (1973), trans. Richard Miller (New York: Hill and Wang, 1975), 66-67.

[28] Roland Barthes, "The Grain of the Voice," in *Image, Music, Text,* selected and trans., Stephen Heath (New York: Hill and Wang, 1977), 182, 185.

[29] As Seng reports (257), Johnson's music for "Full Fathom Five" survives in two manuscripts and one collection of songs: in Birmingham City Reference Library MS. 57,316; in Folger Library MS. 747.1 (fols. 9v-13v); and in John Wilson's *Cheerful Ayres or Ballads,* 1660 (sigs. B3v-B4). The Arden edition gives a facsimile of the song as it appears in Wilson's collection (157). For my analysis I have used Ian Spink's edition of the song (reprinted in Orgel's Oxford edition), which appears in Johnson's *Ayres, Songs and Dialogues,* vol. 17 of *The English Lute-Songs,* 2nd ser., 2nd rev. ed. (London: Stainer and Bell, 1974), 24-25.

[30] For a representative article, see "The Mirror of Analogy: *The Tempest*," by Reuben Brower, in *Fields of Light* (New York: Oxford University Press, 1951); rpt. in *The Tempest,* ed. Robert Langbaum (New York: Nal-Signet, 1963), 182-205, esp. 182 and 184-85.

[31] Lindley, 49.

[32] A slightly more technical explanation of what happens here is that the section begins (in m. 10) in G major, then introduces a flatted vii° chord of that key (the diminished F-sharp AC replaces the major FAC). Johnson may have conceived of this as a shift from Ionian to Mixolydian mode, but to modern ears the shift produces for two bars (m. 11-12) what sounds first (in relation to G) like a flatted vii° of G, then like C major (in which FAC is the subdominant chord).

[33] There is, of course, formal, harmonic resolution at the song's end, but I suspect that this is undermined at least in effect by the singing of the burden at the song's end. Johnson's text doesn't indicate this, but the burden may be performed as is indicated by the stage directions for Ariel's first song, "dispersedly", which may mean either not in harmony or not synchronized (i.e., it's not sung by all singers at the same time).

[34] Barthes, "The Grain of the Voice," 181.

[35] Among the most provocative uses of this material is that of Lisa Jardine, Chapter 1 of *Still Harping on Daughters: Women and Drama in the Age of Shakespeare,* 2nd ed. (New York: Columbia University Press, 1989), 9-36; and Madelon Sprengnether, "The Boy Actor and Femininity in *Antony and Cleopatra,* in *Shakespeare's Personality,* ed. Norman N. Holland,

Sidney Homan and Bernard J. Paris (Berkeley: University of California Press, 1989), 191-205.

[36] John Northbrooke, *A Treatise Against Dicing, Dancing, Plays and Interludes With Other Idle Pastimes* (1577), ed. J. Payne Collier (London: Shakespeare Society, 1843).

[37] Stephen Gosson, *The Schoole of Abuse* (1579) (London: Shakespeare Society, 1841).

[38] Gosson, 16.

[39] Gosson, 16.

[40] Gosson, 18.

[41] Gosson, 18.

[42] Gosson, 48. Northbrooke similarly instructs women to absent themselves from plays (95).

[43] Gosson, 48-51.

[44] Gosson, 18-19. Linda Phyllis Austern has done very helpful work on music in relation to women and the feminine in early modern culture. Especially germane in this context are " 'Sing Againe Syren' The Female Musician and Sexual Enchantement in Elizabethan Life and Literature," in *Renaissance Quarterly* 42 (1989): 420-48 and "'Alluring the Auditorie to Effeminacie': Music and the Idea of the Feminine in Early Modern England," in *Music and Letters* 74 (1993): 343-54.

[45] Barthes, "Grain," 188.

[46] M. C. Bradbrook, *Elizabethan Stage Conditions: A Study of Their Place in the Interpretation of Shakespeare's Plays* (Cambridge: Cambridge University Press, 1932), 110.

[47] Orgel, Introd., 27.

[48] Ariel is referred to as "him" in the text.

[49] Most who have taught this play to undergraduates will acknowledge the frequency with which they refer to Ariel as "she," against information given in the text. The play's performance history is also interesting in this regard: Ariel's part was played only by men through the seventeenth century, then became exclusively a part for women, until the 1930's (Orgel, 70).

[50] Orgel, 27.

[51] Paul Brown links it to James I's use of music in masque—as an "harmonics of power"—to celebrate his coercive power. Interestingly, Brown also discovers through Caliban's own speech about music ("sounds and sweet airs") a "quality in the island beyond the requirements of the coloniser's powerful harmonics," but this quality, this "site of resistance" can only be represented in the discourse of the colonialism it is resisting (Caliban may be cursing but is still speaking Prospero's language). My point is that music in this play constitutes a truly other discourse, one that resists not only Prospero's control, but his language as well. See Brown, 63-65.

[52] The phrase summarizes the concept suggested by Luce Irigaray in referring to women as *interdit,* "in between signs, between the realized meanings, between the lines." *See Speculum of the Other Woman;* (1974), 20; I have quoted from Toril Moi, *Sexual/Textual Politics: Feminist Literary Theory* (London, New York: Routledge, 1985), 133.

[53] Hélène Cixous with Catherine Clément, *La Jeune Née* (Paris: UGE 10/18), 172. See also Cixous's related text, "The Laugh of the Medusa," where she writes that "in women's speech as in their writing, that element which never stops resonating . . . is the song: first music from the first voice of love which is alive in every woman" (trans. Keith Cohen and Paula Cohen, *Signs: Journal of Women in Culture and Society* 1:4 [1976], 881).

[54] *La Jeune Née,* 173.

[55] Coppelia Kahn, "The Absent Mother in *King Lear,*" in *Rewriting the Renaissance,* ed. Margaret W. Ferguson, Maureen Quilligan, and Nancy J. Vickers (Chicago and London: University of Chicago Press, 1986), 35.

[56] See Orgel, 19.

[57] Orgel, 20.

[58] Janet Adelman, *Suffocating Mothers* (New York, London: Routledge, 1992), 237-38.

[59] Houston Baker has termed it "the venerable Western trope" ("Caliban's Triple Play," in *"Race," Writing and Difference,* ed. Henry Louis Gates, Jr. (Chicago: University of Chicago Press, 1986), 389.

[60] Baker, 389.

[61] Stephen Greenblatt, "Learning to Curse: Aspects of Linguistic Colonialism in the Sixteenth Century," in *First Images of America: The Impact of the New World on the Old,* ed. Fredi Chiapelli, 2 vols. (Berkeley: University of California Press, 1976), 2:575.

[62] Greenblatt thus finds it fitting that no one, still, is certain of the meaning of Caliban's word, "scamels" (575).

[63] Houston A. Baker Jr., *Modernism and the Harlem Renaissance* (Chicago: University of Chicago Press, 1987), 45.

[64] Baker, "Caliban's Triple Play," 389.

[65] Baker, 390.

[66] Baker, 391.

[67] Baker, 394.

[68] Baker, 391-92.

[69] OED.

Source: "Other Voices: The Sweet, Dangerous Air(s) of Shakespeare's *Tempest*," in *Shakespeare Studies,* Vol. XXIV, 1996, pp. 241-74.

Redeeming *The Tempest*: Romance and Politics

Jonathan Hart, *University of Alberta*

Since the Romantics the criticism of Shakespeare's *The Tempest* has been allegorical. Perhaps taking their cue from Coleridge, who said that the appeal of the play was to the imagination, subsequent critics appealed to the fantastic and to aesthetic allegories. Schlegel identified Ariel with air and Caliban with earth; Campbell saw *The Tempest* as the Shakespeare's farewell to his art; Lowell equated Caliban with brute understanding, Ariel with fancy and Prospero with imagination. When I was an undergraduate the Romantic reading of this play as the playwright's farewell to his art was still going strong. But for some time another kind of allegory was going on, that is the political allegory. Once a minority position, the political allegory has, in the last decade, overtaken the aesthetic allegory. My task is to find a version of *The Tempest* that acknowledges the political and aesthetic dimensions of the play but that discovers a middle ground between them. Although allegorical interpretation may be unavoidable in regard to *The Tempest,* I want to minimize it, as others have mined this vein, and to try to point up its stresses and intricacies as a means of moving along to a different type of critique. This attempt, then, is to redeem *The Tempest* from too much redemption.[1]

As the traditional aesthetic allegory of this play has been synthesized into the history of Shakespearean criticism, I want briefly to outline the shift to political allegory, particularly in light of post colonialism, before proceeding to my own analysis. Between about ninety and a hundred and twenty years ago, a shift seems to have happened in interpretations of *The Tempest*. Whereas in 1873 Daniel Wilson thought that *The Tempest* was a social Darwinist work, in 1904 W. T. Stead objected to the imperialism and sided with indigenous cultures. In this century a central debate over the use of canons as a means of promoting tradition and empire has occurred in English-speaking countries. Shakespeare has been at the heart of that debate as in those countries he occupies the centre of literature and education in the humanities. In traditional criticism, Prospero's art and power were sometimes identified with Shakespeare's and Europe's while Caliban was sometimes associated with the physical, moral and political dependency of non-European peoples. As an understandable reaction to this European position, some writers in Africa and the Caribbean set out to use *The Tempest* for their own literary and political purposes. Between 1957 and 1973, most African and large Caribbean colonies won their independence. Dissenting intellectuals and writers from these regions

decided to appropriate *The Tempest* as a means of supporting decolonization and creating an alternative literary tradition.[2] In *The Tempest* African and Caribbean writers saw hints of pre-European traditions and European colonization. These 'proleptic' signs suggested raw material for retrieving repressed traditions and inventing new ones. In Europe itself, as I have suggested, there was already opposition to the imperial view, so that, as usual, there were not two monolithic sides to this debate, Europe on the one hand and Africa and the Caribbean on the other. For forty years or more—in Spanish, French and English—African and Caribbean writers and critics have, directly and indirectly, appropriated or discussed the appropriation of Shakespeare's play. For instance, in 1961 Aimé Césaire's *'Une Tempête': d'après 'La Tempête' de Shakespeare— Adaption pour un théâtre nègre* is published in Paris.[3] During the 1970s, *The Tempest* is not used as much as a tool of opposition in decolonizing cultures. From the mid-1970s, the interest in colonization in the Renaissance, and in *The Tempest,* begins among scholars later known as new historicists. This tradition of dissent from within continues among scholars of European descent and seems to have culminated with the five-hundredth anniversary of Columbus' arrival in America. In this most recent manifestation white North American scholars, like the white American-born élite of the Spanish colonies, or criollos, of the late eighteenth century, find themselves in the position of identifying with Amerindians as a means of vindicating the wrongs done to, and prejudices against, those peoples in the past and as a declaration of independence from their own European past.[4] While this position is understandable and even laudable, it is difficult to avoid contradiction and to erase the European contact with the first Americans so readily and with an exercise of conscience.

My aim here is to do something much more modest. The aesthetic and political allegorists have created a vast body of secondary literature: in this brief space, I wish to set out the intricate problems of interpretation in the play. This argument is cautionary, as much to me as to any other critic. The recognition here sought is not a new world of religious, aesthetic or political redemption from the sins of our parents but more a chronicle of the difficulties and contradictions in interpreting what appears on the surface to be a well-wrought and self-contained comedy or romance.

The ethical and aesthetic dimensions of *The Tempest* have been and will be part of the reception of the play, but it is the interplay of the two that demonstrates how intricate the task at hand is. Rather than side with Prospero or Caliban, who both feel wronged, the one that he has lost Milan and the other that he has lost his island, I will look at them both, as well as at Ariel, who is a frustrated figure caught between rebellion and obedience, and at other characters. *The Tempest* is of the historical moment and is a putative space away from the cares of Milan and Europe. Moreover, the island is a place that lives in the sources of the European past in double exposure with the New World. The play contains much narrative, so that story as meditation, report and description stands in for many actions. The Shakespearean play that represents the so-called classical unities most looks forward to a new world.

Perhaps the nub of the problem of interpretation of *The Tempest* derives from the stresses between the rules of genre and the historical changes that have transformed the audience for the play. Frank Kermode notes this stress: "In romance there survives that system of ideal correspondences and magic patterns which in actuality could not survive the scrutiny of an informed and modern eye."[5] For contemporary critics, it has become increasingly difficult in the face of political and ideological issues arising from *The Tempest* to concentrate on the genre of the play, which some have called a comedy, others a tragicomedy and still others a romance. Although the generic or aesthetic dimension seems to be obscured at the moment, it would be surprising if it disappeared entirely. Rather, like the neglect of the political and historical aspects, the generic question will endure dismissal and oversight.

If *The Tempest* is considered to be a romance, it does not fit entirely Northrop Frye's characterization of the genre even if he thought that it was a romance. Romance, according to Frye, dominates the Elizabethan and Jacobean periods of English literature, for instance by taking over Sidney's *Arcadia,* Spenser's *The Faerie Queene* and the plays of Shakespeare's last phase. This genre was successful even though it was scorned for its extravagance, neglect of the unities, incredible actions and characters, and attention to 'nature.'[6] Unlike *The Winter's Tale, The Tempest* more or less obeys the classical unities, but, as Frye implies, it is extravagant, represents unbelievable characters and actions and focuses a great deal on nature. To nature it adds the nurture of art. Romance, in its narrative and dramatic forms, suggests the intricate relation between, and refraction of, classicism and popular culture. Like *Cymbeline, The Tempest* hints at *translatio imperii,* taking up the westering journey and the movement of empire found in Virgil's *Aeneid.*[7] Romance and the imperial theme, as Wilson Knight argued, do meet.

The temptation in contemporary criticism of *The Tempest* is to seek out Caliban as a hero and to see in

Prospero the idealization of Europe at the brink of empire. My view is that the stress between the ideals and wish-fulfillment of romance on the one hand and the political objections of modernity and post-modernity on the other suggests additional productive ways to view this play. What my reading attempts is an interpretation that takes into account the aesthetic question of genre and the political question of authority and rebellion but through the literary and dramatic text of *The Tempest* itself and not through external sources. When discussing historical analogues and contexts, the essay will do so from and through Shakespeare's play and not the other way around.

My supposition is to discuss the problems as they arise from act to act in order to show how bound up the aesthetic or generic dimension is with the political or historical one. The play opens with the Ship-master and the Boatswain trying to save the ship from the storm. In the first line the Master asks the Boatswain to speak to the mariners briskly or the ship will run aground. After the Master exits and the Mariners enter at line 4, the Boatswain, who has not replied to the Master, follows the order by giving the appropriate instructions to the mariners. At line 9, Alonso, Sebastian, Antonio, Ferdinand, Gonzalo and others enter: here begins the disobedience after only a few lines in which the chain of command seems to have been working. As far as the Boatswain is concerned Alonzo, the King of Naples, is in the way in the fight for survival: 'Hence! What cares these roarers for the name of King? To cabin: silence! trouble us not' (I.1.16-18). When Gonzalo, the old counsellor, reminds the Boatswain that he has the king aboard, the Boatswain, with some sarcasm and under pressure to work while the storm is raging, says he loves no one more than himself and reminds Gonzalo of his apparent impotence:

> *You are a counsellor; if you can command these elements to silence, and work the peace of the presence, we will not hand a rope more; use your authority: if you cannot, give thanks you have lived so long, and make yourself ready in your cabin for the mischance of the hour, if it so hap. Cheerly, good hearts! Out of our way, I say.*
>
> (I.1.20-7)

Authority is a matter of context, convention and use. The king and his counsellor have no authority in the storm because they hinder, rather than help, the survival of the crew. Gonzalo may pun on the gallows the Boatswain will face, but the nobles are almost comic in the way they presume to assert authority where they have it in name only. By insisting on authority, Gonzalo is showing up its fissures. Fate may, as Gonzalo wishes, save them and hang the Boatswain. The Boatswain's authority in seamanship is not respected. He has four lines of peace before Sebastian, Antonio and Gonzalo re-emerge in another comic brawl with him. He meets them with more sarcasm and they counter with condescending insults. Antonio concludes that 'We are less afraid to be drowned than thou art' (I.1.44-5) and adds later that 'We are merely cheated of our lives by drunkards' (55). Gonzalo and the others show their nobility by joining the king and the prince in their prayers. Even though the nobles seem to have asserted their honour and courage, Gonzalo ends the opening scene with the contradictory: 'The wills above be done! but I would fain die a dry death' (I.1.65-6).

The audience is reminded of motifs of romance in the opening words of Act One, scene two, which Miranda speaks to Prospero: 'If by your Art, my dearest father, you have / Put the wild waters in this roar, allay them' (I.2.1-2). The child orders the father, even if it is after a conditional clause. The motifs of magic, suffering and survival, regeneration and wish-fulfillment occur in Prospero's magical storm and Miranda's desire that it cease (see I.2.3-20). Part of the genre of romance (which is closely related to epic and comedy) is the quest for identity. In this play, Prospero and Miranda have been ship-wrecked and both have had new identities thrust upon them, he knowingly and she not. So Prospero has promised to tell about Miranda's past. She reminds him that 'You have often/Begun to tell me what I am, but stopp'd' (33-4). He now tells her the story of her early life in a dialogue where he leads her to see 'the dark backward and abysm of time' (50). Prospero chronicles his brother Antonio's perfidious usurpation of Prospero's dukedom (66-139). His 'library/ Was dukedom large enough,' so that Prospero neglected his Milan until his brother, with the help of the King of Naples, took it by expelling Prospero and Miranda (109-10). The personification of the winds that Prospero creates is supposed to move Miranda and the audience in the theatre to lamentation and indignation over the wrong (149-51). So too is the appeal to Miranda as a cherubim and to Divine Providence as the reason for their survival (152-9). Prospero tells her how Gonzalo helped save them by sneaking them food and books, which allowed him to study on the island (160-74). Miranda wants to know the reason for Prospero's storm, and he thanks Fortune for bringing his enemies to him, and then casts his daughter into a sleep (175-86).

The first appearance of Ariel is one of obedience. He carries out Prospero's art. When Prospero asks Ariel to come, the spirit replies: 'All hail, great master! grave sir, hail! I come/ To answer thy best pleasure' (189-90). When Prospero inquires whether he has performed the tempest as he was bade, he enumerates, amid his master's exclamations of joy, its execution, so that the audience is also well informed. Like Prospero's narrative, Ariel's is a device to compress the action of the play, to let the classical unities obtain in a way that Shakespeare had not done since *Comedy of Errors*.[8] In

fact, in keeping with romance, Ariel assures Prospero that his actions were regenerative as those tossed in the water now have fresher garments than before (218-19). In this account, Ariel makes the only allusion to the Bermoothes or Bermuda. In a nook, where Prospero once summoned him 'at midnight to fetch dew/ From the still-vexed Bermoothes,' Ariel has hidden the ship, while he has put all the other ships on the Mediterranean 'Bound sadly home for Naples' (228-9, 235). Bermuda is an allusion in a subordinate clause, a kind of association with storms in a story-fragment, and with no grid of where the island is located. Here is the only direct and obvious evidence of the New World in the play and it is in passing, and perhaps not far for a spirit who can go from here to there, from Mediterranean to Bermuda, in a glance.[9] Even Ariel is rebellious, as he reminds Prospero of his promise of granting him liberty (242-50). Prospero reacts to what he views as ingratitude by reminding Ariel of the torments that Sycorax had devised for him and of the way Prospero rescued him. The phrase, 'Thou liest, malignant thing,' illustrates the vehemence that Prospero shows to Ariel and the quickness with which his mood can swing (257). According to Prospero's account, he found a tyranny on the island. For a crime, Sycorax was banished from Algiers and, pregnant, was brought to the island, where Ariel was her servant. As Ariel would not enact her terrible commands, she imprisoned him in pain in a cloven pine for a dozen years, during which time she died. Only Caliban had a 'human shape' on the island when Prospero found it, and only Prospero's 'Art' could free Ariel from his howling captivity (284, 291, see 256-93). Even after Ariel responds, 'I thank thee, master,' Prospero threatens to do unto him what Sycorax had. After Ariel swears his obedience, Prospero gives up the threats and promises to free Ariel in two days. He also commands Ariel to make himself invisible in his next enactment of Prospero's magic. Prospero claims the barely inhabited island from the bestial yet human Caliban as if it were *terra nullius* or, in John Winthrop's words, *vacuum domicilium*. Just as the Portuguese had claimed 'discovery' of populated areas of the African coast in the fifteenth century, so too had the Spanish, English and French used the legal fiction of *terra nullius,* that nomadic Amerindians ranged but did not inhabit the land as Europeans did, so their land could be possessed.[10] If we are sympathetic to Prospero, we can say that he usurped the remnants of a penal colony, founded as the result of some unnamed crime, and became the *de facto* ruler through justice. On the other hand, his magic is a deterrent and becomes the force of law, especially in relation to Caliban, the son of the tyrannous Sycorax of Prospero's official version, but also to Ariel.

After Ariel leaves, Prospero wakes up Miranda in order to find Caliban, whom Prospero calls 'slave' to his face five times in this scene (310, 315, 321, 346,

376). As in the opening scene, a conflict between classes occurs here, but in its most unsavory manifestation (at least for a modern audience), that is in the relation between master and slave. Prospero understands Caliban's indispensability, whereas Miranda feels repugnance.[11] Ariel makes a brief entrance as a water nymph, as if to provide a contrast with Caliban (318-20). According to Prospero, Caliban is the offspring of a witch and an incubus, a fiend whose mother is in many ways a witch from the classics.[12] Prospero and Caliban curse each other (323-32). Caliban claims the island was his: he was a king who has now become Prospero's only subject. He curses Prospero, whom he once loved and showed the fruits of the island, for detaining him in a rock. For Prospero, this state arose because Caliban attempted to rape Miranda, an attempt that Caliban wishes Prospero had not thwarted. Miranda (some editors make it Prospero) curses Caliban as 'Abhorred slave' and upbraids him for his betrayal of trust (353-64). Here, then, is an irreconcilable dispute over the history of the island, a meeting of two sides who are incommensurate, whether this irreconcilable difference possesses any dimension of an allegory of the New World. Caliban makes his position clear: 'You taught me language; and my profit on't/Is, I know how to curse' (365-6). He then proceeds to do just that chiasmically, for he curses Prospero (and Miranda) for teaching him their language. But even then Shakespeare weighs the debate rhetorically in Prospero's favour, making Caliban almost too much of a *tabula rasa*. As in the case of Ariel, Prospero threatens Caliban with physical pain if he does not obey him. Even if there is no direct evidence that this Old World island is also of the New World, it seems that the berry drink Caliban remembers as a gift of Prospero is like the one the Bermuda castaways drank in Sylvester Jourdain's *A Discovery of the Bermudas* (1610) and that Caliban must obey Prospero, who could control Sycorax's god, Sestebos, whom, as Richard Eden mentions in *History of Travaile* (1577), in his description of Magellan's voyage, the Patagonians summoned for help.[13] But, like Ariel's stopover in Bermuda, Caliban's allusion, which is more unconscious, is part of a diffuse context of Shakespeare's reading rather than a distinct fictional world based in the New World.

The next segment of the scene involves Ariel leading Ferdinand to Prospero and Miranda (377-504). His songs of wild waves and drowning remind Ferdinand of his father, who was apparently lost in the storm (377-411). Miranda considers Ferdinand a spirit, and, as Prospero has planned it, she thinks the young man 'A thing divine' (421). For Ferdinand, Miranda is a wonder, and more wonderful still for speaking his language (429-33). His wish fulfilment is that of the traveller who hopes to find a paradise that speaks his language and bears his names. The Europeans began to rename the New World, but Ferdinand does not

need to in this scene that Prospero has made for him. Prospero is so pleased that in asides he promises to set Ariel free for his good work: he also calls Ferdinand a spy who wants to usurp his island and tests him in case he takes Miranda too lightly for having wooed her so easily (422-69). Nor does Prospero fail to test Miranda as he says that she has seen two men, Ferdinand and Caliban, and this young man needs to be obedient (469-501). The scene closes with Prospero promising freedom to Ariel if he does exactly 'All points of my command,' which Ariel promises 'To th' syllable' (503). Prospero controls the freedom of all the other characters in the play.

The political themes of authority and rebellion or freedom and slavery continue to interact with the romance themes of survival, regeneration and wonder. In Act Two, scene one, Gonzalo tries to cheer Alonzo with thoughts on the miracle of their preservation, while the king will not be so easily humoured. Sebastian and Antonio make fun of Gonzalo's efforts and wit in a satirical running commentary made in asides, until they mock the old counsellor directly as Hamlet does with Polonius. Gonzalo notes the freshness of the garments as Ariel had (II.1.1-68). The first one hundred and eighty-five lines of this scene involve a diversion in which Antonio and Sebastian send up Gonzalo, thereby showing their youthful impatience with him, indirectly their opposition to Alonzo, whom Gonzalo serves, and their impatient and sharp characters as opposed to Gonzalo's well-meaning but official character. The marriage between Claribel and the King of Tunis, to which Gonzalo alludes, is the pretext for the journey in which Prospero has trapped them by means of the storm. Gonzalo's comparison of the couple to 'widow Dido' and Aeneas causes Antonio, Sebastian and Adrian much merriment. They were not married but were lovers—and Aeneas abandoned Dido to found Rome and to become part of the translation of empire. As Adrian points out, Gonzalo confuses Carthage with Tunis. In Antonio's and Sebastian's response the subsequent allusion to the miraculous harp of Amphion, which raised the walls of Thebes, reveals that Gonzalo's gaffe has made a new city. Antonio and Sebastian also make fun of his wondrous geography, mocking him for making magical mistakes (66-97). Just as Gertrude grows impatient with Polonius' logorrheia, so too does Alonzo tire of the surfeit of words. He is lost in his grief and he will not abide Gonzalo's verbal insistence (102-09). Not even Francisco's hopeful description of Ferdinand's possible escape from the storm will placate the doleful Alonzo. It is his distraction that has allowed Gonzalo to be the butt of the jokes for so long in this scene as the men wile away the time until the king's grief abates. Alonzo's brother, Sebastian, blames the king for marrying his daughter to an African, for not listening to all of them who argued against the marriage and for not heeding his daughter, who 'Weigh'd between loathness and obedience' (126). Besides this aspect of obedience, the theme of widows recurs, as Sebastian reminds him of the men lost at sea, but his bluntness earns him Gonzalo's gentle rebuke—to think of the king's feelings (118-36).

When Gonzalo speaks of his ideal commonwealth, he draws on Montaigne's *Des Cannibales,* which John Florio published in translation in 1603 (143ff).[14] Montaigne, and therefore Gonzalo, draws on reports of cannibals in the New World. Those critics who emphasize the New World in *The Tempest* have seized on something important in the play. The notion of Europe's connection with Africa and America occurs in passing, in brief allusions and in sources. It is a significant subtext that Shakespeare uses but does not stress explicitly. For ethical and political reasons, critics have increasingly felt the need to focus on the theme of colonizer and colonized. The ideal commonwealth, which Gonzalo borrows from Montaigne, is something Antonio and Sebastian scorn in their continued mockery of the old man. Whether Shakespeare is satirizing Montaigne's natural commonwealth is unclear. Nature is abundant and sufficient to ensure human happiness. Is Gonzalo a good man who is wrong about the ideal state or are Antonio and Sebastian as misguided in their mockery as they are in their plot against Alonzo? It is true that Gonzalo would need the authority not to admit sovereignty, which would be a trick of government this world has not yet seen. Sebastian and Gonzalo treat Gonzalo as an upstart king of his dreams, and tell him they laugh at him (139-79). They willingly literalize Gonzalo's words, beginning with his first words about the commonwealth that equate 'plantation' with planting and forgetting its equivalence with colonization, so to ridicule his ideas. But Gonzalo is good-natured as he asks his two mockers to laugh him to sleep (180-5). It is, however, Ariel who lulls Gonzalo and then Alonzo to sleep with solemn music (179-93).

It does not take Antonio long to tempt Sebastian with Alonzo's crown (193-203). Sebastian thinks that Antonio is speaking a language of sleep in this torpid place. Antonio says that Ferdinand is dead and that Claribel is in Tunis and therefore out of the way from Naples, so that Sebastian could be king; he also replies to Sebastian's remark that Antonio supplanted Prospero and to his question about conscience by representing himself as happy and without regret (204-75). The audience experiences dramatic irony as it knows that Ferdinand is alive and that Prospero has orchestrated the storm to trap Antonio and to redeem his lost kingdom. Whereas Antonio is hyperbolic, Sebastian is not. He would kill Alonzo while Sebastian killed Gonzalo. But, as Ariel says, Prospero has foreseen this rebellion, so that Sebastian's agreement will get him nowhere. Ariel awakens Gonzalo with song, and the two guards, who had promised Alonzo his safety, have to

lie about drawing swords against bulls or lions (276-320). The scene ends with Ariel promising to report his work to Prospero, and his wish: 'So, King, go safely on to seek thy son' (322).

Ariel may be obedient, but Caliban, like Sebastian, is not and is open to suggestion. Yet another rebellion is simmering. Caliban opens Act Two, scene two with a curse on Prospero (II.2.1-4). Caliban mistakes Trinculo for one of Prospero's spirits, and Trinculo does not know whether Caliban is a man or a fish. In England, Trinculo says, a monster makes a man rich: there, when people 'will not give a doit to relieve a lame beggar, they will lay out ten to see a dead Indian' (32-4). From Frobisher onward (1576), the English brought many Indians home and exhibited them. Montaigne spoke with some Amerindians who visited France. As Indians became more familiar, they replaced the wild man in masques and pageants.[15] This comic incident of the fishiness of Caliban demonstrates that, through allusion, he was at least in part associated with the Amerindian in Shakespeare's mind. When Stephano enters with his bawdy sailor's song, Caliban mistakes him as well for one of Prospero's tormenting spirits. Stephano misapprehends the four-legged beast under the gabardine, that is Trinculo and Caliban: 'Have we devils here? Do you put tricks upon's with salvages and men of Ind, ha?' (58-9). Stephano wonders how the 'monster of the isle' learned 'our language,' an astonishment not unlike Ferdinand's when he hears Miranda speak (66-8). Like Trinculo, Stephano is thinking of how a show of this 'monster' will make him rich at home (69-80). On stage the humour is more apparent as the monster that Stephano is talking about is Trinculo and Caliban under cover, and Stephano thinks it the devil when it calls him by name (99-100). In an aside, Caliban considers Stephano a god who 'bears celestial liquor' (118). Stephano admits that he escaped the storm on a butt of sack, a comic gesture for a drunkard but also a detail from the Bermuda narratives.[16] Rather than swear on the Bible, Caliban declares uninvited: 'I'll swear, upon that bottle, to be thy true subject; for the liquor is not earthly' (126-7). Here is a parodic oath of allegiance, a type of comic inversion of the obedience Caliban once gave to Prospero. Shakespeare represents a kind of parodic first encounter between Amerindian and European:

> Caliban   Hast thou not dropp'd from heaven?
>
> Stephano   Out o' the moon, I do assure thee: I was the man i'th'moon when time was.
>
> Caliban   I have seen thee in her, and I do adore thee.
>
> (137-40)

Other Europeans had thought that they had beguiled the Natives so, but that might have been hubris on their part.[17] The famous Letter of Columbus concerning the first voyage represents the first contact with the Amerindians in similar fashion: 'And they do not know any creed and are not idolaters; only they all believe that power and good are in the heavens, and they are very firmly convinced that I, with these ships and men, came from heaven.'[18] It is questionable whether the Natives thought of the Europeans in the grandiose ways that the Europeans represent for themselves.

Trinculo insults Caliban as 'A most poor credulous monster!' while Caliban asks Stephano to 'be my god' and swears to be his subject (146, see 142-59). Thus Caliban promises to serve Stephano as he had served Prospero by exploiting the island's resources for him. Amid these promises and his curse of Prospero, whom he calls a tyrant, Trinculo comments: 'A most ridiculous monster, to make a wonder of a poor drunkard!' (165-6). Once again, dramatic irony limits the usurpation of new authority. The audience knows that the king and company live even as Stephano tells Trinculo the contrary and that 'we will inherit here' (175). Trinculo thinks that Caliban is drunk (179). Although Caliban sings that he will make no more dams for fish, he has promised to fish for Stephano (161, 180). In this drunken scene of mistaken identity, there is comedy from the ironic blindness with which Caliban and Stephano end it:

> Caliban   *'Ban, 'Ban, Cacaliban*
> *Has a new master:—get a new man.*
> *Freedom, high-day! high-day, freedom!*
> * freedom,*
> *high-day, freedom!*
> Stephano   *O brave monster! lead the way.*
>
> (183-8)

Here the class delusions of Stephano are as great as the illusions of Caliban.

Act Three, scene one represents Ferdinand as he performs his labours cheerfully for Miranda, though he is not without criticism for Prospero (1-14). She bids Ferdinand rest and circumvent her father's orders because Prospero is studying but he is actually observing them at a distance unseen. She tells Ferdinand her name against her father's wishes. They swear their love and Prospero asks heaven to shower its grace on this pair. Prospero is less happy with their promise to marry than they are (15-96). Like Caliban and Stephano, the lovers are full of wonder, but their oaths will see them farther than the two rebels because in the context of romance, they are the young who will regenerate the world through marriage. Their obedience in comedy would not be so necessary as they could circumvent the senex, but here in romance, the magus helps their love with his spell, which also heals the impotent king.[19]

Shakespeare surrounds the love scene in the middle of the play with the antics of Stephano and Caliban and the satirical comments of Trinculo. Folly continues to be Trinculo's theme: 'They say there's but five upon this isle: we are three of them; if th'other two be brain'd like us, the state totters' (III.4.6). Both Caliban and Stephano are reeling with drink. Of Trinculo, Caliban says, 'I'll not serve him, he is not valiant' (22-3). He appeals to Stephano when Trinculo abuses him, and Stephano warns the offender: 'if you prove a mutineer,—the next tree!' (33-4). Ariel plays tricks on the three so that when he says 'Thou liest' to Caliban's lament, that Prospero is a tyrant who cheated him of the island, Ariel is mistaken for Trinculo and this brings about new threats from Stephano (40f). By repeating this phrase at key times, Ariel disrupts Caliban's plot to deliver Prospero to Stephano and raises the new master's ire against Trinculo. Caliban wants Stephano to possess and burn Prospero's books, 'for without them/He's but a sot, as I am' and promises that Stephano will have Miranda in bed and produce 'brave brood' (90-103). Stephano declares that Miranda will be his queen after he kills Prospero and that Caliban and Trinculo will be vice-roys. Ariel's invisible presence makes this all unlikely and increases the dramatic irony. Thoughts of Prospero's death by violence make Caliban 'full of pleasure,' and Stephano cannot remember the song Caliban wants but comes up with a nonsensical catch that ends 'Thought is free' (114, 120). Stephano and Trinculo are afraid of Ariel's music, so that Caliban must tell them not to be afraid of this island so 'full of noises' (131-2). As in the scene before the pledges of Ferdinand and Miranda, Caliban leads Stephano, to make the inversion complete.

Not surprisingly, the next scene represents more rebellious thoughts. Gonzalo is tired and Alonzo out of hope: Antonio and Sebastian plot to kill them. Now Prospero and Ariel put on a banquet for them and play more tricks. This time Prospero's asides point out the evil in Alonzo's party. He leaves the banquet behind, but Alonzo does not want to touch it. Gonzalo, however, tries to reassure him that this feast is not more strange than 'men/Whose heads stood in their breasts' (III.3.47). This Mandevillian motif also occurs in Walter Ralegh's *The Discovery of Guiana* (1595) and in Othello's Anthropophagi, so that it combines old world fiction with new world rumour (I.3.144-5).[20] When Alonzo decides to eat, Ariel, as a Harpy, makes the banquet vanish. Ariel appeals to himself as an agent of Destiny and Fate. He reminds the three that they 'From Milan did supplant good Prospero' and tells Alonzo that for such actions the ministers have taken away his son and leave the father to perdition (70). Ariel vanishes; the spirits reappear and carry out the table; Prospero praises Ariel's role as harpy and speaks of his control over his enemies and his impending visit to Ferdinand, whom they suppose drowned. Another case of dramatic irony shows the limitations of those who oppose Prospero: the conventions of romance check political rebellion. Alonzo thinks the events 'monstrous,' that the wind seemed to call out the name of Prospero and make him so aware of his guilt that he will seek his son in the deep. Sebastian and Antonio think that they are fighting fiends. Realizing that Alonzo, Antonio and Sebastian are desperate and that 'their great guilt,/ Like poison given to work a great time after,/Now 'gins to bite the spirits,' Gonzalo sends Adrian to restrain the three (104-06).

Shakespeare has been contrasting the loyalty and honour of Ferdinand with the treachery of Caliban, Sebastian and Antonio. In Act Four, scene one, he intensifies this comparison. Prospero tells Ferdinand that he has passed his tests and now has won Miranda's hand, a daughter who 'will outstrip all praise' (IV.1.10). Still, Prospero threatens Ferdinand not to break Miranda's virginity before the marriage ceremony, and Ferdinand swears by his honour that he will not (13-32). Prospero, the trickster, still needs Ariel to perform tricks, so that he can regain Milan and ensure the dynastic marriage for his daughter. After checking the young couple's resolve, Prospero arranges for the masque. It is stylized, its verse in rhymed couplets. Iris, Juno's messenger, speaks of Ceres, the goddess of the harvest, in appropriately pastoral imagery. Juno descends. Ceres asks Iris why Juno has summoned her, and Iris replies that 'A contract of true love to celebrate;/ And some donation freely to estate/ On the blest lovers' (84-6). Ceres wonders whether Venus or Cupid now attends Juno as they plotted to allow Dis or Pluto, the ruler of the underworld, to carry off Ceres' daughter Proserpine to be his queen. Thus, Ceres has foresworn their company, and Iris assures her that Venus and Cupid will not carry out their vows to put a 'wanton charm' on the young couple, for they are defeated (95). Juno asks Ceres to go with her to bless the couple's marriage, and they do with images of increase and agricultural bounty. Ferdinand praises this 'most majestic vision' and asks Prospero whether these are spirits, which the magician says he has summoned. The audience response or interruption, so common in Shakespearean plays-within-plays, ends with Ferdinand's praise of Prospero's ability to make this place 'Paradise,' and Prospero's call for silence for fear that the spell will be broken (118-27). On behalf of Juno, Iris calls forth the Naiads, or chaste nymphs, to 'celebrate/ A contract of true love' (132-3). This emphasis on chastity amplifies Prospero's lesson to Ferdinand and Miranda. The reapers join the nymphs in a dance, but at the height of harmony, which would usually end a comedy, Prospero ends the vision because of his memory of Caliban's conspiracy (139-44). The political theme will not let the romance theme alone.

Miranda tells Ferdinand that she has never seen Prospero so distempered, and to cheer up his new-found and unsolemnized son-in-law, Prospero comments with his famous speech, beginning 'Our revels now are ended' (148f. See V.1.309). The spirits dissolve just as the masque did, but from that dissolution Prospero makes his well-known generalization about human life, 'We are such stuff/As dreams are made on; and our little life/Is rounded with a sleep' (156-8). This metatheatrical moment calls attention to the metaphysics and aesthetic experience of drama. The politics of ingratitude, which Caliban and Antonio represent for Prospero, break in on the theatrical illusion but do so in the self-conscious space of the theatre.

After Miranda and Ferdinand have gone, Ariel enters and says that he did not want to anger Prospero by mentioning Caliban. Ariel left Caliban and his cohorts up to their chins in a foul lake and in their conspiracy. Prospero dismisses the idea of Caliban as 'A devil, a born devil, on whose nature/Nurture can never stick' (188-9). He thinks that the outward decline of his body reflects the inward decline of his mind. There is now great dissension among the three conspirators, and even Stephano has begun to threaten Caliban. Caliban wants Stephano to kill Prospero, but his king is drawn to what his monster knows to be a trashy wardrobe. It is as if Stephano and Trinculo cannot measure up to Caliban. Prospero and Ariel drive the three conspirators out. Prospero wants them to feel pain, and he reminds Ariel one more time that he will soon be free (264-5).

The fifth and final act shows Prospero in control as he had planned. Ariel tells him about Alonso and his other prisoners and says that Gonzalo's tears have moved him and should therefore move Prospero, who is human. The magician orders his spirit to release his prisoners from the spell. Alone, Prospero chronicles his power as a magician and concludes: 'But this rough magic/I here abjure;' he says he will break his staff and drown his book (V.1.50-7). Ariel brings Alonso and the others to Prospero, and he notes how the charm dissolves. The nub of Prospero's meditation is the loyalty of Gonzalo and the unnaturalness of his own brother Antonio, who resembles Caliban in this: 'I do forgive thee,/ Unnatural though thou art' (78-9). This act of forgiveness is spoken for the benefit of Prospero and the audience because Antonio is still spell-bound. Prospero will dress as he did as Duke of Milan (86). Politics lie behind his art of magic.

Ariel sings while attiring him in ducal dress. Prospero says he will miss Ariel and promises him freedom once more. The last bit of magical business that Prospero wants Ariel to perform is to wake up the crew and bring them to him. Gonzalo and Alonso awaken to Prospero, dressed as the Duke of Milan. Understandably, Alonso is confused whether Prospero is an apparition or the person himself, but he gives up Milan's tribute. Here is the ultimate recognition scene in which Alonso asks pardon for his wrongs (112-19).

Prospero's generous welcome yields to his reproach for his brother, Antonio, who is blind to recognition of his faults and does not answer or make amends (129-34). But Alonso deflects the confrontation by asking Prospero to tell his story (134). The greatest moment of dramatic irony occurs in this scene. Alonso has lost his son, and Prospero says he has lost his daughter. The audience knows his double meaning: Alonso does not. He wishes that they were both alive to be King and Queen of Naples. Prospero will not tell his story in full 'For 'tis a chronicle of day by day,/ Not a relation for a breakfast, nor/Befitting this first meeting' (163-5). When speaking about the recovery of his dukedom, Prospero uncovers the final piece in the comic cogito or discovery. As the stage direction indicates, 'cognitio *he discovers* FERDINAND *and* MIRANDA *playing at chess*' (171). This game of chess as moment of recognition is wonderful theatre and is also a romance motif. Like the resurrection of Hermione in *The Winter's Tale,* this scene is, as Sebastian says, 'A most high miracle!' (177). More than the similar scene in *The Winter's Tale,* this scene involves two-way recognition. Alonso learns that Ferdinand is alive, but the son also sees that the father still lives. And Miranda discovers her 'brave new world,' even if it is new to her and not to Prospero (183-4). Ferdinand and Gonzalo, who says he is speechless with inward weeping, claim that it is Providence that has brought Miranda and Ferdinand together.

Gonzalo summarizes the comic triumph of this romance. Through this good counsellor, Shakespeare represents, for the characters if not for the audience, the comic catastrophe, how events driving towards tragedy, reverse themselves to a happy ending:

> *Was Milan thrust from Milan, that his issue*
> *Should become Kings of Naples? O, rejoice*
> *Beyond a common joy! and set it down*
> *With gold on lasting pillars: in one voyage*
> *Did Claribel her husband find at Tunis,*
> *And Ferdinand, her brother, found a wife*
> *Where he himself was lost, Prospero his*
>   *dukedom*
> *In a poor isle, and all of us ourselves*
> *When no man was his own.*

                  (205-13)

Alonso and Gonzalo bless the much-blessed couple as if to amplify the blessings of Prospero and Juno and Ceres in the masque. But Shakespeare keeps his lightness of touch by having Gonzalo confront the foulmouthed Boatswain, who arrives after an absence since the first scene of the play. The Boatswain ignores the confrontation and is glad to see his king safe. The chaos, which began with the storm that made him question the use of his ruler and the counsellor on deck, is over. In asides that punctuate this part of the scene, Prospero praises Ariel's work. In response to the Boatswain's wondrous tale about what happened to the crew in the storm, Alonso gives another perspective on events: 'This is as strange a maze as e'er men trod; / And there is in this business more than nature/Was ever conduct of' (242-4). He asks for an oracle to make all clear, and Prospero says he will later give every detail of events.

The final loose end is the three rebels, Caliban, Stephano and Trinculo. Ariel drives these drunkards on stage. After Sebastian and Antonio return to their sardonic repartee (this time about these three) as if nothing happened, Prospero tells of Caliban's origins and how he plotted to take Prospero's life (263-74). This parodic Saturnalia must have an end. In a kind of comic accommodation, but with some political tensions in our day, Prospero says of the three drunken plotters: 'Two of these fellows you / Must know and own; this thing of darkness I / Acknowledge mine' (274-6). Prospero is probably referring to darkness as evil because he has called him 'this demi-devil' (V.1.272), but some critics, like E. K. Chambers, have thought that Prospero is referring to Caliban's skin.[21] Despite Prospero's assertion that Caliban's ill shape reflects his ill manners, he sees that Caliban looks 'To have my pardon' (293). Perhaps part of the logic of the comic ending of romance, which may be generally seen as part of general comedy, Caliban asks forgiveness and seems to be assimilated into the comic triumph. He will obey Prospero and go promptly to his cell: 'and I'll be wise hereafter, / And seek for grace. What a thrice-double ass/ Was I, to take this drunkard for a god, / And worship this dull fool!' (294-7). The comic imperative can also allow Sebastian, who was part of Antonio's plot to kill Alonso and Gonzalo, to correct Alonso, who asks the three drunkards to take their luggage, saying that they stole it. Prospero invites everyone to his cell to rest for a night and to hear the story of his life. Unlike the end of *Cymbeline,* where Shakespeare represents a long narrative to enlighten the characters about events the audience already knows, here the narrative is but a promise for the future. In the morning Prospero hopes to go to Naples, to see the nuptial solemnized and give every third thought to his grave. Alonso continues to do what he has done in this scene: he speaks about the strangeness of the events, a reminiscent theme of the endings of Shakespearean comedy and romance, something, for instance, much evident in *A Midsummer Night's Dream*:: 'I long/ To hear the story of your life, which must/Take the ear strangely' (311-13). Once again, Prospero promises to 'deliver all' and he hopes for good winds. His last act is to set Ariel free (313-18).

But of course that is how the body of the play ends. The Epilogue, which Prospero speaks, is famous for his request that the audience set him free from the island through its applause. The breath of the audience in his extended metaphor will blow his ship and make his project succeed, because his magic has left him. Prospero is out of character and out of magic. He needs the audience's mercy and prayer to free him from his faults. His last two lines are 'As you from crimes would pardon'd be/, Let your indulgence set me free' (19-20). This is metatheatrical pleading along the lines of Rosalind's Epilogue at the end of *As You Like It*. Here is the imperfect perfection beyond the bounds of the body of the play: the audience rounds off the illusion of drama with a mediation back into the world. I have tried to take the middle way and look at the intertwined themes of romance and politics, the two allegories of Shakespeare's taking leave of his art and of the politics of colonizer and colonized. These two allegories, especially Shakespeare's return to Stratford, are understandable ways of reading the need for pardon in the play and in the Epilogue. But as an audience, we have to remember that we too have faults, aesthetic and political, for which we need pardon and understanding.

Notes

[1] For a discussion of earlier criticism of the play. All citations and quotations from *The Tempest* are from *William Shakespeare, The Tempest,* ed. Frank Kermode (1954. London: Methuen, 1958).

See Kermode, Introduction, *The Tempest,* lxxxi. I thank Jean-Marie Maguin, Angela Maguin, and Charles Whitworth for their invitation to give an earlier version of this essay as a seminar at their Centre d'Études et de Recherches sur la Renaissance Anglaise, Université Paul Valéry (Montpellier III) in March 1994.

[2] Aimé Césaire, *'Une Tempête:' d'après 'La Tempête' de Shakespeare—Adaptation pour un théâtre nègre* (Paris: Éditions du Seuil, 1961). See Thomas A. Hale, "Sur *Une tempête* d'Aimé Césaire," *Études Littéraires* 6 (1973): 21-34. For early debates of imperialism and Shakespeare, see:

Daniel Wilson, *Caliban: the Missing Link* (London: Macmillan, 1873) and W. T. Stead, "First Impressions of the Theatre," *Review of Reviews* 30 (October 1904): 360-7. For discussions of this postcolonial use of Shakespeare, Charlotte H. Bruner, "The Meaning of Caliban in Black Literature Today," *Comparative Literature Studies* 13 (1976): 240-53; Trevor R. Griffiths, "'This Island's Mine:' Caliban and Colonialism," *Yearbook of English Studies* 13 (1983): 159-80; Diana Brydon, "Re-writing *The Tempest*," *World Literature Written in English [WLWE]* 23 (1984): 75-88; Peter Hulme, *'Prospero and Caliban,' Colonial Encounters: Europe and the Native Caribbean 1492-1797,* London: Routledge, 1986. 89-134; Rob Nixon, "Caribbean and African Appropriations of *The Tempest*," *Critical Inquiry* 13.3 (1987): 557-78; Laura Donaldson, "The Miranda Complex: Colonialism and Question of Femi-

nist Reading," *Diacritics* (1988): 65-77; Jonathan Hart, "Traces, Resistances and Contradictions: Canadian and International Perspectives on Post-Colonial Theories," *Arachne,* 1.1 (1994): esp. 77-8.

[3] See also Frantz Fanon, *Peau noire, masques blancs* (Paris: Seuil, 1952); George Lamming, *The Pleasures of Exile* (London: M. Joseph, 1960); C. L. R. James, *The Black Jacobins: Toussaint Louverture and the San Domingo Revolution,* (New York: Vintage, 1963); Dominique O. Mannoni, *Prospero and Caliban: The Psychology of Colonization,* trans. Pamela Powesland (New York: Praeger, 1964); Edward Braithwaite, *Islands* (Oxford: Oxford UP, 1969); Lemuel Johnson, *Highlife for Caliban* (Ann Arbor: Ardis, 1973). Roberto Fernandez Retamar, "Caliban: Notes Toward a Discussion of Culture in Our America," *Massachusetts Review* 15 (1974): 7-72.

[4] See Anthony Pagden, *Spanish Imperialism and the Political Imagination,* New Haven: Yale UP, 1990 10-11.

[5] Kermode lvi.

[6] Northrop Frye, Foreword to George M. Logan and Gordon Teskey eds., *Unfolded Tales: Essays in Renaissance Romance* (Ithaca, NY: Cornell UP, 1989) ix.

[7] Geoffrey H. Hartman, *The Fate of Reading And Other Essays,* (Chicago: University of Chicago Press, 1975); Northrop Frye, *A Natural Perspective: The Development of Shakespearian Comedy,* (New York: Harcourt, Brace & World, 1965) 88; see A. Kent Hieatt, "*Cymbeline* and the Intrusion of Lyric into Romance Narrative: *Sonnets, A Lover's Complaint,* Spenser's *Ruins of Rome,*" 117-18 and Patricia Parker, "Romance and Empire: Anachronistic *Cymbeline,*" 189-208 both in G. Logan and G. Teskey eds., *Unfolded Tales* (Ithaca: Cornell UP, 1989) 191-207.

[8] See Jonathan Hart, "Introduction: Narrative, Narrative Theory, Drama: The Renaissance," Special Issue/ Numéro Spécial. *Renaissance Narrative and Drama/ Récit et Théâtre à la Renaissance,* ed. Jonathan Hart, *Canadian Review of Comparative Literature/ Revue Canadienne de Littérature Comparée* 18 2/3 (1991): 117-18, 145-65.

[9] Here I use the word 'direct' advisedly. There is other evidence of the 'American' dimension of this play. If at one time, too little emphasis was placed on the New World in *The Tempest,* in recent years this dimension has eclipsed all other aspects. What I have been suggesting is a balance between the aesthetic and political elements. In arguing for that intricate relation, it may seem that I am playing down the utopian or new-world thematics, but such a position is only apparent because elsewhere I have recognized the im-

portance of the play for colonialism and post-colonial-ism. Now, in response to so much discussion of this dimension, I am now saying that we should look at as many views of *The Tempest,* as possible [see Hart, "Perspectives" *Arachne* 1 (1994) 78, Griffiths, "'This Island's Mine,'" *Yearbook of English Studies* 13 (1983): 159-80]. In his recent Oxford edition of the play, Stephen Orgel provides a useful reminder that it is too easy to underestimate utopia and the New World in this drama which Malone first called attention to in 1808 [Stephen Orgel, Introduction, William Shake-speare, *The Tempest* (1987. Oxford: Oxford UP, 1994) 31-6)]. For instance, in the body of this essay, I mention Gonzalo's utopian speech (II.1.145-62). Both Kermode and Orgel remind us that this speech is taken almost verbatim from Florio's translation of Montaigne's "Of the Cannibals" and echoes Renaissance thought about the relation of Europe to the New World. Shakespeare uses Strachey's account of Bermuda. The playwright associated with members of the Virginia Company like Southampton, Pembroke, Christopher Brooke, Dudley Digges and others. Other allusions to the New World exist besides "the still-vexed Bermudas" as E. E. Stoll argued in 1927 [Orgel 31-2; Charles Mills Gayley, *Shakespeare and the Founders of Liberty in America* (New York: Macmillan, 1917); Leslie Hotson *I, William Shakespeare, Do Appoint Thomas Russell, Esquire* (London: Cape, 1937), 203-36; E. E. Stoll, "Certain Fallacies and Irrelevancies in the Literary Scholarship of the Day," *Studies in Philology* 24 (1927) 487]. Charles Frey, as Orgel notes, suggests that travel narratives gave Shakespeare models of behaviour in the exchange between European and Native (Orgel 33; Charles Frey, "*The Tempest* and the New World," *Shakespeare Quarterly* 30 (1979) 34; Philip Brockbank, "*The Tempest:* Conventions of Art and Empire," *Later Shakespeare,* ed. J. R. Brown and B. Harris (London: Arnold, 1966) 183-201). From the time of Columbus into the seventeenth century, free love, utopia and cannibalism recur in the New World narratives in word and iconography. As reading Thomas Harriot shows, there is a the typology between Old World savages, such as the ancient Britons, and New World Natives (Orgel 34, Harriot, Thomas. *A Briefe and True Report of the New Found Land of Virginia* (London, 1590) sig Er). A tension exists in Shakespeare's play between notions of the Natives as predatory (Purchas, John Smith) and the ideas that the Europeans are thus (Montaigne) (see Orgel 35-6, Stephen Greenblatt, "Learning to Curse," *First Images of America,* ed. Fredi Chiapelli (Berkeley: U of California P, 1976) 561-80).

¹⁰ L. C. Green, L. C. and Olive P. Dickason, *The Law of Nations and the New World* (Edmonton: U of Alberta P, 1989) 221, 235, see 87; Neal Salisbury, "Squanto: Last of the Patuxets," David G. Sweet and Gary B. Nash ed. *Struggle and Survival in Colonial America* (Berkeley: U of California P, 1981) 239-40).

¹¹ See Sidney Lee, "The American Indian in Elizabethan England," *Scribners* 42 (1907): 313-30.

¹² Kermode xl.

¹³ See Kermode xxxii, 141.

¹⁴ See Kermode 145-7.

¹⁵ This practice of kidnapping the aboriginal peoples of the New World begins with Columbus and, for the English, appears to have occurred earlier than Kermode (62) says. For instance, in *Sixteenth Century North America: The Land and the People as Seen by the Europeans* [Berkeley: U of California P, 1971], Carl Ortwin Sauer notes the practice amongst the Portuguese: The two ships of Gaspar and Miguel Vaz Corte Real, returning from the coast of Newfoundland, brought back to Lisbon "several score of natives, male and female, described in attentive detail. They were Indians, not Eskimos, and are thought to have been Beothuks, inhabitants of Newfoundland" (13). Sauer talks about voyages from Bristol to north of Newfoundland. In March 1501 Henry VII gave letters patent to six men of Bristol, three of whom being originally from the Azores, including John Fernandes, to explore any seas yet unknown to Christians. Two voyages occurred, the ships of the second "returning with three savages, presumably Eskimos" (15).

¹⁶ See Kermode 122.

¹⁷ Kermode xxxvii, 66; see Cawley, "Shakespeare's Use of the Voyagers," *PMLA* 41 (1926): 688-726.

¹⁸ *The Four Voyages of Columbus: A History in Eight Documents, Including Five By Christopher Columbus, In The Original Spanish, With English Translations* Cecil Jane trans. and ed. (1930, 1933. New York: Dover, 1988) 8-10. See Jonathan Hart, "Images of the Native in Renaissance Encounter Narratives," *Ariel* 25 (October 1994): 55-76. Other related papers that I gave at Cambridge, Warwick, Deakin, and Melbourne from April to mid-July 1994 provide other points of view on the European and Native encounter; see Hart "Mediation in the Exchange Between Europeans and Native Americans in the Early Modern Period," special issue, *CRCL/RCLC* 22 (1995), 319-43 and "Strategies of Promotion: The Prefatory Matter of Oviedo, Thevet and Hakluyt," *Imagining Culture: Essays in Early Modern History and Literature,* Jonathan Hart, ed. (New York and London: Garland Publishing, forthcoming 1996).

¹⁹ See Northrop Frye, *Natural Perspective* (1965) 87.

²⁰ See Kermode xxxii, 88.

²¹ E.K. Chambers, *William Shakespeare: A Study of*

Facts and Problems (Oxford: Clarendon P, 1930) vol.
1. 94, cited in Kermode xxxviii.

———————

Source: "Redeeming *The Tempest*: Romance and Politics," in *Cahiers Elisabéthains,* No. 49, April, 1996,
pp. 23-38.

Introduction to *The Sonnets*

Anthony Hecht, *Georgetown University*

It may be that the single most important fact about Shakespeare's Sonnets—at least statistically—is that they regularly outsell everything else he wrote. The plays are taught in schools and universities, and a large annual sale is thereby guaranteed for *Hamlet, Macbeth, Romeo and Juliet,* and *A Midsummer Night's Dream*. But the Sonnets are still more widely read. There are several diverse factions among their readership, many of which are not scholarly. Some people are eager for a glimpse into what they suppose is Shakespeare's private life; they hope for scandal. There are those who treat the Sonnets as biographical fiction; they yearn to decode the poems and reveal a narrative of exciting, intimate relationships. And there are readers whose overriding preoccupation with sexual politics makes them determined that no one shall view the Sonnets in any way that differs from their own.

In all likelihood, however, the largest group within this readership is made up of young lovers, for whom these sonnets compose a compact and attractive *vade mecum*. The poems speak directly to their condition, being rich and emotionally complex, and they describe states of perfect happiness, but also submission, self-abnegation, jealousy, fear, desperation, and self-hatred.

It is possible to argue that there exists no work of comparable brevity and excellence that digests such intimate emotional experience. What is more, the Sonnets are written with an astonishing self-consciousness, a deep sense that love opens enormous vistas of novel reflection, not all of it flattering. Loving another human being, we find that our motives are no longer disinterested; everything we do or feel is no longer purely a personal matter, but is strangely compromised by our relationship with this other person; our hopes and fears are not only generated by another, but by how we wish to be thought of and how we have come to feel about ourselves. Initially, when we fall in love, this does not appear as any sort of danger, or indeed as anything to be deplored. Our own happiness seems enormously enlarged by being both shared with and caused by another. That is only the beginning of what, for a thoughtful person, becomes an increasingly complicated state of mind, with almost infinite permutations, most of them unforeseeable. How do we react, for example, when the person we love commits a transgression that really wounds us? If the relationship is not immediately halted, it is necessary to palliate the fault, first and foremost to ourselves, and then to the beloved. The simple first step is to fall back upon reassuring proverbial wisdom ('To err is human' or 'No one is perfect'), and, while acknowledging our pain, to temper our feelings with the suspicion that, in our idolatry of the beloved, we may have imagined an impossible perfection which it would be ludicrous to expect anyone to live up to, and which may itself have put an insupportable burden on the person we love. We begin to blame ourselves for what may have been unrealistic expectations. And if we are deeply enamoured, we wish to spare the beloved any additional anguish of guilt that would be entailed by our explicit blame. Yet this kind of generous thinking can end in the danger of our viewing ourselves as supine and servile, and lead to an active form of self-hatred. So to guard against that danger and against any tendency to blame the beloved, we may find ourselves determined to assert our unconditional love—which is, after all, as we desperately tell ourselves, what love ought to be—and to rebuke any third party who might criticise the beloved, a rebuke designed as much to confirm our own commitment as to silence the critic. I have known both heterosexual and homosexual instances of this kind of devotion which, to an outsider, is likely to seem perverse, obstinate, and full of misery. Consider, for example, the following:

> No more be grieved at that which thou hast done:
> Roses have thorns, and silver fountains mud,
> Clouds and eclipses stain both moon and sun,
> And loathsome canker lives in sweetest bud.
> All men make faults, and even I in this,
> Authòrising thy trespass with compare,
> Myself corrupting salving thy amiss,
> Excusing thy sins more than their sins are;
> For to thy sensual fault I bring in sense—
> Thy adverse party is thy advocate—
> And 'gainst myself a lawful plea commence:
> Such civil war is in my love and hate
>   That I an àccessary needs must be
>   To that sweet thief which sourly robs from me.
>
>   (Sonnet 35)

The first line presupposes a penitent attitude on the part of the beloved. Whatever the offence that is referred to as 'thy sensual fault', it is clearly something that would cause a deeper sense of guilt than could be cleared away with a simple apology. What was done is serious enough for the speaker to think of himself as offering absolution—an absolution based on the universal imperfection of all sublunary, terrestrial things that figure in the catalogue of the following three lines. It should be noted that the moon and sun, beyond the orbit of imperfection, are not themselves contaminated, but are viewed through imperfections nearer at hand. These imperfections are traditionally explained as a consequence of the fall from grace in the Garden of Eden and of man's first disobedience. (Milton himself was to write of that paradise, 'Flow'rs of all hue, and without thorn the rose'.[2]) This fallen world is thus a kind of paradox, where 'loathsome canker lives in sweetest bud'. What is being said here is complex. 'Loathsome canker' is strong language, potentially wounding to the beloved: will it seem vengeful? The speaker may hope that its tone of indictment will be sufficiently mitigated by the description 'sweetest bud'. The fifth line is more tactful, and finds fault first of all with the speaker himself for so much as venturing to excuse the beloved, and for doing so by means of metaphorical examples. There is good reason for him to apologise. The instances that he cites from nature are consequences of our fallen state and are now unalterable. To describe the faults of the beloved in the same terms is to risk saying something like: 'There's no point in your apologising, because you can't *help* doing what you do'—which makes the beloved a primitive or perverse creature and completely invalidates the sincerity of the grief mentioned in the first line. The speaker goes on, in the seventh and eighth lines, to balance any offence he may have given by proclaiming himself the worse sinner of the two, both for making too much of the trespass in the first place, and then for taking upon himself the role of the priest offering absolution, as if he himself were without taint.

The ninth line is pivotal and richly suggestive. William Empson has described it as containing at least three possible lines of thought: (1) 'I bring in reason, arguments to justify [your sensual fault]'; (2) 'I bring in feelings about it, feel it more important than it really was (and therefore excuse it more than it needs)'; (3) 'I bring extra sensuality to it; I enjoy thinking about it and making arguments to defend it, so that my sensuality sympathizes with yours.'[3] It can also bear this further meaning: 'To the sensuality of your fault I bring in (to my regret) my own sensuality, which may well, alas, have been the initial cause of your arousal, though now it is not directed at me—in other words, I am myself the unwitting author of your new-found promiscuity.'

Lines 10 and 11 are a very ingenious paradox:

> Thy adverse party is thy advocate—
> And 'gainst myself a lawful plea commence.

They may be a way of lessening slightly the gravity of the moral predicament in which both parties are now deeply enmeshed. But in addition, the paradox turns the whole focus of complaint and indictment against the speaker himself, leaving the beloved out of the picture to such a degree that with the twelfth line the love and hate are not merely balanced; we are entitled to feel that the *hatred* is as much self-directed as it is directed at the sensual fault of the beloved, and the *love* is that which is not only directed towards the beloved but generates the requisite (and, to the speaker, degrading) absolution. This 'civil war' is, in Marlowe's words, an 'intestine broil',[4] and it is highly complex. (1) Love and hate are at war. (2) The speaker is at war with himself, as well as with the beloved. (3) He is furthermore at war with the impulses of war and the impulses of hate. This warfare may end in total disaster. It seems almost, in fact, on its way to that very end in the concluding couplet, which, among other things, seems to say that the very distraction of the speaker may be driving his beloved from him; or that his generous willingness to forgive transgressions has encouraged the beloved to feel that no harm has been done; and either alternative would be a highly undesirable state of affairs. These two possibilities are mutually exclusive, and this leaves the speaker in an agonising and insoluble predicament. What is finally so effective about this poem is its stunning dramatic power. It hovers among alternatives, all of them anguishing, delicate in its manoeuvring, tense in its anxiety not to place too much blame on the beloved, but unable to conceal the torment from which the poem sprang. The 'sweet' and 'sour' of the last line echo the mixed imperfections that began the poem, in which the loathsome canker must find out and infect the sweetest bud.[5] The bitterness here is not wholly veiled by the cosmic explanation that *everything* is corrupt. The human drama is based on the terrible truth that thinking about and imagining infidelity is at least as poisonous as any proof of it, and as sickening to the contemplator. *Othello* and *The Winter's Tale* are extended illustrations of this, if any confirmation were needed. Moreover, the speaker's drama in Sonnet 35 is enhanced by the fact that we are allowed—indeed, virtually invited—to feel that he is discovering the complexity of his situation as the poem develops. The first line is grammatically and syntactically independent. It can be conceived as spoken in the uncomplicated spirit of charity, sympathy, and good will. The illustrative examples of imperfection in the lines that immediately follow are fairly conventional, and might initially seem to confirm the permissiveness and generosity of the first line, did they not almost unwittingly introduce the appalling note of universal corruption. And from there on we move into increasing darkness and unending corridors of guilt.

It seems to me impossible not to find deeply moving and compelling the complicated and tormenting emotions latent in this poem, though it may be added that such riches are, or might be, implicit in any love poetry that is searching enough. In England in the 1590s there was a vogue of sonnet-writing in which poets admonished themselves, in the words of Philip Sidney, to look in their hearts and write.[6] Such introspection and honesty are not easy in any age, and it is the general consensus that, of all the sonneteers, Shakespeare was beyond question the most penetrating. He was also the one who seemed most perfectly to adapt the form itself to his analytic or diagnostic and deeply dramatic purposes.

It may be as well at this point to say something about the sonnet as a literary form; this is not so simple a matter as commentators have supposed. In the 1870s Walter Pater argued that some parts of the early play *Love's Labour's Lost* resembled the Sonnets: 'This connexion of *Love's Labours Lost* with Shakespere's poems is further enforced by the actual insertion in it of three sonnets and a faultless song.'[7] The song, of course, is the one that ends the play: 'When daisies pied and violets blue'. But as to the three sonnets, only two of them count as such by our modern and conventional definition; the third is a poem in tetrameter couplets twenty lines long. So it should be said here that there are at least two distinct definitions of the sonnet. One of them is not formally precise; it is given by the *Oxford English Dictionary* as simply 'A short poem or piece of verse'—in early use especially, one 'of a lyrical and amatory character'. Though *OED* calls this loose definition rare and indeed obsolete, it was current in English between 1563 and 1820, and it is worth remembering that Donne's *Songs and Sonets* (1633) contained not a single poem composed in the conventional fourteen-line form. Giroux nevertheless continues to refer to *Love's Labour's Lost* as 'the sonnet play'. He would have done much better to have cited *Romeo and Juliet,* which employs far more sonnets, as well as sonnet fragments.[8] Indeed, Shakespeare seems in that play to have counted upon his audience's familiarity with some aspects of the sonnet form, and with that form's association with amatory verse.

Under the formal modern definition, the sonnet is a fourteen-line poem, usually written in pentameter verse, though Sidney, for example, sometimes used hexameters, and there have been other variations. The fourteen-line sonnet can be divided into two sorts, the Italian or Petrarchan on the one hand, and the Shakespearean on the other. The Italian poet Petrarch (1304-74) did not invent the Petrarchan form; it was used earlier by Dante (1265-1321) and his circle, but Petrarch's use of this form of sonnet to celebrate his beloved Laura made it widely known, and it was much imitated, notably in France by Ronsard (1524-85) and Du Bellay (*c.* 1522-60). The Petrarchan sonnet is composed of an octave—an initial passage of eight lines, rhyming ABBAABBA—followed by a sestet—six lines requiring only that each line have a rhyming mate. In addition to the separation of octave from sestet by

rhyme-scheme, there is almost invariably a subtle but dramatic shift, a change of tone or point of view, introduced by the sestet and bringing to the poem a sort of 're-vision' or revelation. The severe restriction placed on the rhyming words in the octave—only two rhyme sounds for eight lines—is not difficult to overcome in Italian, which has an abundance of rhyming words; despite the fact that it is very much more difficult to deal with in English, the Petrarchan sonnet has become the preferred form, used by Milton, Wordsworth, and many more recent poets.

The Shakespearean sonnet, too, is named after its most famous practitioner, but as a form it was already firmly established, and was used by Shakespeare's predecessors and contemporaries, including Spenser, Surrey, Sidney, Giles Fletcher, Samuel Daniel, Michael Drayton, Thomas Lodge, Richard Lynche, William Smith, and Bartholomew Griffin. It consists of three quatrains rhyming ABAB, CDCD, EFEF, and concluding with a rhymed couplet, GG. This form is particularly easy to 'catch by ear' and identify when spoken aloud. The final six lines of a sonnet, even though written in Shakespearean form, can become its sestet, and Shakespeare often seemed to think of his sonnets in terms of the Italian division, including the dramatic or rhetorical relationship of octave to sestet. This is clearly the case in Sonnet 35, discussed above, and Shakespeare enjoyed the rather luxurious advantage of being able to write his sonnets in the spirit of either the form named after him or the Petrarchan fashion,[9] as can be shown by comparing Sonnet 73 and Sonnet 18:

> That time of year thou mayst in me behold
> When yellow leaves, or none, or few, do hang
> Upon those boughs which shake against the cold,
> Bare ruined choirs, where late the sweet birds sang.
> In me thou seest the twilight of such day
> As after sunset fadeth in the west,
> Which by and by black night doth take away,
> Death's second self, that seals up all in rest.
> In me thou seest the glowing of such fire
> That on the ashes of his youth doth lie,
> As the death-bed whereon it must expire,
> Consumed with that which it was nourished by.
>> This thou perceiv'st, which makes thy love more strong,
>> To love that well which thou must leave ere long.
>
> (Sonnet 73)

This sonnet is a perfect example of the Shakespearean form. Three quatrains, each with its own governing figure of decline, serve as incremental parts of a discourse; each parallels and reinforces the others with beauty and delicacy of detail, and describes the inexorable truth of the natural world's mutability. William Empson's imaginative account of the fourth line is famous:

> there is no pun, double syntax, or dubiety of feeling, in

> Bare ruined choirs, where late the sweet
>   birds sang,

but the comparison holds for many reasons; because ruined monastery choirs are places in which to sing, because they involve sitting in a row, because they are made of wood, are carved into knots and so forth, because they used to be surrounded by a sheltering building crystallised out of the likeness of a forest, and coloured with stained glass and painting like flowers and leaves, because they are now abandoned by all but the grey walls coloured like the skies of winter, because the cold and Narcissistic charm suggested by choir-boys suits well with Shakespeare's feeling for the object of the Sonnets, and for various sociological and historical reasons (the protestant destruction of monasteries; fear of puritanism), which it would be hard now to trace out in their proportions; these reasons, and many more relating the simile to its place in the Sonnet, must all combine to give the line its beauty, and there is a sort of ambiguity in not knowing which of them to hold most clearly in mind.[10]

But these boughs are either themselves (by metaphoric transmutation) the bare ruined choirs, which shake against the 'cold', used as a noun; or else 'cold' is an adjective modifying bare ruined choirs themselves. This is not merely grammatical quibbling. Empson places a certain weight on the physical presence of a ruined church, cathedral, or monastery, and derives from these stones a good deal of religious controversy and historical ferment, to say nothing of the putative narcissism of the beloved—an imputation expounded at greater length in 'They that have power', an essay on Sonnet 94 in *Some Versions of Pastoral*[11].

The decline of the year, of the day, of the fire, involving the repetition of autumnal, russet and golden colours, even in the fire, is also graduated in brevity, gaining force thereby. The second quatrain is emotionally more ambiguous than the first, since death is explicitly mentioned, but its terrors are tempered by the soothing comparison with sleep, and more especially a sleep that 'seals up all in rest'. This note of tranquillity is close to Macbeth's 'Come, seeling night, / Scarf up the tender eye of pitiful day' (3.2.46-7).[12] The four lines progress from twilight to dark, and we are permitted to regard that conclusion as either a consum-

mation devoutly to be wished or else as the end of all the pleasures, beauties and joys of this mortal world. But the final quatrain is dramatically and emotionally the most dense and meaningful. The fire, once brilliant, has dimmed; its ashes now serve to extinguish the very flame that, when those ashes were wood, they fed. What is implied, of course, is that the vigour and liberties of our youth are precisely what serve to bring us, by the excess of that youthful folly and energy, to our demise. We are thus self-executed. This is not altogether remote from the notion (to be found in Donne's 'Farewell to Love') that every sexual experience abbreviates our lives by one day. This sense that youth, injudiciously or wantonly expended, brings about its own forfeiture, is restated in other terms in Sonnet 94, where Shakespeare writes of those who 'rightly do inherit heaven's graces / And husband nature's riches from expense'. These are people who maintain their youth and beauty seemingly for ever because they are by temperament 'Unmoved, cold, and to temptation slow'.

And then we come to the deeply unnerving couplet. A number of critics have observed that 'To love that well' means either to treasure your own youth, or to love the poem's speaker, whose old age and imagined death have been the subject of this poem. Either alternative presents problems of emotional complexity. If the beloved is being instructed to husband his own youth and beauty, there is the double pathos of his being instructed by the decay of the poet before him, and of the poet's making himself into a seemingly disinterested object lesson. In addition, this act of husbandry is cruelly doomed, since youth is something 'thou must leave ere long'. If, on the other hand, the beloved is being praised for the nobility of loving someone whom he is destined soon to lose, the poignancy is greatly increased, and the continued love, especially in the face of a ravaged lover, is quietly heroic. Something of the deep risk of all mortal attachments is expressed, and we once again realise that to avoid such attachments may be the safer and more prudent course, but it is not to live life to its fullest, whereas to love means to expose oneself to every possible kind of grief. On being told his newly married wife is dead, Pericles exclaims:

> O you gods!
> Why do you make us love your goodly
>   gifts
> And snatch them straight away?
> *(Per.* 3.1.22-4)

Something of Ben Jonson's anguished cry upon the death of his first son—'O, could I lose all father, now'—haunts the ending of the poem.

Sonnet 18 offers a direct contrast to Sonnet 73 in form and structure.

Shall I compare thee to a summer's day?
Thou art more lovely and more temperate:
Rough winds do shake the darling buds of
   May,
And summer's lease hath all too short a
   date;
Sometime too hot the eye of heaven shines,
And often is his gold complexion dimmed;
And every fair from fair sometime declines,
By chance or nature's changing course
   untrimmed:
But thy eternal summer shall not fade,
Nor lose possession of that fair thou ow'st,
Nor shall Death brag thou wand'rest in his
   shade,
When in eternal lines to time thou grow'st.
    So long as men can breathe or eyes can
      see,
    So long lives this, and this gives life to
      thee.

                (Sonnet 18)

This sonnet is decisively Petrarchan, notwithstanding its Shakespearean rhyme-scheme. To begin with, it is rhetorically divided into octave and sestet, the change between the two parts balanced on the fulcrum of the word 'But' at the beginning of the ninth line. The poem is widely and deservedly admired. Great riches of implication are packed into the interrogatory first line, which is a single sentence. A summer's day is itself full of meanings both lovely and ominous. It represents the season of growth, fertility, flowers, juvenescence, love, when days are not only luxurious in themselves but at their longest of all the seasons of the year. But that fact itself reminds us of a single day's brevity, no matter how long it lasts by count of daylight hours. We are already made conscious of the portents of decline and imperfection that are inevitably to follow. And how may it be said that some human being is 'like' a summer's day? This person is declared to be superior to any of them, since even the best of them have their faults. There is, I think, a danger, in reading the octave, of forgetting that the descriptive terms drawn from the world of nature are in fact metaphors for human imperfection and mutability. The third line, for example, is filled with the most delicate and tender solicitude for the fragility of beauty—and not just the beauty of buds. We are disposed to think of Hamlet's description of his father as 'so loving to my mother / That he might not beteem the winds of heaven / Visit her face too roughly' (*Ham.* 1.2.140-2). Even the most seemingly benign forces of nature, the 'eye of heaven', can induce drought and parch the skin; in Sonnet 62 Shakespeare describes himself as 'Beated and chopped with tanned antiquity'. The octave concludes with a vital distinction between 'chance' and 'nature's changing course'. Of these two forces, the latter is predictable, the former not; both are perilous. The sequential progress of the seasons is inexorable, and that it should present itself as a law of nature in the last line of the octave was implicit in the first line. But chance is another matter. In medieval times it was personified, notably by Boethius and Dante, as the pagan goddess Fortuna. Her vagaries and fickleness were proverbial, but a belief in her power provided a wonderful solution to an otherwise vexing theological problem. How could a beneficent and omnipotent God visit calamity or misfortune upon the meek, the pious, and the innocent? Speculation along these lines invited all the perils of heresy and atheism. But Fortuna, with her authority strictly confined to mundane and earthly matters, could be as capricious as she liked, and thereby exculpate God from any charge of negligence or malignity. This solution can, however, be viewed in many ways, not all of them comforting. The licensed rule of chance, undiscriminating as death itself, was reassuring to those in unfavourable circumstances, as a guarantee that if things get bad enough they could only take a turn for the better. Kent reassures himself in this way—not altogether justifiably—when he is put in the stocks: 'Fortune, good night; smile once more; turn thy wheel' (*Lear* 2.2.173). That turning of the wheel of chance also assured men that no temporal greatness was durable, and that the mighty would surely fall. If this was a consolation to the powerless, it was a serious admonition to the powerful, urging clemency and charity upon them in that season when they were in a position to confer such favours. But when chance turns to havoc, as it does in Donne's *The First Anniversarie,* very little in the way of consolation or admonition is offered:

'Tis all in pieces, all cohaerence gone;
All just supply, and all Relation:
Prince, Subject, Father, Sonne, are things
   forgot,
For every man alone thinkes he hath got
To be a Phoenix, and that there can bee
None of that kinde, of which he is, but
   hee.[13]

King Lear abounds in this sort of apocalyptic chaos of vanity and disorder, and it is this chaos that is quietly implied in Sonnet 18 by the word 'chance'.

Then comes the brilliantly defiant sestet, in which the poet promises to immortalise his beloved in deathless verse. It needs immediately to be said that this is not personal vanity, nor even a shrewd intuition on Shakespeare's part, but a poetic convention that can be traced back to classical antiquity. It can be found in Homer and Virgil, and J. B. Leishman noted that 'passages on the immortalizing power of poetry are very frequent in Pindar's Odes'.[14] This tradition was so strong among the Pléiade—the group of poets who acclimatised the sonnet form in France—that Ronsard in one of his sonnets threatened to withhold immortality from one particular unnamed lady unless she acceded to his decidedly carnal desire. The convention is to be found in Spenser's 'Epithalamion':

> Song made in lieu of many ornaments,
> With which my love should duly have bene
>   dect . . .
> Be unto her a goodly ornament,
> And for short time an endlesse moniment[15]

and in Shakespeare's own Sonnet 55:

> Not marble nor the gilded monuments
> Of princes shall outlive this pow'rful rhyme.

If Shakespeare is undoubtedly invoking an ancient convention in asserting the poet's capacity to confer immortality, it is not the only convention he employs in his sonnets. We commonly assume that, whatever else love may be, it is at the very least a spontaneous and undeniable impulse, but it was not always thought to be so, and in the Renaissance, views about it were much more complicated. One modern critic has declared flatly: 'L'amour? une invention du douziéme siécle.'[16] What could seem more pedantically offensive to our habits of feeling and thought? But the fact is that in classical literature, love is almost invariably regarded as an aberration, a dangerous taking leave of one's senses, most likely to lead to catastrophe and generally to be deplored. Many of the greatest Greek tragedies—*Oedipus Rex, Medea, Hippolytus, The Bacchae*—treat love as a tragic madness; so does Virgil in the episode of Dido in the *Aeneid*. The whole calamity of the Trojan war was brought about by a surrender to this insane impulse, which is treated in the *Iliad* as altogether unworthy and trifling in comparison with grave matters of war and heroism. The hero Odysseus, in the *Odyssey,* rejects all manner of solicitations from Calypso, Circe, and the Sirens; all these kinds of love are dangerous and to be avoided. Romantic love was historically a late development, and first manifested itself in Provence during the age of medieval feudalism, to which it bears a kind of metaphoric resemblance.

In the poetry developed by the troubadours and poets of Languedoc, the poet-lover always humbles himself in a submissive relationship to his beloved, a posture that duplicates the relation of a vassal towards his feudal lord. Indeed, as C. S. Lewis has pointed out, the lover addresses his beloved as *midons,* 'which etymologically represents not "my lady" but "my lord" '. Lewis notes that 'The lover is always abject. Obedience to his lady's lightest wish, however whimsical, and silent acquiescence in her rebukes, however unjust, are the only virtues he dares to claim.'[17] He goes on to assert that 'an unmistakable continuity connects the Provençal love song with the love poetry of the later Middle Ages, and thence, through Petrarch and many

others, with that of the present day'.[18] Anyone reading Shakespeare's Sonnet 57—'Being your slave, what should I do but tend / Upon the hours and times of your desire?'—would do well to remember the strength and antiquity of this tradition. It is a tradition virtually insisted upon in the final couplet of that sonnet:

> So true a fool is love that in your will
> (Though you do any thing) he thinks no ill.

This is more than merely abject; 'true' in these lines means not only genuinely and certifiably a fool but also 'faithful'. The implication is that fidelity not merely exposes one to folly but requires it.

These matters of tradition and convention lead us directly to the insoluble question of just what in the Sonnets may be said to be (as Wordsworth claimed they were)[19] a key with which Shakespeare unlocked his heart, and what may instead be attributed to a traditional posture belonging to the kind of fourteen-line love poem that he inherited. Are we to regard these poems as anything other than the surviving pages of an intimate diary, transcribing the poet's exact and authentic feelings on every topic he addresses? There are always readers who seek, not art, but something documentary and unassailably factual; when these two categories seem mysteriously intermingled, they will always prize the second over the first. Susan Sontag has said that

> Between two fantasy alternatives, that Holbein the Younger had lived long enough to have painted Shakespeare or that a prototype of the camera had been invented early enough to have photographed him, most Bardolators would choose the photograph. This is not just because it would presumably show what Shakespeare really looked like, for even if the hypothetical photograph were faded, barely legible, a brownish shadow, we should probably still prefer it to another glorious Holbein. Having a photograph of Shakespeare would be like having a nail from the True Cross.[20]

Those who cherish the Sonnets for their documentary value are inclined to dismiss as irrelevant, if not actually wrong, T. S. Eliot's pronouncement in 'Tradition and the Individual Talent':

> the poet has, not a 'personality' to express, but a particular medium, which is only a medium and not a personality, in which impressions and experiences combine in peculiar and unexpected ways. Impressions and experiences which are important for the man may take no place in the poetry, and those which become important in the poetry may play quite a negligible part in the man, the personality . . . One error, in fact, of eccentricity in poetry is to seek for new human emotions to express; and in this search for novelty in the wrong place it discovers the perverse. The

business of the poet is not to find new emotions, but to use the ordinary ones and, in working them up into poetry, to express feelings which are not in actual emotions at all. *And emotions which he has never experienced will serve his turn as well as those familiar to him.* [My italics][21]

Those who reject this view in so far as it applies to the Sonnets most often declare that Eliot's formula is based on the nervous self-protection of an unusually fastidious and evasive man. But such an explanation fails to take into account the fact that Eliot has done very little more than reformulate some observations of Coleridge in *Biographia Literaria* (XV, 2), so this view is not quite so idiosyncratic as has sometimes been asserted. Indeed, though the Sonnets were not published until much later, already in 1598 Francis Meres, in *Palladis Tamia: Wit's Treasury,* referred to the circulation of Shakespeare's 'sugred Sonnets among his private friends',[22] and it is reasonable to suppose that the poet would only have countenanced this kind of intimate distribution of his work if he felt it to be within the bounds of good taste. This is a question to which I shall return.

A word or two should perhaps be said here about metre and diction as they apply to these poems. Iambic pentameter—'When I do count the clock that tells the time'—is the most familiar metrical pattern in English verse. It is employed by Chaucer in *The Canterbury Tales,* by Shakespeare and Marlowe in their plays, by Milton, by Wordsworth, by the Victorians Tennyson and Browning, by Frost, Stevens, and the poets of today. It is the metre of most of the sonnets in English from Sir Thomas Wyatt to Richard Wilbur. Each line is composed of five feet, and each foot is composed, generally speaking, of two syllables, with the strong accent on the second of these, as in the naturally iambic words 'today' or 'because'. Any moderate acquaintance with the body of English poetry will so habituate a reader to this metre that it will become something that can be recognised involuntarily, as a dancer will recognise the rhythms of a waltz, a foxtrot, or a tango, each with its identifiable idiom and pattern. In the same way, a reader of poetry will in due course become habituated to the sound and weight of a line of five iambic feet, though knowing that any given line will probably deviate in some regard from complete regularity. Such deviations are licensed by convention, and conventions change with the passing of time. Deviations of stress are useful and attractive for a number of reasons. They supply the rhythmical variety that is essential in a long poem or a five-act play. They make possible a flexibility of syntax and a directness of colloquial speech that a strictly regular metre would distort. They serve as a kind of counterpoint or syncopation, if the 'ideal' pattern of the regular iambic line is kept in mind, varying from that ideal in the way a jazz musician will

improvise riffs on an established harmony and measure, or the way Elizabethan composers wrote what were called 'Divisions upon a Ground'. As readers, we welcome the introduction of non-iambic feet into a poem nominally iambic in character because we can hear in such poems the authentic sound of a human voice speaking in an idiom we can regard as reasonably 'natural'. There are many degrees and styles of such naturalness, and these too vary from period to period. But metrical flexibility allows a poet to avoid inverted word order and other peculiarities, and permits the words of a poem to speak with a true sense of emotional urgency, whether of anger, rapture, grief, or devotion.

It must be said that Shakespeare's Sonnets are in general metrically regular, especially by comparison with the great liberties he took with metre in the later plays. He often uses feminine endings (an extra, unaccented eleventh syllable at the end of a line), and twelve of the fourteen lines of Sonnet 87 ('Farewell, thou art too dear for my possessing') end in this way, most of these endings being composed of the participial *-ing*.

Clearly, matters of metre are intimately connected with questions of diction, and the diction of Shakespeare's Sonnets is worth noticing for its comparative spareness and simplicity—a sometimes deceptive simplicity. It is as far from the harsh brass choirs of Donne's Holy Sonnets, on the one hand, as it is from the stately elegance and learning of sonnets by Spenser and Sidney on the other. Just as Shakespeare made use of classical mythology only in the most chary and tentative way, so he employed a diction that not only distinguishes his work from that of his fellow sonneteers but from the language of his own work as a dramatist, both early and late. Drama presents human beings speaking to one another in something approximating the manner of ordinary human discourse, whereas we often think of poetry as violating the normal modes of speech. Furthermore, one would suppose that when, in the course of his plays, Shakespeare turns to 'heightened' forms of speech, he would reserve such heightening for the chief utterances of his major characters, as when Macbeth says:

> No; this my hand will rather
> The multitudinous seas incarnadine,
> Making the green one red.
>
> (*Mac.* 2.2.58-60)

But it is merely a nameless Second Gentleman, never to reappear, who observes at the beginning of the second act of *Othello:*

> I never did like molestation view
> On the enchafed flood.
>
> (*Oth.* 2.1.16-17)

The fact that Shakespeare can allot language like this to persons of no dramatic consequence whatever means that he is not attempting, by such musical flourishes, to convey character, but is simply treating with exuberant and exploratory relish the resources of the English language.

The solid facts about the Sonnets that can be called undisputed are few. In 1599 William Jaggard published two of the Sonnets (138 and 144) in a collection of poems called *The Passionate Pilgrim,* in which a number of other poems, some of them now firmly identified as being by other hands, were also attributed to Shakespeare. The 1590s were the time of the great vogue for sonnets in England, but Shakespeare's Sonnets did not appear until 1609, when they were published by Thomas Thorpe in a volume usually believed to have been unauthorised by Shakespeare. Thorpe possibly hoped to cash in, belatedly, on what was by then a waning interest in the form. His edition was mysteriously and indeed notoriously dedicated to 'THE.ONLIE.BEGETTER.OF.THESE. INSUING.SONNETS.M^R.W.H., and there has been a great deal of argument over this man's identity. . .There has been at least as much conjecture about the order of the poems as about the dedication, some critics proposing that they should be linked by rhyme, or by words that connect one sonnet with another. Some of the sonnets are clearly linked in rhetorical structure as part of a developed argument; several in Thorpe's sequence are clustered round a specific theme. This order, fretted over and argued about, has not yet been superseded by any other that wins wide consent, and it has some elements of design and logic to recommend it. It is generally assumed that the first 126 sonnets are addressed to a young man; the remainder concern a woman. Both involve poems of unusual intimacy, sometimes openly bawdy and erotic in character, though the humour is similar to that of the off-colour jokes that can be found in many of the plays. The poems concerned with the man are, for the most part, more respectful than those about the woman, but even the first group takes liberties that would be admissible between friends in the plays, but are less likely between a poet and his titled patron—if indeed they are to be taken as addressed to the Earl of Southampton. Shakespeare had dedicated other poems to Southampton in words of conventional servility, though it has been correctly noted that the language Shakespeare used in his prose dedication of *The Rape of Lucrece* to Southampton is very closely echoed in Sonnet 26. Southampton, of course, is one of the leading candidates for the 'young man'—along with William Herbert, Earl of Pembroke—among those who wish to decode the sequence into a personal narrative.

The question of the historical identity of the man is interestingly linked to another question. A group of the earliest sonnets in the sequence is concerned to urge the young man to marry and beget children who will perpetuate his beauty. 'What man in the whole world', asks C. S. Lewis, 'except a father or potential father-in-law, cares whether any other man gets married?' He regards this repeated recommendation of marriage as 'inconsistent . . . with a real homosexual passion. It is not even very obviously consistent with normal friendship. It is indeed hard to think of any real situation in which it would be natural.'[23] Lewis's remarks here seem amusingly suspicious of the benefits of marriage, since he finds it improbable that one friend should recommend it to another; but far more important is his comment that it is hard to think of a 'real situation' in which such a recommendation would be natural. *Are* we to imagine a real situation behind the poems? Is Shakespeare always writing *in propria persona*? Some critics have proposed that these 'marital' sonnets were commissioned to be passed on to the young nobleman as if coming from his mother.

The problem is not confined simply to the question of the young man's identity, or that of the so-called Dark Lady who is the subject of the later sonnets. Some critics with a strong narrative bent have come up with a detailed plot of sexual betrayal and infidelity which supposes that Shakespeare is simultaneously attached both to the young man and to the woman, and makes the fatal mistake of introducing them to each other, which leads, as in a third-rate film script, to their instant infatuation with each other, their abandonment of the playwright, and their exclusive erotic interest in each other. Followers of this line of argument suggest that Shakespeare acknowledged the double desertion in Sonnet 40—'Take all my loves, my love, yea, take them all'—and Samuel Butler adds the excruciating twist, perhaps suggested to him by Rostand's *Cyrano,* that some of the sonnets addressed to the Dark Lady were written by Shakespeare for the young man to pass on as his own.

There is at least one further major puzzle that seems beyond the reach of any solution. This has to do with the sexual orientation of the poet, and the quality and degree of his intimacy with the young man. (The quality and degree of his intimacy with the woman is unambiguous.) About these matters almost no one feels neutral. Many of Shakespeare's plays have been construed to demonstrate an explicit or implicit homosexual bias on the playwright's part. The relationship between Horatio and Hamlet, between Antonio and Bassanio, and between Iago and Othello—to say nothing of Orsino's erotic interest in Viola disguised as a boy and played by a boy actor, as well as Olivia's interest in Viola, who she thinks really is the boy she pretends to be, or the relationship between Falstaff and Hal[24]—all these seem homoerotic to some readers. And these arguments are invariably advanced by appealing to the 'evidence' of the Sonnets.

There was an established tradition in Europe that placed a higher value on the love relationship between men than on love between the sexes. Towards the end of the *Morte D'Arthur* (Book xx, ch. 9), Malory has King Arthur speak in a mood close to despair:

> 'And therefore,' said the king, 'wit you well my heart was never so heavy as it is now, and much more am I sorrier for my good knights' loss than for the loss of my fair queen; for queens I might have enow, but such a fellowship of good knights shall never be together in no company.'[25]

Montaigne, in his essay 'On Friendship' (by which he means the friendship between men), says something not dissimilar:

> To compare the affection toward women unto it [i.e. friendship], although it proceed from our own free choice [as distinguished from the bonds of child and parent], a man cannot; nor may it be placed in this rank. [Venus's] fire, I confess it . . . to be more active, more fervent, and more sharp. But it is a rash and wavering fire, waving and divers, the fire of an ague subject to fits and stints, and that hath but slender hold-fast [i.e. grasp] of us. In true friendship is a general and universal heat, all pleasure and smoothness, that hath no pricking or stinging in it, which the more it is in lustful love, the more is it but a ranging and mad desire in following that which flies us.[26]

'The exaltation of friendship over love was a widespread Neoplatonic commonplace . . . popularized in the writings of John Lyly'[27]—and not in Lyly's works alone, or in Montaigne's. There was the biblical story of David and Jonathan; the Homeric account of Achilles and Patroclus; the classical legend of Damon and Pythias; and, if more authority were needed, Aristotle's argument that relations between men who are friends must of necessity be closer than any possible relationship between men and women because men bear a closer resemblance to one another—an argument advanced in *The Merchant of Venice* by Portia herself in speaking of the 'love' between Bassanio, her 'lord', and his friend, Antonio. There is, moreover, a theological basis for the devotion of Antonio and Bassanio to each other. The play pointedly confronts the Old Testament (Law) with the New Testament (Love), and the latter is figuratively dramatised as an enactment of John 15.13: 'Greater love than this hath no man, when any man bestoweth his life for his friends' (Geneva Bible). Such love is expressly 'greater' than connubial love, and *The Merchant of Venice* exhibits much wit in giving each a due and proportionate place in its dramatic fable.

Since it was at times a part of Shakespeare's poetic strategy to invert, parody or burlesque sonnets in the conventional Petrarchan tradition—see, for instance, Sonnet 130: 'My mistress' eyes are nothing like the sun'—it may be useful to illustrate this device by citing just such a model along with Shakespeare's irreverent treatment of the same conventions. The following sonnet by Sir Thomas Wyatt is in fact a translation of Petrarch's sonnet, *In vita* CIX, 'Amor, che nel penser mio vive e regna':

> The longe love, that in my thought doeth
>   harbar
> And in myn hert doeth kepe his residence,
> Into my face preseth with bolde pretence,
> And therin campeth, spreding his baner.
> She that me lerneth to love and suffre,
> And willes that my trust and lustes
>   negligence
> Be rayned by reason, shame and reverence,
> With his hardines taketh displeasure.
> Wherewithall, unto the hertes forrest he
>   fleith,
> Leving his enterprise with payn and cry;
> And ther him hideth, and not appereth.
> What may I do when my maister fereth
> But in the feld with him to lyve and dye?
> For goode is the liff, ending faithfully.[28]

This remarkable poem draws its central metaphoric structure from a tradition that reaches back to the *Roman de la Rose,* which had been partly translated into English by Chaucer. The image is that of a faithful knight dedicated to the service of love, and obedient to the rebuke and correction of a sternly chaste but beautiful mistress, and thus destined to love and suffer simultaneously. But the image of knight-errantry, with all its military embellishments, goes back to the classical identification of love and war, the love of Venus and Mars, the proverbial association that links these forces in the expression, 'All's fair in love and war.' Wyatt's translation of Petrarch is lovingly compounded of a double allegiance: to Love, the involuntary passion that shows itself like a banner in the flushed face of the lover in the first quatrain—and to the beloved, to whom the lover submits in meek obedience, shame, and contrition in the second quatrain. It then becomes the complex duty of the lover to be faithful both to his passion and to his mistress; his loyalty to the former is expressed as a vassal's fidelity to his sovereign lord, and a resignation to accept death itself if that should be called for.

This very set of metaphors—military in character, involving notions of fidelity to the point of death, loyalty, treason, betrayal, and triumph—figures, with deliberate allowance made for the irony of its deployment, in what is probably Shakespeare's most outrageously libidinous sonnet:

> Love is too young to know what conscience
>   is,
> Yet who knows not conscience is born of
>   love?

Then, gentle cheater, urge not my amiss,
Lest guilty of my faults thy sweet self
    prove.
For thou betraying me, I do betray
My nobler part to my gross body's treason:
My soul doth tell my body that he may
Triumph in love; flesh stays no farther
    reason,
But rising at thy name doth point out thee
As his triumphant prize. Proud of this pride,
He is contented thy poor drudge to be,
To stand in thy affairs, fall by thy side.
    No want of conscience hold it that I call
    Her 'love' for whose dear love I rise
        and fall.

(Sonnet 151)

It does not take a long acquaintance with this poem to realise that it is laden with puns, most of them leeringly sexual. Critics have ransacked the *OED* and precedents from Elizabethan literature in tracing the various meanings buried in this wordplay, but there has been very little agreement about whether this is to be regarded as a poem to be admired or simply a crude and embarrassing piece of youthful sexual raillery. Moreover, not only has the quality of the poem been left in doubt, but its meaning as well. For while the puns have been glossed, it is often left unclear which meanings apply to particular words as they make their multiple appearances from line to line. In addition, there has been little if any discussion of the rhetorical structure and premise of the poem.

It posits a dramatic context, an anterior situation, known to the person addressed, the beloved, and to be inferred by us, the readers. It is a defence against a prior accusation, a self-exculpation, a *tu quoque* argument, but presented in a spirit of bawdy good humour, and free from any sense of guilt or of wounded feelings. Indeed, our whole task as readers is to determine the nature of the charge against which the poem has been composed as if it were a legal brief for the defence. The brief wittily employs all the ancient metaphors of vassalage and faithful military service, of warfare, treason, and triumph that had been part of the Petrarchan conventions, but which are here adapted to carnal purposes where before they had served the most discarnate and spiritual ends.

The first two lines both contain the words 'love' and 'conscience'. To make any sense of them whatever requires a recognition that a different meaning applies to those words in each of the lines. 'Love' in the opening line is Cupid, too young to know or care about the damage he inflicts with his weapons of bow and arrow (the military imagery of weapons is implied right at the start), too young to feel the pang of sexual arousal himself, and thus unaware of the pain he causes others—hence, without conscience. But in the second line 'conscience' as carnal knowledge is begotten by the passion of love (the root meaning here is *con scire*, 'to know together', in the biblical sense: 'And Adam knew Heva his wife, who conceiving, bare Cain' (Gen. 4.1 in the Bishops' Bible)). For reasons that I hope presently to make clear, I am at variance with critics who regard the phrase 'gentle cheater' as an oxymoron, especially when they argue that 'cheater' implies fraud, deceit or infidelity. The *OED* cites these very lines to illustrate its first definition of 'cheater': 'The officer appointed to look after the king's escheats; an escheator' (though this meaning became obsolete after the seventeenth century, when the modern sense implying 'fraud' replaced it). An escheater was 'an officer appointed yearly by the Lord Treasurer to take notice of the escheats in the county to which he is appointed, and to certify them into the Exchequer'; the office is therefore one concerned to demand forfeits from those who have defaulted from their obligations, usually financial. In the present case, the 'gentle cheater' is an 'assessor' of some sexual malfeasance, which the sonnet will shortly make somewhat clearer; and the epithet seems to be used without complication in an affectionate and jocular spirit.

The phrase 'urge not my amiss' is densely compressed and probably cannot be construed in isolation from the line that follows: 'Lest guilty of my faults thy sweet self prove'. I would claim in defence of my reading of 'gentle cheater' that it chimes harmoniously with 'sweet self', as any suggestion of sexual treason would not. The third and fourth lines, taken together, are a central crux of the poem, and can plausibly be interpreted in contradictory and mutually exclusive ways. If 'urge' is understood as 'incite', we may read the lines as meaning: 'Do not incite me to some known but unspecified offence (1) lest you be to blame for my fault by inciting me, or (2) lest you turn out upon further inquiry to be guilty of the very same fault yourself.' If, on the other hand, 'urge' means 'accuse' or 'allege', the lines mean: 'Do not charge me with this unspecified fault, lest in some way you turn out to be responsible for it.' There is a further possible complication. In the seventeenth-century orthography of Thorpe's edition, the fourth line is printed: 'Least guilty of my faults thy sweet selfe proue'. And if 'Least' is taken in the modern sense, as distinct from a legitimate spelling of 'Lest', the line would mean: 'Distance yourself as emphatically as possible from my ways and errors.' But this meaning cannot be fitted intelligibly into the rest of the sonnet.

All this leaves us tantalisingly uncertain about what the fault may be, though the entire remainder of the poem is devoted to it, in the form of a legal defence and exculpation, commencing with the first word of the fifth line—'For'—as the beginning of a demonstration and proof of innocence in regard to the charge. From the evidence of the argument for the defence, the charge appears ambiguously to be that the lover has either made sexual demands of too great and burdensome a kind, or else is sexually backward, shy, and indifferent in performance.

The fifth line, with its punning use of 'betray' and 'betraying', is not without its own complexities and puzzles. It has been proposed by some critics that 'betraying' means an overt act of infidelity, and that what is being claimed is something like: 'Every time you are unfaithful to me, I become sexually aroused.' This seems to me at best unlikely, though it is of course possible. Far more plausible is the suggestion that 'betraying' is used here to mean 'seducing', as when Cleopatra says:

> I will betray
> Tawny-finn'd fishes; my bended hook shall
>   pierce
> Their slimy jaws; and as I draw them up,
> I'll think them every one an Antony,
> And say, 'Ah, ha! y'are caught.'
>
> (*Ant.* 2.5.11-15)

In contrast to 'betraying', 'betray' here means the treasonable conveyance of the soul ('my nobler part') to the gross and carnal powers of the body. The body itself commits treason by subverting the soul from its chief goal and purpose. The 'I' in the fifth line betrays his own soul by subjecting it to the base authority of his body, so much corrupting the soul that it grants permission to the body to pursue its own lewd ends. And having gained this permission from the soul, the body seeks no further check upon its lusts (such checks as might be offered either by the soul or by outside authority), 'But rising at thy name doth point out thee / As his triumphant prize'. It should be noted here that the 'I' who has been advancing the whole argument of the poem has, rather interestingly, disappeared in this description of the warfare between soul and body. This familiar convention of spiritual and bodily conflict dates back at least as far as St Paul's Epistle to the Galatians 5.17: 'For the flesh lusteth against the Spirit, and the Spirit against the flesh: and these are contrary one to the other' (Geneva Bible). This conflict was played out in such poems as Andrew Marvell's 'A Dialogue between the Soul and the Body' and 'A Dialogue, between the Resolved Soul and Created Pleasure',[29] and may be found in other poems as well. In the present case, however, the conflict is circumvented or simply avoided by the total capitulation of soul to body.

The 'rising' of the ninth line and the 'pride' of the tenth refer to the tumescence of male sexual arousal; flesh is said to be 'proud' when it swells. The wit here lies in the fact that this truth pertains equally to body and to spirit: a man swollen with pride is guilty of spiritual sin. But these acknowledgements of vigor-

ous sexual reaction are now excused—and indeed glorified—as a testament to the obedience and duty of a vassal to his *midons,* his absolute sovereign, the disposer of his fortunes good and bad, his very life and death. It is 'flesh' which is the subject of lines 8-14, and by flesh is meant the male sexual organ, which is personified as faithful even unto death, rising and falling at the behest of the beloved. For this reason it seems to me highly unlikely that the word 'cheater' in the third line can contain any overtones of perfidy on the part of the beloved—a meaning which would involve the notion that the speaker is sexually aroused only by the infidelity of his beloved. This is, as I acknowledged, possible, though it raises the whole ludicrous puzzle of frequency. For a man to say of himself that he is instantly aroused by a woman's beauty is at least understandable. To defend his reputation by saying he is aroused only by infidelity on the part of the woman he loves must mean he is aroused at far less frequent intervals, as well as in more curious circumstances, and it becomes thereby a somewhat feebler defence.

There is much more to this sonnet than has been here too briefly summarised, but we must return to the nature of the 'amiss' mentioned in the third line. Has the speaker been accused of sexual negligence, indifference, or impotence? Or of making too insistent carnal demands upon the beloved? The poem can, astonishingly, be read both ways, and in both cases the same argument for the defence works. If she has said to him that he has failed to gratify her sexual appetite, his response is that her 'betrayal' or seductive looks instantly result in sexual arousal on his part, so he is blameless. If, on the other hand, she has accused him of being too insistent upon satisfying his own carnal appetites, his response is that she herself must be blamed for his behaviour by the initial betrayal (i.e. seduction) that leads him to the further betrayal of his soul to his body. No doubt all this is forensic jesting, and the sort of banter not uncommon between lovers. Those who feel the point is overworked should consider once again how much in the way of traditional Petrarchan devices, metaphors of war and treason, images of vassalage and fidelity, are, as I think, brilliantly crowded into a mere fourteen lines. This may not be one of Shakespeare's greatest sonnets, but it is surely one of his wittiest.[30]

Sonnet 151, though full of puns and complicated wordplay, is still a comparatively simple poem in terms of its tone, and it probably intends a simple and comparatively straightforward meaning, if only we were so situated as to know the nature of the 'amiss' with which it is concerned. Far more complicated in terms both of tone and meaning is Sonnet 87:

> Farewell, thou art too dear for my
>   possessing,
> And like enough thou know'st thy estimate:

The charter of thy worth gives thee
  releasing;
My bonds in thee are all determinate.
For how do I hold thee but by thy granting,
And for that riches where is my deserving?
The cause of this fair gift in me is wanting,
And so my patent back again is swerving.
Thy self thou gav'st, thy own worth then
  not knowing,
Or me, to whom thou gav'st it, else
  mistaking;
So thy great gift, upon misprision growing,
Comes home again, on better judgement
  making.
    Thus have I had thee as a dream doth
      flatter,
    In sleep a king, but waking no such
      matter.

The genius of this poem consists in its absolute command of tonal complexity throughout, by which it is left brilliantly ambiguous—through tact and diplomacy, with bitterness and irony, or with matter-of-fact worldliness—just which of the two parties involved is to be blamed for the impasse and end of what had once been a deeply binding relationship. The pretext of the poem is one of self-mortification characteristic of the traditional early love sonnets discussed above. The lover insists upon his own unworthiness, particularly as regards the exalted, unapproachable condition of the beloved. Although there is a pun on the word 'dear' in the first line—a pun made the more explicit by the possibly commercial language of the second line—puns are not the building blocks of this poem as they are of others. The lover begins in what seems initially to be a spirit of generous renunciation: the line can mean both (1) 'I am prepared to give you up' and (2) 'I appear not to have much choice in the matter, so I am giving you up.' Taken in conjunction with the first line, however, the second line of the poem seems to include or suggest the following possible meanings:

(1) You know how much I love you.
(2) You know how much you deserve to be
    loved.
(3) You have a very high opinion of
    yourself.
(4) You know how much others love you.
(5) You know the value of the opinions of
    (a) me
    (b) yourself
    (c) others
    (d) all of us.

The poem continues to manoeuvre between these modes of worldliness and unworldliness in a way that, by its skill, speaks of two different kinds of pain, and at the same time makes the pain almost tolerable by the sheer act of lively intelligence that went into the making of the poem, which is clearly no raw, unmediated transcription of experience. By the time we reach the end of the second line, the poem has begun to seethe with implied hostility, governed nevertheless by conventions of propriety and the decorum of charity. We cannot fail to notice the pervasive language of law and commerce, those two ledger-keeping modes of coming to terms with the world; and we cannot fail to feel the irony of the application of those modes to questions of love.

The speaker here seems to be giving the beloved a writ of freedom to depart, and justifying that departure by several different kinds of 'reason', generally practical and intended as plausible. The words 'estimate', 'charter', 'bonds', 'riches', 'gift', 'patent', 'misprision', and 'judgement' all speak, as might a shrewd auctioneer, from a market-place perspective. Beneath the surface of supposedly self-abnegating relinquishment, we detect a flavour of bitterness and scarcely repressed resentment. This may be most openly expressed, and at the same time best concealed, by the lines

  For how do I hold thee but by thy granting,
  And for that riches where is my deserving?

We do not love anyone on the basis of merit, or rank, or wealth, or for other worldly advantages. Love mixed with or tainted by calculation is highly suspect—is indeed not love at all. It follows then that if the beloved is willing to accept as a legitimate excuse for withdrawing from the relationship any of the various 'worldly' and practical excuses proposed by the lover, then the lover cannot but conclude that the love has not been mutual, whatever he may have thought it to begin with; that the beloved, surveying the prospect or prospects, has both reason and right to seek elsewhere, since no real love seems to be involved. The very word 'misprision' means both a misunderstanding or mistake, and also a clerical error of the ledger-keeping sort. The final irony of the poem lies in the fact that both parties were deeply deceived—the beloved by either underestimating himself or overestimating the lover, and the lover by having believed that he was loved.

This mutual deception and self-deception are re-examined by Shakespeare in Sonnet 138:

  When my love swears that she is made of
    truth,
  I do believe her, though I know she lies,
  That she might think me some untutored
    youth,
  Unlearnèd in the world's false subtleties.
  Thus vainly thinking that she thinks me
    young,
  Although she knows my days are past the
    best,

Simply I credit her false-speaking tongue:
On both sides thus is simple truth
   suppressed.
But wherefore says she not she is unjust?
And wherefore say not I that I am old?
O love's best habit is in seeming trust,
And age in love loves not t'have years told.
     Therefore I lie with her, and she with me,
     And in our faults by lies we flattered be.

Sonnet 93 deals with the subject even more directly—'So shall I live, supposing thou art true, / Like a deceivèd husband . . . ' Sonnet 138 is a private meditation, with no express addressee, and may perhaps exhibit a certain candour of insight that direct address might forbid in the name of tact. But each is concerned with love as illusion, as self-deception, as bitterly unreal—in ways that remind us that the world of *A Midsummer Night's Dream* is not altogether as taintless as it might at first appear.

This capacity for illusion and self-deception concerns not only matters of love but our very sense of ourselves, of our worth—our self-image and self-respect. This issue raises its head in the sonnets about the 'rival poet'. These are usually regarded as a group made up of Sonnets 78-80 and 82-86. But even in so 'early' a sonnet as the celebrated 29—'When in disgrace with Fortune and men's eyes'—we find the quatrain:

Wishing me like to one more rich in hope,
Featured like him, like him with friends
   possessed,
Desiring this man's art, and that man's
   scope,
With what I most enjoy contented least . . .

Such vulnerability, modesty, uncertainty, are touching in their own right, and a small solace to lesser poets in their moods of tormenting self-doubt.

I have earlier raised the topic of how literally and precisely we should allow ourselves to read these poems as documentary transcriptions of personal events. This calls for a few further words. A number of philosophers, beginning perhaps with Plato, have argued on a variety of grounds that poetry is a tissue of lies. This was Stephen Gosson's view in *The School of Abuse* (1579), and John Skelton, maintaining that religious poetry is 'true', touches upon the same conventional topic when he asks:

Why have ye then disdain
At poets, and complain
How poets do but feign?[31]

This view, that poets are only feigning, did not differ greatly from ideas that were forcibly advanced during the period of the Enlightenment, when the domain of truth was confined more and more strictly to what could be known with scientific precision. It is a view still voiced in certain quarters to this day. But we may approach the question in another way—one that centres on the nature of poetic form and the demands it makes on the materials it must employ and put into artistic order. The raw materials of poetry can be recalcitrant; the demands of form can be severe. How are these conflicting elements to be reconciled? Here is W.H. Auden's especially persuasive answer to that question:

> In the process of composition, as every poet knows, the relation between experience and language is always dialectical, but in the finished product it must always appear to the reader to be a one-way relationship. In serious poetry thought, emotion, event, must always appear to dictate the diction, meter, and rhyme in which they are embodied; vice versa, in comic poetry it is the words, meter, rhyme, which must appear to create the thoughts, emotions, and events they require.[32]

If what Auden says is right (and it seems to me almost indisputable), then the question of the documentary nature of the Sonnets is largely irrelevant. This will no doubt leave some readers feeling cheated. But the Sonnets are, first and last, poems, and it should be our task to read, evaluate, and enjoy them as such. Devoted attention to each of them in its own right will yield striking discoveries. They are not all equally inventive or moving. Some are little more than conventional; others are wonderfully original and ingenious. Scarcely any lacks true merit, many of them are beyond compare, and in bulk they are without question the finest single group of sonnets in the language. They contain puzzles which will probably never be wholly answered, and this may be a part of their enigmatic charm. But most of all they speak with powerful, rich, and complex emotion of a very dramatic kind, and we cannot fail to hear in them a voice of passion and intelligence.

Notes

[2] Milton, *Paradise Lost,* IV, 256.

[3] William Empson, *The Structure of Complex Words,* 1951, pp. 272-3.

[4] Christopher Marlowe, *Hero and Leander,* 1, 251, in *Works,* II, 438.

[5] Compare Sonnet 94: 'For sweetest things turn sourest by their deeds.'

[6] See the first sonnet in Sidney's *Astrophil and Stella.*

[7] Walter Pater, *Appreciations,* 1889, p. 167. A similar identification is made more recently by Robert Giroux,

The Book Known as Q, 1982, pp. 140-1, citing Pater and referring to *Love's Labour's Lost* as 'the sonnet play'.

[8] See Prologue to Act 1; 1.2.45-50; 1.2.88-93; 1.5.93-110; Prologue to Act 2; 5.3.12-17; 5.3.305-10.

[9] It should be added that while these two canonical varieties of the sonnet predominate among Shakespeare's ventures in the form, there are individual sonnets that deviate from both; for rhetorical purposes, or under the pressure of overwhelming feelings, the 'divisions' of some sonnets are at odds with both the Petrarchan and the Shakespearean convention. See, for example, Sonnets 66, 145, and 154.

[10] William Empson, *Seven Types of Ambiguity,* 2nd edn, 1947, pp. 2-3.

[11] William Empson, *Some Versions of Pastoral,* 1935, pp. 89-115.

[12] This is pointed out by Stephen Booth (ed.), *Shakespeare's Sonnets,* rev. edn, 1978, p. 259.

[13] John Donne, *The First Anniversarie,* lines 213-18, in *The Epithalamions, Anniversaries and Epicedes,* ed. W. Milgate, 1978, p. 28.

[14] J. B. Leishman, *Themes and Variations in Shakespeare's Sonnets,* 1961, p. 27.

[15] Edmund Spenser, *Epithalamion,* lines 427-32, in *Works, Minor Poems,* II, 252.

[16] Charles Seignobos, quoted by Maurice Valency, *In Praise of Love,* 1958, p. I. Much the same claim is made by C. S. Lewis, *The Allegory of Love,* 1936, p. 2: 'Every one has heard of courtly love, and every one knows that it appears quite suddenly at the end of the eleventh century in Languedoc.'

[17] Lewis, *Allegory of Love,* p. 2.

[18] *Ibid.,* p. 3.

[19] William Wordsworth, 'Scorn not the Sonnet', a sonnet published in 1827.

[20] Susan Sontag, *On Photography,* 1977, p. 154.

[21] T. S. Eliot, *Selected Essays 1917-32,* 1932, pp. 9-10.

[22] E. K. Chambers, *William Shakespeare: A Study of Facts and Problems,* 2 vols., 1930, II, 194.

[23] C. S. Lewis, *English Literature in the Sixteenth Century Excluding Drama,* 1954, p. 503.

[24] See W. H. Auden, 'The Prince's Dog', in *The Dyer's Hand and Other Essays,* 1962, pp. 182-208.

[25] Sir Thomas Malory, *Le Morte D'Arthur,* ed. Janet Cowen, 2 vols., 1969, II, 473.

[26] *The Essays of Michael, Lord of Montaigne,* trans. John Florio (1603), 3 vols., 1928, I, 195-209.

[27] See David Bevington (ed.), *The Complete Works of Shakespeare,* 1980, p. 1582.

[28] R. A. Rebholz (ed.), *The Complete Poems of Sir Thomas Wyatt,* 1978, pp. 76-7.

[29] Elizabeth Story Donno (ed.), *Andrew Marvell: The Complete Poems,* 1972, pp. 25-8 and 103-4.

[30] Anyone who wants to see how carefully constructed, how densely packed, a sonnet of Shakespeare's can be, and who would also like to see how a sensitive and painstaking reader with responsible critical intelligence can unpack those meanings and reveal that design, cannot do better than read Roman Jakobson on Shakespeare's Sonnet 129, in Roman Jakobson and Lawrence G. Jones, *Shakespeare's Verbal Art in 'Th'expense of spirit',* The Hague, 1970.

[31] John Skelton, 'A Replication Against Certain Young Scholars Abjured of Late', in John Scattergood (ed.), *John Skelton: The Complete English Poems,* 1983, p. 384.

[32] W.H. Auden (ed.), *Selected Poetry and Prose of Byron,* 1966, p. xix.

Source: An introduction to *The Sonnets,* edited by G. Blakemore Evans, Cambridge University Press, 1996, pp. 1-28.

"The care . . . of subjects' good": *Pericles,* James I, and the Neglect of Government

Stuart M. Kurland, *Duquesne University*

Critics have generally found the story of Pericles, Prince of Tyre, interesting—if at all—for the strange and marvelous adventures that befall the romance hero as he wanders the ancient Mediterranean world. Yet Pericles is also a prince—a prince who seems curiously uninterested in the fate of his kingdom of Tyre once he takes ship, in Act I, to escape the vengeance of the tyrant Antiochus, a prince who seems oblivious to the important issues of government and statecraft depicted in the diverse realms he visits. Pericles' obliviousness is the more striking since it appears in the context of a virtual education in government provided by a diverse group of rulers: the incestuous and cruel Antiochus, the ineffective but kindly Cleon, the "good Simonides," the licentious but miraculously transformed Lysimachus. Pericles' remoteness and general passivity are striking too because of the contrast with them provided by the energetic conduct of the daughter who will inherit his authority, the "absolute" Marina. Pericles' only daughter confronts and overcomes comparable adversity at the hands of fate, enough to consume all of Act IV and rate prominent mention alongside Pericles on the Quarto title page, which calls attention both to "the whole Historie, aduentures, and fortunes of the said Prince: As also, The no lesse strange, and worthy accidents, in the Birth and Life, of his Daughter MARIANA [sic]."[1]

These political aspects of *Pericles,* I will argue, are best appreciated in the context of early Jacobean politics, notably the problems associated with King James I's disinclination to stay in London to dispatch government business—that is, to govern and to be seen as governing. While James remained in the country whenever he could, hunting and traveling restlessly from one rural seat to another, his ministers were left to conduct affairs of state by correspondence. Observers commented on the problems caused by the King's apparent inattention to government business, which was the more notable in contrast with the picture of involvement presented by Elizabeth I. It might seem farfetched to see in Pericles and Marina an allegory of rule in the early Jacobean period, but, as I will suggest, the contemporaneous perception of royal indifference to good government provides a context for viewing Shakespeare's interest around 1606 in such a "mouldy" tale as the ancient history of Apollonius of Tyre, his politicization of aspects of that tale in *Pericles, Prince of Tyre,* and the play's surprising contemporary popularity.

I

Let us begin with the travels of Pericles, who flees Antioch secretly after he discovers the tyrant Antiochus' secret incest in the opening scenes. Convinced that his discovery will result in certain death, Pericles returns home to Tyre and falls into a deep depression about the suffering that will surely befall his subjects. When Helicanus advises Pericles to "travel for a while" and offers himself as caretaker, Pericles immediately embraces the suggestion—"The care I had and have of subjects' good/On thee I lay, whose wisdom's strength can bear it" (I.ii.106, 118-19)—and takes ship. Guided by ancient Gower and his dumb shows, the audience of *Pericles* accompanies the romance hero in his wanderings, sailing from Tyre to Tharsus, from Tharsus to Pentapolis, from Pentapolis to Ephesus, from Ephesus to Tharsus—and, eventually, after a gap of many years, enduring a period of aimless drifting in the Mediterranean and Aegean seas that brings him to Mytilene and then to Ephesus, where he and his reunited family make plans to return to Pentapolis.

The impression of constant movement, frenzied and disjointed, is compounded by sudden scene shifts while Pericles is off stage—for example, during Pericles' entertainment in Pentapolis after his shipwreck the scene returns to Tyre, where Pericles' lords urge Helicanus to take the crown for himself (II.iv. 17-58). More significant, during Pericles' virtual disappearance from the story in Act IV, we follow the fortunes of his daughter Marina, who is brought from Tharsus to Mytilene, where they will eventually be reunited.[2]

Sometimes these movements are quite deliberate, as when Pericles and his wife Thaisa take ship for Tyre to reclaim his crown (III.Chorus.39-41). But often, as with Pericles' wanderings in Act IV, they seem deliberately aimless. Periodically, outside forces interrupt and redirect events. There are human agents: an assassin in the service of an incestuous tyrant, a jealous mother, a band of opportunistic pirates. And there are natural or supernatural forces, equally appropriate to romance, notably three storms at sea (which cause Pericles to wash up in Pentapolis, to bury a comatose Thaisa at sea off Ephesus, and to find harborage and Marina in Mytilene), and, memorably, the vision of the goddess Diana (V.i.238-47), which leads directly to Pericles' reunion with Thaisa.[3] Whether deliberate or aimless in themselves, the product of human or non-human forces, Pericles' continual, random movements suggest an unsettled life, a life without direction or purpose.

This sense of purposelessness is inseparable from Pericles' casual attitude towards rule: his apparent disinclination or inability to exercise his authority responsibly in Tyre. As Pericles traverses the known world, Tyre is governed by a regent of uncommon dedication—"A figure of truth, of faith, of loyalty," as Gower observes in the Epilogue (l. 8)—yet the lengthy regency nevertheless results in a "mutiny" by the lords (III.Cho.29), who, uncertain about the fate of the prince and fearful of the consequences for a headless commonwealth, urge the regent to assume the crown.

The impression of drift in Pericles' movements is reinforced by a number of inconsistencies, even absurdities, in the treatment of geographical detail that become clear when his course is plotted on a map.[4] Though seemingly inconsequential in themselves, these lapses may undermine an attentive audience's confidence in Pericles' ability to control himself and his world. After Pericles deciphers Antiochus' riddle and returns to Tyre, for example, his choice of Tharsus for a refuge (I.ii.115-17) seems to place him in unnecessary danger, since to get there he must retrace his course along the Syrian coast near Antioch. Learning in Tharsus that Antiochus has in fact sent an assassin after him, Pericles again "put[s] forth to seas" and survives a shipwreck off Pentapolis (II.Cho.22-34), likely the cluster of five cities on and near Rhodes, off southwest Asia Minor in the Aegean Sea.[5] From Pentapolis, Pericles, after wooing and marrying Thaisa, returns with his pregnant wife to Tyre and along the way encounters another storm off Ephesus in western Asia Minor—that is, having traveled some distance in the wrong direction.[6] Concluding that she has died in childbirth off Ephesus and concerned about caring for the newborn, Pericles considers changing directions; he is now, unaccountably, off the coast of Tharsus on the other end of the eastern Mediterranean (III.i.72-79)—an impossibility. Such a course change would make no sense if he is sailing off the coast of Ephesus, since from there the distance to Tharsus and Tyre, his original destination, is approximately equal.[7]

These discrepancies, which may underscore our sense of Pericles' lack of control over his environment, can be accounted for in various ways. Many of them derive directly from the Apollonius of Tyre tradition that the play dramatizes—a tradition which has been well documented by Elizabeth Archibald.[8] Shakespeare could be casual about geography, as the Bohemian seacoast in *The Winter's Tale* reminds us.[9] And, of course, there is clearly dramatic warrant for such departures from strict realism as eliding the distance between Ephesus and Tharsus or skipping over Marina's childhood under Dionyza's care—inconsistencies that would likely go

unnoticed in performance. But we ought also to keep in mind that the lack of realism is a feature that characterizes romance, a form whose characteristic self-consciousness about its lack of realism paradoxically allows it to be useful for a dramatist interested in exploring sensitive political issues.

II

Let us turn to the record of a very different set of travels, the progresses and hunting trips that marked the residence of King James I in England during the period of *Pericles'* composition, around 1606-08.[10] Endeavoring to "sample" James' "wanderings" in the course of one year, 1605, D. H. Willson writes that the King left Royston for Whitehall for the Christmas season 1604-05, returned to Royston in mid-January 1605, and then moved to Huntingdon and Hinchinbrook.

> He came to London early in February but soon returned to Royston, travelled thence to Ware, Newmarket and Thetford, then back to Newmarket and Royston, then to London about the middle of March. For some four months he remained in the vicinity of the capital, moving between Greenwich, Richmond, Windsor and Oatlands, hunting as he went. A progress in July and August took him towards Oxford. Thence he came to Windsor and to Hampton Court for part of September. In October he was again at Royston, Huntingdon, Hinchinbrook and Ware, and though he came to London to open Parliament in November, he returned to Royston for most of the remainder of the year.[11]

In various contemporary accounts, the King's hectic itinerary is a constant theme: during the first half of 1606, for example, James' movements can be traced from Enfield to London (he stayed primarily at Greenwich and Whitehall, with trips to Woking and Newmarket), then to Royston and on to Newmarket, and again to "London and its neighbourhood" (with brief stays at Havering, Theobalds, and Cheshunt).[12]

M. S. Giuseppi, editor of the Salisbury papers, quotes James writing in 1607 to his chief minister, Robert Cecil, Viscount Cranborne and later Earl of Salisbury, that "the confusion of business before my parting made me to forget those principal things whereof I should then have put you in remembrance," a comment that Giuseppi says "sums up very well the disorder introduced into the administration both by his peregrinations and also by his entire mode of life."[13] On a number of occasions, the business of government was delayed or disrupted as a result of James' disinclination to stay in London: the Salisbury papers refer to a lost box that may have contained letters, a delivery boy who hurt himself and lay in the fields overnight until found, and complaints about the slow conveyance of important papers from the Privy Council. "On other occasions Salisbury's letters are reported to have arrived soon after six in the morning but the King was already on horseback. . . . The King remembers that he had forgotten sundry things in his last letter; . . . he puts off reading those from Salisbury, lies abed late, or is in no disposition to sign anything owing to a swollen ankle."[14]

Modern historians have been divided about just how disruptive James' habits were. According to Willson's unsympathetic portrait, after the accession in 1603 his "Councillors soon discovered that the transaction of business was rendered difficult by the peculiar habits of the King, and especially by his fondness for country life. . . . [T]he nervous and perpetual wanderings of this peripatetic Prince never ceased; year in and year out, for weeks and months on end, he loitered in the country or journeyed from one hunting-seat to the next though business demanded his presence in London." James' passion for hunting was well known. But he also sought to avoid London, which he "heartily disliked, much preferring the retired privacy and careless ease of the country. He wished to escape from business, from perplexing diversity of counsel, from the merciless importunity of suitors." On balance, according to Willson, James' "sylvan existence caused many difficulties in government."[15]

This view, that the business of government suffered because "[g]overnment was conducted largely by correspondence,"[16] has been challenged by Maurice Lee, Jr., who nonetheless acknowledges that James' reputation suffered from "his devotion to the chase, which made him appear uncaring and irresponsible." Lee quotes a dispatch from the Venetian ambassador soon after the accession in which James was reported to be "bewitched" by his ministers: "He is 'lost in bliss' and leaves everything to them, while he indulges in the pursuit of stags, 'to which he is quite foolishly devoted'."[17] And Lee acknowledges that "many English courtiers and officials were disconcerted by the king's lifestyle and habits of business."[18] But James felt that "[d]ay-to-day attention to the government of England was not necessary for him" and could be left to Salisbury and his other ministers. As an "experienced king," James could keep up with necessary business by relying on his servants and using his own time efficiently. "And he could, and did, keep in touch: he was seldom very far from London." According to Lee, "James might justifiably have resented any charge that he neglected his duties. His unbusinesslike lifestyle and the disorderly nature of his court, both so very different from Elizabeth's, concealed the amount of attention he paid to business and have given him a reputation for laziness that is far from deserved."[19] According to this view, "it is possible to exaggerate the delays and disruption of business routine entailed by James's lifestyle. Cecil found ways to get the nec-

essary business done—through . . . [one of the members] of James's peripatetic entourage."[20]

Whatever the disagreements among modern historians—who will no doubt continue to reassess the abilities, character, and habits of James I[21]—for our purposes the pertinent issue is how James' habits appeared to interested contemporaries, especially observers outside the court. Writing prior to the coronation, Thomas Wilson reported, "Sometymes he [James] comes to Counsell, but most tyme he spends in fieldes and parkes and chaces, chasinge away idlenes by violent exercise and early risinge, wherin the Sune seldom prevents him."[22] A Privy Councillor accompanying James at Royston in late 1604 complained of exhaustion from trying to keep up with him in the field and with official business in his lodgings: "since my departure from London I think I have not had two hours of twenty-four of rest but Sundays, for in the morning we are on horseback by eight, and so continue in full career from the death of one hare to another, until four at night; then, for the most part, we are five miles from home; by that time I find at my lodging sometimes one, most commonly two packets of letters, all which must be answered before I sleep, for here is none of the Council but myself, no, not a Clerk of the Council nor Privy Signet. . . . "[23] John Chamberlain reported in early 1605 that at Royston the King "findes such felicitie in that hunting life, that he hath written to the counsaile, that yt is the only meanes to maintain his health, (which being the health and welfare of us all) he desires them to undertake the charge and burden of affaires, and foresee that he be not interrupted nor troubled with too much busines. . . . Though he seeke to be very private and retired where he is, yet he is much importuned with petitions . . . [in behalf of nonconforming clergy] and with foolish prophesies of daungers to insue."[24]

There were complaints about James' habits, including a letter from the Archbishop of York to Salisbury, transcripts of which circulated, in which he gently criticized James' devotion to hunting. According to the Earl of Worcester, reading the letter James "was merry at the first, till as I guessed he came to the wasting of the treasure, and the immoderate exercise of hunting. He began then to alter countenance, and, in the end, said it was the foolishest letter that he ever read." James commended Salisbury for his "excellent answer, paying him soundly, but in good and fair terms."[25] And there was an anonymous message delivered in an unusual manner. Hunting near Royston, James was displeased to find that "one of the King's special hounds, called Jowler," was missing; the next day the dog was found with a paper attached to his neck: "Good Mr. Jowler, we pray you speak to the King (for he hears you every day, and so doth he not us) that it will please his Majesty to go back to London, for else the country will be undone; all our provision is spent already, and we are not able to entertain him longer." Unfortunately for the hard-pressed local inhabitants, the message "was taken for a jest, and so passed over, for his Majesty intend[ed] to lie there yet a fortnight."[26]

To the Privy Council, James sent assurances "that I shall never take longer vacancy from them for the necessary maintenance of my health than other kings will consume upon their physical diets and going to their whores."[27] He expressed a similar sentiment in an undated letter: "if my continual presence in London be so necessary as my absence for my health makes the councillors to be without authority or respect, one word shall bring me home and make me work till my breath work out, if that be the greatest weal for the kingdom. But I cannot think that course so needful. . . . "[28]

Various testimonials to the King's fondness for hunting and disinclination to be disturbed while engaged in his private pastimes can be found in contemporary accounts. On one occasion, near Thetford, James "was driven out of the field with press of company, which came to see him; but therein he took no great delight, therefore came home, and played at cards." Residents were then forbidden, by proclamation, to "presume to come to him on hunting days; but those that come to see him, or prefer petitions, shall do it going forth, or coming home."[29] In fall 1605 Chamberlain relayed an account of the King's visit to Oxford that concludes: "Other newes here hath ben litle or none but hunting and such like journies. The King went lately to Roiston his old garrison, and is now at Huntington or thereabout: the Quene lies at Hampton Court, and the counsaile sit much at White-hall about ordering the houshold. . . . "[30]

Another, clearly unsympathetic, account of James' entertainment at Oxford contrasts his inattention to "the public business" while there with Elizabeth's conduct during a progress of 1592: "whilst the Queen was at Oxford, some time was allowed for the Lords to sit in Council, during which all other exercise ceased; but during the King's days of enchantment there, there was no time left for Counsel (that I have observed), but the public business seems to have been forgotten."[31] In late October, Chamberlain reported that "The King findes such varietie of sports that he cannot easilie leave Roiston and those quarters: he is now fallen into a great humor of catching larkes and takes as much delight in yt or more then in hunting."[32]

In sum, various contemporary accounts—both those of government officials concerned about getting business done and of outside observers interested in how England was being governed—preserve the impression that there were misgivings about James' manner of living, notably his constant movements from one place to another and his apparent preference for the excite-

ment of the hunt over the tedium of governing. I believe such concerns animate the politics of *Pericles*.

III

If we focus on the pragmatic issue at the heart of governance, the central question of the monarch's apparent concern for and attention to the maintenance of the commonweal,[33] Pericles is surely lacking as a prince. Pericles is hardly the first representation in Shakespeare's work of a monarch who appears disengaged from the responsibilities of rule. Besides Lear, who wishes—like Richard II—to enjoy the ceremonial aspects of monarchy without the responsibility that goes with them, we might add a number of rulers from the seemingly non-political plays of the Jacobean period: Duke Vincentio, Cymbeline, Leontes, Prospero. Even in the most overtly political plays of Shakespeare, which clearly show the personal and political limitations of a Richard II or Lear, we tend to see only brief glimpses of the actual business of government, of the processes by which options are considered, decisions are reached, and authority is exercised. In *Pericles* we find several brief and pragmatic discussions, notably between Pericles and Helicanus, about the responsibilities of rule, and we find some discussion among the lords of Tyre about whether the good of the state requires that Pericles' authority be conferred permanently on the regent Helicanus. Still, it is Pericles' *failure* to rule that lies at the heart of the play and reminds us of other irresponsible rulers in Shakespeare's late plays.[34]

Although the play's hero is explicitly identified as "Pericles, Prince of Tyre" in the Stationers' Register entry and on the Quarto title page,[35] Pericles often appears more like a private gentleman than a king. The extreme case comes after his shipwreck in Pentapolis, when he reveals nothing of his identity to the fishermen who assist him beyond the obvious fact that he is fallen in fortune (II.i.52-165) and introduces himself at court as simply "A gentleman of Tyre" (II.iii.81). Pericles maintains this humble persona throughout the courtship of Princess Thaisa, despite King Simonides' suspicions that he is of royal birth (II.v.77-79), until messengers from Tyre arrive by chance and reveal his true identity (III.Cho.26-38). By this time, Pericles has already taken a bride and set up housekeeping, incognito, at her father's court.

When Pericles appears on shipboard at the end of the play he is identified as the King of Tyre, but in behavior and appearance he is anything but regal: his despondency is so great he has not spoken in three months, "nor taken sustenance/ But to prorogue his grief" (V.i.23-26), and he appears in sackcloth, unwashed and unbarbered (IV.iv.27-29). Nor does his conduct elsewhere appear royal. During his long flight from Antiochus, he loses touch with Helicanus and his other lords despite his avowed intention to remain in contact (I.ii.116-17), with the result that the lords presume him dead and, out of concern for the well-being of a state left "without a head—/ Like goodly buildings left without a roof," press Helicanus to take the crown for himself (II.iv.26-39).

Although the shipwreck off Pentapolis may be seen to contribute to Pericles' difficulty in maintaining contact, once he recovers he still fails to initiate contact with his subjects in Tyre—and he is finally found only because of his subjects' persistence. Summoned home by the news that Antiochus is dead (so the threat to Tyre is eased) and that his subjects plan to crown Helicanus if he does not return within a year (a device of Helicanus "The mutiny . . . t'appease" [III.Cho.29]), Pericles is thus compelled to turn his thoughts homeward, to the kingdom he has neglected. As Gower succinctly puts it, "Brief, he must hence depart to Tyre" (l. 39). After a second storm on the voyage to Tyre causes him to lose Thaisa off Ephesus and head for Tharsus to leave the infant Marina, Pericles continues on only because he is impelled by the expiration of his year and the knowledge that Tyre "stands/ In a litigious peace" (III.iii.1-3).

Pericles' care for his country is overwhelmed by his personal grief, which is strikingly evident in his resolve to leave his hair uncut until Marina marries "Though I show ill in't" (III.iii.27-30). A tidy appearance does not make a prince, of course, but after Pericles' return to Tyre, where Gower invites us to imagine him "Welcom'd and settled to his own desire" (IV.Cho.1-2), the play leaves him, and we are left to wonder whether he now pays any more attention to the state than he does to his appearance—or to his growing daughter and heir, whom he ignores for fourteen years, during which it is unclear what occupies his time (a similarly problematic feature of Apollonius of Tyre).[36] Gower insists that Marina is "all his life's delight" (IV.iv.12), but Pericles' neglect is again suggested by the fact that she does not recognize him when they meet in Mytilene. When Pericles learns of his daughter's supposed death, like Apollonius,[37] he sinks into overwhelming despair: Pericles leaves Tharsus "in sorrow all devour'd," swearing to wear sackcloth and "Never to wash his face, nor cut his hairs" (IV.iv.25-28). Literally and metaphorically, the despondent Pericles drifts, his "courses," as Gower says, "ordered/ By Lady Fortune" until the storm that drives him into Mytilene and the reunion with Marina (IV.iv.46-48, V.Chor.13-15). There is nothing regal about Pericles or his suffering.

While these events involving Pericles transpire, his lords, especially the regent Helicanus (and, to a lesser extent, Escanes), fill the political vacuum in Tyre. The contrast between Helicanus' sense of duty and Pericles' apparent indifference to his responsibilities is often

striking. Helicanus, ruling selflessly during the period of Pericles' travels, refuses to take the crown for himself despite the persistent entreaties of the lords (II.iv.17-58). Since a textual problem mars the scene in which Pericles returns from Antioch and determines to flee, his motives appear somewhat garbled. Also garbled are Helicanus' comments on the importance of good counsel and the corrupting influence of flattery, a speech which "seems quite uncalled for" in the context in which it appears.[38] According to Stephen Dickey, in denouncing flatterers Helicanus is guilty of flattery himself, and his advice is hardly disinterested: counseling Pericles to flee and leave the government to him, Helicanus encourages Pericles' "first abdication of responsibility."[39] But such a reading overlooks Helicanus' actual exercise of power, which consistently seeks to protect the prince's interest, and the legitimacy of the monarchical system, notably in Helicanus' unwillingness to accept the crown despite the lords' entreaties.

The figure of Helicanus is elaborated from a hint in Gower, where the name appears, and Escanes is entirely the dramatist's invention.[40] Escanes is an ancient lord, "Advanc'd in time to great and high estate" by Helicanus, who serves as regent when Helicanus attends Pericles on the voyage to Tharsus to see Marina (IV.iv.13-16). According to Archibald, "The emphasis on kingship [in earlier versions of the Apollonius story] is developed in a number of later versions, most obviously in *Pericles,* where there are frequent observations on the proper role of rulers." Indeed, with a number of additions to its sources, *Pericles* "highlights questions about kingship and authority which are merely latent in [*Historia Apollonii*]."[41] As has been noted, Helicanus and his discussions of rule with Pericles go beyond what may be found in the play's sources.[42] Both Helicanus and, to a lesser extent, Escanes are significant in the politics of the play: loyal counselors seemingly more alert to the best interests of the prince and state than the prince is. In summing up the political moral of the play, which is "without parallel in any earlier version of the story,"[43] in the Epilogue Gower underscores the virtue of Pericles' chief surrogate: "In Helicanus may you well descry/ A figure of truth, of faith, of loyalty" (ll. 7-8).

Pericles' first action in the play, his quest to win a royal bride by solving the riddle of Antiochus, obviously has a political dimension, though this is concealed by the formulaic, chivalric language Pericles uses.[44] Gower introduces the scene by stressing the physical attractiveness of the unnamed princess, Antiochus' daughter, which "Made many princes thither frame,/ To seek her as a bed-fellow;/ In marriage-pleasures play-fellow" (I.Cho.32-34). Gower's emphasis on the sexual rather than the dynastic aspects of a royal match seems shared by Pericles despite his flattering insistence that he "would be son to great Antiochus" (I.i.27) and his later declaration to Helicanus that he "sought the purchase of a glorious beauty,/ From whence an issue I might propagate,/ Are arms to princes and bring joys to subjects" (I.ii.72-74). The heads of earlier suitors hanging on Antiochus' walls bear silent witness to the imprudence of Pericles' willingness to wager his life on the solution of a riddle. Left unspoken is the danger to his realm (the succession unprovided for) by this daring. Pericles changes directions, of course, and ceases to pursue the match, but he does so only after discovering the incest scarcely concealed by the riddle and recoiling in horror from the object of his former desire. His inability to make more of an admittedly disadvantageous situation is confirmed by his failure to assuage the tyrant's suspicions: even before Pericles flees, Antiochus knows that his secret has been discovered (I.i.110; I.i[b].144), a consequence less of Antiochus' insight or suspiciousness than of Pericles' clumsy rhetoric: "Great king,/ Few love to hear the sins they love to act . . ." (I.i.92-93).

Pericles is profoundly affected by the episode in Antioch in one respect, the fearfulness for himself and his subjects that leads him to flee Antiochus' vengeance and his responsibilities in Tyre. In another respect, however, he seems wholly unaffected: when occasion again presents itself to woo a royal bride, after he is shipwrecked in Pentapolis, he pursues the hand of Thaisa with an enthusiasm undiminished by his experience in Antioch:

> *1 Fish.* [King Simonides] hath a fair daughter, and tomorrow is her birthday; and there are princes and knights come from all parts of the world to joust and tourney for her love.
>
> *Per.* Were my fortunes equal to my desires, I could wish to make one there. (II.i.106-09)

The fisherman asks, "Why, wilt thou tourney for the lady?" and Pericles responds, modestly, "I'll show the virtue I have borne in arms" (II.i.143-44), though in thanking Fortune for restoring his armor ("after all thy crosses/ Thou giv'st me somewhat to repair myself" [II.i.120-21]) he stresses two more times the chance he has been given to raise his fortunes (II.i.141-42, 164-65).

Pericles expresses admiration for the King of Pentapolis, "the good Simonides," who, he learns, "deserves so to be call'd for his peacable [*sic*] reign and good government." But although Pericles observes that "He is a happy king, since he gains from his subjects the name of good by his government" (II.i.98-103), we see little of Simonides' rule or Pericles' understanding of what makes Simonides successful. At the tournament to celebrate Thaisa's birthday, which brings many well-born young suitors, both Simonides and Thaisa demonstrate courtly virtues of hospitality and courtesy,

but there is nothing here to reinforce the impression that the fishermen convey of Simonides' political virtue. Interestingly, in lauding Simonides the fishermen also point out the limitations of his government. In an episode of "social comment" not found in the play's sources,[45] the fishermen observe the similarity between life at sea, where whales devour small fish, and life among men, where "the great ones eat up the little ones"—especially "rich misers," the sort "who never leave gaping till they swallow'd the whole parish" (II.i.28-34). As Pericles looks on, commenting in an aside, "A pretty moral," one of the fishermen says, "if the good King Simonides were of my mind—" (ll. 35, 43-44), which suggests that Simonides is not of such a mind, that he may be aware of the inequities in his kingdom but is unwilling to embrace the radical solution that seems appropriate to this laborer—i.e., "purg[ing] the land of these drones, that rob the bee of her honey" (ll. 46-47) and, implicitly, redistributing their wealth to the workers who originally created it. Pericles' unenlightened response, aside, is rather general:

> How from the finny subject of the sea
> These fishers tell the infirmities of men;
> And from their wat'ry empire recollect
> All that may men approve or men detect!
>
> (II.i.48-51)

But Pericles seems oblivious to the political implications of this parable, which is not found in the source, and nothing is said again about the political inadequacies implicit in Simonides' toleration of an oppressive economic order, though the fishermen continue to dwell on the grievances of the poor (one compares Pericles' armor hanging in the net, which he assumes is a fish, to "a poor man's right in the law; 'twill hardly come out") and their own need (which he underscores in comically asking Pericles to remember them if he finds success at court [II.i.115-17, 147-51]).

With the upper classes at the tournament, Simonides demonstrates a hospitable concern for the happiness and well-being of all, including *The mean Knight,"* Pericles (II.ii.58 *s.d.*), independent of any knowledge of his birth. Pericles has termed himself simply a "gentleman" educated "in arts and arms" (II.iii.81-82), but his courtly conduct proves his worth to the assembled company: Thaisa falls in love, and, as noted above, Simonides concludes that Pericles "May be (nor can I think the contrary)/ As great in blood as I myself" (II.v.77-79).[46] Except for Simonides' clumsy involvement in Thaisa's courtship, where he first favors the unknown Pericles, then tests him by feigning anger and accusing him of treason, and finally endorses Thaisa's choice (II.iii.54-110, II.v.32-92), and the courtesy mentioned above, we are given no hint of his governing ability. He is termed "the good Simonides" so often (twice by the humble fishermen and three times by the knights who court his daughter) that without other evidence we accept it as true.

The romance motif of the seemingly humble suitor's unwillingness to reveal his true identity, evident in Apollonius of Tyre as well,[47] is significant here because it echoes Pericles' quest in Act I to win the daughter of Antiochus. In both instances, Pericles hopes to prevail on his own merit. The "good Simonides" and the tyrant Antiochus offer contrasting models of kingship (and fatherhood),[48] and their daughters present contrasting models of royal feminine virtue, yet there are similarities in the two episodes,[49] notably the attitude Pericles reveals in his quest for a royal bride. Unlike the riddle contest in Antioch, the tournament in Pentapolis holds no special danger for the unsuccessful aspirants for Thaisa's favor beyond the physical hazards of the competition itself—a suitable risk for a martial prince—yet as a political act it retains a considerable and perhaps unacceptable element of chance and thus uncertainty. Kingship is not without risk, of course, and Pericles' effort to restore his fortunes by winning a royal bride may be seen as justifiable, at least in the world of romance.[50] Still, it is worth noting that Pericles has a penchant for throwing himself unthinkingly into situations that are ultimately political, situations where success or failure depends on the skill and wit of the prince, and on the vagaries of fortune, rather than on prudent political calculation. Old Hamlet's single combat with Old Norway, admirable though it may be, is the stuff of legend, not of late Renaissance statecraft.

Such daring is of course the stuff of romance, but excepting these two occasions it must be emphasized that Pericles is a curiously passive hero, "the plaything of Fortune and the gods."[51] He does relieve the famine-stricken residents of Tharsus, but his conduct and motivation have been questioned, notably by Dickey, who observes that "this is not his kingdom, and the gesture, however commendable, is a bribe for asylum in his flight from Antiochus."[52]

We never see Pericles acting with similar resolution in behalf of his own people. After giving himself up to "dull-ey'd melancholy" at the thought of Antiochus' power and the suffering his armies might inflict on the innocent citizens of Tyre (I.ii.3, 25-32, 90-95), Pericles acts most demonstratively in the name of his people in refusing to act, following Helicanus' advice to leave the government to a surrogate (ll. 101-10). Pericles claims that time will reveal the wisdom of what Dickey terms his "abdication of responsibility": he tells Helicanus, "in our orbs we'll live so round and safe,/ That time of both this truth shall ne'er convince,/ Thou showd'st a subject's shine, I a true prince" (I.ii.122-24).[53] As noted above, despite his initial good intentions Pericles fails to return to his responsibilities, or to give any sign of contemplating a return, until he is

found, still disguised as a simple gentleman, by the lords who worry about the fate of a headless realm.

The general point Dickey makes about Pericles' aid to Tharsus is compelling despite the negative connotations in his use of the term "bribe" to characterize Pericles' generosity: the assistance he provides the citizens of Tharsus does place them in the position of owing him a reciprocal obligation, in this case protection.[54] When Pericles later decides to leave the infant Marina in the care of Cleon and Dionyza (III.i.78-80), his assumption that his earlier generosity imposes serious obligations is made explicit by Cleon:

> Fear not, my lord, but think
> Your grace, that fed my country with your
>   corn,
> For which the people's prayers still fall
>   upon you,
> Must in your child be thought on.
>   (III.iii.17-20)

As a ruler, Cleon falls somewhere between the evil Antiochus and "the good Simonides," yet his passivity mirrors Pericles' own, and he ultimately suffers the consequences of his weakness. Cleon's dispute with Dionyza over her plot to kill their charge, Marina (IV.iii), the root cause of their destruction, is not hinted at in the source.[55] As Governor of Tharsus, Cleon acknowledges that he had apparently been unable to curb the excesses of his people, whose pride is responsible for their distress:

> This Tharsus, o'er which I have the
>   government,
> A city on whom plenty held full hand,
>
>   . . . . .
>
> Whose men and dames so jetted and
>   adorn'd,
> Like one another's glass to trim them by—
> Their tables were stor'd full to glad the
>   sight,
> And not so much to feed on as delight:
> All poverty was scorn'd, and pride so great,
> The name of help grew odious to repeat.
>   (I.iv.21-22, 27-31)

Indeed, until Pericles arrives with succor, Cleon can only bemoan his, and his people's, fate (I.iv.1-19), and he is helpless to confront the danger he imagines at the sight of Pericles' sails, portending Tharsus' overthrow by "some neighbouring nation,/ Taking advantage of our misery" (I.iv.65-66).

Cleon's passivity is seen most memorably in his reluctant acceptance of Dionyza's plot to murder Marina. Protesting first that he would give anything "to undo the deed," then that "Of all the faults beneath the heavens, the gods/ Do like this worst," and finally that even acquiescing in the deed after the fact would be dishonorable (IV.iii.6, 20-21, 25-28), Cleon nevertheless cooperates—as Dionyza predicted he would (ll. 49-51)—in covering up the crime. The result is a horrible death at the hands of the outraged citizens of Tharsus: "For wicked Cleon and his wife, when fame/ Had spread his cursed deed," according to Gower, "to rage the city turn,/ That him and his they in his palace burn" (Epilogue.11-14). As Gower comments, this is the gods' punishment for murder "although not done, but meant."

Significantly, Cleon's fate echoes "the due and just reward" for the "monstrous lust" of Antiochus and his daughter, who were shriveled up while riding in a carriage "even to loathing" by a "fire from heaven" (Epi.2, 15-16; II.iv.7-10).[56] Cleon's death also bears out the punishment that Cleon ironically assured Pericles would be appropriate if ingratitude prevented him and Dionyza from caring properly for Marina (III.iii.20-25). Gower stresses Cleon's responsibility, even though Dionyza planned and carried out the attempted murder without his knowledge (Epi.11-14).[57] Thus Cleon's weakness and passivity may explain but do not justify his acquiescence in evil, a moral underscored by the juxtaposition with Antiochus, who was the active initiator of both the corruption of the daughter who is incinerated alongside him and the gruesome deaths of her would-be suitors.

Pericles, giving way to grief after learning of the supposed death of his daughter, remains insensible to the world beyond his sorrow, including the other rulers, both positive or negative, the play depicts.[58] Most important is the Governor of Mytilene, Lysimachus, whose "behaviour . . . is highly ambiguous,"[59] a regular visitor to the brothel until he is transformed by Marina's conversation into a figure worthy of becoming her husband. Despite his ignorance of Lysimachus' past, Pericles warmly receives him as a potential suitor for Marina and reassures him that he will "prevail" in his unnamed suit: "Were it to woo my daughter; for it seems/ You have been noble towards her" (V.i.259-61). On the subject of marriage, Pericles is as impetuous a judge for his daughter—whom he cannot be said to know—as he had been for himself. Unlike Pericles, the audience can see that Lysimachus' intentions in visiting the brothel are less honorable than he suggests after the fact—that is, after Marina moved him to change his ways. Lysimachus declares after he hears Marina speak, "Had I brought hither a corrupted mind,/ Thy speech had alter'd it." A few lines later he adds: "For me, be you thoughten/ That I came with no ill intent" (IV.vi.103-04, 108-09). However, as Archibald observes, Lysimachus "is presented as a hardened debauchee" whose conversion is unconvincingly hasty.[60]

The key to Lysimachus' transformation is Marina's emphasis, which is not in the play's sources, on his political responsibility as governor: "Do you know this house to be a place of such resort, and will come into't? I hear say you're of honourable parts and are the governor of this place" (IV.vi.78-80). Despite Lysimachus' consciousness of his authority, to which he alludes more than once, Archibald notes that "by continuing her attack she shames him into forswearing his old haunts."[61] The reformed Lysimachus offers Marina gold, and more gold, and promises her his help; eventually, of course, he seeks to marry her (IV.vi.104, 113, 116; V.i.67-69, 258-59), a comic device, like Duke Vincentio's proposal to Isabella in *Measure for Measure,* that also has a political and dynastic dimension. Together they will reign in Tyre, and, presumably, continue to rule Mytilene, where Lysimachus is governor, while Pericles and Thaisa will return to Pentapolis (V.iii.79-82), which Marina will presumably inherit when her father dies.

IV

Although Marina is a political figure primarily in the indirect sense that she is Pericles' heir and Lysimachus' betrothed, she still provides a model of initiative and principled resourcefulness that contrasts with the purposelessness and drift (and, on occasion, the misdirected energy) that characterize her father throughout the play.[62] Refusing to succumb to the debased life of the brothel, Marina displays an astonishing ability to act affirmatively and make the best of her situation.

Marina's influence on the characters around her is profound. She transforms not only Lysimachus, who leaves the brothel cursing the "damned door-keeper" Boult and "saying his prayers" (IV.vi.118, 140), but also the common denizens of the brothel, including Boult as he is about to rape her to remove the impediment of her virginity (IV.vi.152-99). She escapes the brothel and sets up a school with noble pupils, "Who pour their bounty on her" (V.Chor.1-11).[63] And, of course, Marina breaks through her father's despair and restores Pericles to himself, herself becoming, as he tells her, "Thou that beget'st him that did thee beget" (V.i.195). Moreover, she leads the revitalized Pericles, finally, to act purposefully, in ways appropriate to his station: first to call for "fresh garments," his "robes" of office (V.i.213, 221); and then to take arms against "savage Cleon" (V.i.215). Even though Pericles' plan "to strike/ The inhospitable Cleon" is prevented by the vision of Diana commanding him to Ephesus, where he will be reunited with Thaisa (V.i.238-51), thanks to Marina we begin to glimpse a new Pericles.

Thus in Marina we see a positive model to counterbalance the Pericles we have seen throughout the course of the play. The contrast between Pericles' virtual abdication of rule and Marina's ability and willingness to act affirmatively may be the key to the relevance of the "mouldy tale" of Apollonius of Tyre for a Jacobean audience. Throughout the early years of James I's reign in England, his restless travels from one rural haunt to another and his obvious unwillingness to remain in London at the seat of government drew comments from those who expected a king to reign and rule. Unlike Pericles, James could be an intensely active and personal ruler, but the popular impression that he was inattentive to state affairs was exacerbated by his devotion to the hunt and the difficulties inherent in the resulting government by correspondence. Especially as the reign wore on, the initial enthusiasm that greeted James' accession was increasingly tempered with a wistful regard for the resolute and engaged Elizabeth.

In *Pericles,* the responsibilities of kingship are a recurring motif. Dutiful surrogates continually fill the vacuum left by a prince who is either literally missing or missing in spirit, so preoccupied is he with his personal travails. Fortune, which is responsible for Pericles' travails and travels in the romance world of the play, eventually restores what has been lost, including Pericles' interest in the world outside himself and, by implication, in rule: he and Thaisa will "spend our following days" in Pentapolis, succeeding the dead Simonides, while Marina and Lysimachus will rule in Tyre (V.iii.77-82). It is hard to imagine Pericles dedicating himself wholeheartedly to earning the sobriquet "the good Pericles," for instance by painstakingly redressing the grievances of subjects like the three fishermen who rescued him from the sea. It is much easier to imagine Marina applying herself to the government of Tyre with the same dedication she showed in reforming the brothel in Mytilene. For the first audiences of *Pericles,* aware of King James' apparent unwillingness to place the demands of government before his personal desires, the example of Marina might have offered a more compelling model of rule.

Notes

[1] F. D. Hoeniger, ed., *Pericles,* New Arden Edition (London: Methuen, 1963), p. xxiv; all quotations from the play in my text are from this edition. I would like to thank Duquesne University for a Presidential Scholarship to work on this project in Summer 1994. I am also grateful for the support, tangible and intangible, of my wife Donna. In revising the essay for publication, I have benefited from the suggestions of more than one anonymous reader.

[2] Following the fortunes of Marina in Act IV, in Tharsus and then Mytilene, the scene continues to shift. It is in Tharsus that Cleon and Dionyza plan their deception and Pericles later learns of Marina's supposed death (IV.iii-iv).

[3] The storm specified in earlier versions of the Apollonius of Tyre story is less explicit in the immediate source for this passage, Gower's *Confessio Amantis;* in the play, Gower as Chorus says in a close paraphrase that Pericles was "driven before the winds" to Mytilene (V.Cho.14); see also Hoeniger's note to this line and Elizabeth Archibald, *Apollonius of Tyre: Medieval and Renaissance Themes and Variations* (Woodbridge, Suffolk: D. S. Brewer, 1991), p. 11.

[4] Recent considerations of geography and Renaissance texts have been offered by Richard Helgerson, who treats English chorography in *Forms of Nationhood: The Elizabethan Writing of England* (Chicago: Univ. of Chicago Press, 1992), and Steven Mullaney, who discusses the social and political topography of London in *The Place of the Stage: License, Play, and Power in Renaissance England* (Chicago: Univ. of Chicago Press, 1988). The latter considers *Pericles* briefly in chap. 6. See Constance C. Relihan, "Liminal Geography: *Pericles* and the Politics of Place," *Philological Quarterly,* 71 (1992), 281-99, for an interesting discussion of *Pericles* and its use of remote "geographic settings" (p. 282).

[5] Two places called Pentapolis may be relevant here, both of which have the advantage of being relatively distant from Antioch and danger. One—apparently the Pentapolis specified in the earliest surviving Apollonius of Tyre text but not in *Pericles'* immediate sources, Gower and Twine—lies in North Africa; the other—a more probable site, geographically, for the shipwreck—is in southwest Asia Minor, on the Aegean Sea, not far from Ephesus and Mytilene, significant sites in the story. The earliest surviving text of *Apollonius* identifies Pentapolis with Cyrene in North Africa—Apollonius "ad Pentapolitanas Cyrenaeorum terras adfirmabatur navigare" ("decided to sail to Pentapolis in Cyrene"); quoted by Archibald, *Apollonius of Tyre,* pp. 122-23. This is an identification not made in the play's immediate sources, Gower and Twine (see *Narrative and Dramatic Sources of Shakespeare,* ed. Geoffrey Bullough, VI [London: Routledge and Kegan Paul; New York: Columbia Univ. Press, 1966], 384-86, 394, 434, 439). Still, it seems geographically improbable (see *Webster's Geographical Dictionary,* rev. ed. [Springfield, Mass.: Merriam, 1969], *passim*). Classical texts generally did not treat geographical matters with great precision, according to my colleague Jerry Clack, Professor of Classics at Duquesne University.

Although Ephesus is relatively near the Pentapolis in Asia Minor, Gower's account is unhelpful in determining the issue, since he says that the storm comes up when "half the flood/ Hath their keel cut" (III.Cho.45-46). This general statement might be more or less accurate in describing the distance from the African Pentapolis to Tyre if Pericles had been blown very far off course to the north, skirting Crete and heading into the Aegean, by a storm that Gower says came out of "the grisled north" (III.Cho.47-50). The storm must occur near Ephesus, since that is where the chest containing Thaisa washes up after Cerimon and the others have weathered a "turbulent and stormy night" (III.ii.4). The play's time cues are quite specific: the chest washed up in the early morning "even now" (l. 49), and since, in Cerimon's judgment, "She hath not been entranc'd above five hours," she could not have drifted far (l. 96).

[6] In earlier versions of *Apollonius of Tyre,* though not in Gower or Twine, the hero and his bride learn of the destruction of Antiochus and set sail for Antioch to assume the vacant throne. The nature of Apollonius' claim to the crown of Antioch is unexplained, which poses obvious problems, as Archibald notes (*Apollonius of Tyre,* pp. 67-68). "There are many gaps and inconsistencies in the plot," according to Archibald, "but in the course of a thousand years of popularity, very few attempts at improvement were made. Medieval and Renaissance writers and readers were far less sensitive to illogicalities which strike modern critics so forcibly" (ibid., p. 63).

[7] Pericles' comments about the newborn's welfare seem to ignore the presence of the nurse, Lychorida, who will remain with her. Pericles' failure to visit his growing daughter in Tharsus, or have her visit in Tyre, cannot be accounted for by the distances involved. This problematic feature of the play can be traced to the earliest versions of the Apollonius story (see ibid., p. 68).

[8] According to Archibald, "On the whole the play is remarkably faithful to the traditional plot" (ibid., p. 215).

[9] I was myself reminded of this by G. Foster Provost, Emeritus Professor of English at Duquesne University.

[10] Here I follow Hoeniger's dating (*Pericles,* pp. lxiii-lxv).

[11] D. H. Willson, *King James VI and I* (London: Jonathan Cape, 1956), p. 179.

[12] *Calendar of the Manuscripts of the Most Honourable The Marquess of Salisbury,* ed. M. S. Giuseppi *et al.,* Historical Manuscripts Commission Reports, 9, 24 vols. (London: HMSO, 1883-1976), XVIII, v; hereafter cited as *HMC Salisbury.*

[13] Ibid., XVIII, v.

[14] Ibid., XIX, viii. Sir Thomas Lake, who was accompanying James at Royston in 1604, wrote Cecil that an important dispatch the King was expecting "was not so soon come, which arrived about six in the morning or a little before, but the King had before sent to me to know if any letters were come. It seemed strange to me that your own being dated at 6 last night should not come hither till six in the morning. The messenger lays the fault upon the posts. Immediately I delivered it to his Majesty in his bed, who called for pen and ink, and has written this answer enclosed with his own hand."

Lake goes on to report an incident demonstrating "what disorder I find here." The King "was resolved to have gone on and gave out warrant for post horses. . . . [However,] there was no man about the King of authority to command horses to be ready or to give warrant for them, so as the King was fain to sign warrants of his own hand." The King's warrants were then disobeyed—a fact that Lake says he "concealed" from James. "Whether this contempt grows for lack of the ordinary officers, or of any other cause I know not. . . . " The letter is endorsed, by Lake, "For his Majesty's special affairs. . . . Haste, haste, Post Haste, for Life, Life, Life" (Lake to Cecil, 2 April 1604, in *HMC Salisbury,* XVI, 50).

For instances of efforts in 1604 by Lake and others to facilitate government correspondence while the King was hunting, see *HMC Salisbury* XVI, 209, 219, 263.

[15] Willson, *King James VI and I,* pp. 178-79, 183, 185.

[16] Ibid., p. 185.

[17] Maurice Lee, Jr., *Great Britain's Solomon: James VI and I in His Three Kingdoms* (Urbana: Univ. of Illinois Press, 1990), p. 111, citing *Calendar of State Papers and Manuscripts Relating to English Affairs Existing in the Archives and Collections of Venice,* ed. H. F. Braun and A. B. Hind (London, 1900-12), X, 70-71.

[18] Lee, *Great Britain's Solomon,* p. 111.

[19] Ibid., p. 111.

[20] Ibid., p. 147.

[21] For a brief survey of the traditional negative view of James by English historians and recent challenges to those views, see ibid., pp. xi-xv.

[22] Thomas Wilson to Sir Thomas Parry, 22 June 1603, in *The Progresses, Processions, and Magnificent Festivities, of King James the First,* ed. John Nichols (London, 1828), I, 188.

[23] "The Earl of Worcester to The Earl of Shrewsbury," 4 December 1604, in Edmund Lodge, *Illustrations of*

British History, Biography, and Manners, 2nd ed. (1838; rpt. Westmead: Gregg, 1969), III, 110 (Letter 43).

[24] John Chamberlain to Ralph Winwood, 26 January 1605, in *The Letters of John Chamberlain,* ed. Norman Egbert McClure, American Philosophical Society Memoirs, 12 (Philadelphia: American Philosophical Society, 1939), I, 201 (Letter 69). In the King's letter to the Privy Council, summarized by Chamberlain, "James formalizes the arrangements for the government of England during his absences in pursuit of the stag and the hare" (9 January 1605, in *Letters of King James VI & I,* ed. G. P. V. Akrigg [Berkeley and Los Angeles: Univ. of California Press, 1984], p. 246 [Letter 114]). James assures the Council that if needed he would return willingly: "we will sooner undergo the peril (or rather the overthrow) of our own health than suffer this state . . . to feel any inconvenience in the constitution thereof by our long absence or by omissions of those cares which any of our progenitors have taken either for the safety, the justice, or honour of the same in general or particular. . . . " Thus he has "resolved (as our business and the season of the year may permit us) to remove sometimes to places distant from this city and our houses nearest to it, with some small company to attend us in our sports and private journeys, only used for preservation of our health" (ibid., pp. 246-47).

[25] "To Lord Cranborne," 25 February 1604 [1605], in Lodge, *Illustrations,* III, 131 (Letter 49); see *Letters of King James VI and I,* p. 256, n. 2). The Archbishop of York's letter reads, in part, "as I confess I am not to deal in state matters, yet, as one that honoureth and loveth his most excellent Majesty with all my heart, I wish less wastening of the treasure of the realm, and more moderation in the lawful exercise of hunting, both that poor men's corn may be less spoiled, and other his Majesty's subjects more spared" ("To Lord Cranborne," 18 December 1604, in Lodge, *Illustrations,* III, 116 [Letter 45]). Salisbury responds, after commenting wryly on the wide circulation of the Archbishop's letter ("seeing you have so uncivil clerks as they are like to make my letter as common as they have made your own . . ."), concerning hunting, "That as it was a praise in the good Emperor Trajan to be disposed to such manlike and active recreations, so ought it be a joy to us to behold our King of so able a constitution . . ." ("To the Archbishop of York," February 1604, in ibid., III, 129-30 [Letter 48]).

[26] "Edmund Lascelles to the Earl of Shrewsbury," 4 December 1604, in Lodge, *Illustrations,* III, 108 (Letter 42).

[27] "To Robert Cecil, Viscount Cranborne," [February 1605], in *Letters of King James VI and I,* p. 255 (Letter 118).

[28] "To the Council," [1604?], in *Letters of King James VI and I,* p. 223 (Letter 102).

[29] "The Earl of Worcester to Lord Cranborne," 3 May 1604 [*sic;* 3 Mar. 1605], in Lodge, *Illustrations,* III, 138 (Letter 53).

[30] John Chamberlain to Ralph Winwood, 12 October 1605, in *The Letters of John Chamberlain,* I, 209 (Letter 73).

[31] *The Progresses,* ed. Nichols, I, 531n.

[32] John Chamberlain to Dudley Carleton, 24 October 1605, in *The Letters of John Chamberlain,* I, 212 (Letter 74).

[33] In a stimulating essay, ("'Eating the Mother': Property and Propriety in *Pericles,*" in *Creative Imitation: New Essays on Renaissance Literature in Honor of Thomas M. Greene,* ed. David Quint *et al.,* Medieval and Renaissance Texts and Studies, 95 [Binghamton: Medieval and Renaissance Texts and Studies, 1992], pp. 331-53), Constance Jordan has examined *Pericles* and its politics in terms of early modern political theory, notably "the contemporary debate on the proper form of government and specifically of the monarchy" (p. 331). Jordan focuses on the rich implications of the incest metaphor embodied in the tyrant Antiochus: "When the image of incest is understood by reference to the language describing the nature of political rule, both domestic and civil—specifically one in which the monarch is to behave as a father to his children, the subjects, and as a husband to his wife, the commonwealth—it provides a basis for understanding the play's continuous appeal to ideas of legitimate government" (p. 332).

Jordan's sensitivity to the subtlety with which political metaphor and topicality can be interwoven stands in contrast with the more mechanical topical reading offered by an earlier writer, T. S. Graves, who suggested that the Tharsus episode should be read in the light of a contemporary effort to procure English grain to relieve a dearth in Italy ("On the Date and Significance of *Pericles,*" *Modern Philology,* 13 [1916], 177-88).

[34] See Stephen Dickey, "Language and Role in *Pericles,*" *English Literary Renaissance,* 16 [1986], 550-66, for the observation that "[o]ne of the things Pericles constantly retreats from is the task of governing. Like ancestor Lear and descendent Prospero, Pericles, if not actually incompetent as a ruler, does relinquish political power for psychological leverage over other characters" (p. 556).

[35] *Pericles,* ed. Hoeniger, pp. xxiii-xxiv.

[36] Archibald, *Apollonius of Tyre,* pp. 68-69. When Pericles returns to Tharsus to see his daughter, ac-

cording to Gower, he is "Attended on by many a lord and knight" (IV.iv.9-12), which suggests that he has resumed his rightful position in Tyre, though the play is silent about how he has governed or how Tyre has profited from his return.

37 Archibald, *Apollonius of Tyre,* p. 16.

38 See Hoeinger, ed., *Pericles,* pp. xxxiii-xxxiv; *s.d.* at beginning of Act I, Scene ii; Appendix C (pp. 180-83); and the note to I.ii.35-51 (p. 22).

39 According to Dickey, Helicanus' denunciation of flattery "is itself flattery of the most persuasive sort." Finding Helicanus' motives "questionable," Dickey notes that he "endorse[s] Pericles' fears" and "enhances them"; he "introduces the idea of Pericles' departure and hastily volunteers his services as replacement. . . . " Helicanus thus willingly participates in Pericles' "first abdication of responsibility" by conspiring with Pericles in a "charade" that "affords Pericles an excuse for quitting his rule while maintaining that it is done in the best interests of his subjects," a charade that involves "the two principals cuing each other toward a conclusion desirable to both" ("Language and Role," pp. 556-57).

40 Hoeniger, ed., *Pericles,* p. xv; *Narrative and Dramatic Sources,* ed. Bullough, VI, 361; Archibald, *Apollonius of Tyre,* p. 214.

41 Archibald, *Apollonius of Tyre,* pp. 21-22.

42 Hoeniger, ed., *Pericles,* p. xv; *Narrative and Dramatic Sources,* ed. Bullough, VI, 360-61. Bullough maintains that "The responsibility for the Prince's long absence from his city is . . . not his alone, and proper arrangements are made for its government during his absence. Unlike Apollonius Pericles is not governed only by selfish fear, but is a 'true prince' with a sense of duty. Some attempt is thus made to transfer the fairy tale into terms of Renaissance political interests" (VI, 361).

43 Archibald, *Apollonius of Tyre,* p. 101.

44 Dickey, "Language and Role," pp. 553-56; cf. Maurice Hunt, *Shakespeare's Romance of the Word* (Lewisburg: Bucknell Univ. Press, 1990), pp. 21-26.

45 *Narrative and Dramatic Sources,* ed. Bullough, VI, 361.

46 On the play's minor departures from the Apollonius tradition in this episode, see Archibald, *Apollonius of Tyre,* pp. 10, 66-67, 214-15. For his part, Pericles associates Simonides sitting in state with his own father at the height of his power (II.iii.37-42). Seen in this light, Pericles' courtship of Thaisa complicates easy generalizations about the incest motif in the play.

47 Archibald, *Apollonius of Tyre,* p. 10.

48 *Narrative and Dramatic Sources,* ed. Bullough, VI, 373.

49 See Dickey, "Language and Role," p. 559.

50 Politically or financially advantageous marriages are important in a number of Shakespeare's other plays, in various genres; one may think of such objects of marital desire as Portia in *Merchant of Venice,* Elizabeth of York in *Richard III,* Gertrude in *Hamlet,* Octavia in *Antony and Cleopatra.* or, in romance, Imogen in *Cymbeline.*

51 Hoeniger, ed., *Pericles,* pp. lxxx-lxxxi.

52 Dickey, "Language and Role," p. 556.

53 Ibid. Pericles' confidence that things will work out with his exile seems unduly optimistic. Contemplating the threat to Tyre he perceives from Antiochus, and wishing to assure himself that his proposed flight will not worsen the situation, Pericles asks Helicanus, "But should he wrong my liberties in my absence?" and receives the assurance, "We'll mingle our bloods together in the earth,/ From whence we had our being and our birth" (I.ii.112-14). Despite this declaration of resolve, worthy of the English lords whom Henry V leaves behind when he sets off to conquer France (*Henry V* I.ii.136-220), these are presumably the same defenders whose ability to withstand Antiochus had been troubling Pericles:

> With hostile forces he'll o'erspread the land,
> And with th'ostent of war will look so huge,
> Amazement shall drive courage from the
>   state,
> Our men be vanquish'd ere they do resist. . . .
>   (I.ii.25-28)

On Pericles' physical and metaphorical absences from Tyre, it is worth noting that we get few glimpses of him in his own kingdom among his own subjects. He appears in Tyre after fleeing Antioch, at the start of the play, and remains briefly, consumed by worry about the threat he perceives from Antiochus. Later, in the long interval between Marina's birth and Dionyza's plot on her life, we see nothing of Pericles or his restored rule in Tyre. After Cleon and Dionyza build a monument to Marina, Gower reports Pericles' return to Tharsus with a large retinue, a detail that does more to set up his exchange with them than illuminate his rule (IV.iv.9-12).

54 On Jacobean attitudes towards the acceptance of gifts by courtiers and government officials, see Linda Levy Peck, *Court Patronage and Corruption in Early Stuart England* (1990; rpt. New York: Routledge,

1993), *passim*. On Renaissance attitudes towards the reciprocity of benefits, see John M. Wallace, "The Senecan Context of *Coriolanus*," *Modern Philology*, 90 (1993), 465-78.

55 Hoeinger, ed., *Pericles,* p. xv.

56 Archibald, *Apollonius of Tyre,* p. 215.

57 See Hoeinger, ed., *Pericles,* p. 162 (n. to Epi.12).

58 The plot requires that Pericles remain wholly ignorant of Lord Cerimon, who revived Thaisa after she had washed ashore and then facilitated her new life at Diana's temple, though the audience sees him as a model of private benevolence and wisdom as well as, apparently, the dominant figure in Ephesus.

59 *Narrative and Dramatic Sources,* ed. Bullough, VI, 366.

60 Archibald, *Apollonius of Tyre,* p. 70.

61 Ibid., pp. 21, 215.

62 Thaisa is also a figure of some resolution, or at least constancy, in that she dedicates herself wholeheartedly to a new life as a nun at Diana's temple. A certain passivity reminiscent of Pericles is also evident, however: after awakening in Ephesus she assumes she will never see Pericles again (III.iv.7-9), even though the evidence for concluding her spouse has perished is less compelling than it was for Pericles, and she chooses to remain in Ephesus to take on her "vestal livery" rather than continue on to Tyre (or return to her father in Pentapolis). Like Pericles, Thaisa assumes she will "never more have joy" (l. 10).

63 On Marina's accomplishments, contrasted with the greater emphasis on her counterpart's intellect and learning in Apollonius of Tyre, see Elizabeth Archibald, "'Deep clerks she dumbs': The Learned Heroine in *Apollonius of Tyre* and *Pericles*," *Comparative Drama,* 22 (1988), 289-303.

_____

Source: "'The care...of subjects' good': *Pericles, James I, and the Neglect of Government*," in *Comparative Drama,* Vol. 30, No. 2, Summer, 1996, pp. 220-44.

"Thou maist have thy *Will*": The Sonnets of Shakespeare and His Stepsisters

Josephine A. Roberts, *Louisiana State University*

One of the dangers in teaching Shakespeare's sonnets is that undergraduates may quickly become overwhelmed by the array of unanswered and unanswerable questions that surround the 1609 Quarto. When they come to the sonnets with the expectation of hearing the unmediated voice of the Bard, they confront instead a group of shifting and mysterious figures—the fair young friend(s), the rival poet, and the dark lady. If they share Wordsworth's conviction that "Shakespeare unlocked his heart" in the sonnets,[1] they may follow in the wake of many earlier generations of readers who have searched in vain for a key.

To lead students into more fruitful approaches to the sonnets, I prefer to teach the sequence in conjunction with lyrics by contemporary women poets, including Elizabeth I, Aemilia Lanyer, and Lady Mary Wroth. By using a paratactic method—juxtaposing sonnets on related subjects, such as absence, night, lust, betrayal, or constancy—it is possible to see how these poets differ in their treatment of conventional motifs.[2] It is also valuable to explore how Shakespeare and the women authors radically transform their Petrarchan heritage, for most of these poets are writing after the extraordinary outpouring of English sonnet sequences in the 1590s. They confront the common problem of how to write in a genre in which the female beloved is generally silent, distant, and unattainable.

One strategy to use in teaching the sonnets is to divide the class into teams, each responsible for researching and discussing a critical perspective on the poetry. Although the particular approaches listed below could easily be changed or expanded, the advantage of having students working together is the opportunity it gives them to discuss the poetry in small groups, to formulate their own interpretations, and then to share their results with the class; often the groups offer vastly different readings of the same poem, especially Sonnets 20, 93, or 116. In the first week of study on the sonnets, I generally meet with each of the teams outside of class to discuss the readings (and in some cases to provide additional reading materials, such as xeroxes of the 1609 Quarto or Wroth's manuscript poems). During the second and third weeks, the teams give their class presentations. The students working on physical features of the texts generally speak last because their topic is the least familiar and requires some extra time for preparation.

SUBJECTIVITY OF THE SONNETS

Rather than open the study of Shakespeare's sequence by analyzing Thomas Thorpe's dedication to the 1609 Quarto (this topic is actually explored by the last group), we begin with a discussion of Queen Elizabeth's "On Monsieur's Departure":

> I grieve and dare not show my discontent,
> I love and yet am forced to seem to hate,
> I do, yet dare not say I ever meant,
> I seem stark mute but inwardly do prate.
>   I am and not, I freeze and yet am burned,
>   Since from myself another self I turned.
>
> My care is like my shadow in the sun,
> Follows me flying, flies when I pursue it,
> Stands and lies by me, doth what I have done.
> His too familiar care doth make me rue it.
>   No means I find to rid him from my breast,
>   Till by the end of things it be supprest.
>
> Some gentler passion slide into my mind,
> For I am soft and made of melting snow;
> Or be more cruel, love, and so be kind.
> Let me or float or sink, be high or low.
>   Or let me live with some more sweet
>   content,
>   Or die and so forget what love ere meant.[3]

Perhaps the first questions to consider are who is the "I" of the poem and who is "another self" from whom the speaker has turned away? Initially the reader may assume that "another self" is the unnamed "Monsieur" of the title, and that the poem invokes the Petrarchan idea of the beloved as mirror image of oneself. Yet other possibilities immediately occur: could the speaker be referring to the spurning of love (rather than a particular person) or to a part of her own nature that must be suppressed?

Students quickly discover that the identity of "Monsieur" cannot be established with certainty either, for while two manuscripts identify him as the French Duc d'Anjou, who departed from England in 1582, a third copy (titled "Sonetto") appears among papers connected with Robert Devereux, earl of Essex.[4] These two possibilities invoke radically different situations: in the case of d'Anjou, Elizabeth's poem may well be a politic display of affection for a man whom privately she never intended to marry. On the other hand, if the dashing and charismatic Essex is veiled under the title of "Monsieur," then the "I" may hint at deeper recesses of emotion. The poem plays on the mysterious identity of "Monsieur" in the second stanza, where the speaker laments, "No means I find to rid him from my breast"; here "him" can refer either to the lover or to the allegorical figure of "care" that haunts the speaker. Leicester Bradner, a modern editor of Elizabeth's poetry, classifies "On Monsieur's Departure" as one of six poems of "undoubted authorship" based on its manuscript tradition but is deeply troubled by the implications of the final stanza. Bradner states, "I cannot believe that the Queen would ever have committed to writing personal feelings of this kind, particularly as they show her in a light which would not have pleased her."[5] What he may have found especially incredible is the eroticism of the last line, with its dual meanings of *die* as orgasm and oblivion. Yet one of the characteristic features of this poem is its exploration of a divided self, torn between conflicting impulses of affirmation and surrender. Indeed, the editor's uneasiness in attributing it to Elizabeth may reflect a larger problem encountered when dealing with Shakespeare's sonnets, when some readers assume that the "I" of the poem must be read autobiographically.

In reading "On Monsieur's Departure," students begin to discover alternative methods of interpretation that emphasize the persona's changing states of mind. I often assign to one group of students the introductory chapter of Joel Fineman's *Shakespeare's Perjured Eye* as critical reading.[6] Although undergraduates typically find Fineman's book difficult, they quickly grasp his important thesis concerning how Shakespeare contrasts a poetic of praise for the fair young man with a poetic of paradox in the sonnets explicitly addressed to the dark lady. Out of this fissure in poetics, Shakespeare fashions the persona of the later sonnets, "disrupted, at the same time as it is constituted, by its doubled language and its divided desire."[7] In their own readings of the sonnets, students search for examples of contrasting poems that illustrate, on the one hand, the orthodox poetry of praise and, on the other, the later, fractured sense of self. Frequently groups will select Shakespeare's Sonnet 133 for discussion:

> Me from myself thy cruel eve hath taken,
> And my next self thou harder hast
>   engrossed.
> Of him, myself, and thee, I am forsaken—
> A torment thrice threefold thus to be
>   crossed.
>
>   (ll. 5-8)[8]

From "On Monsieur's Departure" students will be familiar with the image of "myself" as both 'my true nature' and 'my beloved friend,' but Shakespeare's sonnet enhances the complexity with its *eye/I* pun and

its emphasis on a triple abandonment. Students also explore how subjectivity is created in the sonnets, as in this case, by means of the persona's continual shifts between past and present, then and now, and here and there.

One of Fineman's most significant claims is that Shakespeare introduces "a subjectivity altogether novel in the history of lyric."[9] Because my students examine the sonnets of Shakespeare alongside those of contemporary women poets, they are in a position to test this assertion. They are able, for example, to consider how the persona in Wroth's sequence is neither fixed nor unchanging but moves from an initial position as a passive and powerless dreamer at the beginning of *Pamphilia to Amphilanthus* to emerge in the final sonnet as a fully conscious, assertive poet who renounces "the discource of Venus, and her sunn."[10] Yet saying farewell to the language of love is not the same as forsaking passion, as the speakers of both sequences suggest.

Finally, I invite the group to consider what happens when Shakespeare's sonnets are read aloud, how the "I" of performance compounds interpretation of the subjective "I" of the text. Students may consider, for instance, the effect of reading Shakespeare's Sonnet 116 in its place within the sequence versus its performance in isolation at a wedding service. Or they may consider its very different impact in Emma Thompson's 1995 film adaptation of *Sense and Sensibility,* when Marianne tearfully delivers the same sonnet as she overlooks the estate of the man who has betrayed her.

THE NATURE OF SONNET COLLECTIONS

The concept of a sonnet sequence suggests to most readers a clearly defined linear progression; yet while Shakespeare's sonnets are sequentially numbered in the 1609 Quarto, how the order was determined—whether by the author, by the editor, by the printer, or by chance—is unknown. Because of this uncertainty, much criticism on the sonnets has been devoted to rearranging the poems into various configurations. As early as 1640, John Benson reordered Shakespeare's sonnets, interspersed them with lyrics and third-person narratives by other poets, and affixed generic titles, such as "An Intreatie for Her Acceptance" and "A Perjurie."[11] Subsequent critics have proposed various rearrangements of the sonnets into related groups that would produce a straightforward narrative, although significantly no reordering has ever won widespread acceptance.[12]

Rather than asking students to consider particular controversies over sonnet order, I encourage them to explore more general questions dealing with the design of sonnet collections. Many modern reordering schemes are directed toward producing a linear pattern, but what alternative models exist in sonnet sequences written by Shakespeare's contemporaries? Fortunately there is evidence to suggest how early modern poets approached the task of arrangement.

In the case of Mary Wroth's sonnets, the Folger manuscript of *Pamphilia to Amphilanthus* (V.a.104) provides a corrected fair copy of her songs and sonnets, as well as later poems interspersed throughout the text of the prose romance *Urania*. Students can examine Wroth's reordering of the sequence and the process of selecting, revising, and substantially rearranging the poems in the printed version of her sonnet sequence published in 1621. Wroth's two collections can be compared to see how the author heightened the emotional conflicts of the persona and to what extent she relied on clusters or contrasting groups of sonnets, using circular patterns rather than clear-cut narratives.

Her collection "A Crowne of Sonetts dedicated to Love" (a group of fourteen sonnets in which the last line of one sonnet serves as the first line of the next) also offers a specific model of design: the labyrinth.[13] Deriving from Petrarch's *Rime* 211, the idea of the labyrinth or maze of love was an Elizabethan commonplace, prevalent in literature as well as in gardens and all types of ornamental design. Its associations with the myth of Ariadne, who rescued Theseus only to be later betrayed by him, reinforces the connection between the labyrinth and tragically frustrated love. Recent studies have shown that labyrinths could be categorized into two main types of design: those that have a single point of entry and exit and those that have multiple pathways and points of egress.[14] In the case of Wroth's own crown of sonnets, the speaker wanders through a maze of repeated efforts to pay homage to Cupid but emerges with a renewed feeling of entrapment: "Soe though in Love I fervently doe burne, / In this strange labourinth how shall I turne?"[15] Interestingly, some of Wroth's greatest changes in her ordering of the *Pamphilia to Amphilanthus* sequence occur immediately after the appearance of the self-contained crown of fourteen sonnets.

Further evidence that Shakespeare's contemporaries designed their collections according to nonlinear principles occurs in the manuscript of Robert Sidney's sonnets.[16] Although these poems did not appear in print until 1984, the manuscript reveals Sidney's intense interest in the arrangement of his sonnets, for he numbers them in two different series, excluding some of the lyrics in his notebook. He also provides an alternative sequence of thirteen poems, in the center of which he places his own uncompleted crown of sonnets.[17] While they remain a part of the larger sequence, this group of thirteen poems may be read entirely separately as an exploration of the speaker's

"unlucky" experience in love. P. J. Croft suggests that the multiple numbering systems reflect the author's interest in tracing the "shifting moods of love."[18]

In turning to Shakespeare's collection, students may apply the concept of the labyrinth by considering how the persona follows, abandons, retreats, and advances along numerous paths in search of love. Instead of placing emphasis on narrative events, students focus more on the dilemma of the poet-lover. This approach has the advantage of freeing readers from trying to construct, with few individualizing details, a characterization of the fair young friend, who "steals men's eyes and women's souls amazeth" (20.8).[19] Northrop Frye points to the fact that all our knowledge of the friend is mediated through the voice of the poet-lover: "we are forced to conclude that Shakespeare has lavished a century of the greatest sonnets in the language on an unresponsive oaf as stupid as a doorknob and as selfish as a weasel."[20] Yet the poet, trapped in a maze of love, sees only intermittently through the walls of his own self-deceptions.

As they explore the design of Shakespeare's collection, students consider the relationships between poems addressed to the fair young friend and those addressed to the dark lady, with special attention to how later sonnets repeat an image or idea included earlier (such as lying in Sonnets 115 and 138, or love and lust in Sonnets 116 and 129). They may also consider the relationship between sonnet sequences and other genres with which they were originally published. For example, the 1609 Quarto prints Shakespeare's sonnets together with "A Lover's Complaint," a long poem written in the voice of a deceived woman. As Katherine Duncan-Jones has shown, there are ample precedents for combining a sonnet sequence featuring a male persona with a ventriloquized female complaint.[21] This arrangement can be contrasted with Wroth's sonnet sequence, which appears at the end of the first part of her long prose romance *The Countess of Montgomery's Urania*. Throughout this fiction the central character, Pamphilia, conceals her inmost feelings of love, fear, and grief from her closest friends; only in the appended sonnet sequence does she reveal the extent of her emotional suffering.

CONSTRUCTIONS OF GENDER

A key problem faced by both Shakespeare and early modern women poets was how to write in a tradition marked by highly polarized gender roles, where the Petrarchan poet-lover is a distinctly masculine subject fashioned in relation to a female other. In considering poets' responses to this challenge, students must deal with the fact that it is often difficult to determine whether a sonnet is addressed to a man or a woman. Critics have traditionally assumed that Shakespeare's Sonnets 1-126 are addressed to one or more men and

127-52 to a woman, but the question of the addressee's gender is open for debate in the case of many individual poems.[22]

Shakespeare's Sonnet 93, for example, deals with the problem of how to discern the beloved's genuine feelings beneath the surface of "love's face":

> So shall I live, supposing thou art true,
> Like a deceivèd husband—so love's face
> May still seem love to me, though altered
>   new:
> Thy looks with me, thy heart in other place.
>
> (ll. 1-4)

In his 1780 edition of the sonnets, Edmond Malone interpreted the poem as Shakespeare's allusion to his wife's adultery, reading the simile "like a deceivèd husband" as biographical fact. But this poem is typical of many of the sonnets addressed to the young man in that it uses the words "sweet" and "sweetness."[23] The speaker himself identifies with the role of husband, pondering whether to believe in the fidelity of his beloved, who is finally cast in the role of woman, regardless of actual sex: "How like Eve's apple doth thy beauty grow, / If thy sweet virtue answer not thy show" (ll. 13-14). As Stephen Booth suggests, the last line plays on the idea of the deceptive appearance of the apple, which may conceal falsehood and corruption within its core, but it also hints more darkly at the assignment of gender roles, for if a beloved woman might deceive, why might not a beloved man?

As students explore the problems of gendered address in the sonnets, they also consider more generally the issue of homoeroticism. Some of my students read excerpts from Bruce R. Smith's *Homosexual Desire in Shakespeare's England* to learn more about early modern attitudes toward same-sex love.[24] It is important, I think, to encourage students to discuss the issue, with a particular focus on the interpretation of Sonnet 20. In the debate over whether Shakespeare's sonnets express a denial of sexual desire toward the young man or a veiled admission of it, this sonnet is crucial. It is valuable for students to consider the poem's historical reception, ranging from George Steevens's homophobic outrage in 1780—"It is impossible to read this fulsome panegyrick, addressed to a male object, without an equal mixture of disgust and indignation"—to Edmond Malone's reply: "[S]uch addresses to men, however indelicate, were customary in our author's time, and neither imported criminality nor were esteemed indecorous."[25] Between these two extremes there is certainly room for a variety of interpretations of the poet's relationship with the fair friend as it evolves and changes over time.

In the case of Wroth's sonnets, the issue of gendered address is even more problematic because Wroth's

persona avoids speaking to her beloved directly. Although Amphilanthus's name appears in the title, he is never explicitly mentioned in the sequence, and indeed Wroth's poems apostrophize such abstractions as Night, Absence, Hope, Grief, and Time far more often they address the beloved. Part of the persona's evasiveness may be explained in the context of the social constraints on a woman of Shakespeare's time from dealing frankly with the subject of desire. Yet Wroth develops techniques to circumvent these obstacles, as in the following sonnet:

> Deare fammish nott what you your self gave
>   food;
>   Destroy nott what your glory is to save;
>   Kill nott that soule to which you spiritt
>   gave;
>   In pitty, nott disdaine your triumph
>   stood. . . . [26]

On the one hand, the poem can be read as an open confession to her lover, but it can just as easily be interpreted as an address to the god Cupid, with an allusion to Petrarch's *Trionfi* in line 4. The mythological veil allows the persona to speak with the same bluntness as the male lover Astrophil in crying "Your sight is all the food I doe desire."[27] Occasionally a poem that begins as an apostrophe may undergo a subtle shift of address, as in the sonnet beginning "You blessed starrs," which moves from a description of the heavens to refer to the "Light of my joye, fixt stedfast nor will move."[28]

Rather than attack her lover directly for his infidelity, Wroth's speaker links him to the mischievous Cupid, who evades control by his mother, Venus, and describes the various punishments the child undergoes.[29] At times the speaker seems exhausted by the futile effort involved in concealment, as when she issues a plea to her beloved (masked as Cupid): "I should nott have bin made this stage of woe / Wher sad disasters have theyr open showe."[30]

To what extent does the persona of Wroth's sequence identify herself as a woman rather than a disembodied lover? When students begin to read the sequence closely, they are apt to notice how frequently Wroth assigns a feminine gender to the abstractions she addresses. For example, she speaks of Night as a female friend: "My thoughts are sad; her face as sad doth seeme: / My paines are long; Her houers taedious are."[31] The female bonding with Night intensifies in a later sonnet, as Naomi J. Miller notes, when the speaker actually sees herself as part of a larger community of "oprest" lovers, emphasizing the female perspective of the speaker in contrast to "mens phant'sies."[32] The speaker's fellowship with feminized Night reappears when she invokes the name of darkness (which "doth truly sute with mee oprest") as it covers a carpet woven of dead leaves: "If trees, and leaves for absence, mourners bee / Noe mervaile that I grieve, who like want see."[33]

Wroth's speaker often identifies with images of oppression, as in the sonnet comparing her adoration of her beloved to that of the Indians, "scorched with the sunne."[34] But perhaps her most graphic reference to the female body occurs in the following sonnet:

> Faulce hope which feeds butt to destroy,
>   and spill
>   What itt first breeds; unaturall to the
>   birth
>   Of thine owne wombe; conceaving butt
>   to kill,
>   And plenty gives to make the greater
>   dearth.[35]

Here she describes false hope in an image of miscarriage, which "feeds butt to destroy," and links it in the next stanza to an example of the political ruler who rewards and advances his subjects only to betray them. By moving from the body natural to the body politic, she hints at the tyrannical power of delusory hope to entrap the lover.[36] Like Shakespeare, Wroth emphasizes the speaker's struggle with self-deception, to resist the temptation that in "our faults by lies we flattered be" (138.14).

INTERROGATING THE DARK LADY

Although the term *dark lady* appears in nearly all discussions of the sonnets, significantly Shakespeare's speaker never refers to her as a lady and only once as "dark" (147.14).[37] It is not surprising, however, that the phrase has such widespread currency, for the dark lady has become emblematic of female evil. She stands in opposition to nearly every cultural value associated with the idealized Petrarchan beloved, who is fair, chaste, and unattainable. While James Winny has questioned whether the sonnets may refer to more than one woman, the mistress who pursues the fair young man in Sonnets 40-42 gives every indication of being the same active and aggressive wooer of the later Sonnets 133-35.[38] The speaker intimates her married status ("In act thy bed-vow broke" [152.3]) and strongly implies that she is a source of disease and contagion (137.14; 144.14).

One key question for students to consider is whether the so-called dark lady functions primarily as a character (comparable to Cleopatra or Cressida) or as a universal symbol or both. As in the case of the fair young man, all knowledge of her is filtered through the voice of the poet-lover, who freely admits his own prejudices, lust, and obsession. On the one hand, he praises her unadorned black beauty because it stands opposed to false show (127), but the same blackness

comes to serve as a sign of her interior evil ("In nothing art thou black save in thy deeds" [131.13]).

The multiple implications of blackness are disturbing to some students, who find that older editions of the sonnets offer an unsatisfactory one-word annotation of "black" as brunette. Indeed, earlier sonnet collections, such as *Astrophil and Stella,* had explored the dynamics of fairness versus blackness in relation to physical appearance (for example, Stella's dark eyes— "She even in blacke doth make all beauties flow" [7.11]). But if the clash between dark and light is a conventional motif, in Shakespeare's collection it assumes complex dimensions, for the love associated with the young man is described as "fair, kind, and true" (105.9), whereas love for the woman is characterized in polar oppositions.

That blackness might suggest more than hair color is certainly an idea pursued by women poets contemporary with Shakespeare, who explore the racial implications of the term. Wroth's sonnet "Like to the Indians, scorched with the sunne" sets forth the contrast between the dark skin of the Indians and Pamphilia's fairness, unexpectedly to the advantage of the natives, who worship with hope, whereas Wroth's persona is pale with grief and despair. Similarly, in Elizabeth Cary's play *The Tragedy of Mariam* (1613) the central female figures, in competition with each other, are characterized as fair and black: Herod makes the racial implications of blackness explicit when he compares his sister Salome to Mariam: "Go your ways, / You are to her a sun-burnt blackamoor."[39] Students quickly see how in Shakespeare's sonnets "blackness is neither a purely aesthetic nor a moral category but the site for crucial negotiations of sexual politics and cultural and racial difference."[40] At the end of Kim F. Hall's important study *Things of Darkness* is a collection of lyrical poems that illustrates the highly charged nature of the tropes of blackness. Her book also provides invaluable visual material for exploring how modern Western notions of race were developing during the same period in which Shakespeare was writing his poems.

As further background to the sonnets, students may explore some of the misogynist ideas current in Shakespeare's time, such as the diatribes against cosmetics, often regarded as a symbol of female pride, falsehood, and lasciviousness. The speaker's claim that in the present age "each hand hath put on nature's pow'r, / Fairing the foul with art's false borrowed face" (127.5-6) can be considered in the light of Donne's paradoxical encomium "That Women ought to paint."[41] They may consider how the speaker's principal accusation against the dark lady—her sexual aggression—can be viewed in the context of the treatment of women in the conduct books, where they are repeatedly enjoined to practice modesty and discretion; the illustrated frontispiece of Richard Brathwait's *The English Gentle-woman* (1631), together with its accompanying explanation of the emblems, offers students a highly accessible means of measuring how far the dark lady departs from the prevailing definition of the submissive, careful wife.[42]

Students also enjoy researching some of the folklore and proverbs concerning women that relate specifically to the dense verbal texture of Shakespeare's sonnets. With the aid of Tilley's *Dictionary of the Proverbs,* they can discover the multiplicity of adages related to the subject of women's will. They range from the simple—"Women will have their wills"—to the complex—"Will will have will (wilt) though will woe win."[43] They quickly begin to recognize the presence of bawdy innuendo surrounding the word *will,* which Booth demonstrates might refer more generally to lust, as well as specifically to both the male and female sex organs.[44] The proverbs repeatedly imply a view of woman as carnally insatiable, an idea expressed most forcefully by Edgar in *King Lear* when he reads over Goneril's seductive letter to Edmund and exclaims against her lasciviousness: "O indistinguish'd space of woman's will!" (4.6.271). Occasionally the proverbs point to the sexual double standard ignored by Edgar: "Women must have their wills while they live because they make none when they die."[45] This proverb plays on the fact that few women held land or property in their own names unless they were rich widows. Once students become familiar with the range of *will*'s Elizabethan connotations and the negative associations of the term with women, they are in a better position to interpret Shakespeare's elaborate wordplay in the later sonnets (especially 134-36 and 143).

Despite the speaker's description of the dark lady as "my female evil" (144.5), some contemporary poets attempted to counteract this cultural stereotype of women. One of the most important works to confront the issue was Aemilia Lanyer's *Salve Devs Rex Ivdaeorvm* (1611), published only two years after Shakespeare's sonnets. Lanyer carefully constructs her book as a defense of women, with a series of nine dedications to powerful female patrons, including Queen Anne: Princess Elizabeth; Lady Arbella Stuart; Mary Sidney, countess of Pembroke; Lucy Harington, countess of Bedford; Margaret Russell, countess dowager of Cumberland (Lanyer's principal patron); and others. Even more important, Lanyer extends her praise of womankind from the highborn to the "Vertvovs Reader," addressed in the prose preface, to whom she speaks frankly about the need to defend the reputation of women. She anticipates the argument of her major poem by stressing the importance of women at each stage of Christ's life, "from the time of his conception, till the houre of his death."[46] By linking examples of wise and virtuous women from the Old Testament with those

of the New, Lanyer creates a vision of womankind that is designed to "inforce all good Christians and honourable minded men to speake reverently of our sexe."[47]

Central to the structure of Lanyer's poem is the dramatic monologue spoken by the character of Pilate's wife and identified on the title page as "Eues Apologie in defence of Women." Students are naturally attracted to this section of the poem because it is a highly imaginative recreation of what Pilate's wife may have said to warn her husband against condemning Christ to death.[48] The monologue is framed with the melancholy recognition that Pilate did not heed his wife's dream, and that it was he, not she, who would act willfully.

Pilate's wife insists that the crucifixion is an action undertaken by men alone, and that this historical event frees women from the taint of Eve's fall. Pilate's wife insists that Eve was tricked by Satan's temptation because, in her innocence, she was unprepared to detect guile or cunning. By contrast, "*Adam* can not be excusde" because, as Lanyer argues, he was not deceived:

> If *Eue* did erre, it was for knowledge sake,
> The fruit beeing faire perswaded him to fall:
> > No subtill Serpents falshood did betray him,
> > If he would eate it, who had powre to stay him?[49]

Thus Lanyer's division of responsibility for the Fall does not completely exonerate Eve, but it does place the major burden on Adam's shoulders. Rather than presenting Eve as a vain and self-centered seductress, Lanyer offers a portrait of a loyal, devoted wife, "whose fault was onely too much loue" in sharing the apple with her husband.[50]

Lanyer modulates the voice of Pilate's wife with increasing fervor as she mounts this defense of her first mother; the argument reaches its climax in line 809, when she argues that any evil in Eve must derive ultimately from Adam and then turns to remind Pilate that Eve's sin was small by comparison to his. On this basis she will make her claim for equality: "Your fault beeing greater, why should you disdaine / Our beeing your equals, free from tyranny?" Pilate's wife thus goes beyond merely removing the "staine / Vpon our Sexe" caused by Eve's fall, for she defiantly denounces men's claim to rule.[51]

What were the precedents for Lanyer's extraordinary dramatic monologue? Three apocryphal gospels include positive references to Pilate's wife, who was named Procula (or Procla) and was eventually made a saint in the Eastern Orthodox church.[52] But Lanyer may have been familiar with a more immediate dramatic tradition developed in the fifteenth-century English cycle plays. Pilate's wife appears as a character in three of the surviving mysteries—the *Ludus Coventriae* (or N-Town plays), the Cornish *Ordinalia,* and the York cycle. In each of these cycles, the dream of Pilate's wife comes directly from Satan, who seeks to forestall Christ's crucifixion.[53] The episode is most extensively dramatized in the York cycle, where Procula is a vain woman, proud of her husband's position: "Wife to Sir Pilate here, prince without peer. / All well of all womanhood I am, witty and wise."[54] Satan warns her in the dream that if Pilate puts Christ to death, she will lose all of her riches, and so she hastily sends a messenger to stop him. In the York play Pilate's wife serves as Satan's unwitting agent and instrument; in fact Procula becomes a second Eve in the way in which she falls through pride.

Lanyer's poem is all the more remarkable because it opposes the earlier medieval dramatic tradition of Pilate's wife. Instead of offering a demonic dream inspired by Satan, Lanyer presents the dream of Pilate's wife as a divinely inspired vision. She creates a highly sympathetic portrait of the wife who genuinely wants to help her husband see the truth and to spare the life of Christ ("Condemne not him that must thy Sauiour be").[55] Most important, Lanyer seeks to vindicate both Pilate's wife and Eve and, in so doing, to break the misogynistic identification of woman with evil.

As students begin to recognize the degree of Lanyer's innovation in creating "Eues Apologie in defence of Women," they may be surprised to learn that the first editor of Lanyer's poems, A. L. Rowse, seriously proposed her as a candidate for Shakespeare's dark lady, and that he regarded *Salve Deus* as a reply to the sonnets.[56] They will discover the irony that the author who wrote most powerfully against the myth of "female evil" was cast into the literal role. In order to make her fit the part of Shakespeare's mistress, Rowse provided his own modern stereotyping of what he believed to be Lanyer's loose character; but despite his best efforts, he failed to uncover any documentary evidence that the two authors even knew each other. Yet in calling attention to Lanyer's poetry, Rowse performed a valuable service: her *Salve Deus Rex Ivdaeorvm* can be read as a counterdiscourse to Shakespeare's own literary creation of the dark lady.[57]

MATERIALITY OF THE TEXTS

The task of the last group is to examine the physical features of the 1609 Quarto, to consider where the text comes from and how the process of transmission from manuscript to print affects interpretation of the verse. Students begin with Thomas Thorpe's vexing dedication, which they may analyze by comparing it with other similar prefaces.[58] While they will certainly

disagree over its meaning—whether the "onlie begetter" of the sonnets refers to the author, the person addressed, or the intermediary who obtained the handwritten copy for Thorpe—the advantage of considering the dedication is that it provides a reminder of the lost manuscript(s) that forms the basis of the printed text. Unlike the other groups, which work exclusively with a modern edition of the sonnets, this last group also consults a xerox of the 1609 Quarto so that they can become familiar with some of the physical features of spelling, punctuation, and capitalization that are part of the original text.

Because most undergraduates know little about the nature of Elizabethan printing houses and their practices, it is important to warn them against assuming that the typographical oddities of the Quarto are authorial. In fact, meticulous analysis of the Quarto has revealed that the punctuation of the sonnets is the work not of the poet but of two compositors in George Eld's printshop.[59] The frequent and heavy use of punctuation throughout the 1609 Quarto appears to be at variance with what we know of Shakespeare's own habit of light punctuation in the portion of the manuscript play *Sir Thomas More* attributed to him: but since no autograph copy of the sonnets survives, it is impossible to tell to what extent the printed text departs from the original.

Fortunately students can see the process of transmission at work in Wroth's sonnets when they compare a xerox of the Folger's autograph manuscript with the 1621 printed text of *Pamphilia to Amphilanthus.* They quickly notice how the manuscript provides a punctuation that is mainly rhetorical (rather than grammatical) and that indicates where the pauses belong in reading aloud. A good example is illustrated below, where the author's absence of punctuation suggests that there is no break between the first and second quatrains: "then hopes still bee / bred in my brest" (ll. 4-5). However, the compositors of the 1621 text inserted a period at the end of the first quatrain, breaking the enjambement of the line and disrupting its meaning. After comparing only one or two of Wroth's poems in manuscript and print, students can see how radically the compositors, working with a printing-house style, could change the text before them.

When students return to the 1609 Quarto, they may regard the material text with a greater degree of skepticism, but they also express a heightened sensitivity to the nuances of meaning conveyed by accidentals. This group often analyzes the 1609 text of Sonnet 20, with its reference to the "Master Mistris of my passion." They consider what difference it makes that these words are capitalized and unhyphenated in the printed text. When they compare the poem with modern critical editions, they can see how some editors treat "Master" as a lowercase subordinate adjective, while others treat it as a hyphenated appositive to "Mistris." The ambiguities of syntax cannot easily be resolved, and the material approach to the text often calls attention to shades of meaning overlooked when the poem is discussed by earlier groups. The Quarto version of Sonnet 126 is also a good candidate for analysis, since students discover that the printed text inserts two sets of parentheses following the 12-line sonnet. Because this poem is often regarded as marking the division between the poems addressed to the fair young friend and those to the dark lady, it is particularly valuable to consider what the brackets might mean. Are they simply an indication that the printer thought something was missing, or do they reflect the author's expression of loss or incompletion?

Even more curious are the italicized words found in the 1609 Quarto. Again, textual study of Eld's printing house has shown that his books often contain italicized proper names as well as a selection of italicized common nouns.[60] For this reason it is impossible to know whether the italicized *Will* found in several of the sonnets (134-36 and 143) derives from the printer or the author. But surely the italicized name in the 1609 Quarto calls attention to the complexity of the wordplay. For example, Sonnet 143 begins with an epic simile, in which the speaker compares his lover to a distressed housewife, torn between running after her chickens and attending to her crying baby. This poem appears late in the sequence and so is generally assumed to be addressed to the dark lady (although students working on gender construction may point out that a satirical address to the fair young friend is at least a possibility). In the sestet the poet-lover casts himself in the role of the baby chasing after the mother: "So will I pray that thou maist have thy *Will,* / If thou turne back and my loude crying still" (1609 Q, ll. 13-14). Part of the comedy of the sonnet depends on the reversal of roles (the dark lady domesticated, the eternizing poet reduced to babbling babe), but the speaker's frustrated desire is summed up in the multiple meanings of his own name. Here class discussion can draw on nearly all of the critical approaches, including the persona's fractured sense of identity, what it means to satisfy another's will and yet remain *Will.*

This complex wordplay has its counterpart in Wroth's Sonnet P55, which concludes the first subgroup of poems in *Pamphilia to Amphilanthus.* While a number of Wroth's lyrics involve wordplay on "worth" as well as "will," this sonnet is especially rich in the way it alternates between the concepts of will as earthly, passionate desire and will as a driving aspect of the immortal soul.[61] The speaker describes the fires of love as all-consuming, able to purify her heart "to theyr best pleasing will"; but in the last line, the speaker asserts her own control over love in an affirmation of both desire and constancy: "Yett love I will till I butt ashes prove."[62] Interestingly, in the Folger manuscript

the author does not italicize "will" or call attention to what might be a pun on the name of her lover, William Herbert. Instead she emphasizes the persona's identity as Pamphilia, "all-loving," with the signature surrounded by the repeated sign of *s fermé* (a symbol of herself as a member of the Sidney family).[63] The simple italics in the 1621 printed text give only a hint of Wroth's arrangement of the persona's name, encircled by the author's larger identity. Thus the manuscript *Pamphilia* reflects the complex representation of subjectivity, in which the persona and author are not equated.

There are numerous advantages to teaching Shakespeare's sonnets alongside the works of his female contemporaries. Many of the material features of the 1609 Quarto which are most puzzling to students become clearer and easier to understand when they are viewed in the light of authors such as Wroth, for whom we have surviving autograph manuscripts. How Shakespeare treats gender in the sonnets can be studied in relation to the way in which women deal with some of the same problems of trying to create a new poetics by finding alternatives to the older Petrarchan tradition, with its starkly opposed gender roles. Students can compare how Shakespeare and contemporary women poets engaged in the process of fashioning subjectivity, using a variety of creative methods. In the case of Elizabeth I, Aemilia Lanyer, and Lady Mary Wroth, we are only beginning to recognize the magnitude of their accomplishments. Above all, the technique of parataxis tends to undercut bardolatry by showing that Shakespeare's creation of subjectivity in the sonnets was not an isolated stroke of genius. The juxtaposition with women authors by no means diminishes Shakespeare's achievement in creating some of the greatest poetry in English—"Thou maist have thy *Will*"—but it enhances our understanding of it.

Notes

[1] William Wordsworth, "Scorn not the Sonnet" (1827) in *Wordsworth: Poetical Works,* ed. Thomas Hutchinson (London: Oxford UP, 1969), 206.

[2] For a discussion of parataxis and its application to the study of women's writing, see Laurie A. Finke, *Feminist Theory, Women's Writing* (Ithaca, NY: Cornell UP, 1992), 28.

[3] *The Poems of Queen Elizabeth I,* ed. Leicester Bradner (Providence, RI: Brown UP, 1964), 5.

[4] Bradner, ed., 73. Other useful discussions of the poem include Ellen M. Caldwell, "John Lyly's *Gallathea:* A New Rhetoric of Love for the Virgin Queen" in *Women in the Renaissance: Selections from* English Literary Renaissance, Kirby Farrell, Elizabeth H. Hageman, and Arthur F. Kinney, eds. (Amherst: U of

Massachusetts P, 1988), 69-87; and Leonard Forster, *The Icy Fire: Five Studies in European Petrarchism* (Cambridge: Cambridge UP, 1969), 122-47.

⁵ Bradner, ed., xiii.

⁶ See Joel Fineman, *Shakespeare's Perjured Eye: The Invention of Poetic Subjectivity in the Sonnets* (Berkeley: U of California P, 1986), 1-48.

⁷ Fineman, 84.

⁸ Quotations of Shakespeare's sonnets follow Stephen Booth's edition, *Shakespeare's Sonnets* (New Haven, CT, and London: Yale UP, 1977).

⁹ Fineman, 48.

¹⁰ *Pamphilia to Amphilanthus* in *The Poems of Lady Mary Wroth,* ed. Josephine A. Roberts (Baton Rouge: Louisiana State UP, 1983), P103.9. Quotations of Wroth's poetry and numeric citations of her sonnets follow this edition, which uses as copy-text the Folger Shakespeare Library autograph manuscript of *Pamphilia to Amphilanthus* with the order of the poems revised to reflect the arrangement of the 1621 printed edition.

¹¹ For an account of the impact of Benson's 1640 miscellany, entitled *Poems: Written by Wil. Shakespeare, Gent.,* see Margreta de Grazia, "The Motive for Interiority: Shakespeare's *Sonnets* and *Hamlet." Style* 23 (1989): 430-44; and her *Shakespeare Verbatim: The Reproduction of Authenticity and the 1790 Apparatus* (Oxford: Clarendon Press, 1991), 163-73.

¹² For interesting discussions of attempts to rearrange the sonnets, see Brents Stirling, *The Shakespeare Sonnet Order: Poems and Groups* (Berkeley and Los Angeles: U of California P, 1968); J. W. Lever, *The Elizabethan Love Sonnet* (London: Methuen, 1956); and John Padel, *New Poems by Shakespeare: Order and meaning restored to the Sonnets* (London: Herbert Press, 1981).

¹³ One of my students, Elena Khalturina, called my attention to the importance of the "crown of sonnets" in twentieth-century Russian poetry, where the crown typically consists of fourteen sonnets, followed by a fifteenth, or magistral, sonnet that combines the first lines of all the previous sonnets.

¹⁴ See Penelope Reed Doob, *The Idea of the Labyrinth from Classical Antiquity through the Middle Ages* (Ithaca, NY: Cornell UP, 1990), 46-63.

¹⁵ Wroth, P90.13-14.

¹⁶ British Library Add. MS 58435.

¹⁷ See *The Poems of Robert Sidney,* ed. P. J. Croft (Oxford: Clarendon Press, 1984), 124.

¹⁸ Croft, ed., 112.

¹⁹ Note the pun here on *amaze* and *a maze.*

²⁰ Northrop Frye, "How True a Twain" in *The Riddle of Shakespeare's Sonnets,* Edward Hubler, ed. (New York: Basic Books, 1962), 23-53, esp. 27.

²¹ Katherine Duncan-Jones, "Was the 1609 *Shakespeares Sonnets* Really Unauthorized?" *Review of English Studies* 34 (1983): 151-71.

²² See de Grazia, "The Scandal of Shakespeare's Sonnets," *Shakespeare Survey* 46 (1994): 35-49, esp. 40-41; and Heather Dubrow, *Echoes of Desire: English Petrarchism and its Counter-discourses* (Ithaca, NY, and London: Cornell UP, 1995), 122-25.

²³ See Shakespeare's Sonnets 4.10; 13.4-8; 29.13; 35.14; 76.9; 89.10; and 95.1.

²⁴ See Bruce R. Smith, *Homosexual Desire in Shakespeare's England: A Cultural Poetics* (Chicago and London: U of Chicago P, 1991), 225-70. On the sonnets, see also Joseph Pequigney, *Such is My Love: A Study of Shakespeare's Sonnets* (Chicago and London: U of Chicago P, 1985); Eve Kosofsky Sedgwick, *Between Men: English Literature and Male Homosocial Desire* (New York: Columbia UP, 1985), 28-48; and Martin Green, *The Labyrinth of Shakespeare's Sonnets: An Examination of Sexual Elements in Shakespeare's Language* (London: Charles Skilton, 1974).

²⁵ Quoted in Smith, 230.

²⁶ Wroth, P15.1-4.

²⁷ Wroth, P15.9. In this passage Wroth invokes Astrophil's famous line: "'But ah,' Desire still cries, 'give me some food'" (*The Poems of Sir Philip Sidney,* ed. William A. Ringler Jr. [Oxford: Clarendon Press, 1962], *Astrophil and Stella,* 71.9 and 14).

²⁸ Wroth, P47.1 and 10.

²⁹ See Wroth, P58, P64, P70, and P96.

³⁰ Wroth, P48.12-13.

³¹ Wroth, P13.9-10.

³² Wroth, P17.11 and 3. See Naomi J. Miller, "Rewriting Lyric Fictions: The Role of the Lady in Lady Mary Wroth's *Pamphilia to Amphilanthus*" in *The Renaissance Englishwoman in Print: Counterbalancing the*

Canon, Anne M. Haselkorn and Betty S. Travitsky, eds. (Amherst: U of Massachusetts P, 1990), 295-310, esp. 299-300.

[33] Wroth, P22.3 and 13-14.

[34] Wroth, P25.1.

[35] Wroth, P40.1-4.

[36] For the political implications of P40 (Wroth's Sonnet 35), see Nona Fienberg, "Mary Wroth and the Invention of Female Poetic Subjectivity" in *Reading Mary Wroth: Representing Alternatives in Early Modern England,* Naomi J. Miller and Gary Waller, eds. (Knoxville: U of Tennessee P, 1991), 175-90, esp. 183.

[37] See Pequigney, 144.

[38] See James Winny, *The Master-Mistress: A Study of Shakespeare's Sonnets* (London: Chatto and Windus, 1968), 91.

[39] Elizabeth Cary, Lady Falkland, *The Tragedy of Mariam, the Fair Queen of Jewry,* ed. Barry Weller and Margaret W. Ferguson (Berkeley and Los Angeles: U of California P, 1994), 131.

[40] Kim F. Hall, *Things of Darkness: Economies of Race and Gender in Early Modern England* (Ithaca, NY: Cornell UP, 1995), 116.

[41] John Donne, *Paradoxes and Problems* (1633) in *John Donne: Selected Prose,* ed. Helen Gardner and Timothy Healy (Oxford: Clarendon Press, 1967), 1-22, esp. 7-8.

[42] For reproductions of Brathwait's frontispiece, see *Renaissance Woman: A Sourcebook: Constructions of Femininity in England,* Kate Aughterson, ed. (London: Routledge, 1995), figs. 4-5; and the cover and frontispiece of *Attending to Women in Early Modern England,* Betty S. Travitsky and Adele F. Seeff, eds. (Newark: U of Delaware P; London and Toronto: Associated University Presses, 1994).

[43] Morris Palmer Tilley, *A Dictionary of the Proverbs in England in the Sixteenth and Seventeenth Centuries* (Ann Arbor: U of Michigan P, 1950), 749 and 726.

[44] For a discussion of six distinct meanings of *will,* see Booth, ed., 466-67.

[45] Tilley, 748.

[46] Aemilia Lanyer, *Salve Devs Rex Ivdaeorvm* (London, 1611), f3[r-v].

[47] Lanyer, f3[v].

[48] The character of Pilate's wife is mentioned in only one biblical verse, Matthew 27:19: "When he was set down on the judgment seat, his wife sent unto him, saying, Have thou nothing to do with that just man: for I have suffered many things this day in a dream because of him."

[49] Lanyer, D[1][r-v]. Lanyer's argument may be based on an interpretation of 1 Timothy 2:14: "And Adam was not deceived, but the woman being deceived was in the transgression."

[50] Lanyer, D[1][v].

[51] Lanyer, D2[r] and D[1][v].

[52] The three apocrypha include the *Gospel of Nicodemus, or Acts of Pilate,* the *Paradosis Pilate, or Trial and Condemnation of Pilate,* and the *Letter of Pilate to Herod.* These texts are reprinted in *The Apochryphal New Testament,* ed. J. K. Elliott (Oxford: Clarendon Press, 1993), 164-85, 208-11, and 222-23.

[53] In the *Ludus Coventriae,* Satan's warning to Pilate's wife is given in dumb show; see *The N-Town Play,* ed. Stephen Spector, 2 vols. (Oxford: Oxford UP for the Early English Text Society, 1991), 1:317. In the Cornish *Ordinalia,* Beelzebub tells Pilate's wife that she and her family will be punished if Christ is put to death; see *The Cornish Ordinalia: A Medieval Dramatic Trilogy,* trans. Markham Harris (Washington, DC: Catholic U of America P, 1969), 138. The most developed characterization of Pilate's wife appears in the York cycle: see *York Mystery Plays: A Selection in Modern Spelling,* ed. Richard Beadle and Pamela M. King (Oxford: Clarendon Press, 1984), 154-66.

[54] "Christ before Pilate 1: The Dream of Pilate's Wife" in Beadle and King, eds., 154-74, esp. 156.

[55] Lanyer, C[4][v].

[56] See A. L. Rowse, *The Poems of Shakespeare's Dark Lady* (London: Jonathan Cape, 1978).

[57] The beginning stanzas of Lanyer's poem offer "An Invective against outward beauty unaccompanied by virtue" (marginalia, l. 185), in which Lanyer mentions a number of examples, including Lucrece, Cleopatra, Rosamund, and Matilda. Janel Mueller calls attention to this passage as a reflection of Lanyer's interest in "how female moral agency is represented in recent English secular poetry and drama"; see "The Feminist Poetics of Aemilia Lanyer's 'Salve Deus Rex Judaeorum'" in *Feminist Measures: Soundings in Poetry and Theory,* Lynn Keller and Cristanne Miller, eds. (Ann Arbor: U of Michigan P, 1994), 208-36, esp. 214.

[58] On the Thorpe dedication, see Donald W. Foster, "Master W. H., R.I.P.," *PMLA* 102 (1987): 42-54. A facsimile of the 1609 Quarto is readily available in Booth's edition of the sonnets.

[59] See MacD. P. Jackson, "Punctuation and the Compositors of Shakespeare's *Sonnets,* 1609," *The Library,* 5th ser., 30 (1975): 1-24.

[60] See Alice Walker's study of the quarto of *Troilus and Cressida* printed by Eld in 1609, the same year in which he published Shakespeare's sonnets: "The Textual Problem of 'Troilus and Cressida'." *Modern Language Review* 45 (1950): 459-64, esp. 461-62.

[61] Sonnets that pun on *Wroth/worth* include P15, P25, P35, and P84: the puns on *will* are more numerous: P3, P6, P7, P8, P12, P15, P20, P30, P40, P47, P49, P55, P64, P69, P89, and P103.

[62] Wroth, P55.6 and 14.

[63] For other examples of Wroth's use of the same symbol, see *Lady Mary Wroth's Love's Victory: The Penshurst Manuscript,* ed. Michael G. Brennan (London: Roxburghe Club, 1988), 16.

———————————

Source: "'Thou maist have thy *Will*': The Sonnets of Shakespeare and His Stepsisters," in *Shakespeare Quarterly,* Vol. 47, No. 4, Winter, 1996, pp. 407-23.

Cumulative Index to Topics

The Cumulative Index to Topics identifies the principal topics of discussion in the criticism of each play and non-dramatic poem. The topics are arranged alphabetically. Page references indicate the beginning page number of each essay containing substantial commentary on that topic.

All's Well That Ends Well

appearance vs. reality **7**: 37, 76, 93; **26**: 117
audience perspective **7**: 81, 104, 109, 116, 121
bed-trick **7**: 8, 26, 27, 29, 32, 41, 86, 93, 98, 113, 116, 126; **13**: 84; **26**: 117; **28**: 38
Bertram
    characterization **7**: 15, 27, 29, 32, 39, 41, 43, 98, 113; **26**: 48; **26**: 117
    conduct **7**: 9, 10, 12, 16, 19, 21, 51, 62, 104
    physical desire **22**: 78
    transformation or redemption **7**: 10, 19, 21, 26, 29, 32, 54, 62, 81, 90, 93, 98, 109, 113, 116, 126; **13**: 84
comic elements **26**: 97, 114
dark elements **7**: 27, 37, 39, 43, 54, 109, 113, 116; **26**: 85
Decameron (Boccaccio), compared with **7**: 29, 43
displacement **22**: 78
education **7**: 62, 86, 90, 93, 98, 104, 116, 126
elder characters **7**: 9, 37, 39, 43, 45, 54, 62, 104
gender issues **7**: 9, 10, 67, 126; **13**: 77, 84; **19**: 113; **26**: 128
Helena
    as agent of reconciliation, renewal, or grace **7**: 67, 76, 81, 90, 93, 98, 109, 116
    as dualistic or enigmatic character **7**: 15, 27, 29, 39, 54, 58, 62, 67, 76, 81, 98, 113, 126; **13**: 66; **22**: 78; **26**: 117
    as "female achiever" **19**: 113
    pursuit of Bertram **7**: 9, 12, 15, 16, 19, 21, 26, 27, 29, 32, 43, 54, 76, 116; **13**:

77; **22**: 78
virtue and nobility **7**: 9, 10, 12, 16, 19, 21, 27, 32, 41, 51, 58, 67, 76, 86, 126; **13**: 77
improbable or implausible elements **7**: 8, 45
irony, paradox, and ambiguity **7**: 27, 32, 58, 62, 67, 81, 86, 109, 116
language and imagery **7**: 12, 29, 45, 104, 109, 121
Lavatch **26**: 64
love **7**: 12, 15, 16, 51, 58, 67, 90, 93, 116
merit vs. rank **7**: 9, 10, 19, 37, 51, 76
"mingled yarn" **7**: 62, 93, 109, 126
morality plays, influence of **7**: 29, 41, 51, 98, 113; **13**: 66
Parolles
    characterization **7**: 8, 9, 43, 76, 81, 98, 109, 113, 116, 126; **22**: 78; **26**: 48, 73, 97; **26**: 117
    exposure **7**: 9, 27, 81, 98, 109, 113, 116, 121, 126
    Falstaff, compared with **7**: 8, 9, 16
reconciliation or regeneration **7**: 90, 93, 98
religious or spiritual elements **7**: 15, 45, 54, 67, 76, 98, 109, 116
romance or folktale elements **7**: 32, 41, 43, 45, 54, 76, 104, 116, 121; **26**: 117
sexuality **7**: 67, 86, 90, 93, 98, 126; **13**: 84; **19**: 113; **22**: 78; **28**: 38
social and political context **13**: 66; **22**: 78
staging issues **19**: 113; **26**: 15, 19, 48, 52, 64, 73, 85, 92, 93, 94, 95, 97, 114, 117, 128
structure **7**: 21, 29, 32, 45, 51, 76, 81, 93, 98, 116; **22**: 78; **26**: 128
youth vs. age **7**: 9, 45, 58, 62, 76, 81, 86, 93, 98, 104, 116, 126; **26**: 117

Antony and Cleopatra

All for Love (John Dryden), compared with **6**: 20, 21; **17**: 12, 94, 101
ambiguity **6**: 53, 111, 161, 163, 180, 189, 208, 211, 228; **13**: 368
androgyny **13**: 530
Antony
    characterization **6**: 22, 23, 24, 31, 38, 41, 172, 181, 211; **16**: 342; **19**: 270; **22**: 217; **27**: 117
    Cleopatra, relationship with **6**: 25, 27, 37, 39, 48, 52, 53, 62, 67, 71, 76, 85, 100, 125, 131, 133, 136, 142, 151, 161, 163, 165, 180, 192; **27**: 82
    death scene **25**: 245
    dotage **6**: 22, 23, 38, 41, 48, 52, 62, 107, 136, 146, 175; **17**: 28
    nobility **6**: 22, 24, 33, 48, 94, 103, 136, 142, 159, 172, 202; **25**: 245
    political conduct **6**: 33, 38, 53, 107, 111, 146, 181
    public vs. private personae **6**: 165
    self-knowledge **6**: 120, 131, 175, 181, 192
    as superhuman figure **6**: 37, 51, 71, 92, 94, 178, 192; **27**: 110
    as tragic hero **6**: 38, 39, 52, 53, 60, 104, 120, 151, 155, 165, 178, 192, 202, 211; **22**: 217; **27**: 90
Cleopatra
    Antony, relationship with **6**: 25, 27, 37, 39, 48, 52, 53, 62, 67, 71, 76, 85, 100, 125, 131, 133, 136, 142, 151, 161, 163, 165, 180, 192; **25**: 257; **27**: 82
    contradictory or inconsistent nature **6**: 23, 24, 27, 67, 76, 100, 104, 115, 136, 151,

Beaumont and Fletcher's romances, compared with **4:** 46, 52, 138

Belarius **4:** 48, 89, 141

British nationalism **4:** 19, 78, 89, 93, 129, 141, 159, 167; **32:** 373; **36:** 129

Cloten **4:** 20, 116, 127, 155; **22:** 302, 365; **25:** 245; **36:** 99, 125, 142, 155

combat scenes **22:** 365

comic elements **4:** 35, 56, 113, 141; **15:** 111, 122

dramatic structure **4:** 17, 18, 19, 20, 21, 22, 24, 38, 43, 48, 53, 64, 68, 89, 116, 129, 141; **22:** 302, 365; **25:** 319; **36:** 115, 125

dreams **4:** 162, 167

dualisms **4:** 29, 64, 73

Elizabethan dramatic conventions **4:** 53, 124

Guiderius and Arviragus **4:** 21, 22, 89, 129, 141, 148; **25:** 319; **36:** 125, 158

Iachimo **25:** 245, 319; **36:** 166

Imogen **4:** 21, 22, 24, 29, 37, 45, 46, 52, 56, 78, 89, 108; **15:** 23, 32, 105, 121; **19:** 411; **25:** 245, 319; **28:** 398; **32:** 373; **36:** 129, 142, 148

Imogen's reawakening (Act IV, scene ii) **4:** 37, 56, 89, 103, 108, 116, 150; **15:** 23; **25:** 245

irony **4:** 64, 77, 103

language and imagery **4:** 43, 48, 61, 64, 70, 73, 93, 108; **13:** 401; **25:** 245; **28:** 373, 398; **36:** 115, 158, 166, 186

Lucretia, analogies to **36:** 148

misperception **19:** 411; **36:** 99, 115

mythic elements **28:** 373; **36:** 142

negative appraisals **4:** 20, 35, 43, 45, 48, 53, 56, 68; **15:** 32, 105, 121

patriarchy **32:** 373; **36:** 134

Posthumus **4:** 24, 30, 53, 78, 116, 127, 141, 155, 159, 167; **15:** 89; **19:** 411; **25:** 245, 319; **36:** 142

psychological elements **36:** 134

regeneration, renewal, or reconciliation **4:** 38, 64, 73, 93, 105, 113, 116, 129, 138, 141, 162, 170

religious or spiritual elements **4:** 22, 29, 78, 93, 105, 108, 115, 116, 127, 134, 138, 141, 159; **36:** 158, 186

romance elements **4:** 17, 20, 46, 68, 77, 141, 148, 172; **15:** 111; **25:** 319; **28:** 373

self-conscious or artificial nature of play **4:** 43, 52, 56, 68, 124, 134, 138; **36:** 99

sexuality **4:** 170, 172; **25:** 319; **32:** 373

Shakespeare's lyric poetry, compared with **13:** 401

sources **4:** 17, 18; **13:** 401; **28:** 373

staging issues **15:** 6, 23, 75, 105, 111, 121, 122; **22:** 365

subversiveness **22:** 302

tragic elements **25:** 319; **28:** 373; **36:** 129

trickster, motif of **22:** 302

vision scene (Act V, scene iv) **4:** 17, 21, 28, 29, 35, 38, 78, 105, 108, 134, 150, 167

wager plot **4:** 18, 24, 29, 53, 78, 155; **22:** 365; **25:** 319

Hamlet

ambiguity or mystery, role of **1:** 92, 160, 198, 227, 230, 234, 247, 249; **21:** 72; **35:** 241

appearance vs. reality **1:** 95, 116, 166, 169, 198; **35:** 82, 126, 132, 144, 238

audience response **28:** 325; **32:** 238; **35:** 167

autobiographical elements **1:** 98, 115, 119; **13:** 487

classical Greek tragedies, compared with **1:** 74, 75, 130, 184, 212; **13:** 296; **22:** 339

Claudius **13:** 502; **16** 246; **21:** 259, 347, 361, 371; **28:** 232, 290; **35:** 104, 182

closet scene (Act III, scene iv) **16:** 259; **21:** 151, 334, 392; **35:** 204, 229

costume **21:** 81

death, decay, or corruption **1:** 144, 153, 188, 198, 221, 242; **13:** 502; **28:** 280, 311; **35:** 241

dumbshow and play scene (Act III, scene ii) **1:** 76, 86, 134, 138, 154, 160, 207; **13:** 502; **21:** 392; **35:** 82

Elizabethan culture, relation to **1:** 76, 148, 151, 154, 160, 166, 169, 171, 176, 184, 202, 209, 254; **13:** 282, 494; **19:** 330; **21:** 407, 416; **22:** 258

Elizabethan and Jacobean politics, relation to **28:** 232; **28:** 290, 311; **35:** 140

fencing scene (Act V, scene ii) **21:** 392

Fortinbras **21:** 136, 347; **28:** 290

gender issues **35:** 144

genre **1:** 176, 212, 237

Gertrude **21:** 259, 347, 392; **28:** 311; **32:** 238; **35:** 182, 204, 229

Ghost **1:** 75, 76, 84, 85, 128, 134, 138, 154, 171, 218, 231, 254; **16:** 246; **21:** 17, 44, 112, 151, 334, 371, 377, 392; **25:** 288; **35:** 152, 157, 174, 237

gravedigger scene (Act V, scene i) **21:** 392; **28:** 280

Hamlet

  delay **1:** 76, 83, 88, 90, 94, 98, 102, 103, 106, 114, 115, 116, 119, 120, 148, 151, 166, 171, 179, 188, 191, 194, 198, 221, 268; **13:** 296, 502; **21:** 81; **25:** 209, 288; **28:** 223; **35:** 82, 174, 212, 215, 237

  divided nature **16:** 246; **28:** 223; **32:** 288; **35:** 182, 215; **37:** 241

  elocution of the character's speeches **21:** 96, 104, 112, 127, 132, 172, 177, 179, 194, 245, 254, 257

  madness **1:** 76, 81, 83, 95, 102, 106, 128, 144, 154, 160, 234; **21:** 35, 50, 72, 81, 99, 112, 311, 339, 355, 361, 371, 377, 384; **35:** 117, 132, 134, 140, 144, 212

  melancholy **21:** 99, 112, 177, 194; **35:** 82, 95, 117

  as negative character **1:** 86, 92, 111, 171, 218; **21:** 386; **25:** 209; **35:** 167

  reaction to his father's death **22:** 339; **35:** 104, 174

  reaction to Gertrude's marriage **1:** 74, 120, 154, 179; **16:** 259; **21:** 371; **22:** 339; **35:** 104, 117

  romantic aspects of the character **21:** 96

  as scourge or purifying figure **1:** 144, 209, 242; **25:** 288; **35:** 157

  sentimentality vs. intellectuality **1:** 75, 83, 88, 91, 93, 94, 96, 102, 103, 115, 116, 120, 166, 191; **13:** 296; **21:** 35, 41, 44, 72, 81, 89, 99, 129, 132, 136, 172, 213, 225, 339, 355, 361, 371, 377, 379, 381,

386; **25:** 209

soliloquies **1:** 76, 82, 83, 148, 166, 169, 176, 191; **21:** 17, 31, 44, 53, 89, 112, 268, 311, 334, 347, 361, 384, 392; **25:** 209; **28:** 223

theatrical interpretations **21:** 11, 31, 78, 101, 104, 107, 160, 177, 179, 182, 183, 192, 194, 197, 202, 203, 208, 213, 225, 232, 237, 249, 253, 254, 257, 259, 274, 311, 339, 347, 355, 361, 371, 377, 380

virility **21:** 213, 301, 355

Hamlet with Alterations (David Garrick adaptation) **21:** 23, 334, 347

idealism vs. pragmatism **16** 246; **28:** 325

Laertes **21:** 347, 386; **28:** 290; **35:** 182

language and imagery **1:** 95, 144, 153, 154, 160, 188, 198, 221, 227, 249, 259, 270; **22:** 258, 378; **28:** 311; **35:** 144, 152, 238, 241

madness **19:** 330; **35:** 104, 126, 134, 140, 144

marriage **22:** 339

nunnery scene (Act III, scene i) **21:** 157, 381, 410

Ophelia **1:** 73, 76, 81, 82, 91, 96, 97, 154, 166, 169, 171, 218, 270; **13:** 268; **16:** 246; **19:** 330; **21:** 17, 41, 44, 72, 81, 101, 104, 107, 112, 136, 203, 259, 347, 381, 386, 392, 416; **28:** 232, 325; **35:** 104, 126, 140, 144, 182, 238

Polonius **21:** 259, 334, 347, 386, 416; **35:** 182

prayer scene (Act III, scene iii) **1:** 76, 106, 160, 212, 231

psychoanalytic interpretation **1:** 119, 148, 154, 179, 202; **21:** 197, 213, 361; **25:** 209; **28:** 223; **35:** 95, 104, 134, 237; **37:** 241

religious or mythic content **1:** 98, 102, 130, 184, 191, 209, 212, 231, 234, 254; **21:** 361; **22:** 258; **28:** 280; **32:** 238; **35:** 134

revenge **1:** 74, 194, 209, 224, 234, 254; **16:** 246; **22:** 258; **25:** 288; **28:** 280; **35:** 152, 157, 167, 174, 212

Richard II, compared with **1:** 264

rites and ceremonies **13:** 268; **28:** 232

sources **1:** 76, 81, 113, 125, 128, 130, 151, 191, 202, 224, 259

staging issues **13:** 494, 502; **21:** 11, 17, 31, 35, 41, 44, 50, 53, 78, 81, 89, 101, 112, 127, 139, 142, 145, 148, 151, 157, 160, 172, 182, 183, 202, 203, 208, 225, 232, 237, 242, 245, 249, 251, 259, 268, 270, 274, 283, 284, 301, 311, 334, 347, 355, 361, 371, 377, 379, 380, 381, 384, 386, 392, 407, 410, 416

structure **22:** 378; **28:** 280, 325; **35:** 82, 104, 215

textual variants **13:** 282; **16:** 259; **21:** 11, 23, 72, 101, 127, 129, 139, 140, 142, 145, 202, 208, 259, 270, 284, 347, 361, 384; **22:** 258; **32:** 238

topical elements **13:** 282

unity or consistency **1:** 75, 76, 87, 103, 113, 125, 128, 142, 148, 160, 184, 188, 198, 264; **16:** 259; **35:** 82, 215

unnatural ordering **22:** 378

widowhood and remarriage, themes of **32:** 238

Henry IV, Parts 1 and 2

carnival elements **28:** 203; **32:** 103
characterization **1:** 321, 328, 332, 333, 336, 344, 365, 383, 385, 389, 391, 397, 401; **19:** 195
comic elements **1:** 286, 290, 314, 327, 328, 336, 353; **19:** 195; **25:** 109
contractual and economic relations **13:** 213
contrasting dramatic worlds **14:** 56, 60, 61, 84, 105
deception **1:** 397, 406, 425
Elizabethan culture, relation to **19:** 195
Elizabethan politics, relation to **22:** 395; **28:** 203
Falstaff
    characterization **1:** 287, 298, 312, 333; **25:** 245; **28:** 203
    as comic figure **1:** 287, 311, 327, 344, 351, 354, 357, 410, 434
    as coward or rogue **1:** 285, 290, 296, 298, 306, 307, 313, 317, 323, 336, 337, 338, 342, 354, 366, 374, 391, 396, 401, 433; **14:** 7, 111, 125, 130, 133; **32:** 166
    dual personality **1:** 397, 401, 406, 434
    female attributes **13:** 183
    Iago, compared with **1:** 341, 351
    Marxist interpretation **1:** 358, 361
    as parody of the historical plot **1:** 314, 354, 359
    as positive character **1:** 286, 287, 290, 296, 298, 311, 312, 321, 325, 333, 344, 355, 357, 389, 401, 408, 434
    rejection by Hal **1:** 286, 287, 290, 312, 314, 317, 324, 333, 338, 344, 357, 366, 372, 374, 379, 380, 389, 414; **13:** 183; **25:** 109
    as satire of feudal society **1:** 314, 328, 361; **32:** 103
    as scapegoat **1:** 389, 414
    stage interpretations **14:** 4, 6, 7, 9, 15, 116, 130, 146
    as subversive figure **16:** 183; **25:** 109
    as Vice figure **1:** 342, 361, 366, 374
flattery **22:** 395
gender issues **13:** 183; **25:** 151
Hal
    as the central character **1:** 286, 290, 314, 317, 326, 338, 354, 366, 374, 396
    dual personality **1:** 397, 406; **25:** 109, 151
    as Everyman **1:** 342, 366, 374
    fall from humanity **1:** 379, 380, 383
    general assessment **1:** 286, 287, 289, 290, 314, 317, 326, 327, 332, 357, 397; **25:** 245; **32:** 212
    as ideal ruler **1:** 289, 309, 317, 321, 326, 337, 342, 344, 374, 389, 391, 434; **25:** 109
    as a negative character **1:** 312, 332, 333, 357; **32:** 212
    Richard II, compared with **1:** 332, 337
historical content **1:** 310, 328, 365, 366, 370, 374, 380, 387, 421, 424, 427, 431; **16:** 172; **19:** 157; **25:** 151; **32:** 136
Hotspur **25:** 151; **28:** 101
kingship **1:** 314, 318, 337, 366, 370, 374, 379, 380, 383, 424; **16:** 172; **19:** 195; **28:** 101

language and imagery **13:** 213; **16:** 172; **25:** 245; **28:** 101
as morality play **1:** 323, 324, 342, 361, 366, 373, 374; **32:** 166
Mortimer **25:** 151
Neoclassical rules **1:** 286, 287, 290, 293
Oldcastle, references to **22:** 114; **32:** 166
as part of Shakespeare's historical epic **1:** 309, 314, 328, 374, 379, 424, 427
politics **28:** 101
psychoanalytic interpretation **13:** 457; **28:** 101
rebellion **22:** 395; **28:** 101
relationship to other Shakespearean plays **1:** 286, 290, 309, 329, 365, 396; **28:** 101
relationship of Parts 1 and 2 **32:** 136
religious or mythic content **1:** 314, 374, 414, 421, 429, 431, 434; **32:** 103
    as autonomous works **1:** 289, 337, 338, 347, 348, 373, 387, 393, 411, 418, 424
    comparison **1:** 290, 295, 329, 348, 358, 393, 411, 419, 429, 431, 441
    unity of both parts **1:** 286, 290, 309, 314, 317, 329, 365, 373, 374, 396, 402, 404, 419
staging issues **32:** 212
textual issues **22:** 114
time and change, motif of **1:** 372, 393, 411
Turkish elements **19:** 170
two fathers **14:** 86, 101, 105, 108
violence **25:** 109

Henry V

battle of Agincourt **5:** 197, 199, 213, 246, 257, 281, 287, 289, 293, 310, 318; **19:** 217; **30:** 181
Canterbury and churchmen **5:** 193, 203, 205, 213, 219, 225, 252, 260; **22:** 137; **30:** 215, 262
characterization **5:** 186, 189, 192, 193, 199, 219, 230, 233, 252, 276, 293; **30:** 227, 278
Chorus, role of **5:** 186, 192, 226, 228, 230, 252, 264, 269, 281, 293; **14:** 301, 319, 336; **19:** 133; **25:** 116, 131; **30:** 163, 202, 220
class relations **28:** 146
colonialism **22:** 103
comic elements **5:** 185, 188, 191, 192, 217, 230, 233, 241, 252, 260, 276; **19:** 217; **28:** 121; **30:** 193, 202,
economic relations **13:** 213
Elizabethan culture, relation to **5:** 210, 213, 217, 223, 257, 299, 310; **16:** 202; **19:** 133, 233; **28:** 121, 159; **30:** 215, 262; **37:** 187
English language and colonialism **22:** 103; **28:** 159
epic elements **5:** 192, 197, 246, 257, 314; **30:** 181, 220, 237, 252
Falstaff **5:** 185, 186, 187, 189, 192, 195, 198, 210, 226, 257, 269, 271, 276, 293, 299; **28:** 146
Fluellen **30:** 278; **37:** 105
French aristocrats and the Dauphin **5:** 188, 191, 199, 205, 213, 281; **22:** 137; **28:** 121
French language, Shakespeare's use of **5:** 186, 188, 190; **25:** 131

gender issues **13:** 183; **28:** 121, 146, 159
Henry
    brutality and cunning **5:** 193, 203, 209, 210, 213, 219, 233, 239, 252, 260, 271, 287, 293, 302, 304; **30:** 159,
    characterization in *1* and *2 Henry IV* contrasted **5:** 189, 190, 241, 304, 310; **19:** 133; **25:** 131; **32:** 157
    chivalry **37:** 187
    courage **5:** 191, 195, 210, 213, 228, 246, 257, 267
    disguise **30:** 169, 259
    education **5:** 246, 267, 271, 289; **14:** 297, 328, 342; **30:** 259
    emotion, lack of **5:** 209, 212, 233, 244, 264, 267, 287, 293, 310
    as heroic figure **5:** 192, 205, 209, 223, 244, 252, 257, 260, 269, 271, 299, 304; **28:** 121, 146; **30:** 237, 244, 252; **37:** 187
    humor **5:** 189, 191, 212, 217, 239, 240, 276
    intellectual and social limitations **5:** 189, 191, 203, 209, 210, 225, 226, 230, 293; **30:** 220
    interpersonal relations **5:** 209, 233, 267, 269, 276, 287, 293, 302, 318; **19:** 133; **28:** 146
    mercy **5:** 213, 267, 289, 293
    mixture of good and bad qualities **5:** 199, 205, 209, 210, 213, 244, 260, 304, 314; **30:** 262, 273
    piety **5:** 191, 199, 209, 217, 223, 239, 257, 260, 271, 289, 310, 318; **30:** 244; **32:** 126
    public vs. private selves **22:** 137; **30:** 169, 207
    self-doubt **5:** 281, 310
    slaughter of prisoners **5:** 189, 205, 246, 293, 318; **28:** 146
    speech **5:** 212, 230, 233, 246, 264, 276, 287, 302; **28:** 146; **30:** 163, 227
historical content **5:** 185, 188, 190, 192, 193, 198, 246, 314; **13:** 201; **19:** 133; **25:** 131; **30:** 193, 202, 207, 215, 252
homoerotic elements **16:** 202
Hotspur **5:** 189, 199, 228, 271, 302
hypocrisy **5:** 203, 213, 219, 223, 233, 260, 271, 302
imperialism **22:** 103; **28:** 159
Irish affairs **22:** 103; **28:** 159
irony **5:** 192, 210, 213, 219, 223, 226, 233, 252, 260, 269, 281, 299, 304; **14:** 336; **30:** 159, 193,
Katherine **5:** 186, 188, 189, 190, 192, 260, 269, 299, 302; **13:** 183; **19:** 217; **30:** 278
kingship **5:** 205, 223, 225, 233, 239, 244, 257, 264, 267, 271, 287, 289, 299, 302, 304, 314, 318; **16:** 202; **22:** 137; **30:** 169, 202, 259, 273
language and imagery **5:** 188, 230, 233, 241, 264, 276; **9:** 203; **19:** 203; **25:** 131; **30:** 159, 181, 207, 234 **30:** 159, 181, 207, 234
Machiavellianism **5:** 203, 225, 233, 252, 287, 304; **25:** 131; **30:** 273
MacMorris **22:** 103; **28:** 159; **30:** 278
Marlowe's works, compared with **19:** 233
metadramatic elements **13:** 194; **30:** 181,

Topic Index

Topic Index

The Tempest

ISBN 0-7876-1135-2

90000

REFERENCE